THE NAVY OF
WORLD WAR II
1922–1947

THE U.S. NAVY WARSHIP SERIES

The Sailing Navy, 1775–1854
Civil War Navies, 1855–1883
The New Navy, 1883–1922
The Navy of World War II, 1922–1947

THE NAVY OF WORLD WAR II 1922–1947

Paul H. Silverstone

New York London

Routledge
Taylor & Francis Group
270 Madison Avenue
New York, NY 10016

Routledge
Taylor & Francis Group
2 Park Square
Milton Park, Abingdon
Oxon OX14 4RN

Routledge is an imprint of Taylor & Francis Group, an Informa business

Printed in the United States of America on acid-free paper
10 9 8 7 6 5 4 3 2 1

International Standard Book Number-13: 978-0-415-97898-9 (Hardcover)

Library of Congress Cataloging-in-Publication Data

Silverstone, Paul H.
The Navy of World War II, 1922-1947 / Paul H. Silverstone.
p. cm. -- (The U.S. Navy warship series)
Includes bibliographical references and index.
ISBN 978-0-415-97898-9 (alk. paper)
1. United States. Navy--Lists of vessels. 2. United States. Navy--History--World War, 1939-1945. 3. Warships--United States--History--20th century. I. Title.

VA61.S547 2007
940.54'5973--dc22 2006036705

Visit the Taylor & Francis Web site at
http://www.taylorandfrancis.com

and the Routledge Web site at
http://www.routledge.com

CONTENTS

INTRODUCTION

In 1945, at the end of World War II, the U.S. Navy stood at its peak in size and power. Huge numbers of ships had been built from the largest *Iowa*-class battleships to wooden submarine chasers. Thousands of merchant ships were constructed, of which the Navy used hundreds as auxiliaries of all types.

The attack on Pearl Harbor opened hostilities with the devastation of the fleet, magnified by the surprise nature of the attack. Conditions close to war were already in effect in the Atlantic Ocean, and Adolf Hitler made it simpler for the United States to enter the global conflict by declaring war three days later.

Major ships were hurriedly transferred to the Pacific Ocean using the Panama Canal. No doubt, there were many who thanked the foresight of Theodore Roosevelt decades earlier. Nevertheless, during the early battles of 1942 disasters continued with the loss of the Philippines, Malaya, Singapore, and the Dutch East Indies. Thousands of Allied troops were killed or captured, and many ships were sunk. Japanese forces roamed the western Pacific virtually unopposed, their attacks reaching as far as Ceylon and Northern Australia. The battles in the Coral Sea and then the decisive Battle of Midway were the first setbacks for Japan. In August 1942 the two enemies clashed in the Solomon Islands, which were destined to become a ferocious battleground that would cost the lives of many men and dozens of ships.

The clash came on the island of Guadalcanal, where the Japanese were building an airfield. American landings started an intense battle for the island, into which more ships and men were drawn. Following the disaster at Savo Island, a series of naval battles were fought—in the Eastern Solomon Islands, at Cape Esperance, and at Santa Cruz—culminating in the actions in November called the Battle of Guadalcanal. Both sides suffered serious losses in cruisers and destroyers.

During the next year the American forces made their way up the Solomon Island chain, landing and fighting on Vella Lavella, Rendova, Kolombangara, Choiseul, New Georgia, and, finally, Bougainville—names of places previously unknown to most. Naval fighting occurred at Kula Gulf, Empress Augusta Bay, the Bismarck Sea, and Cape St. George. Other fighting took place in New Guinea, and an intense air campaign caused havoc to Japanese shipping in these confined waters.

During this time, shipyards and training stations in the United States were busy producing the fleet that emerged in 1943 and grew into the carrier task forces and amphibious forces, which turned the tide and eventually dominated the Pacific. Meanwhile, the underwater war was growing, as an increasing number of newly built submarines carried out the destruction of the Japanese Navy and Merchant Marine.

The American war in the Pacific was, early on, divided into two commands: an Army command under General Douglas MacArthur in the Southwest Pacific, and a Navy command under Admiral Chester W. Nimitz in the Central Pacific. Thus a two-pronged attack was conceived. MacArthur's forces moved from the Solomons up the northern coast of New Guinea to reach the Philippines. The Navy under Nimitz moved west through the Gilbert and Marshall Islands to the Mariana Islands and eventually Okinawa.

In November 1943, the first amphibious landings in the Central Pacific occurred in the Gilbert Islands. Tarawa and the Makin Islands entered Marine Corps history. Two months later the next move was made in the Japanese-governed Marshall Islands, with landings on Kwajalein and Eniwetok. Meanwhile, the first of the great carrier raids was launched against the Japanese naval fortress of Truk in the Caroline Islands.

Breaking out of the Solomons, MacArthur's forces started moving on New Britain and then along the northern coast of New Guinea; landings were made at the once obscure points, Arawe, Cape Gloucester, Saidor, Aitape, Wakde, Biak, Noemfoor, and Morotai, each getting closer to his objective, the Philippines.

In June 1944, the Central Pacific exploded with the defining Battle of the Philippine Sea, which destroyed Japan's carrier fleet and wiped out most of its experienced pilots. This battle has gone down in history with the impolitic name of "The Great Marianas

Turkey Shoot." Landings were made in the Mariana Islands at Saipan, Guam, and Tinian.

American strategy was to bypass many Japanese fortified strong points, such as Rabaul and Truk, which the enemy was unable to resupply.

Carrier raids reached farther into the areas of the Pacific that the Japanese had considered "their" waters. The Bonin and Ryukyu Islands, and Formosa, were attacked. Landings were made on Morotai and Palau. All this set the stage for MacArthur's return to the Philippines with the landings on Leyte in October 1944. Japan made its last great effort to stop the advance with the landmark Battle of Leyte Gulf, using a three-pronged attack on the American landing forces. It was a failure, although nearly successful when a Japanese battle fleet broke through to attack lightly armed American escort carriers off Samar. At Surigao Strait was fought the last action between battleships in naval history, the U.S. Navy represented by survivors of Pearl Harbor.

After gaining control of Leyte, U.S. forces made more landings in the Philippines, notably at Mindoro and on Luzon at Lingayen Gulf. Japanese forces fought bitterly for Manila, destroying most of the city.

It was during this time that the Japanese started using suicide planes in great numbers, called *kamikaze* ("divine wind"). American losses mounted from these attacks. In February 1945 the first great carrier raids were made on the Japanese home islands, including those on Tokyo. At the same time, landings were made on Iwo Jima. Gaining this island's airfield brought Japan itself within close range of American B-29 bombers.

In April the island of Okinawa was attacked and the grueling ground action continued for two and one-half months. Kamikaze attacks on the huge amphibious support fleet reached a high point, and casualties soared.

Preparations were then made for the invasion of Kyushu, the southernmost island of Japan (named Operation Olympic), to be followed by landings on Honshu (named Operation Coronet). But on 6 August 1945, the first atomic bomb was dropped on the city of Hiroshima, followed three days later by another on Nagasaki. This led to the momentous day of surrender on 15 August. An instrument of surrender was signed on the battleship *Missouri* in Tokyo Bay on 2 September 1945, ending the war.

The U. S. Navy lost 36, 950 officers and enlisted men killed and 37,778 wounded in action. Some women were casualties. Six nurses were killed on the USS *Comfort* in 1945 and 16 became Japanese prisoners of war.

The vast expanse of the Pacific Ocean led to a major increase and development in support vessels that enabled the fleet to take its bases with it. Major operating bases were set up at islands such as Ulithi and Manus using ships built to provide every service needed, repairs including major battle damage repairs, replacement parts, supplies, fuel, and ammunition.

In the Atlantic, the principal combat was the war against the German U-boats. Enemy submarines operated off the east coast of the United States within sight of shore and merchant losses were heavy. Trans-Atlantic convoys were vulnerable because there were too few escort vessels and a large area of the ocean was out of range of aircraft protection. Losses were heavy here also; during the first six months of 1942, 4.1 million tons of shipping were sunk, followed by 3.5 million during the next six months. The desperate situation changed in 1943 as large numbers of hastily built destroyer escorts, frigates, and corvettes became available, and with the advent of the escort carrier, which provided air cover in Mid-Atlantic. New weapons, intelligence, and tactics enabled the Allies to gain the upper hand. During April 1943, when over 400 U-boats were in service, the Germans lost 41 boats. The convoys bringing the troops and supplies needed for the assault on Europe were made safer.

Amphibious operations started in North Africa in November 1942, which initiated the Axis retreat. In July 1943 the invasion of Italy began with landings on the island of Sicily, followed by the first on the European continent at Salerno. These had the effect of knocking Italy out of the war, and the Italian fleet sailed to Malta to surrender. These landings set the stage for the greatest invasion in history on 6 June 1944 in Normandy: D-Day. Over 6,000 ships and craft of all sizes were involved in this historic enterprise. The extraordinary success of this operation firmly planted Allied troops on the mainland of Europe.

The sleepy Navy of the 1920s and 1930s, gradually letting go of the ships acquired during World War I, was transformed by the stirrings of conflict around the world. The London Treaty of 1930 redefined the sizes and capabilities of the various types of warships. After the economic disasters of 1929 to 1931, the new administration of Franklin D. Roosevelt commenced construction of new ships for the Navy, in part as an effort to provide work for the unemployed.

When James C. Fahey brought out his first edition of *Ships and Aircraft of the U.S. Fleet* in 1939, some of the ships destined to lead the Navy in the coming war were already listed. By 1941, in the second "Two-Ocean Fleet" edition, hundreds of new ships on order (part of Roosevelt's 1940 programs) appeared, including the *Alaska*, *Atlanta*, *Baltimore*, *Cleveland*, *Essex*, *Fletcher*, and *Iowa* classes, and the *Balao* and *Gato* classes of submarines, all of which became the backbone of the new Navy. This vast expansion was not limited to major combatant ships, but also included smaller patrol and mine vessels as well as dozens of auxiliary ships.

During the war, the industrial capacity of the United States was completely mobilized. We look at the maritime side of this mobilization, specifically the Navy and Coast Guard. Aside from the Navy-built ships, scores of merchant hulls were converted for use as auxiliaries, both as specialized types such as tenders and also as carriers of supplies and men. Specialized landing ships were developed—particularly the tank landing ship (LST), which was built in large numbers.

This fourth volume in the *U.S. Navy Warship Series* is an attempt to cover all the commissioned ships of the Navy during World War II. But despite the book's size, this still has not been possible, and numbers of smaller unnamed ships, although commissioned, have been omitted or listed in an abbreviated format. In particular, those excluded are the many small numbered craft, wood submarine chasers (SC and PCS), the motor minesweepers (YMS), the coastal minesweepers (AMc), the coastal yachts (PYc), motor torpedo boats (PT, PTC), smaller landing ships (LSM, LCI, LCS, LCT), the rescue tugs (ATR), the coastal transports (APc), and all district craft (designations beginning with Y), as well as Coast Guard patrol boats. It is hoped that providing a listing of these units will come at a later time. Lend-lease ships built for foreign navies are included where they were given U.S. Navy numbers.

The task of listing all these ships has been made easier by the Navy system of nomenclature and numbering. Finding the details of these ships has also been made easier by the vast literature available on the war and its ships, but also more difficult because of the vastness of it.

The majority of the pictures used in this book are official U.S. Navy photographs. Despite the number of photographs included, it has been impossible to illustrate every type and class. Changes made during the period are illustrated for major types but it has been necessary to eliminate many excellent photographs.

I appreciate greatly the assistance of Ernest Arroyo, Charles R. Haberlein, the late Martin Holbrook, William Jurens, Norman Polmar, William Rau, William A. Schell, the late Ted Stone, Chris Wright, and the resources of the Naval Photo Club, the Steamship Historical Society of America, the U.S. Navy History Division, the International Naval Research Organization, the U.S. Ship Cancellation Society, and the World Ship Society.

EXPLANATION OF DATA

The ships of the U.S. Navy for this period are listed according to the type of vessel as designated by the Navy. Combatant vessels are listed first, with auxiliaries following. Listings are also given for some other government departments, the Coast Guard, and the Coast and Geodetic Survey. In most cases, a ship is listed only once, under its initial classification, and later changes will be noted.

In this book, information for ships built or acquired before 1922 is provided only where it pertains to the period after that year. Full particulars and earlier history may be found in the third volume of this series.*

Particulars are given for each ship as follows.

Number. The official Navy number according to the official nomenclature.

Name. Navy name as completed with former names (naval or merchant) given below. Further changes of name, if any, are indicated in the Service Record, with new Navy names in **bold type**.

Builder. The builder's name, or the place where the ship was built (the latter in parentheses). The full name and location of most builders are given in appendix 4.

Construction Dates. For Navy-built ships, dates given are for laying down of keel, launching, and commissioning. For acquired vessels, dates given are date of launching, acquisition by Navy, and commissioning. If the ship was completed as converted or for a foreign navy, the date is in *italics*.

Tonnage. For Navy-built ships, tonnage is light displacement and/or full-load displacement. For acquired ships it is gross tonnage (GRT), actually a measurement of volume rather than weight.

Dimensions. Standard dimensions given in feet (') and inches (") are: length x beam x draft. Where known, length is specified as overall (oa); between perpendiculars (bp)—that is, between foreside of stem and aftside of rudder post; or on the waterline (wl). Where no type of length is given, registered dimensions are provided.

Machinery. Mode of propulsion, number of propellers, type and maker of engines, number and type of boilers (where known), and horsepower and speed are given. For submarines, the surface and submerged figures are separated by a slash (/).

Endurance. The maximum distance a ship could steam at the speed indicated.

Complement. Normal figure for officers and crew. For some ships, where sources vary, a range (50/75) is given. There was often a large variance in peacetime and wartime complements.

Armament. Original number and type of guns is given first. Later significant changes made are given with date, either by listing the entire complement of guns or by indicating modifications as additions or subtractions from the previous armament shown. The date reflects the date of survey rather than when changes were actually made. Minor variations are not necessarily given. Guns are described by size of bore (in inches) and caliber. For the Coast Guard, wartime armament is given.

Armor. Thickness of armor for the areas noted.

Notes. Additional information pertaining to design, construction, later modifications, or acquisition, or earlier historical notes of interest not included in other categories. In 1920 all Navy ships were assigned a type designation and number; changes are noted as *reclassified* ("Rec"). U.S. Maritime Commission ship type designations are given where applicable. These are divided into three parts. The first represents the type and size of ship, the second the propulsion system, and the third the design. The principal ship type designations are *C* (cargo), *P* (passenger), *N* (coastal cargo), *R* (refrigerator), *T* (tanker), *V* (tug), and *S* (special). The number following represents the size, with 1 being the smallest. The propulsion system is also represented by a letter, with *S* (steam), *D* (diesel), *SE* (turbo-electric); no number following indicates one screw. Liberty ships were prefixed with the letter *E*, and Victory ships with *V*.

* Paul H. Silverstone, *The New Navy, 1883–1922* (New York: Routledge, 2006.

Service Records. A capsule history of each ship's naval service showing assignment by station or squadron and war service including participation in engagements, major damage to vessel or loss. Casualties are given in parentheses. Changes in Navy name are given here in **bold type**, as are final disposition by the Navy, loss, sale, or transfer to another agency or a foreign country. The term *returned* means returned to previous owner—often the War Shipping Administration or the U.S. Maritime Commission. The wartime service of each ship is shown with the number of battle stars it was awarded (e.g., 2*). Actions listed are from the official listing of authorized operations and engagements. The number of battle stars awarded does not equal the number of operations listed because some operations are grouped in the official listings. Submarines received a battle star for each patrol in which a ship sinking was confirmed; surface ships received one for sinking a submarine. *USCG* indicates the ship was manned by the Coast Guard. For submarines, the number of wartime patrols is included.

Ships captured/sunk. Names and dates of merchant ships captured or sunk during the war. Some sinkings were credited to several ships acting together and so appear more than once. For submarines the listings are according to the latest and most authoritative sources. For ships captured by the Japanese, the former nationality and name is given. The numbers after the name indicate gross tonnage and year of build. For naval vessels the type symbol is included.

Most merchant types were returned to the U.S. Maritime Commission after being decommissioned or stricken, for later sale. Many of these were kept in laid up status for many years before being broken up. Some older ships were returned to their previous owners. The specific date for this return is not given here unless there is no other indication of the ship's disposition. The term "sold" covers a sale and all forms of transfer, including to the Martime Commission or War Shipping Agency. A number of smaller vessels were sold into commercial service but their later identities are unknown.

Later history. Brief details of the ship's career after leaving Naval service given include later merchant names and service in other government departments or in foreign navies. Ultimate fate is given where known, or the year the ship disappeared from shipping registers (RR) or was sold to foreign buyers (S/F). Occasionally a date is given for the last published reference (se = still existing). The symbol † indicates that a continuation of the ship's history after 1946 may be found in the next volume.[†]

Some vessels were used as Q-ships, a carryover from World War I, in which an armed ship was disguised as a harmless merchant ship to lure an unsuspecting submarine to surface. This tactic was not very successful in World War II.

† Paul H. Silverstone, *The Navy of the Nuclear Age, 1947–2007* (New York: Routledge, in press).

Pennsylvania (BB 38) and *New Mexico* (BB 40) at a Pacific base, 31 Oct 1943.

ABBREVIATIONS

†	(dagger) see next volume
★	battle stars (with number)
	ship sunk in joint attack with other agents
+	probable sinking (submarines)
#	possible sinking (submarines)
§	question on sinking (submarines)
AA	antiaircraft
acq	acquired
AC	Allis-Chalmers
ASW	Anti-submarine warfare
B&W	Babcock and Wilcox
bbl	barrels
bp	length between perpendiculars
b/r	blockade runner
BS	Busch-Sulzer
BU	broken up
canc	canceled
CB	Cooper Bessemer
CE	Combustion engineering (boilers)
comm	commision, commissioned
CT	conning tower
CTL	constructive total loss
d/e	double-ended (boilers)
decomm	decommissioned
DET	diesel-electric tandem motor drive (DE)
DP	Dual purpose
DUKW	An amphibious truck
F&WS	U.S. Fish and Wildlife Service
f/l	full load
FFU	further fate unknown
FM	Fairbanks Morse
FMR	Fairbanks Morse diesel reverse gear drive (DE)
FW	Foster Wheeler
GE	General Electric
GMT	Diesel-electric tandem motor drive, short hull (DE)
grt	gross registered tonnage
GT	geared turbines
HF/DF	high frequency direction finder ("huff-duff")
HMCS	His Majesty's Canadian Ship
HMS	His Majesty's Ship
HP	High pressure
IHP	Indicated horse power
L	launched
LD	laid down
LP	Low pressure
Marad	US Maritime Administration
MG	Machine guns
m/v	merchant ship
MC	US Maritime Commission
mod(s)	modification(s)
MTB	motor torpedo boat
ND	naval district
NN	Newport News
NOB	Naval operating base
NOTS	Naval Overseas Transportation Service (WWI)
NRT	Naval reserve training
NYd	Navy yard
oa	length overall
o/s	out of service
pdr	pounder
PRC	People's Republic of China
PUC	Presidential Unit Citation
R (year)	stricken from foreign navy
reacq	reacquired
RCN	Royal Canadian Navy
rec	reclassified, reclassification
recomm	recommissioned
RN	Royal Navy
RR(year)	removed from merchant register
RS	Receiving ship

SCAJAP	Shipping Control Administration, Japan
schr	schooner
se	still existing
s/e	single-ended (boiler)
SF	Sea Frontier
S/F	sold to foreign buyers
SHP	shaft horsepower
SP	Section patrol (USN designation WWI)
sqn	squadron
ST	Steam turbines
TB	Torpedo boat
TE	Turbine electric drive
TEV	Turbine electric drive, 5" guns (DE)
TF	task force
TG	task group
tkr	tanker
TT	torpedo tubes
trfd	transferred
TS	Training ship
(U)	unknown
USA	U.S. Army
USAHS	U.S. Army hospital ship
USAT	U.S. Army transport
USC&GS	U.S. Coast and Geodetic Survey
USCG	U.S. Coast Guard
USCGC	U.S. Coast Guard cutter
USLHS	U.S. Lighthouse Service
USMG	U.S. Military Government
USSB	U.S. Shipping Board
VQE	vertical quadruple expansion
VTE	vertical triple expansion
West.	Westinghouse
W-F	White-Forster
WGT	Westinghouse geared turbine drive (DE)
wl	length on waterline
WSA	War Shipping Administration
XCL	auxiliary cruiser
XPG	converted gunboat

U.S. NAVAL ORDNANCE, 1922–1947

W. J. Jurens

INTRODUCTION

The interval between the two world wars represented the last period when the gun was king, while the subsequent employment of "invisible" ordnance such as radar, coupled with the introduction of missiles whose geometric characteristics often revealed relatively little regarding their capabilities, also marked this as the last era when "counting guns" represented even an approximate measure of the offensive capability of a warship. Although disarmament treaties greatly restricted production during the 1920s and 30s, the sheer quantity of ordnance developed and delivered later was unprecedented; the aggregate gunpower of the fleet increased by more than an order of magnitude between 1940 and 1945 alone. By the end of World War II, U.S. Navy ships mounted almost 89,000 gun assemblies, ranging from 0.30 caliber machine guns to the massive 16"/50 triple turrets mounted on the Iowa class battleships. This, combined with the 48,446 antiaircraft and dual-purpose guns mounted on merchant vessels, meant that by 1945 the fleet could, at least in theory, deliver some 18,000 tons of projectiles per minute. By war's end this rate of delivery could, probably, be equaled—though perhaps not sustained—by naval aircraft as well.

The World War II ordnance cornucopia produced a multitude of variant and experimental weapons. Fortunately, the demands of mass production, and the recognition that quantity has a quality all its own, kept the variety of widely deployed weapons relatively small. Even so, the sheer number of items produced precludes comprehensive listings and necessitates both the generalization of tabular values and the complete omission of many weapons of lesser importance, especially those not completed before the end of the war.

William J. Jurens

GUNS

Although many guns—for example, the 3"/50 used on small combatants—were carryovers from or represented only slight variations on guns developed during World War I, a large number of new guns were developed between the wars and during hositilities.

A new low-velocity 86-ton 16"/45, adopted to save weight in treaty limited ships, was designed in 1937. After design errors rendered plans to reuse leftover 128-ton 16"/50 caliber weapons from scrapped and abandoned vessels impracticable, a new 107-ton 16"/50 type, Mk7, was developed for the Iowa class. Curiously, the older 16"/45, though of lesser maximum range, tended to be a slightly more accurate weapon, and—because of the higher trajectory required to reach any given range—was probably a better deck penetrator. The development of 14" guns—a caliber that the Navy found rather disappointing—was largely neglected after 1920. A new and unusually accurate 12"/50 gun was designed for service aboard the Alaska-class cruisers in 1939, entering service in 1944.

Progress with cruiser-caliber guns primarily revolved around improvements in ammunition handling and loading. A new 8" gun was designed about 1922, entering service on the treaty class cruisers in the 1930s. The 8" Mks 12 and 15, designed about 1933, were much lighter in weight than their predecessors and saw service on post-treaty and war-built units. Light cruisers got new guns as well; a new and very successful 6"/47 Mk 16, designed around 1932, went into service on the Brooklyn class in 1937. A dual-purpose version with greatly enhanced ammunition handling capability entered service on the Worcester class a decade later.

Perhaps the most notable new gun designed between the wars was the 5"/38, a near-perfect dual-purpose amalgam of the 5"/51 surface weapon and the 5"/25 antiaircraft gun. The 5"/38 first appeared as a single mount on the Farragut-class destroyers in 1934, with a twin mount appearing three years later. More than 8,000 of these guns, in an assortment of closely related models, were manufactured during World War II alone, with some surviving in use until the turn of the twenty-first century. A new 5"/54 mount, intended for the Midway-class aircraft carriers and the Montana-class battleships, was introduced in April 1945, too late to see war service.

The Navy began development of a new short-range antiaircraft mount in the 1930s. The resulting 1.1" quad mount, intended to bridge the gap between 3" and 5" antiaircraft fire and the "last-ditch" fire of 0.50 caliber machine guns, proved unpopular in service, and it was replaced—at least aboard front-line units—with single, twin, and quad versions of the new Swedish-designed 40-mm Bofors mounts in 1942–43. Similarly, the Swiss-designed 20-mm Oerlikon replaced 0.50 caliber machine guns after 1942.

The production of new designs did not preclude the continued and expanded production of older guns, most of which have been described in previous volumes. Quantities were large; the Navy produced more than 6,500 "old" 3"/50s in 1943 alone.

PROPELLANTS

The United States continued to use single-base ("pyro") propellant formulations throughout this period. Basic propellant chemistry remained unchanged, with most work concentrating on the possibility of removing or reducing flash, which could blind firing crews engaged in firing at night. Although efforts to suppress flash during the 1920s were accompanied by unacceptable increases in smoke, the introduction of a "flashless pellet" that could be added to the propellant charges allowed guns under 6" caliber to operate in flashless mode after 1942. Later, the pellets were blended right into the grains.

Introducing flashless powder into bigger guns took longer. After much experimentation, the Navy's Bureau of Ordnance (BuOrd) finally concluded that effective flash reduction in guns larger than 8" would require adopting a formulation similar to British Cordite-N, an idea that—due to the perceived volatility of cordite—caused some consternation in the fleet when it was suggested late in the war. In fact, BuOrd's solution, type SPGC, a triple-base propellant containing 19 percent nitroglycerine and more than 50 percent nitroguanidine, turned out to be more stable than the old double-base SPD and SPDN propellants it was intended to replace. Introduced in 1944, type SPGC did not see widespread service before the end of the war.

PROJECTILES

As they had been previously, projectiles were generally manufactured in three major types: armor-piercing, common, and high-capacity, each type containing proportionately more explosive filling than the previous. The general trend of projectile design during this period was toward the production of longer, and hence heavier, projectiles. Increasing projectile weight tended to drop initial velocities, increase accuracy, and improve deck penetration, all with little cost in gun erosion. Thus, during this period, the 16" armor piercing bullet—representative of many others—went from 2,100 pounds to 2,240 pounds, and then to 2700 pounds in its final incarnation, and the 8" armor piercing bullet was seen in both 260-pound and 335-pound versions. The basic design of armor piercing bullets changed only slightly over the period, although—insofar as individual manufacturers generally produced designs to their own specifications—a great many more-or-less interchangeable versions were produced. Probably the greatest advances in armor-piercing projectile design lay in improved fuze technology, where substantive improvements in reliability and flexibility were achieved.

The greatest advances in the design of common and antiaircraft projectiles also lay in the installation of better fuzes, in this case radio-controlled proximity fuzes that provided an order-of-magnitude improvement in antiaircraft efficiency. Old-style -fuzes continued to be manufactured long after proximity fuzes were common; for a long time it was forbidden—or at least considered undesirable—to fire proximity-fuzed projectiles over land, lest samples fall into the hands of the enemy. Further, although a triggered fuzed shell was often lethal, projectiles that missed their targets did not explode, and thus gave little sense of their possibly incorrect trajectories. For that reason, the smoke puffs of old-style time-fuzed projectiles remained useful to point out gross errors in target designation or fire control.

ARMOR

The production and design of face-hardened and homogeneous armors had reached maturity by the early 1930s, and armor manufactured in 1945 was essentially identical to that produced in 1922. The huge demands of war production, especially following a prolonged period of more-or-less profound neglect of the armor production industry during the "battleship holiday" of the 1920s and 1930s, placed great strain on armor production facilities which often ran on "24/7" production schedules throughout the war. Although quality generally remained high, in a few cases armor slightly under nominal specifications, though by no means inadequate, was accepted in order to avoid delaying the completion of ships on the ways. The possibility of substituting cast armor for forged armor was pursued throughout the war, and although success was eventually achieved, it came too late for application during hostilities. Progress in fuzing a hard face to a ductile back—a revision to a technique abandoned some 40 years earlier—permitted the production of face-hardened plates less than an inch thick by 1944, but these also arrived too late to see combat.

ROCKETS

Although rockets had long been employed in support roles (e.g., for signalling and in line guns), their application to weapons did not commence until about 1940. Although early work concentrated on using rockets to increase the striking velocity of bombs, it was soon found that merely adding an equivalent weight of high explosive had equal or more desirable effects, and these programs were soon dropped. The development of 4.2" rocket motors for "Mousetrap," the diminutive version of the "Hedgehog" antisubmarine device, proved more promising, with production reaching 30,000 units per month midwar, dropping off thereafter as other weapons—and changes in antisubmarine tactics—took over. Serious development of a forward-firing aircraft mounted rocket—initially seen as an antisubmarine weapon—commenced about 1943 but proceeded relatively slowly thereafter. By 1944 a 3.5"-diameter solid-fuel rocket had been developed that could disable a submarine 60 feet below the surface. This weapon, which also turned out to be effective against light armor, personnel, and shipping, was augmented by a 5"-diameter version, in August 1944. "Tiny Tim," an 11.5"-diameter 1,300-pound monster, arrived early in 1945, but was rarely employed in action.

A good deal of work also revolved around the development of so-called "barrage rockets", which could be launched from light landing craft in support of amphibious operations. The most popular version, which employed a 2.25" "mousetrap" motor to propel a 4.5" diameter 20 lb general purpose bomb to a range of 1,100 yards was available in time for the invasion of North Africa in 1942. Expenditures were enormous; production numbers exceeded 500,000 in 1944 alone. Spin-stabilized versions of this weapon eventually reached ranges of 5,000 yards

TORPEDOES, MINES, AND DEPTH CHARGES

The Navy deployed three major torpedo types prior to the war: one for surface ships, one for submarines, and one for aircraft. The Mk 15, a derivative of the earlier Mk 11, was deployed on surface ships and was a rugged and fairly reliable performer. Submarines deployed Mks 10, 14, and 18, the latter an electric torpedo based loosely on the German G7e. Aircraft generally deployed variants of Mk 13. Problems with defective exploders and unreliable control mechanisms were not corrected until 1943, a fiasco that robbed the Americans of many valuable targets.

Many special torpedoes were produced in lesser quantities.. Mk 24 "Fido," initially classified as a mine for security purposes—and possibly because the mine branch was more familiar with relevant technologies—was an air-launched acoustic homer primarily used against U-boats. Mk 27 "Cutie," essentially an enlarged "Fido," was a submarine-launched swim-out version used against surface ships—primarily escorts.

The United States entered the war with relatively large inventories of conventional Mk 3, 4, 6, and 7 "ash can" type depth charges. Most war-work concentrated on making new (and old) charges sink straighter and faster, and on improving fuzing. The 420 lb Mk 6, in production until mid-1944, was the most popular weapon, sinking at 8–12' per second, and carrying a 300-pound charge to 600'. The larger Mk 7 carried a 600-pound charge. The aluminum-cased 520-pound Mk 8, which entered service in mid-1944, was dimensionally similar to the Mk 6; but unreliable magnetic proximity fuzes resulted in its quick withdrawal. Mk 9, a 340-pound teardrop-shaped weapon with a 200-pound charge, sank at up to 20' per second but was rendered unnecessary by the amazing success of "Hedgehog", which also killed off depth charges Mk 11 and Mk 12. In order to maintain interchangeability, most depth charges ended up at about 18" in diameter by about 28" in length. Initially aircraft deployed with slightly modified surface ship charges, later carrying the specially designed Mk 17, a 325-pound, 15"-diameter weapon carrying a 234-pound charge. Mk 10, perhaps the most interesting innovation, was a two-gallon paint can that carried 25 pounds of explosive. Introduced in 1943, it was primarily intended for disposition in harbors.

Ahead-thrown weapons were developed as well, the most important being "Hedgehog", an adaptation of a British spigot mortar. The Hedgehog Mk 10 projected 24 charges in an elliptical pattern 280 yards ahead of the hunting ship; the Mk 11 had slightly lesser range and fired a circular pattern instead. Excessively large recoil forces with Hedgehog spurred development of the diminutive Mk 20 "Mousetrap", which used rockets to propel four—and in the Mk 22, sixteen—charges to similar distances. Both Hedgehog and Mousetrap fired 65-pound contact-fuzed projectiles carrying about 35 pounds of explosive, and sinking at about 22 feet per second. Both weapons debuted in 1943.

At the beginning of World War II, most mines in inventory were variants of the old spherical 1,400-pound Mk 6, left over from World War I. Moored mines included the 1,760-pound Mk 10, designed between the wars for delivery by submarines and carrying a 300-pound charge -- later versions carried 420-pound charges and could be dropped by aircraft and PT boats as well. The Mk 11, designed for the submarine Argonaut, was never deployed in combat; Mk 10s were used instead. The Mk 23 was a small surface-laid moored weapon with a two-pound charge designed to cut sweep cables. Mk 7, a variant of the Mk 6, carried a 500-pound charge, and was designed to drift at about 35 feet.

Ground mines included the magnetically fired Mk 12, which weighed between 1,390 and 1,700 pounds and carried 1,060 to 1,200 pounds of TNT or Torpex. Mods 1 and 4, designed for aircraft delivery, were rarely used and Mod 2 for surface ships was not used at all. Mod 3 was deployed by submarines. The Mine Mk 13, which looked like a 1,000-pound bomb, carried a 375-pound charge; Mod 1 was for depths up to 60 feet, Mod 4 was for shallower depths, and Mod 5—the "odd man out"—was acoustically rather than magnetically activated. The Mk 18, laid by surface ships, carried a 1,300-pound charge. The Mk 25, laid by aircraft, carried an 1,100-pound charge. The Mk 36 Mod 1 was a small mine designed for aircraft, carrying a 475-pound charge. The Mk 36, also for aircraft delivery, carried a 600-pound charge.

FIRE CONTROL

Fire Control

The Navy developed a very large number of gun directors during the period of interest, the most notable being the dual-purpose Mk 37, designed to control 5" guns; the Mk 34, which controlled 6" and 8" guns aboard cruisers; and Mk 38, which controlled the main batteries of the new 'fast battleships' and the rebuilt Pearl Harbor veterans. Most of the larger units required a crew of about seven. Pre-war directors were originally designed as optical-only devices, but radar control was added as soon as it became available. Directors Mk 51 and Mk 52 controlled smaller guns on destroyer escorts. Light antiaircraft batteries—that is, 1.1", 20-mm, and 40-mm guns—were most often controlled via one-man units such as the Mk 14 and Mk 51.

Radar, almost unknown prior to 1941, was ubiquitous by 1945. The Navy's Bureau of Ships tended to control search and navigational radars—which are not discussed here—while the Bureau of Ordnance controlled fire-control radars. Serious work on fire-control gear, which required equipment that could operate at wavelengths of 10cm or less, i.e., at frequencies exceeding 3 GHz, began in 1940. The first really effective surface fire-control unit, Mk 3, introduced late in 1941 and used with great success in the Solomon Islands, was a main-battery director that could spot 16" salvos out to about 20,000 yards. Mk 8, with better electronics and a much more useful display, superceded Mk 3 in 1942–43. In 1945, the by-then-venerable Mk 8 was in turn replaced by the Mk 13, which could spot 16" splashes past the maximum range of the guns. The Mk 26 was used on smaller ships; 40-mm mounts were generally controlled via the gun director Mk 51, a one-man hand-operated item using the gunsight Mk 14.

Antiaircraft fire-control radars needed to measure altitude as well as range and bearing. Mk 4, basically an enhanced Mk 3, entered service in 1941. Radar Mk 12, the only other unit in widespread use, was introduced in 1944. Unfortunately, neither unit was particularly good at dealing with low-flying aircraft, which—as operations off Okinawa showed—remained a threat throughout the war.

Although radar's uncanny ability to measure ranges accurately led to spectacular improvements in gunfire accuracy, radar was (and to some extent remains) inherently poor at target identification, target designation, and spotting in deflection. For those reasons, optical spotting and observation remained critically important throughout the war. In contrast, aircraft spotting, with the possible exception of spotting for shore bombardment and target practices, did not. Operational experience, the presence of more versatile carrier-based aircraft, and the advent of radar ranging generally rendered aircraft spotters obsolete, with the result being that battleship and cruiser-borne aircraft were little employed for spotting after 1943. Attempts to mount spotting and/or scouting aircraft aboard destroyers were entirely unsuccessful.

About 35 sonar types, both active and passive, were developed between the wars for installation on surface ships, submarines, and ashore. Installations of active sonars began about 1934, and most early units were delivered in relatively small quantities. Anti-submarine sonars between the wars were rudimentary by current standards, with detection ranges below 1,000 yards. Most active units were installed on destroyers and smaller vessels; experimental installations on most cruisers were removed prewar. Early war plans called for mounting two units per ship, but production problems meant that most ended up with only one. Smaller ships typically mounted a variant of type QB, while older destroyers got some model of QC or (later) QGB. The Sumner/Gearings mounted type QGA.

AIRCRAFT

Aircraft development during this period was extremely rapid, with few types remaining in service more than six or seven years. As with ships, the general trend lay toward fewer units, each of increased size and capability. The Navy entered the war with the relatively crude TBD "Devastator" torpedo bomber in front-line service, replaced in mid-1942 with the much larger TBM/TBF "Avenger." The most popular—or at least the most used—fighter early in the war was the Grumman F4F "Wildcat," which was quickly replaced by the larger F6F "Hellcat" in 1943–44. The much-admired (and very effective) SBD "Dauntless" dive bomber was obsolescent by midwar and phased out by the larger (and by most accounts less popular) SB2C "Helldiver." Marine units ashore often used variants of the F4U "Corsair" fighter, but these proved to be quite difficult to handle at sea and they were rarely employed aboard carriers before 1944.

Most aircraft were equipped with 0.50-caliber machine guns augmented by a medley of "dumb bombs" or torpedoes, as appropriate. Guided weapons were also used. "Pelican," a rudimentary (and ultimately unsuccessful) guided bomb that homed on reflected radio signals, was developed in 1942 to fight U-boats. "Gargoyle," a joystick-controlled glide bomb inspired by the German HS-293, was still in development at the end of the war. The most successful unit was "Bat," a 1,600-pound radar-controlled "fire-and-forget smart bomb" deployed in May 1945. Dropped from a PB4Y "Privateer"—essentially a naval version of the B-24 bomber—and equipped with an active radar homing system, Bat could carry a 1,000-pound warhead 10 to 15 miles.

From 1923 through 1935 the Navy operated a small number of enormous rigid airships, primarily as long range high speed scouts. These proved too fragile to operate in heavy weather, and all were gone—most destroyed in crashes—by 1935. During the war, the Navy deployed more than 100 non-rigid "K" type blimps, primarily on antisubmarine patrol.

William J. Jurens
Associate Editor and Staff Draftsman
Journal *Warship International*

William J. Jurens has been an associate editor and staff draftsman for the journal Warship International since 1986, and is a Silver Member of the United States Naval Institute. He has been a member of the Society of Naval Architects and Marine Engineers Marine Forensics Panel (SD-7) since 1995, and has published several papers on the loss and wreck examination of various warships, including "The Loss of HMS Hood—A Re-examination" (1987), and "A Marine Forensic Analysis of HMS Hood and DKM Bismarck" (2002). He has, to date, acted as a consultant and contributor in the production of four television programs concerning the loss of HMS Hood, DKM Bismarck, and the British battle cruisers sunk at Jutland, and participated in the investigation into the explosion aboard the USS Iowa in 1989. He has also published a number of papers on ordnance and ballistics, most notably "The Evolution of Battleship Gunnery in the U.S. Navy, 1920–1945" (1991). He regularly collaborates with well-known authors on the production of full-length books dealing with historical naval technology. Jurens currently teaches engineering graphics at Winnipeg Technical College in Winnipeg, Manitoba.

Table 1 U.S. Navy Guns, 1922–1945

Gun	Weight (lbs)	Length (inches)	Initial Velocity (ft/sec)	Projectile Weight (lbs)	Charge Weight (lbs)	Range (yds) at Elevation (deg)
16"/50 Mk 7	267,900	816	2,690	1,900 HC	664	41,600@45
			2,500	2,700 AP	664	42,350@45
16"/45 Mk 6	192,300	736	2,625	1,900 HC2,	544	40,180@45
			2,520	2,240 AP	544	40,200@45
			2,300	2,700 AP	544	36,900@45
8"/55 Mk 9, 10, 11, 13, 14	67,200	449	2,800	260 HE	90	31,860@41
			2,800	260 AP	90	31,860@41
8"/55 Mk 12, 15	38,500	449	2,700	260 HE	86	29,800@41
			2,500	335 AP	86	30,050@41
6"/47 Mk 16	9,632	232.3	2,500	130 AP	32	26,100@47
			2,800	105 HE	32	23,500@47
5"/38 Mk 12	7,170	224.0	2,500	55.0	15.5	17,300@45
5"/54 Mk 16	5,360	249.0	2,650	69.3	18.5	25,800@45
1.1"/75	750	119.6	2,650	0.91	0.27	c. 7,800@45
40mm/56	1,150	98.4	2,890	2.00	0.70	c.10,500@45
20mm/70	150	87	2,750	0.27	0.06	c. 4,800@45
0.50 cal. machine gun	c. 90	c. 63	2,850	0.11	0.03	c. 7,500@45

Notes: "HC" = high capacity; "AP" = armor piercing; "HE" = high explosive. The 0.50 caliber machine gun was produced in both air-cooled and water-cooled versions, with slightly different metrics. Most of the smaller weapons (e.g., the antiaircraft guns) could (and did) fire a fairly wide assortment of fixed rounds, and tabular values have been rounded. AA ceilings were about 19,000' for the 1.1", 22,300' for the 40 mm, 10,000' for the 20 mm, and (at least theoretically) 15,000' for the 20 min, and (at least theoretically) 15,000' for the 0.50. The 5/38" could reach 37,000 feet.

Table 2 U.S. Navy Torpedoes, 1922–1945

Model	Diameter (inches)	Length (inches)	Weight (lbs)	Charge Weight (lbs)	Speed (knts) at Range (yds)	"In Use" Dates
Mk13 (aircraft)	22.5	161	2,216	600	6,300@33.5	1936–1950
Mk 14 (submarine)	21.0	246	3,209	643	9,000@31	1931–1980
					4,500@46	
Mk 15 (surface)	21.0	288	3,841	825	15,000@26	1935–1975
					10,000@33	
					60,00@45	
Mk18 (submarine)	21.0	245	3,154	575	4,000@29	1943–1950
Mk 23 (submarine)	21.0	246	3,209	643	4,500@46	1931–1980
Mk 24 "Fido"(aircraft)	19.0	84	680	92	4,000@12	1942–1948
Mk 27 "Cutie"(submarine)	19.0	90	720	95	5,000@12	1943–1946

Notes: Weapons are listed by Mark number. Missing Mark numbers represent unsuccessful weapons or weapons that did not see extensive service. The Mk 23 was the Mk 14 with the low-speed setting omitted. World War II production of major weapons totaled 63,900: 17,000 Mk 13s, 13,000 Mk 14s, 9,700 Mk 15s, 9,600 Mk 18s, 9,600 Mk 23s, 4,000 Mk 24s, and 1,000 Mk 27s. Robert Gannon's "Hellions of the Deep" covers the development of homing weapons in detail.

Table 3 U.S. Navy Aircraft 1922–1945

Name	Type	Number Procured	Gross Weght (lbs)	Span (ft) Length (ft)	Range (naut. miles)	Speed (knots)	Dates in use
Grumman F2F	Fighter	56	3,847	28' 6" 21' 5"	850	200	1935–1940
Grumman F3F	Fighter	164	4,795	32' 0" 23' 2"	850	230	1936–1941
Grumman F4F "Wildcat"	Fighter	7,899	8,000	38' 0" 28' 9"	725	285	1940–1945
Grumman F6F "Hellcat"	Fighter	12,275	15,500	42' 10" 33' 7"	1,100	330	1943–1953
Chance-Vought F4U "Corsair"	Fighter	12,570	14,250	41' 0" 33' 4"	1,515	390	1942–1955
Douglas SBD "Dauntless"	Dive Bomber	5,376	10,900	41' 6" 33' 0"	950	212	1939–1945
Curtiss SB2C "Helldiver"	Dive Bomber	6,650	16,600	49' 9 "36' 8"	1,000	250	1942–1950
Douglas TBD "Devastator"	Torpedo Bomber	130	10,200	50' 0" 35' 0"	620	180	1936–1942
Grumman TBF/ TBM "Avenger"	Torpedo Bomber	9,836	16,500	54' 2" 41' 0"	955	239	1942–1954
Curtiss SOC 'Seagull"	Scout-observation	303	5,437	36' 0" 31' 5"	590	147	1935–1946
Curtiss SBC "Helldiver"	Fighter	257	7,632	34' 0" 28' 4"	535	205	1937–1942
Consolidated PBY "Catalina"	Flying Boat	3,062	28,400–35,500	104' 0" 63' 10"	1,830–2,600	155	1936–1949
SWOD Mk 9 "Bat"	"Smart Bomb"	Unknown	1,600	11' 11" 10' 0"	12.5	Unknown	1945–1947
ZR-1 "Shenandoah"	Airship	1	0	680' 2" 78' 9"	3,980	51	1923–1925
ZR-3 "Los Angeles"	Airship	1	0	658' 4" 104' 5"	5,770	65	1924–1939
ZRS-4, ZRS-5 "Akron," "Macon"	Airship	2	0	785' 0" 132' 9"	5,940	76	1931–1935
Type K	Airship	133	0	251' 8" 61' 6"	2,000	67	1939–1955

Notes: Only the most significant types are listed. Aircraft primarily produced for other services (e.g., the B-24, which was the PB4Y in Navy service) are omitted. Airships, being lighter than air, have been assigned a nominal weight of zero. Particularly during World War II, many aircraft models went through five or six model changes, and were produced by a number of manufacturers, so minor variations were common. Dates of withdrawal from service are approximate. The best general reference is Swanborough and Bowers, *United States Navy Aircraft since 1911*, in various editions; the Naval Historical Center Web site contains valuable information as well.

CHRONOLOGY 1922–1947

1922	Feb 6	Washington Naval Treaty signed
	Mar 20	*Langley*, first aircraft carrier, commissioned
1925	May 6	Marines land in Nicaragua (withdrawn Jan 1933)
1930	Apr 22	London Naval Treaty signed
1934	Aug 15	Last Marines withdrawn from Haiti
1936	Sep 18	Squadron sent to Spain to evacuate United States nationals
1937	Dec 13	USS *Panay* sunk by Japanese aircraft in China
1939	Sep 1	World War II begins; Germany invades Poland
	Sep 6	Neutrality Patrol established
1940	Sep 3	"Destroyer for bases" agreement with Britain
1941	Mar 11	Lend-Lease Act effective; Atlantic Charter meeting
	Jul 7	U.S. forces land in Iceland
	Sep 4	USS *Greer* attacked by German submarine
	Sep 27	First Liberty Ship, *Patrick Henry*, launched
	Oct 17	USS *Kearny* torpedoed by German submarine
	Oct 31	USS *Reuben James* sunk by German submarine
	Nov 1	Coast Guard placed under Navy control
	Nov 5	Six U.S. transports (Convoy WS-12x) sail from Halifax, N.S., carrying British troops to Singapore
	Nov 14	U.S. Marines ordered to leave China
	Dec 7	Japanese attack on Pearl Harbor
	Dec 8	U.S. Naval forces commence departure from the Philippines
	Dec 10	Guam surrenders; Japanese land in Luzon and Malaya
	Dec 11	Germany and Italy declare war on the United States
	Dec 23	Wake Island surrenders; Japanese land in Borneo
	Dec 25	Hong Kong surrenders
1942	Jan 2	Japanese capture Manila
	Jan 11	Japan declares war on the Netherlands
	Jan 16	Japanese invade Burma
	Jan 23	Japanese occupy Rabaul and Bougainville
	Jan 24	Battle of Makassar Strait
	Feb 9	USS *Lafayette* (ex–*Normandie*) burns in New York
	Feb 15	Singapore surrenders
	Feb 19	Japanese carrier raid on Darwin, Australia; Japanese land on Bali; Battle of Badoeng Strait
	Feb 27	Battle of the Java Sea
	Mar 30	Pacific divided into separate commands under Nimitz and MacArthur
	Apr 9	U.S. forces on Bataan surrender

	Apr 18	Doolittle raid on Tokyo
	May 4–8	Battle of the Coral Sea
	May 6	Corregidor surrenders
	Jun 2	Japanese strike Alaska
	Jun 2–6	Battle of Midway
	Jul 21	Japanese land at Buna, New Guinea
	Aug 7	U.S. forces land on Guadalcanal
	Aug 9	Battle of Savo Island
	Aug 23	Battle of the Eastern Solomons
	Oct 12	Battle of Cape Esperance
	Oct 26	Battle of Santa Cruz
	Nov 8	Allied landings in Morocco and Algeria
	Nov 12–15	Battle of Guadalcanal
	Nov 30	Battle of Tassafaronga
1943	Jan 29	Battle of Rennell Island
	Feb 2	Battle of the Bismarck Sea
	Feb 9	End of land action on Guadalcanal
	Mar 26	Battle of the Komandorski Islands
	Apr 18	Admiral Yamamoto killed
	May 11	Landings on Attu
	Jun 30	Landings on Rendova Island
	Jul 6	Battle of Kula Gulf
	Jul 10	Landings in Sicily
	Jul 13	Battle of Kolombangara
	Jul 28	Japanese evacuate Kiska
	Aug 15	Landings on Vella Lavella
	Sep 9	Landings at Salerno, Italy
	Sep 11	Italian fleet surrenders at Malta
	Oct 6	Battle of Vella Lavella
	Nov 1	Landing at Cape Torokina, Bougainville
	Nov 2	Battle of Empress Augusta Bay
	Nov 19	Landings in Gilbert Islands, Tarawa and Makin
	Nov 23	Battle of Cape St. George, Bougainville
	Dec 15	Landings at Arawe, New Britain
	Dec 26	Landings at Cape Gloucester, New Britain
1944	Jan 2	Landings at Saidor, New Guinea
	Jan 22	Landings at Anzio, Italy
	Feb 1	Landings on Kwajalein, Marshall Islands
	Feb 17	Carrier attack on Truk, Caroline Islands
	Feb 19	Landings on Eniwetok, Marshall Islands
	Feb 23	Carrier attack on Saipan, Tinian, Guam, Mariana Islands
	Feb 29	Landings on Admiralty Islands
	Mar 30	Carrier attack on Palau and Yap, Caroline Islands
	Apr 19	Carrier attack on Sabang, Sumatra
	Apr 21	Landings at Aitape, New Guinea
	May 17	Landings at Wakde, Dutch New Guinea
	May 27	Landings on Biak Island, Dutch New Guinea
	Jun 4	German submarine *U-505* captured at sea by U.S. forces
	Jun 6	Landings in Normandy (D-Day)
	Jun 15	Landings on Saipan (through 9 Jul)
	Jun 19	Battle of the Philippine Sea
	Jul 2	Landings on Noemfoor Island
	Jul 21	Landings on Guam (through 10 Aug)
	Jul 24	Landings on Tinian (through 1 Aug)
	Aug 4	Carrier attack on Bonin Islands
	Aug 15	Landings in Southern France
	Sep 15	Landings on Morotai Island; landings on Peleliu Island, Palau (through 27 Dec)
	Sep 23	Landings on Ulithi Island, which became the main forward Pacific base
	Oct 10	Carrier strike on Okinawa and Ryukyu Islands

	Oct 12	Carrier strike on Formosa
	Oct 20	Landings on Leyte, Philippines
	Oct 24–26	Battle of Leyte Gulf; Battle of Surigao Strait; Battle off Samar; Battle of Cape Engaño
	Dec 7	Landings at Ormoc Bay, Leyte
	Dec 15	Landings on Mindoro
	Dec 18	Major typhoon hits Third Fleet
1945	Jan 3–22	Carrier strikes on Formosa, Ryukyus, Luzon, Saigon, Hong Kong
	Jan 9	Landings at Lingayen, Luzon
	Feb 16	Landings on Corregidor
	Feb 16–1 Mar	Carrier strikes on Tokyo area, Japan
	Feb 19	Landings on Iwo Jima (through 16 Mar)
	Mar 18–22	Carrier strikes on Kyushu Island, Japan
	Mar 23	Carrier strikes and bombardments commence on Okinawa
	Apr 1	Landings on Okinawa (through 21 Jun)
	Apr 7	Abortive attack by Japanese force led by battleship *Yamato*
	Apr 11	Death of President Franklin Delano Roosevelt
	Apr 30	Death of Adolf Hitler
	May 1	Landings at Tarakan, Borneo
	May 7	Germany surrenders
	Jun 10	Landings at Brunei, Borneo
	Jul 1	Landings at Balikpapan, Borneo
	Jul 10–Aug 15	Carrier strikes on Japan
	Aug 6	First atomic bomb dropped on Hiroshima
	Aug 9	Second atomic bomb dropped on Nagasaki
	Aug 15	Japan surrenders
	Sep 2	Surrender ceremony on USS *Missouri* in Tokyo Bay
1946	Jul 1	First atomic bomb test at Bikini (Able)
	Jul 26	Second atomic bomb test at Bikini (Baker)
1947	Jan–Mar	Operation High Jump, Antarctica
	May 1	Submarine *Cusk* launches first guided missile

A fast carrier task force at anchor in Majuro Lagoon. At left forward is an *Independence*-class light carrier, *Enterprise* at right, and four *Essex* class carriers. At left is a *South Dakota*-class battleship, and behind is an *Iowa*-class battleship.

DISPOSITION OF COMBATANT SHIPS, 7 DECEMBER 1941

ATLANTIC OCEAN—U.S. EAST COAST

Casco Bay, Me.: BB *Arkansas, Texas*
Portland, Me.: BB *North Carolina*
Portsmouth, N.H.: SS *Grampus, Grayback, Grenadier, O-6*
Boston: CL *Philadelphia*; DD *Mustin, Noa, Overton, Truxtun, Walke*
Newport, R.I.: CA *Augusta*; DD *Sampson*
New London, Conn.: DD *Herbert*; SS *Mackerel, Marlin, O-2, O-3, O-4, O-7, O-8, O-10, R-1, R-5, R-6, R-9, R-12, R-15, R-17, R-18, R-19, S-20, S-21, S-26, S-32, S-33, S-48*
Philadelphia: SS *S-1, S-31, S-44*
Norfolk, Va.: BB *New Mexico*; CV *Hornet, Long Island, Yorktown*; DD *Hughes, O'Brien, Sims*
Charleston, S.C.: DD *Warrington*
Key West, Fla.: DD *Biddle*; SS *R-2, R-4, R-10, R-11, R-13, R-14, R-20*
Off Cape Cod, Mass.: DD *Roper*
Off East Coast: CL *Atlanta* (trials); DD *Dahlgren*
At sea returning to Norfolk, Va.: CV *Ranger*; DD *Bristol, Ellyson, Emmons, Ingraham, Lang, Rhind, Trippe*
On patrol off Atlantic Coast: SS *R-7*
En route to Key West, Fla.: SS *R-16*

ATLANTIC OCEAN

Argentia, Newfoundland: BB *New York*; DD *Decatur, Dickerson, Dupont, Eberle, Ellis, Ericsson, Grayson, Greer, McCormick, Monssen*; SS *S-30* (patrol), *S-45* (patrol), *S-47*
Hvalfjordur, Iceland: BB *Idaho, Mississippi*; CA *Tuscaloosa, Wichita*; DD *Anderson, Gwin, Hammann, Kearny, Livermore, Meredith, Morris*
At sea off Iceland: DD *Ludlow, Woolsey*
At sea escorting lend-lease shipments: DD *Babbitt, Bainbridge, Benson, Bernadou, Broome, Buck, Cole, Dallas, Edison, Gleaves, Charles F. Hughes, Hilary P. Jones, Jacob Jones, Lansdale, Lea, Leary, Macleish, Madison, Mayo, Niblack, Nicholson, Roe, Schenck, Simpson, Sturtevant, Tarbell, Upshur, Wilkes*
Bermuda: CL *Brooklyn, Nashville*; CV *Wasp*; DD *Russell, Stack, Sterett, Wilson*; SS *S-42, S-45, S-46*
At sea escorting convoy to South Africa: CA *Quincy, Vincennes*; DD *Mayrant, McDougal, Moffett, Rowan, Wainwright, Winslow*

CARIBBEAN SEA

Canal Zone: CL *Trenton*; DD *Barry, Borie, Breckinridge, Goff, J. Fred Talbott, Tattnall*; SS *Barracuda, Bass, Bonita, S-22, S-24, S-29*
At sea escorting prize to Puerto Rico: CL *Omaha*; DD *Somers*
Trinidad: CL *Cincinnati, Memphis, Milwaukee*; DD *Jouett*
Gulf of Mexico: BB *Washington*; DD *Swanson*
Caribbean: DD *Davis*
Convoy escort, Caribbean: DD *Badger, Barney, Blakeley*
At sea enroute New London, Conn., to San Francisco: DD *Lawrence*

PACIFIC OCEAN—U.S. WEST COAST

Bremerton, Wash.: BB *Colorado*; DD *Fox, Gilmer, Kane*
San Francisco/Mare Island: DD *Cushing, King, Perkins, Smith*; SS *Cuttlefish, Nautilus, Tuna, S-23, S-27, S-28*
San Diego: CL *Concord*; CV *Saratoga*; DD *Clark, Crane, Crosby, Dent, Hatfield, Humphreys, Kennison, Kilty, Preston, Rathburne, Talbot, Waters*; SS *S-34, S-35*
On patrol off West Coast: SS *S-18*

PACIFIC OCEAN

Pearl Harbor: BB *Arizona, California, Maryland, Nevada, Oklahoma, Pennsylvania, Tennessee, West Virginia*; CA

New Orleans, San Francisco; CL *Detroit, Helena, Honolulu, Phoenix, Raleigh, St. Louis*; DD *Allen, Aylwin, Bagley, Blue, Case, Cassin, Chew, Conyngham, Cummings, Dale, Dewey, Downes, Farragut, Helm, Henley, Hull, Jarvis, MacDonough, Monaghan, Mugford, Patterson, Phelps, Reid, Schley, Selfridge, Shaw, Ralph Talbot, Tucker, Ward, Worden*; SS *Cachalot, Dolphin, Narwhal, Tautog*

Lahaina Roads: SS *Gudgeon*

At sea off Pearl Harbor: CA *Minneapolis*; DD *Litchfield*; SS *Plunger, Thresher*

At sea transporting aircraft to Midway: CA *Astoria, Chicago, Portland*; CV *Lexington*; DD *Drayton, Flusser, Lamson, Mahan, Porter*

At sea escorting ships to the Philippines: CA *Pensacola*

At sea escorting transport to Pearl Harbor: CA *Louisville*

At sea returning to Pearl Harbor from Wake Island: CA *Chester, Northampton, Salt Lake City*; CV *Enterprise*; DD *Balch, Benham, Craven, Dunlap, Ellet, Fanning, Gridley, Maury, McCall*

On patrol: SS *Argonaut* (Midway), *Tambor* (Wake Island), *Triton* (Wake Island), *Trout* (Midway)

En route to Pearl Harbor: SS *Pollack, Pompano*

Johnston Island: CA *Indianapolis*

At sea en route to Valparaiso: CL *Richmond*

En route to San Diego: SS *Gar, Grayling*

FAR EAST

Philippines: CA *Houston* (Panay); CL *Boise* (Cebu); DD *Bulmer, John D. Ford, Pope, Peary*; SS *Pike, Perch, Permit, Pickerel (on patrol), Porpoise, S-36, S-37, S-38, S-39 (on patrol), S-40, S-41, Sailfish, Salmon (on patrol), Sargo, Saury, Sculpin, Seadragon, Seal, Sealion, Searaven, Seawolf, Shark, Skipjack, Snapper, Spearfish, Stingray, Sturgeon, Swordfish, Tarpon*

Tarakan, Borneo: CL *Marblehead*; DD *Barker, Paul Jones, Parrott, Pillsbury, Stewart*

En route, Balikpapan to Singapore: DD *Alden, Edsall, John D. Edwards, Whipple*

The wreck of *Arizona*, 7 Dec 1941. The forward tripod mast has collapsed following a massive explosion that destroyed the forward part of the ship.

Cassin (DD 372), 8 Dec 1941, capsized in drydock, leaning against the *Downes*, which remained upright. Both destroyers were rebuilt with new hulls.

1 BATTLESHIPS

Following the signing of the Washington Naval Treaty in 1922, all the remaining pre-dreadnoughts and the first four of the dreadnoughts were broken up, except for the *North Dakota*, retained as a mobile target ship. Also gone were the ships under construction and not yet launched, the *Washington*, the six super-dreadnoughts of the *South Dakota* class, and the six battle cruisers of the *Lexington* class.

The strength of the U.S. Navy became symbolized by the "Big Five," the five newest battleships of the *Colorado* and *Tennessee* classes. Alike except for the caliber of their main armament, they carried, like all American battleships, the ubiquitous cage masts that served readily to identify their nationality. But change was already underway. Starting with the earliest surviving class, they were being modernized, and the most striking evidence was the elimination of cage masts and installation of catapults. Boilers completed for the canceled ships were installed.

The oil-burning battleships (BB 36–42) that remained on the list were modernized during the 1920s and 1930s. Secondary battery was relocated, torpedo tubes removed, main battery elevation increased, catapults placed on turrets, new fire controls equipment added, and a single funnel moved slightly aft. In 1925 the *Florida* and *Utah* lost their mainmasts, and their two funnels were replaced by one. Similar changes were performed on each later class as its turn came, and starting with the *New York* and *Texas*, in 1925, tripods replaced the old cage masts. Successively, the *Nevada* and *Pennsylvania* classes were also modernized, with huge tripods and large tops.

The London Treaty of 1930 imposed new rules, leading to the decommissioning of three battleships: the *Florida*, *Utah*, and *Wyoming*. The last two were demilitarized and turned into a target ship and gunnery training ship, respectively.

The planners were busy designing new battleships, to be commenced in 1937 as permitted by the treaty. Meanwhile, from 1930 to 1934 the three *New Mexico*–class ships were modernized, emerging with a new profile with a massive tower superstructure.

Figure 1.1: *Pennsylvania* (BB 38) firing a broadside, 1920s. Notice the two cage masts, and guns lining the casemates in the hull.

In 1937 the first new battleships since World War I, the *North Carolina* and *Washington*, were laid down to replace the *Arkansas* and *New York*. They were considerably longer than their predecessors, with a distinctive tower superstructure, two funnels, and three triple turrets with new 16" guns. They were fast, making over 27 knots.

The next four, the *South Dakota* class, differed in having a pyramidal aspect, with the same armament on a shorter hull. The arrangement of armor, which included an innovative internally sloped belt, was different. The new battleships were armed with a new version of 16" gun with somewhat improved fire-control systems.

Six larger battleships displacing 45,000 tons to become the *Iowa* class were ordered in 1939–40. The main armament and armor remained the same and the larger size was devoted to increasing speed to 33 knots. As on the *South Dakota*–class ships, the armor arrangement was quite different, being internal rather than flush to the side of the hull. The six ships of the *Montana* class, which reverted to an external armor belt, were ordered in 1940, with a displacement of 58,000 tons and an additional 16" turret. The changes in naval warfare made these ships superfluous, and none was ever started.

In 1941, attention was turned toward the war in Europe, and the Navy had eight battleships in the Atlantic Ocean, including the two new ships of the *North Carolina* class. The *Arkansas, New York,* and *Texas* stayed in the Atlantic and, with the rebuilt *Nevada,* were present at Normandy. The *New Mexico*–class ships and all the new battleships went to the Pacific Ocean, where they remained. The only exceptions were the brief presence of the new *Alabama, South Dakota,* and *Washington* in the waters off Iceland in 1942 and the *Massachusetts* at the landings in Morocco. Also in 1943, the new *Iowa* was stationed off Newfoundland to offset the threat of the *Tirpitz,* and in the fall carried President Franklin Delano Roosevelt to Casablanca for the Teheran Conference.

The attack on Pearl Harbor found eight of the nine Pacific Fleet battleships present, and all were either sunk or damaged. The *Arizona, California, Nevada, Oklahoma,* and *West Virginia* were sunk, with two being complete losses. The *Maryland, Pennsylvania,* and *Tennessee* were somewhat damaged, while the *Colorado* was being overhauled at Bremerton, Washington, in Puget Sound.

As a result of the destruction of the battle line at Pearl Harbor, all the survivors were radically rebuilt, emerging with new profiles. The moderately damaged *Maryland* and *Tennessee,* along with *Colorado,* lost their cage mainmasts. The *Pennsylvania* and the heavily damaged *Nevada* also lost their mainmasts. The *California* and *West Virginia,* and later the *Tennessee,* were rebuilt with a massive central superstructure similar to the new *South Dakota* class. In all, masts and superstructure were cut down to add field of fire for the numerous additional antiaircraft guns. The older guns of the secondary armament were replaced by the superior 5"/38 guns. The addition of radar changed not only the appearance of the ships but their tactics.

During World War II, the battleships progressively lost their place as the capital ships of the fleet and were relegated to duties such as escorting the carrier task forces and preinvasion shore bombardment. The new battleships were fast and ultimately covered with 40mm and 20mm antiaircraft guns. As such, they helped provide protection to the carriers in the continuous raids that took place in the vast reaches of the Pacific Ocean.

The last glorious moment of the battleship took place in October 1944 during the night action in Surigao Strait as part of the Battle of Leyte Gulf. There the old battleships, survivors of Pearl Harbor, fought and sank the attacking Japanese battleships, in the final battleship action.

At the end of the war, only the newest battleships were retained. Five of the oldest veterans, the *Arkansas, Nevada, New York, Pennsylvania,* and *Texas,* were expended as targets in the atomic tests in the Bikini Atoll in 1946. The others were laid up in reserve waiting for a day that never came, and were eventually broken up.

Battleships, as the principal ships of the Navy, were named after states and used the designation *BB.*

Figure 1.2: *Oklahoma* (BB 37), as reconstructed, 1936, with two massive tripod masts. Compare with *Nevada,* which has added level on mainmast.

Figure 1.3: *South Dakota* (BB 57) and *Alabama* (BB 60), summer 1943, operating with British Home Fleet in the Norwegian Sea.

Figure 1.4: *Utah* (BB 31), 28 Oct 1927, following reconstruction. Her cage mainmast has been replaced with a pole mast and the two funnels rebuilt into one. In 1931 she was disarmed and converted to a mobile target ship.

Figure. 1.5: *Wyoming* (BB 32), 1920s, at Honolulu, prior to reconstruction.

Figure 1.6: *Arkansas* (BB 33), 27 Jun 1942, after her last reconstruction at Norfolk Navy Yard. A tripod mast has replaced the old cage foremast; the cage mainmast was replaced in 1927.

Figure 1.7: *Texas* (BB 35), 19 Aug 1942. With the other oldest battleships, it remained in the Atlantic until the European war was ending.

BATTLESHIPS ON THE NAVY LIST, 1922

BB 14 *Nebraska* Stricken 9 Nov 1923; BU Oakland.
BB 15 *Georgia* Stricken 10 Nov 1923; BU Mare I.
BB 17 *Rhode Island* Sold 1 Nov 1923; BU Mare I.
BB 18 *Connecticut* Decomm 1 Mar 1923; sold 1 Nov 1923; BU Oakland.
BB 19 *Louisiana* Sold 1 Nov 1923; BU Baltimore.
BB 20 *Vermont* Stricken 10 Nov 1923; BU 1924 Mare I.
BB 21 *Kansas* Stricken 24 Aug 1923; BU.
BB 22 *Minnesota* Stricken 1 Dec 1921; sold 23 Jan 1924; BU.
BB 25 *New Hampshire* Sold 1 Nov 1923; BU Philadelphia.
BB 26 *South Carolina* Decomm 15 Dec 1921; stricken 10 Nov 1923; sold 24 Apr 1924; BU.
BB 27 *Michigan* Decomm 11 Feb 1922; stricken 10 Nov 1923; sold 23 Jan 1924; BU Philadelphia.
BB 28 *Delaware* Decomm 10 Nov 1923; stricken 19 Nov 1923; sold 5 Feb 1924; BU.
BB 29 *North Dakota* Collided with schooner *T. K. Bentley* off Cape Cod, 4 Jan 1922; decomm 22 Nov 1923; unclassified, converted to mobile target, 28 May 1924; stricken 7 Jan 1931; sold 16 Mar 1931; BU Baltimore.
BB 30 *Florida* Decomm 16 Feb 1931; stricken 6 Apr 1931; BU.
BB 31 *Utah* Out of comm 31 Oct 1925–1 Dec 1925 for modification; converted to target ship, **AG 16**, 1 Jul 1931. Out of comm 1931–1 Apr 1932; torpedoed by Japanese aircraft and capsized at Pearl Harbor, 7 Dec 1941 (64 killed).
1* Pearl Harbor.
BB 32 *Wyoming* Modernized at Philadelphia NYd 1927. Converted to training ship, **AG 17**, 25 Apr 1932. 5" gun explosion near San Clemente, Calif., 18 Feb 1937 (7 killed). Decomm 1 Aug 1947. Stricken 16 Sep 1947. Sold 5 Dec 1947; BU Newark.
BB 33 *Arkansas* Rammed and damaged destroyer *McFarland* off Cape Cod, 19 Sep 1923. Modernized at Philadelphia NYd, 1925–26. Sank m/v *Melrose* in collision off New Jersey, 19 Dec 1940. Neutrality patrol. Rebuilt 6 Mar–26 Jul 1942; refit Sep–Nov 1944. Bikini test ship, damaged in atom bomb aerial explosion test Able, 1 Jul 1946; sunk in underwater explosion, test Baker, 25 Jul 1946.
4* Normandy, Southern France, Iwo Jima, Okinawa. Operation Magic Carpet.
BB 34 *New York* Gunnery TS 1943–44. Slightly damaged by kamikaze, east of Okinawa, 14 Apr 1945. Bikini test ship. Decomm 29 Aug 1946. Sunk as target ship by gunfire and aircraft off Pearl Harbor, 8 Jul 1948.
3* North Africa, Iwo Jima, Okinawa. Operation Magic Carpet.

Figure 1.8: *New York* (BB 34), 14 Nov 1944, retaining much of the reconstructed prewar appearance as it heads for the Pacific.

BB 35 *Texas* In collision with m/v *Steel Seafarer* off Point Arguello, Calif., 13 Sep 1923. Neutrality patrol. Damaged by coastal guns, Cherbourg, 25 Jun 1944 (1 killed). Decomm 21 Apr 1948. Stricken 30 Apr 1948. Decomm 21 Apr 1948 and trfd to State of Texas as museum.
5* North Africa, Normandy, Southern France, Iwo Jima, Okinawa. Operation Magic Carpet.
Later history: Preserved as museum in Galveston, Tex.

BB 36 *Nevada* Modernized Aug 1927–Jan 1930. In collision with *Arizona* off Hawaii, 22 Oct 1941. Damaged by one torpedo and five bombs at Pearl Harbor, 7 Dec 1941 (57 killed). Refloated 12 Feb 1942. Recomm Dec 1942. Damaged by kamikaze, west of Okinawa, 27 Mar 1945 (11 killed), and by five hits from coastal gunfire, 5 Apr 1945 (2 killed). Bikini test ship. Decomm 29 Aug 1946. Sunk as target off Hawaii, 31 Jul 1948.

Figure 1.9: *Nevada* (BB 36) underway, late 1930s. As modernized in 1930, with tripod masts replacing the old cage masts, this is how she appeared on 7 Dec 1941.

Figure 1.10: *Nevada* entering drydock at Pearl Harbor, 18 Feb 1942, after being refloated. She was the only battleship to get underway during the Japanese attack but was grounded after being torpedoed to prevent her sinking and blocking the entrance to the harbor.

Figure 1.11: *Nevada* (BB 36) after reconstruction, 23 Aug 1943. The aft tripod has been replaced with a smaller structure and new twin 5"/38s have been added amidships. Notice the three- and two-gun turrets. Much of the prewar clutter has been removed to provide wide arcs of fire for antiaircraft guns, as was done on all the older ships.

Figure 1.12: *Arizona* (BB 39) after reconstruction, 1930s. The cage masts have been replaced by two massive tripod masts. Corsair scout planes are perched on catapults aft and the no. 3 turret.

7* Pearl Harbor, Attu, Normandy, Southern France, Iwo Jima, Okinawa, Raids on Japan 7–8/45.

BB 37 *Oklahoma* Modernized Sep 1927–Jul 1929. In collision with tug *Goliath* at Puget Sound NYd, 19 Sep 1940. Hit by five torpedoes and capsized at Pearl Harbor, 7 Dec 1941 (429 killed). Righted and refloated, Mar–Sep 1943. Decomm 1 Sep 1944. Sold 5 Dec 1946. Sank under tow from Pearl Harbor to San Francisco, 17 May 1947.
1* Pearl Harbor.

BB 38 *Pennsylvania* Flagship, Pacific Fleet, 1922–41. Modernized Jun 1929–May 1931. Damaged by one bomb in drydock at Pearl Harbor, 7 Dec 1941 (24 killed). Refit Oct 1942–Feb 1943. Slight damage by coastal gunfire, Wake I., 1 Aug 1945. Severely damaged by aircraft torpedo, Buckner Bay, Okinawa, 12 Aug 1945 (20 killed). Bikini test ship. Decomm 29 Aug 1946. Sunk as target off Kwajalein, 10 Feb 1948.

Figure 1.13: *Pennsylvania* (BB 38), 1941, at pier in San Diego, as rebuilt in 1931, with two tripod masts and all casemate guns removed.

Figure 1.14: *Pennsylvania* (BB 38), 1 Feb 1943, following reconstruction after Pearl Harbor. Tripod mainmast has been removed and 5"/38s in twin mounts can be seen amidships.

8* Pearl Harbor, Attu, Gilbert Is., Kwajalein, Eniwetok, Saipan, Guam, Palau, Leyte, Surigao Strait, Lingayen.

BB 39 *Arizona* Modernized 1919–31. Carried President Herbert Hoover to Puerto Rico, Mar 1931. Sank fishing vessel *Umatilla* in collision in Strait of Juan de Fuca, 26 Jul 1934. In collision with destroyer *Davis* off Hawaii, 21 Apr 1941. In collision with *Nevada* off Hawaii, 22 Oct 1941. Hit by eight bombs and one torpedo and blew up at Pearl Harbor, 7 Dec 1941 (1,177 killed, including RADM Isaac Kidd).

1* Pearl Harbor.

Later history: Submerged hulk preserved as memorial at Pearl Harbor; the two aft turrets were almost undamaged and removed to serve as Army coastal batteries in Oahu.

BB 40 *New Mexico* Modernized Mar 1931–Jan 1933. Neutrality patrol. Sank m/v *Oregon* in collision south of Nantucket, Mass., 10 Dec 1941. Damaged by kamikaze that hit bridge, Lingayen Gulf, 6 Jan 1945 (30 killed, including British Gen. Herbert Lumsden). Damaged by U.S. gunfire, west of Okinawa, 12 Apr 1945. Moderately damaged by kamikaze, Okinawa, 12 May 1945 (54 killed). Decomm 19 Jul 1946. Stricken 13 Oct 1947; BU Newark.

6* Attu, Gilbert Is., Kwajalein, Saipan, Guam, Lingayen, Okinawa. Tokyo Bay.

BB 41 *Mississippi* Damaged by powder explosion in no. 2 turret off San Pedro, Calif., 12 Jun 1924 (48 killed). Modernized, Mar 1931–Sep 1933.

Figure 1.15: *Mississippi* (BB 41), 8 Mar 1940, at Puget Sound, showing how this class was completely reconstructed with a more modern profile.

Figure 1.16: *New Mexico* (BB 40), 6 Oct 1943. The massive tower superstructure can be seen to advantage.

Figure 1.17: *Idaho* (BB 42), 2 Jan 1945, rearmed with single 5" mounts amidships, the only battleship with this arrangement.

Neutrality patrol. Damaged by accidental explosion in no. 2 turret off Makin, Gilbert Is., 20 Nov 1943 (43 killed). Damaged by kamikaze, Lingayen, 9 Jan 1945 (23 killed) and again off Okinawa, 5 Jun 1945. Converted to experimental gunnery ship and rec **AG 126**, 15 Feb 1946. †
8* Attu, Gilbert Is., Kwajalein, Palau, Leyte, Surigao Strait, Lingayen, Okinawa. Tokyo Bay.

BB 42 *Idaho* Modernized Sep 1931–Oct 1934. Neutrality patrol. North Atlantic 1941–42. Refit Oct–Dec 1942 and Oct–Dec 1944. Damaged by kamikaze near miss, Okinawa, 12 Apr 1945. Damaged by grounding, Okinawa, 13 Jun 1945. Decomm 3 Jul 1946. Sold 24 Nov 1947; BU Newark.
8* Attu, Gilbert Is., Kwajalein, Saipan, Guam, Palau, Iwo Jima, Okinawa.

BB 43 *Tennessee* Went aground in San Francisco harbor, 11 Jun 1937. Damaged by two bombs at Pearl Harbor, 7 Dec 1941 (5 killed). Rebuilt Sep 1942–May 1943. Minor damaged by two hits from coastal guns, Tinian, 15 Jun 1944 (8 killed). Collided with *California*, 24 Aug 1944. Damaged by coastal guns, Iwo Jima, 17 Feb 1945. Damaged by one kamikaze, Okinawa, 12 Apr 1945 (22 killed). Decomm 14 Feb 1947. †
10* Pearl Harbor, Gilbert Is., Kwajalein, Eniwetok, Saipan, Tinian, Guam, Palau, Leyte, Surigao Strait, Iwo Jima, Okinawa, Raids on Japan 7–8/45.

BB 44 *California* Damaged by two aircraft bombs and two torpedoes at Pearl Harbor and sank, 7 Dec 1941 (102 killed). Refloated 25 Mar

Figure 1.20: *Tennessee* (BB 43), 25 Jan 1945, as reconstructed, at a West Coast yard. The ship bears no resemblance to her former self, having been rebuilt though not damaged at Pearl Harbor.

Figure 1.18: *California* (BB 44) stern quarter, prior to installation of catapults in 1924. Notice the range clock added after World War I, and calibrations on the turret.

Figure 1.21: *Colorado* (BB 45), in a broadside view during the 1930s. She was the only Pacific Fleet battleship not at Pearl Harbor on 7 Dec 1941.

Figure 1.19: *Tennessee* (BB 43) 26 Feb 1942; first reconstruction after Pearl Harbor, cage mainmast replaced by small tower. The ship was later totally reconstructed.

Figure 1.22: *Maryland* (BB 46), 5 Aug 1945. She and *Colorado* retained their cage foremasts throughout the war.

1942. Rebuilt 7 Jun 1942–31 Jan 1944. Minor damage by coastal guns, Saipan, 14 Jun 1944 (1 killed). Collided with *Tennessee*, 24 Aug 1944. Damaged by strafing, Leyte, 27 Oct 1944. Damaged by kamikaze, Lingayen Gulf, 6 Jan 1945 (44 killed). Decomm 14 Feb 1947. †
7* Pearl Harbor, Saipan, Tinian, Guam, Leyte, Surigao Strait, Lingayen, Okinawa, Raids on Japan 7–8/45.

BB 45 *Colorado* Commissioned 30 Aug 1923. Went aground at tip of Manhattan I., New York, 30 Apr 1927. Damaged in collision with m/v *Ruth Alexander* off Los Angeles, Mar 1928. Explosion of 5" AA gun northwest of San Pedro, Calif., 5 Nov 1931 (4 killed). Damaged by 22 hits from coastal guns off Tinian, 24 Jul 1944. Damaged by two kamikazes, Leyte, 27 Nov 1944 (19 killed). Damaged by friendly gunfire, Lingayen, Luzon, 9 Jan 1945 (18 killed). Damaged by explosion, Okinawa, 20 Apr 1945. Decomm 7 Jan 1947. †
7* Gilbert Is., Kwajalein, Eniwetok, Saipan, Tinian, Guam, Leyte, Mindoro, Lingayen, Okinawa. Tokyo Bay, Operation Magic Carpet.

Figure 1.23: *West Virginia* (BB 48), off Alcatraz in San Francisco Bay, during the 1930s. One of the "Big Five," she was the last battleship to be completed after World War I.

Figure 1.24: *West Virginia* (BB 48), Apr 1942, with salvage operations underway. The ship was sunk at her moorings on 7 Dec 1942, having been struck by seven torpedoes on the starboard side. Here her mainmast has already been removed.

BB 46 *Maryland* Carried President Hoover to South America 1928. Damaged by two bombs at Pearl Harbor, 7 Dec 1941 (3 killed). Bow damaged by aircraft torpedo, Saipan, 22 Jun 1944. Damaged by kamikaze, Leyte, 29 Nov 1944 (31 killed). Damaged by kamikaze and bomb, Okinawa, 7 Apr 1945 (16 killed). Decomm 3 Apr 1947. †
7* Pearl Harbor, Gilbert Is., Kwajalein, Saipan, Palau, Leyte, Surigao Strait, Okinawa. Operation Magic Carpet.

BB 48 *West Virginia* Commissioned 1 Dec 1923. Went aground in Hampton Roads, Va., when engines failed, 16 Jun 1924. Sunk by seven torpedoes and two bombs at Pearl Harbor, 7 Dec 1941 (106 killed). Refloated 17 May 1942; rebuilt at Bremerton, Wash. Recomm Jul 1944. Damaged by kamikaze, Okinawa, 1 Apr 1945 (4 killed). Decomm 9 Jan 1947. †
5* Pearl Harbor, Leyte, Surigao Strait, Lingayen, Iwo Jima, Okinawa. Tokyo Bay, Operation Magic Carpet.

Notes:

Florida class: Modernized 1925, cage mainmast replaced by pole, single funnel, oil fuel, catapult on turret. *Utah* rearmed 1939 as training ship, with four 5"/25 and two quad 1.1" guns; four 5"/38 added 1941.

Wyoming class: Modernized, cage mainmast replaced by tripod, single funnel, 1925–27. Catapult on no. 3 turret. Displacement: 27,900 tons, 29,000 f/l; beam: 106'; machinery: four White-Foster boilers, SHP 28,000, 21 knots; endurance: 14,000/10.

Arkansas (1942). Five-inch guns on gun deck removed, tripod foremast fitted. Armament: 12–12"/50, 16–5"/51, 8–3"/50 AA guns; (1945) 6–5"/51, 10–3"/50, 9 quad 40mm, 36–20mm guns; 3 aircraft.

New York class: Modernized, cage masts replaced by tripods, single funnel, 1925–27. Displacement: 28,700 tons, 30,000 f/l; beam increased to 106'; machinery: 6 Bureau Express boilers; endurance: 15,400/10. During wartime, retained tripod foremast, mainmast cut down. Armament: 10–14"/45, 16–5"/51, 8–3"/50 AA guns; (1945) 6–5"/51, 10–3"/50, 10 quad 40mm, 44 to 48 20mm guns; 3 aircraft.

Nevada class: Catapults added 1923. Modernized, cage masts replaced by tripods, 1927–29. Displacement: 30,500 tons, 33,900 f/l; beam increased to 107'11"; machinery: 6 Bureau Express boilers; endurance: 15,700/10. *Nevada* new engines, Parsons turbines originally fitted in *North Dakota*. *Nevada*, 1942: tripod foremast retained, stump tripod mainmast; raked stack extension. Armament: 10–14"/45, 12–5"/51, 8–5"/25 AA guns; (1945, *Nevada*) 16–5"/38, 8 quad 40mm, 40–20mm guns; 2 aircraft.

Pennsylvania class: Modernized, cage masts replaced by tripods, oil fuel, 1928–31. Funnel moved aft. Reengined, received geared turbines built for BB 47. Displacement: 34,400 tons, 39,224 f/l; beam 106'3"; machinery: 6 Bureau Express boilers, SHP 32,000; endurance: 19,900/10; armament: 12–14"/45, 12–5"/51, 8–5"/25 AA guns. *Pennsylvania*, 1942: Tripod mainmast removed, new secondary guns; (1945) 16–5"/38, 10 quad 40mm, 51–20mm guns.

New Mexico class: Catapults added 1923 (BB 41 and BB 42) and 1925 (BB 40). Rebuilt 1930–34, superstructure replaced by tower bridge; oil fuel, new machinery. Displacement: 35,000 tons; beam increased to 106'3"; machinery: all Westinghouse turbines, 6 Bureau Express boilers (*New Mexico*: 4 White-Foster), SHP 40,000; endurance 23,400/9; armament: 12–14"/50, 12–5"/51, 8–5"/25 AA guns; (1945) 6–5"/51, 8–5"/25 (BB 42: 10–5"/38), 10 quad 40mm, 40 to 46 20mm guns; 2 aircraft.

Tennessee class: Catapults added 1924. Modernization postponed in late 1930s. *Tennessee* had cage mainmast removed 1942 and replaced by small tower. Both rebuilt 1942–43. Superstructure replaced by tower bridge, bulges added beam 114'. Armament (1945): 12–14"/50, 16–5"/38, 10 quad 40mm, 43 to 60 20mm guns; 2 aircraft.

BB 45–46: Catapult added 1922 (BB 46), 1925 (BB 45). Both had cage mainmast cut down 1942 and later replaced by small tower. Armament (1945): 8–16"/45, 8–5"/51, 8–5"/25, 8 quad 40mm, 2 twin 40mm, 44 20mm guns; 2 aircraft.

BB 48: Rebuilt 1943–44. Superstructure replaced by tower bridge; bulges added, beam 114'. Armament: (1945) 8–16"/45, 16–5"/38, 10 quad 40mm, 64–20mm guns; 2 aircraft.

Figure 1.25: *North Carolina* (BB 55), 24 Sep 1944, in dazzle camouflage. The clean lines and modern superstructure were a new departure when she was completed in 1941.

Figure 1.26: *Massachusetts* (BB 59), 11 Jul 1944, off Point Wilson, Washington.

North Carolina Class

No.	Name	Builder	Keel Laid	Launched	Comm.
BB 55	*North Carolina*	New York NYd	27 Oct 1937	13 Jun 1940	9 Apr 1941
BB 56	*Washington*	Phila. NYd	14 Jun 1938	1 Jun 1940	15 May 1941

Displacement	35,000 tons; 46,770 f/l
Dimensions	728'9" (oa); 714'6" (wl) x 108'4" x 35'6"
Machinery	4 screws; GE GT; 8 B&W boilers; SHP 121,000; 27.6 knots
Endurance	16,320/15
Complement	2,340
Armament	9–16"/45, 20–5"/38, 15 quad 40mm, 48 to 67 20mm AA guns; 3 aircraft; (1941) 4 quad 1.1" AA
Armor	6" to 12" belt, 9.8" to 16" turrets, 14.7" to 16" barbettes, 1.9" to 11.1" bulkheads, 3.6" to 4.1" decks, 14.7" to 16" CT

Notes: New design with tower foremast, two funnels, long flush deck with two catapults aft. Three triple turrets with new 16" guns; secondary armament in twin turrets.

Service Records:

BB 55 *North Carolina* Torpedoed by submarine *I-15* near Espiritu Santo, 15 Sep 1942 (5 killed). In collision with destroyer *Hailey* off Iwo Jima, 18 Feb 1945. Damaged in error by U.S. gunfire, Okinawa, 6 Apr 1945 (3 killed). Decomm 27 Jun 1947. †

12* Guadalcanal-Tulagi, Eastern Solomons, Gilbert Is., Kwajalein, Raid on Truk, Marianas Raid 2/44, Palau-Yap Raids 3/44, Hollandia, Truk Raid 4/44, Saipan, Philippine Sea, Luzon Raids 10/44, Formosa Raids 1/45, Luzon Raids 1/45, China Coast Raids 1/45, Nansei Shoto Raid 1/45, Honshu Raid 2/45, Iwo Jima, Fleet Raids 1945, Raids on Japan 7–8/45. Operation Magic Carpet.

Ship sunk: AP *Eiho Maru*, west of Roi, 30 Jan 1944.

BB 56 *Washington* Flag of RADM John W. Wilcox, who was lost overboard in North Atlantic, 27 Mar 1942. North Atlantic Mar–Jul 1942. Damaged in collision with battleship *Indiana* south of Kwajalein, 2 Feb 1944. Decomm 27 Jun 1947. †

13* Russian Convoys, Solomons, Battle of Guadalcanal, Gilbert Is., Kavieng Raid 1/44, Kwajalein, Saipan, Philippine Sea, Guam, Palau-Yap Raids 7/44, Palau, Philippines Raids 9/44, Okinawa Raid 10/44, N. Luzon–Formosa Raids 10/44, Visayas Is. Raids 1944, Surigao Strait, Formosa Raids 1/45, Luzon Raids 1/45, China Coast Raids 1/45, Nansei Shoto Raid 1/45, Honshu Raid 2/45, Iwo Jima, Fleet Raids 1945, Okinawa. Operation Magic Carpet.

Figure 1.27: *Indiana* (BB 58), 8 Sep 1942. Overhead view showing layout of armament and superstructure.

South Dakota Class

No.	Name	Builder	Keel Laid	Launched	Comm.
BB 57	*South Dakota*	NY Sbdg	5 Jul 1939	7 Jun 1941	20 Mar 1942
BB 58	*Indiana*	Newport News	20 Nov 1939	21 Nov 1941	30 Apr 1942
BB 59	*Massachusetts*	Beth. Quincy	20 Jul 1939	23 Sep 1941	15 May 1942
BB 60	*Alabama*	Norfolk NYd	1 Feb 1940	16 Feb 1942	16 Aug 1942

Displacement	35,000 tons; 45,216 f/l
Dimensions	680' (oa); 666' (wl) x 108'2" x 36'1"

Machinery	4 screws; GE GT (BB 58, BB 60: West.); 8 B&W boilers (BB 58, BB 60: FW); SHP 130,000; 27.8 knots
Endurance	17,000/15
Complement	2,354
Armament	9–16"/45, 20–5"/38 (BB 57: 16), 14 quad 40mm (BB 57: 17), 38 to 76 20mm AA
Armor	12.2" belt, 9.5" to 18" turrets, 11.5" to 17.3" barbettes, 13.4" bulkheads, 5.3" deck, 7.25" to 15" CT

Notes: New design, shorter hull, single funnel. Superstructure massed amidships in a pyramidal arrangement. Mainmast stepped close abaft funnel. *South Dakota* and *Alabama* operated with the British Home Fleet in 1942 before going to the Pacific.

Service Records:

BB 57 *South Dakota* Damaged by hitting coral reef in Lahai Passage, Tonga Is., 6 Sep 1942. Slightly damaged when hit in turret by aircraft bomb off Santa Cruz, 26 Oct 1942. Damaged in collision with destroyer *Mahan* in Solomon Is., 27 Oct 1942. Damaged by naval gunfire, Battle of Guadalcanal, 15 Nov 1942. Damaged by aircraft bomb, Philippine Sea, 19 Jun 1944 (24 killed). Damaged by powder explosion while loading ammunition off Okinawa, 6 May 1945 (1 killed). Decomm 31 Jan 1947. †
13* Santa Cruz, Battle of Guadalcanal, Gilbert Is., Kwajalein, Raid on Truk, Marianas Raid 2/44, Palau-Yap Raids 3/44, Hollandia, Truk Raid 4/44, Saipan, Philippine Sea, Philippines Raids 9/44, Okinawa Raid 10/44, N. Luzon–Formosa Raids 10/44, Luzon Raids 10/44, Visayas Is. Raids 10/44, Formosa Raids 1/45, Luzon Raids 1/45, Formosa Raids 1/45, China Coast Raids 1/45, Honshu Raid 2/45, Iwo Jima, Fleet Raids 1945, Raids on Japan 7–8/45. Tokyo Bay.

BB 58 *Indiana* Damaged in collision with battleship *Washington* south of Kwajalein, 2 Feb 1944. Minor damage by aircraft bomb, Philippine Sea, 19 Jun 1944. Damaged in typhoon in Philippine Sea, 5 Jun 1945. Decomm 11 Sep 1947. †
9* Marcus I. Raid 1943, Gilbert Is., Kwajalein, Truk Raid 4/44, Philippine Sea, Saipan, Guam, Palau-Yap Raids 7/44, Palau, Philippines Raids 9/44, Honshu Raid 2/45, Iwo Jima, Fleet Raids 1945, Raids on Japan 7–8/45.

BB 59 *Massachusetts* Minor damage by gunfire off Casablanca, 8 Nov 1942. Damaged in typhoon, Okinawa, 5 Jun 1945. Decomm 27 Mar 1947.
11´ North Africa, Gilbert Is., Kwajalein, Raid on Truk, Marianas Raid 2/44, Palau-Yap Raids 3/44, Hollandia, Truk Raid 4/44, Palau, Okinawa Raid 10/44, N. Luzon–Formosa Raids 10/44, Luzon Raids 10/44, Visayas Is. Raids 10/44, Surigao Strait, Formosa Raids 1/45, Luzon Raids 1/45, China Coast Raids 1/45, Nansei Shoto Raid 1/45, Honshu Raid 2/45, Iwo Jima, Fleet Raids 1945, Raids on Japan 7–8/45.

BB 60 *Alabama* North Atlantic May–Aug 1943. Damaged by 5" gun accident, 21 Feb 1944 (5 killed). Damaged in typhoon, Philippine Sea, 5 Jun 1945. Decomm 9 Jan 1947. †
9* Gilbert Is., Kwajalein, Raid on Truk, Marianas Raid 2/44, Palau Raid 3/44, Truk Raid 4/44, Saipan, Philippine Sea, Guam, Palau-Yap Raids 7/44, Bonins-Yap Raids, Hollandia, Palau, Philippines Raids 9/44, Okinawa Raid 10/44, N. Luzon–Formosa Raids 10/44, Luzon Raids 10/44, Visayas Is. Raids 10/44, Surigao Strait, Fleet Raids 1945, Raids on Japan 7–8/45. Operation Magic Carpet.

Iowa Class

No.	Name	Builder	Keel Laid	Launched	Comm.
BB 61	*Iowa*	New York NYd	27 Jun 1940	27 Aug 1942	22 Feb 1943
BB 62	*New Jersey*	Phila. NYd	16 Sep 1940	7 Dec 1942	23 May 1943
BB 63	*Missouri*	New York NYd	6 Jan 1941	29 Jan 1944	11 Jun 1944
BB 64	*Wisconsin*	Phila. NYd	25 Jan 1941	7 Dec 1943	16 Apr 1944
BB 65	*Illinois*	Phila. NYd	15 Jan 1945	—	—
BB 66	*Kentucky*	Norfolk NYd	6 Dec 1944	20 Jan 1950	—

Displacement	45,000 tons; 57,540 f/l
Dimensions	887'3" (oa); 860' (wl) x 108'2" x 37'9"
Machinery	4 screws; GE GT (BB 62, BB 64, BB 65: West.); 8 B&W boilers; SHP 212,000; 32.5 knots
Endurance	16,600/15
Complement	2,788
Armament	9–16"/50, 20–5"/38, 20 quad 40mm, 47 to 52 20mm AA guns; 3 aircraft
Armor	12.2" belt, 2.5" to 17" turrets, 11.6" to 17.3" barbettes, 4.75" to 5" deck, 11.2" bulkheads, 17.3" CT

Notes: The largest battleships built by the Navy. Significantly longer than their predecessors, with long main deck and flush deck, clipper bow, and two huge funnels, with the one forward built into the tower superstructure. The armor was flush with the hull and extended over a greater part of the hull. Only four were completed, and two canceled at the end of the war.

Figure 1.28: *Iowa* (BB 61), 24 Jan 1944; an aerial view as she heads, camouflaged, for the Pacific battle zone.

Figure 1.29: *Missouri* (BB 63), in the Hudson River, New York, on 30 May 1946. The last battleship to be completed. The Japanese surrender ceremony took place on her deck in Tokyo Bay on 2 Sep 1945.

Service Records:

BB 61 *Iowa* North Atlantic Aug–Oct 1943. Carried President Roosevelt to Casablanca conference, Nov 1943. Minor damage by gunfire off Mili I., 18 Mar 1944. †
9* Kwajalein, Raid on Truk, Marianas Raid 2/44, Palau Raid 3/44, Hollandia, Truk Raid 4/44, Saipan, Philippine Sea, Tinian, Guam, Palau-Yap Raids 7/44, Palau, Philippines Raids 9/44, Okinawa Raid 10/44, N. Luzon–Formosa Raids 10/44, Luzon Raids 10/44, Visayas Is. Raids 10/44, Surigao Strait, Fleet Raids 1945, Raids on Japan 7–8/45. Tokyo Bay.

BB 62 *New Jersey* In collision with destroyer *Franks* southeast of Okinawa, 2 Apr 1945. †
9* Kwajalein, Raid on Truk, Palau Raid 3/44, Hollandia, Truk Raid 4/44, Saipan, Philippine Sea, Guam, Palau-Yap Raids 7/44, Palau, Philippines Raids 9/44, Okinawa Raid 10/44, N. Luzon–Formosa Raids 10/44, Luzon Raids 10/44, Visayas Is. Raids 10/44, Surigao Strait, Formosa Raids 1/45, Luzon Raids 1/45, China Coast Raids 1/45, Nansei Shoto Raid 1/45, Honshu Raid 2/45, Iwo Jima, Fleet Raids 1945. Operation Magic Carpet.

BB 63 *Missouri* Slightly damaged by kamikaze off Okinawa, 11 and 16 Apr 1945. Damaged in typhoon, Philippine Sea, 5 Jun 1945. Japanese surrender signed on board in Tokyo Bay, 2 Sep 1945. †
3* Honshu Raid 2/45, Iwo Jima, Honshu Raid 2/45, Fleet Raids 1945, Raids on Japan 7–8/45. Tokyo Bay.

BB 64 *Wisconsin* †
5* Luzon Raids 10/44, Formosa Raids 1/45, Luzon Raids 1/45, China Coast Raids 1/45, Nansei Shoto Raid 1/45, Honshu Raid 2/45, Iwo Jima, Fleet Raids 1945, Raids on Japan 7–8/45. Tokyo Bay, Operation Magic Carpet.

BB 65 *Illinois* Canceled, 11 Aug 1945, 22 percent complete.

BB 66 *Kentucky* Canceled, 17 Feb 1947, 69.2 percent complete.

Figure 1.30: *Wisconsin* (BB 64), a unit of the *Iowa* class, in July 1947.

Montana Class

No.	Name	Builder	Keel Laid	Launched	Comm.
BB 67	*Montana*	Phila. Nyd	—	—	—
BB 68	*Ohio*	Phila. NYd	—	—	—
BB 69	*Maine*	New York NYd	—	—	—
BB 70	*New Hampshire*	New York NYd	—	—	—
BB 71	*Louisiana*	Norfolk NYd	—	—	—

Displacement	60,500 tons; 70,965 f/l
Dimensions	921'3" (oa) 890' (wl) x 121'1" x 36'
Machinery	4 screws, ST, 8 boilers, SHP 172,000, 28 knots
Endurance	15,000/15
Complement	2,355
Armament	12–16"/50, 20–5"/54, 10 quad 40mm AA, 56–20mm guns
Armor	10.2 to 16.1" belt, 18" turrets, 7.75 to 21.3" barbettes, 15.25" and 18" bulkheads, 6.2" deck, 7.4–18" CT

Notes: Improved *Iowa* class with four main turrets. All canceled 21 Jul 1943. None laid down.

2
AIRCRAFT CARRIERS

In 1922 the sole aircraft carrier in the U.S. Navy fleet was the *Langley*, converted from a collier. She was joined in 1927 by two converted battle cruisers, the *Lexington* and the *Saratoga*. With these carriers, the Navy learned how to use air power at sea through extensive maneuvers and annual battle exercises.

Aircraft carrier design following World War I was severely influenced by limitations imposed by the Washington Treaty of 1922 and the London Treaty of 1930. The 1922 treaty provided tonnage limits for carriers, which for the United States was 135,000 tons. Reducing the *Lexington* and *Saratoga* to 33,000 tons each left only 69,000 tons for new construction. Having decided that five additional carriers were required, only 13,800 tons were then available for each new ship.

The *Ranger* was designed with this in mind, resulting in a highly vulnerable ship. With a need for larger ships, the *Enterprise* and *Yorktown* were designed with the idea that keeping within the limits for five ships was not possible, and that three would be the new limit.

Figure 2.1: *Lexington* (CV 2) and *Saratoga* (CV 3), anchored together. The *Saratoga* can be distinguished by the stripe on her funnel.

Size and power, but not protection, were increased. The Naval Limitation Treaty of 1936 limited the tonnage of new carriers to 23,000 tons. Needing another carrier in the minimum building time, the Navy ordered the *Hornet* as a duplicate of the *Yorktown*.

With the outbreak of war in 1939, France and the United Kingdom suspended their participation in the 1936 treaty, thus freeing the United States from its limits. The design for the *Essex* class grew out of these facts. The idea of an armored flight deck was rejected both for considerations of weight and because an open, naturally ventilated hangar deck was desired. The larger ship was required because new airplanes needed a longer flight deck, and increases in aviation fuel capacity, armament, protection, and propulsive power. The new carriers were designed to be fast; a speed of 33 knots was required. As always, the size of American warships was limited by the width of the locks of the Panama Canal, 110'.

In 1943 antiaircraft protection was increased, necessitating an increase in length, which was carried out in the later *Essex* class carriers. To keep the flight deck clear for flight operations, the additional 40mm and 20mm gun mounts were installed on the bow and stern, and along the flight deck on both sides. The urgent need to get new carriers into service meant some were completed without the changes that had been authorized. The changes made necessary by wartime experience eliminated margins originally included for weight and stability.

The war in the Pacific Ocean was a carrier war from the beginning, with the Japanese attack on Pearl Harbor. In April 1942 planes from the carrier *Hornet* under Lt. Col. James H. Doolittle bombed Tokyo, an indication of what was to come. The Battles of the Coral Sea and Midway took place without the opposing fleets meeting. During 1942 four of the Navy's seven carriers were lost; at one point only the *Enterprise* was in service. For a period in 1943 the British carrier *Victorious* operated with the Navy.

In order to fill the gap, ten light cruisers under construction were converted to light carriers. In addition, the escort carriers of the *Sangamon* class were used in fleet operations.

As more *Essex* class ships came into service, the fast carrier task force came into its own. The ships ordered in 1940—the battleships, the *Baltimore-* and *Cleveland-*class cruisers, and *Fletcher-*class destroyers—were designed with high speed and proved proper escorts for the carriers. Ranging the Pacific, they devastated Japanese forces and installations. As the war progressed they made steadily deeper incursions into waters the Japanese felt to be their own. In February 1944 the first attack on the fortress island of Truk in the Caroline Islands was made, and in the months ahead the carriers struck at the Bonin, Mariana, and Ryukyu Islands; Formosa; and the Philippines. In February 1945 the first attacks on Tokyo and Japan proper were made.

Japan could not match American industrial power in terms of ship construction. At the Battle of the Philippine Sea over 600 planes were destroyed, with the loss of many experienced pilots, spelling the end of Japanese naval aviation. At the Battle of Leyte Gulf, the four Japanese carriers sunk off Cape Engano were decoys; they had no planes. In late 1944 the Japanese introduced the new tactic of using planes manned by pilots who deliberately crashed themselves into enemy ships—*kamikaze* (literally, "divine wind"). At Leyte, Luzon, Iwo Jima, and Okinawa, the carriers were the main target of these suicide planes, and suffered heavily. The saga of the *Franklin* losing 724 of her crew, yet with the ship surviving, became legendary.

Task Forces 38 and 58, under Admirals Raymond A. Spruance and William F. Halsey, were composed of the same carriers, alternating command.

As the war ended, the first of the next generation of carriers, the *Midway*, was completed; it was considerably larger, with increased capacity and an armored flight deck.

The development of the escort carrier was most significant in winning the war in the Atlantic against the German U-boats. The first conversion was that of the *Long Island*, followed by that of a number of others built for the United Kingdom under lend-lease. The four *Sangamon-*class carriers were converted oilers, but tankers were more urgently needed and so no more oilers were converted. The 50 *Casablanca-*class ships were built quickly, with the last being commissioned just one year after the very first. Escort carriers made possible the closing of the gap in air protection for Atlantic convoys from land bases. In the Pacific they were useful in providing air protection for landings and for transporting aircraft. Not intended for front-line combat, the escort carriers with their escorting destroyers of Taffy 3 (TG 77.4.3) made naval history when confronted with the main striking force of the Japanese Navy off Samar in Leyte Gulf.

Aircraft carriers were designated CV, and during the war other classifications—CVL, CVB and CVE—were devised. Carriers were named after historic battles and famous ships of the old Navy. Escort carriers were named after bays and battles.

AIRCRAFT CARRIER ON THE NAVY LIST, 1922

CV 1 *Langley* Joined Pacific Fleet 29 Nov 1924. Damaged by generator explosion off Ambrose Light, N.Y., 29 Apr 1927. Damaged by explosion at San Diego, Calif., 20 Dec 1927 (1 killed). Converted to seaplane tender; flight deck cut back to midship, and rec **AV 3**, 14 Jan 1937. Sunk by Japanese aircraft 75 miles southeast of Tjilatjap, Java, 27 Feb 1942. Armament: 4–5"/51 guns.
(14 killed) Survivors picked up by destoyers *Whipple* and *Edsall* and transferred to oiler *Pecos* (About 260 lost with *Pecos*).

Lexington Class

No.	Name	Builder	Keel Laid	Launched	Comm.
CV 2	*Lexington* ex–CC 1 (1 Jul 1922)	Fore River	8 Jan 1921	3 Oct 1925	14 Dec 1927
CV 3	*Saratoga* ex–CC 3 (1 Jul 1922)	NY Sbdg	25 Sep 1920	7 Apr 1925	16 Nov 1927

Displacement	33,000 tons; 47,700 f/l; *Saratoga* (1945): 48,552 f/l.
Dimensions	888' (oa); 850' (wl); 822' (bp) x 105'6" x 24'2"; *Saratoga* (1945): 909'6" (oa); beam 111'9" (oa).
Machinery	4 screws; GE T-E, 16 Yarrow boilers (WF 3); SHP 180,000; 33.9 knots
Endurance	12,000/14; (1945) 9,500/15
Complement	2,176; (1945) 3,375
Armament	8–8"/55, 12–5"/25 AA; *Saratoga* (1942): 8–5"/38, 36–1.1" AA; (1945) 12–5"/38, 2 twin 40mm, 23 quad 40mm, 16–20mm guns
Armor	5" to 7" belt

Notes: Converted from incomplete hulls of canceled battle cruisers. Largest ships built in the United States up to that time, and the only U.S. carriers with integrated hull and flight deck. *Saratoga* had a vertical black recognition stripe on her stack. Flight deck widened forward and AA added, Oct 1940; 8" gun turrets removed in 1942 for coast defense in Hawaii, and replaced in the *Lexington* by 20–20mm AA.

Figure 2.2: *Lexington* (CV 2), 1941. Notice massive funnel, tripod mast, and twin 8" gun turrets.

Figure 2.3: *Saratoga* (CV 3), in 1943, with her island superstructure and funnel cut down. At this time she operated with the British fleet in the Indian Ocean.

Service Records:

CV 2 *Lexington* Provided electric power to the city of Tacoma, Washington, 17 Dec 1929–16 Jan 1930. At sea en route to Midway, 7 Dec 1941. Damaged by two or three aircraft torpedoes and two bombs at Battle of the Coral Sea, causing massive gas vapor explosion, and sunk by U.S. destroyers, 8 May 1942 (216 killed).
2* Salamaua-Lae Raid, Coral Sea.

CV 3 *Saratoga* Went aground on Sunset Beach, Calif., 18 Aug 1932. Torpedoed by submarine *I-6* 500 miles southwest of Oahu, 11 Jan 1942 (6 killed). Torpedoed by Japanese submarine *I-26* southeast of Guadalcanal, moderately damaged, 31 Aug 1942. Operated with British fleet in Indian Ocean, Mar–May 1944. Severely damaged when hit by four kamikazes and two bombs off Iwo Jima, 21 Feb 1945 (123 killed). Carried largest number of troops home (29,204) in Operation Magic Carpet voyages. Sunk as target at Bikini atomic bomb test, 25 Jul 1946.
7* Guadalcanal-Tulagi, Guadalcanal, Eastern Solomons, Buka Raid, 1st Rabaul Raid, 2nd Rabaul Raid, Gilbert Is., Kwajalein, Eniwetok, Sabang Raid, Soerabaja Raid, Honshu Raid 2/45, Iwo Jima. Operation Magic Carpet.

Ranger

No.	Name	Builder	Keel Laid	Launched	Comm.
CV 4	*Ranger*	Newport News	26 Sep 1931	25 Feb 1933	4 Jun 1934

Displacement	14,500 tons; 19,000 f/l
Dimensions	769' (oa); 728' (wl) x 80'1" x 19'8"
Machinery	2 screws; Curtis HP GT and Parsons LP GT; 6 B&W boilers; SHP 53,500; 29.25 knots
Endurance	11,500/15
Complement	1,788; (1945) 2,650
Armament	8–5"/25 AA; (1945) 6 quad 40mm AA, 46–20mm added
Armor	none

Notes: First U.S. aircraft carrier built from the keel up. Open hangar deck, gallery around flight deck. Three funnels on each side aft could be tilted to horizontal position. No underwater protection; too slow for World War II fleet operations. Intended to provide scouting for battleship force.

Figure 2.4: *Ranger* (CV 4), 6 Apr 1935, as completed. Notice the funnels aft lowered horizontally for flight operations. She proved too slow for fleet operations in the Pacific.

Service Record:

CV 4 *Ranger* Neutrality patrol. Damaged by fire at Norfolk, Va., 12 Jul 1939. Action with French warships off Casablanca, 8 Nov 1942. Trained pilots, 1944–45. Decomm 18 Oct 1946. Stricken 29 Oct 1946, sold 28 Jan 1947, BU Chester, Pa.
2* North Africa, Raid on Norway.

Yorktown Class

No.	Name	Builder	Keel Laid	Launched	Comm.
CV 5	*Yorktown*	Newport News	21 May 1934	4 Apr 1936	30 Sep 1937
CV 6	*Enterprise*	Newport News	16 Jul 1934	3 Oct 1936	12 May 1938

Displacement	19,800 tons, 32,060 f/l
Dimensions	827'4" (oa); 770' (wl) x 95'5" x 31'; *Enterprise* beam (1945): 114'
Machinery	4 screws; Curtis HP GT and Parsons LP GT; 9 B&W boilers; SHP 120,000; 32.5 knots
Endurance	12,000/15
Complement	2,921

Figure 2.5: *Yorktown* (CV 5), 1941. Notice biplanes lining the flight deck and large distinguishing *Y* on funnel.

Figure 2.6: *Enterprise* (CV 6), 27 Oct 1945, at New York for the victory celebrations. She took part in every major Pacific operation except Coral Sea.

Armament	8–5"/38, six quad 40mm, 8 twin 40mm, fifty 20mm AA; (1945) 8–5"/38, six quad 40mm, 8 twin 40mm, fifty 20mm guns
Armor	2.5–4" belt, 4" bulkheads, 2–4" CT

Notes: Size and power increased but very light protection. The *Enterprise* had blisters added 1943.

Service Records:

CV 5 *Yorktown* Neutrality patrol. Extensive damage by aircraft bomb, Battle of Coral Sea, 8 May 1942 (66 killed). Damaged by three aircraft bombs at Battle of Midway, later by two torpedoes, 4 Jun 1942 and torpedoed twice by *I-168* on the 6th, sank on 7 Jun 1942 (86 killed).
3* Marshall-Gilberts Raid 1942, Salamaua-Lae Raid, Coral Sea, Midway.

CV 6 *Enterprise* At sea en route to Pearl Harbor, 7 Dec 1941. Minor damage by one bomb near miss, Marshall Is. Raid, 1 Feb 1942. Extensive damage by three aircraft bombs, Eastern Solomons, 24 Aug 1942 (74 killed). Damaged by two aircraft bombs, Battle of Santa Cruz, 26 Oct 1942 (44 killed). Minor damage by aircraft bomb off Kyushu, 18 Mar 1945. Damaged in error by U.S. Naval gunfire off Japan, 20 Mar 1945. Slight damage by Kamikaze, Okinawa, 11 Apr 1945. Severely damaged by kamikaze off Honshu, 13 May 1945 (14 killed). Decomm 17 Feb 1947. †
20* Marshall-Gilberts Raid 1942, Wake I. Raid 1942, Marcus I. Raid 1942, Midway, Guadalcanal-Tulagi, Eastern Solomons, Santa Cruz, Rennell Is., Gilbert Is., Kwajalein, Raid on Truk, Jaluit Attack, Palau-Yap Raids 3/44, Hollandia, Truk Raid 4/44, Saipan, Philippine Sea, Bonins-Yap Raids, Palau, Philippines Raids 9/44, Okinawa Raid 10/44, N. LuzonFormosa Raids 10/44, Luzon Raids 10/44, Surigao Strait, Formosa Raids 1/45, Luzon Raids 1/45, China Coast Raids 1/45, Honshu Raid 2/45, Iwo Jima, Fleet Raids 1945. PUC, Operation Magic Carpet.

Submarine sunk: *I-70*, northeast of Pearl Harbor, 10 Dec 1941.

Wasp

No.	Name	Builder	Keel Laid	Launched	Comm.
CV 7	*Wasp*	Beth. Quincy	1 Apr 1936	4 Apr 1939	25 Apr 1940

Displacement	14,700 tons
Dimensions	741'4" (oa); 688' (wl) x 80'9" x 20'; extreme beam 111'10"
Machinery	2 screws; GT; 6 3-drum boilers; SHP 75,000; 29.5 knots
Endurance	12,000/15
Complement	2,367
Armament	8–5"/38, 4 quad 1.1" AA guns; later 34–20mm AA

Notes: Four catapults and the first deck edge elevator. Small size, not repeated.

Service Record:

CV 7 *Wasp* Neutrality patrol. Damaged in collision with destroyer *Stack* in North Atlantic, 17 Mar 1942. Made two trips with Spitfires to reinforce Malta, Apr–May 1942. Torpedoed by *I-19* south of Guadalcanal, causing gas and ammunition explosion, 15 Sep 1942, and sunk by destroyer *Lansdowne* (193 killed).
2* Reinforcement of Malta, Solomons, Guadalcanal-Tulagi.

Hornet

No.	Name	Builder	Keel Laid	Launched	Comm.
CV 8	*Hornet*	Newport News	25 Sep 1939	14 Dec 1940	20 Oct 1941

Displacement	19,900 tons, 25,600 f/l
Dimensions	824'9" (oa); 761' (wl) x 83'1" 114' x 21'8"; extreme beam
Machinery	4 screws; GT; 9 boilers; SHP 120,000; 32.5 knots
Endurance	12,500/15
Complement	2,900
Armament	8–5"/38, 4 quad 1.1" AA guns, 32–20mm added 1942
Armor	2.5" to 4" belt, 4" bulkheads, 2" to 4" CT, 4" sides

Notes: Repeat *Yorktown*. New directors and CT.

Service Record:

CV 8 *Hornet* Carried 16 Army B-25 bombers for Raid on Tokyo (commanded by Lt. Col. James H. Doolittle), 18 Apr 1942. Damaged by Japanese aircraft, three torpedoes and two bombs, at Battle of Santa Cruz, and sunk by Japanese destroyers after being abandoned, 25 Oct 1942 (111 killed).

3* Midway, Buin Raid 1942, Solomons, Santa Cruz.

Figure 2.7: *Wasp* (CV 7), Jul 1942, after carrying planes to reinforce Malta. Too small, she was sunk two months later.

Figure 2.8: *Hornet* (CV 8), launching a B-26 bomber for the raid on Tokyo, led by Col. James Doolittle, 18 Apr 1942. Other bombers can be seen amassed on the flight deck, aft.

Figure 2.9: *Bunker Hill* (CV 17), 24 May 1943, the third *Essex*–class carrier, as completed, leaving Boston harbor. Notice the deck-edge elevator folded down and the two deck elevators.

Figure 2.10: *Bon Homme Richard* (CV 31), the last of the short-hull *Essex* class to be completed.

Essex Class

No.	Name	Builder	Keel Laid	Launched	Comm.
CV 9	*Essex*	Newport News	28 Apr 1941	31 Jul 1942	31 Dec 1942
CV 10	*Yorktown*	Newport News	1 Dec 1941	21 Jan 1943	15 Apr 1943
	ex–*Bon Homme Richard* (26 Sep 1942)				
CV 11	*Intrepid*	Newport News	1 Dec 1941	26 Apr 1943	16 Aug 1943
CV 12	*Hornet*	Newport News	3 Aug 1942	30 Aug 1943	29 Nov 1943
	ex–*Kearsarge* (24 Jan 1943)				
CV 13	*Franklin*	Newport News	7 Dec 1942	14 Oct 1943	31 Jan 1944
CV 16	*Lexington*	Beth. Quincy	15 Jul 1941	26 Sep 1942	17 Feb 1943
	ex–*Cabot* (16 Jun 1942)				
CV 17	*Bunker Hill*	Beth. Quincy	15 Sep 1941	7 Dec 1942	24 May 1943
CV 18	*Wasp*	Beth. Quincy	18 Mar 1942	17 Aug 1943	24 Nov 1943
	ex–*Oriskany* (13 Nov 1942)				
CV 20	*Bennington*	New York NYd	15 Dec 1942	26 Feb 1944	6 Aug 1944
CV 31	*Bon Homme Richard*	New York NYd	1 Feb 1943	29 Apr 1944	26 Nov 1944

Displacement	27,100 tons; 36,380 f/l
Dimensions	872' (oa); 820' (wl) x 93' x 28'6"; extreme beam 147'6"
Machinery	4 screws; West. GT; 8 B&W boilers; SHP 150,000; 33 knots
Endurance	20,000/15
Complement	3,428
Armament	12–5"/38, 8 quad 40mm, 46–20mm AA
Armor	2.5" to 4" belt, 1.5" hangar deck, 4" bulkheads, 1.5" CT

Notes: Short hull type. Two catapults. In 1945 approved armament was 17 or 18 quad 40mm guns, but this was not fitted in all. The flight deck overhanging the bows proved to be vulnerable to storms in 1944–45.

Service Records:

CV 9 *Essex* Refit Aug–Oct 1944. Damaged by kamikaze off Luzon, 25 Nov 1944 (15 killed). Damaged by U.S. Naval gunfire, off Shikoku, 19 Mar 1945. Damaged by aircraft crash, Okinawa, 27 Mar 1945. In collision with destroyer *Borie* southeast of Okinawa, 2 Apr 1945. Moderate damage by aircraft bomb, Okinawa, 11 Apr 1945 (33 killed). Decomm 9 Jan 1947. †
13* Marcus I. 1943, Wake Raid 1943, 2nd Rabaul Raid, Gilbert Is., Kwajalein, Raid on Truk, Marianas Raids 2/44, Saipan, 1st Bonins Raid, Philippine Sea, Guam, Tinian, Palau, Philippines Raids 9/44, Okinawa Raid 10/44, N. Luzon–Formosa Raids 10/44, Luzon Raids 10/44, Visayas Is. Raids 10/44, Formosa Raids 1/45, Luzon Raids 1/45, Formosa Raids 1/45, China Coast Raids 1/45, Nansei Shoto Raid 1/45, Honshu Raid 2/45, Iwo Jima, Fleet Raids 1945, Raids on Japan 7–8/45. PUC.

CV 10 *Yorktown* Damaged by aircraft bomb off Kyushu, 18 Mar 1945 (5 killed). Decomm 9 Jan 1947. †
11* Marcus I. 1943, Wake Raid 1943, Gilbert Is., Kwajalein, Raid on Truk, Marianas Raids 2/44, Palau-Yap Raids 3/44, Hollandia, Truk Raid 4/44, Saipan, 1st Bonins Raid, Philippine Sea, 2nd Bonins Raid, 3rd Bonins Raid, Guam, Palau-Yap Raids 7/44, Luzon Raids 10/44, Formosa Raids 1/45, Luzon Raids 1/45, Nansei Shoto Raid 1/45, Honshu Raid 2/45, Iwo Jima, Fleet Raids 1945, Raids on Japan 7–8/45. PUC.

CV 11 *Intrepid* Torpedoed by Japanese aircraft off Truk, 17 Feb 1944. Repairs Mar–Jun 1944. Damaged by kamikaze, Leyte, 29 Oct 1944 (10 killed). Severe damage by two kamikazes in Philippine Sea, 25 Nov 1944 (65 killed). Minor damage by kamikaze and U.S. Naval gunfire off Kyushu, 18 Mar 1945 (2 killed). Severely damaged by kamikaze east of Okinawa, 16 Apr 1945 (8 killed). Repairs May–Aug 1945. Decomm 22 Mar 1947. †
5* Kwajalein, Raid on Truk, Palau, Philippines Raids 9/44, Okinawa Raid 10/44, N. Luzon–Formosa Raids 10/44, Luzon Raids 10/44, Visayas Is. Raids 10/44, Fleet Raids 1945.

CV 12 *Hornet* Damaged in typhoon in Philippine Sea, forward flight deck collapsed, 5 Jun 1945. Decomm 15 Jan 1947. †

Figure 2.11: *Franklin* (CV 13) on fire and listing after Kamikaze attack, 19 Mar 1945. She was heavily damaged and lost 724 crewmen. Although repaired, she was never again in active service.

Figure 2.12: USS *Ticonderoga* (CV 14) on commissioning day, 8 May 1944.

7* Palau-Yap Raids 3/44, Hollandia, Truk Raid 4/44, Saipan, 1st Bonins Raid, Philippine Sea, 2nd Bonins Raid, 3rd Bonins Raid, Guam, Palau-Yap Raids 7/44, 4th Bonins Raid, Palau, Philippines Raids 9/44, Morotai, Okinawa Raid 10/44, N. Luzon–Formosa Raids 10/44, Luzon Raids 10/44, Surigao Strait, Formosa Raids 1/45, Luzon Raids 1/45, China Coast Raids 1/45, Nansei Shoto Raid 1/45, Honshu Raid 2/45, Iwo Jima, Fleet Raids 1945. PUC, Operation Magic Carpet.

CV 13 *Franklin* Damaged by aircraft crash east of Philippines, 13 and 15 Aug 1944. Lightly damaged by kamikaze off Formosa, 13 Oct 1944. Damaged by aircraft bomb, Philippine Sea, 15 Oct 1944 (3 killed). Damaged by kamikaze 1,000 miles east of Samar, 27 Oct 1944, and again, extensively, 30 Oct 1944 (56 killed). Severely damaged by two aircraft bombs 50 miles south of Kyushu, 19 Mar 1945 (724 killed). Not returned to service. Decomm 17 Feb 1947. †

4* 3rd Bonins Raid, Guam, Palau-Yap Raids 7/44, 4th Bonins Raid, Bonins-Yap Raids, Palau, Philippines Raids 9/44, Okinawa Raid 10/44, N. Luzon–Formosa Raids 10/44, Luzon Raids 10/44, Fleet Raids 1945.

CV 16 *Lexington* Moderate damage when torpedoed by Japanese aircraft off Wotje, Marshall Is., 4 Dec 1943. Repairs Dec 1943–Feb 1944. Damaged by kamikaze and bomb off Luzon, 5 Nov 1944 (50 killed). Decomm 23 Apr 1947. †

11* Tarawa Raid 1943, Wake Raid 1943, Gilbert Is., Palau-Yap Raids 3/44, Hollandia, Truk Raid 4/44, Saipan, Philippine Sea, Guam, Palau-Yap Raids 7/44, 4th Bonins Raid, Palau, Philippines Raids 9/44, Okinawa Raid 10/44. N. Luzon–Formosa Raids 10/44, Luzon Raids 10/44, Surigao Strait, Formosa Raids 1/45, Luzon Raids 1/45, China Coast Raids 1/45, Nansei Shoto Raid 1/45, Iwo Jima, Honshu Raid 2/45, Raids on Japan 7–8/45. PUC, Operation Magic Carpet.

CV 17 *Bunker Hill* Damaged by aircraft bomb near miss in Philippine Sea, 19 Jun 1944 (2 killed). Refit Nov 1944–Jan 1945. Severely damaged by two kamikazes, Okinawa, 11 May 1945 (389 killed). Decomm 9 Jan 1947. †

11* 2nd Rabaul Raid, Gilbert Is., Kavieng Raid 1943, Kavieng Raid 1/44, Kwajalein, Raid on Truk, Marianas Raids 2/44, Palau-Yap Raids 3/44, Hollandia, Truk Raid 4/44, Saipan, Philippine Sea, Guam, Palau-Yap Raids 7/44, 4th Bonins Raid, Palau, Philippines Raids 9/44, Okinawa Raid 10/44, N. Luzon–Formosa Raids 10/44, Luzon Raids 10/44, Honshu Raid 2/45, Iwo Jima, Fleet Raids 1945. Operation Magic Carpet.

Figure 2.13: *Antietam* (CV 36), 1945; *Essex* class, long-hull type.

CV 18 *Wasp* Damaged by aircraft bomb and near misses, Philippine Sea, 19 Jun 1944. Damaged by aircraft bomb off Shikoku, 19 Mar 1945 (101 killed). Refit Apr–Jul 1945. Damaged in typhoon, forward flight deck collapsed, 25 Aug 1945. Flight deck buckled in Atlantic storm bringing troops home, 28 Dec 1945. Decomm 17 Feb 1947. †

8* Morotai, Saipan, 3rd Bonins Raid, Philippine Sea, Guam, Palau-Yap Raids 7/44, Palau, Philippines Raids 9/44, Okinawa Raid 10/44, N. Luzon–Formosa Raids 10/44, Luzon Raids 10/44, Surigao Strait, Formosa Raids 1/45, Luzon Raids 1/45, China Coast Raids 1/45, Nansei Shoto Raid 1/45, Honshu Raid 2/45, Iwo Jima, Fleet Raids 1945, Raids on Japan 7–8/45. Operation Magic Carpet.

CV 20 *Bennington* Damaged in typhoon in Philippine Sea, bow smashed, 5 Jun 1945. Decomm 8 Nov 1946. †

3* Honshu Raid 2/45, Iwo Jima, Fleet Raids 1945, Raids on Japan 7–8/45.

CV 31 *Bon Homme Richard* Decomm 9 Jan 1947. †

1* Raids on Japan 7–8/45. Operation Magic Carpet.

Ticonderoga Class

No.	Name	Builder	Keel Laid	Launched	Comm.
CV 14	*Ticonderoga*	Newport News	1 Feb 1943	7 Feb 1944	8 May 1944
	ex–*Hancock* (1 May 1943)				
CV 15	*Randolph*	Newport News	10 May 1943	29 Jun 1944	9 Oct 1944
CV 19	*Hancock*	Beth. Quincy	26 Jan 1943	24 Jan 1944	15 Apr 1944
	ex–*Ticonderoga* (1 May 1943)				
CV 21	*Boxer*	Newport News	13 Sep 1943	14 Dec 1944	16 Apr 1945
CV 32	*Leyte*	Newport News	21 Feb 1944	23 Aug 1945	11 Apr 1946
	ex–*Crown Point* (8 May 1945)				
CV 33	*Kearsarge*	New York NYd	1 Mar 1944	5 May 1945	2 Mar 1946
CV 34	*Oriskany*	New York NYd	1 May 1944	13 Oct 1945	25 Sep 1950
CV 35	*Reprisal*	New York NYd	1 Jul 1944	—	—
CV 36	*Antietam*	Phila. NYd	15 Mar 1943	20 Aug 1944	28 Jan 1945
CV 37	*Princeton*	Phila. NYd	14 Sep 1943	8 Jul 1945	18 Nov 1945
	ex–*Valley Forge* (20 Nov 1944)				
CV 38	*Shangri-La*	Norfolk NYd	15 Jan 1943	24 Feb 1944	15 Sep 1944
CV 39	*Lake Champlain*	Norfolk NYd	15 Mar 1943	2 Nov 1944	3 Jun 1945
CV 40	*Tarawa*	Norfolk NYd	1 Mar 1944	12 May 1945	8 Dec 1945
CV 45	*Valley Forge*	Phila. NYd	7 Sep 1944	18 Nov 1945	3 Nov 1946
CV 46	*Iwo Jima*	Newport News	29 Jan 1945	—	—
CV 47	*Philippine Sea*	Beth. Quincy	19 Aug 1944	5 Sep 1945	11 May 1946
	ex–*Wright* (13 Feb 1945)				
CV 50–55	—	—	—	—	—

Displacement	27,100 tons ; 36,380 f/l
Dimensions	888' (oa); 820' (wl) x 93' x 28'6"; extreme beam 147'6"
Machinery	4 screws; West. GT; 8 B&W boilers; SHP 150,000; 33 knots
Endurance	16,900/15
Complement	3,428
Armament	12–5"/38, 18 quad 40mm, 56 to 62 20mm AA guns

Notes: Modified design. Long hull type. CV 32 originally ordered from New York NYd.

Service Records:

CV 14 *Ticonderoga* Severely damaged by aircraft bomb and two kamikazes in South China Sea, 21 Jan 1945 (143 killed). Repairs Jan–Apr 1945. Decomm 9 Jan 1947. †
5* Palau, Philippines Raids 9/44, Luzon Raids 10/44, Formosa Raids 1/45, Luzon Raids 1/45, China Coast Raids 1/45, Fleet Raids 1945, Raids on Japan 7–8/45. Operation Magic Carpet.

CV 15 *Randolph* Moderately damaged by kamikaze at Ulithi, Micronesia, 11 Mar 1945 (25 killed). †
3* Iwo Jima, Honshu Raid 2/45, Fleet Raids 1945, Raids on Japan 7–8/45. Operation Magic Carpet.

CV 19 *Hancock* Slightly damaged by aircraft bomb north of Luzon, 14 Oct 1944. Damaged by kamikaze off Luzon, 25 Nov 1944. Damaged by plane crash and bomb explosion off Formosa, 21 Jan 1945 (52 killed). Severe damage by kamikaze, Okinawa, 7 Apr 1945 (72 killed). Repairs Apr–Jun 1945. Decomm 9 May 1947. †
4* Formosa Raids 1/45, Luzon Raids 1/45, China Coast Raids 1/45, Nansei Shoto Raid 1/45, Honshu Raid 2/45, Iwo Jima, Raids on Japan 7–8/45. Operation Magic Carpet.

CV 21 *Boxer* †

CV 32 *Leyte* †

CV 33 *Kearsarge* †

CV 34 *Oriskany* Construction suspended when 40 percent complete, 12 Aug 1945. Reordered, 8 Aug 1947. †

CV 35 *Reprisal* Canceled 12 Aug 1945 when 52.3 percent complete. Hull used as target. Sold 2 Aug 1949, BU Baltimore.

CV 36 *Antietam* Damaged by explosion at Hunters Point NYd, 19 Nov 1946. †

CV 37 *Princeton* †

CV 38 *Shangri-La* Operation Crossroads. Decomm 7 Nov 1947. †
2* Fleet Raids 1945, Raids on Japan 7–8/45.

CV 39 *Lake Champlain* Set record for crossing the Atlantic, 26 Nov 1945 (four days, eight hours, 51 minutes). Decomm 17 Feb 1947. Operation Magic Carpet. †

CV 40 *Tarawa* †

CV 45 *Valley Forge* †

CV 46 *Iwo Jima* Canceled 12 Aug 1945.

CV 47 *Philippine Sea* †

CV 50–55 Canceled 27 Mar 1945.

Midway Class

No.	Name	Builder	Keel Laid	Launched	Comm.
CVB 41	*Midway*	Newport News	27 Oct 1943	20 Mar 1945	10 Sep 1945
CVB 42	*Franklin D. Roosevelt*	New York Nyd	1 Dec 1943	29 Apr 1945	27 Oct 1945
	ex–*Coral Sea* (8 May 1945)				
CVB 43	*Coral Sea*	Newport News	10 Jul 1944	2 Apr 1946	1 Oct 1947
CV 44	—	Newport News	—	—	—
CVB 56/57	—	Newport News	—	—	—

Displacement	45,000 tons; 60,100 f/l
Dimensions	968' (oa); 900' (wl) x 113' x 35'; extreme beam 136'
Machinery	4 screws, West. GT; 12 B&W boilers; SHP 212,000; 33 knots (CV42:GE)
Endurance	20,000/15
Complement	4,104
Armament	18–5"/54, 21 quad 40mm, 28–20mm AA guns
Armor	7.6" belt; 3.5" flight deck; 6.3" bulkheads, 3.5" to 6.5" CT

Notes: Armored flight deck. CV 42 originally ordered from Newport News,

Figure 2.14: *Belleau Wood* (CVL 24), 22 Dec 1943; *Independence* class. At sea in the Pacific, she was one of nine light cruiser hulls hurriedly converted in 1942 to relieve the shortage of aircraft carriers. Notice the break in the hull forward showing the armor.

Figure 2.15: *Cowpens* (CVL 25) 12 May 1945. Notice the four funnel uptakes and the island outside the flight deck.

reordered 21 Jan 1943; CV 43 and CV 44 canceled 11 Jan 1943; CV 43 reinstated 28 May 1943. Antiaircraft battery relocated below flight deck level.

Service Records:

CVB 41 *Midway* †
CVB 42 *Franklin D. Roosevelt* †
CVB 43 *Coral Sea* †
CVB 44 Canceled 11 Jan 1943.
CVB 56/57 Canceled 28 Mar 1945.

Independence Class

No.	Name	Builder	Keel Laid	Launched	Comm.
CVL 22	*Independence*	NY Sbdg	1 May 1941	22 Aug 1942	14 Jan 1943
	ex-*Amsterdam*, CL 59 (10 Jan 1942)				
CVL 23	*Princeton*	NY Sbdg	2 Jun 1941	18 Oct 1942	25 Feb 1943
	ex-*Tallahassee*, CL 61 (16 Feb 1942)				
CVL 24	*Belleau Wood*	NY Sbdg	11 Aug 1941	6 Dec 1942	31 Mar 1943
	ex-*New Haven*, CL 76 (16 Feb 1942)				
CVL 25	*Cowpens*	NY Sbdg	17 Nov 1941	17 Jan 1943	28 May 1943
	ex-*Huntington*, CL 77 (27 Mar 1942)				
CVL 26	*Monterey*	NY Sbdg	29 Dec 1941	28 Feb 1943	17 Jun 1943
	ex-*Dayton*, CL 78 (27 Mar 1942)				
CVL 27	*Langley*	NY Sbdg	11 Apr 1942	22 May 1943	31 Aug 1943
	ex *Crown Point* (13 Nov 1942), ex-*Fargo*, CL 85 (27 Mar 1942)				
CVL 28	*Cabot*	NY Sbdg	16 Mar 1942	4 Apr 1943	24 Jul 1943
	ex-*Wilmington*, CL 79 (23 Jun 1942)				
CVL 29	*Bataan*	NY Sbdg	31 Aug 1942	1 Aug 1943	17 Nov 1943
	ex-*Buffalo*, CL 99 (2 Jun 1942)				
CVL 30	*San Jacinto*	NY Sbdg	26 Oct 1942	26 Sep 1943	15 Dec 1943
	ex-*Reprisal* (6 Jan 1943), ex-*Newark*, CL 100 (23 Jun 1942)				

Displacement	11,000 tons, 15,100 f/l
Dimensions	622'6" (oa); 600' (wl) x 71'6" x 26'; extreme beam 109'2"
Machinery	4 screws; GE GT; 4 B&W boilers; SHP 100,000; 31.6 knots
Endurance	12,500/15
Complement	1,569
Armament	10 twin 40mm, 2 quad 40mm, 16 to 20 20mm AA guns
Armor	3.75" to 5" bulkheads

Notes: *Cleveland*-class cruiser hulls converted to aircraft carriers while under construction; speed of construction was an important consideration. CV rec CVL, 15 Jun 1943. Originally planned with 2–5"/38. Island built outside the flight deck with four funnel uptakes on starboard side aft.

Service Records:

CVL 22 *Independence* Severely damaged by aircraft torpedo off Tarawa, 20 Nov 1943 (12 killed). Damaged by crash of "friendly" aircraft, Luzon, 25 Nov 1944. Repairs Jan–Jun 1945. Bikini target. Decomm 28 Aug 1946. Sunk as target off Calif., 29 Jan 1951.
8* Marcus I. 1943, Wake Raid 1943, 2nd Rabaul Raid, Gilbert Is., Palau, Philippines Raids 9/44, Formosa Raids 1/45, Luzon Raids 1/45, China Coast Raids 1/45, Nansei Shoto Raid 1/45, Raids on Japan 7–8/45, Okinawa Raid 10/44, N. Luzon–Formosa Raids 10/44, Surigao Strait, Visayas Is. Raids 10/44, Luzon Raids 10/44. Operation Magic Carpet.

CVL 23 *Princeton* Damaged by Japanese aircraft bomb at Battle of Leyte Gulf, 24 Oct 1944; resulting fire led to several explosions, sunk by USS *Reno* (108 killed).
9* Tarawa Raid 1943, Buka Raid, 1st Rabaul Raid, Gilbert Is., Kwajalein, Eniwetok, Palau-Yap Raids 3/44, Hollandia, Truk Raid 4/44, Saipan, Philippine Sea, Guam, Palau, Philippines Raids 9/44, 2nd Rabaul Raid, Okinawa Raid 10/44, N. Luzon–Formosa Raids 10/44, Luzon Raids 10/44, Visayas Is. Raids 10/44, Surigao Strait.

CVL 24 *Belleau Wood* Severely damaged by kamikaze off Leyte, 30 Oct 1944 (92 killed). Repairs and refit Nov 1944–Jan 1945. Damaged in typhoon, Philippine Sea, 5 Jun 1945. Decomm 13 Jan 1947. †
12* Tarawa Raid 1943, Wake Raid 1943, Gilbert Is., Kwajalein, Raid on Truk, Marianas Raids 2/44, Palau-Yap Raids 3/44, Hollandia, Truk Raid 4/44, Morotai, Saipan, 1st Bonins Raid, Philippine Sea, 2nd Bonins Raid, Guam, Palau, Philippines Raids 9/44, Okinawa Raid 10/44, N. Luzon–Formosa Raids 10/44, Luzon Raids 10/44, Surigao Strait, Honshu Raid 2/45, Iwo Jima, Fleet Raids 1945, Raids on Japan 7–8/45. PUC, Operation Magic Carpet.

CVL 25 *Cowpens* Damaged in typhoon, caught fire, lost seven planes, Philippine Sea, 18 Dec 1944 (1 killed). Refit Mar–Jun 1945. Decomm 13 Jan 1947. †
12* Wake Raid 1943, Gilbert Is., Kwajalein, Raid on Truk, Marianas Raids 2/44, Palau-Yap Raids 3/44, Hollandia, Truk Raid 4/44, Saipan, 1st Bonins Raid, Philippine Sea, Palau, Philippines Raids 9/44,

Morotai, Okinawa Raid 10/44, N. Luzon–Formosa Raids 10/44, Luzon Raids 10/44, Surigao Strait, Formosa Raids 1/45, Luzon Raids 1/45, China Coast Raids 1/45, Nansei Shoto Raid 1/45, Honshu Raid 2/45, Iwo Jima, Raids on Japan 7–8/45, Tokyo Bay, Operation Magic Carpet.

CVL 26 *Monterey* Severely damaged by fire in typhoon in Philippine Sea, 18 Dec 1944. Refit Jan–May 1945. Decomm 11 Feb 1947. †
11* Gilbert Is., Kavieng Raid 1943, Kavieng Raid 1/44, Kwajalein, Raid on Truk, Marianas Raids 2/44, Palau-Yap Raids 3/44, Hollandia, Truk Raid 4/44, Saipan, Philippine Sea, 3rd Bonins Raid, Guam, Palau, Philippines Raids 9/44, Morotai, Okinawa Raid 10/44, N. Luzon–Formosa Raids 10/44, Luzon Raids 10/44, Fleet Raids 1945, Raids on Japan 7–8/45. Operation Magic Carpet.
Submarine sunk: *RO-45*, southwest of Truk, 30 Apr 1944.

CVL 27 *Langley* Moderate damage by aircraft bomb in South China Sea, 21 Jan 1945 (3 killed). Hit by bomb off Iwo Jima, 21 Feb 1945. Refit Jun–Jul 1945. Decomm 11 Feb 1947. †
9* Kwajalein, Eniwetok, Palau-Yap Raids 3/44, Hollandia, Truk Raid 4/44, Saipan, 1st Bonins Raid, Philippine Sea, Guam, Palau, Philippines Raids 9/44, Okinawa Raid 10/44, N. Luzon–Formosa Raids 10/44, Luzon Raids 10/44, Visayas Is. Raids 10/44, Formosa Raids 1/45, Luzon Raids 1/45, China Coast Raids 1/45, Nansei Shoto Raid 1/45, Iwo Jima, Honshu Raid 2/45, Fleet Raids 1945. Operation Magic Carpet.

CVL 28 *Cabot* Damaged by two kamikazes off Luzon, 25 Nov 1944. Damaged in typhoon in Philippine Sea, 18 Dec 1944. Refit Mar–Jun 1945. Decomm 11 Feb 1947. †
9* Kwajalein, Raid on Truk, Palau-Yap Raids 3/44, Truk Raid 4/44, Hollandia, Philippine Sea, 3rd Bonins Raid, Saipan, Guam, Palau-Yap Raids 7/44, 4th Bonins Raid, Palau, Philippines Raids 9/44, Okinawa Raid 10/44, N. Luzon–Formosa Raids 10/44, Luzon Raids 10/44, Visayas Is. Raids 10/44, Surigao Strait, Formosa Raids 1/45, Luzon Raids 1/45, China Coast Raids 1/45, Nansei Shoto Raid 1/45, Honshu Raid 2/45, Iwo Jima, Fleet Raids 1945. PUC, Operation Magic Carpet.

CVL 29 *Bataan* Damaged by kamikaze, 17 Apr 1945. Damaged in error by U.S. naval gunfire, off Honshu, 13 May 1945. Decomm 11 Feb 1947. †
6* Hollandia, Truk Raid 4/44, Saipan, 1st Bonins Raid, Philippine Sea, 2nd Bonins Raid, Fleet Raids 1945, Raids on Japan 7–8/45. Tokyo Bay, Operation Magic Carpet.
Submarine sunk: *Kaiten carrier *I-56* east of Okinawa, 18 Apr 1945.

CVL 30 *San Jacinto* Damaged in collision with oiler *Merrimack* off Iwo, 27 Feb 1945. Damaged in typhoon, Philippine Sea, 18 Dec 1944. Minor damage by kamikaze, Okinawa, 6 Apr 1945. Damaged in typhoon in Philippine Sea, 5 Jun 1945. Decomm 1 Mar 1947. †
5* Saipan, Philippine Sea, Guam, Palau-Yap Raids 7/44, 4th Bonins Raid, Bonins-Yap Raids, Palau, Philippines Raids 9/44, Okinawa Raid 10/44, N. Luzon–Formosa Raids 10/44, Luzon Raids 10/44, Formosa Raids 1/45, Luzon Raids 1/45, China Coast Raids 1/45, Nansei Shoto Raid 1/45, Honshu Raid 2/45, Iwo Jima, Fleet Raids 1945, Raids on Japan 7–8/45. PUC.

Saipan Class

No.	Name	Builder	Keel Laid	Launched	Comm.
CVL 48	*Saipan*	NY Sbdg	10 Jul 1944	8 Jul 1945	14 Jul 1946
CVL 49	*Wright*	NY Sbdg	21 Aug 1944	1 Sep 1945	9 Feb 1947

Displacement	14,500 tons; 18,750 f/l
Dimensions	683'7" (oa); 664' (wl) x 76'9" x 25'; extreme beam 108'
Machinery	4 screws; GT; 4 B&W boilers; SHP 120,000; 33 knots
Endurance	11,000/15
Complement	1,787
Armament	5 quad 40–mm, 11 twin 40mm, 16 twin 20mm AA
Armor	2.5" to 4" belt, 2.5" decks, 1.5" to 4" bulkheads

Notes: Improved *Independence* class, hull based on *Baltimore*-class heavy cruisers. Three funnels, two catapults.

Service Records:

CVL 48 *Saipan* †
CVL 49 *Wright* †

ESCORT AIRCRAFT CARRIERS

Escort carriers were originally designated Aircraft Escort Vessels (AVG), and reclassified ACV on 20 Aug 1942 and CVE 15 Jul 1943. AVG 2–5 were reserved for the transports *Wakefield*, *Mount Vernon*, and *West Point* and the liner *Kungsholm*, but conversion would have been too lengthy and was abandoned.

Figure 2.16: *Saipan* (CVL 48), 2 Nov 1946. One of two light carriers built from the keel up, completed after the end of the war. Notice the lowered elevator in the flight deck forward.

Figure 2.17: *Long Island* (CVE 1), later in the war. The first escort carrier converted from a merchant hull in 1941, she was used principally to ferry aircraft; the flight deck is crowded with planes and structures, thus preventing flight operations.

Long Island Class

No.	Name	Builder	Keel Laid	Launched	Comm.
CVE1	*Long Island*	Sun	7 Jul 1939	11 Jan 1940	2 Jun 1941
	ex–*Mormacmail* (1941)				
BAVG1	—	Sun	7 Jun 1939	14 Dec 1939	*17 Nov 1941*
	ex–*Mormacland* (1941)				

Displacement	7,800 tons; 15,400 tons f/l
Dimensions	492'6" (oa); 465' (wl) x 69'6" x 25'6"; extreme beam 102'
Machinery	1 screw; diesel; SHP 8,500, 17.6 knots
Complement	970
Armament	1–5"/38, 2–3"/50

Notes: Flight deck on *Long Island* extended 1941 after completion. Acquired 6 Mar 1941.

Service Record:

CVE 1 *Long Island* Carried first planes to Henderson Field, Guadalcanal, 20 Aug 1942. Decomm 26 Mar 1946. Stricken 12 Apr 1946. Sold 24 Apr 1947.
1* Solomons. Operation Magic Carpet.
Later history: Merchant *Nelly* 1949, renamed *Seven Seas* 1953. Used as hotel 1966. BU 1977 Belgium.

BAVG 1 — To UK, 17 Nov 1941, named HMS *Archer*. Returned 9 Jan 1946. Sold 30 Sep 1947.
Later history: Merchant *Empire Lagan*, renamed *Anna Salen* 1947, *Tasmania* 1955, *Union Reliance* 1961. Damaged in collision at Houston, 7 Nov 1961, BU 1962 New Orleans.

Charger Class

No.	Name	Builder	Keel Laid	Launched	Comm.
BAVG 2	—	Sun	28 Nov 1939	27 Nov 1940	*2 Mar 1942*
	LD as *Rio Hudson*				
BAVG 3	—	Sun	28 Dec 1939	18 Dec 1940	*6 May 1942*
	LD as *Rio Parana*				
CVE 30	*Charger*	Sun	19 Jan 1940	1 Mar 1941	3 Mar 1942
	ex–BAVG 4 (24 Jan 1942), ex–HMS *Charger* (4 Oct 1941), LD as *Rio de la Plata*				
BAVG 5	—	Sun	14 Mar 1940	12 Apr 1941	2 Jul 1942
	LD as *Rio de Janeiro*				

Displacement	15,900 tons f/l
Dimensions	492' (oa); 465' (wl) x 69'6" x 26'3"; extreme beam 111'2"
Machinery	1 screw; diesel; SHP 8,500; 17.6 knots
Complement	856
Armament	1–5"/38, 4–3"/50, 16–40mm AA; CVE 30 *Charger*: 1–5"/51, 2–3"/50, 10–20mm guns

Notes: Lend-lease for UK, *Charger* retained by U.S. Navy.

Service Records:

BAVG 2 — To UK, 2 Mar 1942, named HMS *Avenger*. Torpedoed and sunk by *U-155* west of Gibraltar, 15 Nov 1942.

BAVG 3 — To UK, 6 May 1942, named HMS *Biter*. To France, 9 Apr 1945, renamed *Dixmude*. Sunk as target, 10 Jun 1966.

CVE 30 *Charger* Training, Chesapeake Bay. Decomm 15 Mar 1946. Stricken 28 Mar 1946. Sold 15 Apr 1947.
Later history: Merchant *Fairsea*, 1949.

BAVG 5 — To UK, 2 Jul 1942, named HMS *Dasher*. Sunk by fire and explosion south of Cumbrae, 27 Mar 1943.

Figure 2.18: *Nassau* (CVE 16), 29 Apr 1944, *Bogue*-class escort carrier that served in the Pacific.

Bogue Class

No.	Name	Builder	Keel Laid	Launched	Comm.
BAVG 6	—	Sea-Tac Tacoma	3 Nov 1941	7 Mar 1942	*31 Jan 1943*
CVE 6	*Altamaha* (i)	Ingalls	15 Apr 1941	4 Apr 1942	*31 Oct 1942*
	LD as *Mormacmail*				
CVE 7	*Barnes* (i)	W. Pipe S.F.	7 Apr 1941	27 Sep 1941	*30 Sep 1942*
	LD as *Steel Artisan*				
CVE 8	*Block Island* (i)	Ingalls	12 May 1941	22 May 1942	*9 Jan 1943*
	LD as *Mormacpenn*				
CVE 9	*Bogue*	Sea-Tac Tacoma	1 Oct 1941	15 Jan 1942	26 Sep 1942
	LD as *Steel Advocate*				
CVE 10	*Breton* (i)	Ingalls	28 Jun 1941	19 Jun 1942	*9 Apr 1943*
	LD as *Mormacgulf*				
CVE 11	*Card*	Sea-Tac Tacoma	27 Oct 1941	21 Feb 1942	*8 Nov 1942*
CVE 12	*Copahee*	Sea-Tac Tacoma	18 Jun 1941	21 Oct 1941	15 Jun 1942
CVE 13	*Core*	Sea-Tac Tacoma	2 Jan 1942	15 May 1942	10 Dec 1942
CVE 14	*Croatan* (i)	W. Pipe S.F.	5 Sep 1941	4 Apr 1942	*27 Feb 1943*
CVE 15	*Hamlin*	W.Pipe S.F.	6 Oct 1941	5 Mar 1942	*21 Dec 1942*
CVE 16	*Nassau*	Sea-Tac Tacoma	27 Nov 1941	4 Apr 1942	20 Aug 1942
CVE 17	*St. George*	Ingalls	31 Jul 1941	18 Jul 1942	*14 Jun 1943*
	LD as *Mormacland*				
CVE 18	*Altamaha* (ii)	Sea-Tac Tacoma	19 Dec 1941	25 May 1942	15 Sep 1942
CVE 19	*Prince William* (i)	W. Pipe S.F.	15 Dec 1941	7 May 1942	*28 Apr 1943*

CVE 20	*Barnes* (ii)	Sea-Tac Tacoma	19 Jan 1942	22 May 1942	20 Feb 1943
CVE 21	*Block Island* (ii)	Sea-Tac Tacoma	19 Jan 1942	6 Jun 1942	8 Mar 1943
CVE 22		Sea-Tac Tacoma	2 Feb 1942	20 Jul 1942	*7 Apr 1943*
CVE 23	*Breton* (ii)	Sea-Tac Tacoma	25 Feb 1942	27 Jun 1942	12 Apr 1943
CVE 24	—	Sea-Tac Tacoma	11 Apr 1942	16 Jul 1942	*25 Apr 1943*

Displacement	10,200 tons; 14,200 tons f/l
Dimensions	496' (oa) 465' (wl) x 69'6" x 26'3"; extreme beam 111'2"
Machinery	1 screw, GT, 2 FW D boilers, SHP 8,500, 17 knots
Endurance	26,300/15
Complement	856
Armament	2–5"/38, 10 twin 40mm (CVE 18, CV 20: 8), 27–20mm guns; 28 aircraft

Notes: Converted from C-3 hulls under construction; CVE 31–52 built as carriers from keel up. Island built out over the side so as not to obstruct flight deck.

Service Records:

BAVG 6 — To UK, 31 Jan 1943, named HMS *Tracker.* Returned 29 Nov 1945, sold 14 May 1947.
Later history: Merchant *Corrientes* 1949. BU 1964 Antwerp.

CVE 6 *Altamaha* To UK, 31 Oct 1942, renamed HMS *Battler.* Returned 29 Nov 1945. Stricken 28 Mar 1946, sold 14 May 1946, BU Baltimore.

CVE 7 *Barnes* To UK, 30 Sep 1942, renamed HMS *Attacker.* Returned 5 Jan 1946, sold 28 Oct 1946.
Later history: Merchant *Castel Forte* 1948; renamed *Fairsky* 1958, *Fair Sky, Philippine Tourist* 1979. BU 1980 Hong Kong.

CVE 8 *Block Island* To UK, 9 Jan 1943, renamed HMS *Hunter.* Returned 29 Dec 1945, sold 17 Jan 1947.
Later history: Merchant *Almdijk* 1948. BU 1965 Valencia.

CVE 9 *Bogue* Decomm 30 Nov 1946. †
3* TG 21.12, TG 21.13 (2). PUC, Operation Magic Carpet.
Submarines sunk: *U-569* in Mid-Atlantic, 22 May 1943; *U-217* in Mid-Atlantic, 5 Jun 1943; *U-118* west of Canary Is., 12 Jun 1943; *U-527* south of Azores, 23 Jul 1943; *U-86* off Azores, 29 Nov 1943; *U-172* off Canary Is., 13 Dec 1943; *U-850* west of Madeira, 20 Dec 1943; *U-575* north of Azores, 13 Mar 1944; *I-52* 800 miles southwest of Fayal, Azores, 24 Jun 1944; *U-1229* south of Newfoundland, 20 Aug 1944.

CVE 10 *Breton* To UK, 9 Apr 1943, renamed HMS *Chaser.* Returned 12 May 1946. Sold 20 Dec 1946.
Later history: Merchant *Aagtekerk* 1948, renamed *E-Yung* 1967. Destroyed by fire while under repair at Kaohsiung, Taiwan; beached. 4 Dec 1972. BU Taiwan.

CVE 11 *Card* Decomm 13 May 1946. †
3* TG 21.14. PUC, Operation Magic Carpet.
Submarines sunk: *U-117* in Mid-Atlantic, 7 Aug 1943; *U-664* west of Azores, 9 Aug 1943; *U-525* northwest of Azores, 11 Aug 1943; *U-847* in Sargasso Sea, 27 Aug 1943; *U-460* north of Azores, 4 Oct 1943; *U-402* in Mid-Atlantic, 13 Oct 1943; *U-584* in Mid-Atlantic, 31 Oct 1943.

CVE 12 *Copahee* Decomm 5 Jul 1946. †
1* Saipan, 3rd Bonins Raid. Operation Magic Carpet.

CVE 13 *Core* Decomm 4 Oct 1946. †
1* TG 21.12. Operation Magic Carpet.
Submarines sunk: *U-487* in Mid-Atlantic, 13 Jul 1943; *U-67* in Sargasso Sea, 16 Jul 1943; *U-185* and *U-84* in Mid-Atlantic, 24 Aug 1943; *U-378* in Mid-Atlantic, 20 Oct 1943.

CVE 14 *Croatan* To UK, 27 Feb 1943, renamed HMS *Fencer.* Returned 21 Dec 1946, sold 30 Dec 1947.
Later history: Merchant *Sydney* 1948; renamed *Roma* 1967, *Galaxy Queen* 1971, *Lady Dina* (1972), *Caribia 2* (1973). BU 1974 La Spezia, Italy.

CVE 15 *Hamlin* To UK, 21 Dec 1942, renamed HMS *Stalker.* Returned 29 Dec 1945. Stricken 20 Mar 1946. Sold 18 Dec 1946.
Later history: Merchant *Riouw* (1948), renamed *Lobito* (1967). BU 1975 Gandia, Spain.

CVE 16 *Nassau* Decomm 28 Oct 1946. †
5* Attu, Gilbert Is., Kwajalein, Palau, Philippines Raids 9/44, N. Luzon–Formosa Raids 10/44, Luzon Raids 10/44. Operation Magic Carpet.

CVE 17 *St. George* To UK, 14 Jun 1943, renamed HMS *Pursuer.* Returned 12 Feb 1946, sold 14 May 1946, BU.

CVE 18 *Altamaha* Damaged in typhoon in Philippine Sea, 18 Dec 1944. Decomm 27 Sep 1946. †
1* Formosa Raids 1/45, China Coast Raids 1/45. Operation Magic Carpet.

CVE 19 *Prince William* To UK, 28 Apr 1943, renamed HMS *Striker.* Returned 12 Feb 1946, sold 5 Jun 1946, BU Baltimore.

CVE 20 *Barnes* Decomm 29 Aug 1946. †
3* Gilbert Is., Palau, Philippines Raids 9/44, Luzon Raids 10/44.

CVE 21 *Block Island* Hit by three torpedoes from *U-549* and sank northwest of Canary Is., 29 May 1944.
2* TG 21.16, TG 21.11.
Submarines sunk: *U-220* in Mid-Atlantic, 28 Oct 1943; **U-801* off Cape Verde Is., 17 Mar 1944; *U-1059* southwest of Cape Verde Is., 19 Mar 1944; **U-66* off Cape Verde Is., 1 May 1944.

CVE 22 — To UK, 7 Apr 1943, renamed HMS *Searcher.* Completed by Willamette. Returned 29 Nov 1945, sold 30 Sep 1947.
Later history: Merchant *Captain Theo* 1948, renamed *Oriental Banker* 1964. BU 1976 Kaohsiung, Taiwan.

CVE 23 *Breton* Decomm 30 Aug 1946. †
4* Saipan, Philippine Sea, 2nd Bonins Raid, Okinawa.

CVE 24 — To UK, 25 Apr 1943, renamed HMS *Ravager* (ex-*Charger*). Completed by Willamette. Returned 27 Feb 1946, sold 14 Jan 1947.
Later history: Merchant *Robin Trent* 1948, renamed *Trent* 1972. BU 1973 Kaohsiung, Taiwan.

No.	Name	Builder	Keel Laid	Launched	Comm.
CVE 25	*Croatan* (ii)	Sea-Tac Tacoma	15 Apr 1942	1 Aug 1942	28 Apr 1943

Figure 2.19: *Prince William* (CVE 31), 15 Jul 1943. Her war service consisted of ferrying planes and supplies and training operations.

CVE 31	*Prince William* (ii)	Sea-Tac Tacoma	18 May 1942	23 Aug 1942	29 Apr 1943
CVE 32	*Chatham*	Sea-Tac Tacoma	25 May 1942	19 Sep 1942	*11 Aug 1943*
CVE 33	*Glacier*	Sea-Tac Tacoma	9 Jun 1942	7 Sep 1942	*31 Jul 1943*
CVE 34	*Pybus*	Sea-Tac Tacoma	23 Jun 1942	7 Oct 1942	*6 Aug 1943*
CVE 35	*Baffins*	Sea-Tac Tacoma	18 Jul 1942	18 Oct 1942	*19 Jul 1943*
CVE 36	*Bolinas*	Sea-Tac Tacoma	3 Aug 1942	11 Nov 1942	*2 Aug 1943*
CVE 37	*Bastian*	Sea-Tac Tacoma	25 Aug 1942	15 Dec 1942	*4 Aug 1943*
CVE 38	*Carnegie*	Sea-Tac Tacoma	9 Sep 1942	30 Dec 1942	*13 Aug 1943*
CVE 39	*Cordova*	Sea-Tac Tacoma	22 Sep 1942	27 Dec 1942	*25 Aug 1943*
CVE 40	*Delgada*	Sea-Tac Tacoma	9 Oct 1942	20 Feb 1943	*20 Nov 1943*
CVE 41	*Edisto*	Sea-Tac Tacoma	20 Oct 1942	9 Mar 1943	*7 Sep 1943*
CVE 42	*Estero*	Sea-Tac Tacoma	31 Oct 1942	22 Mar 1943	*3 Nov 1943*
CVE 43	*Jamaica*	Sea-Tac Tacoma	13 Nov 1942	21 Apr 1943	*27 Sep 1943*
CVE 44	*Keweenaw*	Sea-Tac Tacoma	27 Nov 1942	6 May 1943	*22 Oct 1943*
CVE 45	*McClure*	Sea-Tac Tacoma	17 Dec 1942	18 May 1943	*17 Jan 1944*
CVE 46	*Niantic*	Sea-Tac Tacoma	5 Jan 1943	2 Jun 1943	*8 Nov 1943*
CVE 47	*Perdido*	Sea-Tac Tacoma	1 Feb 1943	16 Jun 1943	*31 Jan 1944*
CVE 48	*Sunset*	Sea-Tac Tacoma	23 Feb 1943	15 Jul 1943	*19 Nov 1943*
CVE 49	*St. Andrews*	Sea-Tac Tacoma	12 Mar 1943	2 Aug 1943	*7 Dec 1943*
CVE 50	*St. Joseph*	Sea-Tac Tacoma	25 Mar 1943	21 Aug 1943	*22 Dec 1943*
CVE 51	*St. Simon*	Sea-Tac Tacoma	26 Apr 1943	9 Sep 1943	*31 Dec 1943*
CVE 52	*Vermillion*	Sea-Tac Tacoma	10 May 1943	27 Sep 1943	*20 Jan 1944*
CVE 53	*Willapa*	Sea-Tac Tacoma	21 May 1943	8 Nov 1943	*5 Feb 1944*
CVE 54	*Winjah*	Sea-Tac Tacoma	5 Jun 1943	22 Nov 1943	*18 Feb 1944*

Service Record:

CVE 25 *Croatan* Decomm 20 May 1946. †
2* TG 21.15, TG 22.5. Operation Magic Carpet.
Submarine sunk: **U-490* northwest of Azores, 11 Jun 1944.

CVE 31 *Prince William* Decomm 29 Aug 1946. Operation Magic Carpet. †

CVE 32 *Chatham* To UK, 11 Aug 1943, renamed HMS *Slinger.* Returned 27 Feb 1946. Sold 7 Nov 1946.
Later history: Merchant *Robin Mowbray* 1948. BU 1970 Kaohsiung, Taiwan.

CVE 33 *Glacier* To UK, 31 Jul 1943, renamed HMS *Atheling.* Completed at Puget Sound NYd. Returned 13 Dec 1946. Stricken 7 Feb 1947, sold 26 Nov 1947.
Later history: Merchant *Roma* 1950. BU 1967 Vado, Italy.

CVE 34 *Pybus* To UK, 6 Aug 1943, renamed HMS *Emperor.* Completed at Puget Sound NYd. Returned 12 Feb 1946. Sold 14 May 1946, BU.

CVE 35 *Baffins* To UK, 19 Jul 1943, as HMS *Ameer.* Completed at Puget Sound NYd. Returned 17 Jan 1946. Sold 17 Sep 1946.
Later history: Merchant *Robin Kirk* 1948. BU 1969 Kaohsiung, Taiwan.

CVE 36 *Bolinas* To UK, 2 Aug 1943, as HMS *Begum.* Returned 4 Jan 1946. Sold 16 Apr 1947.
Later history: Merchant *Raki* 1948, renamed *I-Yung* 1966. BU 1974 Kaohsiung, Taiwan.

CVE 37 *Bastian* To UK, 4 Aug 1943, renamed HMS *Trumpeter* (ex-*Lucifer*). Completed at Commercial. Returned 6 Apr 1946. Stricken 21 May 1946, sold 2 May 1947.
Later history: Merchant *Alblasserdijk* 1947, renamed *Irene Valmas* 1966. BU 1971 Castellon, Spain.

CVE 38 *Carnegie* To UK, 13 Aug 1943, renamed HMS *Empress.* Returned 28 Jan 1946. Sold 21 Jun 1946, BU.

CVE 39 *Cordova* To UK, 25 Aug 1943, renamed HMS *Khedive.* Returned 26 Jan 1946. Sold 23 Jan 1947.
Later history: Merchant *Rempang* 1947, renamed *Daphne* 1968. BU 1975 Gandia, Spain.

CVE 40 *Delgada* To UK, 20 Nov 1943, as HMS *Speaker.* Returned 27 Jul 1946. Sold 22 Apr 1947.
Later history: Merchant *Lancero* 1948, renamed *President Osmeña* 1965, *Lucky Three* 1971, *President Osmeña* 1971. BU 1972 Kaohsiung, Taiwan.

CVE 41 *Edisto* To UK, 7 Sep 1943, renamed HMCS *Nabob.* Torpedoed by *U-354* northeast of Tromso, Norway, 23 Aug 1944, CTL. Returned 16 Mar 1945. Sold 28 Oct 1946.
Later history: Merchant *Nabob* 1951, renamed *Glory* 1967. BU 1977 Kaohsiung, Taiwan.

CVE 42 *Estero* To UK, 3 Nov 1943, renamed HMS *Premier.* Returned 12 Apr 1946. Sold 14 Feb 1947.
Later history: Merchant *Rhodesia Star* 1947, renamed *Hongkong Knight* 1967. BU 1974 Kaohsiung, Taiwan.

CVE 43 *Jamaica* To UK, 27 Sep 1943, renamed HMS *Shah.* Returned 6 Dec 1945. Sold 20 Jun 1947.
Later history: Merchant *Salta* 1948. BU 1966 Buenos Aires.

CVE 44 *Keweenaw* To UK, 22 Oct 1943, renamed HMS *Patroller.* Returned 13 Dec 1946. Stricken 7 Feb 1947. Sold 26 Aug 1947.
Later history: Merchant *Almkerk* 1948, renamed *Pacific Reliance* 1968. BU 1974 Kaohsiung, Taiwan.

CVE 45 *McClure* To UK, 17 Jan 1944, renamed HMS *Rajah* (*ex–Prince*). Completed by Willamette. Returned 13 Dec 1946. Stricken 7 Feb 1947. Sold 7 Jul 1947.
Later history: Merchant *Drente* 1948, renamed *Lambros* 1966, *Ulisse* 1969. BU 1975 Savona, Italy.

CVE 46 *Niantic* To UK, 8 Nov 1943, renamed HMS *Ranee.* Returned 21 Nov 1946. Sold 1 Jul 1947.
Later history: Merchant *Friesland* 1948, renamed *Pacific Breeze* 1967. BU 1974 Kaohsiung, Taiwan.

CVE 47 *Perdido* To UK, 31 Jan 1944, renamed HMS *Trouncer.* Returned 3 Mar 1946. Stricken 12 Apr 1946. Sold 6 Mar 1947.
Later history: Merchant *Greystoke Castle*, renamed *Gallic* 1954, *Benrinnes* 1959. BU 1973 Kaohsiung, Taiwan.

CVE 48 *Sunset* To UK, 19 Nov 1943, renamed HMS *Thane.* Torpedoed by *U-1172* off Clyde LV, 15 Jan 1945; CTL. Returned 5 Dec 1945. Sold 26 Oct 1946, BU.

CVE 49 *St. Andrews* To UK, 7 Dec 1943, renamed HMS *Queen.* Returned 31 Oct 1946. Sold 29 Jul 1947.
Later history: Merchant *Roebiah* 1948, renamed *President Marcos* 1966, *Lucky One* 1972. BU 1972 Kaohsiung, Taiwan.

Figure 2.20: *Suwannee* (CVE 27), 26 Jan 1945. A *Sangamon*-class escort carrier, converted in 1942 from a fleet oiler. This class served with carrier task forces in the Pacific.

CVE 50 *St. Joseph* To UK, 22 Dec 1943, renamed HMS *Ruler.* Completed by Willamette. Returned 29 Jan 1946. Sold 13 May 1946, BU.

CVE 51 *St. Simon* To UK, 31 Dec 1943, renamed HMS *Arbiter.* Completed by Willamette. Returned 3 Mar 1946. Sold 30 Jan 1947.
Later history: Merchant *Coracero* 1948, renamed *President Macapagal* 1965, *Lucky Two* 1972. BU 1972 Kaohsiung, Taiwan.

CVE 52 *Vermillion* To UK, 20 Jan 1944, renamed HMS *Smiter.* Completed by Willamette. Returned 6 Apr 1946. Stricken 6 May 1946, sold 28 Jan 1947.
Later history: Merchant *Artillero* 1948, renamed *President Garcia* 1966. Went aground in Saints Bay, Jersey, 13 Jul 1967; refloated and BU Hamburg.

CVE 53 *Willapa* To UK, 5 Feb 1944, renamed HMS *Puncher.* Returned 17 Jan 1946. Stricken 12 Mar 1946, sold 4 Feb 1947.
Later history: Merchant *Muncaster Castle* 1948; renamed *Bardic* 1954, *Bennevis* 1959. BU 1973 Kaohsiung, Taiwan.

CVE 54 *Winjah* To UK, 18 Feb 1944, renamed HMS *Reaper.* Returned 20 May 1946. Stricken 8 Jul 1946, sold 12 Feb 1947.
Later history: Merchant *South Africa Star.* BU 1967 Mihara, Japan.

Sangamon Class

No.	Name	Builder	Keel Laid	Launched	ReComm.
CVE 26	*Sangamon*	Federal	13 Mar 1939	4 Nov 1939	25 Aug 1942
	ex–AO 28 (25 Feb 1942), ex–*Esso Trenton* (1940)				
CVE 27	*Suwannee*	Federal	3 Jun 1939	4 Mar 1939	24 Sep 1942
	ex–AO 33 (25 Feb 1942), ex–*Markay* (1940)				
CVE 28	*Chenango*	Sun	10 Jul 1938	1 Apr 1939	19 Sep 1942
	ex–AO 31 (25 Feb 1942), ex–*Esso New Orleans* (1941)				
CVE 29	*Santee*	Sun	31 May 1938	4 Mar 1939	24 Aug 1942
	ex–AO 29 (25 Feb 1942), ex–*Seakay* (1941)				

Displacement	12,000 tons; 24,275 tons f/l
Dimensions	553' (oa); 525' (wl) x 75' x 32'; extreme beam 114'3"
Machinery	2 screws; GE GT (CVE 28–29: West. GT); 4 B&W boilers; SHP 13,500, 18.3 knots
Endurance	23,900/15
Complement	1,080
Armament	2–5"/51, 4 twin 40mm, 12–20mm AA guns; 30 aircraft

Notes: Commercially built tankers acquired as oilers, 1939, and later converted to carriers. *Sangamon* and *Suwannee* converted by Newport News; *Chenango* by Beth. Staten I.; *Santee* by Norfolk NYd. Served with Pacific carrier task forces.

Service Records:

CVE 26 *Sangamon* Damaged by aircraft crash landing off Kwajalein, 25 Jan 1944 (9 killed). Damaged by aircraft bomb, Leyte, 20 Oct 1944. Damaged by kamikaze, Leyte Gulf, 25 Oct 1944 (1 killed). Severe damage by kamikaze off Okinawa, 4 May 1945 (46 killed), not repaired. Decomm 24 Oct 1945. Stricken 1 Nov 1945, sold 11 Feb 1948.
8* North Africa, Gilbert Is., Kwajalein, Eniwetok, Hollandia, Saipan, Philippine Sea, Guam, Visayas Is. Raids 10/44. Leyte, Samar, Okinawa. PUC.
Later history: Merchant *Sangamon* 1948. BU 1960 Osaka.

CVE 27 *Suwannee* Damaged by kamikazes off Samar, 25 Oct and 26 Oct 1944 (146 killed). Damaged by explosion off Okinawa, 24 May 1945. Decomm 8 Jan 1947. †
13* North Africa, Gilbert Is., Kwajalein, Eniwetok, Palau-Yap Raids 3/44, Hollandia, Saipan, Tinian, Morotai, Rennell I., Leyte, Samar, Okinawa, Balikpapan. PUC.
Submarines sunk: French *Sidi-Ferruch* off Fedhala, Morocco, 11 Nov 1942; *I-184* 350 miles east of Guam, 19 Jun 1944.

Figure 2.21: *Lunga Point* (CVE 94).

Figure 2.22: *Admiralty Islands* (CVE 99), a *Casablanca*-class escort carrier. Notice the two lowered elevators in the flight deck.

CVE 28 *Chenango* Damaged by aircraft crash, Okinawa, 9 Apr 1945. Decomm 14 Aug 1946. †
11* North Africa, Rennell I., Gilbert Is., Kwajalein, Eniwetok, Palau-Yap Raids 3/44, Hollandia, Saipan, Guam, Morotai, Leyte, Fleet Raids 1945, Okinawa, Raids on Japan 7–8/45. Operation Magic Carpet.

CVE 29 *Santee* Damaged by kamikaze and submarine torpedo from *I-56*, Leyte Gulf, 25 Oct 1944 (16 killed). Decomm 21 Oct 1946. †
9* North Africa, TG 21.11, Palau-Yap Raids 3/44, Hollandia, Guam, Morotai, Leyte, Samar, Okinawa, Raids on Japan 7–8/45. PUC, Operation Magic Carpet.
Submarines sunk: *U-160* south of Azores, 14 Jul 1943; *U-509* northwest of Madeira, 15 Jul 1943; *U-43* southwest of Azores, 30 Jul 1943.

Casablanca Class

No.	Name	Builder	Keel Laid	Launched	Comm.
CVE 55	*Casablanca* ex–*Alazon Bay* (3 Apr 1943)	Kaiser Vanc.	3 Nov 1942	5 Apr 1943	8 Jul 1943
CVE 56	+*Liscome Bay* ex–*Ameer* (23 Jan 1943)	Kaiser Vanc.	9 Dec 1942	19 Apr 1943	7 Aug 1943
CVE 57	*Coral Sea* ex–*Alikula Bay* (3 Apr 1943)	Kaiser Vanc.	12 Dec 1942	1 May 1943	27 Aug 1943
CVE 58	*Corregidor* ex–*Anguilla Bay* (3 Apr 1943)	Kaiser Vanc.	17 Nov 1942	12 May 1943	31 Aug 1943
CVE 59	*Mission Bay* ex–*Atheling* (3 Apr 1943)	Kaiser Vanc.	28 Dec 1942	26 May 1943	13 Sep 1943
CVE 60	*Guadalcanal* ex–*Astrolabe Bay* (3 Apr 1943)	Kaiser Vanc.	5 Jan 1943	5 Jun 1943	25 Sep 1943
CVE 61	*Manila Bay* ex–*Bucareli Bay* (3 Apr 1943)	Kaiser Vanc.	15 Jan 1943	10 Jul 1943	5 Oct 1943
CVE 62	*Natoma Bay* ex–*Begum* (3 Apr 1943)	Kaiser Vanc.	17 Jan 1943	20 Jul 1943	14 Oct 1943
CVE 63	*Midway* ex–*Chapin Bay* (3 Apr 1943)	Kaiser Vanc.	23 Jan 1943	17 Aug 1943	23 Oct 1943
CVE 64	*Tripoli* ex–*Didrickson Bay* (3 Apr 1943)	Kaiser Vanc.	1 Feb 1943	2 Sep 1943	31 Oct 1943
CVE 65	*Wake Island* ex–*Dolomi Bay* (3 Apr 1943)	Kaiser Vanc.	6 Feb 1943	15 Sep 1943	7 Nov 1943
CVE 66	*White Plains* ex–*Elbour Bay* (3 Apr 1943)	Kaiser Vanc.	11 Feb 1943	27 Sep 1943	15 Nov 1943
CVE 67	*Solomons* ex–*Nassuk Bay* (6 Nov 1943), ex–*Emperor* (28 Jun 1943)	Kaiser Vanc.	19 Apr 1943	6 Oct 1943	21 Nov 1943
CVE 68	*Kalinin Bay*	Kaiser Vanc.	26 Apr 1943	15 Oct 1943	27 Nov 1943
CVE 69	*Kasaan Bay*	Kaiser Vanc.	11 May 1943	24 Oct 1943	4 Dec 1943
CVE 70	*Fanshaw Bay*	Kaiser Vanc.	18 May 1943	1 Nov 1943	9 Dec 1943
CVE 71	*Kitkun Bay* ex–*Empress*	Kaiser Vanc.	31 May 1943	8 Nov 1943	15 Dec 1943
CVE 72	*Tulagi* ex–*Fortaleza Bay* (6 Nov 1943)	Kaiser Vanc.	7 Jun 1943	15 Nov 1943	21 Dec 1943
CVE 73	*Gambier Bay*	Kaiser Vanc.	10 Jul 1943	22 Nov 1943	28 Dec 1943
CVE 74	*Nehenta Bay* ex–*Khedive*	Kaiser Vanc.	20 Jul 1943	28 Nov 1943	3 Jan 1944
CVE 75	*Hoggatt Bay*	Kaiser Vanc.	17 Aug 1943	4 Dec 1943	11 Jan 1944
CVE 76	*Kadashan Bay*	Kaiser Vanc.	2 Sep 1943	11 Dec 1943	18 Jan 1944

+Note: British Admiralty records indicate CVE56 was to be named *Ameer* and not CVE55. (See ADM 209/3 Admiralty Blue List, List of Ship Building, 15 Jul 1943, p.2).

Displacement	6,730 tons; 10,400 tons f/l
Dimensions	512'3" (oa); 490' (wl) x 65'2" x 22'6"; extreme beam 108'1"
Machinery	2 screws; Nordberg Skinner Unaflow, 4 FW/B&W d/e boilers; SHP 9,000; 19.3 knots
Endurance	10,200/15
Complement	860
Armament	1–5"/38, 4 twin 40mm, 20–20mm guns; later, 8 twin 40mm, 20–20mm AA guns

Notes: Two small exhaust uptakes on either side amidships. Fourteen were originally to be transferred to UK under lend-lease (CVE 56, 59, 62, 67, 71, 74, 79, 83, 86, 90, 94, 99, 103, 104).

Service Records:

CVE 55 *Casablanca* Training ship. Operation Magic Carpet. Decomm 10 Jun 1946. Stricken 3 Jul 1946. Sold 23 Apr 1947, BU.

CVE 56 *Liscome Bay* Torpedoed by *I-175* off Makin I. and sank following explosion of after magazines, 24 Nov 1943 (648 killed, including RADM Henry M. Mullinix).
1* Gilbert Is.

CVE 57 *Coral Sea* Renamed ***Anzio***, 15 Sep 1944. Decomm 5 Aug 1946.
6* Gilbert Is., Kwajalein, Eniwetok, Saipan, Guam, Luzon Raids 10/44, Luzon Raids 1/45, Formosa Raids 1/45, Nansei Shoto Raid 1/45, Iwo Jima, Okinawa, Raids on Japan 7–8/45. Operation Magic Carpet.
Submarines sunk: **I-41* east of Samar, 18 Nov 1944; *I-368* west of Iwo Jima, 27 Feb 1945; *RO-43* northwest of Iwo Jima, 26 Feb 1945; *I-361* 400 miles southeast of Okinawa, 30 May 1945; **I-13* 550 miles east of Yokosuka, 16 Jul 1945.

CVE 58 *Corregidor* Damaged in typhoon east of Marshall Is., 20 Apr 1945. Decomm 30 Jul 1946. †
4* Gilbert Is., Kwajalein, Eniwetok, Saipan, Guam. Operation Magic Carpet.

CVE 59 *Mission Bay* North Atlantic. Damaged in collision with dredge in New York harbor, 17 Jun 1944. Decomm 21 Feb 1947. †

CVE 60 *Guadalcanal* Decomm 15 Jul 1946. †
3* TG 21.12, TG 22.3.
Submarines sunk: *U-544* northwest of Azores, 17 Jan 1944; *U-68* northwest of Madeira, 10 Apr 1944; **U-515* north of Madeira, 9 Apr 1944; *captured *U-505* northwest of Dakar, 4 Jun 1944.

CVE 61 *Manila Bay* Damaged by two kamikazes off Luzon, 5 Jan 1945 (22 killed). Decomm 31 Jul 1946. †
8* Bismarcks, Kwajalein, Eniwetok, Saipan, Hollandia, Leyte, Samar, Lingayen, Okinawa. Operation Magic Carpet.

CVE 62 *Natoma Bay* Damaged by kamikaze off Okinawa, 7 Jun 1945 (1 killed). Decomm 20 May 1946. †
7* Kwajalein, Saipan, Leyte, Samar, Lingayen, Iwo Jima, Okinawa. Operation Magic Carpet.

CVE 63 *Midway* Renamed ***Saint Lo***, 15 Sep 1944. Sunk by kamikaze and one bomb off Samar, Battle of Leyte Gulf, 25 Oct 1944 (126 killed).
4* Saipan, Guam, Tinian, Morotai, Okinawa Raid 10/44, Samar.

CVE 64 *Tripoli* Damaged by fire at San Diego, 4 Jan 1944 (1 killed). Operation Magic Carpet. Decomm 22 May 1946. †

CVE 65 *Wake Island* Moderate damage by kamikaze, Okinawa, 3 Apr 1945. Decomm 5 Apr 1946. Stricken 17 Apr 1946, sold 19 Apr 1947, BU.
3* Lingayen, Iwo Jima, Okinawa. Operation Magic Carpet.
Submarine sunk: *U-543* southwest of Tenerife, 2 Jul 1944.

CVE 66 *White Plains* In collision with destroyer *Caldwell* off Marshall Is., 7 Feb 1944. Damaged by naval gunfire and kamikaze west of Samar, Leyte Gulf, 25 Oct 1944. Decomm 10 Jul 1946. †
5* Kwajalein, Saipan, Tinian, Palau, Leyte, Samar. PUC, Operation Magic Carpet.

Figure 2.23: Japanese plane fails to hit *Kitkun Bay* (CVE 71) off Saipan, 18 Jun 1944. This dramatic picture typifies the danger faced by the men of the fleet at sea.

CVE 67 *Solomons* Decomm 15 May 1946. Stricken 5 Jun 1946. Sold 22 Dec 1946, BU Baltimore.
Submarine sunk: *U-860* off St. Helena, 15 Jun 1944.

CVE 68 *Kalinin Bay* Severely damaged by naval gunfire of Japanese warships (15 hits), then by two kamikazes off Samar, Leyte Gulf, 25 Oct 44 (5 killed). Decomm 15 May 1946. Stricken 5 Jun 1946. Sold 8 Dec 1946, BU Baltimore.
5* Kwajalein, Saipan, Guam, Tinian, Palau, Leyte, Samar. PUC, Operation Magic Carpet.

CVE 69 *Kasaan Bay* Decomm 6 Jul 1946. †
1* Southern France. Operation Magic Carpet.

CVE 70 *Fanshaw Bay* Moderate damage by aircraft bomb off Marianas, 17 Jun 1944 (14 killed). Damaged by six hits of gunfire of Japanese cruisers off Samar, Leyte Gulf, 25 Oct 1944 (4 killed). Decomm 14 Aug 1946. †
5* Saipan, Morotai, Leyte, Samar, Okinawa, Raids on Japan 7–8/45. PUC, Operation Magic Carpet.

CVE 71 *Kitkun Bay* Damaged by aircraft bomb off Samar, Leyte Gulf, 25 Oct 1944 (1 killed). Moderate damage by kamikaze, Luzon, 8 Jan 1945 (16 killed). Decomm 19 Apr 1946. Stricken 8 May 1946, sold 18 Nov 1946, BU 1947 Portland, Ore.
6* Saipan, Tinian, Guam, Palau, Leyte, Samar, Lingayen, Raids on Japan 7–8/45. PUC, Operation Magic Carpet.

CVE 72 *Tulagi* Decomm 30 Apr 1946. Stricken 8 May 1946, sold 30 Dec 1946, BU, West Coast U.S.
4* Southern France, Lingayen, Iwo Jima, Okinawa.
Submarine sunk: *I-44*, 220 miles southeast of Okinawa, 29 Apr 1945.

CVE 73 *Gambier Bay* Sunk by gunfire (over 28 hits) of Japanese warships off Samar, Battle of Leyte Gulf, 25 Oct 1944 (124 killed).
4* Saipan, Tinian, Guam, Palau, Leyte, Samar. PUC.

CVE 74 *Nehenta Bay* Damaged in typhoon in Philippine Sea, 18 Dec 1944. Damaged in storm, Philippine Sea, 17 Jan 1945. Decomm 15 May 1946. †
7* Guam, Bonins-Yap Raids, Palau, Philippines Raids 9/44, N. Luzon–Formosa Raids 10/44, Luzon Raids 10/44, Formosa Raids 1/45, Luzon Raids 1/45, Formosa Raids 1/45, China Coast Raids 1/45, Nansei Shoto Raid 1/45, Fleet Raids 1945, Raids on Japan 7–8/45. Operation Magic Carpet.

CVE 75 *Hoggatt Bay* Damaged by accidental explosion, west of Luzon, Philippines, 15 Jan 1945. Decomm 20 Jul 1946. †
5* TG 30.4, TG 12.2, Palau, Philippines Raids 9/44, Luzon Raids 10/44, Leyte, Lingayen, Okinawa. Operation Magic Carpet.

CVE 76 *Kadashan Bay* Severely damaged by kamikaze and bombs west of Luzon, 8 Jan 1945. Decomm 14 Jun 1946. †
2* Palau, Samar, Lingayen. Operation Magic Carpet.

No.	Name	Builder	Keel Laid	Launched	Comm.
CVE 77	*Marcus Island*	Kaiser Vanc.	15 Sep 1943	16 Dec 1943	26 Jan 1944
	ex–*Kanalku Bay* (6 Nov 1943)				
CVE 78	*Savo Island*	Kaiser Vanc.	27 Sep 1943	22 Dec 1943	3 Feb 1944
	ex–*Kaita Bay* (6 Nov 1943)				
CVE 79	*Ommaney Bay*	Kaiser Vanc.	6 Oct 1943	29 Dec 1943	11 Feb 1944
	ex–*Nabob*				
CVE 80	*Petrof Bay*	Kaiser Vanc.	15 Oct 1943	5 Jan 1944	18 Feb 1944
CVE 81	*Rudyerd Bay*	Kaiser Vanc.	24 Oct 1943	12 Jan 1944	25 Feb 1944
CVE 82	*Saginaw Bay*	Kaiser Vanc.	1 Nov 1943	19 Jan 1944	2 Mar 1944
CVE 83	*Sargent Bay*	Kaiser Vanc.	8 Nov 1943	31 Jan 1944	9 Mar 1944
	ex–*Premier*				
CVE 84	*Shamrock Bay*	Kaiser Vanc.	15 Nov 1943	4 Feb 1944	15 Mar 1944
CVE 85	*Shipley Bay*	Kaiser Vanc.	22 Nov 1943	12 Feb 1944	21 Mar 1944
CVE 86	*Sitkoh Bay*	Kaiser Vanc.	28 Nov 1943	19 Feb 1944	28 Mar 1944
	ex–*Shah*				
CVE 87	*Steamer Bay*	Kaiser Vanc.	4 Dec 1943	26 Feb 1944	4 Apr 1944
CVE 88	*Cape Esperance*	Kaiser Vanc.	11 Dec 1943	3 Mar 1944	9 Apr 1944
	ex–*Tananek Bay* (6 Nov 1943)				
CVE 89	*Takanis Bay*	Kaiser Vanc.	16 Dec 1943	10 Mar 1944	15 Apr 1944
CVE 90	*Thetis Bay*	Kaiser Vanc.	22 Dec 1943	16 Mar 1944	21 Apr 1944
	ex–*Queen*				
CVE 91	*Makassar Strait*	Kaiser Vanc.	29 Dec 1943	22 Mar 1944	27 Apr 1944
	ex–*Ulitka Bay*				
CVE 92	*Windham Bay*	Kaiser Vanc.	5 Jan 1944	29 Mar 1944	3 May 1944
CVE 93	*Makin Island*	Kaiser Vanc.	12 Jan 1944	5 Apr 1944	9 May 1944
	ex–*Woodcliff Bay* (17 Dec 1943)				
CVE 94	*Lunga Point*	Kaiser Vanc.	19 Jan 1944	11 Apr 1944	14 May 1944
	ex–*Alazon Bay* (6 Nov 1943), ex–*Rajah*				
CVE 95	*Bismarck Sea*	Kaiser Vanc.	31 Jan 1944	17 Apr 1944	20 May 1944
	ex–*Alikula Bay* (16 May 1944)				
CVE 96	*Salamaua*	Kaiser Vanc.	4 Feb 1944	22 Apr 1944	26 May 1944
	ex–*Anguilla Bay* (6 Nov 1943)				
CVE 97	*Hollandia*	Kaiser Vanc.	12 Feb 1944	28 Apr 1944	1 Jun 1944
	ex–*Astrolabe Bay* (30 May 1944)				

CVE 98	*Kwajalein* ex-*Bucareli Bay*	Kaiser Vanc.	19 Feb 1944	4 May 1944	7 Jun 1944
CVE 99	*Admiralty Islands* ex-*Chapin Bay* (26 Apr 1944), ex-*Ranee*	Kaiser Vanc.	26 Feb 1944	10 May 1944	13 Jun 1944
CVE 100	*Bougainville* ex-*Didrickson Bay*	Kaiser Vanc.	3 Mar 1944	16 May 1944	18 Jun 1944
CVE 101	*Matanikau* ex-*Dolomi Bay*	Kaiser Vanc.	10 Mar 1944	22 May 1944	24 Jun 1944
CVE 102	*Attu* ex-*Elbour Bay*	Kaiser Vanc.	16 Mar 1944	27 May 1944	30 Jun 1944
CVE 103	*Roi* ex-*Alava Bay* (26 Apr 1944), ex-*Ruler*	Kaiser Vanc.	22 Mar 1944	2 Jun 1944	6 Jul 1944
CVE 104	*Munda* ex-*Tonowek Bay* (6 Nov 1943), ex-*Thane*	Kaiser Vanc.	29 Mar 1944	2 Jun 1944	8 Jul 1944

Service Records:

CVE 77 *Marcus Island* Slight damage by kamikaze near miss off Mindoro, 15 Dec 1944. Damaged by fire at Boston, 13 Jul 1946. Decomm 12 Dec 1946. †
4* Palau, Leyte, Samar, Lingayen, Okinawa. Operation Magic Carpet.

CVE 78 *Savo Island* Minor damage by kamikaze, Luzon, 5 Jan 1945. Decomm 12 Dec 1946. †
4* Palau, Leyte, Samar, Lingayen, Fleet Raids 1945. PUC, Operation Magic Carpet.

CVE 79 *Ommaney Bay* Damaged by kamikaze and bombs south of Mindoro and sunk by destroyer *Burns*, 4 Jan 1945 (95 killed).
2* Palau, Samar, Lingayen.

CVE 80 *Petrof Bay* Decomm 31 Jul 1946. †
5* Palau, Samar, Lingayen, Iwo Jima, Fleet Raids 1945. PUC, Operation Magic Carpet.

CVE 81 *Rudyerd Bay* Decomm 11 Jun 1946. †
5* Palau, Philippines Raids 9/44, Luzon Raids 10/44, Lingayen, Luzon Raids 1/45, China Coast Raids 1/45, Nansei Shoto Raid 1/45, Iwo Jima, Fleet Raids 1945. Operation Magic Carpet.

CVE 82 *Saginaw Bay* Decomm 19 Jun 1946. †
5* Palau, Lingayen, Iwo Jima, Okinawa, Leyte. Operation Magic Carpet.

CVE 83 *Sargent Bay* Damaged in collision with DE *Robert F. Keller* in Philippines, 3 Jan 1945. Decomm 23 Jul 1946. †
6* Saipan, Palau, Philippines Raids 9/44, Luzon Raids 10/44, Luzon Raids 1/45, Formosa Raids 1/45, China Coast Raids 1/45, Nansei Shoto Raid 1/45, Iwo Jima, Fleet Raids 1945. Operation Magic Carpet.

CVE 84 *Shamrock Bay* Decomm 6 Jul 1946. †
3* Lingayen, Iwo Jima, Fleet Raids 1945. Operation Magic Carpet.

CVE 85 *Shipley Bay* Damaged in collision with oiler *Cache* off Okinawa, 16 May 1945. Decomm 28 Jun 1946. †
2* Formosa Raids 1/45, Luzon Raids 1/45, Okinawa. Operation Magic Carpet.

CVE 86 *Sitkoh Bay* Decomm 30 Nov 1946. †
3* Palau, Philippines Raids 9/44, N. Luzon–Formosa Raids 10/44, Luzon Raids 10/44, Okinawa. Operation Magic Carpet.

CVE 87 *Steamer Bay* Damaged in collision with destroyer *Hale*, Okinawa, 25 Apr 1945. Damaged by plane crash, Okinawa, 16 Jun 1945. Decomm Jan 1947. †
6* Palau, Philippines Raids 9/44, N. Luzon–Formosa Raids 10/44, Luzon Raids 10/44, Lingayen, Iwo Jima, Fleet Raids 1945, Raids on Japan 7–8/45. Operation Magic Carpet.

CVE 88 *Cape Esperance* Damaged in typhoon in Philippine Sea, caught fire, 18 Dec 1944. Decomm 22 Aug 1946. †
2* Luzon Raids 10/44, Formosa Raids 1/45, China Coast Raids 1/45. Operation Magic Carpet.

CVE 89 *Takanis Bay* Operation Magic Carpet. Decomm 1 May 1946. †

CVE 90 *Thetis Bay* Decomm 7 Aug 1946. †
1* Raids on Japan 7–8/45. Operation Magic Carpet.

CVE 91 *Makassar Strait* Decomm 9 Aug 1946. †
2* Iwo Jima, Okinawa. Operation Magic Carpet.

CVE 92 *Windham Bay* Damaged in typhoon off Okinawa, 5 Jun 1945. Decomm 23 Aug 1946. †
3* Saipan, Iwo Jima, Fleet Raids 1945. Operation Magic Carpet.

CVE 93 *Makin Island* Decomm 19 Apr 1946. Stricken 11 Jul 1946, sold 5 Jan 1947, BU, West Coast U.S.
5* Leyte, Lingayen, Iwo Jima, Okinawa, Raids on Japan 7–8/45.

CVE 94 *Lunga Point* Slightly damaged by kamikaze, Iwo Jima, 21 Feb 1945. Decomm 24 Oct 1946. †
5* Leyte, Lingayen, Iwo Jima, Fleet Raids 1945, Raids on Japan 7–8/45. PUC.

CVE 95 *Bismarck Sea* Hit by two kamikazes and capsized off Iwo Jima, 21 Feb 1945 (218 killed).
3* Leyte, Lingayen, Iwo Jima.

CVE 96 *Salamaua* Severely damaged by two kamikazes, Lingayen, 13 Jan 1945 (15 killed). Damaged in typhoon in Philippine Sea, 5 Jun 1945. Decomm 9 May 1946. Stricken 21 May 1946, sold 28 Dec 1946, BU Portland, Ore. Tokyo Bay.
3* Leyte, Lingayen, Fleet Raids 1945. Operation Magic Carpet.

CVE 97 *Hollandia* Decomm 17 Jan 1947. †
2* Okinawa, Raids on Japan 7–8/45. Operation Magic Carpet.

CVE 98 *Kwajalein* Damaged in typhoon in Philippine Sea, 18 Dec 1944. Decomm 16 Aug 1946. †

Figure 2.24: *Commencement Bay*–class escort carrier *Sicily* (CVE 118).

Figure 2.25: *Commencement Bay* (CVE 105), 20 Oct 1944, as completed. Notice tall and elaborate mast.

2* Guam, Formosa Raids 1/45, Luzon Raids 1/45, China Coast Raids 1/45, Nansei Shoto Raid 1/45. Operation Magic Carpet.

CVE 99 *Admiralty Islands* Decomm 24 Apr 1946. Stricken 8 May 1946, sold 2 Jan 1947, BU Portland, Ore.

3* Iwo Jima, Fleet Raids 1945, Raids on Japan 7–8/45. Operation Magic Carpet.

CVE 100 *Bougainville* Damaged in typhoon, Okinawa, 5 Jun 1945. Decomm 3 Nov 1946. †

2* Iwo Jima, Fleet Raids 1945.

CVE 101 *Matanikau* Operation Magic Carpet. Decomm 11 Oct 1946. †

CVE 102 *Attu* Damaged in typhoon, Okinawa, 5 Jun 1945. Decomm 8 Jun 1946. Stricken 3 Jul 1946, sold 3 Jan 1947.

2* Iwo Jima, Fleet Raids 1945. Operation Magic Carpet.

Later history: Merchant *Gay*. Conversion canceled, BU 1949.

CVE 103 *Roi* Decomm 9 May 1946. Stricken 21 May 1946, sold 31 Dec 1946, BU Portland, Ore.

1* Raids on Japan 7–8/45. Operation Magic Carpet.

CVE 104 *Munda* Decomm 13 Sep 1946. †

1* Raids on Japan 7–8/45. Operation Magic Carpet.

Commencement Bay Class

No.	Name	Builder	Keel Laid	Launched	Comm.
CVE 105	*Commencement Bay*	Todd Tacoma	23 Sep 1943	9 May 1944	27 Nov 1944
	ex-*St. Joseph Bay* (10 Jul 1944)				
CVE 106	*Block Island*	Todd Tacoma	25 Oct 1943	10 May 1944	30 Dec 1944
	ex-*Sunset Bay* (5 Jul 1944)				
CVE 107	*Gilbert Islands*	Todd Tacoma	29 Nov 1943	20 Jul 1944	5 Feb 1945
	ex-*St. Andrews Bay* (26 Apr 1944)				
CVE 108	*Kula Gulf*	Todd Tacoma	16 Dec 1943	15 Aug 1944	12 May 1945
	ex-*Vermillion Bay* (6 Nov 1943)				
CVE 109	*Cape Gloucester*	Todd Tacoma	10 Jan 1944	12 Sep 1944	5 Mar 1945
	ex-*Willapa Bay* (26 Apr 1944)				
CVE 110	*Salerno Bay*	Todd Tacoma	7 Feb 1944	26 Sep 1944	19 May 1945
	ex-*Winjah Bay* (6 Nov 1943)				
CVE 111	*Vella Gulf*	Todd Tacoma	7 Mar 1944	19 Oct 1944	9 Apr 1945
	ex-*Totem Bay* (26 Apr 1944)				
CVE 112	*Siboney*	Todd Tacoma	1 Apr 1944	9 Nov 1944	14 May 1945
	ex-*Frosty Bay* (26 Apr 1944)				
CVE 113	*Puget Sound*	Todd Tacoma	12 May 1944	30 Nov 1944	18 Jun 1945
	ex-*Hobart Bay* (5 Jun 1944)				
CVE 114	*Rendova*	Todd Tacoma	15 Jun 1944	28 Dec 1944	22 Oct 1945
	ex-*Mosser Bay* (6 Nov 1943)				
CVE 115	*Bairoko*	Todd Tacoma	25 Jul 1944	25 Jan 1945	16 Jul 1945
	ex-*Portage Bay* (5 Jun 1944)				
CVE 116	*Badoeng Strait*	Todd Tacoma	18 Aug 1944	15 Feb 1945	14 Nov 1945
	ex-*San Alberto Bay* (6 Nov 1943)				
CVE 117	*Saidor*	Todd Tacoma	29 Sep 1944	17 Mar 1945	4 Sep 1945
	ex-*Saltery Bay* (5 Jun 1944)				
CVE 118	*Sicily*	Todd Tacoma	23 Oct 1944	14 Apr 1945	27 Feb 1946
	ex-*Sandy Bay* (5 Jun 1944)				
CVE 119	*Point Cruz*	Todd Tacoma	4 Dec 1944	18 May 1945	16 Oct 1945
	ex-*Trocadero Bay* (5 Jun 1944)				
CVE 120	*Mindoro*	Todd Tacoma	2 Jan 1945	27 Jun 1945	24 Dec 1945
CVE 121	*Rabaul*	Todd Tacoma	29 Jan 1945	14 Jul 1945	30 Aug 1946 (delivered)
CVE 122	*Palau*	Todd Tacoma	19 Feb 1945	6 Aug 1945	15 Jan 1946
CVE 123	*Tinian*	Todd Tacoma	20 Mar 1945	5 Sep 1945	30 Jul 1946 (delivered)
CVE 124	*Bastogne*	Todd Tacoma	Apr 1945	—	—
CVE 125	*Eniwetok*	Todd Tacoma	Apr 1945	—	—
CVE 126	*Lingayen*	Todd Tacoma	1 May 1945	—	—
CVE 127	*Okinawa*	Todd Tacoma	22 May 1945	—	—
CVE 128–31	—	Todd Tacoma	—	—	—

Figure 2.26: The escort carriers of Task Unit 77.4 taking station off Kossol Passage, Palau Is. At right, *Ommaney Bay* (CVE 79), *Wake Island* (CVE 65), *Steamer Bay* (CVE 87), *Manila Bay* (CVE 61), and *Natoma Bay* (CVE 62). At left are *Makin Island* (CVE 93), *Hoggatt Bay* (CVE 75), and *Tulagi* (CVE 72).

CVE 132–39	—	Kaiser Vanc.	—	—	—

Displacement	10,900 tons; 24,275 tons f/l
Dimensions	557'1" (oa); 525' (wl) x 75' x 32'; extreme beam 105'2"
Machinery	2 screws; AC GT; 4 CE boilers, SHP 16,000; 19.1 knots
Endurance	8,300/15
Complement	1,066
Armament	2–5"/38, three quad 40mm, 12 twin 40mm, 20–20mm AA guns

Notes: Modified *Sangamon* class. Two catapults.

Service Records:

CVE 105 *Commencement Bay* Training Ship. Decomm 30 Nov 1946. †

CVE 106 *Block Island* In collision with DE *O'Flaherty* off Okinawa, 15 Jun 1945. Decomm 28 May 1946, then training ship at Annapolis. †
2* Okinawa, Balikpapan.

CVE 107 *Gilbert Islands* Decomm 21 May 1946. †
3* Okinawa, Balikpapan, Raids on Japan 7–8/45.

CVE 108 *Kula Gulf* Completed by Willamette. Operation Magic Carpet. Decomm 3 Jul 1946. †

CVE 109 *Cape Gloucester* Decomm 5 Nov 1946. †
1* Raids on Japan 7–8/45. Operation Magic Carpet.

CVE 110 *Salerno Bay* Completed by Commercial. Decomm 4 Oct 1947. †

CVE 111 *Vella Gulf* Decomm 9 Aug 1946. †

CVE 112 *Siboney* †

CVE 113 *Puget Sound* Operation Magic Carpet. Decomm 18 Oct 1946. †

CVE 114 *Rendova* †

CVE 115 *Bairoko* †

CVE 116 *Badoeng Strait* Out of commission 20 Apr 1946– 6 Jan 1947. †

CVE 117 *Saidor* Operation Crossroads . Decomm 12 Sep 1947. †

CVE 118 *Sicily* Completed by Willamette. †

CVE 119 *Point Cruz* Decomm 30 Jun 1947. †

CVE 120 *Mindoro* †

CVE 121 *Rabaul* Completed by Commercial. Never commissioned. †

CVE 122 *Palau* †

CVE 123 *Tinian* Never commissioned. †

CVE 124 *Bastogne* Canceled 12 Aug 1945.

CVE 125 *Eniwetok* Canceled 12 Aug 1945.

CVE 126 *Lingayen* Canceled 12 Aug 1945.

CVE 127 *Okinawa* Canceled 12 Aug 1945.

CVE 128–39 Canceled 12 Aug 1945.

3
CRUISERS

After the Washington Treaty of 1922, the U.S. Navy's cruiser fleet included nine obsolescent armored cruisers, three scout cruisers of the *Chester* class, six *Denver*–class small cruisers, and two large *St. Louis*–class cruisers in service, all built before the war; ten cruisers of the *Omaha* class were under construction. The treaty's goal was to end the race in construction of battleships and battle cruisers, but it also limited construction of aircraft carriers and size and armament of cruisers. Cruisers were limited in size to 10,000 tons with a maximum gun caliber of 8".

Reacting to the treaty, the Navy decided to complete the *Omaha*–class cruisers immediately, and to built sixteen new 8" gun cruisers to replace all the older cruisers. At the end of 1924, the U.S. Congress authorized eight new cruisers, which became the *Pensacola* and *Northampton* classes. They had two funnels with tripod masts fore and aft and carried catapults and aircraft amidships. Each was armed with ten or nine 8" guns in three turrets. They were built quickly with the last ship laid down before the first had completed her trials.

The first five of the next eight ships were originally ordered as modified *Northamptons*, but three were then reordered to the new design of the *Tuscaloosa*. These became the *New Orleans* class of six while the other two became the *Portland* class. In 1931 the cruiser classification was divided with the 8" gun ships being designated heavy cruisers (CA).

During the 1930s the seven ships of the *Brooklyn* class were built, followed by two near sisters, the *St. Louis* and *Helena*. These ships had counter sterns with catapults aft and were armed with 15 6" guns in five turrets. A tenth ship of this type, the *Wichita*, was built with nine 8" guns.

New types were developed toward the end of the decade. In 1938, four units of a smaller cruiser designed as flotilla flagships were ordered. These became the fast antiaircraft cruisers of the *Atlanta* class, armed with 16 5" guns. Eleven of these were built.

The *Cleveland* class light cruisers were modified *Brooklyns* with one less 6" turret. The first two were ordered in 1940; 28 were ordered, plus 13 modified ships with a single funnel. Altogether, 29 of this very successful class were built.

The new heavy cruisers of the *Baltimore* class exceeded the old treaty limits and carried nine 8" turrets and catapults aft. Eight of these were originally ordered. During the war six more were ordered plus eleven modified ships with a single funnel. Seventeen were completed, and one, the *Northampton*, was completed as a command ship after the war.

A startling new development was the highly secret large cruisers of the *Alaska* class. Six of these ships were ordered in 1940, designed apparently as a reply to the German *Scharnhorst* class and similar ships reportedly projected by Japan. They were much larger than any cruisers, mounting nine 12" guns in three turrets, with a single funnel and catapults amidships. Often wrongly described as battle cruisers, only two were completed as the need for such ships became unnecessary. A third, the *Hawaii*, remained incomplete for many years after the war but no use could be found for it.

New cruisers were designed and ordered during the war. The *Des Moines*–class heavy cruisers were larger than the *Baltimores* but carried a similar armament; three of the eight ordered were completed. The *Worcester* class light cruisers were also larger than the previous *Clevelands*, and similar to the *Baltimore* class. They were armed with 12 6" guns of a new type in six turrets and a new antiaircraft armament. Two of the four ordered were completed.

During the war the heavy cruisers suffered greatly in the battles for the Solomon Islands, starting with the disaster at Savo Island, where three were sunk. But their sisters survived great damage from Japanese torpedoes and were repaired despite the loss of bows and sterns. The *Omaha*-class cruisers were used mainly in areas away from the main combat. The ships of the *Baltimore* and *Cleveland* classes performed well in the Pacific. Survivors of major damage included the *Canberra*, torpedoed in 1944; the *Pittsburgh*, which lost her bow in a typhoon; and the light cruiser *Houston*, torpedoed twice.

Cruisers were named after cities and used the symbols *CA* for heavy cruisers and *CL* for light cruisers. The symbol *CB* was used for large cruisers, which were named for U.S. territories.

LARGE CRUISERS

Alaska Class

No.	Name	Builder	Keel Laid	Launched	Comm.
CB 1	*Alaska*	NY Sbdg	17 Dec 1941	15 Aug 1943	17 Jun 1944
CB 2	*Guam*	NY Sbdg	2 Feb 1942	21 Nov 1943	17 Sep 1944
CB 3	*Hawaii*	NY Sbdg	20 Dec 1943	3 Nov 1945	—
CB 4	*Philippines*	NY Sbdg	—	—	—
CB 5	*Puerto Rico*	NY Sbdg	—	—	—
CB 6	*Samoa*	NY Sbdg	—	—	—

Displacement	27,000 tons; 34,253 f/l
Dimensions	808'6" (oa); 791'6" (wl) x 91'1" x 32'4"
Machinery	4 screws; GE GT; 8 B&W boilers; SHP 150,000; 33.4 knots
Endurance	12,000/15
Complement	2,251
Armament	9–12"/50, 12–5"/38, 14 quad 40mm, 34–20mm AA guns
Armor	9.5" belt, 2.8" to 3.25" deck, 10.6" bulkhead, 11" to 13" barbettes, 5.25" to 12.6" gunhouses, 4" to 9" CT

Notes: Hull and machinery similar to *Essex* class carriers. Although often referred to as "battle cruisers" they were actually cruisers, albeit large, with 12" guns in three triple turrets. They were designed to confront enemy ships such as the German "pocket battleships" and similar ships thought to be under construction by Japan. No such Japanese ships were built, and only two CBs were completed. Cruiser-type armor and layout, with two catapults amidships. Handsome ships with a tower foremast and single large funnel.

Service Records:

CB 1 *Alaska* Decomm 17 Feb 1947. †
3* Iwo Jima, Honshu Raid 2/45, Fleet Raids 1945, Raids on Japan 7–8/45. Operation Magic Carpet.

CB 2 *Guam* Decomm 17 Feb 1947. †
2* Fleet Raids 1945, Raids on Japan 7–8/45. Operation Magic Carpet.

CB 3 *Hawaii* Construction suspended, 17 Feb 1947; 82.4 percent complete. †

CB 4/6 — Canceled 24 Jun 1943.

Figure 3.1: *Alaska* (CB 1), 1944, a handsome ship with sleek lines and 12" guns. Notice tower foremast, large smokestack, and catapults on either side amidships.

Figure 3.2: The incomplete cruiser *Hawaii* (CB 3), stern looking forward, 3 Jul 1946. Notice the turret and guns in place; the ship was over 80 percent complete when construction stopped.

HEAVY CRUISERS

First–Line Cruisers Acquired prior to 1922

CA 2 *Rochester* Nicaragua 1926–31. Asiatic Fleet 1932–33. Yangtze River 1932. Decomm 29 Apr 1933. Stricken 28 Oct 1938. Hulk sunk as blockship in Subic Bay, Luzon, 24 Dec 1941. (Note: [1924] 4–8"/45, 8–5"/50, 2–3"/50 AA, 2–3 pdr; forefunnel and boilers removed [1927], IHP 7,700.)

CA 4 *Pittsburgh* Out of comm 15 Oct 1921–2 Oct 1922. Flagship, Asiatic Fleet 1927–31. Yangtze River, 1927. Decomm 10 Jul 1931. Stricken 26 Oct 1931, sold 21 Dec 1931 and BU Baltimore. (Note: Refitted 1926 as flagship; forward funnel and boilers removed.)

CA 5 *Huntington* Decomm 1 Sep 1920. Stricken 12 Mar 1930, sold 13 Aug 1930 and BU.

CA 7 *Pueblo* Receiving ship, Brooklyn, 1921–27. Decomm 28 Sep 1927. Stricken 21 Feb 1930, sold 14 Sep 1931 and BU.

CA 8 *Frederick* Decomm 14 Feb 1922. Stricken 13 Nov 1929, sold 11 Feb 1930 and BU.

CA 9 *Huron* Flagship, Asiatic Fleet 1919–26. Yangtze River 1926. Decomm 17 Jun 1927. Stricken 15 Nov 1929, sold 11 Feb 1930; BU. Hulked in Powell River, British Columbia; hulk sank 18 Feb 1961.

CA 11 *Seattle* Out of comm 14 Feb 1921–1 Mar 1923. Went aground in Puget Sound, 21 Sep 1923. Decomm 15 Sep 1927. Receiving ship, New York 1927. Unclassified, rec **IX 39**, 1 Jul 1931. Decomm 28 Jun 1946. Stricken 19 Jul 1946, sold 3 Dec 1946 and BU Philadelphia.

CA 12 *Charlotte* Decomm 18 Feb 1921. Stricken 15 Jul 1930, sold 29 Sep 1930; BU.

CA 13 *Missoula* Decomm 2 Feb 1921. Stricken 15 Jul 1930, sold 29 Sep 1930.

CA 18 *St. Louis* Decomm 3 Mar 1922. Stricken 20 Mar 1930, sold 13 Aug 1930 and BU.

CA 19 *Charleston* Decomm 4 Dec 1923. Stricken 25 Nov 1929, sold 6 Mar 1930. Hulked in Powell River, British Columbia.

Figure 3.3: *Pittsburgh* (CA 4), during the 1920s. In 1926 her forward funnel was removed, the only ship of the class so changed. She was the flagship of the Asiatic Fleet.

Figure 3.4: *Salt Lake City* (CA 25), Jan 1944, drying signal flags.

Pensacola Class

No.	Name	Builder	Keel Laid	Launched	Comm.
CA 24	*Pensacola*	New York NYd	27 Oct 1926	25 Apr 1929	6 Feb 1930
CA 25	*Salt Lake City*	NY Sbdg	9 Jun 1927	23 Jan 1929	11 Dec 1929

Displacement	9,100 tons; 13,700 f/l
Dimensions	585'8" (oa); 570' (wl) x 65'3" x 22'5"
Machinery	4 screws; Parsons GT; 8 WF boilers; SHP 107,000; 32.8 knots
Endurance	10,000/15
Complement	1,193/653
Armament	10–8"/55, 4–5"/25 AA, 2–3 pdr guns; 6–21" TT; (1945) 10–8"/55, 8–5"/25 DP, 6 quad 40mm, 20–20mm
Armor	2.5–4" belt, 2.5" bulkheads, 1" deck, .75" barbettes, 2.5" gunhouses, 1.25" CT

Notes: Reclassified from CL, 1 Jul 1931; 8" guns in twin and triple turrets. Two funnels, two tripod masts. Last cruisers built without aircraft hangars. Small platform fitted to foremast after completion. Tripod mainmast at first cut down, and by 1945 replaced by small tower with light pole mast fitted abaft funnel.

Service Records:

CA 24 *Pensacola* Severely damaged by torpedo from Japanese destroyers at Battle of Tassafaronga, 30 Nov 1942 (125 killed). Moderately damaged by eight hits from shore gunfire at Iwo Jima, 17 Feb 1945 (17 killed). Damaged in collision with *LST*-277 off Okinawa, 31 Mar 1945. Bikini target ship. Decomm 26 Aug 1946. Sunk as target off Portland, Ore., 10 Nov 1948.
13* Salamaua-Lae Raid, Midway, Buin Raid, Santa Cruz, Battle of Guadalcanal, Tassafaronga, Gilbert Is., Kwajalein, Palau-Yap Raids, Kurile Is., Marcus I. Raid 10/44, Luzon Raids 10/44, Iwo Jima Bombard., Iwo Jima, Okinawa. Operation Magic Carpet.

CA 25 *Salt Lake City* Damaged by gunfire, three hits, Battle of Cape Esperance, 11 Oct 1942. Damaged by gunfire, five hits, Battle of Komandorski Is., 26 Mar 1943. Bikini target ship. Decomm 29 Aug 1946. Sunk as target off Southern California, 25 May 1948.
11* Marshall-Gilbert Raids, Wake I. Raid, 1942 Marcus I. Raid, Guadalcanal-Tulagi, Cape Esperance, Komandorski Is., Attu, Gilbert Is., Kwajalein, Palau-Yap Raids 3/44, Marcus I. Raid 10/44, Luzon Raids 10/44, Iwo Jima Bombard., Iwo Jima, Okinawa, Raids on Japan 7–8/45. Operation Magic Carpet.

Northampton Class

No.	Name	Builder	Keel Laid	Launched	Comm.
CA 26	*Northampton*	Beth. Quincy	12 Apr 1928	5 Sep 1929	17 May 1930
CA 27	*Chester*	NY Sbdg	6 Mar 1928	3 Jul 1929	24 Jun 1930
CA 28	*Louisville*	Puget Sd NYd	4 Jul 1928	1 Sep 1930	15 Jan 1931
CA 29	*Chicago*	Mare I NYd	10 Sep 1928	10 Apr 1930	9 Mar 1931
CA 30	*Houston*	Newport News	1 May 1928	7 Sep 1929	17 Jun 1930

Figure 3.5: *Augusta* (CA 31), 31 Mar 1941. The after tripod was later replaced by a light mast around the second funnel.

Figure 3.6: *Chester* (CA 27), 12 Jun 1944, retains her after tripod mast.

CA 31	*Augusta*	Newport News	2 Jul 1928	1 Feb 1930	30 Jan 1931

Displacement	9,050 tons; 10,559 f/l (CA 27: 9,200; CA 29: 9,300)
Dimensions	600'3" (oa); 582' (wl) x 66'1" x 23'
Machinery	4 screws; Parsons GT; 8 WF boilers; SHP 107,000; 32.5 knots
Endurance	10,000/15
Complement	1,030/621
Armament	9–8"/55, 4–5"/25 AA, 2–3 pdr guns, 6–21" TT; 4 more 5" added 1938; (1945) 9–8"/55, 8–5"/25DP, 5 quad and 4 twin 40mm AA
Armor	3" belt, 1.5" to 2.5" bulkheads, 1" to 2" deck, 1.5" barbettes, 2.5" gunhouses, 1.25" CT

Notes: Ordered as CL 26–31; rec Aug 1931. Three triple turrets, two tripod masts; catapults amidships. CA 29–31 designed as fleet flagships. *Northampton* had raised forefunnel, cut down in 1942. TT removed 1935. Heavy tripod mainmast removed 1943, replaced by light tripod further forward; tripod foremast cut down.

Service Records:

CA 26 *Northampton* Damaged in collision with destroyer *Craven* north of Oahu, 14 Dec 1941. Twice torpedoed by Japanese destroyer *Oyashio* and capsized at Battle of Tassafaronga, 30 Nov 1942 (58 killed).
6* Marshall-Gilbert Raids, Wake I. Raid, 1942 Marcus I. Raid, Midway, Buin Raid, Santa Cruz, Battle of Guadalcanal, Tassafaronga.

CA 27 *Chester* Moderately damaged by aircraft bomb off Wotje, Marshall Is. Raid, 1 Feb 1942 (8 killed). Damaged by torpedo of *I-176*, north of Espiritu Santo, 20 Oct 1942 (11 killed). Damaged in collision with USS *Estes*, Iwo Jima, 19 Feb 1945. Decomm 10 Jun 1946. †
11* Marshall-Gilbert Raids, Coral Sea, Gilbert Is., Kwajalein, Palau-Yap Raids 3/44, Kurile Is., Marcus I. Raid 10/44, Luzon Raids 10/44, Iwo Jima Bombard., Iwo Jima, Okinawa, Raids on Japan 7–8/45. Operation Magic Carpet.

CA 28 *Louisville* Damaged by naval gunfire, Kwajalein, 31 Jan 1944. Damaged by two kamikazes off Luzon, 5 Jan (1 killed) and on bridge, 6 Jan 1945 (32 killed, including RADM Theodore Chandler). Damaged by kamikaze, Okinawa, 5 Jun 1945. Decomm 17 Jun 1946. †
13* Marshall-Gilbert Raids, Battle of Guadalcanal, Rennell I., Attu, Kwajalein, Eniwetok, Palau-Yap Raids 3/44, Hollandia, Truk Raid 4/44, Saipan, Tinian, Guam, Palau, Luzon Raids 10/44, Leyte, Surigao Strait, Lingayen, Okinawa.

CA 29 *Chicago* Damaged in collision with m/v *Silver Palm* off Point Sur, Calif., 24 Oct 1933 (3 killed). Damaged by destroyer torpedo, Savo I., 9 Aug 1942 (2 killed). Damaged by two aircraft torpedoes off Rennell I., 29 Jan; struck by four more torpedoes while in tow, 30 Jan 1943 and capsized (62 killed).
3* Coral Sea, Guadalcanal-Tulagi, Savo I., Rennell I.

CA 30 *Houston* Damaged in collision with French gunboat *Francis-Garnier* at Shanghai, 1 Apr 1933. In collision with destroyer *Peary* at Shanghai, 7 Oct 1933. Carried President Franklin Delano Roosevelt on Caribbean cruise, Jul 1934; also 14 Jul 1938 and Jan 1939. Damaged by aircraft bomb north of Bali, turret no. 3 out of action, 4 Feb 1942. Sunk by gunfire and torpedoes of Japanese cruisers *Mogami* and *Mikuma* in Sunda Strait, 27 28 Feb 1942 (~700 killed).
2* Philippines, Java Sea. PUC.

CA 31 *Augusta* Asiatic Fleet 1933–40. Hit by stray Japanese shell at Shanghai, 20 Aug 1937 (1 killed). Neutrality patrol. Carried President Roosevelt to Argentia meeting with Churchill, Aug 1941. Action with French warships off Casablanca, 8 Nov 1942. Damaged by engine room explosion at Philadelphia, 20 Nov 1944 (3 killed). Carried President Harry S. Truman to Potsdam Conference, Jul 1945. Decomm 16 Jul 1946. †
3* North Africa, Normandy, Southern France. Operation Magic Carpet.

Portland Class

No.	Name	Builder	Keel Laid	Launched	Comm.
CA 33	*Portland*	Beth. Quincy	17 Feb 1930	21 May 1932	23 Feb 1933
CA 35	*Indianapolis*	NY Sbdg	31 Mar 1930	7 Nov 1931	15 Nov 1932

Displacement	9,800 tons; 11,574 f/l (CA 35: 9,950)
Dimensions	610'3" (oa); 592' (wl) x 66'1" x 24'
Machinery	4 screws; Parsons GT; 8 Yarrow boilers (C 35: WF); SHP 107,000; 32.7 knots
Endurance	10,000/15
Complement	1,229/952
Armament	9–8"/55, 8–5"/25 AA, 2–3 pdr; (1945) 6 quad 40mm (CA 35); 4 quad and 4 twin 40mm (CA 33), 12–20mm in both added
Armor	3.25" to 5" belt, 2" to 5.75" bulkheads, 2.5" deck, 1.5" barbettes, 2.5" gunhouses, 1.25" CT

Notes: Designed as flagships. Two raked funnels, catapult amidships. Tripod foremast, small tower and pole mast aft. Light tripod added forward of second funnel 1943, and prominent director aft.

Figure 3.7: *Portland* (CA 33), 30 Jul 1944. The after tripod mast has been replaced by a light mast around the second funnel.

Service Records:

CA 33 *Portland* Damaged by torpedo and gunfire (two hits), Battle of Guadalcanal, 13 Nov 1942. Damaged in Atlantic Ocean storm bringing troops home, 17 Dec 1945 (3 killed). Decomm 12 Jul 1946. †
16* Coral Sea, Midway, Guadalcanal-Tulagi, Eastern Solomons, Santa Cruz, Battle of Guadalcanal, Gilbert Is., Kwajalein, Eniwetok, Palau-Yap Raids 3/44, Hollandia, Truk Raid 4/44, Palau, Philippines Raids 9/44, Leyte, Surigao Strait, Luzon Raids 10/44, Mindoro, Lingayen, Mariveles-Corregidor, Okinawa. Operation Magic Carpet.

CA 35 *Indianapolis* In collision with ammunition ship *Shasta* off Iwo Jima, 19 Feb 1945. Moderate damage by kamikaze, Okinawa, 31 Mar 1945 (9 killed). Torpedoed twice by *I-58* and sank in Philippine Sea, 30 Jul 1945 (883 killed).
10* Salamaua-Lae Raid, Attu, Gilbert Is., Kwajalein, Eniwetok, Palau-Yap Raids 3/44, Saipan, Philippine Sea, Guam, Tinian, Palau, Surigao Strait, Honshu Raid 2/45, Iwo Jima, Fleet Raids 1945.

Figure 3.8: *Tuscaloosa* (CA 37) 1942, serving in the North Atlantic. Notice the searchlight platform between the funnels, later removed, and the Curtiss Seagull scout plane on the catapult.

Figure 3.9: *New Orleans* (CA 32), 8 Mar 1945, late in the war, recovered from her bow damage earlier. The bridge has been cut back and deck hamper removed to provide for antiaircraft fire.

New Orleans Class

No.	Name	Builder	Keel Laid	Launched	Comm.
CA 32	*New Orleans*	New York NYd	14 Mar 1931	12 Apr 1933	15 Feb 1934
CA 34	*Astoria*	Puget Sd NYd	1 Sep 1930	16 Dec 1933	28 Apr 1934
CA 36	*Minneapolis*	Phila. NYd	27 Jun 1931	6 Sep 1933	19 May 1934
CA 37	*Tuscaloosa*	NY Sbdg	3 Sep 1931	15 Nov 1933	17 Aug 1934
CA 38	*San Francisco*	Mare I NYd	9 Sep 1931	9 Mar 1933	10 Feb 1934
CA 39	*Quincy*	Beth. Quincy	15 Nov 1933	19 Jun 1935	9 Jun 1936
CA 44	*Vincennes*	Beth. Quincy	2 Jan 1934	21 May 1936	24 Feb 1937

Displacement	9,950 tons; 13,500 f/l (CA 37 *Tuscaloosa*: 9,975)
Dimensions	588' (oa); 578' (wl) x 61'9" x 24'4"
Machinery	4 screws; West. GT; 8 B&W boilers; SHP 107,000; 32 knots
Endurance	10,000/15
Complement	1,121/751
Armament	(1945) 9–8"/55, 8–5"/25; (1944) 6 quad 40mm, 28–20mm added (CA 32: 18mm to 20mm)
Armor	3" to 5" belt, 1.5" to -3" bulkheads, 2.25" deck, 5" barbettes, 2.75" to 8" gunhouses, 5" CT

Notes: CA 32–36 ordered as improved *Northamptons*; CA 32, CA 34, CA 36 reordered to CA 37 design. Improved protection. Tower bridge similar to rebuilt *New Mexico*–class battleships. Two catapults, aircraft hangar amidships; searchlight tower between funnels. *Quincy* and *Vincennes* built to modified design. Bridges rebuilt 1943. *Minneapolis* had 40mm mount on no. 2 turret, Jun 1945. *New Orleans* had port catapult removed 1945.

Service Records:

CA 32 *New Orleans* Torpedoed by destroyer and lost bow at battle of Tassafaronga, 30 Nov 1942 (28 killed). Damaged by carrier plane crash in Caroline I. area, 22 Apr 1944. Decomm 10 Feb 1947. †
17* Pearl Harbor, Coral Sea, Midway, Guadalcanal-Tulagi, Eastern Solomons, Tassafaronga, Wake I. Raid 1943, Gilbert Is., Kwajalein, Raid on Truk, Marianas Raid 2/44, Palau-Yap Raids 3/44, Hollandia, Truk Raid 4/44, Saipan, Philippine Sea, Guam, Tinian, Bonins-Yap Raids, Palau, Philippines Raids 9/44, Okinawa Raid 10/44, N. Luzon-Formosa Raids 10/44, Luzon Raids 10/44, Surigao Strait, Okinawa. Operation Magic Carpet.

CA 34 *Astoria* Received over 65 hits from gunfire of Japanese warships and capsized off Savo I., 9 Aug 1942 (216 killed).
3* Coral Sea, Midway, Guadalcanal-Tulagi.

CA 36 *Minneapolis* Torpedoed twice, lost bow during battle of Tassafaronga, 30 Nov 1942. Minor damage by aircraft bomb near miss, Philippine Sea, 19 Jun 1944. Minor damage by kamikaze, Lingayen, 6 Jan 1945. Decomm 10 Feb 1947. †
16* Marshall-Gilbert Raids, Salamaua-Lae Raid, Coral Sea, Midway, Guadalcanal-Tulagi, Eastern Solomons, Tassafaronga, Wake I. Raid 1943, Gilbert Is., Kwajalein, Raid on Truk, Marianas Raid 2/44, Palau-Yap Raids 3/44, Hollandia, Truk Raid 4/44, Saipan, Philippine Sea, Guam, Palau, Leyte, Surigao Strait, Luzon Raids 10/44, Lingayen, Mariveles-Corregidor, Okinawa. Operation Magic Carpet.

CA 37 *Tuscaloosa* Carried President Roosevelt to Maine, Aug 1939, and on cruise to Panama, Feb 1940. Action with French warships off Casablanca, 8 Nov 1942. Decomm 13 Feb 1946. †
7* Russian convoys, Morocco, Norway Raid 10/43, Normandy, Southern France, Iwo Jima, Okinawa. Operation Magic Carpet.

Figure 3.10: *Wichita* (CA 45), 2 Dec 1942; 8" gun version of the *Brooklyn* class. A Curtiss SOC-3 scout seaplane is being hoisted at the stern.

CA 38 *San Francisco* In collision with minelayer *Breese* in New Hebrides, 30 Sep 1942. Damaged by crashing aircraft off Guadalcanal, 12 Nov 1942 (15 killed). Damaged by 45 hits from gunfire, Battle of Guadalcanal, 13 Nov 1942 (80 killed, including RADM Daniel Callaghan and Capt. Cassin Young). Damaged in storm, Iwo Jima, 24 Feb 1945. Decomm 10 Feb 1946. †

17* Pearl Harbor, Salamaua-Lae Raid, Guadalcanal-Tulagi, Cape Esperance, Battle of Guadalcanal, Attu, Wake I. Raid 1943, Gilbert Is., Kwajalein, Raid on Truk, Palau-Yap Raids 3/44, Hollandia, Truk Raid 4/44, Saipan, Philippine Sea, Guam, Luzon Raids 10/44, Formosa Raids 1/45, Luzon Raids 1/45, Formosa Raids 1/45, China Coast Raids 1/45, Nansei Shoto Raid 1/45, Honshu Raid 2/45, Iwo Jima, Okinawa.

CA 39 *Quincy* Spanish Civil War (Sqn 40T), Jul–Sep 1936. Neutrality patrol. Received over 36 hits from gunfire and two torpedoes by Japanese warships and capsized off Savo I., 9 Aug 1942 (370 killed).

1* Guadalcanal-Tulagi.

CA 44 *Vincennes* Neutrality patrol. Carried 200 tons of French gold from Casablanca to New York, 10 Jun–20 Jun 1940. Received over 57 hits from gunfire and one torpedo from Japanese warships and capsized off Savo I., 9 Aug 1942 (332 killed).

2* Midway, Guadalcanal-Tulagi.

Wichita

No.	Name	Builder	Keel Laid	Launched	Comm.
CA 45	*Wichita*	Phila. NYd	28 Oct 1935	16 Nov 1937	16 Feb 1939

Displacement	10,000 tons; 13,700 f/l
Dimensions	608'4" (oa); 600' (wl) x 61'9" x 25'
Machinery	4 screws; Parsons GT; 8 B&W boilers; SHP 100,000; 33.7 knots
Endurance	10,000/15
Complement	1,343/843
Armament	9–8"/55, 8–5"/38; (1944) 6 quad 40mm, 18–20mm added
Armor	4" to 6" belt, 2.25" deck, 6" bulkheads, 7" barbettes, 1.5" to 8" gunhouses, 2.25" to 6" CT

Notes: *Brooklyn*-class cruiser with 8" guns. Flush-deck hull, pole masts, catapults aft.

Service Record:

CA 45 *Wichita* Neutrality patrol. Ran aground in gale at Hvalfjordur, Iceland, 10 Jan 1942. Convoy escort, Arctic Sea, 1942. Slight damage by shore gunfire off Casablanĉa, 8 Nov 1942; action with French warships off Casablanca. Damaged by one hit by coastal gunfire, Okinawa, 27 Apr 1945. Damaged in error by U.S. gunfire, Okinawa, 12 May 1945 (1 killed). Decomm 3 Feb 1947. †

13* Russian convoys, Morocco, Rennell I., Attu, Kwajalein, Raid on Truk, Palau-Yap Raids 3/44, Hollandia, Truk Raid 4/44, Saipan, Philippine Sea, Guam, Palau, Philippines Raids 9/44, Morotai, Okinawa Raid 10/44, N. Luzon–Formosa Raids 10/44, Luzon Raids 10/44, Surigao Strait, Okinawa, Raids on Japan 7–8/45. Operation Magic Carpet.

Figure 3.11: *Canberra* (CA 70), serving with the Pacific Fleet shortly before being torpedoed off Formosa, Oct 1944. A *Fletcher*-class destroyer is visible at left.

Figure 3.12: *Columbus* (CA 74), 27 Oct 1945, a *Baltimore*-class heavy cruiser, in the Hudson River, New York.

Baltimore Class

No.	Name	Builder	Keel Laid	Launched	Comm.
CA 68	*Baltimore*	Beth. Quincy	26 May 1941	28 Jul 1942	15 Apr 1943
CA 69	*Boston*	Beth. Quincy	30 Jun 1941	26 Aug 1942	30 Jun 1943
CA 70	*Canberra*	Beth. Quincy	3 Sep 1941	19 Apr 1943	14 Oct 1943
	ex–*Pittsburgh* (12 Oct 1942)				

CA 71	*Quincy*	Beth. Quincy	9 Oct 1941	22 Jun 1943	15 Dec 1943
	ex–*St. Paul* (16 Oct 1942)				
CA 72	*Pittsburgh*	Beth. Quincy	3 Feb 1943	22 Feb 1944	10 Oct 1944
	ex–*Albany* (26 Nov 1942)				
CA 73	*Saint Paul*	Beth. Quincy	3 Feb 1943	16 Sep 1944	17 Feb 1945
	ex–*Rochester* (26 Nov 1942)				
CA 74	*Columbus*	Beth. Quincy	28 Jun 1943	30 Nov 1944	8 Jun 1945
CA 75	*Helena*	Beth. Quincy	9 Sep 1943	28 Apr 1945	4 Sep 1945
	ex–*Des Moines* (6 Nov 1944)				
CA 130	*Bremerton*	NY Sbdg	1 Feb 1943	2 Jul 1944	29 Apr 1945
CA 131	*Fall River*	NY Sbdg	12 Apr 1943	13 Aug 1944	1 Jul 1945
CA 132	*Macon*	NY Sbdg	14 Jun 1943	15 Oct 1944	26 Aug 1945
CA 133	*Toledo*	NY Sbdg	13 Sep 1943	6 May 1945	27 Oct 1946
CA 135	*Los Angeles*	Phila. NYd	28 Jul 1943	20 Aug 1944	22 Jul 1945
CA 136	*Chicago*	Phila. NYd	28 Jul 1943	20 Aug 1944	10 Jan 1945

Displacement	13,600 tons; 17,200 f/l
Dimensions	673'5" (oa); 664' (wl) x 70'10" x 26'10"
Machinery	4 screws; GE GT; 4 B&W boilers; SHP 120,000; 34 knots
Endurance	10,000/15
Complement	1,772
Armament	9–8"/55, 12–5"/38, 12 quad 40mm AA, 26–20mm AA
Armor	2" to 6" belt, 2.5" deck, 5" to 6" bulkheads, 6" to 3" barbettes, 1.5" to 8" gunhouses, 1.5" to 6" CT (CA 74–75, CA 130–36: 3" to 6.5" CT)

Notes: Flush-deck hull, pole masts, two raked stacks. Catapults and crane at stern; *Baltimore* had two cranes.

Service Records:

CA 68 *Baltimore* Carried President Roosevelt to Pearl Harbor and Alaska, Jul 1944. Damaged in typhoon in Philippine Sea, 5 Jun 1945. Decomm 8 Jul 1946. †
9* Gilbert I., Kwajalein, Raid on Truk, Eniwetok, Marianas Raid 2/44, Palau-Yap Raids 3/44, Hollandia, Truk Raid 4/44, Saipan, 1st Bonins Raid, Philippine Sea, 2nd Bonins Raid, Luzon Raids 10/44, Formosa Raids 1/45, Luzon Raids 1/45, China Coast Raids 1/45, Formosa Raids 1/45, China Coast Raids 1/45, Formosa Raids 1/45, Nansei Shoto Raid 1/45, Iwo Jima Bombard., Iwo Jima, Honshu Raid 2/45, Fleet Raids 1945. Operation Magic Carpet.

CA 69 *Boston* Decomm 29 Oct 1946. †
10* Kwajalein, Eniwetok, Palau-Yap Raids 3/44, Hollandia, Truk Raid 4/44, Morotai, Saipan, 1st Bonins Raid, Philippine Sea, 2nd Bonins Raid, 3rd Bonins Raid, Guam, Palau-Yap Raids 7/44, Palau, Philippines Raids 9/44, Okinawa Raid 10/44, N. Luzon–Formosa Raids 10/44, Luzon Raids 10/44, Surigao Strait, Formosa Raids 1/45, Luzon Raids 1/45, China Coast Raids 1/45, Nansei Shoto Raid 1/45, Honshu Raid 2/45, Iwo Jima, Raids on Japan 7–8/45. Tokyo Bay.

CA 70 *Canberra* Severely damaged by aircraft torpedo off Formosa, 13 Oct 1944 (23 killed). Decomm 7 Mar 1947. †
7* Eniwetok, Palau-Yap Raids 3/44, Hollandia, Truk Raid 4/44, Morotai, Saipan, 1st Bonins Raid, Philippine Sea, 2nd Bonins Raid, 3rd Bonins Raid, Guam, Palau-Yap Raids 7/44, Palau, Philippines Raids 9/44, Okinawa Raid 10/44, N. Luzon–Formosa Raids 10/44, Luzon Raids 10/44.

Figure 3.13: *Albany* (CA 123), May 1947, in New York. A modified *Baltimore*-class cruiser with single funnel.

CA 71 *Quincy* Carried President Roosevelt to Yalta Conference, 23 Jan–27 Feb 1945. Damaged in typhoon, Okinawa, 5 Jun 1945. Decomm 19 Oct 1946. †
4* Normandy, Southern France, Fleet Raids 1945, Raids on Japan 7–8/45. Tokyo Bay.

CA 72 *Pittsburgh* Damaged, lost bow, in typhoon in Philippine Sea, 5 Jun 1945. Repaired, and decomm 7 Mar 1947. †
2* Honshu Raid 2/45, Iwo Jima, Fleet Raids 1945.

CA 73 *Saint Paul* Slightly damaged in collision with Chinese landing ship *144* at Shanghai, 21 Dec 1945. †
1* Raids on Japan 7–8/45. Tokyo Bay.

CA 74 *Columbus* †
1* Raids on Japan 7–8/45.

CA 75 *Helena* †

CA 130 *Bremerton* †

CA 131 *Fall River* Operation Crossroads. †

CA 132 *Macon* †

CA 133 *Toledo* †

CA 135 *Los Angeles* †

CA 136 *Chicago* Tokyo Bay. Decomm 6 Jun 1947. †
1* Raids on Japan 7–8/45.

Oregon City Class

No.	Name	Builder	Keel Laid	Launched	Comm.
CA 122	*Oregon City*	Beth. Quincy	8 Apr 1944	9 Jun 1945	16 Feb 1946
CA 123	*Albany*	Beth. Quincy	6 Mar 1944	30 Jun 1945	15 Jun 1946
CA 124	*Rochester*	Beth. Quincy	29 May 1944	28 Aug 1945	20 Dec 1946
CA 125	*Northampton*	Beth. Quincy	31 Aug 1944	—	—
CA 126	*Cambridge*	Beth. Quincy	16 Dec 1944	—	—
CA 127	*Bridgeport*	Beth. Quincy	13 Jan 1945	—	—
CA 128	*Kansas City*	Beth. Quincy	9 Jul 1945	—	—
CA 129	*Tulsa*	Beth. Quincy	—	—	—

CA 137	*Norfolk*	Phila. NYd	27 Dec 1944	—	—
CA 138	*Scranton*	Phila. NYd	27 Dec 1944	—	—

Displacement	13,700 tons
Dimensions	673'5" x 70'10" x 26'4"
Machinery	4 screws; GT; SHP 120,000; 33 knots
Endurance	10,000/15
Complement	1,969
Armament	9–8"/55, 12–5"/38, 11 quad and 2 twin 40mm AA
Armor	6" belt, 8" turrets, 2.5" deck, 6" CT

Notes: *Baltimore* class with single large funnel, smaller silhouette. *Oregon City* had no cruising turbines. Two catapults aft, single crane.

Service Records:

CA 122 *Oregon City* Decomm 15 Dec 1947. †
CA 123 *Albany* †
CA 124 *Rochester* †
CA 125 *Northampton* Suspended, 12 Aug 1945, 56.2 percent complete. †
CA 126 *Cambridge* Canceled 12 Aug 1945.
CA 127 *Bridgeport* Canceled 12 Aug 1945.
CA 128 *Kansas City* Canceled 12 Aug 1945.
CA 129 *Tulsa* Canceled 12 Aug 1945.
CA 137 *Norfolk* Canceled 12 Aug 1945.
CA 138 *Scranton* Canceled 12 Aug 1945.

Des Moines Class

No.	Name	Builder	Keel Laid	Launched	Comm.
CA 134	*Des Moines*	Beth. Quincy	28 May 1945	27 Sep 1946	16 Nov 1948
CA 139	*Salem*	Beth. Quincy	4 Jul 1945	25 Mar 1947	14 May 1949
CA 140	*Dallas*	Beth. Quincy	15 Oct 1945	—	—
CA 141	—	Beth. Quincy	—	—	—
CA 142	—	Beth. Quincy	—	—	—
CA 143	—	Beth. Quincy	—	—	—
CA 148	*Newport News*	Newport News	1 Oct 1945	6 Mar 1947	29 Jan 1949
CA 149	—	Newport News	—	—	—
CA 150	*Dallas*	NY Sbdg	—	—	—
CA 151	—	NY Sbdg	—	—	—
CA 152	—	NY Sbdg	—	—	—
CA 153	—	NY Sbdg	—	—	—

Displacement	17,000 tons; 20,950 f/l
Dimensions	716'6" (oa); 700' (wl) x 76'6" x 22'
Machinery	4 screws; GE ST, 4 B&W boilers; SHP 120,000; 33 knots
Endurance	10,500/15
Complement	1,769
Armament	9–8"/55, 12–5"/38, 12 quad 40mm, 20–20mm (designed); 9–8"/55, 24–3"/50, 12–20mm (completed)
Armor	4" to 6" belt, 3.5" deck, 5" bulkheads, 6.3" barbettes, 2" to 8" gunhouses, 4" to 6.5" CT

Notes: CA 134 and CA 143 originally ordered from NY Sbdg, and CA 148–49 from Cramp. Two catapults aft. Modified *Baltimore* class.

Service Records:

CA 134 *Des Moines* †
CA 139 *Salem* †
CA 140 *Dallas* Canceled 6 Jun 1946.
CA 141–43 Canceled 7 Jan 1946.
CA 148 *Newport News* †
CA 149 — Canceled 12 Aug 1945.
CA 150 *Dallas* Canceled 28 Mar 1945.
CA 151–53— Canceled 28 Mar 1945.

LIGHT CRUISERS

Second-Line Cruisers Acquired prior to 1922

— *Boston* see IX 2
— *Baltimore* see CM 1
— *Philadelphia* see IX 24
— *San Francisco* see CM 2
CL 1 *Chester* Decomm 10 Jun 1921. Renamed ***York***, 16 Jul 1928. Stricken 21 Jan 1930, sold 13 May 1930 and BU.
CL 2 *Birmingham* Decomm 1 Dec 1923. Stricken 21 Jan 1930, sold 13 May 1930 and BU.
CL 3 *Salem* Decomm 16 Aug 1921. Stricken 13 Nov 1929, sold 11 Feb 1930 and BU San Francisco.
CL 14 *Chicago* Decomm 30 Sep 1923. Barracks ship, Pearl Harbor, 1923–35. Unclassified, **IX 5**, renamed ***Alton***, 16 Jul 1928. Stricken 16 Aug 1935. Foundered in tow between Honolulu and San Francisco, 8 Jul 1936.
CL 15 *Olympia* Decomm 9 Dec 1922. Rec unclassified, **IX 40**, 30 Jun 1931. Museum at Philadelphia. Stricken 2 Jan 1957, trfd 11 Sep 1957. **Later history:** Museum at Philadelphia.
CL 16 *Denver* Central America 1922–29. Nicaragua 1926–30. Decomm 14 Feb 1931. Stricken 12 Mar 1931, sold 13 Sep 1933.
CL 17 *Des Moines* Decomm 9 Apr 1921. Stricken 13 Dec 1929, sold 11 Mar 1930; BU Baltimore.
CL 18 *Chattanooga* Decomm 19 Jul 1921. Stricken 13 Dec 1929, sold 11 Mar 1930; BU Baltimore.
CL 19 *Galveston* Out of comm 30 Nov 1923–5 Feb 1924. Nicaragua, 1926–30. Decomm 2 Sep 1930. Stricken 1 Nov 1930, sold 13 Sep 1933; BU Philadelphia.
CL 20 *Tacoma* Wrecked off Vera Cruz, Mexico, 16 Jan 1924 (4 killed).
CL 21 *Cleveland* Nicaragua, 1926–29. Decomm 1 Nov 1929. Stricken 13 Dec 1929, sold 7 Mar 1930; BU Baltimore.

Figure 3.14: USS *Concord* (CL 10), of the *Omaha* class, in 1925, with experimental number on the bow. The tall masts, later eliminated, were for radio transmission.

Figure 3.15: *Trenton* (CL 11), an *Omaha*-class light cruiser, in 1945.

Figure 3.16: *Marblehead* (CL 12), 31 May 1934, cruising with a sister ship. Notice the main guns in turrets and sponsons both fore and aft, and catapults crammed in amidships.

CL 22 *New Orleans* Decomm 16 Nov 1922. Stricken 13 Nov 1929, sold 11 Feb 1930; BU San Francisco.

CL 23 *Albany* Decomm 10 Oct 1922. Stricken 3 Nov 1929, sold 11 Feb 1930; BU San Francisco.

Omaha Class

No.	Name	Builder	Laid Down	Launched	Comm.
CL 4	*Omaha*	Todd Tacoma	12 Dec 1918	14 Dec 1920	24 Feb 1923
CL 5	*Milwaukee*	Todd Tacoma	28 Dec 1918	24 Mar 1921	20 Jun 1923
CL 6	*Cincinnati*	Todd Tacoma	15 May 1920	23 May 1921	1 Jan 1924
CL 7	*Raleigh*	Beth. Quincy	16 Aug 1920	25 Oct 1922	6 Feb 1924
CL 8	*Detroit*	Beth. Quincy	10 Nov 1920	29 Jun 1922	31 Jul 1923
CL 9	*Richmond*	Cramp	16 Feb 1920	29 Sep 1921	2 Jul 1923
CL 10	*Concord*	Cramp	29 Mar 1920	15 Dec 1921	3 Nov 1923
CL 11	*Trenton*	Cramp	18 Aug 1920	16 Apr 1923	19 Apr 1924
CL 12	*Marblehead*	Cramp	4 Aug 1920	9 Oct 1923	8 Sep 1924
CL 13	*Memphis*	Cramp	14 Oct 1920	17 Apr 1924	4 Feb 1925

Displacement	7,050 tons; 9,700 f/l
Dimensions	555'6" (oa); 550' (wl) x 55'4" x 20'
Machinery	4 screws; 4 to 6 Westinghouse-Parsons turbines; reduction gear (CL 7–8: Curtis; CL 9–13: Parsons); 12 Yarrow boilers (CL 13: White-Forster); SHP 90,000; 35 knots
Endurance	9,000/15
Complement	458
Armament	12–6"/53, 2–3"/50 AA, 2–3 pdr, 10–21" TT; 4 TT removed 1920s, 2–3" AA added (4 in *Concord*) 1930s; (1945) 10–6"/53, 6–3"/50, 3 twin 40mm, 12–20mm, 2 triple 21" TT (except CL 8 *Detroit*: 8–6"; and CL 6–8 *Cincinnati, Raleigh,* and *Detroit*: 8–3"; CL 13 *Memphis*: 7–3"; CL 6 *Cincinnati*: also 2–40mm single.
Armor	3" belt, 1.5" upper deck and bulkheads, 1.25" CT

Notes: Four funnels in pairs, two catapults aft of funnels. Tripod foremast, pole mainmast. Searchlight platform around aft pair of funnels. Two twin turrets; other 6" guns in sponsons. Could carry 224 mines as built, but mine-laying tracks removed 1924. Served as destroyer leaders. Two aft 6" guns removed in *Cincinnati, Detroit, Marblehead* , *Raleigh,* and *Richmond* during 1930s. Had very high masts as built, later shortened. *Concord* wore number 10 on bow, 1925.

Service Records:

CL 4 *Omaha* Went aground off Castle I. Light, Bahamas, 19 Jul 1937; refloated 29 Jul. Spanish Civil War (Sqn 40T), Apr 1938–Jun 1939. Neutrality patrol. Decomm 1 Nov 1945. Stricken 28 Nov 1945. BU Feb 1946 Philadelphia.
1* Southern France.
Ships sunk: German m/v *Odenwald* (5,098/23) in South Atlantic, 6 Nov 1941 (captured); b/r *Rio Grande* (6,062/39) and *Burgenland* (7,320/28) scuttled in South Atlantic, 4–5 Jan 1944.

CL 5 *Milwaukee* Sank schr *Benjamin van Brunt* in collision, 20 Sep 1925. In collision with destroyer *Simpson* in Caribbean, 8 May 1934. Discovered greatest depth in Atlantic Ocean, 30,246' (Milwaukee Depth), 14 Feb 1939. South Atlantic. To USSR, 20 Apr 1944, at Kola, renamed *Murmansk*. Returned 16 Mar 1949. Stricken 18 Mar 1949. Sold 10 Dec 1949; BU Wilmington, Del.
Ship sunk: *Anneliese Essberger* (5,173/35), 21 Nov 1942 off Trinidad.

CL 6 *Cincinnati* Struck submerged reef off Guafo I., Chile, 26 Feb 1924. Neutrality patrol. Decomm 1 Nov 1945. Stricken and sold 27 Feb 1946; BU Philadelphia.
1* Southern France.

CL 7 *Raleigh* Nicaragua 1927. Spanish Civil War (Sqn 40T), Sep 1936–Apr 1938. Damaged by aircraft torpedo and one bomb at Pearl Harbor, 7 Dec 1941. Decomm 2 Nov 1945. Stricken 28 Nov 1945, sold 27 Feb 1946; BU Philadelphia.
3* Pearl Harbor, Attu, Kurile Is.

CL 8 *Detroit* Slightly damaged in collision with cruiser *Milwaukee* en route to Panama, 3 Feb 1926. Damaged in typhoon, Okinawa, 5 Jun 1945. Decomm 11 Jan 1946. Stricken and sold 27 Feb 1946; BU Baltimore.
6* Pearl Harbor, Attu, Kurile Is., Iwo Jima, Fleet Raids 1945, Raids on Japan 7–8/45. Tokyo Bay. Operation Magic Carpet.

CL 9 *Richmond* Yangtze River 1927. Decomm 21 Dec 1945. Stricken 21 Jan 1946, sold 18 Dec 1946; BU Baltimore.
3* Komandorski Is., Attu, Kurile Is.

Figure 3.17: *Nashville* (CL 43), 25 Mar 1945. Note modifications made during the war.

Figure 3.18: *Honolulu* (CL 48), at Mare I., 30 Jan 1942, shows the appearance of the *Brooklyn* class early in the war with prominent searchlight tower between the funnels and catapults aft. Notice distinctive arrangement of turrets forward.

Figure 3.19: *Savannah* (CL 42), Apr 1945; a *Brooklyn* class cruiser after refit showing 5"/38 turrets amidships and new tall directors.

CL 10 *Concord* Damaged by gasoline explosion in Southeast Pacific, 7 Oct 1943 (22 killed). Decomm 12 Dec 1945. Stricken 21 Jan 1946, sold 21 Jan 1947; BU Baltimore.
1* Kurile Is.

CL 11 *Trenton* Damaged by powder explosion in forward turret off Norfolk, Va., 20 Oct 1924 (14 killed). Nicaragua 1927. Spanish Civil War (Sqn 40T), Jun 1939–Jul 1940. Decomm 20 Dec 1945. Stricken 21 Jan 1946, sold 29 Dec 1946; BU Baltimore.
1* Kurile Is.

CL 12 *Marblehead* Nicaragua 1927. Yangtze River, 1927. Damaged in collision with m/v *Evansville* northwest of Nantucket, 15 Nov 1929. China 1937–39. Asiatic Fleet 1938–42. Damaged by three aircraft bombs in Madoera Strait, 4 Feb 1942 (15 killed). South Atlantic. Decomm 1 Nov 1945. BU 27 Feb 1946, Philadelphia.
2* Philippines, Southern France.

CL 13 *Memphis* Carried Charles Lindbergh from Southampton, England, to Washington, D.C., Jun 1927. Nicaragua 1932. Neutrality patrol. South Atlantic. Decomm 17 Dec 1945, sold 18 Dec 1946; BU Baltimore.

Brooklyn Class

No.	Name	Builder	Keel Laid	Launched	Comm.
CL 40	*Brooklyn*	New York NYd	12 Mar 1935	30 Nov 1936	30 Sep 1937
CL 41	*Philadelphia*	Phila. NYd	28 May 1935	17 Nov 1936	23 Sep 1937
CL 42	*Savannah*	NY Sbdg	31 May 1934	8 May 1937	10 Mar 1938
CL 43	*Nashville*	NY Sbdg	24 Jan 1935	2 Oct 1937	6 Jun 1938
CL 46	*Phoenix*	NY Sbdg	15 Apr 1935	12 Mar 1938	3 Oct 1938
CL 47	*Boise*	Newport News	1 Apr 1935	3 Dec 1936	12 Aug 1938
CL 48	*Honolulu*	New York NYd	10 Sep 1935	26 Aug 1937	15 Jun 1938

Displacement	10,000 tons; 14,000 f/l
Dimensions	608'4" (oa); 600' (wl) x 61'9" x 24'7"
Machinery	4 screws; Parsons GT; 8 B&W boilers; SHP 100,000; 32.5 knots
Endurance	10,000/15
Complement	1,284/868
Armament	15–6"/47, 8–5"/25; (1945) 4 quad and 4 twin 40mm, 14 to 28 20mm guns (except CL 42 *Savannah* and CL 48 *Honolulu*: 8–5"/38; CL 41 *Philadelphia*: 2 quad and 6 twin 40mm; CL 42–43 *Savannah* and *Nashville*: 6 twin 40mm; CL 40 *Brooklyn*: 2 quad 40mm.
Armor	2" to 5" belt, 2" deck, 2" to 5" bulkheads, 6" barbettes, 3" to 6.5" gunhouses

Notes: Radically different from previous designs. Two pole masts; aviation placed aft with aircraft stored below deck. New 6" guns in five turrets; 5" AA in light gunhouses, no TT. Searchlight tower between funnels removed during the war. *Savannah* rebuilt 1945, new bridge, 5" in twin turrets.

Service Records:

CL 40 *Brooklyn* Neutrality patrol. Slightly damaged by shore gunfire at Fedala, Morocco, 8 Nov 1942; sank destroyer *Boulonnais*. Slightly damaged by mine, off Sicily, 14 Jul 1943. Decomm 3 Jan 1947. †
4* North Africa, Sicily, Anzio, Southern France.

CL 41 *Philadelphia* Carried President Roosevelt on cruise, 30 Apr–8 May 1938. Neutrality patrol. Damaged in collision with transport *Edward Rutledge* in Hampton Roads, 15 Sep 1942. Damaged by radio-controlled bomb near miss, Salerno, 11 Sep 1943. Damaged in

collision with destroyer *Laub* off Anzio, 22 May 1944. Decomm 3 Feb 1947. †
5* North Africa, Sicily, Salerno, Anzio, Southern France. Operation Magic Carpet.

CL 42 *Savannah* Hull holed by anchor during gale off San Pedro, Calif., 27 Sep 1939. Neutrality patrol. Severely damaged by radio-controlled bomb, Salerno, 11 Sep 1943 (197 killed). Decomm 3 Feb 1947. †
3* Sicily, Salerno, Anzio, Southern France. Operation Magic Carpet.
Ship sunk: captured b/r *Karin* in South Atlantic, 11 Mar 1943.

CL 43 *Nashville* Carried $25 million in gold bullion from England to United States, Sep 1939. Neutrality patrol. Damaged by grounding at Midway I., 8 May 1942. Damaged by explosion in forward turret off Kolombangara, 13 May 1943 (18 killed). Minor damage by aircraft bomb near miss off Biak, 4 Jun 1944. Damaged when kamikaze and bombs hit bridge off Negros I., 13 Dec 1944 (133 killed). Decomm 24 Jun 1946. †
10* Solomons, Marcus I. Raid 1943, Wake I. Raid 1943, Cape Gloucester, Admiralty Is., Hollandia, Wakde, Biak I., Morotai, Leyte, Mindoro, Brunei Bay, Balikpapan. Operation Magic Carpet.

CL 46 *Phoenix* Damaged by two aircraft bomb near misses off Biak, 4 Jun 1944 (1 killed). Decomm 3 Jul 1946.
9* Pearl Harbor, Cape Gloucester, Admiralty Is., Hollandia, Wakde, Biak I., Noemfoor I. , Cape Sansapor, Morotai, Leyte, Surigao Strait, Mindoro, Lingayen, Mariveles-Corregidor, Tarakan, Brunei Bay, Balikpapan.

CL 47 *Boise* Struck uncharted shoal in Sape Strait, Dutch East Indies, 21 Jan 1942. Severely damaged by six hits from gunfire at Cape Esperance, 12 Oct 1942 (107 killed). Decomm 1 Jul 1946. †
11* Philippines, Cape Esperance, Sicily, Salerno, Hollandia, Wakde, Biak I., Noemfoor I., Cape Sansapor, Morotai, Leyte, Surigao Strait, Mindoro, Lingayen, Tarakan, Brunei Bay, Balikpapan, Mariveles-Corregidor. Operation Magic Carpet.

CL 48 *Honolulu* Damaged by aircraft bomb near miss at Pearl Harbor, 7 Dec 1941. Damaged by torpedo and lost bow, Battle of Kolombangara, 13 Jul 1943. Severely damaged by aircraft torpedo, Leyte, 20 Oct 1944 (60 killed). In collision with submarine *Argonaut* off New Jersey, 11 Jan 1946. Decomm 3 Feb 1947. †
8* Pearl Harbor, Tassafaronga, Solomons, New Georgia landings, Kula Gulf, Kolombangara, Green I. Ldgs., Saipan, Guam, Palau, Leyte.

Figure 3.20: *St. Louis* (CL 49), 5 Oct 1944, in San Pedro Bay, Calif.; it closely resembled the *Brooklyn* class but with no space between the mainmast and after funnel. The layout of the catapults aft is clearly shown.

St. Louis Class

No.	Name	Builder	Keel Laid	Launched	Comm.
CL 49	*St. Louis*	Newport News	10 Dec 1936	15 Apr 1938	19 May 1939
CL 50	*Helena*	New York NYd	9 Dec 1936	27 Aug 1938	18 Sep 1939

Displacement	10,000 tons; 13,900 f/l
Dimensions	607'4" (oa); 600' (wl) x 61'8" x 25'10"
Machinery	4 screws; Parsons GT; 8 B&W boilers; SHP 100,000; 32.5 knots
Endurance	10,000/15
Complement	1,216/888
Armament	15–6"/47, 8–5"/38; (1945) 4 quad and 4 twin 40mm, 10–20mm added
Armor	2" to 5" belt, 3.75" to 5" bulkheads, 2" deck, 6" barbettes, 1.25" to 6" gunhouses, 2.25" to 5" CT

Notes: Modified *Brooklyn* class. Mainmast close to second funnel. New 5" guns.

Service Records:

CL 49 *St. Louis* Damaged by torpedo, lost bow, battle of Kolombangara, 13 Jul 1943. Damaged by aircraft bomb and three near misses, Green I., Bismarck Arch., 14 Feb 1944 (23 killed). Damaged by two kamikazes off Leyte, 27 Nov 1944 (16 killed). Decomm 20 Jun 1946. †
11* Pearl Harbor, Marshall-Gilbert Raids, Solomons, Cape Torokina, New Georgia landings, Kula Gulf, Kolombangara, Green I. Ldgs., Saipan, Guam, Leyte, Fleet Raids 1945, Raids on Japan 7–8/45. Operation Magic Carpet.

CL 50 *Helena* Damaged by one aircraft torpedoed at Pearl Harbor, 7 Dec 1941 (34 killed). Minor damage by naval gunfire, Battle of Guadalcanal, 13 Nov 1942. Torpedoed three times and sunk by Japanese destroyers at Battle of Kula Gulf, 6 Jul 1943 (168 killed).
7* Pearl Harbor, Cape Esperance, Battle of Guadalcanal, Solomons, New Georgia landings, Kula Gulf.

Atlanta Class

No.	Name	Builder	Keel Laid	Launched	Comm.
CL 51	*Atlanta*	Federal	22 Apr 1940	6 Sep 1941	24 Dec 1941
CL 52	*Juneau*	Federal	27 May 1940	25 Oct 1941	14 Feb 1942

Figure 3.21: *San Diego* (CL 53), of the *Atlanta* class, 14 Jun 1942, was one of the first group with wing turrets aft.

Figure 3.22: *Reno* (CL 96), 25 Jan 1944, shortly after completion. Aft view shows the turrets on three levels and absence of wing turrets in earlier ships.

CL 53	*San Diego*	Beth. Quincy	27 Mar 1940	26 Jul 1941	10 Jan 1942
CL 54	*San Juan*	Beth. Quincy	15 May 1940	6 Sep 1941	28 Feb 1942
CL 95	*Oakland*	Beth. S. Fran.	15 Jul 1941	23 Oct 1942	17 Jul 1943
CL 96	*Reno*	Beth. S. Fran.	1 Aug 1941	23 Dec 1942	28 Dec 1943
CL 97	*Flint*	Beth. S. Fran.	23 Oct 1942	25 Jan 1944	31 Aug 1944
	ex–*Spokane* (26 Nov 1942).				
CL 98	*Tucson*	Beth. S. Fran.	23 Dec 1942	3 Sep 1944	3 Feb 1945
CL 119	*Juneau*	Federal	15 Sep 1944	15 Jul 1945	14 Feb 1946
CL 120	*Spokane*	Federal	15 Nov 1944	22 Sep 1945	17 May 1946
CL 121	*Fresno*	Federal	12 Feb 1945	5 Mar 1946	27 Nov 1946

Displacement	6,000 tons; 8,600 f/l
Dimensions	541'6" (oa); 530' (wl) x 53'2" x 26'8"
Machinery	2 screws, West. GT; 4 B&W boilers; SHP 75,000, 31.8 knots
Endurance	8,500/15
Complement	810/873
Armament	16–5"/38, 16–1.1" AA, 4 quad 21" TT; (1945) 1 quad and 3 twin 40mm, 15–20mm (CL 54 *San Juan*: 2 twin 40mm and 9–20mm) added; CL 95–98: 12–5"/38, 4 quad and 4 twin 40mm, 16–20mm, 4 quad 21" TT; CL 119–21: 8 twin 40mm, no quad, 12–5"/38, 4 quad and 6 twin 40mm AA
Armor	1.1" to 3.75" belt, 1.25" deck, 3.75" bulkheads, 1" to 2.5" gunhouses, 1.25" to 2.5" CT

Notes: Antiaircraft cruisers. Flush deck, with destroyer lines. Dual purpose guns in six twin turrets (eight in CL 51–54). CL 51–54 had round bridge and wing turrets aft. TT removed in *Reno* 1945. CL 119–21 originally ordered from Beth. S. Fran. In CL 119–21, two forward and two aft turrets were on same level.

Service Records:

CL 51 *Atlanta* Torpedoed by destroyer *Akatsuki* and hit in error by gunfire from cruiser *San Francisco* at Battle of Guadalcanal, 12 Nov 1942 and scuttled on 13 Nov (169 killed, incl. RADM Norman Scott).
5* Midway, Guadalcanal-Tulagi, Eastern Solomons, Battle of Guadalcanal. PUC.

CL 52 *Juneau* Torpedoed and sunk by Japanese submarine *I-26* after torpedo damage by enemy warships off Guadalcanal, 13 Nov 1942 (~650 killed).
4* Buin Raid, Santa Cruz, Solomons, Battle of Guadalcanal.

CL 53 *San Diego* Decomm 4 Nov 1946. †
15* Buin Raid, Santa Cruz, Battle of Guadalcanal, Rennell I., Buka Raid, 1st Rabaul Raid, 2nd Rabaul Raid 1943, Gilbert Is., Kwajalein, Raid on Truk, Jaluit attack, Saipan, 1st Bonins Raid, Philippine Sea, Guam, Palau, Philippines Raids 9/44, Okinawa Raid 10/44, N. Luzon–Formosa Raids 10/44, Luzon Raids 10/44, Surigao Strait, Luzon Raids 10/44, Formosa Raids 1/45, Luzon Raids 1/45, China Coast Raids 1/45, Nansei Shoto Raid 1/45, Honshu Raid 2/45, Iwo Jima, Fleet Raids 1945, Raids on Japan 7–8/45. Tokyo Bay. Operation Magic Carpet.

CL 54 *San Juan* Minor damage by aircraft bomb, Battle of Santa Cruz, 26 Oct 1942. Damaged by dive bomber north of Espiritu Santo, 6 Jan 1943. Damaged in typhoon, Okinawa, 5 Jun 1945. Decomm 9 Nov 1946. †
13* Guadalcanal-Tulagi, Santa Cruz, Buka Raid, 1st Rabaul Raid, 2nd Rabaul Raid 1943, Gilbert Is., Kwajalein, Eniwetok, Palau-Yap Raids, Hollandia, Truk Raid 4/44, Saipan, 1st Bonins Raid, Philippine Sea, 2nd Bonins Raid, 3rd Bonins Raid, Guam, Palau-Yap Raids 7/44, Luzon Raids 10/44, Formosa Raids 1/45, Luzon Raids 1/45, China Coast Raids 1/45, Nansei Shoto Raid 1/45, Iwo Jima, Honshu Raid 2/45, Fleet Raids 1945, Raids on Japan 7–8/45. Tokyo Bay. Operation Magic Carpet.

CL 95 *Oakland* †
9* Gilbert Is., Kwajalein, Raid on Truk, Marianas Raid 2/44, Palau-Yap Raids, Hollandia, Truk Raid 4/44, Saipan, 1st Bonins Raid, Philippine Sea, 2nd Bonins Raid, 3rd Bonins Raid, Guam, Palau-Yap Raids 7/44, 4th Bonins Raid, Palau, Philippines Raids 9/44, Okinawa Raid 10/44, Luzon Raids 10/44, Surigao Strait, Fleet Raids 1945, Raids on Japan 7–8/45. Tokyo Bay. Operation Magic Carpet.

CL 96 *Reno* Minor damage by kamikaze, north of Luzon, 14 Oct 1944. Severely damaged by torpedo from *I-41* southwest of Samar, 4 Nov 1944 (2 killed). Decomm 4 Nov 1946. †
3* Saipan, 1st Bonins Raid, Philippine Sea, Guam, Palau-Yap Raids 7/44, 4th Bonins Raid, Palau, Philippines Raids 9/44, Leyte, Okinawa Raid 10/44, N. Luzon–Formosa Raids 10/44, Luzon Raids 10/44, Visayas Is. Raids 10/44, Surigao Strait. Operation Magic Carpet.

Figure 3.23: *Mobile* (CL 63), of the *Cleveland* class, 14 Apr 1943, newly completed. Notice the rounded bridge distinctive of earlier units of the class.

Figure 3.24: *Pasadena* (CL 65), of the *Cleveland* class, in 1944 with a blimp overhead.

Figure 3.25: *Birmingham* (CL 62), of the *Cleveland* class, on 20 Feb 1943; similar to ships of the *Brooklyn* class, but with only four turrets.

CL 97 *Flint* Decomm 6 May 1947. †
4* Formosa Raids 1/45, Luzon Raids 1/45, China Coast Raids 1/45, Honshu Raid 2/45, Iwo Jima, Fleet Raids 1945, Raids on Japan 7–8/45. Operation Magic Carpet.
CL 98 *Tucson* †
1* Raids on Japan 7–8/45.
CL 119 *Juneau* †
CL 120 *Spokane* †
CL 121 *Fresno* †

Cleveland Class

No.	Name	Builder	Keel Laid	Launched	Comm.
CL 55	*Cleveland*	NY Sbdg	1 Jul 1940	1 Nov 1941	15 Jun 1942
CL 56	*Columbia*	NY Sbdg	19 Aug 1940	17 Dec 1941	29 Jul 1942
CL 57	*Montpelier*	NY Sbdg	2 Dec 1940	12 Feb 1942	9 Sep 1942
CL 58	*Denver*	NY Sbdg	26 Dec 1940	4 Apr 1942	15 Oct 1942
CL 59	*Amsterdam*	NY Sbdg	1 May 1941	—	—
CL 60	*Santa Fe*	NY Sbdg	7 Jun 1941	10 Jun 1942	24 Nov 1942
CL 61	*Tallahassee*	NY Sbdg	2 Jun 1941	—	—
CL 62	*Birmingham*	Newport News	17 Feb 1941	20 Mar 1942	29 Jan 1943
CL 63	*Mobile*	Newport News	14 Apr 1941	15 May 1942	24 Mar 1943
CL 64	*Vincennes*	Beth. Quincy	7 Mar 1942	17 Jul 1943	21 Jan 1944
	ex-*Flint* (16 Oct 1942)				
CL 65	*Pasadena*	Beth. Quincy	6 Feb 1943	28 Dec 1943	8 Jun 1944
CL 66	*Springfield*	Beth. Quincy	13 Feb 1943	9 Mar 1944	8 Sep 1944
CL 67	*Topeka*	Beth. Quincy	21 Apr 1943	19 Aug 1944	23 Dec 1944
CL 76	*New Haven*	NY Sbdg	11 Aug 1941	—	—
CL 77	*Huntington*	NY Sbdg	17 Nov 1941	—	—
CL 78	*Dayton*	NY Sbdg	29 Dec 1941	—	—
CL 79	*Wilmington*	NY Sbdg	16 Mar 1942	—	—
CL 80	*Biloxi*	Newport News	9 Jul 1941	23 Feb 1943	31 Aug 1943
CL 81	*Houston*	Newport News	4 Aug 1941	19 Jun 1943	20 Dec 1943
	ex-*Vicksburg* (12 Oct 1942)				
CL 82	*Providence*	Beth. Quincy	27 Jul 1943	28 Dec 1944	15 May 1945
CL 83	*Manchester*	Beth. Quincy	25 Sep 1944	5 Mar 1946	29 Oct 1946
CL 84	*Buffalo*	Federal	—	—	—
CL 85	*Fargo*	NY Sbdg	—	—	—
CL 86	*Vicksburg*	Newport News	26 Oct 1942	14 Dec 1943	12 Jun 1944
	ex-*Cheyenne* (26 Nov 1942)				
CL 87	*Duluth*	Newport News	9 Nov 1942	13 Jan 1944	18 Sep 1944
CL 88	—	Federal	—	—	—
CL 89	*Miami*	Cramp	2 Aug 1941	8 Dec 1942	28 Dec 1943
CL 90	*Astoria*	Cramp	6 Sep 1941	6 Mar 1943	17 May 1944
	ex-*Wilkes-Barre* (16 Oct 1942)				
CL 91	*Oklahoma City*	Cramp	8 Dec 1942	20 Feb 1944	22 Dec 1944
CL 92	*Little Rock*	Cramp	6 Mar 1943	27 Aug 1944	17 Jun 1945
CL 93	*Galveston*	Cramp	20 Feb 1944	22 Apr 1945	24 May 1946 (delivered)
CL 94	*Youngstown*	Cramp	4 Sep 1944	—	—
CL 99	*Buffalo*	NY Sbdg	—	—	—
CL 100	*Newark*	NY Sbdg	—	—	—
CL 101	*Amsterdam*	Newport News	3 Mar 1943	25 Apr 1944	8 Jan 1945
CL 102	*Portsmouth*	Newport News	28 Jun 1943	20 Sep 1944	25 Jun 1945
CL 103	*Wilkes-Barre*	NY Sbdg	14 Dec 1942	24 Dec 1943	1 Jul 1944
CL 104	*Atlanta*	NY Sbdg	25 Jan 1943	6 Feb 1944	3 Dec 1944
CL 105	*Dayton*	NY Sbdg	8 Mar 1943	19 Mar 1944	7 Jan 1945

Displacement	10,000 tons; 14,400 f/l
Dimensions	608'4" (oa); 600' (wl) x 66'4" x 25'3"
Machinery	4 screws; GE GT; 4 B&W boilers; SHP 100,000; 31.6 knots
Endurance	11,000/15
Complement	1,285/1255
Armament	12–6"/47, 12–5"/38, 4 quad and 6 twin 40mm, 10 to 23 20mm
Armor	2" to 5" belt, 2" deck, 3.75" to 5" bulkheads, 6" barbettes, 1.5" to 6" gunhouses, 2.25" to 5" CT

Notes: Modified *Brooklyn* class with only four turrets and four additional 5" guns. Two funnels, two pole masts; flush deck hull. CL 85–87 originally ordered from Federal.

Service Records:

CL 55 *Cleveland* Decomm 7 Feb 1947. †
13* North Africa, Rennell I., Solomons, New Georgia landings, Kolombangara, Buka Bombard., Shortland I. Raid, Saipan, Philippine Sea, Tinian, Palau, Empress Augusta Bay, Lingayen, Ldgs. on Palawan, Mindanao Ldgs., Visayan Is. Ldgs., Mariveles-Corregidor, Brunei Bay, Balikpapan, Raids on Japan 7–8/45.

CL 56 *Columbia* Moderately damaged by two kamikazes in Lingayen Gulf, 6 Jan 1945 (13 killed) and by a third kamikaze on 9 Jan (24 killed). Decomm 30 Nov 1946. †
10* Rennell I., New Georgia landings, Kolombangara, Empress Augusta Bay, Cape Torokina, Palau, Solomons, Leyte, Surigao Strait, Lingayen, Balikpapan, Raids on Japan 7–8/45.

CL 57 *Montpelier* Slightly damaged by aircraft bomb, Empress Augusta Bay, 2 Nov 1943. Damaged by three kamikazes, Leyte, 27 Nov 1944. Decomm 24 Jan 1947. †
13* Rennell I., Solomon Is., New Georgia landings, Green I. Ldgs., Buka Bombard., Shortland I. Raid, Cape Torokina, Saipan, Philippine Sea, Guam, Tinian, Leyte, Lingayen, Ldgs. on Palawan, Mindanao Ldgs., Mariveles-Corregidor, Brunei Bay, Balikpapan, Raids on Japan 7–8/45.

CL 58 *Denver* Slightly damaged by gunfire at Empress Augusta Bay, 2 Nov 1943. Damaged by aircraft torpedo off Bougainville, 13 Nov 1943 (20 killed). Damaged by aircraft bomb near miss, Leyte, 28 Oct 1944. Decomm 7 Feb 1947. †
11* Solomons, New Georgia landings, Empress Augusta Bay, Cape Torokina, 3rd Bonins Raid, Guam, Palau-Yap Raids 7/44, 4th Bonins Raid, Palau, Leyte, Surigao Strait, Mindoro, Lingayen, Buka Bombard., Shortland I. Raid, Subic Bay, Ldgs. at Nasugbu, Ldgs. on Palawan, Mariveles-Corregidor, Brunei Bay, Balikpapan, Raids on Japan 7–8/45.

CL 59 *Amsterdam* Reordered as **CV 22**, 16 Feb 1942.

CL 60 *Santa Fe* Decomm 19 Oct 1946. †
13* Attu, Tarawa Raid 1943, Wake I. Raid 1943, Gilbert Is., Kwajalein, Raid on Truk, Marianas Raid 2/44, Palau-Yap Raids 3/44, Hollandia, Truk Raid 4/44, Saipan, Philippine Sea, 3rd Bonins Raid, Guam, Palau-Yap Raids 7/44, 4th Bonins Raid, Palau, Philippines Raids 9/44, Okinawa Raid 10/44, N. Luzon–Formosa Raids 10/44, Luzon Raids 10/44, Visayas Is. Raids 10/44, Formosa Raids 1/45, Luzon Raids 1/45, China Coast Raids 1/45, Nansei Shoto Raid 1/45, Honshu Raid 2/45, Iwo Jima, Fleet Raids 1945. Operation Magic Carpet.

CL 61 *Tallahassee* Reordered as **CV 23**, 16 Feb 1942.

CL 62 *Birmingham* Damaged by aircraft torpedo and two bombs off Cape Torokina, Bougainville, 8 Nov 1943. Severely damaged by explosion of carrier *Princeton* at Leyte Gulf, 24 Oct 1944. (~200 killed) Damaged by kamikaze, Okinawa, 4 May 1945 (51 killed). Decomm 2 Jan 1947. †
9* Sicily, Tarawa Raid 1943, Wake I. Raid 1943, Saipan, Philippine Sea, Tinian, Guam, Philippines Raids 9/44, Okinawa Raid 10/44, N. Luzon–Formosa Raids 10/44, Luzon Raids 10/44, Iwo Jima, Okinawa.

CL 63 *Mobile* Damaged by accidental explosion in 5" mount, northeast of Wotje I., Marshall Is., 4 Dec 1943. Damaged by explosion, Okinawa, 18 Apr 1945. Decomm 9 May 1947. †
11* Marcus I. Raid 1943, Tarawa Raid 1943, Wake I. Raid 1943, Gilbert Is., Kwajalein, Raid on Truk, Bismarck Archipelago, Marianas Raid 2/44, Palau-Yap Raids, Hollandia, Truk Raid 4/44, Saipan, Philippine Sea, 3rd Bonins Raid, Guam, Palau-Yap Raids 7/44, 4th Bonins Raid, Philippines Raids 9/44, Okinawa Raid 10/44, N. Luzon–Formosa Raids 10/44, Luzon Raids 10/44, Visayas Is. Raids 10/44, Cape Engano, Okinawa. Operation Magic Carpet.

CL 64 *Vincennes* Decomm 10 Sep 1946. †
6* Saipan, 1st Bonins Raid, Philippine Sea, Guam, Tinian, Palau, Philippines Raids 9/44, 4th Bonins Raid, Okinawa Raid 10/44, N. Luzon–Formosa Raids 10/44, Luzon Raids 10/44, Visayas Is. Raids 10/44, Formosa Raids 1/45, Luzon Raids 1/45, China Coast Raids 1/45, Honshu Raid 2/45, Iwo Jima, Okinawa. Operation Magic Carpet.

CL 65 *Pasadena* Slightly damaged by enemy naval gunfire, south of Honshu, 26 Feb 1945. Damaged in error by U.S. gunfire, Okinawa, 6 Apr 1945. †
5* Palau, Philippines Raids 9/44, Luzon Raids 10/44, Formosa Raids 1/45, Luzon Raids 1/45, China Coast Raids 1/45, Formosa Raids 1/45, Nansei Shoto Raid 1/45, Honshu Raid 2/45, Iwo Jima, Fleet Raids 1945, Raids on Japan 7–8/45. Tokyo Bay.

CL 66 *Springfield* †
2* Fleet Raids 1945, Raids on Japan 7–8/45. Tokyo Bay.

CL 67 *Topeka* †
2* Raids on Japan 7–8/45, Fleet Raids 1945. Operation Magic Carpet.

CL 76 *New Haven* Reordered as **CV 24**, 16 Feb 1942.

CL 77 *Huntington* Reordered as **CV 25**, 27 Mar 1942.

CL 78 *Dayton* Reordered as **CV 26**, 27 Mar 1942.

CL 79 *Wilmington* Reordered as **CV 28**, 2 Jun 1942.

CL 80 *Biloxi* Damaged in error by naval gunfire, Iwo Jima, 20 Feb 1945. Damaged by single kamikaze off Okinawa, 27 Mar 1945. Decomm 29 Oct 1946. †
9* Eniwetok, Raid on Truk, Marianas Raid 2/44, Palau-Yap Raids 3/44, Hollandia, Truk Raid 4/44, Saipan, Philippine Sea, 3rd Bonins Raid, Guam, Palau-Yap Raids 7/44, 4th Bonins Raid, Bonins-Yap Raids, Palau, Philippines Raids 9/44, Okinawa Raid 10/44, N. Luzon–Formosa Raids 10/44, Luzon Raids 10/44, Surigao Strait, Luzon Raids 10/44, Formosa Raids 1/45, Luzon Raids 1/45, Formosa Raids 1/45, China Coast Raids 1/45, Honshu Raid 2/45, Iwo Jima, Honshu Raid 2/45, Okinawa.

CL 81 *Houston* Torpedoed by Japanese aircraft, 300 miles east of Formosa, 14 Oct 1944, and again while in tow, on 16 Oct, southeast of Formosa. Decomm 15 Dec 1947. †
3* Saipan, 1st Bonins Raid, Philippine Sea, Guam, 4th Bonins Raid, Palau, Philippines Raids 9/44, Okinawa Raid 10/44, N. Luzon–Formosa Raids 10/44, Luzon Raids 10/44.

CL 82 *Providence* †

CL 83 *Manchester* †

CL 84 *Buffalo* Canceled 16 Dec 1940.

CL 85 *Fargo* Reordered as **CV 27**, 27 Mar 1942.

CL 86 *Vicksburg* In collision, Okinawa, 11 Jun 1945. Decomm 30 Jun 1947. †
2* Iwo Jima, Fleet Raids 1945. Operation Magic Carpet.

CL 87 *Duluth* Damaged in typhoon, Okinawa, 5 Jun 1945. †
2* Fleet Raids 1945, Raids on Japan 7–8/45.

CL 88—Canceled 16 Dec 1940.

CL 89 *Miami* Damaged in typhoon in Philippine Sea, 18 Dec 1944. Decomm 30 Jun 1947. †
6* Saipan, 1st Bonins Raid, Philippine Sea, 3rd Bonins Raid, Guam, 4th Bonins Raid, Palau, Philippines Raids 9/44, Okinawa Raid 10/44, N. Luzon–Formosa Raids 10/44, Luzon Raids 10/44, Visayas Is. Raids 10/44, Surigao Strait, Formosa Raids 1/45, Luzon Raids 1/45, China Coast Raids 1/45, Nansei Shoto Raid 1/45, Honshu Raid 2/45, Iwo Jima, Fleet Raids 1945.

CL 90 *Astoria* †
5* Luzon Raids 10/44, Formosa Raids 1/45, Luzon Raids 1/45, Formosa Raids 1/45, China Coast Raids 1/45, Nansei Shoto Raid 1/45, Iwo Jima, Fleet Raids 1945, Raids on Japan 7–8/45.

CL 91 *Oklahoma City* Decomm 30 Jun 1947. †
2* Okinawa, Raids on Japan 7–8/45.

Figure 3.26: *Wilkes-Barre* (CL 103), of the *Cleveland* class. Notice the squared off bridge of the later units.

CL 92 *Little Rock* †
CL 93 *Galveston* Laid up incomplete 1946. †
CL 94 *Youngstown* Canceled 12 Aug 1945, 54.1 percent complete.
CL 99 *Buffalo* Reordered as **CV 29**, 2 Jun 1942.
CL 100 *Newark* Reordered as **CV 30**, 2 Jun 1942.
CL 101 *Amsterdam* Decomm 30 Jun 1947. †
1* Raids on Japan 7–8/45.
CL 102 *Portsmouth* †
CL 103 *Wilkes-Barre* Decomm 9 Oct 1947. †
4* Formosa Raids 1/45, Luzon Raids 1/45, China Coast Raids 1/45, Nansei Shoto Raid 1/45, Honshu Raid 2/45, Iwo Jima, Fleet Raids 1945, Raids on Japan 7–8/45. Tokyo Bay.
CL 104 *Atlanta* Damaged in typhoon, Philippine Sea, 5 Jun 1945. †
2* Fleet Raids 1945, Raids on Japan 7–8/45. Operation Magic Carpet.
CL 105 *Dayton* †
1* Raids on Japan 7–8/45.

Fargo Class

No.	Name	Builder	Keel Laid	Launched	Comm.
CL 106	*Fargo*	NY Sbdg	23 Aug 1943	25 Feb 1945	9 Dec 1945
CL 107	*Huntington*	NY Sbdg	4 Oct 1943	8 Apr 1945	23 Feb 1946
CL 108	*Newark*	NY Sbdg	17 Jan 1944	14 Dec 1945	—
CL 109	*New Haven*	NY Sbdg	28 Feb 1944	—	—
CL 110	*Buffalo*	NY Sbdg	3 Apr 1944	—	—
CL 111	*Wilmington*	Cramp	5 Mar 1945	—	—
CL 112	*Vallejo*	NY Sbdg	—	—	—
CL 113	*Helena*	NY Sbdg	—	—	—
CL 114	*Roanoke*	NY Sbdg	—	—	—
CL 115	—	NY Sbdg	—	—	—
CL 116	*Tallahassee*	Newport News	31 Jan 1944	—	—
CL 117	*Cheyenne*	Newport News	29 May 1944	—	—
CL 118	*Chattanooga*	Newport News	9 Oct 1944	—	—

Displacement	10,000 tons; 14,230 f/l
Dimensions	611'2" (oa); 600' (wl) x 66'6" x 20'
Machinery	4 screws; GT GE; 4 B&W boilers; SHP 100,000; 31.6 knots
Endurance	11,000/15
Complement	992
Armament	12–6"/47, 12–5"/38, 6 quad and 2 twin 40mm, 18–20mm
Armor	2" to 5" belt, 2" deck, 3.75" to 5" bulkheads, 6" barbettes, 1.5" to 6" gunhouses, 2.25" to 5" CT

Notes: Modified *Cleveland* class with single funnel. Only two completed. CL 111 originally ordered from NY Sbdg.

Service Records:

CL 106 *Fargo* †
CL 107 *Huntington* †
CL 108 *Newark* Canceled 12 Aug 1945, 67.8 percent complete. Launched for use in underwater explosive tests in Chesapeake Bay. Sold 2 Apr 1949; BU Philadelphia.
CL 109 *New Haven* Canceled 12 Aug 1945.
CL 110 *Buffalo* Canceled 12 Aug 1945.
CL 111 *Wilmington* Canceled 12 Aug 1945.
CL 112 *Vallejo* Canceled 5 Oct 1944.
CL 113 *Helena* Canceled 5 Oct 1944.
CL 114 *Roanoke* Canceled 5 Oct 1944.
CL 115 — Canceled 5 Oct 1944.
CL 116 *Tallahassee* Canceled 12 Aug 1945, 56.1 percent complete.
CL 117 *Cheyenne* Canceled 12 Aug 1945, 41.5 percent complete.
CL 118 *Chattanooga* Canceled, 12 Aug 1945, 31.5 percent complete.

Worcester Class

No.	Name	Builder	Keel Laid	Launched	Comm.
CL 144	*Worcester*	NY Sbdg	29 Jan 1945	4 Feb 1947	26 Jun 1948
CL 145	*Roanoke*	NY Sbdg	15 May 1945	16 Jun 1947	4 Apr 1949
CL 146	*Vallejo*	NY Sbdg	16 Jul 1945	—	—
CL 147	*Gary*	NY Sbdg	—	—	—

Displacement	14,700 tons; 17,970 f/l
Dimensions	679'6" (oa); 664' (wl) x 70'8" x 21'6"
Machinery	4 screws; GT GE; 4 B&W boilers; SHP 120,000; 33 knots
Endurance	8,000/15
Complement	1,560
Armament	12–6"/47, 24 3"/50 AA
Armor	3" to 5" belt, 4" bulkheads, 3.5" desk, 5" barbettes, 2" to 6.5" gunhouses, 4" to 5" CT

Notes: New 6" guns in twin turrets.

Service Records:

CL 144 *Worcester* †
CL 145 *Roanoke* †
CL 146 *Vallejo* Canceled 12 Aug 1945.
CL 147 *Gary* Canceled 12 Aug 1945.
CL 154 —

CL 155 —
CL 156 —
CL 157 —
CL 158 —
CL 159 —

Displacement	7,370 tons; 11,050 f/l
Dimensions	591'6" (oa); 580" (wl) x 55'6 x **(U)**
Machinery	SHP 100,000; 34.5 knots
Endurance	6,000/20
Complement	692
Armament	12–5"/54, 28–40mm, 24–20mm
Armor	3.12" belt, 1.25" deck

Notes: Antiaircraft cruisers. Never ordered. Design never made final.

4
DESTROYERS

During World War I the U.S. Navy embarked on the construction of a single type of destroyer; by 1922, 265 ships had been completed. These nearly identical vessels were the ubiquitous flush-deck destroyers, so called because of the straight unbroken deck from stem to stern. During the interwar years the "four-pipe" flush-deckers were the only destroyers in service and, together with the battleships' cage masts, became symbolic of the Navy of that period.

With so many destroyers built and authorized funds cut, dozens rode out their careers laid up in the backwaters of Navy yards on both U.S. coasts. Some were operated with reduced crews. A ship would serve several years and then be laid up and replaced by another from the reserve. Fourteen were converted into minelayers. Some 20 prewar destroyers were used by the Coast Guard in the 1920s to prevent smuggling of liquor. In 1923 the Navy suffered a grievous loss when 6 destroyers were wrecked off California. Following the signing of the London Naval Treaty of 1930, dozens of flush-deckers were scrapped, along with 46 older units.

The first new postwar destroyers were the 8 ships of the *Farragut* class. Authorized in 1931, they had a heavier armament and quadruple torpedo tubes. These were followed by the 16 ships of the *Mahan* class. The Navy also built some larger destroyers, the eight *Porter*-class destroyer "leaders"; they had 5" guns in twin mounts.

The next destroyers built in the 1930s followed a basic pattern with single stack, four or five 5" guns and a heavy torpedo armament. The tripod masts of the *Mahan* and *Porter* classes were abandoned in favor of a single pole mast.

By the late 1930s new designs were favored: first the *Benson* and *Livermore* classes with two funnels and five guns, followed by the larger *Fletcher* class. It was the *Fletchers* that bore the brunt of the latter half of the Pacific war as they came into service, and eventually 175 were built. The succeeding *Allen M. Sumner*–class destroyers were improved *Fletchers* with 5" guns in twin mounts, and the *Gearing*-class destroyers were longer *Sumners*.

American Naval officers understood that the next war would be in the Pacific, and designed their ships with the ability to operate over vast distances. The destroyers built at this time had a high endurance, and also the ability to refuel at sea.

In 1941, 136 flush-deckers were in service; at the end of the war many were still active as escort DDs. Many were converted to other duties, as minelayers (DM), minesweepers (DMS), seaplane tenders (AVD), and high-speed transports (APD).

At this time the Navy used many of the newer destroyers in the Atlantic. Many remained to protect large units, leaving convoy protection to the older boats, patrol vessels and Coast Guard cutters. Ships of the *Craven*, *Somers*, and *Benson* classes were used in the European theater, and some of the new *Sumner* class were at Normandy.

The 13 flush-deck destroyers in the Philippines were evacuated immediately after Pearl Harbor, and a number were lost in action against the Japanese in early 1942. The newer boats built in the 1930s bore the brunt of the action in the Pacific from Pearl Harbor on until the arrival of the bigger *Fletcher* class. Twenty-three of these were lost in the brutal actions in the Solomon Islands campaigns.

The *Fletchers* became the necessary escorts for the fast carrier task forces that dominated the Pacific war from 1943 on. Although they had been built with high speed and the ability to operate over long distances, they really lacked sufficient endurance for this purpose. In 1944–45 they were joined by the *Sumner* class, and these units suffered heavily from kamikaze attacks in the Philippines and Okinawa. Sixty-four destroyer types were lost during the Okinawa campaign.

At the end of the war all the prewar destroyers were stricken from the list of naval vessels, some being used as part of the target fleet for the atomic bomb explosions at Bikini in 1946.

Destroyers are designated by the symbol *DD* and are named after deceased distinguished Navy and Marine Corps officers and heroes, as well as civilians who have been of service to the Navy.

Figure 4.1: *Warrington* (DD 383), a so-called destroyer leader, as built. Notice twin gun mounts and four banks of torpedo tubes.

DESTROYERS ON THE NAVY LIST, 1922

Paulding Class

DD 22 *Paulding* Decomm Aug 1919. On loan to USCG, CG-17, 28 Apr 1924–18 Oct 1930. Rammed and sank submarines-4 in a collision off Provincetown, Mass., 17 Dec 1927. Stricken 28 Jun 1934; BU.
DD 23 *Drayton* Decomm 17 Nov 1919. Name canceled 1 Jul 1933. Stricken 8 Mar 1935, sold 28 Jun 1935; BU.
DD 24 *Roe* Decomm 1 Dec 1919. On loan to USCG, CG-18, 7 Jun 1924–18 Oct 1930. Stricken 28 Jun 1934; BU.
DD 25 *Terry* Decomm 13 Nov 1919. On loan to USCG, CG-19, 7 Jun 1924–18 Oct 1930. Sold 2 May 1934. Stricken 28 Jun 1934; BU.
DD 26 *Perkins* Decomm 5 Dec 1919. Name canceled 1 Nov 1933. Stricken 8 Mar 1935, sold 28 Jun 1935; BU.
DD 27 *Sterett* Decomm 9 Dec 1919. Stricken 8 Mar 1935, sold 28 Jun 1935; BU Norfolk, Va.
DD 28 *McCall* Decomm 12 Dec 1919. On loan to USCG, CG-14, 7 Jun 1924–18 Oct 1930. Stricken 28 Jun 1934; BU.
DD 29 *Burrows* Decomm 12 Dec 1919. On loan to USCG, CG-10, 28 Apr 1924–2 May 1931. Stricken 5 Jul 1934; BU.
DD 30 *Warrington* Decomm 31 Jan 1920. Stricken 20 Mar 1935, sold 28 Jun 1935; BU Norfolk, Va.
DD 31 *Mayrant* Decomm 12 Dec 1919. Stricken 8 Mar 1935, sold 28 Jun 1935; BU Norfolk, Va.
DD 32 *Monaghan* Decomm 4 Nov 1919. On loan to USCG, CG-15, 7 Jun 1924–8 May 1931. Name canceled 1 Jul 1933. Stricken 5 Jul 1934; BU.
DD 33 *Trippe* Decomm 6 Nov 1919. On loan to USCG, CG-20, 7 Jun 1924–2 May 1931. Stricken 5 Jul 1934, sold 22 Aug 1934; BU Brooklyn.
DD 34 *Walke* Decomm 12 Dec 1919. Name canceled 1 Jul 1933. Stricken 20 Mar 1935; BU Philadelphia.
DD 35 *Ammen* Decomm 11 Dec 1919. On loan to USCG, CG-8, 28 Apr 1924–22 May 1931. Name canceled 1 Jul 1933. Stricken 5 Jul 1934; BU.
DD 36 *Patterson* Decomm 1919. On loan to USCG, CG-16, 28 Apr 1924–18 Oct 1930. Name canceled 1 Jul 1933. Stricken 28 Jun 1934; BU.
DD 37 *Fanning* Decomm 24 Nov 1919. On loan to USCG, CG-11, 7 Jun 1924–24 Nov 1930. Stricken 28 Jun 1934; BU.
DD 38 *Jarvis* Decomm 26 Nov 1919. Stricken 8 Mar 1935, sold 23 Apr 1935; BU.
DD 39 *Henley* Decomm 12 Dec 1919. On loan to USCG, CG-12, 16 May 1924–8 May 1931. Stricken 5 Jul 1934, sold 22 Aug 1934; BU Philadelphia.
DD 40 *Beale* Decomm 25 Oct 1919. On loan to USCG, CG-9, 28 Apr 1924–18 Oct 1930. Stricken 28 Jun 1934; BU Philadelphia.
DD 41 *Jouett* Decomm 24 Nov 1919. On loan to USCG, CG-13, 28 Apr 1924–22 May 1931. Stricken 5 Jul 1934; BU Brooklyn.
DD 42 *Jenkins* Decomm 31 Oct 1919. Stricken 8 Mar 1935; BU.

Cassin Class

DD 43 *Cassin* Decomm 7 Jun 1922. On loan to USCG, CG-1, 28 Apr 1924–30 Jun 1933. Name canceled 1 Jul 1933. Stricken 5 Jul 1934, sold 22 Aug 1934; BU.
DD 44 *Cummings* Decomm 23 Jun 1922. On loan to USCG, CG-3, 7 Jun 1924–23 May 1932. Name canceled 1 Jul 1933. Stricken 5 Jul 1934, sold 22 Aug 1934; BU.
DD 45 *Downes* Decomm 6 Jun 1922. On loan to USCG, CG-4, 28 Apr 1924–2 May 1931. Name canceled 1 Jul 1933. Stricken 5 Jul 1934, sold 22 Aug 1934; BU.
DD 46 *Duncan* Decomm 9 Aug 1921. Stricken 8 Mar 1935, sold 23 Apr 1935; BU.
DD 47 *Aylwin* Decomm 23 Feb 1921. Name canceled 1 Jul 1933. Stricken 8 Mar 1935, sold 23 Apr 1935; BU.
DD 48 *Parker* Decomm 6 Jun 1922. Stricken 8 Mar 1935, sold 23 Apr 1935; BU.
DD 49 *Benham* Decomm 7 Jul 1922. Stricken 8 Mar 1935, sold 23 Apr 1935; BU.
DD 50 *Balch* Decomm 20 Jun 1922. Name canceled 1 Jul 1933. Stricken 8 Mar 1935, sold 23 Apr 1935; BU.

O'Brien Class

DD 51 *O'Brien* Decomm 9 Jun 1922. Stricken 8 Mar 1935, sold 23 Apr 1935; BU Philadelphia.
DD 52 *Nicholson* Decomm 26 May 1922. Stricken 7 Jan 1936, sold 30 Jun 1936.
DD 53 *Winslow* Decomm 5 Jun 1922. Name canceled, 1 Jul 1933. Stricken 7 Jan 1936, sold 30 Jun 1936; BU.
DD 54 *McDougal* Decomm 26 May 1922. On loan to USCG, CG-6, 7 Jun 1924–0 Jun 1933. Stricken 5 Jul 1934, sold 22 Aug 1934; BU.
DD 55 *Cushing* Decomm 7 Aug 1920. Name canceled 1 Jul 1933. Stricken 7 Jan 1936, sold 30 Jun 1936; BU.
DD 56 *Ericsson* Decomm 16 Jun 1922. On loan to USCG, CG-5, 7 Jun 1924–23 May 1932. Stricken 5 Jul 1934, sold 22 Aug 1934; BU.

Tucker Class

DD 57 *Tucker* Decomm 16 May 1921. On loan to USCG, CG-23, 25 Mar 1926–30 Jun 1933. Name canceled 1 Nov 1933. Stricken 24 Oct 1936, sold 10 Dec 1936.
DD 58 *Conyngham* Decomm 23 Jun 1922. On loan to USCG, CG-2, 7 Jun 1924–30 Jun 1933. Name canceled 1 Nov 1933. Stricken 5 Jul 1934, sold 22 Aug 1934: BU.
DD 59 *Porter* Decomm 23 Jun 1922. On loan to USCG, CG-7, 7 Jun 1924–30 Jun 1933. Name canceled 1 Jul 1933. Stricken 5 Jul 1934, sold 22 Aug 1934; BU.
DD 60 *Wadsworth* Decomm 3 Jun 1922. Stricken 7 Jan 1936, sold 30 Jun 1936; BU.
DD 62 *Wainwright* Decomm 19 May 1922. On loan to USCG, CG-24, 2 Apr 1926–27 Apr 1934. Stricken 5 Jul 1934, sold 22 Aug 1934; BU Brooklyn.

Sampson Class

DD 63 *Sampson* Decomm 15 Jun 1921. Stricken 7 Jan 1936, sold 8 Sep 1936; BU Baltimore.
DD 64 *Rowan* Decomm 19 Jun 1922. Stricken 7 Jan 1936, sold 20 Apr 1939.
DD 65 *Davis* Decomm 20 Jun 1922. On loan to USCG, CG-21, 25 Mar 1926–5 Jul 1934. Sank rumrunner *Shuben Acadia* in collison south of Montauk Pt., NY, 12 Jun 1931. Sold 22 Aug 1934; BU.

DD 66 *Allen*: Out of comm 22 Jun 1922–23 Jun 1925. Reserve training. Out of comm Mar 1928–23 Aug 1940. Decomm 15 Oct 1945. Stricken 1 Nov 1945, sold 26 Sep 1946; BU Baltimore.
1* Pearl Harbor. Rearmed 1940.

DD 67 *Wilkes* Decomm 5 Jun 1922. On loan to USCG, CG-25, 25 Mar 1926–27Apr 1934. Stricken 5 Jul 1934, sold 22 Aug 1934; BU.

DD 68 *Shaw* Decomm 21 Jun 1922. On loan to USCG, CG-22, 25 Mar 1926–30 Jun 1933. Name canceled 1 Nov 1933. Stricken 5 Jul 1934, sold 22 Aug 1934; BU.

Caldwell Class

DD 69 *Caldwell* Decomm 27 Jun 1922. Stricken 7 Jan 1936, sold 30 Jun 1936.

DD 70 *Craven* Decomm 15 Jun 1922–9 Aug 1940. Name canceled 31 May 1935. Renamed ***Conway***, 30 Nov 1938. To UK, 23 Oct 1940.
Later history: Renamed HMS *Lewes*. Scuttled off Sydney, Australia, 25 May 1946.

DD 71 *Gwin* Decomm 28 Jun 1922. Stricken 25 Jan 1937, sold 16 Mar 1939; BU Baltimore.

DD 72 *Conner* Out of comm 21 Jun 1922–23 Aug 1940. To UK, 23 Oct 1940.
Later history: Renamed HMS *Leeds*. BU 1949 Grays, England.

DD 73 *Stockton* Out of comm 26 Jun 1922–16 Aug 1940. To UK, 23 Oct 1940.
Later history: Renamed HMS *Ludlow*. Beached off Fidra I., 6 Jun 1945, and sunk as target.

DD 74 *Manley* Out of comm 14 Jun 1922–1 May 1930. Damaged in hurricane 300 miles east of Sable I., 25 Sep 1937. Spanish Civil War (Sqn 40T), Nov 1937–Oct 1938. Rec **AG 28**, 28 Nov 1938, converted to transport. Rec **APD 1**, 2 Aug 1940. Rec **DD 74**, 25 Jun 1945. Decomm 19 Nov 1945. Stricken 5 Dec 1945, sold 26 Nov 1946; BU Philadelphia.
5* Solomons, Kwajalein, Saipan, Leyte, Mariveles-Corregidor, Ldgs. at Nasugbu.

Wickes Class

DD 75 *Wickes* Out of comm 15 May 1922–26 Apr 1930. Nicaragua 1932. Out of comm 6 Apr 1937–30 Sep 1939. To UK 23 Oct 1940.
Later history: Renamed HMS *Montgomery*. RCN 1942–43. BU 1945 Dunston, UK.

DD 76 *Philip* Out of comm 29 May 1922–25 Feb 1930. Nicaragua 1931–32. Out of comm 2 Apr 1937–30 Sep 1939. To UK, 23 Oct 1940.
Later history: Renamed HMS *Lancaster*. BU 1947 Blyth, UK.

Figure 4.2: *Williams* (DD 108) under way at San Diego, early 1920s. In 1940 she was transferred to the Royal Navy and renamed HMS *St. Clair*.

Figure 4.3: *Breckinridge* (DD 148), 8 Mar 1945, as converted for escort duties.

DD 78 *Evans* Out of comm 29 May 1922–1 Apr 1930 and 31 Mar 1937–30 Sep 1939. Neutrality Patrol. To UK, 23 Oct 1940.
Later history: Renamed HMS *Mansfield*. BU 1945 Baltimore.

DD 79 *Little* Out of comm 5 Jul 1922– 4 Nov 1940. Converted to transport and rec **APD 4**, 2 Aug 1940. Sunk by Japanese destroyer *Yudachi* off Lunga Point, Guadalcanal, 5 Sep 1942 (22 killed).
2* Guadalcanal-Tulagi, Solomons.

DD 80 *Kimberly* Decomm 30 Jun 1922. Stricken 25 Jan 1937 and sold; BU Baltimore.

DD 81 *Sigourney* Out of comm 26 Jun 1922–23 Aug 1940. To UK, 26 Nov 1940.
Later history: Renamed HMS *Newport*. Norwegian Navy 1942–43. BU 1947 Granton, UK.

DD 82 *Gregory* Out of comm 7 Jul 1922–4 Nov 1940. Converted to transport and rec **APD 3**, 2 Aug 1940. Sunk by Japanese destroyer *Yudachi* off Lunga Point, Guadalcanal, 5 Sep 1942 (11 killed).
2* Guadalcanal-Tulagi, Solomons.

DD 83 *Stringham* Out of comm 2 Jun 1922–11 Dec 1940. Converted to transport and rec **APD 6**, 2 Aug 1940. Damaged by fire at Manus, 3 Oct 1944. Rammed by destroyer *LaVallette* at Guam, 7 May 1945. Rec **DD 83**, 25 Jun 1945. Decomm 9 Nov 1945. Stricken 5 Dec 1945, sold 29 Mar 1946; BU Philadelphia.
9* Solomons, Vella Lavella, Treasury Is. Ldgs., Cape Torokina, Cape Gloucester, Saidor, Green I. Ldgs., Saipan, Tinian, Palau, Okinawa.

DD 84 *Dyer* Decomm 7 Jun 1922. Stricken 7 Jan 1936, sold 8 Sep 1936; BU Baltimore.

DD 85 *Colhoun* Out of comm 28 Jun 1922–11 Dec 1940. Converted to transport and rec **APD 2**, 2 Aug 1940. Sunk by Japanese aircraft off Guadalcanal, 30 Aug 1942 (51 killed).
1* Guadalcanal-Tulagi, Solomons.

DD 86 *Stevens* Decomm 19 Jun 1922. Stricken 7 Jan 1936, sold 8 Sep 1936; BU Baltimore.

DD 87 *McKee* Decomm 16 Jun 1922. Stricken 7 Jan 1936, sold 8 Sep 1936; BU Baltimore.

DD 88 *Robinson* Out of comm 3 Aug 1922–23 Aug 1940. To UK, 26 Nov 1940.
Later history: Renamed HMS *Newmarket*. BU 1945 Llanelli, UK.

DD 89 *Ringgold* Out of comm 17 Jun 1922–23 Aug 1940. To UK, 26 Nov 1940.
Later history: Renamed HMS *Newark*. BU 1947 Bo'ness, UK.

DD 90 *McKean* Out of comm 19 Jun 1922–11 Dec 1940. Converted to transport and rec **APD 5**, 2 Aug 1940. Torpedoed and sunk by Japanese aircraft off Bougainville, 17 Nov 1943 (114 killed).
4* Guadalcanal-Tulagi, Solomons, New Georgia, Vella Lavella, Treasury Is. Ldgs., Choiseul Ldgs., Cape Torokina.

DD 91 *Harding* Decomm 1 Jul 1922. Stricken 7 Jan 1936, sold 29 Sep 1936.

DD 92 *Gridley* Decomm 22 Jun 1922. Name canceled 31 May 1935. Stricken 25 Jan 1937, sold 18 Apr 1939.

DD 93 *Fairfax* Out of comm 19 Jun 1922–1 May 1930. To UK, 26 Nov 1940.
Later history: Renamed HMS *Richmond.* To USSR Jul 1944, Renamed *Zhivuchiy.* Returned 1949 and BU Grangemouth, UK.

DD 94 *Taylor* Out of comm 21 Jun 1922–1 May 1930. Decomm 23 Sep 1938. Stricken 6 Dec 1938. Damage ControlHulk No. 40, 1940. Bow used to repair *Blakeley,* 1942. Sold 8 Aug 1945; BU.

DD 95 *Bell* Decomm 21 Jun 1922. Stricken 25 Jan 1937, sold 18 Apr 1939.

DD 103 *Schley* Out of comm 1 Jun 1922–3 Oct 1940. Converted to transport and rec **APD 14**, 2 Jan 1943. Rec **DD 103**, 5 Jul 1945. Decomm 9 Nov 1945. Stricken 5 Dec 1945, sold 29 Mar 1946; BU Philadelphia.
11* Pearl Harbor, Solomons, New Georgia, Kwajalein, Eniwetok, Admiralty Is., Hollandia, Biak, Cape Sansapor, Morotai, Leyte, Ormoc, Mindoro, Okinawa, Mariveles-Corregidor.

DD 104 *Champlin* Decomm 7 Jun 1922. Stricken 19 May 1936. Sunk as target off San Diego, 12 Aug 1936.

DD 105 *Mugford* Decomm 7 Jun 1922. Name canceled 31 May 1935. Stricken 19 May 1936, sold 29 Sep 1936; BU.

DD 106 *Chew* Out of comm 1 Jun 1922–14 Oct 1940. Hawaii. Decomm 15 Oct 1945. Stricken 1 Nov 1945, sold 4 Oct 1946.
1* Pearl Harbor (2 killed).

DD 107 *Hazelwood* Out of comm 7 Jul 1922–1 Apr 1925. Decomm 15 Nov 1930. Rec **IX 36**, 5 Nov 1930. Rec **DD 107**, 11 Aug 1931. Stricken 5 Jun 1935, sold 30 Aug 1935; BU.

DD 108 *Williams* Out of comm 7 Jun 1922–6 Nov 1939. To UK, 24 Sep 1940.
Later history: Renamed HMCS *St. Clair.* Sold 1946, sank in tow to BU at Halifax.

DD 109 *Crane* Out of comm 7 Jun 1922–18 Dec 1939. U.S. West Coast. Decomm 14 Nov 1945. Stricken 19 Dec 1945, sold 1 Nov 1946.

DD 113 *Rathburne* Out of comm 12 Feb 1923–8 Feb 1930. Converted to transport and rec **APD 25**, 20 May 1944. Damaged by kamikaze, Okinawa, 27 Apr 1945. Rec **DD 113**, 10 Jul 1945. Decomm 2 Nov 1945. Stricken 28 Nov 1945, sold 21 Nov 1946; BU.
6* Palau, Leyte, Lingayen, Iwo Jima, Okinawa, Subic Bay.

DD 114 *Talbot* Out of comm 31 Mar 1923–31 May 1930. Damaged by explosion at San Diego, 21 Jan 1930. Converted to transport and rec **APD 7**, 31 Oct 1942. In collision with battleship *Pennsylvania* in Mid-Pacific, 6 Jun 1944. Rec **DD 114**, 16 Jul 1945. Decomm 9 Oct 1945. Stricken 24 Oct 1945, sold 30 Jan 1946; BU Baltimore.
8* New Georgia, Vella Lavella, Treasury Is. Ldgs., Cape Torokina, Green I. Ldgs., Hollandia, Saipan, Leyte, Mariveles-Corregidor, Ldgs. at Nasugbu, Okinawa.

DD 115 *Waters* Out of comm 28 Dec 1922–4 Jun 1930. Converted to transport and rec **APD 8**, 31 Oct 1942. Rec **DD 115**, 2 Aug 1945. Decomm 12 Oct 1945. Stricken 24 Oct 1945, sold 21 Nov 1946; BU.
7* Solomons, New Georgia, Vella Lavella, Treasury Is. Ldgs., Cape Torokina, Green I. Ldgs., Saipan, Guam, Iwo Jima, Okinawa.

DD 116 *Dent* Out of comm 7 Jun 1922–15 May 1930. Converted to transport and rec **APD 9**, 31 Oct 1942. Went aground off New Guinea, 22 Dec 1943. Decomm 4 Dec 1945. Stricken 3 Jan 1946, sold 13 Jun 1946.
5* Solomons, New Georgia, Vella Lavella, Treasury Is. Ldgs., Cape Torokina, Hollandia, Saipan.

DD 117 *Dorsey* Out of comm 9 Mar 1923–1 Mar 1930. Converted to minesweeper and rec **DMS 1**, 19 Nov 1940. Damaged by kamikaze, Okinawa, 26 Mar 1945 (3 killed). Wrecked in typhoon at Okinawa, 9 Oct 1945. Decomm 8 Dec 1945. Hulk destroyed, 11 Jan 1946.
6* Cape Torokina, Lingayen, Iwo Jima, Okinawa, Raids on Japan 7–8/45, Minesweeping 1945.

DD 118 *Lea* Out of comm 22 Jun 1922–1 May 1930 and 7 Apr 1937–30 Sep 1939. Damaged in collision with destroyer *Sicard* off Hawaii, 12 May 1935. Neutrality Patrol. Damaged in collision with m/v *Elihu Yale* off the Azores, 31 Dec 1943. Decomm 20 Jul 1945. Stricken 13 Aug 1945, sold 30 Nov 1945; BU Baltimore.
3* Convoy TAG-18, Convoy ON-67, TG 21.12. PUC.

DD 119 *Lamberton* Out of comm 30 Jun 1922–15 Nov 1930. Rec **AG 21**, 16 Apr 1932, converted to target towing ship. Converted to minesweeper and rec **DMS 2**, 19 Nov 1940. In collision with destroyer *Chandler* in fog, Aleutians, 2 Jul 1942. Rec **AG 21**, 5 Jun 1945. Decomm 13 Dec 1946. Stricken 28 Jan 1947, sold 9 May 1947; BU Terminal I.
1* Attu.

DD 120 *Radford* Decomm 9 Jun 1922. Rec **AG 22**, 16 Apr 1932, conversion to target vessel canceled and rec **DD 120**, 27 Jun 1932. Stricken 19 May 1936, sunk as target off San Diego, 5 Aug 1936.

DD 121 *Montgomery* Out of comm 6 Jun 1922–20 Aug 1931. Converted to minelayer and rec **DM 17**, 5 Jan 1931. Out of comm 7 Dec 1937–25 Sep 1939. Damaged in collision with minelayer *Preble* off Savo I., Solomons, 25 Aug 1943. Damaged by mine at Ngulu, 17 Oct 1944 (4 killed). Decomm 23 Apr 1945. Stricken 28 Apr 1945, sold 11 Mar 1946.
4* Pearl Harbor, Solomons, New Georgia, Palau.

DD 122 *Breese* Out of comm 17 Jun 1922–1 Jun 1931. Converted to minelayer and rec **DM 18**, 5 Jan 1931. Out of comm 12 Nov 1937–25 Sep 1939. Damaged in collision with cruiser *San Francisco* in New Hebrides, 30 Sep 1942. Decomm 15 Jan 1946. Stricken 7 Feb 1946, sold 20 May 1946.
10* Pearl Harbor, Solomons, New Georgia, Cape Torokina, Leyte, Lingayen, Iwo Jima, Okinawa, Raids on Japan 7–8/45, Minesweeping 1945.

DD 123 *Gamble* Out of comm 17 Jun 1922–24 May 1930. Converted to minelayer and rec **DM 15**, 13 Jun 1930. Out of comm 22 Dec 1937–25 Sep 1939. Damaged by Japanese bombers off Iwo Jima, 18 Feb 1945 (5 killed), not repaired. Scuttled off Saipan, 16 Jul 1945.
7* Pearl Harbor, Solomons, New Georgia, Cape Torokina, Iwo Jima.
Submarine sunk: *I-123* southeast of Savo I., 29 Aug 1942.

DD 124 *Ramsay* Out of comm 30 Jun 1922–2 Jun 1930. Converted to minelayer and rec **DM 16**, 13 Jun 1930. Out of comm 14 Dec 1937–25 Sep 1939. Rec **AG 98**, 5 Jun 1945. Decomm 19 Oct 1945. Stricken 13 Nov 1945, sold 21 Nov 1946.
3* Pearl Harbor, Attu, Kwajalein.

DD 125 *Tattnall* Out of comm 15 Jun 1922–1 May 1930. Converted to transport and rec **APD 19**, 24 Jul 1943. Damaged by aircraft bomb, Okinawa, 20 May 1945. Decomm 17 Dec 1945. Stricken 8 Jan 1946, sold 17 Oct 1946; BU Seattle.
3* Elba Ldgs., Southern France, Okinawa.

DD 126 *Badger* Out of comm 27 May 1922–6 Jan 1930. Spanish Civil War (Sqn 40T), Oct 1938–Mar 1939. Neutrality Patrol. Decomm 20 Jul 1945. Stricken 13 Aug 1945, sold 30 Nov 1945.
1* TG 21.12.
Submarine sunk: *U-613* north of Azores, 23 Jul 1943.

DD 127 *Twiggs* Out of comm 24 Jun 1922–20 Feb 1930 and 6 Apr 1937–30 Sep 1939. To UK, 23 Oct 1940.
Later history: Renamed HMS *Leamington*; to USSR Jul 1944 Renamed *Zhguchiy.* Returned 1950 and BU Newport, Wales.

DD 128 *Babbitt* Out of comm 15 Jun 1922–4 Apr 1930. Neutrality Patrol. Rec **AG 102**, 10 Jun 1945. Decomm 25 Jan 1946. Stricken 25 Feb 1946, sold 20 May 1946.
1* Convoy SC-121.

DD 130 *Jacob Jones* Out of comm 24 Jun 1922–1 May 1930. Spanish Civil War (Sqn 40T), Oct 1938–Mar 1939. Neutrality Patrol. Torpedoed twice by *U-578* and sank off Cape May, N.J., 28 Feb 1942 (138 killed).

DD 131 *Buchanan* Out of comm 7 Jun 1922–10 Apr 1930 and 9 Apr 1937–30 Sep 1939. To UK, 9 Sep 1940.
Later history: Renamed HMS *Campbeltown.* Blown up to destroy locks at St. Nazaire, France, 28 Mar 1942.

DD 132 *Aaron Ward* Out of comm 17 Jun 1922–24 May 1930 and 1 Apr 1937–30 Sep 1939. To UK, 9 Sep 1940.
Later history: Renamed HMS *Castleton.* BU 1948 Bo'ness, UK.

DD 133 *Hale* Out of comm 22 Jun 1922–1 May 1930 and 9 Apr 1937–30 Sep 1939. To UK, 9 Sep 1940.

Later history: Renamed HMS *Caldwell*. Laid up Mar 1945. BU 1945 Granton, UK.

DD 134 *Crowninshield* Out of comm 7 Jul 1922–12 May 1930 and 8 Apr 1937–30 Sep 1939. Neutrality Patrol. To UK, 9 Sep 1940.

Later history: Renamed HMS *Chelsea*; to USSR 1944, renamed *Derzkiy*. Returned 1949; BU Bo'ness, UK.

DD 135 *Tillman* Out of comm 3 Jul 1922–1 May 1930. Decomm 15 Jun 1939. To UK, 26 Nov 1940.

Later history: Renamed HMS *Wells*. BU 1946 Troon, Scotland.

DD 136 *Boggs* Out of comm 29 Jun 1922–19 Dec 1931. Rec **IX 36**, 11 Aug 1931, target service. Rec **AG 19**, 5 Sep1931. Converted to minesweeper and rec **DMS 3**, 19 Nov 1940. Hawaii. Rec **AG 19**, 5 Jun 1945. Decomm 20 Mar 1946. Stricken 12 Apr 1946, sold 6 Nov 1946.

DD 137 *Kilty* Out of comm 5 Jun 1922–18 Dec 1939. Rec **IX 37**, 11 Aug 1931. Rec **AG 20**, 5 Sep 1931. Rec **DD 137**, 16 Apr 1932. Converted to transport and rec **APD 15**, 2 Jan 1943. Rec **DD 137**, 20 Jul 1945. Decomm 2 Nov 1945. Stricken 16 Nov 1945, sold 28 Aug 1946; BU Philadelphia.

10* New Georgia, Vella Lavella, Treasury Is. Ldgs., Choiseul Ldgs., Cape Torokina, Cape Gloucester, Saidor, Green I. Ldgs., Hollandia, Biak, Cape Sansapor, Morotai, Leyte, Mindoro, Ldgs. at Nasugbu, Mariveles-Corregidor, Okinawa.

DD 138 *Kennison* Out of comm 22 Jun 1922–18 Dec 1939. U.S. West Coast. Rec **AG 83**, 1 Oct 1944, target ship. Decomm 21 Nov 1945. Stricken 5 Dec 1945, sold 18 Nov 1946; BU Philadelphia.

DD 139 *Ward* Out of comm 21 Jul 1921–15 Jan 1941. Sank Japanese midget submarine at Pearl Harbor entrance before air attack, 7 Dec 1941. Converted to transport and rec **APD 16**, 2 Jan 1943. Sunk by Japanese aircraft off Ormoc, Leyte, 7 Dec 1944. (None killed)

9* Pearl Harbor, Solomons, Vella Lavella, Treasury Is. Ldgs., Choiseul Ldgs., Cape Torokina, Cape Gloucester, Saidor, Green I. Ldgs., Hollandia, Biak, Cape Sansapor, Morotai, Leyte, Ormoc.

DD 140 *Claxton* Out of comm 18 Jun 1922–22 Jan 1930. Damaged in hurricane 300 miles east of Sable I., 25 Sep 1937. Spanish Civil War (Sqn 40T), Nov 1937–Oct 1938. To UK, 26 Nov 1940.

Later history: Renamed HMS *Salisbury*. BU 1945 Baltimore.

DD 141 *Hamilton* Out of comm 20 Jul 1922–20 Jan 1930. Converted to minesweeper and rec **DMS 18**, 11 Oct 1941. Rec **AG 111**, 5 Jun 1945. Decomm 16 Oct 1945. Stricken 1 Nov 1945, sold 21 Nov 1946; BU.

9* Convoy TAG-18, North Africa, Kwajalein, Admiralty Is., Hollandia, Saipan, Guam, Palau, Leyte, Lingayen, Iwo Jima. (Note: Forward boiler replaced by stabilization tanks, 1938.)

DD 142 *Tarbell* Out of comm 8 Jun 1922–29 May 1930 and 15 Jan 1937–4 Oct 1939. Neutrality patrol. Decomm 20 Jul 1945. Stricken 13 Aug 1945, sold 30 Nov 1945; BU Baltimore.

DD 143 *Yarnall* Out of comm 29 May 1922–19 Apr 1930 and 30 Dec 1936–4 Oct 1939. Went aground off Norfolk, Va., 25 Nov 1939. To UK, 23 Oct 1940.

Later history: Renamed HMS *Lincoln*. Norwegian Navy 1942. RCN 1942–43. To USSR 1944, Renamed *Druzhniy*. BU 1952 Charleston, UK.

DD 144 *Upshur* Out of comm 15 May 1922–2 Jun 1930 and 22 Dec 1936–4 Oct 1939. Neutrality Patrol, North Atlantic Convoys. Rec **AG 103**, 30 Jun 1945. Decomm 2 Nov 1945. Stricken 16 Nov 1945, sold 26 Sep 1947; BU Philadelphia.

DD 145 *Greer* Out of comm 22 Jun 1922–31 Mar 1930 and 13 Jan 1937–4 Oct 1939. Neutrality Patrol, Atlantic Convoys. Attacked by U-boat 175 miles southwest of Iceland, 4 Sep 1941; first American warship to attack a U-boat in World War II. Damaged in collision with destroyer *Barney* off Curacao, 18 Sep 1942. Sank armed yacht *Moonstone* in collision off Delaware Capes, 16 Oct 1943. In collision with oiler *Rapidan* at Norfolk, Va., 30 Nov 1943. Decomm 19 Jul 1945. Stricken 13 Aug 1945, sold 30 Nov 1945; BU Baltimore.

1* Convoy SC-121.

DD 146 *Elliot* Out of comm 22 May 1922–8 Feb 1930. Converted to minesweeper and rec **DMS 4**, 19 Nov 1940. Rec **AG 104**, 5 Jun 1945. Decomm 12 Oct 1945. Stricken 24 Oct 1945, sold 28 Jan 1946; BU.

1* Attu.

DD 147 *Roper* Out of comm 14 Dec 1922–18 Mar 1930. Converted to transport and rec **APD 20**, 20 Oct 1943. Damaged in collision with transport *Arthur Middleton*, 400 miles southeast of Okinawa, 30 Mar 1945. Damaged by kamikaze, Okinawa, 25 May 1945. Decomm 15 Sep 1945. Stricken 11 Oct 1945, sold 31 Mar 1946; BU.

4* Elba Ldgs., Southern France, Okinawa.

Submarine sunk: *U-85* off Cape Hatteras, 14 Apr 1942.

DD 148 *Breckinridge* Out of comm 20 Jun 1922–1 May 1930 and 23 Dec 1936–4 Oct 1939. Rec **AG 112**, 30 Jun 1945. Decomm 30 Nov 1945. Stricken 19 Dec 1945, sold 31 Oct 1946.

1* Convoy UGS-37.

DD 149 *Barney* Out of comm 30 Jun 1922–1 May 1930 and 9 Nov 1936–4 Oct 1939. Damaged in collision with destroyer *Greer* off Curacao, 18 Sep 1942 (2 killed). Rec **AG 113**, 30 Jun 1945. Decomm 30 Nov 1945. Stricken 19 Dec 1945, sold 13 Oct 1946; BU.

1* Convoy UGS-37.

DD 150 *Blakeley* Out of comm 29 Jun 1922–16 Oct 1939. Torpedoed by *U-156* off Martinique, lost bow, 25 May 1942 (6 killed). Repaired with bow from decomm DD 94. Decomm 21 Jul 1945. Stricken 13 Aug 1945, sold 30 Nov 1945.

1* Convoy UGS-37.

DD 151 *Biddle* Out of comm 20 Jun 1922–1 May 1930 and 11 Nov 1936–16 Oct 1939. Recomm 16 Oct 1939. Rec **AG 114**, 30 Jun 1945. Decomm 5 Oct 1945. Stricken 24 Oct 1945, sold 3 Dec 1946.

1* Convoy UGS-37.

DD 152 *DuPont* Neutrality Patrol. Out of comm 19 Apr 1922–1 May 1930 and 14 Jan 1937–16 Oct 1939. Damaged in collision with British m/v *Thorshovdi*, North Atlantic, 24 Nov 1941. Rec **AG 80**, 25 Sep 1944. Decomm 2 May 1946. Stricken 5 Jun 1946, sold 12 Mar 1947.

3* Convoy UGS-6, TG 21.13. PUC.

Submarine sunk: **U-172* west of Canary Is., 13 Dec 1943.

DD 153 *Bernadou* Out of comm 1 Jul 1922–1 May 1930 and 8 Jan 1937–16 Oct 1939. Neutrality Patrol. Landed assault troops at Safi, Morocco, 8 Nov 1942. Decomm 17 Jul 1945. Stricken 13 Aug 1945, sold 30 Nov 1945.

5* Convoy ON-67, North Africa, Sicily, Salerno, Convoy UGS-40. PUC.

DD 154 *Ellis* Out of comm 17 Jun 1922–1 May 1930 and 16 Dec 1936–16 Oct 1939. In collision with destroyer *McFarland* off Magdalena Bay, Mexico, 5 Nov 1934. Neutrality Patrol, North Atlantic Convoys. Rec **AG 115**, 30 Jun 1945. Decomm 31 Oct 1945. Stricken 16 Nov 1945, sold 20 Jun 1947.

1* Convoy UGS-40.

DD 155 *Cole* Out of comm 10 Jul 1922–1 May 1930 and 7 Jan 1937–16 Oct 1939. Neutrality patrol. Landed assault troops at Safi, Morocco, 8 Nov 1942. Rec **AG 116**, 30 Jun 1945. Decomm 1 Nov 1945. Stricken 16 Nov 1945, sold 6 Oct 1947.

3* North Africa, Sicily, Salerno, Okinawa. PUC.

DD 156 *J. Fred Talbott* Out of comm 18 Jan 1923–1 May 1930. Rec **AG 81**, 25 Sep 1944. Decomm 21 May 1946. Stricken 19 Jun 1946, sold 6 Nov 1946; BU Baltimore.

DD 157 *Dickerson* Out of comm 25 Jun 1922–1 May 1930. Attacked in error by gunfire from m/v *Liberator* off Norfolk, Va., 19 Mar 1942 (4 killed). Converted to transport and rec **APD 21**, 21 Aug 1943. Damaged by kamikaze off Okinawa, 2 Apr, and sunk 21 Apr 1945 (58 killed).

6* Green I. Ldgs., Hollandia, Saipan, Guam, Lingayen, Iwo Jima, Okinawa.

DD 158 *Leary* Out of comm 29 Jun 1922–1 May 1930. Neutrality Patrol. Torpedoed three times by *U-275* and sank in North Atlantic, 24 Dec 1943 (97 killed).

1* TG 21.14.

Figure 4.4: *Leary* (DD 158), 20 Nov 1943, as modified for escort duty, with one funnel and eight torpedo tubes removed.

DD 159 *Schenck* Out of comm 29 Jun 1922–1 May 1930. Neutrality patrol. Damaged in collision with m/v *Exterminator* at Iceland, 13 Mar 1943. Rec **AG 82**, 25 Sep 1944. Decomm 17 May 1946. Stricken 5 Jun 1946, sold 25 Nov 1946; BU Baltimore.
1* TG 21.14.
Submarine sunk: *U-645* north of Azores, 24 Dec 1943.

DD 160 *Herbert* Out of comm 27 Jun 1922–1 May 1930. Converted to transport and rec **APD 22**, 1 Dec 1943. Decomm 25 Sep 1945. Stricken 24 Oct 1945, sold 23 May 1946; BU Baltimore.
6* Hollandia, Biak, Cape Sansapor, Morotai, Leyte, Ormoc, Mindoro, Iwo Jima, Okinawa, Minesweeping 1945.

DD 161 *Palmer* Out of comm 31 May 1922–7 Aug 1940. Converted to minesweeper and rec **DMS 5**, 19 Nov 1940. Damaged by gunfire off Casablanca, 8 Nov 1942. Sunk by mine and Japanese aircraft in Lingayen Gulf, 7 Jan 1945 (28 killed).
5* North Africa, Kwajalein, Saipan, 2nd Bonins Raid, 3rd Bonins Raid, Guam, Leyte, Lingayen.

DD 162 *Thatcher* Out of comm 7 Jun 1922–18 Dec 1939. To UK, 24 Sep 1940.
Later history: Renamed HMCS *Niagara*. BU 1947 Hamilton, Ont.

DD 163 *Walker* Decomm 7 Jun 1922. Stricken 28 Mar 1938. Converted to water barge and rec **YW 57**, 30 Mar 1939. Renamed ***DCH-1*** as damage control hulk, 11 Jul 1940. Rec **IX 44**, 17 Feb 1941. Scuttled in tow en route San Diego to Honolulu, 28 Dec 1941.

DD 164 *Crosby* Out of comm 7 Jun 1922–18 Dec 1939. Sank fishing vessel *Lone Eagle* in collision off Point Arguello, Calif., 3 Apr 1940. Converted to transport and rec **APD 17**, 22 Feb 1943. Decomm 28 Sep 1945. Stricken 24 Oct 1945, sold 23 May 1946.
10* New Georgia, Treasury Is. Ldgs., Choiseul Ldgs., Cape Torokina, Cape Gloucester, Saidor, Green I. Ldgs., Hollandia, Biak, Cape Sansapor, Morotai, Leyte, Ormoc, Mindoro, Okinawa, Mariveles-Corregidor.

DD 165 *Meredith* Decomm 28 Jun 1922. Stricken 7 Jan 1936, sold 29 Sep 1936; BU.

DD 166 *Bush* Decomm 21 Jun 1922. Stricken 7 Jan 1936, sold 8 Sep 1936; BU Baltimore.

DD 167 *Cowell* Out of comm 27 Jun 1922–17 Jun 1940. To UK, 23 Sep 1940.
Later history: Renamed HMS *Brighton*. To USSR 24 Jul 1944, renamed *Zharkiy*. Returned 1949; BU Bo'ness, UK.

DD 168 *Maddox* Out of comm 14 Jun 1922–17 Jun 1940. To UK, 23 Sep 1940.
Later history: Renamed HMS *Georgetown*. To USSR Aug 1944, renamed *Zhestkiy*. BU 1952 Inverkeithing, Scotland.

DD 169 *Foote* Out of comm 6 Jul 1922–2 Jul 1940. To UK, 23 Sep 1940.
Later history: Renamed HMS *Roxborough*. To USSR 24 Aug 1944, renamed *Doblestnyy*. Returned 1949; BU Dunston, UK.

DD 170 *Kalk* Out of comm 10 Jul 1922–17 Jun 1940. To UK, 23 Sep 1940.
Later history: Renamed HMS, then HMCS *Hamilton*. BU 1945 Baltimore.

DD 175 *Mackenzie* Out of comm 27 May 1922–6 Nov 1939. To UK, 24 Sep 1940.
Later history: Renamed HMCS *Annapolis*. BU 1945 Baltimore.

DD 176 *Renshaw* Decomm 27 May 1922. Stricken 19 May 1936, sold 29 Sep 1936.

DD 177 *O'Bannon* Decomm 27 May 1922. Stricken 19 May 1936, sold 29 Sep 1936, used as breakwater.

DD 178 *Hogan* Out of comm 27 May 1922–7 Aug 1940. Converted to minesweeper and rec **DMS 6**, 19 Nov 1940. Rec **AG 105**, 5 Jun 1945. Sunk as target off San Diego, 8 Nov 1945.
6* North Africa, Kwajalein, Hollandia, Saipan, Guam, Lingayen, Iwo Jima.

DD 179 *Howard* Out of comm 27 May 1922–29 Aug 1940. Converted to minesweeper and rec **DMS 7**, 19 Nov 1940. Rec **AG 106**, 5 Jun 1945. Decomm 30 Nov 1945. Stricken 19 Dec 1945, sold 13 Jun 1946; BU Philadelphia.
6* North Africa, Saipan, Tinian, Leyte, Lingayen, Iwo Jima.

DD 180 *Stansbury* Out of comm 27 May 1922–29 Aug 1940. Converted to minesweeper and rec **DMS 8**, 19 Nov 1940. Damaged by mine off Casablanca, 8 Nov 1942. Rec **AG 107**, 5 Jun 1945. Decomm 11 Dec 1945. Stricken 3 Jan 1946, sold 26 Oct 1946; BU.
3* North Africa, Kwajalein, Saipan, Guam.

DD 181 *Hopewell* Out of comm 17 Jul 1922–17 Jun 1940. To UK, 23 Sep 1940.
Later history: Renamed HMS *Bath*. Norwegian Navy, 1941. Torpedoed and sunk by *U-204* in North Atlantic southwest of Ireland, 19 Aug 1941.

DD 182 *Thomas* Out of comm 30 Jun 1922–17 Jun 1940. To UK 23 Sep 1940.
Later history: Renamed HMS *St. Albans*. Norwegian Navy, 1941. To USSR 24 Aug 1944, renamed *Dostoynyy*. Returned 28 Feb 1949; BU Charlestown, UK.

DD 183 *Haraden* Out of comm 17 Jul 1922–4 Dec 1939. To UK, 23 Sep 1940.
Later history: Renamed HMCS *Columbia*. Hulked 1944. BU 1945 Hamilton, Ont.

DD 184 *Abbot* Out of comm 5 Jul 1922–17 Jun 1940. To UK 23 Sep 1940.
Later history: Renamed HMS *Charlestown*. BU 1948 Sunderland.

DD 185 *Bagley* Out of comm 12 Jul 1922–17 Jun 1940. Name canceled 31 May 1935. Renamed **Doran**, 22 Dec 1939. To UK, 23 Sep 1940.
Later history: Renamed HMS *St. Marys*. BU 1945 Rosyth.

Figure 4.5: *John D. Ford* (DD 228), at Mare I., 7 Aug 1942, refitted but little changed. She was a survivor of the destroyer flotillas in the Far East at the outbreak of the war.

Figure 4.6: *Farenholt* (DD 332), a typical flush-deck destroyer, was scrapped in 1931.

Clemson Class

DD 186 *Clemson* Out of comm 30 Jun 1922–12 Jul 1940. Converted to seaplane tender and rec **AVP 17**, 15 Nov 1939. Rec **AVD 4**, 2 Aug 1940. Caribbean, Brazil 1940–42. Rec **DD 186**, 1 Dec 1943. Converted to transport and rec **APD 31**, 7 Mar 1944. Damaged in collision with battleship *Pennsylvania* and transport *Latimer*, Lingayen Gulf, 10 Jan 1945. Rec **DD 186**, 17 Jul 1945. Decomm 12 Oct 1945. Sold 21 Nov 1946.

9* TG 21.12, TG 21.13, Saipan, Guam, Palau, Leyte, Lingayen, Okinawa. PUC.

Submarine sunk: **U-172* west of Canary Is., 13 Dec 1943.

DD 187 *Dahlgren* Out of comm 30 Jun 1922–25 Oct 1932. Damaged in collision with destroyer *Tarbell* west of San Diego, 24 Jan 1933. Experimental ship 1937. (Note: Two aft funnels trunked into one.) Rec **AG 91**, 1 Mar 1945. Decomm 14 Dec 1945. Stricken 8 Jan 1946, sold 17 Jun 1946.

DD 188 *Goldsborough* Out of comm 14 Jul 1922–1 Jul 1940. Converted to seaplane tender and rec **AVP 18**, 15 Nov 1939. Rec **AVD 5**, 2 Aug 1940. Neutrality Patrol. Rec **DD 188**, 1 Dec 1943. Converted to transport and rec **APD 32**, 7 Mar 1944. Damaged by coastal gunfire, Leyte, 18 Oct 1944 (2 killed). Rec **DD 188**, 10 Jul 1945. Decomm 11 Oct 1945. Stricken 24 Oct 1945, sold 21 Nov 1946; BU.

5* Saipan, Tinian, Leyte, Iwo Jima, Okinawa.

DD 189 *Semmes* Decomm 17 Jul 1922. On loan to USCG, CG-20, 20 Apr 1932–14 Jun 1934. Rec **AG 24**, 1 Jul 1935 as sonar experimental ship. (Most armament removed.) Damaged in collision with British trawler *Senateur Duhamel* which sank, off Norfolk, 6 May 1942. Decomm 2 Jun 1946. Stricken 3 Jul 1946, sold 25 Nov 1946; BU Philadelphia.

DD 190 *Satterlee* Out of comm 11 Jul 1922–18 Dec 1939. To UK, 9 Oct 1940.

Later history: Renamed HMS *Belmont.* Torpedoed and sunk by *U-82* southeast of Nova Scotia, 31 Jan 1942.

DD 191 *Mason* Out of comm 3 Jul 1922–4 Dec 1939. To UK, 9 Oct 1940.

Later history: Renamed HMS *Broadwater.* Torpedoed and sunk by *U-101* south of Iceland, 19 Oct 1941.

DD 193 *Abel P. Upshur* Decomm 7 Aug 1922. Training ship, Mar 1928. On loan to USCG, CG-15, 5 Nov 1930–21 May 1934. Recomm 4 Dec 1939. To UK, 9 Sep 1940.

Later history: Renamed HMS *Clare.* BU 1947 Troon, Scotland.

DD 194 *Hunt* Decomm 11 Aug 1922. On loan to USCG, CG-18, 13 Sep 1930–28 May 1934. Recomm 26 Jan 1940. To UK, 9 Oct 1940.

Later history: Renamed HMS *Broadway.* BU 1948 Charlestown, UK.

DD 195 *Welborn C. Wood* Decomm 8 Aug 1922. On loan to USCG, CG-19, 1 Oct 1930–28 May 1934. Recomm 4 Sep 1939. To UK, 9 Oct 1940.

Later history: Renamed HMS *Chesterfield.* BU 1948 Dunston, UK.

DD 196 *George E. Badger* Decomm 11 Aug 1922. On loan to USCG, CG-16, 1 Oct 1930–21 May 1934. Converted to seaplane tender and rec **AVP 16**, 1 Oct 1939. Recomm 8 Jan 1940. Rec **AVD 3**, 2 Aug 1940. Neutrality Patrol. Rec **DD 196**, 4 Nov 1943. Converted to transport and rec **APD 33**, 10 Apr 1944. Rec **DD 196**, 20 Jul 1945. Decomm 3 Oct 1945, sold 3 Jun 1946; BU.

8* TG 21.12, TG 21.13, Palau, Leyte, Lingayen, Iwo Jima, Okinawa. PUC.

Submarine sunk: **U-172* west of Canary Is., 13 Dec 1943.

DD 197 *Branch* Out of comm 11 Aug 1922–4 Dec 1939. To UK, 9 Oct 1940.

Later history: Renamed HMS *Beverley.* Torpedoed and sunk by *U-188* in North Atlantic, 11 Apr 1943, after collision with m/v *Cairnvalona* on 9 Apr.

DD198 *Herndon* Decomm 6 Jun 1922. On loan to USCG, CG-17, 13 Sep 1930–28 May 1934. Damaged in collision in fog with m/v *Lemuel Burrows* south of Montauk, N.Y., 15 Jan 1932. Recomm 4 Dec 1939. To UK, 9 Sep 1940.

Later history: Renamed HMS *Churchill.* To USSR 24 Aug 1944, renamed *Deyatelnyy.* Torpedoed and sunk by *U-956* off Cape Tereberskii, 16 Jan 1945.

DD 199 *Dallas* Out of comm 26 Jun 1922–14 Apr 1925 and 23 Mar 1939–25 Sep 1939. Neutrality Patrol. Landed assault troops at Port Lyautey, Morocco, 10 Nov 1942. Renamed ***Alexander Dallas***, 31 Mar 1945. Decomm 28 Jul 1945. Stricken 13 Aug 1945, sold 30 Nov 1945.

4* North Africa, Sicily, Salerno, Convoy UGS-40. PUC.

DD 206 *Chandler* Out of comm 20 Oct 1922–31 Mar 1930. Converted to minesweeper and rec **DMS 9**, 19 Nov 1940. Damaged in collision with minesweeper *Lamberton* in fog in Aleutians, 27 Jul 1942. Damaged by fire, west of Saipan, 23 Jul 1944. Rec **AG 108**, 5 Jun 1945. Decomm 21 Nov 1945. Stricken 5 Dec 1945, sold 18 Nov 1946.

8* Attu, Kwajalein, Eniwetok, Saipan, Tinian, Leyte, Lingayen, Iwo Jima.

Submarine sunk: **I-185* northeast of Saipan, 22 Jun 1944.

DD 207 *Southard* Out of comm 7 Feb 1922–6 Jan 1930. Converted to minesweeper and rec **DMS 10**, 19 Nov 1940. Damaged by kamikaze, Lingayen, 6 Jan 1945. Damaged by kamikaze, Okinawa, 27 Mar 1945. Damaged in typhoon at Okinawa, 17 Sep 1945; wrecked on reef during another typhoon and lost, 9 Oct 1945. Decomm 5 Dec 1945. Destroyed 14 Jan 1946.

10* Guadalcanal-Tulagi, Solomons, Battle of Guadalcanal, Leyte, Cape Torokina, Palau, Lingayen, Leyte, Okinawa, Raids on Japan 7–8/45.

Submarine sunk: *I-172* off Cape Recherche, 10 Nov 1942 (probable).

DD 208 *Hovey* Out of comm 1 Feb 1923–20 Feb 1930. Converted to minesweeper and rec **DMS 11**, 19 Nov 1940 and recomm. Hit by kamikaze and torpedoed and sunk off Lingayen, 7 Jan 1945 (24 killed).

8* Guadalcanal-Tulagi, Solomons, Battle of Guadalcanal, Cape Torokina, Hollandia, Palau, Leyte, Lingayen.

DD 209 *Long* Out of comm 30 Dec 1922–29 Mar 1930. Converted to minesweeper and rec **DMS 12**, 19 Nov 1940. Damaged in collision with destroyer *Monaghan* in fog off Aleutians, 27 Jul 1942. Sunk by kamikazes off Lingayen, 6 Jan 1945 (1 killed).

9* Attu, Kwajalein, Admiralty Is., Hollandia, Saipan, Palau, Guam, Leyte, Lingayen.

DD 210 *Broome* Out of comm 30 Dec 1922–5 Feb 1930. Neutrality Patrol, Atlantic Convoys. Rec **AG 96**, 23 May 1945. Decomm 20 May 1946. Sold 20 Nov 1946.

DD 211 *Alden* Out of comm 24 Jan 1923–8 May 1930. China 1937–39. Damaged in collision with high-speed transport *Hayter* off Norfolk, 31 Jan 1945. Decomm 15 Jul 1945. Stricken 13 Aug 1945, sold 30 Nov 1945; BU Baltimore.

3* Philippines 1941–42, Java Sea, Convoy UGS-36.

DD 212 *Smith Thompson* Radio relay ship at Yokohama after earthquake, 1923. Nicaragua 1926–27. Mediterranean 1927–28. Asiatic Fleet 1929–36. Yangtze River 1930–32. Damaged in collision with destroyer *Whipple* in South China Sea, 14 Apr 1936. Stricken 19 May 1936, sunk as target off Subic Bay, 25 Jul 1936.

DD 213 *Barker* Nicaragua 1927. Yangtze River 1930–32. China 1937–39. Damaged by near misses during action off Banka, 15 Feb 1942. Decomm 18 Jul 1945. Stricken 13 Aug 1945. Sold 30 Nov 1945.

2* Philippines 1941–42, TG 21.12.

DD 214 *Tracy* Nicaragua 1926–27. Yangtze River 1930. Converted to minelayer and rec **DM 19**, 30 Jun 1937. Decomm 19 Jan 1946. Stricken 7 Feb 1946, sold 20 May 1946; BU.
7* Pearl Harbor (3 killed), Guadalcanal-Tulagi, Guadalcanal, Cape Torokina, Iwo Jima, Okinawa, Minesweeping 1945.

DD 215 *Borie* Nicaragua 1927. Yangtze River 1930–32. Damaged by ramming *U-405*, which sank, in Mid-Atlantic, 1 Nov 1943, and was sunk by destroyer *Barry* (27 killed).
3* TG 21.14. PUC.

DD 216 *John D. Edwards* Nicaragua 1927. Asiatic Fleet 1929–42. Yangtze River 1930–32. China 1937–39. Decomm 28 Jul 1945. Stricken 3 Aug 1945, sold 30 Nov 1945; BU Baltimore.
3* Philippines 1941–42, Badoeng Strait, Java Sea, Convoy UGS-36.

DD 217 *Whipple* Far East, 1921–25, 1929–42. Nicaragua, 1926–27. Yangtze River 1930–32. In collision with m/v *Rosalie Moller* off Shanghai, 6 Feb 1932. Damaged in collision with destroyer *Smith Thompson* in South China Sea, 14 Apr 1936. China 1937–39. Damaged in collision with Dutch cruiser *De Ruyter* in Prigi Bay, Java, 12 Feb 1942. North Atlantic Convoys. Rec **AG 117**, 6 Jun 1945. Decomm 9 Nov 1945. Stricken 5 Dec 1945, sold 30 Sep 1947; BU Philadelphia.
2* Philippines 1941–42, Convoy UGS-36.

DD 218 *Parrott* Asiatic Fleet 1923–42. Yangtze River 1927–32. China 1937–39. Damaged when rammed by m/v *John Morton* in Elizabeth River, Norfolk, Va., and beached, 2 May 1944. Decomm 14 Jun 1944. Stricken 18 Jul 1944, sold 5 Apr 1947; BU.
2* Philippines 1941–42, Makassar Strait, Badoeng Strait.

DD 219 *Edsall* Asiatic Fleet 1923–42. Yangtze River 1927–32. China 1937–39. Sunk by gunfire from Japanese surface warships south of Java, 1 Mar 1942 (~150 killed; no survivors).
2* Philippines 1941–42.
Submarine sunk: **I-124* in Western Clarence Strait off Darwin, Australia, 20 Jan 1942.

DD 220 *MacLeish* Neutrality Patrol. Asiatic Fleet 1925–38. Yangtze River 1927–31. Out of comm 11 Mar 1938–25 Sep 1939. Atlantic Convoys. Rec **AG 87**, 5 Jan 1945. Decomm 8 Mar 1946. Stricken 13 Nov 1946, sold 18 Dec 1946; BU Baltimore.
1* TG 21.11.

DD 221 *Simpson* Asiatic Fleet 1925–32. Yangtze Guantanamo River, 1927–32. Damaged in collision with cruiser *Milwaukee* off Guantanamo, 7 May 1934. Neutrality Patrol. Conversion to **APD 27** canceled 1943. Rec **AG 97**, 23 May 1945. Decomm 27 May 1946. Stricken 19 Jun 1946, sold 21 Nov 1946; BU Philadelphia.

DD 222 *Bulmer* Eastern Mediterranean 1923. Asiatic Fleet 1925–42. Yangtze River 1927–32. China 1937–39. Rec **AG 86**, 5 Jan 1945. Decomm 16 Aug 1946. Stricken 25 Sep 1946. Sold 19 Feb 1947.
2* Philippines 1941–42, TG 21.12.

DD 223 *McCormick* Eastern Mediterranean 1922–24. Asiatic Fleet 1925–32. Yangtze River 1927–31. Out of comm 14 Oct 1938–26 Sep 1939. Neutrality Patrol. Rec **AG 118**, 30 Jun 1945. Decomm 4 Oct 1945. Stricken 24 Oct 1945, sold 15 Dec 1946; BU Baltimore.

DD 224 *Stewart* Asiatic Fleet 1922–42. Yangtze River 1926–32. China 1937–39. Damaged by Japanese gunfire, Badoeng Strait, 20 Feb 1942. Fell off keel blocks in drydock at Surabaya and damaged by bomb, 22 Feb 1942. Drydock scuttled, 2 Mar 1942.
2* Philippines 1941–42, Badoeng Strait.
Later history: Raised by Japanese Feb 1943 and recomm as *Patrol Boat No.102.* Recomm in Navy as **DD 224**, 29 Oct 1945. Stricken 17 Apr 1946. Decomm 23 May 1946 and sunk as a target off San Francisco, 24 May.

DD 225 *Pope* Asiatic Fleet 1921–42. Yangtze River 1926–32. China 1937–39. Damaged in collision with destroyer *Pillsbury* in Manila Bay, 16 Oct 1941. Sunk by Japanese cruisers *Ashigara* and *Maya* in Java Sea, 1 Mar 1942. (~90 killed).
2* Philippines 1941–42, Makassar Strait, Badoeng Strait. PUC.

DD 226 *Peary* Asiatic Fleet 1922–42. Yangtze River 1926–32. Damaged in collision with cruiser *Houston* at Shanghai, 7 Oct 1933. China 1937–39. Damaged by one aircraft bomb at Cavite, Philippines, 10 Dec 1941 (8 killed). Sunk by five aircraft bombs at Darwin, North Australia, 19 Feb 1942 (80 killed).
1* Philippines 1941–42.

DD 227 *Pillsbury* Asiatic Fleet 1922–42. Yangtze River 1926–32. China 1937–39. Damaged in collision with destroyer *Pope* in Manila Bay, 16 Oct 1941. Sunk by Japanese cruisers *Atago* and *Takao* south of Java, 1 Mar 1942 (149 killed; no survivors).
2* Philippines 1941–42, Badoeng Strait.

DD 228 *John D. Ford* Asiatic Fleet 1922–42. Yangtze River 1926–32. China 1937–39. Damaged by gunfire, Makassar Strait, 24 Jan 1942. Damaged in collision with British tanker at Gibraltar, 29 Mar 1944. Rec **AG 119**, 30 Jun 1945. Decomm 2 Nov 1945. Stricken 16 Nov 1945, sold 30 Sep 1947; BU Philadelphia.
4* Philippines 1941–42, Makassar Strait, Badoeng Strait, Java Sea, Convoy UGS-36. PUC.

DD 229 *Truxtun* Asiatic Fleet 1922–32. Yangtze River 1926–32. Neutrality Patrol. Wrecked in storm in Placentia Bay, Nfld, 18 Feb 1942 (110 killed).

DD 230 *Paul Jones* Asiatic Fleet 1923–42. Yangtze River 1926–32. China 1937–39. Rec **AG 120**, 30 Jun 1945. Decomm 5 Nov 1945. Stricken 28 Nov 1945, sold 5 Oct 1947; BU Norfolk, Va.
2* Philippines 1941–42, Makassar Strait, Java Sea.

DD 231 *Hatfield* Mediterranean 1922–23. Nicaragua 1927. Spanish Civil War (Sqn 40T), Sep 1936–Nov 1937. Out of comm 28 Apr 1938–25 Sep 1939. Alaska 1941–44. Rec **AG 84**, 1 Oct 1944. Decomm 13 Dec 1946. Stricken 28 Jan 1947, sold 9 May 1947; BU Terminal I.

DD 232 *Brooks* Went aground off Portsmouth, NH, 5 Jul 1924. Nicaragua 1926. Out of comm 20 Jan 1931–18 Jun 1932 and 9 Sep 1938–25 Apr 1939. Converted to transport and rec **APD 10**, 1 Dec 1942. Damaged by kamikaze, Lingayen Gulf, 6 Jan 1945 (3 killed). Decomm 2 Aug 1945. Stricken 17 Sep 1945, sold 30 Jan 1946.
6* Finschhafen, Lae Ldgs., Saidor, Admiralty Is., Hollandia, Saipan, Cape Gloucester, Leyte, Ormoc, Mindoro, Lingayen.

DD 233 *Gilmer* Went aground off Portsmouth, NH, 5 Jul 1924. Nicaragua 1926. Out of comm 31 Aug 1938–25 Sep 1939. Converted to transport and rec **APD 11**, 22 Jan 1943. Damaged by kamikaze, Kerama Retto, Okinawa, 26 Mar 1945 (1 killed). Stricken 23 Feb 1946. Decomm 5 Feb 1946. Sold 3 Dec 1946; BU.
7* Lae Ldgs., Finschhafen, Cape Gloucester, Saidor, Admiralty Is., Hollandia, Saipan, Tinian, Iwo Jima, Okinawa.
Submarine sunk: **I-6* off Tinian, 14 Jul 1944.

DD 234 *Fox* In collision with British cruiser *Ceres* in the Bosporus, 4 Apr 1923. Out of comm 2 Feb 1931–18 Jun 1932 and 16 Sep 1938–25 Sep 1939. U.S. West Coast. Rec **AG 85**, 1 Oct 1944. Decomm 29 Nov 1945. Stricken 19 Dec 1945, sold 12 Nov 1946; BU.

DD 235 *Kane* Nicaragua 1927. Out of comm 31 Dec 1930–1 Apr 1932. Spanish Civil War (Sqn 40T), Sep 1936–Nov 1937. Out of comm 28 Apr 1938–23 Sep 1939. Converted to transport and rec **APD 18**, 2 Jan 1943. Decomm 24 Jan 1946. Stricken 25 Feb 1946, sold 13 Jun 1946; BU Philadelphia.
7* Attu, Kwajalein, Eniwetok, Admiralty Is., Hollandia, Saipan, Guam, Leyte, Okinawa.

DD 236 *Humphreys* Nicaragua 1926. Out of comm 10 Jan 1930–13 Jun 1932 and 14 Sep 1938–26 Sep 1939. Converted to transport and rec **APD 12**, 1 Dec 1942. Rec **DD 236**, 20 Jul 1945. Decomm 26 Oct 1945. Stricken 13 Nov 1945, sold 26 Aug 1946; BU Terminal I.
7* Lae Ldgs., Finschhafen, Arawe, Cape Gloucester, Saidor, Admiralty Is., Hollandia, Leyte, Lingayen, Iwo Jima, Okinawa.

DD 237 *McFarland* Nicaragua 1927. Damaged in collision with battleship *Arkansas* off Cape Cod, 19 Sep 1923 (1 killed). Out of comm 30 Jan 1931–13 Jun 1932 and 10 Jun 1935–5 Oct 1940. In collision with destroyer *Ellis* in Magdalena Bay, Mexico, 5 Nov 1934. Converted to seaplane tender and rec **AVD 14**, 2 Aug 1940. Damaged by dive bombers, Guadalcanal, 16 Oct 1942 (27 killed). Rec **DD 237**, 1 Dec 1943. Conversion to **APD 26** canceled. Decomm 8 Nov 1945. Stricken 19 Dec 1945, sold 29 Oct 1946; BU Bordentown, N.J.
2* Pearl Harbor, Solomons. PUC.

DD 238 *James K. Paulding* Nicaragua 1926–27. Decomm 10 Feb 1931. Stricken 25 Jan 1937, sold 16 Mar 1939.

DD 239 *Overton* Nicaragua 1927. Out of comm 20 Nov 1937–26 Sep 1939. Neutrality Patrol. Converted to transport and rec **APD 23**, 21 Aug 1943. Decomm 30 Jul 1945. Stricken 13 Aug 1945, sold 30 Nov 1945; BU Baltimore.

8* TG 21.11, Kwajalein, Saipan, Tinian, Leyte, Lingayen, Iwo Jima, Okinawa.

DD 240 *Sturtevant* Out of comm 30 Jan 1931–9 Mar 1932. Nicaragua 1932. Out of comm 20 Nov 1935–26 Sep 1939. Neutrality Patrol. Sunk by mines off Key West, Fla., 26 Apr 1942 (15 killed).

DD 241 *Childs* Sank schr *A. Ernest Mills* in collision off Hampton Roads, Va., lost bow, 5 Apr 1929. Converted to seaplane tender and rec **AVP 14**, 1 Jul 1938. Rec **AVD 1**, 1 Oct 1940. Asiatic Sqn 1940, Australia 1942–44. Decomm 10 Dec 1945. Stricken 3 Jan 1946, sold 23 May 1946.

1* Philippines 1942

DD 242 *King* Nicaragua 1927. Out of comm 10 Mar 1931–13 Jun 1932 and 21 Sep 1938–26 Sep 1939. U.S. West Coast and Alaska. Decomm 23 Oct 1945. Stricken 16 Nov 1945, sold 29 Sep 1946; BU Baltimore.

1* Attu.

DD 243 *Sands* Out of comm 13 Feb 1931–21 Jul 1932 and 15 Sep 1938–26 Sep 1939. Converted to transport and rec **APD 13**, 30 Oct 1942. Decomm 10 Oct 1945. Stricken 11 Nov 1945, sold 23 May 1946; BU.

9* Rennell I., Lae Ldgs., Finschhafen, Arawe, Cape Gloucester, Saidor, Admiralty Is., Hollandia, Palau, Leyte, Lingayen, Iwo Jima, Okinawa.

DD 244 *Williamson* Nicaragua 1927. Converted to seaplane tender and rec **AVP 15**, 1 Jul 1938. Rec **AVD 2**, 2 Aug 1940. Damaged by depth charge explosion off Dutch Harbor, 25 Aug 1942. Rec **DD 244**, 1 Dec 1943. Conversion to **APD 27** canceled. Damaged by collision, Iwo Jima, 21 Feb 1945. Decomm 8 Nov 1945. Stricken 19 Dec 1945, sold 17 Oct 1946; BU Bordentown, N.J.

4* Attu, Guam, Iwo Jima, Okinawa.

DD 245 *Reuben James* Nicaragua 1927. Out of comm 20 Jan 1931–9 Mar 1932. Conversion to **AVP 16** canceled, 1938. Went aground on Lobos Cay, Cuba, 30 Nov 1939. Damaged in collision with tug *Wicomico*, which sank, in Hampton Roads, Va., 15 Feb 1940. Neutrality Patrol. Torpedoed and sunk by *U-562* northeast of Newfoundland, 31 Oct 1941 (115 killed).

DD 246 *Bainbridge* Nicaragua 1927. Out of comm 23 Dec 1930–5 Sep 1933 and 20 Nov 1937–26 Sep 1939. Neutrality Patrol. Decomm 21 Jul 1945. Sold 30 Nov 1945 Philadelphia.

1* TG 21.11.

DD 247 *Goff* Nicaragua 1927. Out of comm 13 Jan 1931–2 Mar 1932. Decomm 21 Jul 1945. Stricken 13 Aug 1945, sold 30 Nov 1945; BU Philadelphia.

2* TG 21.14. PUC.

DD 248 *Barry* Nicaragua, 1926–27. Out of comm 30 Dec 1932–20 Jun 1933. Converted to transport and rec **APD 29**, 15 Jan 1944. Damaged by kamikaze, Okinawa, 24 May 1945. Decomm 21 Jun 1945 and sunk by kamikaze while in tow as a decoy.

4* TG 21.14, Southern France, Okinawa. PUC.

DD 249 *Hopkins* Converted to minesweeper and rec **DMS 13**, 19 Nov 1940. Hit by kamikaze, Okinawa, 4 May 1945. Decomm 21 Dec 1945. Sold 8 Nov 1946; BU Hillsdale, N.J.

10* Guadalcanal-Tulagi, Solomons, New Georgia, Cape Torokina, Saipan, Guam, Lingayen, Iwo Jima, Okinawa, Minesweeping 1945. Tokyo Bay.

DD 250 *Lawrence* Nicaragua 1927. Out of comm 6 Jan 1931–13 Jun 1932 and 13 Sep 1938–26 Sep 1939. Alaska and U.S. West Coast. Decomm 24 Oct 1945. Stricken 13 Nov 1945, sold 1 Oct 1946; BU Baltimore.

DD 251 *Belknap* Out of comm 28 Jun 1922–22 Nov 1940. Converted to seaplane tender and rec **AVD 8**, 2 Aug 1940. Neutrality Patrol. Rec **DD 251**, 14 Nov 1943. Converted to transport and rec **APD 34**, 22 Jun 1944. Damaged by kamikaze, Lingayen, 11 Jan 1945 (38 killed). Decomm 4 Aug 1945. Stricken 13 Aug 1945, sold 30 Nov 1945; BU.

3* TG 21.12, Leyte, Lingayen. PUC.

DD 252 *McCook* Out of comm 30 Jun 1922–18 Dec 1939. To UK, 24 Sep 1940.

Later history: Renamed HMCS *St. Croix*. Torpedoed and sunk by *U-305* south of Iceland, 20 Sep 1943.

DD 253 *McCalla* Out of comm 30 Jun 1922–18 Dec 1939. To UK, 23 Oct 1940.

Later history: Renamed HMS *Stanley*. Torpedoed and sunk by *U-574* east of Azores, 19 Dec 1941.

DD 254 *Rodgers* Out of comm 10 Jul 1922–17 Jun 1940. To UK, 23 Oct 1940.

Later history: Renamed HMS *Sherwood*. Laid up 1943 and used as target in Humber Estuary.

DD 255 *Osmond Ingram* Out of comm 24 Jun 1922–22 Nov 1940. Converted to seaplane tender and rec **AVD 9**, 2 Aug 1940. Rec **DD 255**, 4 Nov 1943. Converted to transport and rec **APD 35**, 22 Jun 1944. Decomm 8 Jan 1946. Stricken 21 Jan 1946, sold 17 Jun 1946; BU.

6* TG 21.12, TG 21.13, Southern France, Okinawa. PUC.

DD 256 *Bancroft* Out of comm 11 Jul 1922–18 Dec 1939. To UK, 24 Sep 1940.

Later history: Renamed HMCS *St. Francis*. Depot ship 1944. Sank in tow after collision with m/v *Winding Gulf* off Rhode Island, 14 Jul 1945.

DD 257 *Welles* Out of comm 15 Jun 1922–6 Nov 1939. To UK, 9 Sep 1940.

Later history: Renamed HMS *Cameron*. Severely damaged by German aircraft bombs in drydock at Portsmouth, England, 5 Dec 1940. Salved; BU 1944 Falmouth, UK.

DD 258 *Aulick* Out of comm 27 May 1922–18 Jun 1939. To UK 9 Oct 1940.

Later history: Renamed HMS *Burnham*. BU 1948 Pembroke, Wales.

DD 259 *Turner* Decomm 7 Jun 1922. Stricken 5 Aug 1936. Converted to water barge and rec **YW 56**, 23 Oct 1936. Rec **IX 98** and renamed ***Moosehead***, 10 Feb 1943. Stricken 17 Apr 1946, sold 20 Feb 1947; BU.

DD 260 *Gillis* Out of comm 26 May 1922–28 Jun 1940. Converted to seaplane tender and rec **AVD 12**, 2 Aug 1940. Recomm 25 Mar 1941. Aleutians. Decomm 15 Oct 1945. Stricken 1 Nov 1945, sold 29 Jan 1946.

2* Attu, Okinawa.

DD 261 *Delphy* Wrecked on Honda Point, Calif., 8 Sep 1923, broke in two (3 killed).

DD 262 *McDermut* Decomm 22 May 1930. Stricken 11 Nov 1931, sold 25 Feb 1932; BU.

DD 263 *Laub* Mediterranean 1919. Out of comm 15 Jun 1922–18 Dec 1939. To UK, 9 Oct 1940.

Later history: Renamed HMS *Burwell*. BU 1947 Milford Haven, Wales.

DD 264 *McLanahan* Out of comm 10 Jun 1922–18 Dec 1939. To UK, 9 Oct 1940.

Later history: Renamed HMS *Bradford*. Accommodation ship *Ffoliott*, Jun 1943. BU 1946 Troon, Scotland.

DD 265 *Edwards* Out of comm 8 Jun 1922–18 Dec 1939. Neutrality Patrol. To UK, 9 Oct 1940.

Later history: Renamed HMS *Buxton*. Static training ship, 1943. BU 1946 Baltimore.

DD 266 *Greene* Out of comm 17 Jun 1922–28 Jun 1940. Converted to seaplane tender and rec **AVD 13**, 6 Apr 1941. Converted to transport and rec **APD 36**, 1 Feb 1944. Went aground in typhoon at Okinawa and lost, 9 Oct 1945. Stricken 5 Dec 1945. Destroyed 11 Feb 1946.

3* TG 21.12, Southern France, Okinawa. PUC.

DD 267 *Ballard* Out of comm 17 Jun 1922–28 Jun 1940. Converted to seaplane tender and rec **AVD 10**, 2 Aug 1940. Recomm 2 Jan 1941. Decomm 5 Dec 1945. Sold 23 May 1946.

2* Saipan, Palau.

DD 268 *Shubrick* Haiti 1919–20. Out of comm 8 Jun 1922–18 Dec 1939. To UK, 26 Nov 1940.

Later history: Renamed HMS *Ripley*. Laid up 1944. BU 1945 Sunderland, England.

DD 269 *Bailey* Out of comm 15 Jun 1922–30 Sep 1939. To UK, 26 Nov 1940.

Later history: Renamed HMS *Reading*. BU 1945 Inverkeithing, Scotland.

DD 270 *Thornton* Out of comm 24 May 1922–5 Mar 1941. Converted to seaplane tender and rec **AVD 11**, 2 Aug 1940. Damaged by collision with oilers *Ashtabula* and *Escalante*, Okinawa, 5 Apr 1945, not repaired. Decomm 2 May 1945. Stricken 13 Aug 1945 and destroyed.
3* Pearl Harbor, Solomons, Okinawa.

DD 271 *Morris* Decomm 15 Jun 1922. Stricken 19 May 1936, sold 29 Sep 1936.

DD 272 *Tingey* Decomm 24 May 1922. Stricken 19 May 1936, sold 29 Sep 1936; BU.

DD 273 *Swasey* Out of comm 10 Jun 1922–18 Dec 1939. To UK 26 Nov 1940.
Later history: Renamed HMS *Rockingham*. Sunk by mine off Aberdeen, Scotland, 27 Sep 1944.

DD 274 *Meade* Out of comm 25 May 1922–18 Dec 1939. To UK, 26 Nov 1940.
Later history: Renamed HMS *Ramsey*. BU 1947 Bo'ness, UK.

DD 275 *Sinclair* Out of comm 25 May 1920–27 Sep 1923. Decomm 1 Jun 1929. Rec **IX 37**, 5 Nov 1930 and renamed ***Light Target No. 3***. Conversion canceled because of faulty boilers and rec **DD 275**, 11 Aug 1931. Stricken 5 Jun 1935, sold 30 Aug 1935; BU Oakland.

DD 276 *McCawley* Out of comm 7 Jun 1922–27 Sep 1923. Decomm 1 Apr 1930. Stricken 13 Aug 1930, sold 2 Sep 1931.

DD 277 *Moody* Out of comm 15 Jun 1922–27 Sep 1923. Decomm 2 Jun 1930. Stricken 3 Nov 1930, sold 30 Jun 1931.
Later history: Sunk as motion picture prop, 21 Feb 1933.

DD 278 *Henshaw* Out of comm 15 Jun 1922–27 Sep 1923. Decomm 11 Mar 1930. Stricken 22 Jul 1930, sold 14 Nov 1930.

DD 279 *Meyer* Decomm 15 May 1929. Stricken 25 Nov 1930, sold 25 Feb 1932. BU Mare I. NYd.

DD 280 *Doyen* Out of comm 8 Jun 1922–26 Sep 1923. Decomm 25 Feb 1930. Stricken 12 Jul 1930, sold 20 Dec 1930.

DD 281 *Sharkey* Decomm 1 May 1930. Stricken 22 Oct 1930, sold 17 Jan 1931; BU Baltimore.

DD 282 *Toucey* Decomm 1 May 1930. Stricken 22 Oct 1930, sold 17 Jan 1931; BU Baltimore.

DD 283 *Breck* Europe 1926–27. Decomm 1 May 1930. Stricken 22 Oct 1930, sold 17 Jan 1931; BU Baltimore.

DD 284 *Isherwood* Decomm 1 May 1930. Stricken 22 Oct 1930, sold 17 Jan 1931; BU Baltimore.

DD 285 *Case* Decomm and stricken 22 Oct 1930, sold 17 Jan 1931; BU Baltimore.

DD 286 *Lardner* Decomm 1 May 1930. Stricken 22 Oct 1930, sold 17 Jan 1931.

DD 287 *Putnam* Decomm 21 Sep 1929. Stricken 22 Oct 1930, sold 17 Jan 1931.
Later history: Merchant *Teapa*. BU 1955.

DD 288 *Worden* Europe 1924. Decomm 1 May 1930. Stricken 22 Oct 1930, sold 17 Jan 1931.
Later history: Merchant *Tabasco*. Lost by grounding on Alacran Reef north of Progreso, Gulf of Mexico, 17 Apr 1933.

DD 289 *Flusser* Nicaragua 1927. Decomm 1 May 1930. Stricken 22 Oct 1930, sold 17 Jan 1931; BU Baltimore.

DD 290 *Dale* Decomm 1 May 1930. Stricken 22 Oct 1930, sold 17 Jan 1931 sold.
Later history: Merchant *Masaya*. Sunk by Japanese aircraft in Oro Bay, New Guinea, 28 Mar 1943.

DD 291 *Converse* Decomm 1 May 1930. Stricken 22 Oct 1930, sold 17 Jan 1931; BU Baltimore.

DD 292 *Reid* Nicaragua 1927. Decomm 1 May 1930. Stricken 22 Oct 1930, sold 17 Jan 1931; BU Baltimore.

DD 293 *Billingsley* Decomm 1 May 1930. Stricken 22 Oct 1930, sold 17 Jan 1931; BU Baltimore.

DD 294 *Charles Ausburn* Carried experimental seaplane, 1923. Decomm 1 May 1930. Stricken 22 Oct 1930, sold 17 Jan 1931, BU Baltimore.

Figure 4.7: A panoramic view of the wrecked destroyers at Point Arguello, Calif., 8 Sep 1923. In the center from front to back are the *Fuller*, *Woodbury*, *Young* (capsized), and *Chauncey*. At left can be seen the *Nicholas* and *S. P. Lee*.

Figure 4.8: *Chauncey* (DD 296) wrecked on 8 Sep 1923; the *Woodbury* is in the background.

DD 295 *Osborne* Nicaragua 1927. Decomm 1 May 1930. Stricken 22 Oct 1930, sold 17 Jan 1931.
Later history: Merchant *Matagalpa*. Burned at Sydney, Australia, 27 Jun 1942, BU.

DD 296 *Chauncey* Wrecked on Honda Point, Calif., 8 Sep 1923 (all saved).

DD 297 *Fuller* Wrecked on Honda Point, Calif., broke in two, 8 Sep 1923 (all saved).

DD 298 *Percival* Decomm 26 Apr 1930. Stricken 18 Nov 1930, sold 19 Mar 1931; BU.

DD 299 *John Francis Burnes* Decomm 25 Feb 1930. Stricken 22 Jul 1930, sold 10 Jun 1931; BU.

DD 300 *Farragut* Went aground on Honda Point, Calif., 8 Sep 1923. Decomm 1 Apr 1930. Stricken 22 Jul 1930, sold 31 Oct 1931; BU.

DD 301 *Somers* Damaged by rocks at Honda Point, Calif., 8 Sep 1923. Rammed by *Zeilin* during maneuvers off Point Loma, Calif., damaged, 16 Nov 1927. Decomm 10 Apr 1930. Stricken 18 Nov 1930, sold 19 May 1931; BU Mare I.

DD 302 *Stoddert* Out of comm 20 May 1930–6 Apr 1931. Rec **IX 35**, 5 Nov 1930 as ***Light Target No. 1***. Rec DD 302, 24 Apr 1931. Rec **AG 18**, 30 Jun 1931. Rec **DD 302**, 16 Apr 1932. Decomm 10 Jan 1933. Stricken 5 Jun 1935, sold 30 Aug 1935.

DD 303 *Reno* Decomm 18 Jan 1930. Stricken 8 Jul 1930, sold 27 Jan 1931; BU.

DD 304 *Farquhar* Damaged in collision with a battleship during maneuvers off Panama, 15 Feb 1923. Decomm 20 Feb 1930. Stricken 18 Nov 1930, sold 22 Apr 1932; BU.

DD 305 *Thompson* Decomm 4 Apr 1930. Stricken 22 Jul 1930, sold 10 Jun 1931.
Later history: Floating restaurant. Sunk as target in San Francisco Bay, Feb 1944.

DD 306 *Kennedy* Decomm 1 May 1930. Stricken 18 Nov 1930, sold 19 Mar 1931; BU.

DD 307 *Paul Hamilton* Decomm 20 Jan 1930. Stricken 8 Jul 1930, sold 27 Jan 1931, BU.

DD 308 *William Jones* In collision with destroyer *Percival* off Coronado, Calif., 31 Jan 1926. Decomm 24 May 1930. Stricken 13 Aug 1930, sold 25 Feb 1932 BU.

DD 309 *Woodbury* Wrecked on Honda Point, Calif., 8 Sep 1923 (all saved).

DD 310 *S. P. Lee* Wrecked on Honda Point, Calif., 8 Sep 1923. (all saved).

DD 311 *Nicholas* Wrecked on Honda Point, Calif., 8 Sep 1923 (all saved).

DD 312 *Young* Wrecked on Honda Point, Calif., capsized, 8 Sep 1923 (20 killed).

DD 313 *Zeilin* Damaged in collision with USS *Henderson* in Puget Sound off Port Angeles, Wash., 27 Jul 1923. Damaged colliding with destroyer *Somers* during maneuvers off Point Loma, Calif., 16 Nov 1927. Decomm 22 Jan 1930. Stricken 8 Jul 1930, sold 20 Dec 1930; BU.

DD 314 *Yarborough* Nicaragua 1927. Decomm 29 May 1930. Stricken 3 Nov 1930, sold 20 Dec 1930; BU.

DD 315 *La Vallette* Went aground north of San Francisco, 2 Jul 1924. Nicaragua 1927. Decomm 19 Apr 1930. Stricken 22 Jul 1930, sold 10 Jun 1931; BU.

DD 316 *Sloat* Nicaragua 1927. Decomm 2 Jun 1930. Stricken 28 Jan 1935, sunk as target off San Diego 26 Jun 1935.

DD 317 *Wood* Nicaragua 1927. Decomm 31 Mar 1930. Stricken 22 Jul 1930, sold 14 Nov 1930; BU.

DD 318 *Shirk* Nicaragua 1927. Decomm 8 Feb 1930. Stricken 22 Jul 1930, sold 27 Jan 1931. BU Mare I.

DD 319 *Kidder* Nicaragua 1927. Decomm 18 Mar 1930. Stricken 22 Jul 1930, sold 31 Oct 1930; BU Alameda, Calif.

DD 320 *Selfridge* Nicaragua 1927. Decomm 8 Feb 1930. Stricken 3 Nov 1930, sold 2 Sep 1931; BU Oakland.

DD 321 *Marcus* Nicaragua 1927. Decomm 31 May 1930. Stricken 28 Jan 1935, sunk as target off San Diego, 25 Jun 1935.

DD 322 *Mervine* Nicaragua 1927. Decomm 4 Jun 1930. Stricken 3 Nov 1930, sold 2 Sep 1931; BU Mare I.

DD 323 *Chase* Decomm 15 May 1930. Stricken 13 Aug 1930, sold 19 Mar 1931.

DD 324 *Robert Smith* In collision with carrier *Langley* off San Pedro, Calif., 1 Mar 1925. Nicaragua 1927. Decomm 1 Mar 1930. Stricken 12 Jul 1930, sold 10 Jun 1931.

DD 325 *Mullany* Nicaragua 1927. Decomm 1 May 1930. Stricken 18 Nov 1930, sold 19 Mar 1931.

DD 326 *Coghlan* Went aground off Beaufort, N.C., 11 Jan 1924. Nicaragua 1927. Decomm 1 May 1930. Sold 17 Jan 1931.

DD 327 *Preston* Nicaragua 1927. Decomm 1 May 1930. Used in hull strength tests at Norfolk NYd, 1931. Stricken 6 Nov 1931, sold 23 Aug 1932.

DD 328 *Lamson* Decomm 1 May 1930. Stricken 22 Oct 1930, sold 17 Jan 1931; BU Baltimore.

DD 329 *Bruce* Decomm 1 May 1930. Used in hull strength tests at Norfolk NYd, 1931. Stricken 6 Nov 1931, sold 23 Aug 1932.

DD 330 *Hull* Decomm 31 Mar 1930. Stricken 22 Jul 1930, sold 10 Jun 1931.

DD 331 *MacDonough* Decomm 8 Jan 1930. Stricken 8 Jul 1930, sold 20 Dec 1930; BU.

DD 332 *Farenholt* In collision with destroyer *Litchfield* off Cape Flattery, Wash., 11 Aug 1924. Decomm 20 Feb 1930. Stricken 12 Jul 1930, sold 10 Jun 1931.

DD 333 *Sumner* Decomm 29 Mar 1930. Stricken 18 Nov 1930. Barracks ship and structural strength test ship 1930–34. sold 12 Jun 1934; BU.

DD 334 *Corry* Decomm 24 Apr 1930. Stricken 22 Jul 1930, sold 18 Oct 1930; BU Mare I.

DD 335 *Melvin* Nicaragua 1927. Decomm 8 May 1930. Stricken 3 Nov 1930, sold 2 Sep 1931; BU Mare I.

DD 336 *Litchfield* Damaged in collision with destroyer *Farenholt* off Cape Flattery, Wash., 11 Aug 1924. Nicaragua 1927. Hawaii. Rec **AG 95**, 31 Mar 1945. Decomm 5 Nov 1945. Stricken 28 Nov 1945, sold 29 Mar 1946; BU Philadelphia.

DD 337 *Zane* Damaged in collision with m/v *Tse Kiang* in Whangpo River, China, 6 Jun 1922. Out of comm 1 Feb 1923–25 Feb 1930. Converted to minesweeper and rec **DMS 14**, 19 Nov 1940. Damaged by gunfire from Japanese destroyers, Sealark Channel, off Guadalcanal, 25 Oct 1942 (3 killed). Damaged by grounding, 30 Jun 1943, during Ldgs. on New Georgia, Solomons. Rec **AG 109**, 5 Jun 1945. Decomm 14 Dec 1945. Stricken 8 Jan 1946, sold 22 Oct 1946; BU.
6* Pearl Harbor, Guadalcanal-Tulagi, Solomons, New Georgia, Kwajalein, Eniwetok, Saipan, 2nd Bonins Raid, 3rd Bonins Raid, Guam.

DD 338 *Wasmuth* Out of comm 26 Jul 1922–11 Mar 1930. Converted to minesweeper and rec **DMS 15**, 19 Nov 1940. Damaged by explosion of own depth charges in storm off Alaska and sank, 27 Dec 1942.
1* Pearl Harbor.

DD 339 *Trever* Out of comm 17 Jan 1923–2 Jun 1930. Converted to minesweeper and rec **DMS 16**, 19 Nov 1940. Rec **AG 110**, 5 Jun 1945. Decomm 23 Nov 1945. Stricken 5 Dec 1945, sold 12 Nov 1946.
5* Pearl Harbor, Guadalcanal-Tulagi, Solomons, New Georgia, Cape Torokina.

DD 340 *Perry* Out of comm 17 Jan 1923–1 Apr 1930. Converted to minesweeper and rec **DMS 17**, 19 Nov 1940. Sank after hitting two mines off Peleliu, 12–13 Sep 1944 (7 killed).
6* Pearl Harbor, Attu, Kwajalein, Hollandia, Saipan, Guam, Palau.

DD 341 *Decatur* Out of comm 17 Jan–26 Sep 1923. Neutrality Patrol. Cnversion to **APD 30** canceled Decomm 28 Jul 1945. Stricken 13 Aug 1945. Sold 30 Nov 1945; BU Baltimore.
2* TG 21.14, Convoy UGS-36.

DD 342 *Hulbert* Damaged by explosion at Philadelphia, 28 Feb 1923 (6 killed). Yangtze River 1926–27. Out of comm 17 Oct 1934–2 Aug 1940. Converted to seaplane tender and rec **AVP 19**, 15 Nov 1939. Rec **AVD 6**, 2 Aug 1940. Blown ashore during storm at Attu, 30 Jun 1943. Rec **DD 342**, 1 Dec 1943. Conversion to **APD 28** canceled. Decomm 2 Nov 1945. Stricken 28 Nov 1945. Sold 17 Oct 1946; BU Philadelphia.
2* Pearl Harbor, Attu.

DD 343 *Noa* Asiatic Fleet 1922–29. Yangtze River 1927. Out of comm 11 Nov 1934–1 Apr 1940. Fitted with experimental seaplane XSOC-1. which replaced after TT, then removed, Apr 1940. Converted to transport and rec **APD 24**, 10 Aug 1943. Sunk in collision with destroyer *Fullam* off Palau, 12 Sep 1944.
5* Cape Gloucester, Saidor, Green I. Ldgs., Hollandia, Saipan, Guam, Palau.

DD 344 *William B. Preston* Asiatic Fleet 1922–29. Yangtze River 1926–27. Out of comm 15 Oct 1934–14 Jun 1940. Converted to seaplane tender and rec **AVP 20**, 15 Nov 1939. Rec **AVD 7**, 2 Aug 1940. Damaged by Japanese aircraft bombs at Darwin, Australia, 19 Feb 1942 (13 killed). Decomm 6 Dec 1945. Stricken 3 Jan 1946, sold 6 Nov 1946; BU Philadelphia.
1* Philippines 1941–42.

DD 345 *Preble* Asiatic Fleet 1922–29. Yangtze River, 1926–27. Converted to minelayer and rec **DM 20**, 30 Jun 1937. Damaged in collision with minelayer *Montgomery* off Savo I., 25 Aug 1943. Rec **AG 99**, 5 Jun 1945. Decomm 7 Dec 1945. Stricken 3 Jan 1946, sold 26 Oct 1946 BU Philadelphia.

8* Pearl Harbor, Guadalcanal, Solomons, New Georgia, Kwajalein, Palau, New Georgia, Leyte, Lingayen.

DD 346 *Sicard* Asiatic Fleet 1922–29. Yangtze River, 1926–27. Damaged in collision with destroyer *Lea* off Diamond Head, 12 May 1935 (1 killed). Converted to minelayer and rec **DM 21**, 30 Jun 1937. Damaged in collision with destroyer *McDonough* north of Adak, Aleutians, 10 May 1943. Rec **AG 100**, 5 Jun 1945. Decomm 21 Nov 1945. Stricken 19 Dec 1945, sold 22 Jun 1946; BU.

2* Pearl Harbor (1 killed), Cape Torokina.

DD 347 *Pruitt* Asiatic Fleet 1922–29. Yangtze River, 1926–27. Converted to minelayer and rec **DM 22**, 30 Jun 1937. Rec **AG 101**, 5 Jun 1945. Decomm 16 Nov 1945. Stricken 5 Dec 1945. BU 1946 Philadelphia.

3* Pearl Harbor (1 killed), Attu, Cape Torokina.

Notes: For further details, see Paul H. Silverstone, *The New Navy, 1883–1922* (New York: Routledge, 2006).

Twenty-seven destroyers (DD 118, 126, 128, 130, 142, 144, 145, 152–55, 157–160, 199, 210, 220, 221, 223, 229, 239, 240, 245, 246, 341) converted for escort duties 1941; 6 TT and 4" guns replaced by 6–3"/50, Y gun replaced by 3" AA. HF/DF and hedgehog added.

Extra fuel tanks replaced no. 1 boiler to make up for inadequate steaming endurance (except DD 210, 221, 246, 248, and 341).

DD 220 and 223 had remaining TT replaced by 40mm guns.

DD 187 *Dahlgren*: Engineering experimental ship 1937, with new geared turbines and two ultra-high-pressure boilers. Aft funnels trunked. Returned to destroyer duties 1941.

DD 343 *Noa* carried experimental seaplane 1940.

Fifty destroyers transferred to the United Kingdom in 1940 in the destroyers-for-bases exchange. Fourteen had been converted to minelayers in 1919 (DM), four more in 1930–31, and four more in 1937. Eighteen were converted to high speed minesweepers in 1940 (DMS). DD 74 *Manley* was converted to an experimental high speed transport in 1938. This was successful, and five more were converted in 1940. Eventually, thirty were converted during the war. Fourteen became seaplane tenders (AVD) in 1940.

Figure 4.9: *Charles Ausburn* (DD 294), with an experimental catapult on the bow, 1923. A Naval Aircraft Factory TS-1 floatplane fighter can be seen mounted forward.

Figure 4.10: USS *Farragut* (DD 348). The namesake of the class in her prewar appearance.

Farragut Class

No.	Name	Builder	Keel Laid	Launched	Comm.
DD 348	*Farragut*	Beth. Quincy	20 Sep 1932	15 Mar 1934	18 Jun 1934
	ex-*Smith* (13 Aug 1933), ex-*Farragut* (15 Jul 1933)				
DD 349	*Dewey*	Bath	16 Dec 1932	28 Jul 1934	4 Oct 1934
	ex-*Phelps* (13 Aug 1933), ex-*Dewey* (15 Jul 1933).				
DD 350	*Hull*	New York NYd	7 Mar 1933	31 Jan 1934	11 Jan 1935
DD 351	*MacDonough*	Boston NYd	15 May 1933	22 Aug 1934	15 Mar 1935
DD 352	*Worden*	Puget Sd NYd	29 Dec 1932	27 Oct 1934	15 Jan 1935
DD 353	*Dale*	New York NYd	10 Feb 1934	23 Jan 1935	17 Jun 1935
DD 354	*Monaghan*	Boston NYd	21 Nov 1933	9 Jan 1935	19 Apr 1935
DD 355	*Aylwin*	Phila NYd	23 Sep 1933	10 Jul 1934	1 Mar 1935

Displacement 1,365 tons; 1,726 f/l

Dimensions 341'3" (oa); 334'(wl) x 34'2" x 15'6"

Figure 4.11: *Worden* (DD 352), of the *Farragut* class, on 21 Nov 1942, has had her mainmast removed.

Machinery	2 screws; Parsons GT; 4 Yarrow boilers; SHP 42,800; 36.5 knots
Endurance	7,700/12
Complement	182
Armament	5–5"/38, 2 quad 21" TT; (1945) 4–5"/38, 2 twin 40mm, 5–20mm guns, 2 quad 21" TT

Notes: First new destroyers built in 18 years. Two funnels, two pole masts. Quadruple TT mounts. *Dewey* forefunnel raised in 1935 briefly. Mainmast and fifth gun removed 1942.

Service Records:

DD 348 *Farragut* Damaged in collision with destroyer *Aylwin* off Pearl Harbor, 19 Mar 1941. Decomm 23 Oct 1945. Stricken 28 Jan 1947. Sold 14 Aug 1947.
14* Pearl Harbor, Coral Sea, Guadalcanal-Tulagi, Eastern Solomons, Komandorski Is., Gilbert Is., Kwajalein, Eniwetok, Palau-Yap Raids 3/44, Saipan, Guam, Hollandia, Truk Raid 4/44, Formosa Raids 1/45, China Coast Raids 1/45, Nansei Shoto Raid 1/45, Iwo Jima, Fleet Raids 1945, Okinawa.
Submarine sunk: **I-31* off Attu, 27 Apr 1943 (possible).

DD 349 *Dewey* Severely damaged in typhoon in Philippine Sea, lost forward funnel, 18 Dec 1944. Decomm 19 Oct 1945. Stricken 1 Nov 1945. Sold 20 Dec 1946.
13* Pearl Harbor, Salamaua-Lae Raid, Coral Sea, Guadalcanal-Tulagi, Eastern Solomons, Attu, Gilbert Is., Kwajalein, Eniwetok, Marianas Raids 2/44, Palau-Yap Raids 3/44, Hollandia, Truk Raid 4/44, Philippine Sea, Saipan, Guam, Iwo Jima, Okinawa, Fleet Raids 1945.

DD 350 *Hull* Foundered in typhoon in Philippine Sea, 18 Dec 1944 (202 killed).
10* Pearl Harbor, Salamaua-Lae Raid, Guadalcanal-Tulagi, Solomons, Attu, Wake I. Raid 1943, Gilbert Is., Kwajalein, Eniwetok, Truk Raid 4/44, Saipan, Philippine Sea, Guam.

DD 351 *MacDonough* Damaged in collision with minelayer *Sicard* off Attu, in Aleutians, 10 May 1943. Decomm 22 Oct 1945. Stricken 1 Nov 1945. Sold 20 Dec 1946; BU.
13* Pearl Harbor, Salamaua-Lae Raid, Guadalcanal-Tulagi, Eastern Solomons, Guadalcanal, Gilbert Is., Kwajalein, Eniwetok, Palau-Yap Raids 3/44, Hollandia, Truk Raid 4/44, Saipan, Philippine Sea, Guam, Leyte, Formosa Raids 1/45, Luzon Raids 1/45, Formosa Raids 1/45, China Coast Raids 1/45, Nansei Shoto Raid 1/45.
Submarine sunk: **RO-45*, southwest of Truk, 1 May 1944.

DD 352 *Worden* In collision with destroyer *Reid* off Calif. coast, 2 Aug 1937. Wrecked on Amchitka I., Aleutians, 12 Jan 1943 (14 killed).
4* Pearl Harbor, Midway, Guadalcanal-Tulagi, Eastern Solomons.

DD 353 *Dale* Decomm 16 Oct 1945. Stricken 1 Nov 1945. Sold 20 Dec 1946.
12* Pearl Harbor, Salamaua-Lae Raid, Komandorski Is., Attu, Gilbert Is., Kwajalein, Eniwetok, Palau-Yap Raids 3/44, Hollandia, Truk Raid 4/44, Saipan, Philippine Sea, Guam, Formosa Raids 1/45, Nansei Shoto Raid 1/45, Iwo Jima, Fleet Raids 1945, Okinawa, Balikpapan.

DD 354 *Monaghan* Damaged in collision with minesweeper *Long* in bad weather off Kiska, 27 Jul 1942. Foundered in typhoon in Philippine Sea, 18 Dec 1944 (~250 killed).
12* Pearl Harbor, Coral Sea, Midway, Komandorski Is., Attu, Gilbert Is., Kwajalein, Eniwetok, Palau-Yap Raids 3/44, Hollandia, Truk Raid 4/44, Saipan, Philippine Sea, Guam, Luzon Raids 10/44.
Submarines sunk: Midget sub at Pearl Harbor, 7 Dec 1941; *I-7* by gunfire off Kiska, 22 Jun 1943.

DD 355 *Aylwin* Damaged in collision with destroyer *Farragut* off Pearl Harbor, 19 Mar 1941. Damaged in typhoon, Philippine Sea, 18 Dec 1944 (2 lost). Decomm 16 Oct 1945. Stricken 1 Nov 1945, sold 20 Dec 1946; BU Brooklyn.
13* Pearl Harbor, Coral Sea, Midway, Attu, Gilbert Is., Kwajalein, Eniwetok, Palau-Yap Raids 3/44, Hollandia, Truk Raid 4/44, Saipan, Philippine Sea, Guam, China Coast Raids 1/45, Formosa Raids 1/45, Nansei Shoto Raid 1/45, Iwo Jima, Fleet Raids 1945.

Porter Class

No.	Name	Builder	Keel Laid	Launched	Comm.
DD 356	*Porter*	NY Sbdg	18 Dec 1933	12 Dec 1935	25 Aug 1936
DD 357	*Selfridge*	NY Sbdg	18 Dec 1933	18 Apr 1936	25 Nov 1936
DD 358	*McDougal*	NY Sbdg	18 Dec 1933	17 Jul 1936	23 Dec 1936
DD 359	*Winslow*	NY Sbdg	18 Dec 1933	21 Sep 1936	17 Feb 1937
DD 360	*Phelps*	Beth. Quincy	2 Jan 1934	18 Jul 1935	26 Feb 1936
DD 361	*Clark*	Beth. Quincy	2 Jan 1934	15 Oct 1935	20 May 1936
DD 362	*Moffett*	Beth. Quincy	2 Jan 1934	11 Dec 1935	28 Aug 1936
DD 363	*Balch*	Beth. Quincy	16 May 1934	24 Mar 1936	20 Oct 1936

Figure 4.12: *Phelps* (DD 360), of the *Porter* class, shows the prewar appearance of the class with two tripod masts and four twin gun mounts.

Figure 4.13: *Moffett* (DD 362), 12 Sep 1944, as modified. Tripod masts have been replaced by light poles and one twin gun mount removed.

Displacement	1,850 tons; 2,132 f/l
Dimensions	381' (oa); 372' (wl) x 36'10" x 16'6"
Machinery	2 screws; Parsons GT; 4 Express boilers; SHP 50,000; 37 knots
Endurance	7,800/12
Complement	240
Armament	8–5"/38, 8–1.1" AA, 2 quad 21" TT; (1945) 5–5"/38, 4 quad 40mm, 2 twin 40mm, 6–20mm AA guns; 2–21" quad TT

Notes: "Leaders" with more powerful armament and power plant. Two funnels, tripod masts, 5" guns in dual mounts. Carried eight reload torpedoes. During the war, altered twice: 5" superfiring turrets replaced by 40mm aft; single 5" gun forward; tripod masts and aft superstructure removed, replaced by pole foremast.

Service Records:

DD 356 *Porter* Torpedoed by *I-21* off Santa Cruz Is. and sunk by gunfire from destroyer *Shaw*, 26 Oct 1942 (15 killed).
1* Santa Cruz.

DD 357 *Selfridge* Torpedoed by Japanese destroyer and lost bow, Battle of Vella Lavella, 6 Oct 1943 (49 killed). Decomm 15 Oct 1945. Stricken 1 Nov 1945, sold 20 Dec 1946; BU.
4* Pearl Harbor, Guadalcanal-Tulagi, Vella Lavella, Saipan, Philippine Sea, Guam.

DD 358 *McDougal* Neutrality Patrol. South Atlantic. Rec **AG 126**, 17 Sep 1945. Decomm 24 Jun 1946, in service as training ship. †

DD 359 *Winslow* Neutrality Patrol. South Atlantic. Converted to experimental AA ship. Rec **AG 127**, 17 Sep 1945. †

DD 360 *Phelps* Damaged by coastal gunfire, Saipan, 18 Jun 1944 and again, 5 hits, 20 Jun 1944. Decomm 6 Nov 1945. Stricken 28 Jan 1947, sold 7 Aug 1947; BU.
12* Pearl Harbor, Salamaua-Lae Raid, Coral Sea, Midway, Guadalcanal-Tulagi, Eastern Solomons, Attu, Gilbert Is., Kwajalein, Eniwetok, Palau-Yap Raids 3/44, Saipan.
Submarine sunk: **RO-40* northwest of Kwajalein, 16 Feb 1944.

DD 361 *Clark* U.S. West Coast 1943, Atlantic Convoys. Decomm 23 Oct 1945. Stricken 16 Nov 1945. Sold 29 Mar 1946 BU Philadelphia.
2* Salamaua-Lae Raid, Battle of Guadalcanal.

DD 362 *Moffett* Neutrality patrol. South Atlantic. Decomm 2 Nov 1945. Stricken 28 Jan 1947, sold 16 May 1947; BU Baltimore.
2*
Submarines sunk: **U-128* off Pernambuco, Brazil, 17 May 1943; *U-604*, later scuttled, 11 Aug 1943.

DD 363 *Balch* Decomm 19 Oct 1945. Stricken 1 Nov 1945. BU 29 Mar 1946, Philadelphia.
6* Marshall-Gilberts Raid 1942, Wake I. Raid 1942, Midway, Guadalcanal-Tulagi, Eastern Solomons, Attu, Wakde, Biak.

Figure 4.14: *Reid* (DD 369) shows the prewar appearance of the *Mahan* class as built with tripod foremast and pole mast aft.

Figure 4.15: *Mahan* (DD 364), 21 Jun 1944, with pole mainmast and greatly reduced torpedo tube armament.

Mahan Class

No.	Name	Builder	Keel Laid	Launched	Comm.
DD 364	*Mahan*	Beth. Staten I	12 Jun 1934	15 Oct 1935	18 Sep 1936
DD 365	*Cummings*	Beth. Staten I	26 Jun 1934	11 Dec 1935	25 Nov 1936
DD 366	*Drayton*	Bath	20 Mar 1934	26 Mar 1936	1 Sep 1936
DD 367	*Lamson*	Bath	20 Mar 1934	17 Jun 1936	21 Oct 1936
DD 368	*Flusser*	Federal	4 Jun 1934	28 Sep 1935	1 Oct 1936
DD 369	*Reid*	Federal	25 Jun 1934	11 Jan 1936	2 Nov 1936
DD 370	*Case*	Boston NYd	19 Sep 1934	14 Sep 1935	15 Sep 1936
DD 371	*Conyngham*	Boston NYd	19 Sep 1934	14 Sep 1935	4 Nov 1936
DD 372	*Cassin*	Phila. NYd	1 Oct 1934	28 Oct 1935	21 Aug 1936
DD 373	*Shaw*	Phila. NYd	1 Oct 1934	28 Oct 1935	28 Sep 1936
DD 374	*Tucker*	Norfolk NYd	15 Aug 1934	26 Feb 1936	23 Jul 1936
DD 375	*Downes*	Norfolk NYd	15 Aug 1934	22 Apr 1936	15 Jan 1937
DD 376	*Cushing*	Puget Sd NYd	15 Aug 1934	31 Dec 1935	28 Aug 1936
DD 377	*Perkins*	Puget Sd NYd	15 Nov 1934	31 Dec 1935	18 Sep 1936
DD 378	*Smith*	Mare I NYd	27 Oct 1934	20 Feb 1936	19 Sep 1936
DD 379	*Preston*	Mare I NYd	27 Oct 1934	22 Apr 1936	27 Oct 1936

Displacement	1,450 tons; 1,726 f/l
Dimensions	341'3" (oa); 334' (wl) x 34'8" x 17'
Machinery	2 screws; GE GT; 4 express boilers; SHP 46,000; 37 knots
Endurance	6,500/12
Complement	204
Armament	5–5"/38 AA, 3 quad 21" TT; (1945) 4–5"/38, 2 twin 40mm, 5–20mm, 3 quad 21" TT

Notes: High-pressure boilers; two funnels. Tripod foremast, pole mainmast. *Cassin* and *Downes* rebuilt 1942 with new hulls and salvaged machinery; torpedo tubes on center line. *Shaw* also rebuilt 1942. Tripod mast replaced by pole; mainmast removed 1942.

Service Records:

DD 364 *Mahan* Damaged in collision with battleship *South Dakota* en route to Noumea, 27 Oct 1942. Hit by three kamikazes off Ormoc, Leyte, and sunk by U.S. forces, 7 Dec 1944 (10 killed).
5* Marshall-Gilberts Raid 1942, Santa Cruz, Lae Ldgs., Finschhafen, Arawe, Saidor, Admiralty Is., Leyte, Ormoc.
Ship sunk: PG **Hakkaisan Maru*, southwest of Tamana, Gilbert Is., 22 Oct 1942.

DD 365 *Cummings* Decomm 14 Dec 1945. Stricken 28 Jan 1947. Sold 17 Jul 1947.
7* Pearl Harbor, Kwajalein, Eniwetok, Sabang Raid, Soerabaja Raid, Rennell I., Marcus I. Raid 10/44, Philippines Raids 9/44, Luzon Raids 10/44, Iwo Jima Bombard., Iwo Jima.

DD 366 *Drayton* Damaged in collision with destroyer *Flusser* off Hawaii, 4 Oct 1942. Damaged by aircraft bomb and kamikaze off Leyte, 5 Dec 1944 (8 killed). Decomm 9 Oct 1945. Stricken 24 Oct 1945. Sold 20 Dec 1946.
11* Tassafaronga, Solomons, Lae Ldgs., Finschhafen, Arawe, Cape Gloucester, Saidor, Admiralty Is., Palau, Leyte, Ormoc, Lingayen, Tarakan, Balikpapan, Visayan Is. Ldgs.

DD 367 *Lamson* Damaged by aircraft bomb, Cape Gloucester, 26 Dec 1943. Damaged by kamikaze, Leyte, and near miss, 7 Dec 1944 (25 killed). Foundered after atom bomb aerial explosion, test Able at Bikini, 2 Jul 1946.
5* Tassafaronga, Solomons, Lae Ldgs., Finschhafen, Arawe, Cape Gloucester, Saidor, Leyte, Ormoc.
Ship sunk: PG **Hakkaisan Maru*, southwest of Tamana, Gilbert Is., 22 Oct 1942.

DD 368 *Flusser* Spanish Civil War (Sqn 40T), Dec 1936–Feb 1937. Damaged in collision with destroyer *Drayton* off Hawaii, 4 Oct 1942. Damaged in collision off Cotabato, Mindanao, 22 Apr 1945. Damaged by collision, Balikpapan, 15 Jul 1945. Bikini target. Decomm 16 Dec 1946. Stricken 7 Apr 1947. Sold 6 Jan 1948.
8* Lae Ldgs., Finschhafen, Solomons, Arawe, Cape Gloucester, Saidor, Admiralty Is., Leyte, Ormoc, Lingayen, Ldgs. on Palawan I., Ldgs. at Nasugbu, Mindanao Ldgs., Visayan Is. Ldgs., Balikpapan.

DD 369 *Reid* In collision with destroyer *Worden* off Calif., 2 Aug 1937. Minor damage by aircraft bombs, off Biak, New Guinea, 3 Jun 1944. Hit by two kamikazes off Ormoc, Leyte, and capsized, 11 Dec 1944 (~150 killed).
7* Pearl Harbor, Solomons, Lae Ldgs., Finschhafen, Arawe, Cape Gloucester, Saidor, Cape Gloucester, Admiralty Is., Hollandia, Wakde, Biak, Noemfoor I., Leyte, Ormoc.
Submarine sunk: *RO-61* south of Atka, Aleutians, 31 Aug 1942.

DD 370 *Case* Decomm 13 Dec 1945. Stricken 28 Jan 1947. Sold 31 Dec 1947.
7* Pearl Harbor, Kwajalein, Eniwetok, Palau-Yap Raids 3/44, Hollandia, Truk Raid 4/44, Marcus I. Raid 10/44, Saipan, 1st Bonins Raid, Philippine Sea, Guam, 4th Bonins Raid, Luzon Raids 10/44, Iwo Jima Bombard., Iwo Jima.
Submarine sunk: Midget sub off Ulithi, Micronesia, 20 Nov 1944.

DD 371 *Conyngham* Damaged in collision with transport *Fuller* off Guadalcanal, 2 Nov 1942. Damaged by three aircraft bomb near misses, off Arawe, New Guinea, 4 Sep 1943. Sank *PT-77* and *PT-79* in error off Talin Point, Luzon, 1 Feb 1945. Bikini target. Decomm 20 Dec 1946. Stricken 13 Jun 1948. Sunk as target off Calif., 2 Jul 1948.
14* Pearl Harbor, Midway, Santa Cruz, Guadalcanal, Solomons, Lae Ldgs., Finschhafen, Arawe, Cape Gloucester, Saidor, Saipan, Philippine Sea, Guam, Tinian, Leyte, Ormoc, Lingayen, Balikpapan, Ldgs. at Nasugbu, Ldgs. on Palawan I., Mindanao Ldgs., Visayan Is. Ldgs., Mariveles-Corregidor.

DD 372 *Cassin* Sunk by three bombs and explosion of *Downes* in drydock at Pearl Harbor, 7 Dec 1941. Rebuilt at Mare I. NYd, laid down 20 Nov 1942, launched 21 Jun 1943, recomm 5 Feb 1944. Decomm 17 Dec 1945. Stricken 28 Jan 1947. Sold 25 Nov 1947.

Figure 4.16: The rebuilt *Downes* (DD 375) differs from the rest of her class, with pole mainmast and greater space between superstructure and funnel. Engines and guns of the original destroyer sunk at Pearl Harbor were put in a new hull built at Mare I. *Cassin* was similarly rebuilt.

6* Pearl Harbor, Marcus I. Raid 10/44, Guam, Luzon Raids 10/44, Iwo Jima, Iwo Jima Bombard., Saipan, Guam, Palau, Philippines Raids 9/44.

DD 373 *Shaw* In collision with oiler *Sabine*, Hawaii, 21 Nov 1941. Sunk by three aircraft bombs in drydock at Pearl Harbor, lost bow, 7 Dec 1941 (24 killed). Refloated and rebuilt, recomm Aug 1942. Damaged by grounding at Noumea, 10 Jan 1943. Damaged by three aircraft bomb near misses, Cape Gloucester, 26 Dec 1943 (3 killed). Damaged by grounding off Bohol, Philippines, 2 Apr 1945. Decomm 2 Oct 1945. Stricken 4 Oct 1945. Sold 12 Jul 1946; BU.
11* Pearl Harbor, Santa Cruz, Solomons, Finschhafen, Arawe, Cape Gloucester, Saipan, Guam, Leyte, Ormoc, Mindoro, Lingayen, Ldgs. on Palawan I., Ldgs. at Nasugbu, Visayan Is. Ldgs.

DD 374 *Tucker* Sunk by mine off Espiritu Santo, New Hebrides, 4 Aug 1942 (6 killed).
1* Pearl Harbor.

DD 375 *Downes* Sunk by aircraft bombs and flooding of drydock at Pearl Harbor, 7 Dec 1941 (12 killed). Decomm 20 Jan 1942. Rebuilt at Mare I. NYd, laid down 13 Oct 1942, launched 20 May 1943, recomm 15 Nov 1943. Decomm 17 Dec 1945. Stricken 28 Jan 1947. Sold 18 Nov 1947; BU.
4* Pearl Harbor, Saipan, Marcus I. Raid 10/44, Luzon Raids 10/44.

DD 376 *Cushing* Sunk by seventeen hits of gunfire from battleship *Hiyei* and destroyer *Terutsuki*, Battle of Guadalcanal, 13 Nov 1942 (69 killed).
3* Santa Cruz, Guadalcanal, Battle of Guadalcanal.

DD 377 *Perkins* Rammed and sunk in collision with m/v *Duntroon* off Buna, New Guinea, 19 Nov 1943 (4 killed).
4* Coral Sea, Tassafaronga, Solomons, Lae Ldgs., Finschhafen.

DD 378 *Smith* Damaged by Japanese aircraft crash at Battle of Santa Cruz, 26 Oct 1942 (57 killed). Damaged by aircraft bomb off Finschhafen, 20 Oct 1943. Damaged in collision with destroyer *Hutchins*, off Madang, New Guinea, 1 Jan 1944. Damaged by one hit by coastal gunfire, Balikpapan, 30 Jun–1 Jul 1945. Damaged by depth charge explosion, Balikpapan, 5 Jul 1945. Decomm 28 Jun 1946. Stricken 25 Feb 1947. Sold 20 Aug 1947.
6* Santa Cruz, Lae Ldgs., Finschhafen, Arawe, Cape Gloucester, Saidor, Cape Gloucester, Admiralty Is., Leyte, Ormoc, Ldgs. on Palawan I., Visayan Is. Ldgs., Tarakan, Balikpapan.

DD 379 *Preston* Sunk by five hits by gunfire from Japanese cruiser *Nagara*, Battle of Guadalcanal, 14 Nov 1942 (116 killed).
2* Santa Cruz, Battle of Guadalcanal.

Figure 4.17: *Fanning* (DD 385) before the war.

Figure 4.18: *Dunlap* (DD 384), 10 May 1942. Notice the raised forward funnel.

Dunlap Class

No.	Name	Builder	Keel Laid	Launched	Comm.
DD 384	*Dunlap*	Beth. Staten I	10 Apr 1935	18 Apr 1936	12 Jun 1937
DD 385	*Fanning*	Beth. Staten I	10 Apr 1935	18 Sep 1936	8 Oct 1937

Displacement	1,490 tons; 2,345 f/l
Dimensions	341'4" (oa); 334' (wl) x 35'5" x 17'2"
Machinery	2 screws; GE GT; 4 B&W and FW boilers; SHP 46,000; 37 knots
Complement	251
Armament	5–5"/38, 3 quad 21" TT; (1945) 4–5"/38, 8–40mm, 5–20mm, 3 quad 21" TT

Notes: *Mahan* type with pole foremast only.

Service Records:

DD 384 *Dunlap* Decomm 14 Dec 1945. Stricken 28 Jan 1947. Sold 31 Dec 1947.
6* Marshall-Gilberts Raid 1942, Wake I. Raid 1942, Vella Gulf, Kwajalein, Eniwetok, Sabang Raid, Soerabaja Raid, Marcus I. Raid 10/44, Luzon Raids 10/44, Iwo Jima Bombard.

DD 385 *Fanning* Damaged in collision with destroyer *Gridley* in storm northwest of Samoa, 22 Jan 1942. Decomm 14 Dec 1945. Stricken 28 Jan 1947. Sold 6 Jan 1948.
4* Kwajalein, Eniwetok, Sabang Raid, Soerabaja Raid, Marcus I. Raid 10/44, Luzon Raids 10/44, Iwo Jima Bombard.

Somers Class

No.	Name	Builder	Keel Laid	Launched	Comm.
DD 381	*Somers*	Federal	27 Jun 1935	13 Mar 1937	1 Dec 1937
DD 383	*Warrington*	Federal	10 Oct 1935	15 May 1937	9 Feb 1938
DD 394	*Sampson*	Bath	8 Apr 1936	16 Apr 1937	19 Aug 1938
DD 395	*Davis*	Bath	28 Jul 1936	30 Jul 1938	9 Nov 1938
DD 396	*Jouett*	Bath	26 Mar 1936	24 Sep 1938	25 Jan 1939

Displacement	1,850 tons; 2,905 f/l
Dimensions	381'6" (oa); 372' (wl) x 36'11" x 18'
Machinery	2 screws; GE GT; 4 B&W boilers; SHP 52,000; 37.5 knots
Endurance	6,000/15
Complement	294
Armament	8–5"/38, 8–1.1" AA, 3 quad 21" TT; 2 (1945) 6–5"/38 (DD 395–96: 5–5"), 3 twin 40mm, 6 to 8 20mm guns, 2 quad 21" TT

Figure 4.19: *Sampson* (DD 394), of the *Somers* class, 27 Aug 1944.

Figure 4.20: *Jouett* (DD 396), 20 Apr 1944. The "B" mount was later replaced with a single 5" gun.

Notes: "Leaders" with single funnel, single pole mast. Two twin turrets removed; DD 395 *Davis* and DD 396 *Jouett* mounted single 5" superfiring gun aft.

Service Records:

DD 381 *Somers* Neutrality Patrol. Sank German corvette *UJ-6082* off Île du Levant, Southern France, 15 Aug 1944. Decomm 28 Oct 1945. Stricken 28 Jan 1947. Sold 16 May 1947; BU Baltimore.
2* Normandy, Southern France.
Ships sunk: German b/r *Odenwald* (5,098/23) captured in South Atlantic, 6 Nov 1941; German b/r *Anneliese Essberger* (5,173/35), which sank, off Trinidad, 21 Nov 1942; German b/r *Weserland* (6,528/22), which sank, 1 Jan 1944.

DD 383 *Warrington* Neutrality Patrol. Foundered in hurricane off Bahamas, 13 Sep 1944 (248 killed).
2* Cape Torokina, Wakde, Biak.

DD 394 *Sampson* Neutrality Patrol. U.S. West Coast 1942–43, Atlantic 1944–45. Decomm 1 Nov 1945. Stricken 28 Nov 1945; BU 29 Mar 1946, Philadelphia.
1* Biak.

DD 395 *Davis* In collision with battleship *Arizona*, Hawaii, 21 Apr 1941. Neutrality Patrol. Damaged by mine in Seine Bay, Normandy, 21 Jun 1944. Decomm 19 Oct 1945. Stricken 1 Nov 1945. Sold 24 Nov 1947.
1* Normandy.

DD 396 *Jouett* Neutrality Patrol. Decomm 1 Nov 1945. BU 29 Mar 1946, Philadelphia.
3* Normandy, Southern France.
Submarine sunk: **U-128* off Pernambuco, Brazil, 17 May 1943.
Ships sunk: German b/r *Rio Grande* (6062/39), 4 Jan 1944; German b/r *Burgenland* (7,320/28), 6 Jan 1944.

Gridley Class

No.	Name	Builder	Keel Laid	Launched	Comm.
DD 380	*Gridley*	Beth. Quincy	3 Jun 1935	1 Dec 1936	24 Jun 1937
DD 382	*Craven*	Beth. Quincy	3 Jun 1935	25 Feb 1937	2 Sep 1937
DD 400	*McCall*	Beth. S. Fran.	17 Mar 1936	20 Nov 1937	22 Jun 1938
DD 401	*Maury*	Beth. S. Fran.	24 Mar 1936	14 Feb 1938	5 Aug 1938

Displacement	1,500 tons; 2,350 f/l
Dimensions	340'10" (oa); 334' (wl) x 35'10" x 17'3"
Machinery	2 screws; Beth. GT; 4 Yarrow boilers; SHP 44,000; 37 knots
Endurance	6,500/12
Complement	251
Armament	4–5"/38, 4–1.1" AA guns, 4–21" quad TT; (1945) 6 to 8 20mm replaced 1.1"

Figure 4.21: *Craven* (DD 382), of the *Gridley* class, during the war.

Notes: Bethlehem design. Single funnel, pole mast.

Service Records:

DD 380 *Gridley* Damaged in collision with destroyer *Fanning* in storm northwest of Samoa, 22 Jan 1942. Decomm 18 Apr 1946. Stricken 25 Feb 1947. Sold 20 Aug 1947.
10* New Georgia, Gilbert Is., Kwajalein, Eniwetok, Palau-Yap Raids 3/44, Hollandia, Truk Raid 4/44, Saipan, 1st Bonins Raid, Philippine Sea, 2nd Bonins Raid, 3rd Bonins Raid, Guam, Palau-Yap Raids 7/44, 4th Bonins Raid, Bonins-Yap Raids, Palau, Philippines Raids 9/44, Okinawa Raid 10/44, N. Luzon–Formosa Raids 10/44, Luzon Raids 10/44, Lingayen.
Submarine sunk: **I-46* 125 miles northeast of Surigao, 28 Oct 1944.

DD 382 *Craven* Damaged in collision with cruiser *Northampton* north of Oahu, 14 Dec 1941. Decomm 19 Apr 1946. Stricken 25 Feb 1947. Sold 2 Oct 1947.
9* Marshall-Gilberts Raid 1942, Wake I. Raid 1942, Solomons, Vella Gulf, Kwajalein, Eniwetok, Palau-Yap Raids 3/44, Hollandia, Truk Raid 4/44, Saipan, 1st Bonins Raid, Philippine Sea, 2nd Bonins Raid, 3rd Bonins Raid, Guam, Palau-Yap Raids 7/44, 4th Bonins Raid, Bonins-Yap Raids, Palau, Philippines Raids 9/44, Okinawa Raid 10/44, N. Luzon–Formosa Raids 10/44, Luzon Raids 10/44.

DD 400 *McCall* Decomm 30 Nov 1945. Stricken 28 Jan 1947, sold 14 Nov 1947; BU.
9* Marshall-Gilberts Raid 1942, Kwajalein, Eniwetok, Palau-Yap Raids 3/44, Hollandia, Truk Raid 4/44, Saipan, 1st Bonins Raid, Philippine Sea, 2nd Bonins Raid, 3rd Bonins Raid, Guam, Palau-Yap Raids 7/44, 4th Bonins Raid, Bonins-Yap Raids, Palau, Philippines Raids 9/44, Okinawa Raid 10/44, N. Luzon–Formosa Raids 10/44, Luzon Raids 10/44, Surigao Strait, Lingayen, Iwo Jima.

DD 401 *Maury* Decomm 19 Oct 1945. Stricken 1 Nov 1945. Sold 13 Jun 1946; BU Philadelphia.
16* Marshall-Gilberts Raid 1942, Wake I. Raid 1942, Midway, Guadalcanal-Tulagi, Eastern Solomons, Santa Cruz, Tassafaronga, Solomons, New Georgia, Kolombangara, Vella Gulf, Gilbert Is., Kwajalein, Eniwetok, Palau-Yap Raids 3/44, Hollandia, Truk Raid 4/44, Saipan, 1st Bonins Raid, Philippine Sea, 2nd Bonins Raid, 3rd Bonins Raid, Guam, Palau-Yap Raids 7/44, 4th Bonins Raid, Bonins-Yap Raids, Palau, Philippines Raids 9/44, Okinawa Raid 10/44, N. Luzon–Formosa Raids 10/44, Luzon Raids 10/44, Surigao Strait, Lingayen. PUC.

Bagley Class

No.	Name	Builder	Keel Laid	Launched	Comm.
DD 386	*Bagley*	Norfolk NYd	31 Jul 1935	3 Sep 1936	12 Jun 1937
DD 387	*Blue*	Norfolk NYd	25 Sep 1935	27 May 1937	14 Aug 1937
DD 388	*Helm*	Norfolk NYd	25 Sep 1935	27 May 1937	16 Oct 1937
DD 389	*Mugford*	Boston NYd	28 Oct 1935	31 Oct 1936	16 Aug 1937
DD 390	*Ralph Talbot*	Boston NYd	28 Oct 1935	31 Oct 1936	14 Oct 1937
DD 391	*Henley*	Mare I NYd	28 Oct 1935	12 Jan 1937	14 Aug 1937
DD 392	*Patterson*	Puget Sd NYd	23 Jul 1935	6 May 1937	22 Sep 1937
DD 393	*Jarvis*	Puget Sd NYd	21 Aug 1935	6 May 1937	27 Oct 1937

Figure 4.22: *Blue* (DD 387), of the *Bagley* class, on 11 Apr 1942. Notice the prominent funnel trunks of the navy yard design.

Displacement	1,500 tons; 2,350 f/l
Dimensions	340'10" (oa); 334' (wl) x 35'10" x 17'3"
Machinery	2 screws; Beth. GT; 4 Yarrow boilers; SHP 50,000, 40 knots
Endurance	6,100/15
Complement	251
Armament	4–5"/38, 4–1.1" AA guns, 4–21" quad TT; (1945) 1–40mm, 6–20mm replaced 1.1"

Notes: Similar to *Gridley* class with prominent boiler uptakes. One funnel, pole foremast. Navy yard design.

Service Records:

DD 386 *Bagley* Decomm 14 Jun 1946. Stricken 25 Feb 1947. Sold 3 Oct 1947.
12* Pearl Harbor, Salamaua-Lae Raid, Guadalcanal-Tulagi, Arawe, Cape Gloucester, Saidor, Saipan, Philippine Sea, Guam, Tinian, Bonins-Yap Raids, Palau, Philippines Raids 9/44, Okinawa Raid 10/44, Luzon Raids 10/44, Surigao Strait, Leyte, Lingayen, Iwo Jima, Okinawa.

DD 387 *Blue* Torpedoed by Japanese destroyer *Kawakaze* off Guadalcanal, lost stern, 22 Aug 1942, scuttled next day (9 killed).
5* Pearl Harbor, Marshall-Gilberts Raid 1942, Wake I. Raid 1942, Guadalcanal-Tulagi, Solomons.

DD 388 *Helm* Damaged by near misses from bombs at Pearl Harbor, 7 Dec 1941. Slight damage when hit by kamikaze, west of Luzon, 5 Jan 1945. Decomm 26 Jun 1946. Bikini target. Stricken 25 Feb 1947. Sold 2 Oct 1947; BU Oakland.
11* Pearl Harbor, Guadalcanal-Tulagi, Cape Gloucester, Saidor, Saipan, 1st Bonins Raid, Philippine Sea, 2nd Bonins Raid, 3rd Bonins Raid, Guam, Palau-Yap Raids 7/44, 4th Bonins Raid, Bonins-Yap Raids, Palau, Philippines Raids 9/44, Okinawa Raid 10/44, N. Luzon–Formosa Raids 10/44, Luzon Raids 10/44, Surigao Strait, Lingayen, Iwo Jima, Okinawa.
Submarine sunk: **I-46* 125 miles northeast of Surigao, 28 Oct 1944.

DD 389 *Mugford* Damaged by aircraft bomb off Guadalcanal, 7 Aug 1942 (18 killed). Damaged by two aircraft bombs near misses, Cape Gloucester, 26 Dec 1943 (1 killed). Damaged by kamikaze in Surigao Strait, Leyte, 5 Dec 1944 (8 killed). Bikini target ship. Decomm 29 Aug 1946. Stricken 5 Apr 1948. Sunk as target off Kwajalein, 22 Mar 1948.
7* Pearl Harbor, Guadalcanal-Tulagi, Lae Ldgs., Finschhafen, Arawe, Cape Gloucester, Saipan, Philippine Sea, Tinian, Guam, Bonins-Yap Raids, Palau, Philippines Raids 9/44, Okinawa Raid 10/44, N. Luzon–Formosa Raids 10/44, Luzon Raids 10/44, Surigao Strait.

DD 390 *Ralph Talbot* Damaged by five hits from gunfire of Japanese warships off Savo I., 9 Aug 1942 (12 killed). Moderate damage by kamikaze, Okinawa, 27 Apr 1945 (5 killed). Bikini target ship. Decomm 29 Aug 1946. Stricken 5 Apr 1948. Sunk as target off Kwajalein, 8 Mar 1948.
12* Pearl Harbor, Marshall-Gilberts Raid 1942, Wake I. Raid 1942, Guadalcanal-Tulagi, New Georgia, Kolombangara, Cape Gloucester, Saidor, Cape Gloucester, Saipan, Philippine Sea, Bonins-Yap Raids, Palau, Philippines Raids 9/44, Okinawa Raid 10/44, N. Luzon–Formosa Raids 10/44, Luzon Raids 10/44, Surigao Strait, Leyte, Iwo Jima, Okinawa.

DD 391 *Henley* In collision with m/v *Washingtonian* off San Diego, 23 Sep 1938. Torpedoed and sunk by Japanese submarine *Ro-108* off Finschhafen, New Britain, 3 Oct 1942 (17 killed).
4* Pearl Harbor, Guadalcanal-Tulagi, Solomons, Finschhafen.

DD 392 *Patterson* Damaged by one hit from gunfire of Japanese warships off Savo I., 9 Aug 1942 (10 killed). Damaged in collision with destroyer *McCalla* south of Choiseul I., Solomons, lost bow, 29 Sep 1943 (3 killed). Decomm 8 Nov 1945. Stricken 25 Feb 1947. Sold 18 Aug 1947; BU Philadelphia.
13* Pearl Harbor, Eastern Solomons, Salamaua-Lae Raid, Guadalcanal-Tulagi, New Georgia, Saipan, Philippine Sea, Tinian, Guam, Bonins-Yap Raids, Palau, Philippines Raids 9/44, Okinawa Raid 10/44, N. Luzon–Formosa Raids 10/44, Luzon Raids 10/44, Surigao Strait, Leyte, Iwo Jima, Okinawa.
Submarine sunk: *Ro-35* 170 miles southeast of San Cristobal, 25 Aug 1943 (possible).

DD 393 *Jarvis* Damaged by aircraft torpedo off Tulagi, 8 Aug 1942, and sunk by bombs on 9 Aug (247 killed; no survivors).
3* Pearl Harbor, Guadalcanal-Tulagi.

Benham Class

No.	Name	Builder	Keel Laid	Launched	Comm.
DD 397	*Benham*	Federal	1 Sep 1936	16 Apr 1938	2 Feb 1939
DD 398	*Ellet*	Federal	3 Dec 1936	11 Jun 1938	17 Feb 1939
DD 399	*Lang*	Federal	5 Apr 1937	27 Aug 1938	30 Mar 1939
DD 402	*Mayrant*	Boston NYd	15 Apr 1937	14 May 1938	19 Sep 1939
DD 403	*Trippe*	Boston NYd	15 Apr 1937	14 May 1938	1 Nov 1939
DD 404	*Rhind*	Phila. NYd	22 Sep 1937	28 Jul 1938	10 Nov 1939
DD 405	*Rowan*	Norfolk NYd	25 Jun 1937	5 May 1938	23 Sep 1939
DD 406	*Stack*	Norfolk NYd	25 Jun 1937	5 May 1938	20 Nov 1939
DD 407	*Sterett*	Charleston NYd	2 Dec 1936	27 Oct 1938	15 Aug 1939
DD 408	*Wilson*	Puget Sd NYd	22 Mar 1937	12 Apr 1939	5 Jul 1939

Figure 4.23: *Stack* (DD 406), of the *Benham* class, on 27 May 1944. Notice the wartime lower profile; aft guns unshielded.

Figure 4.24: *Rhind* (DD 404), of the *Benham* class, on 6 Aug 1942.

Displacement	1,500 tons; 2,350 f/l
Dimensions	341'4 (oa); 334' (wl) x 35'6" x 17'3"
Machinery	2 screws; West. GT; 3 B&W boilers; SHP 50,000; 38.8 knots
Endurance	6,500/12
Complement	251
Armament	4–5"/38, 4–1/1" AA, 4–21" quad TT; (1945) 1.1" replaced by 2 twin 40mm, 4–20mm, 2–21" quad TT

Notes: Gibbs and Cox design. One funnel, pole foremast. Later units modified with aft guns in enclosed mounts. Two TT mounts removed.

Service Records:

DD 397 *Benham* Torpedoed by Japanese warships at Battle of Guadalcanal, lost bow and sunk by destroyer *Gwin*, 15 Nov 1942. (None killed)
5* Midway, Guadalcanal-Tulagi, Eastern Solomons, Solomons, Battle of Guadalcanal.

DD 398 *Ellet* Decomm 29 Oct 1945. Stricken 13 Nov 1945. Sold 1 Aug 1947; BU San Francisco.
10* Midway, Guadalcanal-Tulagi, Eastern Solomons, New Georgia, Kwajalein, Eniwetok, Palau-Yap Raids 3/44, Saipan, 1st Bonins Raid, Philippine Sea, Guam, Palau-Yap Raids 7/44, 4th Bonins Raid, Rennell I., Iwo Jima Bombard.
Submarine sunk: *I-20* 150 miles northeast of Espiritu Santo, New Hebrides, 3 Sep 1944 (probable).

DD 399 *Lang* Damaged by collision, Okinawa, 28 Apr 1945. Decomm 16 Oct 1945. Stricken 13 Nov 1945. Sold 20 Dec 1946; BU.
11* Reinforcement of Malta, Solomons, Guadalcanal-Tulagi, Vella Gulf, Kwajalein, Raid on Truk, Marianas Raids 2/44, Saipan, Philippine Sea, Guam, Palau-Yap Raids 7/44, Morotai, Leyte, Lingayen, Okinawa.

DD 402 *Mayrant* Neutrality Patrol. Damaged by German aircraft bomb near miss off Palermo, Sicily, 26 Jul 1943 (5 killed). Bikini target ship. Decomm 28 Aug 1946. Sunk as target off Kwajalein, 4 Apr 1948.
3* Casablanca, North Africa, Convoy UGS-6, Sicily.

DD 403 *Trippe* Neutrality Patrol. Damaged in collision with destroyer *Benson* off Casco Bay, Me., 19 Oct 1942. Bikini target ship. Decomm 28 Aug 1946. Sunk as target off Kwajalein, 3 Feb 1948.
6* Tunisia, Convoy UGS-6, Sicily, Salerno, Anzio.
Submarine sunk: **U-73* by gunfire off Oran, 16 Dec 1943.

DD 404 *Rhind* Neutrality Patrol. Slightly damaged by near misses off Palermo, Sicily, 26 Jul 1943. Bikini target ship. Decomm 26 Aug 1946. Sunk as target off Kwajalein, 22 Mar 1948.
4* North Africa, Casablanca, Convoy UGS-6, Sicily, Salerno.

DD 405 *Rowan* Neutrality Patrol. Torpedoed and sunk by German MTB off Salerno, 11 Sep 1943 (202 killed).
5* Arctic Convoys, North Africa, Convoy UGS-6, Sicily, Salerno.

DD 406 *Stack* Neutrality Patrol. Damaged in collision with carrier *Wasp* in North Atlantic off Casco Bay, Me., 17 Mar 1942. Bikini target ship. Decomm 29 Aug 1946. Sunk as target off Kwajalein, 24 Apr 1948.
12* Guadalcanal-Tulagi, Guadalcanal, Solomons, Vella Gulf; Buka Raid, 1st Rabaul Raid, 2nd Rabaul Raid, Gilbert Is., Kwajalein, Raid on Truk, Eniwetok, Cape Sansapor, Morotai, Leyte, Lingayen, Okinawa.

DD 407 *Sterett* Neutrality Patrol. Damaged by 11 hits of gunfire from Japanese warships at Battle of Guadalcanal, 13 Nov 1942. (32 killed). Severe damage by kamikaze off Okinawa, 9 Apr 1945 (none killed). Decomm 2 Nov 1945. Stricken 25 Feb 1947, sold 10 Aug 1947; BU Philadelphia.
12* Reinforcement of Malta, Guadalcanal, Battle of Guadalcanal, Solomons, Vella Gulf; Buka Raid, 1st Rabaul Raid, 2nd Rabaul Raid, Gilbert Is., Kwajalein, Raid on Truk, Marianas Raids 2/44, Saipan, 1st Bonins Raid, Philippine Sea, Guam, Palau-Yap Raids 7/44, Lingayen, Okinawa. PUC.

DD 408 *Wilson* Damaged by kamikaze and bomb, Okinawa, 16 Apr 1945 (5 killed). Bikini target. Decomm 29 Aug 1946. Sunk as target off Kwajalein, 8 Mar 1948.
11* Guadalcanal-Tulagi, Solomons, New Georgia; Buka Raid, 1st Rabaul Raid, 2nd Rabaul Raid, Gilbert Is., Kwajalein, Raid on Truk, Marianas Raids 2/44, Saipan, 1st Bonins Raid, Philippine Sea, Guam, Palau-Yap Raids 7/44, Lingayen, Okinawa.

Sims Class

No.	Name	Builder	Keel Laid	Launched	Comm.
DD 409	*Sims*	Bath	13 Jul 1937	8 Apr 1939	1 Aug 1939
DD 410	*Hughes*	Bath	15 Sep 1937	17 Jun 1939	21 Sep 1939
DD 411	*Anderson*	Federal	15 Nov 1937	4 Feb 1939	19 May 1939
DD 412	*Hammann*	Federal	17 Jan 1938	4 Feb 1939	11 Aug 1939
DD 413	*Mustin*	Newport News	20 Dec 1937	8 Dec 1938	15 Sep 1939
DD 414	*Russell*	Newport News	20 Dec 1937	8 Dec 1938	3 Nov 1939
DD 415	*O'Brien*	Boston NYd	31 May 1938	20 Oct 1939	2 Mar 1940
DD 416	*Walke*	Boston NYd	31 May 1938	20 Oct 1939	27 Apr 1940
DD 417	*Morris*	Norfolk NYd	7 Jun 1938	1 Jun 1939	5 Mar 1940
DD 418	*Roe*	Charleston NYd	23 Apr 1938	21 Jun 1939	5 Jan 1940

Figure 4.25: *Wainwright* (DD 419), of the *Sims* class, as completed, 31 May 1940. Notice that two 5" guns are not in shields to save top weight. The no. 3 gun and one bank of torpedo tubes were later removed.

DD 419	*Wainwright*	Norfolk NYd	7 Jun 1938	1 Jun 1939	15 Apr 1940
DD 420	*Buck*	Phila. NYd	6 Apr 1938	22 May 1939	15 May 1940

Displacement	1,720 tons; 2,465 f/l
Dimensions	348'4" (oa); 341'4" (wl) x 36'1" x 17'4"
Machinery	2 screws; West. GT; 3 B&W boilers; SHP 50,000; 35 knots
Endurance	4,700/15
Complement	251
Armament	5–5"/38, 4–1.1" AA, 3 quad 21" TT; (1945) 4–5"/38, 2 twin and 3 single 40mm, 4–20mm guns, 2 quad 21" TT.

Notes: Five gun battery reinstated and 12 TT as in *Mahan* class. New fire control system. One funnel, pole foremast. Immediately altered to reduce top weight and one TT mount removed. Exposed guns fitted with half-shields, 1940. Later, no. 3 gun removed.

Service Records:

DD 409 *Sims* Neutrality Patrol. Sunk by three aircraft bombs, Battle of Coral Sea, 7 May 1942 (237 killed).
2* Marshall-Gilberts Raid 1942, Coral Sea.

DD 410 *Hughes* Neutrality Patrol. Damaged in collision with British m/v *Chumleigh* at Reykjavik, 27 Aug 1941. Damaged in error by U.S. gunfire west of Solomon Is., 25 Oct 1942. Damaged by collision, Santa Cruz, 26 Oct 1942. Severely damaged by kamikaze in Surigao Strait, 10 Dec 1944. Bikini target. Decomm 28 Aug 1946. Sunk as target, 16 Oct 1948.
14* Marshall-Gilberts Raid 1942, Midway, Solomons; Buin Raid, Santa Cruz, Battle of Guadalcanal, Attu, Gilbert Is., Kwajalein, Eniwetok, Palau-Yap Raids 3/44, Wakde, Biak, Noemfoor I., Cape Sansapor, Morotai, Rennell I., Leyte, Ormoc, Kurile Is.

DD 411 *Anderson* Neutrality Patrol. Damaged by one hit from coastal battery off Wotje, Marshall Is., 30 Jan 1944. Damaged by grounding off Kwajalein, Marshall Is., 1 Feb 1944. Damaged by kamikaze off Leyte, 1 Nov 1944 (16 killed). Bikini target ship. Sunk in atom bomb aerial explosion test Able at Bikini, 1 Jul 1946.
10* Coral Sea, Midway, Santa Cruz, Battle of Guadalcanal, Solomons, Gilbert Is., Kwajalein, Cape Sansapor, Morotai, Leyte, Kurile Is.

DD 412 *Hammann* Neutrality Patrol. Torpedoed and sunk by submarine *I-168* at Battle of Midway, 6 Jun 1942 (102 killed).
2* Coral Sea, Midway.

DD 413 *Mustin* Neutrality Patrol. Damaged in collision with destroyer *Morris* off Hawaii, 8 Aug 1942. Bikini target ship. Decomm 29 Aug 1946. Sunk as target in Marshall Is., 18 Apr 1948.
13* Buin Raid, Santa Cruz, Battle of Guadalcanal, Guadalcanal, Attu, Gilbert Is., Kwajalein, Eniwetok, Palau-Yap Raids 3/44, Wakde, Biak, Noemfoor I., Cape Sansapor, Morotai, Rennell I., Leyte, Lingayen, Okinawa.

DD 414 *Russell* Neutrality Patrol. Decomm 15 Nov 1945. Stricken 28 Nov 1945. Sold 28 Sep 1947; BU Terminal I.
16* Marshall-Gilberts Raid 1942, Salamaua-Lae Raid, Coral Sea, Midway; Buin Raid, Santa Cruz, Battle of Guadalcanal, Solomons, Gilbert Is., Kwajalein, Rennell I., Hollandia, Wakde, Biak, Noemfoor I., Cape Sansapor, Leyte, Lingayen, Okinawa, Subic Bay.

DD 415 *O'Brien* Neutrality Patrol. Minor damage in collision with destroyer *Case* off Calif., Feb 1942. Torpedoed by submarine *I-15* north of Espiritu Santo, 15 Sep 1942. Foundered off Samoa as result of damage, 19 Oct 1942 (none lost).
1* Santa Cruz.

DD 416 *Walke* Neutrality Patrol. Sunk by torpedo and gunfire from Japanese warships at Battle of Guadalcanal, bow blown off, 14 Nov 1942 (81 killed).
3* Marshall-Gilberts Raid 1942, Salamaua-Lae Raid, Coral Sea, Battle of Guadalcanal.

DD 417 *Morris* Neutrality Patrol. Damaged in collision with destroyer *Mustin* off Hawaii, 8 Aug 1942. Damaged by kamikaze off Okinawa, 6 Apr 1945 (13 killed). Decomm 9 Nov 1945. Stricken 28 Nov 1945. Sold 2 Aug 1947; BU Hillside, N.J.
15* Coral Sea, Midway, Guadalcanal; Buin Raid, Santa Cruz, Battle of Guadalcanal, Solomons, Rennell I., Attu, Gilbert Is., Kwajalein, Eniwetok, Palau-Yap Raids 3/44, Wakde, Biak, Noemfoor I., Cape Sansapor, Morotai, Leyte, Lingayen, Okinawa.

DD 418 *Roe* Neutrality Patrol. Damaged in collision with destroyer *Swanson* off Porto Empedocle, Sicily, 10 Jul 1943. Decomm 30 Oct 1945. Stricken 16 Nov 1945. Sold 1 Aug 1947.
6* North Africa, Sicily, Admiralty Is., Hollandia, Wakde, Biak, Noemfoor I., Philippines Raids 9/44, Iwo Jima Bombard.

DD 419 *Wainwright* Neutrality Patrol. Bikini target. Decomm 29 Aug 1946. Sunk as target off Kwajalein, 5 Jul 1948.
7* Arctic Convoys, North Africa, Casablanca, Convoy UGS-6, Sicily, Salerno, Anzio.
Submarine sunk: **U-593* north of Constantine, Algeria, 13 Dec 1943.

DD 420 *Buck* Neutrality Patrol. Damaged in collision with m/v *Awatea* southeast of Nova Scotia, in North Atlantic, lost stern, 22 Aug 1942 (7 killed). Torpedoed and sunk by *U-616* off Salerno, broke in two, 9 Oct 1943 (166 killed).
3* Sicily.
Submarine sunk: Italian *Argento* off Pantellaria, 3 Aug 1943.

Benson Class

No.	Name	Builder	Keel Laid	Launched	Comm.
DD 421	*Benson*	Beth. Quincy	16 May 1938	15 Nov 1939	25 Jul 1940
DD 422	*Mayo*	Beth. Quincy	16 May 1938	26 Mar 1940	18 Sep 1940
DD 423	*Gleaves*	Bath	16 May 1938	9 Dec 1939	14 Jun 1940
DD 424	*Niblack*	Bath	8 Aug 1938	18 May 1940	1 Aug 1940
DD 425	*Madison*	Boston NYd	19 Dec 1938	20 Oct 1939	6 Aug 1940
DD 426	*Lansdale*	Boston NYd	19 Dec 1938	20 Oct 1939	17 Sep 1940
DD 427	*Hilary P. Jones*	Charleston NYd	16 Nov 1938	14 Dec 1939	6 Sep 1940
DD 428	*Charles F. Hughes*	Puget Sd NYd	3 Jan 1939	16 May 1940	5 Sep 1940
DD 459	*Laffey*	Beth. S. Fran.	13 Jan 1941	30 Oct 1941	31 Mar 1942

Figure 4.26: *Gleaves* (DD 423), an early *Benson*-class destroyer, on 31 May 1942. Notice the gun mount in the no. 3 position, later removed.

DD 460	*Woodworth*	Beth. S. Fran.	13 Jan 1941	29 Nov 1941	30 Apr 1942
DD 491	*Farenholt*	Beth. Staten I.	11 Dec 1940	19 Nov 1941	2 Apr 1942
DD 492	*Bailey*	Beth. Staten I.	29 Jan 1941	19 Dec 1941	11 May 1942
DD 598	*Bancroft*	Beth. Quincy	1 May 1941	31 Dec 1941	30 Apr 1942
DD 599	*Barton*	Beth. Quincy	20 May 1941	31 Jan 1942	29 May 1942
DD 600	*Boyle*	Beth. Quincy	31 Dec 1941	15 Jun 1942	15 Aug 1942
DD 601	*Champlin*	Beth. Quincy	31 Jan 1942	25 Jul 1942	12 Sep 1942
DD 602	*Meade*	Beth. Staten I.	25 Mar 1941	15 Feb 1942	22 Jun 1942
DD 603	*Murphy*	Beth. Staten I.	19 May 1941	29 Apr 1942	27 Jul 1942
DD 604	*Parker*	Beth. Staten I.	9 Jun 1941	12 May 1942	31 Aug 1942
DD 605	*Caldwell*	Beth. S. Fran.	24 Mar 1941	15 Jan 1942	10 Jun 1942
DD 606	*Coghlan*	Beth. S. Fran.	28 Mar 1941	12 Feb 1942	10 Jul 1942
DD 607	*Frazier*	Beth. S. Fran.	5 Jul 1941	17 Mar 1942	30 Jul 1942
DD 608	*Gansevoort*	Beth. S. Fran.	16 Jun 1941	11 Apr 1942	25 Aug 1942
DD 609	*Gillespie*	Beth. S. Fran.	16 Jun 1941	8 May 1942	18 Sep 1942
DD 610	*Hobby*	Beth. S. Fran.	30 Jun 1941	4 Jun 1942	18 Nov 1942
DD 611	*Kalk*	Beth. S. Fran.	30 Jun 1941	18 Jul 1942	10 Oct 1942
DD 612	*Kendrick*	Beth. S. Pedro	1 May 1941	2 Apr 1942	12 Sep 1942
DD 613	*Laub*	Beth. S. Pedro	1 May 1941	28 Apr 1942	24 Oct 1942
DD 614	*Mackenzie*	Beth. S. Pedro	29 May 1941	27 Jun 1942	21 Nov 1942
DD 615	*McLanahan*	Beth. S. Pedro	29 May 1941	7 Sep 1942	19 Dec 1942
DD 616	*Nields*	Beth. Quincy	15 Jun 1942	1 Oct 1942	15 Jan 1943
DD 617	*Ordronaux*	Beth. Quincy	25 Jul 1942	9 Nov 1942	13 Feb 1943

Displacement	1,620 tons; 2,525 f/l
Dimensions	348'3" (oa); 341' (wl) x 36'1" x 17'6"
Machinery	2 screws; Beth. GT; 4 B&W boilers; SHP 50,000; 35 knots
Endurance	6,500/12
Complement	276
Armament	5–5"/38, 10–.50 AA, 2 quint 21" TT; (1945) 4–5"/38, 2 twin 40mm, 7 to 8 20mm AA, 1 quint 21" TT

Notes: DD 421–22 designed by Bethlehem; DD 423–24 by Gibbs and Cox. *Benson* class can be recognized by flat funnels; *Livermore* class had round funnels. Designed with five guns, two quintuple torpedo tubes, later reduced to add AA guns. DD 616–617 originally ordered from Beth. S. Fran. Two funnels, pole mast. Searchlight tower aft cut down 1942.

Service Records:

DD 421 *Benson* Neutrality Patrol. Damaged in collision with destroyer *Trippe* in North Atlantic, 19 Oct 1942. Decomm 18 Mar 1946. †
4* Sicily, Salerno, Convoy UGS-40, Southern France.

DD 422 *Mayo* Neutrality Patrol. Damaged by mine explosion off Anzio, 24 Jan 1944 (7 killed). Decomm 18 Mar 1946. †
2* Salerno, Anzio. Tokyo Bay.

DD 423 *Gleaves* Neutrality Patrol. Decomm 8 May 1946. †
5* Sicily, Salerno, Anzio, Southern France.
Submarine sunk: **U-616* off Cartagena, Spain, 17 May 1944.

DD 424 *Niblack* Neutrality Patrol. Decomm 25 Apr 1946. †
5* Sicily, Salerno, Anzio, Southern France.
Submarine sunk: **U-960* Northwest of Algiers, 19 May 1944.

DD 425 *Madison* Neutrality Patrol. Decomm 13 Mar 1946. †
5* Reinforcement of Malta, Convoy UC-1, Anzio, Southern France. Tokyo Bay.
Submarine sunk: **U-450* off Ostia, 10 Mar 1944.

DD 426 *Lansdale* Neutrality Patrol. Torpedoed and sunk by German aircraft off Algiers, broke in two, 20 Apr 1944 (47 killed).
4* Convoy UC-1, Convoy UGS-37, Convoy UGS-38, Anzio.

DD 427 *Hilary P. Jones* Neutrality Patrol. Damaged by guided bomb, Anzio, 15 Feb 1944. Destroyed four enemy MTBs off Southern France, 20 Aug 1944. Decomm 6 Feb 1947. Tokyo Bay. †
4* Convoy UC-1, Anzio, Southern France. Tokyo Bay.

DD 428 *Charles F. Hughes* Neutrality Patrol. Destroyed four enemy MTBs off Southern France, 20 Aug 1944. Decomm 18 Mar 1946. †
4* Convoy UC-1, Anzio, Southern France. Tokyo Bay.

DD 459 *Laffey* Sunk by gunfire from Japanese battleship *Hiyei*, and torpedo, Battle of Guadalcanal, 13 Nov 1942 (59 killed).
3* Cape Esperance, Guadalcanal, Battle of Guadalcanal. PUC.

DD 460 *Woodworth* Collided with destroyer *Buchanan* at Kolombangara, 13 Jul 1943. Decomm 11 Apr 1946. †
7* Guadalcanal, Solomons, Arawe; Buka Raid, 1st Rabaul Raid, 2nd Rabaul Raid, Green I. Ldgs., Rabaul and Kavieng Bombard., Okinawa Raid 10/44, N. Luzon–Formosa Raids 10/44, Luzon Raids 10/44, Okinawa, Raids on Japan 7–8/45.

DD 491 *Farenholt* Damaged by four hits from gunfire, Cape Esperance, 11 Oct 1942 (3 killed). Damaged by one hit, coastal gunfire, off Kavieng, New Ireland, 25 Feb 1944. Decomm 26 Apr 1946. †
11* Guadalcanal-Tulagi, Cape Esperance, Solomons, New Georgia; Buka Raid, 1st Rabaul Raid, 2nd Rabaul Raid, Cape Torokina, Green I. Ldgs., Rabaul and Kavieng Bombard., Guam, Palau, Philippines Raids 9/44, Solomons, Morotai, Luzon Raids 10/44, Okinawa, Raids on Japan 7–8/45.

DD 492 *Bailey* Damaged by five hits of gunfire from Japanese warships in Battle of Komandorski Is., Bering Sea, 26 Mar 1943 (5 killed). Damaged by aircraft strafing, Palau, 1 Oct 1944 (9 killed). Decomm 2 May 1946. †
9* Komandorski Is., Gilbert Is., Kwajalein, Eniwetok, Saipan, Tinian, Palau, Leyte, Tarakan, Balikpapan, Mindanao Ldgs.

DD 598 *Bancroft* Damaged by collision, at Olongapo, Luzon, 31 Jul 1945. Decomm 1 Feb 1946. †
8* Attu, Tarawa Raid, Gilbert Is., Kwajalein, Palau-Yap Raids 3/44, Hollandia, Saipan, Tarakan.

DD 599 *Barton* Sunk by two torpedoes from Japanese destroyer *Amatsukaze*, Battle of Guadalcanal, broke in two, 13 Nov 1942 (175 killed).
4* Buin Raid, Santa Cruz, Guadalcanal, Battle of Guadalcanal.

DD 600 *Boyle* Decomm 29 Mar 1946. †
4* Casablanca, North Africa, Sicily, Anzio, Southern France.

DD 601 *Champlin* Decomm 31 Jan 1947. †
6* Convoy UGS-6, Sicily, Anzio, Southern France.

Submarines sunk: *U-130* west of Azores, 12 Mar 1943; *U-856* in North Atlantic, 7 Apr 1944 (one [commanding officer] killed; ramming damage).

DD 602 *Meade* Decomm 17 Jun 1946. †
9* Solomons, Rennell I., Attu, Gilbert Is., Kwajalein, Palau-Yap Raids 3/44, Hollandia, Truk Raid 4/44, Tinian, Guam, Mindanao Ldgs.
Submarine sunk: **I-35*, off Tarawa, Gilbert Is., 22 Nov 1943.

DD 603 *Murphy* Hit by shore gunfire off Fedala, Morocco, 8 Nov 1942 (3 killed). Cut in two in collision with tanker *Bulkoil* off New York, bow sank, 21 Oct 1943 (38 killed). Decomm 9 Mar 1946. †
4* North Africa, Sicily, Normandy, Southern France.

DD 604 *Parker* Decomm 31 Jan 1947. †
4* North Africa, Sicily, Convoy KMF-25A, Anzio, Southern France.

DD 605 *Caldwell* Damaged in collision with escort carrier *White Plains* off Marshall Is., 7 Feb 1944. Severely damaged by kamikaze and bombs south of Ormoc. 12 Dec 1944 (33 killed). Minor damaged by mine, Brunei Bay, 27 Jun 1945. Decomm 24 Apr 1946. †
8* Attu, Tarawa Raid, Wake I. Raid 1943, Gilbert Is., Kwajalein, Palau-Yap Raids 3/44, Hollandia, Truk Raid 4/44, Leyte, Ormoc, Tarakan.

DD 606 *Coghlan* Slightly damaged by gunfire, Battle of Komandorski Is., 26 Mar 1943. Decomm 31 Mar 1947. †
8* Komandorski Is., Attu, Tarawa Raid, Tarawa Raid, Gilbert Is., Kwajalein, Eniwetok, Saipan, Tinian, Leyte, Ormoc, Lingayen.

DD 607 *Frazier* Decomm 15 Apr 1946. †
12* Rennell I., Attu, Gilbert Is., Kwajalein, Palau-Yap Raids 3/44, Hollandia, Truk Raid 4/44, Mindanao Ldgs., Mariveles-Corregidor, Lingayen, Balikpapan.
Submarines sunk: *I-9* off Kiska, 13 Jun 1944 (probable): damaged by ramming *I-35*, off Tarawa, Gilbert Is., 22 Nov 1943.

DD 608 *Gansevoort* Severely damaged by kamikaze off Southern Mindoro, 30 Dec 1944. Decomm 1 Feb 1946. †
4* Solomons, Attu, Gilbert Is., Leyte.

DD 609 *Gillespie* Decomm 17 Apr 1946. †
9* Cape Gloucester, Saidor, Admiralty Is., Hollandia, Wakde, Biak, Noemfoor I., Cape Sansapor, Palau, Philippines Raids 9/44, Iwo Jima, Fleet Raids 1945, Okinawa, Raids on Japan 7–8/45.

DD 610 *Hobby* Decomm 1 Feb 1946. †
10* Convoy UGS-6, Cape Gloucester, Saidor, Admiralty Is., Hollandia, Wakde, Biak, Noemfoor I., Cape Sansapor; Palau, Luzon Raids 10/44, Formosa Raids 1/45, China Coast Raids 1/45, Nansei Shoto Raid 1/45, Iwo Jima, Okinawa.

DD 611 *Kalk* Damaged by aircraft bomb off Biak, New Guinea, 12 Jun 1944. Decomm 3 May 1946. †
8* Cape Gloucester, Saidor, Admiralty Is., Hollandia, Wakde, Biak, Palau, Philippines Raids 9/44, Formosa Raids 1/45, Luzon Raids 1/45, Nansei Shoto Raid 1/45, Iwo Jima, Okinawa, Fleet Raids 1945, Raids on Japan 7–8/45. Tokyo Bay.

Figure 4.27: *Gansevoort* (DD 608), of the *Benson* class, on 17 Aug 1945, built with only four guns.

DD 612 *Kendrick* Damaged by German aircraft torpedo in stern off Oran, 2 Sep 1943. Decomm 31 Mar 1947. †
3* Sicily, Anzio, Southern France.

DD 613 *Laub* Damaged in collision with cruiser *Philadelphia* off Anzio, Italy, 23 May 1944. Decomm 2 Feb 1946. †
4* Tunisia, Sicily, Convoy KMF-25A, Anzio.

DD 614 *Mackenzie* Decomm 4 Feb 1946. †
4* Sicily, Anzio, Southern France.
Submarine sunk: *U-182* off Tristan da Cunha, 16 May 1943.

DD 615 *McLanahan* Damaged by one hit from shore gunfire off San Remo, 11 Feb 1945 (1 killed). Decomm 2 Feb 1946. †
4* Sicily, Convoy KMF-25A, Anzio, Southern France.

DD 616 *Nields* Decomm 25 Mar 1946. †
3* Sicily, Southern France.
Submarines sunk: Italian *Gorgo* off Oran, 21 May 1943; **U-616* off Cartagena, Spain, 17 May 1944.

DD 617 *Ordronaux* Decomm Jan 1947. †
3* Sicily, Anzio, Southern France.

Figure 4.28: *Gwin* (DD 433), of the *Livermore* class, 27 Mar 1941, with round funnels. Notice gun in the no. 3 position.

Figure 4.29: *Wilkes* (DD 441), of the *Livermore* class, with the 5" no. 3 gun removed. Another ship is visible behind, aft.

Figure 4.30: *Swanson* (DD 443), of the *Livermore* class, 16 Apr 1943, with wartime modifications. Compare with the photo of the *Gwin* (Figure 4.28).

Livermore Class

No.	Name	Builder	Keel Laid	Launched	Comm.
DD 429	*Livermore*	Bath	6 Mar 1939	3 Aug 1940	7 Oct 1940
DD 430	*Eberle*	Bath	12 Apr 1939	14 Sep 1940	4 Dec 1940
DD 431	*Plunkett*	Federal	1 Mar 1939	9 Mar 1940	17 Jul 1940
DD 432	*Kearny*	Federal	1 Mar 1939	9 Mar 1940	13 Sep 1940
DD 433	*Gwin*	Boston NYd	1 Jun 1939	25 May 1940	15 Jan 1941
DD 434	*Meredith*	Boston NYd	1 Jun 1939	24 Apr 1940	1 Mar 1941
DD 435	*Grayson*	Charleston NYd	17 Jul 1939	7 Aug 1940	14 Feb 1941
DD 436	*Monssen*	Puget Sd NYd	12 Jul 1939	16 May 1940	14 Mar 1941
DD 437	*Woolsey*	Bath	9 Oct 1939	12 Feb 1941	7 May 1941
DD 438	*Ludlow*	Bath	18 Dec 1939	11 Nov 1940	5 Mar 1941
DD 439	*Edison*	Federal	18 Mar 1940	23 Nov 1940	31 Jan 1941
DD 440	*Ericsson*	Federal	18 Mar 1940	23 Nov 1940	13 Mar 1941
DD 441	*Wilkes*	Boston NYd	1 Nov 1939	31 May 1940	22 Apr 1941
DD 442	*Nicholson*	Boston NYd	1 Nov 1939	31 May 1940	3 Jun 1941
DD 443	*Swanson*	Charleston NYd	15 Nov 1939	2 Nov 1940	29 May 1941
DD 444	*Ingraham*	Charleston NYd	15 Nov 1939	15 Feb 1941	17 Jul 1941

Displacement	1,630 tons; 2,525 f/l
Dimensions	349'4" (oa); 341' (wl) x 36'1" x 17'6"
Machinery	2 screws; GE GT; 4 B&W boilers; SHP 50,000; 37.4 knots
Endurance	6,500/12
Complement	276
Armament	5–5"/38, 2 twin 40mm, 8–20mm guns, 2–21" quint TT (DD 453 and up: 1–21" quint TT)

Notes: Flat sided funnels. Two funnels, pole foremast. One 5" gun and aft superstructure removed to save weight.

Service Records:

DD 429 *Livermore* Neutrality Patrol. Ran aground off Iceland, 24 Nov 1941. Decomm 24 Jan 1947. †
3* North Africa, Anzio, Southern France.

DD 430 *Eberle* Neutrality Patrol. Decomm 3 Jun 1946. †
3* North Africa, Anzio, Southern France.
Ship sunk: German b/r *Karin* in South Atlantic, 10 Mar 1943 (7 killed; boarding party).

DD 431 *Plunkett* Neutrality Patrol. Damaged by aircraft bomb, Anzio, 24 Jan 1944 (61 killed). Decomm 3 May 1946. †
5* Sicily, Salerno, Anzio, Normandy, Southern France.

DD 432 *Kearny* Neutrality Patrol. Torpedoed by *U-568* southwest of Iceland, 17 Oct 1941 (11 killed). Decomm 7 Mar 1946. †
3* North Africa, Anzio, Southern France.

DD 433 *Gwin* Neutrality Patrol. Moderately damaged by two hits from gunfire of Japanese destroyers at Battle of Guadalcanal, 15 Nov 1942. Damaged by one hit by shore gunfire off Munda, 30 Jun 1943 (3 killed). Torpedoed by Japanese destroyer at Battle of Kolombangara, and sunk by U.S. destroyer *Ralph Talbot*, 13 Jul 1943.
5* Midway, Guadalcanal-Tulagi, Solmons, Battle of Guadalcanal, New Georgia, Kolombangara.

DD 434 *Meredith* Neutrality Patrol. Sunk by two aircraft torpedoes and two bombs south of Guadalcanal, 15 Oct 1942 (185 killed; 51 from tug *Vireo*).
1* Solomons.

DD 435 *Grayson* Neutrality Patrol. Damaged in collision, south of Rennell I., Solomons, 21 Oct 1942. Damaged *I-5* in depth charge attack, 25 Aug 1942. Decomm 4 Feb 1947. †
13* Guadalcanal-Tulagi, Eastern Solomons, Solomons, Buka Raid, 1st Rabaul Raid, 2nd Rabaul Raid, Admiralty Is., Hollandia, Wakde, Biak, Noemfoor I., Cape Sansapor, Hollandia, Palau, Philippines Raids 9/44, Morotai, Surigao Strait, Okinawa Raid 10/44, N. Luzon–Formosa Raids 10/44, Luzon Raids 10/44.

DD 436 *Monssen* Neutrality Patrol. Hit over 37 times by Japanese destroyers at Battle of Guadalcanal, 13 Nov 1942, and blew up next day (130 killed).
4* Guadalcanal-Tulagi, Eastern Solomons, Solomons, Battle of Guadalcanal.

DD 437 *Woolsey* Neutrality Patrol. Decomm 6 Feb 1947. †
7* North Africa, Sicily, Salerno, Anzio, Southern France.
Submarines sunk: **U-173* off Casablanca, 16 Nov 1942; **U-73* off Oran, 16 Dec 1943; **U-960* north of Oran, 19 May 1944.

DD 438 *Ludlow* Neutrality Patrol. Hit by gunfire from French warships off Casablanca, 8 Nov 1942. Slightly damaged by coastal gunfire, Anzio, 8 Feb 1944. Decomm 20 May 1946. †
6* North Africa, Casablanca, Sicily, Salerno, Anzio, Southern France.
Submarine sunk: **U-960* northwest of Algiers, 19 May 1944.

DD 439 *Edison* Neutrality Patrol. Decomm 18 May 1946. †
6* Convoy ON-67, Casablanca, North Africa, Sicily, Salerno, Anzio, Southern France.

DD 440 *Ericsson* Neutrality Patrol. Collided with Icelandic trawler *Greedir*, which sank, off Hvalfjordur, Iceland, 13 Feb 1942. Decomm 15 Mar 1946. †
3* North Africa, Anzio, Southern France.

DD 441 *Wilkes* Neutrality Patrol. Went aground off Argentia, Newfoundland, 18 Feb 1942. Damaged in collision with tanker *Davila* off Maine, 8 Apr 1942. Damaged by grounding, near Bizerte, 4 Jul 1943. Decomm 4 Mar 1946. †
10* North Africa, Casablanca, Sicily, Admiralty Is., Hollandia, Wakde, Biak, Noemfoor I., Cape Sansapor, Bonins-Yap Raids, Palau, Philippines Raids 9/44, Surigao Strait, Okinawa Raid 10/44, N. Luzon–Formosa Raids 10/44, Luzon Raids 10/44, Okinawa, Raids on Japan 7–8/45.

DD 442 *Nicholson* Neutrality Patrol. Damaged by one hit from shore gunfire, Los Negros, Admiralty Is., 4 Mar 1944 (3 killed). Decomm 26 Feb 1946. †

10* Convoy ON-67, Sicily, Salerno, Cape Gloucester, Admiralty Is., Hollandia, Wakde, Biak, Noemfoor I., Cape Sansapor, Bonins-Yap Raids, Palau, Philippines Raids 9/44, E1–3, Okinawa Raid 10/44, Surigao Strait, N. Luzon–Formosa Raids 10/44, Luzon Raids 10/44, Okinawa, Raids on Japan 7–8/45.

DD 443 *Swanson* Neutrality Patrol. Damaged in collision with destroyer *Roe* off Porto Empedocle, Sicily, 10 Jul 1943. Decomm 10 Dec 1945. †
8* North Africa, Casablanca, Sicily, Cape Gloucester, Admiralty Is., Hollandia, Biak, Noemfoor I., Cape Sansapor, Bonins-Yap Raids, Palau, Philippines Raids 9/44, Surigao Strait, Okinawa Raid 10/44, N. Luzon–Formosa Raids 10/44, Luzon Raids 10/44.
Submarine sunk: **U-173* off Casablanca, 16 Nov 1942.

DD 444 *Ingraham* Sunk in collision with oiler *Chemung* in fog off Nova Scotia, 22 Aug 1942 (218 killed).

No.	Name	Builder	Keel Laid	Launched	Comm.
DD 453	*Bristol*	Federal	2 Dec 1940	26 Jul 1941	21 Oct 1941
DD 454	*Ellyson*	Federal	2 Dec 1940	26 Jul 1941	28 Nov 1941
DD 455	*Hambleton*	Federal	16 Dec 1940	26 Sep 1941	22 Dec 1941
DD 456	*Rodman*	Federal	16 Dec 1940	26 Sep 1941	27 Jan 1942
DD 457	*Emmons*	Bath	14 Nov 1940	23 Aug 1941	5 Dec 1941
DD 458	*Macomb*	Bath	3 Sep 1940	23 Sep 1941	26 Jan 1942
DD 461	*Forrest*	Boston NYd	6 Jan 1941	14 Jun 1941	13 Jan 1942
DD 462	*Fitch*	Boston NYd	6 Jan 1941	14 Jun 1941	3 Feb 1942
DD 463	*Corry*	Charleston NYd	4 Sep 1940	28 Jul 1941	18 Dec 1941
DD 464	*Hobson*	Charleston NYd	14 Nov 1940	8 Sep 1941	22 Jan 1942
DD 483	*Aaron Ward*	Federal	11 Feb 1941	22 Nov 1941	4 Mar 1942
DD 484	*Buchanan*	Federal	11 Feb 1941	22 Nov 1941	21 Mar 1942
DD 485	*Duncan*	Federal	31 Jul 1941	20 Feb 1942	16 Apr 1942
DD 486	*Lansdowne*	Federal	31 Jul 1941	20 Feb 1942	29 Apr 1942
DD 487	*Lardner*	Federal	15 Sep 1941	20 Mar 1942	13 May 1942
DD 488	*McCalla*	Federal	15 Sep 1941	20 Mar 1942	27 May 1942
DD 489	*Mervine*	Federal	3 Nov 1941	3 May 1942	17 Jun 1942
DD 490	*Quick*	Federal	3 Nov 1941	3 May 1942	3 Jul 1942
DD 493	*Carmick*	Sea-Tac Seattle	29 May 1941	8 Mar 1942	28 Dec 1942
DD 494	*Doyle*	Sea-Tac Seattle	26 May 1941	17 Mar 1942	27 Jan 1943
DD 495	*Endicott*	Sea-Tac Seattle	1 May 1941	5 Apr 1942	25 Feb 1943
DD 496	*McCook*	Sea-Tac Seattle	1 May 1941	30 Apr 1942	15 Mar 1943
DD 497	*Frankford*	Sea-Tac Seattle	5 Jun 1941	17 May 1942	31 Mar 1943

Service Records:

DD 453 *Bristol* Torpedoed and sunk by *U-371* off Algiers, broke in two, 13 Oct 1943 (52 killed).
3* North Africa, Casablanca, Sicily, Salerno.

DD 454 *Ellyson* Damaged in collision with destroyer *Hambleton* in North Atlantic, 17 May 1942. Converted to minesweeper and rec **DMS 19**, 15 Nov 1944. Damaged by kamikaze, Okinawa, 3 Apr 1945. †
7* North Africa, Normandy, Southern France, Okinawa, Raids on Japan 7–8/45, Minesweeping 1945. Tokyo Bay.
Submarine sunk: **U-616* off Cartagena, Spain, 17 May 1944.

DD 455 *Hambleton* Damaged in collision with destroyer *Ellyson* in North Atlantic, 17 May 1942. Torpedoed by *U-173* off Fedala, cut in two, 11 Nov 1942 (20 killed). Converted to minesweeper and rec **DMS 20**, 15 Nov 1944. Damaged in collision with *YMS-96* off Okinawa, 12 Apr 1945. Damaged by kamikaze, Okinawa, 22 Jun 1945. †
7* North Africa, Normandy, Southern France, Okinawa, Raids on Japan 7–8/45, Minesweeping 1945. Tokyo Bay.
Submarine sunk: **U-616* off Cartagena, Spain, 17 May 1944.

DD 456 *Rodman* Converted to minesweeper and rec **DMS 21**, 15 Nov 1944. Damaged by three kamikazes off Okinawa, 6 Apr 1945 (16 killed). †
5* North Africa, Normandy, Southern France, Okinawa.
Submarine sunk: **U-616* off Cartagena, Spain, 17 May 1944.

DD 457 *Emmons* Converted to minesweeper and rec **DMS 22**, 15 Nov 1944. Hit by five kamikazes off Okinawa, 6 Apr 1945 and sunk by U.S. forces (64 killed).
4* North Africa, Normandy, Southern France, Okinawa.
Submarine sunk: **U-616* off Cartagena, Spain, 17 May 1944.

DD 458 *Macomb* Converted to minesweeper and rec **DMS 23**, 15 Nov 1944. Damaged by kamikaze, Okinawa, 3 May 1945 (7 killed). †
5* North Africa, Southern France, Okinawa, Minesweeping 1945. Tokyo Bay.
Submarine sunk: **U-616* off Cartagena, Spain, 17 May 1944.

DD 461 *Forrest* Damaged by collision, off Marseille, 1 Oct 1944. Converted to minesweeper and rec **DMS 24**, 15 Nov 1944. Damaged by kamikaze, Okinawa, 27 May 1945 (5 killed), not repaired. Decomm 30 Nov 1945. Stricken 9 Dec 1945. Sold 5 Nov 1946.
6* North Africa, Norway Raid, Task Group 21.12, Normandy, Southern France, Okinawa.

DD 462 *Fitch* Converted to minesweeper and rec **DMS 25**, 15 Nov 1944. Damaged by running on coral reef at Ulithi, Micronesia, ... Mar 1945. †
5* North Africa, Norway Raid, Normandy, Southern France, Minesweeping 1945. Tokyo Bay.

DD 463 *Corry* Sunk by mine off Utah Beach, Normandy, broke in two, 6 Jun 1944 (22 killed).
4* North Africa, Norway Raid, TG 21.16, Normandy.
Submarine sunk: **U-801* off Cape Verde Is., 17 Mar 1944.

DD 464 *Hobson* Converted to minesweeper and rec **DMS 26**, 15 Nov 1944. Damaged by kamikaze bomb, Okinawa, 16 Apr 1945. †
6* North Africa, Norway Raid, Normandy, Southern France, Okinawa.
Submarine sunk: **U-575* north of Azores, 13 Mar 1944.

DD 483 *Aaron Ward* Damaged by nine hits from naval gunfire, Battle of Guadalcanal, 13 Nov 1942 (15 killed). Hit by aircraft bomb and near misses off Guadalcanal and sank in tow, 7 Apr 1943 (27 killed).
2* Battle of Guadalcanal, Solomons.

DD 484 *Buchanan* Damaged in error by gunfire of U.S. warships, Battle of Guadalcanal, 12 Nov 1942 (5 killed). Ran aground off Guadalcanal, 30 Apr 1943. Damaged in collision with destroyer *Woodworth*, off Kolombangara, 13 Jul 1943. Damaged by two hits by coastal gunfire, Kavieng, New Ireland, 24 Feb 1944. Damaged in typhoon, Philippine Sea, 18 Dec 1944. Decomm 21 May 1946. †
16* Guadalcanal-Tulagi, Cape Esperance, Battle of Guadalcanal, Solomons, New Georgia, Kolombangara, Green I. Ldgs., Rabaul and Kavieng Bombard., Buka Raid, 1st Rabaul Raid, Palau, Philippines Raids 9/44, Luzon Raids 10/44, Luzon Raids 1/45, Formosa Raids 1/45, China Coast Raids 1/45, Iwo Jima, Okinawa, Raids on Japan 7–8/45. PUC.
Submarine sunk: *Ro-37* 130 miles southeast of San Cristobal, 22 Jan 1944.

DD 485 *Duncan* Sunk by at least 14 hits of gunfire from Japanese warships, Battle of Cape Esperance, 12 Oct 1942 (48 killed).
1* Cape Esperance.

DD 486 *Lansdowne* Decomm 2 May 1946. †
12* Solomons, Okinawa, Raids on Japan 7–8/45, Attu; Buka Raid, 1st Rabaul Raid, 2nd Rabaul Raid, Cape Torokina, Green I. Ldgs., Rabaul and Kavieng Bombard., Palau-Yap Raids 3/44, Saipan, 1st Bonins Raid, Philippine Sea, Guam, Tinian. Tokyo Bay.
Submarine sunk: *U-153* off Colon, Panama, 13 Jul 1942.

DD 487 *Lardner* Ran aground off Palau Is., 29 Jan 1945. Decomm 16 May 1946. †

10* Tassafaronga, Solomons, Buka Raid, 1st Rabaul Raid, 2nd Rabaul Raid, Cape Torokina, Green I. Ldgs., Rabaul and Kavieng Bombard., Palau-Yap Raids 3/44, Saipan, 1st Bonins Raid, Philippine Sea, Guam, Tinian, Solomons, Okinawa, Raids on Japan 7–8/45. Tokyo Bay.

DD 488 *McCalla* Damaged in collision with destroyer *Patterson*, south of Choiseul I., Solomons, 29 Sep 1943. Decomm 17 May 1946. †
10* Cape Esperance, Guadalcanal, Battle of Guadalcanal, Solomons, New Georgia, Saipan, 1st Bonins Raid, Philippine Sea, Guam, 4th Bonins Raid, Palau, Philippines Raids 9/44, Morotai, Okinawa Raid 10/44, N. Luzon–Formosa Raids 10/44, Luzon Raids 10/44, Ldgs. on Palawan I., Raids on Japan 7–8/45.
Submarine sunk: *I-15* southwest of San Cristobal, 2 Nov 1942.

DD 489 *Mervine* Converted to minesweeper and rec **DMS 31**, 30 May 1945. †
3* North Africa, Sicily, Convoy KMF-25A, Minesweeping 1945.

DD 490 *Quick* Converted to minesweeper and rec **DMS 32**, 23 Jun 1945. †
4* North Africa, Sicily, Minesweeping 1945.
Submarine sunk: **U-173* off Casablanca, 16 Nov 1942.

DD 493 *Carmick* Struck submerged object north of Boston, 16 Jun 1943. Converted to minesweeper and rec **DMS 33**, 23 Jun 1945. †
3* Normandy, Southern France, Minesweeping 1945.

DD 494 *Doyle* Converted to minesweeper and rec **DMS 34**, 23 Jun 1945. †
2* Normandy, Southern France.

DD 495 *Endicott* Damaged in collision with m/v *Exhibitor* off British coast, 24 May 1944. Sank German corvette *UJ-6081* off La Ciotat, France, 17 Aug 1944. Converted to minesweeper and rec **DMS 35**, 30 May 1945. †
2* Southern France, Minesweeping 1945.

DD 496 *McCook* Damaged by two near misses in air Raid at Weymouth, England, 28 May 1944. Converted to minesweeper and rec **DMS 36**, 30 May 1945. Damaged in typhoon at Wakamiya, Japan, 14 Dec 1945. †
3* Normandy, Southern France, Minesweeping 1945.

DD 497 *Frankford* Sank three enemy boats off Southern France, 18 Aug 1944. Decomm 4 Mar 1946. †
2* Normandy, Southern France.

No.	Name	Builder	Keel Laid	Launched	Comm.
DD 618	*Davison*	Federal	26 Feb 1942	19 Jul 1942	11 Sep 1942
DD 619	*Edwards*	Federal	26 Feb 1942	19 Jul 1942	18 Sep 1942
DD 620	*Glennon*	Federal	25 Mar 1942	26 Aug 1942	8 Oct 1942
DD 621	*Jeffers*	Federal	25 Mar 1942	26 Aug 1942	5 Nov 1942
DD 622	*Maddox*	Federal	7 May 1942	15 Sep 1942	31 Oct 1942
DD 623	*Nelson*	Federal	7 May 1942	15 Sep 1942	26 Nov 1942
DD 624	*Baldwin*	Sea-Tac Seattle	19 Jul 1941	14 Jun 1942	30 Apr 1943
DD 625	*Harding*	Sea-Tac Seattle	22 Jul 1941	28 Jun 1942	25 May 1943
DD 626	*Satterlee*	Sea-Tac Seattle	10 Sep 1941	17 Jul 1942	1 Jul 1943
DD 627	*Thompson*	Sea-Tac Seattle	22 Sep 1941	10 Aug 1942	10 Jul 1943
DD 628	*Welles*	Sea-Tac Seattle	27 Sep 1941	7 Sep 1942	16 Aug 1943
DD 632	*Cowie*	Boston NYd	18 Mar 1941	27 Sep 1941	1 Jun 1942
DD 633	*Knight*	Boston NYd	18 Mar 1941	27 Sep 1941	23 Jun 1942
DD 634	*Doran*	Boston NYd	14 Jun 1941	10 Dec 1941	4 Aug 1942
DD 635	*Earle*	Boston NYd	14 Jun 1941	10 Dec 1941	1 Sep 1942
DD 636	*Butler*	Phila. NYd	16 Sep 1941	12 Feb 1942	15 Aug 1942
DD 637	*Gherardi*	Phila. NYd	16 Sep 1941	12 Feb 1942	15 Sep 1942
DD 638	*Herndon*	Norfolk NYd	26 Aug 1941	2 Feb 1942	20 Dec 1942
DD 639	*Shubrick*	Norfolk NYd	17 Feb 1942	18 Apr 1942	7 Feb 1943
DD 640	*Beatty*	Charleston NYd	1 May 1941	20 Dec 1941	7 May 1942
DD 641	*Tillman*	Charleston NYd	1 May 1941	20 Dec 1941	4 Jun 1942
DD 645	*Stevenson*	Federal	23 Jul 1942	11 Nov 1942	15 Dec 1942
DD 646	*Stockton*	Federal	24 Jul 1942	11 Nov 1942	11 Jan 1943
DD 647	*Thorn*	Federal	15 Nov 1942	28 Feb 1943	1 Apr 1943
DD 648	*Turner*	Federal	15 Nov 1942	28 Feb 1943	15 Apr 1943

Figure 4.31: *Earle* (DD 635), of the *Livermore* class, later in the war.

Service Records:

DD 618 *Davison* Converted to minesweeper and rec **DMS 37**, 23 Jun 1945. †
3* Sicily, Convoy KMF-25A, Minesweeping 1945.

DD 619 *Edwards* Decomm 11 Apr 1946. †
14* Rennell I., Attu, Wake I. Raid 1943; Buka Raid, 1st Rabaul Raid, 2nd Rabaul Raid, Gilbert Is., Hollandia, Palau-Yap Raids 3/44, Truk Raid 4/44, Saipan, Palau, Ormoc, Lingayen, Mindanao Ldgs.
Submarine sunk: **I-31* off Attu, 27 Apr 1943 (possible).

DD 620 *Glennon* Damaged by mine off Utah Beach, Normandy, 8 Jun, grounded, and sunk by 11 hits from shore batteries, 10 Jun 1944 (25 killed).
2* Sicily, Normandy.

DD 621 *Jeffers* Converted to minesweeper and rec **DMS 27**, 15 Nov 1944. Damaged by kamikaze and piloted bomb, Okinawa, 12 Apr 1945. †
7* Tunisia, Sicily, Normandy, Southern France, Okinawa, Raids on Japan 7–8/45, Minesweeping 1945. Tokyo Bay.

DD 622 *Maddox* Sunk by German dive bomber with two bombs off Gela, Sicily, capsized, 10 Jul 1943 (211 killed).
2* Sicily.

DD 623 *Nelson* Severely damaged by MTB torpedo, Normandy, lost stern, 12 Jun 1944 (24 killed). Decomm 6 May 1946. †
2* Sicily, Normandy.

DD 624 *Baldwin* Decomm 20 Jun 1946. †
3* Normandy, Southern France, Minesweeping 1945.

DD 625 *Harding* Damaged by grounding, Normandy, 7 Jun 1944. Sank three enemy boats off Southern France, 18 Aug 1944. Converted to minesweeper and rec **DMS 28**, 15 Nov 1944. Damaged by aircraft bomb near miss, Okinawa, 6 Apr 1945. Damaged by kamikaze, Okinawa, 16 Apr 1945 (22 killed). Decomm 2 Nov 1945. Stricken 16 Nov 1945. Sold 14 Apr 1947; BU.
3* Normandy, Southern France, Okinawa.

DD 626 *Satterlee* Decomm 16 Mar 1946. †
2* Normandy, Southern France.

DD 627 *Thompson* Converted to minesweeper and rec **DMS 38**, 30 May 1945.
3* Normandy, Southern France, Minesweeping 1945. †

DD 628 *Welles* Decomm 4 Feb 1946. †
8* Cape Gloucester, Admiralty Is., Hollandia, Biak, Noemfoor I., Cape Sansapor, Palau, Leyte, Surigao Strait, Luzon Raids 10/44, Formosa Raids 1/45, Luzon Raids 1/45, China Coast Raids 1/45, Nansei Shoto Raid 1/45, Iwo Jima, Fleet Raids 1945, Okinawa.

DD 632 *Cowie* Converted to minesweeper and rec **DMS 39**, 30 May 1945. Decomm 21 Apr 1947. †
3* North Africa, Sicily, Minesweeping 1945.

DD 633 *Knight* Converted to minesweeper and rec **DMS 40**, 30 May 1945. Decomm 19 Mar 1947. †
4* North Africa, Sicily, Salerno, Minesweeping 1945.

DD 634 *Doran* Converted to minesweeper and rec **DMS 41**, 30 May 1945. Decomm 29 Jan 1947. †
3* North Africa, Sicily, Minesweeping 1945.

DD 635 *Earle* Converted to minesweeper and rec **DMS 42**, 30 May 1945. Decomm 17 May 1947. †
2* Sicily, Minesweeping.

DD 636 *Butler* Converted to minesweeper and rec **DMS 29**, 15 Nov 1944. Damaged by kamikaze, Okinawa, 28 Apr 1945 (9 killed). Damaged by aircraft bombs, Okinawa, 24 May 1945 (9 killed). Decomm 8 Nov 1945. Stricken 28 Nov 1945, sold 10 Jan 1948; BU.
4* Sicily, Salerno, Southern France, Okinawa.

DD 637 *Gherardi* Converted to minesweeper and rec **DMS 30**, 15 Nov 1944. †
5* Sicily, Normandy, Southern France, Okinawa, Raids on Japan 7–8/45, Minesweeping 1945. Tokyo Bay.

DD 638 *Herndon* Decomm 8 May 1946. †
3* Sicily, Normandy, Southern France.

DD 639 *Shubrick* Damaged by German aircraft bomb at Palermo, 4 Aug 1943 (17 killed). Severely damaged by kamikaze, Okinawa, 28 May 1945 (35 killed). Decomm 16 Nov 1945, not repaired. Stricken 28 Nov 1945, sold 28 Sep 1947; BU.
4* Sicily, Normandy, Southern France, Okinawa.

DD 640 *Beatty* Torpedoed and sunk by German aircraft off Philippeville, Algeria, broke in two, 6 Nov 1943 (11 killed).
2* North Africa, Sicily, Convoy KMF-25A.

DD 641 *Tillman* Decomm 6 Feb 1947. †
3* North Africa, Sicily, Convoy KMF-25A.

DD 645 *Stevenson* In collision with m/v *Berwindvale* off Newport, R.I., 12 Apr 1943. Decomm 27 Apr 1946. †
7* Admiralty I., Hollandia, Wakde, Biak, Noemfoor I., Cape Sansapor, Palau, Iwo Jima, Fleet Raids 1945, Raids on Japan 7–8/45.

DD 646 *Stockton* Slight damage by one hit from coastal gunfire, Biak, 28 May 1944. Decomm 16 May 1946. †
8* Admiralty Is., Hollandia, Wakde, Biak, Noemfoor I., Cape Sansapor, Palau, Iwo Jima, Fleet Raids 1945, Okinawa, Raids on Japan 7–8/45.
Submarine sunk: **I-8* off Okinawa, 31 Mar 1945.

DD 647 *Thorn* Struck uncharted reef in Admiralty Is., 10 Apr 1944. Decomm 6 May 1946. †
7* Admiralty Is., Palau, Leyte, Surigao Strait, Luzon Raids 10/44, Formosa Raids 1/45, Luzon Raids 1/45, China Coast Raids 1/45, Nansei Shoto Raid 1/45, Iwo Jima, Fleet Raids 1945, Okinawa, Raids on Japan 7–8/45.

DD 648 *Turner* Sank or damaged a U-boat in North Atlantic, convoy GUS-18, 23 Oct 1943. Sunk by internal ammunition explosion off Ambrose Light, N.Y., 3 Jan 1944 (153 killed).

Percival Class

No.	Name	Builder	Keel Laid	Launched	Comm.
DD 452	*Percival*	Federal	—	—	—
DD 482	*Watson*	Federal	—	—	—

Machinery	DD 452: 4 GE GT; 4 B&W boilers; DD 482: GM diesel-electric; HP 60,000 .

Notes: Experimental types: DD 452 *Percival* with high-pressure boilers; DD 453 *Watson* all diesel machinery. *Percival*'s machinery used in DD 828. Never laid down. Canceled 7 Jan 1946.

Stevenson Class

No.	Name	Builder	Keel Laid	Launched	Comm.
DD 503	*Stevenson*	Federal	—	—	—
DD 504	*Stockton*	Federal	—	—	—
DD 505	*Thorn*	Federal	—	—	—
DD 506	*Turner*	Federal	—	—	—

Displacement	1,175 tons
Dimensions	300' x 34'6" x 9'9"
Machinery	SHP 12,000; 24.5 knots
Endurance	5,000/15
Armament	4–5"/38, 8–1.1" AA

Notes: Experimental forerunner of the DE design. Canceled 10 Feb 1941.

Fletcher Class

No.	Name	Builder	Keel Laid	Launched	Comm.
DD 445	*Fletcher*	Federal	2 Oct 1941	3 May 1942	30 Jun 1942
DD 446	*Radford*	Federal	2 Oct 1941	3 May 1942	22 Jul 1942
DD 447	*Jenkins*	Federal	27 Nov 1941	21 Jun 1942	31 Jul 1942
DD 448	*La Vallette*	Federal	27 Nov 1941	21 Jun 1942	12 Aug 1942
DD 449	*Nicholas*	Bath	3 Mar 1941	19 Feb 1942	4 Jun 1942
DD 450	*O'Bannon*	Bath	3 Mar 1941	14 Mar 1942	26 Jun 1942
DD 451	*Chevalier*	Bath	30 Apr 1941	11 Apr 1942	20 Jul 1942
DD 465	*Saufley*	Federal	27 Jan 1942	19 Jul 1942	29 Aug 1942
DD 466	*Waller*	Federal	12 Feb 1942	15 Aug 1942	1 Oct 1942
DD 467	*Strong*	Bath	30 Apr 1941	17 May 1942	7 Aug 1942
DD 468	*Taylor*	Bath	28 Aug 1941	7 Jun 1942	28 Aug 1942
DD 469	*De Haven*	Bath	27 Sep 1941	28 Jun 1942	21 Sep 1942

Figure 4.32: *Hazelwood* (DD 531), 24 Jun 1943, as completed; this is a typical *Fletcher*-class configuration.

Figure 4.33: *Halford* (DD 480), 25 Apr 1943, as completed with experimental catapult, which was removed later.

DD 470	*Bache*	Beth. Staten I.	19 Nov 1941	7 Jul 1942	14 Nov 1942
DD 471	*Beale*	Beth. Staten I.	19 Dec 1941	24 Aug 1942	23 Dec 1942
DD 472	*Guest*	Boston NYd	27 Sep 1941	20 Feb 1942	15 Dec 1942
DD 473	*Bennett*	Boston NYd	10 Dec 1941	16 Apr 1942	9 Feb 1943
DD 474	*Fullam*	Boston NYd	10 Dec 1941	16 Apr 1942	2 Mar 1943
DD 475	*Hudson*	Boston NYd	20 Feb 1942	3 Jun 1942	13 Apr 1943
DD 476	*Hutchins*	Boston NYd	27 Sep 1941	20 Feb 1942	17 Nov 1942

Displacement	2,050 tons; 2.750 f/l
Dimensions	376'5" (oa); 369' (wl) x 39'7" x 17'9"
Machinery	2 screws; GT; 4 B&W boilers; SHP 60,000; 37.8 knots
Endurance	6,500/18
Complement	329
Armament	5–5"/38, 2–40mm, 6–20mm AA guns, 2 quint 21" TT; (1945) 5–5"/38, 4 to 5 twin 40mm, 6 to 11 20mm guns, 2 quint 21" TT

Notes: First destroyers designed without treaty restrictions. Very successful design, flush hull, broad beam. Earlier units had rounded bridges, later ones squared off design.

DD 476–81 were planned with a catapult in place of the after TT and no. 3 gun, but only three (*Pringle, Stevens* and *Halford*) so completed. Results were disappointing, and they were reconverted to original design in Oct 1943.

Fifty-three units (DD 445–48, 473, 478, 499, 502, 520, 521, 528, 530, 531, 534–39, 541, 550, 554, 556, 563, 577, 578, 580, 581, 583, 586, 589, 590, 592, 643, 657, 661, 665, 668–76, 681, 682, 685, 686, 800, 802, 804) modernized 1945 with increased AA.

Service Records:

DD 445 *Fletcher* Damaged by one hit from coastal gunfire at Mariveles, Luzon, 14 Feb 1945 (8 killed). Decomm 15 Jan 1947. †
15* Battle of Guadalcanal, Tassafaronga, Solomons, Gilbert Is., Kwajalein, Eniwetok, Hollandia, Biak, Noemfoor I., Cape Sansapor, Leyte, Ormoc, Mindoro, Lingayen, Tarakan, Ldgs. on Palawan I., Subic Bay, Ldgs. at Nasugbu, Mariveles-Corregidor.
Submarine sunk: **I-18* 200 miles south of San Cristobal, 11 Feb 1943.

DD 446 *Radford* Moderate damage by mine, at Mariveles, Luzon, 14 Feb 1945 (3 killed). Decomm 17 Jan 1946. †
12* Solomons, New Georgia, Kula Gulf, Kolombangara, Gilbert Is., Kwajalein, Hollandia, Biak, Noemfoor I., Cape Sansapor, Mindoro, Lingayen, Mariveles-Corregidor, Subic Bay. PUC.
Submarine sunk: *I-19* (or *I-40*) west of Makin I., 25 Nov 1943.

DD 447 *Jenkins* Damaged by shore gunfire at Lingayen, 9 Jan 1945. Moderate damage by mine off Tarakan, Borneo, 30 Apr 1945. Decomm 1 May 1946. †
14* North Africa, Casablanca, Solomons, New Georgia, Kula Gulf, Kolombangara, Gilbert Is., Kwajalein, Hollandia, Biak, Noemfoor I., Cape Sansapor, Morotai, Solomons, Leyte, Lingayen, Tarakan, Ldgs. on Palawan I., Mariveles-Corregidor.
Submarine sunk: **RO-115* 125 miles southwest of Manila, 31 Jan 1945.

DD 448 *La Vallette* Torpedoed by Japanese aircraft off Rennell I., 30 Jan 1943 (22 killed). Severely damaged by mine in Mariveles harbor, Luzon, 14 Feb 1945 (6 killed). Decomm 16 Apr 1946. †
10* Rennell I., Marcus I. Raid 1943, Gilbert Is., Kwajalein, Eniwetok, Hollandia, Biak, Noemfoor I., Cape Sansapor, Morotai, Leyte, Mindoro, Lingayen, Mariveles-Corregidor.

DD 449 *Nicholas* Damaged by accidental gun explosion off Kolombangara, Solomons, 13 May 1943. Decomm 12 Jun 1946. †
16* Solomons, New Georgia, Kula Gulf, Kolombangara, Vella Lavella, Gilbert Is., Hollandia, Morotai, Leyte, Ormoc, Lingayen, Mariveles-Corregidor, Visayan Is. Ldgs., Tarakan, Fleet Raids 1945, Raids on Japan 7–8/45. PUC. Tokyo Bay.
Submarines sunk: *I-11* east of Marshall Is., 17 Feb 1944.(Possible)*: I-38* near Ngulu I., 85 miles south of Yap I., 12 Nov 1944.

DD 450 *O'Bannon* Minor damage in error by U.S. gunfire, Battle of Guadalcanal, 13 Nov 1942. Damaged in collision with destroyer *Chevalier*, Battle of Vella Lavella, 6 Oct 1943. Decomm 21 May 1946. †
17* Battle of Guadalcanal, Solomons, New Georgia, Kula Gulf, Kolombangara, Rennell I., Vella Lavella, Vella Lavella, Hollandia, Morotai, Leyte, Ormoc, Mindoro, Lingayen, Mariveles-Corregidor, Ldgs. on Palawan, Tarakan, Fleet Raids 1945, Raids on Japan 7–8/45. PUC.
Submarines sunk: *RO-34* off Russell I., 5 Apr 1943; **RO-115* 125 miles southwest of Manila, 31 Jan 1945.

DD 451 *Chevalier* Damaged by Japanese destroyers off Bairoko, 5 Jul 1943. Torpedoed by Japanese destroyer *Yugumo* off Vella Lavella, 6 Oct 1943, rammed by *O'Bannon* and sunk by U.S. destroyer on 7 Oct (54 killed).
3* Rennell I., Solomons, New Georgia, Vella Lavella.

DD 465 *Saufley* Damaged by three aircraft bomb near misses, Vella Lavella, Solomons, 1 Oct 1943 (2 killed). Damaged by two kamikazes and near misses, Leyte, 29 Nov 1944 (1 killed). Decomm 12 Jun 1946. †
16* Solomons, Tinian, New Georgia, Vella Lavella, Treasury Is. Ldgs., Cape Torokina, Green I. Ldgs., Saipan, Guam, Lingayen, Balikpapan, Subic Bay, Ldgs. at Nasugbu, Mindanao Ldgs., Mariveles-Corregidor, Minesweeping 1945.
Submarines sunk: *RO-101* 100 miles east of San Cristobal, 15 Sep 1943; *I-2* northwest of New Hanover I., 7 Apr 1944.

DD 466 *Waller* Damaged in collision with destroyer *Philip* off Vella Lavella, 17 Aug 1943. Minor damage by mine off Shanghai, 9 Oct 1945. Decomm 10 Jun 1946. †
12* Rennell I., Solomons, New Georgia, Vella Lavella, Treasury Is. Ldgs., Cape Torokina, Green I. Ldgs., Saipan, Guam, Tinian, Lingayen, Ldgs. on Palawan I., Mindanao Ldgs., Tarakan, Balikpapan, Raids on Japan 7–8/45, Minesweeping 1945.
Submarine sunk: **I-46* off Leyte, 28 Nov 1944 (possible).

DD 467 *Strong* Torpedoed and sunk by Japanese destroyers off Bairoko, 5 Jul 1943 (46 killed).
2* Solomons, New Georgia.
Submarine sunk: **RO-34* off Kolombangara, 5 Apr 1943 (not confirmed).

DD 468 *Taylor* Damaged in error by gunfire from cruiser *Oakland*, Marshall Is., 4 Dec 1943. Decomm 31 May 1946. †
15* Rennell I., Solomons, New Georgia, Kolombangara, Vella Lavella, Gilbert Is., Hollandia, Morotai, Morotai, Leyte, Lingayen, Mariveles-Corregidor, Visayan Is. Ldgs., Mindanao Ldgs., Tarakan, Okinawa, Raids on Japan 7–8/45. Tokyo Bay.
Submarines sunk: *RO-107* off Kolombangara, 12 Jul 1943 (probable): *RO-111* 200 miles northwest of Kavieng, 10 Jun 1944.

DD 469 *De Haven* Sunk by three aircraft bombs off Cape Esperance, 1 Feb 1943 (167 killed).
1* Guadalcanal. †

DD 470 *Bache* Severely damaged by kamikaze, Okinawa, 13 May 1945 (41 killed). Decomm 4 Feb 1946. †
8* Attu, Cape Gloucester, Saidor, Admiralty Is., Hollandia, Wakde, Biak, Noemfoor I., Wewak-Aitape, Cape Sansapor, Leyte, Surigao Strait, Iwo Jima, Okinawa.

DD 471 *Beale* Damaged in collision with oiler *Yahara*, Okinawa, 6 Jun 1945. Decomm 11 Apr 1946. †
6* Cape Gloucester, Saidor, Admiralty Is., Hollandia, Wakde, Biak, Noemfoor I., Wewak-Aitape, Cape Sansapor, Morotai, Surigao Strait, Okinawa, Raids on Japan 7–8/45.

DD 472 *Guest* Slightly damaged by kamikaze, Okinawa, 24 May 1945. Decomm 4 Jun 1946. †
8* Cape Torokina, Solomons, Green I. Ldgs., Saipan, Guam, Palau, Philippines Raids 9/44, Iwo Jima, Okinawa.
Submarine sunk: **I-171* west of Buka I., 1 Feb 1944 (not confirmed).

DD 473 *Bennett* Minor damage by aircraft bomb, Iwo Jima, 28 Feb 1945. Severely damaged by kamikaze, Okinawa, 7 Apr 1945 (3 killed). Decomm 18 Apr 1946. †
9* Solomons, Cape Torokina, Green I. Ldgs., Rabaul and Kavieng Bombard., Guam, Palau, Iwo Jima, Okinawa.

DD 474 *Fullam* Damaged by grounding off Cape Torokina, Solomons, 1 Nov 1943. Damaged in collision with transport *Noa* which sank, off Palau, 12 Sep 1944. Decomm 15 Jan 1947. †
7* Solomons, Cape Torokina, Green I. Ldgs., Saipan, Guam, Palau, Philippines Raids 9/44, Iwo Jima, Okinawa.

DD 475 *Hudson* Damaged in error by U.S. fire, west of Guam, Philippine Sea, 19 Jun 1944. Slight damage by kamikaze, Okinawa, 22 Apr 1945. Damaged in collision, Okinawa, while assisting burning carrier *Sangamon*, 4 May 1945. Decomm 31 May 1946. †
9* Cape Torokina, Green I. Ldgs., Saipan, Guam, Palau.
Submarines sunk: **I-171* west of Buka I., 1 Feb 1944 (not confirmed); *RO-49* west of Okinawa, 5 Apr 1945.

DD 476 *Hutchins* Damaged by gun misfire while testing guns at Pearl Harbor, 23 Jun 1943 (9 killed). Damaged in collision with destroyer *Smith*, off Saidor, New Guinea, 1 Jan 1944. Damaged by kamikaze, Okinawa, 6 Apr 1945. Moderate damage by suicide boat/depth charges off Okinawa, 27 Apr 1945. Decomm 30 Nov 1945. Stricken 19 Dec 1945, sold 10 Jan 1948; BU Oakland.
6* Cape Gloucester, Saidor, Admiralty Is., Wakde, Biak, Noemfoor I., Wewak-Aitape, Cape Sansapor, Morotai, Leyte, Surigao Strait, Iwo Jima, Okinawa.

No.	Name	Builder	Keel Laid	Launched	Comm.
DD 477	*Pringle*	Charleston NYd	31 Jul 1941	2 May 1942	15 Sep 1942
DD 478	*Stanly*	Charleston NYd	15 Sep 1941	2 May 1942	15 Oct 1942
DD 479	*Stevens*	Charleston NYd	30 Dec 1941	24 Jun 1942	1 Feb 1943
DD 480	*Halford*	Puget Sd NYd	3 Jun 1941	29 Oct 1942	10 Apr 1943
DD 481	*Leutze*	Puget Sd NYd	3 Jun 1941	29 Oct 1942	4 Mar 1944
DD 498	*Philip*	Federal	7 May 1942	13 Oct 1942	21 Nov 1942
DD 499	*Renshaw*	Federal	7 May 1942	13 Oct 1942	5 Dec 1942
DD 500	*Ringgold*	Federal	25 Jun 1942	11 Nov 1942	30 Dec 1942
DD 501	*Schroeder*	Federal	25 Jun 1942	11 Nov 1942	1 Jan 1943
DD 502	*Sigsbee*	Federal	22 Jul 1942	7 Dec 1942	23 Jan 1943
DD 507	*Conway*	Bath	5 Nov 1941	16 Aug 1942	9 Oct 1942
DD 508	*Cony*	Bath	24 Dec 1941	30 Aug 1942	30 Oct 1942
DD 509	*Converse*	Bath	23 Feb 1942	30 Aug 1942	20 Nov 1942
DD 510	*Eaton*	Bath	17 Mar 1942	20 Sep 1942	4 Dec 1942
DD 511	*Foote*	Bath	14 Apr 1942	11 Oct 1942	22 Dec 1942
DD 512	*Spence*	Bath	18 May 1942	27 Oct 1942	8 Jan 1943
DD 513	*Terry*	Bath	8 Jun 1942	22 Nov 1942	27 Jan 1943
DD 514	*Thatcher*	Bath	29 Jun 1942	6 Dec 1942	10 Feb 1943
DD 515	*Anthony*	Bath	17 Aug 1942	20 Dec 1942	26 Feb 1943
DD 516	*Wadsworth*	Bath	18 Aug 1942	10 Jan 1943	16 Mar 1943
DD 517	*Walker*	Bath	31 Aug 1942	31 Jan 1943	3 Apr 1943
DD 518	*Brownson*	Beth. Staten I.	15 Feb 1942	24 Sep 1942	3 Feb 1943
DD 519	*Daly*	Beth. Staten I.	29 Apr 1942	24 Oct 1942	10 Mar 1943
DD 520	*Isherwood*	Beth. Staten I.	12 May 1942	24 Nov 1942	12 Apr 1943
DD 521	*Kimberly*	Beth. Staten I.	27 Jul 1942	4 Feb 1943	22 May 1943
DD 522	*Luce*	Beth. Staten I.	24 Aug 1942	6 Mar 1943	21 Jun 1943
DD 523/524/525	—	Beth. Staten I.	—	—	—

Service Records:

DD 477 *Pringle* Slight damage by kamikaze, south of Mindoro, 30 Dec 1944. Sunk by kamikaze off Okinawa, broke in two, 16 Apr 1945 (65 killed).
10* Solomons, New Georgia, Vella Lavella, Treasury Is. Ldgs., Cape Torokina, Green I. Ldgs., Saipan, Tinian, Guam, Mindoro, Iwo Jima, Okinawa.

DD 478 *Stanly* Damaged by piloted (Baka) bomb, Okinawa, 12 Apr 1945. Decomm Oct 1945. †
9* Solomons, Buka Bombard., Shortland Is. Raid, Empress Augusta Bay, Cape Torokina, Rabaul and Kavieng Bombard., Palau-Yap Raids 3/44, Saipan, 1st Bonins Raid, Philippine Sea, Guam, Tinian, Mindoro, Iwo Jima, Okinawa. PUC.

DD 479 *Stevens* Decomm 2 Jul 1946. †
9* Marcus I. Raid 1943, Tarawa Raid, Wake I. Raid 1943, Kwajalein, Hollandia, Guam, Morotai, Leyte, Mindoro, Mindanao Ldgs., Brunei, Balikpapan.

DD 480 *Halford* Decomm 15 May 1946. †
13* Solomons, Green I. Ldgs., Marcus I. Raid 1943, Wake I. Raid 1943, Saipan, Guam, Palau, Leyte, Surigao Strait, Ormoc, Mindoro, Lingayen.

DD 481 *Leutze* Damaged by aircraft bombs, Leyte Gulf, 24 Oct 1944. Minor damage by one hit from coastal gunfire, Iwo Jima, 17 Feb 1945. Severely damaged by kamikaze, Okinawa, 6 Apr 1945 (8 killed). Decomm 6 Dec 1945, unrepaired. Stricken 3 Jan 1946, sold 11 Feb 1947; BU Bordentown, N.J.
5* Palau, Leyte, Surigao Strait, Lingayen, Iwo Jima, Okinawa.

DD 498 *Philip* Damaged in collision with destroyer *Waller* off Vella Lavella, 17 Aug 1943. Decomm Jan 1947. †
9* New Georgia, Vella Lavella, Solomons, Treasury Is. Ldgs., Cape Torokina, Green I. Ldgs., Saipan, Tinian, Mindoro, Lingayen, Mindanao Ldgs., Brunei, Tarakan, Balikpapan.

DD 499 *Renshaw* Torpedoed by submarine *RO-43* in Mindanao Sea, severely damaged, 21 Feb 1945 (19 killed). Decomm Feb 1947. †
8* Solomons, New Georgia, Vella Lavella, Treasury Is. Ldgs., Cape Torokina, Green I. Ldgs., Saipan, Guam, Tinian, Lingayen.

DD 500 *Ringgold* Slight damage by coastal batteries, Tarawa, 20 Nov 1943. In collision with destroyer *Yarnall* northwest of Ulithi, Micronesia, 3 Mar 1945. Decomm 23 Mar 1946. †
10* Marcus I. Raid 1943, Tarawa Raid, Wake I. Raid 1943, Gilbert Is., Kwajalein, Eniwetok, Hollandia, Guam, Morotai, Leyte, Honshu Raids 2/45, Iwo Jima, Fleet Raids 1945, Raids on Japan 7–8/45.

DD 501 *Schroeder* Damaged in typhoon, Philippine Sea, 5 Jun 1945. Decomm 29 Apr 1946. †
10* Marcus I. Raid 1943, Wake I. Raid 1943, Gilbert Is., Kwajalein, Hollandia, Guam, Morotai, Leyte, Honshu Raids 2/45, Iwo Jima, Fleet Raids 1945, Raids on Japan 7–8/45.

DD 502 *Sigsbee* Severely damaged by kamikaze, Okinawa, 14 Apr 1945 (23 killed). Decomm 1 May 1946. †
10* Marcus I. Raid 1943, Wake I. Raid 1943, Gilbert Is., Kwajalein, Hollandia, Guam, Morotai, Lingayen, Leyte, Honshu Raids 2/45, Iwo Jima, Fleet Raids 1945.

DD 507 *Conway* Decomm 25 Jun 1946. †
11* Rennell I., Solomons, New Georgia, Vella Lavella, Treasury Is. Ldgs., Ldgs. on Choiseul, Cape Torokina, Green I. Ldgs., Saipan, Guam, Lingayen, Mariveles-Corregidor, Mindanao Ldgs., Visayan Is. Ldgs., Brunei.

DD 508 *Cony* Damaged by two aircraft bombs off Treasury Is., 27 Oct 1943 (8 killed). Decomm 18 Jun 1946. †
11* Solomons, Vella Lavella, Treasury Is. Ldgs., Saipan, Tinian, Palau, Leyte, Surigao Strait, Lingayen, Mindanao Ldgs., Brunei, Balikpapan, Minesweeping 1945.

DD 509 *Converse* Decomm 23 Apr 1946. †
11* Solomons, Buka Bombard., Shortland Is. Raid, Empress Augusta Bay, Cape Torokina, Cape St. George, Rabaul and Kavieng Bombard., Palau-Yap Raids 3/44, Hollandia, Truk Raid 4/44, Saipan, 1st Bonins Raid, Philippine Sea, Guam, Tinian, Mariveles-Corregidor, Leyte, Lingayen, Okinawa. PUC.

DD 510 *Eaton* Decomm 21 Jun 1946. †
11* Solomons, Vella Lavella, Treasury Is. Ldgs., Cape Torokina, Green I. Ldgs., Saipan, Tinian, Lingayen, Mindanao Ldgs., Mariveles-Corregidor, Brunei, Balikpapan.
Submarine sunk: *I-20* off Vella Lavella, ?1 Oct 1943 (possible).

DD 511 *Foote* Torpedoed by Japanese destroyer in Battle of Empress Augusta Bay, lost stern, 2 Nov 1943 (3 killed). Slightly damaged by kamikaze near miss, Mindoro, 21 Dec 1944. Decomm 18 Apr 1946. †
4* Cape Torokina; Buka Bombard., Shortland Is. Raid, Empress Augusta Bay, Leyte, Lingayen, Okinawa.

DD 512 *Spence* Damaged by gunfire and collision with destroyer *Thatcher* in Battle of Empress Augusta Bay, 2 Nov 1943. Foundered in typhoon in Philippine Sea, 18 Dec 1944 (~300 killed; 24 survivors).
8* Cape Torokina; Buka Raid, Solomons, Shortland Is. Raid, Empress Augusta Bay, Cape St. George, Rabaul and Kavieng Bombard., Palau-Yap Raids 3/44, Hollandia, Truk Raid 4/44, Saipan, 1st Bonins Raid, Philippine Sea, Guam, Tinian, Luzon Raids 10/44.

DD 513 *Terry* Minor damage by coastal gunfire, Iwo Jima, 1 Mar 1945 (11 killed). Decomm Jan 1947. †
7* Vella Lavella, Solomons, Cape Torokina, Green I. Ldgs., Saipan, Guam, Philippine Sea, Iwo Jima, Raids on Japan 7–8/45.

DD 514 *Thatcher* Damaged in collision with destroyer *Spence* at Battle of Empress Augusta Bay, 2 Nov 1943. Damaged by two kamikazes, Okinawa, 20 May 1945 (14 killed), and hit again, 19 Jul 1945. Decomm 23 Nov 1945. Stricken 5 Dec 1945. Sold 28 Jan 1948; BU.
12* Marcus I. Raid 1943; Buka Bombard., Palau-Yap Raids 3/44, Hollandia, Truk Raid 4/44, Saipan, 1st Bonins Raid, Philippine Sea, Guam, Tinian, Palau, Philippines Raids 9/44, Luzon Raids 10/44, Formosa Raids 1/45, Luzon Raids 1/45, Formosa Raids 1/45, China Coast Raids 1/45, Nansei Shoto Raid 1/45, Visayan Is. Ldgs., Mariveles-Corregidor, Okinawa.

DD 515 *Anthony* Moderate damage by kamikaze, Okinawa, 27 May 1945 (66 killed). Decomm 17 Apr 1946. †
7* Solomons, Green I. Ldgs., Cape Torokina, Saipan, Philippine Sea, Guam, Iwo Jima, Okinawa, Raids on Japan 7–8/45.

DD 516 *Wadsworth* Minor damage by kamikaze near miss, Okinawa, 22 Apr 1945, and again, 28 Apr 1945. Decomm 18 Apr 1946. †
7* Solomons, Cape Torokina, Green I. Ldgs., Saipan, Guam, Iwo Jima, Okinawa, Raids on Japan 7–8/45. PUC.
Submarine sunk: *I-182* off Espiritu Santo, 1 Sep 1943.

DD 517 *Walker* Decomm 31 May 1946. †
6* Kwajalein, Guam, Saipan, Leyte, Fleet Raids 1945, Raids on Japan 7–8/45.
Submarine sunk: *RO-39* off Wotje , 2 Feb 1944 (possible).

DD 518 *Brownson* Sunk by two aircraft bombs and near miss off Cape Gloucester, 27 Dec 1943 (108 killed).
1* Cape Gloucester.

DD 519 *Daly* Sank PC *Cha-10* off Wewak, 19 Mar 1944. Moderate damage by kamikaze, Okinawa, 28 Apr 1945 (3 killed). Decomm 18 Apr 1946. †
8* Cape Gloucester, Saidor, Admiralty Is., Hollandia, Wakde, Biak, Noemfoor I., Cape Sansapor, Morotai, Leyte, Surigao Strait, Iwo Jima, Okinawa, Raids on Japan 7–8/45.

DD 520 *Isherwood* Severely damaged by kamikaze, Okinawa, 22 Apr 1945 (42 killed). Decomm 1 Feb 1946. †
5* Kurile Is., Leyte, Lingayen, Subic Bay, Okinawa.

DD 521 *Kimberly* Damaged by kamikaze, Kerama Retto, Okinawa, 25 Mar 1945 (4 killed). Decomm 5 Feb 1947. †
5* Gilbert Is., Kurile Is., Leyte, Lingayen, Okinawa.

DD 522 *Luce* Sunk by two kamikazes off Okinawa, capsized, 3 May 1945 (149 killed).
5* Kurile Is., Leyte, Lingayen, Subic Bay, Okinawa.

DD 523/525 — Canceled 16 Dec 1940.

No.	Name	Builder	Keel Laid	Launched	Comm.
DD 526	*Abner Read*	Beth. S. Fran.	30 Oct 1941	18 Aug 1942	5 Feb 1943
DD 527	*Ammen*	Beth. S. Fran.	29 Nov 1941	17 Sep 1942	20 Mar 1943
DD 528	*Mullany*	Beth. S. Fran.	15 Jan 1942	10 Oct 1942	23 Apr 1943
	ex-*Beatty* (28 May 1941)				
DD 529	*Bush*	Beth. S. Fran.	12 Feb 1942	27 Oct 1942	10 May 1943
DD 530	*Trathen*	Beth. S. Fran.	17 Mar 1942	22 Oct 1942	28 May 1943

Figure 4.34: *Yarnall* (DD 541), 17 Jan 1944, of the *Fletcher* class.

DD 531	*Hazelwood*	Beth. S. Fran.	11 Apr 1942	20 Nov 1942	18 Jun 1943
DD 532	*Heermann*	Beth. S. Fran.	8 May 1942	5 Dec 1942	6 Jul 1943
DD 533	*Hoel*	Beth. S. Fran.	4 Jun 1942	19 Dec 1942	29 Jul 1943
DD 534	*McCord*	Beth. S. Fran.	17 Mar 1942	10 Jan 1943	19 Aug 1943
DD 535	*Miller*	Beth. S. Fran.	18 Aug 1942	7 Mar 1943	31 Aug 1943
DD 536	*Owen*	Beth. S. Fran.	17 Sep 1942	21 Mar 1943	20 Sep 1943
DD 537	*The Sullivans*	Beth. S. Fran.	10 Oct 1942	4 Apr 1943	30 Sep 1943
	ex–*Putnam* (6 Feb 1943).				
DD 538	*Stephen Potter*	Beth. S. Fran.	27 Oct 1942	28 Apr 1943	21 Oct 1943
DD 539	*Tingey*	Beth. S. Fran.	22 Oct 1942	28 May 1943	25 Nov 1943
DD 540	*Twining*	Beth. S. Fran.	20 Nov 1942	11 Jul 1943	1 Dec 1943
DD 541	*Yarnall*	Beth. S. Fran.	5 Dec 1942	25 Jul 1943	30 Dec 1943
DD 542/543	—	Beth. S. Fran.	—	—	—
DD 544	*Boyd*	Beth. S. Pedro	2 Apr 1942	29 Oct 1942	8 May 1943
DD 545	*Bradford*	Beth. S. Pedro	28 Apr 1942	12 Dec 1942	12 Jun 1943
DD 546	*Brown*	Beth. S. Pedro	27 Jun 1942	21 Feb 1943	10 Jul 1943
DD 547	*Cowell*	Beth. S. Pedro	7 Sep 1942	18 Mar 1943	23 Aug 1943
DD 548/549		Beth. S. Pedro	—	—	—

Service Records:

DD 526 *Abner Read* Damaged by mine off Kiska, lost stern, 18 Aug 1943 (70 killed). Damaged by grounding off Buna, New Guinea, 28 Feb 1944. Sunk by Japanese aircraft bomb and kamikaze off Samar, capsized, 1 Nov 1944 (22 killed).
4* Attu, Hollandia, Wakde, Biak, Noemfoor I., Morotai, Leyte.

DD 527 *Ammen* Severely damaged by kamikaze off Leyte, 1 Nov 1944 (5 killed). Slightly damaged by aircraft bomb near miss, Okinawa, 21 Apr 1945. Decomm 15 Apr 1946. †
8* Attu, Cape Gloucester, Saidor, Admiralty Is., Hollandia, Wakde, Biak, Noemfoor I., Wewak-Aitape, Leyte, Okinawa, Raids on Japan 7–8/45.

DD 528 *Mullany* Severely damaged by kamikaze, Okinawa, 6 Apr 1945 (30 killed). Decomm 14 Feb 1946. †
7* Cape Gloucester, Saidor, Admiralty Is., Hollandia, Wakde, Biak, Morotai, Leyte, Iwo Jima, Okinawa.

DD 529 *Bush* Slightly damaged by aircraft bomb, Leyte, 1 Nov 1944. Sunk by three kamikazes off Okinawa, broke in two, 6 Apr 1945 (94 killed).
7* Cape Gloucester, Saidor, Admiralty Is., Morotai, Leyte, Mindoro, Lingayen, Iwo Jima, Okinawa.

DD 530 *Trathen* Damaged in error by gunfire, Okinawa, 11 Apr 1945 (3 killed). Decomm 18 Jan 1946. †
8* Wake I. Raid 1943, Kwajalein, Eniwetok, Wakde, Biak, Noemfoor I., Palau, Leyte, Samar, Formosa Raids 1/45, Luzon Raids 1/45, Formosa Raids 1/45, China Coast Raids 1/45, Nansei Shoto Raid 1/45, Honshu Raids 2/45, Iwo Jima, Fleet Raids 1945.

DD 531 *Hazelwood* Severely damaged by kamikaze, Okinawa, 29 Apr 1945 (77 killed). Decomm 18 Jan 1946. †
10* Tarawa Raid, Gilbert Is., Kwajalein, Eniwetok, Palau, Leyte, Samar, Formosa Raids 1/45, Luzon Raids 1/45, Formosa Raids 1/45, China Coast Raids 1/45, Nansei Shoto Raid 1/45, Honshu Raids 2/45, Iwo Jima, Okinawa.
Ships sunk: YP *Fuji Mari, Koki Maru, Seiun Maru No. 5*, north of Iwo Jima, 25 Feb 1945.

DD 532 *Heermann* Seriously damaged by two hits of gunfire from Japanese cruisers off Samar, Leyte Gulf, 25 Oct 1944. Decomm 12 Jun 1946. †
9* Gilbert Is., Kwajalein, Eniwetok, Palau, Leyte, Samar, Honshu Raids 2/45, Iwo Jima, Fleet Raids 1945, Raids on Japan 7–8/45. PUC.
Submarine sunk: *Kaiten carrier *I-56* east of Okinawa, 18 Apr 1945.

DD 533 *Hoel* Sunk by over 40 hits from Japanese battleship *Kongo* and other warships off Samar, Battle of Leyte Gulf, 25 Oct 1944 (253 killed).
5* Gilbert Is., Kwajalein, Eniwetok, Palau, Leyte, Samar. PUC.

DD 534 *McCord* Decomm 15 Jan 1947. †
10* Kwajalein, Eniwetok, Tinian, Palau, Leyte, Samar, Luzon Raids 10/44, Formosa Raids 1/45, Luzon Raids 1/45, China Coast Raids 1/45, Nansei Shoto Raid 1/45, Honshu Raids 2/45, Iwo Jima.
Submarine sunk: *Kaiten carrier *I-56* east of Okinawa, 18 Apr 1945.

DD 535 *Miller* Decomm 19 Dec 1945. †
10* Kwajalein, Eniwetok, Palau-Yap Raids 3/44, Hollandia, Truk Raid 4/44, Saipan, Philippine Sea, Guam, Tinian, Palau-Yap Raids 7/44, Philippines Raids 9/44, Okinawa Raid 10/44, N. Luzon–Formosa Raids 10/44, Surigao Strait, Luzon Raids 10/44, Formosa Raids 1/45, Luzon Raids 1/45, Nansei Shoto Raid 1/45, China Coast Raids 1/45, Honshu Raids 2/45, Iwo Jima, Fleet Raids 1945.

DD 536 *Owen* Decomm 10 Dec 1946. †
9* Kwajalein, Raid on Truk, Palau-Yap Raids 3/44, Hollandia, Truk Raid 4/44, Saipan, Philippine Sea, 3rd Bonins Raid, Guam, Palau-Yap Raids 7/44, Palau, Philippines Raids 9/44, Luzon Raids 10/44, Surigao Strait, Formosa Raids 1/45, Luzon Raids 1/45, China Coast Raids 1/45, Nansei Shoto Raid 1/45, Honshu Raids 2/45, Iwo Jima, Fleet Raids 1945.

DD 537 *The Sullivans* Decomm 10 Jan 1946. †
9* Kwajalein, Palau-Yap Raids 3/44, Truk Raid 4/44, Raid on Truk, Saipan, Philippine Sea, 3rd Bonins Raid, Guam, Palau-Yap Raids 7/44, Palau, Philippines Raids 9/44, Okinawa Raid 10/44, N. Luzon–Formosa Raids 10/44, Luzon Raids 10/44, Surigao Strait, Formosa Raids 1/45, Luzon Raids 1/45, China Coast Raids 1/45, Nansei Shoto Raid 1/45, Honshu Raids 2/45, Okinawa.

DD 538 *Stephen Potter* Damaged in storm off Iwo Jima, 26 Feb 1945. Decomm 21 Sep 1945. †
10* Kwajalein, Raid on Truk, Hollandia, Saipan, 3rd Bonins Raid, Guam, Palau-Yap Raids 7/44, Philippines Raids 9/44, Okinawa Raid 10/44, N. Luzon–Formosa Raids 10/44, Luzon Raids 10/44, Visayas Is. Raids 10/44, Formosa Raids 1/45, Luzon Raids 1/45, China Coast Raids 1/45, Nansei Shoto Raid 1/45, Iwo Jima, Honshu Raids 2/45, Fleet Raids 1945.
Submarine sunk: **RO-45* southwest of Truk, 1 May 1944.

DD 539 *Tingey* Decomm Mar 1946. †
8* Hollandia, Truk Raid 4/44, Saipan, Philippine Sea, 3rd Bonins Raid, Guam, Palau-Yap Raids 7/44, Palau, Philippines Raids 9/44, Okinawa Raid 10/44, N. Luzon–Formosa Raids 10/44, Luzon Raids 10/44, Visayas Is. Raids 10/44, Surigao Strait, Formosa Raids 1/45, Luzon Raids 1/45, China Coast Raids 1/45, Nansei Shoto Raid 1/45, Honshu Raids 2/45, Iwo Jima, Fleet Raids 1945.

DD 540 *Twining* Decomm 14 Jun 1946. †
8* Tinian, Palau, Philippines Raids 9/44, Okinawa Raid 10/44, N. Luzon–Formosa Raids 10/44, Luzon Raids 10/44, Visayas Is. Raids 10/44, Formosa Raids 1/45, Luzon Raids 1/45, China Coast Raids

1/45, Nansei Shoto Raid 1/45, Honshu Raids 2/45, Iwo Jima, Fleet Raids 1945, Visayan Is. Ldgs., Raids on Japan 7–8/45. Tokyo Bay.

DD 541 *Yarnall* Damaged in collision with Destroyer *Ringgold* in Philippine Sea off Ulithi, Micronesia, lost bow, 5 Mar 1945 (1 killed). Decomm 15 Jan 1947. †
7* Saipan, Tinian, Guam, Palau, Philippines Raids 9/44, Leyte, N. Luzon–Formosa Raids 10/44, Luzon Raids 10/44, Visayas Is. Raids 10/44, Surigao Strait, Formosa Raids 1/45, Luzon Raids 1/45, China Coast Raids 1/45, Nansei Shoto Raid 1/45, Iwo Jima, Honshu Raids 2/45, Fleet Raids 1945. Tokyo Bay.

DD 542–43 — Canceled, 16 Dec 1940.

DD 544 *Boyd* Damaged by coastal batteries, Nauru I., 8 Dec 1943. Decomm 15 Jan 1947. †
11* Wake I. Raid 1943, Gilbert Is., Truk Raid 4/44, Hollandia, Morotai, Saipan, 1st Bonins Raid, Philippine Sea, 2nd Bonins Raid, 3rd Bonins Raid, Guam, Palau-Yap Raids 7/44, 4th Bonins Raid, Palau, Philippines Raids 9/44, Okinawa Raid 10/44, N. Luzon–Formosa Raids 10/44, Luzon Raids 10/44, Surigao Strait, Iwo Jima Bombard., Okinawa, Raids on Japan 7–8/45.
Ship sunk: YP *Tatsutagawa Maru*, east of Ogasawara, 15 Jun 1944.

DD 545 *Bradford* Damaged in collision, Iwo Jima, 19 Feb 1945. Decomm 11 Jul 1946. †
12* Tarawa Raid, Wake I. Raid 1943, Gilbert Is., Kavieng Raid 1943, Kavieng Raid 1/44, Kwajalein, Raid on Truk, Marianas Raids 2/44, Palau-Yap Raids 3/44, Truk Raid 4/44, Saipan, 1st Bonins Raid, Philippine Sea, 2nd Bonins Raid, 3rd Bonins Raid, Guam, Palau-Yap Raids 7/44, 4th Bonins Raid, Hollandia, Philippines Raids 9/44, Iwo Jima, Okinawa, Raids on Japan 7–8/45, Minesweeping 1945.
Submarine sunk: *I-19* off Makin I., 25 Nov 1943.

DD 546 *Brown* Damaged by kamikaze, Okinawa, 10 May 1945. Decomm 1 Aug 1946. †
13* Wake I. Raid 1943, Gilbert Is., Kavieng Raid 1943, Kavieng Raid 1/44, Kwajalein, Raid on Truk, Marianas Raids 2/44, Palau-Yap Raids 3/44, Hollandia, Morotai, Truk Raid 4/44, Saipan, 1st Bonins Raid, Philippine Sea, 2nd Bonins Raid, 3rd Bonins Raid, Guam, Palau-Yap Raids 7/44, 4th Bonins Raid, Palau, Philippines Raids 9/44, Okinawa Raid 10/44, N. Luzon–Formosa Raids 10/44, Surigao Strait, Luzon Raids 10/44, Okinawa, Raids on Japan 7–8/45, Minesweeping 1945.

DD 547 *Cowell* Damaged by collision with carrier *Saratoga*, north of Luzon, 14 Oct 1944. Slightly damaged by kamikaze, Okinawa, 4 May 1945 and slightly damaged by kamikaze, Okinawa, 25 May 1945. Decomm 22 Jul 1946. †
11* Gilbert Is., Kavieng Raid 1943, Kavieng Raid 1/44, Kwajalein, Raid on Truk, Marianas Raids 2/44, Palau-Yap Raids 3/44, Hollandia, Truk Raid 4/44, Saipan, 1st Bonins Raid, Philippine Sea, 2nd Bonins Raid, 3rd Bonins Raid, Guam, Palau-Yap Raids 7/44, Palau, Philippines Raids 9/44, Morotai, Okinawa Raid 10/44, N. Luzon–Formosa Raids 10/44, Luzon Raids 10/44, Okinawa, Raids on Japan 7–8/45. PUC.

DD 548/549 — Canceled, 16 Dec 1940.

No.	Name	Builder	Keel Laid	Launched	Comm.
DD 550	*Capps*	Gulf	12 Jun 1941	31 May 1942	23 Jun 1943
DD 551	*David W. Taylor*	Gulf	12 Jun 1941	4 Jul 1942	18 Sep 1943
DD 552	*Evans*	Gulf	21 Jul 1941	4 Oct 1942	11 Dec 1943
DD 553	*John D. Henley*	Gulf	21 Jul 1941	15 Nov 1942	2 Feb 1943
DD 554	*Franks*	Sea-Tac Seattle	8 Mar 1942	7 Dec 1942	30 Jul 1943
DD 555	*Haggard*	Sea-Tac Seattle	27 Mar 1942	9 Feb 1943	31 Aug 1943
DD 556	*Hailey*	Sea-Tac Seattle	11 Apr 1942	9 Mar 1943	30 Sep 1943
DD 557	*Johnston*	Sea-Tac Seattle	6 May 1942	25 Mar 1943	27 Oct 1943
DD 558	*Laws*	Sea-Tac Seattle	19 May 1942	22 Apr 1943	18 Nov 1943
DD 559	*Longshaw*	Sea-Tac Seattle	16 Jun 1942	4 Jun 1943	4 Dec 1943
DD 560	*Morrison*	Sea-Tac Seattle	30 Jun 1942	4 Jul 1943	18 Dec 1943
DD 561	*Prichett*	Sea-Tac Seattle	20 Jul 1942	31 Jul 1943	15 Jan 1944
DD 562	*Robinson*	Sea-Tac Seattle	12 Aug 1942	28 Aug 1943	31 Jan 1944
DD 563	*Ross*	Sea-Tac Seattle	7 Sep 1942	10 Sep 1943	21 Feb 1944
DD 564	*Rowe*	Sea-Tac Seattle	7 Dec 1942	30 Sep 1943	13 Mar 1944
DD 565	*Smalley*	Sea-Tac Seattle	9 Feb 1943	27 Oct 1943	31 Mar 1944
DD 566	*Stoddard*	Sea-Tac Seattle	10 Mar 1943	19 Nov 1943	15 Apr 1944
DD 567	*Watts*	Sea-Tac Seattle	26 Mar 1943	31 Dec 1943	29 Apr 1944
DD 568	*Wren*	Sea-Tac Seattle	24 Apr 1943	29 Jan 1944	20 May 1944
DD 569	*Aulick*	Consol. Orange	14 May 1941	2 Mar 1942	27 Oct 1942
DD 570	*Charles Ausburne*	Consol. Orange	14 May 1941	16 Mar 1942	24 Nov 1942
DD 571	*Claxton*	Consol. Orange	25 Jun 1941	1 Apr 1942	8 Dec 1942
DD 572	*Dyson*	Consol. Orange	25 Jun 1941	15 Apr 1942	30 Dec 1942
DD 573	*Harrison*	Consol. Orange	25 Jul 1941	7 May 1942	25 Jan 1943
DD 574	*John Rodgers*	Consol. Orange	25 Jul 1941	7 May 1942	9 Feb 1943
DD 575	*McKee*	Consol. Orange	2 Mar 1942	2 Aug 1942	31 Mar 1943
DD 576	*Murray*	Consol. Orange	16 Mar 1942	16 Aug 1942	20 Apr 1943
DD 577	*Sproston*	Consol. Orange	1 Apr 1942	31 Aug 1942	19 May 1943
DD 578	*Wickes*	Consol. Orange	15 Apr 1942	13 Sep 1942	16 Jun 1943
DD 579	*William D. Porter*	Consol. Orange	7 May 1942	27 Sep 1942	6 Jul 1943
DD 580	*Young*	Consol. Orange	7 May 1942	11 Oct 1942	31 Jul 1943

Service Records:

DD 550 *Capps* Decomm 15 Jan 1947. †
7* Norway Raid, Kwajalein, Saipan, Philippine Sea, 2nd Bonins Raid, Guam, Philippines Raids 9/44, Luzon Raids 10/44, Iwo Jima, Okinawa.

DD 551 *David W. Taylor* Severely damaged by mine off Chichi Jima, Bonin Is., 5 Jan 1945 (4 killed). Decomm 17 Aug 1946. †

8* Kwajalein, Saipan, 3rd Bonins Raid, Tinian, Guam, Bonins-Yap Raids, Palau, Philippines Raids 9/44, Luzon Raids 10/44, Okinawa, Raids on Japan 7–8/45.
Submarine sunk: **I-10* northeast of Saipan, 4 Jul 1944.

DD 552 *Evans* Severely damaged by four kamikazes, Okinawa, 11 May 1945 (32 killed). Decomm 7 Nov 1945. Stricken 28 Nov 1945, sold 11 Feb 1947; BU.
5* Saipan, Philippine Sea, 2nd Bonins Raid, Guam, Palau, Philippines Raids 9/44, Luzon Raids 10/44, Iwo Jima, Okinawa. PUC.

DD 553 *John D. Henley* Decomm 30 Apr 1946. †
6* Saipan, Philippine Sea, 2nd Bonins Raid, 3rd Bonins Raid, Guam, Bonins-Yap Raids, Palau, Philippines Raids 9/44, Okinawa Raid 10/44, N. Luzon–Formosa Raids 10/44, Luzon Raids 10/44, Iwo Jima, Okinawa, Raids on Japan 7–8/45.

DD 554 *Franks* Damaged in collision with battleship *New Jersey* off Okinawa, 2 Apr 1945. Decomm 31 May 1946. †
9* Gilbert Is., Kwajalein, Guam, Saipan, Palau, Leyte, Samar, Luzon Raids 10/44, Formosa Raids 1/45, Luzon Raids 1/45, Honshu Raids 2/45, Iwo Jima, Fleet Raids 1945.
Submarine sunk: **I-176* 150 miles north of Cape Alexander, off Buka, 17 May 1944.

DD 555 *Haggard* Damaged by accidental explosion off Kwajalein, Marshall Is., 1 Feb 1944. Severely damaged by kamikaze, Okinawa, 29 Apr 1945 (11 killed). Decomm 1 Nov 1945. Stricken 16 Nov 1945. Sold 4 Mar 1946; BU Norfolk, Va.
9* Kwajalein, Eniwetok, Saipan, Guam, Palau, Leyte, Samar, Luzon Raids 10/44, Formosa Raids 1/45, Luzon Raids 1/45, China Coast Raids 1/45, Nansei Shoto Raid 1/45, Honshu Raids 2/45, Iwo Jima, Fleet Raids 1945.
Submarines sunk: **I-176* 150 miles north of Cape Alexander, off Buka, 17 May 1944; *RO-41* 320 miles southeast of Okinawa, 23 Mar 1945 (damaged by ramming).

DD 556 *Hailey* In collision with battleship *Washington* off Iwo Jima, 18 Feb 1945. Decomm 27 Jan 1946. †
6* Kwajalein, Eniwetok, Saipan, Palau, Leyte, Samar, Formosa Raids 1/45, Luzon Raids 1/45, China Coast Raids 1/45, Honshu Raids 2/45, Iwo Jima, Fleet Raids 1945.

DD 557 *Johnston* Sunk by numerous hits of gunfire from Japanese warships off Samar during Battle of Leyte Gulf, 25 Oct 1944 (183 killed).
6* Solomons, Kwajalein, Eniwetok, Guam, Palau, Leyte, Samar. PUC.
Submarine sunk: **I-176* 150 miles north of Cape Alexander, off Buka, 17 May 1944.

DD 558 *Laws* Decomm 10 Dec 1946. †
9* Palau-Yap Raids 3/44, Hollandia, Truk Raid 4/44, Saipan, Tinian, Palau, Philippines Raids 9/44, Okinawa Raid 10/44, N. Luzon–Formosa Raids 10/44, Luzon Raids 10/44, Visayas Is. Raids 10/44, Surigao Strait, Formosa Raids 1/45, Luzon Raids 1/45, China Coast Raids 1/45, Honshu Raids 2/45, Iwo Jima, Okinawa.

DD 559 *Longshaw* Damaged by kamikaze, Okinawa, 7 Apr 1945. Went aground off Naha, Okinawa and destroyed by shore gunfire, 18 May 1945 (86 killed).
9* Palau-Yap Raids 3/44, Hollandia, Truk Raid 4/44, Saipan, Guam, Tinian, Palau, Philippines Raids 9/44, Okinawa Raid 10/44, N. Luzon–Formosa Raids 10/44, Luzon Raids 10/44, Visayas Is. Raids 10/44, Surigao Strait, Formosa Raids 1/45, Luzon Raids 1/45, China Coast Raids 1/45, Nansei Shoto Raid 1/45, Honshu Raids 2/45, Iwo Jima, Okinawa.

DD 560 *Morrison* Damaged by explosion of the sinking carrier *Princeton*, Leyte, 24 Oct 1944. Sunk by four kamikazes off Okinawa, capsized, 4 May 1945 (152 killed).
8* Hollandia, Truk Raid 4/44, Saipan, Tinian, Palau, Philippines Raids 9/44.
Submarine sunk: **I-8* off Okinawa, 31 Mar 1945.

DD 561 *Prichett* Damaged in error by naval gunfire, Philippine Sea, 12 Oct 1944. Damaged by aircraft bombs, Okinawa, 1 Apr 1945 and 3 Apr 1945. Moderate damage by kamikaze, Okinawa, 28 Jul 1945. Decomm 14 Mar 1946. †
8* Truk Raid 4/44, Saipan, Tinian, Guam, Palau, Philippines Raids 9/44, Okinawa Raid 10/44, N. Luzon–Formosa Raids 10/44, Visayas Is. Raids 10/44, Luzon Raids 10/44, Formosa Raids 1/45, Luzon Raids 1/45, Nansei Shoto Raid 1/45, Honshu Raids 2/45, Iwo Jima, Okinawa.

DD 562 *Robinson* Decomm 12 Jun 1946. †
8* Saipan, Guam, Tinian, Palau, Leyte, Surigao Strait, Lingayen, Mindanao Ldgs., Balikpapan, Minesweeping 1945.

DD 563 *Ross* Severely damaged by two mines off Dinagat in Leyte Gulf, 19 Oct 1944 (23 killed). Decomm 4 Jun 1946. †
5* Saipan, Tinian, Palau, Leyte, Raids on Japan 7–8/45. Tokyo Bay.

DD 564 *Rowe* Decomm 31 Jan 1947. †
3* Kurile Is., Okinawa, Raids on Japan 7–8/45.

DD 565 *Smalley* Decomm Jan 1947. †
3* Kurile Is., Okinawa, Raids on Japan 7–8/45.

DD 566 *Stoddard* Decomm Jan 1947. †
3* Kurile Is., Okinawa, Raids on Japan 7–8/45.

DD 567 *Watts* Decomm 12 Apr 1946. †
3* Kurile Is., Okinawa, Raids on Japan 7–8/45.

DD 568 *Wren* Decomm 13 Jul 1946. †
3* Kurile Is., Okinawa, Raids on Japan 7–8/45. Tokyo Bay.

DD 569 *Aulick* Severely damaged by grounding on reef off New Caledonia, 9 Mar 1943. Damaged by three hits from coastal gunfire, Leyte, 19 Oct 1944 (1 killed). Damaged by two kamikazes and bomb, Leyte, 29 Nov 1944 (32 killed). Decomm 18 Apr 1946. †
5* Guam, Palau, Leyte, Surigao Strait, Okinawa, Mindanao Ldgs.

DD 570 *Charles Ausburne* Decomm 18 Apr 1946. †
11* Solomons, Buka Bombard., Cape Torokina, Cape St. George, Rabaul and Kavieng Bombard., Palau-Yap Raids 3/44, Hollandia, Truk Raid 4/44, Saipan, 1st Bonins Raid, Philippine Sea, Guam, Leyte, Mindanao Ldgs., Visayan Is. Ldgs., Lingayen, Okinawa. PUC.

DD 571 *Claxton* Damaged in stern by coastal gunfire off Bougainville, 4 Feb 1944. Moderate damage by kamikaze, Leyte, 1 Nov 1944 (5 killed). Decomm 18 Apr 1946. †
8* Solomons, Buka Bombard., Shortland Is. Raid, Empress Augusta Bay, Cape Torokina, Cape St. George, Palau, Leyte, Surigao Strait, Lingayen, Mariveles-Corregidor, Ldgs. at Nasugbu, Mindanao Ldgs., Visayan Is. Ldgs., Okinawa. PUC.

DD 572 *Dyson* Damaged in typhoon, Philippine Sea, 18 Dec 1944. Damaged by collision, Okinawa, 5 Jun 1945. Decomm 31 Mar 1947. †
11* Solomons, Empress Augusta Bay, Cape Torokina, Cape St. George, Rabaul and Kavieng Bombard., Palau-Yap Raids 3/44, Hollandia, Truk Raid 4/44, Saipan, 1st Bonins Raid, Philippine Sea, Guam, Luzon Raids 10/44, Luzon Raids 1/45, Formosa Raids 1/45, China Coast Raids 1/45, Nansei Shoto Raid 1/45, Mindanao Ldgs., Visayan Is. Ldgs., Mariveles-Corregidor, Okinawa. PUC.

DD 573 *Harrison* Damaged in storm south of Honshu, 25 Feb 1945. Minor damage by kamikaze, Okinawa, 6 Apr 1945. Decomm 1 Apr 1946. †
11* Marcus I. Raid 1943, Tarawa Raid, Wake I. Raid 1943, Gilbert Is., Kwajalein, Hollandia, Guam, Morotai, Leyte, Honshu Raids 2/45, Iwo Jima, Fleet Raids 1945, Raids on Japan 7–8/45.

DD 574 *John Rodgers* Damaged in typhoon, Philippine Sea, 5 Jun 1945. Decomm 25 May 1946. †
12* Marcus I. Raid 1943, Tarawa Raid, Wake I. Raid 1943, Gilbert Is., Kwajalein, Hollandia, Guam, Morotai, Leyte, Honshu Raids 2/45, Iwo Jima, Fleet Raids 1945, Raids on Japan 7–8/45.

DD 575 *McKee* Damaged in typhoon, Philippine Sea, 5 Jun 1945. Decomm 25 Feb 1946. †
11* Marcus I. Raid 1943, Tarawa Raid, Wake I. Raid 1943, 2nd Rabaul Raid, Gilbert Is., Kwajalein, Hollandia, Guam, Leyte, Honshu Raids 2/45, Iwo Jima, Raids on Japan 7–8/45.

DD 576 *Murray* Damaged by aircraft torpedo off Okinawa, 27 Mar 1945 (1 killed). Decomm 27 Mar 1946. †
11* Wake I. Raid 1943, Cape St. George, Gilbert Is., Kwajalein, Eniwetok, Hollandia, Guam, Morotai, Leyte, Honshu Raids 2/45, Iwo Jima, Fleet Raids 1945, Raids on Japan 7–8/45.
Ships sunk: YP *Fuji Maru, Koki Maru, Seiun Maru No.5*, north of Iwo Jima, 25 Feb 1945.

DD 577 *Sproston* Minor damage by aircraft bomb near miss, Okinawa, 3 Apr 1945. Decomm 18 Jan 1946. †
5* Kurile Is., Leyte, Lingayen, Subic Bay, Okinawa.

DD 578 *Wickes* Minor damaged by aircraft bomb, west of Luzon, 10 Jan 1945. Decomm 20 Dec 1945.
5* Kurile Is., Leyte, Lingayen, Mariveles-Corregidor, Okinawa.

DD 579 *William D. Porter* Fired live torpedo in error at battleship *Iowa* carrying President Roosevelt, in North Atlantic, 14 Nov 1943. Damaged in error by gunfire, Okinawa, 27 Apr 1945. Sunk by kamikaze and bomb off Okinawa, capsized, 10 Jun 1945. (none lost)
4* Kurile Is., Leyte, Lingayen, Okinawa.

DD 580 *Young* Decomm Jan 1947. †
5* Kurile Is., Leyte, Lingayen, Mindanao Ldgs., Subic Bay, Mariveles-Corregidor.

No.	Name	Builder	Keel Laid	Launched	Comm.
DD 581	*Charrette*	Boston NYd	20 Feb 1942	3 Jun 1942	18 May 1943
DD 582	*Conner*	Boston NYd	16 Apr 1942	18 Jul 1942	8 Jun 1943
DD 583	*Hall*	Boston NYd	16 Apr 1942	18 Jul 1942	6 Jul 1943
DD 584	*Halligan*	Boston NYd	9 Nov 1942	19 Mar 1943	19 Aug 1943
DD 585	*Haraden*	Boston NYd	9 Nov 1942	19 Mar 1943	16 Sep 1943
DD 586	*Newcomb*	Boston NYd	19 Mar 1943	4 Jul 1943	10 Nov 1943
DD 587	*Bell*	Charleston NYd	30 Dec 1941	24 Jun 1942	4 Mar 1943
DD 588	*Burns*	Charleston NYd	9 May 1942	8 Aug 1942	3 Apr 1943
DD 589	*Izard*	Charleston NYd	9 May 1942	8 Aug 1942	15 May 1943
DD 590	*Paul Hamilton*	Charleston NYd	20 Jan 1943	7 Apr 1943	25 Oct 1943
DD 591	*Twiggs*	Charleston NYd	20 Jan 1943	7 Apr 1943	4 Nov 1943
DD 592	*Howorth*	Puget Sd NYd	26 Nov 1941	10 Jan 1943	3 Apr 1944
DD 593	*Killen*	Puget Sd NYd	26 Nov 1941	10 Jan 1943	4 May 1944
DD 594	*Hart*	Puget Sd NYd	10 Aug 1943	25 Sep 1944	4 Nov 1944
	ex–*Mansfield* (21 Mar 1944)				
DD 595	*Metcalf*	Puget Sd NYd	10 Aug 1943	25 Sep 1944	18 Nov 1944
DD 596	*Shields*	Puget Sd NYd	10 Aug 1943	25 Sep 1944	8 Feb 1945
DD 597	*Wiley*	Puget Sd NYd	10 Aug 1943	25 Sep 1944	22 Feb 1945
DD 629	*Abbot*	Bath	21 Sep 1942	17 Feb 1943	23 Apr 1943
DD 630	*Braine*	Bath	12 Oct 1942	7 Mar 1943	11 May 1943
DD 631	*Erben*	Bath	28 Oct 1942	21 Mar 1943	28 May 1943
DD 642	*Hale*	Bath	23 Nov 1942	4 Apr 1943	15 Jun 1943
DD 643	*Sigourney*	Bath	7 Dec 1942	24 Apr 1943	29 Jun 1943
DD 644	*Stembel*	Bath	21 Dec 1942	8 May 1943	16 Jul 1943

Service Records:

DD 581 *Charrette* Decomm 15 Jan 1947. †
13* Wake I. Raid 1943, Gilbert Is., Kavieng Raid 1943, Kavieng Raid 1/44, Kwajalein, Raid on Truk, Palau-Yap Raids 3/44, Hollandia, Truk Raid 4/44, Saipan, 1st Bonins Raid, Philippine Sea, 2nd Bonins Raid, 3rd Bonins Raid, Guam, Palau-Yap Raids 7/44, 4th Bonins Raid, Palau, Philippines Raids 9/44, Morotai, Okinawa Raid 10/44, N. Luzon–Formosa Raids 10/44, Luzon Raids 10/44, Surigao Strait, Lingayen, Brunei, Balikpapan.
Submarine sunk: **I-175* (or *I-21*?) 100 miles northwest of Jaluit, 4 Feb 1944.
Ship sunk: YP *Tatsutagawa Maru*, east of Ogasawara, 15 Jun 1944.

DD 582 *Conner* Captured Japanese hospital ship *Tachibana Maru* carrying contraband, 2 Aug 1945. Decomm 5 Jul 1946. †
12* Wake I. Raid 1943, Gilbert Is., Kavieng Raid 1943, Kavieng Raid 1/44, Kwajalein, Raid on Truk, Marianas Raids 2/44, Palau-Yap Raids 3/44, Hollandia, Truk Raid 4/44, Saipan, 1st Bonins Raid, Philippine Sea, 2nd Bonins Raid, 3rd Bonins Raid, Guam, Palau, Philippines Raids 9/44, Morotai, Okinawa Raid 10/44, N. Luzon–Formosa Raids 10/44, Luzon Raids 10/44, Visayas Is. Raids 10/44, Surigao Strait, Mindoro, Lingayen, Brunei, Balikpapan.

DD 583 *Hall* Damaged by three hits from coastal gunfire, Wotje I., Marshall Is., 4 Apr 1944 (1 killed). Decomm 10 Dec 1946. †
8* Kwajalein, Eniwetok, Hollandia, 2nd Bonins Raid, 3rd Bonins Raid, Bonins-Yap Raids, Palau, Philippines Raids 9/44, Okinawa Raid 10/44, N. Luzon–Formosa Raids 10/44, Luzon Raids 10/44, Lingayen, Iwo Jima, Okinawa.

DD 584 *Halligan* Sunk by mine off Okinawa, grounded on reef, 26 Mar 1945 (152 killed).
6* Kwajalein, Eniwetok, Saipan, Leyte, Lingayen, Iwo Jima, Okinawa.

DD 585 *Haraden* Severely damaged by kamikaze in Sulu Sea off Mindanao, 13 Dec 1944 (16 killed). Decomm 2 Jul 1946. †
5* Kwajalein, Eniwetok, Saipan, Leyte, Lingayen, Mindanao Ldgs.

DD 586 *Newcomb* Damaged by kamikaze near miss in Lingayen Gulf, 6 Jan 1945. Severely damaged by four kamikazes, Okinawa, 6 Apr 1945 (43 killed). Decomm 20 Nov 1945. Stricken 28 Mar 1946. Sold 24 Oct 1947.
8* Saipan, Palau, Leyte, Surigao Strait, Lingayen, Iwo Jima, Okinawa.
Submarine sunk: **I-185* northeast of Saipan, 22 Jun 1944.

DD 587 *Bell* Damaged in collision south of Mindoro, 4 Jan 1945. Decomm 14 Jun 1946. †
12* Wake I. Raid 1943, Kavieng Raid 1943, Kavieng Raid 1/44, Kwajalein, Raid on Truk, Marianas Raids 2/44, Palau-Yap Raids 3/44, Hollandia, Morotai, Truk Raid 4/44, Saipan, 1st Bonins Raid, Philippine Sea, 2nd Bonins Raid, 3rd Bonins Raid, Guam, Palau-Yap Raids 7/44, 4th Bonins Raid, Palau, Philippines Raids 9/44, Okinawa Raid 10/44, N. Luzon–Formosa Raids 10/44, Luzon Raids 10/44, Surigao Strait, Lingayen, Balikpapan, Brunei.
Submarine sunk: **RO-115* 125 miles southwest of Manila., 31 Jan 1945.

DD 588 *Burns* Sank four-ship convoy off Ujae Atoll, 30 Jan 1944. Decomm 25 Jun 1946. †
11* Wake I. Raid 1943, Gilbert Is., Kwajalein, Raid on Truk, Palau-Yap Raids 3/44, Hollandia, Truk Raid 4/44, 1st Bonins Raid, Philippine Sea, 2nd Bonins Raid, 3rd Bonins Raid, Saipan, Guam, Palau-Yap Raids 7/44, 4th Bonins Raid, Palau, Philippines Raids 9/44, Morotai, Okinawa Raid 10/44, N. Luzon–Formosa Raids 10/44, Luzon Raids 10/44, Surigao Strait, Lingayen, Brunei, Balikpapan.
Ships sunk: *Akibasan Maru*, YP *Nichiei Maru*, 30 Jan 1944; PC *CH-24* off Truk, 17 Feb 1944.

DD 589 *Izard* Decomm 31 May 1946. †
10* Wake I. Raid 1943, Gilbert Is., Kwajalein, Raid on Truk, Marianas Raids 2/44, Palau-Yap Raids 3/44, Hollandia, Truk Raid 4/44, Saipan, 1st Bonins Raid, Philippine Sea, 2nd Bonins Raid, 3rd Bonins Raid, Guam, Palau-Yap Raids 7/44, 4th Bonins Raid, Palau, Philippines Raids 9/44, Morotai, Okinawa Raid 10/44, N. Luzon–Formosa Raids 10/44, Luzon Raids 10/44, Surigao Strait, Lingayen, Iwo Jima.

DD 590 *Paul Hamilton* Minor damage by aircraft bomb, Mindoro, 15 Dec 1944. Decomm 24 Sep 1945. †
7* Saipan, Philippine Sea, Guam, Tinian, Philippines Raids 9/44, N. Luzon–Formosa Raids 10/44, Luzon Raids 10/44, Mindoro, Lingayen, Iwo Jima, Okinawa.
DD 591 *Twiggs* Minor damage by kamikaze and bomb, Okinawa, 28 Apr 1945. Sunk by aircraft torpedo and kamikaze off Okinawa, 16 Jun 1945 (193 killed).
4* Leyte, Lingayen, Iwo Jima, Okinawa.
DD 592 *Howorth* Slight damage by kamikazes, Mindoro, 15 Dec 1944. Moderate damage by three kamikazes, Okinawa, 6 Apr 1945 (9 killed). Decomm 30 Apr 1946. †
5* Morotai, Leyte, Lingayen, Iwo Jima, Okinawa.
DD 593 *Killen* Damaged by aircraft bomb, Leyte, 1 Nov 1944 (15 killed). Decomm 9 Jul 1946. †
2* Leyte, Surigao Strait, Brunei, Balikpapan.
DD 594 *Hart* Decomm 31 May 1946. †
2* Okinawa, Brunei, Balikpapan.
DD 595 *Metcalf* Decomm Mar 1946. †
3* Okinawa, Brunei, Balikpapan.
DD 596 *Shields* Decomm 14 Jun 1946. †
DD 597 *Wiley* Decomm 15 May 1946. †
DD 629 *Abbot* Damaged in collision with carrier *Cowpens* off Hawaii, 18 Oct 1943. Decomm 21 May 1946. †
8* Kwajalein, Hollandia, Saipan, Guam, Leyte, Lingayen, Ldgs. on Palawan I., Mindanao Ldgs., Visayan Is. Ldgs., Mariveles-Corregidor, Raids on Japan 7–8/45.
DD 630 *Braine* Damaged by one hit by coastal gunfire off Tinian, 14 Jun 1944. Severe damage by two kamikazes off Okinawa, 27 May 1945. Decomm 26 Jul 1946. †
9* Cape Torokina, Green I. Ldgs., Wake I. Raid 1943, Saipan, Leyte, Lingayen, Mariveles-Corregidor, Mindanao Ldgs., Okinawa.
DD 631 *Erben* Decomm 31 May 1946. †
6* Gilbert Is., Kwajalein, Guam, Leyte, Fleet Raids 1945, Raids on Japan 7–8/45.
DD 642 *Hale* Damaged by aircraft bomb near miss, Okinawa, 11 Apr 1945. Damaged in collision with escort carrier *Steamer Bay*, Okinawa, 25 Apr 1945. Decomm 15 Jan 1947. †
6* Gilbert Is., Kwajalein, Guam, Leyte, Fleet Raids 1945, Raids on Japan 7–8/45.
DD 643 *Sigourney* Damaged by grounding off Torokina, Bougainville, 10 Dec 1943. Decomm 20 Mar 1946. †
9* Solomons, Cape Torokina, Green I. Ldgs., Saipan, Tinian, Palau, Leyte, Surigao Strait, Lingayen, Mindanao Ldgs.
DD 644 *Stembel* Decomm 31 May 1946. †
9* Kwajalein, Raid on Truk, Hollandia, Guam, Leyte, Lingayen, Iwo Jima, Fleet Raids 1945, Raids on Japan 7–8/45.

Figure 4.35: *Kidd* (DD 661), 12 Jun 1944, in the Pacific. She was named after RADM Isaac Kidd, killed at Pearl Harbor.

Figure 4.36: *Van Valkenburgh* (DD 656), a *Fletcher*-class destroyer.

No.	Name	Builder	Keel Laid	Launched	Comm.
DD 649	*Albert W. Grant*	Charleston NYd	30 Dec 1942	29 May 1943	24 Nov 1943
DD 650	*Caperton*	Bath	11 Jan 1943	22 May 1943	30 Jul 1943
DD 651	*Cogswell*	Bath	1 Feb 1943	5 Jun 1943	17 Aug 1943
DD 652	*Ingersoll*	Bath	18 Feb 1943	28 Jun 1943	31 Aug 1943
DD 653	*Knapp*	Bath	8 Mar 1943	10 Jul 1943	16 Sep 1943
DD 654	*Bearss*	Gulf	14 Jul 1942	25 Jul 1943	12 Apr 1944
DD 655	*John Hood*	Gulf	12 Oct 1942	25 Oct 1943	7 Jun 1944
DD 656	*Van Valkenburgh*	Gulf	15 Nov 1942	19 Dec 1943	2 Aug 1944
DD 657	*Charles J. Badger*	Beth. Staten I.	24 Sep 1942	3 Apr 1943	23 Jul 1943
DD 658	*Colahan*	Beth. Staten I.	24 Oct 1942	3 May 1943	23 Aug 1943
DD 659	*Dashiell*	Federal	1 Oct 1942	6 Feb 1943	20 Mar 1943
DD 660	*Bullard*	Federal	16 Oct 1942	28 Feb 1943	9 Apr 1943
DD 661	*Kidd*	Federal	16 Oct 1942	28 Feb 1943	23 Apr 1943
DD 662	*Bennion*	Boston NYd	19 Mar 1943	4 Jul 1943	14 Dec 1943
DD 663	*Heywood L. Edwards*	Boston NYd	4 Jul 1943	6 Oct 1943	26 Jan 1944
DD 664	*Richard P. Leary*	Boston NYd	4 Jul 1943	6 Oct 1943	23 Feb 1944
DD 665	*Bryant*	Charleston NYd	30 Dec 1942	29 May 1943	4 Dec 1943
DD 666	*Black*	Federal	14 Nov 1942	28 Mar 1943	21 May 1943
DD 667	*Chauncey*	Federal	14 Nov 1942	28 Mar 1943	31 May 1943
DD 668	*Clarence K. Bronson*	Federal	9 Dec 1942	18 Apr 1943	11 Jun 1943
DD 669	*Cotten*	Federal	8 Feb 1943	12 Jun 1943	24 Jul 1943
DD 670	*Dortch*	Federal	2 Mar 1943	20 Jun 1943	7 Aug 1943
DD 671	*Gatling*	Federal	3 Mar 1943	20 Jun 1943	19 Aug 1943
DD 672	*Healy*	Federal	4 Mar 1943	4 Jul 1943	3 Sep 1943
DD 673	*Hickox*	Federal	12 Mar 1943	4 Jul 1943	10 Sep 1943
DD 674	*Hunt*	Federal	31 Mar 1943	1 Aug 1943	22 Sep 1943
DD 675	*Lewis Hancock*	Federal	31 Mar 1943	1 Aug 1943	29 Sep 1943

DD 676	*Marshall*	Federal	19 Apr 1943	29 Aug 1943	16 Oct 1943
DD 677	*McDermut*	Federal	14 Jun 1943	17 Oct 1943	19 Nov 1943
DD 678	*McGowan*	Federal	30 Jun 1943	14 Nov 1943	20 Dec 1943
DD 679	*McNair*	Federal	30 Jun 1943	14 Nov 1943	30 Dec 1943
DD 680	*Melvin*	Federal	6 Jul 1943	17 Oct 1943	24 Nov 1943

Service Records:

DD 649 *Albert W. Grant* Seriously damaged by naval gunfire in Surigao Strait Battle, with over 20 hits, including some by U.S. forces, 24 Oct 1944 (38 killed). Decomm 16 Jul 1946. †
7* Hollandia, Truk Raid 4/44, Saipan, Tinian, Palau, Leyte, Surigao Strait, Brunei, Balikpapan.

DD 650 *Caperton* †
10* Gilbert Is., Kwajalein, Raid on Truk, Marianas Raids 2/44, Palau-Yap Raids 3/44, Hollandia, Truk Raid 4/44, Saipan, Philippine Sea, Guam, Palau-Yap Raids 7/44, 4th Bonins Raid, Philippines Raids 9/44, Okinawa Raid 10/44, N. Luzon–Formosa Raids 10/44, Luzon Raids 10/44, Surigao Strait, Formosa Raids 1/45, Luzon Raids 1/45, China Coast Raids 1/45, Nansei Shoto Raid 1/45, Okinawa, Raids on Japan 7–8/45. Tokyo Bay.

DD 651 *Cogswell* Decomm 30 Apr 1946. †
9* Kwajalein, Raid on Truk, Marianas Raids 2/44, Palau-Yap Raids 3/44, Hollandia, Truk Raid 4/44, Saipan, Philippine Sea, Guam, Palau-Yap Raids 7/44, 4th Bonins Raid, Philippines Raids 9/44, Okinawa Raid 10/44, N. Luzon–Formosa Raids 10/44, Luzon Raids 10/44, Visayas I. Raids 10/44, Surigao Strait, Mindoro, Luzon Raids 1/45, Formosa Raids 1/45, China Coast Raids 1/45, Okinawa, Raids on Japan 7–8/45. Tokyo Bay.

DD 652 *Ingersoll* Decomm 19 Jul 1946. †
9* Kwajalein, Raid on Truk, Marianas Raids 2/44, Palau-Yap Raids 3/44, Hollandia, Truk Raid 4/44, Saipan, Philippine Sea, Guam, Palau-Yap Raids 7/44, 4th Bonins Raid, Palau, Philippines Raids 9/44, Okinawa Raid 10/44, N. Luzon–Formosa Raids 10/44, Luzon Raids 10/44, Visayas Is. Raids 10/44, Surigao Strait, Formosa Raids 1/45, Luzon Raids 1/45, China Coast Raids 1/45, Nansei Shoto Raid 1/45, Okinawa, Raids on Japan 7–8/45. Tokyo Bay.

DD 653 *Knapp* Decomm 5 Jul 1946. †
8* Kwajalein, Raid on Truk, Marianas Raids 2/44, Palau-Yap Raids 3/44, Hollandia, Truk Raid 4/44, Saipan, Philippine Sea, Guam, Palau-Yap Raids 7/44, 4th Bonins Raid, Palau, Philippines Raids 9/44, N. Luzon–Formosa Raids 10/44, Luzon Raids 10/44, Visayas Is. Raids 10/44, Surigao Strait, Formosa Raids 1/45, Luzon Raids 1/45, Formosa Raids 1/45, China Coast Raids 1/45, Nansei Shoto Raid 1/45, Mindoro, Raids on Japan 7–8/45. Tokyo Bay.

DD 654 *Bearss* Decomm 31 Jan 1947. †
1* Kurile Is.

DD 655 *John Hood* Decomm 3 Jul 1946. †
1* Kurile Is.

DD 656 *Van Valkenburgh* Decomm 12 Apr 1946. †
3* Iwo Jima, Okinawa, Raids on Japan 7–8/45.

DD 657 *Charles J. Badger* Severely damaged by kamikaze boat off Okinawa, 9 Apr 1945. Decomm 21 May 1946. †
5* Kurile Is., Leyte, Lingayen, Okinawa, Subic Bay.

DD 658 *Colahan* Damaged by grounding off Kwajalein, Marshall Is., 31 Jan 1944. Damaged in storm off Iwo Jima, 24 Feb 1945. Decomm 14 Jun 1946. †
8* Kwajalein, Guam, Palau, Philippines Raids 9/44, Okinawa Raid 10/44, N. Luzon–Formosa Raids 10/44, Luzon Raids 10/44, Visayas Is. Raids 10/44, Surigao Strait, Luzon Raids 10/44, Formosa Raids 1/45, Luzon Raids 1/45, China Coast Raids 1/45, Nansei Shoto Raid 1/45, Honshu Raids 2/45, Iwo Jima, Fleet Raids 1945, Raids on Japan 7–8/45. Tokyo Bay.

DD 659 *Dashiell* Damaged by grounding, Gilbert Is., 20 Nov 1943. Minor damage by bomb near miss and kamikazes, Okinawa, 14 Apr 1945. Damaged in typhoon, Philippine Sea, 5 Jun 1945. Decomm 30 Mar 1946. †
10* Marcus I. Raid 1943, Tarawa Raid, Wake I. Raid 1943, Gilbert Is., Hollandia, Guam, Morotai, Leyte, Mindoro, Mariveles-Corregidor, Fleet Raids 1945, Raids on Japan 7–8/45.

DD 660 *Bullard* Slightly damaged by kamikaze, Okinawa, 11 Apr 1945. Decomm 20 Dec 1946. †
9* 2nd Rabaul Raid, Wake I. Raid 1943, Admiralty Is., Gilbert Is., Hollandia, Kwajalein, Saipan, Guam, Fleet Raids 1945, Raids on Japan 7–8/45.

DD 661 *Kidd* Severely damaged by kamikaze, Okinawa, 11 Apr 1945 (38 killed). Decomm 10 Dec 1946. †
4* 2nd Rabaul Raid, Gilbert Is., Kwajalein, Saipan, Guam, Leyte, Fleet Raids 1945.

DD 662 *Bennion* Damaged by one hit by coastal gunfire, Leyte, 20 Oct 1944. Minor damage by kamikaze, Okinawa, 28 Apr 1945 and again, 30 Apr 1945. Decomm 20 Jun 1946. †
8* Saipan, Tinian, Palau, Leyte, Surigao Strait, Lingayen, Iwo Jima, Okinawa, Raids on Japan 7–8/45. PUC.

DD 663 *Heywood L. Edwards* Damaged in collision with destroyer *Bryant*, Iwo Jima, 24 Feb 1945. Damaged in error by gunfire, Okinawa, 24 May 1945. Decomm 1 Jul 1946. †
7* Saipan, Tinian, Palau, Philippines Raids 9/44, Leyte, Surigao Strait, Lingayen, Iwo Jima, Okinawa.

DD 664 *Richard P. Leary* Minor damage by kamikaze, Lingayen, Luzon, 6 Jan 1945. Decomm 10 Dec 1946. †
6* Saipan, Palau, Leyte, Surigao Strait, Lingayen, Iwo Jima, Okinawa.

DD 665 *Bryant* Minor damage by kamikaze near miss, Mindoro, 22 Dec 1944. Damaged in collision with destroyer *Heywood L. Edwards*, Iwo Jima, 24 Feb 1945. Heavily damaged by kamikaze, Okinawa, 16 Apr 1945 (36 killed). Decomm 15 Jan 1947. †
7* Saipan, Tinian, Palau, Leyte, Surigao Strait, Lingayen, Iwo Jima, Okinawa.

DD 666 *Black* Decomm 5 Aug 1946. †
6* Kwajalein, Guam, Leyte, Fleet Raids 1945, Raids on Japan 7–8/45.

DD 667 *Chauncey* Decomm 19 Dec 1945. †
7* 2nd Rabaul Raid, Gilbert Is., Kwajalein, Saipan, Guam, Leyte, Fleet Raids 1945, Raids on Japan 7–8/45.

DD 668 *Clarence K. Bronson* Decomm 16 Jul 1946. †
9* Kwajalein, Raid on Truk, Marianas Raids 2/44, Palau-Yap Raids 3/44, Hollandia, Truk Raid 4/44, Saipan, Philippine Sea, Guam, Palau-Yap Raids 7/44, 4th Bonins Raid, Philippines Raids 9/44, Okinawa Raid 10/44, N. Luzon–Formosa Raids 10/44, Luzon Raids 10/44, Visayas Is. Raids 10/44, Surigao Strait, Formosa Raids 1/45, Luzon Raids 1/45, China Coast Raids 1/45, Nansei Shoto Raid 1/45, Honshu Raids 2/45, Iwo Jima, Fleet Raids 1945. Tokyo Bay.

DD 669 *Cotten* Decomm 15 Jul 1946. †
9* Gilbert Is., Raid on Truk, Palau-Yap Raids 3/44, Truk Raid 4/44, Saipan, Philippine Sea, Guam, Hollandia Palau-Yap Raids 7/44, 4th Bonins Raid, Philippines Raids 9/44, Okinawa Raid 10/44, N. Luzon–Formosa Raids 10/44, Luzon Raids 10/44, Visayas Is. Raids 10/44, Surigao Strait, Formosa Raids 1/45, Luzon Raids 1/45, China Coast Raids 1/45, Nansei Shoto Raid 1/45, Honshu Raids 2/45, Iwo Jima. Tokyo Bay.
Submarine sunk: *RO-38* west of Tarawa, 24 Nov 1943.

DD 670 *Dortch* Damaged by strafing, Iwo Jima, 17 Feb 1945. Decomm 19 Jul 1946. †
8* Kwajalein, Raid on Truk, Marianas Raids 2/44, Palau-Yap Raids 3/44, Hollandia, Truk Raid 4/44, Saipan, Philippine Sea, Guam, Palau-Yap Raids 7/44, 4th Bonins Raid, Philippines Raids 9/44, Okinawa Raid 10/44, N. Luzon–Formosa Raids 10/44, Luzon Raids 10/44, Visayas Is. Raids 10/44, Surigao Strait, Formosa Raids 1/45, Luzon Raids 1/45, China Coast Raids 1/45, Nansei Shoto Raid 1/45, Honshu Raids 2/45, Iwo Jima. Tokyo Bay.
Ship sunk: YP *Ajukawa Maru*, off Iwo Jima, 18 Feb 1945 (3 killed).

DD 671 *Gatling* Damaged by explosion of carrier *Princeton*, Leyte, 24 Oct 1944. Decomm 16 Jul 1946. †
8* Kwajalein, Raid on Truk, Marianas Raids 2/44, Palau-Yap Raids 3/44, Hollandia, Truk Raid 4/44, Saipan, Philippine Sea, Guam, Palau-Yap Raids 7/44, 4th Bonins Raid, Palau, Philippines Raids 9/44, Okinawa Raid 10/44, N. Luzon–Formosa Raids 10/44, Luzon Raids 10/44, Visayas Is. Raids 10/44, Formosa Raids 1/45, Luzon Raids 1/45, China Coast Raids 1/45, Nansei Shoto Raid 1/45, Honshu Raids 2/45, Iwo Jima. Tokyo Bay.

DD 672 *Healy* Decomm 11 Jul 1946. †
8* Kwajalein, Raid on Truk, Marianas Raids 2/44, Palau-Yap Raids 3/44, Hollandia, Truk Raid 4/44, Saipan, Philippine Sea, Guam, Palau-Yap Raids 7/44, 4th Bonins Raid, Philippines Raids 9/44, Okinawa Raid 10/44, N. Luzon–Formosa Raids 10/44, Luzon Raids 10/44, Visayas Is. Raids 10/44, Surigao Strait, Luzon Raids 10/44, Formosa Raids 1/45, Luzon Raids 1/45, China Coast Raids 1/45, Nansei Shoto Raid 1/45, Honshu Raids 2/45, Iwo Jima. Tokyo Bay.

DD 673 *Hickox* Damaged in typhoon, Philippine Sea, 18 Dec 1944. Decomm 10 Dec 1946. †
9* Kwajalein, Jaluit attack, Raid on Truk, Palau-Yap Raids 3/44, Hollandia, Truk Raid 4/44, Saipan, Philippine Sea, 3rd Bonins Raid, Guam, Palau-Yap Raids 7/44, Palau, Philippines Raids 9/44, Okinawa Raid 10/44, N. Luzon–Formosa Raids 10/44, Luzon Raids 10/44, Visayas Is. Raids 10/44, Surigao Strait, Formosa Raids 1/45, China Coast Raids 1/45, Honshu Raids 2/45, Iwo Jima, Fleet Raids 1945.

DD 674 *Hunt* Minor damage by kamikaze, Okinawa, 14 Apr 1945. Decomm 15 Dec 1945. †
9* Kwajalein, Raid on Truk, Jaluit attack, Palau-Yap Raids 3/44, Hollandia, Truk Raid 4/44, Saipan, Philippine Sea, 3rd Bonins Raid, Guam, Palau-Yap Raids 7/44, Palau, Philippines Raids 9/44, Okinawa Raid 10/44, N. Luzon–Formosa Raids 10/44, Luzon Raids 10/44, Visayas Is. Raids 10/44, Surigao Strait, Formosa Raids 1/45, Honshu Raids 2/45, Iwo Jima, Fleet Raids 1945.

DD 675 *Lewis Hancock* Decomm 10 Jan 1946. †
9* Kwajalein, Raid on Truk, Jaluit attack, Palau-Yap Raids 3/44, Hollandia, Truk Raid 4/44, Saipan, Philippine Sea, 3rd Bonins Raid, Guam, Palau-Yap Raids 7/44, Palau, Philippines Raids 9/44, Okinawa Raid 10/44, N. Luzon–Formosa Raids 10/44, Luzon Raids 10/44, Visayas Is. Raids 10/44, Surigao Strait, Formosa Raids 1/45, Luzon Raids 1/45, Honshu Raids 2/45, Iwo Jima, Fleet Raids 1945.

DD 676 *Marshall* Decomm Dec 1945. †
8* Palau-Yap Raids 3/44, Hollandia, Truk Raid 4/44, Saipan, Philippine Sea, 3rd Bonins Raid, Guam, Palau-Yap Raids 7/44, Philippines Raids 9/44, Okinawa Raid 10/44, N. Luzon–Formosa Raids 10/44, Luzon Raids 10/44, Surigao Strait, Formosa Raids 1/45, Luzon Raids 1/45, China Coast Raids 1/45, Honshu Raids 2/45, Iwo Jima, Fleet Raids 1945.

DD 677 *McDermut* Damaged by U.S. gunfire in error, Okinawa, 16 Apr 1945 (5 killed). Damaged by gunfire, south of Paramushiru, Kurile Is., 11 Aug 1945. Decomm 15 Jan 1947. †
10* Palau-Yap Raids 3/44, Truk Raid 4/44, Saipan, Guam, Tinian, Palau, Leyte, Surigao Strait, Mindoro, Lingayen, Fleet Raids 1945, Raids on Japan 7–8/45, Kurile Is., Minesweeping 1945.

DD 678 *McGowan* Decomm 30 Apr 1946. †
9* Saipan, Guam, Tinian, Palau, Leyte, Surigao Strait, Honshu Raids 2/45, Iwo Jima, Fleet Raids 1945, Raids on Japan 7–8/45, Kurile Is., Minesweeping 1945.

DD 679 *McNair* Decomm 28 May 1946. †
8* Saipan, Guam, Palau, Leyte, Surigao Strait, Honshu Raids 2/45, Iwo Jima, Fleet Raids 1945, Raids on Japan 7–8/45, Kurile Is., Minesweeping 1945.

DD 680 *Melvin* Decomm 31 May 1946. †
10* Saipan, Guam, Palau, Leyte, Surigao Strait, Honshu Raids 2/45, Iwo Jima, Fleet Raids 1945, Raids on Japan 7–8/45, Kurile Is., Minesweeping 1945.
Submarines sunk: *RO-36* east of Saipan, 13 Jun 1944; **RO-114* west of Tinian, 17 Jun 1944.

No.	Name	Builder	Keel Laid	Launched	Comm.
DD 681	*Hopewell*	Beth. S. Pedro	29 Oct 1942	2 May 1943	30 Sep 1943
DD 682	*Porterfield*	Beth. S. Pedro	12 Dec 1942	13 Jun 1943	30 Oct 1943
DD 683	*Stockham*	Beth. S. Fran.	19 Dec 1942	25 Jun 1943	11 Feb 1944
DD 684	*Wedderburn*	Beth. S. Fran.	10 Jan 1943	1 Aug 1943	9 Mar 1944
DD 685	*Picking*	Beth. Staten I.	24 Nov 1942	1 Jun 1943	21 Sep 1943
DD 686	*Halsey Powell*	Beth. Staten I.	4 Feb 1943	30 Jun 1943	25 Oct 1943
DD 687	*Uhlmann*	Beth. Staten I.	6 Mar 1943	30 Jul 1943	22 Nov 1943
DD 688	*Remey*	Bath	22 Mar 1943	25 Jul 1943	30 Sep 1943
DD 689	*Wadleigh*	Bath	5 Apr 1943	7 Aug 1943	19 Oct 1943
DD 690	*Norman Scott*	Bath	26 Apr. 1943	28 Aug 1943	5 Nov 1943
DD 691	*Mertz*	Bath	10 May 1943	11 Sep 1943	19 Nov 1943
DD 792	*Callaghan*	Beth. S. Pedro	21 Feb 1943	1 Aug 1943	27 Nov 1943
DD 793	*Cassin Young*	Beth. S. Pedro	18 Mar 1943	12 Sep 1943	31 Dec 1943
DD 794	*Irwin*	Beth. S. Pedro	2 May 1943	31 Oct 1943	14 Feb 1944
DD 795	*Preston*	Beth. S. Pedro	13 Jun 1943	12 Dec 1943	20 Mar 1944
DD 796	*Benham*	Beth. Staten I.	3 Apr. 1943	30 Aug 1943	20 Dec 1943
DD 797	*Cushing*	Beth. Staten I.	3 May 1943	30 Sep 1943	17 Jan 1944
DD 798	*Monssen*	Beth. Staten I.	1 Jun 1943	30 Oct 1943	14 Feb 1944
DD 799	*Jarvis*	Todd Seattle	7 Jun 1943	14 Feb 1944	3 Jun 1944
DD 800	*Porter*	Todd Seattle	6 Jul 1943	13 Mar 1944	24 Jun 1944
DD 801	*Colhoun*	Todd Seattle	3 Aug 1943	10 Apr. 1944	8 Jul 1944
DD 802	*Gregory*	Todd Seattle	31 Aug 1943	8 May 1944	29 Jul 1944
DD 803	*Little*	Todd Seattle	13 Sep 1943	22 May 1944	19 Aug 1944
DD 804	*Rooks*	Todd Seattle	27 Oct 1943	6 Jun 1944	2 Sep 1944

Service Records:

DD 681 *Hopewell* Damaged by four hits from coastal gunfire, Mariveles, Luzon, 14 Feb 1945. Decomm 15 Jan 1947.
9* Solomons, Kwajalein, Hollandia, Morotai, Leyte, Lingayen, Mariveles-Corregidor, Raids on Japan 7–8/45.

DD 682 *Porterfield* Damaged by naval gunfire, south of Honshu, sinking picket boat, 26 Feb 1945 (1 killed). Slightly damaged by kamikaze, Okinawa, 26 Mar 1945. Damaged in error by gunfire, Okinawa, 9 Apr 1945. Decomm 15 Jul 1946.
10* Kwajalein, Palau-Yap Raids 3/44, Hollandia, Truk Raid 4/44, Saipan, Tinian, Guam, Palau, Philippines Raids 9/44, Okinawa Raid 10/44, N. Luzon–Formosa Raids 10/44, Luzon Raids 10/44, Visayas Is. Raids 10/44, Surigao Strait, Formosa Raids 1/45, Luzon Raids 1/45, China

Coast Raids 1/45, Nansei Shoto Raid 1/45, Honshu Raids 2/45, Iwo Jima, Honshu Raids 2/45, Okinawa.

DD 683 *Stockham* Damaged in typhoon, Philippine Sea, 5 Jun 1945. Decomm Nov 1947. †
8* Saipan, Guam, Tinian, Palau, Philippines Raids 9/44, Okinawa Raid 10/44, N. Luzon–Formosa Raids 10/44, Luzon Raids 10/44, Visayas Is. Raids 10/44, Surigao Strait, Formosa Raids 1/45, China Coast Raids 1/45, Nansei Shoto Raid 1/45, Honshu Raids 2/45, Iwo Jima, Raids on Japan 7–8/45. Tokyo Bay.

DD 684 *Wedderburn* Decomm 4 Apr 1946. †
7* Guam, Palau, Philippines Raids 9/44, Okinawa Raid 10/44, N. Luzon–Formosa Raids 10/44, Luzon Raids 10/44, Visayas Is. Raids 10/44, Surigao Strait, Formosa Raids 1/45, Luzon Raids 1/45, China Coast Raids 1/45, Nansei Shoto Raid 1/45, Iwo Jima, Honshu Raids 2/45, Fleet Raids 1945, Raids on Japan 7–8/45. Tokyo Bay.

DD 685 *Picking* Decomm 20 Dec 1945. †
5* Kurile Is., Leyte, Lingayen, Mariveles-Corregidor, Subic Bay, Okinawa.

DD 686 *Halsey Powell* Damaged in storm off Iwo Jima, 26 Feb 1945. Severely damaged by kamikaze southeast of Kyushu, 20 Mar 1945 (12 killed). Decomm 10 Dec 1946. †
7* Saipan, Tinian, Guam, Palau, Philippines Raids 9/44, Okinawa Raid 10/44, N. Luzon–Formosa Raids 10/44, Luzon Raids 10/44, Visayas Is. Raids 10/44, Surigao Strait, Formosa Raids 1/45, Luzon Raids 1/45, China Coast Raids 1/45, Honshu Raids 2/45, Iwo Jima, Fleet Raids 1945. Tokyo Bay.

DD 687 *Uhlmann* Damaged in collision with destroyer *Benham* off Hawaii, 24 Apr 1944. Damaged by collision with three destroyers during typhoon at Ulithi, Micronesia, 3 Oct 1944. Decomm 14 Jun 1946. †
7* Palau, Philippines Raids 9/44, Okinawa Raid 10/44, N. Luzon–Formosa Raids 10/44, Luzon Raids 10/44, Visayas Is. Raids 10/44, Formosa Raids 1/45, Luzon Raids 1/45, China Coast Raids 1/45, Nansei Shoto Raid 1/45, Honshu Raids 2/45, Iwo Jima, Fleet Raids 1945, Raids on Japan 7–8/45. Tokyo Bay.
Submarine sunk: *Kaiten carrier *I-56* east of Okinawa, 18 Apr 1945.

DD 688 *Remey* Damaged by kamikaze, 12 Apr 1945. Decomm 10 Dec 1946. †
10* Kwajalein, Saipan, Tinian, Palau, Leyte, Surigao Strait, Luzon Raids 10/44, Mindoro, Lingayen, Honshu Raids 2/45, Iwo Jima, Honshu Raids 2/45, Fleet Raids 1945, Raids on Japan 7–8/45, Kurile Is.

DD 689 *Wadleigh* Severely damaged by mine off Peleliu, 16 Sep 1944 (3 killed). Decomm Jan 1947. †
6* Saipan, Tinian, Palau, Fleet Raids 1945, Raids on Japan 7–8/45. Tokyo Bay.
Submarine sunk: **RO-114* west of Tinian, 17 Jun 1944.

DD 690 *Norman Scott* Damaged by six hits by shore gunfire off Tinian, 24 Jul 1944 (22 killed). Damaged by collision with oiler *Cimarron* southeast of Okinawa, 4 Apr 1945. Decomm 30 Apr 1946. †
5* Saipan, Tinian, Honshu Raids 2/45, Iwo Jima, Fleet Raids 1945, Raids on Japan 7–8/45.

DD 691 *Mertz* Decomm 23 Apr 1946. †
10* Palau-Yap Raids 3/44, Saipan, Guam, Tinian, Palau, Leyte, Surigao Strait, Honshu Raids 2/45, Iwo Jima, Fleet Raids 1945, Raids on Japan 7–8/45, Kurile Is.
Submarines sunk: **RO-56* east of Okinawa, 9 Apr 1945; *Kaiten carrier *I-56* east of Okinawa, 18 Apr 1945.

DD 792 *Callaghan* Minor damage by kamikaze, Okinawa, 26 Mar 1945. Sunk by kamikaze and bomb off Okinawa, 28 Jul 1945 (47 killed).
8* Palau-Yap Raids 3/44, Hollandia, Truk Raid 4/44, Saipan, Guam, Palau, Philippines Raids 9/44, Okinawa Raid 10/44, N. Luzon–Formosa Raids 10/44, Luzon Raids 10/44, Visayas Is. Raids 10/44, Surigao Strait, Formosa Raids 1/45, Luzon Raids 1/45, China Coast Raids 1/45, Nansei Shoto Raid 1/45, Honshu Raids 2/45, Iwo Jima, Okinawa.

DD 793 *Cassin Young* Minor damaged by aircraft strafing, north of Luzon, 14 Oct 1944. Severely damaged by kamikaze, Okinawa, 12 Apr 1945 (1 killed). Damaged by kamikaze and bomb, Okinawa, 29 Jul 1945 (22 killed). Decomm 28 May 1946. †
4* Okinawa Raid 10/44, N. Luzon–Formosa Raids 10/44, Luzon Raids 10/44, Visayas Is. Raids 10/44, Surigao Strait, Formosa Raids 1/45, Luzon Raids 1/45, China Coast Raids 1/45, Nansei Shoto Raid 1/45, Honshu Raids 2/45, Iwo Jima, Okinawa.

DD 794 *Irwin* Damaged by explosion of carrier *Princeton*, Leyte, 24 Oct 1944. Decomm 21 May 1946. †
6* Saipan, Tinian, Guam, Palau, Philippines Raids 9/44, Okinawa Raid 10/44, N. Luzon–Formosa Raids 10/44, Luzon Raids 10/44, Visayas Is. Raids 10/44, Honshu Raids 2/45, Iwo Jima, Okinawa.

DD 795 *Preston* Damaged in storm off Iwo Jima, 26 Feb 1945. Decomm 24 Apr 1946. †
6* Guam, Palau, Philippines Raids 9/44, Okinawa Raid 10/44, N. Luzon–Formosa Raids 10/44, Luzon Raids 10/44, Visayas Is. Raids 10/44, Surigao Strait, Luzon Raids 10/44, Formosa Raids 1/45, Luzon Raids 1/45, China Coast Raids 1/45, Nansei Shoto Raid 1/45, Honshu Raids 2/45, Iwo Jima, Okinawa.

DD 796 *Benham* Damaged in collision with destroyer *Uhlmann* off Hawaii, 24 Apr 1944. Damaged in typhoon, Philippine Sea, 18 Dec 1944. Damaged in storm off Iwo Jima, 26 Feb 1945. Damaged by kamikaze and in error by gunfire, Okinawa, 17 Apr 1945. Decomm 18 Oct 1946. †
8* Saipan, Tinian, Guam, Palau, Philippines Raids 9/44, Okinawa Raid 10/44, N. Luzon–Formosa Raids 10/44, Luzon Raids 10/44, Visayas Is. Raids 10/44, Formosa Raids 1/45, Luzon Raids 1/45, China Coast Raids 1/45, Nansei Shoto Raid 1/45, Iwo Jima, Honshu Raids 2/45, Fleet Raids 1945, Raids on Japan 7–8/45. Tokyo Bay.

DD 797 *Cushing* Decomm 3 Feb 1947. †
6* Palau, Philippines Raids 9/44, Okinawa Raid 10/44, N. Luzon–Formosa Raids 10/44, Luzon Raids 10/44, Visayas Is. Raids 10/44, Surigao Strait, Formosa Raids 1/45, Luzon Raids 1/45, Formosa Raids 1/45, China Coast Raids 1/45, Nansei Shoto Raid 1/45, Iwo Jima, Honshu Raids 2/45, Fleet Raids 1945, Raids on Japan 7–8/45. Tokyo Bay.

DD 798 *Monssen* Decomm 30 Apr 1946. †
8* Saipan, Guam, Palau, Leyte, Surigao Strait, Honshu Raids 2/45, Iwo Jima, Honshu Raids 2/45, Fleet Raids 1945, Raids on Japan 7–8/45, Kurile Is.
Submarine sunk: **RO-56* east of Okinawa; 9 Apr 1945.

DD 799 *Jarvis* Decomm 29 Jun 1946. †
1* Kurile Is.

DD 800 *Porter* Decomm 3 Jul 1946. †
1* Kurile Is.

DD 801 *Colhoun* Damaged in collision, Iwo Jima, 27 Feb 1945. Minor damage by one hit from coastal gunfire, Iwo Jima, 1 Mar 1945 (1 killed). Damaged by three kamikazes off Okinawa, 6 Apr 1945 (34 killed) and sunk by destroyer *Cassin Young*.
2* Iwo Jima, Okinawa.

DD 802 *Gregory* Damaged by kamikaze and bombs off Okinawa, 8 Apr 1945. Decomm 15 Jan 1947. †
2* Iwo Jima, Okinawa.

DD 803 *Little* Sunk by four kamikazes off Okinawa, broke in two, 3 May 1945 (30 killed).
2* Iwo Jima, Okinawa.

DD 804 *Rooks* Decomm 11 Jun 1946. †
3* Iwo Jima, Okinawa, Raids on Japan 7–8/45.

Allen M. Sumner Class

No.	Name	Builder	Keel Laid	Launched	Comm.
DD 692	*Allen M. Sumner*	Federal	7 Jul 1943	15 Dec 1943	26 Jan 1944
DD 693	*Moale*	Federal	5 Aug 1943	16 Jan 1944	28 Feb 1944
DD 694	*Ingraham*	Federal	4 Aug 1943	16 Jan 1944	10 Mar 1944
DD 695	*Cooper*	Federal	30 Aug 1943	9 Feb 1944	27 Mar 1944
DD 696	*English*	Federal	19 Oct 1943	27 Feb 1944	4 May 1944

Figure 4.37: *Meredith* (DD 726), of the *Sumner* class, 29 Mar 1944, as completed. She was sunk at Normandy in June of the same year.

Figure 4.38: *Hugh W. Hadley* (DD 774), 11 Dec 1944. Notice the twin 5" gun mounts.

DD 697	*Charles S. Sperry*	Federal	19 Oct 1943	13 Mar 1944	17 May 1944
DD 698	*Ault*	Federal	15 Nov 1943	26 Mar 1944	31 May 1944
DD 699	*Waldron*	Federal	16 Nov 1943	26 Mar 1944	7 Jun 1944
DD 700	*Haynsworth*	Federal	16 Dec 1943	15 Apr. 1944	22 Jun 1944
DD 701	*John W. Weeks*	Federal	17 Jan 1944	21 May 1944	21 Jul 1944
DD 702	*Hank*	Federal	17 Jan 1944	21 May 1944	28 Aug 1944
DD 703	*Wallace L. Lind*	Federal	14 Feb 1944	14 Jun 1944	8 Sep 1944
DD 704	*Borie*	Federal	29 Feb 1944	4 Jul 1944	21 Sep 1944
DD 705	*Compton*	Federal	28 Mar 1944	17 Sep 1944	4 Nov 1944
DD 706	*Gainard*	Federal	29 Mar 1944	17 Sep 1944	23 Nov 1944
DD 707	*Soley*	Federal	18 Apr 1944	8 Sep 1944	8 Dec 1944
DD 708	*Harlan R. Dickson*	Federal	23 May 1944	17 Dec 1944	15 Feb 1945
DD 709	*Hugh Purvis*	Federal	23 May 1944	17 Dec 1944	1 Mar 1945
DD 722	*Barton*	Bath	24 May 1943	10 Oct 1943	30 Dec 1943
DD 723	*Walke*	Bath	7 Jun 1943	27 Oct 1943	21 Jan 1944
DD 724	*Laffey*	Bath	28 Jun 1943	21 Nov 1943	8 Feb 1944
DD 725	*O'Brien*	Bath	12 Jul 1943	8 Dec 1943	25 Feb 1944
DD 726	*Meredith*	Bath	26 Jul 1943	21 Dec 1943	14 Mar 1944
DD 727	*De Haven*	Bath	9 Aug 1943	9 Jan 1944	31 Mar 1944
DD 728	*Mansfield*	Bath	28 Aug 1943	29 Jan 1944	14 Apr 1944
DD 729	*Lyman K. Swenson*	Bath	11 Sep 1943	12 Feb 1944	2 May 1944
DD 730	*Collett*	Bath	11 Oct 1943	5 Mar 1944	16 May 1944
DD 731	*Maddox*	Bath	28 Oct 1943	19 Mar 1944	2 Jun 1944
DD 732	*Hyman*	Bath	22 Nov 1943	8 Apr 1944	16 Jun 1944
DD 733	*Mannert L. Abele*	Bath	9 Dec 1943	23 Apr 1944	4 Jul 1944
DD 734	*Purdy*	Bath	22 Dec 1943	7 May 1944	18 Jul 1944
DD 735	*Robert H. Smith*	Bath	10 Jan 1944	25 May 1944	4 Aug 1944
DD 736	*Thomas E. Fraser*	Bath	31 Jan 1944	10 Jun 1944	*22 Aug 1944*
DD 737	*Shannon*	Bath	14 Feb 1944	24 Jun 1944	*8 Sep 1944*
DD 738	*Harry F. Bauer*	Bath	6 Mar 1944	9 Jul 1944	*22 Sep 1944*
DD 739	*Adams*	Bath	20 Mar 1944	23 Jul 1944	*10 Oct 1944*
DD 740	*Tolman*	Bath	10 Apr 1944	13 Aug 1944	*27 Oct 1944*
DD 741	*Drexler*	Bath	24 Apr 1944	3 Sep 1944	14 Nov 1944

Displacement	2,200 tons; 2,315 f/l
Dimensions	376'6" (oa); 369' (wl) x 40'10' x 15'8"
Machinery	2 screws; West. GT; 4 B&W boilers; SHP 60,000; 36.5 knots
Endurance	6,500/15
Complement	345
Armament	6–5"/38, 2 quad and 2 twin 40mm, 11 20mm AA, 2–21" quint TT

Notes: Similar hull to *Fletcher* class. New twin 5" mounts, twin rudders. Twelve completed as minelayers (DM).

Service Records:

DD 692 *Allen M. Sumner* Damaged by aircraft bomb near miss, Ormoc Bay, 3 Dec 1944. Moderate damage by kamikaze, Lingayen Gulf, 6 Jan 1945 (14 killed). Operation Crossroads. †
2* Luzon Raids 10/44, Lingayen, Mindoro.

DD 693 *Moale* Damaged by naval gunfire, Ormoc Bay, 3 Dec 1944. Bow damaged in storm off Iwo Jima, 24 Feb 1945. Operation Crossroads. †
5* Luzon Raids 10/44, Mindoro, Lingayen, Honshu Raids 2/45, Iwo Jima, Okinawa, Raids on Japan 7–8/45.
Ships sunk: YP **Nanshin Maru No. 35*, **Kyowa Maru No. 3*, **Fukuitsu Maru No. 5* south of Honshu, 18 Feb 1945.

DD 694 *Ingraham* Damaged in collision with destroyer *Barton*, Iwo Jima, 16 Feb 1945. Severely damaged by kamikaze and bomb, Okinawa, 3 May 1945 (14 killed). Operation Crossroads. †
4* Luzon Raids 10/44, Mindoro, Lingayen, Honshu Raids 2/45, Iwo Jima, Okinawa.
Ships sunk: YP **Nanshin Maru No. 35*, **Kyowa Maru No. 3*, **Fukuitsu Maru No. 5* south of Honshu, 18 Feb 1945.

DD 695 *Cooper* Torpedoed and sunk by Japanese destroyer *Take* in Ormoc Bay, broke in two, 3 Dec 1944 (191 killed).
1* Luzon Raids 10/44.

DD 696 *English* †
4* Formosa Raids 1/45, Luzon Raids 1/45, China Coast Raids 1/45, Nansei Shoto Raid 1/45, Honshu Raids 2/45, Iwo Jima, Fleet Raids 1945, Okinawa, Raids on Japan 7–8/45.

DD 697 *Charles S. Sperry* †
4* Nansei Shoto Raid 1/45, Raids on Japan 7–8/45, Luzon Raids 1/45, Formosa Raids 1/45, China Coast Raids 1/45, Honshu Raids 2/45, Iwo Jima, Fleet Raids 1945.

DD 698 *Ault* †
5* Palau, Philippines Raids 9/44, Formosa Raids 1/45, Luzon Raids 1/45, Formosa Raids 1/45, China Coast Raids 1/45, Nansei Shoto Raid 1/45, Iwo Jima, Honshu Raids 2/45, Fleet Raids 1945, Raids on Japan 7–8/45. Tokyo Bay.

DD 699 *Waldron* †
4* Formosa Raids 1/45, Luzon Raids 1/45, China Coast Raids 1/45, Nansei Shoto Raid 1/45, Honshu Raids 2/45, Iwo Jima, Fleet Raids 1945, Raids on Japan 7–8/45.
Ship sunk: YP *Ajukawa Maru* off Iwo Jima, 17 Feb 1945.

DD 700 *Haynsworth* Severely damaged by kamikaze, Okinawa, 6 Apr 1945 (7 killed). †
3* Formosa Raids 1/45, Luzon Raids 1/45, China Coast Raids 1/45, Nansei Shoto Raid 1/45, Honshu Raids 2/45, Iwo Jima, Fleet Raids 1945.
Ships sunk: YP *Nanshin Maru No. 36, Wafu Maru,* 17 Feb 1945.

DD 701 *John W. Weeks* Damaged by coastal gunfire, Iwo Jima, 19 Feb 1945. Damaged in storm off Iwo Jima, 26 Feb 1945. Damaged in error by gunfire, east of Nojima, Honshu, 9 Aug 1945. †
4* Formosa Raids 1/45, Luzon Raids 1/45, China Coast Raids 1/45, Nansei Shoto Raid 1/45, Honshu Raids 2/45, Iwo Jima, Fleet Raids 1945, Raids on Japan 7–8/45.

DD 702 *Hank* Slightly damaged by Kamikaze near miss, Okinawa, 11 Apr 1945 (3 killed). †
4* Formosa Raids 1/45, Luzon Raids 1/45, China Coast Raids 1/45, Nansei Shoto Raid 1/45, Iwo Jima Bombard., Honshu Raids 2/45, Fleet Raids 1945, Raids on Japan 7–8/45.

DD 703 *Wallace L. Lind* †
4* Luzon Raids 1/45, Formosa Raids 1/45, China Coast Raids 1/45, Nansei Shoto Raid 1/45, Iwo Jima, Lingayen, Fleet Raids 1945, Raids on Japan 7–8/45. Tokyo Bay.

DD 704 *Borie* Damaged by collision with carrier *Essex,* southeast of Okinawa, 2 Apr 1945. Severely damaged by kamikaze, southeast of Sendai, Honshu, 9 Aug 1945 (48 killed). †
4* Honshu Raids 2/45, Iwo Jima, Fleet Raids 1945, Raids on Japan 7–8/45.

DD 705 *Compton* †
1* Okinawa.

DD 706 *Gainard* †
1* Okinawa.

DD 707 *Soley* Decomm 15 Apr 1947. †

DD 708 *Harlan R. Dickson* †

DD 709 *Hugh Purvis* †

DD 722 *Barton* Damaged by one hit from coastal gunfire, Cherbourg, 25 Jun 1944. Damaged in collision with destroyer *Ingraham,* Iwo Jima, 16 Feb 1945. Operation Crossroads. Decomm 22 Jan 1947. †
6* Normandy, Luzon Raids 10/44, Ormoc, Mindoro, Iwo Jima, Honshu Raids 2/45, Okinawa, Raids on Japan 7–8/45.
Ships sunk: YP **Nanshin Maru No. 35,* **Kyowa Maru No. 3,* **Fukuitsu Maru No. 5* south of Honshu, 18 Feb 1945.

DD 723 *Walke* Damaged by kamikaze and bomb off Lingayen, 6 Jan 1945 (1 killed). Operation Crossroads. Decomm 30 Jun 1947. †
6* Normandy, Luzon Raids 10/44, Ormoc, Mindoro, Lingayen, Okinawa, Raids on Japan 7–8/45.

DD 724 *Laffey* Hit by coastal gunfire off Cherbourg, 25 Jun 1944. Severely damaged by seven kamikazes and two bombs off Okinawa, 16 Apr 1945 (32 killed). Damaged in collision with *PC-815* north of San Diego, 11 Sep 1945. Operation Crossroads. Decomm 30 Jun 1947. †
5* Normandy, Luzon Raids 10/44, Ormoc, Mindoro, Lingayen, Iwo Jima, Honshu Raids 2/45, Okinawa. PUC.

DD 725 *O'Brien* Damaged by one hit by coastal gunfire, Cherbourg, 25 Jun 1944 (13 killed). Moderate damage by kamikaze, Lingayen, 6 Jan 1945. Severely damaged by kamikaze at Okinawa, 27 Mar 1945 (50 killed). Operation Crossroads. Decomm 4 Oct 1947. †
6* Normandy, Luzon Raids 10/44, Ormoc, Mindoro, Lingayen, Iwo Jima, Honshu Raids 2/45, Okinawa, Mindanao Ldgs..

DD 726 *Meredith* Sunk by mine off Normandy, 8–9 Jun 1944 (32 killed).
1* Normandy.

DD 727 *De Haven* Damaged in typhoon, Philippine Sea, 5 Jun 1945. †
5* Luzon Raids 10/44, Formosa Raids 1/45, Luzon Raids 1/45, China Coast Raids 1/45, Nansei Shoto Raid 1/45, Honshu Raids 2/45, Iwo Jima, Fleet Raids 1945, Raids on Japan 7–8/45. Tokyo Bay.

DD 728 *Mansfield* †
5* Luzon Raids 10/44, Formosa Raids 1/45, Luzon Raids 1/45, China Coast Raids 1/45, Nansei Shoto Raid 1/45, Iwo Jima, Honshu Raids 2/45, Fleet Raids 1945, Raids on Japan 7–8/45.

DD 729 *Lyman K. Swenson* †
5* Surigao Strait, Luzon Raids 10/44, Formosa Raids 1/45, Luzon Raids 1/45, China Coast Raids 1/45, Nansei Shoto Raid 1/45, Honshu Raids 2/45, Iwo Jima, Fleet Raids 1945, Raids on Japan 7–8/45.

DD 730 *Collett* †
6* N. Luzon–Formosa Raids 10/44, Luzon Raids 10/44, Formosa Raids 1/45, Luzon Raids 1/45, Nansei Shoto Raid 1/45, Honshu Raids 2/45, Iwo Jima, Fleet Raids 1945, Raids on Japan 7–8/45.
Submarine sunk: *Kaiten carrier *I-56* east of Okinawa, 18 Apr 1945.

DD 731 *Maddox* Damaged in typhoon, Philippine Sea, 18 Dec 1944. Moderate damage by kamikaze off Formosa, 21 Jan 1945 (7 killed). Damaged in typhoon, Philippine Sea, 5 Jun 1945. †
4* Luzon Raids 10/44, Formosa Raids 1/45, Luzon Raids 1/45, China Coast Raids 1/45, Fleet Raids 1945, Raids on Japan 7–8/45.

DD 732 *Hyman* Severely damaged by kamikaze, Okinawa, 6 Apr 1945 (10 killed). †
2* Iwo Jima, Okinawa.

DD 733 *Mannert L. Abele* Sunk by glider (baka) bomb and kamikaze off Okinawa, broke in two, 12 Apr 1945 (79 killed).
2* Iwo Jima, Okinawa.

DD 734 *Purdy* Moderate damage by kamikaze off Okinawa, 12 Apr 1945 (15 killed). †
1* Okinawa.

DD 735 *Robert H. Smith* Rec **DM 23**, 19 Jul 1944. Damaged by kamikaze, Okinawa, 25 Mar 1945. Decomm 29 Jan 1947. †
5* Lingayen, Iwo Jima, Okinawa, Raids on Japan 7–8/45, Minesweeping 1945.

DD 736 *Thomas E. Fraser* Rec **DM 24**, 19 Jul 1944. Damaged by collision, Okinawa, 15 Jul 1945. †
3* Iwo Jima, Okinawa, Raids on Japan 7–8/45. Tokyo Bay.

DD 737 *Shannon* Rec **DM 25**, 19 Jul 1944. Damaged by kamikaze, Okinawa, 29 Apr 1945. †
4* Iwo Jima, Okinawa, Raids on Japan 7–8/45, Minesweeping 1945.

DD 738 *Harry F. Bauer* Rec **DM 26**, 19 Jul 1944. Damaged by aircraft torpedo, Okinawa, 6 Apr 1945. Damaged by kamikaze, Okinawa, 29 Apr 1945, and again 10 May 1945, and on 6 Jun 1945. †
4* Iwo Jima, Okinawa, Raids on Japan 7–8/45, Minesweeping 1945. PUC.

DD 739 *Adams* Rec **DM 27**, 19 Jul 1944. Slight damage by kamikaze, Okinawa, 27 Mar 1945, then in collision with a salvage vessel. Damaged by kamikaze and bombs, Okinawa, 1 Apr 1945. Decomm 19 Jan 1947. †
2* Okinawa, Minesweeping 1945.

DD 740 *Tolman* Rec **DM 28**, 19 Jul 1944. Went aground on Nagunna Reef, south of Okinawa, 19 Apr 1945. Decomm 29 Jan 1947. †
1* Okinawa.

DD 741 *Drexler* Sunk by kamikaze and bomb off Okinawa, 8 May 1945 (164 killed)..
1* Okinawa.

No.	Name	Builder	Keel Laid	Launched	Comm.
DD 744	*Blue*	Beth. Staten I.	30 Jun 1943	28 Nov 1943	20 Mar 1944
DD 745	*Brush*	Beth. Staten I.	30 Jul 1943	28 Dec 1943	17 Apr 1944
DD 746	*Taussig*	Beth. Staten I.	30 Aug 1943	25 Jan 1944	20 May 1944
DD 747	*Samuel N. Moore*	Beth. Staten I.	30 Sep 1943	23 Feb 1944	24 Jun 1944
DD 748	*Harry E. Hubbard*	Beth. Staten I.	30 Oct 1943	24 Mar 1944	22 Jul 1944
DD 749	*Henry A. Wiley*	Beth. Staten I.	28 Nov 1943	21 Apr 1944	*31 Aug 1944*
DD 750	*Shea*	Beth. Staten I.	28 Dec 1943	20 May 1944	*30 Sep 1944*
DD 751	*J. William Ditter* ex-*William Ditter*	Beth. Staten I	25 Jan 1944	4 Jul 1944	*28 Oct 1944*
DD 752	*Alfred A. Cunningham*	Beth. Staten I.	23 Feb 1944	3 Aug 1944	23 Nov 1944
DD 753	*John R. Pierce*	Beth. Staten I.	24 Mar 1944	1 Sep 1944	30 Dec 1944
DD 754	*Frank E. Evans*	Beth. Staten I.	21 Apr 1944	3 Oct 1944	3 Feb 1945
DD 755	*John A. Bole*	Beth. Staten I.	20 May 1944	1 Nov 1944	3 Mar 1945
DD 756	*Beatty*	Beth. Staten I.	4 Jul 1944	30 Nov 1944	31 Mar 1945
DD 757	*Putnam*	Beth. S. Fran.	11 Jul 1943	26 Mar 1944	12 Oct 1944
DD 758	*Strong*	Beth. S. Fran.	25 Jul 1943	23 Apr 1944	8 Mar 1945
DD 759	*Lofberg*	Beth. S. Fran.	4 Nov 1943	12 Aug 1944	26 Apr 1945
DD 760	*John W. Thomason*	Beth. S. Fran.	21 Nov 1943	30 Sep 1944	11 Oct 1945
DD 761	*Buck*	Beth. S. Fran.	1 Feb 1944	11 Mar 1945	28 Jun 1945
DD 762	*Henley*	Beth. S. Fran.	8 Feb 1944	8 Apr 1945	8 Oct 1945
DD 770	*Lowry*	Beth. S. Pedro	1 Aug 1943	6 Feb 1944	28 Jul 1944
DD 771	*Lindsey*	Beth. S. Pedro	12 Sep 1943	5 Mar 1944	*20 Aug 1944*
DD 772	*Gwin*	Beth. S. Pedro	31 Oct 1943	9 Apr 1944	*30 Sep 1944*
DD 773	*Aaron Ward*	Beth. S. Pedro	12 Dec 1943	5 May 1944	*28 Oct 1944*
DD 774	*Hugh W. Hadley*	Beth. S. Pedro	6 Feb 1944	16 Jul 1944	25 Nov 1944
DD 775	*Willard Keith*	Beth. S. Pedro	5 Mar 1944	29 Aug 1944	27 Dec 1944
DD 776	*James C. Owens*	Beth. S. Pedro	9 Apr 1944	1 Oct 1944	17 Feb 1945
DD 777	*Zellars*	Todd Seattle	24 Dec 1943	19 Jul 1944	25 Oct 1944
DD 778	*Massey*	Todd Seattle	14 Jan 1944	19 Aug 1944	24 Nov 1944
DD 779	*Douglas H. Fox*	Todd Seattle	31 Jan 1944	30 Sep 1944	26 Dec 1944
DD 780	*Stormes*	Todd Seattle	15 Feb 1944	4 Nov 1944	27 Jan 1945
DD 781	*Robert K.Huntington*	Todd Seattle	29 Feb 1944	5 Dec 1944	3 Mar 1945
DD 857	*Bristol*	Todd Seattle	5 May 1944	29 Oct 1944	17 Mar 1945

Service Records:

DD 744 *Blue* Damaged in typhoon, Philippine Sea, 5 Jun 1945. Decomm 14 Feb 1947. †
6* Bonins-Yap Raids, Palau, Philippines Raids 9/44, Luzon Raids 10/44, Formosa Raids 1/45, Luzon Raids 1/45, Formosa Raids 1/45, China Coast Raids 1/45, Honshu Raids 2/45, Iwo Jima, Fleet Raids 1945, Raids on Japan 7–8/45. Tokyo Bay.

DD 745 *Brush* Damaged in typhoon, Philippine Sea, 5 Jun 1945. †
5* Surigao Strait, Luzon Raids 10/44, Formosa Raids 1/45, Luzon Raids 1/45, China Coast Raids 1/45, Nansei Shoto Raid 1/45, Honshu Raids 2/45, Iwo Jima, Fleet Raids 1945, Raids on Japan 7–8/45.

DD 746 *Taussig* Slightly damaged by aircraft bomb, Okinawa, 6 Apr 1945. Damaged in typhoon, Philippine Sea, 5 Jun 1945. †
6* Palau, Philippines Raids 9/44, Luzon Raids 10/44, Formosa Raids 1/45, Luzon Raids 1/45, China Coast Raids 1/45, Nansei Shoto Raid 1/45, Iwo Jima, Honshu Raids 2/45, Fleet Raids 1945, Raids on Japan 7–8/45.

DD 747 *Samuel N. Moore* Damaged in typhoon, Philippine Sea, 5 Jun 1945. †
5* Luzon Raids 10/44, Formosa Raids 1/45, Luzon Raids 1/45, China Coast Raids 1/45, Nansei Shoto Raid 1/45, Honshu Raids 2/45, Iwo Jima, Fleet Raids 1945, Raids on Japan 7–8/45.

DD 748 *Harry E. Hubbard* Decomm 15 Jan 1947. †
1* Okinawa.

DD 749 *Henry A. Wiley* Rec **DM 29**, 19 Jul 1944. Decomm 29 Jan 1947. †
4* Iwo Jima, Okinawa, Raids on Japan 7–8/45, Minesweeping 1945. PUC.

DD 750 *Shea* Rec **DM 30**, 19 Jul 1944. Damaged by kamikaze, Okinawa, 22 Apr 1945. Damaged by piloted (baka) bomb, Okinawa, 3 May 1945 (27 killed). †
1* Okinawa.

DD 751 *J. William Ditter* Rec **DM 31**, 19 Jul 1944. Severely damaged by kamikaze, Okinawa, 6 Jun 1945 (10 killed). Decomm 28 Sep 1945. Stricken 11 Oct 1945, sold 12 Jul 1946; BU.
1* Okinawa.

DD 752 *Alfred A.Cunningham* Decomm 12 May 1947. †
1* Okinawa.

DD 753 *John R. Pierce* Decomm 24 Jan 1947. †

DD 754 *Frank E. Evans* †
1* Okinawa.

DD 755 *John A. Bole* †
1* Okinawa.

DD 756 *Beatty* †

DD 757 *Putnam* †
3* Iwo Jima, Okinawa, Raids on Japan 7–8/45.

DD 758 *Strong* Decomm 9 May 1947. †

DD 759 *Lofberg* †

DD 760 *John W. Thomason* †

DD 761 *Buck* †

DD 762 *Henley* †

DD 770 *Lowry* Damaged in error by U.S. gunfire, Lingayen, 6 Jan 1945. Light damage by kamikaze, Okinawa, 3 May 1945. Damaged by kaiten from *I-58* in Philippine Sea, 26 Jul 1945. Operation Crossroads. Decomm 30 Jun 1947. †

4* Mindoro, Lingayen, Honshu Raids 2/45, Iwo Jima, Okinawa, Raids on Japan 7–8/45.

DD 771 *Lindsey* Rec **DM 32**, 19 Jul 1944. Severely damaged by two kamikazes and lost bow off Okinawa, 12 Apr 1945 (57 killed). Decomm 25 May 1946. †
2* Iwo Jima, Okinawa.

DD 772 *Gwin* Rec **DM 33**, 19 Jul 1944. Damaged by kamikaze, Okinawa, 4 May 1945 (4 killed). Decomm 3 Sep 1946. †
4* Iwo Jima Bombard., Okinawa, Raids on Japan 7–8/45, Minesweeping 1945. Tokyo Bay.

DD 773 *Aaron Ward* Rec **DM 34**, 19 Jul 1944. Severely damaged by three kamikazes, Okinawa, 3 May 1945 (45 killed). Decomm 25 Sep 1945, not repaired. Stricken 11 Oct 1945, sold 12 Jul 1946. †
1* Okinawa. PUC.

DD 774 *Hugh W. Hadley* Severely damaged by piloted (baka) bomb and two kamikazes, Okinawa, 11 May 1945 (28 killed). Decomm 15 Dec 1945. Stricken 8 Jan 1946, sold 2 Sep 1947; BU.
1* Okinawa.

DD 775 *Willard Keith* Decomm Jun 1947. †
2* Okinawa, Raids on Japan 7–8/45.

DD 776 *James C. Owens* †
2* Okinawa, Raids on Japan 7–8/45.

DD 777 *Zellars* Severely damaged by kamikaze and bomb, Okinawa, 2 Apr 1945 (29 killed). †
1* Okinawa.

DD 778 *Massey* †
2* Okinawa, Raids on Japan 7–8/45.

DD 779 *Douglas H. Fox* Moderate damage by kamikaze and bomb, Okinawa, 17 May 1945 (7 killed). †
1*Okinawa.

DD 780 *Stormes* Moderate damaged by kamikaze and bomb, Okinawa, 25 May 1945 (21 killed). †
1* Okinawa.

DD 781 *Robert K. Huntington* Tokyo Bay. Operation Crossroads. †

DD 857 *Bristol* Damaged in collision with oiler *Ashtabula* off Iwo Jima, 5 Aug 1945. †
1* Raids on Japan 7–8/45.

Gearing Class

No.	Name	Builder	Keel Laid	Launched	Comm.
DD 710	*Gearing*	Federal	10 Aug 1944	18 Feb 1945	3 May 1945
DD 711	*Eugene A. Greene*	Federal	17 Aug 1944	18 Mar 1945	8 Jun 1945
DD 712	*Gyatt*	Federal	7 Sep 1944	15 Apr 1945	2 Jul 1945
DD 713	*Kenneth D. Bailey*	Federal	21 Sep 1944	17 Jun 1945	31 Jul 1945
DD 714	*William R. Rush*	Federal	19 Oct 1944	8 Jul 1945	21 Sep 1945
DD 715	*William M. Wood*	Federal	2 Nov 1944	29 Jul 1945	24 Nov 1945
DD 716	*Wiltsie*	Federal	13 Mar 1945	31 Aug 1945	12 Jan 1946
DD 717	*Theodore E.Chandler*	Federal	23 Apr 1945	10 Oct 1945	22 Mar 1946
DD 718	*Hamner*	Federal	25 Apr 1945	24 Nov 1945	12 Jul 1946
DD 719	*Epperson*	Federal	20 Jun 1945	22 Dec 1945	19 Mar 1949
DD 720	*Castle*	Federal	11 Jul 1945	16 Feb 1946	—
DD 721	*Woodrow R. Thompson*	Federal	1 Aug 1945	16 Mar 1946	—
DD 742	*Frank Knox*	Bath	8 May 1944	17 Sep 1944	11 Dec 1944
DD 743	*Southerland*	Bath	27 May 1944	5 Oct 1944	22 Dec 1944
DD 763	*William C. Lawe*	Beth. S. Fran.	12 Mar 1944	21 May 1945	18 Dec 1946
DD 764	*Lloyd Thomas*	Beth. S. Fran.	26 Mar 1944	5 Oct 1945	21 Mar 1947
DD 765	*Keppler*	Beth. S. Fran.	23 Apr 1944	24 Jun 1946	23 May 1947
DD 766	*Lansdale*	Beth. S. Fran.	2 Apr 1944	20 Dec 1946	—
DD 767	*Seymour D. Owens*	Beth. S. Fran.	3 Apr 1944	24 Feb 1947	—
DD 768	*Hoel*	Beth. S. Fran.	21 Apr 1944	—	—
DD 769	*Abner Read*	Beth. S. Fran.	21 May 1944	—	—

Figure 4.39: *Gearing* (DD 710), 29 May 1946. The nameship of her class, a lengthened version of the *Sumner* class. Notice the two-gun mount and depth charge racks on stern. Aft bank of tubes has been removed.

Figure 4.40: *George K. Mackenzie* (DD 836), 1945. A typical *Gearing*-class destroyer as completed, with only one bank of torpedo tubes.

Displacement	2,425 tons; 3,479 f/l
Dimensions	391' (oa); 383' (wl) x 40'1" x 18'6"
Machinery	2 screws; GE GT; 4 B&W boilers; SHP 60,000; 34.6 knots
Endurance	4,500/20
Complement	345
Armament	6–5"/38, 2 quad and 2 twin 40mm AA, 20–20mm AA, 1 or 2–21" quint TT

Notes: *Sumner* class with added section in hull. Very wet forward. DD 719, 766, 767, 791, 824, 825, 827 delivered incomplete. DD 850–56 originally ordered from Beth. S. Fran., and DD 809–28 from Federal. DD 742–43, 805–8, 829–35, 873–83 converted to radar pickets (DDR) with tripod mainmast added in place of one bank of TT. Completion of *Timmerman* (828) was delayed for experimental purposes.

Service Records:

DD 710 *Gearing* †
DD 711 *Eugene A. Greene* †
DD 712 *Gyatt* †
DD 713 *Kenneth D. Bailey* †
DD 714 *William R. Rush* †
DD 715 *William M. Wood* †
DD 716 *Wiltsie* †
DD 717 *Theodore E. Chandler* †
DD 718 *Hamner* †
DD 719 *Epperson* †
DD 720 *Castle* Construction suspended 11 Feb 1946. †
DD 721 *Woodrow R. Thompson* Construction suspended 11 Feb 1946. †
DD 742 *Frank Knox* In collision with destroyer *Higbee* off Oahu, 15 Nov 1946. †
1* Raids on Japan 7–8/45. Tokyo Bay.
DD 743 *Southerland* †
1* Raids on Japan 7–8/45. Tokyo Bay.
DD 763 *William C. Lawe* †
DD 764 *Lloyd Thomas* †
DD 765 *Keppler* †
DD 766 *Lansdale* Construction suspended, 7 Jan 1946. †
DD 767 *Seymour D. Owens* Construction suspended 7 Jan 1946. †
DD 768 *Hoel* Canceled 1 Sep 1946.
DD 769 *Abner Read* Canceled 1 Sep 1946.

Figure 4.42: *Dennis J. Buckley* (DD 808), 24 Apr 1945, completed as a radar picket with radar mast between the funnels.

No.	Name	Builder	Keel Laid	Launched	Comm.
DD 782	*Rowan*	Todd Seattle	25 Mar 1944	29 Dec 1944	31 Mar 1945
DD 783	*Gurke*	Todd Seattle	1 Jul 1944	15 Feb 1945	12 May 1945
	ex-*John A. Bole* (15 Jun 1944)				
DD 784	*McKean*	Todd Seattle	15 Sep 1944	31 Mar 1945	9 Jun 1945
DD 785	*Henderson*	Todd Seattle	27 Oct 1944	28 May 1945	4 Aug 1945
DD 786	*Richard B. Anderson*	Todd Seattle	1 Dec 1944	7 Jul 1945	26 Oct 1945
DD 787	*James E. Kyes*	Todd Seattle	27 Dec 1944	4 Aug 1945	8 Feb 1946
DD 788	*Hollister*	Todd Seattle	18 Jan 1945	9 Oct 1945	26 Mar 1946
DD 789	*Eversole*	Todd Seattle	28 Feb 1945	8 Jan 1946	10 May 1946
DD 790	*Shelton*	Todd Seattle	31 May 1945	8 Mar 1946	21 Jun 1946
DD 791	*Seaman*	Todd Seattle	10 Jul 1945	20 May 1946	—
DD 805	*Chevalier*	Bath	12 Jun 1944	29 Oct 1944	9 Jan 1945
DD 806	*Higbee*	Bath	26 Jun 1944	12 Nov 1944	27 Jan 1945
DD 807	*Benner*	Bath	10 Jul 1944	30 Nov 1944	13 Feb 1945
DD 808	*Dennis J. Buckley*	Bath	24 Jul 1944	20 Dec 1944	2 Mar 1945
DD 809–12	—	Bath	—	—	—
DD 813–14	—	Beth. Staten I.	—	—	—
DD 815	*Charles H. Roan*	Consol. Orange	—	—	—
DD 816	*Timmerman*	Consol. Orange	—	—	—
DD 817	*Corry*	Consol. Orange	5 Apr 1945	28 Jul 1945	27 Feb 1946
DD 818	*New*	Consol. Orange	14 Apr 1945	18 Aug 1945	5 Apr 1946
DD 819	*Holder*	Consol. Orange	23 Apr 1945	25 Aug 1945	18 May 1946
DD 820	*Rich*	Consol. Orange	16 May 1945	5 Oct 1945	3 Jul 1946
DD 821	*Johnston*	Consol. Orange	5 Jun 1945	19 Oct 1945	23 Aug 1946
DD 822	*Robert H. McCard*	Consol. Orange	20 Jun 1945	9 Nov 1945	23 Oct 1946
DD 823	*Samuel B. Roberts*	Consol. Orange	27 Jun 1945	30 Nov 1945	22 Dec 1946
DD 824	*Basilone*	Consol. Orange	7 Jul 1945	21 Dec 1945	26 Jul 1949
DD 825	*Carpenter*	Consol. Orange	30 Jul 1945	28 Dec 1945	15 Dec 1949

Figure 4.41: *Frank Knox* (DD 742), 20 Mar 1945, as radar picket, one of the few *Gearing*-class destroyers to serve in the war.

Service Records:

DD 782 *Rowan* †
DD 783 *Gurke* †
DD 784 *McKean* †
DD 785 *Henderson* †
DD 786 *Richard B. Anderson* †
DD 787 *James E. Kyes* †
DD 788 *Hollister* †
DD 789 *Eversole* †
DD 790 *Shelton* †
DD 791 *Seaman* Construction suspended, 1946. Delivered incomplete 25 Jun 1946. †
DD 805 *Chevalier* †
1* Raids on Japan 7–8/45.
DD 806 *Higbee* Damaged in collision with destroyer *Frank Knox* off Oahu, 15 Nov 1946. †
1* Raids on Japan 7–8/45.
DD 807 *Benner* †
1* Raids on Japan 7–8/45.
DD 808 *Dennis J. Buckley* †
DD 809–14 Canceled 11 Aug 1945.
DD 815 *Charles H. Roan* Canceled 11 Aug 1945.
DD 816 *Timmerman* Canceled 11 Aug 1945.
DD 817 *Corry* †
DD 818 *New* †
DD 819 *Holder* †
DD 820 *Rich* †
DD 821 *Johnston* †
DD 822 *Robert H. McCard* †
DD 823 *Samuel B. Roberts* †
DD 824 *Basilone* Delivered incomplete. †
DD 825 *Carpenter* Delivered incomplete. Completed by Newport News. †

No.	Name	Builder	Keel Laid	Launched	Comm.
DD 826	*Agerholm*	Bath	10 Sep 1945	30 Mar 1946	20 Jun 1946
DD 827	*Robert A. Owens*	Bath	1 Oct 1945	15 Jul 1946	5 Nov 1949
DD 828	*Timmerman*	Bath	1 Oct 1945	19 May 1951	26 Sep 1952
DD 829	*Myles C. Fox*	Bath	14 Aug 1944	13 Jan 1945	20 Mar 1945
DD 830	*Everett F. Larson*	Bath	4 Sep 1944	28 Jan 1945	6 Apr 1945
DD 831	*Goodrich*	Bath	18 Sep 1944	25 Feb 1945	24 Apr 1945
DD 832	*Hanson*	Bath	7 Oct 1944	11 Mar 1945	11 May 1945
DD 833	*Herbert J. Thomas*	Bath	30 Oct 1944	25 Mar 1945	29 May 1945
DD 834	*Turner*	Bath	13 Nov 1944	8 Apr 1945	12 Jun 1945
DD 835	*Charles P. Cecil*	Bath	2 Dec 1944	22 Apr 1945	29 Jun 1945
DD 836	*George K. Mackenzie*	Bath	21 Dec 1944	13 May 1945	13 Jul 1945
DD 837	*Sarsfield*	Bath	15 Jan 1945	27 May 1945	31 Jul 1945
DD 838	*Ernest G. Small*	Bath	30 Jan 1945	14 Jun 1945	21 Aug 1945
DD 839	*Power*	Bath	26 Feb 1945	30 Jun 1945	13 Sep 1945
DD 840	*Glennon*	Bath	12 Mar 1945	14 Jul 1945	4 Oct 1945
DD 841	*Noa*	Bath	26 Mar 1945	30 Jul 1945	2 Nov 1945
DD 842	*Fiske*	Bath	9 Apr 1945	8 Sep 1945	28 Nov 1945
DD 843	*Warrington*	Bath	23 Apr 1945	27 Sep 1945	20 Dec 1945
DD 844	*Perry*	Bath	14 May 1945	25 Oct 1945	17 Jan 1946
DD 845	*Bausell*	Bath	28 May 1945	19 Nov 1945	7 Feb 1946
DD 846	*Ozbourn*	Bath	16 Jun 1945	22 Dec 1945	5 Mar 1946
DD 847	*Robert L. Wilson*	Bath	2 Jul 1945	5 Jan 1946	28 Mar 1946
DD 848	*Witek*	Bath	16 Jul 1945	2 Feb 1946	23 Apr 1946
DD 849	*Richard E. Kraus*	Bath	31 Jul 1945	2 Mar 1946	23 May 1946
DD 850	*Joseph P. Kennedy Jr.*	Beth. Quincy	2 Apr 1945	26 Jul 1945	15 Dec 1945
DD 851	*Rupertus*	Beth. Quincy	2 May 1945	21 Sep 1945	8 Mar 1946
DD 852	*Leonard F. Mason*	Beth. Quincy	6 Aug 1945	4 Jan 1946	28 Jun 1946
DD 853	*Charles H. Roan*	Beth. Quincy	27 Sep 1945	15 Mar 1946	12 Sep 1946
DD 854	*Robert A. Owens*	Beth. Staten I.	7 Jul 1945	—	—
DD 855	—	Beth. Staten I.	6 Aug 1945	—	—
DD 856	—	Beth. Staten I.	—	—	—

Service Records:

DD 826 *Agerholm* †
DD 827 *Robert A. Owens* Delivered incomplete. Completed by Newport News. †
DD 828 *Timmerman* Construction suspended 1946. Experimental unit. †
DD 829 *Myles C. Fox* †
DD 830 *Everett F. Larson* †
DD 831 *Goodrich* †
DD 832 *Hanson* †
DD 833 *Herbert J. Thomas* †
DD 834 *Turner* Operation Crossroads. †
DD 835 *Charles P. Cecil* Operation Crossroads. †
DD 836 *George K. Mackenzie* †
DD 837 *Sarsfield* †
DD 838 *Ernest G. Small* Went aground on Block I., N.Y., 3 Apr 1947. †
DD 839 *Power* †
DD 840 *Glennon* †
DD 841 *Noa* †
DD 842 *Fiske* †
DD 843 *Warrington* †
DD 844 *Perry* †
DD 845 *Bausell* †
DD 846 *Ozbourn* †
DD 847 *Robert L. Wilson* †
DD 848 *Witek* Rec **EDD 848**, Jul 1946. †
DD 849 *Richard E. Kraus* †
DD 850 *Joseph P. Kennedy Jr.* †
DD 851 *Rupertus* †
DD 852 *Leonard F. Mason* †
DD 853 *Charles H. Roan* †
DD 854 *Robert A. Owens* Canceled 11 Aug 1945.
DD 855–56 — Canceled 11 Aug 1945.

No.	Name	Builder	Keel Laid	Launched	Comm.
DD 858	*Fred T. Berry*	Beth. S. Pedro	16 Jul 1944	28 Jan 1945	12 May 1945
DD 859	*Norris*	Beth. S. Pedro	29 Aug 1944	25 Feb 1945	9 Jun 1945
DD 860	*McCaffery*	Beth. S. Pedro	1 Oct 1944	12 Apr 1945	26 Jul 1945

DD 861	*Harwood*	Beth. S. Pedro	29 Oct 1944	22 May 1945	28 Sep. 1945
DD 862	*Vogelgesang*	Beth. Staten I.	3 Aug 1944	15 Jan 1945	28 Apr 1945
DD 863	*Steinaker*	Beth. Staten I.	1 Sep. 1944	13 Feb 1945	26 May 1945
DD 864	*Harold J. Ellison*	Beth. Staten I	3 Oct 1944	14 Mar 1945	23 Jun 1945
DD 865	*Charles R. Ware*	Beth. Staten I.	1 Nov 1944	12 Apr 1945	21 Jul 1945
DD 866	*Cone*	Beth. Staten I.	30 Nov 1944	10 May 1945	18 Aug 1945
DD 867	*Stribling*	Beth. Staten I.	15 Jan 1945	8 Jun 1945	29 Sep. 1945
DD 868	*Brownson*	Beth. Staten I.	13 Feb 1945	7 Jul 1945	17 Nov 1945
DD 869	*Arnold J. Isbell*	Beth. Staten I.	14 Mar 1945	6 Aug 1945	5 Jan 1946
DD 870	*Fechteler*	Beth. Staten I.	12 Apr 1945	19 Sep. 1945	2 Mar 1946
DD 871	*Damato*	Beth. Staten I.	10 May 1945	21 Nov 1945	27 Apr 1946
DD 872	*Forrest Royal*	Beth. Staten I.	8 Jun 1945	17 Jan 1946	29 Jun 1946
DD 873	*Hawkins*	Consol. Orange	14 May 1944	7 Oct 1944	10 Feb 1945
DD 874	*Duncan*	Consol. Orange	22 May 1944	27 Oct 1944	25 Feb 1945
DD 875	*Henry W. Tucker*	Consol. Orange	29 May 1944	8 Nov 1944	12 Mar 1945
DD 876	*Rogers*	Consol. Orange	3 Jun 1944	20 Nov 1944	26 Mar 1945
DD 877	*Perkins*	Consol. Orange	19 Jun 1944	7 Dec 1944	5 Apr 1945
DD 878	*Vesole*	Consol. Orange	3 Jul 1944	29 Dec 1944	23 Apr 1945
DD 879	*Leary*	Consol. Orange	11 Aug 1944	20 Jan 1945	7 May 1945
DD 880	*Dyess*	Consol. Orange	17 Aug 1944	26 Jan 1945	21 May 1945
DD 881	*Bordelon*	Consol. Orange	9 Sep. 1944	3 Mar 1945	5 Jun 1945
DD 882	*Furse*	Consol. Orange	23 Sep. 1944	9 Mar 1945	10 Jul 1945
DD 883	*Newman K. Perry*	Consol. Orange	10 Oct 1944	17 Mar 1945	26 Jul 1945
DD 884	*Floyd B. Parks*	Consol. Orange	30 Oct 1944	31 Mar 1945	31 Jul 1945
DD 885	*John R. Craig*	Consol. Orange	17 Nov 1944	14 Apr 1945	20 Aug 1945
DD 886	*Orleck*	Consol. Orange	28 Nov 1944	12 May 1945	15 Sep. 1945
DD 887	*Brinkley Bass*	Consol. Orange	20 Dec 1944	26 May 1945	1 Oct 1945
DD 888	*Stickell*	Consol. Orange	5 Jan 1945	26 May 1945	31 Oct 1945
DD 889	*O'Hare*	Consol. Orange	27 Jan 1945	22 Jun 1945	29 Nov 1945
DD 890	*Meredith*	Consol. Orange	27 Jan 1945	28 Jun 1945	31 Dec 1945
DD 891 –893	—	Federal	—	—	—
DD 894 –895	—	Consol. Orange	—	—	—
DD 896 –904	—	Bath	—	—	—
DD 905 –908	—	Boston NYd	—	—	—
DD 909 –916	—	Beth. Staten I.	—	—	—
DD 917–24	—	Consol. Orange	—	—	—
DD 925–26	—	Charleston NYd	—	—	—

Service Records:

DD 858 *Fred T. Berry* †
DD 859 *Norris* †
DD 860 *McCaffery* †
DD 861 *Harwood* †
DD 862 *Vogelgesang* †
DD 863 *Steinaker* †
DD 864 *Harold J. Ellison* †
DD 865 *Charles R. Ware* †
DD 866 *Cone* †
DD 867 *Stribling* †
DD 868 *Brownson* †
DD 869 *Arnold J. Isbell* †
DD 870 *Fechteler* †
DD 871 *Damato* †
DD 872 *Forrest Royal* †
DD 873 *Hawkins* †
DD 874 *Duncan*†
DD 875 *Henry W. Tucker* †
DD 876 *Rogers* †
DD 877 *Perkins* Tokyo Bay. †
DD 878 *Vesole* †
DD 879 *Leary* †
DD 880 *Dyess* †
DD 881 *Bordelon* †
DD 882 *Furse* Operation Crossroads. †
DD 883 *Newman K. Perry* Operation Crossroads. †
DD 884 *Floyd B. Parks* †
DD 885 *John R. Craig* †
DD 886 *Orleck* †
DD 887 *Brinkley Bass* †
DD 888 *Stickell* †
DD 889 *O'Hare* †
DD 890 *Meredith* †
DD 891–93 — Canceled 8 Mar 1945.
DD 894–95 — Canceled 27 Mar 1945.
DD 896–904 — Canceled 8 Mar 1945.
DD 905–26 — Canceled 27 Mar 1945.

EX–ENEMY SHIPS

DD 934 *Hanatsuki* Japanese destroyer, launched 10 Oct 1944. Taken as prize 28 Aug 1947. BU 1948.

DD 935 *T-35* German torpedo boat, launched 1941. Taken as prize Jul 1945. Trfd to France 1948. BU 1953.

DD 939 *Z-39* German destroyer, launched 2 Dec 1941. Taken as a prize Jul 1945 and used for materials experiments. Trfd to France 1947 for replacement parts. BU Feb 1964.

5
DESTROYER ESCORTS

Destroyer escorts were designed for the United Kingdom's Royal Navy requirements, with a length of 300', a speed of 30 knots, dual-purpose main armament, and an open bridge. The first units were ordered as BDE 1–50.

Originally, more diesel engines were available and the design called for two engines equaling 12,000 horsepower for 24 knots. But too many were ordered for the diesel manufacturers, so the installation was halved, with 6,000 horsepower for 19 knots. There were difficulties finding engines for so many ships and later units used alternatives such as geared turbines.

Figure 5.1: *Dionne* (DE 261), 21 May 1945, a short-hull destroyer escort, type GMT.

Evarts Class (GMT)

No.	Name	Builder	Keel Laid	Launched	Comm.
BDE 1	—	Boston NYd	5 Apr 1942	27 Jun 1942	*13 Feb 1943*
BDE 2	—	Boston NYd	5 Apr 1942	27 Jun 1942	*18 Feb 1943*
BDE 3	—	Boston NYd	22 Sep 1942	23 Nov 1942	*15 Mar 1943*
BDE 4	—	Boston NYd	22 Sep 1942	23 Nov 1942	*27 Mar 1943*
DE 5	*Evarts*	Boston NYd	17 Oct 1942	7 Dec 1942	5 Apr 1943
DE 6	*Wyffels*	Boston NYd	17 Oct 1942	7 Dec 1942	21 Apr 1943
DE 7	*Griswold*	Boston NYd	27 Nov 1942	9 Jan 1943	28 Apr 1943
DE 8	*Steele*	Boston NYd	27 Nov 1942	9 Jan 1943	4 May 1943
DE 9	*Carlson*	Boston NYd	27 Nov 1942	9 Jan 1943	10 May 1943
DE 10	*Bebas*	Boston NYd	27 Nov 1942	9 Jan 1943	15 May 1943
DE 11	*Crouter*	Boston NYd	8 Dec 1942	26 Jan 1943	25 May 1943
BDE 12	—	Boston NYd	8 Dec 1942	26 Jan 1943	*2 Jun 1943*
DE 13	*Brennan*	Mare I. NYd	28 Feb 1942	22 Aug 1942	20 Jan 1943
	ex–HMS *Bentinck* (25 Jan 1943)				
DE 14	*Doherty*	Mare I. NYd	28 Feb 1942	29 Aug 1942	6 Feb 1943
	ex–HMS *Berry* (6 Jan 1943)				
DE 15	*Austin*	Mare I. NYd	14 Mar 1942	25 Sep 1942	13 Feb 1943
	ex–HMS *Blackwood* (25 Jan 1943)				
DE 16	*Edgar G. Chase*	Mare I. NYd	14 Mar 1942	26 Sep 1942	20 Mar 1943
	ex–HMS *Burges* (Feb 1943)				

Figure 5.2: *Canfield* (DE 262), 16 May 1945, short hull type, *Evarts* class.

DE 17	*Edward C. Daly*	Mare I. NYd	1 Apr 1942	21 Oct 1942	3 Apr 1943
	ex–HMS *Byard* (19 Feb 1943)				
DE 18	*Gilmore*	Mare I. NYd	1 Apr 1942	22 Oct 1942	17 Apr 1943
	ex–HMS *Calder* (19 Feb 1943)				
DE 19	*Burden R. Hastings*	Mare I. NYd	15 Apr 1942	20 Nov 1942	1 May 1943
	ex–HMS *Duckworth* (25 Jan 1943)				
DE 20	*Le Hardy*	Mare I. NYd	15 Apr 1942	21 Nov 1942	15 May 1943
	ex–HMS *Duff* (19 Feb 1943)				
DE 21	*Harold C. Thomas*	Mare I. NYd	30 Apr 1942	18 Dec 1942	31 May 1943
	ex–HMS *Essington* (1943)				
DE 22	*Wileman*	Mare I. NYd	30 Apr 1942	19 Dec 1942	11 Jun 1943
	ex–HMS *Foley* (1943)				
DE 23	*Charles R. Greer*	Mare I. NYd	7 Sep 1942	18 Jan 1943	25 Jun 1943
DE 24	*Whitman*	Mare I. NYd	7 Sep 1942	19 Jan 1943	3 Jul 1943
DE 25	*Wintle*	Mare I. NYd	1 Oct 1942	18 Feb 1943	10 Jul 1943
DE 26	*Dempsey*	Mare I. NYd	1 Oct 1942	19 Feb 1943	24 Jul 1943
DE 27	*Duffy*	Mare I. NYd	29 Oct 1942	16 Apr 1943	5 Aug 1943
DE 28	*Emery*	Mare I. NYd	29 Oct 1942	17 Apr 1943	14 Aug 1943
	ex–*Eisner* (14 Jul 1943)				
DE 29	*Stadtfeld*	Mare I. NYd	26 Nov 1942	17 May 1943	26 Aug 1943
DE 30	*Martin*	Mare I. NYd	26 Nov 1942	18 May 1943	4 Sep 1943
DE 31	*Sederstrom*	Mare I. NYd	24 Dec 1942	15 Jun 1943	11 Sep 1943
	ex–*Gillette* (30 Jul 1943)				
DE 32	*Fleming*	Mare I. NYd	24 Dec 1942	16 Jun 1943	18 Sep 1943
DE 33	*Tisdale*	Mare I. NYd	23 Jan 1943	28 Jun 1943	11 Oct 1943
DE 34	*Eisele*	Mare I. NYd	23 Jan 1943	29 Jun 1943	18 Oct 1943
DE 35	*Fair*	Mare I. NYd	24 Feb 1943	27 Jul 1943	23 Oct 1943
DE 36	*Manlove*	Mare I. NYd	24 Feb 1943	28 Jul 1943	8 Nov 1943

Displacement	1,140 tons; 1,430 f/l
Dimensions	289'5" (oa); 283'6" (wl) x 35'1" x 8'3"
Machinery	2 screws; diesel-electric; SHP 6,000; 19 knots
Endurance	6,000/12
Complement	198
Armament	3–3"/50, 2–40mm, 9–20mm AA (originally 1 quad 1.1")

Notes: "Short hull" type, GMT. Originally designed to Admiralty specifications for lend-lease transfer to the United Kingdom as BDE 1–50, but 44 were retained by the Navy; altogether, 31 transferred to the United Kingdom. Ninety-seven were built.

Service Records:

BDE 1 — To UK 13 Feb 1943., renamed HMS *Bayntun*. Returned 22 Aug 1945. Sold 22 Feb 1947.

BDE 2 — To UK 18 Feb 1943, renamed HMS *Bazely*. Returned 20 Aug 1945. BU 28 May 1946.

BDE 3 — To UK 15 Mar 1943, renamed HMS *Berry*. Returned 15 Feb 1946. Sold 9 Nov 1946.

BDE 4 — To UK 27 Mar 1943, renamed HMS *Blackwood*. Torpedoed by *U-764*, 15 Jan, and sank in tow off Portland, England, 16 Jun 1944.

DE 5 *Evarts* Decomm 2 Oct 1945. Stricken 12 Jul 1946; BU.
1* Convoy UGS-40.

DE 6 *Wyffels* Decomm 28 Aug 1945. To China 28 Aug 1945.
1* Convoy UGS-40.
Later history: Renamed *Tai Kang*. R 1972; BU.

DE 7 *Griswold* Decomm 19 Nov 1945. Stricken 5 Dec 1945. Sold 2 Dec 1946; BU Seattle.
3* Okinawa, Raids on Japan 7–8/45.
Submarine sunk: *I-39* off Guadalcanal, Solomon Is., 23 Dec 1944 (possible).

DE 8 *Steele* Decomm 21 Nov 1945. Stricken 5 Dec 1945. Sold 2 Dec 1946.
2* Saipan, Palau, Philippines Raids 9/44.

DE 9 *Carlson* Decomm 10 Dec 1945. Sold 17 Oct 1946.
2* Okinawa, Raids on Japan 7–8/45. Tokyo Bay.

DE 10 *Bebas* Decomm 18 Oct 1945. Sold 8 Jan 1947.
3* Palau, Philippines Raids 9/44, Okinawa, Raids on Japan 7–8/45.

DE 11 *Crouter* Decomm 30 Nov 1945. Sold 25 Nov 1946.
1* Okinawa.

BDE 12 — To UK 2 Jun 1943, renamed HMS *Burges*. Returned 27 Feb 1946. Sold 19 Nov 1946.

DE 13 *Brennan* Training ship. Decomm 9 Oct 1945. Sold 12 Jul 1946.

DE 14 *Doherty* Decomm 14 Dec 1945. Sold 26 Dec 1946.

DE 15 *Austin* Decomm 21 Dec 1945. Stricken 8 Jan 1946. Sold 9 Jan 1947; BU Terminal I.

DE 16 *Edgar G. Chase* Decomm 16 Oct 1945. Sold 18 Mar 1947.

DE 17 *Edward C. Daly* Decomm 20 Dec 1945. Sold 8 Jan 1947.

DE 18 *Gilmore* Decomm 29 Dec 1945. Sold 1 Feb 1947.
1*
Submarine sunk: *I-180* off Kodiak, Alaska 26 Apr 1944.

DE 19 *Burden R. Hastings* Decomm 25 Oct 1945. Sold 1 Feb 1947.
4* Gilbert Is., Kwajalein, Palau-Yap Raids 3/44.
Submarine sunk: *RO-44* 110 miles east of Eniwetok, 16 Jun 1944.

DE 20 *Le Hardy* Decomm 25 Oct 1945. Sold 26 Dec 1946; BU Terminal I.
2* Gilbert Is., Kwajalein, Eniwetok.

DE 21 *Harold C. Thomas* Decomm 26 Oct 1945. Sold 25 Nov 1946; BU San Francisco.
2* Gilbert Is., Kwajalein.

DE 22 *Wileman* Decomm 16 Nov 1945. Stricken 28 Nov 1945. Sold 8 Jan 1947; BU.
4* Gilbert Is., Kwajalein, Saipan, Guam, Tinian.

DE 23 *Charles R. Greer* Decomm 2 Nov 1945. Sold 1 Feb 1947.
2* Gilbert Is., Kwajalein.

DE 24 *Whitman* Decomm 1 Nov 1945. Stricken 16 Nov 1945. Sold 31 Jan 1947; BU Terminal I.
4* Gilbert Is., Kwajalein, Saipan, Guam, Tinian.

DE 25 *Wintle* Damaged in collision with DE *Dempsey* off Pearl Harbor, 3 Jan 1944. Decomm 15 Nov 1945. Stricken 28 Nov 1945. Sold 25 Aug 1947; BU.
3* Gilbert Is., Kwajalein, Palau.

DE 26 *Dempsey* Collided with DE *Wintle* off Pearl Harbor, 3 Jan 1944. Decomm 22 Nov 1945. Sold 18 Apr 1947.
3* Palau, Gilbert Is., Kwajalein.

DE 27 *Duffy* Decomm 9 Nov 1945. Sold 27 Jul 1947.
2* Gilbert Is., Kwajalein.

DE 28 *Emery* Decomm 15 Nov 1945. Sold 21 Jul 1947.
4* Gilbert Is., Kwajalein, Palau, Iwo Jima.

DE 29 *Stadtfeld* Decomm 15 Nov 1945. Stricken 28 Nov 1945. Sold 22 Jul 1947; BU.
4* Gilbert Is., Kwajalein, Palau, Iwo Jima.

DE 30 *Martin* Decomm 19 Nov 1945. Stricken 5 Dec 1945, sold 3 Jun 1947; BU Wilmington, Calif.
1* Kwajalein.

DE 31 *Sederstrom* Damaged in collision with escort carrier *Sangamon*, Okinawa, 25 Mar 1945. Decomm 15 Nov 1945. Stricken 28 Nov 1945. Sold 21 Jan 1948; BU.
5* Kwajalein, Saipan, Guam, Tinian, Iwo Jima, Okinawa.

DE 32 *Fleming* Decomm 10 Nov 1945. Sold 29 Jan 1948.
4* Kwajalein, Okinawa, Guam.
Submarine sunk: *I-362* 320 miles northeast of Truk, 18 Jan 1945.

DE 33 *Tisdale* Decomm 17 Nov 1945. Stricken 28 Nov 1946. Sold 2 Feb 1948.
4* Kwajalein, Saipan, Tinian, Guam, Okinawa.

DE 34 *Eisele* Decomm 16 Nov 1945. Sold 29 Jan 1948.
2* Guam, Okinawa.

DE 35 *Fair* Decomm 17 Nov 1945. To U.S. War Department, 20 May 1947. Sold for BU 1949.
5* Kwajalein, Saipan, Philippine Sea, 2nd Bonins Raid, Guam, Tinian, Okinawa.
Submarine sunk: **I-175* (or *RO-39*) 100 miles northwest of Jaluit, 4 Feb 1944.

DE 36 *Manlove* Slight damage by exploding aircraft off Okinawa, 11 Apr 1945. Decomm 16 Nov 1945. Sold 4 Dec 1947; BU.
5* Guam, Tinian, Okinawa, Kwajalein, Saipan.
Submarine sunk: **I-32* south of Wotje, 24 Mar 1944.

No.	Name	Builder	Keel Laid	Launched	Comm.
DE 37	*Greiner*	Puget Sound NYd	7 Sep 1942	20 May 1943	18 Aug 1943
DE 38	*Wyman*	Puget Sound NYd	7 Sep 1942	3 Jun 1943	1 Sep 1943
DE 39	*Lovering*	Puget Sound NYd	7 Sep 1942	18 Jun 1943	17 Sep 1943
DE 40	*Sanders*	Puget Sound NYd	7 Sep 1942	18 Jun 1943	1 Oct 1943
DE 41	*Brackett*	Puget Sound NYd	12 Jan 1943	1 Aug 1943	18 Oct 1943
DE 42	*Reynolds*	Puget Sound NYd	12 Jan 1943	1 Aug 1943	1 Nov 1943
DE 43	*Mitchell*	Puget Sound NYd	12 Jan 1943	1 Aug 1943	7 Nov 1943
DE 44	*Donaldson*	Puget Sound NYd	12 Jan 1943	1 Aug 1943	1 Dec 1943
DE 45	*Andres*	Phila. NYd	12 Feb 1942	24 Jul 1942	15 Mar 1943
	ex–HMS *Capel* (25 Jan 1943)				
BDE 46	—	Phila. NYd	12 Feb 1942	24 Jul 1942	*12 Apr 1943*
DE 47	*Decker*	Phila. NYd	1 Apr 1942	24 Jul 1942	3 May 1943
DE 48	*Dobler*	Phila. NYd	1 Apr 1942	24 Jul 1942	17 May 1943
DE 49	*Doneff*	Phila. NYd	1 Apr 1942	24 Jul 1942	10 Jun 1943
DE 50	*Engstrom*	Phila. NYd	1 Apr 1942	24 Jul 1942	21 Jun 1943
DE 256	*Seid*	Boston NYd	10 Jan 1943	22 Feb 1943	11 Jun 1943
DE 257	*Smartt*	Boston NYd	10 Jan 1943	22 Feb 1943	18 Jun 1943
DE 258	*Walter S. Brown*	Boston NYd	10 Jan 1943	22 Feb 1943	25 Jun 1943
DE 259	*William C. Miller*	Boston NYd	10 Jan 1943	22 Feb 1943	2 Jul 1943
DE 260	*Cabana*	Boston NYd	27 Jan 1943	10 Mar 1943	9 Jul 1943
DE 261	*Dionne*	Boston NYd	27 Jan 1943	10 Mar 1943	16 Jul 1943
DE 262	*Canfield*	Boston NYd	23 Feb 1943	6 Apr 1943	22 Jul 1943
DE 263	*Deede*	Boston NYd	23 Feb 1943	6 Apr 1943	29 Jul 1943
DE 264	*Elden*	Boston NYd	23 Feb 1943	6 Apr 1943	4 Aug 1943
DE 265	*Cloues*	Boston NYd	23 Feb 1943	6 Apr 1943	10 Aug 1943
DE 266	*Wintle*	Boston NYd	11 Mar 1943	22 Apr 1943	*16 Aug 1943*
DE 267	*Dempsey*	Boston NYd	11 Mar 1943	22 Apr 1943	*30 Aug 1943*
DE 268	*Duffy*	Boston NYd	7 Apr 1943	19 May 1943	*28 Aug 1943*
DE 269	*Eisner*	Boston NYd	7 Apr 1943	19 May 1943	*3 Sep 1943*
DE 270	*Gillette*	Boston NYd	7 Apr 1943	19 May 1943	*8 Sep 1943*
DE 271	*Fleming*	Boston NYd	7 Apr 1943	19 May 1943	*13 Sep 1943*
DE 272	*Lovering*	Boston NYd	23 Apr 1943	4 Jun 1943	*18 Sep 1943*
DE 273	*Sanders*	Boston NYd	23 Apr 1943	4 Jun 1943	*23 Sep 1943*
DE 274	*O'Toole*	Boston NYd	20 May 1943	8 Jul 1943	*28 Sep 1943*
DE 275	*Reybold*	Boston NYd	20 May 1943	8 Jul 1943	*4 Oct 1943*
DE 276	*George*	Boston NYd	20 May 1943	8 Jul 1943	*9 Oct 1943*
DE 277	*Herzog*	Boston NYd	20 May 1943	8 Jul 1943	*14 Oct 1943*
DE 278	*Tisdale*	Boston NYd	5 Jun 1943	17 Jul 1943	*19 Oct 1943*
DE 279	*Trumpeter*	Boston NYd	5 Jun 1943	17 Jul 1943	*23 Oct 1943*
DE 280	—	Boston NYd	9 Jul 1943	13 Aug 1943	*29 Oct 1943*

Service Records:

DE 37 *Greiner* Decomm 19 Nov 1945. Stricken 5 Dec 1945. Sold 11 Feb 1947; BU.
3* Gilbert Is., Saipan, Fleet Raids 1945.

DE 38 *Wyman* Decomm 17 Dec 1945. Stricken 8 Jan 1946. Sold 16 Apr 1947; BU Terminal I.
6* TG 12.2, Philippines Raids 9/44, Iwo Jima, Fleet Raids 1945, Okinawa.
Submarines sunk: *I-5* (or *RO-48*) 360 miles east of Guam, 19 Jul 1944; **I-55*, 300 miles east of Tinian, 28 Jul 1944.

DE 39 *Lovering* Decomm 16 Oct 1945. Stricken 1 Nov 1945. Sold 31 Dec 1946.
3* Eniwetok, Iwo Jima, Fleet Raids 1945, Okinawa.

DE 40 *Sanders* Decomm 19 Dec 1945. Stricken 8 Jan 1946. Sold 8 May 1947; BU Terminal I.
4* Philippine Sea, Saipan, Iwo Jima, Fleet Raids 1945, Okinawa, Palau.

DE 41 *Brackett* Decomm 23 Nov 1945. Sold 22 May 1947.
3* Kwajalein, Saipan, Fleet Raids 1945.

DE 42 *Reynolds* Decomm 5 Dec 1945. Stricken 19 Dec 1945. Sold 28 Apr 1947.
8* Kwajalein, TG 12.2, Palau, Formosa Raids 1/45, China Coast Raids 1/45, Nansei Shoto Raid 1/45, Iwo Jima, Fleet Raids 1945, Raids on Japan 7–8/45.
Submarine sunk: **I-55* 300 miles east of Tinian, 28 Jul 1944.

DE 43 *Mitchell* Decomm 29 Dec 1945. Stricken 29 Dec 1945, sold 11 Dec 1946. BU Seattle.
9* Saipan, Guam, Tinian, Palau, Philippines Raids 9/44, Luzon Raids 10/44, Formosa Raids 1/45, China Coast Raids 1/45, Nansei Shoto Raid 1/45, Iwo Jima, Fleet Raids 1945, Balikpapan, Raids on Japan 7–8/45.

DE 44 *Donaldson* Damaged in typhoon, Philippine Sea, 18 Dec 1944 (3 killed). Again damaged in typhoon, 5 Jun 1945. Decomm 5 Dec 1945. Sold 2 Jul 1946.
7* TG 12.2, Palau, Luzon Raids 10/44, Formosa Raids 1/45, China Coast Raids 1/45, Nansei Shoto Raid 1/45, Iwo Jima, Fleet Raids 1945, Raids on Japan 7–8/45, Balikpapan.

DE 45 *Andres* Decomm 18 Oct 1945. Stricken 1 Nov 1945. Sold 14 Feb 1946.

BDE 46 — To UK 12 Apr 1943, renamed HMS *Drury* (ex–*Cockburn*). Returned 20 Aug 1945. Comm 20 Aug–22 Oct 1945. Sold 19 Jun 1946.

DE 47 *Decker* To China 28 Aug 1945.
1* Convoy UGS-40.
Later history: Renamed *Tai Ping*. Torpedoed and sunk by Chinese (PRC) MTB's Off Tachen Is., 14 Nov 1954.

DE 48 *Dobler* Decomm 2 Oct 1945. Sold 12 Jul 1946.
1* Convoy UGS-40.

DE 49 *Doneff* Decomm 19 Dec 1945. Sold 26 Dec 1946.

DE 50 *Engstrom* Decomm 19 Dec 1945. Sold 26 Dec 1946.

DE 256 *Seid* Damaged in typhoon north of Noumea, 7 Jan 1944. Decomm 14 Dec 1945. Stricken 8 Jan 1946. Sold 8 Jan 1947; BU San Francisco.
2* Palau, Philippines Raids 9/44, Okinawa.

DE 257 *Smartt* Decomm 5 Oct 1945. Stricken 24 Oct 1945. Sold 12 Jul 1946.
1* Convoy UGS-40.

DE 258 *Walter S. Brown* Decomm 4 Oct 1945. Stricken 24 Oct 1945. BU 12 Jul 1946 New York.
1* Convoy UGS-40.

DE 259 *William C. Miller* Decomm 21 Dec 1946. Stricken 8 Jan 1946. Sold 18 Apr 1947; BU.
7* Gilbert Is., Kwajalein, Eniwetok, Saipan, Tinian, Iwo Jima, Raids on Japan 7–8/45.
Submarine sunk: **RO-48* 75 miles west of Saipan (possible), 14 Jul 1944; **I-6* off Tinian, 14 Jul 1944.

DE 260 *Cabana* Decomm 9 Jan 1946. Stricken 21 Jan 1946. Sold 13 May 1947.
7* Iwo Jima, Gilbert Is., Kwajalein, Saipan, Guam, Tinian, Palau, Raids on Japan 7–8/45.

DE 261 *Dionne* Decomm 18 Jan 1946. Stricken 7 Feb 1946. Sold 12 Jun 1947.
6* Gilbert Is., Kwajalein, Saipan, Guam, Tinian, Iwo Jima, Raids on Japan 7–8/45.

DE 262 *Canfield* Decomm 21 Dec 1945. Stricken 8 Jan 1946. Sold 12 Jun 1947.
4* Kwajalein, Saipan, Iwo Jima, Raids on Japan 7–8/45. .

DE 263 *Deede* Decomm 9 Jan 1946. Stricken 21 Jan 1946. Sold 12 Jun 1947.
6* Kwajalein, Philippine Sea, 2nd Bonins Raid, Saipan, Tinian, Guam, Palau, Iwo Jima, Raids on Japan 7–8/45.

DE 264 *Elden* Decomm 18 Jan 1946. Stricken 7 Feb 1946. Sold 12 Jun 1947.
6* Kwajalein, Saipan, Guam, Bonins-Yap Raids, Palau, Philippines Raids 9/44, Luzon Raids 10/44, Surigao Strait, Iwo Jima, Raids on Japan 7–8/45.

DE 265 *Cloues* Decomm 26 Nov 1945. Stricken 5 Dec 1945. Sold 22 May 1947.
3* Saipan, Guam, Fleet Raids 1945, Balikpapan.

DE 266 *Wintle* To UK 16 Aug 1943, renamed HMS *Capel*. Torpedoed and sunk by *U-486* off Cherbourg, 26 Dec 1944.

DE 267 *Dempsey* To UK 30 Aug 1943, renamed HMS *Cooke*. Returned 5 Mar 1946. Sold 10 Jun 1947.

DE 268 *Duffy* To UK 28 Aug 1943, renamed HMS *Dacres*. Returned 26 Jan 1946. Sold 14 Dec 1946.

DE 269 *Eisner* To UK 3 Sep 1943, renamed HMS *Domett*. Returned 5 Mar 1946. Sold 3 Jun 1947.

DE 270 *Gillette* To UK 8 Sep 1943, renamed HMS *Foley*. Returned 22 Aug 1945. BU 19 Jun 1946.

DE 271 *Fleming* To UK 13 Sep 1943, renamed HMS *Garlies*. Returned 20 Aug 1945. Sold 18 Jul 1947; BU.

DE 272 *Lovering* To UK 18 Sep 1943, renamed HMS *Gould*. Torpedoed and sunk by *U-358* north of Azores, 1 Mar 1944.

DE 273 *Sanders* To UK 23 Sep 1943, renamed HMS *Grindall*. Returned 20 Aug 1945. BU 28 May 1946.

DE 274 *O'Toole* To UK 28 Sep 1943, renamed HMS *Gardiner*. Returned 12 Feb 1946. Sold 10 Dec 1946; BU.

DE 275 *Reybold* To UK 4 Oct 1943, renamed HMS *Goodall*. Torpedoed by *U-286* off Kola Inlet, 29 Apr and sunk by gunfire, 30 Apr 1945.

DE 276 *George* To UK 9 Oct 1943, renamed HMS *Goodson*. Torpedoed by *U-984* off Cherbourg, 25 Jan 1944, not repaired. Returned 21 Oct 1945. Sold 9 Jan 1947; BU Whitchurch.

DE 277 *Herzog* To UK 14 Oct 1943, renamed HMS *Gore*. Returned 2 May 1946. Sold 10 Jun 1947.

DE 278 *Tisdale* To UK 19 Oct 1943, renamed HMS *Keats*. Returned 27 Feb 1946. Sold 19 Nov 1946.

DE 279 *Trumpeter* To UK 23 Oct 1943, renamed HMS *Kempthorne*. Returned 20 Aug 1945. Stricken 1 Nov 1945. BU 28 May 1946.

DE 280 — To UK 29 Oct 1943, renamed HMS *Kingsmill*. Returned 22 Aug 1945. Sold 17 Feb 1947.

No.	Name	Builder	Keel Laid	Launched	Comm.
DE 301	*Lake*	Mare I. NYd	22 Apr 1943	18 Aug 1943	5 Feb 1944
DE 302	*Lyman*	Mare I. NYd	22 Apr 1943	18 Aug 1943	19 Feb 1944
DE 303	*Crowley*	Mare I. NYd	24 May 1943	22 Sep 1943	25 Mar 1944
DE 304	*Rall*	Mare I. NYd	24 May 1943	23 Sep 1943	8 Apr 1944
DE 305	*Halloran*	Mare I. NYd	21 Jun 1943	14 Jan 1944	27 May 1944
DE 306	*Connolly*	Mare I. NYd	21 Jun 1943	15 Jan 1944	8 Jul 1944
DE 307	*Finnegan*	Mare I. NYd	5 Jul 1943	22 Feb 1944	19 Aug 1944
DE 308	*Creamer* ex–*Register* (10 Sep 1943)	Mare I. NYd	5 Jul 1943	23 Feb 1944	—
DE 309	*Ely*	Mare I. NYd	2 Aug 1943	10 Apr 1944	—
DE 310	*Delbert W. Halsey*	Mare I. NYd	2 Aug 1943	11 Apr 1944	—
DE 311	*Keppler*	Mare I. NYd	23 Aug 1943	—	—
DE 312	*Lloyd Thomas*	Mare I. NYd	23 Aug 1943	—	—
DE 313	*William C. Lawe*	Mare I. NYd	22 Jan 1944	—	—
DE 314	*Willard Keith*	Mare I. NYd	22 Jan 1944	—	—
DE 315	—	Mare I. NYd	1 Mar 1944	—	—
DE 516	—	Boston NYd	9 Jul 1943	13 Aug 1943	*3 Nov 1943*
DE 517	—	Boston NYd	9 Jul 1943	13 Aug 1943	*9 Nov 1943*
DE 518	—	Boston NYd	9 Jul 1943	13 Aug 1943	*15 Nov 1943*
DE 519	—	Boston NYd	18 Jul 1943	30 Aug 1943	*20 Nov 1943*
DE 520	—	Boston NYd	18 Jul 1943	30 Aug 1943	*27 Nov 1943*
DE 521	—	Boston NYd	14 Aug 1943	24 Sep 1943	*3 Dec 1943*
DE 522	—	Boston NYd	14 Aug 1943	24 Sep 1943	*16 Dec 1943*
DE 523	—	Boston NYd	14 Aug 1943	24 Sep 1943	*6 Dec 1943*
DE 524	—	Boston NYd	14 Aug 1943	24 Sep 1943	*23 Dec 1943*
DE 525	—	Boston NYd	25 Sep 1943	2 Nov 1943	*29 Dec 1943*
DE 526	—	Boston NYd	25 Sep 1943	2 Nov 1943	*13 Jan 1944*
DE 527	*O'Toole*	Boston NYd	25 Sep 1943	2 Nov 1943	22 Jan 1944
DE 528	*John J. Powers*	Boston NYd	25 Sep 1943	2 Nov 1943	29 Feb 1944
DE 529	*Mason*	Boston NYd	14 Oct 1943	17 Nov 1943	20 Mar 1944
DE 530	*John M. Bermingham*	Boston NYd	14 Oct 1943	17 Nov 1943	8 Apr 1944

Service Records:

DE 301 *Lake* Decomm 3 Dec 1946. Sold 14 Dec 1946; BU Seattle.
2* Palau, Formosa Raids 1/45, Luzon Raids 1/45, Formosa Raids 1/45, China Coast Raids 1/45, Nansei Shoto Raid 1/45, Iwo Jima, Fleet Raids 1945.

DE 302 *Lyman* Damaged in typhoon in Philippine Sea, 11 Jun 1945. Decomm 5 Dec 1945. Sold 26 Dec 1946; BU Seattle.
5* Palau, Formosa Raids 1/45, Luzon Raids 1/45, Iwo Jima, Fleet Raids 1945, Raids on Japan 7–8/45. Tokyo Bay.

DE 303 *Crowley* Decomm 3 Dec 1945. Sold 21 Dec 1946.
5* Palau, Formosa Raids 1/45, Luzon Raids 1/45, China Coast Raids 1/45, Iwo Jima, Fleet Raids 1945, Okinawa, Raids on Japan 7–8/45.

DE 304 *Rall* Sank midget submarine in Ulithi, Micronesia, harbor, 20 Nov 1944. Severely damaged by kamikaze, Okinawa, 12 Apr 1945 (21 killed). Decomm 11 Dec 1945. Stricken 3 Jan 1946. Sold 18 Mar 1947; BU.
3* Palau, Iwo Jima, Okinawa.

DE 305 *Halloran* Minor damage by bomb near miss off Okinawa, 21 Jun 1945 (3 killed). Decomm 2 Nov 1945. Sold 18 Mar 1947.
3* Luzon Raids 10/44, Iwo Jima, Okinawa.

DE 306 *Connolly* Slightly damaged by kamikaze, Okinawa, 13 Apr 1945. Decomm 22 Nov 1945. Sold 20 May 1946.
2* Iwo Jima, Okinawa.

DE 307 *Finnegan* Damaged in collision, Iwo Jima, 19 Feb 1945. Decomm 27 Nov 1945. Stricken 19 Dec 1945. Sold 20 May 1946.
3* Iwo Jima, Okinawa.
Submarine sunk: Kaiten carrier *I-370* 120 miles south of Iwo Jima, 26 Feb 1945.

DE 308 *Creamer* Canceled 5 Sep 1944. BU 1945 Mare I.

DE 309 *Ely* Canceled 5 Sep 1944. BU 1945 Mare I.

DE 310 *Delbert W. Halsey* Canceled 5 Sep 1944. BU 1945 Mare I.

DE 311 *Keppler* Canceled 13 Mar 1944.

DE 312 *Lloyd Thomas* Canceled 13 Mar 1944.

DE 313 *William C. Lawe* Canceled 13 Mar 1944.

DE 314 *Willard Keith* Canceled 13 Mar 1944.

DE 315 — Canceled 13 Mar 1944.

DE 516 — To UK 3 Nov 1943, renamed HMS *Lawford*. Sunk by German aircraft off Juno Beach, Seine Bay, 8 Jun 1944.

DE 517 — To UK 9 Nov 1943, renamed HMS *Louis*. Returned 20 Mar 1946. Sold 17 Jun 1946.

DE 518 — To UK 15 Nov 1943, renamed HMS *Lawson*. Returned 20 Mar 1946. Sold 31 Jan 1947; BU.

DE 519 — To UK 20 Nov 1943, renamed HMS *Paisley* (ex–*Lindsay*). Returned 20 Aug 1943. BU 19 Jun 1946.

DE 520 — To UK 27 Nov 1943, renamed HMS *Loring*. Returned 7 Jan 1947. Sold 23 Mar 1947; BU Greece.

DE 521 — To UK 3 Dec 1943, renamed HMS *Hoste* (ex–*Mitchell*). Returned 20 Aug 1945. BU 7 May 1946.

DE 522 — To UK 16 Dec 1943, renamed HMS *Moorsom*. Returned 25 Oct 1945. BU 12 Jul 1946.

DE 523 — To UK 6 Dec 1943, renamed HMS *Manners*. Torpedoed by *U-1051* west of Skerries, 26 Jan 1945; bow sank. Returned 8 Nov 1945. BU 7 Jan 1947 Piraeus, Greece.

DE 524 — To UK 23 Dec 1943, renamed HMS *Mounsey*. Returned 25 Feb 1946. Sold 8 Nov 1946; BU.

DE 525 — To UK 29 Dec 1943, renamed HMS *Inglis*. Returned 20 Mar 1946. Sold 3 Sep 1947.

DE 526 — To UK 13 Jan 1944, renamed HMS *Inman*. Returned 1 Mar 1946. Sold 19 Nov 1946; BU.

DE 527 *O'Toole* Decomm 18 Oct 1945. Stricken 1 Nov 1945. Sold 13 Mar 1946; BU.

DE 528 *John J. Powers* Decomm 16 Oct 1945. Stricken 1 Nov 1945. Sold 14 Feb 1946; BU Charleston, S.C.

DE 529 *Mason* Decomm 12 Oct 1945. Stricken 1 Nov 1945. Sold 13 Mar 1947; BU Barber, N.J.

DE 530 *John M. Bermingham* Decomm 16 Oct 1945. Stricken 1 Nov 1945. Sold 13 Mar 1946; BU.

Figure 5.3: *J. Douglas Blackwood* (DE 219), of the *Buckley* class, type TE, with two 5" guns.

Figure 5.4: *Spangenberg* (DE 223), 8 Sep 1944, of the *Buckley* class, type TE.

Buckley Class (TE)

No.	Name	Builder	Keel Laid	Launched	Comm.
DE 51	*Buckley*	Hingham	21 Jul 1942	9 Jan 1943	30 Apr 1943
DE 52	*Bull*	Hingham	29 Jun 1942	2 Mar 1943	*19 May 1943*
DE 53	*Charles Lawrence*	Hingham	1 Aug 1942	16 Feb 1943	31 May 1943
DE 54	*Daniel T. Griffin*	Hingham	7 Sep 1942	25 Feb 1943	9 Jun 1943
DE 55	*Donaldson*	Hingham	15 Sep 1942	6 Mar 1943	*18 Jun 1943*
DE 56	*Donnell*	Hingham	27 Nov 1942	13 Mar 1943	26 Jun 1943
DE 57	*Fogg*	Hingham	4 Dec 1942	20 Mar 1943	7 Jul 1943
DE 58	*Formoe*	Hingham	11 Dec 1942	27 Mar 1943	*15 Jul 1943*
DE 59	*Foss*	Hingham	31 Dec 1942	10 Apr 1943	23 Jul 1943
DE 60	*Gantner*	Hingham	31 Dec 1942	17 Apr 1943	29 Jul 1943
DE 61	*Gary*	Hingham	16 Jan 1943	1 May 1943	*4 Aug 1943*
DE 62	*George W. Ingram*	Hingham	6 Feb 1943	8 May 1943	11 Aug 1943
DE 63	*Ira Jeffery* ex–*Jeffery* (29 Jul 1943)	Hingham	13 Feb 1943	15 May 1943	15 Aug 1943
DE 64	*Lamons*	Hingham	22 Feb 1943	22 May 1943	*23 Aug 1943*
DE 65	*Lee Fox*	Hingham	1 Mar 1943	29 May 1943	30 Aug 1943
DE 66	*Amesbury*	Hingham	8 Mar 1943	6 Jun 1943	31 Aug 1943
DE 67	—	Hingham	15 Mar 1943	19 Jun 1943	*7 Sep 1943*
DE 68	*Bates*	Hingham	29 Mar 1943	6 Jun 1943	12 Sep 1943
DE 69	*Blessman*	Hingham	22 Mar 1943	19 Jun 1943	19 Sep 1943
DE 70	*Joseph E. Campbell* ex–*Campbell*	Hingham	29 Mar 1943	26 Jun 1943	23 Sep 1943
DE 71	*Oswald*	Hingham	5 Apr 1943	30 Jun 1943	*29 Sep 1943*
DE 72	*Harmon*	Hingham	12 Apr 1943	10 Jul 1943	*30 Sep 1943*
DE 73	*McAnn*	Hingham	19 Apr 1943	10 Jul 1943	*7 Oct 1943*
DE 74	*Ebert*	Hingham	26 Apr 1943	17 Jul 1943	*13 Oct 1943*
DE 75	*Eisele*	Hingham	3 May 1943	26 Jul 1943	*17 Oct 1943*
DE 76	*Liddle*	Hingham	10 May 1943	31 Jul 1943	*22 Oct 1943*
DE 77	*Straub*	Hingham	10 May 1943	31 Jul 1943	*13 Nov 1943*
DE 78	—	Hingham	17 May 1943	7 Aug 1943	*25 Oct 1943*
DE 79	—	Hingham	24 May 1943	14 Aug 1943	*30 Oct 1943*
DE 80	—	Hingham	2 Jun 1943	21 Aug 1943	*31 Oct 1943*
DE 81	—	Hingham	2 Jun 1943	21 Aug 1943	*8 Nov 1943*
DE 82	—	Hingham	9 Jun 1943	28 Aug 1943	*13 Nov 1943*
DE 83	—	Hingham	9 Jun 1943	11 Sep 1943	*17 Nov 1943*

DE 84	—	Hingham	23 Jun 1943	18 Sep 1943	*20 Nov 1943*
DE 85	—	Hingham	23 Jun 1943	18 Sep 1943	*23 Nov 1943*
DE 86	—	Hingham	30 Jun 1943	25 Sep 1943	*26 Nov 1943*
DE 87	—	Hingham	5 Jul 1943	2 Oct 1943	*29 Nov 1943*
DE 88	—	Hingham	24 Aug 1943	1 Sep 1943	*16 Oct 1943*
DE 89	—	Hingham	14 Jul 1943	2 Oct 1943	*30 Nov 1943*
DE 90	—	Hingham	21 Jul 1943	9 Oct 1943	*8 Dec 1943*
DE 91	—	Hingham	10 Aug 1943	14 Oct 1943	*3 Nov 1943*
DE 92	—	Hingham	4 Aug 1943	23 Oct 1943	*14 Dec 1943*
DE 93	—	Hingham	4 Aug 1943	23 Oct 1943	*16 Dec 1943*
DE 94	—	Hingham	11 Aug 1943	30 Oct 1943	*20 Dec 1943*
DE 95	—	Hingham	18 Aug 1943	30 Oct 1943	*22 Dec 1943*
DE 96	—	Hingham	25 Aug 1943	31 Oct 1943	*24 Dec 1943*
DE 97	—	Hingham	25 Aug 1943	31 Oct 1943	*28 Dec 1943*
DE 98	—	Hingham	1 Sep 1943	1 Nov 1943	*23 Dec 1943*

Displacement	1,400 tons; 1,740 f/l
Dimensions	306' (oa); 300' (wl) x 36'9" x 13'6"
Machinery	2 screws; turbo-electric drive; 2 D Express boilers; SHP 12,000; 24 knots
Endurance	6,000/12
Complement	213
Armament	3–3"/50, 2–40mm AA, 8–20mm AA, 1 triple 21" TT

Notes: Type TE (turbo-electric drive); 154 built, forty-six units completed for Royal Navy under lend-lease; British units had no TT. DE 198–237 originally ordered from Newport News; DE 665–76 from Charleston NYd. Thirty-four were converted to high speed transports (APD), six were completed as such, and conversion of seven was canceled. DE 51, 57, 153, 221, 223, 577, and 578 converted to radar pickets (DER) 1945, with tripod mast aft of funnel. DE 217–19, 678–80, 696–98 and 700–701 refitted with two 5"/38 guns, 1945.

Service Records:

DE 51 *Buckley* Decomm 3 Jul 1946. †
3* TG 21.11.
Submarines sunk: *U-66*, off West Africa, 6 May 1944 (damaged by ramming); **U-879* off Boston, 19 Apr 1945.

DE 52 *Bull* To UK 19 May 1943, renamed HMS *Bentinck*. Returned 5 Jan 1946. Sold 26 May 1946.

DE 53 *Charles Lawrence* Rec **APD 37**, 23 Oct 1944. Decomm 21 Jun 1946. †

DE 54 *Daniel T. Griffin* Rec **APD 38**, 23 Oct 1944. Damaged by collision, Okinawa, 6 Apr 1945. Decomm 30 May 1946. †
1* Okinawa.

DE 55 *Donaldson* To UK 18 Jun 1943, renamed HMS *Byard*. Returned 12 Dec 1945. Sold 8 Dec 1946.

DE 56 *Donnell* Torpedoed by *U-473* in North Atlantic, 3 May 1944 (29 killed), stern blown off, not repaired; accommodation ship. Rec **IX 182**, 15 Jul 1944. Floating power plant at Cherbourg. Decomm 23 Oct 1945. Stricken 10 Nov 1945. Sold 29 Apr 1946.

DE 57 *Fogg* Torpedoed by *U-870* north of Azores, 20 Dec 1944, lost stern (14 killed). Converterd to radar picket 1945. Decomm 27 Oct 1947. †

DE 58 *Formoe* To UK 15 Jul 1943, renamed HMS *Calder*. Returned 19 Oct 1945, sold 15 Jan 1948.

DE 59 *Foss* Used as floating power station, Portland, Me., 1947–48. †

DE 60 *Gantner* Rec **APD 42**, 23 Feb 1945. †

DE 61 *Gary* To UK 4 Aug 1943, renamed HMS *Duckworth*. Returned 17 Dec 1945. Sold 29 May 1946; BU Philadelphia.

DE 62 *George W. Ingram* Rec **APD 43**, 23 Feb 1945. Decomm 15 Jan 1947. †
Submarine sunk: **U-172* in N.Atlantic, 13 Dec 1943 (possible).

DE 63 *Ira Jeffery* Rec **APD 44**, 23 Feb 1945. Decomm 18 Jun 1946. †

DE 64 *Lamons* To UK 23 Aug 1943, renamed HMS *Duff*. Damaged by mine off Dutch coast, 30 Nov 1944, not repaired. Returned 22 Aug 1945. Sold 26 Oct 1946; BU Netherlands.

DE 65 *Lee Fox* Damaged in hurricane off Bermuda, 17 Oct 1943. Damaged by projectile explosion in forecastle off Cape Cod, 11 Dec 1943. Rec **APD 45**, 31 Jul 1944. Decomm 13 May 1946. †

DE 66 *Amesbury* Rec **APD 46**, 31 Jul 1944. Conv. Feb-May 1945. Decomm 3 Jul 1946. †
1* Normandy.

DE 67 — To UK 7 Sep 1943, renamed HMS *Essington*. Returned 19 Oct 1945. Sold 22 Dec 1947.

DE 68 *Bates* Rec **APD 47**, 31 Jul 1944. Sunk by kamikazes and bomb off Okinawa, 25 May 1945 (21 killed).
3* Normandy, Iwo Jima, Okinawa.

DE 69 *Blessman* Rec **APD 48**, 31 Jul 1944. Damaged by aircraft bomb, Iwo Jima, 18 Feb 1945 (47 killed). Decomm 28 Aug 1946. †
3* Normandy, Lingayen, Iwo Jima.

DE 70 *Joseph E. Campbell* Rec **APD 49**, 24 Nov 1944. Decomm 15 Nov 1946. †
1* Convoy UGS-37, Okinawa.
Submarine sunk: **U-371* off Constantine, Algeria, 4 May 1944.

DE 71 *Oswald* To UK 29 Sep 1943, renamed HMS *Affleck*. Torpedoed by *U-486* off Cherbourg, 26 Dec 1944, not repaired. Returned 22 Aug 1945. Sold 24 Jan 1947.
Later history: Hulk *Nuestra Señora de la Luz*, at Tenerife. RR 1970s.

DE 72 *Harmon* To UK 30 Sep 1943, renamed HMS *Aylmer*. Returned 5 Nov 1945. Sold 20 Jun 1947.

DE 73 *McAnn* To UK 7 Oct 1943, renamed HMS *Balfour*. Returned 25 Oct 1945. Sold 28 Oct 1946.

DE 74 *Ebert* To UK 13 Oct 1943, renamed HMS *Bentley*. Returned 5 Nov 1945. Sold 20 Jun 1947.

DE 75 *Eisele* To UK 17 Oct 1943, renamed HMS *Bickerton*. Torpedoed by *U-354* northwest of North Cape and sunk by destroyer, 22 Aug 1944.

DE 76 *Liddle* To UK 22 Oct 1943, renamed HMS *Bligh*. Returned 12 Nov 1945. Sold 13 Jun 1946.

DE 77 *Straub* To UK 13 Nov 1943, renamed HMS *Braithwaite*. Returned 13 Nov 1945. Sold 30 May 1946.

DE 78 — To *UK 25* Oct 1943, renamed HMS *Bullen*. Torpedoed and sunk by U-775 northwest of Scotland, 6 Dec 1944.

DE 79 — To UK 30 Oct 1943, renamed HMS *Byron*. Returned 24 Nov 1945. Sold 25 Oct 1947.

DE 80 — To UK 31 Oct 1943, renamed HMS *Conn*. Returned 26 Nov 1945. Sold 21 Jan 1948.

DE 81 — To UK 8 Nov 1943, renamed HMS *Cotton*. Returned 5 Nov 1945. Sold 22 Dec 1947.

DE 82 — To UK 13 Nov 1943, renamed HMS *Cranstoun*. Returned 3 Dec 1945. Sold 20 Nov 1947.

DE 83 — To UK 17 Nov 1943, renamed HMS *Cubitt*. Returned 4 Mar 1946. Sold 7 Mar 1947.

DE 84 — To UK 20 Nov 1943, renamed HMS *Curzon*. Returned 27 Mar 1946. Sold 4 Nov 1946.

DE 85 — To UK 23 Nov 1943, renamed HMS *Dakins*. Damaged by mine off Ostende, 25 Dec 1944, not repaired. Sold 6 Jan 1947; BU Netherlands.

DE 86 — To UK 26 Nov 1943, renamed HMS *Deane*. Returned 4 Mar 1946. Sold 7 Nov 1946.

DE 87 — To UK 29 Nov 1943, renamed HMS *Ekins*. Damaged by mine off Ostende, 16 Apr 1945, not repaired. Returned 15 Jul 1945. Sold 26 Oct 1946; BU Netherlands.

DE 88 — To UK 16 Oct 1943, renamed HMS *Fitzroy*. Returned 5 Jan 1946. Sold 23 May 1946.

DE 89 — To UK 30 Nov 1943, renamed HMS *Redmill*. Torpedoed by *U-1105* west of Mayo, Ireland, 27 Apr 1945, not repaired. Returned 20 Jan 1947. Sold 29 Jan 1947.

DE 90 — To UK 8 Dec 1943, renamed HMS *Retalick*. Returned 25 Oct 1945. Sold 7 May 1946.

DE 91 — To UK 3 Nov 1943, renamed HMS *Halsted* (ex–*Reynolds*). Torpedoed by German torpedo boats *Jaguar* and *Möwe* off Cherbourg, 11 Jun 1944, not repaired. Returned 24 Dec 1945. Sold 21 Mar 1947; BU Netherlands.

DE 92 — To UK 14 Dec 1943, renamed HMS *Riou*. Returned 28 Feb 1946. Sold 21 Apr 1947.

DE 93 — To UK 16 Dec 1943, renamed HMS *Rutherford*. Returned 25 Oct 1945. Sold 7 May 1946; BU.

DE 94 — To UK 20 Dec 1943, renamed HMS *Cosby* (ex–*Reeves*). Returned 4 Mar 1946. Sold 5 Nov 1946.

DE 95 — To UK 22 Dec 1943, renamed HMS *Rowley*. Returned 12 Nov 1945. Sold 14 Jun 1946.

DE 96 — To UK 24 Dec 1943, renamed HMS *Rupert*. Returned 20 Mar 1946. Sold 17 Jun 1946.

DE 97 — To UK 28 Dec 1943, renamed HMS *Stockham*. Returned 15 Feb 1946. Sold 9 Apr 1947; BU.

DE 98 — To UK 23 Dec 1943, renamed HMS *Seymour*. Returned 5 Jan 1946. Sold 10 Dec 1946.

No.	Name	Builder	Keel Laid	Launched	Comm.
DE 153	*Reuben James*	Norfolk NYd	7 Sep 1942	6 Feb 1943	1 Apr 1943
DE 154	*Sims*	Norfolk NYd	7 Sep 1942	6 Feb 1943	24 Apr 1943
DE 155	*Hopping*	Norfolk NYd	15 Dec 1942	10 Mar 1943	21 May 1943
DE 156	*Reeves*	Norfolk NYd	7 Feb 1943	22 Apr 1943	9 May 1943
DE 157	*Fechteler*	Norfolk NYd	7 Feb 1943	22 Apr 1943	1 Jul 1943
DE 158	*Chase*	Norfolk NYd	16 Mar 1943	24 Apr 1943	18 Jul 1943
DE 159	*Laning*	Norfolk NYd	23 Apr 1943	4 Jul 1943	1 Aug 1943
DE 160	*Loy*	Norfolk NYd	23 Apr 1943	4 Jul 1943	12 Sep 1943
DE 161	*Barber*	Norfolk NYd	27 Apr 1943	20 May 1943	10 Oct 1943
DE 198	*Lovelace*	Norfolk NYd	22 May 1943	4 Jul 1943	7 Nov 1943
DE 199	*Manning*	Charleston NYd	15 Feb 1943	1 Jun 1943	1 Oct 1943
DE 200	*Neuendorf*	Charleston NYd	15 Feb 1943	1 Jun 1943	18 Oct 1943
DE 201	*James E. Craig*	Charleston NYd	15 Apr 1943	22 Jul 1943	1 Nov 1943
DE 202	*Eichenberger*	Charleston NYd	15 Apr 1943	22 Jul 1943	17 Nov 1943
DE 203	*Thomason*	Charleston NYd	5 Jun 1943	23 Aug 1943	10 Dec 1943
DE 204	*Jordan*	Charleston NYd	5 Jun 1943	23 Aug 1943	17 Dec 1943
DE 205	*Newman*	Charleston NYd	8 Jun 1943	9 Aug 1943	26 Nov 1943
DE 206	*Liddle*	Charleston NYd	12 Jun 1943	9 Aug 1943	6 Dec 1943
DE 207	*Kephart*	Charleston NYd	12 May 1943	6 Sep 1943	7 Jan 1944
DE 208	*Cofer*	Charleston NYd	12 May 1943	6 Sep 1943	19 Jan 1944
DE 209	*Lloyd*	Charleston NYd	26 Jul 1943	23 Oct 1943	11 Feb 1944
DE 210	*Otter*	Charleston NYd	26 Jul 1943	23 Oct 1943	21 Feb 1944
DE 211	*Hubbard*	Charleston NYd	11 Aug 1943	11 Nov 1943	6 Mar 1944
DE 212	*Hayter*	Charleston NYd	11 Aug 1943	11 Nov 1943	16 Mar 1944
DE 213	*William T. Powell*	Charleston NYd	26 Aug 1943	27 Nov 1943	28 Mar 1944
DE 214	*Scott*	Phila. NYd	1 Jan 1943	3 Apr 1943	20 Jul 1943
DE 215	*Burke*	Phila. NYd	1 Jan 1943	3 Apr 1943	20 Aug 1943
DE 216	*Enright*	Phila. NYd	22 Feb 1943	29 May 1943	21 Sep 1943
DE 217	*Coolbaugh*	Phila. NYd	22 Feb 1943	29 May 1943	15 Oct 1943
DE 218	*Darby*	Phila. NYd	22 Feb 1943	29 May 1943	15 Nov 1943
DE 219	*J. Douglas Blackwood*	Phila. NYd	22 Feb 1943	29 May 1943	15 Dec 1943
DE 220	*Francis M. Robinson*	Phila. NYd	22 Feb 1943	29 May 1943	15 Jan 1944
DE 221	*Solar*	Phila. NYd	22 Feb 1943	29 May 1943	15 Feb 1944
DE 222	*Fowler*	Phila. NYd	5 Apr 1943	3 Jul 1943	15 Mar 1944
DE 223	*Spangenberg*	Phila. NYd	5 Apr 1943	3 Jul 1943	15 Apr 1944

Service Records:

DE 153 *Reuben James* Decomm 11 Oct 1947. †
1*
Submarine sunk: *U-879 off Boston, 19 Apr 1945.

DE 154 *Sims* Rec **APD 50**, 25 Sep 1944. Damaged by kamikaze, Okinawa, 18 May 1945 and 24 May 1945 (none killed). Tokyo Bay. Decomm 24 Apr 1946. †
1* Okinawa.

DE 155 *Hopping* Rec **APD 51**, 25 Sep 1944. Damaged by coastal gunfire, Okinawa, 9 Apr 1945 (2 killed). Decomm 5 May 1947. †
1* Okinawa.

DE 156 *Reeves* Rec **APD 52**, 25 Sep 1944. Tokyo Bay. Decomm 30 Jul 1946.†
1* Okinawa.

DE 157 *Fechteler* Torpedoed and sunk by *U-967* northwest of Oran, Algeria, broke in two, 5 May 1944 (29 killed).
1* Convoy UGS-38.

DE 158 *Chase* Rec **APD 54**, 28 Nov 1944. Severely damaged by kamikaze at Okinawa, 20 May 1945, not repaired (none killed). Decomm 15 Jan 1946. Stricken 7 Feb 1946. Sold 13 Nov 1946.
2* Convoy UGS-38, Okinawa.

DE 159 *Laning* Rec **APD 55** 28 Nov 1944. Decomm 28 Jun 1946. †
1* Convoy UGS-38.

DE 160 *Loy* Rec **APD 56**, 23 Oct 1944. Damaged by kamikaze, Okinawa, 27 May 1945 (3 killed). Decomm 21 Feb 1947. †
1* Okinawa.

DE 161 *Barber* Rec **APD 57**, 23 Oct 1944. Decomm 22 May 1946. †
3* Task Group 21.15, Okinawa.
Submarine sunk: *U-488 northwest of Cape Verde Is., 26 Apr 1944.

DE 198 *Lovelace* Decomm 22 May 1946. †
3* Hollandia, Wakde, Biak, Leyte.

DE 199 *Manning* Decomm 15 Jan 1947. †
4* Hollandia, Wakde, Leyte, Lingayen.

DE 200 *Neuendorf* Damaged in collision, off Iloilo City, Philippines, 24 Jun 1945. Decomm 14 May 1946. †
3* Hollandia, Wakde, Leyte.

DE 201 *James E. Craig* Decomm 2 Jul 1946. †
4* Hollandia, Wakde, Biak, Noemfoor I., Palau, Leyte.

DE 202 *Eichenberger* Decomm 14 May 1946. †
4* Hollandia, Wakde, Biak, Palau, Leyte.
DE 203 *Thomason* Decomm 22 May 1946. †
3* Wakde, Leyte.
Submarine sunk: *RO-55* off Iba, Luzon, 7 Feb 1945.
DE 204 *Jordan* Damaged in collision with m/v *John Sherman* in North Atlantic, 18 Sep 1945. Decomm 19 Dec 1945. Stricken 8 Jan 1946. Sold 10 Jul 1947; BU.
DE 205 *Newman* Rec **APD 59**, 5 Jul 1944. Decomm 18 Feb 1946. †
5* Leyte, Mindoro, Balikpapan, Ldgs. on Palawan I., Subic Bay, Visayan Is. Ldgs.
DE 206 *Liddle* Rec **APD 60**, 5 Jul 1944. Damaged by kamikaze off Ormoc, Leyte, 7 Dec 1944 (40 killed). Decomm 18 Jun 1946. †
4* Leyte, Ormoc, Balikpapan, Mindanao Ldgs.
DE 207 *Kephart* Rec **APD 61**, 5 Jul 1944. Decomm 21 Jun 1946. †
5* Leyte, Ormoc, Mindoro, Subic Bay, Visayan Is. Ldgs., Balikpapan.
DE 208 *Cofer* Rec **APD 62**, 5 Jul 1944. Decomm 28 Jun 1946. †
8* Leyte, Ormoc, Mindoro, Brunei, Balikpapan, Ldgs. on Palawan, Subic Bay, Visayan Is. Ldgs.
DE 209 *Lloyd* Rec **APD 63**, 5 Jul 1944. Decomm 1 Jul 1946. †
5* Leyte, Ormoc, Mindoro, Balikpapan, Ldgs. on Palawan, Subic Bay, Visayan Is. Ldgs.
DE 210 *Otter* Decomm Jan 1947. †
1*
Submarine sunk: **U-248* in North Atlantic, 16 Jan 1945.
DE 211 *Hubbard* Rec **APD 53**, 1 Jun 1945. Decomm 15 Mar 1946. †
2*
Submarines sunk: **U-248* in North Atlantic, 16 Jan 1945; **U-546* northwest of Azores, 24 Apr 1945.
DE 212 *Hayter* Rec **APD 80**, 1 Jun 1945. Decomm 19 Mar 1946. †
1*
Submarine sunk: **U-248* in North Atlantic, 16 Jan 1945.
DE 213 *William T. Powell* Converted to DER 1945. †
DE 214 *Scott* Conversion to **APD 64** canceled, 10 Sep 1945. Decomm 3 Mar 1947. †
DE 215 *Burke* Rec **APD 65**, 24 Jan 1945. †
1* Okinawa. Tokyo Bay.
DE 216 *Enright* Damaged in collision with m/v in North Atlantic, 16 Apr 1944. Rec **APD 66**, 24 Jan 1945. Decomm 21 Jun 1946. †
1* Okinawa.
DE 217 *Coolbaugh* †
3* Leyte, Samar, Lingayen, Iwo Jima.
DE 218 *Darby* Decomm 28 Apr 1947. †
2* Lingayen, Iwo Jima.
DE 219 *J. Douglas Blackwood* Decomm 20 Apr 1946. †
3* Palau, Lingayen, Iwo Jima.
DE 220 *Francis M. Robinson* †
1*
Submarine sunk: *RO-501* (*U-1224*) 400 miles southwest of Azores, 13 May 1944.
DE 221 *Solar* Conversion to DER canceled 1945. Destroyed by ammunition explosion at Earle, N.J., 30 Apr 1946 (165 killed). Hulk sunk at sea, 9 Jun 1946.
DE 222 *Fowler* Decomm 28 Jun 1946. †
1*
Submarine sunk: **U-869* off Rabat, Morocco, 28 Feb 1945.
DE 223 *Spangenberg* Converted to DER 1945. Decomm 18 Jul 1947. †

No.	Name	Builder	Keel Laid	Launched	Comm.
DE 563	—	Hingham	15 Sep 1943	16 Oct 1943	*14 Jan 1944*
DE 564	—	Hingham	22 Sep 1943	6 Nov 1943	*30 Dec 1943*
DE 565	—	Hingham	22 Sep 1943	13 Nov 1943	*31 Dec 1943*
DE 566	—	Hingham	29 Sep 1943	20 Nov 1943	*10 Jan 1944*
DE 567	—	Hingham	6 Oct 1943	20 Nov 1943	*14 Jan 1944*
DE 568	—	Hingham	22 Sep 1943	27 Nov 1943	*18 Jan 1944*
DE 569	—	Hingham	6 Oct 1943	27 Nov 1943	*21 Jan 1944*
DE 570	—	Hingham	16 Oct 1943	4 Dec 1943	*25 Jan 1944*
DE 571	—	Hingham	20 Oct 1943	12 Dec 1943	*28 Jan 1944*
DE 572	—	Hingham	27 Oct 1943	18 Dec 1943	*31 Jan 1944*
DE 573	—	Hingham	27 Oct 1943	18 Dec 1943	*7 Feb 1944*
DE 574	—	Hingham	5 Nov 1943	21 Dec 1943	*8 Feb 1944*
DE 575	*Ahrens*	Hingham	5 Nov 1943	21 Dec 1943	12 Feb 1944
DE 576	*Barr*	Hingham	5 Nov 1943	28 Dec 1943	16 Feb 1944
DE 577	*Alexander J. Luke*	Hingham	5 Nov 1943	28 Dec 1943	19 Feb 1944
DE 578	*Robert I. Paine*	Hingham	5 Nov 1943	30 Dec 1943	26 Feb 1944
DE 633	*Foreman*	Beth. S. Fran.	9 Mar 1943	1 Aug 1943	22 Oct 1943
DE 634	*Whitehurst*	Beth. S. Fran.	21 Mar 1943	5 Sep 1943	19 Nov 1943
DE 635	*England*	Beth. S. Fran.	4 Apr 1943	26 Sep 1943	10 Dec 1943
DE 636	*Witter*	Beth. S. Fran.	28 Apr 1943	17 Oct 1943	29 Dec 1943
DE 637	*Bowers*	Beth. S. Fran.	28 May 1943	31 Oct 1943	27 Jan 1944
DE 638	*Willmarth*	Beth. S. Fran.	25 Jun 1943	21 Nov 1943	13 Mar 1944
DE 639	*Gendreau*	Beth. S. Fran.	1 Aug 1943	12 Dec 1943	17 Mar 1944
DE 640	*Fieberling*	Beth. S. Fran.	19 Mar 1944	2 Apr 1944	11 Apr 1944
DE 641	*William C. Cole*	Beth. S. Fran.	5 Sep 1943	29 Dec 1943	12 May 1944
DE 642	*Paul G. Baker*	Beth. S. Fran.	26 Sep 1943	12 Mar 1944	25 May 1944
DE 643	*Damon M. Cummings*	Beth. S. Fran.	17 Oct 1943	18 Apr 1944	29 Jun 1944
DE 644	*Vammen*	Beth. S. Fran.	1 Aug 1943	21 May 1944	27 Jul 1944
DE 665	*Jenks*	Dravo Pitt.	12 May 1943	11 Sep 1943	19 Jan 1944
DE 666	*Durik*	Dravo Pitt.	22 Jun 1943	9 Oct 1943	24 Mar 1944
DE 667	*Wiseman*	Dravo Pitt.	26 Jul 1943	6 Nov 1943	4 Apr 1944
DE 668	*Yokes*	Dravo Pitt.	22 Aug 1943	27 Nov 1943	18 Dec 1944
DE 669	*Pavlic*	Dravo Pitt.	21 Sep 1943	18 Dec 1943	29 Dec 1944
DE 670	*Odum*	Dravo Pitt.	15 Oct 1943	19 Jan 1944	12 Jan 1945
DE 671	*Jack C. Robinson*	Dravo Pitt.	10 Nov 1943	8 Jan 1944	2 Feb 1945
DE 672	*Bassett*	Dravo Pitt.	28 Nov 1943	15 Jan 1944	23 Feb 1945
DE 673	*John P. Gray*	Dravo Pitt.	18 Dec 1943	18 Mar 1944	15 Mar 1945

Service Records:

DE 563 — To UK 14 Jan 1944, renamed HMS *Spragge*. Returned 28 Feb 1946. Sold 18 Nov 1947
DE 564 — To UK 30 Dec 1943, renamed HMS *Stayner*. Returned 24 Nov 1945. Sold 7 Nov 1947.
DE 565 — To UK 31 Dec 1943, renamed HMS *Thornborough*. Sold 29 Jan 1947; BU Greece.
DE 566 — To UK 10 Jan 1944, renamed HMS *Trollope*. Torpedoed and went aground off Arromanches, 6 Jul 1944, not repaired. Returned 10 Oct 1944, Stricken 13 Nov 1944. BU 1951 Troon, Scotland.
DE 567 — To UK 14 Jan 1944, renamed HMS *Tyler*. Returned 12 Nov 1945. Sold 23 May 1946; BU Philadelphia.

DE 568 — To UK 18 Jan 1944, renamed HMS *Torrington*. Returned 11 Jun 1946. Sold 7 Nov 1947.

DE 569 — To UK 21 Jan 1944, renamed HMS *Narbrough*. Returned 4 Feb 1946. Sold 14 Dec 1946.

DE 570 — To UK 25 Jan 1944, renamed HMS *Waldegrave*. Returned 3 Dec 1945. Sold 8 Dec 1946.

DE 571 — To UK 28 Jan 1944, renamed HMS *Whitaker*. Torpedoed by *U-483* off Malin Head, Northern Ireland, 1 Nov 1944, not repaired. Returned 10 Mar 1945. Sold 9 Jan 1947; BU Whitchurch, England.

DE 572 — To UK 31 Jan 1944, renamed HMS *Holmes*. Returned 3 Dec 1945. Sold 16 Oct 1947.

DE 573 — To UK 7 Feb 1944, renamed HMS *Hargood*. Returned 4 Mar 1946. Sold 7 Mar 1947.

DE 574 — To UK 8 Feb 1944, renamed HMS *Hotham*. Returned 13 Mar 1956. BU 1956 Netherlands.

DE 575 *Ahrens* Decomm 24 Jun 1946. †
2* TG 21.11.
Submarine sunk: **U-549* southwest of Madeira, 29 May 1944.

DE 576 *Barr* Torpedoed by *U-549* northwest of Canary Is., 29 May 1944 (17 killed). Rec **APD 39**, 31 Jul 1944. Decomm 12 Jul 1946. †
3* TG 21.11, Iwo Jima, Okinawa. Tokyo Bay.

DE 577 *Alexander J. Luke* Went aground off Boston, 2 Mar 1944. Converted to DER Jun-Dec 1945. †

DE 578 *Robert I. Paine* Converted to DER 1945. Decomm 21 Nov 1947. †
1* TG 21.11.

DE 633 *Foreman* Slight damage by kamikaze, Okinawa, 27 Mar 1945. Moderate damage by aircraft bomb off Kerama Retto, 3 Apr 1945. Decomm 28 Jun 1946. †
5* Solomons, Wakde, Leyte, Okinawa, Raids on Japan 7–8/45.

DE 634 *Whitehurst* Severely damaged by kamikaze, Okinawa, 12 Apr 1945 (42 killed). Used as floating power station, Manila, 1945 and Guam. Decomm 27 Nov 1946. †
6* Palau-Yap Raids 3/44, Solomons, Hollandia, Wakde, Leyte, Okinawa.
Submarine sunk: *I-45* 120 miles northeast of Surigao, 28 Oct 1944.

DE 635 *England* Sank six submarines within ten days, May 1944. Damaged by kamikaze, Okinawa, 27 Apr 1945. Severely damaged by kamikaze and bomb off Okinawa, 9 May 1945 (37 killed). Rec **APD 41**, conversion canceled, 10 Jul 1945. Decomm 15 Oct 1945. Sold 26 Nov 1946.
10* TG 30.4, Solomons, Leyte, Okinawa. PUC.
Submarines sunk: *I-16* 140 miles northeast of Cape Alexander, 19 May 1944; *RO-106* 250 miles, 22 May 1944; *RO-104* 250 miles, 23 May 1944; *RO-116*, 24 May 1944; *RO-108*, 26 May 1944; **RO-105*, 31 May 1944; all northwest of New Ireland.

Figure 5.5: *England* (DE 635), 9 Feb 1944, a *Buckley* class destroyer escort, which distinguished herself by sinking six Japanese submarines in 12 days.

DE 636 *Witter* Moderate damage by kamikaze, Okinawa, 6 Apr 1945 (6 killed). Rec **APD 58**, conversion and repairs canceled, 15 Aug 1945. Decomm 22 Oct 1945. Stricken 16 Nov 1945. Sold 2 Dec 1946; BU Philadelphia.
4* Solomons, Wakde, Leyte, Okinawa.

DE 637 *Bowers* Severely damaged by kamikaze and bomb, Okinawa, 17 Apr 1945 (65 killed). Rec **APD 40**, 25 Jun 1945 Decomm 10 Feb 1947. †
4* Solomons, Wakde, Leyte, Okinawa.

DE 638 *Willmarth* Decomm 26 Apr 1946. †
4* Solomons, Leyte, Okinawa, Raids on Japan 7–8/45.

DE 639 *Gendreau* Damaged by one hit by coastal gunfire, Okinawa, 10 Jun 1945 (2 killed). †
2* Okinawa, Raids on Japan 7–8/45.

DE 640 *Fieberling* Slight damage by kamikaze, Okinawa, 6 Apr 1945. †
1* Okinawa.

DE 641 *William C. Cole* Slightly damaged by kamikaze, Okinawa, 24 May 1945. †
1* Okinawa.

DE 642 *Paul G. Baker* Decomm 3 Feb 1947. †
1* Okinawa.

DE 643 *Damon M. Cummings* Decomm 3 Feb 1947. †
1* Okinawa.

DE 644 *Vammen* Damaged by underwater explosion off Okinawa, 1 Apr 1945. Damaged in collision, Okinawa, 19 May 1945. Decomm 3 Feb 1947. †
1* Okinawa.

DE 665 *Jenks* Conversion to **APD 67** canceled, 1944. Decomm 26 Jun 1946. †
2* TG 22.3. PUC.

DE 666 *Durik* Conversion to **APD 68** canceled, 1944. Decomm 15 Jun 1946. †

DE 667 *Wiseman* Used as floating power station, Manila, 1945. Decomm 31 May 1946. †

DE 668 *Yokes* Rec **APD 69**, 27 Jun 1944. Decomm 19 Aug 1946. †
1* Okinawa.

DE 669 *Pavlic* Rec **APD 70**, 27 Jun 1944. Tokyo Bay. Decomm 15 Nov 1946. †

DE 670 *Odum* Rec **APD 71**, 27 Jun 1944. Decomm 15 Nov 1946. †

DE 671 *Jack C. Robinson* Rec **APD 72**, 27 Jun 1944. Decomm 13 Dec 1946. †
1* Okinawa.

DE 672 *Bassett* Rec **APD 73**, 27 Jun 1944. Decomm 29 Apr 1946. †

DE 673 *John P. Gray* Rec **APD 74**, 27 Jun 1944. Decomm 29 Apr 1946. †

No.	Name	Builder	Keel Laid	Launched	Comm.
DE 675	*Weber*	Beth. Quincy	22 Feb 1943	1 May 1943	30 Jun 1943
DE 676	*Schmitt*	Beth. Quincy	22 Feb 1943	29 May 1943	24 Jul 1943
DE 677	*Frament*	Beth. Quincy	1 May 1943	28 Jun 1943	15 Aug 1943
DE 678	*Harmon*	Beth. Quincy	31 May 1943	25 Jul 1943	31 Aug 1943
DE 679	*Greenwood*	Beth. Quincy	29 Jun 1943	21 Aug 1943	25 Sep 1943
DE 680	*Loeser*	Beth. Quincy	27 Jul 1943	11 Sep 1943	10 Oct 1943
DE 681	*Gillette*	Beth. Quincy	24 Aug 1943	25 Sep 1943	27 Oct 1943
DE 682	*Underhill*	Beth. Quincy	16 Sep 1943	15 Oct 1943	15 Nov 1943
DE 683	*Henry R. Kenyon*	Beth. Quincy	29 Sep 1943	30 Oct 1943	30 Nov 1943

DE 693	*Bull*	Defoe	15 Dec 1942	25 Mar 1943	12 Aug 1943
DE 694	*Bunch*	Defoe	22 Feb 1943	29 May 1943	21 Aug 1943
DE 695	*Rich*	Defoe	27 Mar 1943	22 Jun 1943	1 Oct 1943
DE 696	*Spangler*	Defoe	28 Apr 1943	15 Jul 1943	31 Oct 1943
DE 697	*George*	Defoe	22 May 1943	14 Aug 1943	20 Nov 1943
DE 698	*Raby*	Defoe	7 Jun 1943	4 Sep 1943	7 Dec 1943
DE 699	*Marsh*	Defoe	23 Jun 1943	25 Sep 1943	12 Jan 1944
DE 700	*Currier*	Defoe	21 Jul 1943	14 Oct 1943	1 Feb 1944
DE 701	*Osmus*	Defoe	17 Aug 1943	4 Nov 1943	23 Feb 1944
DE 702	*Earl V. Johnson*	Defoe	7 Sep 1943	24 Nov 1943	18 Mar 1944
DE 703	*Holton*	Defoe	28 Sep 1943	15 Dec 1943	1 May 1944
DE 704	*Cronin*	Defoe	19 Oct 1943	5 Jan 1944	5 May 1944
DE 705	*Frybarger*	Defoe	8 Nov 1943	25 Jan 1944	18 May 1944
DE 789	*Tatum*	Consol. Orange	22 Apr 1943	7 Aug 1943	22 Nov 1943
DE 790	*Borum*	Consol. Orange	28 Apr 1943	14 Aug 1943	30 Nov 1943
DE 791	*Maloy*	Consol. Orange	10 May 1943	18 Aug 1943	13 Dec 1943
DE 792	*Haines*	Consol. Orange	17 May 1943	26 Aug 1943	27 Dec 1943
DE 793	*Runels*	Consol. Orange	7 Jun 1943	4 Sep 1943	3 Jan 1944
DE 794	*Hollis*	Consol. Orange	5 Jul 1943	11 Sep 1943	24 Jan 1944
DE 795	*Gunason*	Consol. Orange	9 Aug 1943	16 Oct 1943	1 Feb 1944
DE 796	*Major*	Consol. Orange	16 Aug 1943	23 Oct 1943	12 Feb 1944
DE 797	*Weeden*	Consol. Orange	18 Aug 1943	27 Oct 1943	19 Feb 1944
DE 798	*Varian*	Consol. Orange	27 Aug 1943	6 Nov 1943	29 Feb 1944
DE 799	*Scroggins*	Consol. Orange	4 Sep 1943	6 Nov 1943	30 Mar 1944
DE 800	*Jack W. Wilke*	Consol. Orange	18 Oct 1943	18 Dec 1943	7 Mar 1944

Service Records:

DE 675 *Weber* Rec **APD 75**, 15 Dec 1944. Decomm 10 Jun 1947. †
1* Okinawa.

DE 676 *Schmitt* Rec **APD 76**, 24 Jan 1945. †
1* Balikpapan.

DE 677 *Frament* Damaged in collision with Italian submarine *Settembrini*, which sank off Azores Is., 15 May 1944. Rec **APD 77**, 15 Dec 1944. Decomm 30 May 1946. †
1* Okinawa.

DE 678 *Harmon* Decomm 25 Mar 1947. †
3* Palau, Lingayen, Iwo Jima.

DE 679 *Greenwood* †
2* Lingayen, Iwo Jima.

DE 680 *Loeser* Decomm 28 Mar 1947. †
2* Lingayen, Iwo Jima.

DE 681 *Gillette* Decomm 3 Feb 1947. †

DE 682 *Underhill* Struck submerged object at Bizerte, 24 Jul 1944. Sunk by human torpedo (kaiten) northeast of Luzon, broke in two, 24 Jul 1945 (113 killed).

DE 683 *Henry R. Kenyon* Decomm 3 Feb 1947. †

DE 693 *Bull* Rec **APD 78**, 31 Jul 1944. Decomm 5 Jun 1947. †
3* Lingayen, Iwo Jima, Okinawa.

DE 694 *Bunch* Rec **APD 79**, 31 Jul 1944. Decomm 31 May 1946. †
2* Okinawa, Minesweeping 1945.

DE 695 *Rich* Sunk by three mines off Utah Beach, Normandy, 8 Jun 1944 (91 killed).
1* Normandy.

DE 696 *Spangler* †
2* TG 30.4, Iwo Jima.

DE 697 *George* †
2* TG 30.4.

DE 698 *Raby* †
3* TG 30.4.
Submarine sunk: **I-48* northeast of Yap, 23 Jan 1945.

DE 699 *Marsh* Converted to provide mobile power 1945, used at Guam and Kwajalein. †
1* Southern France.

DE 700 *Currier* †
2* Iwo Jima.

DE 701 *Osmus* Decomm 15 Mar 1947. †
1* TG 30.4.

DE 702 *Earl V. Johnson* Damaged by underwater explosion, Philippine Sea, 4 Aug 1945. Decomm 18 Jun 1946. †

DE 703 *Holton* Decomm 31 May 1946. †

DE 704 *Cronin* Decomm 31 May 1946. †

DE 705 *Frybarger* Decomm 30 Jun 1947. †

DE 789 *Tatum* Rec **APD 81**, 15 Dec 1944. Damaged by kamikaze, Okinawa, 29 May 1945. Decomm 15 Nov 1946. †
2* Southern France, Okinawa.

DE 790 *Borum* Conversion to **APD 82** canceled, date. Decomm 15 Jun 1946. †
1* Normandy.

DE 791 *Maloy* Conversion to **APD 83** canceled, date. Rec **EDE 791**, 14 Aug 1946. †
1* Normandy.

DE 792 *Haines* Rec **APD 84**, 15 Dec 1944. Decomm 29 Apr 1946. †
1* Southern France.

DE 793 *Runels* Rec **APD 85**, 24 Jan 1945. Decomm 10 Feb 1947. †
1* Southern France. Tokyo Bay.

DE 794 *Hollis* Rec **APD 86**, 24 Jan 1945. Went aground in typhoon at Okinawa, 9 Oct 1945. Decomm 5 May 1947. †
1* Southern France. Tokyo Bay.

DE 795 *Gunason* †

DE 796 *Major* Tokyo Bay. †

DE 797 *Weeden* Decomm 9 May 1946. †

DE 798 *Varian* Decomm 15 Mar 1946. †
2* **Submarines sunk:** **U-248* in North Atlantic, 16 Jan 1945; *U-546* northwest of Azores, 24 Apr 1945.

DE 799 *Scroggins* Decomm 15 Jun 1946. †

DE 800 *Jack W. Wilke* †

Cannon Class (DET)

No.	Name	Builder	Keel Laid	Launched	Comm.
DE 99	*Cannon*	Dravo Wilm.	14 Nov 1942	25 May 1943	26 Sep 1943
DE 100	*Christopher*	Dravo Wilm.	7 Dec 1942	19 Jun 1943	23 Oct 1943
DE 101	*Alger*	Dravo Wilm.	2 Jan 1943	8 Jul 1943	12 Nov 1943
DE 102	*Thomas*	Dravo Wilm.	16 Jan 1943	31 Jul 1943	21 Nov 1943
DE 103	*Bostwick*	Dravo Wilm.	6 Feb 1943	30 Aug 1943	1 Dec 1943
DE 104	*Breeman*	Dravo Wilm.	20 Mar 1943	4 Sep 1943	12 Dec 1943
DE 105	*Burrows*	Dravo Wilm.	24 Mar 1943	2 Oct 1943	19 Dec 1943
DE 106	*Corbesier*	Dravo Wilm.	24 Apr 1943	11 Nov 1943	*2 Jan 1944*
DE 107	*Cronin*	Dravo Wilm.	13 May 1943	27 Nov 1943	*23 Jan 1944*

Figure 5.6: *Baron* (DE 166), 21 Oct 1944, of the *Cannon* class, type DET.

Figure 5.7: *Riddle* (DE 185), 16 Dec 1944, of the *Cannon* class, type DET.

No.	Name	Builder	Keel Laid	Launched	Comm.
DE 108	*Crosley*	Dravo Wilm.	23 Jun 1943	17 Dec 1943	*11 Feb 1944*
DE 109	—	Dravo Wilm.	7 Sep 1943	1 Jan 1944	*29 Feb 1944*
DE 110	—	Dravo Wilm.	25 Sep 1943	22 Jan 1944	*18 Mar 1944*
DE 111	—	Dravo Wilm.	23 Oct 1943	11 Feb 1944	*9 Apr 1944*
DE 112	*Carter*	Dravo Wilm.	19 Nov 1943	29 Feb 1944	3 May 1944
DE 113	*Clarence L. Evans*	Dravo Wilm.	23 Dec 1943	22 Mar 1944	25 Jun 1944
DE 114–28	—	Dravo Wilm.	—	—	—

Displacement	1,240 tons; 1,620 f/l
Dimensions	306" (oa); 300' (wl) x 36'8" x 8'9"
Machinery	2 screws; diesel-electric; boilers; SHP 6,000; 21 knots
Endurance	10,800/12
Complement	186/213
Armament	3–3"/50, 2–40mm AA, 8–20mm AA, 3–21"TT

Notes: Type DET (diesel-electric tandem motor drive). Seventy-two completed, of which six were completed for France under lend-lease, and eight transferred to Brazil. Resembled *Edsall* (FMR) class with different machinery.

Service Records:

DE 99 *Cannon* Decomm 19 Dec 1944 and trfd to Brazil.
Later history: Renamed *Baependi.* R1974.

DE 100 *Christopher* Decomm 19 Dec 1944 and trfd to Brazil.
Later history: Renamed *Benavente.* R1964.

DE 101 *Alger* Decomm 10 Mar 1945 and trfd to Brazil.
Later history: Renamed *Babitonga.* R1964.

DE 102 *Thomas* Completed by Norfolk NYd. Decomm 13 Mar 1946. †
4* TG 21.16.
Submarines sunk: **U-709* north of Azores, 1 Mar 1944; **U-233* off Halifax, Nova Scotia, 5 Jul 1944; **U-548* off Cape Hatteras, 30 Apr 1945.

DE 103 *Bostwick* Decomm 30 Apr 1946. †
3* TG 21.16.
Submarines sunk: **U-709* north of Azores, 1 Mar 1944; **U-548* off Cape Hatteras, 30 Apr 1945.

DE 104 *Breeman* Completed by Norfolk NYd. Decomm 26 Apr 1946. †
1* TG 21.16.

DE 105 *Burrows* Decomm 14 Jun 1946. †

DE 106 *Corbesier* To France 2 Jan 1944, renamed *Sénégalais,* renamed Yser 1963. R1964.

DE 107 *Cronin* To France 23 Jan 1944, renamed *Algérien,* renamed *Oise* 1963. R1964.

DE 108 *Crosley* To France 11 Feb 1944, renamed *Tunisien.* R1963.

DE 109 — To France 29 Feb 1944, renamed *Marocain.* R1963.

DE 110 — To France 18 Mar 1944, renamed *Hova.* R1963.

DE 111 — To France 9 Apr 1944, renamed *Somali,* renamed *Arago* 1968. R1976

DE 112 *Carter* Decomm 10 Apr 1946. †
1*
Submarine sunk: **U-518* northwest of Azores, 22 Apr 1945.

DE 113 *Clarence L. Evans* Decomm 29 May 1947. †

DE 114–28 — Canceled 10 Feb 1943.

No.	Name	Builder	Keel Laid	Launched	Comm.
DE 162	*Levy*	Federal	19 Oct 1942	28 Mar 1943	13 May 1943
DE 163	*McConnell*	Federal	19 Oct 1942	28 Mar 1943	28 May 1943
DE 164	*Osterhaus*	Federal	11 Nov 1942	18 Apr 1943	12 Jun 1943
DE 165	*Parks*	Federal	11 Nov 1942	18 Apr 1943	22 Jun 1943
DE 166	*Baron*	Federal	30 Nov 1942	9 May 1943	5 Jul 1943
DE 167	*Acree*	Federal	30 Nov 1942	9 May 1943	19 Jul 1943
DE 168	*Amick*	Federal	30 Nov 1942	27 May 1943	26 Jul 1943
DE 169	*Atherton*	Federal	14 Jan 1943	27 May 1943	29 Aug 1943
DE 170	*Booth*	Federal	30 Jan 1943	21 Jun 1943	19 Sep 1943
DE 171	*Carroll*	Federal	30 Jan 1943	21 Jun 1943	24 Oct 1943
DE 172	*Cooner*	Federal	22 Feb 1943	25 Jul 1943	21 Aug 1943
DE 173	*Eldridge*	Federal	22 Feb 1943	25 Jul 1943	27 Aug 1943
DE 174	*Marts*	Federal	26 Apr 1943	8 Aug 1943	3 Sep 1943
DE 175	*Pennewill*	Federal	26 Apr 1943	8 Aug 1943	15 Sep 1943
DE 176	*Micka*	Federal	3 May 1943	22 Aug 1943	23 Sep 1943
DE 177	*Reybold*	Federal	3 May 1943	22 Aug 1943	29 Sep 1943
DE 178	*Herzog*	Federal	17 May 1943	5 Sep 1943	6 Oct 1943
DE 179	*McAnn*	Federal	17 May 1943	5 Sep 1943	11 Oct 1943
DE 180	*Trumpeter*	Federal	7 Jun 1943	19 Sep 1943	16 Oct 1943
DE 181	*Straub*	Federal	7 Jun 1943	19 Sep 1943	25 Oct 1943
DE 182	*Gustafson*	Federal	5 Jul 1943	3 Oct 1943	1 Nov 1943
DE 183	*Samuel S. Miles* ex–*Miles*	Federal	5 Jul 1943	3 Oct 1943	4 Nov 1943

DE 184	*Wesson*	Federal	29 Jul 1943	17 Oct 1943	11 Nov 1943
DE 185	*Riddle*	Federal	29 Jul 1943	17 Oct 1943	17 Nov 1943
DE 186	*Swearer*	Federal	12 Aug 1943	31 Oct 1943	24 Nov 1943
DE 187	*Stern*	Federal	12 Aug 1943	31 Oct 1943	1 Dec 1943
DE 188	*O'Neill*	Federal	26 Aug 1943	14 Nov 1943	6 Dec 1943
DE 189	*Bronstein*	Federal	26 Aug 1943	14 Nov 1943	13 Dec 1943
DE 190	*Baker*	Federal	9 Sep 1943	28 Nov 1943	23 Dec 1943
	ex–*Raby* (3 Sep 1943)				
DE 191	*Coffman*	Federal	9 Sep 1943	28 Nov 1943	27 Dec 1943
DE 192	*Eisner*	Federal	23 Sep 1943	12 Dec 1943	1 Jan 1944
DE 193	*Garfield Thomas*	Federal	23 Sep 1943	12 Dec 1943	24 Jan 1944
	ex–*William G. Thomas*				
DE 194	*Wingfield*	Federal	7 Oct 1943	30 Dec 1943	28 Jan 1944
DE 195	*Thornhill*	Federal	7 Oct 1943	30 Dec 1943	1 Feb 1944
DE 196	*Rinehart*	Federal	21 Oct 1943	9 Jan 1944	12 Feb 1944
DE 197	*Roche*	Federal	21 Oct 1943	9 Jan 1944	21 Feb 1944

Service Records:

DE 162 *Levy* Decomm 4 Apr 1947. †
5* Hollandia, Truk Raid 4/44, Guam, Saipan, Bonins-Yap Raids, Palau, Philippines Raids 9/44, Okinawa Raid 10/44, N. Luzon–Formosa Raids 10/44, Luzon Raids 10/44.

DE 163 *McConnell* Decomm 29 Jun 1946. †
3* Guam, Palau, Philippines Raids 9/44, Bonins-Yap Raids, N. Luzon–Formosa Raids 10/44, Luzon Raids 10/44.

DE 164 *Osterhaus* Decomm 26 Jun 1946. †
3* Saipan, Guam, Palau, Philippines Raids 9/44, Luzon Raids 10/44.

DE 165 *Parks* Decomm .. Mar 1946. †
4* Hollandia, Truk Raid 4/44, Saipan, Guam, Palau, Philippines Raids 9/44, N. Luzon–Formosa Raids 10/44.

DE 166 *Baron* Decomm 26 Apr 1946. †
3* Truk Raid 4/44, Hollandia, Saipan, Guam.

DE 167 *Acree* Decomm 1 Apr 1946. †
5* Truk Raid 4/44, Saipan, Guam, Tinian, Hollandia, Philippines Raids 9/44.

DE 168 *Amick* Completed by Norfolk NYd. Decomm 16 May 1947. †

DE 169 *Atherton* Completed by Norfolk NYd. Decomm 10 Dec 1945. †
1*
Submarine sunk: **U-853* off Block I., N.Y., 6 May 1945.

DE 170 *Booth* Decomm 4 Mar 1946. †

DE 171 *Carroll* Decomm 19 Jun 1946. †

DE 172 *Cooner* Decomm 25 Jun 1946. †

DE 173 *Eldridge* Decomm 17 Jun 1946. †

DE 174 *Marts* Decomm 20 Mar 1945 and trfd to Brazil.
Later history: Renamed *Bocaina.* R1975.

DE 175 *Pennewill* Decomm 1 Aug 1944 and trfd to Brazil.
Later history: Renamed *Bertioga.* R1964

DE 176 *Micka* Decomm 14 Jun 1946. †

DE 177 *Reybold* Decomm 15 Aug 1944 and trfd to Brazil.
Later history: Renamed *Baurú.* R1973, Museum at Rio de Janeiro.

DE 178 *Herzog* Decomm 1 Aug 1944 and trfd to Brazil.
Later history: Renamed *Beberibe.* R1968

DE 179 *McAnn* Decomm 15 Aug 1944 and trfd to Brazil.
Later history: Renamed *Bracui'.* R1973, Museum at Rio de Janeiro.

DE 180 *Trumpeter* Decomm 14 Jun 1946. †

DE 181 *Straub* Decomm 17 Oct 1947. †

DE 182 *Gustafson* Damaged in collision with cruiser *Omaha* in South Atlantic, 22 Nov 1944. Decomm 26 Jun 1946. †
1*
Submarine sunk: *U-857* off Boston, 7 Apr 1945 (possible).

DE 183 *Samuel S. Miles* Damaged by kamikaze near miss, Okinawa, 11 Apr 1945 (1 killed). Decomm 28 Mar 1946. †
8* Palau-Yap Raids 3/44, Hollandia, Truk Raid 4/44, Saipan, Guam, Palau, Philippines Raids 9/44, Formosa Raids 1/45, Luzon Raids 1/45, China Coast Raids 1/45, Nansei Shoto Raid 1/45, Iwo Jima, Okinawa.
Submarine sunk: *I-177* northeast of Angaur, Palau, 3 Oct 1944.

DE 184 *Wesson* Moderate damage by kamikaze and bomb, Okinawa, 7 Apr 1945 (8 killed). Decomm 24 Jun 1946. †
7* Saipan, Guam, Tinian, Palau, Philippines Raids 9/44, N. Luzon–Formosa Raids 10/44, Luzon Raids 10/44, Formosa Raids 1/45, Iwo Jima, Okinawa.

DE 185 *Riddle* Moderate damage by kamikaze, Okinawa, 12 Apr 1945 (1 killed). Decomm 8 Jun 1946. †
12* Eniwetok, Palau-Yap Raids 3/44, Hollandia, Truk Raid 4/44, Saipan, Palau, Philippines Raids 9/44, N. Luzon–Formosa Raids 10/44, Luzon Raids 10/44, Formosa Raids 1/45, China Coast Raids 1/45, Iwo Jima, Okinawa.
Submarine sunk: **I-10* northeast of Saipan., 4 Jul 1944.

DE 186 *Swearer* Decomm 25 Feb 1946. †
9* Palau-Yap Raids 3/44, Truk Raid 4/44, Saipan, Guam, Tinian, Palau, Philippines Raids 9/44, Luzon Raids 10/44, Formosa Raids 1/45, China Coast Raids 1/45, Nansei Shoto Raid 1/45, Iwo Jima, Okinawa.

DE 187 *Stern* Decomm 26 Apr 1946. †
3* Formosa Raids 1/45, Luzon Raids 1/45, China Coast Raids 1/45, Nansei Shoto Raid 1/45, Iwo Jima, Okinawa.

DE 188 *O'Neill* Damaged by kamikaze off Okinawa, 26 May 1945 (2 killed). Decomm 2 May 1946. †
4* Palau, Formosa Raids 1/45, Luzon Raids 1/45, China Coast Raids 1/45, Nansei Shoto Raid 1/45, Iwo Jima, Okinawa.

DE 189 *Bronstein* Decomm 5 Nov 1945. †
4* TG 21.16. PUC.
Submarines sunk: **U-709* north of Azores, 1 Mar 1944; *U-603* in Mid-Atlantic, 1 Mar 1944; **U-801* off Cape Verde Is., 17 Mar 1944.

DE 190 *Baker* Decomm 4 Mar 1946. †
1*
Submarine sunk: **U-233* off Halifax, Nova Scotia, 5 Jul 1944.

DE 191 *Coffman* Decomm 30 Apr 1946. †
1*
Submarine sunk: **U-548* off Cape Hatteras, 30 Apr 1945.

DE 192 *Eisner* Decomm 5 Jul 1946. †

DE 193 *Garfield Thomas* Decomm 27 Mar 1947. †

DE 194 *Wingfield* Decomm 15 Jun 1946. †

DE 195 *Thornhill* Decomm 17 Jun 1946. †

DE 196 *Rinehart* Decomm 17 Jul 1946. †

DE 197 *Roche* Damaged by mine northwest of Eniwetok, 22 Aug 1945 (3 killed); towed to Tokyo, not repaired. Scuttled off Yokosuka, 11 Mar 1946.

No.	Name	Builder	Keel Laid	Launched	Comm.
DE 739	*Bangust*	W. Pipe S. Pedro	11 Feb 1943	6 Jun 1943	30 Oct 1943
DE 740	*Waterman*	W. Pipe S. Pedro	24 Feb 1943	20 Jun 1943	30 Nov 1943
DE 741	*Weaver*	W. Pipe S. Pedro	13 Mar 1943	4 Jul 1943	31 Dec 1943
DE 742	*Hilbert*	W. Pipe S. Pedro	23 Mar 1943	18 Jul 1943	4 Feb 1944
DE 743	*Lamons*	W. Pipe S. Pedro	10 Apr 1943	1 Aug 1943	29 Feb 1944
DE 744	*Kyne*	W. Pipe S. Pedro	16 Apr 1943	15 Aug 1943	4 Apr 1944
DE 745	*Snyder*	W. Pipe S. Pedro	28 Apr 1943	29 Aug 1943	5 May 1944
DE 746	*Hemminger*	W. Pipe S. Pedro	5 May 1943	12 Sep 1943	30 May 1944

DE 747	*Bright*	W. Pipe S. Pedro	9 Jun 1943	26 Sep 1943	30 Jun 1944
DE 748	*Tills*	W. Pipe S. Pedro	23 Jun 1943	3 Oct 1943	8 Aug 1944
DE 749	*Roberts*	W. Pipe S. Pedro	7 Jul 1943	14 Nov 1943	2 Sep 1944
DE 750	*McClelland*	W. Pipe S. Pedro	21 Jul 1943	28 Nov 1943	19 Sep 1944
DE 751	*Gaynier*	W. Pipe S. Pedro	4 Aug 1943	30 Jan 1944	—
DE 752	*Curtis W. Howard*	W. Pipe S. Pedro	18 Aug 1943	26 Mar 1944	—
DE 753	*John J. Van Buren*	W. Pipe S. Pedro	31 Aug 1943	16 Jan 1944	—
DE 754	*Willard Keith*	W. Pipe S. Pedro	14 Sep 1943	—	—
DE 755	*Paul G. Baker*	W. Pipe S. Pedro	27 Sep 1943	—	—
DE 756	*Damon M. Cummings*	W. Pipe S. Pedro	—	—	—
DE 757–62	—	W. Pipe S. Pedro	—	—	—
DE 763	*Cates*	Tampa	1 Mar 1943	10 Oct 1943	15 Dec 1943
DE 764	*Gandy*	Tampa	1 Mar 1943	12 Dec 1943	7 Feb 1944
DE 765	*Earl K. Olsen*	Tampa	9 Mar 1943	13 Feb 1944	10 Apr 1944
DE 766	*Slater*	Tampa	9 Mar 1943	13 Feb 1944	1 May 1944
DE 767	*Oswald*	Tampa	1 Apr 1943	25 Apr 1944	12 Jun 1944
DE 768	*Ebert*	Tampa	1 Apr 1943	11 May 1944	12 Jul 1944
DE 769	*Neal A. Scott*	Tampa	1 Jun 1943	4 Jun 1944	31 Jul 1944
DE 770	*Muir*	Tampa	1 Jun 1943	4 Jun 1944	30 Aug 1944
DE 771	*Sutton*	Tampa	23 Aug 1943	6 Aug 1944	22 Dec 1944
DE 772	*Milton Lewis* ex–*Rogers* (18 Jul 1944)	Tampa	23 Aug 1943	6 Aug 1944	—
DE 773	*George M. Campbell*	Tampa	14 Oct 1943	15 Oct 1944	—
DE 774	*Russell M. Cox*	Tampa	14 Oct 1943	—	—
DE 775–88	—	Tampa	—	—	—

Service Records:

DE 739 *Bangust* Decomm 17 Nov 1946. †
11* Kwajalein, Palau-Yap Raids 3/44, Saipan, Philippine Sea, Guam, Tinian, Palau, Philippines Raids 9/44, N. Luzon–Formosa Raids 10/44, Luzon Raids 10/44, Formosa Raids 1/45, China Coast Raids 1/45, Nansei Shoto Raid 1/45, Iwo Jima, Fleet Raids 1945, Raids on Japan 7–8/45.
Submarine sunk: *RO-42* 90 miles northeast of Roi, Kwajalein, 10 Jun 1944.

DE 740 *Waterman* Damaged in typhoon in Philippine Sea, 18 Dec 1944. Decomm 31 May 1946. †
8* Saipan, 3rd Bonins Raid, Guam, Tinian, Palau, Philippines Raids 9/44, N. Luzon–Formosa Raids 10/44, Luzon Raids 10/44, Surigao Strait, Luzon Raids 1/45, Formosa Raids 1/45, China Coast Raids 1/45, Nansei Shoto Raid 1/45, Iwo Jima, Fleet Raids 1945, Raids on Japan 7–8/45.

DE 741 *Weaver* Decomm 29 May 1947. †
9* Palau-Yap Raids 3/44, Saipan, Philippine Sea, 2nd Bonins Raid, Tinian, Guam, Palau, Philippines Raids 9/44, Luzon Raids 10/44, Luzon Raids 1/45, Formosa Raids 1/45, China Coast Raids 1/45, Nansei Shoto Raid 1/45, Iwo Jima, Fleet Raids 1945, Raids on Japan 7–8/45. Tokyo Bay.

DE 742 *Hilbert* Damaged in typhoon, Philippine Sea, 5 Jun 1945. Decomm 19 Jun 1946. †
8* Saipan, Philippine Sea, Guam, Tinian, Palau, Philippines Raids 9/44, Luzon Raids 10/44, Formosa Raids 1/45, China Coast Raids 1/45, Nansei Shoto Raid 1/45, Iwo Jima, Fleet Raids 1945, Raids on Japan 7–8/45.

DE 743 *Lamons* Decomm 14 Jun 1946. †
9* Saipan, 2nd Bonins Raid, 3rd Bonins Raid, Guam, Tinian, Palau, Philippines Raids 9/44, N. Luzon–Formosa Raids 10/44, Luzon Raids 10/44, Nansei Shoto Raid 1/45, Iwo Jima, Fleet Raids 1945, Balikpapan, Raids on Japan 7–8/45.

DE 744 *Kyne* Decomm 14 Jun 1946. †
6* Palau, Luzon Raids 1/45, Formosa Raids 1/45, China Coast Raids 1/45, Iwo Jima, Fleet Raids 1945, Balikpapan, Raids on Japan 7–8/45.

DE 745 *Snyder* Decomm Dec 1946. †
1* Okinawa.

DE 746 *Hemminger* Decomm 17 Jun 1946. †
1* Okinawa.

DE 747 *Bright* Severely damaged by kamikaze bomb, Okinawa, 13 May 1945 (none killed). Decomm 19 Apr 1946. †
1* Okinawa.

DE 748 *Tills* Decomm 14 Jun 1946. †
1* Okinawa.

DE 749 *Roberts* Decomm 3 Mar 1947. †
1* Okinawa.

DE 750 *McClelland* Decomm 15 May 1946. †
3* Iwo Jima, Okinawa, Raids on Japan 7–8/45.

DE 751 *Gaynier* Construction suspended, 6 Jun 1944. Canceled 1 Sep 1944.

DE 752 *Curtis W. Howard* Canceled 1 Sep 1944

DE 753 *John J. Van Buren* Canceled 1 Sep 1944

DE 754–62 — Canceled 2 Oct 1943.

DE 763 *Cates* Decomm 28 Mar 1947. †

DE 764 *Gandy* Decomm 17 Jun 1946. †
1*
Submarine sunk: *U-550* southeast of Cape Cod, 16 Apr 1944 (damaged by ramming).

DE 765 *Earl K. Olsen* Decomm 17 Jun 1946. †

DE 766 *Slater* Decomm 26 Sep 1947. †

DE 767 *Oswald* Decomm 30 Apr 1946. †

DE 768 *Ebert* Decomm 14 Jun 1946. †

Figure 5.8: *Kretchmer* (DE 329), 26 Jul 1944, of the *Edsall* class, type FMR. Torpedo tubes replaced by antiaircraft guns.

DE 769 *Neal A. Scott* Decomm 30 Apr 1946. †
1*
Submarine sunk: **U-518* northwest of Azores, 22 Apr 1945.
DE 770 *Muir* Decomm Sep 1947. †
DE 771 *Sutton* Decomm Sep 1947. †
DE 772 *Milton Lewis* Canceled 1 Sep 1944. Hull towed to Charleston and BU.
DE 773 *George M. Campbell* Canceled 1 Sep 1944.
DE 774 *Russell M. Cox* Canceled 1 Sep 1944.
DE 775–88 Canceled 2 Oct 1943.

Edsall Class (FMR)

No.	Name	Builder	Keel Laid	Launched	Comm.
DE 129	*Edsall*	Consol. Orange	2 Jul 1942	1 Nov 1942	10 Apr 1943
DE 130	*Jacob Jones*	Consol. Orange	16 Jun 1942	29 Nov 1942	29 Apr 1943
DE 131	*Hammann*	Consol. Orange	10 Jul 1942	13 Dec 1942	17 May 1943
	ex–*Langley* (1 Aug 1942)				
DE 132	*Robert E. Peary*	Consol. Orange	30 Jun 1942	3 Jan 1943	31 May 1943
DE 133	*Pillsbury*	Consol. Orange	18 Jul 1942	10 Jan 1943	7 Jun 1943
DE 134	*Pope*	Consol. Orange	14 Jul 1942	12 Jan 1943	25 Jun 1943
DE 135	*Flaherty*	Consol. Orange	7 Nov 1942	17 Jan 1943	26 Jun 1943
DE 136	*Frederick C. Davis*	Consol. Orange	9 Nov 1942	24 Jan 1943	14 Jul 1943
DE 137	*Herbert C. Jones*	Consol. Orange	30 Nov 1942	19 Jan 1943	21 Jul 1943
DE 138	*Douglas L. Howard*	Consol. Orange	8 Dec 1942	24 Jan 1943	29 Jul 1943
DE 139	*Farquhar*	Consol. Orange	14 Dec 1942	13 Feb 1943	5 Aug 1943
DE 140	*J. R. Y. Blakely*	Consol. Orange	16 Dec 1942	7 Mar 1943	16 Aug 1943
DE 141	*Hill*	Consol. Orange	21 Dec 1942	28 Feb 1943	16 Aug 1943
DE 142	*Fessenden*	Consol. Orange	4 Jan 1943	9 Mar 1943	25 Aug 1943
DE 143	*Fiske*	Consol. Orange	4 Jan 1943	14 Mar 1943	25 Aug 1943
DE 144	*Frost*	Consol. Orange	13 Jan 1943	21 Mar 1943	30 Aug 1943
DE 145	*Huse*	Consol. Orange	11 Jan 1943	23 Mar 1943	30 Aug 1943
DE 146	*Inch*	Consol. Orange	19 Jan 1943	4 Apr 1943	8 Sep 1943
DE 147	*Blair*	Consol. Orange	19 Jan 1943	6 Apr 1943	13 Sep 1943
DE 148	*Brough*	Consol. Orange	22 Jan 1943	10 Apr 1943	18 Sep 1943
DE 149	*Chatelain*	Consol. Orange	25 Jan 1943	21 Apr 1943	22 Sep 1943
DE 150	*Neunzer*	Consol. Orange	29 Jan 1943	27 Apr 1943	27 Sep 1943
DE 151	*Poole*	Consol. Orange	13 Feb 1943	8 May 1943	29 Sep 1943
DE 152	*Peterson*	Consol. Orange	28 Feb 1943	15 May 1943	29 Sep 1943

Displacement	1,200 tons; 1,590 f/l
Dimensions	306' (oa); 300' (wl) x 36'10" x 8'7"
Machinery	2 screws; FM diesel; boilers; SHP 6,000; 21 knots
Endurance	6,000/12
Complement	209
Armament	3–3"/50, 2–40mm twin AA, 8–20mm AA, 1 triple 21" TT (DE 251 *Camp*: 2–5"/38; 1945)

Notes: Type FMR (geared diesel, FM reverse gear drive). Similar to *Cannon* (DET) class with different machinery. Seventy-two completed.

Service Records:

DE 129 *Edsall* Decomm 11 Jun 1946. †
DE 130 *Jacob Jones* Decomm 26 Jul 1946. †
DE 131 *Hammann* Decomm 24 Oct 1945 . †
DE 132 *Robert E. Peary* Decomm 13 Jun 1947. †
DE 133 *Pillsbury* Decomm 1947. †
5* TG 21.12, TG 22.3. PUC.
Submarines sunk: **U-515* north of Madeira, 9 Apr 1944; *capture of *U-505* northwest of Dakar, 4 Jun 1944; **U-546* northwest of Azores, 24 Apr 1945.
DE 134 *Pope* Decomm 17 May 1946. †
3* TG 21.12, TG 22.3. PUC.
DE 135 *Flaherty* Decomm 17 Jun 1946. †
3* TG 21.12, TG 22.3. PUC.
Submarines sunk: **U-515* north of Madeira, 9 Apr 1944; **U-546* northwest of Azores, 24 Apr 1945.
DE 136 *Frederick C. Davis* Torpedoed and sunk by *U-546* in Western Atlantic, broke in two, 24 Apr 1945 (115 killed).
4* TG 21.12, Convoy KMF-25A, Anzio, Southern France.
DE 137 *Herbert C. Jones* Damaged by two glider bomb near misses off Anzio, 15 Feb 1944. Decomm 2 May 1947. †
3* Convoy KMF-25A, Anzio, Southern France.
DE 138 *Douglas L. Howard* Decomm 17 Jun 1946. †
DE 139 *Farquhar* Decomm 14 Jun 1946. †
1*
Submarine sunk: *U-881* south of Newfoundland, 6 May 1945.
DE 140 *J. R. Y. Blakely* Decomm 14 Jun 1946. †
DE 141 *Hill* Decomm 7 Jun 1946. †
DE 142 *Fessenden* Decomm 24 Jun 1946. †
2* Convoy UGS-38.
Submarine sunk: *U-1062* southwest of Cape Verde, 30 Sep 1944.
DE 143 *Fiske* Torpedoed and sunk by *U-804* north of Azores Is., broke in two, 2 Aug 1944 (30 killed).
1* Convoy UGS-38.
DE 144 *Frost* Decomm 18 Jun 1946. †
7* TG 21.15, TG 22.5. PUC.
Submarines sunk: **U-488* northwest of Cape Verde Is., 26 Apr 1944; **U-490* northwest of Azores, 11 Jun 1944; **U-154* off Madeira, 3 Jul 1944; **U-1235* in Mid-Atlantic, 15 Apr 1945; **U-880* in Mid-Atlantic, 16 Apr 1945.
DE 145 *Huse* Decomm 27 Mar 1946. †
5* TG 21.15, TG 22.5.
Submarines sunk: **U-856* south of Halifax; 7 Apr 1944; **U-488* northwest of Cape Verde Is., 26 Apr 1944; **U-490* northwest of Azores, 11 Jun 1944.
DE 146 *Inch* Decomm 17 May 1946. †
4* TG 21.15, TG 22.5.

Submarines sunk: **U-490* northwest of Azores, 1 Jun 1944; **U-154* off Madeira, 3 Jul 1944.

DE 147 *Blair* Decomm 28 Jun 1946. †

DE 148 *Brough* Decomm 22 Mar 1946. †

DE 149 *Chatelain* Decomm 14 Jun 1946. †

5* TG 21.12, TG 22.3. PUC.

Submarines sunk: **U-515* north of Madeira, 9 Apr 1944; *captured *U-505* off Azores, 4 Jun 1944; **U-546* northwest of Azores, 24 Apr 1945.

DE 150 *Neunzer* Decomm Jan 1947. †

1*

Submarine sunk: **U-546* northwest of Azores, 24 Apr 1945.

DE 151 *Poole* USCG crew. Decomm Jan 1947. †

DE 152 *Peterson* USCG crew. Decomm 1 May 1946. †

1*

Submarine sunk: **U-550* south of Halifax, Nova Scotia, 16 Apr 1944.

No.	Name	Builder	Keel Laid	Launched	Comm.
DE 238	*Stewart*	Brown	15 Jul 1942	22 Nov 1942	31 May 1943
DE 239	*Sturtevant*	Brown	15 Jul 1942	3 Dec 1942	16 Jun 1943
DE 240	*Moore*	Brown	20 Jul 1942	21 Dec 1942	1 Jul 1943
DE 241	*Keith*	Brown	4 Aug 1942	21 Dec 1942	19 Jul 1943
	ex–*Scott* (8 Dec 1942)				
DE 242	*Tomich*	Brown	15 Sep 1942	28 Dec 1942	27 Jul 1943
DE 243	*J. Richard Ward*	Brown	30 Sep 1942	6 Jan 1943	5 Jul 1943
	ex–*James R. Ward*				
DE 244	*Otterstetter*	Brown	9 Nov 1942	19 Jan 1943	6 Aug 1943
DE 245	*Sloat*	Brown	21 Nov 1942	21 Jan 1943	16 Aug 1943
DE 246	*Snowden*	Brown	7 Dec 1942	19 Feb 1943	23 Aug 1943
DE 247	*Stanton*	Brown	7 Dec 1942	21 Feb 1943	7 Aug 1943
DE 248	*Swasey*	Brown	30 Dec 1942	18 Mar 1943	31 Aug 1943
DE 249	*Marchand*	Brown	30 Dec 1942	20 Mar 1943	8 Sep 1943
DE 250	*Hurst*	Brown	27 Jan 1943	14 Apr 1943	30 Aug 1943
DE 251	*Camp*	Brown	27 Jan 1943	16 Apr 1943	16 Sep 1943
DE 252	*Howard D. Crow*	Brown	6 Feb 1943	26 Apr 1943	27 Sep 1943
DE 253	*Pettit*	Brown	6 Feb 1943	28 Apr 1943	23 Sep 1943
DE 254	*Ricketts*	Brown	16 Mar 1943	10 May 1943	5 Oct 1943
DE 255	*Sellstrom*	Brown	16 Mar 1943	12 May 1943	12 Oct 1943
DE 316	*Harveson*	Consol. Orange	9 Mar 1943	22 May 1943	12 Oct 1943
DE 317	*Joyce*	Consol. Orange	8 Mar 1943	26 May 1943	30 Sep 1943
DE 318	*Kirkpatrick*	Consol. Orange	15 Mar 1943	5 Jun 1943	23 Oct 1943
DE 319	*Leopold*	Consol. Orange	24 Mar 1943	12 Jun 1943	18 Oct 1943
DE 320	*Menges*	Consol. Orange	22 Mar 1943	15 Jun 1943	26 Oct 1943
DE 321	*Mosley*	Consol. Orange	6 Apr 1943	26 Jun 1943	30 Oct 1943
DE 322	*Newell*	Consol. Orange	5 Apr 1943	29 Jun 1943	30 Oct 1943
DE 323	*Pride*	Consol. Orange	12 Apr 1943	3 Jul 1943	13 Nov 1943
DE 324	*Falgout*	Consol. Orange	26 May 1943	24 Jul 1943	15 Nov 1943
DE 325	*Lowe*	Consol. Orange	24 May 1943	28 Jul 1943	22 Nov 1943
DE 326	*Gary*	Consol. Orange	15 Jun 1943	21 Aug 1943	27 Nov 1943
DE 327	*Brister*	Consol. Orange	14 Jun 1943	24 Aug 1943	30 Nov 1943
	ex–*O'Toole* (23 Jul 1943)				
DE 328	*Finch*	Consol. Orange	29 Jun 1943	28 Aug 1943	13 Dec 1943
DE 329	*Kretchmer*	Consol. Orange	28 Jun 1943	31 Aug 1943	27 Dec 1943
DE 330	*O'Reilly*	Consol. Orange	29 Jul 1943	2 Oct 1943	28 Dec 1943
DE 331	*Koiner*	Consol. Orange	26 Jul 1943	5 Oct 1943	27 Dec 1943
DE 332	*Price*	Consol. Orange	24 Aug 1943	30 Oct 1943	12 Jan 1944
DE 333	*Strickland*	Consol. Orange	23 Aug 1943	2 Nov 1943	10 Jan 1944
DE 334	*Forster*	Consol. Orange	31 Aug 1943	13 Nov 1943	25 Jan 1944
DE 335	*Daniel*	Consol. Orange	30 Aug 1943	16 Nov 1943	24 Jan 1944
DE 336	*Roy O. Hale*	Consol. Orange	13 Sep 1943	20 Nov 1943	3 Feb 1944
DE 337	*Dale W. Peterson*	Consol. Orange	25 Oct 1943	22 Dec 1943	17 Feb 1944
DE 338	*Martin H. Ray*	Consol. Orange	27 Oct 1943	29 Dec 1943	28 Feb 1944

Service Records:

DE 238 *Stewart* Decomm Jan 1947. †

DE 239 *Sturtevant* Decomm 24 Mar 1946. †

DE 240 *Moore* Decomm 30 Jun 1947. †

DE 241 *Keith* Decomm 20 Sep 1946. †

1*

Submarine sunk: **U-546* northwest of Azores, 24 Apr 1945.

DE 242 *Tomich* Decomm 20 Sep 1946. †

1* Convoy UGS-36.

DE 243 *J. Richard Ward* Decomm 13 Jun 1946. †

DE 244 *Otterstetter* Decomm 21 Sep 1946. †

DE 245 *Sloat* Decomm .. Jan 1947. †

1* Convoy UGS-36.

DE 246 *Snowden* Decomm 29 Mar 1946. †

3* TG 21.15, TG 22.5.

Submarine sunk: **U-488* northwest of Cape Verde Is., 26 Apr 1944.

DE 247 *Stanton* Decomm 2 Jun 1947. †

3* Convoy UGS-37.

Submarines sunk: **U-1235* in Mid-Atlantic, 5 Apr 1945; **U-880* in Mid-Atlantic, 16 Apr 1945.

DE 248 *Swasey* Decomm 15 Jan 1946. †

2* Convoy UGS-37, TG 22.5.

DE 249 *Marchand* USCG crew. Rammed while assisting burning m/v *El Coston* off Bermuda, 25 Feb 1945. Decomm 25 Apr 1947. †

DE 250 *Hurst* USCG crew. Decomm 1 May 1946. †

DE 251 *Camp* USCG crew. Damaged in collision with m/v tkr *Santa Cecilia* south of Ireland, 18 Nov 1944 (1 killed). Decomm 1 May 1946. †

DE 252 *Howard D. Crow* USCG crew. Decomm 22 May 1946. †

DE 253 *Pettit* USCG crew. Decomm 6 May 1946. †

DE 254 *Ricketts* USCG crew. Decomm 17 Apr 1946. †

DE 255 *Sellstrom* Decomm 13 Jun 1946. †
1* Convoy UGS-36. USCG crew.
DE 316 *Harveson* USCG crew. Damaged in collision with m/v *William T. Barry* off Virginia Capes, 15 Dec 1943. Decomm 9 May 1947.
DE 317 *Joyce* USCG crew. Decomm 1 May 1946. †
1*
Submarine sunk: **U-550* south of Halifax, Nova Scotia, 16 Apr 1944.
DE 318 *Kirkpatrick* USCG crew. Decomm 1 May 1946. †
DE 319 *Leopold* USCG crew. Torpedoed by *U-255* south of Iceland (convoy CU-16), broke in two and sunk by U.S. forces, 10 Mar 1944 (171 killed).
DE 320 *Menges* USCG crew. Torpedoed in stern by *U-371* in Gulf of Bougie, 3 May 1944 (3 killed). Repaired with stern of damaged *Holder* at New York NYd. Decomm Jan 1947. †
2* Convoy UGS-38.
Submarine sunk: **U-866* southeast of Halifax, Nova Scotia, 18 Mar 1945.
DE 321 *Mosley* USCG crew. Decomm 15 Mar 1946. †
2* Convoy UGS-38.
Submarine sunk: **U-866* southeast of Halifax, Nova Scotia, 18 Mar 1945.
DE 322 *Newell* USCG crew. Decomm 20 Nov 1945. †
1* Convoy UGS-38.
DE 323 *Pride* USCG crew. Decomm 26 Apr 1946. †
3* Convoy UGS-38.
Submarines sunk: **U-371* off Constantine, Algeria, 4 May 1944; **U-866* southeast of Halifax, Nova Scotia, 18 Mar 1945.
DE 324 *Falgout* †
1* Convoy UGS-38. USCG crew. Decomm 18 Apr 1947.
DE 325 *Lowe* †
2* Convoy UGS-38. USCG crew. Decomm 1 May 1946.
Submarine sunk: **U-866* southeast of Halifax, Nova Scotia, 18 Mar 1945.
DE 326 *Gary* Renamed ***Thomas J. Gary***, 1 Jan 1945. Decomm 7 Mar 1947. †
DE 327 *Brister* Decomm 4 Oct 1946. †
DE 328 *Finch* Decomm 4 Oct 1946. †
DE 329 *Kretchmer* Decomm 20 Sep 1946. †
DE 330 *O'Reilly* Damaged by striking reef in Buckner Bay, Okinawa, 23 Oct 1945. Decomm 15 Jun 1946. †
DE 331 *Koiner* Decomm 4 Oct 1946. †
DE 332 *Price* Decomm 16 May 1947. †
1* Convoy UGS-37.
DE 333 *Strickland* Decomm 15 Jun 1946. †
1* Convoy UGS-37.
DE 334 *Forster* Decomm 15 Jun 1946. †
1* Convoy UGS-37.
DE 335 *Daniel* Decomm 12 Apr 1946. †
DE 336 *Roy O. Hale* Decomm 11 Jul 1946. †
DE 337 *Dale W. Peterson* Decomm 27 Mar 1946. †
DE 338 *Martin H. Ray* Decomm Mar 1946. †

No.	Name	Builder	Keel Laid	Launched	Comm.
DE 382	*Ramsden*	Brown	26 Mar 1943	24 May 1943	19 Oct 1943
DE 383	*Mills*	Brown	26 Mar 1943	26 May 1943	12 Oct 1943
DE 384	*Rhodes*	Brown	19 Apr 1943	29 Jun 1943	25 Oct 1943
DE 385	*Richey*	Brown	19 Apr 1943	30 Jun 1943	30 Oct 1943
DE 386	*Savage*	Brown	30 Apr 1943	15 Jul 1943	29 Oct 1943
DE 387	*Vance*	Brown	30 Apr 1943	16 Jul 1943	1 Nov 1943
DE 388	*Lansing*	Brown	15 May 1943	2 Aug 1943	10 Nov 1943
DE 389	*Durant*	Brown	15 May 1943	3 Aug 1943	16 Nov 1943
DE 390	*Calcaterra*	Brown	28 May 1943	16 Aug 1943	17 Nov 1943
DE 391	*Chambers*	Brown	28 May 1943	17 Aug 1943	22 Nov 1943
DE 392	*Merrill*	Brown	1 Jul 1943	29 Aug 1943	27 Nov 1943
DE 393	*Haverfield*	Brown	1 Jul 1943	30 Aug 1943	29 Nov 1943
DE 394	*Swenning*	Brown	17 Jul 1943	13 Sep 1943	1 Dec 1943
DE 395	*Willis*	Brown	17 Jul 1943	14 Sep 1943	10 Dec 1943
DE 396	*Janssen*	Brown	4 Aug 1943	4 Oct 1943	18 Dec 1943
DE 397	*Wilhoite*	Brown	4 Aug 1943	5 Oct 1943	16 Dec 1943
DE 398	*Cockrill*	Brown	31 Aug 1943	29 Oct 1943	24 Dec 1943
DE 399	*Stockdale*	Brown	31 Aug 1943	30 Oct 1943	31 Dec 1943
DE 400	*Hissem*	Brown	6 Oct 1943	26 Dec 1943	13 Jan 1944
DE 401	*Holder*	Brown	6 Oct 1943	27 Dec 1943	18 Jan 1944

Service Records:

DE 382 *Ramsden* USCG crew. Decomm 13 Jun 1946. †
1* Convoy UGS-36.
DE 383 *Mills* USCG crew. Decomm 14 Jun 1946. †
1* Convoy UGS-36.
DE 384 *Rhodes* USCG crew. Decomm 13 Jun 1946. †
1* Convoy UGS-36.
DE 385 *Richey* USCG crew.
DE 386 *Savage* USCG crew. Decomm 13 Jun 1946. †
1* Convoy UGS-36.
DE 387 *Vance* USCG crew. Decomm 27 Feb 1946. †
DE 388 *Lansing* USCG crew. Decomm 25 Apr 1946. †
DE 389 *Durant* USCG crew. Decomm 27 Feb 1946. †
DE 390 *Calcaterra* USCG crew. Decomm 1 May 1946. †
DE 391 *Chambers* USCG crew. Decomm 22 Apr 1946. †
DE 392 *Merrill* USCG crew. Decomm 1 May 1946. †
DE 393 *Haverfield* Decomm 30 Jun 1947. †
1* PUC.
Submarine sunk: **U-575* north of Azores, 13 Mar 1944.
DE 394 *Swenning* Decomm 18 Jun 1946. †
DE 395 *Willis* Decomm 14 Jun 1946. †
1* Okinawa. PUC.
DE 396 *Janssen* Decomm 12 Apr 1946. †
1* PUC.
Submarine sunk: **U-546* northwest of Azores, 24 Apr 1945.
DE 397 *Wilhoite* Decomm 19 Jun 1946. †
1* Convoy UGS-40. PUC.
DE 398 *Cockrill* Decomm 21 Jun 1946. †

Figure 5.9: *McNulty* (DE 581), 5 Apr 1944, of the *Rudderow* class, type TEV, with 5" guns.

DE 399 *Stockdale* Decomm 15 Jun 1946. †
1* Convoy UGS-37.
DE 400 *Hissem* Decomm 15 Jun 1946. †
1* Convoy UGS-37.
DE 401 *Holder* Torpedoed by German aircraft northeast of Algiers, 11 Apr 1944. Decomm 13 Sep 1944. Stricken 23 Sep 1944. Stern used to repair *Menges*. BU 19 Jun 1947.
1* Convoy UGS-37.

Rudderow Class (TEV)

No.	Name	Builder	Keel Laid	Launched	Comm.
DE 224	*Rudderow*	Phila. NYd	15 Jul 1943	14 Oct 1943	15 May 1944
DE 225	*Day*	Phila. NYd	15 Jul 1943	14 Oct 1943	10 Jun 1944
DE 226	*Crosley*	Phila. NYd	16 Oct 1943	12 Feb 1944	22 Oct 1944
DE 227	*Cread*	Phila. NYd	16 Oct 1943	12 Feb 1944	29 Jul 1945
DE 228	*Ruchamkin*	Phila. NYd	14 Feb 1944	14 Jun 1944	16 Sep 1945
DE 229	*Kirwin*	Phila. NYd	14 Feb 1944	15 Jun 1944	4 Nov 1945
DE 230	*Chaffee*	Charleston NYd	26 Aug 1943	27 Nov 1943	9 May 1944
DE 231	*Hodges*	Charleston NYd	9 Sep 1943	9 Dec 1943	27 May 1944
DE 232	*Kinzer*	Charleston NYd	9 Sep 1943	9 Dec 1943	1 Nov 1944
DE 233	*Register*	Charleston NYd	27 Oct 1943	20 Jan 1944	11 Jan 1945
DE 234	*Brock*	Charleston NYd	27 Oct 1943	20 Jan 1944	9 Feb 1945
DE 235	*John Q. Roberts*	Charleston NYd	15 Nov 1943	11 Feb 1944	8 Mar 1945
DE 236	*William M. Hobby*	Charleston NYd	15 Nov 1943	2 Feb 1944	4 Apr 1945
DE 237	*Ray K. Edwards*	Charleston NYd	1 Dec 1943	19 Feb 1944	11 Jun 1945
DE 281	*Arthur L. Bristol*	Charleston NYd	1 Dec 1943	19 Feb 1944	25 Jun 1945
DE 282	*Truxtun*	Charleston NYd	13 Dec 1943	9 Mar 1944	9 Jul 1945
DE 283	*Upham*	Charleston NYd	13 Dec 1943	9 Mar 1944	23 Jul 1945
DE 284	*Vogelgesang*	Charleston NYd	1944	—	—
DE 285	*Weeks*	Charleston NYd	1944	—	—
DE 286	*Sutton*	Hingham	—	—	—
DE 287	*William M. Wood*	Hingham	—	—	—
DE 288	*William R. Rush*	Hingham	—	—	—
DE 289	—	Hingham	—	—	—
DE 290	*Williams*	Hingham	—	—	—
DE 291–300	—	Hingham	—	—	—

Displacement	1,450 tons; 1,810 f/l
Dimensions	306' (oa); 300' (wl) x 37' x 13'9"
Machinery	2 screws; turbo-electric; SHP 12,000; 24 knots
Endurance	6,000/12
Complement	204
Armament	2–5"/38, 2–40mm twin, 10–20mm, 1–21" triple TT; (as APD) 1–5"/38, 3 twin 40mm, 6–20mm, no TT

Notes: Type TEV (turbo-electric drive). Seventy-two completed, including fifty as high speed transports (APD), which carried 162 troops. DE 286–300, 665–87 originally ordered from Charleston NYd; DE 645–64 from Beth. Quincy; DE 706–20 from Phila. NYd; DE 688–92 from Norfolk NYd; and DE 721–22 from Dravo Pitt.

Service Records:

DE 224 *Rudderow* Decomm 15 Jan 1947. †
1* Lingayen.
DE 225 *Day* Decomm 16 May 1946. †
2* Lingayen, Subic Bay.
DE 226 *Crosley* Rec **APD 87**, 17 Jul 1944. Decomm 15 Nov 1946. †
1* Okinawa.
DE 227 *Cread* Rec **APD 88**, 17 Jul 1944. Decomm 15 Mar 1946. †
DE 228 *Ruchamkin* Rec **APD 89**, 17 Jul 1944. Decomm 27 Feb 1946. †
DE 229 *Kirwin* Rec **APD 90**, 17 Jul 1944. Decomm 6 Apr 1946. †
DE 230 *Chaffee* Damaged by aerial torpedo off Lingayen, 23 Jan 1945. Decomm 15 Apr 1946. Stricken 17 Aug 1946. Sold 29 Jun 1948.
2* Lingayen, Balikpapan.
DE 231 *Hodges* Slightly damaged by kamikaze, Lingayen, 9 Jan 1945. Decomm 22 Jun 1946. †
1* Lingayen.
DE 232 *Kinzer* Rec **APD 91**, 17 Jul 1944. Decomm 18 Dec 1946. †
1* Okinawa.
DE 233 *Register* Rec **APD 92**, 17 Jul 1944. Damaged by kamikaze, Okinawa, 20 May 1945. Decomm 31 Mar 1946. †
1* Leyte.
DE 234 *Brock* Rec **APD 93**, 17 Jul 1944. Decomm 5 May 1946. †
1* Okinawa.
DE 235 *John Q. Roberts* Rec **APD 94**, 17 Jul 1944. Decomm 30 May 1946. †
DE 236 *William M. Hobby* Rec **APD 95**, 17 Jul 1944. Decomm 6 Apr 1946. †
DE 237 *Ray K. Edwards* Rec **APD 96**, 17 Jul 1944. Decomm 30 Aug 1946. †
DE 281 *Arthur L. Bristol* Rec **APD 97**, 17 Jul 1944. Decomm 29 Apr 1946. †
DE 282 *Truxtun* Rec **APD 98**, 17 Jul 1944. Decomm 15 Mar 1946. †
DE 283 *Upham* Rec **APD 99**, 17 Jul 1944. Decomm 25 Apr 1946. †
DE 284 *Vogelgesang* Canceled 10 Jun 1944.
DE 285 *Weeks* Canceled 10 Jun 1944.
DE 286–300 Canceled 12 Mar 1944.

No.	Name	Builder	Keel Laid	Launched	Comm.
DE 579	*Riley*	Hingham	20 Oct 1943	29 Dec 1943	13 Mar 1944
DE 580	*Leslie L. B. Knox*	Hingham	7 Nov 1943	8 Jan 1944	13 Mar 1944
DE 581	*McNulty*	Hingham	17 Nov 1943	8 Jan 1944	31 Mar 1944
DE 582	*Metivier*	Hingham	24 Nov 1943	12 Jan 1944	7 Apr 1944
DE 583	*George A. Johnson*	Hingham	24 Nov 1943	12 Jan 1944	15 Apr 1944
DE 584	*Charles J. Kimmel*	Hingham	1 Dec 1943	15 Jan 1944	20 Apr 1944
DE 585	*Daniel A. Joy*	Hingham	1 Dec 1943	15 Jan 1944	28 Apr 1944
DE 586	*Lough*	Hingham	8 Dec 1943	22 Jan 1944	2 May 1944
DE 587	*Thomas F. Nickel*	Hingham	15 Dec 1943	22 Jan 1944	9 Jun 1944
DE 588	*Peiffer*	Hingham	21 Dec 1943	26 Jan 1944	15 Jun 1944
DE 589	*Tinsman*	Hingham	21 Dec 1943	29 Jan 1944	26 Jun 1944
DE 590	*Ringness*	Hingham	23 Dec 1943	5 Feb 1944	25 Oct 1944

DE 591	*Knudson*	Hingham	23 Dec 1943	5 Feb 1944	25 Nov 1944
DE 592	*Rednour*	Hingham	30 Dec 1943	12 Feb 1944	30 Dec 1944
DE 593	*Tollberg*	Hingham	30 Dec 1943	12 Feb 1944	31 Jan 1945
DE 594	*William J. Pattison*	Hingham	4 Jan 1944	15 Feb 1944	27 Feb 1945
DE 595	*Myers*	Hingham	15 Jan 1944	15 Feb 1944	26 Mar 1945
DE 596	*Walter B. Cobb*	Hingham	15 Jan 1944	23 Feb 1944	25 Apr 1945
DE 597	*Earle B. Hall*	Hingham	19 Jan 1944	1 Mar 1944	15 May 1945
DE 598	*Harry L. Corl*	Hingham	19 Jan 1944	1 Mar 1944	5 Jun 1945
DE 599	*Belet*	Hingham	26 Jan 1944	3 Mar 1944	15 Jun 1945
DE 600	*Julius A. Raven*	Hingham	26 Jan 1944	3 Mar 1944	28 Jun 1945
DE 601	*Walsh*	Hingham	27 Feb 1945	27 Apr 1945	11 Jul 1945
DE 602	*Hunter Marshall*	Hingham	9 Mar 1945	5 May 1945	17 Jul 1945
DE 603	*Earheart*	Hingham	20 Mar 1945	12 May 1945	26 Jul 1945
DE 604	*Walter S. Gorka*	Hingham	3 Apr 1945	26 May 1945	7 Aug 1945
DE 605	*Rogers Blood*	Hingham	12 Apr 1945	2 Jun 1945	22 Aug 1945
DE 606	*Francovich*	Hingham	19 Apr 1945	5 Jun 1945	6 Sep 1945
DE 607–16	—	Hingham	—	—	—
DE 617–32	—	Hingham	—	—	—
DE 645–64	—	Hingham	—	—	—

Service Records:

DE 579 *Riley* Decomm 15 Jan 1947. †
2* Lingayen, Subic Bay.
DE 580 *Leslie L. B. Knox* Decomm 15 Jun 1946. †
3* Lingayen, Subic Bay, Visayan Is. Ldgs.
DE 581 *McNulty* Decomm 2 Jul 1946. †
2* Lingayen, Subic Bay.
DE 582 *Metivier* Decomm 1 Jun 1946. †
3* Lingayen, Okinawa, Subic Bay.
DE 583 *George A. Johnson* Decomm 31 May 1946. †
2* Lingayen, Subic Bay.
DE 584 *Charles J. Kimmel* Decomm 15 Jan 1947. †
1* Lingayen.
DE 585 *Daniel A. Joy* †
2* Leyte, Lingayen.
DE 586 *Lough* Sank *PT-77* and *PT-79* in error off Nasugbu, Luzon, 2 Feb 1945. Decomm 24 Jun 1946. †
3* Leyte, Lingayen, Ldgs. at Nasugbu.
DE 587 *Thomas F. Nickel* Decomm 31 May 1946. †
1* Lingayen.
DE 588 *Peiffer* Decomm 1 Jun 1946. †
1* Lingayen.
DE 589 *Tinsman* Decomm 11 May 1946. †
2* Lingayen, Ldgs. at Nasugbu.
DE 590 *Ringness* Rec **APD 100**, 17 Jul 1944. Decomm Apr 1946. †
1* Okinawa.
DE 591 *Knudson* Rec **APD 101**, 17 Jul 1944. Slightly damaged by aircraft bomb, Okinawa, 25 Mar 1945. Decomm 4 Nov 1946. †
1* Okinawa.
DE 592 *Rednour* Rec **APD 102**, 17 Jul 1944. Damaged by kamikaze, Okinawa, 27 May 1945 (3 killed). Decomm 24 Jul 1946. †
1* Okinawa.
DE 593 *Tollberg* Rec **APD 103**, 17 Jul 1944. Decomm 20 Dec 1946. †
1* Okinawa.
DE 594 *William J. Pattison* Rec **APD 104**, 7 Jul 1944. Tokyo Bay. Decomm 5 Jul 1946. †
DE 595 *Myers* Rec **APD 105**, 17 Jul 1944. Decomm 31 Jan 1947. †
DE 596 *Walter B. Cobb* Rec **APD 106**, 17 Jul 1944. Decomm 29 Mar 1946. †
DE 597 *Earle B. Hall* Rec **APD 107**, 17 Jul 1944. Decomm 27 Sep 1946. †
DE 598 *Harry L. Corl* Rec **APD 108**, 17 Jul 1944. Decomm 21 Jun 1946. †
DE 599 *Belet* Rec **APD 109**, 17 Jul 1944. Decomm 22 May 1946. †
DE 600 *Julius A. Raven* Rec **APD 110**, 17 Jul 1944. Decomm 31 May 1946. †
DE 601 *Walsh* Rec **APD 111**, 17 Jul 1944. Decomm 26 Apr 1946. †
DE 602 *Hunter Marshall* Rec **APD 112**, 17 Jul 1944. Decomm 30 May 1946. †
DE 603 *Earheart* Rec **APD 113**, 17 Jul 1944. Decomm 29 Apr 1946. †
DE 604 *Walter S. Gorka* Rec **APD 114**, 17 Jul 1944. Decomm Jan 1947. †
DE 605 *Rogers Blood* Rec **APD 115**, 17 Jul 1944. Decomm 19 Mar 1946. †
DE 606 *Francovich* Rec **APD 116**, 17 Jul 1944. Decomm 29 Apr 1946. †
DE 607–16 — Canceled 10 Jun 1944.
DE 617–32 — Canceled 12 Mar 1944.
DE 645–64 — Canceled 12 Mar 1944.

No.	Name	Builder	Keel Laid	Launched	Comm.
DE 674	*Joseph M. Auman*	Consol. Orange	8 Nov 1943	2 May 1944	25 Apr 1945
DE 684	*De Long*	Beth. Quincy	19 Oct 1943	23 Nov 1943	31 Dec 1943
DE 685	*Coates*	Beth. Quincy	8 Nov 1943	12 Dec 1943	24 Jan 1944
DE 686	*Eugene E. Elmore*	Beth. Quincy	27 Nov 1943	23 Dec 1943	4 Feb 1944
DE 687	*Kline*	Beth. Quincy	27 May 1944	27 Jun 1944	18 Oct 1944
DE 688	*Raymon W. Herndon*	Beth. Quincy	12 Jun 1944	15 Jul 1944	3 Nov 1944
DE 689	*Scribner*	Beth. Quincy	29 Jun 1944	1 Aug 1944	20 Nov 1944
DE 690	*Alex Diachenko*	Beth. Quincy	18 Jul 1944	15 Aug 1944	8 Dec 1944
DE 691	*Horace A. Bass*	Beth. Quincy	3 Aug 1944	12 Sep 1944	21 Dec 1944
DE 692	*Wantuck*	Beth. Quincy	17 Aug 1944	25 Sep 1944	30 Dec 1944
DE 706	*Holt*	Defoe	28 Nov 1943	15 Feb 1944	9 Jun 1944
DE 707	*Jobb*	Defoe	20 Dec 1943	4 Mar 1944	4 Jul 1944
DE 708	*Parle*	Defoe	8 Jan 1944	25 Mar 1944	29 Jul 1944
DE 709	*Bray*	Defoe	27 Jan 1944	15 Apr 1944	4 Sep 1944
DE 710	*Gosselin*	Defoe	17 Feb 1944	4 May 1944	31 Dec 1944
DE 711	*Begor*	Defoe	6 Mar 1944	25 May 1944	14 Mar 1945
DE 712	*Cavallaro*	Defoe	28 Mar 1944	15 Jun 1944	13 Mar 1945
DE 713	*Donald W. Wolf*	Defoe	17 Apr 1944	22 Jul 1944	14 Apr 1945
DE 714	*Cook*	Defoe	7 May 1944	26 Aug 1944	25 Apr 1945
DE 715	*Walter X. Young*	Defoe	27 May 1944	30 Sep 1944	1 May 1945
DE 716	*Balduck*	Defoe	17 Jun 1944	27 Oct 1944	7 May 1945
DE 717	*Burdo*	Defoe	26 Jul 1944	25 Nov 1944	2 Jun 1945
DE 718	*Kleinsmith*	Defoe	30 Aug 1944	27 Jan 1945	12 Jun 1945
DE 719	*Weiss*	Defoe	4 Oct 1944	17 Feb 1945	7 Jul 1945
DE 720	*Carpellotti*	Defoe	31 Oct 1944	10 Mar 1945	30 Jul 1945
DE 721	*Don O. Woods*	Consol. Orange	1 Dec 1943	9 Feb 1944	28 May 1945

DE 722	*Beverly W. Reid*	Consol. Orange	5 Jan 1944	4 Mar 1944	25 Jun 1945
DE 723	*Walter X. Young*	Dravo Pitt.	—	—	—
DE 724–38	—	Dravo Pitt.	—	—	—
DE 905–59	—	Hingham	—	—	—
DE 960–95	—	Charleston NYd	—	—	—
DE 996–1005	—	Defoe	—	—	—

Service Records:

DE 674 *Joseph M. Auman* Rec **APD 117**, 17 Jul 1944. Decomm 10 Jul 1946. †

DE 684 *De Long* Rec **APD 137**, 15 Aug 1945; conversion canceled, 10 Sep 1945 and rec **DE 684**. Decomm 25 Apr 1947. †

DE 685 *Coates* Rec **APD 138**, 15 Aug 1945; conversion canceled, 10 Sep 1945 and rec **DE 685**. Decomm 16 Apr 1946. †

DE 686 *Eugene E. Elmore* Decomm 31 May 1946. †
4* TG 21.11, Lingayen, Subic Bay.
Submarine sunk: **U-549* southwest of Madeira, 29 May 1944.

DE 687 *Kline* Rec **APD 120**, 17 Jul 1944. Decomm 10 Mar 1947. †
2* Okinawa, Brunei Bay, Balikpapan.

DE 688 *Raymon W. Herndon* Rec **APD 121**, 17 Jul 1944. Decomm 15 Nov 1946. †
1* Okinawa.

DE 689 *Scribner* Rec **APD 122**, 17 Jul 1944. Decomm 15 Nov 1946. †
1* Okinawa.

DE 690 *Alex Diachenko* Rec **APD 123**, 17 Jul 1944, renamed ***Diachenko***, 1 Mar 1945. †
2* Balikpapan, Mindanao Ldgs.

DE 691 *Horace A. Bass* Rec **APD 124**, 17 Jul 1944. Slightly damaged by kamikaze, Okinawa, 30 Jul 1945. Tokyo Bay. †
2* Okinawa.
Submarine sunk: *RO-109* southeast of Okinawa, 25 Apr 1945.

DE 692 *Wantuck* Rec **APD 125**, 17 Jul 1944. Tokyo Bay. †
1* Okinawa.

DE 706 *Holt* Decomm 2 Jul 1946. †
2* Leyte, Mindoro, Lingayen.

DE 707 *Jobb* Decomm 13 May 1946. †
3* Leyte, Mindoro, Ldgs. on Palawan, Mindanao Ldgs.

DE 708 *Parle* Decomm 10 Jul 1946. †

DE 709 *Bray* Damaged in collision with submarine *Cuttlefish* off Boston, 8 Dec 1944. Rec **APD 139**, 16 Jul 1945. Decomm 10 May 1946. †

DE 710 *Gosselin* Rec **APD 126**, 17 Jul 1944. Tokyo Bay. †
1* Okinawa.

DE 711 *Begor* Rec **APD 127**, 17 Jul 1944. Operation Crossroads. †

DE 712 *Cavallaro* Rec **APD 128**, 17 Jul 1944. Decomm 17 May 1946. †

DE 713 *Donald W. Wolf* Rec **APD 129**, 17 Jul 1944. Decomm 15 May 1946. †

DE 714 *Cook* Rec **APD 130**, 17 Jul 1944. Decomm 31 May 1946. †

DE 715 *Walter X. Young* Rec **APD 131**, 17 Jul 1944. Decomm 2 Jul 1946. †

DE 716 *Balduck* Rec **APD 132**, 17 Jul 1944. Decomm 31 May 1946. †

DE 717 *Burdo* Rec **APD 133**, 17 Jul 1944. †

DE 718 *Kleinsmith* Rec **APD 134**, 17 Jul 1944. †

DE 719 *Weiss* Rec **APD 135**, 17 Jul 1944. †

DE 720 *Carpellotti* Rec **APD 136**, 17 Jul 1944. †

DE 721 *Don O. Woods* Rec **APD 118**, 17 Jul 1944. Decomm 18 Jun 1946. †

DE 722 *Beverly W. Reid* Rec **APD 119**, 17 Jul 1944. Decomm 5 May 1947. †

DE 723–24 Canceled 12 Mar 1944.

DE 725–38 Canceled 2 Oct 1943.

DE 905–1005 Canceled 15 Sep 1943.

Figure 5.10: USS *McCoy Reynolds* (DE 440), 3 Jul 1944, of the *John C. Butler* class, type WGT.

Figure 5.11: USS *Joseph E. Connolly* (DE 450), of the *John C. Butler* class, type WGT.

John C. Butler Class (WGT)

No.	Name	Builder	Keel Laid	Launched	Comm.
DE 339	*John C. Butler*	Consol. Orange	5 Oct 1943	12 Nov 1943	31 Mar 1944
DE 340	*O'Flaherty*	Consol. Orange	4 Oct 1943	14 Dec 1943	8 Apr 1944
DE 341	*Raymond*	Consol. Orange	3 Nov 1943	8 Jan 1944	15 Apr 1944
DE 342	*Richard W. Suesens*	Consol. Orange	1 Nov 1943	11 Jan 1944	26 Apr 1944
DE 343	*Abercrombie*	Consol. Orange	8 Nov 1943	14 Jan 1944	1 May 1944
DE 344	*Oberrender*	Consol. Orange	8 Nov 1943	18 Jan 1944	11 May 1944
DE 345	*Robert Brazier*	Consol. Orange	16 Nov 1943	22 Jan 1944	18 May 1944

DE 346	*Edwin A. Howard*	Consol. Orange	15 Nov 1943	25 Jan 1944	25 May 1944
DE 347	*Jesse Rutherford*	Consol. Orange	22 Nov 1943	29 Jan 1944	31 May 1944
DE 348	*Key*	Consol. Orange	14 Dec 1943	12 Feb 1944	5 Jun 1944
DE 349	*Gentry*	Consol. Orange	13 Dec 1943	15 Feb 1944	14 Jun 1944
DE 350	*Traw*	Consol. Orange	19 Dec 1943	12 Feb 1944	20 Jun 1944
DE 351	*Maurice J. Manuel*	Consol. Orange	22 Dec 1943	19 Feb 1944	30 Jun 1944
DE 352	*Naifeh*	Consol. Orange	29 Dec 1943	29 Feb 1944	4 Jul 1944
DE 353	*Doyle C. Barnes*	Consol. Orange	11 Jan 1944	4 Mar 1944	13 Jul 1944
DE 354	*Kenneth M. Willett*	Consol. Orange	10 Jan 1944	7 Mar 1944	19 Jul 1944
DE 355	*Jaccard*	Consol. Orange	25 Jan 1944	18 Mar 1944	26 Jul 1944
DE 356	*Lloyd E. Acree*	Consol. Orange	24 Jan 1944	21 Mar 1944	1 Aug 1944
DE 357	*George E. Davis*	Consol. Orange	15 Feb 1944	8 Apr 1944	11 Aug 1944
DE 358	*Mack*	Consol. Orange	14 Feb 1944	11 Apr 1944	16 Aug 1944
DE 359	*Woodson*	Consol. Orange	7 Mar 1944	20 Apr 1944	24 Aug 1944
DE 360	*Johnnie Hutchins*	Consol. Orange	6 Mar 1944	2 May 1944	28 Aug 1944
DE 361	*Walton*	Consol. Orange	21 Mar 1944	20 May 1944	4 Sep 1944
DE 362	*Rolf*	Consol. Orange	20 Mar 1944	23 May 1944	7 Sep 1944
DE 363	*Pratt*	Consol. Orange	11 Apr 1944	1 Jun 1944	18 Sep 1944
DE 364	*Rombach*	Consol. Orange	10 Apr 1944	6 Jun 1944	20 Sep 1944
DE 365	*McGinty*	Consol. Orange	3 May 1944	5 Aug 1944	25 Sep 1944
DE 366	*Alvin C. Cockrell*	Consol. Orange	1 May 1944	8 Aug 1944	7 Oct 1944
DE 367	*French*	Consol. Orange	1 May 1944	17 Jun 1944	9 Oct 1944
DE 368	*Cecil J. Doyle*	Consol. Orange	12 May 1944	1 Jul 1944	16 Oct 1944
DE 369	*Thaddeus Parker*	Consol. Orange	23 May 1944	26 Aug 1944	25 Oct 1944
DE 370	*John L. Williamson*	Consol. Orange	22 May 1944	29 Aug 1944	31 Oct 1944
DE 371	*Presley*	Consol. Orange	6 Jun 1944	19 Aug 1944	7 Nov 1944
DE 372	*Williams*	Consol. Orange	5 Jun 1944	22 Aug 1944	11 Nov 1944
DE 373	*William C. Lawe*	Consol. Orange	—	—	—
DE 374	*Lloyd Thomas*	Consol. Orange	—	—	—
DE 375	*Keppler*	Consol. Orange	—	—	—
DE 376	*Kleinsmith*	Consol. Orange	—	—	—
DE 377	*Henry W. Tucker*	Consol. Orange	—	—	—
DE 378	*Weiss*	Consol. Orange	—	—	—
DE 379	*Francovich*	Consol. Orange	—	—	—
DE 380–81	—	Consol. Orange	—	—	—

Displacement	1,350 tons; 1,745 f/l
Dimensions	306' (oa); 300' (wl) x 36'8" x 9'5"
Machinery	2 screws; Westinghouse GT; SHP 12,000; 24 knots
Endurance	6,000/12
Complement	215
Armament	2–5"/38, 2–40mm twin AA, 10–20mm AA guns, 1–21" triple TT

Notes: Type WGT (Westinghouse geared turbine). Eighty-one completed. DE 508–15 originally ordered from Puget Sound NYd; DE 425–37 from Brown. Two (DE 539–40) suspended 1945.

Service Records:

DE 339 *John C. Butler* Slightly damaged by two kamikazes, Okinawa, 20 May 1945. Decomm 26 Jun 1946. †
5* Morotai, Leyte, Samar, Lingayen, Iwo Jima, Okinawa. PUC.

DE 340 *O'Flaherty* Damaged in collision with CVE *Block Island*, Okinawa, 15 Jun 1945. Decomm Jan 1947. †
4* Guam, Lingayen, Iwo Jima, Okinawa.

DE 341 *Raymond* Decomm 24 Jan 1947. †
5* Morotai, Leyte, Samar, Lingayen, China Coast Raids 1/45, Formosa Raids 1/45, Iwo Jima, Nansei Shoto Raid 1/45, Okinawa, Fleet Raids 1945. PUC.

DE 342 *Richard W. Suesens* In collision with minesweeper *Valor* which sank in Buzzards Bay, 29 Jun 1944. Minor damage by kamikaze, Lingayen Gulf, 12 Jan 1945. Decomm 15 Jan 1947. †
5* Leyte, Samar, Lingayen, Ldgs at Nasugbu, Okinawa, Raids on Japan 7–8/45.

DE 343 *Abercrombie* Decomm 15 Jun 1946. †
4* Leyte, Samar, Mindoro, Okinawa, Raids on Japan 7–8/45.

DE 344 *Oberrender* Severely damaged by kamikaze off Okinawa, 9 May 1945 (8 killed), not repaired. Decomm 11 Jul 1945 and stricken 22 Jul 1945. Sunk by gunfire, 6 Nov 1945.
3* Leyte, Lingayen, Okinawa.

DE 345 *Robert Brazier* Decomm 16 Sep 1946. †
1* Mindanao Ldgs.

DE 346 *Edwin A. Howard* Damaged in collision with DE *Leland E. Thomas* southeast of Leyte, 5 Jan 1945. Decomm 25 Sep 1946. †
1* Balikpapan.

DE 347 *Jesse Rutherford* Decomm 21 Jun 1946. †
1* Balikpapan.

DE 348 *Key* Decomm 9 Jul 1946. †
1* Balikpapan.

DE 349 *Gentry* Decomm 2 Jul 1946. †

DE 350 *Traw* Decomm 7 Jun 1946. †

DE 351 *Maurice J. Manuel* Decomm 20 May 1946. †

DE 352 *Naifeh* Decomm 27 Jun 1946. †

DE 353 *Doyle C. Barnes* Decomm 15 Jan 1947. †

DE 354 *Kenneth M. Willett* Decomm 24 Oct 1946. †

DE 355 *Jaccard* Decomm 30 Sep 1946. †
1*
DE 356 *Lloyd E. Acree* Decomm 10 Oct 1946. †
DE 357 *George E. Davis* Decomm 26 Aug 1946. †
DE 358 *Mack* Damaged by grounding in Mangarin Bay, Philippines, 13 Mar 1945. Damaged in collision with disabled *FS-274* off San Fernando, Philippines, 10 Jan 1946. Decomm 11 Dec 1946. †
DE 359 *Woodson* Decomm 15 Jan 1947. †
DE 360 *Johnnie Hutchins* Decomm 14 May 1946. †
Submarines sunk: Two midget submarines north of Luzon, 9 Aug 1945.
DE 361 *Walton* Damaged in collision with an LCT off Jinsen (Inchon), Korea, 26 Sep 1945. Decomm 31 May 1946. †
DE 362 *Rolf* Decomm 3 Jun 1946. †
DE 363 *Pratt* Decomm 14 May 1946. †
DE 364 *Rombach* †
DE 365 *McGinty* Decomm 15 Oct 1947. †
DE 366 *Alvin C. Cockrell* Decomm 2 Jul 1946. †
DE 367 *French* Decomm 29 May 1946. †
DE 368 *Cecil J. Doyle* Decomm 2 Jul 1946. †
DE 369 *Thaddeus Parker* Decomm 31 May 1946. †
1* Okinawa.
DE 370 *John L. Williamson* Decomm 14 Jun 1946. †
DE 371 *Presley* Sank *PT-77* and *PT-79* in error off Nasugbu, Luzon, 2 Feb 1945. Decomm 20 Jun 1946. †
DE 372 *Williams* Damaged in typhoon off Marianas, 29 Sep 1945. Decomm 4 Jun 1946. †
DE 373–81 — Canceled 6 Jun 1944.

No.	Name	Builder	Keel Laid	Launched	Comm.
DE 402	*Richard S. Bull*	Brown	18 Aug 1943	16 Nov 1943	26 Feb 1944
DE 403	*Richard M. Rowell*	Brown	18 Aug 1943	17 Nov 1943	9 Mar 1944
DE 404	*Eversole*	Brown	15 Sep 1943	3 Dec 1943	21 Mar 1944
DE 405	*Dennis*	Brown	15 Sep 1943	4 Dec 1943	20 Mar 1944
DE 406	*Edmonds*	Brown	1 Nov 1943	17 Dec 1943	3 Apr 1944
DE 407	*Shelton*	Brown	1 Nov 1943	18 Dec 1943	4 Apr 1944
DE 408	*Straus*	Brown	18 Nov 1943	30 Dec 1943	6 Apr 1944
DE 409	*La Prade*	Brown	18 Nov 1943	31 Dec 1943	20 Apr 1944
DE 410	*Jack Miller*	Brown	29 Nov 1943	10 Jan 1944	13 Apr 1944
DE 411	*Stafford*	Brown	29 Nov 1943	11 Jan 1944	19 Apr 1944
DE 412	*Walter C. Wann*	Brown	6 Dec 1943	19 Jan 1944	2 May 1944
DE 413	*Samuel B. Roberts*	Brown	6 Dec 1943	20 Jan 1944	28 Apr 1944
DE 414	*Le Ray Wilson*	Brown	20 Dec 1943	28 Jan 1944	10 May 1944
DE 415	*Lawrence C. Taylor*	Brown	20 Dec 1943	29 Jan 1944	13 May 1944
DE 416	*Melvin R. Nawman*	Brown	3 Jan 1944	7 Feb 1944	16 May 1944
DE 417	*Oliver Mitchell*	Brown	3 Jan 1944	8 Feb 1944	14 Jun 1944
DE 418	*Tabberer*	Brown	12 Jan 1944	18 Feb 1944	23 May 1944
DE 419	*Robert F. Keller*	Brown	12 Jan 1944	19 Feb 1944	17 Jun 1944
DE 420	*Leland E. Thomas*	Brown	21 Jan 1944	28 Feb 1944	19 Jun 1944
DE 421	*Chester T. O'Brien*	Brown	21 Jan 1944	29 Feb 1944	3 Jul 1944
DE 422	*Douglas A. Munro*	Brown	31 Jan 1944	8 Mar 1944	11 Jul 1944
DE 423	*Dufilho*	Brown	31 Jan 1944	9 Mar 1944	21 Jul 1944
DE 424	*Haas*	Brown	23 Feb 1944	20 Mar 1944	2 Aug 1944
DE 425–37	—	Brown	—	—	—

Service Records:

DE 402 *Richard S. Bull* Decomm Mar 1946. †
5* Morotai, Leyte, Samar, Lingayen, Iwo Jima, Okinawa.
DE 403 *Richard M. Rowell* Sank U.S. submarine *Seawolf* in error, north of Morotai, 4 Oct 1944. Dismasted in storm, 14 Oct 1944. Damaged by strafing, Leyte Gulf, 25 Oct 1944. Decomm 2 Jul 1946. †
6* Morotai, Leyte, Samar, Lingayen, Iwo Jima, Okinawa.
Submarine sunk: *I-54* off Leyte, 24 Oct 1944.
DE 404 *Eversole* Torpedoed twice by Japanese submarine *I-45* off Leyte, broke in two and sank, 28 Oct 1944 (over 40 killed).
2* Morotai, Leyte, Samar.
DE 405 *Dennis* Damaged by four hits by naval gunfire of Japanese warships off Samar, 25 Oct 1944. Decomm 31 May 1946. †
5* Morotai, Leyte, Samar, Iwo Jima, Okinawa. PUC.
DE 406 *Edmonds* Decomm 31 May 1946. †
5* Morotai, Leyte, Lingayen, Iwo Jima, Okinawa.
DE 407 *Shelton* Torpedoed by Japanese submarine *RO-41* north of Morotai, sunk by U.S. in tow, 3 Oct 1944 (13 killed).
1* Morotai.
DE 408 *Straus* Decomm 15 Jan 1947. †
3* Saipan, Philippines Raids 9/44, Okinawa, Fleet Raids 1945.
DE 409 *La Prade* Decomm 11 May 1946. †
1* Okinawa, Fleet Raids 1945.
DE 410 *Jack Miller* Decomm 1 Jun 1946. †
2* Philippines Raids 9/44, Okinawa, Fleet Raids 1945.
DE 411 *Stafford* Damaged by kamikaze, in Northwest Manila Bay, 5 Jan 1945 (2 killed). Decomm Jan 1947. †
2* Lingayen, Okinawa.
DE 412 *Walter C. Wann* Slightly damaged by kamikaze near miss, Okinawa, 12 Apr 1945. Decomm 31 May 1946. †
4* Leyte, Samar, Lingayen, Okinawa, Raids on Japan 7–8/45.
DE 413 *Samuel B. Roberts* Sunk by over 20 hits of gunfire from Japanese warships off Samar, 25 Oct 1944 (89 killed).
1* Leyte, Samar. PUC.
DE 414 *Le Ray Wilson* Moderate damage by kamikaze at Lingayen, Luzon, 10 Jan 1945 (6 killed). Decomm 15 Jan 1947. †
4* Leyte, Samar, Lingayen, Okinawa, Raids on Japan 7–8/45.
DE 415 *Lawrence C. Taylor* Decomm 23 Apr 1946. †
7* Luzon Raids 10/44, Formosa Raids 1/45, Luzon Raids 1/45, Nansei Shoto Raid 1/45, Iwo Jima, Okinawa, Raids on Japan 7–8/45.
Submarines sunk: **I-41* east of Samar, 18 Nov 1944 (possible); **I-13* 550 miles east of Yokosuka, 16 Jul 1945.
DE 416 *Melvin R. Nawman* Damaged in typhoon in Philippine Sea, 18 Dec 1944. Damaged by collision with *LST-807*, Iwo Jima, 22 Feb 1945. Decomm 23 Apr 1946. †
4* Luzon Raids 10/44, Iwo Jima, Okinawa, Raids on Japan 7–8/45.
DE 417 *Oliver Mitchell* Decomm 24 Apr 1946. †
5* Luzon Raids 10/44, Formosa Raids 1/45, Iwo Jima, Okinawa, Raids on Japan 7–8/45.
DE 418 *Tabberer* Damaged in typhoon, Philippine Sea, 18 Dec 1944. Decomm 24 Apr 1946. †
4* Luzon Raids 10/44, Iwo Jima, Okinawa, Raids on Japan 7–8/45.
DE 419 *Robert F. Keller* Damaged in collision with escort carrier *Sargent Bay*, in Philippines, 3 Jan 1945. Decomm 24 Apr 1946. †
*5 Luzon Raids 10/44, Formosa Raids 1/45, China Coast Raids 1/45, Nansei Shoto Raid 1/45, Iwo Jima, Okinawa, Raids on Japan 7–8/45.

DE 420 *Leland E. Thomas* Damaged in collision with DE *Edwin A. Howard* southeast of Leyte, 5 Jan 1945. Decomm 3 May 1946.
1* Mindanao Ldgs, Balikpapan.
DE 421 *Chester T. O'Brien* Decomm 2 Jul 1946. †
DE 422 *Douglas A. Munro* Decomm 15 Jan 1947. †
DE 423 *Dufilho* Decomm 14 May 1946. †
DE 424 *Haas* Decomm 31 May 1946. †
DE 425–37 — Canceled 13 Mar 1944.

No.	Name	Builder	Keel Laid	Launched	Comm.
DE 438	*Corbesier*	Federal	4 Nov 1943	13 Feb 1944	31 Mar 1944
DE 439	*Conklin*	Federal	4 Nov 1943	13 Feb 1944	21 Apr 1944
DE 440	*McCoy Reynolds*	Federal	18 Nov 1943	22 Feb 1944	2 May 1944
DE 441	*William Seiverling*	Federal	2 Dec 1943	7 Mar 1944	1 Jun 1944
DE 442	*Ulvert M. Moore*	Federal	2 Dec 1943	7 Mar 1944	18 Jul 1944
DE 443	*Kendall C. Campbell*	Federal	16 Dec 1943	19 Mar 1944	31 Jul 1944
DE 444	*Goss*	Federal	16 Dec 1943	19 Mar 1944	26 Aug 1944
DE 445	*Grady*	Federal	3 Jan 1944	2 Apr 1944	11 Sep 1944
DE 446	*Charles E. Brannon*	Federal	13 Jan 1944	23 Apr 1944	1 Nov 1944
DE 447	*Albert T. Harris*	Federal	13 Jan 1944	16 Apr 1944	29 Nov 1944
DE 448	*Cross*	Federal	19 Mar 1944	4 Jul 1944	8 Jan 1945
DE 449	*Hanna*	Federal	22 Mar 1944	4 Jul 1944	27 Jan 1945
DE 450	*Joseph E. Connolly*	Federal	6 Apr 1944	6 Aug 1944	28 Feb 1945
DE 451	*Woodrow R. Thompson*	Federal	May 1944	—	—
DE 452	*Steinaker*	Federal	1944	—	—
DE 453–56	—	Federal	—	—	—
DE 457–77	—	Federal	—	—	—
DE 478–507	—	Federal	—	—	—
DE 508	*Gilligan* ex-*Donaldson* (23 Jun 1943)	Federal	18 Nov 1943	22 Feb 1944	12 May 1944
DE 509	*Formoe*	Federal	3 Jan 1944	2 Apr 1944	5 Oct 1944
DE 510	*Heyliger*	Federal	27 Apr 1944	6 Aug 1944	24 Mar 1945
DE 511	—	Federal	1944	—	—
DE 512–15	—	Federal	—	—	—

Service Records:

DE 438 *Corbesier* Decomm 2 Jul 1946. †
2* Fleet Raids 1945.
Submarine sunk: **I-48* northeast of Yap, 23 Jan 1945.
DE 439 *Conklin* Damaged by typhoon, Philippine Sea, 5 Jun 1945. Decomm 17 Jan 1946. †
3* Fleet Raids 1945.
Submarines sunk: **I-37* in Northwest Kossol Passage, 19 Nov 1944; **I-48* northeast of Yap, 23 Jan 1945.
DE 440 *McCoy Reynolds* Decomm 31 May 1946. †
4* Palau, Fleet Raids 1945.
Submarines sunk: *RO-47* 80 miles west of Yap, 26 Sep 1944; **I-37* in Northwest Kossol Passage, 19 Nov 1944.
DE 441 *William Seiverling* Decomm 21 Mar 1947. †
5* Leyte, Lingayen, Iwo Jima, Okinawa, Raids on Japan 7–8/45. Tokyo Bay.
DE 442 *Ulvert M. Moore* Decomm 24 May 1946. †
5* Lingayen, Iwo Jima, Okinawa, Raids on Japan 7–8/45. Tokyo Bay.
Submarine sunk: **RO-115* 125 miles southwest of Manila, 31 Jan 1945.
DE 443 *Kendall C. Campbell* Decomm 31 May 1946. †
4* Lingayen, Iwo Jima, Okinawa, Raids on Japan 7–8/45. Tokyo Bay.
DE 444 *Goss* Decomm 15 Jun 1946. †
4* Lingayen, Iwo Jima, Okinawa, Raids on Japan 7–8/45. Tokyo Bay.
DE 445 *Grady* Decomm 2 Jul 1946. †
3* China Coast Raids 1/45, Formosa Raids 1/45, Nansei Shoto Raid 1/45, Iwo Jima.
DE 446 *Charles E. Brannon* Decomm 21 May 1946. †
1* Tarakan.
DE 447 *Albert T. Harris* Decomm 26 Jul 1946. †
2* Mindanao.
DE 448 *Cross* Decomm 14 Jun 1946. †
1* Okinawa.
DE 449 *Hanna* Decomm 31 May 1946. †
DE 450 *Joseph E. Connolly* Decomm 20 Jun 1946. †
1* Raids on Japan 7–8/45.
DE 451–56 — Canceled 6 Jun 1944.
DE 457–77 — Canceled 12 Mar 1944.
DE 478–507 — Canceled 2 Oct 1943.
DE 508 *Gilligan* Moderate damage by kamikaze, Lingayen, 12 Jan 1945 (12 killed). Damaged by dud aircraft torpedo, Okinawa, 27 May 1945. Decomm 2 Jul 1946. †
1* Mindoro, Okinawa.
DE 509 *Formoe* Decomm 27 May 1946. †
2* Tarakan, Visayan Is. Ldgs.
DE 510 *Heyliger* Decomm 20 Jun 1946. †
DE 511 — Canceled 6 Jun 1944.
DE 512–15 — Canceled 12 Mar 1944.

No.	Name	Builder	Keel Laid	Launched	Comm.
DE 531	*Edward H. Allen*	Boston NYd	31 Aug 1943	7 Oct 1943	16 Dec 1943
DE 532	*Tweedy*	Boston NYd	31 Aug 1943	7 Oct 1943	12 Feb 1944
DE 533	*Howard F. Clark*	Boston NYd	8 Oct 1943	8 Nov 1943	25 May 1944
DE 534	*Silverstein*	Boston NYd	8 Oct 1943	8 Nov 1943	14 Jul 1944
DE 535	*Lewis*	Boston NYd	3 Nov 1943	7 Dec 1943	5 Sep 1944
DE 536	*Bivin*	Boston NYd	3 Nov 1943	7 Dec 1943	31 Oct 1944
DE 537	*Rizzi*	Boston NYd	3 Nov 1943	7 Dec 1943	30 Jun 1945
DE 538	*Osberg*	Boston NYd	3 Nov 1943	7 Dec 1943	10 Dec 1945
DE 539	*Wagner*	Boston NYd	8 Nov 1943	27 Dec 1943	22 Nov 1955
DE 540	*Vandivier*	Boston NYd	8 Nov 1943	27 Dec 1943	11 Oct 1955
DE 541	*Sheehan*	Boston NYd	8 Nov 1943	17 Dec 1943	—
DE 542	*Oswald A. Powers*	Boston NYd	8 Nov 1943	17 Dec 1943	—
DE 543	*Groves*	Boston NYd	9 Dec 1943	27 Jun 1944	—
DE 544	*Alfred Wolf*	Boston NYd	9 Dec 1943	—	—
DE 545	*Harold J. Ellison*	Boston NYd	1944	—	—
DE 546	*Myles C. Fox*	Boston NYd	1944	—	
DE 547	*Charles R. Ware*	Boston NYd	—	—	—
DE 548	*Carpellotti*	Boston NYd	—	—	—

DE 549	*Eugene A. Greene*	Boston NYd	—	—	—
DE 550	*Gyatt*	Boston NYd	—	—	—
DE 551	*Benner*	Boston NYd	—	—	—
DE 552	*Kenneth D. Bailey*	Boston NYd	—	—	—
DE 553	*Dennis J. Buckley*	Boston NYd	—	—	—
DE 554	*Everett F. Larson*	Boston NYd	—	—	—
DE 555	*Rogers Blood*	Boston NYd	—	—	—
DE 556	*William R. Rush*	Boston NYd	—	—	—
DE 557	*William M. Wood*	Boston NYd	—	—	—
DE 555–62	—	Boston NYd	—	—	—
DE 801–32	—	Boston NYd	—	—	—
DE 833–40	—	Mare I. NYd	—	—	—
DE 841–72	—	Brown	—	—	—
DE 873–86	—	Dravo Pitt	—	—	—
DE 887–98	—	Western Pipe	—	—	—
DE 899–904	—	Federal	—	—	—

Service Records:

DE 531 *Edward H. Allen* Decomm 10 May 1946.†
DE 532 *Tweedy* Decomm 10 May 1946. †
DE 533 *Howard F. Clark* Decomm 15 Jul 1946. †
3* Lingayen, Iwo Jima, Okinawa, Fleet Raids 1945.
DE 534 *Silverstein* Decomm 15 Jan 1947. †
2* Iwo Jima, Okinawa, Fleet Raids 1945. †
DE 535 *Lewis* Decomm 31 May 1946. †
4* China Coast Raids 1/45, Formosa Raids 1/45, Nansei Shoto Raid 1/45, Iwo Jima, Okinawa, Fleet Raids 1945.
DE 536 *Bivin* Decomm 15 Jan 1947. †
DE 537 *Rizzi* Decomm 18 Jun 1946. †
DE 538 *Osberg* Decomm Dec 1947. †
DE 539 *Wagner* Construction suspended, 61.5% complete, 17 Feb 1947. †
DE 540 *Vandivier* Construction suspended, 17 Feb 1947. †
DE 541 *Sheehan* Canceled 7 Jan 1946. Sold 2 Jul 1946; BU Quincy, Mass.
DE 542 *Oswald A. Powers* Canceled 7 Jan 1946. BU Quincy, Mass.
DE 543 *Groves* Canceled 5 Sep 1944. Sold 23 Mar 1947; BU.
DE 544 *Alfred Wolf* Canceled 5 Sep 1944. Sold 23 Mar 1947; BU on ways.
DE 545–62 — Canceled 10 Jun 1944.
DE 801–904 — Canceled 15 Sep 1943.

6 SUBMARINES

At the time of the Washington Conference, the U.S. Navy was still completing many of the submarines ordered during World War I. The success of the German U-boat campaign and the advances made by the Germans in submarine technology was the spur to the great attention paid to submarine development after the war. Among the ideas considered were minelayers, transport and supply vessels, and long-range cruiser submarines.*

The experimentation with large fleet submarines produced first the inadequate *T* class, and then the *V-1* class, which had been laid down in 1921, although authorized as far back as 1916.

In 1924 construction was started on the *V-4* (later *Argonaut*), which was to be the largest U.S. submarine built until 1955. The design was inspired by the German commerce-raiding submarine *U-142*. Designed as a minelayer and armed with 6" guns, the *V-4* was unwieldy and slow when submerged. The *V-5* and *V-6*, which followed, were also disappointments. In 1930, the keel was laid for the smaller *V-7* (later *Dolphin*), to be the forerunner of the fleet submarines built thereafter.

The older submarines were kept on the list but laid up and many of them were scrapped after 1930 following the London Naval Treaty. The experimental installation of a scout plane on the *S-1* was disappointing.

The *R* and *S* classes were the backbone of the submarine force during the 1920s. The rivalry between the Electric Boat and Simon Lake companies was settled decisively as the Navy found that the latter's boats were inferior. Most of the Simon Lake-built boats had short careers and were removed from the Navy List by the 1930s.

In 1931 the Navy reverted to the practice of giving submarines names, which had been abandoned in 1911 in favor of numerical series. The *V* boats were all given names, as were all future boats.

The Navy was still looking for the optimum size, and the *Cachalot* class proved too small, but with the first P boats the best match was found. Two boats each were built by the Navy at Portsmouth, N.H. and by the Electric Boat Company. They were the first all-electric submarines with eight torpedo tubes and a range of 11,000 miles at 10 knots. American submarines were built with the Pacific Ocean and its vast distances in mind. The new boats had all-welded hulls which avoided leakage caused by riveted joints. The competition between the yards stimulated the rapid improvement in submarine design.

The succeeding second *S*, *T*, and *G* classes were all improvements on the basic design. The number of torpedo tubes was increased to eight and the number of torpedoes carried was also increased. Engine problems led to a generally reliable engine built by General Motors.

In 1939 the new submarine *Squalus* sank during diving trials off Portsmouth, New Hampshire. The disaster proved the value of the McCann diving bell, and 33 men were rescued.

These developments led to the huge submarine construction programs of the war years. Three yards built submarines—the Electric Boat Company, and the Portsmouth and Mare I. Naval Shipyards—and capacity was quickly increased at all three. Production was expanded by using prefabrication and working on a round-the-clock basis. Boats were launched without superstructure to vacate the ways quickly. A new yard was built at Manitowoc, Wisconsin, and the boats built there were brought down the Mississippi River in floating drydocks. Another shipbuilder, William Cramp and Sons in Philadelphia, was opened to submarine construction, but so many problems arose that the Navy eventually canceled the contracts in 1944 and removed boats for completion at other yards.

The new boats had ten tubes, and diving depth was increased to 300' and eventually 400'. Hull plating was increased from 9/16" to 7/8" thickness, producing extra strength. During the war, the 3" deck guns were replaced by 5" guns, which were placed forward of the conning towers. These were reduced in size as they made good targets and were streamlined. Antiaircraft guns were added.

*John D. Alden, *The Fleet Submarine in the U.S. Navy* (London: Arms and Armour Press, 1979), p. 14.

At the start of the Pacific war in 1941, American submarine commanders found their torpedoes were defective. Their trajectory was uncertain, running too deep or broaching, and often failing to explode when the target was struck. This problem was corrected.

Tactics improved, often using methods successfully employed by German U-boats in the Atlantic. Submarines were also used to rescue downed fliers, to aid guerrilla groups in the Philippines, and for intelligence missions. But the true success of the American submarine force is shown by the almost total destruction of the Japanese merchant marine. More than five million tons were sunk by submarines, 55 percent of the total lost. The stars of this victory were named *Barb, Flasher, Rasher, Silversides, Tang,* and *Tautog,* but while many patrols were crowned with success, all were fraught with danger. The cost of this victory was 52 submarines lost, along with 3,505 men.

Submarines used the designation *SS* and were named after sea creatures. The *SF* and *SC* designations were eliminated in favor of the original hull numbers for all submarines except the minelayer *Argonaut.* They were distinguished by their class numbers painted on the conning tower, but in 1939 this was changed to using the SS hull numbers in order to avoid confusion between the "old" and "new" *S* classes. During the war the numbers were painted out.

SUBMARINES ON THE NAVY LIST, 1922

SS 29 *H-2* Decomm 23 Oct 1922. Stricken 18 Dec 1930, sold 1 Sep 1931, BU.

SS 30 *H-3* Decomm 23 Oct 1922. Stricken 18 Dec 1930, sold 14 Sep 1931, BU.

SS 147 *H-4* Decomm 25 Oct 1922. Stricken 26 Feb 1931, sold 14 Sep 1931.

SS 148 *H-5* Decomm 20 Oct 1922. Stricken 26 Feb 1931, sold 28 Nov 1933.

SS 149 *H-6* Decomm 23 Oct 1922. Stricken 26 Feb 1931, sold 28 Nov 1933.

SS 150 *H-7* Decomm 23 Oct 1922. Stricken 26 Feb 1931, sold 28 Nov 1933.

SS 151 *H-8* Decomm 17 Nov 1922. Stricken 26 Feb 1931, sold 28 Nov 1933.

SS 152 *H-9* Decomm 3 Nov 1922. Stricken 26 Feb 1931, sold 28 Nov 1933.

SS 32 *K-1* Decomm 7 Mar 1923. Stricken 18 Dec 1930, sold 25 Jun 1931, BU.

SS 33 *K-2* Decomm 9 Mar 1923. Stricken 18 Dec 1930, sold 3 Jun 1931, BU.

SS 34 *K-3* Decomm 20 Feb 1923. Stricken 18 Dec 1930, sold 3 Jun 1931, BU.

SS 35 *K-4* Decomm 19 May 1923. Stricken 18 Dec 1930, sold 3 Jun 1931, BU.

SS 36 *K-5* Decomm 20 Feb 1923. Stricken 18 Dec 1930, sold 3 Jun 1931, BU.

SS 37 *K-6* Decomm 21 May 1923. Stricken 18 Dec 1930, sold 3 Jun 1931, BU.

SS 38 *K-7* Decomm 12 Feb 1923. Stricken 18 Dec 1930, sold 3 Jun 1931, BU.

SS 39 *K-8* Decomm 24 Feb 1923. Stricken 18 Dec 1930, sold 3 Jun 1931, BU.

SS 41 *L-2* Decomm 4 May 1923. Stricken 18 Dec 1930, BU 1933.

SS 42 *L-3* Decomm 11 Jun 1923. Stricken 18 Dec 1930, BU 1933.

SS 44 *L-5* Decomm 5 Dec 1922. Stricken 20 Mar 1925, sold 21 Dec 1925. BU Newark, N.J.

SS 45 *L-6* Decomm 25 Nov 1922. Stricken 20 Mar 1925, sold 21 Dec 1925.

SS 46 *L-7* Decomm 15 Nov 1922. Stricken 20 Mar 1925, sold 21 Dec 1925.

SS 48 *L-8* Decomm 15 Nov 1922. Stricken 20 Mar 1925. Sunk as target off Narragansett Bay, 26 May 1926.

SS 49 *L-9* Decomm 4 May 1923. Stricken 18 Dec 1930, BU 1933.

SS 51 *L-11* Decomm 28 Nov 1923. Stricken 18 Dec 1930, BU 1933.

SS 53 *N-1* Decomm 30 Apr 1926. Stricken 18 Dec 1930, BU 1931.

SS 54 *N-2* Decomm 30 Apr 1926. Stricken 18 Dec 1930, BU.

SS 55 *N-3* Damaged in collision with tanker *Montrose* off New London, Conn., 16 Aug 1923. Decomm 30 Apr 1926. Stricken 18 Dec 1930, BU.

SS 52 *T-1* Rec **SF 1**. Decomm 5 Dec 1922. Stricken 19 Sep 1930, BU 1931.

SS 60 *T-2* Rec **SF 2**. Decomm 16 Jul 1923. Stricken 19 Sep 1930, BU 1931.

SS 61 *T-3* Rec **SF 3**. Out of comm 11 Nov 1922–1 Oct 1925. Decomm 14 Jul 1927. Stricken 19 Sep 1930, BU 1931.

SS 62 *O-1* Used for experiments 1930–31. Decomm 11 Jun 1931. Stricken 18 May 1938; BU.

SS 63 *O-2* Out of comm 25 Jun 1931–3 Feb 1941. Decomm 26 Jul 1945. Stricken 11 Aug 1945. Sold 16 Nov 1945; BU.

SS 64 *O-3* Went aground off Portsmouth, N.H., 4 Feb 1930. Out of comm 6 Jun 1931–3 Feb 1941. Decomm 11 Sep 1945. Stricken 11 Oct 1945. Sold 4 Sep 1946; BU.

Figure 6.1: *Holland* (AS 3) with her submarines in 1941. The submarines are (left to right) *Sailfish, Seal, Stingray, Perch, Pollack, Cachalot, Cuttlefish, Skipjack, Sturgeon, Snapper,* and *Sargo.*

Figure 6.2: *O-6* (SS 67), 23 Apr 1942, with the *O-4* at right. They were used for training during the war.

SS 65 *O-4* Out of comm 3 Jun 1931–29 Jan 1941. Decomm 20 Sep 1945. Stricken 11 Oct 1945. Sold 2 Jan 1946; BU.

SS 66 *O-5* Sunk in collision with m/v *Abangarez* in Limon Bay, Canal Zone, 28 Oct 1923 (5 killed).

SS 67 *O-6* Out of comm 9 Jun 1931–4 Feb 1941. Decomm 11 Sep 1945. Stricken 11 Oct 1945. Sold 4 Sep 1946; BU Quincy, Mass.

SS 68 *O-7* Out of comm 1 Jul 1931–12 Feb 1941. Decomm 2 Jul 1945. Stricken 11 Jul 1945. Sold 22 Jan 1946; BU Philadelphia.

SS 69 *O-8* Out of comm 27 May 1931–28 Apr 1941. Decomm 11 Sep 1945. Stricken 11 Oct 1945. Sold 4 Sep 1946; BU Quincy, Mass.

SS 70 *O-9* Out of comm 25 Jun 1931–14 Apr 1941. Foundered in training accident off Isle of Shoals, N.H., 20 Jun 1941 (34 killed).

SS 71 *O-10* Out of comm 25 Jun 1931–10 Mar 1941. Decomm 10 Sep 1945. Stricken 11 Oct 1945. Sold 21 Aug 1946; BU Quincy, Mass.

SS 72 *O-11* Decomm 21 Jun 1924. Stricken 9 May 1930; BU.

SS 73 *O-12* Decomm 17 Jun 1924. Stricken 29 Jul 1930, sold.

Later history: Wilkins-Ellsworth Trans-Arctic Expedition ship *Nautilus*. Scuttled off Norway, 30 Nov 1931.

SS 74 *O-13* Decomm 11 Jun 1924. Stricken 9 May 1930. Sold 30 Jul 1930; BU.

SS 75 *O-14* Decomm 17 Jun 1924. Stricken 9 May 1930; BU.

SS 76 *O-15* Decomm 11 Jun 1924. Stricken 9 May 1930; BU.

SS 77 *O-16* Decomm 21 Jun 1924. Stricken 9 May 1930; BU.

SS 78 *R-1* Went aground off Barbers Point, Oahu, 28 Oct 1924. Out of comm 1 May 1931–23 Sep 1940. Decomm 20 Sep 1945. Stricken 10 Nov 1945. Sold 13 Mar 1946; BU.

SS 79 *R-2* Decomm 10 May 1945. Stricken 2 Jun 1945. Sold 28 Mar 1946; BU Philadelphia.

SS 80 *R-3* Out of comm 10 Aug 1934–19 Aug 1940. Decomm, to UK, 4 Nov 1941.

Later history: Renamed HMS *P-511*. Returned 20 Dec 1944; broke loose in Thames River, became total loss, 22 Nov 1947. BU Feb 1948 Troon, Scotland.

SS 81 *R-4* Decomm 18 Jun 1945. Stricken 11 Jul 1945. Sold 12 Dec 1946; BU Philadelphia.

SS 82 *R-5* Damaged in collision with *R-16* off Pearl Harbor, Dec 1924. Out of comm 30 Jun 1932–19 Aug 1940. Decomm 14 Sep 1945. Stricken 11 Oct 1945. Sold 22 Aug 1946; BU Quincy, Mass.

SS 83 *R-6* Sank alongside dock at San Pedro, Calif., 26 Sep 1922 (2 killed); refloated 13 Oct. Out of comm 4 May 1931–15 Nov 1940. Decomm 27 Sep 1945. Stricken 11 Oct 1945. Sold 13 Mar 1946.

SS 84 *R-7* Out of comm 2 May 1931–22 Jul 1940. Decomm 14 Sep 1945. Stricken 11 Oct 1945. Sold 4 Sep 1946; BU Quincy, Mass.

SS 85 *R-8* Damaged in collision with USS *Widgeon*, 1925. Decomm 2 May 1931. Sank while laid up at Philadelphia, 26 Feb 1936. Stricken 12 May 1936. Sunk as target by aircraft off Cape Henry, Va., 19 Aug 1936.

SS 86 *R-9* Out of comm 2 May 1931–14 Mar 1941. Decomm 25 Sep 1945. Stricken 11 Oct 1945. Sold 1 Feb 1946.

SS 87 *R-10* Decomm 18 Jun 1945. Stricken 11 Jul 1945. Sold 22 Jan 1946; BU Philadelphia.

SS 88 *R-11* Decomm 5 Sep 1945. Stricken 11 Oct 1945. Sold 13 Mar 1946.

SS 89 *R-12* Out of comm 7 Dec 1932–16 Oct 1940. Foundered in training accident off Key West, Fla., 12 Jun 1943 (42 killed).

SS 90 *R-13* Decomm 14 Sep 1945. Stricken 11 Oct 1945. Sold 13 Mar 1946.

SS 91 *R-14* Decomm 7 May 1945. Stricken 19 May 1945. Sold 28 Oct 1945; BU Philadelphia.

SS 92 *R-15* Out of comm 7 May 1931–1 Apr 1941. Decomm 17 Sep 1945. Stricken 11 Oct 1945. Sold 13 Mar 1946.

SS 93 *R-16* Damaged in collision with *R-5* off Pearl Harbor, Dec 1924. Out of comm 12 May 1931–1 Jul 1940. Decomm 5 Jul 1945. Stricken 25 Jul 1945. Sold 22 Jan 1946; BU Philadelphia.

SS 94 *R-17* Out of comm 15 May 1931–16 Mar 1941. Decomm 9 Mar 1942, trfd to UK.

Later history: Renamed HMS *P-512*. Returned 6 Sep 1944; used as target ship. Stricken 22 Jun 1945. Sold 16 Nov 1945; BU Philadelphia.

SS 95 *R-18* Out of comm 13 May 1931–8 Jan 1941. Decomm 19 Sep 1945. Stricken 11 Oct 1945. Sold 4 Sep 1946; BU Quincy, Mass.

SS 96 *R-19* Out of comm 15 May 1931–6 Jan 1941. Decomm, to UK, 9 Mar 1942.

Later history: Renamed HMS *P-514*. Sunk in collision with HMCS *Georgian* in Western Atlantic, 21 Jun 1942.

SS 97 *R-20* Out of comm 15 May 1931–22 Jan 1941. Decomm 27 Sep 1945. Stricken 11 Oct 1945. Sold 13 Mar 1946.

SS 98 *R-21* Decomm 21 Jun 1924. Stricken 9 May 1930. Sold 30 Jul 1930; BU.

SS 99 *R-22* Decomm 29 Apr 1925. Stricken 9 May 1930. Sold 30 Jul 1930; BU Philadelphia.

SS 100 *R-23* Decomm 24 Apr 1925. Stricken 9 May 1930; BU.

SS 101 *R-24* Decomm 11 Jun 1925. Stricken 9 May 1930; BU.

SS 102 *R-25* Decomm 21 Jun 1924. Stricken 9 May 1930; BU.

SS 103 *R-26* Decomm 12 Jun 1925. Stricken 9 May 1930; BU.

SS 104 *R-27* Decomm 24 Apr 1925. Stricken 9 May 1930; BU.

SS 105 *S-1* Experimental airplane catapult mounted aft, 1923–26. Out of comm 20 Oct 1937–16 Oct 1940. To UK, 20 Apr 1942.

Later history: Renamed HMS *P-552*. Returned 16 Oct 1944, sold 20 Jul 1945; BU 1946 Durban, South Africa.

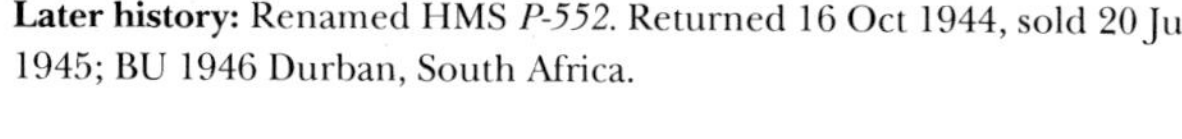

Figure 6.3: *R-12* (SS 89), before the war. She was lost in a training accident off Key West, Fla., in 1943.

Figure 6.4: *S-11* (SS 116), 4 Oct 1935, with old-style number on the conning tower. Submarine hull numbers were used after 1940.

Figure 6.5: *S-38* (SS 143), 1943, probably at San Diego after modernization. In the left background is the attack transport *Harris*.

Figure 6.6: *S-20* (SS 125), 2 Feb 1944. Her appearance was changed in the 1920s with a raised bow and external blisters, an experiment not repeated. Unlike the rest of the S class she remained in the United States during the war.

SS 106 *S-2* Asiatic Fleet 1921–29. Decomm 25 Nov 1930. Stricken 26 Feb 1931, sold 14 Sep 1931; BU.

SS 107 *S-3* Asiatic Fleet 1921–23. Decomm 24 Mar 1931. Stricken 23 Jan 1937; BU.

SS 109 *S-4* Asiatic Fleet 1921–24. Sunk in collision with USCG destroyer *Paulding* off Provincetown, Mass., 17 Dec 1927 (all 40 killed). Refloated 17 Mar 1928, used as experimental hull. Recomm 16 Oct 1928. Decomm 7 Apr 1933. Stricken 15 Jan 1936, scuttled 15 May 1936 off Hawaii.

SS 111 *S-6* Asiatic Fleet 1921–24. Went aground off Jonesport, Me., 3 Jul 1928. Decomm 10 Apr 1931. Stricken 25 Jan 1937; BU.

SS 112 *S-7* Asiatic Fleet 1921–24. Decomm 2 Apr 1931. Stricken 25 Jan 1937; BU.

SS 113 *S-8* Asiatic Fleet 1921–24. Decomm 11 Apr 1931. Stricken 25 Jan 1937; BU.

SS 114 *S-9* Asiatic Fleet 1921–24. Decomm 15 Apr 1931. Stricken 25 Jan 1937; BU.

SS 115 *S-10* Decomm 17 Jul 1936. Stricken 21 Jul 1936. Sold 13 Nov 1936; BU.

SS 116 *S-11* Out of comm 30 Sep 1936–6 Sep 1940. Six patrols, off Panama. Decomm 2 May 1945. Stricken 19 May 1945. Sold 28 Oct 1945; BU Philadelphia.

SS 117 *S-12* In collision with a railway float in East River, New York City, 28 Oct 1926. Damaged in collision with *S-18* at New London, Conn., 31 May 1928. Out of comm 30 Sep 1936–4 Nov 1940. Six patrols, off Panama. Decomm 18 May 1945. Stricken 19 May 1945. Sold 28 Oct 1945; BU Philadelphia.

SS 118 *S-13* Out of comm 30 Sep 1936–28 Oct 1940. Four patrols. Decomm 10 Apr 1945. Stricken 19 May 1945. Sold 28 Oct 1945; BU Philadelphia.

SS 119 *S-14* Asiatic Fleet 1921–24. Collided with *S-16* off Balboa, Canal Zone, 17 Dec 1931. Out of comm 22 May 1935–10 Dec 1940. Four patrols. Decomm 18 May 1945. Stricken 22 Jun 1945. Sold 16 Nov 1945; BU Philadelphia.

SS 120 *S-15* Asiatic Fleet 1921–24. Out of comm 26 Apr 1935–3 Jan 1941. Three patrols. Decomm 11 Jun 1946. Stricken 3 Jul 1946. Sold 4 Dec 1946; BU Baltimore.

SS 121 *S-16* Asiatic Fleet 1921–24. Collided with *S-14* off Balboa, Canal Zone, 17 Dec 1931. Out of comm 22 May 1935–2 Dec 1940. Six patrols. Decomm 4 Oct 1944. Stricken 13 Nov 1944. Sunk as target off Key West, Fla., 3 Apr 1945.

SS 122 *S-17* Asiatic Fleet 1921–24. Out of comm 29 Mar 1935–16 Dec 1940. Seven patrols. Decomm 4 Oct 1944. Stricken 13 Nov 1944. Sunk as target off New London, Conn., 5 Apr 1945.

SS 123 *S-18* Damaged in collision with *S-12* at New London, Conn., 31 May 1928. Decomm 29 Oct 1945. Stricken 13 Nov 1945. Sold 9 Nov 1946; BU San Francisco.
1*. Eight patrols.

SS 124 *S-19* Comm 24 Aug 1921. In yard 1922–23, recomm 6 Jan 1923. Went aground off Nausett, Mass., 13 Jan 1925, refloated 18 Mar. Decomm 10 Feb 1934. Stricken 12 Dec 1936. Scuttled off Pearl Harbor, 18 Dec 1936.

SS 125 *S-20* Decomm 16 Jul 1945. Stricken 25 Jul 1945. Sold 22 Jan 1946; BU Philadelphia.

SS 126 *S-21* Comm 24 Aug 1921. In yard 1922–23, recomm 14 Sep 1923. In collision with m/v tkr *Birkenhead* off Key West, Fla., 3 Feb 1927. Three patrols. Decomm, to UK 14 Sep 1942.
Later history: Renamed HMS *P-553*. Returned 11 Jul 1944, sunk as target in Casco Bay, Me., 23 Mar 1945.

SS 127 *S-22* Three patrols. Decomm, to UK 19 Jun 1942.
Later history: Renamed HMS *P-554*. Returned 11 Jul 1944, sold 16 Nov 1945; BU Philadelphia.

SS 128 *S-23* Decomm 2 Nov 1945. Stricken 16 Nov 1945. Sold 9 Nov 1946; BU San Francisco.
1*; six patrols, Alaska.

SS 129 *S-24* Four patrols. Decomm, to UK 10 Aug 1942.
Later history: Renamed HMS *P-555*. Sunk as target off Portland, UK, 25 Aug 1947.

SS 130 *S-25* Damaged in collision with USS *Ortolan* off San Pedro, Calif., 15 Oct 1925. Decomm, to UK 4 Nov 1941.
Later history: Renamed HMS *P-551*. To Poland, renamed *Jastrzab*, 1942. Sunk in error by HMS *St. Albans* and *Seagull* off Northern Norway, 2 May 1942.

SS 131 *S-26* Two patrols. Sunk in collision with *PC-460* in Gulf of Panama, 24 Jan 1942 (46 killed).

SS 132 *S-27* One patrol. Wrecked on Amchitka I., Aleutians, 19 Jun 1942. Stricken 22 Dec 1944.

SS 133 *S-28* Missing during training exercises off Oahu, 3 Jul 1944 (50 killed).
1*; seven patrols, Alaska.
Ship sunk: XPG +*Katsura Maru No. 2* (1,368/37) 19 Sep 1943.

SS 134 *S-29* Sank yacht *Miladi* in collision on trials off Provincetown, 12 Jul 1924. Three patrols. Decomm, to UK 5 Jun 1942.
Later history: Renamed HMS *P-556*. Sold 24 Jan 1947; BU Portsmouth, UK.

SS 135 *S-30* Out of comm 15 Aug 1921–21 Nov 1923, reengined. Neutrality patrol. Decomm 9 Oct 1945. Stricken 24 Oct 1945. Sold 5 Dec 1946; BU San Francisco.
2*; nine patrols, Alaska.
Ship sunk: *Jinbu Maru* (5,228/94) 11 Jun 1943.

* joint attack; +probable sinking; #possible sinking; § question on sinking

SS 136 *S-31* Out of comm 4 Oct 1922–8 Mar 1923, reengined. Philippines 1925–32. Out of comm 7 Dec 1932–18 Sep 1940. Decomm 19 Oct 1945. Stricken 1 Nov 1945. Sold 6 Dec 1946; BU San Francisco.
1*; eight patrols.
Ship sunk: *Keizan Maru* (2,864/40) 26 Oct 1942.

SS 137 *S-32* Out of comm 25 Sep 1922–21 Feb 1923, reengined. Philippines 1925–32. Out of comm 7 Dec 1937–18 Sep 1940. Decomm 19 Oct 1945. Stricken 1 Nov 1945. Sold 19 Apr 1946; BU Oakland.
5*; eight patrols, 1942–43, Alaska.

SS 138 *S-33* Out of comm 15 Jun 1922–21 Dec 1922, reengined. Philippines, 1926–32. Out of comm 1 Dec 1937–16 Oct 1940. Neutrality patrol. Decomm 23 Oct 1945. Stricken 1 Nov 1945. Sold 5 Dec 1946; BU San Francisco.
1*; eight patrols, 1942–43.

SS 139 *S-34* Out of comm 25 Oct 1922–23 Apr 1923, reengined. Went aground in fog at entrance to San Francisco Harbor, 20 Aug 1924. Philippines 1925–32. Decomm 23 Oct 1945. Stricken 1 Nov 1945. Sold 23 Nov 1946; BU.
1*; seven patrols, 1942–43, Alaska.

SS 140 *S-35* Out of comm 25 Oct 1922–7 May 1923, reengined. Philippines 1925–32. Damaged by weather and fire in Aleutians, 21 Dec 1942. Decomm 19 Mar 1945. Stricken 21 Feb 1946. Sunk as target, 4 Apr 1946.
1*; eight patrols, 1942–43, Alaska.
Ship sunk: *Banshu Maru No.* 7 (5,430/—) 2 Jul 1943.

SS 141 *S-36* Asiatic Fleet 1925–42. Wrecked on Taka Bakang Reef, Makassar Strait, 20 Jan 1942.
1* Philippines 1942; two patrols.

SS 142 *S-37* Damaged by fire at San Pedro, Calif., 10 Oct 1923 (3 killed). Asiatic Fleet 1925–42. Decomm 6 Feb 1945. Stricken 23 Feb 1945. Sunk as aerial target, 20 Feb 1945.
5* Philippines 1942, Badoeng Strait, Eastern Solomons; seven patrols.
Ships sunk: DD *Natsushio* 8 Feb 1942, *Tenzan Maru* (2,776/29) 8 Jul 1942.

SS 143 *S-38* Sank by the stern at Anchorage, Alaska, while alongside USS *Ortolan,* 17 Jul 1923. Asiatic Fleet 1924–42. Decomm 14 Dec 1944. Stricken 20 Feb 1945, sunk as aerial target.
3* Philippines 1942; nine patrols, 1942.
Ships sunk: Norwegian *Hydra II* (1,375/19) off Mindoro 12 Dec 1941 (in error), *Hayo Maru* (5,445/21) 22 Dec 1941, *Meiyo Maru* (5,628/39) 8 Aug 1942.

SS 144 *S-39* Asiatic Fleet 1924–42. Went aground off Rossel I., Louisiade Archipelago, 14 Aug 1942. Stricken 22 Dec 1944.
2* Philippines 1942; five patrols.
Ship sunk: AO *Erimo,* 4 Mar 1942.

SS 145 *S-40* Asiatic Fleet 1924–42. Decomm 29 Oct 1945. Stricken 13 Nov 1945. Sold 19 Nov 1946; BU San Francisco.
1*; nine patrols.

SS 146 *S-41* Asiatic Fleet 1924–42. Decomm 13 Feb 1945. Stricken 25 Feb 1946. Sold 15 Nov 1946; BU San Francisco.
4* Philippines 1942, Solomons; eight patrols.
Ship sunk: Barkentine *Seiki Maru* (1,036/—) 28 May 1943.

SS 153 *S-42* Damaged when surfacing under *S-26* off San Diego, 31 Mar 1928. Decomm 25 Oct 1945. Stricken 13 Nov 1945. Sold 23 Nov 1946; BU.
1*; six patrols.
Ship sunk: CM *Okinoshima,* 11 May 1942.

SS 154 *S-43*: Neutrality patrol. Three patrols. Decomm 10 Oct 1945. Stricken 13 Nov 1945. Sold 7 Dec 1946; BU San Francisco.

SS 155 *S-44* Sunk by Japanese destroyer *Ishigaki* in Kurile Is., 7 Oct 1943 (55 killed).
2*; five patrols.
Ships sunk: AR *Shoei Maru* (5,644/37) 12 May 1942, XPG *Keijo Maru* (2,626/40) 21 Jun 1942; CA *Kako* off New Ireland 10 Aug 1942.

SS 156 *S-45* Four patrols. Decomm 30 Oct 1945. Stricken 13 Nov 1945. Sold 6 Dec 1946; BU San Francisco.

* joint attack; +probable sinking; #possible sinking; § question on sinking

Figure 6.7: *S-43* (SS 154), 24 Jan 1944, at San Francisco after modernization.

Figure 6.8: *S-48* (SS 159), 16 May 1935, the largest of the *S*-class submarines, remained on the U.S. East Coast during the war.

SS 157 *S-46* Decomm 2 Nov 1945. Stricken 13 Nov 1945. Sold 19 Nov 1946; BU.
1*; five patrols.

SS 158 *S-47* Neutrality patrol. Decomm 25 Oct 1945. Stricken 13 Nov 1945. Sold 22 Nov 1946; BU.
3* Solomons, Biak; seven patrols.

SS 159 *S-48* Went aground off Portsmouth, N.H., 29 Jan 1925; refloated 7 Feb. Out of comm 7 Jul 1925–8 Dec 1928, under repair 1926–28. Out of comm 16 Sep 1935–10 Dec 1940. Training, U.S. East Coast. Decomm 29 Aug 1945. Stricken 17 Sep 1945. Sold 22 Nov 1946; BU Philadelphia.

SS 160 *S-49* Damaged by battery explosion at New London, Conn., 20 Apr 1926 (4 killed). Decomm 2 Aug 1927. Stricken 21 Mar 1931. Sold 25 May 1931.
Later history: Used as exhibition ship, renamed *C.* Reacquired as hulk for testing mines, 1943.

SS 161 *S-50* Damaged by battery explosion at sea off Virgin Is., 6 Feb 1924. Decomm 20 Aug 1927. Stricken 21 Mar 1931; BU.

SS 162 *S-51* Sunk in collision with m/v *City of Rome* off Block I., N.Y., 25 Sep 1925 (33 killed). Raised 5 Jul 1926. Stricken 27 Jan 1930. Sold 4 Jun 1930; BU Brooklyn, N.Y.

Notes: *T-3* (*T* class) tested experimental German diesel engines, BHP 3,000, installed 1925–27.

N class used for training at New London, Connecticut. *O* class used for training at New London and at Portsmouth, N.H., during World War II.

R class used for patrols off U.S. East Coast and in Gulf of Mexico, then for training at Key West. *R-6* fitted with experimental snorkel, 1945.

S class designed for Atlantic operations; these ships were inadequate for Arctic and Pacific operations and had multiple material defects. Electric Boat units had to be rebuilt. *S-1* had a small housing aft of conning tower to carry a small seaplane, 1923–26, but results were disappointing. *S-14* to *S-17* were reengined with M.A.N. diesels, 1925, speed increased to 15.5 knots. *S-20* modernized 1931, with raised bow and external blisters and experimental new engines (dimensions: 222'5" (oa) x 24' x 17'4"; displacement: 987/1,165 tons, complement: 43); this rebuilding was not repeated in other units. *S-48* reconstructed 1928, engines replaced with German M.A.N. diesels (dimensions: 267' x 21'6" x 12'5"; displacement: 1,180/1,460 tons; HP 2,000/1,500; speed: 14.2 knots; endurance: 11,000/11. During World War II, the *S* class fitted with radar, AA gun, 3" replaced by 4" gun, some were given air conditioning, conning towers cut down. Only *S-20* and *S-48* remained in U.S. waters. *S-23, S-28, S-30* to *S-35, S-37* to *S-41* modernized at San Diego 1942–43. *S-42* to *S-47* rebuilt 1943–44.

Figure 6.10: *V-3* (later *Bonita*) (SS 165), 7 Mar 1930. The *V-1* class was the first postwar submarine design. Notice distinctive bow.

V-1 (Barracuda) Class

No.	Name	Builder	Keel Laid	Launched	Comm.
SF 4	*V-1*	Portsmouth NYd	20 Oct 1921	17 Jul 1924	1 Oct 1924
SF 5	*V-2*	Portsmouth NYd	20 Oct 1921	27 Dec 1924	26 Sep 1925
SF 6	*V-3*	Portsmouth NYd	16 Nov 1921	9 Jun 1925	22 May 1926

Displacement	2,119/2,506 tons
Dimensions	341'6" (oa) 326' (wl) x 27'7" x 15'2"
Machinery	2 screws; diesel: SHP 6,700, 21 knots; electric: SHP 2,400, 9 knots; 6,200, 18 knots
Endurance	6,000/11; depth: 20'
Complement	87
Armament	1–5"/51 gun, 6–21" TT (1,928: 1–3"/50)

Notes: Deficient in reserve buoyancy. Often out of service for engine repairs. Busch-Sulzer engines. Had partial double hull and unusual shark-nose bow. Conversion to submarine transports canceled 1942. Converted to cargo carriers, 1943; TT, deck gun and main engines removed, not successful.

Service Records:

SF 4 *V-1* Renamed ***Barracuda***, 19 Feb 1931. Rec **SS 163**, 1 Jul 1931. Out of comm 14 May 1937–5 Sep 1940. Conversion to **APS 2** canceled 1942. Six patrols, southwest of Panama. Training 1943–45. Decomm 3 Mar 1945. Stricken 10 Mar 1945. Sold 16 Nov 1945; BU Wilmington, Del.

SF 5 *V-2* Renamed ***Bass***, 19 Feb 1931. Rec **SS 164**, 1 Jul 1931. Out of comm 9 Jun 1937–5 Sep 1940. Four patrols off Panama. Conversion to **APS 3** canceled 1942. Damaged by fire at sea off Balboa, Panama, 17 Aug 1942 (26 killed). Experimental training 1943–44. Decomm 3 Mar 1945. Stricken 10 Mar 1945. Sunk as target off Block I., N.Y., 12 Mar 1945.

SF 6 *V-3* Renamed ***Bonita***, 19 Feb 1931. Rec **SS 165**, 1 Jul 1931. Out of comm 4 Jun 1937–5 Sep 1940. Seven patrols in Southeast Pacific. Training 1944–45. Decomm 3 Mar 1945. Conversion to **APS 4** canceled 1942. Stricken 10 Mar 1945. Sold 28 Oct 1945; BU Philadelphia.

Figure 6.9: *Bass* (SS 164), on 30 Mar 1943, after conversion to a cargo carrier, at Philadelphia.

V-4 (Argonaut)

No.	Name	Builder	Keel Laid	Launched	Comm.
SF 7	*V-4*	Portsmouth NYd	1 May 1925	10 Nov 1927	2 Apr 1928

Displacement	2,710/4,080 tons; (1939) 3,046/4,164
Dimensions	381' (oa) 358' (wl) x 33'10" x 16'4"
Machinery	2 screws; diesel: SHP 3,175, 15 knots; electric: SHP 2,400, 8 knots
Endurance	8,000/10; depth: 300'
Complement	88
Armament	2–6"/53 guns, 4–21" TT, 80 mines

Notes: Minelayer. Largest submarine built in the United States. Full double hull. Only built-for-the-purpose minelaying submarine built for the Navy. Not very successful; unwieldy and slower than designed when submerged. Reached depth of 318'. Reengined 1942, and two additional TT mounted on deck. Converted to a transport for Carlson's Raid on Makin I.

Service Record:

SF 7 *V-4* Renamed ***Argonaut***, 19 Feb 1931. Rec **SM 1 (SS 166)** 1 Jul 1931. Carlson's Raid on Makin I., 16–18 Aug 1942. Converted to submarine transport, rec **APS 1**, 22 Sep 1942. Sunk by Japanese destroyers *Isokaze* and *Maikaze* southeast of New Britain, 10 Jan 1943 (105 killed).

2* Pearl Harbor, Makin Raid; three patrols.

*joint attack; +probable sinking; #possible sinking; § question on sinking

Figure 6.11: *V-5* (SS 167; later, *Narwhal*), in 1930, a cruiser type submarine with two 6" guns; not very successful.

V-5 (Narwhal) Class

No.	Name	Builder	Keel Laid	Launched	Comm.
SC 1	*V-5*	Portsmouth NYd	10 May 1927	17 Dec 1929	15 May 1930
	ex–SF 8 (11 Feb 1925)				
SC 2	*V-6*	Mare I. NYd	2 Aug 1927	15 Mar 1930	1 Jul 1930
	ex–SF 9 (11 Feb 1925)				

Displacement	2,730/3,900 tons; (1943) 3,158/4,040 tons.
Dimensions	370'7" (oa) x 33'4" x 16'11"
Machinery	2 screws; diesel geared drive/diesel; SHP 6,000/1,600; 17 knots/8 knots
Endurance	9,380/10; depth: 300"
Complement	89
Armament	2–6"/53, 6–21" TT

Notes: Cruiser submarines. Similar to *V-4* with minelaying capability replaced by torpedo tubes. Too big, clumsy and slow diving, easy to detect. *Nautilus* reengined 1942, *Narwhal* 1943; 4 external TT added. Both fitted to carry Marine assault/commando troops.

Service Records:

SC 1 *V-5* Renamed ***Narwhal*** 19 Feb 1931. Rec **SS 167**, 1 Jul 1931. Disembarked Army scouts on Attu, May 1943. Bombarded Matsuwa I., Kuriles, 15 Jul 1943. Bombarded Bula, Ceram I., 13 Jun 1944. Carried cargo and passengers to and from occupied areas, 1943–45. Decomm 23 Apr 1945. Stricken 19 May 1945. Sold 16 Nov 1945; BU Wilmington, Del.
15* Pearl Harbor, Midway, Attu; 15 patrols.
Ships sunk: *Taki Maru* (1,244/16) 4 Mar 1942, *Kofuji Maru* (134/—) 24 Jul 1942, *Koan Maru* (884/—), *Meiwa Maru* (2,921/—) 1 Aug 1942; *Bifuku Maru* (2,559/99) 8 Aug 1942, *Hokusho Maru* (4,211/37) 11 Sep 1943, *Himeno Maru* (834/—) 5 Dec 1943 (ex–U.S. *Dos Hermanos*), PR *Karatsu* (ex–USS *Luzon*) damaged 3 Mar 1944.

SC 2 *V-6* Renamed ***Nautilus*** 19 Feb 1931. Rec **SS 168**, 1 Jul 1931. Carlson's Raid on Makin I., 16–18 Aug 1942. Damaged by explosion at sea off San Diego, Calif., 8 Mar 1934. Disembarked Army scouts on Attu, May 1943. Damaged in error by gunfire of destroyer *Ringgold* off Tarawa, 19 Nov 1943. Carried cargo and passengers to and from occupied areas, 1943–45. Decomm 30 Jun 1945. Stricken 19 May 1945. Sold 16 Nov 1945; BU Wilmington, Del.
14* Midway, Makin Raid, Solomons, Gilbert Is., Attu, Leyte Ldgs.; 14 patrols. PUC.
Ships sunk: *CV *Soryu* 4 Jun 1942, DD *Yamakaze* 25 Jun 1942, *Tamon Maru No. 6* (4,994/—) 28 Sep 1942, *Tosei Maru* (2,432/20) 1 Oct 1942, §*Kenun Maru* (4,643/—) 24 Oct 1942, *Yoshinogawa Maru* (1,430/—) 9 Jan 1943, *America Maru* (6,070/98) 6 Mar 1944, DD *Akizuki* west of Tulagi damaged 19 Jan 1943.

*joint attack; +probable sinking; #possible sinking; § question on sinking

Dolphin

No.	Name	Builder	Keel Laid	Launched	Comm.
SS 169	*Dolphin*	Portsmouth NYd	14 Jun 1930	6 Mar 1932	1 Jun 1932 ;
	ex–*V-7* (19 Feb 1931); ex–SC 3 (1 Jul 1931), ex–SF 10 (2 Mar 1929)				

Displacement	1,718/2,240 tons
Dimensions	319'3" (oa) x 27'11" x 16'6"
Machinery	2 screws; diesel direct, SHP 3,500/1,750, 17.5/8 knots
Endurance	4,900/10; depth: 300'
Complement	63
Armament	1–4"/50, 6–21" TT

Notes: Desire for reduced size produced what became the forerunner of World War II fleet types. Used for training after 1942.

Service Record:

SS 169 *Dolphin* Decomm 12 Oct 1945. Stricken 24 Oct 1945. Sold 26 Aug 1946; BU Quincy, Mass.
2* Pearl Harbor, Midway; four patrols.

Figure 6.12: *Dolphin* (SS 169), wearing prewar pendant number D-1, was the forerunner of the wartime fleet type of submarine.

Figure 6.13: *Argonaut* (SM 1), 18 Jul 1942, a submarine minelayer, after alterations at Mare I. She was the largest submarine built in the United States until 1958.

Figure 6.14: *Cachalot* (SS 170), during the 1930s, wearing pendant number C-1.

Cachalot Class

No.	Name	Builder	Keel Laid	Launched	Comm.
SS 170	*Cachalot*	Portsmouth NYd	21 Oct 1931	19 Oct 1933	1 Dec 1933
	ex–*V-8* (19 Feb 1931); ex–SC 4 (1 Jul 1931), ex–SF 11 (2 Mar 1929)				
SS 171	*Cuttlefish*	Electric Boat	7 Oct 1931	21 Nov 1933	8 Jun 1934
	ex–*V-9* (19 Feb 1931); ex–SC 5 (1 Jul 1931), ex–SF 12 (2 Mar 1929)				

Displacement	1,110/1,680 tons
Dimensions	271'11" (oa) x 24'11" x 13'10"; 171: 274' (oa) x 24'9"
Machinery	2 screws; diesel geared drive: SHP 3,070, 17 knots; electric: HP 1,600; 8 knots
Endurance	6,000/10; depth: 250'
Complement	45/55
Armament	1–3"/50, 6–21" TT

Notes: Size further reduced, but too small, with inadequate speed and range. First use of welding in a submarine by the Electric Boat Company. *Cuttlefish* was the first submarine with air conditioning. Training at New London, Conn., after 1943.

Service Records:

SS 170 *Cachalot* Decomm 17 Oct 1945. Stricken 3 Jul 1946. Sold 26 Jan 1947; BU Philadelphia.
3* Pearl Harbor, Midway, four patrols.

SS 171 *Cuttlefish* Decomm 24 Oct 1945. Stricken 3 Jul 1946. Sold 12 Feb 1947; BU Philadelphia.
2* Midway, three patrols.

Porpoise Class

No.	Name	Builder	Keel Laid	Launched	Comm.
SS 172	*Porpoise*	Portsmouth NYd	27 Oct 1933	20 Jun 1935	15 Aug 1935
SS 173	*Pike*	Portsmouth NYd	20 Dec 1933	12 Sep 1935	12 Dec 1935

Displacement	1,310/1,960 tons
Dimensions	301' (oa) x 24'11" x 15'11"
Machinery	2 screws; diesel-electric reduction: SHP 5,200; 19.5 knots; electric: HP 2,085, 8 knots
Endurance	6,000/10; depth: 250'
Complement	54
Armament	1–3"/50, 6–21" TT; (1942) 2 TT added.

Notes: First all-electric submarines. Enlarged *Cachalot* with full double-hull. Two bow deck TT added 1942, reengined. Used for training after 1943.

Service Records:

SS 172 *Porpoise* Training SS after Sep 1943. Decomm 15 Nov 1945. Strike canceled 13 Nov 1945. In service as training ship 8 May 1947. †
5* Philippines 1942, Midway; seven patrols.
Ships sunk: *Renzan Maru* (4,999/17, ex–British *Hatterlock*) 1 Jan 1943, *Koa Maru* (2,024/—) 4 Apr 1943, *Mikage Maru No. 20* (2,718/40) 19 Jul 1943.

SS 173 *Pike* Training SS after Nov 1943. Decomm 15 Nov 1945. NRT Sep 1946. †
4* Philippines 1942, Midway; eight patrols.
Ship sunk: *Shoju Maru* (2,022/20) 5 Aug 1943.

Shark Class

No.	Name	Builder	Keel Laid	Launched	Comm.
SS 174	*Shark*	Electric Boat	24 Oct 1933	21 May 1935	25 Jan 1936
SS 175	*Tarpon*	Electric Boat	22 Dec 1933	4 Sep 1935	12 Mar 1936

Displacement	1,315/1,990 tons
Dimensions	298' (oa) x 25'1" x 17'
Machinery	2 screws; diesel-electric reduction: SHP 5,200; 20.2 knots; electric: HP 2,085, 8.25 knots
Endurance	6,000/10; depth: 250'
Complement	54/73
Armament	1–3"/50, 8–21" TT; later, 1–3"/50

Notes: Different hull from *Porpoise*, first all-welded hull, partial double-hull. Two bow TT added in *Tarpon*, 1942, conning tower cut down.

Service Records:

SS 174 *Shark* Damaged when surfacing under carrier *Yorktown* off Honolulu, 13 Sep 1940. Sunk by Japanese warships, probably destroyer *Yamakaze*, east of Menado, Celebes, 11 Feb 1942 (58 killed).
1* Philippines 1942, two patrols.

SS 175 *Tarpon* Went aground off Flores I., Dutch East Indies, 23 Feb 1942. Decomm 15 Nov 1945. NRT 9 Apr 1947. †
7* Philippines 1942, Midway, Marshall Is., Guam; 12 patrols.
Ships sunk: *Fushimi Maru* (10,935/14) 1 Feb 1943, AP *Tatsuta Maru* (16,975/30) 8 Feb 1943, German CLX *Michel* (4,740/39) in Sea of Izu 17 Oct 1943.

Perch Class

No.	Name	Builder	Keel Laid	Launched	Comm.
SS 176	*Perch*	Electric Boat	25 Feb 1935	9 May 1936	19 Nov 1936
SS 177	*Pickerel*	Electric Boat	25 Mar 1935	7 Jul 1936	26 Jan 1937
SS 178	*Permit*	Electric Boat	6 Jun 1935	5 Oct 1936	17 Mar 1937
	ex–*Pinna* (13 Aug 1935)				
SS 179	*Plunger*	Portsmouth NYd	17 Jul 1935	8 Jul 1936	19 Nov 1936
SS 180	*Pollack*	Portsmouth NYd	1 Oct 1935	15 Sep 1936	15 Jan 1937
SS 181	*Pompano*	Mare I. NYd	14 Jan 1936	11 Mar 1937	12 Jun 1937

Displacement	1,330/2,005 tons
Dimensions	300'6" (oa) x 25'1" x 16'11"

* joint attack; +probable sinking; #possible sinking; § question on sinking

Figure 6.15: *Plunger* (SS 179), of the *Perch* class, during the 1930s, wearing pendant P-8.

Machinery	2 screws; diesel-electric reduction: SHP 5,200, 19.25 knots; electric: HP 2,368, 8.75 knots
Endurance	11,000/10; depth: 250'
Complement	54/73
Armament	1–3"/50, 8–21" TT; (1943) 1–20mm added

Notes: Near duplicates of *Shark*. SS 179–81 were the last riveted submarines. Engines of *Plunger* and *Pollack* were rebuilt and eventually replaced in 1942. *Pompano* was delayed for one year by defective engine, 1937, reengined Nov 1942. First submarines designed with air conditioning. Two-bow deck TT added 1942 in *Pickerel* and *Permit*.

Service Records:

SS 176 *Perch* Scuttled in Java Sea after being damaged by Japanese destroyers *Ushio* and *Sazanami*, 3 Mar 1942 (9 died as POWs).
1* Philippines 1942, two patrols.

SS 177 *Pickerel* Missing off Northern Honshu, Apr 1943 (74 killed). (Probably sunk by minelayer *Shirakami* and patrol boat *Bunzan Maru*, 3 Apr 1943.)
3* Philippines 1942; seven patrols.
Ships sunk: XPG *Kanko Maru* (2,929/38) 10 Jan 1942, PC #*No. 13*, 3 Apr 1943, *Tateyama Maru* (1,990/—) 15 Mar 1943, #*Fukuei Maru* (1,113/—) 1 Apr 1943.

SS 178 *Permit* Decomm 15 Nov 1945. †
10* Philippines 1942, 4th Bonins Raid; 14 patrols.
Ships sunk: *Hokuto Maru* (2,267/23) 4 Feb 1943, *Hisashima Maru* (2,742/—) 8 Mar 1943, *Banshu Maru No. 33* (787/—) 6 Jul 1943, *Showa Maru* (2,212/20) 7 Jul 1943, Soviet trawler *No. 20*, 9 Jul 1943 (in error), AO *Shiretoko* damaged 13 Sep 1943.

SS 179 *Plunger* Slipped off blocks in drydock and fell over, Pearl Harbor, 17 Feb 1942. Hit reef and damaged in Solomon Is., 2 Nov 1942. Decomm 15 Nov 1945. Reserve TS May 1946. †
14* Pearl Harbor, Guadalcanal, Eastern New Guinea, Midway, Gilbert Is., 1st Bonins Raid, 12 patrols.
Ships sunk: *Eizan Maru* (4,702/—) 18 Jan 1942, *Unkai Maru No. 5* (3,282/00) 30 Jun 1942, *Unyo Maru No. 3* (2,997/18) 2 Jul 1942, AO *Iro* damaged west of Jaluit 28 Feb 1943, AW *Taihosan Maru* (1,805/37) 12 Mar 1943, *Tatsutake Maru* (7,068/39) *Kinai Maru* (8,360/30) 10 May 1943, *Niitaka Maru* (2,478/04) 12 Jul 1943, *Seitai Maru* (3,404/18) 20 Aug 1943, *Ryokai Maru* (4,655/11) 22 Aug 1943, *Toyo Maru No. 5* (2,193/18) *Toyo Maru No. 8* (2,191/18) 2 Feb 1944, *Kimishima Maru* (5,193/38) 23 Feb 1944.

SS 180 *Pollack* Decomm 21 Sep 1945. Stricken 29 Oct 1946. Sold 2 Feb 1947; BU Philadelphia.
10* Pearl Harbor, Midway, 11 patrols.
Ships sunk: *Unkai Maru No. 1* (2,225/32) 7 Jan 1942, *Teian Maru* (5,387/28 ex-Yugoslav *Tomislav*) 9 Jan 1942, *Fukushu Maru* (1,454/03), *Baikal Maru* (5,266/21) 11 Mar 1942,; §*Asama Maru* (4,891/01) 26 Jan 1943, XPG *Terushima Maru* (3,110/37) 18 May 1943, XCL *Bangkok Maru* (5,350/37) 20 May 1943, *Taifuku Maru* (3,520/39) 27 Aug 1943, *Tagonoura Maru* (3,521/—) 3 Sep 1943, *Hakuyo Maru* (1,327/29) 20 Mar 1944, PC *PC-54*, 25 Mar 1944, *Tosei Maru* (2,814/—) 3 Apr 1944, DD *Asanagi* 22 May 1944.

SS 181 *Pompano* Missing east of Honshu, Sep 1943 (76 killed).
7* Pearl Harbor, Midway; seven patrols.
Ships sunk: Tkr *Tokyo Maru* (902/37) 25 May 1942, *Atsuta Maru* (7,983/09) 30 May 1942, §unknown (4,000/—) 12 Aug 1942, *Nankai Maru* (451/—) 1 Sep 1943, +*Akama Maru* (5,600/—) 3 Sep 1943, §*Taiko Maru* (2,958/19) ?25 Sep 1943.

*joint attack; +probable sinking; #possible sinking; § question on sinking

Salmon Class

No.	Name	Builder	Keel Laid	Launched	Comm.
SS 182	*Salmon*	Electric Boat	15 Apr 1936	12 Jun 1937	15 Mar 1938
SS 183	*Seal*	Electric Boat	25 May 1936	25 Aug 1937	30 Apr 1938
SS 184	*Skipjack*	Electric Boat	22 Jul 1936	23 Oct 1937	30 Jun 1938
SS 185	*Snapper*	Portsmouth NYd	23 Jul 1936	24 Aug 1937	15 Mar 1938
SS 186	*Stingray*	Portsmouth NYd	1 Oct 1936	6 Oct 1937	15 Mar 1938
SS 187	*Sturgeon*	Mare I. NYd	27 Oct 1936	15 Mar 1938	25 Jun 1938

Displacement	1,435/2,210 tons
Dimensions	308' (oa) x 26'2" x 17'6"
Machinery	2 screws; gear electric drive: SHP 6,140, 21.4 knots; electric: HP 2,860, 9 knots
Endurance	11,000/10; depth: 250'
Complement	59/75
Armament	1–3"/50, 8–21" TT

Notes: Similar to *Perch* class, but interior arrangements differed. Torpedo capacity increased to 24. SS 182–84 reengined 1944.

Service Records:

SS 182 *Salmon* Damaged by gunfire and depth charges off Kyushu, 30 Oct 1944, not repaired. Decomm 24 Sep 1945. Stricken 11 Oct 1945. Sold 4 Apr 1946; BU.
9* Philippines 1942, 11 patrols. PUC.

Figure 6.16: *Seal* (SS 183), 22 Jun 1944, with the deck gun moved to forward position. The conning tower has been substantially cut down.

Ships sunk: AR *Asahi* (xBB) 25 May 1942, *Ganges Maru* (4,382/18) 28 May 1942, AR *Oregon Maru* (5,873/20) 17 Nov 1942, *Wakanoura Maru* (2,411/85) 10 Aug 1943, tkr **Takane Maru* (10,021/—) 30 Oct 1944.

SS 183 *Seal* Damaged when rammed by enemy ship off Palau, 16 Nov 1942. Decomm 15 Nov 1945. NRT, 19 Nov 1947. †
10* Philippines 1942, Marshall Is., twelve patrols.
Ships sunk: *Soryu Maru* (856/23) 23 Dec 1941, **Tatsufuku Maru* (1,946/—) 28 May 1942, *Boston Maru* (5,477/19) 16 Nov 1942, tkr *San Clemente Maru* (7,354/37) 4 May 1943, *Tosei Maru* (531/—) 24 Aug 1944, DD *Namikaze* (irreparable damage) 8 Sep 1944, *Shonan Maru* (5,859/—) 9 Sep 1944, *Hakuyo Maru* (5,742/20) 25 Oct 1944, +*Gassan Maru* (887/—) 13 Nov 1944.

SS 184 *Skipjack* Bikini target ship, sunk in second test, raised. Decomm 11 Dec 1946. Stricken 13 Sep 1948. Sunk as target off San Clemente, Calif., 11 Aug 1948.
7* Philippines 1942, Solomons, raid on Truk, 2/44, Marianas Raids 2/44; ten patrols.
Ships sunk: *Kanan Maru* (2,567/20) 6 May 1942, *Bujun Maru* (4,804/29) 8 May 1942, *Tazan Maru* (5,478/19) 17 May 1942, *Shunko Maru* (6,781/19) 14 Oct 1942, AV *Okitsu Maru* (6,666/39) 26 Jan 1944, DD *Suzukaze* 26 Jan 1944.

SS 185 *Snapper* Damaged by aircraft bomb near Truk, 9 Jun 1944 (1 killed). Decomm 17 Nov 1945. Stricken 30 Apr 1948, sold 18 May 1949; BU.
6* Philippines 1942; ten patrols.
Ships sunk: #*Tokai Maru* (8,359/30) 27 Aug 1943, PF *Mutsure* 2 Sep 1943, *Kenryu Maru* (4,575/35) 29 Nov 1943, *Seian Maru* (1,990/11) and CMc *Ajiro* 1 Oct 1944.

SS 186 *Stingray* Decomm 17 Oct 1945. Stricken 3 Jul 1946. Sold 6 Jan 1947; BU Philadelphia.
12* Philippines 1942, Solomons, Saipan, Philippine Sea, 16 patrols.
Ships sunk: *Harbin Maru* (5,167/15) 10 Jan 1942, XPG *Saikyo Maru* (1,292/36) 28 Jun 1942, §*Tamon Maru* (8,156/19) 2 May 1943, *Ikushima Maru* (3,943/36) 30 Mar 1944.

SS 187 *Sturgeon* Decomm 15 Nov 1945. Stricken 30 Apr 1948, sold 12 Jun 1948; BU.
10* Philippines 1942, Dutch Indies, Solomons, eleven patrols.
Ships sunk: *Choko Maru* (842/41) 30 Mar 1942, PF §unknown 3 Apr 1942, *Montevideo Maru* (7,267/26) 1 Jul 1942 (1,035 POWs lost), AKV *Katsuragi Maru* (8,033/31) 1 Oct 1942, *Erie Maru* (5,493/20) 11 Jan 1944, DD *Suzutsuki* damaged 16 Jan 1944, *Chosen Maru* (3,110/11) 24 Jan 1944, *Seiryu Maru* (1,904/26) 11 May 1944, *Toyama Maru* (7,089/15) 29 Jun 1944, *Tairin Maru* (6,862/44) 3 Jul 1944.

Figure 6.17: *Seadragon* (SS 194), 24 May 1945, at Hunters Point, Calif. Numbers were not worn during the war.

Figure 6.18: *Sealion* (SS 195), of the new *S* class, about 1940. She was damaged by Japanese bombs at Cavite, Luzon, on December 10, 1941, and had to be scuttled to prevent capture.

Sargo Class

No.	Name	Builder	Keel Laid	Launched	Comm.
SS 188	*Sargo*	Electric Boat	12 May 1937	6 Jun 1938	7 Feb 1939
SS 189	*Saury*	Electric Boat	28 Jun 1937	20 Aug 1938	3 Apr 1939
SS 190	*Spearfish*	Electric Boat	9 Sep 1937	29 Oct 1938	1 Jul 1939
SS 191	*Sculpin*	Portsmouth NYd	7 Sep 1937	27 Jul 1938	16 Jan 1939
SS 192	*Squalus*	Portsmouth NYd	18 Oct 1937	14 Sep 1938	1 Mar 1939
SS 193	*Swordfish*	Mare I. NYd	27 Oct 1937	1 Apr 1939	22 Jul 1939
SS 194	*Seadragon*	Electric Boat	18 Apr 1938	21 Apr 1939	23 Oct 1939
SS 195	*Sealion*	Electric Boat	20 Jun 1938	25 May 1939	27 Nov 1939
SS 196	*Searaven*	Portsmouth NYd	9 Aug 1938	21 Jun 1939	2 Oct 1939
SS 197	*Seawolf*	Portsmouth NYd	27 Sep 1938	15 Aug 1939	1 Dec 1939

Displacement	1,460/2,350 tons
Dimensions	310'6" (oa) x 26'10" x 16'7"
Machinery	2 screws; geared electric drive, SHP 6,140, 21 knots/ electric, HP 2740, 8.75 knots
Endurance	11,000/10; depth: 250'
Complement	59/78
Armament	1–3"/50, 8–21" TT

Notes: Repeat *Salmon* class. Corning tower cut down, gun moved forward. SS 194–97 all electric drive. *Seadragon* christened on 11 Apr 1939 but stuck on ways until 21 April. SS 188–90, 194, reengined 1944.

Service Records:

SS 188 *Sargo* Decomm 22 Jun 1946. Stricken 19 Jul 1946. Sold 19 May 1947; BU Oakland.
8* Philippines 1942, Solomons, 12 patrols.
Ships sunk: *Teibo Maru* (4,472/23, ex-Danish *Nordbo*) 25 Sep 1942, *Konan Maru* (5,226/18) 13 Jun 1943, *Taga Maru* (2,868/39) 9 Nov 1943, *Kosei Maru* (3,551/37) 11 Nov 1943, AE *Nichiro Maru* (6,534/39) 17 Feb 1944, AO *Sata* damaged 17 Feb 1944, *Uchide Maru* (5,275/19) 29 Feb 1944, *Wazan Maru* (4,851/18, ex-British *Vitorlock*) 26 Apr 1944.

* joint attack; +probable sinking; #possible sinking; § question on sinking

SS 189 *Saury* Damaged by depth charge attack east of Okinawa, 31 Jul 1944. Decomm 22 Jun 1946. Stricken 19 Jul 1946. Sold 19 May 1947; BU Oakland.
7* Philippines 1942, Makassar Strait, Bonins-Marianas 1944, Palau, 11 patrols.
Ships sunk: AKV *Kanto Maru* (8,606/30) 11 Sep 1942, *Kagi Maru* (2,343/07) 26 May 1943, tkr *Akatsuki Maru* (10,216/38) 28 May 1943, *Takamisan Maru* (1,992/28), *Shoko Maru* (5,385/—) 30 May 1943.

SS 190 *Spearfish* Effected last evacuation of officers and nurses from Corregidor, 3 May 1942. Decomm 22 Jun 1946. Stricken 19 Jul 1946. Sold 19 May 1947; BU Oakland.
10* Philippines 1942, Marshall Is., Solomons, 12 patrols.
Ships sunk: §Unknown 17 Apr 1942, +*Toba Maru* (6,995/16) 25 Apr 1942, *Tamashima Maru* (3,560/40) 30 Jan 1944, *Toyoura Maru* (2,510/13), AF *Mamiya* 6 May 1944.

SS 191 *Sculpin* Sunk by Japanese destroyer *Yamagumo* off Truk, 19 Nov 1943 (12 killed, including Capt. John Cromwell, and 51 as POWs).
8* Philippines 1942, Solomons; nine patrols.
Ships sunk: DD *Suzukaze* damaged off Kendari, Celebes 4 Feb 1942, *Naminoue Maru* (4,731/36) 7 Oct 1942, *Sumiyoshi Maru* (1,921/36) 14 Oct 1942, *Sagami Maru* (135/—) 19 Jun 1943, *Sekko Maru* (3,183/17) 9 Aug 1943.

SS 192 *Squalus* Foundered on trials off Portsmouth, N.H., 23 May 1939 (26 lost). Salved 13 Sep 1939. Renamed ***Sailfish***, 9 Feb 1940. Recomm 15 May 1940. Decomm 27 Oct 1945. Stricken 20 Apr 1948, sold 18 Jun 1948; BU Philadelphia.
9* Philippines 1942, Leyte; 12 patrols.
Ships sunk: *Kamogawa Maru* (6,440/38) 2 Mar 1942, *Shinju Maru* (3,617/—) 15 Jun 1943, *Iburi Maru* (3,291/38) 25 Jun 1943, CVE *Chuyo* 4 Dec 1943, *Totai Maru* (3,195/18) 13 Dec 1943, *Uyo Maru* (6,376/41) 21 Dec 1943, *Toan Maru* (2,110/43) 24 Aug 1944, DD *Harukaze* damaged in Luzon Strait 4 Nov 1944.

SS 193 *Swordfish* Evacuated Philippine President Manuel Quezon y Molinas from Mariveles to Panay, 20 Feb 1942. Missing south of Kyushu, Jan 1945 (89 killed), probably sunk by Japanese *CDS No. 4*, 5 Jan, or by mine, 9 Jan.
8* Philippines 1942, Solomons, 2nd Bonins Raid; 13 patrols.
Ships sunk: *Nikkoku Maru* (2,728/—) 13 Dec 1941, *Atsutasan Maru* (8,662/37) 16 Dec 1941, XPG *Myoken Maru* (4,124/38) 24 Jan 1942, +**Tatsufuku Maru* (1,946/—) 29 May 1942, *Burma Maru* (4,584/17) 12 Jun 1942, *Myoho Maru* (4,122/39) 19 Jan 1943, *Nishiyama Maru* (3,016/21) 22 Aug 1943, *Tenkai Maru* (3,203/17) 5 Sep 1943, *Yamakuni Maru* (6,921/38) 14 Jan 1944, XPG *Delhi Maru* (2,182/22) 16 Jan 1944, XPG *Kasagi Maru* (3,140/28) 27 Jan 1944, DD *Matsukaze* 9 Jun 1944, *Kanseishi Maru* (4,804/29) 15 Jun 1944.

SS 194 *Seadragon* Damaged by Japanese aircraft bombs at Cavite, 10 Dec 1941. Out of comm 15 Nov 1945–8 Feb 1946. Decomm 29 Oct 1946. Stricken 30 Apr 1948, sold 2 Jul 1948; BU Philadelphia.
11* Philippines 1942, Surigao Strait, 12 patrols.
Submarine sunk: *I-4* off Rabaul 20 Dec 1942.
Ships sunk: *Tamagawa Maru* (6,441/38) 2 Feb 1942, *Hiyama Maru* (6,171/—) or *Nichizan Maru* 12 Jul 1942, *Shinyo Maru* (4,163/38) 13 Jul 1942, *Hakodate Maru* (5,302/19) 16 Jul 1942, *Shigure Maru* (1,579/20) (2,445/—) 10 Oct 1942, AF *Irako* damaged 20 Jan 1944, *Taiju Maru* (6,886/44) 23 Apr 1944, *Eiko Maru* (1,843/03), *Daiten Maru* (6,442/42), *Kokuryu Maru* (7,369/37) 24 Oct 1944.

SS 195 *Sealion* Sunk by Japanese aircraft bombs at Cavite, 10 Dec 1941 (5 killed). Wreck blown up, 25 Dec 1941.
1* Philippines 1942.

SS 196 *Searaven* Damaged by fire off Timor, 23 Apr 1942, towed to Albany, Western Australia, by *Snapper*. Bikini target ship. Decomm 11 Dec 1946. Sunk as target off San Clemente, Calif., 11 Sep 1948.
10* Philippines 1942, Marshall Is., raid on Truk 2/44, Marianas Raids 2/44; three patrols.
Ships sunk: *Nissei Maru* (833/—) 17 Nov 1942, *Shirahane Maru* (5,693/18) 14 Jan 1943, YP *Ganjitsu Maru No. 1* (216/26) 14 Jan 1943, tkr *Toa Maru* (10,052/34) 25 Nov 1943, AM *Noshiro Maru No. 2* (216/23) 17 Apr 1944, *Rizan Maru* (4,747/—) 21 Sep 1944, DD *Momi* damaged 27 Sep 1944.

SS 197 *Seawolf* Brought supplies to Corregidor, 28 Jan 1942. Sunk in error by DE *Richard M. Rowell* and aircraft off Morotai, 3 Oct 1944 (99 killed).
13* Philippines 1942, Badoeng Strait, Philippine Sea; 15 patrols.
Ships sunk: CL *Naka* damaged off Christmas I. 1 Apr 1942, XPG *Nampo Maru* (1,206/40) 15 Jun 1942, *Hachigen Maru* (3,113/—) 14 Aug 1942, *Showa Maru* (1,349/—) 25 Aug 1942 (salved), *Gifu Maru* (2,933/21) 2 Nov 1942, *Sagami Maru* (7,189/39) 3 Nov 1942, XPG *Keiko Maru* (2,925/38) 8 Nov 1942, *Kaihei Maru* (4,575/34) 15 Apr 1943, AG *Banshu Maru* No. 5 (389/—) 19 Apr 1943, ODD *No. 39* (*xTade*) 23 Apr 1943, *Shojin Maru* (4,739/ 18) 20 Jun 1943, *Shoto Maru* (5,254/19), *Kokko Maru* (5,486/—), also TB *Sagi* damaged 31 Aug 1943; *Fusei Maru* (2,256/21, ex-British *Fansang*) 1 Sep 1943, *Wuhu Maru* (3,222/—) 29 Oct 1943, *Kaifuku Maru* (3,177/17) 4 Nov 1943, *Asuka Maru* (7,523/25), *Getsuyo Maru* (6,440/34) 10 Jan 1944; *Yahiko Maru* (5,747/26) 11 Jan 1944, *Yamazuru Maru* (3,651/38) 14 Jan 1944, **Tarushima Maru* (4,865/35) 17 Jan 1944.

Tambor Class

No.	Name	Builder	Keel Laid	Launched	Comm.
SS 198	*Tambor*	Electric Boat	16 Jan 1939	20 Dec 1939	3 Jun 1940
SS 199	*Tautog*	Electric Boat	1 Mar 1939	27 Jan 1940	3 Jul 1940
SS 200	*Thresher*	Electric Boat	27 Apr 1939	27 Mar 1940	27 Aug 1940
SS 201	*Triton*	Portsmouth NYd	5 Jul 1939	25 Mar 1940	15 Aug 1940
SS 202	*Trout*	Portsmouth NYd	28 Aug 1939	21 May 1940	15 Nov 1940
SS 203	*Tuna*	Mare I. NYd	19 Jul 1939	2 Oct 1940	2 Jan 1941
SS 206	*Gar*	Electric Boat	27 Dec 1939	7 Nov 1940	14 Apr 1941
SS 207	*Grampus*	Electric Boat	14 Feb 1940	23 Dec 1940	23 May 1941
SS 208	*Grayback*	Electric Boat	3 Apr 1940	31 Jan 1941	30 Jun 1941
SS 209	*Grayling*	Portsmouth NYd	15 Dec 1939	4 Sep 1940	1 Mar 1941
SS 210	*Grenadier*	Portsmouth NYd	2 Apr 1940	29 Nov 1940	1 May 1941
SS 211	*Gudgeon*	Mare I. NYd	22 Nov 1939	25 Jan 1941	21 Apr 1941

Displacement	1,475/2,370 tons
Dimensions	307'3" (oa) x 27'3" x 16'9"
Machinery	2 screws; diesel-electric: SHP 6,400; 20 knots; electric: HP 2,740, 8.75 knots
Endurance	11,000/10; depth: 250'
Complement	60/80
Armament	1–3"/50, 1–40mm AA, 10-21" TT

Notes: Six TT forward. 5"/51 gun replaced 3" in SS 198–200, 203, 206, 208 in 1944.

Service Records:

SS 198 *Tambor* Damaged by depth charges off Midway 5 Jun 1942. Decomm 10 Dec 1945. NRT. †
11* Wake I. Raid 1942, Midway, Guadalcanal; 12 patrols.
Ships sunk: *Kitami Maru* (394/30) 16 Apr 1942, AN *Shofuku Maru* (891/41) 7 Aug 1942, *Shinsei Maru No. 6* (4,928/38) 21 Aug 1942, *Chikugo Maru* (2,461/07) 3 Nov 1942, *Eisho Maru* (2,486/17, ex-Panamanian *Folozu*) 29 May 1943, *Eika Maru* (1,248/96) 2 Jun 1943, *Shuntai Maru* (2,253/20) 29 Jan 1944, tkr *Ariake Maru* (5,149/—), tkr

*joint attack; +probable sinking; #possible sinking; § question on sinking

Goyo Maru (8,496/39) 3 Feb 1944; tkr *Ronsan Maru* (2,735/29) 12 Feb 1944, *Chiyo Maru* (657/35) 26 May 1944, *Toei Maru* (2,324/01) 13 Aug 1944.

SS 199 *Tautog* Decomm 8 Dec 1945. NRT. †
14* Pearl Harbor; 13 patrols.
Submarine sunk: *I-28* southeast of Truk 17 May 1942.
Ships sunk: *Shoka Maru* (4,467/35) 25 May 1942, *Ohio Maru* (5,872/20) 6 Aug 1942, unknown (5,000/—) 27 Oct 1942, *Banshu Maru No. 2* (998/—) 25 Dec 1942, *Yashima Maru* (1,873/—) 22 Jan 1943, DD *Isonami*, *Penang Maru* (5,214/13) 9 Apr 1943, *Shinei Maru* (973/17) 6 Jun 1943, *Meiten Maru* (4,474/38) 20 Jun 1943, SC §*No. 30* 4 Nov 1943, *Saishu Maru* (2,082/97) 3 Jan 1944, *Usa Maru* (3,943/—) 4 Jan 1944, *Ryua Maru* (1,915/—), *Shojin Maru* (1,925/—) 13 Mar 1944; DD *Shirakumo*, *Nichiren Maru* (5,460/20) 16 Mar 1944, *Ryoyo Maru* (5,973/31) 2 May 1944, *Fushimi Maru* (4,935/37) 3 May 1944, *Miyazaki Maru* (3,944/—) 8 May 1944, *Banei Maru No. 2* (1,186/17) 12 May 1944, *Matsu Maru* (887/—) 8 Jul 1944, *Konei Maru* (1,922/17, ex-Italian *Furiere Consolini*) 2 Aug 1944, LST No. 15 17 Jan 1945, AGP *Shuri Maru* (1,857/28) 20 Jan 1945.

SS 200 *Thresher* Out of comm 13 Dec 1945–6 Feb 1946. Decomm 12 Jul 1946. Stricken 23 Dec 1947. Sold 18 Mar 1948; BU Everett, Mass.
15* Pearl Harbor, Iwo Jima, Okinawa; 15 patrols.
Ships sunk: *Sado Maru* (3,039/—) 10 Apr 1942, AGP *Shinsho Maru* (4,836/36) 9 Jul 1942, #unknown (3,000/—) 31 Oct 1942, *Hachian Maru* (2,733/03, ex-British *Kinshan*) 29 Dec 1942, *Kuwayama Maru* (5,724/—) 21 Feb 1943, tkr *Toen Maru* (5,232/17) 2 Mar 1943, *Yoneyama Maru* (5,274/19) sunk, DD *Hokaze* damaged 1 Jul 1943; *Muko Maru* (4,862/37) 13 Nov 1943, *Tatsuno Maru* (6,960/16), *Toho Maru* (4,092/38) 15 Jan 1944; *Kikuzuki Maru* (1,266/—), *Kosei Maru* (2,205/24) 27 Jan 1944; *Sainei Maru* (4,916/—), *Shozan Maru* (2,838/18) 17 Jul 1944; *Gyoku Maru* (6,854/40 ex-British *Empire Lantern*) 18 Sep 1944, *Nissei Maru* (1,468/89) 25 Sep 1944, *Koetsu Maru* (873/—) 26 Sep 1944.

SS 201 *Triton* Sunk by Japanese destroyer *Satsuki* north of Admiralty Is., 15 Mar 1943 (74 killed).
5* Wake I. Raid, Solomons; six patrols.
Submarine sunk: *I-64* 230 miles southeast of Kagoshima 17 May 1942.
Ships sunk: XPG *Shinyo Maru No. 5* (1,498/37) 17 Feb 1942, *Shokyu Maru* (4,484/07) 21 Feb 1942, YP §unknown (1,000/—) 23 Apr 1942, *Calcutta Maru* (5,339/17) 1 May 1942, *Taiei Maru* (2,209/18), *Taigen Maru* (5,660/17) 6 May 1942; DD *Nenohi* at Agattu, Aleutians, 4 Jul 1942, AW *Amakasu Maru No. 1* (1,913/39) 24 Dec 1942, *Omi Maru* (3,393/12) 28 Dec 1942, +*Kiriha Maru* (3,057/19) 6 Mar 1943.

SS 202 *Trout* Delivered ammunition and evacuated 20 tons of gold from Bataan, 6 Feb 1942. Probably sunk by Japanese destroyer *Asashimo* southeast of Okinawa, 29 Feb 1944 (81 killed).
11* Pearl Harbor, Philippines 1942, Midway, 11 patrols. PUC.
Submarine sunk: §*I-182* 9 Sep 1943.
Ships sunk: XPG *Chuwa Maru* (2,719/40) 10 Feb 1942, *Uzan Maru* (5,014/—) 2 May 1942, XPG *Kongosan Maru* (2,119/27) 4 May 1942, AN *Koei Maru* (863/41) 21 Sep 1942, CVE *Taiyo* damaged east of Truk 28 Sep 1942, +unknown (2,984/—) 21 Jan 1943, XPG *Hirotama Maru* (1,911/33) 14 Feb 1943, tkr *Sanraku Maru* (3,000/4?) 15 Jun 1943, Isuzu Maru (2,866/—) 2 Jul 1943, *Ryotoku Maru* (3,483/38), *Yamashiro Maru* (3,429/12) 23 Sep 1943; *Sakito Maru* (7,126/38) 29 Feb 1944.

SS 203 *Tuna* Damaged by Australian aircraft in error off Brisbane, 29 Jul 1943. Bikini target. Decomm 11 Dec 1946. Stricken 21 Oct 1948. Sunk as target off Point Loma, Calif., 24 Sep 1948.
7* Midway, Solomons; 13 patrols.
Ships sunk: §Unknown (4,000/—) 4 Mar 1942, *Toyohara Maru* (805/23) 15 May 1942, *Kurohime Maru* (4,697/20) 30 Mar 1943, *Tosei Maru* (5,484/26) 12 Dec 1943.

SS 206 *Gar* Decomm 11 Dec 1945. †
11* Palau-Yap Raids 3/44, 1st Bonins Raid, 2nd Bonins Raid, Bonins-Yap Raids, Palau; 15 patrols.
Ships sunk: *Chichibu Maru* (1,462/23) 13 Mar 1942, *Heinan Maru* (6,61/41) 8 Dec 1942, YP *Jimbo Maru No. 12* (1,92/—) 2 May 1943, *Kotoku Maru* (164/—) 6 May 1943, XPG *Aso Maru* (703/32) 9 May 1943, *Meikai Maru* (3,197/17), *Indus Maru* (4,361/18) 15 May 1943; *Seizan Maru* (955/18) 20 Aug 1943, *Koyu Maru* (5,325/21) 20 Jan 1944, *Taian Maru* (3,670/36) 23 Jan 1944.

SS 207 *Grampus* Sunk by Japanese warships off New Georgia, 5 Mar 1943 (71 killed).
3* Solomons; six patrols.
Ship sunk: Tkr *Kaijo Maru No. 2* (8,636/37) 1 Mar 1942.

SS 208 *Grayback* Sunk by Japanese aircraft in East China Sea, 27 Feb 1944 (80 killed).
8* Solomons, Bonins-Yap Raids; ten patrols.
Submarine sunk: SS §*I-18* 2 Jan 1943.
Ships sunk: *Ishikari Maru* (3,291/38) 17 Mar 1942, *Yodogawa Maru* (6,441/38) 11 May 1943, DD *Yugure* damaged 16 May 1943, *England Maru* (5,830/19) 17 May 1943, *Kozui Maru* (7,072/37) 14 Oct 1943, *Awata Maru* (7,397/37) 22 Oct 1943, *Gyokurei Maru* (5,588/—) 18 Dec 1943, DD *Numakaze* off Okinawa 19 Dec 1943, *Konan Maru* (2,627/15), AN *Kashiwa Maru* (515/38) 21 Dec 1943, *Taikei Maru* (4,739/—), *Toshin Maru* (1,917/—) 19 Feb 1944; tkr *Nampo Maru* (10,033/43) 24 Feb 1944, *Ceylon Maru* (4,905/04) 27 Feb 1944.

SS 209 *Grayling* Missing near Lingayen Gulf, Sep 1943 (76 killed). (Probably rammed and sunk by transport *Hukuan Maru* west of Luzon, 9 Sep 1943.)
6* Midway, Solomons; eight patrols.
Ships sunk: *Ryujin Maru* (6,243/07) 13 Apr 1942, *Ushio Maru* (749/—) 26 Jan 1943, *Shanghai Maru* (4,103/19) 9 Apr 1943, +*Meizan Maru* (5,480/18) 27 Aug 1943.

SS 210 *Grenadier* Damaged by Japanese aircraft off Penang and scuttled, 22 Apr 1943 (4 died as POWs).
4* Midway; six patrols.
Ships sunk: Soviet *Angarstroi* (4,761/27) 1 May 1942, in error, AP *Taiyo Maru* (14,457/11) 8 May 1942.

SS 211 *Gudgeon* Missing in Marianas Is., Apr 1944 (78 killed). (Probably sunk by Japanese aircraft southwest of Iwo Jima, 18 Apr 1944.)
11* Pearl Harbor, Midway, Solomons, 12 patrols. PUC.
Submarine sunk: SS *I-73* southwest of Oahu 27 Jan 1942.
Ships sunk: Unknown (4,000/—) 26 Mar 1942, *Nissho Maru* (6,526/39) 27 Mar 1942, *Naniwa Maru* (4,858/37) 3 Aug 1942, *Choko Maru* (6,783/20) 21 Oct 1942, *Meigen Maru* (5,434/20) 22 Mar 1943, tkr *Toho Maru* (9997/36) 29 Mar 1943, AP *Kamakura Maru* (17,526/30) 28 Apr 1943, *Sumatra Maru* (5,862/17) 12 May 1943, *Taian Maru* (3,158/17) 28 Sep 1943, *Nekka Maru* (6,784/35) 23 Nov 1943, PF *Wakamiya* 23 Nov 1943.

Mackerel Class

No.	Name	Builder	Keel Laid	Launched	Comm.
SS 204	*Mackerel*	Electric Boat	6 Oct 1939	28 Sep 1940	31 Mar 1941
SS 205	*Marlin*	Portsmouth NYd	28 May 1940	29 Jan 1941	1 Aug 1941

Displacement	SS 204: 825/1,190 tons; SS 205: 800/1,165 tons
Dimensions	SS 204: 243'1" (oa) x 22'1" x 14'6"; SS 205: 238'11" (oa) x 21'8" x 13'6"
Machinery	2 screws; SS 204: HP 1,800/1,500; 14.5/9 knots; SS 205: HP 1,700/1,500; 14.5 9 knots
Endurance	SS 204: 6,500/10; SS 205: 7,400/10; depth: 250'
Complement	42
Armament	1–3"/50, 1–40mm AA, 6–21" TT

Notes: Experimental types. Used for training at New London.

*joint attack; +probable sinking; #possible sinking; § question on sinking

Figure 6.19: *Marlin* (SS 205), Jun 1943, one of two smaller experimental submarines, used for training. The shape of their conning towers differed.

Service Records:

SS 204 *Mackerel* Neutrality patrol. Two patrols. Decomm 9 Nov 1945. Stricken 28 Nov 1945. Sold 24 Apr 1947; BU Philadelphia.

SS 205 *Marlin* Two patrols. Slightly damaged in collision with *SC-642* off Portsmouth, N.H., 26 Jul 1944. Decomm 9 Nov 1945. Stricken 28 Nov 1945. Sold 29 Mar 1946; BU Baltimore.

Gato Class

No.	Name	Builder	Keel Laid	Launched	Comm.
SS 212	*Gato*	Electric Boat	5 Oct 1940	21 Aug 1941	31 Dec 1941
SS 213	*Greenling*	Electric Boat	12 Nov 1940	20 Sep 1941	21 Jan 1942
SS 214	*Grouper*	Electric Boat	28 Dec 1940	27 Oct 1941	12 Feb 1942
SS 215	*Growler*	Electric Boat	10 Feb 1941	22 Nov 1941	20 Mar 1942
SS 216	*Grunion*	Electric Boat	1 Mar 1941	22 Dec 1941	11 Apr 1942
SS 217	*Guardfish*	Electric Boat	1 Apr 1941	20 Jan 1942	8 May 1942

Displacement	1,525/2,415 tons
Dimensions	311'9" (oa) x 27'3" x 15'3"
Machinery	2 screws; diesel-electric: SHP 5,400; 20.25 knots; electric: HP 2,740, 8.75 knots
Endurance	11,000/10; depth: 300'
Complement	60/81
Armament	1–3"/50, then 1–5"/25, 1–40mm AA, 10–21" TT

Notes: Seventy-seven units built. This class built with 9/16" pressure hulls. Capacity 24 torpedoes. *Barb* fitted with rocket-launcher 1945. CT cut down from original silhouette. *Flying Fish* fitted with 2–5"/53 guns 1945. SS 253–264 received new engines 1943–44.

Service Notes:

SS 212 *Gato* Decomm 16 Mar 1946. NRT. †
13* Midway, Solomons, Truk Raid 4/44, 4th Bonins Raid, Bonins-Yap Raids, Iwo Jima, Okinawa, Raids on Japan 7–8/45; 13 patrols. Tokyo Bay. PUC.
Ships sunk: *Kenkon Maru* (4,575/35) 21 Jan 1943, *Nichiun Maru* (2,723/—) 29 Jan 1943, *Suruga Maru* (991/38) 15 Feb 1943, *Columbia Maru* (5,618/27) 30 Nov 1943, *Tsuneshima Maru* (2,926/42) 20 Dec 1943, §*Yamashimo Maru* (6,777/38) 22 Feb 1944, *Daigen Maru No. 3* (5,256/08) 26 Feb 1944, *Okinoyama Maru No. 3* (871/30) 12 Mar 1944, PF *No. 9* 14 Feb 1945, *Tairiku Maru* (2,325/13, ex-Greek *Karavados*) 21 Feb 1945, PC *No. 42* damaged 3 Aug 1945.

* joint attack; +probable sinking; #possible sinking; § question on sinking

Figure 6.20: *Gato* (SS 212), on 30 Dec 1941 at Groton, Conn., looking forward, one day before commissioning.

SS 213 *Greenling* Decomm 16 Oct 1946. NRT Dec 1946.†
10* Midway, Solomons, Marshall Is., 12 patrols.
Ships sunk: XPG *Kinjosan Maru* (3,262/36) 4 May 1942, *Brasil Maru* (12,752/39) 5 Aug 1942, *Palao Maru* (4,495/34) 6 Aug 1942, *Kinkai Maru* (5,852/17) 3 Oct 1942, *Setsuyo Maru* (4,147/—) 4 Oct 1942, *Takusei Maru* (3,515/19) 14 Oct 1942, *Hakonesan Maru* (6,673/29) 18 Oct 1942, ODD *No. 35* (ex-*Tsuta*) 22 Dec 1942, *Ryufuku Maru* or unknown (4,000/—) 30 Dec 1942, *Hiteru Maru* (5,857/—) 30 Dec 1942, *Kinposan Maru* (3,261/36) 16 Jan 1943, *Shoho Maru* (1,936/37) 31 Dec 1943, *Kiri Maru* No. 8 (939/37), tkr *Kota Maru* (975/—) 7 Nov 1944; ODD *No. 46* (ex-*Yugao*) 10 Nov 1944.

SS 214 *Grouper* †
10* Midway, Solomons, Saipan, Palau, Philippines Raids 9/44, Iwo Jima, Okinawa, 12 patrols.
Ships sunk: *Tone Maru* (4,070/20) 21 Sep 1942, *Lisbon Maru* (7,053/20) 1 Oct 1942 (846 POWs lost), *Bandoeng Maru* (4,003/20) 17 Dec 1942, tkr *Nanmei No. 6* (834/—), *Kumanoyama Maru* (2,857/43) 24 Jun 1944.

SS 215 *Growler* Damaged by gunfire when ramming Japanese supply ship *Hayasaki* off New Britain, 7 Feb 1943 (Cdr Howard W. Gilmore killed, "Take her down!"). Sunk by Japanese destroyer *Shigure*, torpedo boat *Chiburi* and frigate *No. 19* off Mindoro, 8 Nov 1944 (85 killed).
8* Midway, Philippine Sea, Solomons; 11 patrols.
Ships sunk: DD *Arare* sunk, *Kasumi* and *Shiranuhi* damaged off Kiska 5 Jul 1942; XPG *Senyo Maru* (2,904/37) 25 Aug 1942, *Eifuku Maru* (5,866/18) 31 Aug 1942, AE *Kashino* 4 Sep 1942, *Taika Maru* (2,204/21) 7 Sep 1942, *Chifuku Maru* (5,857/19) 16 Jan 1943, *Miyadono Maru* (5,196/18) 19 Jun 1943, *Katori Maru* (1,920/38) 29 Jun 1944, DD *Shikinami*, PF *Hirado* 12 Sep 1944.

Figure 6.21: *Grenadier* (SS 210), 27 Dec 1941, with conning tower as originally built and deck gun aft.

SS 216 *Grunion* Missing off Kiska, Aleutians, after 30 Jul 1942 (70 killed). (Probably sunk by gunfire of torpedoed Japanese transport *Kashima Maru* near Kiska, 31 Jul 1942.)
1*; 1 patrol.
Ships sunk: *PC-25* and *PC-27* 15 Jul 1942.
SS 217 *Guardfish:* Torpedoed and sank USS *Extractor* in error off Guam, 24 Jan 1945. Decomm 25 May 1946.
11* Solomons, Finschhafen, Iwo Jima, Okinawa, 12 patrols. Two PUC.
Ships sunk: *Seikai Maru* (3,109/19) 24 Aug 1942, *Teikyu Maru* (2,332/30 ex–Danish *Gustav Diederichsen*) 2 Sep 1942, *Chita Maru* (2,276/23), *Tenyu Maru* (3,738/05), *Kaimei Maru* (5,254/19 ex–Panamanian *Carmar*) 4 Sep 1942; unknown (4,000/—), *Nichiho Maru* (6,363/12) 21 Oct 1942; ODD *No. 1* (ex–*Shimakaze*) 12 Jan 1943, +unknown 22 Jan 1943, DD *Hakaze* 23 Jan 1943, *Suzuya Maru* (901/22) 13 Jun 1943, *Kashu Maru* (5,460/19) 8 Oct 1943, tkr *Kenyo Maru* (1,0022/39) 14 Jan 1944, DD *Umikaze* 1 Feb 1944, *Jinzan Maru* (5,215/19), *Mantai Maru* (5,863/19) 16 Jul 1944; *Hiyama Maru* (2,838/—) 17 Jul 1944, *Teiryu Maru* (6,550/15) 19 Jul 1944, *Miyakawa Maru* No. 2 (873/—) 25 Sep 1944.

No.	Name	Builder	Keel Laid	Launched	Comm.
SS 218	*Albacore*	Electric Boat	21 Apr 1941	17 Feb 1942	1 Jun 1942
SS 219	*Amberjack*	Electric Boat	15 May 1941	6 Mar 1942	19 Jun 1942
SS 220	*Barb*	Electric Boat	7 Jun 1941	2 Apr 1942	8 Jul 1942
SS 221	*Blackfish*	Electric Boat	1 Jul 1941	18 Apr 1942	22 Jul 1942
SS 222	*Bluefish*	Electric Boat	5 Jun 1942	21 Feb 1943	24 May 1943
SS 223	*Bonefish*	Electric Boat	25 Jun 1942	7 Mar 1943	31 May 1943
SS 224	*Cod*	Electric Boat	21 Jul 1942	21 Mar 1943	21 Jun 1943
SS 225	*Cero*	Electric Boat	24 Aug 1942	4 Apr 1943	4 Jul 1943
SS 226	*Corvina*	Electric Boat	21 Sep 1942	9 May 1943	6 Aug 1943
SS 227	*Darter*	Electric Boat	20 Oct 1942	6 Jun 1943	7 Sep 1943

Service Records:

SS 218 *Albacore* Sunk by mine off Northeast Hokkaido, 7 Nov 1944 (86 killed).
9* Eastern New Guinea, Solomons, New Georgia Ldgs., Arawe, Bonins-Yap Raids, Philippine Sea., 11 patrols. PUC.
Ships sunk: CL *Tenryu* 18 Dec 1942, DD *Oshio*, PF unknown 20 Feb 1943; XPG *Heijo Maru* (2,627/41) 4 Sep 1943, *Kenzan Maru* (4,705/19) 25 Nov 1943, XPG *Choko Maru* (2,629/27), DD *Sazanami* 14 Jan 1944, CV *Taiho* 19 Jun 1944, *Shingetsu Maru* (880/—) 5 Sep 1944, SC-165 11 Sep 1944.

SS 219 *Amberjack* Sunk by Japanese torpedo boat *Hayadori* and SC-18 off Rabaul, 14 Feb 1943 (74 killed).
3* Solomons; three patrols.
Ships sunk: *Shirogane Maru* (3,130/38) 19 Sep 1942, XPG Senkai Maru (2,095/26) 7 Oct 1942, tkr *Tonan Maru No. 2* (1,9262/37) 10 Oct 1942 (salved).

SS 220 *Barb* Rescued 14 POW survivors of *Rakuyo Maru*, 17 Sep 1944. Made first rocket attack by submarine, Jun 1945. Decomm 12 Feb 1947. †
8* North Africa, Philippines Raids 9/44, Luzon, Raids on Japan 7–8/45, PUC. 12 patrols (five in Europe).
Ships sunk: Spanish tkr +*Campomanes* (6,276/32) damaged, in error, Bay of Biscay 26 Dec 1942, *Fukusei Maru* (2,219/—) 28 Mar 1944, *Koto Maru* (1,053/39), *Madras Maru* (3,802/19) 31 May 1944; *Toten Maru* (3,823/00), *Chihaya Maru* (1,161/18) 11 Jun 1944; *Takashima Maru* (5,633/—) 13 Jun 1944, *Okuni Maru* (5,633/01), *Hinode Maru No. 20* (281/—) 31 Aug 1944; tkr *Azusa Maru* (10,022/44), CVE *Unyo* southeast of Hong Kong 16 Sep 1944; *Gokoku Maru* (10,438/41) 10 Nov 1944, *Naruo Maru* (4,823/—) 12 Nov 1944, tkr *Tatsuyo Maru* (6,892/44), tkr *Sanyo Maru* (2,854/—), *Anyo Maru* (9,256/13) 8 Jan 1945; *Taikyo Maru* (5,244/—) 23 Jan 1945, *Sapporo Maru No. 11* (2,820/00) 5 Jul 1945, *Toyu Maru* (1,256/—) 15 Jul 1945, PF *No. 112* 18 Jul 1945.

SS 221 *Blackfish* Decomm 11 May 1946. †
8* North Africa, Finschhafen, Arawe, Palau-Yap Raids 3/44, Leyte, Iwo Jima, Okinawa, Raids on Japan 7–8/45; 12 patrols (five in Atlantic).
Ships sunk: German PC *VP-408* (ex–*Haltenbank*, 444/34) in Bay of Biscay 19 Feb 1943, *Kaika Maru* (2,087/—) 16 Jan 1944.

SS 222 *Bluefish* Decomm 12 Feb 1947. †
10* Honshu Raid 2/45, Iwo Jima, Honshu Raid 2/45, Okinawa, nine patrols.
Submarine sunk: *I-351* north of Borneo 14 Jul 1945.
Ships sunk: TB *Kasasagi* 26 Sep 1943, *Akashi Maru* (3,228/18) 27 Sep 1943, tkr *Kyokuei Maru* (10,570/—) 8 Nov 1943, DD *Sanaye* 18 Nov 1943, AO *Ondo* beached off Cavite 18 Nov 1943, tkr *Ichiyu Maru* (5,061/—) 30 Dec 1943, tkr *Hakko Maru* (6,046/—) 4 Jan 1944, tkr *Ominesan Maru* (10,536/43) 4 Mar 1944, *Nanshin Maru* (1,422/30) 16 Jun 1944, *Kanan Maru* (3,312/31) 21 Jun 1944, **Shinpo Maru* (5,135/) 12 Aug 1944, AO *Hayasui* 19 Aug 1944, *SC-50* 9 Jul 1945.

SS 223 *Bonefish* Sunk by Japanese warships in Toyama Bay, 18 Jun 1945 (85 killed).
7* Philippines Raids 9/44, Okinawa; eight patrols.
Ships sunk: *Kashima Maru* (9,908/13) 27 Sep 1943, *Teibi Maru* (10,086/26, ex–French *Bernardin de St. Pierre*) 10 Oct 1943, *Isuzugawa Maru* (4,212/—) 10 Oct 1943, *Suez Maru* (4,646/19) 29 Nov 1943 (~540 POWs lost), *Nichiryo Maru* (2,721/40) 1 Dec 1943, *Tokiwa Maru* (806/—) 26 Apr 1944, DD *Inazuma* 14 May 1944, *Ryuei Maru* (207/—) 7 Jul 1944, tkr *Kokuyo Maru* (10,026/38) 30 Jul 1944, AO *Kamoi* damaged 27 Sep 1944, tkr *Anjo Maru* (2,068/31 ex–Dutch *Angelina*) 28 Sep 1944, *Fushimi Maru* (2,542/02) 14 Oct 1944, *Oshikasan* (or *Oshikayama*) *Maru* (6,892/—) 13 Jun 1945, §*Konzan Maru* (5,488/19) 19 Jun 1945.

SS 224 *Cod* Damaged by torpedo room fire in South China Sea, 26 Apr 1945 (1 killed). Decomm 22 Jun 1946. †
7* Okinawa; seven patrols.
Ships sunk: Tkr *Ogura Maru No. 3* (7,350/16) 23 Feb 1944, *Taisoku Maru* (2,473/18) 27 Feb 1944, ODD *Karukaya*, *Shohei Maru* (7,256/31) 10 May 1944; AN *Seiko Maru* (708/38) 3 Aug 1944, *Shinsei Maru No. 6* (260/—) 11 Aug 1944, LST *No. 129* 14 Aug 1944, *Tatsuhiro Maru* (6,886/44) 5 Oct 1944, AO *Shiretoko* 7 Oct 1944, AM *W-41* 25 Apr 1945.

SS 225 *Cero* Damaged by aircraft bomb miss in Kurile Is., 18 Jul 1945. Decomm 8 Jun 1946. †
7* Cape Sansapor, Okinawa, Raids on Japan 7–8/45; eight patrols.

* joint attack; +probable sinking; #possible sinking; § question on sinking

Ships sunk: *Taijun Maru (2,825/—) 23 May 1944, AO *Tsurumi* 5 Aug 1944, tkr *Taishu Maru* (6,925/44) 29 Apr 1945, *Shinpen Maru* (884/—) 4 May 1945, *Shinnan Maru* (1,025/01, ex–Philippine *Argus*) 13 May 1945.

SS 226 *Corvina* Torpedoed sunk by *I-176* southeast of Truk on first patrol, 16 Nov 1943 (82 killed).

SS 227 *Darter* Stranded off Palawan and destroyed, 24 Oct 1944.
4* Raid on Truk 2/44, Surigao Strait; four patrols.
Ships sunk: *Fujikawa Maru* (2,829/—) 30 Mar 1944, CM *Tsugaru* 29 Jun 1944, CA *Atago* and damaged *Takao* 23 Oct 1944 in Palawan Passage.

No.	Name	Builder	Keel Laid	Launched	Comm.
SS 228	*Drum*	Portsmouth NYd	11 Sep 1940	12 May 1941	1 Nov 1941
SS 229	*Flying Fish*	Portsmouth NYd	6 Dec 1940	9 Jul 1941	10 Dec 1941
SS 230	*Finback*	Portsmouth NYd	5 Feb 1941	25 Aug 1941	31 Jan 1942
SS 231	*Haddock*	Portsmouth NYd	31 Mar 1941	20 Oct 1941	14 Mar 1942
SS 232	*Halibut*	Portsmouth NYd	16 May 1941	3 Dec 1941	10 Apr 1942
SS 233	*Herring*	Portsmouth NYd	14 Jul 1941	15 Jan 1942	4 May 1942
SS 234	*Kingfish*	Portsmouth NYd	29 Aug 1941	2 Mar 1942	20 May 1942
SS 235	*Shad*	Portsmouth NYd	24 Oct 1941	15 Apr 1942	12 Jun 1942
SS 236	*Silversides*	Mare I. NYd	4 Nov 1940	26 Aug 1941	15 Dec 1941
SS 237	*Trigger*	Mare I. NYd	1 Feb 1941	22 Oct 1941	30 Jan 1942
SS 238	*Wahoo*	Mare I. NYd	28 Jun 1941	14 Feb 1942	15 May 1942
SS 239	*Whale*	Mare I. NYd	28 Jun 1941	14 Mar 1942	1 Jun 1942

Service Records:

SS 228 *Drum* Damaged by depth charges south of Caroline Is., 22 Nov 1943. Decomm 16 Feb 1946. NRT †
12* Midway, Palau-Yap Raids 7/44, Solomons, New Georgia Ldgs., Cape Torokina, Surigao Strait, Iwo Jima, Honshu Raid 2/45, Okinawa; 13 patrols.
Ships sunk: AV *Mizuho* 2 May 1942, unknown (4,000/—) 9 May 1942; *Shonan Maru* (5,266/18) 13 May 1942, *Kitakata Maru* (2,380/01) 25 May 1942, *Hague Maru* (5,641/20) 8 Oct 1942, *Hachimanzan Maru* (2,461/—) 9 Oct 1942, *Ryunan Maru* (5,106/11) 20 Oct 1942, CVL *Ryuho* damaged off Hachijo Jima 12 Dec 1942, *Oyama Maru* (3,809/—) 9 Apr 1943, AE *Nisshun Maru* (6,380/41) 18 Apr 1943, *Myoko Maru* (5,037/37) 17 Jun 1943, *Hakutetsu Maru No. 13* (1,334/—) 8 Sep 1943, AS *Hie Maru* (11,621/30) 17 Nov 1943, *Shikisan Maru* (4,725/25) 24 Oct 1944, *Taisho Maru* (6,886/44), *Taihaku Maru* (6,886/44) 26 Oct 1944.

Figure 6.22: *Wahoo* (SS 238), 14 Jul 1943, at Mare I. Notice conning tower reduced in size and deck gun forward. The *Wahoo* was one of the more successful submarines before her loss.

SS 229 *Flying Fish* †
12* Midway, Philippine Sea, Solomons, Okinawa; 12 patrols.
Ships sunk: *Hyuga Maru* (994/42) 16 Feb 1943, *Sapporo Maru No. 12* (2,865/03) 12 Apr 1943, *Amaho Maru* (2,769/98) 17 Apr 1943, *Kasuga Maru* (1,377/16) 24 Apr 1943, *Canton Maru* (2,820/28) 2 Jul 1943, *Nanman Maru* (6,550/21) 27 Oct 1943, *Ginyo Maru* (8,613/21) 16 Dec 1943, tkr *Kyuei Maru* (10,171/43) 27 Dec 1943, *Taijin Maru* (1,937/16) 12 Mar 1944, *Anzan Maru* (5,493/19) 16 Mar 1944, *Minami Maru* (2,398/10, ex–Panamanian *Capella*) 1 Apr 1944, *Taito Maru* (4,466/35), *Osaka Maru* (3,740/22) 25 May 1944, *Taga Maru* (2,220/—) 10 Jun 1945, *Meisei Maru* (1,893/17) 11 Jun 1945.

SS 230 *Finback* †
13* Midway, Philippine Sea, Bonins-Yap Raids, Iwo Jima; 12 patrols.
Ships sunk: *Teison Maru* (7,007/21) 14 Oct 1942, *Yamafuji Maru* (5,359/20), *Africa Maru* (9,475/18) 20 Oct 1942, *Kochi Maru* (2,910/20) 27 May 1943, CM *Kahoku Maru* (3,350/31) 8 Jun 1943, *Genoa Maru* (6,785/19) 11 Jun 1943, *Ryuzan Maru* (4,720/20) 30 Jun 1943, *Kaisho Maru* (6,070/18) 3 Aug 1943, *SC-109* 19 Aug 1943, tkr *Isshin Maru* (10,044/—) 2 Jan 1944, **Suwa Maru* (10,672/14) 5 Apr 1944, *Hakuun Maru No. 2* (860/36), *Hassho Maru* (536/—) 11 Sep 1944; *Jusan Maru* (2,111/18) 16 Dec 1944.

SS 231 *Haddock* Decomm 12 Feb 1947. †
11* Leyte Ldgs., Okinawa, Raids on Japan 7–8/45; 13 patrols. PUC.
Ships sunk: *Tatsuho Maru* (6,334/38) 22 Aug 1942, *Teishun Maru* (2,251/02) 26 Aug 1942, *Tekkai Maru* (1,925/—) 3 Nov 1942, *Venice Maru* (6,571/21) 11 Nov 1942, +unknown 17 Jan 1943, tkr *Arima Maru* (7,389/36) 3 Apr 1943, #*Toyo Maru* (1,916/—) 8 Apr 1943, *Saipan Maru* (5,533/36) 21 Jul 1943, AV *Notoro* damaged 20 Sep 1943, CVE *Unyo* damaged 19 Jan 1944.

SS 232 *Halibut* Severely damaged by depth charge attack in Luzon Strait, 14 Nov 1944; not repaired. Decomm 18 Jul 1945. Stricken 8 May 1946. Sold 10 Jan 1947; BU Camden, N.J.
7* Leyte; ten patrols.
Ships sunk: *Gyokuzan Maru* (1,970/—) 12 Dec 1942, *Shingo Maru* (4,740/17), *Genzan Maru* (5,708/06) 16 Dec 1942; +*Shinkoku Maru* (3,991/41) 20 Feb 1943, §*Nichiyu Maru* (6,817/38) 13 Mar 1943, *Taibun Maru* (6,581/20) 30 Aug 1943, *Shogen Maru* (3,362/10) 6 Sep 1943, *Ehime Maru* (4,653/20) 2 Nov 1943, CV *Junyo* damaged in Bungo Channel 5 Nov 1943, *Taichu Maru* (3,213/97) 12 Apr 1944, *Genbu Maru* (1,872/25), CMc *Kamome* 27 Apr 1944; DD *Akitsuki*, *§*Yamagumo* 25 Oct 1944.

SS 233 *Herring* Sunk by shore gunfire off Matsuwa I., 1 Jun 1944 (84 killed).
5* North Africa; eight patrols (five in Europe).
Submarine sunk: §U-163 15 Mar 1943.
Ships sunk: *Ville du Havre* (5,083/19) off Casablanca 8 Nov 1942, *Hakozaki Maru* (3,948/39) 14 Dec 1943, AKV *Nagoya Maru* (6,072/32) 1 Jan 1944, PF *Ishigaki* 30 May 1944, *Hokuyo Maru* (1,590/19) 31 May 1944, *Iwaki Maru* (3,124/—), *Hiburi Maru* (4,365/—) 1 Jun 1944.

SS 234 *Kingfish* Severely damaged by depth charge attack off Bonin Is., 23 Mar 1943. Decomm 9 Mar 1946. †
9* Iwo Jima, Okinawa; ten patrols.
Ships sunk: *Yomei Maru* (2,860/36) 1 Oct 1942, XPG *Seikyo Maru* (2,608/34) 23 Oct 1942, *Hino Maru* No. 3 (4,391/37) 7 Dec 1942, *Choyo Maru* (5,388/20) 28 Dec 1942, *Takachiho Maru* (8,154/34) 19 Mar 1943, AO *Hayatomo* damaged (CTL) 9 Oct 1943, *Sana Maru* (3,365/13) 20 Oct 1943, tkr *Ryuei Maru* (5,144/43) 3 Jan 1944, tkr **Bokuei Maru* (5,135/43) 3 Jan 1944, tkr *Fushimi Maru No. 3* (4,292/—) 7 Jan 1944, *Ikutagawa Maru* (2,220/—) 24 Oct 1944, *Tokai Maru No. 4* (537/—),

* joint attack; +probable sinking; #possible sinking; § question on sinking

LST No. 138 27 Oct 1944; *Yaei Maru* (1,941/—), *Shibazono Maru* (1,831/03), *Shoto Maru* (572/—) 3 Jan 1945.

SS 235 *Shad* Decomm 24 Apr 1946. NRT. †
6* North Africa, Iwo Jima, Okinawa, Raids on Japan 7–8/45; 11 patrols (five in Atlantic).
Ships sunk: German AM M-4242 (ex–French *Odet II*) (212/08) 4 Jan 1943, German b/r *Nordfels* (1,214/04) damaged 25 Jan 1943, Italian b/r *Pietro Orseolo* (6,344/—) damaged 1 Apr 1943, CL *Ioshima* (ex–Chinese *Ning Hai*) 19 Sep 1944, CM *Fumi Maru No. 2* (304/—) 21 Sep 1944, *Chozan Maru* (3,939/—) 17 May 1945, *Azusa Maru* (1,370/—) 7 Jun 1945.

SS 236 *Silversides* Decomm 17 Apr 1946. NRT Oct 1947. †
12* Solomons, Okinawa, Raids on Japan 7–8/45, Finschhafen; 14 patrols. PUC.
Ships sunk: §Unknown (4,000/—) 28 Jul 1942, *Nikkei Maru* (5,811/—) 8 Aug 1942, tkr *Toei Maru* (10,023/38) 18 Jan 1943, §*Somedono Maru* (5,154/17), *Surabaya Maru* (4,391/19), *Meiu Maru* (8,230/18) 20 Jan 1943; *Hide Maru* (5,256/30) 11 Jun 1943, CM *Tsugaru* damaged off Rabaul 5 Aug 1943, *Tairin Maru* (1,915/—) 18 Oct 1943, tkr *Tennan Maru* (5,407/42), *Kazan Maru* (1,893/36), *Johore Maru* (6,182/32) 24 Oct 1943; *Temposan Maru* (1,970/42), *Shichisei Maru* (1,911/38), *Ryuto Maru* (3,311/12) 29 Dec 1943; *Kofuku Maru* (1,920/—) 16 Mar 1944, *LST §No. 3* 27 Mar 1944, ARC *Okinawa Maru* (2,254/96), *Mikage Maru No. 18* (4,319/37), XPG *Choan Maru No. 2* (2,631/27) 10 May 1944; XPG *Shosei Maru* (998/29) 20 May 1944, *Shoken Maru* (1,949/43), *Horaizan Maru* (1,999/20) 29 May 1944; *Malay Maru* (4,556/—) 25 Jan 1945, YP *Shiratori Maru* (269/—) 12 Apr 1945.

SS 237 *Trigger* Sunk by Japanese aircraft and frigates *Mikura*, *No. 33* and *No. 89* in Nansei Shoto, 28 Mar 1945 (89 killed).
11* N. Luzon–Formosa Raids 10/44, Iwo Jima; 12 patrols. PUC.
Ships sunk: *Holland Maru* (5,869/20) 17 Oct 1942, §*Teifuku Maru* (5,198/21) 22 Dec 1942, DD *Okikaze* 10 Jan 1943, *Momoha Maru* (3,103/18) 15 Mar 1943, *Noborikawa Maru* (2,182/22) 1 Jun 1943, CV *Hiyo* damaged 10 Jun 1943, *Yowa Maru* (6,43542) 18 Sep 1943, AO *Shiriya*, tkr *Shoyo Maru* (7,498/28), *Argun Maru* (6,662/20) 21 Sep 1943; **Yawata Maru* (1,852/35), +*Delagoa Maru* (7,148/19) 2 Nov 1943, *Nachisan Maru* (4,433/31) 13 Nov 1943, *Eizan Maru* (1,681/15) 21 Nov 1943, CMc +*Nasami* 31 Jan 1944, DD *Michishio*, AS *Yasukuni Maru* (11,933/30) 31 Jan 1944, *Miike Maru* (11,739/41), PF *Kasado* damaged 27 Apr 1944, tkr **Takane Maru* (10,021/—) 30 Oct 1944, *Tsukushi Maru No. 3* (1,012/27) 18 Mar 1945, AR #*Odate* 27 Mar 1945.

SS 238 *Wahoo* Sunk by Japanese aircraft and minesweeper *W-18*, patrol craft *SC-15* and *SC-43* in La Perouse Strait, 11 Oct 1943 (80 killed).
6*; seven patrols. PUC.
Ships sunk: *Kamoi Maru* (5,355/37) 10 Dec 1942, DD *Harusame*, damaged west of Wewak 24 Jan 1943, *Ukishima Maru* (4,730/36), *Buyo Maru* (5,447/19), *Fukuei Maru No. 2* (1,901/38) 26 Jan 1943; *Zogen Maru* (1,428/—), *Kowa Maru* (3,217/09) 19 Mar 1943; *Nittsu Maru* (2,183/17), *Hozan Maru* (2,260/18) 21 Mar 1943; unknown (2,427/—) 23 Mar 1943, *Takaosan Maru* (2,076/11) 24 Mar 1943, *Satsuki Maru* (827/—), *Teisho Maru* (9,849/—) 25 Mar 1943, ARC *Yamabato Maru* (2,556/37) 29 Mar 1943, *Tamon Maru No. 5* (5,260/11) 7 May 1943, *Takao Maru* (3,204/20), *Jinmu Maru* (1,912/—) 9 May 1943; §*Hokusei Maru* (1,394/18) 21 Sep 1943, *Masaki Maru No. 2* (1,238/18) 29 Sep 1943, *Konron Maru* (7,908/—) 5 Oct 1943, §*Kanko Maru* (1,288/17) 6 Oct 1943, *Hankow Maru* (2,995/—) 9 Oct 1943.

SS 239 *Whale* Damaged by depth charges in Bungo Strait, 29 Oct 1942. Decomm 5 Jan 1947. NRT. †
11* Palau, Philippines Raids 9/44, Raids on Japan 7–8/45; eleven patrols.
Ships sunk: *Iwashiro Maru* (3,550/39) 13 Jan 1943, *Heiyo Maru* (9,815/30) 17 Jan 1943, *Kenyo Maru* (6,486/38) 23 Mar 1943, XPG *Shoei Maru* (3,580/36) 26 May 1943, AE *Naruto Maru* (7,149/34) 8 Aug 1943, *Denmark Maru* (5,870/20) 16 Jan 1944, **Tarushima Maru* (4,865/38) 17 Jan 1944, *Honan Maru* (5,401/20, ex–British *War Sirdar*) 9 Apr 1944, tkr *Akane Maru* (10,241/—), *Kinugasa Maru* (8,407/36) 6 Oct 1944.

* joint attack; +probable sinking; #possible sinking; § question on sinking

Figure 6.23: *Harder* (SS 257), 19 Feb 1944. Sunk on her sixth patrol under Medal of Honor winner CDR Samuel Dealey.

No.	Name	Builder	Keel Laid	Launched	Comm.
SS 240	*Angler*	Electric Boat	9 Nov 1942	4 Jul 1943	1 Oct 1943
SS 241	*Bashaw*	Electric Boat	4 Dec 1942	25 Jul 1943	25 Oct 1943
SS 242	*Bluegill*	Electric Boat	17 Dec 1942	8 Aug 1943	11 Nov 1943
SS 243	*Bream*	Electric Boat	5 Feb 1943	17 Oct 1943	24 Jan 1944
SS 244	*Cavalla*	Electric Boat	4 Mar 1943	14 Nov 1943	29 Feb 1944
SS 245	*Cobia*	Electric Boat	17 Mar 1943	28 Nov 1943	29 Mar 1944
SS 246	*Croaker*	Electric Boat	1 Apr 1943	19 Dec 1943	21 Apr 1944
SS 247	*Dace*	Electric Boat	22 Jul 1942	25 Apr 1943	23 Jul 1943
SS 248	*Dorado*	Electric Boat	27 Aug 1942	23 May 1943	28 Aug 1943
SS 249	*Flasher*	Electric Boat	30 Sep 1942	20 Jun 1943	25 Sep 1943
SS 250	*Flier*	Electric Boat	30 Oct 1942	11 Jul 1943	18 Oct 1943
SS 251	*Flounder*	Electric Boat	5 Dec 1942	22 Aug 1943	29 Nov 1943
SS 252	*Gabilan*	Electric Boat	5 Jan 1943	19 Sep 1943	28 Dec 1943
SS 253	*Gunnel*	Electric Boat	21 Jul 1941	17 May 1942	20 Aug 1942
SS 254	*Gurnard*	Electric Boat	2 Sep 1941	1 Jun 1942	18 Sep 1942
SS 255	*Haddo*	Electric Boat	1 Oct 1941	21 Jun 1942	9 Oct 1942
SS 256	*Hake*	Electric Boat	1 Nov 1941	17 Jul 1942	30 Oct 1942
SS 257	*Harder*	Electric Boat	1 Dec 1941	19 Aug 1942	2 Dec 1942
SS 258	*Hoe*	Electric Boat	2 Jan 1942	17 Sep 1942	16 Dec 1942
SS 259	*Jack*	Electric Boat	2 Feb 1942	16 Oct 1942	6 Jan 1943
SS 260	*Lapon*	Electric Boat	21 Feb 1942	27 Oct 1942	23 Jan 1943
SS 261	*Mingo*	Electric Boat	21 Mar 1942	30 Nov 1942	12 Feb 1943
SS 262	*Muskallunge*	Electric Boat	7 Apr 1942	13 Dec 1942	15 Mar 1943
SS 263	*Paddle*	Electric Boat	1 May 1942	30 Dec 1942	29 Mar 1943
SS 264	*Pargo*	Electric Boat	21 May 1942	24 Jan 1943	26 Apr 1943

Service Records:

SS 240 *Angler* Struck uncharted object in Exmouth Gulf, 24 Jun 1944. Decomm 12 Feb 1947. †
6* Leyte, Raids on Japan 7–8/45; seven patrols.
Ships sunk: §AN *Shuko Maru* (889/39) 29 Jan 1944, *Otori Maru* (2,105/—) 20 May 1944, *Nanrei Maru* (2,407/24) 14 Oct 1944.

SS 241 *Bashaw* †
5* Palau-Yap Raids 3/44, Philippines Raids 9/44, Leyte; six patrols.
Ships sunk: *Yamamiya Maru* (6,440/44) 25 Jun 1944, *Yanagigawa Maru* (2,813/43) 8 Sep 1944, ARS *Miho Maru* (632/24) 9 Sep 1944, **Gyosan Maru* (5,698/22) 21 Nov 1944, tkr *Ryoei Maru* (10,016/44), tkr *Seishin Maru* (5,239/—) 5 Mar 1945.

SS 242 *Bluegill* Decomm 1 Mar 1946. †
4* Leyte; six patrols.
Ships sunk: CL *Yubari* near Palau 27 Apr 1944, *Asosan Maru* (8,812/35) 1 May 1944, *Miyaura Maru* (1,856/19) 20 May 1944, *Yamatama Maru* (*Sanju Maru*) (4,642/18) 7 Aug 1944, §*SC-12, Kojun Maru* (1,931/24) 13 Aug 1944, *Arabia Maru* (9,480/18); *Chinzei Maru* (1,999/—), *Hakushika Maru* (8,150/17) 18 Oct 1944; tkr *Honan Maru* (5,542/20) 28 Mar 1945.

SS 243 *Bream* Decomm 31 Jan 1946. †
4* Leyte; six patrols.
Ships sunk: *Yuki Maru* (5,704/19) 16 Jun 1944, CA *Aoba* damaged in Manila Bay 23 Oct 1944, **Kagu Maru* (6,806/36) 4 Nov 1944, CA *Kumano* damaged west of Lingayen 6 Nov 1944, AS *Teishu Maru* (1,230/38) 29 Apr 1945.

SS 244 *Cavalla* Decomm 16 Mar 1946. †
4* Philippine Sea, Palau, Philippines Raids 9/44, Raids on Japan 7–8/45; six patrols. Tokyo Bay. PUC.
Ships sunk: CV *Shokaku* in Philippine Sea 19 Jun 1944, DD *Shimotsuki* northeast of Singapore 25 Nov 1944, AN *Shunsen Maru* (971/20), AN *Kanko Maru* (909/41) 5 Jan 1945.

SS 245 *Cobia* Decomm 22 May 1946. †
4* 4th Bonins Raid; six patrols.
Ships sunk: *Daiji Maru* (2,813/43) 13 Jul 1944, XPG *Unkai Maru No. 10* (855/39), *Nisshu Maru* (7,785/17) 18 Jul 1944, CMc *Yurishima* 14 Jan 1945, tkr §*Nanshin Maru No. 22* (834/—), AR *Hakusa* 8 Jun 1945.

SS 246 *Croaker* Decomm 15 May 1946. †
3* ; six patrols.
Ships sunk: CL *Nagara* 7 Aug 1944, XPG *Daigen Maru No. 7* (1,289/37) 14 Aug 1944, *Taito Maru* (267/32) 16 Aug 1944, *Yamateru* (*Sansho*) *Maru* (6,862/44) 17 Aug 1944, *Shinki Maru* (2,211/—) 9 Oct 1944, *Hakuran Maru* (887/—) 23 Oct 1944, *Gassan Maru* (4,515/38), *Mikage Maru* (2,761/97) 24 Oct 1944.

SS 247 *Dace* Decomm 12 Feb 1947. †
7* Truk Raid 2/44, Cape Sansapor, Surigao Strait, Luzon; seven patrols.
Ships sunk: Tkr *Kyoei Maru No. 2* (1,157/40) 27 Jul 1944, tkr *Nittetsu Maru* (5,993/—), *Eikyo Maru* (6,948/44) 14 Oct 1944, CA *Maya* in Palawan Passage 23 Oct 1944, AF *Nozaki* 28 Dec 1944, *Hakuyo Maru* (1,391/29) 10 Jun 1945.

SS 248 *Dorado* Sunk in error by U.S. aircraft in Caribbean, 12 Oct 1943 (76 killed).

SS 249 *Flasher* Decomm 16 Mar 1946. †
6*; six patrols.
Ships sunk: Tkr *Yoshida Maru* (2,920/41) 18 Jan 1944, *Taishin Maru* (1,723/18) 5 Feb 1944, *Minryo Maru* (2,193/38), *Hokuan Maru* (3,712/38) 14 Feb 1944; French PR *Tahure, Song Giang Go* (1,065/22) 29 Apr 1944; *Teisen Maru* (5,050/17) 3 May 1944, AO *Notoro* damaged, *Nippo Maru* (6,079/38, ex-Swedish *Ningpo*) 29 Jun 1944; *Koto Maru No. 2* (3,557/37) 7 Jul 1944, CL *Oi* in South China Sea 19 Jul 1944, tkr *Otorisan(yama) Maru* (5,280/—) 26 Jul 1944, XPG *Saigon Maru* (5,350/37) 18 Sep 1944, **Ural Maru* (6,374/29) 27 Sep 1944; *Taibin Maru* (6,886/44) 4 Oct 1944, DD *Kishinami*, tkr *Hakko Maru* (10,022/44) 4 Dec 1944, tkr *Omurosan Maru* (9,204/37), tkr *Otowasan Maru* (9,204/36), tkr *Arita Maru* (10,238/—) 22 Dec 1944, *Koho Maru* (850/—) 25 Feb 1945;

SS 250 *Flier* Damaged by grounding off Midway, 12 Jan 1944. Sunk by mine in Balabac Strait, Philippines, 13 Aug 1944 (78 killed).
1*; two patrols.
Ships sunk: *Hakusan Maru* (10,380/23) 4 Jun 1944.

SS 251 *Flounder* Attacked in error by U.S. destroyers *Hank* and *Wallace L. Lind*, 18 Jul 1945. Decomm 12 Feb 1947. †
2* Biak; six patrols.
Submarine sunk: *U-537* in Java Sea 9 Nov 1944.
Ships sunk: AGP *Nihonkai Maru* (2,681/32) 17 Jun 1944, **Gyosan Maru* (5,698/22) 21 Nov 1944.

SS 252 *Gabilan* Decomm 23 Feb 1946. †
4* Raids on Japan 7–8/45; six patrols.
Ships sunk: AM *W-25* 17 Jul 1944, AG *Kaiyo No. 6* (200/—) 31 Oct 1944, CL **Isuzu* 7 Apr 1945, *Kako Maru* (762/—) 14 Apr 1945.

SS 253 *Gunnel* Engines failed on first patrol in North Atlantic, 1942. Decomm 18 May 1946. †
5* North Africa, Okinawa; eight patrols.
Ships sunk: *Koyo Maru* (6,435/43) 15 Jun 1943, *Tokiwa Maru* (6,971/16), XPG +*Hong Kong Maru* (2,797/35) 19 Jun 1943; *Hiyoshi Maru* (4,046/37) 4 Dec 1943, TB *Sagi* 8 Nov 1944, *Shunten Maru* (5,623/28), TB *Hiyodori* 17 Nov 1944; AG *Banshu Maru No. 17* (459/23) 19 Nov 1944.

SS 254 *Gurnard* Decomm 27 Nov 1945. †
6*; nine patrols.
Ships sunk: *Taiko Maru* (1,925/37) 11 Jul 1943, *Taian Maru* (5,655/16), *Dainichi Maru* (5,813/22) 8 Oct 1943; damaged German *Havelland* (6,334/21) 22 Dec 1943 (later renamed *Tatsumi Maru*), *Seizan Maru No. 2* (1,898/37), *Tofuku Maru* (5,857/19) 24 Dec 1943; *Naruo Maru* (215/22) 25 Dec 1943, *Tenshinsan* (*Amatsusan*) *Maru* (6,886/44), *Tajima Maru* (6,995/16), *Aden Maru* (5,824/19) 6 May 1944, tkr *Tatekawa Maru* (10,090/35) 24 May 1944; tkr *Taimei Maru* (6,923/44) 3 Nov 1944.

SS 255 *Haddo* Tokyo Bay. Decomm 16 Feb 1946. †
6* Leyte, Raids on Japan 7–8/45; ten patrols (three in Europe).
Ships sunk: *Kinryu Maru* (4,390/—), *Norfolk Maru* (6,576/21) 21 Aug 1944; PF *Sado* 22 Aug 1944, DD *Asakaze* 23 Aug 1944, AGS *Katsuriki* 21 Sep 1944, tkr *Hishi Maru No. 2* (856/36) 9 Nov 1944, PF *Shimushu* damaged 25 Nov 1944, PF No. 72, *Taiun Maru No. 1* (2,200/—), *Konri Maru* (3,106/20) 1 Jul 1945.

SS 256 *Hake* Decomm 13 Jul 1946. †
7* Leyte, Raids on Japan 7–8/45; nine patrols (two in Europe).
Ships sunk: APV *Nigitsu Maru* (9,547/42) 12 Jan 1944, *Shuko Maru* (889/39) 27 Jan 1944, *Tacoma Maru* (5,772/09), *Nanka Maru* (4,065/06) 1 Feb 1944; tkr *Yamamizu Maru* (5,174/—) 27 Mar 1944, DD *Kazegumo* 8 Jun 1944, *Kinshu Maru* (5,591/19) 17 Jun 1944, *Hibi Maru* (5,874/—) 20 Jun 1944, DD §*Hibiki* damaged in Ryukyu Is. 6 Sep 1944, CL *Isuzu* damaged off Corregidor 19 Nov 1944. Tokyo Bay.

SS 257 *Harder* Sunk by Japanese patrol boat *No. 22* off Caiman Point, Luzon, 24 Aug 1944 (79 killed).
6* Palau-Yap Raids 3/44; six patrols. PUC.
Ships sunk: AV *Sagara Maru* (7,189/40) 23 Jun 1943, +*Koyo Maru* (3,010/19) 9 Sep 1943, *Yoko Maru* (1,050/38) 11 Sep 1943, *Kachisan Maru* (814/—) 19 Sep 1943, *Kowa Maru* (4,520/06), tkr *Daishin Maru* (5,878/19, ex-Norwegian *Nordhav*) 23 Sep 1943; *Udo Maru* (3,936/??), *Hokuko Maru* (5,385/40) 19 Nov 1943; *Nikko Maru* (5,949/??) 20 Nov 1943, DD *Ikazuchi* 13 Apr 1944, *Matsue Maru* (7,061/21) 17 Apr 1944, DD *Minatsuki* 6 Jun 1944, DD *Hayanami* 7 Jun 1944, DD *Tanikaze* 9 Jun 1944, PF *Matsuwa*, PF *Hiburi* 22 Aug 1944.

SS 258 *Hoe* Decomm 7 Aug 1946. †
7*; eight patrols.
Ships sunk: Tkr *Nissho Maru* (10,526/38) 25 Feb 1944, *Kohoku Maru* (2,573/15) 8 Oct 1944, **Macassar Maru* (4,026/20) 7 Oct 1944, PF *Shonan* 25 Feb 1945.

SS 259 *Jack* Decomm 8 Jun 1946. †
7* Okinawa; nine patrols. PUC.
Ships sunk: *Toyo Maru* (4,163/37), *Shozan Maru* (5,859/??) 26 Jun 1943; *Nikyu Maru* (6,529/42) 4 Jul 1943, tkr *Kokuei Maru* (5,154/—), tkr *Nanei Maru* (5,019/—), tkr *Nichirin Maru* (5,162/—), tkr *Ichiyo Maru* (5,106/—) 19 Feb 1944; *Yoshida Maru No. 1* (5,425/19) 26 Apr 1944, tkr *San Pedro Maru* (7,268/27) 25 Jun 1944, *Tsurushima Maru* (4,645/19), *Matsukawa Maru* (3,825/38) 30 Jun 1944; AM *W-28* and *Mexico Maru* (5,785/10) 29 Aug 1944, *Hinaga Maru* (5,396/—) 14 Nov 1944, *Yuzan Maru No. 2* (6,859/44) 15 Nov 1944.

SS 260 *Lapon* Reengined Nov 1943. Decomm 25 Jul 1946. †
4* Leyte; eight patrols.
Ships sunk: *Taichu Maru* (1,906/—) 18 Oct 1943, *Toyokuni Maru* (5,792/—) 8 Mar 1944, *Nichirei Maru* (5,396/—) 9 Mar 1944, *Hokuroku Maru* (8,359/30) 18 Mar 1944, *Wales Maru* (6,586/21), *Bizen Maru*

*joint attack; +probable sinking; #possible sinking; § question on sinking

(4,667/43) 24 May 1944; AGS *Kyodo Maru No. 36* (1,499/29) 18 Jul 1944, tkr *Tenshin Maru* (5,061/—) 31 Jul 1944, *Jungen Go* (ex–Chinese *Shun Yuan*) (1,610/96) 22 Sep 1944, tkr *Hokki Maru* (5,599/19) 27 Sep 1944, *Ejiri Maru* (6,968/44) 10 Oct 1944.

SS 261 *Mingo* Decomm.1 Jan 1947. †
5*; seven patrols.
Ships sunk: DD *Tamanami* 7 Jul 1944, *Manila Maru* (9,486/15) 25 Nov 1944.

SS 262 *Muskallunge* Tokyo Bay. Decomm 29 Jan 1947. †
5* 2nd Bonins Raid, Okinawa; seven patrols.
Ship sunk: *Durban Maru* (7,163/19) 21 Aug 1944.

SS 263 *Paddle* Decomm 1 Feb 1946. †
8* Gilbert Is.; eight patrols.
Ships sunk: *Ataka Maru* (5,248/20, ex–Italian *Ada*) 23 Aug 1943, *Mito Maru* (7,061/21), *Hino Maru No. 1* (2,671/29) 16 Apr 1944; DD *Hokaze* 6 Jul 1944, *Shinyo Maru* (2,518/42?) (667 POWs lost), **Kiyo Maru* (5,061/30) 7 Sep 1944; tkr **Shoei Maru* (2,854/—) 8 Dec 1944.

SS 264 *Pargo* Reengined Jan 1944. Decomm 12 Jun 1946. †
8* Philippines Raids 9/44; eight patrols.
Ships sunk: *Manju Maru* (5,877/19) 29 Nov 1943, *Shoko Maru* (1,933/39) 30 Nov 1943, AN *Eiryu Maru* (758/28) 4 May1944, *Yamagiku Maru* (5,236/20) 28 Jun 1944, AN *Hinoki Maru* (599/39) 10 Sep 1944, CM *Aotaka* 26 Sep 1944, tkr *Yuho Maru* (5,226/43) 26 Nov 1944, PF *Manju* 31 Jan 1945, DD *Nokaze* 20 Feb 1945, *Rashin Maru* (5,454/19) 8 Aug 1945.

Figure 6.25: *Runner* (SS 275), 16 Oct 1942, at Portsmouth, N.H. Stern view showing formation of stern and propeller protectors.

No.	Name	Builder	Keel Laid	Launched	Comm.
SS 265	*Peto*	Manitowoc	18 Jun 1941	30 Apr 1942	21 Nov 1942
SS 266	*Pogy*	Manitowoc	15 Sep 1941	23 Jun 1942	10 Jan 1943
SS 267	*Pompon*	Manitowoc	26 Nov 1941	15 Aug 1942	17 Mar 1943
SS 268	*Puffer*	Manitowoc	16 Feb 1942	22 Nov 1942	27 Apr 1943
SS 269	*Rasher*	Manitowoc	4 May 1942	20 Dec 1942	8 Jun 1943
SS 270	*Raton*	Manitowoc	29 May 1942	24 Jan 1943	13 Jul 1943
SS 271	*Ray*	Manitowoc	20 Jul 1942	28 Feb 1943	27 Jul 1943
SS 272	*Redfin*	Manitowoc	3 Sep 1942	4 Apr 1943	31 Aug 1943
SS 273	*Robalo*	Manitowoc	24 Oct 1942	9 May 1943	28 Sep 1943
SS 274	*Rock*	Manitowoc	23 Dec 1942	20 Jun 1943	26 Oct 1943
SS 275	*Runner*	Portsmouth NYd	8 Dec 1941	30 May 1942	30 Jul 1942
SS 276	*Sawfish*	Portsmouth NYd	20 Jan 1942	23 Jun 1942	26 Aug 1942
SS 277	*Scamp*	Portsmouth NYd	6 Mar 1942	20 Jul 1942	18 Sep 1942
SS 278	*Scorpion*	Portsmouth NYd	20 Mar 1942	20 Jul 1942	1 Oct 1942
SS 279	*Snook*	Portsmouth NYd	17 Apr 1942	15 Aug 1942	24 Oct 1942
SS 280	*Steelhead*	Portsmouth NYd	1 Jun 1942	11 Sep 1942	7 Dec 1942
SS 281	*Sunfish*	Mare I. NYd	25 Sep 1941	2 May 1942	15 Jul 1942
SS 282	*Tunny*	Mare I. NYd	10 Nov 1941	30 Jun 1942	1 Sep 1942
SS 283	*Tinosa*	Mare I. NYd	21 Feb 1942	7 Oct 1942	15 Jan 1943
SS 284	*Tullibee*	Mare I. NYd	1 Apr 1942	11 Nov 1942	15 Feb 1943
SS 361	*Golet*	Manitowoc	27 Jan 1943	1 Aug 1943	30 Nov 1943
SS 362	*Guavina*	Manitowoc	3 Mar 1943	29 Aug 1943	23 Dec 1943
SS 363	*Guitarro*	Manitowoc	7 Apr 1943	26 Sep 1943	16 Jan 1944
SS 364	*Hammerhead*	Manitowoc	5 May 1943	24 Oct 1943	1 Mar 1944

Figure 6.24: *Robalo* (SS 273), 15 Oct 1943, in Lake Michigan, as completed.

* joint attack; +probable sinking; #possible sinking; § question on sinking

Service Records:

SS 265 *Peto* Decomm 25 Jun 1946. †
8* Finschhafen, Admiralty Is., Iwo Jima, Okinawa, Raids on Japan 7–8/45; ten patrols.
Ships sunk: *Tonei Maru* (4,930/42), *Kinkasan Maru* (4,980/11) 1 Oct 1943; *Konei Maru* (2,345/30) 1 Dec 1943, *Kayo Maru* (4,368/23) 4 Mar 1944, *Tatsuaki Maru* (2,766/—) 12 Nov 1944, tkr *Aisakasan Maru* (6,923/44), *Chinkai Maru* (2,827/—) 18 Nov 1944.

SS 266 *Pogy* Decomm 20 Jul 1946. †
8* Okinawa; ten patrols.
Submarine sunk: *I-183* off Cape Ashizuri 28 Apr 1944.
Ships sunk: XPG *Keishin Maru* (1,434/40) 1 May 1943, *Tainan Maru* (1,939/—) 26 May 1943, AKV *Mogamigawa Maru* (7,497/34) 1 Aug 1943, *Maebashi Maru* (7,005/21) 30 Sep 1943, AS *Soyo Maru* (6,081/31) 7 Dec 1943, *Fukkai Maru* (3,829/20) 13 Dec 1943, *Malta Maru* (5,500/19), DD *Minekaze* 10 Feb 1944; *Taijin Maru* (5,154/22), ARC *Nanyo Maru* (3,610/23) 20 Feb 1944; *Horei Maru* (5,588/—) 23 Feb 1944, *Shirane Maru* (2,825/43) 5 May 1944, *Awa* (*Anbo*) *Maru* (4,523/43) 13 May 1944, *Chikuzen Maru* (2,448/07) 27 Jul 1945, *Kotohirasan Maru* (2,270/—) 5 Aug 1945.

SS 267 *Pompon* Decomm 11 May 1946. †
4* Leyte Ldgs., Okinawa; nine patrols.
Ships sunk: *Thames Maru* (5,871/20) 25 Jul 1943, *Shiga Maru* (742/06) 30 May 1944, *Mayachi Maru* (2,159/16) 12 Aug 1944.

SS 268 *Puffer* Decomm 28 Jun 1946. †
9* Iwo Jima, Okinawa; nine patrols.
Ships sunk: ODD *Fuyo* 20 Dec 1943, *Ryuyo Maru* (6,707/20) 1 Jan 1944, *Teiko Maru* (15,105/25, ex–French *D'Artagnan*) 22 Feb 1944, *Shinryu Maru* (3,181/18) 18 May 1944, AO *Ashizuri*, AO *Takasaki* 5 Jun 1944; *Kyo Maru No. 2* (340/38) 7 Aug 1944, **Shinpo Maru* (5,135/—), tkr *Teikon Maru* (5,113/13) 12 Aug 1944; *PF No. 42* 10 Jan 1945.

SS 269 *Rasher* Decomm 22 Jun 1946. †
7* Iwo Jima, Okinawa; nine patrols. PUC.
Ships sunk: *Kogane Maru* (3,132/38) 9 Oct 1943, *Kenkoku Maru* (3,377/20) 13 Oct 1943, tkr *Koryo Maru* (589/36) 31 Oct 1943, tkr *Tango Maru* (2,046/26, ex–Dutch *Talang Akar*) 8 Nov 1943, tkr *Kiyo Maru* (7,251/30) 4 Jan 1944, *Tango Maru* (6,200/26, ex–Dutch *Toendjoek*) (~3000 POWs lost), *Ryusei Maru* (4,797/11) 25 Feb 1944; *Nittai Maru* (6,484/21) 3 Mar 1944, *Nichinan Maru* (2,750/—) 27 Mar 1944, *Choi Maru* (1,074/—) 11 May 1944, XPG *Anshu Maru* (2,601/37) 29 May 1944, AOR *Shioya* 8 Jun 1944, *Koan Maru* (3,183/24) 14 Jun 1944; *Shiroganesan Maru* (4,739/—) 6 Aug 1944, §*Eishin Maru* (542/—), tkr *Teiyo Maru* (9,849/31); CVE *Taiyo* 18 Aug 1944; *Teia Maru* (17,537/32, ex–French *Aramis*) 19 Aug 1944.

SS 270 *Raton* †
6* Cape Torokina, Leyte Ldgs., Okinawa; eight patrols.
Ships sunk: AE *Onoe Maru* (6,667/40), *Kamoi Maru* (2,811/??) 26 Nov 1943; *Hokko Maru* (5,347/18), *Yuri Maru* (6,787/19) 28 Nov 1943; *Heiwa Maru* (5,578/??) 24 Dec 1943,.PF *Iki* 24 May 1944, *PF No. 15* 6 Jun 1944, §*Shiranesan Maru* (4,739/—), *Taikai Maru* (3,812/17) 18 Oct 1944; CA *Kumano* damaged 6 Nov 1944, tkr *Unkai Maru No. 5* (2,841/—), AF *Kurasaki* 14 Nov 1944; *Toryu Maru* (1,992/89) 2 May 1945, *Rekizan Maru* (1,311/18) 12 May 1945, *Eiju Maru* (2,455/97) 16 May 1945.

SS 271 *Ray* Damaged by aerial depth charge attack, 14 Oct 1944. Decomm 12 Feb 1947. †
7* Finschhafen, Leyte Ldgs., Okinawa; eight patrols.
Ships sunk: *Nikkai Maru* (2,562/38) 26 Nov 1943, tkr *Kyoko Maru* (5,792/21) 27 Dec 1943, XPG *Okuyo Maru* (2,904/38) 1 Jan 1944, *Tempei Maru* (6,094/18) 22 May 1944, **Taijun Maru* (2,825/—) 23 May 1944, tkr *Janbi Maru* (5,244/—) 18 Jul 1944, *Koshu Maru* (2,612/11) 4 Aug 1944, *Zuisho Maru* (5,289/12) 14 Aug 1944, tkr *Nansei Maru* (5,878/22, ex–British *Pleiodon*) 18 Aug 1944, tkr *Taketoyo Maru* (6,965/20) 21 Aug 1944, *Toko Maru* (4,180/08) 12 Oct 1944, *Horai Maru No. 7* (865/—) 1 Nov 1944, **Kagu Maru* (6,804/36) 4 Nov 1944, *PF No. 7* 14 Nov 1944.

SS 272 *Redfin* Decomm 1 Nov 1946. †
6* Raids on Japan 7–8/45; seven patrols.
Ships sunk: DD *Amatsukaze* damaged off Spratly Is. 17 Jan 1944, DD *Akigumo* 11 Apr 1944, *Shinyu Maru* (4,621/19) 15 Apr 1944, *Yamagata Maru* (3,807/16) 16 Apr 1944, tkr *Asanagi Maru* (5,142/43) 11 Jun 1944, *Aso Maru* (3,028/23) 24 Jun 1944, tkr *Nichinan Maru No. 2* (5,226/—) 8 Nov 1944.

SS 273 *Robalo* Sunk by mine off Palawan, 26 Jul 1944 (78 killed + 4 as POWs).
2*; three patrols.

SS 274 *Rock* Damaged by gunfire of Japanese destroyers off Truk, 29 Feb 1944. Decomm 1 May 1946. †
4* Surigao Strait; six patrols.
Ship sunk: Tkr +*Takasago Maru No. 7* (834/—) 26 Oct 1944.

SS 275 *Runner* Missing in Kurile Is., Jun 1943 (78 killed). (Probably sunk by mine)
1* Three patrols.
Ships sunk: +*Seinan Maru* (1,338/—) 11 Jun 1943, +*Shinryu Maru* (4,936/37) 26 Jun 1943.

SS 276 *Sawfish* Decomm 26 Jun 1946. †
8* Leyte, Okinawa; ten patrols.
Submarine sunk: *I-29* in Balintang Channel, Luzon Strait 26 Jul 1944.
Ships sunk: Soviet *Ilmen* (2,369/28), Soviet *Kola* (2,654/06) 17 Feb 1943 in error; YP *Shinsei Maru* (148/—) 10 Mar 1943, XPG *Hakkai Maru* (2,921/39) 5 May 1943, CMc *Hirashima* 27 Jul 1943, *Sansei Maru* (3,267/31) 8 Dec 1943, tkr *Tachibana Maru* (6,521/21) 9 Oct 1944, AV *Kimikawa Maru* (6,863/37) 23 Oct 1944.

SS 277 *Scamp* Severely damaged by aircraft bomb in Davao Gulf, 7 Apr 1944. Sunk by Japanese patrol ship *No. 4* and aircraft off Tokyo Bay, 11 Nov 1944 (83 killed) .
7* Solomons, Lae Ldgs., Treasury Is. Ldg.; eight patrols.
Submarine sunk: *I-168* off New Hanover 27 Jul 1943.
Ships sunk: AV *Kamikawa Maru* (6,853/37) 28 May 1943, AO *Kazahaya* damaged 27 Jul 1943, *Kansai Maru* (8,614/30) 18 Sep 1943, *Tokyo Maru* (6,486/36) 10 Nov 1943, CL *Agano* damaged 12 Nov 1943, tkr *Nippon Maru* (9,975/36) 14 Jan 1944.

SS 278 *Scorpion* Sank patrol vessel by gunfire, 29 Apr 1943 (1 killed). Missing in East China Sea, Feb 1944 (76 killed).
3*; four patrols.
Ships sunk: YP *Ebisu Maru No. 5* (131/22) 30 Mar 1943, XPG *Meiji Maru No. 1* (1,934/37) 20 Apr 1943, *Yuzan Maru* (6,380/42) 27 Apr 1943, *Anzan Maru* (3,890/15), *Kokuryu Maru* (6,112/21) 3 Jul 1943; AO *Shiretoko* damaged off Singapore (CTL) 13 Nov 1943.

SS 279 *Snook* Missing in Okinawa area, Apr 1945 (84 killed).
7* Marcus I. Raid 1943, Philippines Raids 9/44; nine patrols.
Ships sunk: *Kinko Maru* (1,268/17), *Daifuku Maru* (3,194/07) 5 May 1943; *Tosei Maru* (4,363/19), *Shinsei Maru No. 3* (1,258/18) 7 May 1943; AO *Ose* damaged 24 Jun 1943, *Koki Maru* (5,290/21), *Liverpool Maru* (5,865/19) 4 Jul 1943; *Yamato Maru* (9,656/15) 13 Sep 1943, *Katsurahama Maru* (715/07) 22 Sep 1943, +*Kotobuki Maru* (5,874/—) 28 Nov 1943, *Yamafuku Maru* (4,928/40); *Shiganoura Maru* (3,512/42) 29 Nov 1943, XPG *Magane Maru* (3,120/40) 23 Jan 1944, *Lima Maru* (6,989/20) 8 Feb 1944, *Nittoku Maru* (3,591/05) 14 Feb 1944, §*Hoshi Maru No. 2* (875/—) 15 Feb 1944, *Koyo Maru* (5,471/19) 23 Feb 1944, *Shinsei Maru No. 1* (5,863/19) 23 Oct 1944, tkr *Kikusui Maru* (3,887/19, ex–Dutch *Iris*), *Arisan Maru* (6,886/44) (~1800 POWs lost) 24 Oct 1944.

SS 280 *Steelhead* Damaged by fire in drydock at San Francisco, 1 Oct 1944. Decomm 29 Jun 1946. †
6* Tarawa Raid, Okinawa; seven patrols.
Ships sunk: AO **Kazahaya* damaged in Caroline Is., 6 Oct 1943, AR *Yamabiko Maru* (6,795/37) 10 Jan 1944, *Dakar Maru* (7,169/20), **Yoshino Maru* (8,990/07), *Fuso Maru* (8,195/08) 31 Jul 1944.

SS 281 *Sunfish* Decomm 26 Dec 1945. †
9* Marshall Is., raid on Truk 2/44, Marianas Raids 2/44, Iwo Jima, Okinawa; 11 patrols.
Ships sunk: *Kosei Maru* (3,262/19) 13 Mar 1943, XPG *Edo Maru* (1,299/37) 13 Aug 1943, *Kozan Maru* (4,180/35) 4 Sep 1943, *Shinyubari Maru* (5,354/36) 23 Feb 1944, *Shinmei Maru* (2,577/02) 5 Jul 1944, *Taihei Maru* (6,284/28) 9 Jul 1944, tkr *Chihaya Maru* (4,701/—) 10 Sep 1944, *Etajima Maru* (6,435/44), *Edogawa Maru* (6,968/44) 13 Sep 1944; *Seisho Maru* (5,463/19) 18 Nov 1944, *Dairen Maru* (3,748/25) 30 Nov 1944, *Manryu Maru* (1,620/??), *PF No. 73*, XPG *Kaiho Maru* (1,093/17), *Taisei Maru* (1,948/—) 16 Apr 1945.

SS 282 *Tunny* Damaged by depth charges in Marianas Is., 26 Aug 1943. Damaged by U.S. aircraft in error off Palau, 30 Mar 1944. Damaged by aircraft bombs in South China Sea, 1 Sep 1944. Decomm 13 Dec 1945. †
9* Palau-Yap Raids 3/44, Saipan, Philippine Sea, Iwo Jima, Okinawa; nine patrols. PUC.
Submarine sunk: +I-42 off Angaur 23 Mar 1944.
Ships sunk: *Kusuyama Maru* (5,306/19) 8 Feb 1943, **Suwa Maru* (10,672/14) 28 Mar 1943, *Toyo Maru No. 2* (4,163/37) 2 Apr 1943, *Kosei Maru* (8,237/19) 7 Apr 1943, XPG *Shotoku Maru* (1,964/38) 28 Jun 1943, AO *Iro* damaged 20 Mar 1944, BB *Musashi* damaged off Palau 29 Mar 1944, *Nichiwa Maru* (4,955/09) 17 May 1944.

* joint attack; +probable sinking; #possible sinking; § question on sinking

SS 283 *Tinosa* †
9* Okinawa; 12 patrols. PUC.
Ships sunk: AO **Kazahaya* 6 Oct 1943, *Kiso Maru* (4,071/20), *Yamato Maru* (4,379/17) 22 Nov 1943; *Shini Maru* (3,811/20) 26 Nov 1943, tkr *Azuma Maru* (6,646/38) 3 Dec 1943, tkr *Koshin Maru* (5,485/24), tkr *Seinan Maru* (5,401/—) 22 Jan 1944; *Odatsuki Maru* (1,988/—) 15 Feb 1944, *Chojo Maru* (2,610/27) 16 Feb 1944, *Taibu Maru* (6,440/44), tkr *Toyohi Maru* (6,436/44) 4 May 1944; tkr *Konsan Maru* (2,733/29), *Kamo Maru* (7,954/08) 3 Jul 1944; *Wakatama Maru* (2,211/—) 9 Jun 1945, *Keito Maru* (880/—) 12 Jun 1945, *Kaisei Maru* (884/—), *Taito Maru* (2,726/17) 20 Jun 1945.

SS 284 *Tullibee* Sunk by own torpedo north of Palau, 26 Mar 1944 (79 killed, 1 survivor).
3*; four patrols.
Ships sunk: *Kaisho Maru* (4,164/38) 22 Aug 1943, *Chicago Maru* (5,866/10) 15 Oct 1943, AN *Hiro Maru* (549/27) 31 Jan 1944.

SS 361 *Golet* Two patrols. Sunk by Japanese warships north of Honshu, 14 Jun 1944 (82 killed).

SS 362 *Guavina* Decomm 8 Jun 1946. †
5* Noemfoor I.; six patrols.
Ships sunk: *Noshiro Maru* (2,333/19) 26 Apr 1944, *Tama Maru* (3,052/18) 4 Jul 1944, *LST No. 3* 15 Sep 1944, *Toyo Maru* (2,704/—) 14 Nov 1944, *Dowa Maru* (1,916/—) 22 Nov 1944, tkr *Taigyo Maru* (6,892/44) 7 Feb 1945, tkr *Eiyo Maru* (8,673/29) 20 Feb 1945.

SS 363 *Guitarro* Decomm 6 Dec 1945. †
4*; five patrols.
Ships sunk: *Shisen Maru* (2,201/—) 30 May 1944, PF *Awaji* 2 Jun 1944, PF *Kusakaki* 7 Aug 1944, *Shinei Maru* (5,135/—) 10 Aug 1944, *Uga Maru* (4,433/—) 21 Aug 1944, tkr *Nanshin Maru No. 27* (834/—) 27 Aug 1944, *Komei Maru* (2,857/44), *Pacific Maru* (5,872/20) 31 Oct 1944, **Kagu Maru* (6,806/36) 4 Nov 1944, CA *Kumano* damaged 6 Nov 1944.

SS 364 *Hammerhead* Decomm 9 Feb 1946. †
7*; seven patrols.
Ships sunk: *Kokusei Maru* (5,396/20, ex-Norwegian *Sheng Hwa*), *Higane Maru* (5,320/—), *Hiyori Maru* (5,320/—) 1 Oct 1944; *Ugo Maru* (3,684/20), *Oyo Maru* (5,458/21) 20 Oct 1944; tkr **Shoei Maru* (2,854/—) 8 Dec 1944, PF *Yaku* 23 Feb 1945, PF *No. 84, No. 18* 29 Mar 1945; tkr *Kinrei Maru* (867/41) 6 May 1945, *Tottori Maru* (5,973/13) 15 May 1945, §*Sakura Maru* (900/—), tkr *Nanmei Maru* No. 5 (834/) 10 Jul 1945.

Balao Class

No.	Name	Builder	Keel Laid	Launched	Comm.
SS 285	*Balao*	Portsmouth NYd	26 Jun 1942	27 Oct 1942	4 Feb 1943
SS 286	*Billfish*	Portsmouth NYd	23 Jul 1942	12 Nov 1942	20 Apr 1943
SS 287	*Bowfin*	Portsmouth NYd	23 Jul 1942	7 Dec 1942	1 May 1943
SS 288	*Cabrilla*	Portsmouth NYd	18 Aug 1942	24 Dec 1942	24 May 1943
SS 289	*Capelin*	Portsmouth NYd	14 Sep 1942	20 Jan 1943	4 Jun 1943
SS 290	*Cisco*	Portsmouth NYd	29 Oct 1942	24 Dec 1942	10 May 1943
SS 291	*Crevalle*	Portsmouth NYd	14 Nov 1942	22 Feb 1943	24 Jun 1943
SS 292	*Devilfish*	Cramp	31 Mar 1942	30 May 1943	1 Sep 1944
SS 293	*Dragonet*	Cramp	28 Apr 1942	18 Apr 1943	6 Mar 1944
SS 294	*Escolar*	Cramp	10 Jun 1942	18 Apr 1943	2 Jun 1944
SS 295	*Hackleback*	Cramp	15 Aug 1942	30 May 1943	7 Nov 1944
SS 296	*Lancetfish*	Cramp	30 Sep 1942	15 Aug 1943	never
SS 297	*Ling*	Cramp	2 Nov 1942	15 Aug 1943	8 Jun 1945
SS 298	*Lionfish*	Cramp	15 Dec 1942	7 Nov 1943	1 Nov 1944
SS 299	*Manta*	Cramp	15 Jan 1943	7 Nov 1943	18 Dec 1944
SS 300	*Moray*	Cramp	21 Apr 1943	14 May 1944	26 Jan 1945
SS 301	*Roncador*	Cramp	21 Apr 1943	14 May 1944	27 Mar 1945
SS 302	*Sabalo*	Cramp	5 Jun 1943	4 Jun 1944	19 Jun 1945
SS 303	*Sablefish*	Cramp	5 Jun 1943	4 Jun 1944	18 Dec 1945
SS 304	*Seahorse*	Mare I. NYd	1 Jul 1942	9 Jan 1943	31 Mar 1943
SS 305	*Skate*	Mare I. NYd	1 Aug 1942	4 Mar 1943	15 Apr 1943
SS 306	*Tang*	Mare I. NYd	15 Jan 1943	17 Aug 1943	15 Oct 1943
SS 307	*Tilefish*	Mare I. NYd	10 Mar 1943	25 Oct 1943	28 Dec 1943

* joint attack; +probable sinking; #possible sinking; § question on sinking

Displacement	1,525/2,415 tons
Dimensions	311'9" (oa) x 27'3" x 15'3"
Machinery	2 screws; diesel electric: SHP 5,400; 20.25 knots; electric: HP 2,740, 8.75 knots
Endurance	11,000/10; depth: 400'
Complement	81
Armament	1–4"/50 or 1–5"/25, 1–40mm AA, 1–20mm guns, 10–21" TT

Notes: Total of 119 units completed. Increased depth capacity; 7/8" pressure hulls. Five-inch gun fitted in newer units after mid-1944. *Entemedor, Sea Dog, Sea Poacher, Sea Robin,* and *Sennet* fitted with 2–5"/25 late in the war. *Chivo* and *Chopper* fitted with rocket launchers 1945.

Service Records:

SS 285 *Balao* Decomm 20 Aug 1946. †
9* Finschhafen, Biak, 4th Bonins Raid, Iwo Jima, Okinawa, Raids on Japan 7–8/45; ten patrols.
Ships sunk: *Nikki Maru* (5,857/—) 22 Feb 1944, *Akiura Maru* (6,803/38), *Shoho Maru* (2,723/—) 28 Feb 1944; *Daigo Maru* (5,244/—) 8 Jan 1945, *Tatsuharu Maru* (6,345/39) 19 Feb 1945, *Hakozaki Maru* (10,413/22) 19 Mar 1945, *Shinto Maru No. 1* (880/—) 26 Mar 1945.

SS 286 *Billfish* Decomm 1 Nov 1946. †
7* Okinawa, Raids on Japan 7–8/45; eight patrols.
Ships sunk: *Kotobuki Maru No. 7* (991/—) 26 May 1945, *Taiu Maru* (2,220/—) 4 Jun 1945, *Kori Maru* (1,091/97) 5 Aug 1945.

SS 287 *Bowfin* Damaged by gunfire in Makassar Strait, 28 Nov 1943. Decomm 12 Feb 1947. †
8* Honshu Raid 2/45, Iwo Jima, Honshu Raid 2/45, Okinawa; nine patrols. PUC.
Ships sunk: Tkr *Kirishima Maru* (8,120/31) 25 Sep 1943, tkr *Ogurasan Maru* (5,069/—), *Tainan Maru* (5,407/—), French *Beryl* (671/20) 26 Nov 1943; French *Gouverneur Général Van Vollenhoven* (691/09) 27 Nov 1943, *Sydney Maru* (5,425/29), tkr *Tonan Maru* (9,866/06) 28 Nov 1943, *Shoyo Maru* (4,408/—) 17 Jan 1944, AO *Kamoi* damaged 28 Jan 1944, *Tsukikawa Maru* (4,470/—) 10 Mar 1944, *Bengal Maru* (5,399/21) 24 Mar 1944, *Shinkyo Maru* (5,139/18) 25 Mar 1944, **Miyama Maru* (4,667/—) 14 May 1944, *Tsushima Maru* (6,754/14) 22 Aug 1944, *Hinode Maru* No. 6 (245/—) 4 Sep 1944, PF *No. 56* 17 Feb 1945, XPG *Chowa Maru* (2,719/40) 1 May 1945, *Daito Maru No. 3* (880/—) 8 May 1945, *Shinyo Maru No. 3* (1,898/17) 11 Jun 1945, *Akiura Maru* (887/—) 13 Jun 1945.

SS 288 *Cabrilla* Decomm 7 Aug 1946. †
6* Leyte; eight patrols.
Ships sunk: CVE *Taiyo* damaged off Chichi Jima 24 Sep 1943, *Tamon Maru No. 8* (2,705/—) 4 Jan 1944, *Sanyo Maru* (8,360/30) 26 May 1944, *Maya Maru* (3,145/25) 17 Jul 1944, tkr *Zuiyo Maru* (7,385/16) and tkr *Kyokuho Maru* (10,059/44) 1 Oct 1944, *Hokurei Maru* (2,407/24) and *Yamamizu Maru* No. 2 (5,154/—) 6 Oct 1944, *Shinyo Maru No. 8* (1,959/41) 7 Oct 1944.

SS 289 *Capelin* Missing off Halmahera I., Dec 1943 (78 lost).
1*; two patrols.
Ships sunk: *Kunitama Maru* (3,127/—) 11 Nov 1943, #*Kizan Maru* (2,841/—) 23 Nov 1943.

SS 290 *Cisco* One patrol. Sunk by Japanese aircraft and gunboat *Karatsu* in Sulu Sea, 28 Sep 1943 (76 killed).

SS 291 *Crevalle* Almost lost in diving accident, 10 Sep 1944 (1 killed). Decomm 20 Jul 1946. †
4* Okinawa; seven patrols.
Ships sunk: *Kyokko Maru* (6,783/20) 15 Nov 1943, XPG *Busho Maru* (2,552/21) 26 Jan 1944, AN *Kashiwa Maru* (976/18) 25 Apr 1944, tkr *Nisshin Maru* (16,801/36) 6 May 1944, *Aki Maru* (11,409/42) 26 Jul 1944, §*Tozan Maru* (8,666/—) 27 Jul 1944, *Hakubasan Maru* (6,650/28) 28 Jul 1944, PF *Ikuna* damaged 10 Apr 1945, *Hokuto Maru* (2,215/23) 9 Jun 1945, *Daiki Maru* (2,217/44), PF *Kasado* damaged 10 Jun 1945; XPG *Hakusan Maru* (2,211/20) 11 Jun 1945.

SS 292 *Devilfish* Damaged by kamikaze off Bonin Is., 20 Mar 1945. Decomm 30 Sep 1946. †
3* Okinawa, Raids on Japan 7–8/45; four patrols.

SS 293 *Dragonet* Damaged by striking rock while submerged off Matsuwa I., 15 Dec 1944. Decomm 16 Apr 1946. †
2* Okinawa, Raids on Japan 7–8/45; three patrols.

SS 294 *Escolar* Completed at Portsmouth NYd. Sunk by mine in Yellow Sea on first patrol, Oct 1944 (82 killed).

SS 295 *Hackleback* Completed at Portsmouth NYd. Decomm 20 Mar 1946. †
1* Okinawa; two patrols.

SS 296 *Lancetfish* Towed to Boston NYd for completion, sunk incomplete at pier by workman's error, 15 Mar 1945; raised but not repaired. Decomm 24 Mar 1945. †

SS 297 *Ling* Completed at Boston NYd. Decomm 26 Oct 1946. †

SS 298 *Lionfish* Completed at Portsmouth NYd. Decomm 16 Jan 1946. †
1* Okinawa; two patrols.

SS 299 *Manta* Completed at Portsmouth NYd. One patrol. Decomm 10 Jun 1946.

SS 300 *Moray* Decomm 12 Apr 1946.†
1* Raids on Japan 7–8/45; 1 patrol.

SS 301 *Roncador* Decomm 1 Jun 1946. †

SS 302 *Sabalo* Decomm 7 Aug 1946. †

SS 303 *Sablefish* †

SS 304 *Seahorse* Damaged by aircraft bomb off Okinawa, 23 Mar 1945. Damaged by gunfire of Japanese patrol vessels, 18 Apr 1945. Decomm 2 Mar 1946. †
9* Truk Raid 4/44, Philippine Sea, Palau, Philippines Raids 9/44, Okinawa, Raids on Japan 7–8/45; eight patrols. PUC.
Submarine sunk: #*I-174* 20 Apr 1944.
Ships sunk: **Yawata Maru* (1,852/35), *Chihaya Maru* (7,089/26, ex–Dutch *Tjisaroea*), *Ume Maru* (5,859/19) 2 Nov 1943; *Daishu Maru* (3,322/19) 22 Nov 1943, unknown (4,000/—) 26 Nov 1943, tkr *San Ramon Maru* (7,309/35) 27 Nov 1943, *Nikko Maru* (784/—) 16 Jan 1944, *Yasukuni Maru* (3,025/20), *Ikoma Maru* (3,156/25) 21 Jan 1944; *Toko Maru* (2,747/—) 30 Jan 1944, *Toei Maru* (4,004/37) 1 Feb 1944, AE *Aratama Maru* (6,784/38), AW *Kizugawa Maru* (1,915/41) 8 Apr 1944; *Misaku* (or *Mimasaka*) *Maru* (4,467/42) 9 Apr 1944, *Akigawa Maru* (5,244/43) 27 Apr 1944, tkr *Medan Maru* (5,135/—), PF *Etorofu* damaged 27 Jun 1944; *Nitto Maru* (2,186/20), *Gyoyu Maru* (2,232/18, ex–British *Joan Moller*) 3 Jul 1944; *Kyodo Maru* No. 28 (1,506/19) 4 Jul 1944, PF *No. 21* 6 Oct 1944.

SS 305 *Skate* Target ship, heavily damaged in atom bomb aerial explosion test Able at Bikini, 1 Jul 1946. Decomm 11 Dec 1946. Sunk as target off California, 5 Oct 1948.
8* Wake I. Raid 1943, raid on Truk 2/44, Okinawa; seven patrols.
Submarine sunk: *I-122*, Sea of Japan, 10 Jun 1945.
Ships sunk: Tkr *Terukawa Maru* (6,429/34) 21 Dec 1943, BB *Yamato* damaged 25 Dec 1943, CL *Agano* 16 Feb 1944, DD *Usugumo* north of Truk 7 Jul 1944, *Miho Maru* (515/13) 15 Jul 1944, *Nippo Maru* (1,942/43) 16 Jul 1944, *Ekisan Maru* (3,690/—), *Hoei Maru* (219/19) 29 Sep 1944; *Yozan Maru* (1,227/18), *Kenjo Maru* (3,142/05) 12 Jun 1945; *Zuiko Maru* (887/—) 12 Jun 1945, *Sanjin Maru* (2,560/19, ex–Norwegian *Norse Carrier*) 14 Jun 1945.

Figure 6.26: *Tang* (SS 306). A most successful submarine, sinking 24 Japanese ships under CDR Richard O'Kane. At right is the tug *Seagull*. The *Tang* was later sunk by the erratic run of her own torpedo.

SS 306 *Tang* Sunk by own torpedo off Formosa, 24 Oct 1944 (78 killed).
4* Truk Raid 2/44, Marianas Raids 2/44, Palau-Yap Raids 3/44, Truk Raid 4/44, Leyte; five patrols. PUC.(2).
Ships sunk: *Gyoten Maru* (6,854/42, ex–British *Empire Pagoda*) 17 Feb 1944, XPG *Fukuyama Maru* (3,581/36) 22 Feb 1944, *Echizen Maru* (2,424/07) 24 Feb 1944, tkr *Choko Maru* (1,794/23) 25 Feb 1944, *Tamahoko Maru* (6,780/19; 559 POWs lost), *Tainan Maru* (3,175/97), tkr *Nasusan Maru* (4,399/31), *Kennichi Maru* (1,938/—) 24 Jun 1944; *Nikkin Maru* (5,705/—) 30 Jun 1944, *Taiun Maru No. 2* (998/11), tkr *Takatori Maru No. 1* (878/28) 1 Jul 1944; *Asukasan Maru* (6,886/44), *Yamaoka Maru* (6,932/44) 4 Jul 1944; *Dori Maru* (1,469/02) 6 Jul 1944, *Roko Maru* (3,328/12) 11 Aug 1944, *Tsukushi Maru* (8,135/—; or 1,835/25) 23 Aug 1944, tkr *Nanko Maru* No. 8 (834/—) 25 Aug 1944, *Joshu Go* (1,658/17) 10 Oct 1944, *Oita Maru* (711/07) 11 Oct 1944, *Toun Maru* (1,915/—), *Wakatake Maru* (1,920/38), *Tatsuju Maru* (1,944/—), *Kori Go* (1,339/—) 23 Oct 1944; tkr *Matsumoto Maru* (7,024/21), *Ebara Maru* (6,957/44) 25 Oct 1944.

SS 307 *Tilefish*
5* Honshu Raid 2/45, Iwo Jima, Okinawa; six patrols.
Ships sunk: TB *Chidori* 22 Dec 1944, AM *W-15* 5 Mar 1945.

No.	Name	Builder	Keel Laid	Launched	Comm.
SS 308	*Apogon*	Portsmouth NYd	9 Dec 1942	10 Mar 1943	16 Jul 1943
	ex–*Abadejo* (24 Sep 1942)				
SS 309	*Aspro*	Portsmouth NYd	27 Dec 1942	7 Apr 1943	31 Jul 1943
	ex–*Acedia* (24 Sep 1942)				
SS 310	*Batfish*	Portsmouth NYd	27 Dec 1942	5 May 1943	21 Aug 1943
	ex–*Acoupa* (24 Sep 1942)				
SS 311	*Archerfish*	Portsmouth NYd	22 Jan 1943	28 May 1943	4 Sep 1943
SS 312	*Burrfish*	Portsmouth NYd	24 Feb 1943	18 Jun 1943	14 Sep 1943
	ex–*Arnillo* (24 Sep 1942)				

*joint attack; +probable sinking; #possible sinking; § question on sinking

SS 313	*Perch*	Electric Boat	5 Jan 1943	12 Sep 1943	7 Jan 1944
SS 314	*Shark*	Electric Boat	28 Jan 1943	17 Oct 1943	14 Feb 1944
SS 315	*Sealion*	Electric Boat	25 Feb 1943	31 Oct 1943	8 Mar 1944
SS 316	*Barbel*	Electric Boat	11 Mar 1943	14 Nov 1943	3 Apr 1944
SS 317	*Barbero*	Electric Boat	25 Mar 1943	12 Dec 1943	29 Apr 1944
SS 318	*Baya*	Electric Boat	8 Apr 1943	2 Jan 1944	20 May 1944
SS 319	*Becuna*	Electric Boat	29 Apr 1943	30 Jan 1944	27 May 1944
SS 320	*Bergall*	Electric Boat	13 May 1943	16 Feb 1944	12 Jun 1944
SS 321	*Besugo*	Electric Boat	27 May 1943	27 Feb 1944	19 Jun 1944
SS 322	*Blackfin*	Electric Boat	10 Jun 1943	12 Mar 1944	4 Jul 1944
SS 323	*Caiman*	Electric Boat	24 Jun 1943	30 Mar 1944	17 Jul 1944
	ex–*Blanquillo* (24 Sep 1942)				
SS 324	*Blenny*	Electric Boat	8 Jul 1943	9 Apr 1944	27 Jul 1944

Service Records:

SS 308 *Apogon* Damaged in collision with Japanese freighter *Nichiran Maru No. 3* south of Formosa, 12 Jul 1944. Decomm 1 Oct 1945. Bikini target ship. Sunk during test Baker at Bikini, 26 Jul 1946.
6* Marianas Raids 2/44; eight patrols.
Ships sunk: XPG *Daido Maru* (2,962/35) 4 Dec 1943, *Hachirogata Maru* (1,999/43) 27 Sep 1944, *Hakuai Maru* (2,614/98) 18 Jun 1945.

SS 309 *Aspro* Decomm 30 Jan 1946. †
7* Truk Raid 2/44, Noemfoor I., Lingayen, Raids on Japan 7–8/45; seven patrols.
Submarine sunk: *I-43* 280 miles southeast of Guam 15 Feb 1944.
Ships sunk: *Miyama Maru* (4,667/—) 14 May 1944, *Jokuja Maru* (6,440/43) 15 May 1944, XPG *Peking Maru* (2,288/37) 28 Jul 1944, *Azuchisan Maru* (6,888/44) 2 Oct 1944, **Macassar Maru* (4,026/20) 7 Oct 1944, LSA **Shinshu Maru* (8,170/35) 3 Jan 1945.

SS 310 *Batfish* Decomm 6 Apr 1946. †
9* Palau, Leyte Ldgs., Iwo Jima, Raids on Japan 7–8/45; seven patrols.
Submarines sunk: *RO-112* off Camiguin I. 1 Feb 1945, *RO-113* off Babuyan 12 Feb 1945.
Ships sunk: *Hidaka Maru* (5,486/—) 20 Jan 1944, *Nagaragawa Maru* (990/17) 22 Jun 1944, *Isuzugawa Maru* (226/—) 1 Jul 1944, DD *Samidare* 26 Aug 1944,

SS 311 *Archerfish* Decomm 12 Jun 1946. †
7* Palau-Yap Raids, 1st Bonins Raid, 2nd Bonins Raid, 3rd Bonins Raid, Raids on Japan 7–8/45; seven patrols. PUC. Tokyo Bay.
Ships sunk: PF *No. 24* 28 Jun 1944, CV *Shinano* 29 Nov 1944.

SS 312 *Burrfish* Decomm 10 Oct 1946. †
5* Truk Raid 2/44, Iwo Jima, Okinawa; six patrols.
Ship sunk: German tkr *Rossbach* (5,894/17) 7 May 1944.

SS 313 *Perch* Damaged by depth charges in South China Sea, 14 May 1944. Decomm 15 Jan 1947. †
4* Saipan, Raids on Japan 7–8/45; seven patrols.

SS 314 *Shark* Sunk by Japanese destroyer *Harukaze* off Formosa, 24 Oct 1944 (87 killed).
1* Bonins-Marianas 1944; three patrols.
Ships sunk: *Chiyo Maru* (4,700/—) 2 Jun 1944, *Katsukawa Maru* (6,886/44) 4 Jun 1944, *Tamahime Maru* (3,080/18) *Takaoka Maru* (7,006/20) 5 Jun 1944.

SS 315 *Sealion* Decomm 2 Feb 1946. †
5* Philippines Raids 9/44, Leyte; six patrols. PUC.
Ships sunk: *Sansei Maru* (2,386/36) 28 Jun 1944, *Setsuzan Maru* (1,922/25, ex–Norwegian *Helios*) 6 Jul 1944, *Tsukushi Maru No. 2* (2,417/26), *Taian Maru* No. 2 (1,034/—) 11 Jul 1944; CM *Shirataka* 31 Aug 1944, *Nankai Maru* (8,416/33), *Rakuyo Maru* (9,419/21) (~1159 POWs lost) 12 Sep 1944; BB *Kongo*, DD *Urakaze* 21 Nov 1944; AF *Mamiya* 20 Dec 1944, Thai AO *Samui* 17 Mar 1945.

SS 316 *Barbel* Sunk by Japanese aircraft southwest of Palawan, 4 Feb 1945 (81 killed).
3* Leyte; four patrols.
Ships sunk: *Miyako Maru* (970/14) 5 Aug 1944, *Yagi Maru* (1,937/—), *Boko Maru* (2,333/04, ex–British *Sagres*) 9 Aug 1944; *Koan Maru* (223/—) 13 Aug 1944; *Bushu Maru* (1,222/18) 25 Sep 1944, *Sugiyama Maru* (4,379/14), *Misaki Maru* (4,422/07) 14 Nov 1944.

SS 317 *Barbero* Damaged by aircraft bomb in South China Sea, 27 Dec 1944. Decomm 25 Apr 1946. †
2* Western Carolines 1944; two patrols.
Ships sunk: *Kuramasan Maru* (1,995/27) 2 Nov 1944, *Shimotsu Maru* (2,854/—) 8 Nov 1944, PC *No. 30* 24 Dec 1944, *Junpo Maru* (4,277/11) 25 Dec 1944.

SS 318 *Baya* Decomm 14 May 1946. †
4* Western Carolines 1944; five patrols.
Ships sunk: Tkr *Palembang Maru* (5,236/18, ex–Philippine *Mindanao*) 4 Mar 1945, AN *Kainan Maru* (524/40) 21 Mar 1945, tkr *Yosei Maru* (2,500/28, ex–Dutch *Josefina*) 13 May 1945, TB *Kari* 16 Jul 1945.

SS 319 *Becuna* †
4* Western Carolines 1944, Leyte Ldgs.; five patrols.
Ships sunk: Tkr **Tokuwa Maru* (1,943/—) 9 Oct 1944, Tkr *Nichiyoku Maru* (1,945/—) 22 Feb 1945. †

SS 320 *Bergall* Damaged by Japanese cruiser *Myoko* and destroyer *Ushio* off Malay coast, 13 Jun 1945 and towed to Exmouth Bay by submarine *Angler*. †
4*; five patrols.
Ships sunk: *Shinshu Maru* (4,182/33) 13 Oct 1944, tkr *Nichiho* (*Nippo*) *Maru* (10,528/44), tkr *Itsukushima Maru* (10,007/37) 27 Oct 1944; CA *Myoko* damaged in South China Sea, not repaired 13 Dec 1944, AMC *Wa-102* (ex–HMS *Waglan*) 27 Jan 1945, PF *No. 53* 7 Feb 1945. †

SS 321 *Besugo* †
4* Leyte Ldgs.; five patrols.
Submarine sunk: German *U-183* in Java Sea 23 Apr 1945.
Ships sunk: DD *Suzutsuki* damaged 16 Oct 1944, PF *No. 132* 24 Oct 1944, LST *No. 151* 22 Nov 1944, tkr *Nichiei Maru* (10,020/38) 6 Jan 1945, PF *No. 144* 2 Feb 1945, AM *W-12* 6 Apr 1945. †

SS 322 *Blackfin* †
3* Leyte Ldgs., Raids on Japan 7–8/45; five patrols.
Ships sunk: *Unkai Maru No. 12* (2,745/42), *Caroline Maru* (320/36) 1 Nov 1944; DD *Shigure* 24 Jan 1945. †

SS 323 *Caiman* †
2*; four patrols.

SS 324 *Blenny* †
4* Leyte; four patrols.
Ships sunk: PF No. 28 14 Dec 1944, tkr *Kenzui Maru* (4,156/—) 23 Dec 1944, tkr *Amato Maru* (10,238/—) 26 Feb 1945, *Yamakuni Maru* (500/—), tkr *Nanshin Maru No. 21* (834/—), tkr *Hosen Maru* (1,039/—) 20 Mar 1945; *Hokoku Maru* (ex–Chinese *Li Liang*) (520/) 30 May 1945, PG *Nankai* (ex–Dutch *Regulus*) 16 Jul 1945. †

* joint attack; +probable sinking; #possible sinking; § question on sinking

No.	Name	Builder	Keel Laid	Launched	Comm.
SS 325	*Blower*	Electric Boat	15 Jul 1943	23 Apr 1944	10 Aug 1944
SS 326	*Blueback*	Electric Boat	29 Jul 1943	7 May 1944	28 Aug 1944
SS 327	*Boarfish*	Electric Boat	12 Aug 1943	21 May 1944	23 Sep 1944
SS 328	*Charr*	Electric Boat	26 Aug 1943	28 May 1944	23 Sep 1944
	ex–*Bocaccio* (24 Sep 1942)				
SS 329	*Chub*	Electric Boat	16 Sep 1943	18 Jun 1944	21 Oct 1944
	ex–*Chubb* (24 May 1944), ex–*Bonaci* (24 Sep 1942)				
SS 330	*Brill*	Electric Boat	23 Sep 1943	25 Jun 1944	26 Oct 1944
SS 331	*Bugara*	Electric Boat	21 Oct 1943	2 Jul 1944	15 Nov 1944
SS 332	*Bullhead*	Electric Boat	21 Oct 1943	16 Jul 1944	4 Dec 1944
SS 333	*Bumper*	Electric Boat	4 Nov 1943	6 Aug 1944	9 Dec 1944
SS 334	*Cabezon*	Electric Boat	18 Nov 1943	27 Aug 1944	30 Dec 1944
SS 335	*Dentuda*	Electric Boat	18 Nov 1943	10 Sep 1944	30 Dec 1944
	ex–*Capidoli* (24 Sep 1942)				
SS 336	*Capitaine*	Electric Boat	2 Dec 1943	1 Oct 1944	26 Jan 1945
SS 337	*Carbonero*	Electric Boat	16 Dec 1943	19 Oct 1944	7 Feb 1945
SS 338	*Carp*	Electric Boat	23 Dec 1943	12 Nov 1944	28 Feb 1945

No.	Name	Builder	Keel Laid	Launched	Comm.
SS 339	*Catfish*	Electric Boat	6 Jan 1944	19 Nov 1944	19 Mar 1945
SS 340	*Entemedor*	Electric Boat	3 Feb 1944	17 Dec 1944	6 Apr 1945
	ex–*Chickwick* (24 Sep 1942)				
SS 341	*Chivo*	Electric Boat	21 Feb 1944	14 Jan 1945	28 Apr 1945
SS 342	*Chopper*	Electric Boat	2 Mar 1944	4 Feb 1945	25 May 1945
SS 343	*Clamagore*	Electric Boat	16 Mar 1944	25 Feb 1945	28 Jun 1945
SS 344	*Cobbler*	Electric Boat	3 Apr 1944	1 Apr 1945	8 Aug 1945
SS 345	*Cochino*	Electric Boat	13 Apr 1944	20 Apr 1945	25 Aug 1945
SS 346	*Corporal*	Electric Boat	27 Apr 1944	10 Jun 1945	9 Nov 1945
SS 347	*Cubera*	Electric Boat	11 May 1944	17 Jun 1945	19 Dec 1945
SS 348	*Cusk*	Electric Boat	25 May 1944	28 Jul 1945	5 Feb 1946
SS 349	*Diodon*	Electric Boat	1 Jun 1944	10 Sep 1945	18 Mar 1946
SS 350	*Dogfish*	Electric Boat	22 Jun 1944	27 Oct 1945	29 Apr 1946
SS 351	*Greenfish*	Electric Boat	29 Jun 1944	21 Dec 1945	7 Jun 1946
	ex–*Doncella* (24 Sep 1942)				
SS 352	*Halfbeak*	Electric Boat	6 Jul 1944	19 Feb 1946	22 Jul 1946
	ex–*Dory* (24 Sep 1942)				
SS 353	*Dugong*	Electric Boat	—	—	—
SS 354	*Eel*	Electric Boat	—	—	—
SS 355	*Espada*	Electric Boat	—	—	—
SS 356	*Jawfish*	Electric Boat	—	—	—
	ex–*Fanegal* (24 Sep 1942)				
SS 357	*Ono*	Electric Boat	—	—	—
	ex–*Friar* (24 Sep 1942)				
SS 358	*Garlopa*	Electric Boat		—	—
SS 359	*Garrupa*	Electric Boat	—	—	—
SS 360	*Goldring*	Electric Boat	—	—	—

Service Records:

SS 325 *Blower* Three patrols. †

SS 326 *Blueback* †
2*; three patrols.
Ship sunk: SC-2 27 Jun 1945.

SS 327 *Boarfish* †
1*; four patrols.
Ships sunk: Tkr *Enki Maru* (6,968/44), **Daietsu Maru* (6,890/44) 31 Jan 1945.

SS 328 *Charr* †
Three patrols.
Ship sunk: CL **Isuzu* off Soembawa I. 7 Apr 1945.

SS 329 *Chub* †
3*; three patrols.
Ship sunk: AM W-34 21 May 1945.

SS 330 *Brill* †
1*; three patrols.

SS 331 *Bugara* †
3* Iwo Jima, Okinawa; three patrols.

SS 332 *Bullhead* Sunk by Japanese aircraft off Bali, 6 Aug 1945 (84 killed).
2* Fleet Raids 1945; three patrols.

SS 333 *Bumper* †
1*; two patrols.
Ship sunk: *Tkr Kyoei Maru No. 3* (1,189/41) 20 Jul 1945.

SS 334 *Cabezon* †
1*; 1 patrol.
Ship sunk: *Zaosan Maru* (2,631/06) 19 Jun 1945.

SS 335 *Dentuda* Bikini target. Decomm 11 Dec 1946. NRT. †
1*Okinawa.; 1 patrol.

SS 336 *Capitaine* †
1*; two patrols.

SS 337 *Carbonero* †
1*; two patrols.

* joint attack; +probable sinking; #possible sinking; § question on sinking

SS 338 *Carp* †
1* Raids on Japan 7–8/45; 1 patrol.

SS 339 *Catfish* †
1* Raids on Japan 7–8/45; 1 patrol.

SS 340 *Entemedor* One patrol. †

SS 341 *Chivo* †

SS 342 *Chopper* †

SS 343 *Clamagore* †

SS 344 *Cobbler* †

SS 345 *Cochino* †

SS 346 *Corporal* †

SS 347 *Cubera* †

SS 348 *Cusk* †

SS 349 *Diodon* †

SS 350 *Dogfish* †

SS 351 *Greenfish* †

SS 352 *Halfbeak* †

SS 353 *Dugong* Canceled 23 Oct 1944.

SS 354 *Eel* Canceled 23 Oct 1944.

SS 355 *Espada* Canceled 23 Oct 1944.

SS 356 *Jawfish* Canceled 29 Jul 1944.

SS 357 *Ono* Canceled 29 Jul 1944.

SS 358 *Garlopa* Canceled 29 Jul 1944.

SS 359 *Garrupa* Canceled 29 Jul 1944.

SS 360 *Goldring* Canceled 29 Jul 1944.

No.	Name	Builder	Keel Laid	Launched	Comm.
SS 365	*Hardhead*	Manitowoc	7 Jul 1943	12 Dec 1943	18 Apr 1944
SS 366	*Hawkbill*	Manitowoc	7 Aug 1943	9 Jan 1944	17 May 1944
SS 367	*Icefish*	Manitowoc	4 Sep 1943	20 Feb 1944	10 Jun 1944
SS 368	*Jallao*	Manitowoc	29 Sep 1943	12 Mar 1944	8 Jul 1944
SS 369	*Kete*	Manitowoc	25 Oct 1943	9 Apr 1944	31 Jul 1944
SS 370	*Kraken*	Manitowoc	13 Dec 1943	30 Apr 1944	8 Sep 1944
SS 371	*Lagarto*	Manitowoc	12 Jan 1944	28 May 1944	14 Oct 1944
SS 372	*Lamprey*	Manitowoc	22 Feb 1944	18 Jun 1944	17 Nov 1944
SS 373	*Lizardfish*	Manitowoc	14 Mar 1944	16 Jul 1944	30 Dec 1944
SS 374	*Loggerhead*	Manitowoc	1 Apr 1944	13 Aug 1944	9 Feb 1945
SS 375	*Macabi*	Manitowoc	1 May 1944	19 Sep 1944	29 Mar 1945
SS 376	*Mapiro*	Manitowoc	30 May 1944	9 Nov 1944	30 Apr 1945
SS 377	*Menhaden*	Manitowoc	21 Jun 1944	20 Dec 1944	22 Jun 1945
SS 378	*Mero*	Manitowoc	22 Jul 1944	17 Jan 1945	17 Aug 1945
SS 379	*Needlefish*	Manitowoc	—	—	—
SS 380	*Nerka*	Manitowoc	—	—	—

Service Records:

SS 365 *Hardhead* Decomm 10 May 1946. †
6* Leyte; six patrols.
Ships sunk: CL *Natori* 18 Aug 1944, tkr *Banei Maru* (5,226/44) 8 Nov 1944, PF *No. 38* 25 Nov 1944, tkr *Nanshin Maru No. 19* (834/—) 2 Feb 1945, *Araosan Maru* (6,886/44) 6 Apr 1945, *SC-1942*, *SC-113* and *SC-117* 23 Jul 1945.

SS 366 *Hawkbill* Decomm 20 Sep 1946.
6* Western Carolines 1944, Leyte; five patrols.
Ships sunk: Tkr *Tokuwa Maru* (1,943/—) 9 Nov 1944, DD *Momo* 15 Dec 1944, SC-4, SC-114 14 Feb 1945; *Daizen Maru* (5,396/—) 20 Feb 1945, CM *Hatsutaka* 16 May 1945.

SS 367 *Icefish* Decomm 21 Jun 1946. †
4* Surigao Strait, Iwo Jima, Okinawa; five patrols.
Ships sunk: *Tenshin Maru* (4,236/18) 24 Oct 1944, *Taiyo Maru* (4,168/13) 26 Oct 1944.

SS 368 *Jallao* Decomm 30 Sep 1946. †
4* Surigao Strait, Iwo Jima, Okinawa; four patrols.

Figure 6.27: *Icefish* (SS 367) 1946. Notice number on the bow.

Figure 6.28: *Mapiro* (SS 376). The war ended during her first patrol.

Ships sunk: CL **Tama* 25 Oct 1944, *Teihoku Maru* (5,795/35, ex-French *Persée*) 11 Aug 1945.

SS 369 *Kete* Missing in central Pacific, Mar 1945 (87 killed).
1* Iwo Jima; two patrols.
Ships sunk: *Keizan Maru* (2,116/18), *Sanka Maru* (2,495/18), *Dokan Maru* (2,270/—) 10 Mar 1945.

SS 370 *Kraken* Decomm 4 May 1946. †
1*; four patrols.
Ship sunk: *Sail Tachibana Maru No. 58* 20 Jun 1945.

SS 371 *Lagarto* Sunk by Japanese minelayer *Hatsutaka* in Gulf of Siam, 3 May 1945 (85 killed).
2* Iwo Jima; two patrols.
Submarine sunk: *+I-371* off Bungo Strait 2 Feb 1945.
Ship sunk: *Tatsumomo Maru* (880/—) 24 Feb 1945.

SS 372 *Lamprey* Decomm 3 Jun 1946. †
4* Iwo Jima, Okinawa; three patrols.

SS 373 *Lizardfish* Decomm 24 Jun 1946. †
1*; two patrols.
Ship sunk: SC-37 5 Jul 1945.

SS 374 *Loggerhead* Two patrols. Decomm 6 Jun 1946. †

SS 375 *Macabi* One patrol. Decomm 16 Jun 1946. †

SS 376 *Mapiro* One patrol. Decomm 16 Mar 1946. †

SS 377 *Menhaden* Decomm 31 May 1946. †

SS 378 *Mero* Decomm 15 Jun 1946. †

SS 379 *Needlefish* Canceled 29 Jul 1944.

SS 380 *Nerka* Canceled 29 Jul 1944.

*joint attack; +probable sinking; #possible sinking; § question on sinking

No.	Name	Builder	Keel Laid	Launched	Comm.
SS 381	*Sand Lance*	Portsmouth NYd	12 Mar 1943	25 Jun 1943	9 Oct 1943
	ex-*Ojanco* (24 Sep 1942), ex-*Orca* (5 Sep 1942)				
SS 382	*Picuda*	Portsmouth NYd	15 Mar 1943	12 Jul 1943	16 Oct 1943
	ex-*Obispo* (24 Sep 1942)				
SS 383	*Pampanito*	Portsmouth NYd	15 Mar 1943	12 Jul 1943	6 Nov 1943
SS 384	*Parche*	Portsmouth NYd	9 Apr 1943	24 Jul 1943	20 Nov 1943
SS 385	*Bang*	Portsmouth NYd	30 Apr 1943	30 Aug 1943	4 Dec 1943
SS 386	*Pilotfish*	Portsmouth NYd	15 May 1943	30 Aug 1943	16 Dec 1943
SS 387	*Pintado*	Portsmouth NYd	7 May 1943	15 Sep 1943	1 Jan 1944
SS 388	*Pipefish*	Portsmouth NYd	31 May 1943	12 Oct 1943	22 Jan 1944
SS 389	*Piranha*	Portsmouth NYd	21 Jun 1943	27 Oct 1943	5 Feb 1944
SS 390	*Plaice*	Portsmouth NYd	28 Jun 1943	15 Nov 1943	12 Feb 1944
SS 391	*Pomfret*	Portsmouth NYd	14 Jul 1943	27 Oct 1943	19 Feb 1944
SS 392	*Sterlet*	Portsmouth NYd	14 Jul 1943	27 Oct 1943	4 Mar 1944
	ex-*Pudiano* (24 Sep 1942)				
SS 393	*Queenfish*	Portsmouth NYd	27 Jul 1943	30 Nov 1943	11 Mar 1944
SS 394	*Razorback*	Portsmouth NYd	9 Sep 1943	27 Jan 1944	3 Apr 1944
SS 395	*Redfish*	Portsmouth NYd	9 Sep 1943	27 Jan 1944	12 Apr 1944
SS 396	*Ronquil*	Portsmouth NYd	9 Sep 1943	27 Jan 1944	22 Apr 1944
SS 397	*Scabbardfish*	Portsmouth NYd	27 Sep 1943	27 Jan 1944	29 Apr 1944
SS 398	*Segundo*	Portsmouth NYd	14 Oct 1943	5 Feb 1944	9 May 1944
SS 399	*Sea Cat*	Portsmouth NYd	30 Oct 1943	21 Feb 1944	16 May 1944

Service Records:

SS 381 *Sand Lance* Damaged by premature torpedo explosion, 6 Aug 1944. Decomm 14 Feb 1946. †
5* Okinawa, Raids on Japan 7–8/45; five patrols.
Ships sunk: *Kaiko Maru* (3,548/41) 28 Feb 1944, *Akashisan Maru* (4,541/35) 3 Mar 1944, Soviet *Belorussia* (2,920/36) 3 Mar 1944 in error, CL *Tatsuta Kokuyo Maru* (4,667/43) 13 Mar 1944, *Kenan Maru* (3,129/41) 3 May 1944, *Mitakesan Maru* (4,441/37) 11 May 1944, *Koho Maru* (4,291/—) 14 May 1944, *Taikoku Maru* (2,633/43), *Fukko Maru* (3,834/24) 17 May 1944; XPG *Taiko Maru* (2,984/37) 14 Jul 1944, AE §*Seia Maru* (6,659/—) 1 Aug 1944, AM *Yoshino Maru* (220/—) 14 May 1945.

SS 382 *Picuda* Decomm 25 Sep 1946. †
6* Philippines Raids 9/44, Luzon, Okinawa; six patrols.
Ships sunk: *Shinkyo Maru* (5,139/18) 2 Mar 1944, *Hoko Maru* (1,504/23) 11 Mar 1944, *Atlantic Maru* (5,872/20) 30 Mar 1944, PG

Hashidate 22 May 1944, DD *Yunagi*, tkr *Kotoku Maru* (1,943/—) 25 Aug 1944; *Tokushima Maru* (5,975/13) 16 Sep 1944, *Awaji Maru* (1,948/44) 21 Sep 1944, LSD *Mayasan Maru* (9,433/42) 17 Nov 1944, tkr *Shugo Maru* (6,933/44), *Fukuju Maru* (5,291/19) 23 Nov 1944; *Clyde Maru* (5,497/20) 29 Jan 1945.

SS 383 *Pampanito* Rescued 127 POW survivors of *Rakuyo Maru*, 12 Sep 1944. Decomm 15 Dec 1945. †
6* Palau-Yap Raids 3/44, Philippines Raids 9/44; six patrols.
Ships sunk: *Kachidoki Maru* (10,509/21, ex–American *President Harrison*) (~500 POWs lost), tkr *Zuiho Maru* (5,135/—) 12 Sep 1944; *Shinko Maru No. 1* (1,200/—) 19 Nov 1944, tkr *Engen Maru* (6,968/44) 6 Feb 1945, XPG *Eifuku Maru* (3,520/39) 8 Feb 1945.

SS 384 *Parche* Bikini target ship 1946. Decomm 11 Dec 1946. NRT. †
5* Okinawa, Raids on Japan 7–8/45; six patrols. PUC.
Ships sunk: *Taiyoku Maru* (5,244/—), *Shoryu Maru* (6,475/19) 4 May 1944; tkr *Koei Maru* (10,238/—), *Manko Maru* (4,471/35), **Yoshino Maru* (8,990/07) 31 Jul 1944; *Okinoyama Maru* (984/17) 7 Feb 1945, AM W-3 9 Apr 1945, §*Togo Maru* (302/23) 15 Apr 1945, *Hizen Maru* (946/—) 21 Jun 1945, XPG *Kamitsu Maru* (2,723/37), *Eikan Maru* (6,903/—) 26 Jun 1945.

SS 385 *Bang* Decomm 12 Feb 1947. †
6* Philippine Sea, Leyte, Iwo Jima, Okinawa; six patrols.
Ships sunk: *Takegawa Maru* (1,930/38) 29 Apr 1944, tkr *Nittatsu Maru* (2,859/—) 30 Apr 1944, *Kinrei Maru* (5,947/—) 4 May 1944, *Tokiwasan Maru* (1,804/37), *Shoryu Maru* (1,916/—) 9 Sep 1944; tkr *Tosei Maru No. 2* (507/—), PF No. 30 damaged 19 Sep 1944; *Sakae Maru* (2,878/02), *Amakusa Maru* (2,340/01) 23 Nov 1944;

SS 386 *Pilotfish* Bikini target ship. Decomm 29 Aug 1946. Stricken 25 Feb 1947. Sunk as target 16 Oct 1948.
5* Philippine Sea, 4th Bonins Raid, Bonins-Yap Raids, Iwo Jima, Okinawa; six patrols. Tokyo Bay.
Ship sunk: +*Ina Maru* (853/43) 1 Sep 1944.

SS 387 *Pintado* Decomm 6 Mar 1946. †
5* Philippine Sea, Leyte, Okinawa, Raids on Japan 7–8/45; six patrols. PUC.
Ships sunk: *Toho Maru* (4,716/18) 1 Jun 1944, *Kashimasan Maru* (2,825/42), *Havre Maru* (5,652/20) 6 Jun 1944; *Shonan Maru* (5,401/—) 6 Aug 1944, tkr *Tonan Maru No. 2* (19,262/37) 22 Aug 1944, DD *Akikaze* 3 Nov 1944, LST *No. 12* and LST *No. 104* 13 Dec 1944.

SS 388 *Pipefish* Damaged by aircraft bomb off Hainan, 30 Nov 1944. Decomm 19 Mar 1946. †
6* Saipan, Philippine Sea, Bonins-Yap Raids, Iwo Jima, Okinawa, Raids on Japan 7–8/45; six patrols.
Ships sunk: *Hakutetsu Maru* No. 7 (1,018/36) 12 Sep 1944, PF *No. 64* 3 Dec 1944.

SS 389 *Piranha* Decomm 31 May 1946. †
5* Philippines Raids 9/44, Iwo Jima, Okinawa; five patrols.
Ships sunk: Tkr *Nichiran Maru* (6,504/38) 12 Jul 1944, *Seattle Maru* (5,773/09) 16 Jul 1944, *Kiso Maru* (6,890/—) 16 Jun 1945.

SS 390 *Plaice* Decomm 11 Nov 1947. †
6* 1st Bonins Raid, 2nd Bonins Raid, 3rd Bonins Raid, Iwo Jima, Raids on Japan 7–8/45; six patrols.
Ships sunk: *Hyakufuku Maru* (986/28) 30 Jun 1944, AN *Kogi Maru* (857/40) 5 Jul 1944, SC-50 18 Jul 1944, PF *No. 10* 27 Sep 1944, DD *Maki* damaged 9 Dec 1944.

SS 391 *Pomfret* †
5* Philippines Raids 9/44, Honshu Raid 2/45, Iwo Jima, Okinawa, Raids on Japan 7–8/45; six patrols.
Ships sunk: *Tsuyama Maru* (6,962/16) 2 Oct 1944, *Atlas Maru* (7,347/20), *Hamburg Maru* (5,271/20) 2 Nov 1944; *Shoho Maru* (1,356/??) 25 Nov 1944.

SS 392 *Sterlet* †
6* 4th Bonins Raid, Honshu Raid 2/45, Iwo Jima, Okinawa, Raids on Japan 7–8/45; five patrols.
Ships sunk: *Miyagi Maru* (248/—) 4 Aug 1944, *Tama Maru No. 6* (275/36) 9 Aug 1944, tkr *Jinei Maru* (10,241/—) 25 Oct 1944, tkr **Talame Maru* (10,021/—) 30 Oct 1944, *Tateyama Maru* (1,148/—) 1 Mar 1945, *Kuretake Maru* (1,924/—), *Tenryo Maru* (2,231/38) 29 May 1945.

SS 393 *Queenfish* Rescued 18 POW survivors of *Rakuyo Maru*, 17 Sep 1944. †
6* Philippines Raids 9/44, Iwo Jima, Okinawa, Raids on Japan 7–8/45; five patrols.
Ships sunk: Tkr *Chiyoda Maru* (4,700/—) 31 Aug 1944, TB *Manazuru* damaged, *Toyoka Maru* (7,097/15), *Manshu Maru* (3,054/12) 9 Sep 1944; *Keijo Maru* (1,051/03), *Hakko Maru* (1,948/43) 8 Nov 1944; XPG *Chojusan Maru* (2,131/28) 9 Nov 1944, AKV *Akitsu Maru* (9,186/41) 15 Nov 1944, tkr *Manju Maru* (6,516/21) 8 Jan 1945, *Awa Maru* (11,249/43) 1 Apr 1945 (safe-conduct ship sunk in error).

SS 394 *Razorback* †
5* Palau, Philippines Raids 9/44, Iwo Jima, Okinawa; five patrols.
Ships sunk: Tkr **Kenjo Maru* (6,933/44) 7 Dec 1944, ODD *Kuretake* 30 Dec 1944. Tokyo Bay.

SS 395 *Redfish* †
2*; two patrols. PUC.
Ships sunk: *Batopaha Maru* (5,953/42) 25 Aug 1944, tkr *Ogura Maru* No. 2 (7,311/34) 16 Sep 1944, *Mizuho Maru* (8,506/12) 21 Sep 1944, *Hozan Maru* (2,345/07) 23 Nov 1944, CV **Junyo* damaged, not repaired 9 Dec 1944, CV *Unryu* southeast of Shanghai 19 Dec 1944.

SS 396 *Ronquil* †
6* Iwo Jima, Okinawa; five patrols.
Ships sunk: §*Yoshida Maru No. 3* (4,646/18), *Fukurei Maru* (5,969/—) 24 Aug 1944.

SS 397 *Scabbardfish* †
5* Leyte, Iwo Jima, Okinawa, Raids on Japan 7–8/45; five patrols.
Submarine sunk: *I-365* southeast of Yokosuka 28 Nov 1944.
Ships sunk: AS *Jingei* damaged, northwest of Okinawa 19 Sep 1944, *Kisaragi Maru* (875/44) 16 Nov 1944, *Hokkai Maru* (407/34) 21 Nov 1944.

SS 398 *Segundo* †
4* Palau, Philippines Raids 9/44, Iwo Jima, Okinawa; five patrols. Tokyo Bay.
Ships sunk: Tkr **Kenjo Maru* (6,933/44), +*Yasukuni Maru* (5,974/—) ?6 Dec 1944, *Shinto Maru* (1,215/—) 6 Dec 1944, *Shori Maru* (3,087/07) 11 Mar 1945, sail *Anto Maru No. 94* (1,250/—) 2 Jun 1945, *Fukui Maru No. 2* (1,578/17) 11 Jun 1945.

SS 399 *Sea Cat* †
3* Iwo Jima, Okinawa; four patrols. Tokyo Bay.

No.	Name	Builder	Keel Laid	Launched	Comm.
SS 400	*Sea Devil*	Portsmouth NYd	18 Nov 1943	28 Feb 1944	24 May 1944
SS 401	*Sea Dog*	Portsmouth NYd	1 Nov 1943	28 Mar 1944	3 Jun 1944
SS 402	*Sea Fox*	Portsmouth NYd	2 Nov 1943	28 Mar 1944	13 Jun 1944
SS 403	*Atule*	Portsmouth NYd	2 Dec 1943	6 Mar 1944	21 Jun 1944
SS 404	*Spikefish*	Portsmouth NYd	29 Jan 1944	26 Apr 1944	30 Jun 1944
	ex–*Shiner* (24 Sep 1942)				
SS 405	*Sea Owl*	Portsmouth NYd	7 Feb 1944	7 May 1944	17 Jul 1944
SS 406	*Sea Poacher*	Portsmouth NYd	23 Feb 1944	20 May 1944	31 Jul 1944
SS 407	*Sea Robin*	Portsmouth NYd	1 Mar 1944	25 May 1944	7 Aug 1944

* joint attack; +probable sinking; #possible sinking; § question on sinking

SS 408	*Sennet*	Portsmouth NYd	8 Mar 1944	6 Jun 1944	22 Aug 1944
SS 409	*Piper*	Portsmouth NYd	15 Mar 1944	26 Jun 1944	23 Aug 1944
	ex–*Awa* (31 Jan 1944)				
SS 410	*Threadfin*	Portsmouth NYd	18 Mar 1944	26 Jun 1944	30 Aug 1944
	ex–*Sole* (23 Sep 1942)				
SS 411	*Spadefish*	Mare I. NYd	27 May 1943	8 Jan 1944	9 Mar 1944
SS 412	*Trepang*	Mare I. NYd	24 Jun 1943	23 Mar 1944	22 May 1944
	ex–*Senorita* (24 Sep 1942)				
SS 413	*Spot*	Mare I. NYd	24 Aug 1943	19 May 1944	3 Aug 1944
SS 414	*Springer*	Mare I. NYd	30 Oct 1943	3 Aug 1944	18 Oct 1944
SS 415	*Stickleback*	Mare I. NYd	1 Mar 1944	1 Jan 1945	29 Mar 1945
SS 416	*Tiru*	Mare I. NYd	17 Apr 1944	16 Sep 1947	1 Sep 1948
SS 425	*Trumpetfish*	Cramp	23 Aug 1943	13 May 1945	29 Jan 1946
SS 426	*Tusk*	Cramp	23 Aug 1943	8 Jul 1945	11 Apr 1946
SS 427	*Turbot*	Cramp	13 Nov 1943	12 Apr 1946	—
SS 428	*Ulua*	Cramp	13 Nov 1943	23 Apr 1946	—

Service Records:

SS 400 *Sea Devil* †
5* Leyte Ldgs., Iwo Jima, Okinawa, Raids on Japan 7–8/45; five patrols.
Submarine sunk: *I-364* 300 miles southeast of Yokosuka 15 Sep 1944.
Ships sunk: Tkr *Akigawa Maru* (6,859/44), *Hawaii Maru* (9,467/15) 2 Dec 1944; CV **Junyo* damaged SW of Homozaki, not repaired 9 Dec 1944, *Taijo Maru* (6,366/44), *Edogawa Maru* (1,972/—), *Nisshin Maru* (1,179/16) 2 Apr 1945; *Wakamiyasan Maru* (2,211/44) 14 Jun 1945.

SS 401 *Sea Dog* †
2* Okinawa; four patrols.
Ships sunk: XPG *Tomitsu Maru* (2,933/37) AF *Muroto* 22 Oct 1944, *Toko Maru* (6,850/ ?) 16 Apr 1945, *Sagawa Maru* (1,186/18), *Shoyo Maru* (2,211/—) 9 Jun 1945; *Kofuku Maru* (753/19) 11 Jun 1945, *Shinsen Maru* (880/—), +*Kaiwa Maru* (1,045/18) 12 Jun 1945; *Koan Maru* (884/37) 15 Jun 1945, *Kokai Maru* (1,272/18), +*Shinei Maru No. 3* (958/18) 19 Jun 1945.

SS 402 *Sea Fox* †
4* Iwo Jima, Okinawa, Raids on Japan 7–8/45; four patrols.

SS 403 *Atule* Arctic Operation Nanook, Jul 1946. Decomm 8 Sep 1947. †
4* Leyte, Iwo Jima, Okinawa, Raids on Japan 7–8/45; four patrols.
Ships sunk: *Asama Maru* (16,975/29) 1 Nov 1944, AM W-38 20 Nov 1944, ODD *No. 38* (ex–*Yomogi*), AG *Manju Maru* (ex–*Santos Maru*) (7,266/25) 25 Nov 1944; *Taiman Maru No. 1* (6,888/44) 24 Jan 1945, PF No. 4 13 Aug 1945.

SS 404 *Spikefish* †
3* Iwo Jima, Okinawa; four patrols.
Submarine sunk: *I-373* 190 miles southeast of Shanghai 13 Aug 1945.

SS 405 *Sea Owl* †
5* Iwo Jima, Okinawa, Raids on Japan 7–8/45; three patrols.
Submarine sunk: §*RO-56* 17 Apr 1945.
Ship sunk: PF *No. 41* 9 Jun 1945.

SS 406 *Sea Poacher* †
4* Iwo Jima, Raids on Japan 7–8/45; four patrols.
Ship sunk: *Kiri Maru No. 2* (334/35) 23 Jul 1945.

SS 407 *Sea Robin* †
3*; three patrols.
Ships sunk: Tkr *Tarakan Maru* (5,135/43) 6 Jan 1945, *Suiten Maru* (1,805/12) 3 Mar 1945, *Shoyu Maru* (853/—), AN *Nagara Maru* (856/40), XPG *Manyo Maru* (2,904/37) 5 Mar 1945; *Sakishima Maru* (1,224/18) 10 Jul 1945.

SS 408 *Sennet* Damaged by YP *Kotoshiro Maru* No. 8 and sank it south of Japan, 13 Feb 1945. †
4* Iwo Jima, Okinawa; four patrols.
Ships sunk: CMc *Naryu* 16 Feb 1945, *Hagane Maru* (1,901/38) 19 Apr 1945, ARC *Hatsushima* 28 Apr 1945, *Unkai Maru No. 15* (1,208/18), *Hagikawa Maru* (2,995/—), *Hakuei Maru* (2,863/—) 28 Jul 1945; *Yuzan Maru* (6,039/19) 30 Jul 1945.

SS 409 *Piper* †
4* Honshu Raid 2/45, Iwo Jima, Honshu Raid 2/45, Okinawa, Raids on Japan 7–8/45; three patrols.

SS 410 *Threadfin* †
3* Okinawa; three patrols.
Ships sunk: *Issei Maru* (1,864/29) 30 Jan 1945, PF *Mikura* 28 Mar 1945, AM *W-39* 20 Jul 1945.

SS 411 *Spadefish* Decomm 3 May 1946. †
4* Philippines Raids 9/44, Okinawa; five patrols. PUC.
Ships sunk: LSD *Tamatsu Maru* (9,589/43) 19 Aug 1944, tkr *Hakko Maru No. 2* (10,023/44) 22 Aug 1944, *Nichiman Maru* (1,922/17), *Nichian Maru* (6,197/12), *Shinten Maru* (1,254/17), *Shokei Maru* (2,557/38) 8 Sep 1944; *Gyokuyo Maru* (5,396/ , ex–British *Bennevis*) 14 Nov 1944, CVE *Shinyo* 17 Nov 1944, *SC-156* 18 Nov 1944, *Daiboshi Maru No. 6* (3,925/02) 29 Nov 1944, PF *Kume*, *Sanuki Maru* (7,158/39) 28 Jan 1945; *Tairai Maru* (4,273/25) 4 Feb 1945, *Shohei Maru* (1,092/03) 6 Feb 1945, *Doryo Maru* (2,274/44) 23 Mar 1945, *Ritsu Go* (ex–Chinese *Lee Tung*) (1,853/—) 9 Apr 1945, *Hinode Maru No. 17* (235/19) 11 Apr 1945, *Daigen Maru No. 2* (1,999/17), *Unkai Maru No. 8* (1,293/24), *Jintsu Maru* (994/21) 10 Jun 1945; Soviet *Transbalt* (10,335/99) 13 Jun 1945 (in error), *Seizan Maru* (2,018/18) 14 Jun 1945, XCM *Eijo Maru* (2,274/44) 17 Jun 1945. †

SS 412 *Trepang* Decomm 27 Jun 1946.
5* Honshu Raid 2/45, Iwo Jima, Okinawa, Raids on Japan 7–8/45; five patrols.
Ships sunk: §*Takunan Maru* (750/41) 1 Oct 1944, LST *No. 105* 11 Oct 1944, DD *Fuyutsuki* damaged 12 Oct 1944 , *Banshu Maru No. 31* (748/42), *Jinyo Maru* (6,862/44), *Fukuyo Maru* (5,463/20) 6 Dec 1944; *Uzuki Maru* (875/—) 24 Feb 1945, XPG *Nissho Maru No. 2* (1,386/41) 3 Mar 1945, LST *No. 146* 28 Apr 1945, *Miho Maru* (4,667/44) 30 Apr 1945, AM *W-20* 4 May 1945, *Koun Maru No. 2* (606/—) 7 Jul 1945.

SS 413 *Spot* Damaged by naval gunfire off Formosa, 17 Mar 1945. Decomm 19 Jun 1946. †
4* Iwo Jima, Okinawa, Raids on Japan 7–8/45; three patrols.
Ships sunk: **Ikomasan Maru* (3,173/16) 16 Mar 1945, *Nanking Maru* (3,005/14) 17 Mar 1945.

SS 414 *Springer* Decomm 14 Sep 1946. †
3* Iwo Jima, Okinawa, Raids on Japan 7–8/45; three patrols.
Ships sunk: LST *No. 18* 18 Mar 1945, PC *No. 17* 28 Apr 1945, PF *Oka* 2 May 1945, PF *No. 25* 3 May 1945.

SS 415 *Stickleback* 1 patrol. Decomm 26 Jun 1946–6 Sep 1946. †

SS 416 *Tiru* Construction suspended 30 Jan 1946. Completed to new design, GUPPY. †

SS 425 *Trumpetfish* Sank SS *I-400* as target, 1946. †

SS 426 *Tusk* Commenced conversion to GUPPY (Greater Underwater Propulsive Power) design, Oct 1947. †

SS 427 *Turbot* Canceled 12 Aug 1945. Towed to Portsmouth NYd for testing. Machinery test hulk. BU after 1978.

SS 428 *Ulua* Canceled 12 Aug 1945. Towed to Portsmouth NYd for testing underwater explosive test hulk. Sold 15 Oct 1958; BU Portsmouth, Va.

*joint attack; +probable sinking; #possible sinking; § question on sinking

Tench Class

No.	Name	Builder	Keel Laid	Launched	Comm.
SS 417	*Tench*	Portsmouth NYd	1 Apr 1944	7 Jul 1944	6 Oct 1944
SS 418	*Thornback*	Portsmouth NYd	5 Apr 1944	7 Jul 1944	13 Oct 1944
SS 419	*Tigrone*	Portsmouth NYd	8 May 1944	20 Jul 1944	25 Oct 1944
SS 420	*Tirante*	Portsmouth NYd	28 Apr 1944	9 Aug 1944	6 Nov 1944
SS 421	*Trutta*	Portsmouth NYd	22 May 1944	18 Aug 1944	16 Nov 1944
	ex-*Tomatate* (24 Sep 1942)				
SS 422	*Toro*	Portsmouth NYd	27 May 1944	23 Aug 1944	8 Dec 1944
SS 423	*Torsk*	Portsmouth NYd	7 Jun 1944	6 Sep 1944	16 Dec 1944
SS 424	*Quillback*	Portsmouth NYd	27 Jun 1944	1 Oct 1944	29 Dec 1944
SS 429	*Unicorn*	Cramp	—	—	—
SS 430	*Vendace*	Cramp	—	—	—
SS 431	*Walrus*	Cramp	—	—	—
SS 432	*Whitefish*	Cramp	—	—	—
SS 433	*Whiting*	Cramp	—	—	—
SS 434	*Wolffish*	Cramp	—	—	—
SS 435	*Corsair*	Electric Boat	1 Mar 1945	3 May 1946	8 Nov 1946
SS 436	*Unicorn*	Electric Boat	25 Apr 1945	1 Aug 1946	—
SS 437	*Walrus*	Electric Boat	21 Jun 1945	20 Sep 1946	—
SS 438–57	—	Electric Boat	—	—	—
SS 458–63	—	Manitowoc	—	—	—
SS 464	*Chicolar*	Manitowoc	—	—	—
SS 465–74	—	Manitowoc	—	—	—

Displacement	1,570/2,415 tons
Dimensions	311'8" (oa) x 27'3" x 15'3"
Machinery	2 screws; diesel-electric; SHP 5,400; 20.25 knots; HP 2,740; 8.75 knots
Endurance	11,000/10; depth: 400'
Complement	81
Armament	1–5"/25, 1–40mm AA, 1–20mm AA guns 10–21" TT

Notes: Twenty-five completed. Hull more streamlined, otherwise similar to *Balao* class. SS 417–24 originally ordered from Mare I. NYd, 458–63 from Electric Boat, and 537–44 from Cramp. *Requin* fitted with rocket-launcher 1945. *Sarda* had extralong CT.

Service Records:

SS 417 *Tench* Decomm . Jan 1947. †
3* Iwo Jima, Okinawa, Raids on Japan 7–8/45; three patrols.
Ships sunk: *Mikamisan Maru* (861/—) 2 Jun 1945, *Ryujin Maru* (517/??) 4 Jun 1945, *Shinroku Maru* (2,857/44) or *Kamishika Maru* (2,857/—) 9 Jun 1945, tkr *Shoei Maru No. 6* (834/—) 10 Jun 1945.

SS 418 *Thornback* Sank CG-74327 in collision off Portsmouth, N.H., 10 Nov 1944. Decomm 6 Apr 1946. †
1* Raids on Japan 7–8/45; 1 patrol.

*joint attack; +probable sinking; #possible sinking; § question on sinking

SS 419 *Tigrone* Decomm 30 Mar 1946. †
2* Okinawa, Raids on Japan 7–8/45; three patrols. Tokyo Bay.

SS 420 *Tirante* Decomm 6 Jul 1946. †
2* Okinawa; two patrols. PUC.
Ships sunk: AN *Fuji Maru* (703/32) 25 Mar 1945, *Nase Maru* (1,218/17) 28 Mar 1945, *Tama Maru* (396/39) 8 Apr 1945, tkr *Nikko Maru* (5,057/03) 9 Apr 1945, *Jusan Maru* (3943/??), PF *No. 31*, PF *Nomi* 14 Apr 1945; *Hakuju Maru* (2,220/—) 11 Jun 1945, *Saitsu Maru* (1,045/11) 8 Jul 1945.

SS 421 *Trutta* Decomm 2 Feb 1946. †
2* Okinawa, Raids on Japan 7–8/45; two patrols.

SS 422 *Toro* Out of comm 7 Feb 1946–13 May 1947. †
2* Okinawa, Raids on Japan 7–8/45; two patrols.

SS 423 *Torsk* †
2* Okinawa. Two patrols.
Ships sunk: *Kaiho Maru* (873/—) 13 Aug 1945, PF *No. 13* and PF *No. 47* 14 Aug 1945.

SS 424 *Quillback* †
1* Okinawa; 1 patrol.

SS 429 *Unicorn* Canceled 29 Jul 1944.
SS 430 *Vendace* Canceled 29 Jul 1944.
SS 431 *Walrus* Canceled 29 Jul 1944.
SS 432 *Whitefish* Canceled 29 Jul 1944.
SS 433 *Whiting* Canceled 29 Jul 1944.
SS 434 *Wolffish* Canceled 29 Jul 1944.
SS 435 *Corsair* †
SS 436 *Unicorn* Canceled 7 Jan 1946. Reinstated for partial completion, 26 Feb 1946. †
SS 437 *Walrus* Canceled 7 Jan 1946.
SS 438–63 — Canceled 29 Jul 1944.
SS 464 *Chicolar* Canceled 29 Jul 1944.
SS 465–74 — Canceled 29 Jul 1944.

No.	Name	Builder	Keel Laid	Launched	Comm.
SS 475	*Argonaut*	Portsmouth NYd	28 Jun 1944	1 Oct 1944	15 Jan 1945
SS 476	*Runner*	Portsmouth NYd	10 Jul 1944	17 Oct 1944	6 Feb 1945
SS 477	*Conger*	Portsmouth NYd	11 Jul 1944	17 Oct 1944	14 Feb 1945
SS 478	*Cutlass*	Portsmouth NYd	22 Jul 1944	5 Nov 1944	17 Mar 1945

Figure 6.29: *Sea Leopard* (SS 483), rearmed with two deck guns.

SS 479	*Diablo*	Portsmouth NYd	11 Aug 1944	1 Dec 1944	31 Mar 1945
SS 480	*Medregal*	Portsmouth NYd	21 Aug 1944	15 Dec 1944	14 Apr 1945
SS 481	*Requin*	Portsmouth NYd	24 Aug 1944	1 Jan 1945	28 Apr 1945
SS 482	*Irex*	Portsmouth NYd	2 Oct 1944	26 Jan 1945	14 May 1945
SS 483	*Sea Leopard*	Portsmouth NYd	7 Nov 1944	2 Mar 1945	11 Jun 1945
SS 484	*Odax*	Portsmouth NYd	4 Dec 1944	10 Apr 1945	11 Jul 1945
SS 485	*Sirago*	Portsmouth NYd	3 Jan 1945	11 May 1945	13 Aug 1945
SS 486	*Pomodon*	Portsmouth NYd	29 Jan 1945	12 Jun 1945	9 Nov 1945
SS 487	*Remora*	Portsmouth NYd	5 Mar 1945	12 Jul 1945	3 Jan 1946
SS 488	*Sarda*	Portsmouth NYd	12 Apr 1945	24 Aug 1945	19 Apr 1946
SS 489	*Spinax*	Portsmouth NYd	14 May 1945	20 Nov 1945	20 Sep 1946
SS 490	*Volador*	Portsmouth NYd	15 Jun 1945	17 Jan 1946	1 Oct 1948
SS 491	*Pompano*	Portsmouth NYd	16 Jul 1945	—	—
SS 492	*Grayling*	Portsmouth NYd	—	—	—
SS 493	*Needlefish*	Portsmouth NYd	—	—	—
SS 494	*Sculpin*	Portsmouth NYd	—	—	—
SS 495–515	—	Portsmouth NYd	—	—	—
SS 516	*Wahoo*	Mare I. NYd	15 May 1944	—	—
SS 517	—	Mare I. NYd	29 Jun 1944	—	—
SS 518–21	—	Mare I. NYd	—	—	—
SS 522	*Amberjack*	Boston NYd	8 Feb 1944	15 Dec 1944	4 Mar 1946
SS 523	*Grampus*	Boston NYd	8 Feb 1944	15 Dec 1944	26 Oct 1949
SS 524	*Pickerel*	Boston NYd	8 Feb 1944	15 Dec 1944	4 Apr 1949
SS 525	*Grenadier*	Boston NYd	8 Feb 1944	15 Dec 1944	10 Feb 1951
SS 526	*Dorado*	Boston NYd	—	—	—
SS 527	*Comber*	Boston NYd	—	—	—
SS 528	*Sea Panther*	Boston NYd	—	—	—
SS 529	*Tiburon*	Boston NYd	—	—	—
SS 530–36	—	Cramp	—	—	—
SS 537–44	—	Boston NYd	—	—	—
SS 545–47	—	Electric Boat	—	—	—
SS 548–50	—	Portsmouth NYd	—	—	—
SS 551–62	—	—	—	—	—

Service Records:

SS 475 *Argonaut* Collided with cruiser *Honolulu* off New Jersey, 11 Jan 1946. †
1* Raids on Japan 7–8/45; 1 patrol.

SS 476 *Runner* †
1*; two patrols. Tokyo Bay.
Ship sunk: AM *W-27* 10 Jul 1945.

SS 477 *Conger* †
SS 478 *Cutlass* One patrol. †
SS 479 *Diablo* †
SS 480 *Medregal* †
SS 481 *Requin* †
SS 482 *Irex* †
SS 483 *Sea Leopard* †
SS 484 *Odax* †
SS 485 *Sirago* †
SS 486 *Pomodon* †
SS 487 *Remora* †
SS 488 *Sarda* †
SS 489 *Spinax* †
SS 490 *Volador* Suspended 30 Jan 1946. Resumed Aug 1947.
SS 491 *Pompano* Canceled 12 Aug 1945.
SS 492 *Grayling* Canceled 12 Aug 1945.
SS 493 *Needlefish* Canceled 12 Aug 1945.
SS 494 *Sculpin* Canceled 12 Aug 1945.
SS 495–15 Canceled 29 Jul 1944.
SS 516 *Wahoo* Canceled 7 Jan 1946.
SS 517–21 Canceled 29 Jul 1944.
SS 522 *Amberjack* GUPPY Jan 1947. †
SS 523 *Grampus* Suspended 17 Jan 1946. †
SS 524 *Pickerel* Suspended 17 Jan 1946. †
SS 525 *Grenadier* Suspended 17 Jan 1946. †
SS 526 *Dorado* Canceled 29 Jul 1944.
SS 527 *Comber* Canceled 29 Jul 1944.
SS 528 *Sea Panther* Canceled 29 Jul 1944.
SS 529 *Tiburon* Canceled 29 Jul 1944.
SS 530–44 Canceled 29 Jul 1944.
SS 545–62 Canceled 26/28 Mar 1945.

GERMAN U-BOATS IN U.S. CUSTODY

At the end of the war in Europe a number of German U-boats came into U.S. custody, some of which were allocated under Allied agreement.

Boat	Type	Disposition
U-234	XB	Surrendered at Portsmouth, N.H., 16 May 1945. Sunk by submarine *Greenfish* northeast of Cape Cod, 20 Nov 1947.
U-505	XIC	Captured at sea, 4 Jun 1944. Put on display at Museum of Science & Industry, Chicago, 1955.
U-530	IXC	Surrendered at Mar del Plata, Argentina, 10 Jul 1945. Torpedoed in test northeast of Cape Cod, 28 Nov 1947.
U-805	IXC	Surrendered off Portsmouth, N.H., 14 May 1945. Sunk as target off U.S. East Coast, 8 Feb 1946.
U-858	IXC	Surrendered off Delaware, 14 May 1945. Sunk as target off New England, end of 1947.
U-873	IXD	Surrendered at Portsmouth, N.H., 16 May 1945; BU 1948.

U-889	IXC	Surrendered at Shelburne, Nova Scotia, 15 May 1945. Transferred to U.S., 10 Jan 1946. Sunk as torpedo target off New England, end of 1947.
U-977	VIIC	Arrived at Mar del Plata, Argentina, 17 Aug 1945. Transferred to USN, 13 Nov 1945. Torpedoed as target by submarine *Atule*, off Cape Cod, Mass., 13 Nov 1946.
U-1105	VIIC	Surrendered at Loch Eriboll, Scotland, 10 May 1945. Transferred to USN, 1946. Sunk during explosive trials in Chesapeake Bay, 18 Nov 1948. Salvaged and sunk again, 19 Sep 1949.
U-1228	IXC	Surrendered at Portsmouth, N.H., 17 May 1945. Sunk as target off U.S. East Coast, 5 Feb 1946.
U-1406	XVIIB	Scuttled at Cuxhaven, Germany, 5 May 1945. Raised and taken to the United States, 1945. Used for trials and BU 1948.
U-2513	XXI	Surrendered at Horten, Norway, 8 May 1945. Transferred to United States, Aug 1945. President Harry S. Truman embarked and traveled underwater on board off Key West, Fla., 1 Nov 1946. Used in evaluation tests 1946–49. Sunk by destroyer *Robert A. Owens* during Weapon Alfa tests off Key West, 7 Oct 1951
U-3008	XXI	Comm 24 Jul 1946. Out of service 18 Jun 1948. BU 1956 Puerto Rico.

JAPANESE SUBMARINES

The Japanese submarines *I-14, I-201, I-203, I-400,* and *I-401* were taken to Pearl Harbor for testing in late 1945, and sunk as targets there, 21 May–4 Jun 1946.

7
MINE VESSELS

MINELAYERS

Minelayers on the Navy List, 1922

CM 1 *Baltimore* Decomm 15 Sep 1922. Stricken 14 Oct 1937. Sold 16 Feb 1942.

CM 2 *San Francisco* Decomm 24 Dec 1921. Renamed ***Yosemite***, 1 Jan 1931. Stricken 8 Jun 1937. BU 1939, Baltimore.

CM 3 *Aroostook* Seaplane tender. (Armament: 1-5"/51, 2-3"/50.) Decomm 10 Mar 1931. Rec **AK 44**, 20 May 1941. Stricken 5 Feb 1943, to U.S. War Department.
Later history: Merchant *Bunker Hill*, 1946; floating casino *Lux*, 1947. BU 1948, Napa, Calif.

CM 4 *Shawmut* Seaplane tender. (Armament, 1938: 1-3"/50; <1945> 1-5"/38, 4-3"/50, 2 twin 40mm, 8-20mm guns.) Renamed ***Oglala***, 1 Jan 1928. Sunk by torpedo explosion at Pearl Harbor, 7 Dec 1941. Refloated and rebuilt as repair ship. Rec **ARG 1**, 15 Jun 1943. Recomm 28 Feb 1944. Decomm 11 Jul 1946. Stricken 13 Nov 1946. Sold 10 Mar 1947; BU 1965 Richmond, Calif.
1* Pearl Harbor.

Figure 7.1: *Terror* (CM 5), the Navy's only built-for-the-purpose minelayer. Notice the standard 5" gun mounts. Two sisters completed as landing ships.

Terror Class

No.	Name	Builder	Keel Laid	Launched	Comm.
CM 5	*Terror*	Phila. NYd	3 Sep 1940	6 Jun 1941	15 Sep 1942
CM 6	*Catskill*	Willamette	12 Jul 1941	19 May 1942	
CM 7	*Ozark*	Willamette	12 Jul 1941	15 Jun 1942	

Displacement	5,875 tons , 8,640 f/l
Dimensions	454'10" (oa); 440" (wl) x 60'2" x 19'7"
Machinery	2 screws; GE GT; 4 CE boilers; SHP 11,000; 20.3 knots
Endurance	7,000/15
Complement	481
Armament	4-5"/38, 16-1.1"; 1.1" replaced by 4 quad 40mm, 14-20mm AA

Notes: Carried 900 mines. *Catskill* and *Ozark* completed as landing ships. Minelayers were named for Civil War monitors.

Service Records:

CM 5 *Terror* Damaged by kamikaze, Okinawa, 1 May 1945 (48 killed). Decomm 1 Sep 1947. †
4* Gilbert Is., Guam, Iwo Jima, Okinawa.

CM 6 *Catskill* Rec **AP 106**, 1 May 1943. Rec **LSV 1**, 21 Apr 1944. (See p. 200)

CM 7 *Ozark* Rec **AP 107**, 1 May 1943. Rec **LSV 2**, 21 Apr 1944. (See p. 200)

No.	Name	Builder	Launched	Acquired	Comm.
CM 8	*Keokuk*	Cramp	22 Sep 1914	28 Jul 1941	28 Feb 1942
	ex-CMc 6 (15 Aug 1941), ex-AN 5 (18 May 1942); ex-*Columbia Heights* (1941), ex-*Henry M. Flagler*(1941)				
CM 11	*Salem*	Cramp	25 Sep 1916	8 Jun 1942	9 Aug 1942
	ex-*Joseph R. Parrott* (1942)				
CM 12	*Weehawken*	Cramp	6 Nov 1920	15 Jun 1942	30 Sep 1942
	ex-*Estrada Palma* (1942)				

Figure 7.2: *Weehawken* (CM 12), 7 Nov 1943, a converted car ferry; notice mine rails on the stern.

Figure 7.3: *Keokuk* (CM 8), 1 Nov 1942. Formerly the car ferry *Henry M. Flagler*, she was used later as a net cargo ship.

Displacement	6,525 tons f/l; CM 11 *Salem*: 2,406 grt; CM 12 *Weehawken*: 2,639grt; CM 8 *Keokuk*: 5,300 tons; 6,150 f/l; 2,699 grt
Dimensions	350' (oa); 337'3" (wl) x 57' x 17'6" (CM 8: 353' [oa])
Machinery	2 screws; VTE; 4 Scotch s/e boilers; SHP 2,700; 12 knots
Complement	290
Armament	3-3"/50, 2 twin 40mm, 10-20mm AA

Notes: Converted car ferries. CM 11 *Salem* used as net cargo ship 1944-5. CM 12 *Weehawken* converted at Bethlehem, Hoboken, N.J.

Service Records:

CM 8 *Keokuk* Rec **AKN 4**, 1 Nov 1943. Damaged by Kamikaze, Iwo Jima, 21 Feb 1945 (17 killed). Decomm 5 Dec 1945. Sold 7 Mar 1947.

5* Sicily, Saipan, Palau, Iwo Jima, Okinawa.

Later history: Merchant *Henry M. Flagler* 1947, renamed *Flagler Odeca* 1961, *Henry M. Flagler* 1964, *Freight Transporter* 1964. Foundered in tow 16 Dec 1971 en route to BU in Spain.

CM 11 *Salem* In collision with British *LCI-166* at Brooklyn NYd, 10 Nov 1942. Renamed ***Shawmut***, 15 Aug 1945. Decomm 6 Dec 1945. Stricken 3 Jan 1946. Sold 7 Mar 1947.

2* Sicily, Okinawa.

Later history: Merchant *Joseph R. Parrott*. BU 1969, Bilbao, Spain.

CM 12 *Weehawken* Went aground in typhoon at Okinawa, 9 Oct 1945 and lost. Stricken 3 Jan 1946. Hulk destroyed, 16 Feb 1946.

2* Sicily, Okinawa.

CM 9 *Monadnock* CMc 4, 15 Jun 1942

CM 10 *Miantonomah* CMc 5, 15 Jun 1942

COASTAL MINELAYERS

No.	Name	Rec	Date
CMc 1	*Siren*	Rec PY 13	15 Nov 1940
CMc 2	*Niagara*	Rec PG 52	15 Nov 1940
CMc 6	*Keokuk*	Rec CM 8	15 Aug 1941

No.	Name	Builder	Launched	Acquired	Comm.
CMc 3	*Wassuc*	New Jersey DD	1924	20 Dec 1940	15 May 1941
	ex-*Yale* (1940)				

Displacement	1,400 tons; 1,830 f/l; 1,670 grt
Dimensions	230'6" (oa); 222' wl x 42' x 12'6"
Machinery	2 screws; VTE; 2 Scotch boilers; SHP 2,000; 13 knots
Complement	93
Armament	2-3"/50; (1945) 1-3"/50, 4-20mm

Notes: Coastal passenger ship. Converted at New York NYd. Mine training and experimental vessel.

Service Record:

CMc 3 *Wassuc* Decomm 8 Nov 1945. Stricken 28 Nov 1945. Trfd to MC 25 Jul 1946, sold 3 Aug 1948; BU 1948 Baltimore.

Figure 7.4: *Wassuc* (CMc 3) on 31 Jul 1944, a converted passenger steamer was used for training.

Figure 7.5: The minelayer *Miantonomah* (CM 10), 10 Oct 1942, at Norfolk Navy Yard. Notice mine chutes built into the stern.

Figure 7.6: *Picket* (ACM 8) was an Army mine planter acquired by the Navy in 1945.

No.	Name	Builder	Launched	Acquired	Comm.
CMc 4	*Monadnock* ex–*Cavalier* (1941)	Pusey	1938	9 Jun 1941	2 Dec 1941
CMc 5	*Miantonomah* ex–*Quaker* (1941)	Pusey	1938	5 May 1941	13 Nov 1941

Displacement	3,110 tons; 4,070 f/l; 3,056 grt
Dimensions	292' (oa); 280' (wl) x 48'6" x 19'8"
Machinery	1 screw; GE GT; 2 B&W boilers; SHP 4,000; 17.5 knots
Complement	200
Armament	CMc 4 *Monadnock*: 2-3"/50, 2 twin 40mm AA; (1945) 2-3"/50, 10-20mm.

Note: Carried 752 mines.

Service Records:

CMc 4 *Monadnock* Rec **CM 9**, 15 Jun 1942. Rec **ACM 10**, 10 Jul 1945. Decomm 3 Jun 1946. Stricken 3 Jul 1946.
3* North Africa, Lingayen, Okinawa.
Later history: Merchant *Cavalier* 1947, renamed *Karukara* 1949, *Monte de la Esperanza*, 1952. BU 1966 Santander.

CMc 5 *Miantonomah* Rec **CM 10**, 15 May 1942. Sunk by mine off Le Havre, 25 Sep 1944 (58 killed).
2* North Africa, Normandy.

AUXILIARY MINELAYERS

No.	Name	Builder	Launched	Acquired	Comm.
ACM 1	*Chimo* ex–*Col. Charles W. Bundy* (MP 15)	Marietta	2 Feb 1943	7 Apr 1944	7 Apr 1944
ACM 2	*Planter* ex–*Col. George W. Ricker* (MP 16)	Marietta	23 Feb 1943	4 Apr 1944	4 Apr 1944
ACM 3	*Barricade* ex–*Col. John P. Story* (MP 8)	Marietta	16 Jul 1942	7 Apr 1944	7 Apr 1944
ACM 5	*Barbican* ex–*Col. George Armistead* (MP 3)	Marietta	18 Aug 1942	5 Jan 1945	24 Mar 1945
ACM 6	*Bastion* ex–*Col. Henry J. Hunt* (MP 2)	Marietta	2 Dec 1941	4 Jan 1945	9 Apr 1945
ACM 7	*Obstructor* ex–*Lt. William J. Sylvester* (MP 5)	Marietta	24 Mar 1942	4 Jan 1945	1 Apr 1945
ACM 8	*Picket* ex–*Gen. Henry Knox* (MP 1)	Marietta	1941	2 Jan 1945	8 Mar 1945
ACM 9	*Trapper* ex–*Maj. Gen. Arthur Murray* (MP 9)	Marietta	15 Aug 1942	2 Jan 1945	15 Mar 1945

Displacement	1,320 tons f/l
Dimensions	188'2" (oa); 168'8" (wl) x 37' x 12'6"
Machinery	2 screws; Skinner Unaflow; 2 CE boilers; SHP 1,200; 12.5 knots
Complement	69
Armament	1-40mm, 4-20mm AA

Notes: Sixteen "mine planters" were built for the Army. Eight others were transferred to the Navy in 1949. The remaining two, *Gen. Samuel M. Mills* (MP 4) and *Brig. Gen. Henry L. Abbott* (MP 6) were not acquired by the Navy.

Service Records:

ACM 1 *Chimo* Decomm 21 May 1946. Sold 28 Sep 1948.
2* Normandy, Minesweeping 1945.
Later history: Merchant *Chimo* 1949, renamed *Day Island,* 1963. Foundered west of Bulen Bay, 8 Dec 1977.

ACM 2 *Planter* Decomm 22 May 1946. Stricken 23 Dec 1947. Trfd to MC 9 Apr 1948.
1* Southern France.
Later history: Merchant *Planter* 1949, renamed *San Juan* 1963, *Purple Aster, Tiger Fish 2.*

ACM 3 *Barricade* Decomm and trfd to USCG 28 Jun 1946.
1* Southern France.
Later history: Renamed USCGC *Magnolia* (WAGL 328).

ACM 5 *Barbican* Decomm and trfd to USCG, 12 Jun 1946.
Later history: Renamed USCGC *Ivy* (WAGL 329).

ACM 6 *Bastion* Decomm and trfd to USCG, 18 Jun 1946.
Later history: Renamed USCGC *Jonquil* (WAGL 330).

ACM 7 *Obstructor* Decomm and trfd to USCG, 28 Jun 1946.
1* Minesweeping 1945.
Later history: Renamed USCGC *Heather* (WAGL 331).

ACM 8 *Picket* Tokyo Bay. Decomm and trfd to USCG, 24 Jun 1946.
Later history: Renamed USCGC *Willow* (WAGL 332).

ACM 9 *Trapper* Decomm and trfd to USCG, 20 Jun 1946.
Later history: Renamed USCGC *Yamacraw* (WARC 333).

No.	Name	Former	Date
ACM 4	*Buttress*	ex–PCE 878	15 Jun 1944
ACM 10	*Monadnock*	ex–CMc 4	10 Jul 1945

LIGHT MINELAYERS

On the Navy List, 1922

No.	Name	Formerly	
DM 1	*Stribling*	DD 96	Decomm 26 Jun 1922. Stricken 1 Dec 1936, sunk as target off Pearl Harbor, 28 Jul 1937.
DM 2	*Murray*	DD 97	Decomm 1 Jul 1922. Stricken 7 Jan 1936, sold 29 Sep 1936; BU.
DM 3	*Israel*	DD 98	Decomm 7 Jul 1922. Stricken 25 Jan 1937, sold 18 Apr 1939; BU Baltimore.
DM 4	*Luce*	DD 99	Out of comm 30 Jun 1922-19 Mar 1930. Decomm 31 Jan 1931. Stricken 7 Jan 1936. Sold 29 Sep 1936; BU.
DM 5	*Maury*	DD 100	Decomm 19 Mar 1930. Stricken 22 Oct 1930, sold 17 Jan 1931; BU Baltimore.
DM 6	*Lansdale*	DD 101	Out of comm 25 Jun 1922-1 May 1930. Decomm 24 Mar 1931. Stricken 25 Jan 1937, sold 16 Mar 1939; BU Baltimore.
DM 7	*Mahan*	DD 102	Decomm 1 May 1930. Stricken 22 Oct 1930, sold 17 Jan 1931; BU Baltimore.
DM 8	*Hart*	DD 110	Asiatic Fleet 1920-30. Yangtze River 1926-27. Decomm 1 Jun 1931. Stricken 11 Nov 1931, sold 25 Feb 1932; BU.
DM 9	*Ingraham*	DD 111	Decomm 29 Jun 1922. Stricken 1 Dec 1936, sunk as target off Pearl Harbor, 23 Jul 1937.
DM 10	*Ludlow*	DD 112	Decomm 24 May 1930. Stricken 18 Nov 1930, sold 19 Mar 1931; BU.
DM 11	*Burns*	DD 171	Decomm 2 Jun 1930. Stricken 18 Nov 1930, sold 22 Apr 1932; BU.
DM 12	*Anthony*	DD 172	Decomm 30 Jun 1922. Stricken 1 Dec 1936, sunk as target off California, 22 Jul 1937.
DM 13	*Sproston*	DD 173	Decomm 15 Aug 1922. Stricken 1 Dec 1936, sunk as target 22 Jul 1937.
DM 14	*Rizal*	DD 174	Asiatic Fleet 1920-30. Yangtze River 1926-30. Decomm 20 Aug 1931. Stricken 11 Nov 1931, sold 25 Feb 1932; BU.

Figure 7.7: *Gamble* (DM 15), a converted flush-deck destroyer. Notice mine chutes on stern.

Figure 7.8: *Montgomery* (DM 17), on 10 May 1943, at Pearl Harbor, with tug *Hoga* (YT 146) alongside. One of the *New Mexico* class battleships can be seen in the distance. *Hoga* is the last survivor of Pearl Harbor still afloat.

No.	Name	Formerly	Reclassified
DM 15	*Gamble*	DD 123	13 Jun 1930
DM 16	*Ramsay*	DD 124	13 Jun 1930
DM 17	*Montgomery*	DD 121	5 Jan 1931
DM 18	*Breese*	DD 122	5 Jan 1931
DM 19	*Tracy*	DD 214	30 Jun 1937
DM 20	*Preble*	DD 345	30 Jun 1937
DM 21	*Sicard*	DD 346	30 Jun 1937
DM 22	*Pruitt*	DD 347	30 Jun 1937
DM 23	*Robert H. Smith*	DD 735	19 Jul 1944
DM 24	*Thomas E. Fraser*	DD 736	19 Jul 1944
DM 25	*Shannon*	DD 737	19 Jul 1944
DM 26	*Harry F. Bauer*	DD 738	19 Jul 1944
DM 27	*Adams*	DD 739	19 Jul 1944
DM 28	*Tolman*	DD 740	19 Jul 1944
DM 29	*Henry A. Wiley*	DD 749	19 Jul 1944
DM 30	*Shea*	DD 750	19 Jul 1944
DM 31	*J. William Ditter*	DD 751	19 Jul 1944
DM 32	*Lindsey*	DD 771	19 Jul 1944
DM 33	*Gwin*	DD 772	19 Jul 1944
DM 34	*Aaron Ward*	DD 773	19 Jul 1944

Armament	DM 15-22: 4-4"/50, 1-3"/23AA; (1945) 3-3"/50, 1 twin 40mm, 5 or 6 20mm. DM 23-34: 6-5"/38, 2 quad 40mm, 2 twin 40mm, 6 or 8 20mm.

Notes: For details, see destroyers. Fast offensive minelayers.

HIGH-SPEED MINESWEEPERS

No.	Name	Formerly	Reclassified
DMS 1	*Dorsey*	DD 117	19 Nov 1940
DMS 2	*Lamberton*	DD 119	19 Nov 1940
DMS 3	*Boggs*	DD 136	19 Nov 1940

DMS 4	*Elliot*	DD 146	19 Nov 1940
DMS 5	*Palmer*	DD 161	19 Nov 1940
DMS 6	*Hogan*	DD 178	19 Nov 1940
DMS 7	*Howard*	DD 179	19 Nov 1940
DMS 8	*Stansbury*	DD 180	19 Nov 1940
DMS 9	*Chandler*	DD 206	19 Nov 1940
DMS 10	*Southard*	DD 207	19 Nov 1940
DMS 11	*Hovey*	DD 208	19 Nov 1940
DMS 12	*Long*	DD 209	19 Nov 1940
DMS 13	*Hopkins*	DD 249	19 Nov 1940
DMS 14	*Zane*	DD 337	19 Nov 1940
DMS 15	*Wasmuth*	DD 338	19 Nov 1940
DMS 16	*Trever*	DD 339	19 Nov 1940
DMS 17	*Perry*	DD 340	19 Nov 1940
DMS 18	*Hamilton*	DD 141	11 Oct 1941
Armament	3-3"/50, 1 twin 40mm, 5 or 7 20mm		

Notes: DMS 1-18: Converted flush-deck destroyers. TT removed, stern modified for sweeping gear; ability to sweep magnetic and acoustic mines added later.

Figure 7.9: *J. William Ditter* (DM 31), 27 Oct 1944, a *Sumner*-class destroyer converted for minelaying, while under construction.

Figure 7.10: *Wasmuth* (DMS 15), 24 Jul 1942, a converted flush-deck destroyer. Notice sweeping gear on stern.

No.	Name	Formerly	Reclassified
DMS 19	*Ellyson*	DD 454	15 Nov 1944
DMS 20	*Hambleton*	DD 455	15 Nov 1944
DMS 21	*Rodman*	DD 456	15 Nov 1944
DMS 22	*Emmons*	DD 457	15 Nov 1944
DMS 23	*Macomb*	DD 458	15 Nov 1944
DMS 24	*Forrest*	DD 461	15 Nov 1944
DMS 25	*Fitch*	DD 462	15 Nov 1944
DMS 26	*Hobson*	DD 464	15 Nov 1944
DMS 27	*Jeffers*	DD 621	15 Nov 1944
DMS 28	*Harding*	DD 625	15 Nov 1944
DMS 29	*Butler*	DD 636	15 Nov 1944
DMS 30	*Gherardi*	DD 637	15 Nov 1944
DMS 31	*Mervine*	DD 489	30 May 1945
DMS 32	*Quick*	DD 490	23 Jun 1945
DMS 33	*Carmick*	DD 493	23 Jun 1945
DMS 34	*Doyle*	DD 494	23 Jun 1945
DMS 35	*Endicott*	DD 495	30 May 1945

Figure 7.11: *Hovey* (DMS 11), 27 May 1943, at Mare Island Navy Yard. Originally a flush-deck destroyer, she was converted to high-speed minesweeper in 1940. Torpedo tubes and one funnel have been removed.

Figure 7.12: *Hambleton* (DMS 20), 18 Dec 1944. Twenty-four *Livermore*-class destroyers were converted to high speed minesweepers in 1944–45. Notice sweeping gear on stern replacing aft gun and lack of torpedo tubes.

DMS 36	*McCook*	DD 496	30 May 1945
DMS 37	*Davison*	DD 618	23 Jun 1945
DMS 38	*Thompson*	DD 627	30 May 1945
DMS 39	*Cowie*	DD 632	30 May 1945
DMS 40	*Knight*	DD 633	30 May 1945
DMS 41	*Doran*	DD 634	30 May 1945
DMS 42	*Earle*	DD 635	30 May 1945
Armament	3-5"/38, 2 twin 40mm, 7-20mm		

Notes: For details, see destroyers. DMS 19-42: *Benson*-class destroyers converted 1944-45. TT and after gun removed; sweeping gear added.

MINESWEEPERS

Minesweepers were named for birds, and then nouns and adjectives of action.

Minesweepers on the Navy List, 1922:

AM 1 *Lapwing* Out of comm 11 Apr 1922-1 Sep 1932. Rec **AVP 1**, 22 Jan 1936.

AM 2 *Owl* Rec **AT 137**, 1 Jun 1942. Decomm 26 Jul 1946. Sold 27 Jun 1947; BU Norland, Wash.
1* Normandy.

Figure 7.13: "Bird class" minesweepers at Guantanamo during the 1920s. Right to left are *Mallard*, *Tanager*, and *Whippoorwill*.

Figure 7.14: *Robin* (AM 3), 3 Sep 1941, a "bird class" minesweeper. The forward mast was replaced by a light pole behind the bridge.

Figure 7.15: *Sandpiper* (AM 51), a "bird class" minesweeper, was converted to seaplane tender in 1919, but not reclassified until 1936. The star on the bow identifies her aviation status. Notice the heavy mast forward of the bridge.

AM 3 *Robin* Rec **AT 140**, 1 Jun 1942. Decomm 9 Nov 1945. Stricken 28 Nov 1945. FFU.

AM 4 *Swallow* Wrecked on Kanaga I., Aleutians, 19 Feb 1938 (none lost).

AM 5 *Tanager* Sunk by shore gunfire off Corregidor, 4 May 1942.
1* Philippines 1942.

AM 6 *Cardinal* Wrecked off Chirikof I., Alaska, 6 Jun 1923.

AM 7 *Oriole* Out of comm 3 May 1922-2 May 1938. Rec **AT 136**, 1 Jun 1942. Decomm 6 Feb 1946. Stricken 12 Mar 1946, sold 1947.
Later history: Merchant *Oriole* 1947. BU 1952

AM 8 *Curlew* Went aground on Point Mosquito, Panama, and destroyed, 15 Dec 1925.

AM 9 *Finch* Asiatic Fleet 1921-41. Yangtze River, 1932. China 1937-39. Damaged by aircraft bomb off Corregidor, 9 Apr 1942 and sank on 10 Apr.
1* Philippines 1942.
Later history: Salved by Japanese, renamed *Patrol Vessel No. 103*. Sunk by U.S. aircraft off Cap Padaran, Indochina, 12 Jan 1945.

AM 10 *Heron* Asiatic Station 1920-22. Out of comm 6 Apr 1922-18 Dec 1924, recomm as seaplane tender. Yangtze River, 1931-32. China 1937-39. Rec **AVP 2**, 22 Jan 1936.

AM 13 *Turkey* Out of comm 12 Apr 1922-15 Aug 1938. Rec **AT 143**, 1 Jun 1942. Decomm 6 Nov 1945. Stricken 28 Nov 1945, sold 30 Dec 1946. BU
1* Pearl Harbor.

AM 14 *Woodcock* Out of comm 5 May 1922-21 Feb 1924; recomm as gunboat. Station ship, Haiti, 1924-34. Rec **AT 145**, 1 Jun 1942. Decomm 30 Sep 1946. Stricken 23 Apr 1947. Sold 19 Dec 1947; BU Popes Creek, Md.

AM 15 *Quail* Nicaragua 1926-27. Scuttled off Corregidor, 5 May 1942.
1* Philippines 1942.

AM 16 *Partridge* Rec **AT 138**, 1 Jun 1942. Torpedoed and sunk by German MTB off Normandy, 11 Jun 1942 (32 killed).
1* Normandy.

AM 17 *Eider* Decomm 18 Apr 1922. Conv to gate tender and rec **YNG 20**, 7 Oct 1940. MC, 1 Jul 1947. FFU.

AM 18 *Thrush* Out of comm 3 Apr 1922-31 Oct 1935. Rec **AVP 3**, 22 Jan 1936.

AM 19 *Avocet* Out of comm 3 Apr 1922-8 Sep 1925. Ran aground in typhoon near Chefoo, China, 26 Aug 1928. Yangtze River, 1931. Converted to seaplane tender 1932 and rec **AVP 4**, 22 Jan 1936.

AM 20 *Bobolink* Went aground on Plum I., 27 Sep 1928. Rec **AT 131**, 1 Jun 1942. Decomm 22 Feb 1946. Sold 5 Oct 1946. FFU.
1* Pearl Harbor.

AM 21 *Lark* Asiatic Fleet 1941. Escaped from Java 1942. Rec **AT 168**, 1 Mar 1944. Decomm 7 Feb 1946. Stricken 3 Jul 1946. FFU.
1* Philippines 1942, Leyte.

AM 22 *Widgeon* Out of comm 15 Apr 1922-5 Mar 1923, converted to salvage vessel. Rec **ASR 1**, 12 Sep 1929.

AM 23 *Teal* Converted to aircraft tender 1922. Rec **AVP 5**, 22 Jan 1936.

AM 24 *Brant* Neutrality patrol. Rec **AT 132**, 1 Jun 1942. Rec **ARS 32**, 1 Sep 1942.

AM 25 *Kingfisher* Rec **AT 135**, 1 Jun 1942. Decomm 6 Feb 1946. To MC 3 Jun 1947 and sold. FFU.
1* Gilbert Is.

AM 26 *Rail* Rec **AT 139**, 1 Jun 1942. Decomm 29 Apr 1946. To MC, 17 Jan 1947. FFU.
6* Pearl Harbor, Solomons, New Georgia, Leyte, Lingayen, Subic Bay.

AM 27 *Pelican* Rec **AVP 6**, 22 Jan 1936, converted to seaplane tender.

AM 28 *Falcon* Conv to submarine tender and salvage vessel. Rec **ASR 2**, 12 Sep 1929.

AM 29 *Osprey* To USC&GS, 7 Apr 1922, renamed *Pioneer*. Returned 5 Aug 1941, rec **ARS 2**, 17 Sep 1941, renamed ***Crusader***.

AM 30 *Seagull* Rec **AT 141**, 1 Jun 1942. Decomm 5 Sep 1946. Stricken 15 Oct 1946. To MC, 2 May 1947. FFU.

AM 31 *Tern* Rec **AT 142**, 1 Jun 1942. Decomm 23 Nov 1945. Stricken 5 Dec 1945.
1* Pearl Harbor.
Later history: Merchant *Tern* 1948.

AM 32 *Flamingo* Decomm 5 May 1922. To USC&GS, 23 Jan 1923, renamed *Guide*. Returned 27 Jun 1941, rec **ARS 1**, renamed ***Viking***. Stricken 19 Apr 1953, sold 22 Jul 1953.

AM 33 *Penguin* Out of comm 1 Jun 1922-13 Oct 1923. Converted to gunboat for Far East service, 1924. Yangtze River 1926-27. Guam 1930-41. Damaged by Japanese aircraft at Agana, Guam, and scuttled to prevent capture, 8 Dec 1941 (1 killed).

AM 34 *Swan* Out of comm 13 May 1922-23 Jun 1923 and 21 Dec 1933-2 Apr 1934. Went ashore near Gunet Light, 28 Nov 1928. Converted to seaplane tender 1931. In collision with m/v *President Wilson* in Gaillard Cut, Panama Canal, 20 Aug 1933. Rec **AVP 7**, 22 Jan 1936.

AM 35 *Whippoorwill* Asiatic Fleet 1941-42. Escaped from Java, Mar 1942. Rec **AT 169**, 1 Mar 1944. Decomm 17 Apr 1946. Stricken 10 Jun 1946. To MC, 5 Nov 1946. FFU.
1* Philippines 1942.

AM 36 *Bittern* Asiatic Station 1920-41. Yangtze River, 1932. China 1937-39. Damaged by Japanese air attack at Cavite, Philippines, 10 Dec 1941. Scuttled in Manila Bay, 8 Apr 1942.
1* Philippines 1942.

AM 37 *Sanderling* Decomm 2 May 1922. Foundered in tow between Pearl Harbor and San Diego, 26 Jun 1937.

AM 38 *Auk* To USC&GS, 7 Apr 1922, renamed *Discoverer*. Returned 26 Aug 1941, rec **ARS 3** as ***Discoverer***.

AM 39 *Chewink* Converted to submarine rescue vessel, rec **ASR 3**, 12 Sep 1929.

AM 40 *Cormorant* Ordnance testing vessel, Chesapeake Bay, 1921-27. Rec **AT 133**, 1 Jun 1942. Decomm 29 Mar 1946. Sold 8 Jan 1947.
1* Normandy.

AM 41 *Gannet* Converted to seaplane tender 1931. Rec **AVP 8**, 22 Jan 1936.

AM 43 *Grebe* Station ship, St. Thomas, 1922-31. Out of comm 12 May-15 Nov 1922. Tender to USS *Constitution* on tour of America, 1931-34. Rec **AT 134**, 1 Jun 1942. Went aground south of Fiji, 6 Dec 1942 and sank in hurricane, 2 Jan 1943.
1* Pearl Harbor.

AM 44 *Mallard* Converted to submarine rescue vessel 1928. Rec **ASR 4**, 12 Sep 1929.

AM 45 *Ortolan* Out of comm 3 May–11 Jul 1922, converted to submarine tender 1922. Rec **ASR 5**, 12 Sep 1929.

AM 46 *Peacock* Decomm 14 Feb 1920 and loaned to USSB, converted to salvage tug.
Later history: Merchant *Peacock*. Sunk in collision with m/v *Hindonger* off Cartagena, Colombia, 24 Aug 1940.

AM 47 *Pigeon* Out of comm 25 Apr 1922-13 Oct 1923, converted to gunboat. Yangtze River, 1926-27. Rec **ASR 6,** 12 Sep 1929, converted to submarine salvage vessel.

AM 48 *Redwing* Decomm 14 Apr 1922. USCG 24 May 1924-29 Aug 1941. Rec **ARS 4**, 5 Aug 1941.

AM 51 *Sandpiper* Converted to seaplane tender 1919. Haiti 1919-20. Rec **AVP 9**, 22 Jan 1936.

AM 52 *Vireo* Rec **AT 144**, 1 Jun 1942. Damaged by collision with sinking carrier *Yorktown*, 4 Jun, and then ran aground at Midway, 7 Jun 1942. Abandoned at sea in Solomon Is., 15 Oct 1942, when attacked by aircraft (51 lost on destroyer *Meredith* when sunk); later recovered. Decomm 18 Apr 1946. Stricken 8 May 1946, sold 4 Feb 1947. FFU.
7* Pearl Harbor, Midway, Guadalcanal, Solomons, Cape Sansapor, Leyte, Ormoc.

AM 53 *Warbler* Decomm and loaned to USSB, 16 Jun 1920, merchant *Retriever*. Returned to USN as **ARS 11**, 22 Sep 1941. Stricken 10 Jun 1947, sold 12 Aug 1947; BU.

AM 54 *Willet* Decomm and loaned to USSB, 29 May 1920, merchant *Salvor*. Returned to USN as **ARS 12**, 22 Sep 1941. Stricken 5 Dec 1947, sold 2 Nov 1948.

Armament	(1945) 1-3"/50, 4-20mm guns.

Notes: AM 14 *Woodcock*, AM 33 *Penguin*, and AM 47 *Pigeon* converted to gunboats 1924. Six converted to submarine rescue vessels 1929 (ASR), and nine converted to seaplane tenders, 1936 (AVP). Three lent to USC&GS in 1922 were returned to the Navy in 1942 and used as salvage vessels (ARS). Survivors rec tugs 1942; AT rec ATO 15 May 1944. For further details on ARS, ASR and AVP see later pages.

Raven Class

No.	Name	Builder	Keel Laid	Launched	Comm.
AM 55	*Raven*	Norfolk NYd	28 Jun 1939	24 Aug 1940	11 Nov 1940
AM 56	*Osprey*	Norfolk NYd	28 Jun 1939	24 Aug 1940	16 Dec 1940

Displacement	810 tons; 956 f/l
Dimensions	220'6" (oa); 215' (wl) x 32'2" x 9'4"
Machinery	2 screws; diesel; SHP 3,500; 18.1 knots
Complement	105
Armament	1-3"/50, 2-40mm, 8-20mm AA

Notes: Steel hulls. Useful as convoy escorts.

Service Records:

AM 55 *Raven* Decomm 31 May 1946. †
3* North Africa, Normandy, Southern France.

AM 56 *Osprey* Sunk by mine north of Cherbourg, Normandy, 5 Jun 1944 (6 killed).
2* North Africa, Normandy.

Auk Class

No.	Name	Builder	Keel Laid	Launched	Comm.
AM 57	*Auk*	Norfolk NYd	15 Apr 1941	26 Aug 1941	15 Jan 1942
AM 58	*Broadbill*	Defoe	23 Jul 1941	21 May 1942	13 Oct 1942
AM 59	*Chickadee*	Defoe	21 Aug 1941	20 Jul 1942	9 Nov 1942
AM 60	*Nuthatch*	Defoe	22 May 1942	16 Sep 1942	19 Nov 1942
AM 61	*Pheasant*	Defoe	22 Jul 1942	24 Oct 1942	1 Dec 1942
AM 62	*Sheldrake*	General Eng.	24 Jun 1941	12 Feb. 1942	14 Oct 1942

Figure 7.16: *Auk* (AM 57) shortly after completion on 6 May 1942.

AM 63	*Skylark*	General Eng.	9 Jul 1941	12 Mar 1942	24 Nov 1942
AM 64	*Starling*	General Eng.	11 Jul 1941	11 Apr 1942	21 Dec 1942
AM 65	*Swallow*	General Eng.	19 Jul 1941	6 May 1942	14 Jan 1943
AM 100	*Heed*	General Eng.	14 Feb 1942	19 Jun 1942	27 Feb 1943
AM 101	*Herald*	General Eng.	14 Mar 1942	4 Jul 1942	23 Mar 1943
AM 102	*Motive*	General Eng.	14 Apr 1942	17 Aug 1942	17 Apr 1943
AM 103	*Oracle*	General Eng.	7 May 1942	30 Sep 1942	14 May 1943
AM 104	*Pilot*	Pennsylvania	27 Oct 1941	5 Jul 1942	3 Feb 1943
AM 105	*Pioneer*	Pennsylvania	30 Oct 1941	26 Jul 1942	27 Feb 1943
AM 106	*Portent*	Pennsylvania	15 Nov 1941	16 Aug 1942	3 Apr 1943
AM 107	*Prevail*	Pennsylvania	15 Nov 1941	13 Sep 1942	17 Apr 1943
AM 108	*Pursuit*	Commercial	12 Nov 1941	12 Jun 1942	30 Apr 1943
AM 109	*Requisite*	Commercial	12 Nov 1941	25 Jul 1942	7 Jun 1943
AM 110	*Right*	Commercial	19 Jun 1942	7 Nov 1942	21 Jul 1943
AM 111	*Sage*	Commercial	1 Aug 1942	21 Nov 1942	23 Aug 1943
AM 112	*Seer*	Amer. Lorain	28 Nov 1941	23 May 1942	21 Oct 1942
AM 113	*Sentinel*	Amer. Lorain	28 Nov 1941	4 Jun 1942	3 Nov 1942
AM 114	*Staff*	Amer. Lorain	28 Nov 1941	17 Jun 1942	11 Nov 1942
AM 115	*Skill*	Amer. Lorain	28 Nov 1941	22 Jun 1942	17 Nov 1942
AM 116	*Speed*	Amer. Cleve.	17 Nov 1941	18 Apr 1942	15 Oct 1942
AM 117	*Strive*	Amer. Cleve.	17 Nov 1941	16 May 1942	27 Oct 1942
AM 118	*Steady*	Amer. Cleve.	17 Nov 1941	6 Jun 1942	16 Nov 1942
AM 119	*Sustain*	Amer. Cleve.	17 Nov 1941	23 Jun 1942	9 Nov 1942
AM 120	*Sway*	Mathis	18 Nov 1941	29 Sep 1942	20 Jul 1942
AM 121	*Swerve*	Mathis	27 May 1942	25 Feb 1943	23 Jan 1944
AM 122	*Swift*	Mathis	27 Jun 1942	5 Dec 1942	29 Dec 1943
AM 123	*Symbol*	Savannah	18 Nov 1941	2 Jul 1942	10 Dec 1942
AM 124	*Threat*	Savannah	15 Dec 1941	15 Aug 1942	14 Mar 1943
AM 125	*Tide*	Savannah	16 Mar 1942	7 Sep 1942	9 May 1943
AM 126	*Token*	Gulf Mad.	21 Jul 1941	28 Mar 1942	31 Dec 1942
AM 127	*Tumult*	Gulf Mad.	21 Jul 1941	19 Apr 1942	27 Feb 1943
AM 128	*Velocity*	Gulf Mad.	21 Jul 1941	19 Apr 1942	4 Apr 1943
AM 129	*Vital*	Gulf Mad.	1 Jan 1942	7 Sep 1942	*18 May 1943*
AM 130	*Usage*	Gulf Mad.	1 Jan 1942	4 Oct 1942	*7 Jun 1943*
AM 131	*Zeal*	Gulf Mad.	12 Jan 1942	15 Sep 1942	9 Jul 1943

Displacement	890 tons; 956 f/l
Dimensions	221'1" (oa); 215' (wl) x 32'2" x 10'9"
Machinery	2 screws; diesel; SHP 3,118; 18.1 knots
Complement	105
Armament	1-3"/50, 4-40mm AA or 2-40mm, 8-20mm

Notes: Modified *Raven* class. Fast, able to operate as convoy escorts or with fleet units.

Service Records:

AM 57 *Auk* Decomm 1 Jul 1946. †
3* North Africa, Normandy, Southern France.

AM 58 *Broadbill* Decomm 3 Jun 1946. †
2* Normandy, Southern France.

AM 59 *Chickadee* Decomm 15 May 1946. †
2* Normandy, Southern France.

AM 60 *Nuthatch* Damaged by mine in Seine Bay off Normandy, 15 Jun 1944. Decomm 3 Jun 1946. †
2* Normandy, Southern France.

AM 61 *Pheasant* Damaged by collision, Normandy, 7 Jun 1944. Decomm 15 Jun 1947. Tokyo Bay. †
2* Normandy, Southern France.

AM 62 *Sheldrake* Decomm 31 May 1946. †
4* Guam, Okinawa, Raids on Japan 7-8/45, Minesweeping 1945.

AM 63 *Skylark* Sunk by mine off Okinawa, 28 Mar 1945 (5 killed).
3* Solomons, Guam, Okinawa.

AM 64 *Starling* Decomm 15 May 1946. †
3* Okinawa, Guam, Minesweeping 1945.

AM 65 *Swallow* Sunk by kamikaze off Okinawa, 22 Apr 1945 (2 killed).
2* Tinian, Okinawa.

AM 100 *Heed* Decomm 15 Jan 1947. †
5* Kwajalein, Saipan, Tinian, Okinawa, Minesweeping 1945.

AM 101 *Herald* Severely damaged in storm in Aleutians, 6 Nov 1943. Decomm 31 May 1946. †
2* Saipan, Minesweeping 1945.

AM 102 *Motive* Decomm 15 Jun 1946. †
3* Kwajalein, Saipan, Guam, Minesweeping 1945.

AM 103 *Oracle* Decomm 29 May 1946. †
4* Kwajalein, Eniwetok, Saipan, Minesweeping 1945.

AM 104 *Pilot* Damaged in collision with m/v *Samuel Ashe* off Naples, 18 Feb 1944 (1 killed). Decomm 15 Jan 1947. †
3* Salerno, Anzio, Minesweeping 1945.

AM 105 *Pioneer* Decomm 8 Jul 1946. †
4* Anzio, Southern France, Raids on Japan 7-8/45, Minesweeping 1945.

AM 106 *Portent* Sunk by mine off Anzio, 22 Jan 1944 (18 killed).
1* Anzio.

AM 107 *Prevail* Damaged by aircraft bomb, Anzio, 24 Jan 1944. Decomm 31 May 1946. †
6* Salerno, Anzio, Southern France, Okinawa, Raids on Japan 7-8/45, Minesweeping 1945.

AM 108 *Pursuit* Decomm 30 Apr 1947. †
8* Gilbert Is., Kwajalein, Leyte, Ormoc, Mindoro, Lingayen, Okinawa, Subic Bay.

AM 109 *Requisite* Damaged in collision, Okinawa, 6 Jun 1945. Decomm 23 Dec 1947. †
8* Gilbert Is., Kwajalein, Eniwetok, Leyte, Ormoc, Mindoro, Lingayen, Subic Bay, Okinawa, Raids on Japan 7-8/45, Minesweeping 1945.

AM 110 *Right* Renamed ***Revenge***, 15 May 1943. Decomm 18 Mar 1947. †
6* Gilbert Is., Kwajalein, Leyte, Okinawa, Raids on Japan 7-8/45, Minesweeping 1945. Tokyo Bay.

AM 111 *Sage* Decomm Feb 1947. †
8* Kwajalein, Eniwetok, Leyte, Ormoc, Mindoro, Lingayen, Subic Bay, Okinawa, Raids on Japan 7-8/45, Minesweeping 1945.
Submarine sunk: **RO-40* 45 m. northwest of Kwajalein, 16 Feb 1944.

AM 112 *Seer* Damaged by mine off Hyères, southern France, 10 Sep 1944 (3 killed). Decomm 26 Apr 1947. †
6* Tunisia, Sicily, Salerno, Anzio, Southern France, Minesweeping 1945.

AM 113 *Sentinel* Sunk by German aircraft bombs off Licata, Sicily, 10 Jul 1943 (10 killed).
2* Tunisia, Sicily.

AM 114 *Staff* Damaged by mine south of Sicily off Scoglitti, 15 Jul 1943. Decomm 15 Jan 1947. †
6* Sicily, Normandy, Southern France, Okinawa, Raids on Japan 7-8/45, Minesweeping 1945.

AM 115 *Skill* Torpedoed and sunk by *U-593* in Gulf of Salerno, 25 Sep 1943 (71 killed).
1* Sicily.

AM 116 *Speed* Decomm 7 Jun 1946. †
7* Sicily, Anzio, convoy UGS-36, convoy UGS-38, Southern France, Raids on Japan 7-8/45, Minesweeping 1945.

AM 117 *Strive* Decomm 6 Jun 1946. †
7* Sicily, Salerno, Anzio, Southern France, Okinawa, Raids on Japan 7-8/45, Minesweeping 1945.

AM 118 *Steady* Decomm 18 Jun 1946. †
8* Tunisia, Sicily, Salerno, Anzio, convoy UGS-40, Southern France, Raids on Japan 7-8/45, Minesweeping 1945.

AM 119 *Sustain* Decomm 17 Jun 1946. †
8* Tunisia, Sicily, Salerno, Anzio, convoy UGS-38, convoy UGS-40, Southern France, Okinawa, Raids on Japan 7-8/45, Minesweeping 1945.

AM 120 *Sway* Decomm 15 Jan 1947. †
5* Salerno, Anzio, Southern France, Raids on Japan 7-8/45, Minesweeping 1945.

AM 121 *Swerve* Sunk by mine off Anzio, 9 Jul 1944 (3 killed).
1* Anzio.

AM 122 *Swift* Decomm 4 Jun 1946. †
6* Normandy, Southern France, Raids on Japan 7-8/45, Minesweeping 1945.
Submarine sunk: **U-986* southwest of Ireland, 17 Apr 1944.

AM 123 *Symbol* Damaged by aircraft bomb off Anzio, 10 Jun 1944 (4 killed). Decomm 31 May 1946. †
5* Salerno, Anzio, Southern France, Raids on Japan 7-8/45, Minesweeping 1945.

AM 124 *Threat* Decomm 31 May 1946. †
3* Normandy, Southern France, Raids on Japan 7-8/45, Minesweeping 1945.

AM 125 *Tide* Damaged in collision with *LCI-267* in convoy in North Atlantic, 17 Jul 1943. Sunk by mine off Utah Beach, Normandy, 7 Jun 1944. (Killed 10)
1* Normandy.

AN 126 *Token* †
4* Palau, Leyte, Okinawa, Raids on Japan 7-8/45, Minesweeping 1945. Tokyo Bay.

AM 127 *Tumult* †
5* Palau, Leyte, Okinawa, Raids on Japan 7-8/45, Minesweeping 1945. Tokyo Bay.

AN 128 *Velocity* Decomm 7 Oct 1946. †
5* Palau, Leyte, Okinawa, Raids on Japan 7-8/45, Minesweeping 1945.

AM 129 *Vital* To UK 18 May 1943.
Later history: Renamed HMS *Strenuous*. Returned 10 Dec 1946, sold 23 Apr 1947. Merchant *Evening Star, Pride of the West* 1949. Conversion canceled; BU 1956 Hamburg.

AM 130 *Usage* To UK, 7 Jun 1943.
Later history: Renamed HMS *Tourmaline*. Returned Jan 1947, trfd to Turkey, 25 Mar 1947, renamed *Çardak*. R1976.

AM 131 *Zeal* Decomm 4 Jun 1946. †
4* Palau, Leyte, Okinawa, Raids on Japan 7-8/45, Minesweeping 1945.

No.	Name	Builder	Keel Laid	Launched	Comm.
AM 314	*Champion*	General Eng.	6 Jul 1942	12 Dec 1942	8 Sep 1943
	ex-*Akbar*, BAM 1 (23 Jan 1943)				
AM 315	*Chief*	General Eng.	25 Jul 1942	5 Jan 1943	9 Oct 1943
	ex-*Alice*, BAM 2 (23 Jan 1943)				
AM 316	*Competent*	General Eng.	19 Aug 1942	30 Jan 1943	10 Nov 1943
	ex-*Amelia*, BAM 3 (23 Jan 1943)				
AM 317	*Defense*	General Eng.	2 Oct 1942	18 Feb 1943	10 Jan 1944
	ex-*Amity*, BAM 4 (23 Jan 1943)				
AM 318	*Devastator*	General Eng.	15 Dec 1942	19 Apr 1943	12 Jan 1944
	ex-*Augusta*, BAM 5 (23 Jan 1943)				
AM 319	*Gladiator*	General Eng.	7 Jan 1943	7 May 1943	25 Feb 1944
	ex-*Blaze*, BAM 6 (23 Jan 1943)				
AM 320	*Impeccable*	General Eng.	1 Feb 1943	21 May 1943	24 Apr 1944
	ex-*Brutus*, BAM 7 (23 Jan 1943)				
AM 321	*Overseer*	Associated	7 Sep 1942	25 Jan 1943	Never
	ex-*Elfreda*, BAM 16 (23 Jan 1943)				
AM 322	*Spear*	Associated	27 Oct 1942	25 Feb 1943	31 Dec 1943
	ex-*Errant*, BAM 22 (23 Jan 1943)				

Figure 7.17: *Spear* (AM 322), originally slated to go to the United Kingdom under lend-lease, in San Francisco Bay.

AM 323	*Triumph*	Associated	27 Oct 1942	25 Feb 1943	3 Feb 1944
	ex-*Espoir*, BAM 23 (23 Jan 1943)				
AM 324	*Vigilance*	Associated	28 Nov 1942	5 Apr 1943	28 Feb 1944
	ex-*Exploit*, BAM 24 (23 Jan 1943)				
AM 340	*Ardent*	General Eng.	20 Feb 1943	22 Jun 1943	25 May 1944
	ex-*Buffalo*, BAM 8 (24 May 1943)				
AM 341	*Dextrous*	Gulf Mad.	8 Jun 1942	17 Jan 1943	8 Sep 1943
	ex-*Sepoy*, BAM 30 (1 Jun 1943)				

Service Records:

AM 314 *Champion* Slightly damaged by aircraft bomb, Okinawa, 16 Apr 1945. Decomm 30 Jan 1947. †
3* Saipan, Iwo Jima, Okinawa.

AM 315 *Chief* Damaged by grounding, Kwajalein, 3 Feb 1944. Decomm 17 Mar 1947. †
5* Kwajalein, Saipan, Tinian, Okinawa, Minesweeping 1945.

AM 316 *Competent* Decomm 30 Jan 1947. †
5* Kwajalein, Palau, Okinawa, Raids on Japan 7-8/45, Minesweeping 1945.

AM 317 *Defense* Damaged by two kamikazes, Okinawa, 6 Apr 1945 (none killed). Decomm 31 May 1946. †
2* Iwo Jima, Okinawa.

AM 318 *Devastator* Damaged by kamikaze, Okinawa, 6 Apr 1945. Decomm 30 Jan 1947. †
3* Iwo Jima, Okinawa, Raids on Japan 7-8/45.

AM 319 *Gladiator* Damaged by kamikaze, Okinawa, 12 Apr and 22 Apr 1945 (1 killed). Decomm 2 Oct 1946. †
2* Okinawa, Raids on Japan 7-8/45.

AM 320 *Impeccable* Decomm 27 Mar 1947. †
3* Okinawa, Raids on Japan 7-8/45, Minesweeping 1945.

AM 321 *Overseer* Rec **BAM 16**, 19 Jun 1943.

AM 322 *Spear* Damaged in collision, Okinawa, 6 Jun 1945. Decomm Aug 1946. †
4* Guam, Okinawa, Raids on Japan 7-8/45, Minesweeping 1945.

AM 323 *Triumph* Decomm 30 Jan 1947. †
6* Palau, Ormoc, Mindoro, Lingayen, Subic Bay, Okinawa, Raids on Japan 7-8/45.

AM 324 *Vigilance* Decomm 30 Jan 1947. †
3* Fleet Raids 1945, Raids on Japan 7-8/45, Minesweeping 1945.

AM 340 *Ardent* Decomm 30 Jan 1947. †
4* Iwo Jima, Minesweeping 1945.
Submarine sunk: **I-12* east of Honolulu, 13 Nov 1944.

AM 341 *Dextrous* Decomm 5 Jun 1946. †
5* Salerno, Anzio, Southern France, Raids on Japan 7-8/45, Minesweeping 1945.

Figure 7.18: *Sprig* (AM 384), a later *Auk*-class minesweeper, as completed on 12 Apr 1945.

No.	Name	Builder	Keel Laid	Launched	Comm.
AM 371	*Minivet*	Savannah	19 Jul 1944	8 Nov 1944	29 May 1945
AM 372	*Murrelet*	Savannah	24 Aug 1944	29 Dec 1944	21 Aug 1945
AM 373	*Peregrine*	Savannah	24 Oct 1944	17 Feb 1945	27 Sep 1945
AM 374	*Pigeon*	Savannah	10 Nov 1944	28 Mar 1945	30 Oct 1945
AM 375	*Pochard*	Savannah	10 Feb 1944	11 Jun 1944	27 Nov 1944
AM 376	*Ptarmigan*	Savannah	9 Mar 1944	15 Jul 1944	15 Jan 1945
AM 377	*Quail*	Savannah	12 Apr 1944	20 Aug 1944	5 Mar 1945
AM 378	*Redstart*	Savannah	14 Jun 1944	18 Oct 1944	4 Apr 1945
AM 379	*Roselle*	Gulf Mad.	24 Feb 1944	29 Aug 1944	6 Feb 1945
AM 380	*Ruddy*	Gulf Mad.	24 Feb 1944	29 Aug 1944	28 Apr 1945
AM 381	*Scoter*	Gulf Mad.	4 Apr 1944	26 Sep 1944	17 Mar 1945
AM 382	*Shoveler*	Gulf Mad.	1 Apr 1944	10 Dec 1944	22 May 1945
AM 383	*Surfbird*	Amer. Lorain	15 Feb 1944	31 Aug 1944	25 Nov 1944
AM 384	*Sprig*	Amer. Lorain	15 Feb 1944	15 Sep 1944	4 Apr 1945
AM 385	*Tanager*	Amer. Lorain	29 Mar 1944	9 Dec 1944	28 Jul 1945
AM 386	*Tercel*	Amer. Lorain	16 May 1944	16 Dec 1944	21 Aug 1945
AM 387	*Toucan*	Amer. Cleve.	16 Feb 1944	15 Sep 1944	25 Nov 1944
AM 388	*Towhee*	Amer. Cleve.	21 Mar 1944	6 Jan 1945	18 May 1945
AM 389	*Waxwing*	Amer. Cleve.	24 May 1944	10 Mar 1945	6 Aug 1945
AM 390	*Wheatear*	Amer. Cleve.	29 May 1944	21 Apr 1945	3 Oct 1945

Service Records:

AM 371 *Minivet* Sunk by mine in Tsushima Strait, 29 Dec 1945 (31 killed).
1* Minesweeping 1945.

AM 372 *Murrelet* Decomm 20 Jun 1946. †

AM 373 *Peregrine* †

AM 374 *Pigeon* Decomm 10 Jul 1946. †

AM 375 *Pochard* Decomm 15 Jan 1947. †
3* Okinawa, Raids on Japan 7-8/45, Minesweeping 1945. Tokyo Bay.

AM 376 *Ptarmigan* Decomm 3 Jun 1946. †
1* Minesweeping 1945.

AM 377 *Quail* Decomm 27 Jan 1947. †
1* Minesweeping 1945.

AM 378 *Redstart* Decomm 26 Nov 1946. †
1*Minesweeping 1945.

AM 379 *Roselle* Decomm 20 Jun 1946. †

AM 380 *Ruddy* Decomm 15 Jan 1947. †
1* Minesweeping 1945.

AM 381 *Scoter* Decomm 16 Apr 1947. †
1* Minesweeping 1945.

AM 382 *Shoveler* Decomm 5 Nov 1946. †
1* Minesweeping 1945.

AM 383 *Surfbird* Decomm 5 Jun 1946. †
3* Raids on Japan 7-8/45, Minesweeping 1945.

AM 384 *Sprig* †
1* Minesweeping 1945.
AM 385 *Tanager* †
AM 386 *Tercel* †
AM 387 *Toucan* Decomm 1 Jul 1946. †
3* Okinawa, Raids on Japan 7-8/45, Minesweeping 1945.
AM 388 *Towhee* †
AM 389 *Waxwing* Decomm 12 May 1947. †
AM 390 *Wheatear* †

No.	Builder	Keel Laid	Launched	Comm.
BAM 1-7	See AM 314-20			
BAM 8	See AM 340			
BAM 9	Associated	11 Apr 1942	7 Sep 1942	*8 Jul 1943*
BAM 10	Associated	11 Apr 1942	7 Sep 1942	*28 Jul 1943*
BAM 11	Associated	2 Jun 1942	20 Jun 1943	*30 Aug 1943*
BAM 12	Associated	3 Jun 1942	26 Oct 1942	*22 Oct 1943*
BAM 13	Associated	12 Jul 1942	26 Oct 1942	*13 Nov 1943*
BAM 14	Associated	12 Jul 1942	27 Nov 1942	*22 Nov 1943*
BAM 15	Associated	7 Sep 1942	25 Jan 1943	*7 Dec 1943*
BAM 16	Associated ex–AM 321	7 Sep 1942	25 Jan 1943	*22 Dec 1943*
BAM 17	Savannah	2 Jul 1942	10 Jan 1943	*28 Jul 1943*
BAM 18	Savannah	15 Aug 1942	24 Jan 1943	*28 Aug 1943*
BAM 19	Savannah	7 Sep 1942	10 Mar 1943	*22 Sep 1943*
BAM 20	Savannah	15 Jan 1943	24 May 1943	*22 Oct 1943*
BAM 21	Savannah	30 Jan 1943	27 Jun 1943	*24 Nov 1943*
BAM 22-24	See AM 322-24			
BAM 25	Associated	28 Nov 1942	5 Apr 1943	*24 Mar 1944*
BAM 26	Associated	27 Jan 1943	20 May 1943	*14 Apr 1944*
BAM 27	Associated	27 Jan 1943	20 May 1943	*28 Apr 1944*
BAM 28	Associated	5 Mar 1943	20 Jun 1943	*18 May 1944*
BAM 29	Associated	5 Mar 1943	20 Jun 1943	*12 Aug 1944*
BAM 30	see AM 341			
BAM 31	Gulf Mad.	8 Jun 1942	17 Jan 1943	29 Sep 1943
BAM 32	Gulf Mad.	8 Jun 1942	27 Jan 1943	26 Oct 1943

Notes: *Auk* class. BAM 1-32 ordered 1941, 12 retained by Navy. In exchange, Navy ordered nine *Algerine*-class minesweepers. BAM 22-29 originally ordered from Lake Wash.

Service Records:

BAM 9 To UK 8 Jul 1943 renamed HMS *Catherine.* To Turkey Jan 1947. Turkish *Erdemli.* R 1963.

BAM 10 To UK 28 Jul 1943 renamed HMS *Cato.* Sunk by German torpedo in Seine Bay, Normandy, 6 Jul 1944.

BAM 11 To UK 30 Aug 1943 renamed HMS *Celerity*, renamed *Pique.* To Turkey Jan 1947. Turkish *Eregli.* R 1972.

BAM 12 To UK 22 Oct 1943 renamed HMS *Chamois.* Damaged by mine off Normandy, 21 Jul 1944, not repaired. Returned 11 Dec 1946, sold 23 Apr 1947.
Later history: Merchant *Morning Star.* Conversion abandoned; BU 1950.

BAM 13 To UK 13 Nov 1943 renamed HMS *Chance.* To Turkey Jan 1947. Turkish *Edremit.* R 1965.

BAM 14 To UK 22 Nov 1943 renamed HMS *Combatant.* Sold to Greece, 14 Dec 1946. FFU.

BAM 15 To UK 7 Dec 1943 renamed HMS *Cynthia.* Returned 31 Dec 1946, sold 16 Dec 1947

BAM 16 To UK 22 Dec 1943 renamed HMS *Elfreda.* To Turkey Jan 1947, renamed *Çesme.* R 1976.

BAM 17 To UK 28 Jul 1943 renamed HMS *Gazelle.* Returned 11 Dec 1946, sold 17 Jul 1947; BU.

BAM 18 To UK 28 Aug 1943 renamed HMS *Gorgon.* Sold to Greece, 13 Dec 1946. FFU.

BAM 19 To UK 22 Sep 1943 renamed HMS *Grecian.* To Turkey Jan 1947, renamed *Edincik.* R 1976.

BAM 20 To UK 22 Oct 1943 renamed HMS *Magic.* Sunk by German torpedo in Seine Bay, Normandy, 6 Jul 1944.

BAM 21 To UK 24 Nov 1943 renamed HMS *Pylades.* Sunk by German torpedo in Seine Bay, Normandy, 8 Jul 1944.

BAM 25 To UK 24 Mar 1944 renamed HMS *Fairy.* Returned 11 Dec 1946, sold 26 Sep 1947.

BAM 26 To UK 14 Apr 1944 renamed HMS *Florizel.* Sold 14 Dec 1946.
Later history: Merchant *Aida* 1947, *Lasithi* 1959. BU 1967.

BAM 27 To UK 28 Apr 1944 renamed HMS *Foam.* Returned 11 Dec 1946, sold 26 Aug 1947.

BAM 28 To UK 18 May 1944 renamed HMS *Frolic.* To Turkey Jan 1947, renamed, *Çandarli* R 1985.

BAM 29 To UK 12 Aug 1944 renamed HMS *Garnet*, renamed *Jasper.* Sold 24 Dec 1946.
Later history: Merchant *Pandelis.* BU 1968 Split, Yogoslavia.

BAM 31 To UK 29 Sep 1943 renamed HMS *Steadfast.* Returned and sold 24 Dec 1946.

BAM 32 To UK 26 Oct 1943 renamed HMS *Tattoo.* To Turkey Jan 1947, renamed *Çarsamba* R1983.

Adroit Class

No.	Name	Builder	Keel Laid	Launched	Comm.
AM 82	*Adroit*	Commercial	31 Jul 1941	21 Feb 1942	28 Jul 1942
AM 83	*Advent*	Commercial	18 Aug 1941	12 Mar 1942	15 Aug 1942
AM 84	*Annoy*	Commercial	3 Dec 1941	6 Apr 1942	2 Sep 1942
AM 85	*Conflict*	Commercial	28 Jan 1942	18 Apr 1942	7 Sep 1942
AM 86	*Constant*	Commercial	21 Feb 1942	9 May 1942	21 Sep 1942
AM 87	*Daring*	Commercial	22 Mar 1942	23 May 1942	10 Oct 1942
AM 88	*Dash*	Commercial	6 Apr 1942	20 Jun 1942	27 Oct 1942

Figure 7.19: *Despite* (AM 89) in Oct 1942, one of 18 minesweepers built on subchaser hulls. The experiment was not successful, and all were converted to submarine chasers in 1944. *Despite* became *PC-1593.*

AM 89	*Despite*	Dravo Pitt.	24 Nov 1941	28 Mar 1942	21 Aug 1942
AM 90	*Direct*	Dravo Pitt.	26 Dec 1941	25 Apr 1942	31 Aug 1942
AM 91	*Dynamic*	Dravo Pitt.	16 Jan 1942	26 May 1942	15 Sep 1942
AM 92	*Effective*	Dravo Pitt.	31 Jan 1942	13 Jun 1942	1 Oct 1942
AM 93	*Engage*	Dravo Pitt.	22 Feb 1942	11 Jul 1942	22 Oct 1942
AM 94	*Excel*	Jacobson	19 Dec 1941	20 May 1942	10 Dec 1942
AM 95	*Exploit*	Jacobson	11 May 1942	7 Sep 1942	5 Feb 1943
AM 96	*Fidelity*	Nashville	15 Oct 1941	29 Feb 1942	9 Sep 1942
AM 97	*Fierce*	Nashville	18 Oct 1941	5 Mar 1942	12 Oct 1942
AM 98	*Firm*	Penn-Jersey	21 Oct 1941	29 May 1942	10 Apr 1943
AM 99	*Force*	Penn-Jersey	19 Nov 1941	7 Sep 1942	16 Jun 1943

Displacement	280 tons; 450 f/l
Dimensions	173'8" (oa); 170' (wl) x 23' x 11'7"
Machinery	2 screws; diesel; SHP 1700; 16.8 knots
Complement	65
Armament	1-3"/50, 1-40mm AA

Notes: Minesweepers built on submarine chaser hulls. They had sweeping gear on the stern instead of guns. They were not used as minesweepers, however, and were converted to subchasers with names canceled, 1 Jun 1944.

Service Records:

AM 82 *Adroit* Rec **PC 1586**, 1 Jun 1944. Decomm 14 Dec 1945. Stricken 8 Jan 1946. To MC 18 Mar 1948, sold.
1* Treasury Is. Ldgs.

AM 83 *Advent* Rec **PC 1587**, 1 Jun 1944. Decomm 22 Jan 1946. Stricken 25 Feb 1946. To MC 16 Mar 1948, sold.

AM 84 *Annoy* Rec **PC 1588**, 1 Jun 1944. Decomm 8 Feb 1946. Stricken 12 Mar 1946. To MC 6 May 1948, sold.
1* Iwo Jima.

AM 85 *Conflict* Rec **PC 1589**, 1 Jun 1944. Decomm 31 May 1946. Stricken 1 Aug 1947. To WSA 3 Dec 1947.
2* Solomons, Treasury Is. Ldgs.

AM 86 *Constant* Rec **PC 1590**, 1 Jun 1944. Decomm 19 Jun 1946. †

AM 87 *Daring* Rec **PC 1591**, 1 Jun 1944. Decomm 22 Jan 1946. Stricken 25 Feb 1946. To MC, 18 Mar 1948; BU.
2* Treasury Is. Ldgs., Minesweeping 1945.

AM 88 *Dash* Rec **PC 1592**, 1 Jun 1944. Decomm 10 May 1946. Stricken 1 Aug 1947. To WSA, 19 Dec 1947.

AM 89 *Despite* Rec **PC 1593**, 1 Jun 1944. Decomm 17 Dec 1945. Stricken 8 Jan 1946. To MC, 16 Sep 1946.
1* Southern France.
Later history: Merchant *Mustang.*

AM 90 *Direct* Rec **PC 1594**, 1 Jun 1944. Decomm 9 Nov 1945. To MC, 29 Jul 1946.
1* Southern France.
Later history: Merchant *Allmac.*

AM 91 *Dynamic* Rec **PC 1595**, 1 Jun 1944. Decomm 19 Nov 1945. Stricken 5 Dec 1945. To MC 21 Oct 1946.
1* Southern France.

AM 92 *Effective* Rec **PC 1596**, 1 Jun 1944. Decomm 9 Nov and stricken 28 Nov 1945. Sold 30 Jul 1946.
1* Southern France.

AM 93 *Engage* Rec **PC 1597**, 1 Jun 1944. Decomm 19 Nov 1945. Stricken 5 Nov 1945. Sold 8 Nov 1946, to Dominican Republic.
1* Southern France.
Later history: Renamed *Cibao,* then *Constitucion* 1962. Stricken 1968.

AM 94 *Excel* Rec **PC 1598**, 1 Jun 1944. Decomm 22 Jan 1946. Stricken 12 Dec 1946. Sold 11 Jun 1947.
1* Okinawa.

AM 95 *Exploit* Rec **PC 1599**, 1 Jun 1944. Damaged by grounding off Okinawa, 1 Jun 1945. Rec **PCC 1599**, 20 Aug 1945. Decomm 14 Dec 1945. Sold 19 Mar 1948.
2* Iwo Jima, Okinawa.
Later history: Merchant *Exploit.*

AM 96 *Fidelity* Rec **PC 1600**, 1 Jun 1944. Decomm 1946. Stricken 17 Apr 1946. Sold 15 Jun 1948.
2* Leyte, Lingayen.

AM 97 *Fierce* Rec **PC 1601**, 1 Jun 1944. Rec **PCC 1601**, 20 Aug 1945. Decomm Dec 1945. Sold 15 Jun 1948.
3* Leyte, Lingayen, Okinawa.
Later history: Merchant *Seaborn II.*

AM 98 *Firm* Rec **PC 1602**, 1 Jun 1944. Rec **PCC 1602**, 20 Aug 1945. Decomm 1946. Stricken 21 May 1946. Sold 15 Jun 1948.

AM 99 *Force* Rec **PC 1603**, 1 Jun 1944. Damaged by kamikaze off Okinawa, 26 May 1945 (3 killed). Decomm 21 Jun 1945. Stricken 24 Oct 1945 and destroyed.
3* Leyte, Lingayen, Okinawa.

Admirable Class

No.	Name	Builder	Keel Laid	Launched	Comm.
AM 136	*Admirable*	Tampa	8 Apr 1942	18 Oct 1942	20 Apr 1943
AM 137	*Adopt*	Tampa	8 Apr 1942	18 Oct 1942	31 May 1943
AM 138	*Advocate*	Tampa	8 Apr 1942	1 Nov 1942	*25 Jun 1943*
AM 139	*Agent*	Tampa	8 Apr 1942	1 Nov 1942	*10 Jul 1943*
AM 140	*Alarm*	Tampa	8 Jun 1942	7 Dec 1942	*5 Aug 1943*
AM 141	*Alchemy*	Tampa	8 Jun 1942	7 Dec 1942	*11 Aug 1943*
AM 142	*Apex*	Tampa	8 Jun 1942	7 Dec 1942	*17 Aug 1943*
AM 143	*Arcade*	Tampa	8 Jun 1942	7 Dec 1942	*26 Aug 1943*
AM 144	*Arch*	Tampa	18 Oct 1942	7 Dec 1942	*6 Sep 1943*
AM 145	*Armada*	Tampa	18 Oct 1942	7 Dec 1942	*16 Sep 1943*
AM 146	*Aspire*	Tampa	1 Nov 1942	27 Dec 1942	*29 Sep 1943*
AM 147	*Assail*	Tampa	1 Nov 1942	27 Dec 1942	*5 Oct 1943*
AM 148	*Astute*	Tampa	7 Dec 1942	23 Feb 1943	17 Jan 1944
AM 149	*Augury*	Tampa	7 Dec 1942	23 Feb 1943	17 Mar 1944
AM 150	*Barrier*	Tampa	7 Dec 1942	23 Feb 1943	10 May 1944
AM 151	*Bombard*	Tampa	7 Dec 1942	23 Feb 1943	31 May 1944
AM 152	*Bond*	Willamette	11 Apr 1942	21 Oct 1942	30 Aug 1943
AM 153	*Buoyant*	Willamette	15 Apr 1942	24 Nov 1942	30 Sep 1943

Figure 7.20: USS *Diploma* (AM 221), of the *Admirable* class, 1944.

AM 154	*Candid*	Willamette	27 Apr 1942	14 Oct 1942	31 Oct 1943
AM 155	*Capable*	Willamette	28 Apr 1942	16 Nov 1942	5 Dec 1943
AM 156	*Captivate*	Willamette	12 May 1942	1 Dec 1942	30 Dec 1943
AM 157	*Caravan*	Willamette	16 May 1942	27 Oct 1942	21 Jan 1944
AM 158	*Caution*	Willamette	23 May 1942	7 Dec 1942	10 Feb 1944
AM 159	*Change*	Willamette	23 May 1942	15 Dec 1942	28 Feb 1944
AM 160	*Clamour*	Willamette	26 May 1942	24 Dec 1942	14 Mar 1944
AM 161	*Climax*	Willamette	26 May 1942	9 Jan 1943	24 Mar 1944
AM 162	*Compel*	Willamette	15 Jun 1942	16 Jan 1943	8 Apr 1944
AM 163	*Concise*	Willamette	15 Jun 1942	6 Feb 1943	25 Apr 1944
AM 164	*Control*	Willamette	15 Jun 1942	28 Jan 1943	11 May 1944
AM 165	*Counsel*	Willamette	15 Jun 1942	17 Feb 1943	27 May 1944

Displacement	650 tons, 945 tons f/l
Dimensions	184'6" (oa); 180' (wl) x 33' x 9'9"
Machinery	2 screws; diesel; SHP 1,710; 14.8 knots
Endurance	4,500/12
Complement	104
Armament	1-3"/50, 2 twin 40mm AA (AM 214-15: 2-40mm only) or 1-3"/50, 2-40mm, 6-20mm

Notes: AM 136-65 ordered as AMc 113-42, rec 21 Feb 1942. Similar to PCE adapted for minesweeping. Thirty-four ships transferred to USSR under lend-lease were never returned and were stricken 1 Jan 1983. AM 138-47 transferred on completion. Early units had round bridge. AM 351–355 were to be completed by Commercial but were later canceled.

Service Records:

AM 136 *Admirable* Decomm 12 Jun 1945 and trfd to USSR, 18 Jul 1945.
Later history: Renamed *T-331*. Renamed *Giroskop*, 28 Jun 1947; conv to AGS. R 11 Mar 1958.

AM 137 *Adopt* Decomm and trfd to USSR, 18 Jul 1945.
Later history: Renamed *T-332*. Renamed *Kinel*, 17 Oct 1955. Renamed *BRN-10*, 27 Feb 1956. R 27 Mar 1960.

AM 138 *Advocate* To USSR, 25 Jun 1943.
Later history: Renamed *T-111, Starshiy Leitenant Lekarev*. Renamed *TV-25*, 3 Nov 1956. Renamed *PKZ-35*, 14 May 1963. R 4 Jun 1969. Stricken from USN 1 Jan 1983.

AM 130 *Agent* To USSR, 10 Jul 1943.
Later history: Renamed *T-112, Starshiy Leitenant Vladimirov*. Renamed *TV-21*, 15 Oct 1955. Renamed *VTR-21*, 8 Mar 1966. Renamed *UTS-288*, 20 Apr 1972. R 31 Jan 1991. Stricken from USN 1 Jan 1983.

AM 140 *Alarm* To USSR, 5 Aug 1943.
Later history: Renamed *T-113*. Renamed *BSh-34*, 3 Nov 1956. R Mar 1960. Stricken from USN 1 Jan 1983.

AM 141 *Alchemy* To USSR, 11 Aug 1943.
Later history: Renamed *T-114*. Torpedoed and sunk by *U-365* in Kara Sea, 12 Aug 1944.

AM 142 *Apex* To USSR, 17 Aug 1943.
Later history: Renamed *T-115*. Renamed *Aidar*, 17 Oct 1955. R 28 Feb 1961. Stricken from USN 1 Jan 1983.

AM 143 *Arcade* To USSR, 26 Aug 1943.
Later history: Renamed *T-116*. Renamed *TV-23*, 3 Nov 1956. Renamed *SM-7*, 23 Oct 1962. R 4 May 1963. Possibly sunk as missile target. Stricken from USN, 1 Jan 1983.

AM 144 *Arch* To USSR, 6 Sep 1943.
Later history: Renamed *T-117*. Renamed *TV-22*, 15 Oct 1955. Renamed *VTR-22*, 8 Mar 1966. R 19 Sep 1967.

AM 145 *Armada* To USSR, 16 Sep 1943.
Later history: Renamed *T-118*. Torpedoed and sunk by *U-365* in Kara Sea, 12 Aug 1944.

AM 146 *Aspire* To USSR, 29 Sep 1943.
Later history: Renamed *T-119*. Renamed *TV-24*, 3 Nov 1956. Renamed *VTR-140*, 8 Jun 1966. R 4 Nov 1966. Stricken from USN, 1 Jan 1983.

AM 147 *Assail* To USSR, 5 Oct 1943.
Later history: Renamed *T-120*. Torpedoed and sunk by *U-739* in Kara Sea, 24 Sep 1944.

AM 148 *Astute* Decomm and trfd to USSR, 19 Jul 1945.
Later history: Renamed *T-333*. Renamed *Kurchum*, 17 Oct 1955. Renamed *BRN-9*, 27 Feb 1956. R 18 Jan 1960. Stricken from USN 1 Jan 1983.

AM 149 *Augury* Decomm and trfd to USSR, 19 Jul 1945.
Later history: Renamed *T-334*. Renamed *Gazimur*, 12 Jan 1955. Renamed *BRN-12*, 27 Dec 1956. R 1960s. Stricken from USN 1 Jan 1983.

AM 150 *Barrier* Decomm and trfd to USSR, 19 Jul 1945.
Later history: Renamed *T-335*. Renamed *Istok*, 17 Oct 1955. R 11 Jul 1956. Stricken from USN 1 Jan 1983.

AM 151 *Bombard* Decomm and trfd to USSR, 19 Jul 1945.
Later history: Renamed *T-336*. Renamed *Gidan*, 16 Jun 1954. R 12 Feb 1963. Stricken from USN, 1 Jan 1983.

AM 152 *Bond* Decomm and trfd to USSR, 17 Aug 1945.
Later history: Renamed *T-285*. Renamed *BRN-37*, 3 Dec 1956. R 18 Jan 1960. Stricken from USN, 1 Jan 1983.

AM 153 *Buoyant* Decomm 29 May 1946 and sold to China.
1* Okinawa.
Later history: Renamed *Fei Hsing* (A 1), Chinese Customs.

AM 154 *Candid* Decomm and trfd to USSR, 17 Aug 1945.
Later history: Renamed *T-283*. Renamed *Gorizont*, conv to AGS, 28 Jun 1947. R11 Mar 1958. Stricken from USN 1 Jan 1983.

AM 155 *Capable* Decomm and trfd to USSR, 17 Aug 1945.
Later history: Renamed *T-339*. Renamed *BRN-35*, 3 Dec 1956. R8 Jan 1960. Stricken from USN, 1 Jan 1983.

AM 156 *Captivate* Decomm and trfd to USSR, 17 Aug 1945.
Later history: Renamed *T-338*. Renamed *BRN-34*, 3 Dec 1956. R18 Jan 1960. Stricken from USN, 1 Jan 1983.

AM 157 *Caravan* Decomm and trfd to USSR, 17 Aug 1945.
1* Guam.
Later history: Renamed *T-337*. Renamed *BRN-33*, 3 Dec 1956. R17 Jan 1960. Stricken from USN, 1 Jan 1983.

AM 158 *Caution* Decomm and trfd to USSR, 17 Aug 1945.
Later history: Renamed *T-284*. Renamed *BRN-36*, 3 Dec 1956. R18 Jan 1960. Stricken from USN 1 Jan 1983.

AM 159 *Change* Decomm 3 Jul 1946. †

AM 160 *Clamour*. Decomm 12 Jun 1946. †

AM 161 *Climax* Decomm 31 May 1946. †
2* Iwo Jima, Minesweeping 1945.

AM 162 *Compel* Decomm 12 Jun 1946. †
1* Minesweeping 1945.

AM 163 *Concise* Decomm 31 May 1946. †
1* Minesweeping 1945.

AM 164 *Control* Decomm 6 Jun 1946. †

AM 165 *Counsel* Decomm 15 Jan 1947. †
1* Minesweeping 1945.

No.	Name	Builder	Keel Laid	Launched	Comm.
AM 214	*Craig*	Tampa	7 Dec 1942	21 Mar 1943	1 Aug 1945
AM 215	*Cruise*	Tampa	7 Dec 1942	21 Mar 1943	21 Sep 1945
AM 216	*Deft*	Tampa	27 Dec 1942	28 Mar 1943	16 Apr 1945
AM 217	*Delegate*	Tampa	27 Dec 1942	28 Mar 1943	30 Apr 1945
AM 218	*Density*	Tampa	12 Mar 1943	6 Feb 1944	15 Jun 1944
AM 219	*Design*	Tampa	12 Mar 1943	6 Feb 1944	29 Jun 1944
AM 220	*Device*	Tampa	1 Jul 1943	21 May 1944	7 Jul 1944
AM 221	*Diploma*	Tampa	1 Jul 1943	21 May 1944	15 Jul 1944

Figure 7.21:. *Inflict* (AM 251), an *Admirable*-class minesweeper, on 31 Mar 1945. *Admirable*-class hulls were identical to those of the PCE submarine chasers.

AM 222	*Disdain*	Amer. Lorain	23 Oct 1943	25 Mar 1944	26 Dec 1944
AM 223	*Dour*	Amer. Lorain	24 Oct 1943	25 Mar 1944	4 Nov 1944
AM 224	*Eager*	Amer. Lorain	29 Dec 1943	10 Jun 1944	23 Nov 1944
AM 225	*Elusive*	Amer. Lorain	29 Dec 1943	10 Jun 1944	19 Feb 1945
AM 226	*Embattle*	Amer. Lorain	6 Apr 1944	17 Sep 1944	25 Apr 1945
AM 227	*Embroil*	Amer. Lorain	—	—	—
AM 228	*Enhance*	Amer. Lorain	—	—	—
AM 229	*Equity*	Amer. Lorain	—	—	—
AM 230	*Esteem*	Amer. Lorain	—	—	—
AM 231	*Event*	Amer. Lorain	—	—	—
AM 232	*Execute*	Puget Sound Bridge	29 Mar 1944	22 Jun 1944	15 Nov 1944
AM 233	*Facility*	Puget Sound Bridge	29 Mar 1944	22 Jun 1944	29 Nov 1944
AM 234	*Fancy*	Puget Sound Bridge	12 May 1944	4 Sep 1944	13 Dec 1944
AM 235	*Fixity*	Puget Sound Bridge	12 May 1944	4 Sep 1944	29 Dec 1944
AM 236	*Flame*	Puget Sound Bridge	—	—	—
AM 237	*Fortify*	Puget Sound Bridge	—	—	—
AM 238	*Garland*	Commercial	31 Oct 1943	20 Feb 1944	26 Aug 1944
AM 239	*Gayety*	Commercial	14 Nov 1943	19 Mar 1944	23 Sep 1944
AM 240	*Hazard*	Commercial	20 Feb 1944	21 May 1944	31 Oct 1944
AM 241	*Hilarity*	Commercial	20 Mar 1944	30 Jul 1944	27 Nov 1944
AM 242	*Inaugural*	Commercial	22 May 1944	1 Oct 1944	30 Dec 1944
AM 243	*Illusive*	Tampa	—	—	—
AM 244	*Imbue*	Tampa	—	—	—
AM 245	*Impervious*	Tampa	—	—	—
AM 246	*Implicit*	Savannah	16 Mar 1943	6 Sep 1943	20 Jan 1944
AM 247	*Improve*	Savannah	1 Jun 1943	26 Sep 1943	29 Feb 1944
AM 248	*Incessant*	Savannah	3 Jul 1943	22 Oct 1943	25 Mar 1944
AM 249	*Incredible*	Savannah	9 Sep 1943	21 Nov 1943	17 Apr 1944
AM 250	*Indicative*	Savannah	29 Sep 1943	12 Dec 1943	26 Jun 1944
AM 251	*Inflict*	Savannah	26 Oct 1943	16 Jan 1944	28 Aug 1944
AM 252	*Instill*	Savannah	29 Oct 1943	5 Mar 1944	22 May 1944
AM 253	*Intrigue*	Savannah	17 Dec 1943	8 Apr 1944	31 Jul 1944
AM 254	*Invade*	Savannah	19 Jan 1944	6 Feb 1944	18 Sep 1944

Service Records:

AM 214 *Craig* Renamed ***Crag***, 3 Aug 1944. Completed at Charleston NYd. Decomm 19 Mar 1948. †
1* Minesweeping 1945.

AM 215 *Cruise* Completed at Charleston NYd. Decomm 5 Sep 1946. †

AM 216 *Deft* Decomm 9 Nov 1946. †
1* Minesweeping 1945.

AM 217 *Delegate* Decomm 29 May 1946 and trfd to China.
1* Minesweeping 1945.
Later history: Chinese Customs *Teh Hsing* (A 2), to Chinese Navy, renamed *Yung Ho*; BU 1964.

AM 218 *Density* Decomm 3 Mar 1947. †
3* Okinawa, Raids on Japan 7-8/45, Minesweeping 1945.

AM 219 *Design* Decomm 24 Aug 1946. †
3* Okinawa, Raids on Japan 7-8/45, Minesweeping 1945.

AM 220 *Device* Damaged by collision with minesweeper *Dour*, Okinawa, 19 Jun 1945. Decomm 24 Aug 1946. †
3* Okinawa, Raids on Japan 7-8/45, Minesweeping 1945.

AM 221 *Diploma* Decomm 3 Sep 1946. †
3* Okinawa, Raids on Japan 7-8/45, Minesweeping 1945.

AM 222 *Disdain* Decomm 21 May and trfd to USSR, 22 May 1945.
Later history: Renamed *T-271*. Stricken and renamed *Shtorm*, 7 Aug 1948. BU 1960s Stricken from USN, 1 Jan 1983.

AM 223 *Dour* Damaged by collision with minesweeper *Device*, Okinawa, 19 Jun 1945. Decomm 15 Mar 1947. †
3* Okinawa, Raids on Japan 7-8/45, Minesweeping 1945.

AM 224 *Eager* Decomm 27 Sep 1946. †
1* Minesweeping 1945.

AM 225 *Elusive* Decomm 29 May 1946, trfd to China.
1* Minesweeping 1945.
Later history: Chinese Customs *Ho Hsing* (A 3), to Chinese Navy, renamed *Yung Kang*. BU 1964.

AM 226 *Embattle* Decomm 29 May 1946, trfd to China.
1* Minesweeping 1945.
Later history: Chinese Customs *Yun Hsing* (A 4), to Chinese Navy, renamed *Yung Hsing*. R1964

AM 227 *Embroil* Canceled 6 Jun 1944.

AM 228 *Enhance* Canceled 6 Jun 1944.

AM 229 *Equity* Canceled 6 Jun 1944.

AM 230 *Esteem* Canceled 6 Jun 1944.

AM 231 *Event* Canceled 6 Jun 1944.

AM 232 *Execute* Decomm 6 Aug 1946. †
3* Okinawa, Raids on Japan 7-8/45, Minesweeping 1945.

AM 233 *Facility* Damaged by kamikaze near miss, Okinawa, 6 Apr 1945. Decomm 11 Sep 1946. †
3* Okinawa, Raids on Japan 7-8/45, Minesweeping 1945.

AM 234 *Fancy* Decomm 21 May 1945 and trfd to USSR.
Later history: Renamed *T-272*. Renamed *Vyuga*, 7 Aug 1948. BU 1960s. Stricken from USN 1 Jan 1983.

AM 235 *Fixity* Decomm 6 Nov 1946. To MC, 23 Jan 1948. Sold 29 Nov 1948. †
2* Okinawa, Minesweeping 1945.
Later history: Merchant *Commercial Dixie.*
AM 236 *Flame* Canceled 6 Jun 1944.
AM 237 *Fortify* Canceled 6 Jun 1944.
AM 238 *Garland* Decomm 2 Aug 1946. †
2* Raids on Japan 7-8/45, Minesweeping 1945.
AM 239 *Gayety* Damaged by piloted bomb, Okinawa, 4 May 1945 (none killed). Damaged by aircraft bomb, Okinawa, 27 May 1945 (5 killed). Decomm 7 Jun 1946. †
3* Okinawa, Raids on Japan 7-8/45, Minesweeping 1945.
AM 240 *Hazard* Decomm 27 Jul 1946. †
3* Okinawa, Raids on Japan 7-8/45, Minesweeping 1945.
AM 241 *Hilarity* Decomm 26 Aug 1946. †
2* Okinawa, Minesweeping 1945.
AM 242 *Inaugural* Decomm 9 Sep 1946. †
2* Okinawa, Minesweeping 1945.
AM 243 *Illusive* Canceled 6 Jun 1944.
AM 244 *Imbue* Canceled 6 Jun 1944.
AM 245 *Impervious* Canceled 6 Jun 1944.
AM 246 *Implicit* Decomm 16 Nov 1946. †
2* Southern France, Minesweeping 1945.
AM 247 *Improve* Decomm 6 Nov 1946. Sold 24 Feb 1949.
2* Southern France, Minesweeping 1945.
Later history: Merchant *Ecuador.* Burned and sank at Cristobal, Panama, 16 Mar 1953.
AM 248 *Incessant* Decomm 6 Nov 1946. Sold 13 Dec 1948.
2* Southern France, Minesweeping 1945.
Later history: Merchant *Commercial Ohioan*; se 1955.
AM 249 *Incredible* Decomm 6 Nov 1946. †
2* Southern France, Minesweeping 1945.
AM 250 *Indicative* Decomm 5 Apr 1945 and trfd to USSR 22 May 1945.
Later history: Renamed *T-273.* Stricken 7 Aug 1948 and renamed *Tsiklon.* BU 1960s. Stricken 1 Jan 1983.
AM 251 *Inflict* Decomm 6 Nov 1946. Sold 1948.
3* Okinawa, Raids on Japan 7-8/45, Minesweeping 1945.
Later history: Merchant *Manabi.* Foundered and beached off Cape San Antonio, Cuba, 24 May 1953. Refloated 29 Jun 1954 and BU.
AM 252 *Instill* Decomm 26 Feb 1947. †
AM 253 *Intrigue* Decomm 31 May 1946. †
AM 254 *Invade* Decomm 7 Aug 1946. †

Figure 7.22: *Method* (AM 264) on 11 Jan 1945, with patrol craft *YP-569* alongside.

No.	Name	Builder	Keel Laid	Launched	Comm.
AM 255	*Jubilant*	Amer. Lorain	22 Oct 1942	20 Feb 1943	27 Aug 1943
AM 256	*Knave*	Amer. Lorain	23 Oct 1942	13 Mar 1943	14 Oct 1943
AM 257	*Lance*	Amer. Lorain	26 Oct 1942	10 Apr 1943	4 Nov 1943
AM 258	*Logic*	Amer. Lorain	27 Oct 1942	10 Apr 1943	21 Nov 1943
AM 259	*Lucid*	Amer. Lorain	20 Feb 1943	5 Jun 1943	1 Dec 1943
AM 260	*Magnet*	Amer. Lorain	13 Mar 1943	5 Jun 1943	7 Mar 1944
AM 261	*Mainstay*	Amer. Lorain	10 Apr 1943	31 Jul 1943	24 Apr 1944
AM 262	*Marvel*	Amer. Lorain	12 Apr 1943	31 Jul 1943	9 Jun 1944
AM 263	*Measure*	Amer. Lorain	5 Jun 1943	23 Oct 1943	13 May 1944
AM 264	*Method*	Amer. Lorain	7 Jun 1943	23 Oct 1943	20 Jul 1944
AM 265	*Mirth*	Amer. Lorain	31 Jul 1943	24 Dec 1943	12 Aug 1944
AM 266	*Nimble*	Amer. Lorain	2 Aug 1943	24 Dec 1943	15 Sep 1944
AM 267	*Notable*	Gulf Mad.	17 Sep 1942	12 Jun 1943	23 Dec 1943
AM 268	*Nucleus*	Gulf Mad.	7 Sep 1942	26 Jun 1943	19 Jan 1944
AM 269	*Opponent*	Gulf Mad.	21 Sep 1942	12 Jun 1943	18 Feb 1944
AM 270	*Palisade*	Gulf Mad.	21 Sep 1942	16 Jun 1943	9 Mar 1944
AM 271	*Penetrate*	Gulf Mad.	5 Jan 1943	11 Sep 1943	31 Mar 1944
AM 272	*Peril*	Gulf Mad.	1 Feb 1943	25 Jul 1943	20 Apr 1944
AM 273	*Phantom*	Gulf Mad.	1 Feb 1943	25 Jul 1943	17 May 1944
AM 274	*Pinnacle*	Gulf Mad.	1 Feb 1943	11 Sep 1943	24 May 1944
AM 275	*Pirate*	Gulf Mad.	1 Jul 1943	16 Dec 1943	16 Jun 1944
AM 276	*Pivot*	Gulf Mad.	1 Jul 1943	11 Nov 1943	12 Jul 1944
AM 277	*Pledge*	Gulf Mad.	1 Jul 1943	23 Dec 1943	29 Jul 1944
AM 278	*Project*	Gulf Mad.	1 Jul 1943	20 Nov 1943	22 Aug 1944
AM 279	*Prime*	Gulf Mad.	15 Sep 1943	22 Jan 1944	12 Sep 1944
AM 280	*Prowess*	Gulf Mad.	15 Sep 1943	17 Feb 1944	27 Sep 1944
AM 281	*Quest*	Gulf Mad.	24 Nov 1943	16 Mar 1944	25 Oct 1944
AM 282	*Rampart*	Gulf Mad.	24 Nov 1943	30 Mar 1944	18 Nov 1944

Service Records:

AM 255 *Jubilant* Decomm 18 May 1946. †
AM 256 *Knave* Decomm 1 May 1946. †
AM 257 *Lance* Decomm and trfd to China 28 Aug 1945.
Later history: Renamed *Yung Sheng.* R 1968.
AM 258 *Logic* Decomm and trfd to China 28 Aug 1945.
Later history: Renamed *Yung Shun.* R 1968.
AM 259 *Lucid* Decomm and trfd to China 28 Aug 1945.
Later history: Renamed *Yung Ting* (AGS), then *Yang Ming.* R.
AM 260 *Magnet* Decomm and trfd to China 28 Aug 1945.
Later history: Renamed Chinese *Yung Ning.* Stricken 1963.
AM 261 *Mainstay* Decomm 6 Nov 1946. †
2* Southern France, Minesweeping 1945.
AM 262 *Marvel* Decomm and trfd to USSR 21 May 1945.
Later history: Renamed *T-274.* Stricken 7 Aug 1948 and renamed *Passat.* BU 1960s. Stricken 1 Jan 1983 from USN.

AM 263 *Measure* Decomm and trfd to USSR 21 May 1945.
Later history: Renamed *T-275.* Stricken 7 Aug 1948 and renamed *Buran.* BU 1960s. Stricken 1 Jan 1983 from USN.
AM 264 *Method* Decomm and trfd to USSR 21 May 1945.
Later history: Renamed *T-276.* Stricken 7 Aug 1948 and renamed *Purga.* BU 1960s. Stricken 1 Jan 1983 from USN.
AM 265 *Mirth* Decomm and trfd to USSR, 21 May 1945.
Later history: Renamed *T-277.* Stricken 7 Aug 1948 and renamed *Musson.* BU1960s. Stricken 1 Jan 1983.
AM 266 *Nimble* Decomm 10 Oct 1946. †
3* Okinawa, Raids on Japan 7-8/45, Minesweeping 1945.
AM 267 *Notable* Decomm 29 May 1946 and trfd to China (Customs).
3* Okinawa, Raids on Japan 7-8/45, Minesweeping 1945.
AM 268 *Nucleus* Decomm and trfd to USSR, 21 May 1945.
Later history: Renamed *T-278.* Stricken 7 Aug 1948 and renamed *Uragan.* BU 1960s. Stricken 1 Jan 1983.
AM 269 *Opponent* Decomm 27 Aug 1946. †
3* Okinawa, Raids on Japan 7-8/45, Minesweeping 1945.
AM 270 *Palisade* Decomm and trfd to USSR, 22 May 1945.
Later history: Renamed *T-279.* Damaged by mine off Kham I., 14 Aug 1945, CTL. ? Renamed *PKZ-38,* 21 Sep 1951. Stricken 31 Jul 1957.
AM 271 *Penetrate* Weather patrol, North Atlantic 1944. Decomm and trfd to USSR, 21 May 1945.
Later history: Renamed *T-280.* Stricken 7 Aug 1948 and renamed *Taifun.* BU 1960s. Stricken 1 Jan 1983, not returned.
AM 272 *Peril* Decomm and trfd to USSR, 21 May 1945.
Later history: Renamed *T-281.* Renamed *BRN-32,* 3 Dec 1956. *R18* Jan 1960. Stricken 1 Jan 1983.
AM 273 *Phantom* Decomm 10 Oct 1946. †
3* Okinawa, Raids on Japan 7-8/45, Minesweeping 1945.
AM 274 *Pinnacle* Yalta Conference Jan 1945. Decomm 9 Oct 1946. †
* Southern France, Minesweeping 1945.
AM 275 *Pirate* Decomm 6 Nov 1946. †
4* Okinawa, Raids on Japan 7-8/45, Minesweeping 1945.
AM 276 *Pivot* Decomm 6 Nov 1946. †
4* Okinawa, Raids on Japan 7-8/45, Minesweeping 1945.
AM 277 *Pledge* Decomm 6 Nov 1946. †
1* Okinawa.
AM 278 *Project* Decomm 13 Jun 1946. Stricken 16 Sep 1947. To Philippines 24 May 1948.
1* Minesweeping 1945.
Later history: Renamed *Samar.*
AM 279 *Prime* Decomm 29 May 1946 and trfd to China.
1* Minesweeping 1945-48.
Later history: Chinese Customs *Jung Hsing* (A 8), to Chinese Navy, renamed *Yung Feng.*
AM 280 *Prowess* Decomm Dec 1945 †
AM 281 *Quest* Decomm 2 May 1946. Stricken 29 Sep 1947. To Philippines 30 Jun 1948.
2* Minesweeping 1945.
Later history: Renamed *Pagasa, Santa Maria, Pagasa, Mount Samat* 1967.
AM 282 *Rampart* Decomm and trfd to USSR, 20 May 1945.
Later history: Renamed *T-282.* Renamed *Shkval,* 7 Aug 1948. BU 1960s. Stricken 1 Jan 1983 from USN.

No.	Name	Builder	Keel Laid	Launched	Comm.
AM 283	*Ransom*	General Eng.	24 Apr 1943	18 Sep 1943	5 Aug 1944
AM 284	*Rebel*	General Eng.	10 May 1943	28 Oct 1943	12 Sep 1944
AM 285	*Recruit*	General Eng.	24 May 1943	11 Dec 1943	8 Nov 1944
AM 286	*Reform*	General Eng.	24 Jun 1943	29 Jan 1944	28 Feb 1945
AM 287	*Refresh*	General Eng.	22 Sep 1943	12 Apr 1944	10 Apr 1945
AM 288	*Reign*	General Eng.	30 Oct 1943	29 May 1944	10 May 1946; completed
AM 289	*Report*	General Eng.	14 Dec 1943	8 Jul 1944	12 Jul 1946; completed
AM 290	*Reproof*	General Eng.	1 Feb 1944	8 Aug 1944	—
AM 291	*Risk*	General Eng.	15 Apr 1944	7 Nov 1944	—
AM 292	*Rival*	General Eng.	—	—	—
AM 293	*Sagacity*	General Eng.	—	—	—
AM 294	*Salute*	Commercial	11 Nov 1942	6 Feb 1943	4 Dec 1943
AM 295	*Saunter*	Commercial	23 Nov 1942	20 Feb 1943	22 Jan 1944
AM 296	*Scout*	Commercial	8 Feb 1943	2 May 1943	3 Mar 1944
AM 297	*Scrimmage*	Commercial	22 Feb 1943	16 May 1943	4 Apr 1944
AM 298	*Scuffle*	Commercial	4 May 1943	8 Aug 1943	2 May 1944
AM 299	*Sentry*	Commercial	16 May 1943	15 Aug 1943	30 May 1944
AM 300	*Serene*	Commercial	8 Aug 1943	31 Oct 1943	24 Jun 1944
AM 301	*Shelter*	Commercial	16 Aug 1943	14 Nov 1943	9 Jul 1944
AM 302	*Signet*	Associated	8 Apr 1943	16 Aug 1943	20 Jun 1944
AM 303	*Skirmish*	Associated	8 Apr 1943	16 Aug 1943	30 Jun 1944
AM 304	*Skurry*	Associated	24 May 1943	1 Oct 1943	29 Jul 1944
AM 305	*Spectacle*	Associated	24 May 1943	1 Oct 1943	11 Aug 1944
AM 306	*Spector*	Associated	5 Sep 1943	15 Feb 1944	30 Aug 1944
AM 307	*Staunch*	Associated	5 Sep 1943	15 Feb 1944	9 Sep 1944
AM 308	*Strategy*	Associated	4 Oct 1943	28 Mar 1944	22 Sep 1944
AM 309	*Strength*	Associated	4 Oct 1943	28 Mar 1944	30 Sep 1944
AM 310	*Success*	Associated	18 Feb 1944	11 May 1944	18 Oct 1944
AM 311	*Superior*	Associated	18 Feb 1944	11 May 1944	1 Nov 1944
AM 312-13		Associated	—	—	

Service Records:

AM 283 *Ransom* Slightly damaged by kamikaze bomb, Okinawa, 6 Apr 1945, and again 22 Apr 1945. Decomm 3 Mar 1947. †
3* Okinawa, Raids on Japan 7-8/45, Minesweeping 1945.
AM 284 *Rebel* Decomm 12 Jun 1946. †
4* Iwo Jima, Okinawa, Raids on Japan 7-8/45, Minesweeping 1945.
AM 285 *Recruit* Decomm 15 Aug 1946. †
3* Okinawa, Raids on Japan 7-8/45, Minesweeping 1945.
AM 286 *Reform* Decomm 9 Nov 1946. †
3* Okinawa, Raids on Japan 7-8/45, Minesweeping 1945.
AM 287 *Refresh* Decomm 9 Nov 1946. †
2* Raids on Japan 7-8/45, Minesweeping 1945.
AM 288 *Reign* Never commissioned. †
AM 289 *Report* Never commissioned. †
AM 290 *Reproof* Canceled 1 Nov 1945.
Later history: Completed as merchant *Harcourt Malcolm,* renamed *Cotton Bay* 1953, *Stratford* 1960, *Anastasio* 1966.
AM 291 *Risk* Canceled 1 Nov 1945.
Later history: Completed as merchant *George Gamblin,* renamed *Winding Bay* 1953, *Pinguino* 1962. Foundered after a fire off Ilha Grande, Brazil, 25 Jun 1967.

AM 292 *Rival* Canceled 6 Jun 1944.
AM 293 *Sagacity* Canceled 6 Jun 1944.
AM 294 *Salute* Sunk by mine off Brunei, Borneo, 8 Jun 1945 (4 killed).
5* Ormoc, Mindoro, Lingayen, Brunei, Mariveles-Corregidor, Subic Bay.
AM 295 *Saunter* Damaged by mine in Manila Bay, 26 Feb 1945; not repaired. Decomm 27 Oct 1945. Stricken 13 Nov 1945. Sold 24 Apr 1947.
3* Ormoc, Mindoro, Lingayen, Subic Bay, Mariveles-Corregidor.
AM 296 *Scout* Decomm 26 Feb 1947. †
5* Leyte, Ormoc, Mindoro, Lingayen, Brunei, Balikpapan, Subic Bay, Mariveles-Corregidor.
AM 297 *Scrimmage* Decomm 22 Jun 1946. †
6* Ormoc, Mindoro, Lingayen, Brunei, Mariveles-Corregidor, Subic Bay, Minesweeping 1945.
AM 298 *Scuffle* Ran aground on reef in Brunei Bay, 6 Jun 1945. Decomm 19 Jun 1946. †
5* Lingayen, Brunei, Balikpapan, Mariveles-Corregidor, Subic Bay, Minesweeping 1945.
AM 299 *Sentry* Decomm 19 Jun 1946. †
6* Leyte, Ormoc, Mindoro, Lingayen, Mariveles-Corregidor, Brunei, Balikpapan, Subic Bay, Minesweeping 1945.
AM 300 Serene Decomm 19 Jul 1946. †
3* Iwo Jima, Okinawa, Raids on Japan 7-8/45, Minesweeping 1945.
AM 301 *Shelter* Decomm 7 Jun 1946. †
4* Iwo Jima, Okinawa, Raids on Japan 7-8/45, Minesweeping 1945.
AM 302 *Signet* Decomm 18 Jul 1946. †
4* Iwo Jima, Okinawa, Raids on Japan 7-8/45, Minesweeping 1945.
AM 303 *Skirmish* Slightly damaged by kamikaze, Okinawa, 26 Mar 1945. Slightly damaged by aircraft bomb, Okinawa, 2 Apr 1945 (1 killed). Decomm Dec 1945. †
4* Iwo Jima, Okinawa, Raids on Japan 7-8/45, Minesweeping 1945.
AM 304 *Skurry* Renamed ***Scurry***, 3 Aug 1944. Decomm 29 Jun 1946. †
4* Iwo Jima, Okinawa, Raids on Japan 7-8/45, Minesweeping 1945.
AM 305 *Spectacle* Damaged by kamikaze off Okinawa, 22 May 1945 (29 killed), not repaired. Decomm 19 Oct 1945. Stricken 5 Dec 1945. Sold 9 May 1947.
2* Iwo Jima, Okinawa.
AM 306 *Spector* Renamed ***Specter***, 3 Aug 1944. Decomm 2 Jul 1946. †
4* Iwo Jima, Okinawa, Raids on Japan 7-8/45, Minesweeping 1945.
AM 307 *Staunch* Decomm 29 Jun 1946. †
4* Iwo Jima, Okinawa, Raids on Japan 7-8/45, Minesweeping 1945.
AM 308 *Strategy* Decomm 14 May 1946. †
4* Iwo Jima, Okinawa, Raids on Japan 7-8/45, Minesweeping 1945.
AM 309 *Strength* Decomm 19 Jul 1946. †
3* Iwo Jima, Okinawa, Minesweeping 1945.
AM 310 *Success* Decomm 9 Jul 1946. †
4* Iwo Jima, Okinawa, Raids on Japan 7-8/45, Minesweeping 1945.
AM 311 *Superior* Decomm 22 May 1946. †
3* Okinawa, Raids on Japan 7-8/45, Minesweeping 1945.
AM 312-13— Canceled 7 May 1942.

No.	Name	Builder	Keel Laid	Launched	Comm.
AM 351	*Adjutant*	Willamette	30 Aug 1943	17 Jun 1944	—
AM 352	*Bittern*	Willamette	10 Sep 1943	21 Jun 1944	—
AM 353	*Breakhorn*	Willamette	18 Sep 1943	4 Jul 1944	—
AM 354	*Cariama*	Willamette	12 Oct 1943	1 Jul 1944	—
AM 355	*Chukor*	Willamette	11 Dec 1943	15 Jul 1944	—
AM 356	*Creddock*	Willamette	10 Nov 1943	22 Jul 1944	18 Dec 1945
AM 357	*Dipper*	Willamette	19 Nov 1943	26 Jul 1944	26 Dec 1945
AM 358	*Dotterel*	Willamette	20 Nov 1943	5 Aug 1944	—
AM 359	*Drake*	Willamette	24 Nov 1943	12 Aug 1944	—
AM 360	*Driver*	Willamette	29 Nov 1943	19 Aug 1944	—
AM 361	*Dunlin*	Puget Sound Bridge	29 Jan 1943	26 Aug 1943	16 Feb 1945
AM 362	*Gadwall*	Puget Sound Bridge	24 May 1943	15 Jul 1943	23 Jun 1945
AM 363	*Gavia*	Puget Sound Bridge	8 Jul 1943	18 Sep 1943	23 Jul 1945
AM 364	*Graylag*	Puget Sound Bridge	15 Jul 1943	4 Dec 1943	31 Aug 1945
AM 365	*Harlequin*	Puget Sound Bridge	3 Aug 1943	3 Jun 1944	28 Sep 1945
AM 366	*Harrier*	Puget Sound Bridge	11 Aug 1943	7 Jun 1944	31 Oct 1945
AM 367	*Hummer*	Puget Sound Bridge	—	—	—
AM 368	*Jackdaw*	Puget Sound Bridge	—	—	—
AM 369	*Medrick*	Puget Sound Bridge	—	—	—
AM 370	*Minah*	Puget Sound Bridge	—	—	—
AM 391	*Albatross*	Defoe	1945	—	—
AM 392	*Bullfinch*	Defoe	14 Aug 1945	—	—
AM 393	*Cardinal*	Defoe	19 Oct 1945	—	—
AM 394	*Firecrest*	Defoe	—	—	—
AM 395	*Goldfinch*	Defoe	—	—	—
AM 396	*Grackle*	—	—	—	—
AM 397	*Grosbeak*	—	—	—	—
AM 398	*Grouse*	—	—	—	—
AM 399	*Gull*	—	—	—	—
AM 400	*Hawk*	—	—	—	—
AM 401	*Hummer*	—	—	—	—
AM 402	*Jackdaw*	—	—	—	—
AM 403	*Kite*	—	—	—	—
AM 404	*Longspur*	—	—	—	—
AM 405	*Merganser*	—	—	—	—
AM 406	*Osprey*	—	—	—	—
AM 407	*Partridge*	—	—	—	—
AM 408	*Plover*	—	—	—	—
AM 409	*Redhead*	—	—	—	—
AM 410	*Sanderling*	—	—	—	—
AM 411	*Scaup*	—	—	—	—
AM 412	*Sentinel*	—	—	—	—
AM 413	*Shearwater*	—	—	—	—
AM 414	*Waxbill*	—	—	—	—
AM 415	*Bluebird*	—	—	—	—
AM 416	*Flicker*	—	—	—	—
AM 417	*Linnet*	—	—	—	—
AM 418	*Magpie*	—	—	—	—
AM 419	*Parrakeet*	—	—	—	—
AM 420	*Pipit*	—	—	—	—

Service Records:

AM 351 *Adjutant* Canceled 1 Nov 1945. Sold 20 Dec 1946.
Later history: Completed as merchant barge *North Cape.*
AM 352 *Bittern* Canceled 1 Nov 1945. Sold 1946.
AM 353 *Breakhorn* Canceled 1 Nov 1945. BU 1947.

AM 354 *Cariama* Canceled 1 Nov 1945.
AM 355 *Chukor* Canceled 1 Nov 1945.
AM 356 *Creddock* Decomm 26 Mar 1946. †
AM 357 *Dipper* Decomm 15 Jan 1947. †
AM 358 *Dotterel* Canceled 1 Nov 1945.
AM 359 *Drake* Rec **YDG 11**, 20 Apr 1945, degaussing vessel and name canceled. †
AM 360 *Driver* Canceled 1 Nov 1945.
AM 361 *Dunlin* Decomm 29 May 1946, to China.
3* Okinawa, Raids on Japan 7-8/45, Minesweeping 1945.
AM 362 *Gadwall* Decomm 11 Jun 1946. †
AM 363 *Gavia* Decomm 29 May 1946 and trfd to China.
1* Minesweeping 1945.
Later history: Chinese Customs vessel *Hung Hsing* (A7), to Chinese Navy, renamed *Yung Chun*. BU 1963.
AM 364 *Graylag* Decomm 12 Aug 1946. †
AM 365 *Harlequin* Decomm 27 May 1946. †
AM 366 *Harrier* Decomm 28 Mar 1946. †
AM 367 *Hummer* Canceled 6 Jun 1944.
AM 368 *Jackdaw* Canceled 6 Jun 1944.
AM 369 *Medrick* Canceled 6 Jun 1944.
AM 370 *Minah* Canceled 6 Jun 1944.
AM 391-95 Canceled 1 Nov 1945.
AM 396-420 Canceled 12 Aug 1945.

CONVERTED TRAWLERS

No.	Name	Builder	Launched	Acquired	Comm.
AM 66	*Bullfinch* ex–*Villanova* (1940)	Bath	21 Oct 1937	6 Jul 1940	22 Oct 1940
AM 67	*Cardinal* ex–*Jeanne d'Arc* (1940)	Bath	21 Aug 1937	19 Aug 1940	2 Nov 1940

Displacement	425 tons, 291 grt
Dimensions	136'4" (oa); 122' (wl) x 24' x 9'
Machinery	1 screw; diesel; BHP 700; 10 knots
Complement	About 40
Armament	1-3"/50

Service Records:

AM 66 *Bullfinch* Chesapeake Bay. Decomm 15 Sep 1944. Stricken 23 Sep 1944. Returned 1945.
Later history: Merchant *Villanova*, renamed *Flying Cloud* 1946; se 1980.
AM 67 *Cardinal* Fifth ND. Decomm 8 Sep 1944. Stricken 23 Sep 1944. To Returned 1945.
Later history: Merchant *Jeanne d'Arc*, renamed *Red Jacket* 1946.

No.	Name	Builder	Launched	Acquired	Comm.
AM 68	*Catbird* ex–*Bittern* (1940)	Charleston Sbdg	1938	12 Aug 1940	27 Nov 1940
AM 69	*Curlew* ex–*Kittiwake* (1940)	Charleston Sbdg	1938	6 Aug 1940	7 Nov 1940

Displacement	355 grt
Dimensions	147'10" (oa); 125'8" (wl) x 28'8" x 12"
Machinery	1 screw; diesel; SHP 575, 10.5 knots
Complement	40
Armament	1-3"/50

Figure 7.23: *Cardinal* (AM 67), on 31 Oct 1941, was a converted trawler. A sister, probably the *Bullfinch*, is alongside.

Service Records:

AM 68 *Catbird* Fifteenth ND, Cristobal. Rec **IX 183**, 15 Aug 1944. Out of svc 7 Nov 1945. Stricken 28 Nov 1945. Sold 24 Jan 1947.
Later history: Merchant *Salhus*, renamed *Punta Palma* 1952. BU 1966 La Spezia, Italy.
AM 69 *Curlew* Fifteenth ND. Rec **IX 170**, 1 Jun 1944. Decomm 5 Dec 1945. Stricken 19 Dec 1945, sold 24 Sep 1946.
Later history: Merchant *Ragan*, renamed *Haugar* 1947, *Blue Ocean* 1979.

No.	Name	Builder	Launched	Acquired	Comm.
AM 70	*Flicker* ex–*Delaware* (1940)	Bath	25 Feb 1937	9 Aug 1940	26 Oct 1940

Displacement	510 tons, 303 grt
Dimensions	147'5" (oa); 134'8" (wl) x 25' x 12'
Machinery	1 screw; diesel; BHP 735, 13 knots
Complement	40
Armament	1-3"/23

Service Record

AM 70 *Flicker* Brazil. Rec **IX 165**, 20 Apr 1944. Decomm 3 Jan 1945. Stricken 19 Jan 1945. To U.S. Department of the Interior, 31 Jan 1945.
Later history: Merchant *Delaware*.

No.	Name	Builder	Launched	Acquired	Comm.
AM 71	*Albatross* ex–*Illinois* (1940)	Bath	19 Mar 1931	9 Aug 1940	8 Nov 1940
AM 72	*Bluebird* ex–*Maine* (1940)	Bath	7 Apr 1931	22 Aug 1940	22 Nov 1940

Displacement	465 ton, 256 grt
Dimensions	132'4" (oa); 121'7" (wl) x 24' x 12'
Machinery	1 screw; diesel; BHP 550, 10 knots
Complement	40
Armament	1-3"/50

Figure 7.24: *Flicker* (AM 70) on 20 Jan 1942 at the Norfolk Navy Yard.

Figure 7.25: *Kite* (AM 75), a converted trawler, on 16 Jul 1942.

Service Records:

AM 71 *Albatross* Slightly damaged in collision with iceberg off Greenland, 7 Jan 1943. Damaged in collision with ship off Nova Scotia, 11 Apr 1944. Rec **IX 171**, 1 Jun 1944. Decomm 11 Sep 1944. Stricken 23 Sep 1944. Sold 1945.
Later history: Merchant *Illinois*, renamed *Tem* 1949.

AM 72 *Bluebird* Greenland. Rec **IX 172**, 1 Jun 1944. Decomm 12 Jan 1945. Stricken 19 Jan 1945. Sold 1945.
Later history: Merchant *Rytter* 1947, renamed *Trane* 1952, *Stokkvik* 1955, *Basto* 1957. BU 1970 Hendrik Ido Ambacht, Netherlands.

No.	Name	Builder	Launched	Acquired	Comm.
AM 73	*Grackle* ex–*Notre Dame* (1940)	Bath	2 Dec 1929	16 Sep 1940	4 Feb 1941
AM 77	*Goldfinch* ex–*Fordham* (1940)	Bath	3 Jan 1930	19 Sep 1940	30 Jan 1941

Displacement	525 tons, 255 GRT
Dimensions	132'4" (oa); 1'7" (wl) x 24' x 9'8"
Machinery	1 screw; diesel; BHP 500; 10 knots
Complement	36
Armament	1-3"/50

Service Records:

AM 73 *Grackle* Neutrality patrol. Argentia. Decomm 25 Aug 1944. Stricken 16 Nov 1944. Sold 1946.
Later history: Merchant *Notre Dame*, renamed *Truls* 1948. Lost in ice northeast of Sydney, Nova Scotia, 31 Mar 1954.

AM 77 *Goldfinch* Neutrality patrol. Decomm 18 Aug 1944. Stricken 22 Aug 1944. Sold 1946.
Later history: Merchant *Fordham*, renamed *Titus* 1949, *Beater* 1960. Wrecked in hurricane at Blandford, Nova Scotia, 7 Oct 1962.

No.	Name	Builder	Launched	Acquired	Comm.
AM 74	*Gull* ex–*Boston College* (1940)	Bath	17 Oct 1928	30 Aug 1940	3 Dec 1940
AM 75	*Kite* ex–*Holy Cross* (1940)	Bath	24 Nov 1928	11 Sep 1940	3 Mar 1941
AM 76	*Linnet* ex–*Georgetown* (1940)	Bath	15 Dec 1928	4 Sep 1940	3 Mar 1941

Displacement	229 grt, 241 (74)
Dimensions	124'3" (oa); 115'3" (wl) x 23' x 10'8"
Machinery	1 screw; diesel; SHP 550; 9 knots
Complement	40
Armament	1-3"/50

Service Records:

AM 74 *Gull* Neutrality patrol. Argentia. Decomm 25 Jul 1944. Stricken 22 Aug 1944. Sold 1946.
Later history: Merchant *Gudrun*. Foundered south of Cape Race, Newfoundland, 14 Jan 1954.

AM 75 *Kite* Neutrality patrol. Decomm 14 Aug 1944. Stricken 22 Aug 1944. Sold 1945. FFU.

AM 76 *Linnet* Brazil. Rec **IX 166**, 20 Apr 1944. Decomm 18 Dec 1944. Stricken 20 Jan 1945. Sold 31 Jul 1945.
Later history: Merchant *Cambridge*.

No.	Name	Builder	Launched	Acquired	Comm.
AM 79	*Goshawk* ex–*AMc 4* (25 Nov 1940); ex–*Penobscot* (1940), ex–*Lexington* (1938), ex–*Eckmuhl*	Foundation	1919	3 Sep 1940	3 Mar 1941

Displacement	585 tons, 777 f/l; 522 grt
Dimensions	150' (oa); 140' (wl) x 25' x 13'
Machinery	1 screw; diesel; SHP 450, 9.3 knots
Complement	43
Armament	1-3"/50

Notes: Built for French Navy.

Service Record:

AM 79 *Goshawk* Alaska, Puget Sound. Rec **IX 195**, 10 Oct 1944. Stricken 3 Jan 1946. To MC, 7 May 1946.
Later history: Merchant *Bering Sea*. FFU.

No.	Name	Builder	Launched	Acquired	Comm.
AM 80	*Goldcrest* ex–*Shawmut* (1940)	Beth. Quincy	1928	29 Nov 1940	15 May 1941
AM 81	*Chaffinch* ex–*Trimount* (1940)	Beth. Quincy	1928	2 Dec 1940	16 Jul 1941

Displacement	400 tons; 469 f/l; 235 grt
Dimensions	122'6" (oa); 115' (wl) x 23'1" x 10'11"
Machinery	1 screw; diesel; SHP 600; 11 knots
Complement	36
Armament	1-3"/50

Service Records:

AM 80 *Goldcrest* New York. Decomm 12 Dec 1945. Stricken 3 Jan 1946. To MC, 24 Sep 1946.
Later history: Merchant *Batavia*, renamed *Minnie* 1955, Newton 1960.

AM 81 *Chaffinch* New York. Sank British YP *Pentland Firth* in collision off Sandy Hook, N.J., 19 Sep 1942. Decomm 12 Dec 1945. Stricken 3 Jun 1946. To MC, 23 Sep 1946.
Later history: Merchant *Medan.*

No.	Name	Builder	Launched	Acquired	Comm.
AM 132	*Eagle*	Beth. Quincy	1937	1 Jan 1942	5 Mar 1942
	ex-*Wave* (1942), ex-*Harvard* (1939)				
AM 133	*Hawk*	Beth. Quincy	24 Mar 1936	1 Jan 1942	23 May 1942
	ex-*Gale* (1942), ex-*Princeton* (1939)				
AM 134	*Ibis*	Beth. Quincy	1937	1 Jan 1942	23 May 1942
	ex-*Tide* (1942), ex-*Yale* (1939)				
AM 135	*Merganser*	Beth. Quincy	1937	1 Jan 1942	23 May 1942
	ex-*Ocean* (1942), ex-*Annapolis* (1939)				

Displacement	520 tons, 320 grt, 311 grt
Dimensions	147' (oa); 13'7" pp 128' (wl) x 26'1" x 12'8"
Machinery	1 screw; diesel; SHP 650; 12 knots
Complement	47
Armament	1-4"/50 (AM 132 Captor) or 2-6 pdr

Service Records:

AM 132 *Eagle* Renamed **Captor**, 21 Jan 1942; converted to Q-ship; operated off the Grand Banks, 1942-44. Rec **PYc 42**, 18 Apr 1942. Decomm 4 Oct 1944. Stricken 14 Oct 1944. Returned 1945.
Later history: Merchant *Wave.*

Figure 7.26: *Hawk* (AM 133), 28 Oct 1942, was one of four sister trawlers acquired in 1942. The *Eagle* of this type served as a Q-ship in 1942.

AM 133 *Hawk* 1st ND. Decomm 1 May 1944. Returned 16 Sep 1944.
Later history: Merchant *Gale.* Wrecked on Sable I., Newfoundland, 12 Dec 1945.

AM 134 *Ibis* Newport, R.I. Decomm 1 May 1944. Returned 16 Sep 1944.
Later history: Merchant *Tide.*

AM 135 *Merganser* Woods Hole, Mass. Decomm 1 May 1944. Stricken 16 Sep 1944.
Later history: Merchant *Ocean.*

No.	Name	Disposition	Date
AM 78	*Goldcrest*	Rec PYc4,	19 Dec 1940
AM 166-208		Canceled	9 Apr 1942
AM 209-13		Canceled	10 Apr 1942
AM 342–350		Not used	

Algerine Class

AM 325 *Antares*, AM 326 *Arcturus*, AM 327 *Aries*, AM 328 *Clinton*, AM 329 *Friendship*, AM 330 *Gozo*, AM 331 *Lightfoot*, AM 332 *Melita*, AM 333 *Octavia*, AM 334 *Persian*, AM 335 *Postillion*, AM 336 *Skipjack*, AM 337 *Thisbe*, AM 338 *Truelove*, AM 339 *Welfare*.

Notes: Built under reverse lend-lease but served in British Navy. No U.S. names assigned; names given above are British.

MOTOR MINESWEEPERS

The wood motor minesweepers designated YMS proved to be a most durable and versatile ship. They were designated yard because it was originally assumed they would remain at naval yards and adjacent waters. In total 445 were ordered, and 35 additional were originally ordered as submarine chasers (PCS). Another 80 were built for lend-lease to the United Kingdom; 53 others were also transferred. YMS 1-134 had two funnels; YMS 135-445, 480, and 481 had one; and YMS 446-79 had none. In 1947 the surviving YMSs were reclassified AMS—auxiliary minesweepers—and given names.

Nos.
YMS 1-445
YMS 446-81 (ex–PCS)
BYMS 1-80

Displacement	207 tons, 320 f/l
Dimensions	136' (oa) x 24'6" x 6'
Machinery	2 screws; diesel; HP 1,000; 13 knots
Endurance	2,200/10
Complement	33
Armament	1-3"/50, 2-20mm

Notes: BYMS 1-80 ordered for Royal Navy; 53 others also transferred.

War Losses

YMS 14 Sunk in collision with destroyer *Herndon* at Boston, 11 Jan 1945 (none lost).

YMS 19 Sunk by mine off Angaur, Palau, 24 Sep 1944.

YMS 21 Sunk by mine at Toulon, France, 1 Sep 1944.

Figure 7.27: *YMS-14*, 5 Jun 1943.

Figure 7.28: *YMS-260*, 12 Apr 1943, with one funnel. Earlier boats had two funnels, and later ones had none.

YMS 24 Sunk by mine off St. Tropez, France, 16 Aug 1944. (1 killed)
YMS 30 Sunk by mine off Anzio, 25 Jan 1944 (17 killed).
YMS 39 Sunk by mine off Balikpapan, Borneo 26 Jun 1945.
YMS 48 Damaged by gunfire off Corregidor and sunk by destroyer *Fletcher*, 14 Feb 1945.
YMS 50 Damaged by mine off Balikpapan and sunk by U.S. forces, 18 Jun 1945.
YMS 70 Sunk in storm at Leyte, 17 Oct 1944.
YMS 71 Sunk by mine off Brunei, Borneo, 3 Apr 1945.
YMS 84 Sunk by mine off Balikpapan, Borneo, 9 Jul 1945.
YMS 90 Sunk in typhoon at Okinawa, 9 Oct 1945. Stricken 5 Jun 1946; destroyed 25 Sep 1947.
YMS 98 Sunk in typhoon off Okinawa, 16 Sep 1945.
YMS 385 Sunk by mine at Ulithi, Micronesia, 1 Oct 1944 (9 killed)

Builders

AC&F	BYMS 1-4, 31-36
Associated	YMS 287-96, BYMS 9-14
Astoria Marine	YMS 100-103, 135-42, 422-25
Ballard	YMS 327-33, BYMS 25-28
Barbour	BYMS 29-30, 37-42
Bellingham	YMS 269-76, 342-45, 410-13, 480-81, BYMS 17-20
Burger	YMS 107-12, 155-62
Campbell	YMS 151-54
Colberg	YMS 94-99, 383-88
Dachel-Carter	YMS 163-70, BYMS 15-16
Gibbs	YMS 54-65, 347-57, 464-72, BYMS 43-54
Grebe	YMS 84-85, 171-82, 279-80, 405-9, 418-21
Greenport	YMS 20-31, 183-94, 375-82, 453-59
Harbor Boat	YMS 117-20, 313-16, 393-96, 473
Herreshoff	YMS 18-19
Hiltebrant	YMS 32-37, 195-206, 442-45, 462-63
Jacob	YMS 38-41, 207-15, 358-62, 438-41, 446-48
Kruse & Banks	YMS 121-24, 265-68
Larson	YMS 86-87, 320-25
Martinac	YMS 125-28, 216-20, 277-78, 434-37
Mojean Ericsson	YMS 222-25, 426-29, 479
Nevins	YMS 1-11, 308-12, 397-404
Northwestern	YMS 285-86
Rice	YMS 12-17, 303-7
Sample	YMS 104-6, 226-34
San Diego Marine	YMS 113-16, 143-46, 281-84, 475
Seattle Sbdg	YMS 334-41, BYMS 21-24
South Coast	YMS 88-93, 259-64, 318-19, 449
Stadium	YMS 76-83, 235-240, 390-92, 414-17, 460-61
W. F. Stone	YMS 299-302
Tacoma Boat	YMS 129-32, 241-46, 297-98, 430-33, 477-78
Weaver	YMS 66-75, 247-58, 371-74
Westergard	BYMS 55-64
Western Boat	YMS 133-34, 147-50
Wheeler	YMS 42-53, 363-70, BYMS 5-8, 65-80

8 PATROL VESSELS

GUNBOATS

Gunboats and frigates were named after smaller cities.

Gunboats on the Navy List, 1922

PG 8 *Wilmington* Rec unclassified, **IX 30**.

PG 9 *Helena* South China. Decomm and stricken 27 May 1932. Sold 7 Jul 1932.

PG 10 *Annapolis* Rec unclassified 1 Jul 1921, **IX 1**.

PG 12 *Newport* Rec unclassified 1 Jul 1921, **IX 19**.

PG 14 *Wheeling* Rec unclassified 1 Jul 1921, **IX 28**.

PG 16 *Palos* Rec **PR 1**, 15 Jun 1928.

PG 17 *Dubuque* Rec unclassified, 24 Apr 1922, **IX 9**. Recomm 25 May 1922. Great Lakes, 1922–40. Rec **PG 17**, 4 Nov 1940. Recomm 1 Jul 1941. Gunnery practice ship, Little Creek, Va. Decomm 7 Sep 1945. Sold; BU 1947. (Armament: 1–5"/38, 2–4"/50, 1–3"/50, 3 or 5 20mm guns. Fitted with single stack replacing two thin funnels, 1941.)

PG 18 *Paducah* Rec unclassified, 24 Apr 1922, **IX 23**. Naval reserve training, Great Lakes, 1922–41. Rec **PG 18**, 4 Nov 1940. Decomm 7 Sep 1945. (Armament: 1–5"/38, 2–4"/50, 1–3"/50, 3 or 5 20mm guns.)
Later history: Merchant *Paducah* 1946, illegal Jewish immigrant ship, renamed *Geulah* 1947. BU 1950.

PG 19 *Sacramento* Asiatic Fleet 1922–28, 1932–39. China 1922–28. Nicaragua 1929–31. Yangtze River 1926–27, 1932. China 1937–39. Great Lakes 1939–40. Decomm 6 Feb 1946 and stricken. Sold 23 Aug 1947. (Armament: 2–4"/50, 1–3"/50. Funnel cut down 1938.)
1* Pearl Harbor.
Later history: Merchant *Fermina.*

PG 20 *Monocacy* Rec **PR 2**, 15 Jun 1928.

PG 21 *Asheville* Asiatic Fleet 1922–29. Nicaragua 1929–31. Yangtze River 1926–27, 1932. Asiatic Fleet 1932–42. China 1937–39. Broke shaft while en route to Manila from China, Jul 1941. Sunk by Japanese

Figure 8.1: *Dubuque* (PG 17), an old gunboat built in 1904, as she appeared on 4 Jun 1941. Her two thin funnels have been replaced by a single chunky stack.

Figure 8.2: *Sacramento* (PG 19), 12 May 1941, with funnel cut down.

Figure 8.3: *Tulsa* (PG 22), as seen on 1 Sep 1938 at Cavite Navy Yard, after overhaul when stack was cut down.

Figure 8.4: The gunboat *Erie* (PG 50), as completed, on 19 Oct 1936. Notice the 6" guns in single mounts.

Figure 8.5: *Charleston* (PG 51) served in the North Pacific. She is seen here on 13 Mar 1944, with little change in appearance.

warships south of Java, 1 Mar 1942 (~160 killed; only survivor died as POW).
1* Philippines 1942.

PG 22 *Tulsa* Comm 14 Dec 1923. Caribbean 1924–29. Asiatic Fleet 1929–45. Damaged by explosion at Amoy, China, 1 Jun 1932 (1 killed). Nicaragua 1926–28. China 1929–41. Yangtze River 1932. China 1937–39. Damaged by grounding, Milne Bay, New Guinea, 20 Dec 1942. Renamed ***Tacloban***, 18 Dec 1944. Decomm 6 Mar 1946. Stricken 17 Apr 1946. FFU. (Armament: 5–3"/50, 6–20mm guns. Refit 1938, funnel shortened, wood masts installed.)
3* Philippines 1942, Eastern New Guinea, Leyte.

PG 38 *Elcano* Yangtze River 1926–27. Decomm 30 Jun 1928. Stricken 4 Oct 1928. Sunk as target off China Coast, 4 Oct 1928.

PG 39 *Pampanga* South China. Decomm 6 Nov 1928. Stricken 22 Nov 1928. Sunk as target off China Coast, 21 Nov 1928.

PG 40 *Quiros* China. Decomm 10 Aug 1923. Stricken 16 Oct 1923, sunk as target off China Coast.

PG 42 *Villalobos* Yangtze River 1926–27. Decomm 29 May 1928. Stricken 4 Oct 1928. Sunk as target off China Coast, 9 Oct 1928.

PG 43–48 — Rec **PR 3–8**, 15 Jun 1928.

PG 49 *Fulton* Ex-AS 1, 29 Sep 1930.

Erie Class

No.	Name	Builder	Keel Laid	Launched	Comm.
PG 50	*Erie*	New York NYd	17 Dec 1934	29 Jan 1936	1 Jul 1936
PG 51	*Charleston*	Charleston NYd	27 Oct 1934	26 Feb 1936	8 Jul 1936

Displacement	2,000 tons; 2,920 f/l
Dimensions	328'6" (oa); 308' (wl) x 41'3" x 14'10"
Machinery	2 screws; Parsons GT; 2 B&W boilers; SHP 6,200; 20 knots
Complement	246
Armament	4–6"/47; PG 51 *Charleston*: 4 quad 1.1", 8–20mm guns added.
Armor	2" to 3.5" belt, 1" to 1.25" deck, 4" CT

Notes: Built as small cruisers for service in Central America. Clipper bow, counter stern, four single gun mounts, one seaplane. Similar to *Treasury* class Coast Guard cutters. Aft superstructure cut down in PG 51 *Charleston* 1943.

Service Records:

PG 50 *Erie* Spanish Civil War (Sqn 40T), Oct–Dec 1936. Flagship, Special Service Squadron, Central America, 1938–40. Torpedoed by *U-163,* burned and beached near Willemstad, Curacao, 12 Nov 1942 (7 killed); refloated but sank, 5 Dec 1942.

PG 51 *Charleston* Spanish Civil War (Sqn 40T), Feb–Apr 1937. Went aground at Colon, Panama, 11 Jan 1940. Decomm 10 May 1946. Stricken 25 Mar 1948, trfd to Mass. Maritime Academy.
1* Attu.
Later history: Training ship *Charleston*; se 1957.

RIVER GUNBOATS

River Gunboats on the Navy List, 1922

PG 16 *Palos* Rec **PR 1**, 15 Jun 1928. Stricken 21 May 1937. Sold 3 Jun 1937 and BU Chungking, China.

PG 20 *Monocacy* Yangtze River 1926–27, 1930–32. Rec **PR 2**, 15 Jun 1928. Decomm 31 Jan 1939. Stricken 10 Oct 1939. Scuttled off China Coast, 2 Oct 1939.

Six river gunboats were built in China to replace the antiquated ships captured from Spain in 1898. (PG 43–48 rec PR 3–8, 15 Jun 1928) Late in 1941, with war threatening, Navy ships were withdrawn from China, making the dangerous open sea voyage to Manila. PR 6 *Oahu* and PR 7 *Luzon* departed Shanghai, 28 Nov 1941; PR 8 *Mindanao* departed Hong Kong, 4 Dec 1941, arriving at Manila 10 Dec 1941.

No.	Name	Builder	Keel Laid	Launched	Comm.
PR 3	*Guam*	Kiangnan	17 Oct 1926	28 May 1927	28 Dec 1927
PR 4	*Tutuila*	Kiangnan	17 Oct 1926	14 Jun 1927	2 Mar 1928

Displacement	370 tons
Dimensions	159'5" (oa); 150' (wl) x 27'1" x 5'1"
Machinery	2 screws; VTE; 2 Thornycroft boilers; SHP 1,950; 14.5 knots
Complement	63
Armament	2–3"/23

Notes: Ordered as PG 43–44. Yangtze Patrol.

Service Records:

PR 3 *Guam* Renamed ***Wake***, 23 Jan 1941. Captured by Japanese at Shanghai, 8 Dec 1941.
Later history: Renamed *Tatara*. Recovered, Aug 1945, and trfd to China, renamed *Tai Yuan*. Captured by PRC forces 1949.

PR 4 *Tutuila* At Chungking, China, 1938–42. Damaged in collision with steamer at Chungking, 4 Oct 1939. Went aground on reef at Chungking, 8 May 1940, refloated 13 May. Decomm 18 Jan 1942. To China, 16 Feb 1942.
Later history: Renamed *Mei Yuan*. Scuttled at Shanghai to prevent capture by PRC forces, 1949.

No.	Name	Builder	Keel Laid	Launched	Comm.
PR 5	*Panay*	Kiangnan	18 Dec 1926	10 Nov 1927	10 Sep 1928
PR 6	*Oahu*	Kiangnan	18 Dec 1926	26 Nov 1927	22 Oct 1928

Displacement	450 tons
Dimensions	191'1" (oa); 180" (wl) x 28'1" x 5'3"
Machinery	2 screws; VTE; 2 Thornycroft boilers; SHP 2,250; 15 knots
Complement	65
Armament	2–3"/50

Notes: Ordered as PG 45–46. Yangtze Patrol.

Service Records:

PR 5 *Panay* Damaged when rammed by British m/v *Poyang* at wharf at Hwangshihkang, China, 30 Nov 1929. Sunk by Japanese aircraft off Nanking in Yangtze River, 12 Dec 1937 (3 killed).

PR 6 *Oahu* Transferred to Manila, end of Nov 1941. Sunk by gunfire off Corregidor, 5 May 1942.
1* Philippines 1942.

No.	Name	Builder	Keel Laid	Launched	Comm.
PR 7	*Luzon*	Kiangnan	20 Nov 1926	12 Sep 1927	1 Jun 1928
PR 8	*Mindanao*	Kiangnan	20 Nov 1926	28 Sep 1927	10 Jul 1928

Displacement	560 tons
Dimensions	210'9" (oa); 198' (wl) x 31'1" x 5'7"
Machinery	2 screws; VTE; 2 Thornycroft boilers; SHP 3,150; 16 knots
Complement	82
Armament	2–3"/50

Notes: Ordered as PG 47–48. Yangtze Patrol. Both transferred from China to Manila end Nov 1941.

Figure 8.7: The river gunboat *Panay* (PR 5), seen here on 30 Aug 1928, was sunk by Japanese aircraft in the Yangtze River in 1937.

Figure 8.6: *Guam* (PR 3), a river gunboat built at Shanghai. She was renamed *Wake* in 1941 and captured at Shanghai on 7 Dec of that year.

Figure 8.8: The river gunboat *Luzon* (PR 7) at Shanghai on 21 May 1928. She was the largest of the new boats.

Service Records:

PR 7 *Luzon* Scuttled off Corregidor, 6 May 1942.
1* Philippines 1942.
Later history: Salved by Japan, renamed *Karatsu.* Torpedoed by submarine *Narwhal* in Sulu Sea off Mindanao, 3 Mar 1944, and scuttled at Manila, 3 Feb 1945.

PR 8 *Mindanao* Flag ship, South China Patrol, 1929–41. Damaged by gunfire off Bataan, 10 Apr 1942. Scuttled off Corregidor after being damaged, 2 May 1942.
1* Philippines 1942.

FRIGATES

Asheville Class

No.	Name	Builder	Keel Laid	Launched	Comm.
PG 101	*Asheville* ex–HMCS *Nadur*	Can.Vickers	10 Mar 1942	22 Aug 1942	1 Dec 1942
PG 102	*Natchez* ex–HMCS *Annan*	Can.Vickers	16 Mar 1942	12 Sep 1942	16 Dec 1942
PG 103	—	Can.Vickers	10 Jun 1942	26 Sep 1942	*30 Apr 1943*
PG 104	—	Can.Vickers	4 May 1942	24 Oct 1942	*14 May 1943*
PG 105	—	Can.Vickers	28 Jun 1942	8 Nov 1942	*4 Jun 1943*
PG 106	—	Can.Vickers	23 Aug 1942	5 Dec 1942	*25 Jun 1943*
PG 107	—	Can.Vickers	17 Sep 1942	12 Dec 1942	*19 Jul 1943*
PG 108	—	Can.Vickers	1 Oct 1942	30 Apr 1943	*14 Aug 1943*
PG 109	—	Can.Vickers	31 Oct 1942	30 Apr 1943	*31 Aug 1943*
PG 110	—	Can.Vickers	8 Nov 1942	26 May 1943	*30 Sep 1943*

Displacement	2,360 tons f/l
Dimensions	301'6" (oa); 283' (wl) x 36'6" x 13'8"
Machinery	2 screws; VTE; 2 boilers; SHP 5,500; 20 knots
Endurance	7,500/15
Complement	194
Armament	3–3"/50; 2 twin 40mm, 4–20mm AA

Figure 8.9: *Asheville* (PG 101) was one of ten frigates built in Montreal for the Navy, but only two were acquired. In this photo dated 25 Feb 1943 she wears the number PG 101, changed shortly thereafter to PF 1.

Notes: Canadian river class. PG 103–110 were built by Canadian Vickers and immediately lend–leased to the United Kingdom. PF 1–2 acquired 20 Jul 1942.

Service Records:

PG 101 *Asheville* Rec **PF 1**, 17 Apr 1943. Decomm 14 Jan 1946. Stricken 25 Feb 1946.
Later history: Sold to Argentina, 17 Jun 1946, renamed *Hercules*, 1963 *Juan B. Azopardo.*

PG 102 *Natchez* Rec **PF 2**, 17 Apr 1943. Decomm 11 Oct 1945. 1*
Later history: Sold to Dominican Republic, 29 Jul 1947, renamed *Juan Pablo Duarte.* Ran aground at Puerto Plata, Nov 1949, sold and converted to yacht, renamed *Moineau.* 1952. Reported sunk 1957.
Submarine sunk: **U–548* off Cape Hatteras, 30 Apr 1945.

PG 103 To UK as HMS *Barle.* Returned 27 Feb 1946; BU.

PG 104 To UK as HMS *Cuckmere.* Torpedoed by *U–223* northwest of Algiers, 11 Dec 1943, CTL. Returned 6 Nov 1946; BU.

PG 105 To UK as HMS *Evenlode.* Returned 5 Mar 1946; BU.

PG 106 To UK as HMS *Findhorn.* Returned 20 Mar 1946; BU.

PG 107 To UK as HMS *Inver.* Returned 4 Mar 1946; BU.

PG 108 To UK as HMS *Lossie.* Returned 26 Jan 1946. Sold
Later history: Merchant *Teti* 1947, renamed *Adriatiki* 1955. Wrecked in Aegean Sea, 16 Jan 1968.

PG 109 To UK as HMS *Parret.* Returned 5 Feb 1946; BU.

PG 110 To UK as HMS *Shiel.* Returned 4 Mar 1946; BU.

Tacoma Class

No.	Name	Builder	Keel Laid	Launched	Comm.
PF 3	*Tacoma*	Kaiser Rich.	10 Mar 1943	7 Jul 1943	6 Nov 1943
PF 4	*Sausalito*	Kaiser Rich.	7 Apr 1943	20 Jul 1943	4 Mar 1944
PF 5	*Hoquiam*	Kaiser Rich.	10 Apr 1943	31 Jul 1943	8 May 1944
PF 6	*Pasco*	Kaiser Rich.	7 Jul 1943	17 Aug 1943	15 Apr 1944
PF 7	*Albuquerque*	Kaiser Rich.	20 Jul 1943	14 Sep 1943	20 Dec 1943
PF 8	*Everett*	Kaiser Rich.	31 Jul 1943	29 Sep 1943	22 Jan 1944
PF 9	*Pocatello*	Kaiser Rich.	17 Aug 1943	17 Oct 1943	18 Feb 1944
PF 10	*Brownsville*	Kaiser Rich.	14 Sep 1943	14 Nov 1943	6 May 1944
PF 11	*Grand Forks*	Kaiser Rich.	29 Sep 1943	27 Nov 1943	18 Mar 1944
PF 12	*Casper*	Kaiser Rich.	17 Oct 1943	27 Dec 1943	31 Mar 1944
PF 13	*Pueblo*	Kaiser Rich.	14 Nov 1943	20 Jan 1944	27 May 1944
PF 14	*Grand Island*	Kaiser Rich.	27 Nov 1943	19 Feb 1944	27 May 1944

Figure 8.10: The frigate *Eugene* (PF 40) on 24 May 1944 in San Francisco Bay. She was manned by a Coast Guard crew.

Figure 8.11: The frigate *Woonsocket* (PF 32), 18 Sep 1944, as completed. She served as a weather ship in the North Atlantic.

PF 15	*Annapolis*	Amer. Lorain	20 May 1943	16 Oct 1943	4 Dec 1944
PF 16	*Bangor*	Amer. Lorain	20 May 1943	6 Nov 1943	22 Nov 1944
PF 17	*Key West*	Amer. Lorain	23 Jun 1943	29 Dec 1943	7 Nov 1944
PF 18	*Alexandria*	Amer. Lorain	23 Jun 1943	15 Jan 1944	11 Mar 1945
PF 19	*Huron*	Amer. Cleve.	1 Mar 1943	3 Jul 1943	7 Sep 1944
PF 20	*Gulfport*	Amer. Cleve.	5 May 1943	21 Aug 1943	16 Sep 1944
PF 21	*Bayonne*	Amer. Cleve.	6 May 1943	11 Sep 1943	14 Feb 1945

Displacement	1,430 tons; 2,415 f/l
Dimensions	303'11" (oa); 285'6" (wl) x 37'6" x 13'8"
Machinery	2 screws; VTE; 2 B&W boilers; SHP 5,500; 20.3 knots
Endurance	6,000/12
Complement	176
Armament	3–3"/50; 2 twin 40mm, 9–20mm AA; weather ships: 2–3"/50, 2 twin 40mm, 4–20mm

Notes: All USCG manned. PG 111–210 rec PF 3–102, 15 Apr 1943. Similar to British River class, but all welded. One hundred ordered for Royal Navy, twenty-one transferred as compensation for DEs retained by the Navy. PF 18, 23, 24, 28–33, 56–61, 67, 93, 94, 101, 102 served as weather ships.

Service Records:

PF 3 *Tacoma* USCG crew. To USSR, 17 Aug 1945.
Later history: Renamed *EK-11.* Returned 17 Oct 1949. †

PF 4 *Sausalito* USCG crew. To USSR, 17 Aug 1945.
Later history: Renamed *EK-16.* Returned 1 Nov 1949. †

PF 5 *Hoquiam* USCG crew. To USSR, 17 Aug 1945.
Later history: Renamed *EK-13.* Returned 1 Nov 1949. †

PF 6 *Pasco* USCG crew. To USSR, 17 Aug 1945.
Later history: Renamed *EK-12.* Returned 15 Jul 1950. †

PF 7 *Albuquerque* USCG crew. To USSR, 17 Aug 1945.
Later history: Renamed *EK-14.* Returned 15 Nov 1949. †

PF 8 *Everett* USCG crew. To USSR, 17 Aug 1945.
Later history: Renamed *EK-15.* Returned 15 Nov 1949. †

PF 9 *Pocatello* USCG crew. Weather ship, North Pacific. Decomm 2 May 1946. Sold 22 Sep 1947; BU.

PF 10 *Brownsville* USCG crew. Decomm 15 Apr 1946 and loaned to USCG. Returned 28 Jun 1946. Sold 30 Sep 1947; BU.

PF 11 *Grand Forks* USCG crew. Decomm 16 May 1946. Stricken 19 Jun 1946. Sold 19 May 1947; BU.

PF 12 *Casper* USCG crew. Decomm 16 May 1946. Sold 20 May 1947; BU.

PF 13 *Pueblo* USCG crew. Weather ship, N. California. Decomm 6 Apr 1946. Sold 22 Sep 1947. To Dominican Republic 1948
Later history: Renamed *Presidente Troncoso,* renamed *Gregorio Luperon* 1962. R

PF 14 *Grand Island* USCG crew. Decomm 21 May 1946. Stricken 19 Jun 1946. Sold to Cuba, 16 Jun 1947.
Later history: Renamed *Maximo Gomez.* Sunk in Mariel Bay 1961.

PF 15 *Annapolis* USCG crew. Decomm 29 May 1946. Stricken 19 Jun 1946. To Mexico, 24 Nov 1947.
Later history: Renamed *General Vicente Guerrero,* renamed *Usumacinta.* R 1964.

PF 16 *Bangor* USCG crew. Decomm 15 Apr 1946 and loaned to USCG. Returned 16 Aug 1946. To Mexico, 24 Nov 1947.
Later history: Renamed *General José Maria Morelos,* renamed *Tehuantepec.* R 1964.

PF 17 *Key West* USCG crew. Weather ship, Samoa. Decomm 14 Jun 1946. Sold 18 Apr 1947.
Later history: Merchant *Key West.*

PF 18 *Alexandria* USCG crew. Decomm 10 Apr 1946. Stricken 21 May 1946. Sold 18 Apr 1947; BU.

PF 19 *Huron* USCG crew. Damaged in collision with m/v *James Fenimore Cooper* in North Atlantic, 8 Dec 1944. Decomm 19 Apr 1946. Sold 15 May 1947.
Later history: Merchant *José Marcelino.* BU 1965.

PF 20 *Gulfport* USCG crew. Weather ship, Adak. Decomm 28 May 1946. Stricken 19 Jun 1946. Sold 13 Nov 1947; BU Portland, Ore.

PF 21 *Bayonne* USCG crew. To USSR, 2 Sep 1945.
Later history: Renamed *EK-25.* Returned 14 Nov 1949. †

No.	Name	Builder	Keel Laid	Launched	Comm.
PF 22	*Gloucester*	Butler	4 Mar 1943	12 Jul 1943	19 Feb 1944
PF 23	*Shreveport*	Butler	8 Mar 1943	15 Jul 1943	24 Apr 1944
PF 24	*Muskegon*	Butler	11 May 1943	25 Jul 1943	16 Dec 1943
PF 25	*Charlottesville*	Butler	12 May 1943	30 Jul 1943	10 Apr 1944
PF 26	*Poughkeepsie*	Butler	3 Jun 1943	12 Aug 1943	6 Sep 1944
PF 27	*Newport*	Butler	8 Jun 1943	15 Aug 1943	8 Sep 1944
PF 28	*Emporia*	Butler	14 Jul 1943	30 Aug 1943	7 Oct 1944
PF 29	*Groton*	Butler	15 Jul 1943	14 Sep 1943	5 Sep 1944
PF 30	*Hingham*	Butler	25 Jul 1943	27 Sep 1943	3 Nov 1944
PF 31	*Grand Rapids*	Butler	30 Jul 1943	10 Sep 1943	26 Oct 1944
PF 32	*Woonsocket*	Butler	12 Aug 1943	27 Sep 1943	1 Sep 1944
PF 33	*Dearborn* ex-*Toledo* (18 Aug 1943)	Butler	15 Aug 1943	27 Sep 1943	10 Sep 1944
PF 34	*Long Beach*	Consol. Wilm.	18 Mar 1943	5 May 1943	8 Sep 1943
PF 35	*Belfast*	Consol. Wilm.	26 Mar 1943	20 May 1943	24 Nov 1943
PF 36	*Glendale*	Consol. Wilm.	6 Apr 1943	28 May 1943	1 Oct 1943
PF 37	*San Pedro*	Consol. Wilm.	17 Apr 1943	11 Jun 1943	23 Oct 1943
PF 38	*Coronado*	Consol. Wilm.	6 May 1943	17 Jun 1943	17 Nov 1943
PF 39	*Ogden*	Consol. Wilm.	21 May 1943	23 Jun 1943	20 Dec 1943
PF 40	*Eugene*	Consol. Wilm.	12 Jun 1943	6 Jul 1943	15 Jan 1944

PF 41	*El Paso*	Consol. Wilm.	18 Jun 1943	16 Jul 1943	1 Dec 1943
PF 42	*Van Buren*	Consol. Wilm.	24 Jun 1943	27 Jul 1943	17 Dec 1943
PF 43	*Orange*	Consol. Wilm.	7 Jul 1943	6 Aug 1943	1 Jan 1944
PF 44	*Corpus Christi*	Consol. Wilm.	17 Jul 1943	17 Aug 1943	29 Jan 1944
PF 45	*Hutchinson*	Consol. Wilm.	28 Jul 1943	27 Aug 1943	3 Feb 1944
PF 46	*Bisbee*	Consol. Wilm.	7 Aug 1943	7 Sep 1943	15 Feb 1944
PF 47	*Gallup*	Consol. Wilm.	18 Aug 1943	17 Sep 1943	29 Feb 1944
PF 48	*Rockford*	Consol. Wilm.	28 Aug 1943	27 Sep 1943	6 Mar 1944
PF 49	*Muskogee*	Consol. Wilm.	18 Sep 1943	18 Oct 1943	16 Mar 1944
PF 50	*Carson City*	Consol. Wilm.	28 Sep 1943	13 Nov 1943	24 Mar 1944
PF 51	*Burlington*	Consol. Wilm.	19 Oct 1943	7 Dec 1943	3 Apr 1944

Service Records:

PF 22 *Gloucester* USCG crew. To USSR, 4 Sep 1945.
Later history: Renamed *EK–26.* Returned 31 Oct 1949. †

PF 23 *Shreveport* USCG crew. Weather ship, North Atlantic. Decomm 9 May 1946. Stricken 10 Jun 1946. Sold 15 Aug 1947; BU Chester, Pa.

PF 24 *Muskegon* USCG crew. Weather ship. Trfd to USCG, 15 Mar 1945. Decomm. 27 Aug 1946. To France 26 Mar 1947.
Later history: Renamed *Mermoz,* weather ship. R 1952. BU 1955.

PF 25 *Charlottesville* USCG crew. To USSR, 13 Jul 1945.
2* Western New Guinea, Leyte.
Later history: Renamed *EK–1.* Returned 17 Oct 1949. †

PF 26 *Poughkeepsie* USCG crew. To USSR, 2 Sep 1945.
Later history: Renamed *EK–27.* Returned 31 Oct 1949. †

PF 27 *Newport* USCG crew. To USSR, 4 Sep 1945.
Later history: Renamed EK–28. Returned 14 Nov 1949. †

PF 28 *Emporia* USCG crew. Weather ship, Newfoundland. Trfd to USCG, 14 Mar 1946. Decomm 28 Aug 1946. To France, 26 Mar 1947.
Later history: Renamed *Le Verrier,* weather ship. R 1952.

PF 29 *Groton* USCG crew. Weather ship, Newfoundland. To USCG, 13 Mar 1946. Decomm 25 Sep 1946. To Colombia, 26 Mar 1947.
Later history: Renamed *Almirante Padilla.* R 1965.

PF 30 *Hingham* USCG crew. Weather ship, Newfoundland. Decomm 5 Jun 1946. Sold 15 Aug 1947; BU Chester, Pa.

PF 31 *Grand Rapids* USCG crew. Decomm 10 Apr 1946. Sold 14 Apr 1947; BU Chester, Pa.

PF 32 *Woonsocket* USCG crew. Weather ship, North Atlantic. Decomm 18 Sep 1946. Stricken 14 May 1947. To Peru, 4 Sep 1948.
Later history: Renamed *Galvez.* R 1961.

PF 33 *Dearborn* USCG crew. Weather ship, Bermuda. Decomm 5 Jun 1946. Sold 8 Jul 1947.

PF 34 *Long Beach* USCG crew. To USSR, 13 Jul 1945.
3* Admiralty Is., Hollandia, Morotai.
Later history: Renamed *EK–2.* Returned 17 Oct 1949.

PF 35 *Belfast* USCG crew. To USSR, 13 Jul 1945.
2* Morotai, Leyte.
Later history: Renamed *EK–3.* Damaged in storm off Korsakov, Kamchatka, 18 Dec 1948. Renamed *Samarga,* 31 Dec 1952. Renamed *PKZ–116,* 27 Dec 1956. BU 1960.

PF 36 *Glendale* USCG crew. To USSR, 12 Jun 1945.
5* Admiralty Is., Hollandia, Cape Sansapor, Palau, Morotai, Leyte.
Later history: Renamed *EK–6.* Returned 16 Nov 1949. †

PF 37 *San Pedro* USCG crew. To USSR, 13 Jul 1945.
4* Admiralty Is., Hollandia, Biak, Noemfoor, Cape Sansapor, Morotai, Leyte.
Later history: Renamed *EK–5.* Returned 17 Oct 1949. †

PF 38 *Coronado* USCG crew. To USSR, 13 Jul 1945.
4* Admiralty Is., Hollandia, Biak, Cape Sansapor, Morotai, Leyte.
Later history: Renamed *EK–8.* Returned 16 Oct 1949. †

PF 39 *Ogden* USCG crew. To USSR, 13 Jul 1945.
3* Wakde, Leyte, Hollandia.
Later history: Renamed *EK–10.* Returned 17 Oct 1949. †

PF 40 *Eugene* USCG crew. Decomm 12 Jun 1946. Stricken 19 Jul 1946. To Cuba, 16 Jun 1947.
2* Cape Sansapor, Leyte.
Later history: Renamed *José Marti.* R1976.

PF 41 *El Paso* USCG crew. Decomm 18 Jul 1946. Sold 14 Oct 1947; BU.
3* Hollandia, Wakde, Noemfoor, Morotai, Leyte.

PF 42 *Van Buren* USCG crew. Decomm 6 May 1946. Stricken 19 Jun 1946. Sold 15 Aug 1947; BU Chester, Pa.
3* Hollandia, Biak, Wakde, Cape Sansapor, Leyte.

PF 43 *Orange* USCG crew. Decomm 28 Oct 1946. Stricken 23 Apr 1947. Sold 17 Sep 1947; BU.
2* Noemfoor, Leyte.

PF 44 *Corpus Christi* USCG crew. Decomm 2 Aug 1946. Sold 3 Oct 1947; BU.

PF 45 *Hutchinson* USCG crew. Out of comm 15 Apr 1946–23 Sep 1946. Stricken 29 Oct 1946. To Mexico, 24 Nov 1947.
2* Western New Guinea, Leyte.
Later history: Renamed *California.* R 1964.

PF 46 *Bisbee* USCG crew. To USSR, 27 Aug 1945.
2* Cape Sansapor, Leyte.
Later history: Renamed *EK–17.* Returned 1 Nov 1949. †

PF 47 *Gallup* USCG crew. To USSR, 27 Aug 1945.
3* Cape Sansapor, Morotai, Leyte.
Later history: Renamed *EK–22.* Returned 14 Nov 1949. †

PF 48 *Rockford* USCG crew. To USSR, 27 Aug 1945.
2* Cape Sansapor.
Submarine sunk: **I–12* east of Honolulu, 13 Nov 1944.
Later history: Renamed *EK–18.* Returned 1 Nov 1949. †

PF 49 *Muskogee* USCG crew. To USSR, 27 Aug 1945.
1* Leyte.
Later history: Renamed *EK–19.* Returned 1 Nov 1949. †

PF 50 *Carson City* USCG crew. To USSR, 29 Aug 1945.
2* Morotai, Leyte.
Later history: Renamed *EK–20.* Returned 31 Oct 1949. †

PF 51 *Burlington* USCG crew. To USSR, 13 Jul 1945.
2* Morotai, Leyte.
Later history: Renamed *EK–21.* Returned 14 Nov 1949. †

No.	Name	Builder	Keel Laid	Launched	Comm.
PF 52	*Allentown*	Froemming	23 Mar 1943	3 Jul 1943	24 Mar 1944
PF 53	*Machias*	Froemming	8 May 1943	22 Aug 1943	29 Mar 1944
PF 54	*Sandusky*	Froemming	8 Jul 1943	5 Oct 1943	18 Apr 1944
PF 55	*Bath*	Froemming	23 Aug 1943	14 Nov 1943	1 Sep 1944
PF 56	*Covington*	Globe Sup.	1 Mar 1943	15 Jul 1943	17 Oct 1944
PF 57	*Sheboygan*	Globe Sup.	17 Apr 1943	31 Jul 1943	14 Oct 1944
PF 58	*Abilene*	Globe Sup.	6 May 1943	21 Aug 1943	28 Oct 1944
	ex–*Bridgeport* (28 Jun 1944)				
PF 59	*Beaufort*	Globe Sup.	21 Jul 1943	9 Oct 1943	28 Aug 1944
PF 60	*Charlotte*	Globe Sup.	5 Aug 1943	30 Oct 1943	9 Oct 1944
PF 61	*Manitowoc*	Globe; Duluth	26 Aug 1943	30 Nov 1943	5 Dec 1944
PF 62	*Gladwyne*	Globe; Duluth	14 Oct 1943	7 Jan 1944	21 Nov 1944
	ex–*Worcester* (18 Aug 1944)				

PF 63	*Moberly*	Globe; Duluth	3 Nov 1943	26 Jan 1944	11 Dec 1944
	ex–*Scranton* (28 Jun 1944)				
PF 64	*Knoxville*	L. D. Smith	15 Apr 1943	10 Jul 1943	29 Apr 1944
PF 65	*Uniontown*	L. D. Smith	21 Apr 1943	7 Aug 1943	29 Sep 1944
	ex–*Chattanooga* (18 Aug 1944)				
PF 66	*Reading*	L. D. Smith	25 May 1943	28 Aug 1943	19 Aug 1944
PF 67	*Peoria*	L. D. Smith	4 Jun 1943	2 Oct 1943	2 Jan 1945
PF 68	*Brunswick*	L. D. Smith	16 Jul 1943	6 Nov 1943	3 Oct 1944
PF 69	*Davenport*	L. D. Smith	7 Aug 1943	8 Dec 1943	15 Feb 1945
PF 70	*Evansville*	L. D. Smith	28 Aug 1943	27 Nov 1943	4 Dec 1944
PF 71	*New Bedford*	L. D. Smith	2 Oct 1943	29 Dec 1943	17 Jul 1944

Service Records:

PF 52 *Allentown* USCG crew. To USSR, 13 Jul 1945.
2* Morotai, Leyte.
Later history: Renamed *EK–9.* Returned 15 Oct 1949. †

PF 53 *Machias* USCG crew. To USSR, 13 Jul 1945.
2* Western New Guinea, Leyte.
Later history: Renamed *EK–4.* Returned 17 Oct 1949. †

PF 54 *Sandusky* USCG crew. To USSR, 13 Jul 1945.
2* Western New Guinea, Leyte.
Later history: Renamed *EK–7.* Returned 17 Oct 1949. †

PF 55 *Bath* USCG crew. To USSR, 13 Jul 1945.
Later history: Renamed *EK–29.* Returned 15 Nov 1949. †

PF 56 *Covington* USCG crew. Weather ship, Newfoundland. Loaned to USCG, 16 Mar–17 Sep 1946. Decomm 17 Sep 1946. To Ecuador 28 Aug 1947.
Later history: Renamed *Guayas.* R 1972.

PF 57 *Sheboygan* USCG crew. Weather ship, North Atlantic. Loaned to USCG, 14 Mar–9 Aug 1946. Decomm 9 Aug 1946. Sold to Belgium 20 Mar 1947.
Later history: Renamed *Luitenant ter Zee Victor Billet.* BU 1959.

PF 58 *Abilene* USCG crew. Decomm 21 Aug 1946. Stricken 13 Nov 1946. To Netherlands 5 May 1947
Later history: Renamed *Cirrus,* weather ship. R 1964.

PF 59 *Beaufort* USCG crew. Weather ship. Decomm 19 Apr 1946. Sold 11 Apr 1947, BU.

PF 60 *Charlotte* USCG crew. Weather ship, Newfoundland. Decomm 16 Apr 1946. Sold 13 May 1947.
Later history: Merchant *Bahia.* BU 1965.

PF 61 *Manitowoc* USCG crew. Weather ship, Newfoundland. Loaned to USCG 14 Mar 1946–3 Sep 1946. To France 26 Mar 1947.
Later history: Renamed *Le Brix,* weather ship. R 1952. BU 1958.

PF 62 *Gladwyne* USCG crew. Decomm 15 Apr 1946. Stricken 8 Oct 1946. To Mexico 24 Nov 1947.
Later history: Renamed *Papaloapan.* R 1964.

PF 63 *Moberly* USCG crew. Decomm 12 Aug 1946. Stricken 23 Apr 1947. Sold 2 Dec 1947; BU Hillside, N.J.
1*
Submarine sunk: **U–853* off Block I., N.Y., 6 May 1945.

PF 64 *Knoxville* USCG crew. Decomm 13 Jun 1946. To Dominican Republic, 22 Sep 1947.
Later history: Renamed *Presidente Peynado,* renamed *Capitan General Pedro Santana* 1962. BU 1979.

PF 65 *Uniontown* USCG manned. Decomm 20 Dec 1945. Stricken 8 Jan 1946. Sold to Argentina, 17 Jun 1946
Later history: Renamed *Sarandi.* BU 1968.

PF 66 *Reading* USCG crew. Weather ship, North Atlantic. Decomm 19 Dec 1945. Stricken 8 Jan 1946. Sold to Argentina, 17 Jun 1946.
Later history: Renamed *Heroina.* BU 1966.

PF 67 *Peoria* USCG crew. Decomm 15 May 1946. Stricken 19 Jun 1946. To Cuba, 16 Jun 1947.
Later history: Renamed *Antonio Maceo.* R 1975.

PF 68 *Brunswick* USCG crew. Decomm 3 May 1946. Sold 9 Apr 1947; BU.

PF 69 *Davenport* USCG crew. Decomm 4 Feb 1946. Sold 6 Jun 1946; BU.

PF 70 *Evansville* USCG crew. To USSR, 4 Sep 1945
Later history: Renamed *EK–30.* Returned 17 Feb 1950. †

PF 71 *New Bedford* USCG crew. Decomm 24 May 1946. Sold 16 Nov 1947; BU.

No.	Name	Builder	Keel Laid	Launched	Comm.
PF 72	*Machias*	Walsh–Kaiser	1 Apr 1943	14 Jul 1943	*15 Oct 1943*
PF 73	—	Walsh–Kaiser	3 Apr 1943	26 Jul 1943	*4 Nov 1943*
PF 74	—	Walsh–Kaiser	30 Apr 1943	6 Aug 1943	*24 Nov 1943*
PF 75	—	Walsh–Kaiser	7 Apr 1943	17 Aug 1943	*6 Dec 1943*
PF 76	—	Walsh–Kaiser	11 May 1943	27 Aug 1943	*18 Dec 1943*
PF 77	—	Walsh–Kaiser	23 Apr 1943	6 Sep 1943	*30 Dec 1943*
PF 78	—	Walsh–Kaiser	15 Jul 1943	22 Aug 1943	*20 Jan 1944*
PF 79	—	Walsh–Kaiser	27 Jul 1943	14 Sep 1943	*25 Jan 1944*
PF 80	—	Walsh–Kaiser	7 Aug 1943	21 Sep 1943	*5 Feb 1944*
PF 81	—	Walsh–Kaiser	17 Aug 1943	27 Sep 1943	*12 Aug 1944*
PF 82	—	Walsh–Kaiser	28 Aug 1943	27 Sep 1943	*31 Aug 1944*
PF 83	—	Walsh–Kaiser	7 Sep 1943	6 Oct 1943	*31 Jul 1944*
PF 84	—	Walsh–Kaiser	7 Sep 1943	10 Oct 1943	*25 Jul 1944*
PF 85	—	Walsh–Kaiser	14 Sep 1943	15 Oct 1943	*6 Jul 1944*
PF 86	—	Walsh–Kaiser	22 Sep 1943	20 Oct 1943	*19 Jul 1944*
PF 87	—	Walsh–Kaiser	28 Sep 1943	25 Oct 1943	*18 Jul 1944*
PF 88	—	Walsh–Kaiser	28 Sep 1943	30 Oct 1943	*27 Jun 1944*
PF 89	—	Walsh–Kaiser	7 Oct 1943	5 Nov 1943	*16 Mar 1944*
PF 90	—	Walsh–Kaiser	11 Oct 1943	11 Nov 1943	*24 Jun 1944*
PF 91	—	Walsh–Kaiser	16 Oct 1943	16 Nov 1943	*15 May 1944*
PF 92	—	Walsh–Kaiser	20 Oct 1943	21 Nov 1943	*21 Jun 1944*
PF 93	*Lorain*	Amer. Lorain	25 Oct 1943	18 Mar 1944	15 Jan 1945
	ex–*Roanoke* (7 Feb 1944)				
PF 94	*Milledgeville*	Amer. Lorain	9 Nov 1943	5 Apr 1944	18 Jan 1945
	ex–*Sitka* (7 Feb 1944)				
PF 95	*Stamford*	Amer. Lorain	—	—	—
PF 96	*Macon*	Amer. Lorain	—	—	—
PF 97	*Lorain*	Amer. Lorain	—	—	—
	ex–*Vallejo* (19 Nov 1943)				
PF 98	*Milledgeville*	Amer. Lorain	—	—	—
PF 99	*Orlando*	Amer. Cleve.	2 Aug 1943	1 Dec 1943	15 Nov 1944
PF 100	*Racine*	Amer. Cleve.	14 Sep 1943	15 Mar 1944	22 Jan 1945
PF 101	*Greensboro*	Amer. Cleve.	23 Sep 1943	9 Mar 1944	29 Jan 1945
PF 102	*Forsyth*	Amer. Cleve.	6 Dec 1943	20 May 1944	11 Feb 1945

Service Records:

PF 72 *Machias* To UK 15 Oct 1943, as HMS *Hallowell,* renamed HMS *Anguilla* 1943. Returned 31 May 1946. Sold 13 Jun 1947.
Later history: Merchant *Anguilla.*

PF 73 — To UK 4 Nov 1943, as HMS *Hammond,* renamed HMS *Antigua* 1943. Returned 2 May 1946. BU 1947 Chester, Pa.

PF 74 — To UK 24 Nov 1943, as HMS *Hargood,* renamed HMS *Ascension* 1943. Returned 31 May 1946. Sold 16 Oct 1947; BU Newburgh.

PF 75 — To UK 6 Dec 1943, as HMS *Hotham*, renamed HMS *Bahamas* 1943. Returned 11 Jun 1946. Sold 16 Dec 1947; BU Quincy, Mass.

PF 76 — To UK 18 Dec 1943, as HMS *Halsted*, renamed HMS *Barbados* 1943. Returned 13 Apr 1946. Sold 30 Oct 1947; BU Chester, Pa.

PF 77 — To UK 30 Dec 1943, as HMS *Hannam*, renamed HMS *Caicos*. Returned 12 Dec 1945. Sold to Argentina Jul 1947.
Later history: Renamed *Santisima Trinidad, Trinidad, Comodoro Augusto Lassere* 1964. Stricken 1970.

PF 78 — To UK 20 Jan 1944, as HMS *Harland*, renamed HMS *Cayman* 1943. Returned 23 Apr 1946. Sold 1 Jul 1947; BU New York.

PF 79 — To UK 25 Jan 1944, as HMS *Harman*, renamed HMS *Dominica* 1943. Returned 23 Apr 1946. Sold 27 Mar 1947; BU Chester, Pa.

PF 80 — To UK 5 Feb 1944, as HMS *Harvey*, renamed HMS *Gold Coast* 1944. Returned 2 May 1946. Sold 9 Jul 1947; BU Dorchester, Mass.

PF 81 — To UK 12 Aug 1944, as HMS *Holmes*, renamed HMS *Hong Kong* 1944, renamed HMS *Tobago*. Returned 13 May 1946. Sold.
Later history: Merchant *Tobago*. Conversion abandoned. Scuttled as blockship in Suez Canal, 1 Nov 1956.

PF 82 — To UK 31 Aug 1944, as HMS *Hornby*, renamed HMS *Montserrat* 1944. Returned 11 Jun 1946. Sold 30 Nov 1947; BU Quincy, Mass.

PF 83 — To UK 31 Jul 1944, as HMS *Hoste*, renamed HMS *Nyasaland* 1944. Returned 13 Apr 1946. Sold 10 Nov 1947; BU Chester, Pa.

PF 84 — To UK 25 Jul 1944, as HMS *Howett*, renamed HMS *Papua* 1944. Returned 13 May 1946.
Later history: Merchant *Papua*. Scuttled as blockship in Suez Canal, 1 Nov 1956. BU 1966 incomplete

PF 85 — To UK 6 Jul 1944, as HMS *Pilford*, renamed HMS *Pitcairn*. Returned 11 Jun 1946. Stricken 3 Jul 1946. Sold 8 Nov 1947; BU Quincy, Mass.

PF 86 — To UK 19 Feb 1944, as HMS *Pasley*, renamed HMS *St. Helena*. Returned 23 Apr 1946. BU 1947 Chester, Pa.

PF 87 — To UK 18 Jul 1944, as HMS *Patton*, renamed HMS *Sarawak*. Returned 31 May 1946. BU 1947 Chester, Pa.

PF 88 — To UK 27 Jun 1944, as HMS *Peard*, renamed HMS *Seychelles*. Returned 11 Jun 1946. BU 1947 Chester, Pa.

PF 89 — To UK 16 Mar 1944, as HMS *Phillimore*, renamed HMS *Sierra Leone*, then *Perim*. Returned 22 May 1946; BU 1947 Chester, Pa.

PF 90 — To UK 24 Jun 1944, as HMS *Popham*, renamed HMS *Somaliland*. Returned 31 May 1946; BU.

PF 91 — To UK 15 May 1944 as HMS *Peyton*, renamed HMS *Tortola*. Returned 22 May 1946. Stricken 3 Jul 1946. Sold 17 Jan 1947; BU Philadelphia.

PF 92 — To UK 21 Jun 1944 as HMS *Prowse*, renamed HMS *Zanzibar*. Returned 31 May 1946; BU.

PF 93 *Lorain* USCG crew. Weather ship, North Atlantic. Decomm 14 Mar 1946. To France 26 Mar 1947
Later history: Renamed *Laplace*, weather ship. Sunk by mine off St. Malo, 16 Sep 1950.

PF 94 *Milledgeville* USCG crew. Weather ship. Decomm 21 Aug 1946. Stricken 23 Apr 1947. Sold 9 Apr 1947; BU New Orleans.

PF 95 *Stamford* Canceled 31 Dec 1943.

PF 96 *Macon* Canceled 31 Dec 1943.

PF 97 *Lorain* Canceled 31 Dec 1943.

PF 98 *Milledgeville* Canceled 31 Dec 1943.

PF 99 *Orlando* USCG crew. Decomm 27 Jun 1946. Stricken 19 Jul 1946. Sold 10 Nov 1947; BU Portland, Ore.

PF 100 *Racine* USCG crew. Decomm 27 Jun 1946. Stricken 19 Jul 1946. Sold 2 Dec 1947; BU Hillsdale, N.J.

PF 101 *Greensboro* USCG crew. Weather ship, *Argentia*. Decomm 14 Mar 1946. Stricken 23 Apr 1947. Sold 26 Feb 1948; BU New Orleans.

PF 102 *Forsyth* USCG crew. Decomm 2 Aug 1946. To Netherlands 17 Jul 1947.
Later history: Renamed *Cumulus*, weather ship. R 1964.

CORVETTES

Temptress Class

No.	Name	Builder	Launched	Acquired	Comm.
PG 62	*Temptress* ex–HMS *Veronica*	Smith's Dock	17 Oct 1940	21 Mar 1942	21 Mar 1942
PG 63	*Surprise* ex–HMS *Heliotrope*	Crown	5 Jun 1940	24 Mar 1942	24 Mar 1942
PG 64	*Spry* ex–HMS *Hibiscus*	Harland	6 Apr 1940	2 May 1942	2 May 1942
PG 65	*Saucy* ex–HMS *Arabis*	Harland	14 Feb 1940	30 Apr 1942	30 Apr 1942
PG 66	*Restless* ex–HMS *Periwinkle*	Harland	24 Feb 1940	15 Mar 1942	15 Mar 1942
PG 67	*Ready* ex–HMS *Calendula*	Harland	21 Mar 1940	12 Mar 1942	12 Mar 1942
PG 68	*Impulse* ex–HMS *Begonia*	Cook Welton	18 Sep 1940	16 Mar 1942	16 Mar 1942

Figure 8.12: The corvette *Impulse* (PG 68) was acquired from the United Kingdom by reverse lend-lease.

Figure 8.13: The corvette *Tenacity* (PG 71), seen here in New York Harbor on 26 Jun 1942, was the former British *Candytuft* acquired by reverse lend-lease.

PG 69	*Fury*	Fleming	5 Sep 1940	17 Mar 1942	17 Mar 1942
	ex-HMS *Larkspur*				
PG 70	*Courage*	Harland	20 Apr 1940	18 Mar 1942	3 Apr 1942
	ex-HMS *Heartsease*, ex-*Pansy*				
PG 71	*Tenacity*	Grangemouth	8 Jul 1940	4 Mar 1942	11 Jun 1942
	ex-HMS *Candytuft*				
PG 86	*Action*	Collingwood	6 Jan 1942	28 Jul 1942	22 Nov 1942
	ex-HMS *Comfrey* (13 Aug 1942)				
PG 87	*Alacrity*	Collingwood	6 Jan 1942	4 Sep 1942	10 Dec 1942
	ex-HMS *Cornel*				
PG 88	*Beacon*	Collingwood	27 Apr 1942	31 Oct 1942	*28 May 1943*
	ex-HMS *Dittany*				
PG 89	*Brisk*	Kingston	28 Feb 1942	15 Jun 1942	6 Dec 1942
	ex-HMS *Flax*				
PG 90	*Caprice*	Kingston	16 Jun 1942	28 Sep 1942	*28 May 1943*
	ex-HMS *Honesty*				
PG 91	*Clash*	Midland	1 Jun 1942	18 Nov 1942	*22 Jun 1943*
	ex-HMS *Linaria*				
PG 92	*Haste*	Morton	11 Dec 1941	22 Aug 1942	6 Apr 1943
	ex-HMS *Mandrake*				
PG 93	*Intensity*	Morton	11 Dec 1941	5 Aug 1942	31 Mar 1943
	ex-HMS *Milfoil*				
PG 94	*Might*	Morton	28 Nov 1941	15 Jul 1942	22 Dec 1942
	ex-HMS *Musk* (14 Aug 1942)				
PG 95	*Pert*	Morton	23 Jul 1942	27 Nov 1942	23 Jul 1943
	ex-HMS *Nepeta*				
PG 96	*Prudent*	Morton	14 Aug 1942	4 Dec 1942	16 Aug 1943
	ex-HMS *Privet*				
PG 97	*Splendor*	Kingston	1 Oct 1942	11 Feb 1943	*28 Jul 1943*
	ex-HMS *Rosebay*				
PG 98	*Tact*	Collingwood	12 Jun 1942	14 Nov 1942	*21 Jun 1943*
	ex-HMS *Smilax*				
PG 99	*Vim*	Collingwood	11 Aug 1942	10 Apr 1943	*20 Sep 1943*
	ex-HMS *Statice*				
PG 100	*Vitality*	Midland	26 Jun 1942	24 Mar 1943	*30 Aug 1943*
	ex-HMS *Willowherb*				

Displacement	925 tons, 1,375 tons f/l (PG 62–71); 900 tons (PG 86–100)
Dimensions	205' (oa); 190' (wl) x 33' x 14'7"
Machinery	1 screw, VTE; 2 Scotch boilers; SHP 2,750; 16.5 knots
Complement	90
Armament	1–4"/50, 1–3"/50, 4–20mm AA (PG 62–71); 2–3"/50, 4–20mm AA (PG 86-100)

Notes: Former British corvettes transferred to the Navy under reverse lend–lease because of the Navy's urgent need for escorts. Fifteen ordered in Canada, seven transferred to the United Kingdom. Used as coastal escorts. First group (PG 62–71) had single mast forward of bridge; later units built in Canada (PG 86–100) had mast aft of bridge superstructure.

Service Records:

PG 62 *Temptress* Decomm 20 Aug 1945. Returned to UK, 26 Aug 1945.
Later history: HMS *Veronica*. Merchant *Verolock* 1946. Wrecked in tow off Brittany, 12 Jan 1947, hulk BU 1951 Blyth, England.

PG 63 *Surprise* Decomm 20 Aug 1945. Returned to UK, 26 Aug 1945.
Later history: HMS *Heliotrope*. Merchant *Heliolock*, 1946, renamed *Ziang Teh* 1947, *Lin I* 1950. BU.

PG 64 *Spry* Damaged by fire at Argentia, Nfld, 27 May 1942. Decomm 20 Aug 1945. Returned to UK 26 Aug 1945.
Later history: HMS *Hibiscus*. Merchant *Madonna* 1949. BU 1955 Hong Kong.

PG 65 *Saucy* Damaged by depth charge explosion off Amazon River, 22 Mar 1943. Decomm 20 Aug 1945. Returned to UK 26 Aug 1945.
Later history: HMS *Snapdragon*. Merchant *Katina* 1947, renamed *Tewfik* 1950, BU 1964 Italy.

PG 66 *Restless* Decomm 20 Aug 1945. Returned to UK, 26 Aug 1945.
Later history: HMS *Periwinkle*. Merchant *Perilock* 1947; BU 1953 Hong Kong.

PG 67 *Ready* Decomm 20 Aug 1945. Returned to UK, 23 Aug 1945.
Later history: HMS *Calendula*. Merchant *Villa Cisneros* 1948, *Villa Bens* 1950.

PG 68 *Impulse* Decomm 22 Aug 1945, returned to UK.
Later history: HMS *Begonia*. Merchant *Begonlock* 1946, renamed *Fundiciones Molinao* 1949, *Astiluzu* 1951, *Rio Mero* 1956. Wrecked on passage from Canary Is. to Valencia, 21 Jan 1970.

PG 69 *Fury* Decomm 22 Aug 1945 and returned to UK.
Later history: HMS *Larkspur*. Merchant *Larkslock* 1947. BU 1953 Hong Kong.

PG 70 *Courage* Decomm 22 Aug 1945. Returned to UK, 23 Aug 1945.
Later history: HMS *Heartsease*. Merchant *Roskva* 1951, *Douglas* 1956, *Seabird* 1958. Sunk by Indonesian aircraft north of Celebes while aiding rebels, Dec 1958.

PG 71 *Tenacity* Decomm 22 Aug 1945. Returned to UK, 26 Aug 1945.
Later history: HMS *Candytuft*. Merchant *Candytuft* 1946, *Maw Hwa* 1947.

PG 86 *Action* USCG crew. Decomm 6 Sep 1945. Stricken 17 Sep 1945. Sold 18 Oct 1946.
Later history: Merchant *Action*, renamed *Arne Presthus* 1952, *Star of Mariam* 1967, *Star of Beirut* 1971, *Star of Riwiah* 1972. Lost by grounding in Gulf of Suez, 6 Apr 1972.

PG 87 *Alacrity* USCG crew. Decomm 4 Oct 1945. Stricken 24 Oct 1945. Sold 22 Sep 1947.
Later history: Merchant *Rio Marina*, 1951 *Porto Ferraio*. BU 1971 Italy.

PG 88 *Beacon* To UK, 28 May 1943.
Later history: HMS *Dittany*. Sold 30 Sep 1947, merchant *Olympic Cruiser* 1947, renamed *Otori Maru No. 2*, 1956. BU 1966 Japan.

PG 89 *Brisk* USCG crew. Decomm 9 Oct 1945. To MC, 18 Oct 1946.
Later history: Merchant *Brisk*, renamed *Ariana* 1952, *Arvida Bay* 1955, *Zaida* 1963.

Figure 8.14: USS *St. Augustine* (PG 54), 11 May 1943, was a converted yacht rated as a gunboat.

PG 90 *Caprice* To UK, 28 May 1943.
Later history: HMS *Honesty*. Returned 5 Jan 1946. Sold 10 Dec 1946, not converted; BU 1961 Hamburg.

PG 91 *Clash* To UK, 22 Jun 1943.
Later history: HMS *Linaria*. Returned 27 Jul 1946. Sold 15 Jan 1948, merchant *Porto Offuro*.

PG 92 *Haste* USCG crew. Decomm 3 Oct 1945. Sold 22 Sep 1947.
Later history: Merchant *Porto Azzuro*. BU 1971 Italy.

PG 93 *Intensity* USCG crew. Decomm 3 Oct 1945. Sold 18 Oct 1946.
Later history: Merchant *Olympic Promoter*, renamed *Otori Maru No. 5* 1956. BU 1966 Japan.

PG 94 *Might* USCG crew. Decomm 9 Oct 1945. Stricken 24 Oct 1945. Sold 18 Oct 1946.
Later history: Merchant *Olympic Explorer* 1950, renamed *Otori Maru No. 3* 1956, *Kyo Maru No. 12* 1957.

PG 95 *Pert* USCG crew. Decomm 3 Oct 1945. Stricken 24 Oct 1945. Sold 8 Oct 1946.
Later history: Merchant *Olympic Leader*, renamed *Otori Maru No. 1* 1956, *Kyo Maru No. 15* 1957.

PG 96 *Prudent* USCG crew. Decomm 11 Oct 1945. Stricken 1 Nov 1945. Sold 22 Sep 1947.
Later history: To Italy, renamed *Elbano*, renamed *Staffetta* 1951. R 1972.

PG 97 *Splendor* To UK, 28 Jul 1943.
Later history: HMS *Rosebay*. Returned 20 Mar 1946. Sold 19 Nov 1946. Merchant *Benmark*, renamed *Frida* 1950. BU 1954 Sweden.

PG 98 *Tact* To UK, 21 Jun 1943.
Later history: HMS *Smilax*. Returned 18 Oct 1946. Sold to Argentina, 18 Oct 1946, renamed *Republica*. BU 1968.

PG 99 *Vim* To UK, 20 Sep 1943.
Later history: HMS *Statice*. Returned 21 Jun 1946. Sold 7 May 1947, not converted. BU 1960 Hamburg.

PG 100 *Vitality* To UK, 30 Aug 1943.
Later history: HMS *Willowherb*. Returned 11 Jun 1946. Sold 7 May 1947, not converted. BU 1961 Hamburg.

GUNBOATS (YACHTS)

No.	Name	Builder	Launched	Acquired	Comm.
PG 52	*Niagara*	Bath	7 Jun 1929	16 Oct 1940	20 Jan 1941
	ex-CMc 2 (15 Nov 1940), ex-*Hi-Esmaro* (1940)				

Displacement	1,922 tons f/l
Dimensions	267' (oa) 215' (wl) x 35'4" x 17'
Machinery	2 screws; diesel; HP 3,000; **16** knots
Complement	139
Armament	2–3"/50

Note: Originally built as yacht for U.S. industrialist H. Edward Manville.

Service Record:

PG 52 *Niagara* Rec **AGP 1**, 13 Jan 1943. Damaged by Japanese aircraft bombs near San Cristobal I. and sunk by *PT-147*, 23 May 1943.
1* Solomons.

No.	Name	Builder	Launched	Acquired	Comm.
PG 53	*Vixen*	Germania	1929	13 Nov 1940	25 Feb 1941
	ex-*Orion* (1940)				

Displacement	3,060 tons; 3,774 f/l
Dimensions	333' (oa); 305' (wl) x 46'5" x 16'11"
Machinery	2 screws; diesel; SHP 3,600; 15 knots
Complement	279
Armament	4–3"/50

Notes: Originally built as yacht for U.S. businessman Julius Forstmann. Tall foremast, small mainmast.

Service Record:

PG 53 *Vixen* Neutrality patrol. Flag, submarines, Atlantic Fleet, 1941–42. Flag of Admiral King, 1942. Flag Commander-in-Chief, Atlantic Fleet (Admirals Royal E. Ingersoll and Jonas H. Ingram) 1942–46. Decomm 24 May 1946. Stricken 3 Jul 1946. Sold 21 Jan 1947.
Later history: Merchant *Vixen* 1947, renamed *Orion* 1950, *Argonaftis* 1964, *Regina Maris*; se 2001.

No.	Name	Builder	Launched	Acquired	Comm.
PG 54	*St. Augustine*	Newport News	15 Dec 1928	2 Dec 1940	16 Jan 1941
	ex-*Noparo* (1940)				

Displacement	1,720 tons fl, 1,300 tons grt
Dimensions	272'2" (oa) 217' 6"(wl) x 36' x 14'6"
Machinery	2 screws; TE: 14 knots
Complement	185
Armament	2–3"/50

Note: Purchased as yacht from noted socialite Norman B. Woolworth.

Service Record:

PG 54 *St. Augustine* Neutrality patrol. Sunk in collision with tanker *Camas Meadows* off Cape May, N.J., 6 Jan 1944 (115 killed).

No.	Name	Builder	Launched	Acquired	Comm.
PG 55	*Jamestown*	Pusey	1928	6 Dec 1940	26 May 1941
	ex-*Alder* (1940), ex-*Savarona* (1929)				

Displacement	2,250 tons f/l, 2,076 grt
Dimensions	294' (oa); 280' (wl) x 38'2" x 16'
Machinery	2 screws; diesel; SHP 3,000; 15 knots
Complement	259
Armament	2–3"/50

Notes: Purchased as yacht from Colonel William Boyce Thompson. Tall masts forward and aft replaced by small masts on superstructure.

Service Record:

PG 55 *Jamestown* Converted to MTB tender, end of 1941. Rec **AGP 3**, 13 Jan 1943. Decomm 6 Mar 1946. To MC, 4 Sep 1946. Sold 16 Dec 1946.
3* Solomons, Brunei.

Figure 8.15: *Isabel* (PY 10), seen here on 23 Aug 1934, was a converted yacht that served for many years as flagship in the Far East. During World War I she was rated as a destroyer.

Later history: Merchant *Jamestown* 1947, renamed *Marosanna* 1953. Foundered 240 miles southwest of Panama, 2 Aug 1961.

No.	Name	Builder	Launched	Acquired	Comm.
PG 56	*Williamsburg* ex-*Aras* (1941)	Bath	8 Dec 1930	30 Apr 1941	7 Oct 1941

Displacement	1,730 tons; 1,920 f/l
Dimensions	243'9" (oa); 224' (wl) x 36' x 16'
Machinery	2 screws; diesel; SHP 2,200; 16 knots
Complement	81
Armament	2–3"/50 (removed 1945).

Notes: Originally built as ship for U.S. businessman Hugh J. Chisholm.

Service Record:

PG 56 *Williamsburg* Flagship, naval operations base, Iceland, 1942. Rec **AGC 369**, 10 Nov 1945. Presidential yacht.

No.	Name	Builder	Launched	Acquired	Comm.
PG 57	*Plymouth* ex-*Alva* (1941)	Germania	1931	4 Nov 1941	29 Dec 1941

Displacement	1,500 tons, 2,265 grt
Dimensions	264'5" (oa); 250' (wl) x 46'2" x 19'
Machinery	2 screws; diesel; 15 knots
Complement	155
Armament	1–4"/50, 4–3"/50

Notes: Originally built as yacht for U.S. millionaire William K. Vanderbilt II.

Service Record:

PG 57 *Plymouth* Torpedoed and sunk by *U-566* 90 miles east of Elizabeth City, N.C., 5 Aug 1943 (about 70 killed).

No.	Name	Builder	Launched	Acquired	Comm.
PG 58	*Hilo* ex-*Moana* (1941), *ex-Caroline* (1938)	Bath	18 Jul 1931	28 Nov 1941	11 Jun 1942

Displacement	2,350 tons f/l, 1,839 grt
Dimensions	278'11" (oa); 274'7" (wl) x 38'3" x 17'3"
Machinery	2 screws; diesel; SHP 3,000; 15 knots
Complement	116
Armament	1–3"/50, 8–20mm AA

Notes: Purchased as yacht from U.S. millionaire William B. Leeds.

Service Record:

Converted to MTB tender and rec **AGP 2**, 13 Jan 1943. Decomm 3 Mar 1946. Sold 30 Jun 1946.

2* Eastern New Guinea, Leyte.

Later history: Merchant *Hilo.* BU 1958.

No.	Name	Builder	Launched	Acquired	Comm.
PG 59	*San Bernardino* ex-*Vanda* (1942)	Bath	3 Oct 1928	30 Jan 1942	2 Jun 1942

Displacement	1,768 tons f/l, 1,279 grt
Dimensions	240'2" (oa); 219'8" (wl) x 36'4" x 15'11"
Machinery	2 screws; diesel; SHP 3,000; 17 knots
Complement	107
Armament	2–3"/50, 2–40mm AA

Notes: Originally built as yacht for Boston banker Ernest B. Dane.

Service Record:

PG 59 Weather ship, Hawaiian area. *San Bernardino* Decomm 4 Jan 1946. Stricken 8 May 1946. Sold 15 Oct 1946.

Later history: Merchant *Vanda.* BU 1968 Jacksonville, Fla.

No.	Name	Builder	Launched	Acquired	Comm.
PG 60	*Beaumont* ex-*Carola* (1942), ex-*Chalena*, ex-*Reveler*	Krupp	1930	23 Jan 1942	22 Jun 1942

Displacement	1,434 tons f/l, 1,108 grt
Dimensions	226' (oa); 206' (wl) x 34'1" x 12'8"
Machinery	2 screws; diesel; SHP 2,200; 15.5 knots
Complement	110
Armament	2–3"/50, 2–40mm AA

Notes: Originally built as yacht for U.S. entrepreneur Russell A. Alger Jr.

Service Record:

PG 60 *Beaumont* Weather ship, Hawaii. Decomm 19 Feb 1946. Sold 1947.

Later history: Merchant *Elpetal,* renamed *Jezebel, Talitha G;* se 1993.

No.	Name	Builder	Launched	Acquired	Comm.
PG 61	*Dauntless* ex-*Delphine* (1942)	Great Lakes	2 Apr 1921	21 Jan 1942	11 May 1942

Displacement	1,950 tons f/l, 1,255 grt
Dimensions	257'7" (oa); 250'6" (wl) x 35'2" x 16'3"
Machinery	2 screws; VTE; 3 B&W boilers; 16 knots
Complement	135
Armament	2–3"/50

Notes: Originally built as yacht for U.S. auto manufacturer Horace E. Dodge, who died before its completion. Flagship of commander-in-chief of the U.S. Fleet, Admiral Ernest King, Washington, D.C.

Service Record:

PG 61 *Dauntless* Decomm 11 May 1946. Sold 1946.

Later history: Merchant *Delphine,* renamed *Dauntless* 1968. Currently a luxury yacht available for charter in the Mediterranean.

No.	Name	Builder	Launched	Acquired	Comm.
PG 72	*Nourmahal*	Krupp	1928	3 Mar 1942	

Displacement	1,969 grt; 3,200 f/l
Dimensions	264' (oa) 251'6" (bp) x 42' x 18' 5"
Machinery	2 screws; diesel; HP 3,200, 13.7 knots
Complement	153
Armament	2–4"/50

Notes: Acquired as yacht from U.S. millionaire and philanthropist (William) Vincent Astor.

Service Record:

PG 72 *Nourmahal* To USCG, 29 Dec 1943.

Later history: USCGC *Nourmahal* (WPG 122) To MC, 18 Jul 1948. Burned and capsized at Texas City, Tex., 23 Nov 1964.

No.	Name	Rec	Date
PG85	*Natchez*	AGS 3	2 Jun 1942

CONVERTED YACHTS

Yachts on the Navy List, 1922

PY 1 *Mayflower* Presidential yacht. Decomm 22 Mar 1929. Damaged by fire while under conversion to gunboat for Central American waters, at Philadelphia, 24 Jan 1931. Stricken 23 Mar 1931. Sold 19 Oct 1931.
Later history: Merchant *Mayflower*. Renamed *Butte*, acquired by USCG, renamed *Mayflower* **WPG 183**, 1942. Decomm 1 Jul 1946. Merchant *Mayflower* 1947, *Malla* 1948, *Tabor* 1950. BU 1950, Genoa, Italy.

PY 2 *Hawk* Unclassified, **IX 14**.

PY 3 *Scorpion* Station ship, Constantinople 1908–27. Decomm 27 Oct 1927. Stricken 23 Mar 1929. Sold 25 Jun 1929; BU Baltimore.

PY 5 *Sylph* Decomm 27 Apr 1929. Stricken 29 Apr 1929. Sold 26 Nov 1929.
Later history: Merchant *Sylph*. BU 1958.

PY 6 *Nokomis* Out of comm 25 Feb 1921–Jun 1921. Surveying, Caribbean. Decomm 15 Feb 1938. Stricken 25 May 1938.
Later history: USCGC *Burke*, renamed *Bodkin* 1943. BU 1944.

PY 7 *Aramis* Decomm 6 Oct 1921. Stricken 20 Jul 1933. Sold at Guantanamo, 13 Nov 1933. FFU.

PY 8 *Despatch* Decomm 9 Dec 1921. To State of Florida, 10 May 1928.

PY 9 *Niagara* Out of comm 21 Apr 1922–24 Jun 1924. Surveying, Caribbean. Decomm 3 Mar 1931. Stricken 10 Dec 1931. Sold 13 Sep 1933. BU Philadelphia.

PY 10 *Isabel* Asiatic Squadron and Yangtze Patrol, 1921–41. Yangtze River, 1926–27, 1931–32. China 1937–39. Decomm 11 Feb 1946. Sold 25 Mar 1946; BU. (Armament: 2–3"/50, 4–20mm AA guns.)
1* Philippines 1942.

PY 11 *Wenonah* Stricken 20 Jan 1928. Sold 15 May 1929.
Later history: Merchant *Stranger* 1929, renamed *Blue Water* 1937, HMCS *Wolf* 1940, *Gulf Stream* 1946. Wrecked near Powell River, British Columbia, 11 Oct 1947.

No.	Name	Builder	Launched	Acquired	Comm.
PY 12	*Sylph*	Lawley	1930	16 Jul 1940	1 Oct 1940
	ex-YP 71 (19 Jul 1940), ex-*Intrepid* (1940)				

Tonnage	810 tons, 858 f/l
Dimensions	205' (oa); 150' (wl) x 33'10" x 16'10"
Machinery	1 screw, diesel; SHP 900
Complement	88
Armament	2–3"/50

Figure 8.16: *Ruby* (PY 21), on 8 Mar 1943, a converted yacht.

Service Record:

PY 12 *Sylph* ASW training, New London, Conn. Decomm 19 Dec 1945. Stricken 8 Jan 1946. Sold 31 Dec 1946.
Later history: Merchant *Sylph*. BU 1960.

No.	Name	Builder	Launched	Acquired	Comm.
PY 13	*Siren*	Pusey	1930	16 Oct 1940	15 Nov 1940
	ex-CMc 1 (15 Nov 1940), ex-*Lotosland* (1940)				

Tonnage	720 tons; 800 f/l
Dimensions	196'5" (oa); 168'9" (wl) x 28' x 11'
Machinery	2 screws; diesel; SHP 530, 11.5 knots
Complement	89
Armament	2–3"/50

Service Record:

PY 13 *Siren* Decomm 2 May 1944, in service for training. Out of service, 23 Oct 1945. Stricken 13 Nov 1945. Sold 13 Aug 1946.
1* Convoy TAG–18.
Later history: Merchant *Siren*; se 1963.

No.	Name	Builder	Launched	Acquired	Comm.
PY 14	*Argus*	Germania	1929	25 Oct 1940	13 Feb 1941
	ex-*Haida* (1940)				

Tonnage	890 tons; 1,072 f/l
Dimensions	207'6" (oa); 178' (wl) x 30' x 13'5"
Machinery	2 screws; diesel; SHP 1,100; 14.5 knots
Complement	59
Armament	1–3"/50

Service Record:

PY 14 *Argus* To USC&GS, renamed *Pioneer* 17 Sep 1941–16 Mar 1942. Recomm 18 Apr 1942. San Francisco area. Decomm 15 Apr 1946. Stricken 21 May 1946.
Later history: Merchant *Sarina* 1947, renamed *Rosenkavalier*, *Haida G*; se 2000.

No.	Name	Builder	Launched	Acquired	Comm.
PY 15	*Coral*	Pusey	1913	25 Nov 1940	27 Feb 1941
	ex-*Yankee Clipper* (1940), ex-*Sialia*, ex-SP–543				

Tonnage	726 tons grt
Dimensions	214'6" (oa) 191' (bp) x 26'7" x 13'
Machinery	1 screw, diesel; 1500 hp, 14 knots
Complement	61
Armament	2–3"/50

Service Record:

PY 15 *Coral* Decomm 10 Sep 1943. Stricken 11 Oct 1943, sunk as target. Sold 15 Jul 1947.

No.	Name	Builder	Launched	Acquired	Comm.
PY 16	*Zircon*	Pusey	1929	9 Dec 1940	25 Mar 1941
	ex-*Nakhoda* (1940)				

Tonnage	1,220 tons; 1,400 f/l
Dimensions	235'4" (oa); 196'8" (wl) x 34' x 13'5"
Machinery	2 screws; diesel; SHP 1,450, 14 knots
Complement	104
Armament	2–3"/50

Service Record:

PY 16 *Zircon* Neutrality patrol. Decomm 10 Mar 1946. Stricken 5 Jun 1946. Sold 24 Apr 1947.
Later history: Merchant *Nakhoda* 1947, renamed *New York* (pilot) 1951. Sold 1973.

No.	Name	Builder	Launched	Acquired	Comm.
PY 17	*Jade*	Lawley	1926	26 Dec 1940	16 Mar 1941
	ex-*Doctor Brinkley* (1940), ex-*Caroline* (1938), ex-*Athero II* (1928)				

Tonnage	582 tons grt
Dimensions	159' x 27' x 13'
Machinery	2 screws; diesel; 1600 hp, 14 knots
Complement	26
Armament	1–3"/50

Service Record:

PY 17 *Jade* To Ecuador, 25 May 1943, Returned 29 Jan 1944. Training hulk 1944. Out of svc 30 Dec 1944. Stricken 19 Jan 1945. To MC, 12 Jan 1946.
Later history: Merchant *Santa Maria.* Capsized and sank 600 miles northeast of Guam, 24 Nov 1948.

No.	Name	Builder	Launched	Acquired	Comm.
PY 18	*Turquoise*	Newport News	16 Sep 1922	21 Aug 1940	5 Dec 1940
	ex-PC 459 (20 Jan 1941), ex-*Entropy* (1940), ex-*Kallisto,* ex-*Walucia III,* ex-*Miramichi,* ex-*Ohio*				

Tonnage	513 tons grt
Dimensions	160' x 26' x 11'
Machinery	2 screws; diesel; hp 700
Complement	60
Armament	1–3"/50.

Service Record:

PY 18 *Turquoise*
Later history: To Ecuador, 29 Jan 1944, renamed *Nueve de Octubre,* renamed *Esmeraldas* 1949. Foundered in Guayas River, 7 Sep 1953.

No.	Name	Builder	Launched	Acquired	Comm.
PY 22	*Azurlite*	Krupp	1928	9 Dec 1941	16 Mar 1942
	ex-*Vagabondia* (1941)				

Tonnage	1,080 tons f/l
Dimensions	210'11" (oa); 182'6" (wl) x 34' x 12'6"
Machinery	2 screws; diesel; SHP 1,120; 13.5 knots
Complement	67
Armament	2–3"/50, 4–20mm

Service Record:

PY 22 *Azurlite* Hawaii. Decomm 22 Jan 1946. Stricken 25 Feb 1946. Sold 29 Jan 1947.
Later history: Merchant *Azurlite* 1947, renamed *Pacific Reefer* 1968. FFU.

No.	Name	Builder	Launched	Acquired	Comm.
PY 19	*Carnelian*	Bath	18 Oct 1930	13 May 1941	19 Nov 1941
	ex-*Seventeen* (1941), ex-*Trudione*				
PY 20	*Tourmaline*	Bath	24 May 1930	16 May 1941	19 Sep 1941
	ex-*Sylvia* (1941)				
PY 21	*Ruby*	Bath	17 May 1930	19 Jun 1941	23 Sep 1941
	ex-*Placida* (1941)				

Figure 8.17: The yacht *Cythera* (PY 26), at Philadelphia Navy Yard following conversion, on 2 Mar 1942. She was torpedoed and sunk by a U-boat two months later.

Tonnage	500 tons; 609, 750 and 640 f/l
Dimensions	190' (oa); 154' (wl) x 26'6" x 11'(19), 10'8"(20), 10'11"(21)
Machinery	2 screws; diesel; SHP 385 to 410
Complement	65
Armament	2–3"/50; PY 19: 1–3"

Service Record:

PY 19 *Carnelian* Decomm 4 Jan 1946. Sold 24 Oct 1946.
Later history: Merchant *Seventeen,* renamed *William Johnson.* Scuttled off Barbados, 1965.

PY 20 *Tourmaline* Decomm 18 Jul 1945. Stricken 13 Aug 1945. Sold 1946.
Later history: Merchant *Adelphic,* renamed *Kyknos* 1948.

PY 21 *Ruby* Decomm 25 Jul 1945. Stricken 13 Aug 1945. Sold 26 Dec 1945.
Later history: Merchant *Placida.* Foundered off Cuba, 2 Dec 1956.

No.	Name	Builder	Launched	Acquired	Comm.
PY 23	*Beryl*	Pusey	1929	13 Dec 1941	17 Mar 1942
	ex-*René* (1941)				
PY 25	*Crystal*	Pusey	1929	15 Jan 1942	24 Feb 1942
	ex-*Vida* (1942), ex-*Cambriona*				

Tonnage	1,220 tons; 1,400 f/l
Dimensions	225' (oa); 196'8" (wl) x 34' x 13'5"
Machinery	2 screws; diesel; PY 23: SHP 1,100; PY 25: SHP 1,320
Complement	PY 23: 66; PY 25: 127
Armament	2–3"/50

Service Record:

PY 23 *Beryl* Hawaii. Decomm 25 Jan 1946. Sold 14 Oct 1946.
Later history: Merchant *René,* renamed *Baltimore* 1947.

PY 25 *Crystal* Hawaii. Decomm 6 Mar 1946. Sold 3 Apr 1947.
Later history: Merchant *Crystal.* BU 1966.

No.	Name	Builder	Launched	Acquired	Comm.
PY 24	*Almandite*	Krupp	1927	22 Jan 1942	25 Apr 1942
	ex-*Happy Days* (1942)				

Tonnage	705 tons f/l
Dimensions	185'4" (oa); 165'3" (wl) x 27' x 10'4"

Machinery	2 screws; diesel; SHP 470; 12 knots
Complement	75
Armament	1–3"/50

Service Record:

PY 24 *Almandite* Hawaii. Decomm 22 Jan 1946. Stricken 25 Feb 1946. Sold 5 Dec 1946.

No.	Name	Builder	Launched	Acquired	Comm.
PY 26	*Cythera*	Ramage	20 Sep 1906	31 Dec 1941	3 Mar 1942
	ex–*Cythera* (1941), ex–SP 575				

Tonnage	602 tons grt
Dimensions	214'9" (oa) 79'5" (wl) x 27'6" x 12'
Machinery	1 screw, VTE; 12 knots
Complement	113
Armament	3–3"/50

Service Record:

PY 26 *Cythera* Torpedoed and sunk by *U–402* off North Carolina, 2 May 1942 (66 killed).

No.	Name	Builder	Launched	Acquired	Comm.
PY 27	*Girasol*	Krupp	1926	16 Mar 1942	19 May 1942
	ex–*Firenze* (1942), ex–*Noparo*				

Tonnage	700 tons f/l
Dimensions	170' (oa); 160' (wl) x 27'1" x 10'10"
Machinery	2 screws; diesel; SHP 600; 12 knots
Complement	55
Armament	1–3"/50, 2–20mm

Service Record:

PY 27 *Girasol* Hawaii. Decomm 26 Jan 1946. Stricken 26 Feb 1946. Sold 14 Jul 1947.
Later history: Merchant *Girasol*, renamed *South Seas* 1947.

Figure 8.18: *Eagle 27* (PE 27) and *Eagle 48* (PE 48), sometime in the 1930s. A few of these Ford-built submarine chasers were still in service during World War II.

No.	Name	Builder	Launched	Acquired	Comm.
PY 28	*Marcasite*	Lawley	1928	2 Feb 1942	12 May 1942
	ex–*Ramfis* (1942), ex–*Camargo*				

Tonnage	968 tons grt
Dimensions	225' x 34'2" x 17'
Machinery	1 screw, diesel; 12 knots
Armament	2–3"/50

Service Record:

PY 28 *Marcasite* Hawaii and Northwest Sea Frontier. Decomm 5 Oct 1944. Stricken 14 Oct 1944. Sold 5 Dec 1945.
Later history: Merchant *Comando* 1946, renamed *Westminster* 1947, *Star of Malta* 1952 BU 1966 La Spezia.

No.	Name	Builder	Launched	Acquired	Comm.
PY 29	*Mizpah*	Newport News	20 Mar 1926	16 Mar 1942	26 Oct 1942
	ex–*Mizpah* (1942), ex–*Allegro* (1929), ex–*Sequoia* (1928), ex–*Savarona* (1928)				

Tonnage	771 tons f/l
Dimensions	181' (oa); 174' (wl) x 27' x 10'7"
Machinery	2 screws; diesel; SHP 615
Complement	80
Armament	2–3"/50, 3–20mm

Service Record:

PY 29 *Mizpah* Atlantic. Decomm 15 Jan 1946.
Later history: Merchant *Mizpah*. Scuttled as artificial reef off Palm Beach, Fla., 9 Apr 1968.

No.	Name	Builder	Launched	Acquired	Comm.
PY 31	*Cythera*	Germania	1930	14 Jul 1942	26 Oct 1942
	ex–*Abril* (1942), ex–*Argosy*				

Tonnage	800 tons f/l
Dimensions	205'7" (oa); 187'3" (wl) x 30' x 10'10"
Machinery	2 screws; diesel; SHP 625, 15 knots
Complement	74
Armament	1–3"/50, 4–20mm

Service Record:

PY 31 *Cythera* Gulf SF. Decomm 3 Jan 1944 for training and experiments. Out of service 14 Mar 1946. Sold 1946.
Later history: Merchant *Abril*, renamed *Ben Hecht* 1947, Israeli Navy *Maoz* 1948. *Santa Maria del Mare*; se 2000.

No.	Name	Builder	Launched	Acquired	Comm.
PY 32	*Southern Seas*	Consol. NY	1920	23 Nov 1942	23 Dec 1942
	ex–*Southern Seas* (1942), ex–*Lyndonia*				

Tonnage	1,116 tons f/l
Dimensions	228' (oa); 200' (wl) x 31'3" x 14'3"
Machinery	2 screws; diesel; SHP 750, 11 knots
Complement	47
Armament	20 mmguns

Service Record:

PY 32 *Southern Seas* Former Pan American Airways station ship at New Caledonia. Acquired from the Army after running aground in 1942. Accommodation ship for officers at New Caledonia, then Tarawa, and Kwajalein. Sunk in typhoon at Okinawa, 6 Oct 1945 (13 killed).
1* Gilbert Is.

PATROL EAGLES

Eagle Boats on the Navy List, 1923

PE 1 *Eagle 1* Decomm 15 Jun 1922. Stricken 23 Apr 1930. Sold 11 Jun 1930.
PE 2 *Eagle 2* Decomm 24 Dec 1919. Stricken 23 Apr 1930. Sold 11 Jun 1930.
PE 3 *Eagle 3* Stricken 23 Apr 1930. Sold 11 Jun 1930.
PE 4 *Eagle 4* Stricken 23 Apr 1930. Sold 11 Jun 1930.
PE 5 *Eagle 5* Stricken 23 Apr 1930. Sold 11 Jun 1930.
PE 6 *Eagle 6* Stricken 22 Oct 1930. Sunk as target, 14 Aug 1934.
PE 7 *Eagle 7* Stricken 22 Oct 1930. Sunk as target, 14 Aug 1934.
PE 8 *Eagle 8* Stricken 22 Oct 1930. Sold 1 Apr 1931.
Later history: Merchant *Fortitude*, 1932; se 1935.
PE 9 *Eagle 9* Stricken 24 Mar 1930. Sold 26 May 1930.
PE 10 *Eagle 10* Stricken 2 Jul 1936. Sunk as target, 19 Aug 1937.
PE 11 *Eagle 11* Stricken 7 Sep 1934. Sold 16 Jan 1935.
PE 12 *Eagle 12* Stricken 13 Aug 1935. Sold 30 Dec 1935.
PE 13 *Eagle 13* Stricken 24 Mar 1930. Sold 26 May 1930.
PE 14 *Eagle 14* Decomm 15 Jan 1922. Stricken 22 Oct 1930. Sunk as target, 22 Nov 1934.
PE 15 *Eagle 15* Stricken 2 Feb 1934. Sold 14 Jun 1934.
PE 18 *Eagle 18* Stricken 23 Apr 1930. Sold 11 Jun 1930.
PE 19 *Eagle 19* Decomm 9 Jan 1945. Destroyed, 6 Aug 1946.
PE 22 *Eagle 22* To USCG, 19 Dec 1919–22 Jun 1923. Stricken 2 Jul 1936. Sunk as target, 19 Aug 1937.
PE 23 *Eagle 23* Decomm 24 Jun 1923. Stricken 23 Apr 1930. Sold 11 Jun 1930.
PE 24 *Eagle 24* Stricken 23 Apr 1930. Sold 11 Jun 1930.
PE 26 *Eagle 26* Went aground on Block I., N.Y., 18 Jul 1924. Sold 29 Aug 1938.
PE 27 *Eagle 27* Decomm 5 Sep 1945. Sold 19 Jul 1946.
PE 28 *Eagle 28* Stricken 23 Apr 1930. Sold 11 Jun 1930.
PE 29 *Eagle 29* Stricken 23 Apr 1930. Sold 11 Jun 1930.

Figure 8.19: *PGM 12*, on 28 Apr 1945. A number of submarine chasers were converted to motor gunboats; this is the former *PC 1088*.

PE 31 *Eagle 31* Sold 18 May 1923.
PE 32 *Eagle 32* Decomm 6 Dec 1945. Sold 3 Mar 1947.
PE 33 *Eagle 33* Stricken 23 Apr 1930. Sold 11 Jun 1930.
PE 34 *Eagle 34* Damaged in collision with m/v *Javanese Prince* off San Francisco, 5 Apr 1932. Stricken 27 Apr 1932. Sold 9 Jun 1932.
PE 35 *Eagle 35* Decomm 1 Jun 1931. Stricken 11 Feb 1938. Sold 7 Jun 1938.
PE 36 *Eagle 36* Stricken 6 Aug 1935. Sold 27 Feb 1936.
PE 37 *Eagle 37* Stricken 23 Apr 1930. Sold 11 Jun 1930.
PE 38 *Eagle 38* Decomm 6 Dec 1945. Sold 3 Mar 1947.
PE 39 *Eagle 39* Stricken 11 Feb 1938. Sold 7 Jun 1938.
PE 40 *Eagle 40* Decomm 9 Dec 1922. Stricken 22 Oct 1930. Sunk as target, 19 Nov 1934
PE 41 *Eagle 41* Stricken 23 Apr 1930. Sold 11 Jun 1930.
PE 42 *Eagle 42* Stricken 23 Apr 1930. Sold 11 Jun 1930.
PE 43 *Eagle 43* Stricken 24 Mar 1930. Sold 26 May 1930.
PE 44 *Eagle 44* Stricken 14 May 1938.
PE 45 *Eagle 45* Stricken 23 Apr 1930. Sold 11 Jun 1930.
PE 46 *Eagle 46* Loaned to USSB, 18 Dec 1930–13 Jun 1932. Stricken 2 Jun 1936. Sold 10 Dec 1936.
PE 47 *Eagle 47* Decomm 15 Aug 1931. Stricken 13 Aug 1935. Sold 30 Dec 1935.
PE 48 *Eagle 48* Decomm 16 Mar 1946. Stricken 10 Oct 1946.
PE 49 *Eagle 49* Stricken 9 May 1930. Sold 20 Sep 1930.
PE 50 *Eagle 50* Stricken 23 Apr 1930. Sold 11 Jun 1930.
PE 51 *Eagle 51* Sold 29 Aug 1938.
PE 52 *Eagle 52* Decomm 23 Oct 1936. Sold 29 Aug 1938.
PE 53 *Eagle 53* Stricken 24 Mar 1930. Sold 26 May 1930.
PE 54 *Eagle 54* Stricken 24 Mar 1930. Sold 26 May 1930.
PE 55 *Eagle 55* Decomm 8 Jan 1946. Sold 3 Mar 1947.
PE 56 *Eagle 56* Torpedoed and sunk by *U-853* off Portland, Me., 23 Apr 1945 (54 killed).
PE 57 *Eagle 57* Decomm 12 Dec 1945. Sold 3 Mar 1947.
PE 58 *Eagle 58* Decomm 27 Apr 1934. Sold 30 Jun 1940.
PE 59 *Eagle 59* Stricken 14 May 1938. Sold 29 Aug 1938.
PE 60 *Eagle 60* Decomm and stricken 14 May 1938. Sold 29 Aug 1938.

MOTOR GUNBOATS

Wood Hull Type

PGM 1–8; ex-SC 644, 757, 1035, 1053, 1056, 1071, 1072, 1366.	Reclassified 10 Dec 1943.
Armament	1–3"/23, 1–40mm, 1–60mm mortar

Steel Hull Type

PGM 9–32; ex-PC 1548, 805–6, 1088–91, 1148, 1189, 1255, 1550–59, 1565–68.	Reclassified 16 Aug 1944.
Armament	1–3"/50, 1 twin 40mm, 6–20mm, 1–60mm mortar

Notes: Steel submarine chasers completed as gunboats (except PGM 9, converted), to provide close inshore fire support for landing operations.

Service Records:

PGM 9 Went aground in typhoon at Okinawa, 9 Oct 1945. Destroyed 27 Dec 1945.
PGM 10 Sold 9 Oct 1948
2* Okinawa, Raids on Japan 7–8/45, Minesweeping 1945.
PGM 11 Sold 9 Oct 1948.
2* Okinawa, Raids on Japan 7–8/45, Minesweeping 1945.
PGM 12 To China, 30 Jun 1948. PRC Navy.
1* Minesweeping 1945

Figure 8.20: *PC 797*, April 1945.

PGM 13 To China 30 Jun 1948.
1* Minesweeping 1945
Later history: Renamed *Tung Ling*, then *Ling Kiang*. Sunk by Chinese (PRC) MTB's, 10 Jan 1955.

PGM 14 To China 30 Jun 1948.
Later history: Renamed *Yung Ping*. PRC

PGM 15 To China 30 Jun 1948.
Later history: Renamed *Kantang*. PRC

PGM 16 To Greece 24 Nov 1947.
2* Okinawa, Raids on Japan 7–8/45, Minesweeping 1945.
Later history: Renamed *Antiploiarkhos Laskos*. R1970. Sold 29 Aug 1974 (to UK).

PGM 17 Went aground at Okinawa, 4 May 1945. Destroyed 24 Oct 1945.
1* Okinawa.

PGM 18 Sunk by mine off Okinawa, 21 Apr 1945.
1* Okinawa.

PGM 19 Sold Jan 1948.
2* Okinawa, Raids on Japan 7–8/45, Minesweeping 1945. Tokyo Bay.

PGM 20 To China, 30 Jun 1948.
2* Okinawa, Raids on Japan 7–8/45, Minesweeping 1945.
Later history: Renamed *Pao Ying*, *Ying Chiang*. Torpedoed by PRC MTB's, 20 Jan 1955.

PGM 21 To Greece 24 Nov 1947.
3* Okinawa, Raids on Japan 7–8/45, Minesweeping 1945.
Later history: Renamed *Antiploiarkhis Pezopoulos*.

PGM 22 To Greece 24 Nov 1947
2* Okinawa, Minesweeping 1945.
Later history: Renamed *Ploiarkhis Meletopoulos*. R1971. Sold 29 Aug 1971 (UK).

PGM 23 Sold 2 Dec 1947.
3* Okinawa, Raids on Japan 7–8/45, Minesweeping 1945. Operation Crossroads.

PGM 24 Sold 2 Dec 1947.
3* Okinawa, Raids on Japan 7–8/45, Minesweeping 1945. Operation Crossroads.

PGM 25 To Greece 11 Dec 1947.
3* Okinawa, Raids on Japan 7–8/45, Minesweeping 1945. Operation Crossroads.
Later history: Renamed *Plotarkhis Arslanoglou*. R 1979.

PGM 26 To China 30 Jun 1948.
3* Okinawa, Raids on Japan 7–8/45, Minesweeping 1945.
Later history: Renamed *Hung Tse*, 19.. *Ou Chang*. R 1964.

PGM 27 Went aground in typhoon at Okinawa, 9 Oct 1945. Destroyed 24 Dec 1945.

PGM 28 To Greece Dec 1947.
1* Minesweeping 1945.
Later history: Renamed *Plotarkhis Blessas*. R 1963.

PGM 29 To Greece 11 Dec 1947.
3* Okinawa, Raids on Japan 7–8/45, Minesweeping 1945. Operation Crossroads.
Later history: Renamed *Plotarkhis Chantzikonstandis*.

PGM 30 Sold 10 Apr 1947.
3* Okinawa, Raids on Japan 7–8/45, Minesweeping 1945.

PGM 31 Sold 27 Oct 1947
3* Okinawa, Raids on Japan 7–8/45, Minesweeping 1945. Operstion Crossroads

PGM 32 Sold 27 Oct 1947
3* Okinawa, Raids on Japan 7–8/45, Minesweeping 1945. Operation Crossroads.

SUBMARINE CHASERS

Submarine Chasers on the Navy List, 1924

SC 57	Sold 12 Dec 1935
SC 63	Sold 22 Jul 1931
SC 64	Rec **YW 97**, 30 Nov 1942; sold 11 Mar 1943
SC 102	Stricken 3 Jan 1947
SC 103	Sunk in storm at Buffalo, N.Y., Sep 1939
SC 143	Sold 8 Sep 1936
SC 154	FFU
SC 159	Sold 16 Nov 1926
SC 186	Sold 28 Oct 1926; later **YP–177**
SC 188	Stricken 2 Jul 1924
SC 192	To USSB 15 May 1937
SC 210	Sold 23 Apr 1930
SC 214	Sold 21 Feb 1937
SC 223	Sold 18 Mar 1936
SC 224	Sold 8 Sep 1936
SC 229	To USCG 14 Aug 1942, WPC 335
SC 231	To USCG 18 Aug 1942, WPC 336
SC 252	Sold 8 Sep 1936
SC 271	Sold 18 Jun 1934
SC 285	Sold 25 Mar 1927
SC 306	Trfd to U.S. Department of Justice 17 Dec 1930
SC 320	Sold 7 Jul 1927
SC 326	Sold 8 Nov 1935
SC 328	Sold 8 Nov 1935
SC 330	Sold 8 Oct 1946
SC 341	Sold 5 Apr 1927
SC 353	Sold 18 Mar 1936
SC 412	Sold 7 Aug 1946
SC 419	Sold 27 Apr 1927
SC 428	Loaned to City of Baltimore 1921
SC 431	Sold 9 Dec 1946
SC 432	Sold 27 Jul 1945
SC 433	Foundered in Lake Ontario 29 Jan 1938; stricken 22 Jan 1938
SC 437	Sold 21 Mar 1947
SC 440	BU Aug 1942

Submarine Chasers—Numerical Sequence Table

SC 1–448	World War I program
SC 449–50	Experimental
PC 451–52	Experimental

SC 453	Experimental
PC 454–60	Ex–yachts (rec PYc 46–48, PY 18, PYc 50; PC 457 lost)
PC 461–96	
SC 497–508	
PC 509	Ex–yacht (rec PYc 51)
PC 510	Ex–yacht (rec YP 105)
SC 511–22	
PC 523	Ex–yacht (rec YP 77)
SC 524–41	
PC 542–627	
SC 628–775	
PC 776–825	
PC 826	Ex–yacht (rec PYc 52)
PCE 827–976	
SC 977–1076	
PC 1077–1265	
SC 1266–1375	
PCS 1376–1465	
SC 1466–73	Canadian built
SC 1474–1545	
PC 1546–85	
PC 1586–1603	Ex–AM 82–99

Note: PC–457 sunk in collision with m/v *Norluna* off Puerto Rico, 14 Aug 1941 (2 killed).

Submarine Chasers (Steel)

No.	Builder	Keel Laid	Launched	Comm.
PC 451	Defoe	25 Sep 1939	23 May 1940	12 Aug 1940

Displacement	270 tons, 374 f/l
Dimensions	169'7" (oa); 163' (wl) x 20'9" x 8'7"
Machinery	2 screws; diesel; hp 4,000; 18.5 knots
Complement	65
Armament	2–3"/50, 3–20mm

Notes: Experimental boats. PC452 was to be used as a steam turbine test bed hull.

PC 451 Sank tug *Nancy Moran* in collision off east coast of Florida, 27 Dec 1941. Decomm 21 Dec 1945, sold 5 Dec 1946.

No.	Builder	Keel Laid	Launched	Comm.
PC 452	Defoe	14 Mar 1940	23 Aug 1941	26 Jul 1943

Displacement	342 tons
Dimensions	173'8" (oa) x 23'
Machinery	Delaval turbines

PC 452 Completed at Philadelphia NYd. Rec **IX 211** and renamed ***Castine***, 10 Mar 1945. Sold 23 Jan 1947.

No.	Builder	Keel Laid	Launched	Comm.
PC 461	Lawley	10 Jul 1941	23 Dec 1941	19 Mar 1942
PC 462	Lawley	22 Jul 1941	24 Jan 1942	15 Apr 1942
PC 463	Lawley	1 Aug 1941	27 Feb 1942	29 Apr 1942
PC 464	Lawley	8 Aug 1941	27 Feb 1942	15 May 1942
PC 465	Lawley	19 Aug 1941	28 Mar 1942	25 May 1942
PC 466	Lawley	1 Sep 1941	29 Apr 1942	3 Jun 1942
PC 467	Lawley	22 Oct 1941	29 Apr 1942	20 Jun 1942
PC 468	Lawley	1 Jan 1942	30 May 1942	10 Jul 1942
PC 469	Lawley	30 Jan 1942	10 Jun 1942	13 Jul 1942
PC 470	Lawley	27 Feb 1942	27 Jun 1942	31 Jul 1942
PC 471	Defoe	21 Apr 1941	15 Sep 1941	3 Nov 1941
PC 472	Defoe	1 Jul 1941	14 Nov 1941	9 Dec 1941
PC 473	Defoe	18 Aug 1941	19 Nov 1941	9 Dec 1941
PC 474	Defoe	20 Aug 1941	5 Dec 1941	19 Dec 1941
PC 475	Defoe	11 Sep 1941	16 Dec 1941	27 Dec 1941
PC 476	Defoe	2 Oct 1941	1 Jan 1942	18 Mar 1942
PC 477	Defoe	21 Nov 1941	29 Jan 1942	30 Mar 1942
PC 478	Defoe	17 Dec 1941	20 Feb 1942	1 Apr 1942
PC 479	Defoe	14 Jan 1942	10 Mar 1942	30 Apr 1942
PC 480	Defoe	22 Jan 1942	25 Mar 1942	7 Apr 1942
PC 481	Defoe	3 Feb 1942	31 Mar 1942	30 Apr 1942
PC 482	Defoe	16 Feb 1942	9 Apr 1942	30 Apr 1942
PC 483	Consol. NY	31 Dec 1940	25 Oct 1941	12 Mar 1942
PC 484	Consol. NY	7 Apr 1941	6 Dec 1941	3 Apr 1942
PC 485	Consol. NY	1 May 1941	20 Dec 1941	23 Apr 1942
PC 486	Consol. NY	25 Oct 1941	25 Jan 1942	14 May 1942
PC 487	Consol. NY	6 Dec 1941	28 Feb 1942	2 Jun 1942
PC 488	Sullivan	7 Mar 1941	20 Dec 1941	12 Aug 1942
PC 489	Sullivan	17 Mar 1941	20 Dec 1941	14 Jul 1942
PC 490	Dravo Pitt.	9 May 1941	18 Oct 1941	12 May 1942
PC 491	Dravo Pitt.	9 May 1941	6 Dec 1941	13 Apr 1942
PC 492	Dravo Pitt.	25 Jun 1941	29 Dec 1941	5 May 1942
PC 493	Dravo Pitt.	9 Aug 1941	24 Jan 1942	28 May 1942
PC 494	Dravo Pitt.	9 Aug 1941	24 Jan 1942	23 May 1942
PC 495	Dravo Wilm.	10 Jun 1941	30 Dec 1941	23 Apr 1942
PC 496	L. D. Smith	24 Apr 1941	2 Nov 1941	26 Feb 1942

Figure 8.21: *PC 1262*, a typical steel-hull submarine chaser.

Displacement	280 tons; 450 f/l
Dimensions	173'8" (oa); 170' (wl) x 23' x 10'10"
Machinery	2 screws; diesel; SHP 2,880; 20.2 knots
Complement	65
Armament	1–3"/50, 1–40mm AA, 3–20mm

Notes: Steel hulls. Eighteen built as minesweepers were reclassified PC on 1 Jun 1944. Thirty-two were transferred to France under lend–lease and one each to Greece, the Netherlands and Norway. A number were converted for use as amphibious control vessels and reclassified PC(C). PCs were not named until 1956. PC 815-825 were originally ordered from Commercial 1157–1180 from Defoe, 1231–1236 from Grebe, and 1237–1240 from Penn-Jersey.

Service Records:

PC 461 Decomm 18 Aug 1946. †

PC 462 Rec **PC(C) 462**, 20 Aug 1945. Decomm 14 Dec 1945. Sold 20 Feb 1947.
2* Leyte, Okinawa.

PC 463 Rec **PC(C) 463**, 20 Aug 1945. Went aground in typhoon, Okinawa, 9 Oct 1945. Decomm 16 Aug 1946. †
2* Iwo Jima, Okinawa.

PC 464 Decomm 7 Jun 1946. Stricken 3 Jul 1946. Sold 12 Mar 1947.
1* Leyte.

PC 465 Decomm 1946. †

PC 466 Rec **PC(C) 466**, 20 Aug 1945. Decomm Mar 1947. †
2* Palau, Okinawa. Tokyo Bay.

PC 467 To Norway 16 Sep 1942.
Later history: Renamed *Kong Haakon VII.* R 1952.

PC 468 To Netherlands 6 Aug 1942.
Later history: Renamed *Queen Wilhelmina*; sold to Nigeria, 1963, renamed *Ogoja.* Wrecked off Brass, eastern Nigeria, Oct 1969.

PC 469 USCG crew. Rec **PC(C) 469**, 20 Aug 1945. Decomm Dec 1946. †
3* Convoy TAG–18, Iwo Jima, Okinawa.

PC 470 †
2* Leyte, Lingayen.

PC 471 To France 9 Jun 1944.
Later history: Renamed *L'Éveillé.* BU 1959.

PC 472 To France 30 Jun 1944.
Later history: Renamed *Le Rusé.* BU 1959.

PC 473 To France 7 Jul 1944.
Later history: Renamed *L'Ardent.* Sunk in collision with m/v *Empire Abbey* off Casablanca, 31 Jan 1945.

PC 474 To France 1 Jun 1944.
Later history: Renamed *L'Indiscret.* Stricken 1960, used as training hulk *Dragon.*

PC 475 To France 23 Jun 1944.
Later history: Renamed *Le Résolu.* BU 1951.

PC 476 Stricken 23 Dec 1947. Sold 1 Jul 1948; BU.
2* Solomons, Noemfoor, Morotai.

PC 477 Decomm 15 Aug 1946. Sold 17 Jan 1947; BU.
1* Noemfoor, Cape Sansapor.

PC 478 Decomm 10 May 1946. Stricken 25 Oct 1946, sold 14 Nov 1946; BU Portland, Ore.

PC 479 Decomm 13 May 1946. Stricken 13 Nov 1946, sold 6 Dec 1946.
2* Arawe, Saidor, Cape Gloucester.

PC 480 To France 21 Jul 1944.
Later history: Renamed *L'Emporté.* BU 1959.

PC 481 To France 16 Jun 1944.
Later history: Renamed *L'Effronté.* Sunk as target, 29 Apr 1953.

PC 482 To France 15 Jul 1944.
Later history: Renamed *L'Enjoué.* Torpedoed and sunk by *U–870* off Cape Spartel, 9 Jan 1945.

PC 483 Decomm 18 Jun 1946. †

PC 484 Decomm Mar 1947. †
1* Normandy.

PC 485 Decomm 9 Feb 1946. †

PC 486 †

PC 487 †
1*
Submarine sunk: *I–24* (or *I–9*) off Kiska, 10 Jun 1943 (damaged by ramming).

PC 488 Rec **IX 221**, 25 Apr 1945, renamed ***Eureka.*** Sold 13 Mar 1946.

PC 489 Decomm 21 Dec 1945. Sold 5 Nov 1948; BU.

PC 490 Decomm 12 Mar 1946. †

PC 491 Decomm 4 Mar 1946. Sold 24 Jan 1948. Chinese merchant.

PC 492 Decomm 13 Feb 1946. †

PC 493 Decomm 1 Feb 1946. Sold 10 May 1947 to Thailand. Lost in typhoon in Manila Bay, 1947.

PC 494 Decomm 15 Jan 1946. Sold 11 Feb 1948.

PC 495 Decomm 16 Feb 1946, Stricken 25 Feb 1946, sold 12 Jun 1947, to Thailand 1951.
1* Convoy TAG–18.
Later history: Renamed *Sarasin.* Sunk as target.

PC 496 Sunk by mine off Bizerte, Tunisia, 4 Jun 1943. (5 killed)

No.	Builder	Keel Laid	Launched	Comm.
PC 542	Defoe	26 Feb 1942	20 Apr 1942	22 May 1942
PC 543	Defoe	11 Mar 1942	24 Apr 1942	26 May 1942
PC 544	Defoe	24 Mar 1942	30 Apr 1942	5 Jun 1942
PC 545	Defoe	31 Mar 1942	8 May 1942	27 Jun 1942
PC 546	Defoe	9 Apr 1942	14 May 1942	8 Jul 1942
PC 547	Defoe	16 Apr 1942	22 May 1942	24 Jul 1942
PC 548	Defoe	24 Apr 1942	29 May 1942	2 Aug 1942
PC 549	Defoe	1 May 1942	6 Jun 1942	2 Aug 1942
PC 550	L. D. Smith	6 Jun 1941	8 Mar 1942	28 Apr 1942
PC 551	L. D. Smith	22 Jul 1941	12 Apr 1942	15 May 1942
PC 552	Sullivan	20 May 1941	13 Feb 1942	29 Jul 1942
PC 553	Sullivan	20 Dec 1941	30 May 1942	12 Oct 1942
PC 554	Sullivan	20 Dec 1941	2 May 1942	1 Sep 1942
PC 555	Sullivan	13 Feb 1942	30 May 1942	6 Feb 1943
PC 556	Luders	1 Oct 1941	24 Apr 1942	31 Aug 1942
PC 557	Luders	31 Oct 1941	2 Aug 1942	15 Oct 1942
PC 558	Luders	31 Oct 1941	13 Sep 1942	19 Nov 1942
PC 559	Jeffersonville	14 Oct 1941	12 Feb 1942	12 May 1942
PC 560	Jeffersonville	25 Nov 1941	17 Mar 1942	17 Jun 1942
PC 561	Jeffersonville	30 Jan 1942	1 May 1942	11 Jul 1942
PC 562	Jeffersonville	13 Feb 1942	4 Jun 1942	5 Aug 1942
PC 563	Consol. NY	20 Dec 1941	27 Mar 1942	17 Jun 1942
PC 564	Consol. NY	25 Jan 1942	12 Apr 1942	2 Jul 1942
PC 565	Brown	14 Aug 1941	27 Feb 1942	25 May 1942
PC 566	Brown	14 Aug 1941	21 Mar 1942	15 Jun 1942
PC 567	Brown	15 Sep 1941	11 Apr 1942	27 Jun 1942
PC 568	Brown	15 Sep 1941	25 Apr 1942	13 Jul 1942
PC 569	Albina	11 Sep 1941	22 Jan 1942	9 May 1942
PC 570	Albina	11 Sep 1941	5 Jan 1942	18 Apr 1942
PC 571	Albina	27 Sep 1941	12 Feb 1942	26 May 1942
PC 572	Albina	27 Sep 1941	28 Feb 1942	19 Jun 1942
PC 573	Dravo Wilm.	14 Oct 1941	5 Mar 1942	13 Jun 1942
PC 574	Dravo Wilm.	30 Dec 1941	30 Mar 1942	2 Jul 1942
PC 575	Dravo Wilm.	24 Feb 1942	5 May 1942	8 Aug 1942
PC 576	Dravo Wilm.	3 Apr 1942	13 Jun 1942	10 Sep 1942
PC 577	Dravo Wilm.	6 May 1942	25 Jul 1942	15 Oct 1942

Service Records:

PC 542 To France 30 Sep 1944.
3* Sicily, Salerno, Southern France.
Later history: Renamed *Tirailleur.* BU 1958.

PC 543 To France 8 Jun 1944.
3* Sicily, Salerno, Anzio.
Later history: Renamed *Volontaire.* BU 1964.

PC 544 To Brazil 24 Sep 1942.
Later history: Renamed *Guaporé.* R 1958.

PC 545 USCG crew. To France 17 Oct 1944.
4* Sicily, Salerno, Anzio, Southern France.

Later history: Renamed *Goumier.* Loaned to Morocco 15 Jun 1960, renamed *Agadir.* Returned to France 19 Aug 1964, renamed *Q–390.* Sunk as target 1965.

PC 546 To France 3 Oct 1944.
3* Sicily, Salerno, Southern France.
Later history: Renamed *Franc Tireur.* BU 1953.

PC 547 To Brazil 24 Sep 1942.
Later history: Renamed *Gurupí.* R 1960.

PC 548 Decomm 20 Jun 1946. Stricken 31 Jul 1946. Sunk in nuclear test at Eniwetok.

PC 549 Rec **PC(C) 549**, 20 Aug 1945. Decomm Jan 1946. Sold 23 Apr 1948; BU.
2* Guam, Saipan.

PC 550 To France 15 Jun 1944.
3* Sicily, Salerno, Anzio.
Later history: Renamed *Le Vigilant.* BU 1959.

PC 551 To France 19 Oct 1944.
4* Sicily, Salerno, Anzio, Southern France.
Later history: Renamed *Mameluck.* BU 1958.

PC 552 Decomm 18 Apr 1946. Stricken 5 Jun 1946, sold 6 Dec 1946.
1* Normandy.

PC 553 Decomm 9 Jul 1946. †
1* Normandy.

PC 554 To Brazil 29 Oct 1943.
Later history: Renamed *Goiana.* R 1960.

PC 555 Rec **PC(C) 555**, 20 Aug 1945. Decomm 20 May 1946, sold 12 Feb 1947.
1* Guam.

PC 556 USCG crew. Damaged by aircraft bombs at Naples, 9 May 1944. To France 19 Oct 1944.
4* Sicily, Salerno, Anzio, Southern France.
Later history: Renamed *Carabinier.* R 1958, used as training hulk *Uranium.* BU 1968.

PC 557 To France 25 Oct 1944.
5* Tunisia, Sicily, Salerno, Anzio, Southern France.
Later history: Renamed *Dragon.* BU 1959.

PC 558 Torpedoed and sunk by *U–230* north of Palermo, 9 May 1944 (~35 killed).
3* Sicily, Salerno, Anzio.

PC 559 To France 6 Oct 1944.
5* Tunisia, Convoy TAG–18, Sicily, Salerno, Anzio, Southern France. PUC.
Later history: Renamed *Voltigeur.* Stranded, salved, and hulked 1970.

PC 560 Decomm 28 Jan 1947. †

PC 561 To Brazil 30 Nov 1943.
1* Convoy TAG–18.
Later history: Renamed *Graúna.* R1960

PC 562 Damaged by mine off Sicily, 10 Jul 1953. To France 30 Jun 1944.
1* Sicily.
Later history: Renamed *L'Attentif.* BU 1953

PC 563 Rec **PC(C) 563**, 20 Aug 1945. Decomm 15 Mar 1946. Stricken 29 Nov 1946, sold 17 Jan 1947.
2* Leyte, Okinawa.
Later history: Merchant *Doris Neu.* BU 1948

PC 564 Damaged by gunfire from German minesweepers off Granville, Normandy, 8 Mar 1945. (14 killed) Decomm 1946. †
1* Normandy.

PC 565 Decomm 26 Apr 1946. †
2* Normandy.
Submarine sunk: *U–521* off Delaware coast, 2 Jun 1943.

PC 566 Decomm 8 Jan 1947. †

PC 567 Decomm 12 Jul 1946. †
1* Normandy.

PC 568 Decomm 30 Apr 1946. †
1* Normandy.

PC 569 Sank coastal minesweeper *Bunting* in collision in San Francisco Bay, 3 Jun 1942. Decomm 25 Mar 1947. †

PC 570 Decomm 16 May 1946. Stricken 3 Jul 1946. †

PC 571 Decomm 15 Nov 1946. †

PC 572 †
1* Attu.

PC 573 Decomm 12 Jan 1946. Stricken 3 Jul 1946, sold 23 Jun 1948.

PC 574 Decomm 15 May 1946, sold 6 Nov 1946.

PC 575 Sold to Thailand Mar 1947.
Later history: Renamed *Thayanchon.* R 1982.

PC 576 Decomm 14 Feb 1947. Stricken 5 Mar 1947, sold 21 Jul 1948.
Later history: Merchant *Argos*, renamed *Dolphin.*

PC 577 Decomm 21 Dec 1945. Stricken 8 Jan 1947. Scuttled off Norfolk, Va., 12 Nov 1948.

No.	Builder	Keel Laid	Launched	Comm.
PC 578	Albina	20 Dec 1941	29 Apr 1942	15 Jul 1942
PC 579	Albina	5 Jan 1942	29 Apr 1942	25 Aug 1942
PC 580	Albina	22 Jan 1942	29 Apr 1942	26 Sep 1942
PC 581	Albina	12 Feb 1942	8 Jul 1942	9 Oct 1942
PC 582	Albina	21 Feb 1942	15 Jul 1942	22 Oct 1942
PC 583	Defoe	8 May 1942	12 Jun 1942	2 Sep 1942
PC 584	Defoe	14 May 1942	18 Jun 1942	22 Aug 1942
PC 585	Defoe	22 May 1942	8 Jul 1942	6 Sep 1942
PC 586	Defoe	29 May 1942	15 Jul 1942	5 Oct 1942
PC 587	Defoe	5 Jun 1942	1 Aug 1942	19 Sep 1942
PC 588	L. D. Smith	22 Nov 1941	3 May 1942	22 Jun 1942
PC 589	L. D. Smith	9 Mar 1942	7 Jun 1942	23 Jul 1942
PC 590	L. D. Smith	14 Apr 1942	4 Jul 1942	5 Oct 1942
PC 591	L. D. Smith	8 May 1942	2 Aug 1942	10 Oct 1942
PC 592	Dravo Pitt.	31 Mar 1942	27 Jun 1942	28 Nov 1942
PC 593	Dravo Pitt.	21 Apr 1942	22 Aug 1942	26 Dec 1942
PC 594	Dravo Pitt.	1 May 1942	7 Sep 1942	9 Mar 1943
PC 595	Dravo Pitt.	19 May 1942	9 Oct 1942	30 Apr 1943
PC 596	Commercial	18 Apr 1942	8 Aug 1942	23 Jan 1943
PC 597	Commercial	9 May 1942	7 Sep 1942	15 Feb 1943
PC 598	Commercial	23 May 1942	7 Sep 1942	5 Mar 1943
PC 599	Commercial	2 Aug 1942	26 Sep 1942	15 May 1943
PC 600	Consol. NY	28 Feb 1942	9 May 1942	18 Aug 1942
PC 601	Consol. NY	17 Mar 1942	23 May 1942	1 Sep 1942
PC 602	Consol. NY	12 Apr 1942	13 Jun 1942	16 Sep 1942
PC 603	Consol. NY	9 May 1942	30 Jun 1942	1 Oct 1942
PC 604	Luders	16 Feb 1942	24 Oct 1942	9 Mar 1943
PC 605	Luders	20 Mar 1942	19 Nov 1942	28 May 1943
PC 606	Luders	14 Apr 1942	8 Jan 1943	7 Aug 1943
PC 607	Luders	1 Jul 1942	11 Feb 1943	30 Aug 1943
PC 608	Brown	8 Jan 1942	16 May 1942	18 Aug 1942
PC 609	Brown	8 Jan 1942	30 May 1942	7 Sep 1942
PC 610	Brown	24 Feb 1942	19 Jun 1942	28 Sep 1942
PC 611	Brown	24 Feb 1942	29 Jun 1942	26 Oct 1942
PC 612	Gibbs Gas	30 Jun 1942	7 Sep 1942	1 May 1943
PC 613	Gibbs Gas	7 Jul 1942	27 Oct 1942	2 Jun 1943
PC 614	Gibbs Gas	7 Jul 1942	23 Dec 1942	9 Jul 1943
PC 615	Gibbs Gas	7 Jul 1942	17 Feb 1943	16 Jul 1943
PC 616	Lawley	27 Feb 1942	4 Jul 1942	19 Aug 1942
PC 617	Lawley	29 Mar 1942	18 Jul 1942	28 Aug 1942
PC 618	Lawley	29 Apr 1942	1 Aug 1942	7 Sep 1942
PC 619	Lawley	29 Apr 1942	15 Aug 1942	16 Sep 1942

PC 620	Nashville	27 Feb 1942	12 Aug 1942	8 Jan 1943
PC 621	Nashville	4 Mar 1942	22 May 1942	4 Dec 1942
PC 622	Nashville	22 May 1942	7 Sep 1942	21 Feb 1943
PC 623	Nashville	23 Jun 1942	24 Sep 1942	10 Apr 1943
PC 624	Jeffersonville	19 Mar 1942	4 Jul 1942	22 Aug 1942
PC 625	Jeffersonville	2 May 1942	22 Jul 1942	25 Sep 1942
PC 626	Jeffersonville	5 Jun 1942	18 Aug 1942	13 Oct 1942
PC 627	Jeffersonville	6 Jul 1942	7 Sep 1942	5 Nov 1942

Service Records:

PC 578 Rec **PC(C) 578**, 20 Aug 1945. Decomm 26 Apr 1946. Stricken 8 May 1946, sold 14 Apr 1948. Scuttled off Pearl Harbor.
2* Iwo Jima, Okinawa.
PC 579 †
PC 580 †
PC 581 †
2* Saipan, Tinian, Guam.
PC 582 Damaged by grounding in Philippines, 12 Jul 1945. Rec **PC(C) 582**, 20 Aug 1945. †
2* Saipan, Tinian.
PC 583 Decomm 20 Sep 1946, sold 9 Jul 1948.
Later history: Merchant *Pan American* 1949. FFU.
PC 584 Sunk in typhoon at Okinawa, 9 Oct 1945. Destroyed 14 Dec 1945.
1* Okinawa.
PC 585 Decomm Aug 1946, sold 9 Jul 1948.
PC 586 †
1* Saipan.
PC 587 †
PC 588 Decomm 29 Jul 1946. †
PC 589 Rec **PC(C) 589**, 20 Aug 1945. Decomm Mar 1946. †
1* Palau.
PC 590 USCG crew. Broken in two in typhoon at Okinawa, 9 Oct 1945. Destroyed 23 Feb 1946.
1* Iwo Jima.
PC 591 To France 17 Oct 1944.
3* Sicily, Salerno, Southern France.
Later history: Renamed *Spahi.* BU 1959.
PC 592 †
PC 593 Decomm 23 May 1946. Stricken. To China 27 Aug 1948.
Later history: Renamed *Fu Chiang.* BU
PC 594 Decomm 22 Mar 1946. Stricken 1 Aug 1947, sold 3 Dec 1947. Scuttled off Pearl Harbor.
PC 595 †
PC 596 Decomm 1946. Sold 11 Nov 1946; BU Portland, Ore.
PC 597 Decomm 30 Apr 1947. †
PC 598 Rec **PC(C) 598**, 20 Aug 1945. Sold 29 Nov 1946.
3* Palau, Leyte, Okinawa.
PC 599 Sold 14 Apr 1948.
PC 600 †
PC 601 Decomm 27 Jul 1946. †
PC 602 Decomm Jan 1947. †
PC 603 Decomm 8 Jan 1947. †
PC 604 To Brazil 11 Jun 1943. †
Later history: Renamed *Guaiba.* R 1952
PC 605 To Brazil 11 Jun 1943.
Later history: Renamed *Gurupá.* R 1960
PC 606 Decomm 24 Mar 1947. †
PC 607 To Brazil 19 Oct 1943.
Later history: Renamed *Guajará.* R 1960.
PC 608 Decomm 21 May 1946. †
PC 609 Decomm 20 Feb 1946. Stricken 28 Aug 1946, sold 10 May 1947. To Thailand.
Later history: Renamed *Khamronsin.* R 1956.
PC 610 Decomm Dec 1945. †
1* Balikpapan.
PC 611 Decomm 26 Sep 1946. Stricken 23 Jun 1947, sold 1 Jul 1948; Seattle BU.
PC 612 †
PC 613 Decomm 28 Mar 1946. Stricken 8 May 1946. To Dominican Republic, 10 Dec 1947.
Later history: Renamed *27 de Febrero.* R 1968.
PC 614 †
PC 615 Decomm 13 May 1946. Stricken 17 Jul 1947, sold 21 Jun 1948; BU.
PC 616 †
1* Minesweeping 1945.
PC 617 Decomm 30 Jun 1947. †
1* Normandy.
PC 618 †
1* Normandy.
PC 619 Decomm 28 Apr 1947. †
2* Normandy.
Submarine sunk: **U-986* southwest of Ireland, 17 Apr 1944.
PC 620 Decomm Jan 1947. †
PC 621 Collided with an LST, Sicily, 10 Jul 1943. To France 31 Oct 1944.
4* Sicily, Salerno, Anzio, Southern France.
Later history: Renamed *Fantassin.* BU 1961.
PC 622 To Greece 10 Jun 1943.
Later history: Renamed *Vassilefs Georghios II.* R 1963.
PC 623 Decomm 22 Mar 1946. Stricken 17 Apr 1946, sold 17 Jan 1947.
3* Palau, Leyte, Ldgs at Nasugbu.
PC 624 Went aground east of Palermo, Sicily, 12 Mar 1944. Rec YW 120, 30 Jun 1944. Trfd to France, 22 Nov 1944.
4* Sicily, Salerno, Anzio.
Later history: Renamed *Amphore.* Rec **YW120**, 30 Jun 1944. Trfd. to France, 22 Nov 1944.
Submarine sunk: *U-375* northwest of Malta, 30 Jul 1943.
PC 625 To France 16 Oct 1944.
4* Sicily, Salerno, Anzio, Southern France.
Later history: Renamed *Grenadier.* BU 1958
PC 626 To France 28 Oct 1944.
3* Sicily, Anzio, Southern France.
Later history: Renamed *Lansquenet.* BU 1958.
PC 627 To France 28 Oct 1944.
4* Sicily, Salerno, Anzio, Southern France.
Later history: Renamed *Cavalier.* BU 1951.

No.	Builder	Keel Laid	Launched	Comm.
PC 776	Commercial	10 Aug 1942	27 Oct 1942	28 Mar 1943
PC 777	Commercial	7 Sep 1942	11 Nov 1942	8 Apr 1943
PC 778	Commercial	7 Sep 1942	26 Nov 1942	30 Apr 1943
PC 779	Commercial	26 Sep 1942	7 Dec 1942	31 May 1943
PC 780	Commercial	27 Oct 1942	16 Dec 1942	19 Jun 1943
PC 781	Commercial	11 Nov 1942	24 Dec 1942	9 Jul 1943
PC 782	Commercial	26 Nov 1942	31 Dec 1942	19 Jul 1943
PC 783	Commercial	7 Dec 1942	13 Jan 1943	14 Aug 1943
PC 784	Commercial	16 Dec 1942	18 Jan 1943	17 Sep 1943
PC 785	Commercial	24 Dec 1942	23 Jan 1943	9 Oct 1943
PC 786	Commercial	31 Dec 1942	6 Feb 1943	30 Oct 1943
PC 787	Commercial	13 Jan 1943	12 Feb 1943	13 Nov 1943
PC 788	Commercial	18 Jan 1943	5 Mar 1943	15 Feb 1944
PC 789	Commercial	23 Jan 1943	13 Mar 1943	6 Mar 1944
PC 790	Commercial	6 Feb 1943	22 Mar 1943	23 Mar 1944
PC 791	Commercial	13 Mar 1943	17 Apr 1943	28 Mar 1944
PC 792	Commercial	22 Mar 1943	24 Apr 1943	10 Apr 1944
PC 793	Commercial	17 Apr 1943	22 May 1943	10 May 1944
PC 794	Commercial	24 Apr 1943	29 May 1943	25 May 1944
PC 795	Commercial	22 May 1943	24 Jul 1943	20 Jun 1944
PC 796	Commercial	29 May 1943	3 Jul 1943	19 Jun 1944

PC 797	Commercial	17 Jul 1943	21 Aug 1943	5 Jul 1944
PC 798	Commercial	3 Jul 1943	14 Aug 1943	19 Jul 1944
PC 799	Commercial	24 Jul 1943	14 Aug 1943	3 Aug 1944
PC 800	Commercial	31 Jul 1943	28 Aug 1943	23 Sep 1944
PC 801	Commercial	21 Aug 1943	18 Sep 1943	20 Dec 1944
PC 802	Commercial	14 Aug 1943	25 Sep 1943	6 Jan 1945
PC 803	Commercial	16 Aug 1943	2 Oct 1943	23 Jan 1945
PC 804	Commercial	28 Aug 1943	16 Oct 1943	6 Feb 1945
PC 805	Commercial	18 Sep 1943	27 Oct 1943	*29 Nov 1944*
PC 806	Commercial	27 Sep 1943	30 Oct 1943	13 Dec 1944
PC 807	Commercial	2 Oct 1943	6 Nov 1943	20 Feb 1945
PC 808	Commercial	16 Oct 1943	27 Nov 1943	7 Nov 1945?
PC 809	Commercial	27 Oct 1943	4 Dec 1943	20 Mar 1945
PC 810	Commercial	30 Oct 1943	11 Dec 1943	3 Apr 1945
PC 811	Commercial	6 Nov 1943	18 Dec 1943	17 Apr 1945
PC 812	Commercial	27 Nov 1943	11 Feb 1944	4 May 1945
PC 813	Commercial	11 Dec 1943	27 Mar 1944	19 May 1945
PC 814	Commercial	11 Feb 1944	13 May 1944	5 Jun 1945
PC 815	Albina	10 Oct 1942	5 Dec 1942	20 Apr 1943
PC 816	Albina	5 Dec 1942	8 Jan 1943	9 Jun 1943
PC 817	Albina	8 Jan 1943	4 Mar 1943	13 Jul 1943
PC 818	Albina	4 Mar 1943	30 Mar 1943	3 Aug 1943
PC 819	Albina	30 Mar 1943	19 May 1943	28 Aug 1943
PC 820	Albina	19 May 1943	2 Aug 1943	30 Sep 1943
PC 821	L. D. Smith	1 Sep 1943	23 Oct 1943	23 Jun 1944
PC 822	L. D. Smith	26 Oct 1943	27 Dec 1943	2 Jun 1944
PC 823	L. D. Smith	8 Nov 1943	15 Jan 1944	24 Jul 1944
PC 824	L. D. Smith	6 Mar 1944	10 May 1944	28 Aug 1944
PC 825	L. D. Smith	27 Mar 1944	28 May 1944	20 Sep 1944

Service Records:

PC 776 Decomm 21 May 1946. †
PC 777 Decomm 26 Apr 1946. †
PC 778 †
PC 779 †
1* Iwo Jima.
PC 780 Decomm 14 Aug 1946. †
PC 781 Decomm 14 Aug 1946. †
PC 782 Decomm Jan 1947. †
PC 783 Sold 16 Jun 1948.
PC 784 Decomm 25 Sep 1946. Stricken 5 Mar 1947, sold 17 Mar 1948.
PC 785 †
PC 786 Decomm 22 Jun 1946. †
PC 787 Sold to Indonesia 7 Jun 1948.
Later history: Renamed *Alu Alu.* R 1961.
PC 788 Sold 8 Jul 1948.
PC 789 Decomm 2 May 1946. Stricken 13 Dec 1946, sold 14 Jul 1948.
PC 790 Decomm 10 May 1946. Stricken 23 Dec 1947, sold 7 Jun 1948.
Later history: Merchant *Tribesman,* to Cuba, renamed *Baire* 1956. Sunk by aircraft or scuttled at Isle of Pines, 17 Jun 1961.
PC 791 Sold 7 Jun 1948. †
PC 792 Decomm 14 May 1946. Stricken 13 Dec 1948, sold 1 Jul 1948.
PC 793 Sold 1 Jul 1948.
PC 794 Sold to Mexico 8 Jun 1948.
Later history: Mexican *GC–34.* R 1964.
PC 795 Sold 7 Jun 1948.
PC 796 Sold 8 Jun 1948, to France.
Later history: Renamed *Pnom Penh.* R 1955.
PC 797 Sold 1 Jul 1948, to France.
Later history: Renamed *Hué.* R 1955.
PC 798 Sold 8 Jun 1948. To France.
Later history: Renamed *Luang–Prabang.* R 1954.
PC 799 Decomm 11 Jun 1946. Stricken 17 Jul 1947, sold to South Korea 7 Jul 1948.
Later history: Renamed *Kum Kang San.* R. 1960
PC 800 Sold 19 Apr 1948.
2* Iwo Jima, Okinawa.
PC 801 Decomm 17 Apr 1946, sold 1 Jul 1948.
PC 802 Rec **PC(C) 802**, 20 Aug 1945. Decomm and stricken 1946. Sold, to South Korea, 14 Jul 1948.
1* Okinawa.
Later history: Renamed *Sam Kak San.* R 1960.
PC 803 Rec **PC(C) 803**, 20 Aug 1945. Sold 7 Jul 1948.
1* Okinawa.
PC 804 Rec **PC(C) 804**, 20 Aug 1945. Decomm 17 Apr 1946, sold 14 Jul 1948.
Later history: Merchant *Submarex.* BU 1966.
PC 805 Rec **PGM–10**, 16 Aug 1944.
PC 806 Rec **PGM–11**, 16 Aug 1944.
PC 807 Rec **PC(C) 807**, 20 Aug 1945. Decomm 17 Apr 1946, sold 2 Jul 1948.
PC 808 †
PC 809 To Portugal 15 Mar 1948.
Later history: Renamed *Sal.* R 1968.
PC 810 Decomm Feb 1946. To Korea 1950.
Later history: Renamed *Chirisan.* Sunk by mine, Dec 1951.
PC 811 To Portugal 15 Mar 1948.
Later history: Renamed *Madeira.* R 1969.
PC 812 To Portugal 15 Mar 1948.
Later history: Renamed *Flores, Principe* R 1969.
PC 813 Sold, 8 Jun 1948, to Mexico.
Later history: Renamed *GC–33.* R 1966.
PC 814 Sunk in typhoon at Okinawa, 9 Oct 1945. Destroyed 12 Dec 1945.
PC 815 Sunk in collision with destroyer *Laffey* in fog off San Diego, 11 Sep 1945 (1 killed).
PC 816 Sold 1 Jul 1948.
PC 817 Decomm 22 Jul 1946. †
PC 818 Decomm 8 May 1946. Stricken 5 Mar 1947, sold 7 Jun 1948.
PC 819 Sold 8 Jun 1948, to Mexico.
Later history: Renamed *GC–37.* BU 1966.
PC 820 Decomm 2 May 1946. Stricken 5 Mar 1947, sold 1 Jul 1948, to Mexico
Later history: Renamed *GC–30.* BU 1966.
PC 821 Sold 7 Jun 1948.
PC 822 Decomm 12 Jul 1946. †
PC 823 Decomm 11 Feb 1946, to MC as training ship, sold 10 May 1948.
Later history: Training ship *Ensign Whitehead.* To South Korea Sep 1949, renamed *Pak Tu San.* BU 1960.
PC 824 Sold 8 Jun 1948, to Mexico.
Later history: Renamed *GC–35.* BU 1966.
PC 825 Sold 8 Jun 1948.

No.	Builder	Keel Laid	Launched	Comm.
PC 1077	Albina	18 Feb 1942	29 Jul 1942	14 Dec 1942
PC 1078	Albina	29 Apr 1942	8 Aug 1942	5 Feb 1943
PC 1079	Albina	29 Apr 1942	25 Aug 1942	7 Mar 1943
PC 1080	Albina	29 Apr 1942	27 Aug 1942	29 Mar 1943
PC 1081	Albina	29 Jul 1942	29 Aug 1942	16 Apr 1943
PC 1082	Albina	29 Aug 1942	10 Oct 1942	8 May 1943
PC 1083	Lawley	15 Aug 1942	7 Sep 1942	16 Aug 1943
PC 1084	Lawley	7 Sep 1942	31 Oct 1942	31 Aug 1943
PC 1085	Lawley	6 Jan 1943	27 Mar 1943	19 Oct 1943
PC 1086	Lawley	13 Feb 1943	24 Apr 1943	19 Jan 1944
PC 1087	Lawley	12 Apr 1943	21 Aug 1943	22 May 1944

PC 1088	Lawley	31 Aug 1943	18 Jan 1945	*24 Apr 1945*
PC 1089	Lawley	19 Jan 1945	12 Apr 1945	*14 Jun 1945*
PC 1090	Lawley	12 Apr 1945	15 Jun 1945	*9 Aug 1945*
PC 1091	Lawley	15 Jun 1945	31 Jul 1945	*11 Oct 1945*
PC 1092–1105		—	—	—
PC 1106–7		—	—	—
PC 1108–18		—	—	—
PC 1119	Defoe	12 Jun 1942	18 Aug 1942	18 Dec 1942
PC 1120	Defoe	19 Jun 1942	24 Aug 1942	18 Jan 1943
PC 1121	Defoe	30 Jun 1942	27 Aug 1942	10 Dec 1942
PC 1122	Defoe	11 Jul 1942	7 Sep 1942	1 Jan 1943
PC 1123	Defoe	22 Jul 1942	7 Sep 1942	5 Feb 1943
PC 1124	Defoe	4 Aug 1942	1 Oct 1942	23 May 1943
PC 1125	Defoe	20 Aug 1942	15 Oct 1942	26 May 1943
PC 1126	Defoe	29 Aug 1942	31 Oct 1942	27 May 1943
PC 1127	Defoe	7 Sep 1942	2 Nov 1942	29 May 1943
PC 1128	Defoe	14 Sep 1942	19 Nov 1942	31 May 1943
PC 1129	Defoe	23 Sep 1942	7 Dec 1942	1 Jun 1943
PC 1130	Defoe	8 Oct 1942	10 Dec 1942	19 Jun 1943
PC 1131	Defoe	22 Oct 1942	17 Dec 1942	28 Jul 1943
PC 1132	Defoe	5 Nov 1942	29 Dec 1942	10 Aug 1943
PC 1133	Defoe	25 Nov 1942	9 Jan 1943	24 Aug 1943
PC 1134	Defoe	4 Dec 1942	18 Jan 1943	11 Sep 1943
PC 1135	Defoe	11 Dec 1942	3 Feb 1943	7 Oct 1943
PC 1136	Defoe	17 Dec 1942	5 Mar 1943	16 Nov 1943
PC 1137	Defoe	29 Dec 1942	29 Mar 1943	23 Oct 1943
PC 1138	Defoe	9 Jan 1943	19 Apr 1943	17 Sep 1943
PC 1139	Defoe	25 Jan 1943	10 May 1943	18 Nov 1943
PC 1140	Defoe	8 Feb 1943	14 Jun 1943	22 Jan 1944
PC 1141	Defoe	12 Mar 1943	22 Jun 1943	28 Dec 1943
PC 1142	Defoe	31 Mar 1943	20 Aug 1943	3 Jun 1944
PC 1143	Defoe	17 Apr 1943	25 Sep 1943	16 May 1944
PC 1144	Defoe	7 May 1943	4 Oct 1943	20 May 1944
PC 1145	Defoe	2 Jun 1943	27 Oct 1943	1 Jun 1944
PC 1146	Defoe	21 Sep 1943	15 Nov 1943	13 Jul 1944
PC 1147	Defoe	11 Oct 1943	2 Dec 1943	12 Aug 1944
PC 1148	Defoe	25 Oct 1943	19 Dec 1943	*25 Oct 1944*
PC 1149	Defoe	6 Nov 1943	11 Jan 1944	22 Jun 1944
PC 1150–56	Defoe	—	—	—
PC 1157–66	Lawley	—	—	—

Service Records:

PC 1077 †

PC 1078 †

PC 1079 Rec **PC(C) 1079**, 20 Aug 1945. Decomm Mar 1946. †
3* Saipan, Tinian, Guam.

PC 1080 Rec **PC(C) 1080**, 20 Aug 1945. Decomm 9 Aug 1946. Stricken 28 Aug 1946, sold 16 Jan 1947.
3* Saipan, Tinian, Guam.

PC 1081 Rec **PC(C) 1081**, 20 Aug 1945. Decomm 31 Dec 1946. †
2* Iwo Jima, Okinawa.

PC 1082 Engines shut down and ship drifted for 14 days between Kwajalein and Pearl Harbor, Jul 1946. Decomm 18 Sep 1946, sold 13 Nov 1946; BU Taiwan.

PC 1083 Sold 19 Dec 1946.

PC 1084 Decomm 12 Dec 1945. Stricken 8 Jan 1946, sold 19 Aug 1946.

PC 1085 Sold 10 Dec 1946.

PC 1086 †

PC 1087 Decomm 20 Feb 1947. †

PC 1088 Rec **PGM 12**, 16 Aug 1944.

PC 1089 Rec **PGM 13**, 16 Aug 1944.

PC 1090 Rec **PGM 14**, 16 Aug 1944.

PC 1091 Rec **PGM 15**, 16 Aug 1944.

PC 1092–1105 Canceled 5 Nov 1943.

PC 1106–7 Canceled 25 Sep 1943.

PC 1108–18 Canceled 17 Sep 1943.

PC 1119 Damaged by shore gunfire, Luzon, 16 Feb 1945. Decomm 9 Jan 1947. †
5* Arawe, Saidor, Morotai, Leyte, Mariveles–Corregidor, Subic Bay.

PC 1120 Decomm Jan 1947. †
6* Arawe, Saidor, Biak, Noemfoor, Cape Sansapor, Leyte, Ldgs on Palawan, Tarakan.

PC 1121 Decomm 6 Jan 1946. Stricken 16 Sep 1947. To Philippines 25 Jun 1948.
1* Cape Gloucester.
Later history: Renamed *Camarines Sur.*

PC 1122 Decomm 9 Aug 1946. Stricken 16 Sep 1947. To Philippines 6 May 1948.
5* Arawe, Cape Gloucester, Saidor, Biak, Noemfoor, Morotai, Leyte, Subic Bay.

PC 1123 Sold 27 Aug 1947.
2* Cape Gloucester, Cape Sansapor.
Later history: Merchant *Princess of Negros.*

PC 1124 Damaged by aircraft bombs, Leyte, 24 Nov 1944. (7 killed) Rec **IX 206**, renamed ***Chocura***, 20 Feb 1945. Destroyed by sinking off Admiralty Is., 17 Oct 1945.
1* Cape Sansapor.

PC 1125 Rec **PC(C) 1125**, 20 Aug 1945. †
1* Guam.

PC 1126 Rec **PC(C) 1126**, 20 Aug 1945. Went aground in typhoon at Okinawa, 9 Oct 1945. Decomm 28 Nov 1945. Destroyed 24 Dec 1945.
1* Guam.

PC 1127 Rec **PC(C) 1127**, 20 Aug 1945. Decomm 4 Dec 1946. Stricken 22 Jan 1947, sold 7 Jul 1948.
1* Guam.

PC 1128 Damaged in collision during typhoon, New Caledonia, Jan 1944. Went aground in typhoon at Okinawa, 9 Oct 1945. Decomm 29 Nov 1945. Destroyed 9 Mar 1946.
1* Okinawa.

PC 1129 Sunk by Japanese suicide boat, Lubang Is., Philippines, 31 Jan 1945 (1 killed).
4* Green Is., Palau, Leyte, Subic Bay.

PC 1130 Decomm 2 Nov 1946. †
1* Palau.

PC 1131 To Philippines 17 Jun 1948.
1* Saidor, Arawe.
Later history: Renamed *Bohol.* R 1969.

PC 1132 Decomm 31 May 1946. Stricken 16 Sep 1947. Destroyed 20 May 1948.
1* Noemfoor, Cape Sansapor, Tinian.

PC 1133 Damaged by grounding in Philippines, 26 Mar 1945. To Philippines 26 May 1948.
5* Cape Sansapor, Noemfoor, Leyte, Lingayen, Mariveles–Corregidor. Subic Bay, Visayan Is. Ldgs.
Later history: Renamed *Zamboanga del Sur.* R 1956.

PC 1134 Decomm 23 May 1946. Stricken 16 Sep 1947. To Philippines 27 Apr 1948.
4* Noemfoor, Cape Sansapor, Morotai, Leyte, Balikpapan, Visayan Is. Ldgs.
Later history: Renamed *Batangas.* R1979

PC 1135 †
1*
Submarine sunk: **I–32* south of Wotje, 24 Mar 1944.

PC 1136 Rec **PC(C) 1136**, 20 Aug 1945. Decomm 15 Feb 1946. †
1* Guam.

PC 1137 Rec **PC(C) 1137**, 20 Aug 1945. Decomm 10 Aug 1946. †
1* Palau.

PC 1138 †
PC 1139 Decomm 23 Jul 1946. †
PC 1140 Decomm Jan 1947. †
1* Southern France.
PC 1141 †
PC 1142 Decomm Oct 1946. †
PC 1143 †
PC 1144 †
PC 1145 Decomm 15 Feb 1946. †
PC 1146 †
PC 1147 Sold 30 Apr 1948.
PC 1148 Rec **PGM 16**, 16 Aug 1944.
PC 1149 Decomm 20 Feb 1947. †
PC 1150–66 Canceled 17 Sep 1943.

No.	Builder	Keel Laid	Launched	Comm.
PC 1167	Sullivan	3 Apr 1943	3 Jul 1943	3 Dec 1943
PC 1168	Sullivan	3 Apr 1943	3 Jul 1943	31 Dec 1943
PC 1169	Sullivan	3 Jul 1943	16 Oct 1943	26 Jan 1944
PC 1170	Sullivan	3 Jul 1943	16 Oct 1943	21 Feb 1944
PC 1171	L. D. Smith	12 Mar 1943	15 May 1943	24 Sep 1943
PC 1172	L. D. Smith	29 Mar 1943	5 Jun 1943	6 Oct 1943
PC 1173	L. D. Smith	21 Apr 1943	26 Jun 1943	1 Nov 1943
PC 1174	L. D. Smith	18 May 1943	22 Jul 1943	5 Nov 1943
PC 1175	L. D. Smith	8 Jun 1943	7 Aug 1943	1 Dec 1943
PC 1176	L. D. Smith	28 Jun 1943	28 Aug 1943	20 Nov 1943
PC 1177	L. D. Smith	24 Jul 1943	18 Sep 1943	20 Dec 1943
PC 1178	L. D. Smith	11 Aug 1943	2 Oct 1943	6 Jan 1944
PC 1179	L. D. Smith	20 Sep 1943	6 Nov 1943	22 Jan 1944
PC 1180	L. D. Smith	5 Oct 1943	27 Nov 1943	10 Feb 1944
PC 1181	Gibbs Gas	5 Oct 1942	15 Apr 1943	17 Sep 1943
PC 1182	Gibbs Gas	9 Oct 1942	14 Jun 1943	27 Oct 1943
PC 1183	Gibbs Gas	27 Oct 1942	7 Jul 1943	7 Dec 1943
PC 1184	Gibbs Gas	8 Jan 1943	4 Aug 1943	24 Jan 1944
PC 1185	Gibbs Gas	26 Mar 1943	27 Aug 1943	24 Apr 1944
PC 1186	Gibbs Gas	20 Apr 1943	27 Sep 1943	9 Jun 1944
PC 1187	Gibbs Gas	18 Jun 1943	26 Nov 1943	18 Jul 1944
PC 1188	Gibbs Gas	12 Jul 1943	31 Jan 1944	5 Sep 1944
PC 1189	Gibbs Gas	10 Aug 1943	14 Apr 1944	*24 Nov 1944*
PC 1190	Gibbs Gas	1 Sep 1943	29 Jun 1944	6 Feb 1945
PC 1191	Consol. NY	23 May 1942	25 Jul 1942	2 Nov 1942
PC 1192	Consol. NY	13 Jun 1942	8 Aug 1942	26 Nov 1942
PC 1193	Consol. NY	30 Jun 1942	29 Aug 1942	21 Jan 1943
PC 1194	Consol. NY	25 Jul 1942	19 Sep 1942	8 Feb 1943
PC 1195	Consol. NY	8 Aug 1942	3 Oct 1942	23 Mar 1943
PC 1196	Consol. NY	29 Aug 1942	24 Oct 1942	7 Apr 1943
PC 1197	Consol. NY	19 Sep 1942	14 Nov 1942	22 Apr 1943
PC 1198	Consol. NY	3 Oct 1942	12 Dec 1942	3 May 1943
PC 1199	Consol. NY	24 Oct 1942	2 Jan 1943	17 May 1943
PC 1200	Consol. NY	16 Nov 1942	13 Jan 1943	29 May 1943
PC 1201	Consol. NY	12 Dec 1942	14 Feb 1943	11 Jun 1943
PC 1202	Consol. NY	2 Jan 1943	27 Feb 1943	23 Jun 1943
PC 1203	Consol. NY	23 Jan 1943	14 Mar 1943	17 Jul 1943
PC 1204	Consol. NY	27 Feb 1943	14 Apr 1943	6 Aug 1943
PC 1205	Consol. NY	14 Mar 1943	29 Apr 1943	26 Aug 1943
PC 1206	Consol. NY	9 Jun 1943	21 Jul 1943	27 Oct 1943
PC 1207	Consol. NY	26 Jun 1943	18 Aug 1943	12 Nov 1943
PC 1208	Consol. NY	21 Jul 1943	15 Sep 1943	25 Nov 1943
PC 1209	Consol. NY	18 Aug 1943	7 Oct 1943	1 May 1944
PC 1210	Consol. NY	15 Sep 1943	30 Oct 1943	5 May 1944

Service Records:

PC 1167 †
PC 1168 Rec **PC(C) 1168**, 20 Aug 1945. Decomm 31 Dec 1946. †
1* Southern France.
PC 1169 Rec **PC(C) 1169**, 20 Aug 1945. Decomm 1946. †
1* Southern France.
PC 1170 †
PC 1171 †
PC 1172 †
PC 1173 Decomm Mar 1946. †
1* Southern France.
PC 1174 Decomm 28 Jun 1946. †
1* Southern France.
PC 1175 Decomm 16 Aug 1946. †
PC 1176 Decomm 23 May 1946. †
1* Normandy.
PC 1177 Rec **PC(C) 1177**, 20 Aug 1945. Decomm 27 Jul 1946. †
2* Palau, Okinawa.
PC 1178 Rec **PC(C) 1178**, 20 Aug 1945. Decomm 4 Sep 1946. †
1* Palau.
PC 1179 Decomm 13 May 1946. †
3* Leyte, Lingayen, Okinawa.
PC 1180 Rec **PC(C) 1180**, 20 Aug 1945. Decomm 15 Nov 1946. †
2* Palau, Okinawa.
PC 1181 Decomm 18 Aug 1946. †
PC 1182 Decomm 9 Aug 1946. †
PC 1183 Sold 7 Jun 1948, to Indonesia.
Later history: Renamed *Tenggiri*. R 1976.
PC 1184 Sold 16 Jun 1948.
PC 1185 To Thailand 8 Jun 1948.
Later history: Renamed *Phali*. R
PC 1186 Decomm 22 Jul 1946. †
PC 1187 Sold 1 Jul 1948.
Later history: Merchant *Aleutian Packer*. BU 1960.
PC 1188 Sold 28 Mar 1948.
Later history: Israeli Navy, renamed *Nogah*. Sunk as target, 1970s.
PC 1189 Rec **PGM 17**, 16 Aug 1944.
PC 1190 Sold 10 Jun 1948.
PC 1191 Decomm 12 Jul 1946. †
PC 1192 Decomm 28 Mar 1946. Stricken 8 May 1946, sold 18 Jun 1948.
PC 1193 †
PC 1194 Sold 21 Jun 1948.
PC 1195 Sold 7 Jun 1948.
PC 1196 Decomm Jul 1946. †
PC 1197 Decomm 11 Jan 1946. Stricken 19 Jun 1946, sold 21 Jun 1948.
PC 1198 †
PC 1199 Decomm 10 Jan 1946. Stricken 19 Jun 1946, sold 18 Jun 1948.
PC 1200 Decomm 22 Jan 1946. Stricken 20 Mar 1946. Destroyed as bombing target; Buzzards Bay, 1949.
PC 1201 Decomm 30 Jul 1946. †
PC 1202 To Dominican Republic, 10 Dec 1947.
Later history: Renamed *Capt. Wenceslao Arvelo, Patria*. R 1962.
PC 1203 Stricken 28 Mar 1946. Destroyed 1949.
PC 1204 Sold 18 Jun 1948.
PC 1205 Decomm 28 Sep 1946. Stricken 23 Jun 1947, sold 1 Jul 1948.
PC 1206 Decomm 16 Oct 1946. Stricken 22 May 1947, sold 7 Jul 1948.
PC 1207 Decomm 10 Jan 1946. Stricken 13 Nov 1946, sold 23 Jun 1948.
Later history: Merchant *Sea Belle*. RR 1985.
PC 1208 Decomm 9 Aug 1946. †
PC 1209 †
PC 1210 Sold 8 Jun 1948, to Mexico.
Later history: Renamed *GC-30*. R 1971.

Figure 8.22: *PCE 893.* Many of these patrol chasers were completed without the stack.

No.	Builder	Keel Laid	Launched	Comm.
PC 1211	Luders	11 Aug 1942	12 Mar 1943	16 Aug 1943
PC 1212	Luders	26 Sep 1942	23 Apr 1943	18 Sep 1943
PC 1213	Luders	7 Nov 1942	22 May 1943	6 Oct 1943
PC 1214	Luders	22 Feb 1943	28 Jun 1943	28 Oct 1943
PC 1215	Luders	22 Mar 1943	29 Jul 1943	26 Nov 1943
PC 1216	Luders	29 Apr 1943	29 Aug 1943	31 Dec 1943
PC 1217	Luders	26 May 1943	26 Sep 1943	27 Apr 1944
PC 1218	Luders	2 Jul 1943	24 Oct 1943	29 May 1944
PC 1219	Luders	2 Aug 1943	21 Nov 1943	1 Jul 1944
PC 1220	Luders	7 Sep 1943	22 Dec 1943	29 Jul 1944
PC 1221	Penn–Jersey	29 May 1942	29 Aug 1943	19 Apr 1944
PC 1222	Penn–Jersey	26 Oct 1942	25 Sep 1943	7 Jul 1944
PC 1223	Penn–Jersey	26 Sep 1943	9 Jan 1944	13 Nov 1944
PC 1224	Penn–Jersey	31 Aug 1943	9 Jul 1944	8 Jan 1945
PC 1225	L. D. Smith	10 Jun 1942	7 Sep 1942	12 Jan 1943
PC 1226	L. D. Smith	7 Jul 1942	7 Sep 1942	27 Jan 1943
PC 1227	L. D. Smith	5 Aug 1942	17 Oct 1942	23 Feb 1943
PC 1228	L. D. Smith	7 Sep 1942	18 Nov 1942	21 May 1943
PC 1229	L. D. Smith	7 Sep 1942	19 Dec 1942	11 Jun 1943
PC 1230	L. D. Smith	20 Dec 1942	10 Mar 1943	15 Jul 1943
PC 1231	Sullivan	1 Sep 1942	12 Dec 1942	13 Jul 1943
PC 1232	Sullivan	8 Sep 1942	12 Dec 1942	18 Aug 1943
PC 1233	Sullivan	21 Sep 1942	11 Jan 1943	24 Sep 1943
PC 1234	Sullivan	12 Dec 1942	3 Apr 1943	19 Jun 1943
PC 1235	Sullivan	12 Dec 1942	3 Apr 1943	28 Jul 1943
PC 1236	Sullivan	11 Jan 1943	24 Apr 1943	31 Aug 1943
PC 1237	Consol. NY	14 Feb 1943	3 Apr 1943	26 Jul 1943
PC 1238	Consol. NY	3 Apr 1943	15 May 1943	6 Sep 1943
PC 1239	Consol. NY	14 Apr 1943	9 Jun 1943	27 Sep 1943
PC 1240	Consol. NY	15 May 1943	26 Jun 1943	13 Oct 1943
PC 1241	Nashville	4 Sep 1942	24 Dec 1942	28 May 1943
PC 1242	Nashville	22 Sep 1942	25 Jan 1943	12 Jul 1943
PC 1243	Nashville	9 Dec 1942	15 Mar 1943	12 Sep 1943
PC 1244	Nashville	20 Jan 1943	8 May 1943	5 Oct 1943
PC 1245	Nashville	9 Mar 1943	29 May 1943	30 Oct 1943
PC 1246	Nashville	4 May 1943	3 Jul 1943	29 Nov 1943
PC 1247	Nashville	28 May 1943	7 Aug 1943	20 Dec 1943
PC 1248	Nashville	29 Jun 1943	18 Sep 1943	*18 Jan 1944*
PC 1249	Nashville	4 Aug 1943	6 Nov 1943	*9 Feb 1944*
PC 1250	Nashville	14 Sep 1943	18 Dec 1943	*9 Mar 1944*
PC 1251	Brown	8 Jun 1942	12 Sep 1942	27 Feb 1943
PC 1252	Brown	8 Jun 1942	30 Sep 1942	27 Mar 1943
PC 1253	Brown	11 Jun 1942	14 Oct 1942	1 Apr 1943
PC 1254	Brown	22 Jun 1942	31 Oct 1942	13 Apr 1943
PC 1255	Luders	29 Sep 1943	23 Jan 1944	*28 Nov 1944*
PC 1256	Luders	28 Oct 1943	21 May 1944	27 Oct 1944
PC 1257	Luders	24 Nov 1943	23 Jul 1944	21 Dec 1944
PC 1258	Luders	28 Dec 1943	23 Sep 1944	24 Jan 1945
PC 1259	Luders	28 Jan 1944	7 Oct 1944	6 Mar 1945
PC 1260	L. D. Smith	20 Oct 1942	11 Jan 1943	24 Apr 1943
PC 1261	L. D. Smith	20 Oct 1942	28 Feb 1943	22 May 1943
PC 1262	L. D. Smith	21 Jan 1943	27 Mar 1943	29 Jun 1943
PC 1263	L. D. Smith	2 Mar 1943	19 Apr 1943	28 Jul 1943
PC 1264	Consol. NY	7 Oct 1943	28 Nov 1943	25 Apr 1944
PC 1265	Consol. NY	30 Oct 1943	19 Dec 1943	12 May 1944

Service Records:

PC 1211 Decomm 15 Mar 1946. Stricken 17 Apr 1946, sold 16 Oct 1946.
Later history: Merchant *Blue Arrow*, Spanish Navy *Javier Quiroga* 1954. Stricken 1970; BU Cartagena, Spain.

PC 1212 Decomm 23 Aug 1946. †

PC 1213 Decomm 20 Jul 1946. †

PC 1214 Stricken 28 Aug 1946. Destroyed 1951.

PC 1215 Decomm 25 Mar 1946. Stricken 8 May 1946, sold 28 Jun 1948.

PC 1216 Decomm 10 May 1946. †

PC 1217 Damaged in hurricane off Fla., 13 Sep 1944, sold 24 Mar 1948; BU Staten I., N.Y.

PC 1218 Decomm 10 May 1946. To Thailand 7 Jun 1948.
Later history: Renamed *Sukrip*. R1991.

PC 1219 Sold 5 Apr 1948.

PC 1220 Sold 8 Jun 1948.

PC 1221 Decomm 2 Mar 1946. Stricken 12 Apr 1946, sold 28 Jul 1948.

PC 1222 Sold 22 Apr 1947.
Later history: Merchant *Gosse* 1948, renamed *Marjan* 1959.

PC 1223 Sold 17 Jan 1947.

PC 1224 Sold 8 Jun 1948, to Mexico.
Later history: Renamed *GC–36*. R 1964.

PC 1225 Decomm 18 Jul 1946. †
1* Normandy.

PC 1226 To France 6 Nov 1944.
2* Anzio, Southern France.
Later history: Renamed *Légionnaire*. BU 1958.

PC 1227 To France 18 Nov 1944.
2* Anzio, Southern France.
Later history: Renamed *Lancier*. BU 1960.

PC 1228 Decomm 19 Jul 1946. †

PC 1229 Decomm 7 Aug 1946. †

PC 1230 Rec **PC(C) 1230**, 20 Aug 1945. Decomm Mar 1946. †
1* Palau.

PC 1231 Rec **PC(C) 1231**, 20 Aug 1945. Decomm 28 Jun 1946. †
2* Leyte, Lingayen.

PC 1232 Decomm 15 Aug 1946. †
1* Normandy.

PC 1233 Decomm 20 Sep 1946. †
1* Normandy.

PC 1234 To Uruguay 2 May 1944.
Later history: Renamed *Maldonado.*
PC 1235 To France 26 Oct 1944.
2* Anzio, Southern France.
Later history: Renamed *Hussard.* BU 1965.
PC 1236 To Brazil 15 Nov 1943.
Later history: Renamed *Grajaú.* Stricken 1960.
PC 1237 †
PC 1238 Went aground in typhoon at Okinawa, 9 Oct 1945, sold May 1947; BU.
PC 1239 Went aground in typhoon at Okinawa, 9 Oct 1945. Destroyed 5 Feb 1946.
PC 1240 †
PC 1241 Decomm 15 Jun 1946. Stricken 16 Sep 1947. To Philippines 21 Jan 1948.
Later history: Renamed *Nueva Ecija.*
PC 1242 Decomm 1 Jul 1947. †
1* Minesweeping 1945.
PC 1243 Decomm 1 Apr 1947. Stricken 23 Apr 1947, sold 27 Aug 1947.
Later history: Merchant *Princess of Panay.*
PC 1244 Rec **PC(C) 1244**, 20 Aug 1945.
1* Southern France.
PC 1245 Sold 5 Feb 1948.
PC 1246 Decomm Jan 1947. †
1* Southern France.
PC 1247 Decomm 2 Oct 1946. To China 30 Jun 1948.
Later history: Renamed *Chia Ling.* Renamed *Tokiang.* Stricken 1964.
PC 1248 To France 18 Jan 1944.
Later history: Renamed *Sabre.* BU 1959.
PC 1249 To France 9 Feb 1944.
Later history: Renamed *Pique.* BU 1959.
PC 1250 To France 9 Mar 1944.
Later history: Renamed *Cimeterre.* BU 1963
PC 1251 Rec **PC(C) 1251**, 20 Aug 1945. Decomm 3 Aug 1946. †
1* Palau.
PC 1252 Decomm 26 Jun 1946.
1* Normandy.
PC 1253 †
PC 1254 †
PC 1255 Rec **PGM 18**, 16 Aug 1944.
PC 1256 To Portugal 15 Mar 1948.
Later history: Renamed *Sao Tome.* R 1970.
PC 1257 To Portugal 15 Mar 1948.
Later history: Renamed *Santiago.* R 1967.
PC 1258 Sold 21 Jun 1948.
Later history: Merchant *Boston Belle,* renamed *Ciudad de Rosario* 1961. RR 1980s.
PC 1259 To Portugal 15 Mar 1948.
Later history: Renamed *Sao Vicente.* R 1970.
PC 1260 Rec **PC(C) 1260**, 20 Aug 1945. Decomm 12 Apr 1946. †
1* Palau.
PC 1261 Sunk by mine off Utah Beach, Normandy, 6 Jun 1944. (15 killed)
1* Normandy.
PC 1262 †
1* Normandy.
PC 1263 †
1* Normandy.
PC 1264 Decomm 7 Feb 1946. Stricken 28 Mar 1946, sold 24 Mar 1948; BU Staten I., N.Y.
PC 1265 Decomm 19 Mar 1946. Stricken 1 May 1946, sold 3 Dec 1946.

No.	Builder	Keel Laid	Launched	Comm.
PC 1546	Consol. NY	28 Nov 1943	30 Jan 1944	5 Jun 1944
PC 1547	Consol. NY	4 Dec 1943	8 Feb 1944	7 Jul 1944
PC 1548	Consol. NY	19 Dec 1943	13 Feb 1944	1 Jul 1944
PC 1549	Consol. NY	30 Jan 1944	12 Mar 1944	25 Jul 1944
PC 1550	Consol. NY	13 Feb 1944	11 Apr 1944	*1 Dec 1944*
PC 1551	Consol. NY	12 Mar 1944	7 May 1944	*2 Dec 1944*
PC 1552	Consol. NY	11 Apr 1944	25 May 1944	*22 Nov 1944*
PC 1553	Consol. NY	7 May 1944	25 Jun 1944	*23 Dec 1944*
PC 1554	Consol. NY	25 May 1944	16 Jul 1944	*5 Dec 1944*
PC 1555	Consol. NY	15 Jul 1944	13 Aug 1944	*18 Jan 1945*
PC 1556	Consol. NY	16 Jul 1944	6 Sep 1944	*3 Feb 1945*
PC 1557	Consol. NY	13 Aug 1944	25 Sep 1944	*24 Feb 1945*
PC 1558	Consol. NY	6 Jun 1944	28 Oct 1944	*19 Mar 1945*
PC 1559	Consol. NY	25 Jun 1944	19 Nov 1944	*9 Apr 1945*
PC 1560	L. D. Smith	29 Nov 1943	3 Feb 1944	15 Apr 1944
PC 1561	L. D. Smith	28 Dec 1943	23 Feb 1944	4 May 1944
PC 1562	L. D. Smith	17 Jan 1944	4 Mar 1944	25 May 1944
PC 1563	L. D. Smith	4 Feb 1944	24 Mar 1944	29 Jun 1944
PC 1564	L. D. Smith	24 Feb 1944	19 Apr 1944	4 Aug 1944
PC 1565	L. D. Smith	11 May 1944	16 Jul 1944	*29 Nov 1944*
PC 1566	L. D. Smith	29 May 1944	12 Aug 1944	*27 Dec 1944*
PC 1567	L. D. Smith	18 Jul 1944	23 Sep 1944	*17 Jan 1945*
PC 1568	L. D. Smith	14 Aug 1944	14 Oct 1944	*9 Feb 1945*
PC 1569	L. D. Smith	26 Sep 1944	9 Dec 1944	14 Mar 1945
PC 1570–85	Canceled			
PC 1586–1603				

Service Records:
PC 1546 †
PC 1547 †
PC 1548 Rec **PGM 9**, 4 Feb 1944. Went aground in typhoon at Okinawa, 9 Oct 1945. Destroyed 27 Dec 1945.
PC 1549 To China 30 Jun 1948.
Later history: Chinese *Chien Tang.* R. 1952.
PC 1550 Rec **PGM 19**, 16 Aug 1944.
PC 1551 Rec **PGM 20**, 16 Aug 1944.
PC 1552 Rec **PGM 21**, 16 Aug 1944.
PC 1553 Rec **PGM 22**, 16 Aug 1944.
PC 1554 Rec **PGM 23**, 16 Aug 1944.
PC 1555 Rec **PGM 24**, 16 Aug 1944.
PC 1556 Rec **PGM 25**, 16 Aug 1944.
PC 1557 Rec **PGM 26**, 16 Aug 1944.
PC 1558 Rec **PGM 27**, 16 Aug 1944.
PC 1559 Rec **PGM 28**, 16 Aug 1944.
PC 1560 To France 15 Apr 1944.
Later history: Renamed *Coutelas.* BU 1963.
PC 1561 To France 15 May 1944.
Later history: Renamed *Dague.* BU 1964.
PC 1562 To France 5 Jun 1944.
Later history: Renamed *Javelot.* BU 1951.
PC 1563 To Philippines 3 Mar 1948.
Later history: Renamed *Negros Occidental.* Sunk in typhoon at Guam, Nov 1962.
PC 1564 Decomm 2 Jun 1946. Stricken 16 Sep 1947. To Philippines 2 Jul 1948.
Later history: Renamed *Capiz.* R1979
PC 1565 Rec **PGM 29**, 16 Aug 1944.
PC 1566 Rec **PGM 30**, 16 Aug 1944.
PC 1567 Rec **PGM 31**, 16 Aug 1944.
PC 1568 Rec **PGM 32**, 16 Aug 1944.
PC 1569 Decomm 9 Aug 1946 †.
PC 1570–75 Canceled 23 Sep 1943.
PC 1576–81 Canceled 5 Nov 1943.
PC 1582–85 Canceled 23 Sep 1943
PC 1586–1603 Ex- AM 82–99. Rec 1 Jun 1944

PATROL CHASERS, ESCORT

No.	Builder	Keel Laid	Launched	Comm.
PCE 827	Pullman	14 Oct 1942	2 May 1943	*14 Jul 1943*
PCE 828	Pullman	17 Nov 1942	15 May 1943	*31 Jul 1943*
PCE 829	Pullman	7 Dec 1942	27 May 1943	*16 Aug 1943*
PCE 830	Pullman	24 Dec 1942	13 Jun 1943	*31 Aug 1943*
PCE 831	Pullman	16 Jan 1943	26 Jun 1943	*14 Sep 1943*
PCE 832	Pullman	5 Feb 1943	10 Jul 1943	*27 Sep 1943*
PCE 833	Pullman	26 Feb 1943	2 Aug 1943	*9 Oct 1943*
PCE 834	Pullman	12 Mar 1943	19 Aug 1943	*20 Oct 1943*
PCE 835	Pullman	30 Mar 1943	3 Sep 1943	*30 Oct 1943*
PCE 836	Pullman	12 Apr 1943	17 Sep 1943	*6 Nov 1943*
PCE 837	Pullman	23 Apr 1943	1 Oct 1943	*25 Nov 1943*
PCE 838	Pullman	4 May 1943	13 Oct 1943	*11 Dec 1943*
PCE 839	Pullman	13 May 1943	23 Oct 1943	*18 Dec 1943*
PCE 840	Pullman	24 May 1943	2 Nov 1943	*28 Dec 1943*
PCE 841	Pullman	3 Jun 1943	9 Nov 1943	*13 Jan 1944*
PCE 842	Pullman	12 Jun 1943	14 Nov 1943	29 Jan 1944
PCE 843	Pullman	25 Jun 1943	24 Nov 1943	30 Jan 1944
PCE 844	Pullman	8 Jul 1943	1 Dec 1943	18 Feb 1944
PCE 845	Pullman	24 Jul 1943	13 Dec 1943	1 Mar 1944
PCE 846	Pullman	10 Aug 1943	20 Dec 1943	4 Mar 1944
PCE 847	Pullman	24 Aug 1943	27 Dec 1943	18 Mar 1944
PCE(R) 848	Pullman	7 Sep 1943	21 Jan 1944	30 Mar 1944
PCE(R) 849	Pullman	24 Sep 1943	31 Jan 1944	11 Apr 1944
PCE(R) 850	Pullman	Oct 1943	8 Feb 1944	17 Apr 1944
PCE(R) 851	Pullman	18 Oct 1943	22 Feb 1944	15 May 1944
PCE(R) 852	Pullman	28 Oct 1943	1 Mar 1944	26 May 1944
PCE(R) 853	Pullman	16 Nov 1943	18 Mar 1944	16 Jun 1944
PCE(R) 854	Pullman	24 Nov 1943	27 Mar 1944	4 Jan 1945
PCE(R) 855	Pullman	8 Dec 1943	10 Apr 1944	1 Nov 1944
PCE(R) 856	Pullman	7 Dec 1943	21 Apr 1944	11 Nov 1944
PCE(R) 857	Pullman	21 Dec 1943	4 May 1944	26 Apr 1945
PCE(R) 858	Pullman	3 Jan 1944	13 May 1944	16 May 1945
PCE(R) 859	Pullman	14 Jan 1944	28 Nov 1944	10 Mar 1945
PCE(R) 860	Pullman	25 Jan 1944	30 Jan 1945	31 Mar 1945
PCE(R) 861–66	Pullman	—	—	—

Displacement	640 tons, 903 tons f/l
Dimensions	184'6" (oa); 180' (wl) x 33'1" x 9'5"
Machinery	2 screws; diesel; SHP 2,000; 15.7 knots
Endurance	5,600/9
Complement	99
Armament	1–3"/50, 2 or 3 twin 40mm, 4 or 5–20mm AA; PCE(R) series: 1–3"/50, 2–40mm, 1–20mm

Notes: PC rec PCE, 28 Mar 1943. PCE(R) 842–66 and 935–40 rec PCE, 15 Jul 1943. Originally planned for lend-lease to the United Kingdom, but only PCE 827–41 were transferred as BEC 1–15, had no funnel. PCE848,849, 850 served as headquarters ships.

Service Records:

PCE 827 To UK 14 Jul 1943, renamed HMS *Kilbirnie.* Returned 10 Dec 1946, sold.
Later history: Merchant *Haugesund* 1947, renamed *Lauro Express* 1973, *Sicilia Ponte, Tucalif* 1982. BU 1997.

PCE 828 To UK 31 Jul 1943, renamed HMS *Kilbride.* Returned Nov 1946
Later history: Merchant *Jylland* 1947, renamed *Kibris* 1984, *Akdeniz* 1984, *Princess Lydia* 1988. BU 1988.

PCE 829 To UK 16 Aug 1943, renamed HMS *Kilchattan.* Returned Nov 1946.
Later history: Merchant *Stavanger* 1947, renamed *Kong Sverre* 1973. BU 1981 Hamina, Finland.

PCE 830 To UK 31 Aug 1943, renamed HMS *Kilchrenan.* Returned Nov 1946.
Later history: Merchant *Sunnhordland* 1947, renamed *Kristina Brahe* 1975.

PCE 831 To UK 14 Sep 1943, renamed HMS *Kildary.* Returned Nov 1946.
Later history: Merchant *Rio Agueda* 1947. BU 1980 Durban, South Africa.

PCE 832 To UK 27 Sep 1943, renamed HMS *Kildwick.* Returned Nov 1946.
Later history: Merchant *Sunnfjord* 1947, renamed *Sunnfjord II* 1977, *Kildwick* 1983. Foundered in tow off Feistein Light, Norway, 22 Oct 1983.

PCE 833 To UK 9 Oct 1943, renamed HMS *Kilham.* Returned Nov 1946.
Later history: Merchant *Sognefjord* 1947, renamed *Orion* 1984, *Orion II* 1991, *Orient Explorer* 1997.

PCE 834 To UK 20 Oct 1943, renamed HMS *Kilkenzie.* Returned Nov 1946.
Later history: Merchant *Naddodd* 1947, renamed *Governor Wright* 1952, *Southern Lines* 1954, *Sweet Sail* 1967. BU 1978 Manila.

PCE 835 To UK 30 Oct 1943, renamed HMS *Kilhampton.* Returned Nov 1946.
Later history: Merchant *Georgios F.* BU 1970 Greece.

PCE 836 To UK 6 Nov 1943, renamed HMS *Kilmalcolm.* Returned Nov 1946.
Later history: Merchant *Rio Vouga* 1947, renamed *Rio Star* 1977, *Exportrader* 1979. BU 1980 Durban, South Africa.

PCE 837 To UK 25 Nov 1943, renamed HMS *Kilmarnock.* Returned Nov 1946.
Later history: Merchant *Arion* 1949. Wrecked off Port Lyautey, Morocco, 5 Jan 1951.

PCE 838 To UK 11 Dec 1943, renamed HMS *Kilmartin.* Returned Nov 1946.
Later history: Merchant *Marigoula.* BU 1970 Greece.

PCE 839 To UK 18 Dec 1943, renamed HMS *Kilmelford.* Returned Nov 1946.
Later history: Merchant *Aghios Spyridon* 1950, renamed *St. Matthew* 1971.

PCE 840 To UK 28 Dec 1943, renamed HMS *Kilmington.* Returned Nov 1946.
Later history: Merchant *Athinai* 1947, renamed *Trias* 1955, *Agios Gerassimos* 1961.

PCE 841 To UK 13 Jan 1944, renamed HMS *Kilmore.* Returned Nov 1946.
Later history: Merchant *Despina* 1947, Renamed *Evangelistria* 1970.

PCE 842 Decomm 7 Nov 1947. †

PCE 843 †

PCE 844 Sold to Mexico 24 Nov 1947.
Later history: Renamed *Pedro Sainz de Baranda.* BU 1965.

PCE 845 †

PCE 846 Decomm 11 Jun 1946. †

PCE 847 Decomm 24 Oct 1947. To Mexico 8 Nov 1947.
Later history: Renamed *David Porter.* BU 1965.

PCE(R) 848 Decomm 5 Apr 1946. Stricken 21 May 1946, sold 21 Jan 1947. Tokyo Bay.
2* Leyte, Lingayen.

PCE(R) 849 † Tokyo Bay.
3* Leyte, Lingayen, Tarakan.

PCE(R) 850 † Tokyo Bay.
3* Leyte, Lingayen, Mindanao Ldgs., Visayan Is. Ldgs. Tokyo Bay.

PCE(R) 851 †
3* Leyte, Iwo Jima, Okinawa.

PCE(R) 852 †
3* Leyte, Lingayen, Okinawa.

PCE(R) 853 Decomm Oct 1945. †
3* Leyte, Lingayen, Okinawa.

PCE(R) 854 Sold 24 Oct 1946. †
1* Minesweeping 1945.
Later history: Merchant *Liberty Belle,* renamed *Isla de Tesoro* 1958.

PCE(R) 855 †
1* Okinawa.

PCE(R) 856 Decomm 23 Jun 1946. †
1* Okinawa.

PCE(R) 857 †
PCE(R) 858 To USCG 28 Feb 1946. †
1* Minesweeping 1945.
Later history: USCGC *Jackson* (WPG 120). Sold 23 Dec 1947. Merchant *Jackson* 1950.
PCE(R) 859 Sold 12 Jun 1947.
PCE(R) 860 To USCG 25 Apr 1946.
2* Raids on Japan 7–8/45, Minesweeping 1945.
Later history: USCGC *Bedloe* (WPG 121). Sold 23 Dec 1947. Merchant *Bedloe*, 1949.
PCE(R) 861–66 Canceled 21 Mar 1944.

No.	Builder	Keel Laid	Launched	Comm.
PCE 867	Albina	8 Jul 1942	3 Dec 1942	20 Jun 1943
PCE 868	Albina	11 Aug 1942	29 Jan 1943	31 Aug 1943
PCE 869	Albina	2 Sep 1942	6 Feb 1943	19 Sep 1943
PCE 870	Albina	30 Nov 1942	27 Feb 1943	5 Oct 1943
PCE 871	Albina	2 Dec 1942	10 Mar 1943	29 Oct 1943
PCE 872	Albina	30 Jan 1943	24 Mar 1943	29 Nov 1943
PCE 873	Albina	6 Feb 1943	5 May 1943	15 Dec 1943
PCE 874	Albina	1 Mar 1943	11 May 1943	31 Dec 1943
PCE 875	Albina	10 Mar 1943	27 May 1943	19 Jan 1944
PCE 876	Albina	24 Mar 1943	16 Jul 1943	—
PCE 877	Albina	6 May 1943	11 Aug 1943	14 Feb 1944
PCE 878	Albina	11 May 1943	26 Aug 1943	13 Mar 1944
PCE 879	Albina	27 May 1943	30 Sep 1943	—
PCE 880	Albina	12 Aug 1943	27 Oct 1943	29 Apr 1944
PCE 881	Albina	11 Aug 1943	10 Nov 1943	31 Jul 1944
PCE 882	Albina	26 Aug 1943	3 Dec 1943	23 Feb 1945
PCE 883	Albina	30 Sep 1943	14 Jan 1944	—
PCE 884	Albina	17 Oct 1943	24 Feb 1944	30 Mar 1945
PCE 885	Albina	25 Feb 1944	20 Jun 1944	30 Apr 1945
PCE 886	Albina	29 Mar 1944	10 Jul 1944	31 May 1945
PCE 887–90	Albina	—	—	—
PCE 891	Willamette	28 Oct 1942	24 Apr 1943	15 Jun 1944
PCE 892	Willamette	28 Oct 1942	1 May 1943	8 Jul 1944
PCE 893	Willamette	27 Oct 1942	8 May 1943	25 Jul 1944
PCE 894	Willamette	7 Dec 1942	15 May 1943	10 Aug 1944
PCE 895	Willamette	2 Dec 1942	18 May 1943	30 Oct 1944
PCE 896	Willamette	2 Dec 1942	22 May 1943	27 Nov 1944
PCE 897	Willamette	16 Dec 1942	3 Aug 1943	6 Jan 1945
PCE 898	Willamette	16 Dec 1942	3 Aug 1943	24 Jan 1945
PCE 899	Willamette	11 Jan 1943	11 Aug 1943	17 Mar 1945
PCE–900	Willamette	11 Jan 1943	11 Aug 1943	12 Apr 1945
PCE 901	Willamette	10 May 1943	8 Jul 1943	30 Oct 1944
PCE 902	Willamette	29 Jan 1943	28 Aug 1943	30 Apr 1945
PCE 903	Willamette	18 Feb 1943	6 Sep 1943	16 May 1945
PCE 904	Willamette	18 Feb 1943	9 Sep 1943	31 May 1945
PCE 905–34	Canceled 27 Sep 1943			
PCE(R) 935–40	Canceled 5 Nov 1943			
PCE 941–50	Canceled 5 Nov 1943			
PCE 951–60	Canceled 27 Sep 1943			
PC 961–76	Canceled 5 Nov 1942			

Service Records:

PCE 867 To China 28 Aug 1945.
Later history: Renamed *Yung Tai.* Damaged in action 14 Nov 1965 and BU.
PCE 868 Rec **PCEC 868**, 20 Aug 1945. Rec **PCE 868**, 15 Oct 1945. Decomm 29 Oct 1947, sold to Mexico, 8 Nov 1947.
Later history: Renamed *Virgilio Uribe.* BU 1995.
PCE 869 To China 28 Aug 1945.
Later history: Renamed *Yung Hsiang*, then *Wei Yuan.* R. 1971.
PCE 870 Decomm 18 Oct 1946. †
PCE 871 Decomm 24 Nov 1947, sold to Mexico 24 Nov 1947.
Later history: Renamed *Blas Godinez.* BU 1965.
PCE 872 Rec **PCEC 872**, 20 Aug 1945. Sold 1 Oct 1947, to Cuba.
1* Okinawa.
Later history: Renamed *Caribe.* R.
PCE 873 Rec **PCEC 873**, 20 Aug 1945. Decomm 1947. †
1* Okinawa.
PCE 874 Decomm 25 Nov 1946. †
PCE 875 Decomm 24 Nov 1947, sold to Mexico 24 Nov 1947.
Later history: Renamed *Tomás Marín.* R.
PCE 876 Rec **YDG–8**, 23 Dec 1943, completed as degaussing vessel. Rec **ADG 8**, named ***Lodestone***, 1 Nov 1947. †
PCE 877 Rec **PCEC 877**, 20 Aug 1945. †
2* Iwo Jima, Okinawa. Tokyo Bay.
PCE 878 Completed as minelayer and rec **ACM 4**, named ***Buttress***, 15 Jun 1944. Sold 31 Oct 1947.
Later history: Merchant *Pacific Reefer* 1949, renamed *Aleutian Fjord* 1973, then *Mr. J.*
PCE 879 Rec **YDG–9**, 23 Dec 1943, completed as degaussing vessel. Rec **ADG 9,** named ***Magnet***, 1 Nov 1947. †
PCE 880 †
PCE 881 To Philippines 1 Jun 1948.
Later history: Renamed *Cebu.* R 1975.
PCE 882 †
PCE 883 Rec **YDG–10**, 14 Jun 1944, completed as degaussing vessel. Rec **ADG 10**, named ***Deperm***, 1 Nov 1947. †
PCE 884 To Philippines 1 Jun 1948.
Later history: Renamed *Negros Occidental.* R 1995.
PCE 885 To Philippines 1 Jun 1948.
Later history: Renamed *Leyte.* Lost by grounding 1979.
PCE 886 †
PCE 887–90 Canceled 5 Nov 1943.
PCE 891 Rec **PCE(C) 891**, 20 Aug 1945. Rec **PCE 891**, 15 Oct 1945. To Philippines 1 Jun 1948.
Later history: Renamed *Pangasinan.* R.
PCE 892 Rec **PCE(C) 892**, 20 Aug 1945. Rec **PCE 892**, 15 Oct 1945. Decomm Oct 1947. †
PCE 893 Sold to Cuba 20 Nov 1947.
Later history: Renamed *Siboney.* R.
PCE 894 Decomm 19 Dec 1947. †
PCE 895 †
PCE 896 †
PCE 897 To Philippines 1 Jun 1948.
Later history: Renamed *Iloilo.*
PCE 898 †
PCE 899 †
PCE 900 †
PCE 901 Rec **AG 72**, renamed ***Parris Island***, 28 Apr 1944. Out of service 19 Jun 1947. Stricken 1 Aug 1947; sold 20 Jan 1948.
Later history: Merchant *Parris Island.*
PCE 902 †
PCE 903 †
PCE 904 †
PCE 905–10 Rec AM 232–37.
PCE 911–19 Rec AM 351–59.
PCE 920–34 Canceled 1 Nov 1945.
PCE(R) 935–40 Canceled 5 Nov 1943.
PCE 941–50 Canceled 5 Nov 1943.
PCE 951–60 Canceled 27 Sep 1943.
PC 961–76 Canceled 5 Nov 1942

Figure 8.23: *PCS 1397,* seen here on 4 May 1944 in trials off Newport Beach, California. This is the escort version of the YMS-type minesweeper.

SUBMARINE CHASERS, SWEEPER TYPE

PCS 1376–1465	
Displacement	245 tons, 338 tons f/l'
Dimensions	136' (oa); 130' (wl) x 24'6" x 8'7"
Machinery	2 screws; diesel; SHP 800; 14.1 knots
Complement	57
Armament	1–3"/50, 1–40mm or 1–40mm, 2–20mm

Notes: Fifty-eight completed. PCS 1393–95, 1406–12, 1415–16, 1604–8 were canceled. PCS 1458 rec AGS 6, 27 May 1944. PCS 1388, 1396, 1404, 1457 rec AGS 7–10, 20 Mar 1945. PCS 1389–91, 1399–1403, 1418, 1421, 1429, 1448, 1460–61 rec PCS(C), 20 Aug 1945. PCS rec YMS, 27 Sep 1943. PCS 1464–65 rec AMc 203–4, 10 Jan 1945.

War Losses

PCS(C) 1418 Lost by grounding in typhoon at Okinawa, 9 Oct 1945. Destroyed 15 Dec 1945.

PCS(C) 1461 Lost by grounding in typhoon at Okinawa, 9 Oct 1945. Destroyed 26 Dec 1945.

Builders

Astoria	PCS 1464–65
Ballard	PCS 1457–58
Burger	PCS 1423–24, 1449–50
Colberg	PCS 1402–4
Dachel Carter	PCS 1417–20
Gibbs Gas	PCS 1429–31
Greenport	PCS 1405–12
Harbor Boat	PCS 1441–44
Hiltebrant	PCS 1425–28
Jacob	PCS 1388–95
Mojean	PCS 1455
San Diego Marine	PCS 1445–48
South Coast	PCS 1396–1401
Stadium	PCS 1413–16
W.F. Stone	PCS 1421–22
Tacoma Boat	PCS 1451–52
Western Boat	PCS 1460–61
Wheeler Sbdg	PCS 1375–87

SUBMARINE CHASERS, WOOD

SC 497–508 SC 511–22 SC 524–41 SC 628–775 SC 977–1076 SC 1266–1375 SC 1474–1545	
Displacement	95 tons, 148 f/l
Dimensions	110'10" (oa); 107'5" (wl) x 17' x 6'6"
Machinery	2 screws; diesel; SHP 2,400; 23 knots
Endurance	2,300/12
Complement	28
Armament	1–40mm, 2 to 3 20mm guns

Figure 8.24: *SC 1009,* a typical wood-hull chaser, in trials on 1 Jun 1943.

Figure 8.25: *SC 736,* a wood-hull 110' submarine chaser. Notice the depth charge racks on stern.

Figure 8.26: *SC 1472*, 24 Oct 1943, one of several of the Fairmile design obtained from the United Kingdom.

Figure 8.27: *SC 641*, a wood-hull submarine chaser, on 25 Jul 1943 in the South Pacific.

Notes: SC 644, 757, 1035, 1053, 1056, 1071, 1072, 1366 converted to PGM 1–8, 10 Dec 1943. SC 1494–95, 1500–1501, 1509, 1513–16, 1518–45 canceled. SC 449–50, 453 were experimental types. Fifty were transferred to France, seventy-eight to USSR, and six to Brazil. Seventy-two to USCG as WAVR, 1945.

War Losses

SC 521 Foundered in Santa Cruz Is. area, 10 Jul 1945.
SC 633 Went aground in storm off Palau, 8 Nov 1945; destroyed 4 Apr 1946.
SC 636 Foundered in typhoon at Okinawa 9 Oct 1945.
SC 686 Aground in typhoon at Okinawa; 9 Oct 1945, destroyed 20 Dec 1945.
SC 694 Sunk by German aircraft off Palermo, 23 Aug 1943.
SC 696 Sunk by German aircraft off Palermo, 23 Aug 1943.
SC 700 Destroyed by fire off Vella Lavella, Solomon Is., 10 Mar 1944.
SC 709 Lost by grounding off Cape Breton, Nova Scotia, 21 Jan 1943.
SC 740 Lost by grounding off Great Barrier Reef, 13 Jun 1943
SC 744 Sunk by kamikaze in Tacloban Bay, Leyte, 27 Nov 1944.
SC 751 Lost by grounding off Onslow, Western Australia, 22 Jun 1943.
SC 984 Lost by grounding in New Hebrides, 9 Apr 1944.
SC 999 Went aground in typhoon at Okinawa, 9 Oct 1945; destroyed 14 Dec 1945.
SC 1012 Went aground in typhoon at Okinawa, 9 Oct 1945; destroyed 1 Jan 1946.
SC 1019 Went aground off east coast of Cuba, 22 Apr 1945, sold 1 May 1946.
SC 1024 Sunk in collision with USS *Plymouth* and tanker *Cities Service Fuel* off Cape Hatteras, 2 Mar 1943 (no survivors).
SC 1059 Lost by grounding in Bahamas, 12 Dec 1944.
SC 1067 Foundered off Attu, 10 Nov 1943.
SC 1306 Went aground in typhoon at Okinawa, 9 Oct 1945; destroyed 7 Jan 1946.
PGM 7 (SC 1072) Sunk in collision in Bismarck Sea, 18 Jul 1944.

SC 1466–73	
Displacement	99 tons f/l
Dimensions	111'6" (oa); 108' (wl) x 17'9" x 5'3"
Machinery	2 screws; gas engines
Complement	28
Armament	1–40mm, 2–20mm guns

Note: British Fairmile type, ordered as ML392–399, built in Canada. Reverse Lend-lease.

Figure 8.28: *PT 105* and *PT 106*, Elco-type PT boats, on 12 Jul 1942.

Builders

Abrams	SC 672–73, 678–81, 1333–40
AC&F	SC 450
Amer. Cruiser	SC 511–12, 658–59, 682–87
Annapolis Yt.	SC 521–22, 688–91, 1309–14
Burger	SC 660–61
Calderwood	SC 692–93, 1358–61, 1502–3
Dachel Carter	SC 664–65
Daytona Beach	SC 668–69, 694–97, 1302–8, 1484–87
Delaware Bay	SC 648–49, 698–703, 1325–28
Dingle Boat	SC 1000–1002
Donovan	SC 1029–30, 1504–6
Dooleys Basin	SC 710–11
Elizabeth City	SC 515–18, 638–41, 704–9, 1276–87, 1488–91
Fellows Stewart	SC 1003–12, 1370–75
Fisher Boat	SC 453, 499–500, 662–63, 712–21, 1347–50
Gulf Marine	SC 1057–58
Harbor Boat	SC 722–29

Harris Parsons	SC 1061–62, 1321–24, 1507–9
Hiltebrant	SC 674–75, 730–33
Inland Waterway	SC 670–71, 1059–60
Island Dock	SC 996–99
Kneass	SC 990–95
Knutson	SC 1498–1501
Larson	SC 734–35
Le Blanc	SC 1466–73
Luders	SC 449, 506–506?, 532–35, 1013–22, 1355–57
Mathis	SC 524–29, 630–35, 1023–28, 1067–76
J. E. Matton	SC 985–89
Perkins Vaughan	SC 1065–66, 1298–1301, 1510–16
Peterson	SC 536–39, 642–45, 1031–38, 1517–20
J. Peterson	SC 652–53, 1315–20
Peyton	SC 772–75, 1362–65
Quincy Adams	SC 513–14, 628–29, 744–51, 1266–75, 1474–79
Rice	SC 503–4, 1039–46, 1341–46, 1480–83
Robinson Marine	SC 540–41, 646–48, 752–59
W. A. Robinson	SC 676–77, 760–67, 1288–97
Seabrook	SC 501–2, 768–71
Simms Bros	SC 977–80, 1329–32, 1492–95
Snow	SC 656–57
Ventnor Boat	SC 1047–52
Victory	SC 1063–64
Vineyard Sbdg	SC 519–20, 636–37, 981–84, 1351–54, 1496–97
Weaver	SC 666–67
Westergard	SC 497–98, 530–31, 650–51, 654–55
Wilmington Boat	SC 1053–56, 1366–69
Acquired	SC 523

MOTOR TORPEDO BOATS

No.	Class	Builder	Rec or transfer	Date
PT 1–2	Experimental	Miami Sbdg	rec small boat	24 Dec 1941
PT 3–4	Experimental	Fisher Boat	to UK	—
PT 5–6	Experimental	Higgins	to UK	—
PT 7–8	Experimental	Phila. NYd	to UK	—
PT 9	Experimental	British Power Boat	to UK	—
PT 10–19	PT 10	Elco	to UK	—
PT 20–48	PT 20	Elco	—	—
PT 49–58	—	—	rec BPT 1–10	3 Jul 1941
PT 59–68	PT 20	Elco	—	—
PT 69	Experimental	Huckins	—	—
PT 70	Experimental	Higgins	—	—
PT 71–94	Higgins	Higgins	—	—
PT 95–102	Huckins	Huckins	—	—
PT 103–196	Elco	Elco	—	—
PT 197–254	Higgins	Higgins	—	—
PT 255–264	Huckins	Huckins	—	—
PT 265–313	Higgins	Higgins	—	—
PT 314–367	Elco	Elco	—	—
PT 368–371	Vosper	Canadian Power Bt.	—	—
PT 372–383	Elco	Elco	—	—
PT 384–399	Vosper	Jacob	—	—
PT 400–429	Vosper	Annapolis Yt.	—	—
PT 430–449	Vosper	Herreshoff	—	—
PT 450–485	Higgins	Higgins	—	—
PT 486–563	Elco	Elco	—	—
PT 564	Experimental	Higgins	—	—
PT 565–624	Elco	Elco	—	—
PT 625–660	Higgins	Higgins	—	—
PT 661–730	Vosper	Annapolis Yt.	—	—
PT 731–60	Elco	Elco	—	—
PT 761–90	Elco	Elco	—	—
PT 791–808	Higgins	Higgins	—	—
PTC 1–12	—	Elco	to UK	—
PTC 13–24	—	—	rec PT 33–44	24 Mar 1941
PTC 25–36	—	—	rec PT 57–68	19 Jun 1941
PTC 37–66	Trumpy	Trumpy	rec small boat	1 Aug 1943
BPT 1–10	Elco	Elco	to UK	—
BPT 11–20	—	—	rec PT 59–68	12 Dec 1941
BPT 21–28	Vosper	Trumpy	to UK	—
BPT 29–36	Vosper	Herreshoff	to UK	—
BPT 37–42	Vosper	Jacob	to UK	—
BPT 43–48	Vosper	Harbor Bt	to UK	—
BPT 49–68	Vosper	Trumpy	to UK	—
RPT 1–12	—	—	rec PT 372–383	21 Nov 1942
RPT 13–30	—	—	rec PT 546–563	10 May 1943
RPC 1–16	—	Miami Sbdg	rec small boat	1 Aug 1943
RPC 17–29	—	Miami Sbdg	rec small boat	29 Apr 1943
RPC 30–49	PTC	Miami Sbdg	to USSR	—
RPC 50	—	Miami Sbdg	rec small boat	12 Aug 1943
RPC 51–80	—	—	rec PTC 37–66	31 Mar 1943

Figure 8.29: *PT 428*, a Vosper-type motor torpedo boat, before transfer to the USSR, in 1945.

War Losses

PT 22 Lost in williwaw off Adak I., Alaska, 11 Jun 1943.

PT 28 Lost by grounding in williwaw, Dora Harbor, Unimak I., Alaska, 12 Jan 1943.

PT 31 Lost by grounding in Subic Bay and scuttled, 20 Jan 1942.

PT 32 Scuttled to prevent capture in Sulu Sea, 13 Mar 1942.

Class	Built	Tons	Dimensions	hp	Speed	TT	cpl	Armament
PT 1–2	2	33	59' x 13'9" x 3'2"	—	—	—	—	—
PT 3–4	2	33	58'5" x 13'8" x 3'1"	—	—	—	—	—
PT 5–6	2	53	81'3" x 16'8" x 5'5"	—	—	—	—	—
PT 7–8	2	57	80'7" x 16'8" x 3'3"	—	—	2 TT	—	4 MG
PT 9	1	30	70' x 20' x 4'	3300	44	4 T	12	—
PT 10	10	33	70' x 19'11" x 4'	4050	39	4 T	17	4 MG
PT 20	39	35	77' x 19'11" x 5'6"	4050	39	2 TT	17	4 MG
Elco PT103	273	38	80' x 23 x 5'	4050	41	4 T	17	1–20mm, 4 MG
Higgins PT71	27	43	78' x 19'5" x 5'3"	4050	41	4 T	17	1–20mm, 4 MG
Higgins PT200	194	43	78' x 19'11" x 5'3"	4050	41	4 T	17	2–20mm, 4 MG
Huckins PT95	18	48	78' x 20'8" x 5'	4050	41	4 T	17	1–20mm, 4 MG
Vosper PT368	140	33	70' x 19' x 4'9"	4050	41	2 TT	12	1–20mm, 4 MG
Exp PT 564	1	35	70' x 15'	4050	40	4	12	—
PTC PTC 1–12	12	27	70' x 20' x 4'	—	40	—	11	4 MG
PTC PTC–37	24	25–27	63' x 15'3" x 3'10"	1260	30	—	10	1–20mm, 2 MG

Notes: Engines: 3 screws; PTC 2 screws. PT 7–8 had aluminum hulls. PT 1–4 had 18" TT, others 21". PTC was a subchaser version of the PT. An earlier PT-6 was sold to Finland. PT 368–371 originally ordered by Netherlands in Canada. TT torpedo tubes, T torpedoes carried.

Canceled PT 623–624, 761–790, 797–808

Lead lease:

To UK PT 3–7, 10–19, 88, 90–94, 198, 201, 203–217, PTC 1–12

To USSR PT 85–87, 89, 197, 265–276, 288–294, 400–449, 498–504, 506–508, 552–554, 556, 560–563, 661–687, 731–760, PTC 37–49, 54–66, RPC 1–16, 30–49

PT 33 Lost by grounding at Point Santiago, Subic Bay, Philippines, 15 Dec 1941 (6 killed).
PT 34 Sunk by air attack off Cauit I., near Cebu, Philippines, 9 Apr 1942.
PT 35 Blown up by air attack at Cebu, Philippines, 12 Apr 1942.
PT 37 Sunk by gunfire from Japanese destroyer *Kawakaze*, Guadalcanal, 1 Feb 1943. (16 killed)
PT 41 Sunk by air attack off Lanao, Mindanao, 15 Apr 1942.
PT 43 Sunk by Japanese destroyers off Guadalcanal, 10 Jan 1943.
PT 44 Sunk by Japanese destroyers, off Guadacanal (9 killed), 12 Dec 1942.
PT 63 Sunk by internal explosion at Emirau, New Ireland, 18 Jun 1944.
PT 67 Sunk by explosion, Tufi, New Guinea, 17 Mar 1943.
PT 68 Lost by grounding in Oro Bay, New Guinea, 1 Oct 1943.
PT 73 Lost by grounding off Mindoro, Philippines, 15 Jan 1945.
PT 77 Sunk in error by DE *Lough* and destroyer *Conyngham*, Talin Point, Luzon, 1 Feb 1945 (1 killed).
PT 79 Sunk in error by DE *Lough* and destroyer *Conyngham*, Talin Point, Luzon, 1 Feb 1945 (4 killed).
PT 107 Sunk by explosion of *PT 63* at Emirau, New Ireland, 18 Jun 1944.
PT 109 Sunk by Japanese destroyer *Amagiri* in Blackett Strait, Solomon Is., 2 Aug 1943 (2 killed).
PT 110 Sunk in collision with *PT 114* off Cape Gloucester, 26 Jan 1944.
PT 111 Sunk by Japanese destroyer *Kawakaze* off Guadalcanal, 1 Feb 1943. (2 killed).
PT 112 Sunk by Japanese destroyers *Hatsukaze* and *Tokitsukaze* off Guadalcanal, 10 Jan 1943.
PT 113 Lost by grounding at Buna, New Guinea, 8 Aug 1943.
PT 117 Sunk by air attack off Rendova, Solomon Is., 1 Aug 1943 (4 killed).
PT 118 Lost by grounding off Vella Lavella, Solomon Is., 7 Sep 1943.
PT 119 Sunk by explosion, off Tufi, New Guinea, 17 Mar 1943.
PT 121 Sunk by Australian aircraft in error, Bangula Bay, New Britain, 27 Mar 1944.
PT 123 Sunk by aircraft off Guadalcanal, 1 Feb 1943.
PT 133 Sunk by shore gunfire, Biak, New Guinea, 15 Jul 1944.
PT 135 Lost by grounding, east of Cape Gloucester, New Britain, 12 Apr 1944.
PT 136 Lost by grounding and scuttled, Vitiaz Strait, New Guinea, 17 Sep 1943.
PT 145 Lost by grounding and scuttled, Vitiaz Strait, New Guinea, 4 Jan 1944.
PT 147 Lost by grounding, near Finschhafen, New Guinea, 27 Nov 1943.
PT 153 Lost by grounding, off Munda, New Georgia, 4 Jul 1943.
PT 158 Lost by grounding, off Munda, New Georgia, 5 Jul 1943.
PT 164 Sunk by aircraft off Rendova, Solomon Is., 1 Aug 1943.
PT 165 Sunk by fire en route to Noumea, New Caledonia, 23 May 1943.
PT 166 Sunk by U.S. aircraft in error off Blanche Channel, Solomon Is., 20 Jul 1943.
PT 172 Lost by grounding, off Vella Lavella, Solomon Is., 7 Sep 1943.
PT 173 Sunk by fire en route to Noumea, New Caledonia, 23 May 1943.
PT 193 Lost by grounding, off Noemfoor, New Guinea, 25 Jun 1944.
PT 200 Sunk in collision, off Newport, R.I., 22 Feb 1944.
PT 202 Sunk by mine, Gulf of Frejus, Southern France, 16 Aug 1944.
PT 218 Sunk by mine, Gulf of Frejus, Southern France, 16 Aug 1944.

Figure 8.30: *PT 601*, of the Elco type, 21 Jul 1945. Notice the empty torpedo racks.

PT 219 Floundered in bad weather off Attu, Sep 1943.
PT 239 Burned off Vella Lavella, Solomon Is., 14 Dec 1943.
PT 247 Sunk by shore gunfire, Cape Torokina, Bougainville, 5 May 1944.
PT 251 Sunk by shore gunfire in Empress Augusta Bay, near Bougainville, 26 Feb 1944 (13 killed).
PT 279 Sunk in collision with *PT 282* off Cape Torokina, Bougainville, 11 Feb 1944 (1 killed).
PT 283 Sunk by gunfire, Point Moki, Bougainville, 17 Mar 1944 (4 killed).
PT 300 Sunk by kamikaze off Mindoro, 18 Dec 1944 (10 killed).
PT 301 Sunk by internal explosion, Biak, New Guinea, 7 Nov 1944.
PT 311 Sunk by mine off Corsica, 18 Nov 1944 (10 killed).
PT 320 Sunk by aircraft off Leyte, 5 Nov 1944.
PT 321 Lost by grounding, San Isadoro Bay off Ormoc, Leyte, 11 Nov 1944.
PT 322 Lost by grounding and scuttled, Sansapor, Solomon Is., 23 Nov 1943.
PT 323 Sunk by kamikaze, Ormoc, Leyte, 10 Dec 1944.
PT 337 Sunk by shore gunfire, Hansa Bay, New Guinea, 7 Mar 1944.
PT 338 Lost by grounding, Mindoro, 28 Jan 1945.
PT 339 Lost by grounding, Pur Pur, New Guinea, 27 May 1944.
PT 346 Sunk by aircraft, Cape Pomar, New Britain, 29 Apr 1944.
PT 347 Sunk by aircraft, Cape Pomar, New Britain, 29 Apr 1944.
PT 353 Sunk by Australian aircraft in error, Bangula Bay, New Britain, 27 Mar 1944.
PT 363 Sunk by gunfire, Knoe Bay, Halmahera, Indonesia, 25 Nov 1944 (1 killed).
PT 368 Lost by grounding off Halmahera, Indonesia, 11 Oct 1944.
PT 371 Lost by grounding, at Tagalasa, Halmahera, Molucca Passage, 19 Sep 1944.
PT 493 Damaged by Japanese destroyer and sank in Surigao Strait, 25 Oct 1944(2 killed).
PT 509 Sunk by German MTB off St. Malo, English Channel, 9 Aug 1944 (16 killed).
PT 555 Sunk by mine off Cape Couronne, France, 23 Aug 1944 (5 killed).

9
AMPHIBIOUS VESSELS

LANDING SHIPS DOCK

Ashland Class

No.	Name	Builder	Keel Laid	Launched	Comm.
LSD 1	*Ashland*	Moore	22 Jun 1942	21 Dec 1942	5 Jun 1943
LSD 2	*Belle Grove*	Moore	27 Oct 1942	17 Feb 1943	9 Aug 1943
LSD 3	*Carter Hall*	Moore	27 Oct 1942	4 Mar 1943	18 Sep 1943
LSD 4	*Epping Forest*	Moore	23 Nov 1942	2 Apr 1943	11 Oct 1943
LSD 5	*Gunston Hall*	Moore	28 Dec 1942	1 May 1943	10 Nov 1943
LSD 6	*Lindenwald*	Moore	22 Feb 1943	11 Jun 1943	9 Dec 1943
LSD 7	*Oak Hill*	Moore	9 Mar 1943	25 Jun 1943	5 Jan 1944
LSD 8	*White Marsh*	Moore	7 Apr 1943	19 Jul 1943	29 Jan 1944
LSD 9	—	Newport News	23 Nov 1942	21 May 1943	*14 Sep 1943*
LSD 10	—	Newport News	23 Nov 1942	19 Jul 1943	*19 Oct 1943*
LSD 11	—	Newport News	24 May 1943	18 Nov 1943	*15 Feb 1944*
LSD 12	—	Newport News	23 Jul 1943	29 Dec 1943	*29 Mar 1944*
LSD 13	*Casa Grande*	Newport News	22 Nov 1943	11 Apr 1944	5 Jun 1944
LSD 14	*Rushmore*	Newport News	31 Dec 1943	10 May 1944	3 Jul 1944
LSD 15	*Shadwell*	Newport News	17 Jan 1944	24 May 1944	24 Jul 1944
LSD 16	*Cabildo*	Newport News	24 Jul 1944	22 Dec 1944	15 Mar 1945
LSD 17	*Catamount*	Newport News	7 Aug 1944	27 Jan 1945	9 Apr 1945
LSD 18	*Colonial*	Newport News	21 Aug 1944	28 Feb 1945	15 May 1945
LSD 19	*Comstock*	Newport News	3 Jan 1945	28 Apr 1945	2 Jul 1945
LSD 20	*Donner*	Boston NYd	16 Dec 1944	6 Apr 1945	31 Jul 1945
LSD 21	*Fort Mandan*	Boston NYd	21 Jan 1945	2 Jun 1945	31 Oct 1945
LSD 22	*Fort Marion*	Gulf	15 Sep 1944	22 May 1945	29 Jan 1946

Figure 9.1: *Ashland* (LSD 1), 23 Feb 1946, the first landing ship dock, in San Francisco Bay after the war.

Figure 9.2: *Donner* (LSD 20), landing ship dock, 1948. She is fully loaded, with the dock flooded.

LSD 23	*Fort Snelling*	Gulf	8 Nov 1944	—	—
LSD 24	*Point Defiance*	Gulf	28 May 1945	—	—
	ex–*Hilton Head* (30 Dec 1944)				
LSD 25	*San Marcos*	Phila. NYd	1 Sep 1944	10 Jan 1945	15 Apr 1945
LSD 26	*Tortuga*	Boston NYd	16 Oct 1944	21 Jan 1945	8 Jun 1945
LSD 27	*Whetstone*	Boston NYd	7 Apr 1945	18 Jul 1945	12 Feb 1946

Displacement	9,375 tons f/l; 4,032 tons
Dimensions	457'9" (oa); 454' (wl) x 72'2" x 16'2"
Machinery	2 screws; NN GT; 2 boilers; SHP 7,000; 15.4 knots; LSD 1–9: Skinner Unaflow engines, SHP 7,400; LSD 22–24: West GT, SHP 9,000
Endurance	8,000/15
Complement	326; capacity 240 troops
Armament	1–5"/38, 2 quad 40mm, 2 twin 40mm, 16–20mm AA guns

Notes: Ordered as APM. APM 1–8 rec LSD 1–8 and BAPM 1–7 rec LSD 9–15, 1 Jul 1942. Transfer of LSD 13–15 to United Kingdom was canceled; British names *Portway*, *Swashway*, and *Waterway*. Original planned British names for LSD 9–15 were *Battleaxe*, *Claymore*, *Cutlass*, *Dagger*, *Spear*, *Sword*, and *Tomahawk*. LSD 20–21 originally ordered from Newport News, LSD 22–27 from New York NYd. Designed to transport loaded landing craft to the landing area. The hold was flooded and vessels up to the size of LCI(L) could move in and out under their own power to load and unload. A temporary deck was fitted over the well deck to carry vehicles. These ships were often used to transport small warships such as PTs. LSDs were named for historic sites.

Service Records:

LSD 1 *Ashland* Decomm 30 Aug 1946. †
6* Gilbert Is., Kwajalein, Eniwetok, Saipan, Tinian, Leyte, Lingayen, Iwo Jima.

LSD 2 *Belle Grove* Decomm 30 Aug 1946. †
7* Gilbert Is., Kwajalein, Saipan, Tinian, Leyte, Iwo Jima.

LSD 3 *Carter Hall* Decomm 12 Feb 1947. †
6* Arawe, Admiralty Is., Hollandia, Guam, Morotai, Leyte, Balikpapan.

LSD 4 *Epping Forest* Decomm 25 Mar 1947. †
6* Kwajalein, Hollandia, Guam, Palau, Leyte, Okinawa.

LSD 5 *Gunston Hall* Decomm 7 Jul 1947. †
9* Kwajalein, Admiralty Is., Hollandia, Guam, Palau, Leyte, Mindoro, Iwo Jima, Okinawa. Operation Crossroads.

LSD 6 *Lindenwald* Damaged in error by gunfire, Okinawa, 11 Jun 1945. Decomm 5 Apr 1947. †
5* Kwajalein, Saipan, Okinawa, Leyte, Lingayen.

LSD 7 *Oak Hill* Decomm 17 Mar 1947. †
5* Saipan, Palau, Leyte, Lingayen, Okinawa.

LSD 8 *White Marsh* Decomm Mar 1946. †
5* Saipan, Palau, Leyte, Lingayen, Okinawa.

LSD 9 — To UK, 14 Sep 1943 named HMS *Eastway*. Returned 23 Apr 1946. Sold 19 May 1947.
Later history: To Greece 1953, renamed *Nafkratoussa*. R 1971.

LSD 10 — To UK, 19 Oct 1943 named HMS *Highway*. Returned 23 Apr 1946, sold 17 Mar 1948.
Later history: Merchant *Antonio Maceo*, renamed *Abaco Queen* BU 1960.

LSD 11 — To UK, 15 Feb 1944 named HMS *Northway*. Returned 9 Dec 1946, Sold 19 Mar 1948.
Later history: Merchant *Jose Marti* 1953, renamed *City of Havana*, sold to West German Navy 1962; renamed *WS-1*, merchant *Celtic Ferry* 1966.

LSD 12 — To UK, 29 Mar 1944 named HMS *Oceanway*. Trfd to Greece 13 Feb 1947.
Later history: Renamed *Okeanos*. To France 1952, renamed *Foudre*. Sunk as target 10 Feb 1970.

LSD 13 *Casa Grande* Decomm 23 Oct 1946. †
3* Leyte, Lingayen, Okinawa.

LSD 14 *Rushmore* Decomm 16 Aug 1946. †
2* Leyte, Tarakan.

LSD 15 *Shadwell* Damaged by aircraft torpedo, in Mindanao Sea, Philippines, 24 Jan 1945. Tokyo Bay. Decomm 10 Jul 1947. †

LSD 16 *Cabildo* Decomm 15 Jan 1947. †

LSD 17 *Catamount* Tokyo Bay. †

LSD 18 *Colonial* †

LSD 19 *Comstock* †

LSD 20 *Donner* †

LSD 21 *Fort Mandan* †

LSD 22 *Fort Marion* †

LSD 23 *Fort Snelling* Canceled 17 Aug 1945.
Later history: Completed 1956 as merchant *TMT Carib Queen*. Reacquired by USN as **AK 273**, 1959. †

LSD 24 *Point Defiance* Canceled 17 Aug 1945.

LSD 25 *San Marcos* Operation Crossroads. Decomm 19 Dec 1947. †

LSD 26 *Tortuga* Decomm 18 Aug 1947. †

LSD 27 *Whetstone* †

LANDING SHIPS, VEHICLE

No.	Name	Builder	Keel Laid	Launched	Comm.
LSV 1	*Catskill*	Willamette	12 Jul 1941	19 May 1942	30 Jun 1944
	ex–AP 106 (21 Apr 1944), ex–CM 6 (1 May 1943)				
LSV 2	*Ozark*	Willamette	12 Jul 1941	15 Jun 1942	23 Sep 1944
	ex–AP 107 (21 Apr 1944), ex–CM 7 (1 May 1943)				

Displacement	5,875 tons, 7,600 f/l
Dimensions	455'5" (oa); 440' (wl) x 60'2" x 20'
Machinery	2 screws; GE GT; 4 CE boilers; SHP 11,000; 20.3 knots
Endurance	7,000/15
Complement	564; capacity: 868 troops, 44 DUKW.
Armament	4–5"/38, 4 twin 40mm, 20–20mm AA guns

Notes: Commenced as minelayers and converted while under construction. Designed to transport large numbers of LVTs and DUKWs and troops to the landing area. Stern ramp, two funnels.

Service Records:

LSV 1 *Catskill* Decomm 30 Aug 1946. †
3* Leyte, Lingayen, Okinawa.

LSV 2 *Ozark* Tokyo Bay. Decomm 29 Jun 1946. †
3* Lingayen, Iwo Jima, Okinawa.

Figure 9.3: *Ozark* (LSV 2) on 5 Jan 1946, originally begun as a sister ship of the minelayer *Terror*.

Figure 9.4: *Osage* (LSV 3) on 9 Nov 1945, originally begun as a net laying ship. Notice the snub bow.

Figure 9.5: *LST-946*, 13 Oct 1944, as completed.

No.	Name	Builder	Keel Laid	Launched	Comm.
LSV 3	*Osage*	Ingalls	1 Jun 1943	30 Jun 1943	30 Dec 1944
	ex-AP 108 (21 Apr 1944), ex-AN 3 (1 May 1943)				
LSV 4	*Saugus*	Ingalls	27 Jul 1943	4 Sep 1943	22 Feb 1945
	ex-AP 109 (21 Apr 1944), ex-AN 4 (1 May 1943)				
LSV 5	*Monitor*	Ingalls	21 Oct 1941	29 Jan 1943	18 Mar 1944
	ex-AP 160 (21 Apr 1944), ex-AN 1 (2 Aug 1943)				
LSV 6	*Montauk*	Ingalls	14 Apr 1942	14 Apr 1943	25 May 1944
	ex-AP 161 (21 Apr 1944), ex-AN 2 (2 Aug 1943)				

Displacement	5,625 tons , 9,040 f/l
Dimensions	451'4" (oa); 440' (wl) x 60'3" x 20'
Machinery	2 screws; GE GT; 4 CE boilers; SHP 11,000; 20.3 knots
Complement	564; capacity, LSV 3–4: 1358 troops, 19 LVT, 29 DUKW; capacity, LSV 5–6: 800 troops, 21 LVT, 31 DUKW.
Armament	3–5"/38, 4 twin 40mm, 18–20mm AA guns

Notes: Commenced as large netlayers and converted while under construction. Originally designed to carry and lay a heavy antisubmarine net. LSV 5 *Monitor* completed by Todd Brooklyn. One funnel.

Service Records:

LSV 3 *Osage* Decomm 16 May 1947. †
1* Okinawa.

LSV 4 *Saugus* Decomm 24 Mar 1947. †

LSV 5 *Monitor* Tokyo Bay. Decomm 22 May 1947. †
4* Leyte, Lingayen, Subic Bay. Okinawa.

LSV 6 *Montauk* Converted to net cargo ship and rec **AKN 6**, renamed ***Galilea***, 1 Oct 1946 Decomm . Jul 1947. †
1* Okinawa.

LANDING SHIPS, TANK

No.	Name	Builder	Launched	Comm.
LST 1	—	Dravo Pitt.	7 Sep 1942	14 Dec 1942
LST 2	—	Dravo Pitt.	19 Sep 1942	9 Feb 1943
LST 3	—	Dravo Pitt.	19 Sep 1942	8 Feb 1943
LST 4	—	Dravo Pitt.	9 Oct 1942	14 Feb 1943
LST 5	—	Dravo Pitt.	3 Oct 1942	22 Feb 1943
LST 6	—	Dravo Wilm.	21 Oct 1942	30 Jan 1943
LST 7	—	Dravo Pitt.	31 Oct 1942	2 Mar 1943
LST 8	—	Dravo Pitt.	29 Oct 1942	*22 Mar 1943*
LST 9	—	Dravo Pitt.	14 Nov 1942	*19 Mar 1943*
LST 10	—	Dravo Pitt.	25 Nov 1942	*13 Jan 1943*
LST 11	—	Dravo Pitt.	18 Nov 1942	*22 Mar 1943*
LST 12	—	Dravo Pitt.	7 Dec 1942	*25 Mar 1943*
LST 13	—	Dravo Pitt.	5 Jan 1943	*3 Apr 1943*
LST 14	—	Dravo Pitt.	9 Dec 1942	*26 Mar 1943*
LST 15	—	Dravo Pitt.	30 Jan 1943	*5 Aug 1943*

Displacement	1,625 tons, 4,080 f/l
Dimensions	328' (oa); 316' (wl) x 50' x 14'1"
Machinery	2 screws; GM diesel; SHP 1,700; 11.6 knots
Endurance	24,000/9; 6,000/9 (loaded)
Complement	119
Armament	6–20mm (original); 2 twin 40mm, 4–40mm or 1–3"/50, 1–40mm, 6–20mm guns

Notes: Originally classified ATL. First order for 200 was intended for lend-lease to United Kingdom. 1,052 were built; no names assigned. Bow doors and ramp; fitted to carry LCVP. Originally built with ventilators on deck, later removed to enable stowage of vehicles or an LCT. LST 117–156 originally ordered from St Louis S.B. Co.

LSTs were first used at the Rendova Landings, 30 Jun 1943, and then in Sicily. LST 16, 337, 386, 525, 776, and 906 in the Mediterranean were fitted with a flight deck for small observation planes used for artillery spotting. Ten planes could be carried but there were no landing facilities. Some were fitted for evacuation of wounded and rec LST(H). Later many carried sectional pontoons on each side amidships, to make up "rhino" barges for use when LST could not beach at the shoreline.

Eighty-four were transferred to the United Kingdom on completion, and 36 later, under lend-lease, retained their American numbers. Four were transferred to Greece.

Many were converted for other uses: AGP 10, AKS 4, APB 6, ARB 12, ARL 41, ARST 3, ARV 4. For further details, see those types. Six LST type hulls ordered as APB. In 1946, 100 LSTs were transferred to Shipping Control Authority Japan (SCAJAP) and were Japanese-manned.

Service Records:

LST 1 Decomm 21 May 1946. Stricken 19 Jun 1946; sold 5 Dec 1947; BU Barber, N.J.
4* Sicily, Salerno, Anzio, Normandy.

LST 2 Damaged by coastal gunfire, Normandy, 15 Jun 1944. To UK, 29 Nov 1944–12 Apr 1945. Decomm 11 Apr 1946. Stricken 5 Jun 1946; sold 5 Dec 1947.
4* North Africa, Sicily, Salerno, Normandy.

LST 3 Damaged by German bomber, northeast of Palermo, Sicily, 6 Aug 1943. To UK, 24 Dec 1944–12 May 1946. Stricken 19 Jun 1946, sold 10 Sep 1947; BU Baltimore.
2* Sicily, Southern France.

LST 4 To UK, 24 Dec 1944–12 May 1946. Stricken 19 Jun 1946, sold 10 Sep 1947; BU Baltimore.
4* Sicily, Salerno, Anzio, Southern France.

LST 5 To UK, 18 Nov 1944–29 Nov 1946. Stricken 1 Aug 1947, sold 7 Oct 1947; BU Singapore.
3* Sicily, Salerno, Normandy.

LST 6 Damaged in collision with *LST-326* off Bizerte, Tunisia, 17 Jun 1943. Sunk by mine in Seine River, France, 18 Nov 1944.
3* Sicily, Salerno, Normandy.

LST 7 Decomm 21 May 1946. Stricken 19 Jun 1946, sold 8 Oct 1947; BU.
3* Sicily, Salerno, Normandy.

LST 8 To UK, 22 Mar 1943–4 May 1946. Stricken 3 Jul 1946, sold 5 Dec 1947.

LST 9 To UK, 19 Mar 1943–4 May 1946. Stricken 3 Jul 1946, sold 5 Sep 1948.

LST 10 Completed as repair ship, rec **ARL 1**, renamed ***Achelous***, 13 Jan 1943.

LST 11 To UK, 22 Mar 1943–12 Apr 1946. Stricken 5 Jun 1946, sold 5 Dec 1947.

LST 12 To UK, 25 Mar 1943–5 Jan 1946. Stricken 20 Mar 1946, sold 11 Sep 1947; BU Philipsdale, R.I.

LST 13 To UK, 3 Apr 1943–1 Apr 1946. Converted to fighter direction tender and renamed *FDT-13*, 1944. Stricken 5 Jun 1946, sold 14 Oct 1947; BU Philadelphia.

LST 14 Completed as MTB tender, rec **AGP 5**, renamed ***Varuna***, 25 Jan 1943.

LST 15 Completed as repair ship, rec **ARL 3**, renamed ***Phaon***, 25 Jan 1943.

No.	Builder	Launched	Comm.
LST 16	Dravo Wilm.	19 Dec 1942	17 Mar 1943
LST 17	Dravo Pitt.	8 Jan 1943	19 Apr 1943
LST 18	Dravo Pitt.	15 Feb 1943	26 Apr 1943
LST 19	Dravo Pitt.	11 Mar 1943	15 May 1943
LST 20	Dravo Pitt.	15 Feb 1943	14 May 1943
LST 21	Dravo Wilm.	18 Feb 1943	14 Apr 1943
LST 22	Dravo Pitt.	29 Mar 1943	29 May 1943
LST 23	Dravo Pitt.	13 Mar 1943	22 May 1943
LST 24	Dravo Pitt.	17 Apr 1943	14 Jun 1943
LST 25	Dravo Wilm.	9 Mar 1943	3 May 1943
LST 26	Dravo Pitt.	31 Mar 1943	7 Jun 1943
LST 27	Dravo Pitt.	27 Apr 1943	25 Jun 1943
LST 28	Dravo Pitt.	19 Apr 1943	19 Jun 1943
LST 29	Dravo Pitt.	17 May 1943	10 Jul 1943
LST 30	Dravo Pitt.	3 May 1943	3 Jul 1943
LST 31	Dravo Pitt.	5 Jun 1943	21 Jul 1943
LST 32	Dravo Pitt.	22 May 1943	12 Jul 1943
LST 33	Dravo Pitt.	21 Jun 1943	*4 Aug 1943*
LST 34	Dravo Pitt.	15 Jun 1943	26 Jul 1943
LST 35	Dravo Pitt.	30 Jun 1943	*18 Aug 1943*
LST 36	Dravo Pitt.	21 Jul 1943	*23 Aug 1943*
LST 37	Dravo Pitt.	5 Jul 1943	*18 Aug 1943*
LST 38	Dravo Pitt.	27 Jul 1943	3 Sep 1943
LST 39	Dravo Pitt.	29 Jul 1943	8 Sep 1943
LST 40	Dravo Pitt.	7 Aug 1943	15 Sep 1943
LST 41	Dravo Pitt.	17 Aug 1943	24 Sep 1943
LST 42	Dravo Pitt.	17 Aug 1943	30 Sep 1943
LST 43	Dravo Pitt.	28 Aug 1943	6 Oct 1943
LST 44	Dravo Pitt.	11 Sep 1943	22 Oct 1943
LST 45	Dravo Pitt.	31 Aug 1943	15 Oct 1943
LST 46	Dravo Pitt.	16 Sep 1943	3 Nov 1943
LST 47	Dravo Pitt.	24 Sep 1943	8 Nov 1943
LST 48	Dravo Pitt.	2 Oct 1943	16 Nov 1943
LST 49	Dravo Pitt.	9 Oct 1943	20 Nov 1943
LST 50	Dravo Pitt.	16 Oct 1943	27 Nov 1943
LST 51	Dravo Pitt.	22 Oct 1943	8 Dec 1943
LST 52	Dravo Pitt.	20 Oct 1943	15 Dec 1943
LST 53	Dravo Pitt.	6 Nov 1943	21 Dec 1943
LST 54	Dravo Pitt.	13 Nov 1943	24 Dec 1943
LST 55	Dravo Pitt.	20 Nov 1943	6 Jan 1944
LST 56	Dravo Pitt.	27 Nov 1943	10 Jan 1944
LST 57	Dravo Pitt.	4 Dec 1943	15 Jan 1944
LST 58	Dravo Pitt.	11 Dec 1943	22 Jan 1944
LST 59	Dravo Pitt.	18 Dec 1943	31 Jan 1944
LST 60	Dravo Pitt.	24 Dec 1943	7 Feb 1944

Service Records:

LST 16 USCG. Decomm 8 Mar 1946. Stricken 12 Apr 1946, sold 5 Dec 1947; BU, Barber, N.J.
5* Tunisia, Sicily, Salerno, Anzio, Normandy.

LST 17 USCG. Decomm 15 Jan 1946.
1* Normandy.
Later history: SCAJAP, as Q015. †

LST 18 USCG. Decomm 3 Apr 1946. Stricken 17 Apr 1946, sold 10 Dec 1946.
Later history: Merchant *Rosario* 1948.

LST 19 USCG. Rec **LST(H) 19**, 15 Sep 1945. Decomm 20 Mar 1946. Stricken 1 May 1946, sold 5 Dec 1947; BU Barber, N.J.
4* Gilbert Is., Saipan, Tinian, Palau.

LST 20 USCG. Decomm 3 Apr 1946. Stricken 19 Jun 1946, sold 8 Oct 1947; BU.
4* Gilbert Is., Leyte, Lingayen, Okinawa.

LST 21 USCG. Decomm 25 Jan 1946. Stricken 19 Jun 1946, sold 12 Mar 1948; BU.
1* Normandy.

LST 22 USCG. Decomm 1 Apr 1946. Stricken 17 Apr 1946, sold 3 Feb 1947.
8* Cape Gloucester, Saidor, Admiralty Is. Ldgs., Hollandia, Wakde, Biak, Noemfoor I., Cape Sansapor, Morotai, Leyte, Lingayen.
Later history: Merchant *Hwai Yuan* 1948, renamed *Chung 127*, 1951.

LST 23 USCG. Rec **LST(H) 23**, 15 Sep 1945. Decomm 24 May 1946. Stricken 3 Jul 1946, sold 6 Apr 1948; BU Seattle.
6* Gilbert Is., Kwajalein, Saipan, Tinian, Palau, Lingayen.

LST 24 USCG. Decomm 26 Feb 1946. Stricken 5 Jun 1946, sold 23 Dec 1947.
5* Guam, Morotai, Leyte, Lingayen, Okinawa.
Later history: Merchant barge *Humble ST-5*, renamed *World-Over ST-5* 1964, *Diamond M Offshore ST-5* 1968.

LST 25 USCG. Stricken 8 Oct 1946, sold 31 Mar 1948; BU Seattle.
2* Normandy, Okinawa. Decomm 2 Aug 1946.

LST 26 USCG. Decomm 1 Apr 1946. Stricken 8 May 1946, sold 1 Jul 1946.
5* Cape Gloucester, Hollandia, Wakde, Biak, Noemfoor I., Cape Sansapor, Leyte, Mindanao Ldgs.
Later history: Merchant *A.T.T. No. 2*, 1947.

LST 27 USCG. Decomm 9 Nov 1945. Stricken 28 Nov 1945, sold 15 Dec 1947; BU.
2* Convoy UGS-36, Normandy.

LST 28 Decomm 16 Aug 1946. Stricken 29 Oct 1946, sold 19 May 1948; BU.
2* Convoy UGS-36, Normandy.

LST 29 Decomm 11 Mar 1946. Stricken 8 May 1946, sold 17 Jun 1946.
4* Gilbert Is., Kwajalein, Eniwetok, Guam, Okinawa.

Later history: Merchant barge *Foss 200;* renamed *Pelican* 19., *Del Norte Woodsman* 19.

LST 30 Decomm 6 Mar 1946. Stricken 8 May 1946, sold 1 Apr 1947.
1* Normandy.
Later history: Merchant barge *Cap.* To 1960.

LST 31 Decomm 8 Jan 1946.
5* Gilbert Is., Kwajalein, Eniwetok, Saipan, Tinian, Okinawa.
Later history: SCAJAP, as Q005. †

LST 32 Decomm Jul 1946. †
2* Convoy UGS-36, Southern France.

LST 33 To Greece 18 Aug 1943.
Later history: Renamed *Samos.* R 1977.

LST 34 Decomm 15 Nov 1946. To USMG Ryukyus 18 Jul 1946. Stricken 23 Dec 1947. Ran aground and lost, 9 Jan 1949.
6* Gilbert Is., Kwajalein, Eniwetok, Saipan, Leyte, Lingayen, Okinawa.

LST 35 To Greece 18 Aug 1943.
Later history: Renamed *Chios.* R 1977.

LST 36 To Greece 23 Aug 1943
Later history: Renamed *Lemnos.* R 1977.

LST 37 To Greece 18 Aug 1943.
Later history: Renamed *Lesvos.* Ran aground off Bizerte and sank, 6 Jan 1944.

LST 38 Rec **LST(H) 38,** 15 Sep 1945. Decomm 26 Mar 1946. Stricken 1 May 1946, sold 5 Dec 1947; BU Barber, N.J.
5* Kwajalein, Admiralty Is. Ldgs., Hollandia, Guam, Iwo Jima.

LST 39 Sunk by accidental ammunition explosion at Pearl Harbor, 21 May 1944, not repaired. Stricken 18 Jul 1944. Rec **YF 1079,** 21 Aug 1944. Destroyed 22 Aug 1946.

LST 40 Decomm 18 Feb 1946.
4* Solomons, Saipan, Tinian, Okinawa.
Later history: SCAJAP, as Q066. To USMG Korea, 18 Feb 1947. Stricken 5 Mar 1947.

LST 41 Rec **LST(H) 41,** 15 Sep 1945. Decomm 25 Apr 1946. Stricken 19 Jun 1946, sold 8 Oct 1947; BU.
5* Kwajalein, Hollandia, Guam, Palau, Lingayen.

LST 42 Rec **LST(H) 42,** 15 Sep 1945. Decomm 26 Jul 1946. Stricken 25 Sep 1946, sold 20 Mar 1948; BU Seattle.
4* Kwajalein, Eniwetok, Saipan, Tinian, Palau, Iwo Jima.

LST 43 Sunk by accidental ammunition explosion at Pearl Harbor, 21 May 1944.
1* Kwajalein.

LST 44 Decomm 20 Feb 1946.
1* Normandy.
Later history: SCAJAP, as Q068. Stricken 28 Aug 1947. Destroyed 23 Jul 1947.

LST 45 Decomm 30 Nov 1948. Stricken 22 Dec 1948, sold 25 Feb 1949.
4* Kwajalein, Saipan, Tinian, Okinawa.
Later history: Merchant barge *Foss 204,* renamed *Sanitary 3*

LST 46 Decomm 6 Jun 1946. Stricken 19 Jun 1946, sold 13 Feb 1948.
3* Normandy, Southern France, Okinawa.

LST 47 Decomm 11 Jan 1946
3* Normandy, Southern France, Okinawa.
Later history: SCAJAP, as Q007. †

LST 48 Decomm 8 Feb 1946.
3* Normandy, Southern France, Okinawa.
Later history: SCAJAP, as Q049. Stricken 5 Dec 1947, sold 27 May 1948; BU.

LST 49 Decomm 11 Jun 1946. Stricken 3 Jul 1946, sold 5 Dec 1947.
3* Normandy, Southern France, Okinawa.

LST 50 Decomm 6 Feb 1946.
3* Normandy, Southern France, Okinawa.
Later history: SCAJAP, as Q046. †

LST 51 Decomm 6 Mar 1946.
3* Normandy, Southern France, Okinawa.
Later history: SCAJAP, as Q089. Stricken 31 Oct 1947, sold 20 Apr 1948; BU.

LST 52 Decomm 29 Aug 1946. Bikini target. Sunk as target 19 Apr 1948. Stricken 30 Apr 1948.
1* Normandy.

LST 53 Decomm 1946.
3* Normandy, Southern France, Okinawa.
Later history: SCAJAP, as Q021. †

LST 54 Decomm 5 Nov 1945. Stricken 28 Nov 1945, sold 22 Mar 1948; BU Bayonne, N.J.
1* Normandy.

LST 55 Decomm 11 Dec 1945. Stricken 3 Jan 1946, sold 23 Mar 1948.
1* Normandy.
Later history: Merchant barge *TMT Puerto Rico.* BU 1963.

LST 56 Decomm 23 May 1946. Stricken 3 Jul 1946, sold 5 Dec 1947; BU Barber, N.J.
1* Normandy.

LST 57 Decomm 24 Jan 1946.
1* Normandy.
Later history: SCAJAP, as Q028. †

LST 58 Decomm 7 Nov 1945. Stricken 28 Nov 1945, sold 30 Nov 1947; BU Philadelphia.
1* Normandy.

LST 59 Decomm 23 Jan 1946. Stricken 25 Feb 1946, sold 18 Sep 1947; BU New Orleans.
1* Normandy.

LST 60 Decomm 27 Jun 1946. †
1* Normandy.

No.	Builder	Launched	Comm.
LST 61	Jeffersonville	8 Nov 1942	5 Feb 1943
LST 62	Jeffersonville	23 Nov 1942	*3 Mar 1943*
LST 63	Jeffersonville	19 Dec 1942	*15 Mar 1943*
LST 64	Jeffersonville	8 Jan 1943	*2 Apr 1943*
LST 65	Jeffersonville	7 Dec 1942	*15 Mar 1943*
LST 66	Jeffersonville	16 Jan 1943	12 Apr 1943
LST 67	Jeffersonville	28 Jan 1943	20 Apr 1943
LST 68	Jeffersonville	8 Mar 1943	4 Jun 1943
LST 69	Jeffersonville	20 Feb 1943	20 May 1943
LST 70	Jeffersonville	8 Feb 1943	28 May 1943
LST 71	Jeffersonville	27 Feb 1943	9 Jun 1943
LST 72	Jeffersonville	17 Mar 1943	5 Jun 1943
LST 73	Jeffersonville	29 Mar 1943	8 Jun 1943
LST 74	Jeffersonville	31 Mar 1943	15 Jun 1943
LST 75	Jeffersonville	7 Apr 1943	21 Jun 1943
LST 76	Jeffersonville	14 Apr 1943	26 Jun 1943
LST 77	Jeffersonville	21 Apr 1943	3 Jul 1943
LST 78	Jeffersonville	28 Apr 1943	8 Jul 1943
LST 79	Jeffersonville	8 May 1943	7 Jul 1943
LST 80	Jeffersonville	18 May 1943	12 Jul 1943
LST 81	Jeffersonville	28 May 1943	21 Jul 1943
LST 82	Jeffersonville	9 Jun 1943	*26 Jul 1943*
LST 83	Jeffersonville	14 Jun 1943	*6 Aug 1943*
LST 84	Jeffersonville	26 Jun 1943	14 Aug 1943
LST 85–116	—	—	—
LST 117	Jeffersonville	10 Jul 1943	27 Aug 1943
LST 118	Jeffersonville	21 Jul 1943	6 Sep 1943
LST 119	Jeffersonville	28 Jul 1943	1 Sep 1943

LST 120	Jeffersonville	7 Aug 1943	22 Sep 1943
LST 121	Jeffersonville	16 Aug 1943	29 Sep 1943

Service Records:

LST 61 Decomm 5 Jun 1946. Stricken 19 Jun 1946, sold 2 Jun 1947.
2* Sicily, Normandy.
Later history: Merchant *Southern States* 1948, renamed *Gladys* 1956. BU 1960 Wilmington, Del.

LST 62 To UK 3 Mar 1943–10 Jun 1946. Stricken 19 Jul 1946, sold 12 May 1948; BU Philadelphia.

LST 63 To UK 15 Mar 1943–17 Dec 1945. Stricken 21 Jan 1946, sold 27 May 1948.
Later history: Merchant *Northampton* 1948, renamed *Salvatierra* 1968. Wrecked in San Lorenzo Channel, west coast of Mexico, 19 Jun 1976.

LST 64 To UK 2 Apr 1943–12 Oct 1946. Returned damaged, stranded at Naples 26 Feb 1944. Stricken 5 Dec 1945, sold 3 Jul 1946.
Later history: Merchant *Clarus.*

LST 65 To UK 15 Mar 1943–5 Jan 1946. Stricken 20 Mar 1946, sold 4 May 1948; BU Philadelphia.

LST 66 USCG. Damaged by aircraft bomb, Cape Gloucester, 26 Dec 1943. Decomm 26 Mar 1946. Stricken 1 May 1946, sold 7 Apr 1948; BU Seattle.
9* Cape Gloucester, Saidor, Admiralty Is. Ldgs., Hollandia, Wakde, Biak, Noemfoor I., Cape Sansapor, Morotai, Palau, Leyte, Lingayen, Mindanao Ldgs., Balikpapan.

LST 67 USCG. Decomm 28 Mar 1946. Stricken 8 May 1946, sold 5 Dec 1947; BU Barber, N.J.
7* Finschhafen, Cape Gloucester, Saidor, Admiralty Is. Ldgs., Hollandia, Wakde, Biak, Noemfoor I., Cape Sansapor, Morotai, Leyte, Visayan Is. Ldgs., Tarakan, Balikpapan.

LST 68 USCG. Decomm 7 Mar 1946. Stricken 5 Jun 1946, sold 18 Sep 1947; BU New Orleans.
8* Cape Gloucester, Saidor, Admiralty Is. Ldgs., Hollandia, Biak, Noemfoor I., Cape Sansapor, Morotai, Leyte, Lingayen, Visayan Is. Ldgs., Tarakan, Balikpapan.

LST 69 USCG. Sunk by accidental ammunition explosion at Pearl Harbor, 21 May 1944.
1* Gilbert Is.

LST 70 USCG. Damaged by grounding, Okinawa, 4 Apr 1945. Decomm 1 Apr 1946. Stricken 1 May 1946, sold 1 Jul 1946; BU Seattle.
5* Cape Torokina, Green Is. Ldgs., Guam, Iwo Jima, Okinawa.

LST 71 USCG. Decomm 25 Mar 1946. Stricken 8 May 1946, sold 23 Jan 1948.
3* Treasury Is. Ldgs., Guam, Okinawa.
Later history: Merchant *Dona Rosa* 1948, renamed *Maria Sasso* 1968. BU 1974.

LST 72 Decomm 4 Jun 1946. Stricken 19 Jun 1946; To Philippines 8 Jun 1948
1* Normandy.
Later history: Renamed *San Fernando* 1949. BU1959 Hong Kong.

LST 73 Decomm 13 Jul 1946. Stricken 10 Jun 1947, sold 31 Mar 1948; BU Seattle.
1* Normandy.

LST 74 Decomm 21 Dec 1945. Stricken 21 Jan 1946, sold 22 Sep 1947; BU New Orleans.
2* Convoy UGS-36, Southern France.

LST 75 Decomm 22 Dec 1947 and trfd to Philippines, 30 Dec 1947.
1* Normandy.
Later history: Renamed *Cotabato.* R 1964.

LST 76 To UK 24 Dec 1944–23 Apr 1946. Stricken 19 Jun 1946, sold 21 Apr 1948.
2* Convoy UGS-37, Southern France.
Later history: Merchant *Southern Isles* 1948. Foundered in hurricane 190 miles southeast of Cape Hatteras, 5 Oct 1951.

LST 77 To UK 24 Dec 1944–12 May 1946. Stricken 19 Jun 1946, sold 7 Nov 1947; BU.
2* Convoy UGS-37, Southern France.

LST 78 Decomm 8 Mar 1946. Stricken 8 May 1946, sold 13 Apr 1948; BU Seattle.
4* Gilbert Is., Kwajalein, Guam, Okinawa.

LST 79 To UK 17 Jul 1943. Sunk by German aircraft at Ajaccio, Corsica, 30 Sep 1943.

LST 80 To UK 19 Jul 1943. Sunk by mine off Ostend, 20 Mar 1945.

LST 81 Completed as repair ship, rec **ARL 5**, 20 Jul 1943. To UK 29 Jul 1943–21 May 1946, named *LSE-1.* Stricken 29 Oct 1946.
Later history: To Argentina 20 Aug 1947, renamed *Ingeniero Iribas.* R 1967.

LST 82 Completed as repair ship, rec **ARL 6**, 20 Jul 1943. To UK 2 Aug 1943–21 May 1946, as *LSE-2.* Stricken 29 Oct 1946.
Later history: To Argentina 20 Aug 1947, renamed *Ingeniero Gadda.* R60, merchant *Tierra del Fuego.* RR 1967.

LST 83 Completed as repair ship, rec **ARL 4**, renamed ***Adonis***, 26 Aug 1943.

LST 84 Damaged by U.S. gunfire in error, Saipan, 17 Jun 1944. Rec **LST(H) 84**, 15 Sep 1945. Decomm 2 Mar 1946.
5* Gilbert Is., Kwajalein, Saipan, Tinian, Iwo Jima.
Later history: SCAJAP, as Q080. Stricken 31 Oct 1947, sold 20 Apr 1948; BU Seattle.

LST 85–116 Canceled 16 Sep 1942.

LST 117 Rec **LST(H) 117**, 15 Sep 1945. Decomm 16 Feb 1946.
2* Guam, Leyte.
Later history: SCAJAP, as Q063. †

LST 118 Rec **LST(H) 118**, 15 Sep 1945. Decomm 8 Feb 1946.
3* Hollandia, Guam, Leyte.
Later history: SCAJAP, as Q048. Stricken 29 Sep 1947, sold 28 Apr 1948; BU Seattle.

LST 119 Damaged by coastal gunfire, Saipan, 22 Jun 1944. Decomm 13 May 1946. Stricken 19 Jun 1946; sold as barge 17 May 1948.
2* Kwajalein, Saipan.

LST 120 Decomm 7 Jan 1946.
2* Saipan, Tinian.
Later history: SCAJAP, as Q004. To USMG, Korea, Feb 1947. Stricken 5 Mar 1947. Probably merchant *Munsan.* Lost by grounding at Changsadong while trying to land guerrillas behind enemy lines, 15 Sep 1950.

LST 121 Damaged by collision and grounding, Iwo Jima, 26 Feb 1945. Rec **LST(H) 121**, 15 Sep 1945. Decomm 21 Mar 1946. Stricken 1 May 1946, sold 14 Apr 1946; BU Chester, Pa.
5* Kwajalein, Saipan, Tinian, Palau, Iwo Jima.

No.	Builder	Launched	Comm.
LST 122	Missouri Valley	9 Aug 1943	3 Sep 1943
LST 123	Missouri Valley	14 Aug 1943	7 Sep 1943
LST 124	Missouri Valley	18 Aug 1943	24 Sep 1943
LST 125	Missouri Valley	23 Aug 1943	29 Sep 1943
LST 126	Missouri Valley	28 Aug 1943	2 Oct 1943
LST 127	Missouri Valley	31 Aug 1943	6 Oct 1943
LST 128	Missouri Valley	3 Sep 1943	11 Oct 1943
LST 129	Missouri Valley	8 Sep 1943	23 Oct 1943
LST 130	Missouri Valley	13 Sep 1943	4 Nov 1943
LST 131	Missouri Valley	18 Sep 1943	15 Nov 1943
LST 132	Chicago Bridge	26 Oct 1943	*23 Dec 1943*
LST 133	Chicago Bridge	2 Nov 1943	29 Nov 1943
LST 134	Chicago Bridge	9 Nov 1943	7 Dec 1943
LST 135	Chicago Bridge	16 Nov 1943	*25 Apr 1944*
LST 136	Chicago Bridge	23 Nov 1943	*9 May 1944*
LST 137	Amer. Bridge	19 Dec 1943	26 Jan 1944
LST 138	Amer. Bridge	30 Dec 1943	5 Feb 1944
LST 139	Amer. Bridge	12 Jan 1944	14 Feb 1944

LST 140	Amer. Bridge	8 Jan 1944	9 Feb 1944
LST 141	Amer. Bridge	16 Jan 1944	16 Feb 1944
LST 142–56	—	—	—
LST 157	Missouri Valley	31 Oct 1942	10 Feb 1943
LST 158	Missouri Valley	16 Nov 1942	10 Feb 1943
LST 159	Missouri Valley	21 Nov 1942	*13 Feb 1943*
LST 160	Missouri Valley	30 Nov 1942	*18 Feb 1943*
LST 161	Missouri Valley	7 Dec 1942	*28 Feb 1943*
LST 162	Missouri Valley	3 Feb 1943	*15 Mar 1943*
LST 163	Missouri Valley	4 Feb 1943	*24 Mar 1943*
LST 164	Missouri Valley	5 Feb 1943	*30 Mar 1943*
LST 165	Missouri Valley	2 Feb 1943	*3 Apr 1943*
LST 166	Missouri Valley	1 Feb 1943	22 Apr 1943
LST 167	Missouri Valley	25 Feb 1943	27 Apr 1943
LST 168	Missouri Valley	25 Feb 1943	3 May 1943
LST 169	Missouri Valley	26 Feb 1943	22 May 1943
LST 170	Missouri Valley	27 Feb 1943	31 May 1943
LST 171	Missouri Valley	28 Feb 1943	5 Jun 1943
LST 172	Missouri Valley	12 May 1943	11 Jun 1943
LST 173	Missouri Valley	24 Apr 1943	18 Jun 1943
LST 174	Missouri Valley	21 Apr 1943	15 Jun 1943
LST 175	Missouri Valley	18 Apr 1943	19 May 1943
LST 176	Missouri Valley	15 Apr 1943	12 May 1943
LST 177	Missouri Valley	16 May 1943	22 Jun 1943
LST 178	Missouri Valley	23 May 1943	21 Jun 1943
LST 179	Missouri Valley	30 May 1943	3 Jul 1943
LST 180	Missouri Valley	3 Jun 1943	29 Jun 1943

Service Records:

LST 122 Decomm 4 Jun 1946. Stricken 3 Jul 1946, sold 5 Dec 1947.
5* Kwajalein, Hollandia, Wewak, Guam, Okinawa.

LST 123 Rec **LST(H) 123**, 15 Sep 1945. Decomm 22 Mar 1946. Stricken 1 May 1946, sold 30 Mar 1948; BU Chester, Pa.
3* Guam, Leyte, Lingayen.

LST 124 Decomm 26 Jul 1946. Stricken 28 Aug 1946, sold 13 Dec 1947; BU Seattle.
3* Saipan, Tinian, Okinawa.

LST 125 Decomm 10 Jun 1946. Sunk as target, Bikini, 25 Aug 1946. Stricken 25 Sep 1946.
4* Guam, Leyte, Lingayen, Okinawa.

LST 126 Decomm 17 Jun 1946. Stricken 23 Jun 1947, sold 14 Jun 1948.
3* Kwajalein, Saipan, Leyte.

LST 127 Decomm 11 Mar 1947. Stricken 10 Jun 1947, sold 11 Jun 1948; BU.
4* Kwajalein, Eniwetok, Saipan, Tinian, Palau, Lingayen.

LST 128 Decomm 23 Mar 1946; Stricken 17 Apr 1946.
4* Kwajalein, Saipan, Tinian, Palau.

LST 129 Went aground in storm at Peleliu, Palau, 2 Oct 1944. Rec **IX 198**, renamed ***Cohasset***, 31 Dec 1944. Decomm 20 Jan 1945. Stricken 19 Jun 1946; destroyed 16 May 1946.
3* Saipan, Tinian, Palau.

LST 130 Decomm 10 Mar 1946.
2* Saipan, Okinawa.
Later history: SCAJAP, as Q093. Stricken 5 Dec 1947, sold 27 May 1948; BU Seattle.

LST 131 Decomm 20 May 1946. Stricken 10 Jun 1947, sold 6 Apr 1948; BU Seattle.
3* Saipan, Tinian, Palau.

LST 132 Completed as repair ship, rec **ARB 4**, renamed ***Zeus***, 3 Nov 1943.

LST 133 Damaged by mine, Normandy, 15 Jun 1944. Bikini target. Decomm 29 Aug 1946. Sunk as target, 11 May 1948.

LST 134 Decomm 17 Feb 1946.
3* Normandy, Southern France, Okinawa.
Later history: SCAJAP, as Q064. Stricken 31 Oct 1947, sold 20 Apr 1948; BU Seattle.

LST 135 Completed as MTB tender, rec **AGP 10**, renamed *Orestes*, 3 Nov 1943.

LST 136 Completed as repair ship, rec **ARL 8**, renamed ***Egeria***, 3 Nov 1943.

LST 137 Decomm 20 Nov 1945. Stricken 5 Dec 1945, sold 26 Mar 1948.
1* Normandy.
Later history: Merchant *Laura*. BU 1961.

LST 138 Decomm 20 Nov 1945. Stricken 5 Dec 1945, sold 16 Jun 1947.
1* Normandy.
Later history: Merchant *Altalena*. Destroyed by gunfire at Tel Aviv, 22 Jun 1948.

LST 139 Decomm 25 Mar 1946. Stricken 8 May 1946, sold 22 Apr 1947.
1* Normandy. Later history: Merchant barge *McWilliams 734*, renamed *M.O.P. 376–B* 1948.

LST 140 Decomm 5 Jan 1946. Stricken 12 Mar 1946, sold 18 Sep 1947; BU New Orleans.
2* Convoy UGS-36, Southern France.

LST 141 Decomm 18 Dec 1945. Stricken 7 Feb 1946, sold 25 May 1948; BU.
1* Southern France.

LST 142–56 Canceled 16 Sep 1942.

LST 157 To UK 9 Dec 1944–11 Apr 1946. Stricken 5 Jun 1946, sold 5 Dec 1947.
3* Sicily, Salerno, Normandy.

LST 158 Damaged by German aircraft at Licata, Sicily, beached and abandoned, 11 Jul 1943.
2* Tunisia, Sicily.

LST 159 To UK 3 Mar 1943–23 Apr 1946. Stricken 19 Jun 1946, sold 27 Apr 1948 (for conv).

LST 160 To UK 6 Mar 1943–4 May 1946. Stricken 3 Jul 1946, sold 1 Nov 1947.

LST 161 To UK 15 Mar 1943–5 Jan 1946. Stricken 20 Mar 1946, sold 7 May 1948; BU Philadelphia.

LST 162 To UK 22 Mar 1943–1 Feb 1946. Stricken 19 Jun 1946, sold 9 Oct 1947; BU Philadelphia.

LST 163 To UK 29 Mar 1943–29 Nov 1946. Stricken 1 Aug 1947, sold 29 Jul 1947.
Later history: Merchant *Chip Lam.*

LST 164 To UK 5 Apr 1943–29 Nov 1946. Stricken 1 Aug 1947, sold 7 Oct 1947 (for conv).

LST 165 To UK 6 Apr 1943–20 Mar 1946. Stricken 5 Jun 1946, sold 15 Dec 1947; BU Philadelphia.

LST 166 USCG. Damaged by grounding, Okinawa, 4 Apr 1945. Decomm 3 May 1946. Stricken 19 Jun 1946, sold 3 Nov 1947; BU Seattle.
3* Cape Torokina, Saipan, Okinawa.

LST 167 USCG. Damaged by dive bomber, Vella Lavella, irreparably damaged, 25 Sep 1943 (10 killed). Used for ammunition storage until 1948.
1* Ldgs. on Vella Lavella.

LST 168 USCG. Decomm 14 Mar 1946. Stricken 12 Apr 1946, sold 9 Apr 1948; BU.
8* Finschhafen, Cape Gloucester, Saidor, Admiralty Is. Ldgs., Hollandia, Morotai, Leyte, Mindanao Ldgs., Lingayen, Balikpapan.

LST 169 USCG. Decomm 12 Apr 1946. Stricken 19 Jun 1946, sold 24 Oct 1947; BU.
3* Gilbert Is., Saipan, Leyte.

LST 170 USCG. Damaged by bomber off Finschhafen, New Guinea, 10 Feb 1944. Decomm 6 Apr 1946. Stricken 3 Jul 1946, sold 10 Nov 1947; BU Biloxi, Miss.
7* Cape Gloucester, Saidor, Admiralty Is. Ldgs., Hollandia, Wakde, Biak, Cape Sansapor, Morotai, Leyte, Mindoro, Lingayen, Mindanao Ldgs.

LST 171 Decomm 21 May 1946. Stricken 3 Jul 1946, sold 26 Sep 1947; BU Baltimore.
7* Cape Gloucester, Saidor, Admiralty Is. Ldgs., Hollandia, Biak, Cape Sansapor, Morotai, Leyte, Visayan Is. Ldgs., Tarakan, Balikpapan.

LST 172 Decomm 8 Jun 1946. Stricken 9 Jun 1946, sold 5 Nov 1947.
Later history: Merchant *Chung 110,* later PRC Navy.

LST 173 To UK 24 Dec 1944–23 Apr 1946. Stricken 19 Jun 1946, sold 22 Oct 1947; BU Philadelphia.
2* Convoy UGS-36, Southern France.

LST 174 Decomm 21 Dec 1945. Stricken 21 Jan 1946, sold 29 Jan 1947.
2* Convoy UGS-36, Southern France.
Later history: Merchant *Sui Yuan*, renamed *La Colorada* 1949.

LST 175 USCG. Decomm 1 Mar 1946. Stricken 8 May 1946, sold 11 Dec 1947; BU New Orleans.
1* Normandy.

LST 176 USCG. Decomm 6 Jan 1946.
1*Normandy.
Later history: SCAJAP, as Q002. †

LST 177 Decomm 11 Feb 1946. Stricken 12 Apr 1946; to France 13 Mar 1947.
2* Convoy UGS-36, Southern France.
Later history: Renamed *Laïta*, L-9001. R 1964.

LST 178 To UK 24 Dec 1944–12 Dec 1946. Damaged by mine off Patras, Greece; beached in Egypt, 24 Feb 1945. Stricken 22 Jan 1947; salved by Egypt, Nov 1946.
2* Convoy UGS-36, Southern France.
Later history: Renamed *Aka*. Sunk as blockship in Suez Canal, 1 Nov 1956.

LST 179 Sunk by accidental ammunition explosion at Pearl Harbor, 21 May 1944. Raised and sunk as target, Nov 1945.
1* Gilbert Is.

LST 180 To UK 10 Jul 1943–17 Dec 1945. Stricken 21 Jan 1946, sold 10 Mar 1948.
Later history: Merchant *Leona*. Disabled by explosion in Lake Maracaibo, 31 Oct 1954; scuttled, 28 Mar 1955.

No.	Builder	Launched	Comm.
LST 181	Jeffersonville	3 Jul 1943	21 Aug 1943
LST 182–96	Jeffersonville	—	—
LST 197	Chicago Bridge	13 Dec 1942	5 Feb 1943
LST 198	Chicago Bridge	17 Jan 1943	*15 Feb 1943*
LST 199	Chicago Bridge	7 Feb 1943	*1 Mar 1943*
LST 200	Chicago Bridge	20 Feb 1943	*16 Mar 1943*
LST 201	Chicago Bridge	2 Mar 1943	2 Apr 1943
LST 202	Chicago Bridge	16 Mar 1943	9 Apr 1943
LST 203	Chicago Bridge	25 Mar 1943	22 Apr 1943
LST 204	Chicago Bridge	3 Apr 1943	27 Apr 1943
LST 205	Chicago Bridge	13 Apr 1943	15 May 1943
LST 206	Chicago Bridge	21 Apr 1943	7 Jun 1943
LST 207	Chicago Bridge	29 Apr 1943	9 Jun 1943
LST 208	Chicago Bridge	11 May 1943	8 Jun 1943
LST 209	Chicago Bridge	29 May 1943	10 Jun 1943
LST 210	Chicago Bridge	1 Jun 1943	6 Jul 1943
LST 211	Chicago Bridge	5 Jun 1943	6 Jul 1943
LST 212	Chicago Bridge	12 Jun 1943	6 Jul 1943
LST 213	Chicago Bridge	16 Jun 1943	7 Jul 1943
LST 214	Chicago Bridge	22 Jun 1943	*7 Jul 1943*
LST 215	Chicago Bridge	26 Jun 1943	*12 Jul 1943*
LST 216	Chicago Bridge	4 Jul 1943	*23 Jul 1943*
LST 217	Chicago Bridge	13 Jul 1943	*30 Jul 1943*
LST 218	Chicago Bridge	20 Jul 1943	12 Aug 1943
LST 219	Chicago Bridge	27 Jul 1943	19 Aug 1943
LST 220	Chicago Bridge	3 Aug 1943	26 Aug 1943
LST 221	Chicago Bridge	7 Aug 1943	2 Sep 1943
LST 222	Chicago Bridge	17 Aug 1943	10 Sep 1943
LST 223	Chicago Bridge	24 Aug 1943	17 Sep 1943
LST 224	Chicago Bridge	31 Aug 1943	23 Sep 1943
LST 225	Chicago Bridge	4 Sep 1943	2 Oct 1943
LST 226	Chicago Bridge	14 Sep 1943	8 Oct 1943
LST 227	Chicago Bridge	21 Sep 1943	16 Oct 1943
LST 228	Chicago Bridge	25 Sep 1943	25 Oct 1943
LST 229	Chicago Bridge	5 Oct 1943	3 Nov 1943
LST 230	Chicago Bridge	12 Oct 1943	3 Nov 1943
LST 231	Chicago Bridge	19 Oct 1943	*Nov 1943*
LST 232–36	—	—	—

Service Records:

LST 181 Decomm 4 Mar 1946. Stricken 12 Apr 1946, sold 9 Dec 1946.
7* Cape Gloucester, Admiralty Is. Ldgs., Hollandia, Wakde, Philippine Sea, Noemfoor I., Cape Sansapor, Leyte, Visayan Is. Ldgs., Balikpapan.
Later history: Merchant *M.O.P. 378–B.*

LST 182–96 Canceled 16 Sep 1942.

LST 197 Decomm 5 Apr 1946. Stricken 5 Jun 1946; Sold 31 Oct 1947; BU.
4* Sicily, Salerno, Anzio (17 killed), Normandy.

LST 198 To UK 5 Mar 1943–23 Jan 1946. Stricken 20 Mar 1946, sold 19 Mar 1948.
Later history: Merchant *Lidia* 1948, renamed *Hamdan 10* 1969.

LST 199 To UK 19 Mar 1943. Damaged by mine off Surabaya, Java, 5 Nov 1945. CTL 29 Mar 1946.

LST 200 To UK 25 Mar 1943–27 Feb 1946. Stricken 17 Apr 1946, sold 26 Mar 1948.
Later history: Merchant *Linda* 1948. BU 1957 Ghent.

LST 201 Converted to MTB tender and rec **AGP 20**, renamed ***Pontus***, 21 Jul 1944.
3* Hollandia.

LST 202 USCG. Decomm 11 Apr 1946. Stricken 28 Aug 1946, sold 16 Apr 1948; BU Seattle.
5* Cape Gloucester, Saidor, Admiralty Is. Ldgs., Hollandia, Wakde, Noemfoor I., Cape Sansapor, Morotai, Leyte.

LST 203 USCG. Lost by grounding near Nanumea, Ellice Is., 2 Oct 1943.

LST 204 USCG. Decomm 23 Feb 1946. Stricken 5 Jun 1946, sold 8 Oct 1947; BU.
7* Finschhafen, Cape Gloucester, Saidor, Hollandia, Biak, Noemfoor I., Cape Sansapor, Morotai, Leyte, Lingayen, Mindanao Ldgs.

LST 205 USCG. Rec **LST(H) 205**, 15 Sep 1945. Decomm 2 Apr 1946. Stricken 5 Jun 1946, sold 4 Jun 1948; BU.
4* Gilbert Is., Biak, Saipan, Leyte.

LST 206 USCG. Decomm 6 May 1946. Stricken 5 Jun 1946, sold 7 Apr 1948; BU Seattle.
6* Cape Gloucester, Saidor, Admiralty Is. Ldgs., Hollandia, Wakde, Biak, Cape Sansapor, Morotai, Leyte, Balikpapan.

LST 207 USCG. Decomm 20 Mar 1946. Stricken 17 Apr 1946, sold 19 Dec 1947; BU Barber, N.J.
5* Cape Torokina, Green Is. Ldgs., Guam, Leyte, Okinawa.

LST 208 Damaged in collision with m/v in English Channel, Jul 1944. Decomm 12 Jun 1946. Stricken 3 Jul 1946, sold 5 Dec 1947; BU.
1* Normandy.

LST 209 Decomm 27 Jun 1946. †
1* Normandy.

LST 210 Decomm 8 Dec 1945. Stricken 3 Jan 1946, sold 12 May 1948 (as barge).
3* Convoy UGS-36, Anzio, Southern France.

LST 211 Decomm 20 Nov 1945. Stricken 5 Dec 1945, sold 12 Jan 1948.
2* Convoy UGS-37, Southern France.
Later history: Merchant *Chang Sheng*.

LST 212 Decomm 15 Nov 1945. Stricken 28 Nov 1945, sold 24 Jul 1947.
2* Convoy UGS-37, Normandy.
Later history: Merchant *El Cuis*, renamed *Muriel H* 1948, *Il Ponte* 1958, *Neptune IV* 1963, *Arabdrill I* 1967.

LST 213 Rec **LST(H) 213**, 15 Sep 1945. Decomm 11 Mar 1946.
4* Saipan, Tinian, Leyte, Lingayen.
Later history: SCAJAP, as Q095. Stricken 5 Mar 1947; to USMG Korea 26 Jun 1947. Merchant *Hong Czon*. BU 1958.

LST 214 To UK 24 Jul 1943–20 Jan 1946. Stricken 12 Apr 1946, sold 3 Dec 1947; BU Norfolk, Va.

LST 215 To UK 19 Jul 1943–27 Jul 1946, renamed *LSE-51*. Stricken 29 Oct 1946; Sold 11 Sep 1947.
Later history: Merchant *Pigasos*, renamed *Celik* 1954. BU 1962 Split, Yugoslavia.

LST 216 To UK 4 Aug 1943; renamed *FDT-216*. Torpedoed and sunk by German aircraft off Barfleur, 7 Jul 1944.

LST 217 To UK 5 Aug 1943–16 Apr 1946, renamed *FDT-217*. Stricken 5 Jun 1946, sold 12 Dec 1947; BU.

LST 218 Decomm 19 Jan 1946.
4* Gilbert Is., Kwajalein, Eniwetok, Saipan, Tinian.
Later history: SCAJAP, as Q020. †

LST 219 Damaged by grounding, Lingayen, 18 Jan 1945. Decomm 29 Nov 1948. Stricken 22 Dec 1948, sold 25 Feb 1949.
2* Guam, Leyte.
Later history: Merchant barge *Foss 205*.

LST 220 Decomm Mar 1946. Bikini target. Sunk as target 12 May 1948.
4* Green Is. Ldgs., Hollandia, Guam, Leyte.

LST 221 Decomm 6 May 1946. Stricken 3 Jul 1946, sold 4 Mar 1948.
4* Kwajalein, Eniwetok, Hollandia, Guam, Okinawa.
Later history: Merchant barge *Foss 208*.

LST 222 Rec **LST(H) 222**, 15 Sep 1945. Decomm. Feb 1946.
3* Kwajalein, Saipan, Tinian, Palau.
Later history: SCAJAP, as Q044. †

LST 223 Rec **LST(H) 223**, 15 Sep 1945. To France 13 Mar 1947.
3*Kwajalein, Saipan, Leyte.
Later history: Renamed *Rance, L-9004*. R 1961.

LST 224 Damaged in collision, Iwo Jima, 2 Mar 1945. Decomm 22 Mar 1946. Stricken 17 Apr 1946, sold 9 Apr 1948; BU.
5* Kwajalein, Eniwetok, Saipan, Palau, Iwo Jima.

LST 225 Decomm 30 Jul 1946. Stricken 28 Aug 1946, sold 16 Dec 1947; BU Oakland, Calif.
2* Saipan, Tinian, Palau.

LST 226 Decomm 8 Jun 1946. Stricken 19 Jun 1946, sold 5 Nov 1947.
2* Kwajalein, Palau.
Later history: Merchant *Chung 109*. acq by PRC Navy.

LST 227 Decomm 22 Jan 1946.
6* Kwajalein, Hollandia, Guam, Palau, Lingayen, Okinawa.
Later history: SCAJAP, as Q025. †

LST 228 Lost by grounding in Azores Is. on Bahia Angra I., 19 Jan 1944.

LST 229 Decomm 12 Feb 1946. Stricken 31 Oct 1947, sold 7 Apr 1948; BU.
1* Normandy.
Later history: SCAJAP, as Q054.

LST 230 Decomm 4 Mar 1946.
2* Normandy, Southern France.
Later history: SCAJAP, as Q082. †

LST 231 Completed as repair ship, rec **ARL 7** renamed ***Atlas***, 3 Nov 1943.

LST 232–36 Canceled 16 Sep 1942.

No.	Builder	Launched	Comm.
LST 237	Missouri Valley	13 Jun 1943	*30 Jun 1943*
LST 238	Missouri Valley	13 Jun 1943	*9 Jul 1943*
LST 239	Missouri Valley	18 Jun 1943	*13 Jul 1943*
LST 240	Missouri Valley	25 Jun 1943	27 Jul 1943
LST 241	Missouri Valley	29 Jun 1943	31 Jul 1943
LST 242	Missouri Valley	3 Jul 1943	5 Aug 1943
LST 243	Missouri Valley	9 Jul 1943	9 Aug 1943
LST 244	Missouri Valley	14 Jul 1943	13 Aug 1943
LST 245	Missouri Valley	17 Jul 1943	22 Aug 1943
LST 246	Missouri Valley	22 Jul 1943	23 Aug 1943
LST 247	Missouri Valley	30 Jul 1943	26 Aug 1943
LST 248–52	Missouri Valley	—	—
LST 253–60	Marietta	—	—
LST 261	Amer. Bridge	23 Jan 1943	22 May 1943
LST 262	Amer. Bridge	13 Feb 1943	15 Jun 1943
LST 263	Amer. Bridge	27 Feb 1943	30 Jun 1943
LST 264	Amer. Bridge	13 Mar 1943	16 Jul 1943
LST 265	Amer. Bridge	24 Apr 1943	27 Jul 1943
LST 266	Amer. Bridge	16 May 1943	4 Aug 1943
LST 267	Amer. Bridge	6 Jun 1943	9 Aug 1943
LST 268	Amer. Bridge	18 Jun 1943	19 Aug 1943
LST 269	Amer. Bridge	4 Jul 1943	27 Aug 1943
LST 270	Amer. Bridge	18 Jul 1943	8 Sep 1943
LST 271	Amer. Bridge	25 Jul 1943	1 Sep 1943
LST 272	Amer. Bridge	1 Aug 1943	17 Sep 1943
LST 273	Amer. Bridge	8 Aug 1943	24 Sep 1943
LST 274	Amer. Bridge	15 Aug 1943	28 Sep 1943
LST 275	Amer. Bridge	22 Aug 1943	5 Oct 1943
LST 276	Amer. Bridge	29 Aug 1943	11 Oct 1943
LST 277	Amer. Bridge	5 Sep 1943	24 Oct 1943
LST 278	Amer. Bridge	12 Sep 1943	22 Oct 1943
LST 279	Amer. Bridge	19 Sep 1943	25 Oct 1943
LST 280	Amer. Bridge	26 Sep 1943	2 Nov 1943
LST 281	Amer. Bridge	30 Sep 1943	8 Nov 1943
LST 282	Amer. Bridge	3 Oct 1943	12 Nov 1943
LST 283	Amer. Bridge	10 Oct 1943	18 Nov 1943
LST 284	Amer. Bridge	17 Oct 1943	25 Nov 1943
LST 285	Amer. Bridge	24 Oct 1943	13 Dec 1943
LST 286	Amer. Bridge	27 Oct 1943	11 Dec 1943
LST 287	Amer. Bridge	31 Oct 1943	15 Dec 1943
LST 288	Amer. Bridge	7 Nov 1943	20 Dec 1943
LST 289	Amer. Bridge	21 Nov 1943	31 Dec 1943
LST 290	Amer. Bridge	5 Dec 1943	10 Jan 1944
LST 291	Amer. Bridge	14 Nov 1943	22 Dec 1943
LST 292	Amer. Bridge	28 Nov 1943	5 Jan 1944
LST 293	Amer. Bridge	12 Dec 1943	17 Jan 1944
LST 294	Amer. Bridge	15 Dec 1943	20 Jan 1944
LST 295	Amer. Bridge	24 Dec 1943	7 Feb 1944
LST 296–300	Amer. Bridge	—	—

Service Records:

LST 237 To UK 12 Jul 1943–11 Feb 1946. Stricken 26 Feb 1946, sold 5 Nov 1947.
Later history: Merchant *Chung 113*. Later PRC Navy.

LST 238 To UK 16 Jul 1943–13 Feb 1946. Stricken 12 Mar 1946, sold 13 Mar 1948; BU.

LST 239 To UK 19 Jul 1943–5 Feb 1946. Stricken 5 Jun 1948, sold 26 Apr 1948 (as barge).

LST 240 Decomm 3 May 1946. Stricken 23 Jun 1947, sold 1 Jun 1948; BU Chester, Pa.
2* Kwajalein, Eniwetok, Saipan.

LST 241 Damaged by USN gunfire in error, Okinawa, 6 Apr 1945. Damaged by collision, Okinawa,14 Apr 1945. Decomm 7 Mar 1946. Stricken 5 Jun 1946, sold 19 Sep 1947; BU New Orleans.
6* Gilbert Is., Kwajalein, Hollandia, Guam, Iwo Jima, Okinawa.

LST 242 Rec **LST(H) 242**, 15 Sep 1945. Decomm 9 Feb 1946.
4* Gilbert Is., Kwajalein, Eniwetok, Saipan, Leyte.
Later history: SCAJAP, as Q051. Stricken 31 Oct 1947, sold 31 Mar 1948; BU.

LST 243 Rec **LST(H) 243**, 15 Sep 1945. Decomm 9 Jan 1946.
5* Gilbert Is., Kwajalein, Guam, Palau, Lingayen.
Later history: SCAJAP, as Q006. Stricken 17 Jul 1947, sold 2 Apr 1948; BU.

LST 244 Decomm 28 Mar 1946. Stricken 3 Jul 1946, sold 11 Jun 1948; BU Chester, Pa.
4* Gilbert Is., Kwajalein, Guam, Okinawa.

LST 245 Decomm 1 Apr 1946. Stricken 8 May 1946, sold 15 Apr 1948; BU.
8* Saidor, Cape Gloucester, Admiralty Is. Ldgs., Hollandia, Wakde, Biak, Noemfoor I., Cape Sansapor, Leyte, Lingayen, Morotai, Mindanao Ldgs., Balikpapan.

LST 246 Decomm 14 Feb 1946.
6* Kwajalein, Eniwetok, Saipan, Tinian, Palau, Okinawa.
Later history: SCAJAP, as Q061. Stricken 12 Mar 1948; to Army 26 Jun 1947.

LST 247 Damaged in collision, Iwo Jima, 2 Mar 1945. Rec **LST(H) 247**, 15 Sep 1945. Decomm 27 Jun 1946. Stricken 15 Aug 1946, sold 14 Oct 1947; BU.
1* Guam.

LST 248–60 Canceled 16 Sep 1942 .

LST 261 USCG. Decomm 22 Feb 1946. Stricken 28 Mar 1946, sold 10 Nov 1947; BU Biloxi, Miss.
1* Normandy.

LST 262 USCG. Decomm 14 Jan 1946. Stricken 19 Jun 1946, sold 9 Dec 1947; BU Norfolk, Va.
2* Convoy UGS-36, Normandy.

LST 263 Decomm 29 May 1946. †
2* Convoy UGS-37, Southern France.

LST 264 Decomm 11 Jan 1946. Stricken 19 Jun 1946; Sold 23 Apr 1948 (as barge).
1* Normandy.

LST 265 Decomm 11 Dec 1945. Stricken 3 Jan 1946, sold 20 Feb 1948.
3* Convoy UGS-36, Anzio, Southern France.
Later history: Merchant *Excello*, renamed *Deepwater No.1* 19. barge, *San Juan*, *Seadrill 10*.

LST 266 Damaged by coastal gunfire, Normandy, 15 Jun 1944. Decomm 25 Jun 1947. †
2* Convoy UGS-36, Normandy.

LST 267 Decomm 25 Jun 1946. Stricken 31 Jul 1946, sold 24 Sep 1947; BU.
5* Saipan, Tinian, Palau, Lingayen, Okinawa.

LST 268 Rec **LST(H) 268**, 15 Sep 1945. Decomm 16 Feb 1946.
5* Kwajalein, Tinian, Palau, Lingayen, Okinawa.
Later history: SCAJAP, as Q062. Stricken 31 Oct 1947, sold 24 Mar 1948; BU.

LST 269 Damaged by coastal mortars, Leyte, 21 Oct 1944. Decomm 7 Feb 1946.
4* Hollandia, Guam, Leyte, Ldgs. at Nasugbu.
Later history: SCAJAP, as Q047. Stricken 23 Dec 1947, sold 28 May 1948; BU.

LST 270 Damaged by coastal defense gun, Lingayen Gulf, 11 Jan 1945. †
4* Kwajalein, Aitape, Hollandia, Guam, Leyte.

LST 271 Decomm 22 Apr 1946. Stricken 5 Jun 1946, sold 19 Apr 1948; BU Napa, Calif.
5* Kwajalein, Saipan, Tinian, Palau, Lingayen.

LST 272 Decomm 16 Aug 1946. Stricken 25 Sep 1946, sold 5 Apr 1948; BU.
5* Kwajalein, Eniwetok, Saipan, Tinian, Palau, Lingayen.

LST 273 Damaged by collision, Okinawa, 5 Apr 1945. Decomm 12 Aug 1946. Stricken 8 Oct 1946; Sold 3 Nov 1947; BU.
6* Kwajalein, Eniwetok, Saipan, Tinian, Palau, Lingayen, Okinawa.

LST 274 Decomm 6 May 1946. Stricken 23 Jun 1947, sold 29 Jun 1948.
2* Kwajalein, Saipan.
Later history: Merchant barge *Barge 18*.

LST 275 Decomm 16 Aug 1946. Stricken 25 Sep 1946, sold 5 Apr 1948; BU.
2* Saipan, Tinian.

LST 276 Rec **LST(H) 276**, 15 Sep 1945. Decomm 15 Feb 1946.
5* Kwajalein, Hollandia, Guam, Palau, Lingayen.
Later history: SCAJAP, as Q079. †

LST 277 In collision with cruiser *Pensacola* off Okinawa, 31 Mar 1945. Decomm 12 Feb 1946.
5* Kwajalein, Saipan, Leyte, Okinawa, Ldgs. at Nasugbu.
Later history: SCAJAP, as Q055. †

LST 278 Damaged in storm, Peleliu, Palau Is., 2 Oct 1944. Decomm 22 Jan 1945. Rec **IX 209**, renamed ***Seaward***, 15 Feb 1945. Barracks and post office, Ulithi, Micronesia. Destroyed 15 Oct 1946.
2* Saipan, Tinian, Palau.

LST 279 †
1* Normandy.

LST 280 Damaged by submarine torpedo from *U-621*, Normandy, 14 Jun 1944. To UK 26 Oct 1944–13 Apr 1946. Stricken 5 Jun 1946, sold 5 Dec 1947.
1* Normandy.

LST 281 Decomm 9 Mar 1946.
3* Normandy, Southern France, Okinawa.
Later history: SCAJAP, as Q092. †

LST 282 Damaged by German radio-controlled bomb off St.Tropez, France, 15 Aug 1944, beached and abandoned (~25 killed).
2* Normandy, Southern France.

LST 283 Decomm 13 Jun 1946. Stricken 22 Jan 1947, sold 25 Mar 1947.
2* Normandy, Southern France.
Later history: Merchant *Rawhiti*, renamed *Chimbote* 1952 (Peruvian Navy).

LST 284 Decomm 13 Mar 1946. Stricken 19 Jun 1946, sold 11 Dec 1947; BU New Orleans.
3* Normandy, Southern France, Okinawa.

LST 285 Decomm 27 Jun 1947. Stricken 1 Aug 1947, sold 26 Mar 1948; BU Seattle.
2* Normandy, Southern France.

LST 286 Decomm 26 Mar 1946. Stricken 8 May 1946, sold 15 Apr 1948; BU.
2* Normandy, Southern France.

LST 287 Decomm. †
1* Normandy.

LST 288 Decomm 6 Mar 1946.
3* Normandy, Southern France, Okinawa.
Later history: SCAJAP, as Q085. †

LST 289 Damaged by torpedo in Lyme Bay, English Channel, 28 Apr 1944 (12 killed). To UK 9 Dec 1944–10 Dec 1946. Stricken 15 Oct 1946; sold 30 Jun 1947.
Later history: Merchant *Eendracht* 1948, renamed *Estemar* 1956. BU 1970 Rotterdam.

LST 290 Decomm 15 Nov 1945. Stricken 28 Nov 1945, sold 25 Dec 1946.
1* Normandy.
Later history: Merchant *Hope* 1947, renamed *Guarani* 1951, *Cabral Leme* 1967. BU 1971.

LST 291 Decomm 18 Jun 1947. †
1* Normandy.

LST 292 Decomm 25 Jan 1946. Stricken 12 Apr 1946, sold 21 Jan 1948; BU.
1* Normandy.

LST 293 Decomm 3 Dec 1945. Stricken 19 Dec 1945, sold 1 Jun 1949.
1* Normandy.
Later history: Merchant barge *Hughes No.100;* renamed *Witte 100* 1968.

LST 294 Decomm 18 Dec 1945. Stricken 8 Jan 1946, sold 10 Oct 1947; BU Philadelphia.
1* Normandy.

LST 295 Decomm 28 Dec 1945. Stricken 12 Apr 1946, sold 12 Sep 1947.
1* Normandy.
Later history: Merchant *Oceanic V*, renamed *Ginyo Maru* 1954. BU 1962 Japan.

LST 296–300 Canceled 16 Sep 1942.

No.	Builder	Launched	Comm.
LST 301	Boston NYd	15 Sep 1942	*1 Nov 1942*
LST 302	Boston NYd	15 Sep 1942	*10 Nov 1942*
LST 303	Boston NYd	21 Sep 1942	*20 Nov 1942*
LST 304	Boston NYd	21 Sep 1942	*29 Nov 1942*
LST 305	Boston NYd	10 Oct 1942	*6 Dec 1942*

LST 306	Boston NYd	10 Oct 1942	11 Dec 1942
LST 307	Boston NYd	9 Nov 1942	23 Dec 1942
LST 308	Boston NYd	9 Nov 1942	2 Jan 1943
LST 309	Boston NYd	23 Nov 1942	11 Jan 1943
LST 310	Boston NYd	23 Nov 1942	20 Jan 1943
LST 311	Boston NYd	30 Dec 1942	11 Jan 1943
LST 312	New York NYd	30 Dec 1942	9 Jan 1943
LST 313	New York NYd	30 Dec 1942	13 Jan 1943
LST 314	New York NYd	30 Dec 1942	15 Jan 1943
LST 315	New York NYd	28 Jan 1943	3 Feb 1943
LST 316	New York NYd	28 Jan 1943	3 Feb 1943
LST 317	New York NYd	28 Jan 1943	6 Feb 1943
LST 318	New York NYd	28 Jan 1943	8 Feb 1943
LST 319	Phila NYd	5 Nov 1942	*15 Dec 1942*
LST 320	Phila NYd	5 Nov 1942	*31 Dec 1942*
LST 321	Phila NYd	5 Nov 1942	*31 Dec 1942*
LST 322	Phila NYd	5 Nov 1942	*9 Jan 1943*
LST 323	Phila NYd	5 Nov 1942	*18 Jan 1943*
LST 324	Phila NYd	5 Nov 1942	*23 Jan 1943*
LST 325	Phila NYd	27 Oct 1942	1 Feb 1943
LST 326	Phila NYd	11 Feb 1943	26 Feb 1943
LST 327	Phila NYd	11 Feb 1943	5 Mar 1943
LST 328	Phila NYd	11 Feb 1943	*22 May 1943*
LST 329	Phila NYd	1 Feb 1943	*18 May 1943*
LST 330	Phila NYd	11 Feb 1943	*12 Jun 1943*
LST 331	Phila NYd	11 Feb 1943	11 Mar 1943
LST 332	Phila NYd	24 Dec 1942	6 Feb 1943
LST 333	Norfolk NYd	15 Oct 1942	20 Nov 1942
LST 334	Norfolk NYd	15 Oct 1942	29 Nov 1942
LST 335	Norfolk NYd	15 Oct 1942	6 Dec 1942
LST 336	Norfolk NYd	15 Oct 1942	11 Dec 1942
LST 337	Norfolk NYd	8 Nov 1942	16 Dec 1942
LST 338	Norfolk NYd	8 Nov 1942	20 Dec 1942
LST 339	Norfolk NYd	8 Nov 1942	23 Dec 1942
LST 340	Norfolk NYd	8 Nov 1942	26 Dec 1942
LST 341	Norfolk NYd	8 Nov 1942	28 Dec 1942
LST 342	Norfolk NYd	8 Nov 1942	31 Dec 1942
LST 343	Norfolk NYd	15 Dec 1942	9 Jan 1943
LST 344	Norfolk NYd	15 Dec 1942	14 Jan 1943
LST 345	Norfolk NYd	15 Dec 1942	21 Jan 1943
LST 346	Norfolk NYd	15 Dec 1942	25 Jan 1943
LST 347	Norfolk NYd	7 Feb 1943	7 Feb 1943
LST 348	Norfolk NYd	7 Feb 1943	9 Feb 1943
LST 349	Norfolk NYd	7 Feb 1943	11 Feb 1943
LST 350	Norfolk NYd	7 Feb 1943	13 Feb 1943
LST 351	Norfolk NYd	7 Feb 1943	24 Feb 1943
LST 352	Norfolk NYd	7 Feb 1943	26 Feb 1943
LST 353	Charleston NYd	12 Oct 1942	27 Nov 1942
LST 354	Charleston NYd	13 Oct 1942	27 Nov 1942
LST 355	Charleston NYd	16 Nov 1942	22 Dec 1942
LST 356	Charleston NYd	16 Nov 1942	22 Dec 1942
LST 357	Charleston NYd	14 Dec 1942	8 Feb 1943
LST 358	Charleston NYd	15 Dec 1942	8 Feb 1943
LST 359	Charleston NYd	11 Jan 1943	9 Feb 1943
LST 360	Charleston NYd	11 Jan 1943	9 Feb 1943

Service Records:

LST 301 To UK 6 Nov 1942–20 Mar 1946. Stricken Dec 1947, sold 11 Dec 1947; BU.

LST 302 To UK 14 Nov 1942–5 Jan 1946. Stricken 20 Mar 1946, sold 11 Dec 1947; BU Philadelphia.

LST 303 To UK 21 Nov 1942–14 May 1946. Stricken 3 Jul 1946, sold 5 Dec 1947.

LST 304 To UK 30 Nov 1942–29 Nov 1946. Stricken 1 Aug 1947, sold 7 Oct 1947.
Later history: Merchant *Chit Sein*, renamed *Chong Hsing* 1954, *Libertad* 1957. BU 1965 Singapore.

LST 305 To UK 7 Dec 1942. Torpedoed and sunk by *U-230* off Anzio, 20 Feb 1944.

LST 306 Decomm 13 Jun 1946. †
3* Sicily, Salerno, Normandy.

LST 307 Damaged by coastal gunfire, Normandy, 15 Jun 1944. Decomm 13 Jun 1946. Stricken 31 Jul 1946, sold 30 Mar 1948; BU Seattle.
3* Sicily, Salerno, Normandy.

LST 308 Decomm 17 Oct 1946, sold 5 Dec 1947 (U.S. State Department).

LST 309 Decomm 19 Jun 1946. Stricken 23 Jun 1947, sold 25 Jun 1948.
3* Sicily, Salerno, Normandy.
Later history: Merchant *S-26*, renamed *Île de l'Europe* 1972.

LST 310 Decomm 16 May 1945, but conversion to **ARL 42 *Aeolus*** canceled, 11 Aug 1945. Stricken 12 Mar 1946, sold 28 Jan 1947.
2* Sicily, Normandy.
Later history: Merchant *Mercator* 1948, renamed *Altamar* 1963.

LST 311 To UK 20 Nov 1944–11 Apr 1946. Stricken 5 Jun 1946, sold 5 Dec 1947.
3* Sicily, Salerno, Normandy.

LST 312 Damaged by V-1 bomb at Deptford, England, 8 Jul 1944. Decomm 12 Jul 1946. Stricken 15 Aug 1946, sold 13 Dec 1947; BU.
3* Sicily, Salerno, Normandy.

LST 313 Destroyed by German aircraft bombs off Gela, Sicily, 10 Jul 1943 (many killed).
1* Sicily.

LST 314 Torpedoed and sunk by German MTB off Normandy, 9 Jun 1944.
3* Sicily, Salerno, Normandy.

LST 315 To UK 9 Dec 1944–16 Mar 1946. Stricken 26 Feb 1946; Sold 5 Dec 1947.
3* Sicily, Salerno, Normandy.

LST 316 Decomm 24 May 1945, but conversion to **ARL 43 *Cerberus*** canceled, 11 Aug 1945. Stricken 12 Mar 1946, sold 23 Dec 1946.
3* Sicily, Salerno, Normandy.
Later history: Merchant *Augusta*. BU 1966.

LST 317 Decomm 18 May 1945, but conversion to **ARL 44 *Consus*** canceled, 11 Aug 1945. Stricken 12 Mar 1946, sold 22 Jan 1947.
3* Sicily, Salerno, Normandy.

LST 318 Damaged by German aircraft at Caronia, Sicily, beached and abandoned, 9 Aug 1943.
1* Sicily.

LST 319 To UK 15 Dec 1942–17 Dec 1945. Stricken 21 Jan 1946, sold 9 Mar 1948.
Later history: Merchant *Lucia* 1948. BU 1957 Ghent.

LST 320 To UK 31 Dec 1942–23 Apr 1946. Stricken 19 Jun 1946, sold 4 Oct 1947; BU.

LST 321 To UK 31 Dec 1942–11 Apr 1946. Stricken 10 Jun 1947, sold 5 Nov 1947.

LST 322 To UK 9 Jan 1943–10 Jul 1946. Stricken 29 Oct 1946, sold 6 Jan 1947.
Later history: Merchant *Theodoros*. Lost by grounding on Euboea I., 30 Nov 1948.

LST 323 To UK 18 Jan 1943–26 Jan 1946. Stricken 19 Jun 1946, sold 9 Oct 1947; BU Philadelphia.

LST 324 To UK 22 Jan 1943–11 Jun 1946. Stricken 3 Jul 1946, sold 13 Feb 1948.

LST 325 Decomm 2 Jul 1946. †
2* Sicily, Normandy.

LST 326 USCG. Damaged in collision with *LST-6*, at Bizerte, Tunisia, 17 Jun 1943. To UK 9 Dec 1944–16 Mar 1946. Stricken 26 Feb 1946, sold to France 5 Apr 1946.
3* Sicily, Anzio, Normandy.
Later history: Renamed *Liamone.* R 1949.

LST 327 USCG. Severely damaged by mine in English Channel, 27 Aug 1944. Decomm 19 Nov 1945. Stricken 5 Dec 1945, sold 13 Sep 1947; BU Chester, Pa.
5* Tunisia, Sicily, Salerno, Anzio, Normandy.

LST 328 Completed as repair ship, rec **ARB 2**, renamed ***Oceanus,*** 25 Jan 1943.

LST 329 Completed as repair ship, rec **ARB 1**, renamed ***Aristaeus,*** 25 Jan 1943.

LST 330 Completed as MTB tender, rec **AGP 3**, renamed ***Portunus,*** 25 Jan 1943.

LST 331 USCG. Damaged by coastal gunfire, Normandy, 15 Jun 1944. To UK 20 Nov 1944–16 Mar 1946. Stricken 26 Feb 1946, sold 13 Feb 1948.
4* Tunisia, Sicily, Salerno, Normandy.

LST 332 Decomm 22 May 1945, but conversion to **ARL 45 *Feronia*** canceled. Stricken 12 Mar 1946, sold 17 Oct 1946.
3* Sicily, Salerno, Normandy.
Later history: Merchant *Casa Blanca.*

LST 333 Torpedoed by *U-593* off Algeria, northeast of Cape Corbelin, Algeria, beached and abandoned, 22 Jun 1943 (25 killed).

LST 334 Damaged by dive bombers off Vella Lavella, 30 Sep 1943. Decomm 24 Apr 1946. Stricken 5 Jun 1946, sold 22 Apr 1948; BU.
4* Cape Torokina, Ldgs. on Vella Lavella, Guam, Okinawa.

LST 335 Decomm 22 Dec 1945. Stricken 8 Jan 1946, sold 1 Dec 1947; BU.
3* Sicily, Salerno, Normandy.

LST 336 Damaged by coastal batteries, Salerno, 9 Sep 1943 (3 killed). To UK 27 Nov 1944–7 Mar 1946. Stricken 5 Jun 1946, sold 22 Oct 1947; BU Philadelphia.
3* Sicily, Salerno, Normandy.

LST 337 To UK 2 Dec 1944–16 Mar 1946. Stricken 17 Apr 1946, sold 5 Dec 1947.
3* Sicily, Salerno, Normandy.

LST 338 Decomm 6 May 1946. Stricken 23 Jun 1947, sold 3 Dec 1947
3* Sicily, Salerno, Normandy.
Later history: Merchant *Southern Cities* 1948, renamed *Alberta* 1956. BU 1960 Wilmington, Del.

LST 339 Decomm 13 May 1946. Stricken 23 Jun 1947, sold 16 Oct 1947 BU.
5* New Georgia Ldgs., Ldgs. on Vella Lavella, Cape Torokina, Hollandia, Biak, Noemfoor I., Morotai.

LST 340 Damaged by dive bombers, Guadalcanal, 16 Jun 1943 (1 killed). Damaged by grounding, Tinian, 29 Jul 1944, not repaired. Decomm 24 Oct 1944. Rec **IX 196**, renamed ***Spark,*** 20 Oct 1944. Stricken 1 Sep 1945; destroyed 24 Nov 1945.
3* Solomons, Saipan, Tinian.

LST 341 Decomm 14 Mar 1946. Stricken 12 Apr 1946, sold 12 Sep 1946.
4* New Georgia Ldgs., Ldgs. on Vella Lavella, Cape Torokina, Saipan, Guam, Leyte.
Later history: Merchant *Insco Merchant,* renamed *LST I* 1956, *Gonçalo* 1962. Foundered after grounding south of Recife, Brazil, 2 Sep 1966.

LST 342 Torpedoed and sunk by submarine *Ro-106* west of Guadalcanal, 18 Jul 1943.
1* New Georgia Ldgs.

LST 343 Damaged by grounding, Okinawa, 4 Apr 1945. Decomm 27 Jan 1946.
5* Solomons, New Georgia Ldgs., Cape Torokina, Guam, Okinawa.
Later history: SCAJAP, as Q033. To USMG Korea 21 Feb 1947. Stricken 5 Mar 1947.

LST 344 Decomm 7 Jun 1946. †
3* Sicily, Salerno, Normandy.

LST 345 Decomm 5 Dec 1945. Stricken 3 Jan 1946, sold 23 Mar 1948.
3* Sicily, Salerno, Normandy.
Later history: Merchant *Luisa* 1948, renamed *Aegean Sea* 1958.

LST 346 To UK 20 Nov 1944–2 May 1946. Stricken 19 Jun 1946, sold 5 Dec 1947.
3* Sicily, Salerno, Normandy.

LST 347 To UK 17 Dec 1944. To France 2 Feb 1945.
3* Sicily, Salerno, Normandy.
Later history: Renamed *Vire.* R 1957

LST 348 Torpedoed and sunk by *U-410* southeast of Anzio, 20 Feb 1944 (24 killed).
2* Sicily, Anzio.

LST 349 Lost by grounding on Ponza I. near Gaeta, Italy, 26 Feb 1944.
1* Sicily.

LST 350 Decomm 26 May 1945, but conversion to **ARL 46** *Chandra* canceled, 11 Aug 1945. Stricken 12 Mar 1946. Sold 2 Dec 1946.
3* Sicily, Salerno, Normandy.
Later history: Merchant *Dolores* 1947. BU 1960.

LST 351 To UK 12 Dec 1944–10 Dec 1946. Stricken 15 Oct 1946, sold to Netherlands Jun 1947.
4* Sicily, Salerno, Anzio, Elba, Normandy.

LST 352 To UK 24 Dec 1944–2 Aug 1946. Stricken 29 Oct 1946, sold to Greece Jan 1947.
4* Sicily, Salerno, Anzio, Southern France.

LST 353 Sunk by accidental ammunition explosion at Pearl Harbor, 21 May 1944; six LSTs were sunk (163 killed).
3* Solomons, New Georgia Ldgs., Ldgs. on Vella Lavella, Cape Torokina.

LST 354 Decomm 30 Apr 1946. Stricken 19 Jun 1946, sold 16 Dec 1947; BU.
6* New Georgia Ldgs., Ldgs. on Vella Lavella, Cape Torokina, Green Is. Ldgs., Saipan, Iwo Jima, Okinawa.

LST 355 Decomm 6 Mar 1946.
2* Salerno, Normandy.
Later history: SCAJAP, as Q084. Stricken 31 Oct 1947, sold 10 Apr 1948; BU Seattle.

LST 356 Decomm 21 Sep 1945. †
3* Sicily, Salerno, Normandy.

LST 357 Decomm 8 Jun 1946. Stricken 31 Jul 1946, sold 1 Apr 1948; BU.
3* Sicily, Salerno, Normandy.

LST 358 To UK 24 Dec 1944–27 Feb 1946. Stricken 15/25 Aug 1946, sold 3 Oct 1947; BU Philadelphia.
4* Sicily, Salerno, Anzio, Southern France.

LST 359 Torpedoed and sunk by *U-870* 370 miles northeast of Azores, 20 Dec 1944.
5* Sicily, Salerno, Convoy KMS-31, Anzio, Normandy.

LST 360 Damaged by coastal guns, Normandy, 15 Jun 1944. To UK 29 Nov 1944–10 Jun 1946, renamed *LSE-52.* Stricken 15 Aug 1946, sold 8 Oct 1947; BU.
3* Sicily, Anzio, Normandy.

Figure 9.6: *LST-363,* as completed. Notice ventilators on deck, which were later removed from most units to permit storage of vehicles on deck. *LST-363* was transferred to the United Kingdom under lend-lease.

No.	Builder	Launched	Comm.
LST 361	Beth. Quincy	10 Oct 1942	*16 Nov 1942*
LST 362	Beth. Quincy	10 Oct 1942	*23 Nov 1942*
LST 363	Beth. Quincy	26 Oct 1942	*30 Nov 1942*
LST 364	Beth. Quincy	26 Oct 1942	*7 Dec 1942*
LST 365	Beth. Quincy	11 Nov 1942	*14 Dec 1942*
LST 366	Beth. Quincy	11 Nov 1942	*21 Dec 1942*
LST 367	Beth. Quincy	24 Nov 1942	*29 Dec 1942*
LST 368	Beth. Quincy	24 Nov 1942	4 Jan 1943
LST 369	Beth. Quincy	24 Nov 1942	8 Jan 1943
LST 370	Beth. Quincy	12 Dec 1942	13 Jan 1943
LST 371	Beth. Quincy	12 Dec 1942	16 Jan 1943
LST 372	Beth. Quincy	19 Jan 1943	23 Jan 1943
LST 373	Beth. Quincy	19 Jan 1943	27 Jan 1943
LST 374	Beth. Quincy	19 Jan 1943	29 Jan 1943
LST 375	Beth. Quincy	28 Jan 1943	2 Feb 1943
LST 376	Beth. Quincy	1 Feb 1943	5 Feb 1943
LST 377	Beth. Quincy	1 Feb 1943	8 Feb 1943
LST 378	Beth. Quincy	6 Feb 1943	10 Feb 1943
LST 379	Beth. Quincy	6 Feb 1943	12 Feb 1943
LST 380	Beth. Quincy	10 Feb 1943	15 Feb 1943
LST 381	Beth. Quincy	10 Feb 1943	15 Feb 1943
LST 382	Beth. Quincy	3 Feb 1943	18 Feb 1943
LST 383	Newport News	28 Sep 1942	28 Oct 1942
LST 384	Newport News	28 Sep 1942	2 Nov 1942
LST 385	Newport News	28 Sep 1942	6 Nov 1942
LST 386	Newport News	28 Sep 1942	10 Nov 1942
LST 387	Newport News	28 Sep 1942	17 Nov 1942
LST 388	Newport News	28 Sep 1942	20 Nov 1942
LST 389	Newport News	15 Oct 1942	24 Nov 1942
LST 390	Newport News	15 Oct 1942	28 Nov 1942
LST 391	Newport News	28 Oct 1942	3 Dec 1942
LST 392	Newport News	28 Oct 1942	7 Dec 1942
LST 393	Newport News	11 Nov 1942	11 Dec 1942
LST 394	Newport News	11 Nov 1942	13 Dec 1942
LST 395	Newport News	23 Nov 1942	19 Dec 1942
LST 396	Newport News	23 Nov 1942	23 Dec 1942
LST 397	Newport News	22 Nov 1942	28 Dec 1942
LST 398	Newport News	28 Nov 1942	2 Jan 1943
LST 399	Newport News	28 Nov 1942	4 Jan 1943
LST 400	Newport News	28 Nov 1942	7 Jan 1943

Service Records:

LST 361 To UK 16 Nov 1942–7 Mar 1946. Stricken 5 Jun 1946, sold 11 Oct 1947; BU Philadelphia.

LST 362 To UK 23 Nov 1942. Torpedoed and sunk by *U-744* in Bay of Biscay, 2 Mar 1944.

LST 363 To UK 30 Nov 1942–26 Jan 1946. Stricken 12 Apr 1946, sold 4 Dec 1947; BU Norfolk, Va.

LST 364 To UK 7 Dec 1942. Torpedoed and sunk by German midget submarine off Ramsgate, 22 Feb 1945.

LST 365 To UK 14 Dec 1942–10 Dec 1946. Stricken 15 Oct 1946, sold 5 Jun 1947.

Later history: Merchant *Mowbray Road*, renamed *Adri I* 1952.

LST 366 To UK 21 Dec 1942–26 Jan 1946. Stricken 5 Jun 1946, sold 3 Dec 1947; BU Norfolk, Va.

LST 367 To UK 29 Dec 1942–17 Dec 1945. Stricken 21 Jan 1946, sold 18 Mar 1948; BU.

LST 368 Decomm 16 Mar 1946. Stricken 17 Apr 1946; destroyed 16 Jun 1948.

1* Saidor.

LST 369 To UK 29 Nov 1944–29 Nov 1946. Stricken 1 Aug 1947, sold 7 Oct 1947.

3* Sicily, Salerno, Normandy.

LST 370 Decomm 7 Jan 1946. Stricken 12 Apr 1946, sold 3 Feb 1947.

3* Sicily, Salerno, Normandy.

Later history: Merchant *Ting Yuan*, renamed *La Capirena* 1950.

LST 371 To UK 17 Nov 1944–16 Mar 1946. Stricken 26 Feb 1946, sold 5 Dec 1947.

3* Sicily, Salerno, Normandy.

LST 372 Decomm 9 Jul 1946. Stricken 15 Aug 1946, sold 3 Oct 1947; BU Baltimore.

3* Sicily, Salerno, Normandy.

LST 373 To UK 9 Dec 1944–16 Mar 1946. Stricken 26 Feb 1946, sold 5 Nov 1947.

3* Sicily, Salerno, Normandy.

Later history: Merchant *Chung 118*. BU 1962.

LST 374 Decomm 29 May 1945, but conversion to **ARL 47 *Minerva*** canceled, 11 Aug 1945. Stricken 12 Mar 1946, sold 14 Jan 1947.

2* Sicily, Normandy.

Later history: Merchant *Estrella Austral*, renamed *Mar Austral* 1968. Sunk after collision in Parana River, 14 Jun 1968.

LST 375 Damaged by coastal batteries, Salerno, 9 Sep 1943. Damaged in collision, Normandy, 6 Jun 1944. Decomm 18 Jul 1946. Stricken 10 Jun 1947, sold 12 Apr 1948; BU.

3* Sicily, Salerno, Normandy.

LST 376 Damaged by MTB torpedo, Normandy, and sunk by U.S. forces, 9 Jun 1944.

3* Sicily, Salerno, Normandy.

LST 377 Decomm 7 Jun 1946. Stricken 31 Jul 1946, sold 1 Apr 1948; BU.

4* Sicily, Salerno, Anzio, Normandy.

LST 378 Decomm 20 Feb 1946.

4* Sicily, Salerno, Anzio, Normandy.

Later history: SCAJAP, as Q069. Stricken 5 Mar 1947. To USMG Korea 1 Jun 1947.

LST 379 Decomm 28 Feb 1946. Stricken 20 Mar 1946, sold 12 Apr 1948; BU.

4* Sicily, Salerno, Anzio, Normandy.

LST 380 To UK 20 Nov 1944–13 Apr 1946; Stricken 19 Jul 1946. To USMG Korea 7 Jun 1946.

3* Sicily, Salerno, Normandy.

Later history: Merchant *Wan Li*, renamed *Chung Yu* 1955 (Taiwan Navy).

LST 381 USCG. To UK 19 Dec 1944–10 Jun 1946. Stricken 19 Jul 1946, sold 11 Sep 1947; BU.

3* Sicily, Anzio, Normandy.

LST 382 To UK 29 Nov 1944. To France 26 Feb 1945.

3* Sicily, Salerno, Normandy.

Later history: Renamed *Paillote* 1947.To Cambodia 1954.

LST 383 To UK 20 Nov 1944–4 May 1946. Sold to NEI Customs 10 Jun 1946.

4* Sicily, Salerno, Anzio, Normandy.

Later history: Renamed *LST I*, renamed *Albatros* R.

LST 384 Damaged by V-1 bomb at Deptford, England, 8 Jul 1944. Decomm 22 Apr 1946. Stricken 5 Jun 1946, sold 8 Apr 1948; BU Vancouver, Wash.

4* Sicily, Salerno, Anzio, Normandy.

LST 385 Damaged by coastal batteries, Salerno, 9 Sep 1943.To UK 29 Nov 1944–16 Mar 1946. Stricken 26 Feb 1946, sold 5 Dec 1947.

5* Sicily, Salerno, Convoy KMS-31, Anzio, Normandy.

LST 386 Damaged by mine, Salerno, 9 Sep 1943. To UK 9 Dec 1944–10 Dec 1946. Stricken 15 Oct 1946, sold 5 Jun 1947.

5* Tunisia, Salerno, Sicily, Anzio, Normandy.

Later history: Merchant *Barnes Park*, renamed *Sant'Anna*, 1950, *El Oriental* 1955, *Blas Davenia* 1965. BU 1973.

LST 387 Torpedoed by *U-593* northeast of Cape Corbelin, Algeria, 22 Jun 1943. Decomm 2 May 1946. Stricken 19 Jul 1946, sold 22 Dec 1947; BU Philadelphia.

LST 388 Bikini target. Decomm 1 Feb 1947. Stricken 25 Feb 1947, sold 7 Apr 1948 to South Korea.
4* Tunisia, Sicily, Salerno, Normandy.
Later history: Renamed *Samlangjin.*

LST 389 Damaged by coastal batteries, Salerno, 9 Sep 1943. Decomm 12 Mar 1946. †
3* Sicily, Salerno, Normandy.

LST 390 Damaged by collision, Iwo Jima, 21 Feb 1945. Decomm 12 Mar 1946.
3* Cape Torokina, Saipan, Iwo Jima.
Later history: SCAJAP, as Q096. Stricken 29 Sep 1947, sold 3 Apr 1948; BU Seattle.

LST 391 Damaged by mine, Normandy, 16 Aug 1944. Decomm. †
3* Sicily, Salerno, Normandy.

LST 392 Decomm 12 Apr 1946. Stricken 19 Jun 1946, sold 8 Oct 1947; BU.
4* Tunisia, Sicily, Salerno, Normandy.

LST 393 Decomm 1 Mar 1946. Stricken 14 Mar 1947, sold 20 Mar 1948.
3* Sicily, Salerno, Normandy.
Later history: Merchant *Highway 16.* Restored as LST museum, Muskegon, Mich., May 2002.

LST 394 To UK 24 Dec 1944–12 May 1946; Stricken 19 Jun 1946, sold 10 Dec 1947; BU Norfolk, Va.
2* Sicily, Southern France.

LST 395 Decomm 19 Apr 1946. Stricken 1 May 1946, sold 26 Sep 1947; BU Baltimore.
6* New Georgia Ldgs., Ldgs. on Vella Lavella, Cape Torokina, Hollandia, Biak, Cape Sansapor, Balikpapan, Mindanao Ldgs.

LST 396 Destroyed by accidental gasoline explosion off Vella Lavella, Solomon Is., 18 Aug 1943.
1* New Georgia Ldgs., Ldgs. on Vella Lavella.

LST 397 Decomm 26 Apr 1946. Stricken 5 Jun 1946, sold 30 Sep 1947; BU Baltimore.
7* New Georgia Ldgs., Ldgs. on Vella Lavella, Cape Torokina, Hollandia, Biak, Noemfoor I., Cape Sansapor, Morotai, Leyte, Lingayen, Mindanao Ldgs.

LST 398 Decomm 27 Feb 1946.
4* Solomons, New Georgia Ldgs., Ldgs. on Vella Lavella, Cape Torokina, Guam.
Later history: SCAJAP, as Q029. Stricken 28 Aug 1947, sold 28 Mar 1948; BU Seattle.

LST 399 Damaged by coastal mortar, Treasury Is., 27 Oct 1943. Damaged by collision, Okinawa, 4 Apr 1945 and by grounding, Okinawa, 11 Apr 1945. Decomm 8 Dec 1945.
5* New Georgia Ldgs., Ldgs. on Vella Lavella, Treasury Is. Ldgs., Guam, Iwo Jima, Okinawa.
Later history: SCAJAP, as Q088. †

LST 400 Decomm 1946–47. †
2* Sicily, Normandy.

No.	Builder	Launched	Comm.
LST 401	Beth. Fairfield	16 Oct 1942	*30 Nov 1942*
LST 402	Beth. Fairfield	9 Oct 1942	*9 Dec 1942*
LST 403	Beth. Fairfield	24 Oct 1942	*8 Dec 1942*
LST 404	Beth. Fairfield	28 Oct 1942	*16 Dec 1942*
LST 405	Beth. Fairfield	31 Oct 1942	*28 Dec 1942*
LST 406	Beth. Fairfield	28 Oct 1942	*26 Dec 1942*
LST 407	Beth. Fairfield	5 Nov 1942	*31 Dec 1942*
LST 408	Beth. Fairfield	31 Oct 1942	*23 Dec 1942*
LST 409	Beth. Fairfield	15 Nov 1942	*6 Jan 1943*
LST 410	Beth. Fairfield	15 Nov 1942	*14 Jan 1943*
LST 411	Beth. Fairfield	9 Nov 1942	*31 Dec 1942*
LST 412	Beth. Fairfield	16 Nov 1942	*26 Jan 1943*
LST 413	Beth. Fairfield	10 Nov 1942	*5 Jan 1943*
LST 414	Beth. Fairfield	21 Nov 1942	*19 Jan 1943*
LST 415	Beth. Fairfield	21 Nov 1942	*19 Jan 1943*
LST 416	Beth. Fairfield	30 Nov 1942	*3 Feb 1943*
LST 417	Beth. Fairfield	24 Nov 1942	*29 Jan 1943*
LST 418	Beth. Fairfield	30 Nov 1942	*29 Jan 1943*
LST 419	Beth. Fairfield	30 Nov 1942	*8 Feb 1943*
LST 420	Beth. Fairfield	5 Dec 1942	*15 Feb 1943*
LST 421	Beth. Fairfield	5 Dec 1942	*26 Jan 1943*
LST 422	Beth. Fairfield	10 Dec 1942	*4 Feb 1943*
LST 423	Beth. Fairfield	14 Jan 1943	*24 Feb 1943*
LST 424	Beth. Fairfield	12 Dec 1942	*1 Feb 1943*
LST 425	Beth. Fairfield	12 Dec 1942	*10 Feb 1943*
LST 426	Beth. Fairfield	11 Dec 1942	*16 Feb 1943*
LST 427	Beth. Fairfield	19 Dec 1942	*16 Feb 1943*
LST 428	Beth. Fairfield	22 Dec 1942	*9 Feb 1943*
LST 429	Beth. Fairfield	11 Jan 1943	*20 Feb 1943*
LST 430	Beth. Fairfield	31 Dec 1942	*19 Feb 1943*
LST 431/445	Beth. Fairfield	—	—

Service Records:

LST 401 To UK 30 Nov 1942–7 Mar 1946. Stricken 5 Jun 1946; sold 11 Oct 1947; BU Philadelphia.

LST 402 To UK 9 Dec 1942–24 Sep 1946, as *LSE-53.* Stricken 10 Jun 1947, sold 30 Sep 1947; BU Gibraltar.

LST 403 To UK 8 Dec 1942–11 Apr 1946. Stricken 5 Jun 1946, sold 5 Dec 1947.

LST 404 To UK 16 Dec 1942. Torpedoed by *U-741* off Ryde, and beached in two parts, 15 Aug 1944. Returned 14 Oct 1944. Stricken 21 Oct 1945, sold Nov 1946. Hulk BU Zeebrugge, Belgium.

LST 405 To UK 28 Dec 1942. Damaged in collision with USS *Gen. M. M. Patrick* off Colombo, 25 Oct 1945 and not repaired. Sunk 29 Mar 1946.

LST 406 To UK 26 Dec 1942–13 Apr 1946. Stricken 10 Jun 1947, sold 5 Dec 1947.
Later history: Merchant *Chung 116.* Later PRC Navy.

LST 407 To UK 31 Dec 1942. Beached at Baia, Italy during storm in Mediterranean, 24 Apr 1944, CTL. Returned 6 May 1945; Stricken 11 Jul 1945, sold; BU Italy.

LST 408 To UK 23 Dec 1942–2 May 1946. Stricken 19 Jun 1946, sold 5 Dec 1947.

LST 409 To UK 6 Jan 1943–2 Jul 1946. Stricken 29 Oct 1946, sold 21 Nov 1946.
Later history: Merchant *Spyros*, renamed *Attiki* 1953, *Marianti Tetenes* 1955, *Saipem.* BU 1972.

LST 410 To UK 14 Jan 1943–16 Mar 1946. Stricken 26 Feb 1946, sold 13 Feb 1948.

LST 411 To UK 8 Jan 1943. Sunk by mine off Bastia, Corsica, 1 Jan 1944.

LST 412 To UK 26 Jan 1943–23 Jan 1946. Stricken 20 Mar 1946, sold 16 Dec 1947; BU Philadelphia.

LST 413 To UK 5 Jan 1943–11 Apr 1946. Stricken 10 Jun 1947, sold 5 Dec 1947.

LST 414 To UK 19 Jan 1943. Torpedoed by enemy aircraft off Cani Rocks, Tunisia and beached at Bizerte, 15 Aug 1943.

LST 415 To UK 19 Jan 1943–21 Aug 1945. Torpedoed by German MTBs and beached off Thurrock, England, 16 Jan 1945. Stricken 2 Jun 1945, sold Jan 1948; BU England.

LST 416 To UK 3 Feb 1943–12 Feb 1946. Stricken 5 Jun 1946, sold 23 Apr 1948; FFU.

LST 417 To UK 29 Jan 1943–31 May 1946. Stricken 3 Jul 1946, sold 4 Dec 1947; BU.

LST 418 To UK 29 Jan 1943. Torpedoed and sunk by *U-230* off Anzio, 16 Feb 1944.

LST 419 To UK 8 Feb 1943–4 May 1946. Stricken 8 Jul 1946, sold 5 Dec 1947.

LST 420 To UK 15 Feb 1943. Sunk by mine off Ostend, 7 Nov 1944.

LST 421 To UK 26 Jan 1943–29 Nov 1946. Stricken 1 Aug 1947, sold 7 Oct 1947.
Later history: Merchant *Chong Tong*, renamed *Maung Bama* 1950. BU 1957.

LST 422 To UK 4 Feb 1943. Sunk by mine at Anzio, Italy, 26 Jan 1944.

LST 423 To UK 24 Feb 1943–10 Jun 1946. Stricken 19 Jul 1946, sold 29 Dec 1947; BU Philadelphia.

LST 424 To UK 1 Feb 1943–7 Jan 1946. Stricken 21 May 1946, sold 3 Jul 1946; BU Italy.

LST 425 To UK 10 Feb 1943–30 Aug 1946, as HMS *LSE-50*. Stricken 10 Jun 1947, sold 8 Oct 1947; BU.

LST 426 To UK 16 Feb 1943–23 Apr 1946. Stricken 19 Jun 1946, sold 2 Dec 1947; BU Norfolk, Va.

LST 427 To UK 16 Feb 1943–11 Apr 1946. Stricken 10 Jun 1947, sold 5 Dec 1947.

LST 428 To UK 9 Feb 1943–10 Jun 1946. Stricken 19 Jul 1946, sold 10 Oct 1947; BU Philadelphia.

LST 429 To UK 20 Feb 1943. Destroyed by fire off Tunisia in Mediterranean, 3 Jul 1943.

LST 430 To UK 19 Feb 1943–26 Jan 1946. Stricken 8 May 1946, sold 12 Oct 1947; BU Philadelphia.

LST 431–45 Canceled 16 Sep 1942.

No.	Builder	Launched	Comm.
LST 446	Kaiser Vanc.	18 Sep 1942	30 Nov 1942
LST 447	Kaiser Vanc.	22 Sep 1942	13 Dec 1942
LST 448	Kaiser Vanc.	26 Sep 1942	23 Dec 1942
LST 449	Kaiser Vanc.	30 Sep 1942	31 Dec 1942
LST 450	Kaiser Vanc.	4 Oct 1942	6 Jan 1943
LST 451	Kaiser Vanc.	6 Oct 1942	12 Jan 1943
LST 452	Kaiser Vanc.	10 Oct 1942	16 Jan 1943
LST 453	Kaiser Vanc.	10 Oct 1942	21 Jan 1943
LST 454	Kaiser Vanc.	14 Oct 1942	26 Jan 1943
LST 455	Kaiser Vanc.	17 Oct 1942	30 Jan 1943
LST 456	Kaiser Vanc.	20 Oct 1942	3 Feb 1943
LST 457	Kaiser Vanc.	23 Oct 1942	6 Feb 1943
LST 458	Kaiser Vanc.	26 Oct 1942	10 Feb 1943
LST 459	Kaiser Vanc.	29 Oct 1942	13 Feb 1943
LST 460	Kaiser Vanc.	31 Oct 1942	15 Feb 1943
LST 461	Kaiser Vanc.	3 Nov 1942	18 Feb 1943
LST 462	Kaiser Vanc.	6 Nov 1942	21 Feb 1943
LST 463	Kaiser Vanc.	9 Nov 1942	23 Feb 1943
LST 464	Kaiser Vanc.	12 Nov 1942	25 Feb 1943
LST 465	Kaiser Vanc.	9 Jan 1943	27 Feb 1943
LST 466	Kaiser Vanc.	18 Nov 1942	1 Mar 1943
LST 467	Kaiser Vanc.	21 Nov 1942	3 Mar 1943
LST 468	Kaiser Vanc.	24 Nov 1942	5 Mar 1943
LST 469	Kaiser Vanc.	27 Nov 1942	8 Mar 1943
LST 470	Kaiser Vanc.	30 Nov 1942	9 Mar 1943
LST 471	Kaiser Vanc.	3 Dec 1942	11 Mar 1943
LST 472	Kaiser Vanc.	7 Dec 1942	13 Mar 1943
LST 473	Kaiser Vanc.	9 Dec 1942	16 Mar 1943
LST 474	Kaiser Vanc.	12 Dec 1942	19 Mar 1943
LST 475	Kaiser Vanc.	16 Dec 1942	20 Mar 1943

Service Records:

LST 446 Damaged by accidental explosion, Bougainville, Solomon Is., 1 Jan 1944. Decomm 13 Jul 1946. Stricken 8 Oct 1946, sold 13 Feb 1947.
6* Cape Torokina, Green Is. Ldgs., Solomons, New Georgia Ldgs., Ldgs. on Vella Lavella, Guam, Iwo Jima, Okinawa.
Later history: Merchant *Samana* 1948. BU 1964 Panama City, Fla.

LST 447 Sunk by kamikaze off Kerama Retto, 7 Apr 1945 (5 killed).
6* Cape Torokina, Green Is. Ldgs., Hollandia, Guam, Okinawa.

LST 448 Damaged by Japanese aircraft southeast of Bougainville 1 Oct and sank off VellaLavella, 5 Oct 1943.
2* Ldgs. on Vella Lavella.

LST 449 Damaged by coastal gun, Okinawa, 10 Apr 1945. Decomm 16 Mar 1946. Stricken 28 Mar 1946, sold 27 Jan 1947.
5* Solomons, Cape Torokina, Guam, Iwo Jima, Okinawa.
Later history: Merchant *Don Francisco* 1948, renamed *Anna G.* 1959. BU 1971.

LST 450 Rec **LST(H) 450**, 15 Sep 1945. Decomm 8 Apr 1946. Stricken 17 Apr 1946, sold 16 Apr 1948; BU.
3* Saipan, Tinian, Okinawa.

LST 451 Decomm 22 Jul 1946. Stricken 25 Sep 1946, sold 11 Dec 1947; BU Oakland, Calif.
5* Saipan, Tinian, Leyte, Lingayen, Okinawa.

LST 452 Damaged by coastal defense gun, Leyte, 20 Oct 1944. Decomm 12 Jun 1946. Stricken 3 Jul 1946, sold 5 Dec 1947.
7* Lae Ldgs., Finschhafen, Cape Gloucester, Saidor, Admiralty Is. Ldgs., Hollandia, Biak, Cape Sansapor, Morotai, Leyte, Lingayen, Balikpapan.

LST 453 Converted to repair ship in Australia, May 1943, and rec **ARL 40**, renamed ***Remus***, 15 Aug 1944. Decomm 15 Jul 1946. Stricken 15 Aug 1946, sold 16 Dec 1947; BU.
2* Finschhafen, Arawe.

LST 454 Decomm 25 Mar 1946. Stricken 1 May 1946, sold 3 Oct 1947; BU Baltimore.
8* Lae Ldgs., Finschhafen, Saidor, Admiralty Is. Ldgs., Hollandia, Biak, Morotai, Leyte, Lingayen, Visayan Is. Ldgs., Balikpapan.

LST 455 Damaged by dive bomber, east of Buna, New Guinea, 12 Sep 1943. Converted to repair ship and rec **ARL 41**, renamed ***Achilles***, 21 Apr 1944. Decomm 19 Jul 1946. Stricken 28 Aug 1946. To China 8 Dec 1947.
3* Lae Ldgs., Leyte, Brunei.
Later history: Renamed *Hsing An*. Burned and grounded, 1949 salved PRC *Taku Shan*.

LST 456 Decomm Dec 1946. †
8* Lae Ldgs., Cape Gloucester, Saidor, Admiralty Is. Ldgs., Hollandia, Wakde, Biak, Cape Sansapor, Morotai, Leyte, Lingayen, Mindanao Ldgs., Balikpapan.
Later history: SCAJAP, as Q043.

LST 457 Decomm 15 Mar 1946.
7* Lae Ldgs., Cape Gloucester, Saidor, Admiralty Is. Ldgs., Hollandia, Wakde, Biak, Noemfoor I., Morotai, Leyte, Visayan Is. Ldgs., Balikpapan.
Later history: SCAJAP, as Q098. Stricken 29 Sep 1947, sold 20 Apr 1948; BU.

LST 458 Decomm 15 Apr 1946. Stricken 3 Jul 1946, sold 31 Oct 1947; BU Philadelphia.
6* Lae Ldgs., Cape Gloucester, Saidor, Admiralty Is. Ldgs., Hollandia, Wakde, Biak, Noemfoor I., Cape Sansapor, Morotai, Leyte, Mindanao Ldgs.

LST 459 Decomm 12 Apr 1946. Stricken 19 Jun 1946, sold 31Oct 1947; BU New Orleans.
6* Cape Gloucester, Admiralty Is. Ldgs., Hollandia, Biak, Noemfoor I., Cape Sansapor, Morotai, Leyte, Lingayen, Mindanao Ldgs., Sulu Is.

LST 460 Damaged by kamikaze south of Mindoro, 21 Dec 1944; sank 1 Jan 1945.
6* Ldgs. on Vella Lavella, Treasury Is. Ldgs., Hollandia, Morotai, Leyte, Lingayen.

LST 461 Decomm 2 Sep 1947. Stricken 16 Sep 1947, sold 30 Mar 1948; BU Seattle.
5* Saipan, Tinian, Leyte, Okinawa, Ldgs. at Nasugbu , Lingayen.

LST 462 Decomm 21 Mar 1946. Stricken 1 May 1946, sold 13 Dec 1947; BU.
5* Hollandia, Biak, Noemfoor I., Cape Sansapor, Morotai, Leyte, Lingayen, Balikpapan.

LST 463 Decomm 8 Jun 1946. Stricken 19 Jun 1946, sold 3 Nov 1947; BU Seattle.
9* Cape Gloucester, Saidor, Hollandia, Biak, Noemfoor I., Leyte, Cape Sansapor, Morotai, Lingayen, Mindanao Ldgs., Subic Bay, Okinawa.

LST 464 Rec **LST(H) 464**, 15 Sep 1945. Decomm 16 Apr 1946. Stricken 19 Jun 1946, sold 5 Mar 1948 (as barge).
1* Leyte.

LST 465 Decomm 8 Mar 1946. Stricken 12 Apr 1946; Sold 30 Sep 1947; BU Baltimore.
6* Cape Gloucester, Saidor, Admiralty Is. Ldgs., Hollandia, Wakde, Morotai, Leyte, Lingayen.

LST 466 Decomm 8 Mar 1946. Stricken 12 Apr 1946, sold 4 Jun 1948; BU.
7* Lae Ldgs., Cape Gloucester, Saidor, Admiralty Is. Ldgs., Hollandia, Wakde, Biak, Noemfoor I., Cape Sansapor, Leyte, Lingayen, Tarakan, Balikpapan.

LST 467 Decomm 28 May 1946. Stricken 5 Jun 1946, sold 22 Nov 1946.
8* Lae Ldgs., Cape Gloucester, Hollandia, Wakde, Biak, Noemfoor I., Cape Sansapor, Morotai, Leyte, Lingayen, Palawan Ldgs., Visayan Is. Ldgs., Tarakan.
Later history: Merchant *Ampowercorp* 1947, renamed *Frank J. Humphrey* 1948, *Witshoal II* 1969.

LST 468 Decomm 12 Apr 1946. Stricken 5 Jun 1946, sold 30 Sep 1947; BU Baltimore.
7* Lae Ldgs., Cape Gloucester, Saidor, Admiralty Is. Ldgs., Hollandia, Biak, Noemfoor I., Cape Sansapor, Morotai, Leyte, Lingayen, Mindanao Ldgs.

LST 469 Damaged by *I-174* southeast of Coffs Harbor, Northern Australia, 16 Jun 1943. Decomm 27 Mar 1946. Stricken 1 May 1946, sold 13 Dec 1947; BU.
4* Hollandia, Wakde, Biak, Noemfoor I., Cape Sansapor, Morotai, Leyte, Lingayen.

LST 470 Decomm 4 Mar 1946. Stricken 5 Jun 1946, sold 6 Nov 1947; BU Seattle.
8* Lae Ldgs., Cape Gloucester, Saidor, Admiralty Is. Ldgs., Hollandia, Biak, Cape Sansapor, Morotai, Leyte, Lingayen, Palawan Ldgs., Mindanao Ldgs., Balikpapan.

LST 471 Damaged by torpedo and dive bombers off Buna, New Guinea, 4 Sep 1943. Decomm 26 Feb 1946. Stricken 12 Apr 1946, sold 21 Jan 1948; BU.
5* Lae Ldgs., Leyte, Lingayen, Mindanao Ldgs., Balikpapan.

LST 472 Sunk after damage by kamikaze south of Mindoro, 15 Dec 1944 (6 killed).
6* New Georgia Ldgs., Cape Torokina, Green Is. Ldgs., Hollandia, Wakde, Biak, Noemfoor I., Cape Sansapor, Morotai, Mindoro.

LST 473 Damaged by torpedo and dive bombers off Buna, New Guinea, 4 Sep 1943 (8 killed). Decomm 18 Mar 1946. Stricken 17 Apr 1946, sold 21 Apr 1948; BU.
5* Lae Ldgs., Leyte, Lingayen, Subic Bay, Mindanao Ldgs.

LST 474 Decomm 22 Mar 1946. Stricken 17 Apr 1946, sold 5 Dec 1947; BU Barber, N.J.
8* Lae Ldgs., Cape Gloucester, Saidor, Hollandia, Biak, Morotai, Leyte, Lingayen, Mindanao Ldgs., Balikpapan.

LST 475 Decomm 24 Apr 1946. Stricken 5 Jun 1946, sold 31 Oct 1946 .
6* Lae Ldgs., Cape Gloucester, Saidor, Cape Gloucester, Hollandia, Noemfoor I., Cape Sansapor, Morotai, Leyte, Lingayen.
Later history: Merchant *Bonito*, renamed *Ana Carolina* 1964. BU 1971.

No.	Builder	Launched	Comm.
LST 476	Kaiser Rich.	10 Oct 1942	4 Apr 1943
LST 477	Kaiser Rich.	29 Oct 1942	19 Feb 1943
LST 478	Kaiser Rich.	7 Nov 1942	13 Mar 1943
LST 479	Kaiser Rich.	4 Oct 1942	19 Apr 1943
LST 480	Kaiser Rich.	29 Oct 1942	3 May 1943
LST 481	Kaiser Rich.	2 Dec 1942	15 May 1943
LST 482	Kaiser Rich.	17 Dec 1942	20 Mar 1943
LST 483	Kaiser Rich.	30 Dec 1942	3 May 1943
LST 484	Kaiser Rich.	2 Jan 1943	23 Apr 1943
LST 485	Kaiser Rich.	9 Jan 1943	19 May 1943
LST 486	Kaiser Rich.	16 Jan 1943	29 May 1943
LST 487	Kaiser Rich.	23 Jan 1943	27 Apr 1943
LST 488	Kaiser Rich.	5 Mar 1943	24 May 1943
LST 489	Kaiser Rich.	2 Apr 1943	*30 Jul 1943*
LST 490	Kaiser Rich.	3 Apr 1943	*20 Aug 1943*
LST 491	Missouri Valley	23 Sep 1943	3 Dec 1943
LST 492	Missouri Valley	30 Sep 1943	8 Dec 1943
LST 493	Missouri Valley	4 Oct 1943	13 Dec 1943
LST 494	Missouri Valley	11 Oct 1943	18 Dec 1943
LST 495	Missouri Valley	16 Oct 1943	23 Dec 1943
LST 496	Missouri Valley	22 Oct 1943	27 Dec 1943
LST 497	Missouri Valley	27 Oct 1943	31 Dec 1943
LST 498	Missouri Valley	1 Nov 1943	6 Jan 1944
LST 499	Missouri Valley	5 Nov 1943	10 Jan 1944
LST 500	Missouri Valley	10 Nov 1943	13 Jan 1944

Service Records:

LST 476 Decomm 12 Feb 1946.
5* Gilbert Is., Kwajalein, Hollandia, Guam, Cape Sansapor.
Later history: SCAJAP, as Q053. Stricken 31 Oct 1947, sold 1 Jun 1948; BU Seattle.

LST 477 Damaged by kamikaze, Iwo Jima, 21 Feb 1945 (none killed). Rec **LST(H) 477**, 15 Sep 1945. Decomm 1946.
4* Gilbert Is., Kwajalein, Guam, Iwo Jima.
Later history: SCAJAP, as Q091. Stricken 28 Aug 1947, sold 27 Mar 1948; BU.

LST 478 Decomm 23 Mar 1946.
5* Gilbert Is., Hollandia, Guam, Leyte, Okinawa.
Later history: SCAJAP, as Q100. Stricken 28 Aug 1947, sold 25 Mar 1948; BU Seattle.

LST 479 Decomm 28 Feb 1946. Stricken 28 Mar 1946, sold 16 Apr 1948; BU.
5* Gilbert Is., Kwajalein, Hollandia, Guam, Okinawa.

LST 480 Sunk by accidental ammunition explosion at Pearl Harbor, 21 May 1944.
2* Gilbert Is., Kwajalein.

LST 481 Damaged by coastal gunfire, Tinian, 24 Jul 1944. Decomm 28 Feb 1946. Stricken 12 Apr 1948, sold 16 Apr 1948; BU.
6* Gilbert Is., Kwajalein, Hollandia, Guam, Iwo Jima, Okinawa.

LST 482 Rec **LST(H) 482**, 15 Sep 1945. Decomm 23 Feb 1946.
6* Gilbert Is., Kwajalein, Hollandia, Guam, Leyte, Lingayen.
Later history: SCAJAP, as Q072. †

LST 483 Damaged by coastal mortars, Leyte, 21 Oct 1944. Decomm 10 Feb 1946.
4* Saipan, Tinian, Leyte, Okinawa.
Later history: SCAJAP, as Q050. †

LST 484 Decomm 27 Jul 1946. Stricken 28 Aug 1946, sold 19 Nov 1947; BU Seattle.
5* Gilbert Is., Kwajalein, Eniwetok, Saipan, Tinian, Okinawa.

LST 485 Damaged by coastal mortar, Treasury Is., 27 Oct 1943. Rec **LST(H) 485**, 15 Sep 1945. Decomm 30 Jul 1946. Stricken 28 Aug 1946, sold 29 Mar 1948; BU.
5* Ldgs. on Vella Lavella, Treasury Is. Ldgs., Saipan, Tinian, Okinawa.

LST 486 Damaged by coastal mortars, Leyte, 21 Oct 1944. Decomm 13 Jan 1946.
4* Saipan, Tinian, Leyte, Lingayen.
Later history: SCAJAP, as Q011. Destroyed 23 Jul 1947.

LST 487 Decomm 15 Mar 1946. Stricken 1 May 1946, sold 20 Feb 1948.
5* Saipan, Tinian, Palau, Lingayen, Okinawa.
Later history: Merchant *Dona Rosa*.

LST 488 Rec **LST(H) 488**, 15 Sep 1945. Decomm 11 Jan 1946.
Later history: SCAJAP, as Q009. †
4* Cape Torokina, Guam, Leyte, Lingayen.

LST 489 Completed as repair ship, rec **ARL 2**, renamed ***Amycus***, 13 Jan 1943.
LST 490 Completed as repair ship, rec **ARL 3**, renamed ***Agenor***, 13 Jan 1943.
LST 491 Decomm 12 Jan 1946.
 3* Normandy, Southern France, Okinawa.
 Later history: SCAJAP, as Q010. †
LST 492 Decomm 17 Jun 1946. Stricken 23 Jun 1947, sold 24 Feb 1948.
 3* Normandy, Southern France, Okinawa.
LST 493 Lost by grounding off Plymouth, England, 12 Apr 1945.
 1* Normandy.
LST 494 Decomm 29 Jun 1946. Stricken 28 Aug 1946, sold to Philippines, 12 Aug 1948.
 3* Normandy, Southern France, Okinawa.
LST 495 Decomm 23 Apr 1946. Stricken 5 Jun 1946, sold 8 Apr 1948; BU Seattle.
 3* Normandy, Southern France, Okinawa.
LST 496 Sunk by mine off Omaha Beach, Normandy, 11 Jun 1944.
 1* Normandy.
LST 497 Decomm 18 Dec 1945. Stricken 8 Jan 1946; Sold 30 Jan 1948.
 1* Normandy.
 Later history: Merchant *Robert McMichael* 1949, renamed *Fort Gaspe* 1970. BU 1985 Sorel, Que.
LST 498 Decomm 8 Nov 1945. Stricken 28 Nov 1946, sold 21 Nov 1947; BU Philipsdale, R.I.
 1* Normandy.
LST 499 Sunk by mine off Utah Beach, Normandy, 8 Jun 1944.
 1* Normandy.
LST 500 Decomm 18 Jul 1947. Stricken 1 Aug 1947, sold 20 Apr 1948.
 1* Normandy.
 Later history: Merchant *Southern Districts* 1948. Foundered southwest of Key West, Fla., 6 Dec 1954.

No.	Builder	Launched	Comm.
LST 501	Jeffersonville	22 Sep 1943	26 Nov 1943
LST 502	Jeffersonville	25 Sep 1943	8 Dec 1943
LST 503	Jeffersonville	8 Oct 1943	8 Dec 1943
LST 504	Jeffersonville	19 Oct 1943	18 Dec 1943
LST 505	Jeffersonville	27 Oct 1943	27 Dec 1943
LST 506	Jeffersonville	4 Nov 1943	3 Jan 1944
LST 507	Jeffersonville	16 Nov 1943	10 Jan 1944
LST 508	Jeffersonville	10 Nov 1943	14 Jan 1944
LST 509	Jeffersonville	23 Nov 1943	20 Jan 1944
LST 510	Jeffersonville	30 Nov 1943	31 Jan 1944
LST 511	Chicago Bridge	30 Nov 1943	3 Jan 1944
LST 512	Chicago Bridge	10 Dec 1943	8 Jan 1944
LST 513	Chicago Bridge	17 Dec 1943	*9 May 1944*
LST 514	Chicago Bridge	24 Dec 1943	*23 May 1944*
LST 515	Chicago Bridge	31 Dec 1943	28 Jan 1944
LST 516	Chicago Bridge	7 Jan 1944	31 Jan 1944
LST 517	Chicago Bridge	15 Jan 1944	7 Feb 1944
LST 518	Chicago Bridge	20 Jan 1944	*24 Jun 1944*
LST 519	Chicago Bridge	25 Jan 1944	17 Feb 1944
LST 520	Chicago Bridge	31 Jan 1944	28 Feb 1944
LST 521	Chicago Bridge	5 Feb 1944	9 Feb 1944
LST 522	Chicago Bridge	11 Feb 1944	1 Mar 1944
LST 523	Jeffersonville	6 Dec 1943	3 Feb 1944
LST 524	Jeffersonville	13 Dec 1943	9 Feb 1944
LST 525	Jeffersonville	20 Dec 1943	14 Feb 1944
LST 526	Jeffersonville	27 Dec 1943	17 Feb 1944
LST 527	Jeffersonville	3 Jan 1944	17 Feb 1944
LST 528	Jeffersonville	11 Jan 1944	21 Feb 1944
LST 529	Jeffersonville	17 Jan 1944	29 Feb 1944
LST 530	Jeffersonville	25 Jan 1944	6 Mar 1944

Service Records:

LST 501 Decomm 20 Aug 1947.
 3* Normandy, Southern France, Okinawa.
 Later history: SCAJAP, as Q097. Stricken 29 Sep 1947, sold 7 May 1948; BU Seattle.
LST 502 Decomm 4 Feb 1946.
 3* Normandy, Southern France, Okinawa.
 Later history: SCAJAP, as Q041. Stricken 23 Dec 1947, sold 20 May 1948; BU Seattle.
LST 503 Decomm 11 Jun 1946. †
 1* Normandy.
LST 504 Decomm 22 Jan 1946.
 3* Normandy, Southern France, Okinawa.
 Later history: SCAJAP, as Q016. †
LST 505 Decomm 11 Jun 1946. Stricken 16 Sep 1947, sold 13 Feb 1948.
 3* Normandy, Southern France, Okinawa.
LST 506 Decomm 24 Jul 1947. Stricken 28 Aug 1947, sold 4 Dec 1947.
 1* Normandy.
 Later history: Merchant *Southern Counties* 1948, renamed *Bethcoaster* 1953, *Spadafora* barge.
LST 507 Torpedoed and sunk by Ger MTB in Lyme Bay, 28 Apr 1944 (126 killed).
LST 508 Decomm 2 Aug 1946. Stricken 28 Jan 1947. To France 25 Mar 1947.
 1* Normandy.
 Later history: Renamed *Orne, L-9002.* R62.
LST 509 †
 1* Normandy.
LST 510 Decomm 1 Jul 1946. †
 1* Normandy.
LST 511 Decomm 19 Dec 1945. Stricken 8 Jan 1946, sold 17 Feb 1948.
 1* Normandy.
 Later history: Merchant *Guy Bartholomew* 1949, renamed *Fort Kent* 1969. barge 1982.
LST 512 Decomm 28 Mar 1947. †
 1* Normandy.
LST 513 Completed as repair ship, rec **ARL 9**, renamed ***Endymion***, 3 Nov 1943.
LST 514 Completed as repair ship, rec **ARB 5**, renamed ***Midas***, 3 Nov 1943.
LST 515 †
 1* Normandy.
LST 516 Decomm 28 Feb 1947. †
 1* Normandy.
LST 517 Decomm 21 Dec 1945. Stricken 21 Jan 1946, sold 16 Jan 1947.
 1* Normandy.
 Later history: Merchant *Santa Maria de Lujan* 1948. Lost by grounding off Punta del Este, 21 Jul 1965.
LST 518 Completed as repair ship, rec **ARB 6**, renamed ***Nestor***, 3 Nov 1943.
LST 519 †
 2* Convoy UGS-36, Normandy.
LST 520 Decomm 13 Jan 1946.
 2* Normandy, Okinawa.
 Later history: SCAJAP, as Q013. †
LST 521 Decomm 21 Oct 1945. †
 1* Normandy.
LST 522 Decomm 6 Jun 1946. Stricken 22 Jan 1948, sold 18 Oct 1947.
 1* Normandy.
LST 523 Sunk by mine off Utah Beach, Normandy, 19 Jun 1944.
 1* Normandy.
LST 524 Decomm 4 Feb 1946.
 2* Normandy, Okinawa.
 Later history: SCAJAP, as Q040. Stricken 31 Oct 1947, sold 21 May 1948; BU Seattle.

LST 525 Decomm 25 Oct 1946. Stricken 15 Sep 1947. †
2* Convoy UGS-36, Southern France.
LST 526 Decomm 21 Dec 1945. Stricken 21 Jan 1946, sold 24 Jan 1947.
2* Convoy UGS-36, Southern France.
Later history: Merchant *Jane O.* 1948, renamed *Stanolind 59*, then *Arcati* 1952.
LST 527 Decomm 28 Feb 1946. †
1* Normandy.
LST 528 †
1* Normandy.
LST 529 Decomm 7 Jun 1946. †
1* Normandy.
LST 530 Decomm Jan 1946.
3* Normandy, Okinawa, Tarakan.
Later history: SCAJAP, as Q017. †

No. Name	Builder	Launched	Comm.
LST 531	Missouri Valley	24 Nov 1943	17 Jan 1944
LST 532	Missouri Valley	28 Nov 1943	20 Jan 1944
LST 533	Missouri Valley	1 Dec 1943	27 Jan 1944
LST 534	Missouri Valley	8 Dec 1943	31 Jan 1944
LST 535	Missouri Valley	21 Dec 1943	4 Feb 1944
LST 536	Missouri Valley	27 Dec 1943	9 Feb 1944
LST 537	Missouri Valley	31 Dec 1943	9 Feb 1944
LST 538	Missouri Valley	5 Jan 1944	14 Feb 1944
LST 539	Missouri Valley	10 Jan 1944	17 Feb 1944
LST 540	Missouri Valley	14 Jan 1944	22 Feb 1944
LST 541	Missouri Valley	25 Jan 1944	28 Feb 1944
LST 542	Missouri Valley	28 Jan 1944	29 Feb 1944
LST 543	Missouri Valley	1 Feb 1944	6 Mar 1944
LST 544	Missouri Valley	4 Feb 1944	16 Mar 1944
LST 545	Missouri Valley	12 Feb 1944	23 Mar 1944
LST 546	Missouri Valley	16 Feb 1944	27 Mar 1944
LST 547	Missouri Valley	19 Feb 1944	30 Mar 1944
LST 548	Missouri Valley	22 Feb 1944	3 Apr 1944
LST 549	Missouri Valley	25 Feb 1944	5 Apr 1944
LST 550	Missouri Valley	9 Mar 1944	10 Apr 1944
LST 551	Missouri Valley	11 Mar 1944	14 Apr 1944
LST 552	Missouri Valley	14 Mar 1944	19 Apr 1944
LST 553	Missouri Valley	16 Mar 1944	22 Apr 1944
LST 554	Missouri Valley	18 Mar 1944	27 Apr 1944
LST 555	Missouri Valley	22 Mar 1944	28 Apr 1944
LST 556	Missouri Valley	7 Apr 1944	1 May 1944
LST 557	Missouri Valley	11 Apr 1944	5 May 1944
LST 558	Missouri Valley	14 Apr 1944	8 May 1944
LST 559	Missouri Valley	18 Apr 1944	9 May 1944
LST 560	Missouri Valley	21 Apr 1944	2 May 1944
LST 561	Missouri Valley	25 Apr 1944	15 May 1944
LST 562	Missouri Valley	28 Apr 1944	18 May 1944
LST 563	Missouri Valley	1 May 1944	20 May 1944
LST 564	Missouri Valley	4 May 1944	25 May 1944
LST 565	Missouri Valley	8 May 1944	25 May 1944
LST 566	Missouri Valley	11 May 1944	29 May 1944
LST 567	Missouri Valley	15 May 1944	1 Jun 1944
LST 568	Missouri Valley	18 May 1944	3 Jun 1944
LST 569	Missouri Valley	20 May 1944	5 Jun 1944
LST 570	Missouri Valley	22 May 1944	9 Jun 1944
LST 571	Missouri Valley	25 May 1944	14 Jun 1944
LST 572	Missouri Valley	29 May 1944	19 Jun 1944
LST 573	Missouri Valley	31 May 1944	21 Jun 1944
LST 574	Missouri Valley	5 Jun 1944	26 Jun 1944
LST 575	Missouri Valley	9 Jun 1944	24 Jun 1944
LST 576	Missouri Valley	12 Jun 1944	8 Jul 1944
LST 577	Missouri Valley	16 Jun 1944	10 Jul 1944
LST 578	Missouri Valley	19 Jun 1944	15 Jul 1944
LST 579	Missouri Valley	22 Jun 1944	21 Jul 1944
LST 580	Missouri Valley	26 Jun 1944	25 Jul 1944
LST 581	Missouri Valley	29 Jun 1944	27 Jul 1944
LST 582	Missouri Valley	1 Jul 1944	31 Jul 1944
LST 583	Missouri Valley	5 Jul 1944	2 Aug 1944
LST 584	Missouri Valley	8 Jul 1944	5 Aug 1944
LST 585	Missouri Valley	12 Jul 1944	8 Aug 1944
LST 586	Missouri Valley	15 Jul 1944	15 Aug 1944
LST 587	Missouri Valley	19 Jul 1944	18 Aug 1944
LST 588	Missouri Valley	22 Jul 1944	19 Aug 1944
LST 589	Missouri Valley	26 Jul 1944	24 Aug 1944
LST 590	Missouri Valley	29 Jul 1944	26 Aug 1944
LST 591	Missouri Valley	2 Aug 1944	29 Aug 1944
LST 592	Missouri Valley	5 Aug 1944	1 Sep 1944
LST 593	Missouri Valley	9 Aug 1944	5 Sep 1944
LST 594	Missouri Valley	12 Aug 1944	6 Sep 1944
LST 595	Missouri Valley	16 Aug 1944	14 Sep 1944
LST 596	Missouri Valley	21 Aug 1944	14 Sep 1944
LST 597	Missouri Valley	28 Aug 1944	19 Sep 1944
LST 598	Missouri Valley	29 Aug 1944	22 Sep 1944
LST 599	Missouri Valley	2 Aug 1944	27 Sep 1944

Service Records:

LST 531 Torpedoed and sunk by German MTB in Lyme Bay, 28 Apr 1944 (314 killed).
LST 532 †
1* Normandy.
LST 533 †
1* Normandy.
LST 534 Damaged by kamikaze, Okinawa, 22 Jun 1945 (3 killed). Decomm 2 Nov 1945. Scuttled off Okinawa, 9 Dec 1945.
1* Normandy.
LST 535 Decomm 14 Jan 1946.
2* Normandy, Okinawa.
Later history: SCAJAP, as Q014. †
LST 536 Decomm 23 Jan 1946.
1* Normandy.
Later history: SCAJAP, as Q024. To South Korea 21 Feb 1947.
LST 537 Decomm and trfd to China 29 May 1946.
1* Normandy.
Later history: Renamed *Chung Ting.* R 1993.
LST 538 Damaged by MTB torpedo, Normandy, 11 Jun 1944. To UK 26 Oct 1944–16 Mar 1946. Stricken 16 Mar 1946, sold 5 Dec 1947.
2* Convoy UGS-36, Normandy.
LST 539 Decomm 22 Jun 1946. Stricken 31 Jul 1946, sold 22 Apr 1948; BU.
2* Convoy UGS-37, Normandy.
LST 540 Damaged by grounding, Okinawa, 7 Jun 1945. Decomm 13 Jan 1946.
2* Normandy, Okinawa.
Later history: SCAJAP, as Q022. Lost by accident 20 Aug 1947.
LST 541 Decomm 9 Nov 1945. Stricken 28 Nov 1945, sold 22 Mar 1948.
1* Normandy.

Later history: Merchant barge *L.E.M.*, renamed *Ocean Burning No. 1* 1968.
LST 542 †
1* Normandy.
LST 543 Decomm 31 May 1946. Stricken 17 Jul 1947, sold 5 Dec 1947.
2* Normandy, Okinawa.
LST 544 Decomm 9 Aug 1946. Stricken 25 Sep 1946, sold 23 Jun 1948; BU Portland, Ore.
LST 545 Bikini target. Decomm 29 Aug 1946. Stricken 28 May 1948; sunk as target 12 May 1948.
LST 546 Decomm early 1946.
Later history: SCAJAP, as Q076. †
LST 547 Decomm 28 Feb 1946.
Later history: SCAJAP, as Q077. Stricken 31 Oct 1947, sold 26 May 1948; BU.
LST 548 Decomm 15 Feb 1946.
2* Southern France, Okinawa.
Later history: SCAJAP, as Q067. †
LST 549 Decomm 28 Feb 1946.
4* Morotai, Leyte, Lingayen, Mindanao Ldgs.
Later history: SCAJAP, as Q078. Stricken 5 Dec 1947, sold 23 May 1948; BU.
LST 550 Decomm 13 Jan 1946.
2* Southern France, Okinawa.
Later history: SCAJAP, as Q012. †
LST 551 †
1* Southern France.
LST 552 Damaged by bomber, Leyte, 24 Oct 1944. Decomm 19 Apr 1946. Stricken 1 May 1946, sold 3 Nov 1947; BU Seattle.
4* Palau, Leyte, Subic Bay, Okinawa.
LST 553 Decomm and to Army 13 Feb 1947. Stricken 25 Apr 1947.
5* Palau, Leyte, Lingayen, Subic Bay, Okinawa, Minesweeping 1945.
Later history: Merchant barge *Humboldt Woodsman.*
LST 554 Damaged in storm, Okinawa, 3 Apr 1945.
4* Palau, Leyte, Lingayen, Okinawa. Decomm 20 Jul 1946. Stricken 25 Sep 1946, sold 29 Mar 1948; BU Vancouver, Wash.
LST 555 Damaged by grounding, Okinawa, 12 Apr 1945. Went aground at Wakanura, Japan, 8 Oct 1945. Decomm 6 Jan 1946. Destroyed by gunfire, 26 Jan 1946.
4* Palau, Leyte, Okinawa, Subic Bay.
LST 556 Decomm 14 Mar 1946. Stricken 12 Apr 1946, sold 27 Apr 1948; BU Chester, Pa.
5* Palau, Leyte, Ormoc, Mindoro, Subic Bay, Okinawa.
LST 557 Damaged by coastal gun, Okinawa, 9 Apr 1945. Decomm 29 May 1946 and trfd to China. Stricken 12 Mar 1948.
4* Palau, Leyte, Lingayen, Okinawa.
Later history: Renamed *Chung Hsing.* R 1997.
LST 558 Decomm 13 Feb 1946.
4* Palau, Leyte, Okinawa, Subic Bay.
Later history: SCAJAP, as Q056. Stricken 16 Sep 1947, sold 24 May 1948; BU.
LST 559 Decomm 1 Jun 1946. Stricken 19 Jun 1946, sold 5 Dec 1947.
4* Palau, Leyte, Lingayen, Okinawa.
LST 560 Decomm 17 May 1946. Stricken 19 Jun 1946, sold 12 Sep 1946.
2* Palawan Ldgs., Visayan Is. Ldgs., Brunei.
Later history: Merchant *M.O.B. 377-B.*
LST 561 Decomm 30 Apr 1946. †
1* Southern France.
LST 562 Damaged by collision, Brunei, 19 Jun 1945. Decomm 21 May 1946. Stricken 3 Jul 1946, sold 19 Apr 1948; BU.
2* Morotai, Tarakan.
LST 563 Lost by grounding at Clipperton I., 22 Dec 1944. Stricken 23 Feb 1945.
LST 564 Decomm 8 Mar 1946. Stricken 1 May 1946, sold 3 Mar 1948.
2* Leyte, Okinawa.
Later history: Merchant barge *Stanolind 50*, renamed *Pan American 50*, *Seadrill.*
LST 565 Decomm 13 Jun 1946. Stricken 3 Jul 1946; destroyed 13 Dec 1946.
4* Leyte, Mindoro, Okinawa, Subic Bay.
LST 566 Decomm 11 Mar 1946. †
Later history: SCAJAP, as Q094.
LST 567 Damaged in collision with *LST-610*, Lingayen Gulf, 10 Jan 1945. Decomm 28 Jan 1946.
3* Leyte, Lingayen, Okinawa. Tokyo Bay.
Later history: SCAJAP, as Q032. Stricken 31 Oct 1947, sold 24 May 1948; BU.
LST 568 Went aground in typhoon at Okinawa, 9 Oct 1945. Decomm 4 Mar 1946. Stricken 20 Mar 1946; destroyed 16 Mar 1948.
3* Leyte, Lingayen, Okinawa.
LST 569 Decomm 13 Jun 1946. Stricken 15 Oct 1946, sold 5 Dec 1947.
4* Leyte, Lingayen, Subic Bay, Mindanao Ldgs.
LST 570 Damaged by grounding, Okinawa, 4 Apr 1945. Decomm 14 May 1946. Stricken 19 Jun 1946; Sold 31 Dec 1948; BU Baltimore.
2* Lingayen, Okinawa.
LST 571 Decomm 12 Mar 1946. Stricken 12 Apr 1946, sold 17 Aug 1948.
2* Lingayen, Okinawa.
LST 572 Decomm 8 Mar 1946. †
1* Okinawa.
Later history: SCAJAP, as Q090.
LST 573 Decomm 24 Jan 1946.
3* Leyte, Mindoro, Mindanao Ldgs., Visayan Is. Ldgs.
Later history: SCAJAP, as Q027. Stricken 31 Oct 1947, sold 26 May 1948.
LST 574 Decomm 17 Jun 1946. Stricken 3 Jul 1946, sold 5 Nov 1947 to China.
4* Leyte, Lingayen, Mindanao Ldgs., Brunei.
Later history: Renamed *Chung Yung.* R 1997.
LST 575 Rec **LST(M) 575**, 15 Jan 1945. Converted to barracks ship and rec **APB 41**, renamed ***Wythe***, 31 Mar 1945. Decomm 29 May 1947. †
1* Okinawa.
LST 576 Decomm 14 May 1946. Stricken 9 Jun 1946, sold 7 Oct 1947; BU Charleston, S.C.
2* Lingayen, Okinawa.
LST 577 Torpedoed by submarine *Ro-50* west of Mindanao and sunk by US, 11 Feb 1945 (86 killed).
2* Leyte, Lingayen.
LST 578 Decomm 22 Mar 1946.
3* Leyte, Lingayen, Mindanao Ldgs.
Later history: SCAJAP, as Q099. †
LST 579 Decomm 24 Feb 1946.
4* Leyte, Lingayen, Balikpapan, Mindanao Ldgs.
Later history: SCAJAP, as Q073. †
LST 580 Decomm 29 Jan 1946.
2* Lingayen, Okinawa.
Later history: SCAJAP, as Q035. Stricken 31 Oct 1947, sold 2 May 1948; BU Seattle.
LST 581 Decomm 28 Jan 1946.
1* Okinawa.
Later history: SCAJAP, as Q030. †
LST 582 Decomm 29 Jan 1946.
2* Lingayen, Okinawa.
Later history: SCAJAP, as Q034. Stricken 31 Oct 1947, sold 24 May 1948; BU Seattle.
LST 583 Decomm Mar 1946. †
3* Lingayen, Subic Bay, Mindanao Ldgs.
LST 584 Decomm 12 Apr 1946. Stricken 3 Jul 1946, sold 19 Mar 1948.
2* Mindanao Ldgs., Tarakan.
LST 585 Decomm 31 Jul 1946. Stricken 28 Aug 1946, sold to Dutch East Indies, 5 Oct 1946.
3* Lingayen, Mariveles-Corregidor, Tarakan.
Later history: Renamed *LST IV.* R
LST 586 Decomm 17 Feb 1946.
3* Leyte, Lingayen, Mariveles-Corregidor.
Later history: SCAJAP, as Q065. Stricken 29 Sep 1947, sold 28 May 1948.

LST 587 Decomm. 1946/47.
 2* Iwo Jima, Okinawa.
 Later history: SCAJAP, as Q042. †

LST 588 Decomm 8 Jun 1946. Stricken 3 Jul 1946, sold 9 Oct 1948.
 1* Iwo Jima.

LST 589 Decomm 14 Sep 1946. Sold 17 Dec 1946, stricken 23 Apr 1947.
 Later history: Merchant *Chung 106*, renamed *I Meng Shan* 19.

LST 590 Decomm 2 Feb 1946.
 4* Leyte, Lingayen, Subic Bay, Brunei, Balikpapan, Tarakan.
 Later history: SCAJAP, as Q036. †

LST 591 Decomm 5 Feb 1946.
 2* Mindanao Ldgs., Brunei.
 Later history: SCAJAP, as Q045. Stricken 29 Sep 1947, sold 24 May 1948.

LST 592 Decomm 11 Jun 1946. Stricken 31 Jul 1946, sold 23 Oct 1947; BU Baltimore.
 3* Lingayen, Okinawa, Mindanao Ldgs.

LST 593 Decomm 18 Mar 1946. Stricken 8 May 1946, sold 28 May 1948.
 1* Mindanao Ldgs.

LST 594 Decomm 21 Feb 1946. Stricken 5 Mar 1947.
 Later history: SCAJAP, as Q070. To South Korea 4 Jun 1947

LST 595 Decomm 3 Jan 1946. Stricken 5 Mar 1947.
 2* Visayan Is. Ldgs., Palawan Ldgs., Brunei.
 Later history: SCAJAP, as Q001. To South Korea 31 May 1947, renamed *Chochiwan.* BU 1959.

LST 596 Decomm 12 Jun 1946. Stricken 25 Sep 1946, sold 5 Dec 1947.
 Later history: Merchant *Chung 117.*

LST 597 Decomm 5 Mar 1946. Stricken 29 Sep 1947, sold 31 May 1948.
 2* Palawan Ldgs., Visayan Is. Ldgs., Okinawa.

LST 598 Decomm 10 Jun 1946. Stricken 19 Jul 1946.
 1* Okinawa.

LST 599 Decomm 1 Jun 1946. Stricken 22 Jan 1948, sold 5 Dec 1947.
 1* Okinawa.

No. Name	Builder	Launched	Comm.
LST 600	Chicago Bridge	28 Feb 1944	20 Mar 1944
LST 601	Chicago Bridge	4 Mar 1944	25 Mar 1944
LST 602	Chicago Bridge	9 Mar 1944	31 Mar 1944
LST 603	Chicago Bridge	14 Mar 1944	5 Apr 1944
LST 604	Chicago Bridge	20 Mar 1944	*8 Apr 1944*
LST 605	Chicago Bridge	29 Mar 1944	14 Apr 1944
LST 606	Chicago Bridge	3 Apr 1944	24 Apr 1944
LST 607	Chicago Bridge	7 Apr 1944	24 Apr 1944
LST 608	Chicago Bridge	11 Apr 1944	15 Apr 1944
LST 609	Chicago Bridge	15 Apr 1944	15 May 1944
LST 610	Chicago Bridge	19 Apr 1944	15 May 1944
LST 611	Chicago Bridge	28 Apr 1944	15 May 1944
LST 612	Chicago Bridge	29 Apr 1944	16 May 1944
LST 613	Chicago Bridge	2 May 1944	19 May 1944
LST 614	Chicago Bridge	6 May 1944	22 May 1944
LST 615	Chicago Bridge	9 May 1944	26 May 1944
LST 616	Chicago Bridge	12 May 1944	29 May 1944
LST 617	Chicago Bridge	15 May 1944	1 Jun 1944
LST 618	Chicago Bridge	19 May 1944	3 Jun 1944
LST 619	Chicago Bridge	22 May 1944	5 Jun 1944
LST 620	Chicago Bridge	30 May 1944	17 Jun 1944
LST 621	Chicago Bridge	2 Jun 1944	21 Jun 1944
LST 622	Chicago Bridge	8 Jun 1944	26 Jun 1944
LST 623	Chicago Bridge	12 Jun 1944	29 Jun 1944
LST 624	Chicago Bridge	16 Jun 1944	3 Jul 1944
LST 625	Chicago Bridge	20 Jun 1944	10 Jul 1944
LST 626	Chicago Bridge	27 Jun 1944	15 Jul 1944
LST 627	Chicago Bridge	1 Jul 1944	20 Jul 1944
LST 628	Chicago Bridge	4 Jul 1944	31 Jul 1944
LST 629	Chicago Bridge	8 Jul 1944	28 Jul 1944
LST 630	Chicago Bridge	13 Jul 1944	4 Aug 1944
LST 631	Chicago Bridge	18 Jul 1944	9 Aug 1944
LST 632	Chicago Bridge	21 Jul 1944	12 Aug 1944
LST 633	Chicago Bridge	27 Jul 1944	17 Aug 1944
LST 634	Chicago Bridge	1 Aug 1944	22 Aug 1944
LST 635	Chicago Bridge	7 Aug 1944	26 Aug 1944
LST 636	Chicago Bridge	11 Aug 1944	31 Aug 1944
LST 637	Chicago Bridge	18 Aug 1944	5 Sep 1944
LST 638	Chicago Bridge	23 Aug 1944	8 Sep 1944
LST 639	Chicago Bridge	28 Aug 1944	14 Sep 1944
LST 640	Chicago Bridge	31 Aug 1944	18 Sep 1944
LST 641	Chicago Bridge	4 Sep 1944	22 Sep 1944
LST 642	Chicago Bridge	8 Sep 1944	28 Sep 1944
LST 643	Chicago Bridge	12 Sep 1944	2 Oct 1944
LST 644	Chicago Bridge	15 Sep 1944	*26 Sep 1944*
LST 645	Chicago Bridge	20 Sep 1944	*30 Sep 1944*
LST 646	Chicago Bridge	25 Sep 1944	13 Oct 1944
LST 647	Chicago Bridge	28 Sep 1944	19 Oct 1944
LST 648	Chicago Bridge	3 Oct 1944	21 Oct 1944
LST 649	Chicago Bridge	6 Oct 1944	26 Oct 1944
LST 650	Chicago Bridge	10 Oct 1944	*21 Oct 1944*
LST 651	Chicago Bridge	16 Oct 1944	4 Nov 1944
LST 652	Chicago Bridge	19 Oct 1944	1 Jan 1945

Service Records:

LST 600 Decomm early 1946.
 Later history: SCAJAP, as Q074. †

LST 601 †
 1* Southern France.

LST 602 Decomm Dec 1946. †
 1* Southern France.

LST 603 †
 1* Southern France.

LST 604 Completed as MTB tender, rec **AGP 11**, renamed ***Silenus***, 18 Dec 1943.

LST 605 Decomm 24 May 1946. Stricken 3 Jul 1946, sold 15 Apr 1948; BU Vancouver, Wash.
 4* Leyte, Mindoro, Lingayen, Okinawa.

LST 606 Decomm 13 May 1946. Stricken 19 Jun 1946, sold 19 Apr 1948; BU.
 4* Palau, Leyte, Lingayen, Okinawa.

LST 607 Decomm 11 Jan 1946.
 1* Palau.
 Later history: SCAJAP, as Q008. †

LST 608 Decomm 1 Jan 1946. Stricken 7 Feb 1947.
 3* Leyte, Lingayen, Okinawa.
 Later history: SCAJAP, as Q026. To South Korea 31 May 1947, renamed *Ul San.* BU 1959.

LST 609 Decomm 4 Jan 1946. Stricken 21 Jan 1946, sold 26 Sep 1947; BU Baltimore.
 3* Leyte, Mindoro, Subic Bay, Okinawa.

LST 610 Decomm 28 Jun 1946. To USMG Okinawa 18 Sep 1946. Stricken 23 Dec 1947.
 3* Palau, Leyte, Lingayen.

LST 611 Damaged by aircraft bomb, Leyte, 2 Jan 1945. (4 killed) †
 2* Leyte, Mindoro.

LST 612 Decomm 1 Jun 1946. Stricken 3 Jul 1946, sold 5 Dec 1947.
 3* Leyte, Mindoro, Okinawa.

LST 613 Decomm 6 Jan 1946.
5* Morotai, Leyte, Mindoro, Lingayen, Visayan Is. Ldgs., Tarakan.
Later history: SCAJAP, as Q038. †
LST 614 Decomm 20 Jun 1946. Stricken 29 Oct 1946, sold 13 Feb 1948.
4* Morotai, Leyte, Lingayen, Mindanao Ldgs.
LST 615 Decomm 14 Mar 1946. Stricken 12 Apr 1946, sold 7 Apr 1948; BU Vancouver, Wash.
2* Leyte, Okinawa.
LST 616 Decomm 19 Jan 1946.
1* Okinawa.
Later history: SCAJAP, as Q019. †
LST 617 Decomm 24 May 1946. Stricken 3 Jul 1946, sold 15 Apr 1948; BU Vancouver, Wash.
4* Leyte, Mindoro, Lingayen, Okinawa.
LST 618 Damaged by suicide boat, Lingayen Gulf, 10 Jan 1945. To Army 24 Oct 1946. Stricken 23 Dec 1947.
3* Leyte, Lingayen, Mindanao Ldgs.
LST 619 Decomm 19 Jun 1946. Stricken 31 Oct 1947.
3* Leyte, Mindoro, Visayan Is. Ldgs., Palawan Ldgs.
Later history: SCAJAP, as Q031. Sold 27 May 1948; BU Seattle.
LST 620 Decomm 7 Jun 1946. Stricken 19 Jun 1946. Sold Dec 1947.
1* Okinawa.
Later history: Merchant *Northwest.*
LST 621 Decomm 16 Jun 1946. Stricken 31 Jul 1946, sold 30 Mar 1948; BU Seattle.
1* Okinawa.
LST 622 Decomm 14 Mar 1946. Stricken 12 Apr 1946, sold 13 Apr 1948; BU Seattle.
2* Lingayen, Okinawa.
LST 623 Decomm Dec 1946.
3* Leyte, Lingayen, Palawan Ldgs.
Later history: SCAJAP, as Q075. †
LST 624 Damaged by grounding, Okinawa, 4 Apr 1945. Decomm 14 Feb 1946. Stricken 7 Feb 1947.
3* Lingayen, Ldgs. at Nasugbu, Okinawa
Later history: SCAJAP, as Q057. To South Korea 1 Jun 1947.
LST 625 Decomm 11 Feb 1946.
2* Lingayen, Okinawa.
Later history: SCAJAP, as Q052. †
LST 626 Decomm 2 Mar 1946.
4* Leyte, Lingayen, Mindanao Ldgs., Balikpapan.
Later history: SCAJAP, as Q081. †
LST 627 Decomm 6 Jun 1946. Stricken 15 Jun 1946. Sold to Neth. East Indies, 19 Jun 1946.
2* Lingayen, Okinawa.
Later history: Renamed *LST II,* then *Pelikaan.* R.
LST 628 Decomm 3 Apr 1946. Stricken 3 Jul 1946, sold 5 Dec 1947.
2* Lingayen, Okinawa.
Later history: Merchant barge *Pan American Derrick Barge No. 1.*
LST 629 Decomm 4 Mar 1946.
3* Lingayen, Okinawa, Mindanao Ldgs.
Later history: SCAJAP, as Q083. †
LST 630 Decomm 13 Feb 1946.
3* Mindoro, Lingayen, Mindanao Ldgs.
Later history: SCAJAP, as Q059. †
LST 631 Decomm 24 May 1946. Stricken 3 Jul 1946, sold 15 Apr 1948; BU Seattle.
4* Lingayen, Mindanao Ldgs., Subic Bay, Balikpapan.
LST 632 Decomm 30 May 1946. Stricken 28 Jan 1947. Destroyed 11 Jun 1948.
4* Lingayen, Mariveles-Corregidor, Mindanao Ldgs., Balikpapan.
LST 633 Decomm 15 Feb 1946. Stricken 29 Sep 1947.
1* Okinawa.
Later history: SCAJAP, as Q060. Sold 23 Jun 1948; BU Seattle.
LST 634 Damaged in collision, Iwo Jima, 2 Mar 1945. Decomm 8 Jun 1946. Stricken 19 Jul 1946, sold 23 Jun 1948.
1* Okinawa.
LST 635 Damaged by grounding, Leyte, Philippines, 18 Mar 1945. Decomm 7 Jun 1946, to U.S. State Department 19 Jul 1946.
2* Lingayen, Mindanao Ldgs.
LST 636 Decomm 25 May 1946. Stricken 23 Dec 1947, sold Dec 1947.
2* Lingayen, Mindanao Ldgs.
LST 637 Decomm 23 Mar 1946. Stricken 5 Jun 1946, sold 18 Dec 1947; BU Barber, N.J.
3* Lingayen, Tarakan, Visayan Is. Ldgs.
LST 638 Decomm 8 Jun 1946. Stricken 12 Mar 1948. Destroyed as target, 15 Jun 1948.
3* Visayan Is. Ldgs., Palawan Ldgs., Tarakan.
LST 639 Decomm 1 Jun 1946. Stricken 16 Sep 1947, sold 5 Dec 1947.
3* Visayan Is. Ldgs., Palawan Ldgs., Balikpapan.
LST 640 Decomm 30 Apr 1946. Stricken 19 Jul 1946, sold.
2* Palawan Ldgs., Visayan Is. Ldgs., Brunei.
Later history: Merchant *Lu Yi,* renamed *Wan Yiu* 19., *Chung Chu'an* 1955 (Taiwanese Navy).
LST 641 Damaged in collision, Iwo Jima, 28 Feb 1945. Decomm 13 Jun 1946. Stricken 19 Jul 1946.
2* Iwo Jima, Okinawa.
LST 642 Damaged by grounding, Iwo Jima, 2 Mar 1945. Damaged by collision, Iwo Jima, 5 Mar 1945. Decomm 30 Jun 1947. Abandoned at Barter I., Alaska, 10 Feb 1948.
1* Iwo Jima.
LST 643 Decomm Jan 1946.
1* Okinawa.
Later history: SCAJAP, as Q058. †
LST 644 Completed as repair ship, rec **ARL 14**, renamed *Minos,* 14 Aug 1944.
LST 645 Completed as repair ship, rec **ARL 15**, renamed *Minotaur,* 14 Aug 1944.
LST 646 Damaged by collision, Okinawa, 5 Apr 1945. Decomm 15 Mar 1946. Stricken 17 Apr 1946, sold 11 May 1948; BU.
1* Two Jima.
LST 647 Decomm 2 Feb 1946. Stricken 23 Dec 1947.
1* Okinawa.
Later history: SCAJAP, as Q037, sold 25 May 1948: BU.
LST 648 Decomm 14 Feb 1947. Stricken 25 Feb 1947, to Army. Tokyo Bay.
1* Iwo Jima.
LST 649 1* Okinawa.
Later history: SCAJAP, as Q058. †
LST 650 Completed as repair ship, rec **ARL 18**, renamed ***Pandemus,*** 14 Aug 1944.
LST 651 Decomm 23 Jan 1946. Stricken 5 Dec 1947.
1* Okinawa.
Later history: SCAJAP, as Q023, sold 26 May 1948; BU Seattle.
LST 652 Decomm 5 Mar 1946.
Later history: SCAJAP, as Q086. †

No.	Builder	Launched	Comm.
LST 653	Amer. Bridge	23 Jan 1944	1 Apr 1944
LST 654	Amer. Bridge	30 Jan 1944	20 Mar 1944
LST 655	Amer. Bridge	6 Feb 1944	28 Mar 1944
LST 656	Amer. Bridge	18 Feb 1944	7 Apr 1944
LST 657	Amer. Bridge	25 Feb 1944	10 Apr 1944

Figure 9.7: *LST-666.* Notice the empty davits. She gained six battle stars in the Pacific.

LST 658	Amer. Bridge	13 Mar 1944	17 Apr 1944
LST 659	Amer. Bridge	20 Mar 1944	20 Apr 1944
LST 660	Amer. Bridge	24 Mar 1944	26 Apr 1944
LST 661	Amer. Bridge	30 Mar 1944	28 Apr 1944
LST 662	Amer. Bridge	5 Apr 1944	2 May 1944
LST 663	Amer. Bridge	8 Apr 1944	5 May 1944
LST 664	Amer. Bridge	13 Apr 1944	10 May 1944
LST 665	Amer. Bridge	18 Apr 1944	12 May 1944
LST 666	Amer. Bridge	24 Apr 1944	16 May 1944
LST 667	Amer. Bridge	27 Apr 1944	20 May 1944
LST 668	Amer. Bridge	30 Apr 1944	23 May 1944
LST 669	Amer. Bridge	3 May 1944	27 May 1944
LST 670	Amer. Bridge	6 May 1944	29 May 1944
LST 671	Amer. Bridge	11 May 1944	2 Jun 1944
LST 672	Amer. Bridge	14 May 1944	5 Jun 1944
LST 673	Amer. Bridge	22 May 1944	9 Jun 1944
LST 674	Amer. Bridge	26 May 1944	19 Jun 1944
LST 675	Amer. Bridge	2 Jun 1944	24 Jun 1944
LST 676	Amer. Bridge	6 Jun 1944	20 Jun 1944
LST 677	Amer. Bridge	16 Jun 1944	30 Jun 1944
LST 678	Amer. Bridge	16 Jun 1944	30 Jun 1944
LST 679	Amer. Bridge	20 Jun 1944	15 Jul 1944
LST 680	Amer. Bridge	26 Jun 1944	21 Jul 1944
LST 681	Amer. Bridge	1 Jul 1944	25 Jul 1944

Service Records:

LST 653 Rec **LST(H) 653**, 15 Sep 1945. Decomm 3 Feb 1946. Stricken 5 Mar 1947.
Later history: SCAJAP, as Q039. To South Korea 31 May 1947. Renamed *On Yang*. R 1958.

LST 654 Decomm 12 Jun 1946. Stricken 19 Jul 1946. Sold 12 Jun 1948.

LST 655 Decomm 31 May 1946. Stricken 3 Jul 1946, to U.S. State Department.
2* Southern France, Okinawa.

LST 656 Decomm 29 May 1946, to U.S. State Department. Stricken 3 Jul 1946.
1* Southern France.
Later history: Merchant *Chung 104* 1946.

LST 657 Decomm. Feb 1946.
Later history: SCAJAP, as Q071. †

LST 658 Decomm 1 Jun 1946, to U.S. State Department. Stricken 3 Jul 1946.
4* Palau, Leyte, Lingayen, Okinawa.
Later history: Merchant *Chung 105* 1946.

LST 659 Decomm 7 Jan 1946. Stricken 7 Feb 1947.
1* Southern France.
Later history: SCAJAP, as Q003. To South Korea 25 Mar 1947. Renamed *Chong Ho*. BU 1959.

LST 660 Decomm 26 Apr 1946. Stricken 5 Jun 1946, sold 17 May 1948; BU.
4* Palau, Leyte, Subic Bay, Okinawa.

LST 661 Damaged by storm, Palau Is., 2 Oct 1944. Bikini target. Decomm 29 Aug 1946. Destroyed 25 Jul 1948.
1* Palau.

LST 662 Decomm 19 Dec 1945. Stricken 8 Jan 1946, sold 25 Jun 1946.
3* Palau, Subic Bay, Okinawa.
Later history: Merchant *A.T.T. No. 3*, renamed *Neva* 1950, *Presidente Kubitschek* 1958, *Hamdan 20* 1981.

LST 663 Decomm 29 May 1946. Stricken 19 Jul 1946, sold 11 Dec 1947; BU New Orleans.
3* Palau, Leyte, Okinawa.

LST 664 †
1* Southern France.

LST 665 Decomm 11 Jun 1946. Stricken 3 Jul 1946, sold 12 Dec 1947; BU.
2* Southern France, Palau.

LST 666 Decomm 20 Jun 1946. Stricken 31 Jul 1946, sold 26 Sep 1947; BU Chester, Pa.
6* Morotai, Leyte, Lingayen, Visayan Is. Ldgs., Palawan Ldgs., Subic Bay, Balikpapan.

LST 667 Decomm 5 Jun 1946. Stricken 3 Jul 1946, sold 11 Dec 1947; BU Oakland, Calif.
5* Morotai, Leyte, Lingayen, Visayan Is. Ldgs., Tarakan.

LST 668 Decomm 24 Jun 1946. Stricken 31 Jul 1946, sold 26 May 1948.
4* Morotai, Leyte, Okinawa, Mindanao Ldgs.

LST 669 Decomm 13 Aug 1946. Stricken 25 Sep 1946, sold 10 May 1948.
2* Leyte, Okinawa.

LST 670 Decomm 30 Apr 1946. Stricken 19 Jun 1946, sold 13 Feb 1947.
3* Leyte, Mindoro, Okinawa.
Later history: Merchant *Macoris* 1948, renamed *Santa Madalena* 1952. Foundered after fire off Maranhao, 16 Oct 1953.

LST 671 Decomm 25 Jun 1946. Stricken 15 Aug 1946, sold 26 Sep 1947; BU Baltimore.
3* Leyte, Lingayen, Okinawa.

LST 672 Decomm 26 Jun 1946. Stricken 31 Jul 1946, sold 15 Jun 1948; BU.
2* Leyte, Okinawa.

LST 673 Decomm 10 Jul 1946. Stricken 15 Aug 1946, sold 23 Oct 1947; BU Oakland, Calif.
4* Leyte, Mindoro, Lingayen, Balikpapan, Mindanao Ldgs.

LST 674 Decomm 14 May 1946. Stricken 19 Jun 1946, sold 26 May 1948.
1* Okinawa.

LST 675 Damaged by grounding, Okinawa, 4 Apr 1945. Decomm 25 Aug 1945. Stricken 17 Sep 1945. Destroyed Feb 1946.
2* Lingayen, Okinawa.

LST 676 Rec **LST(M) 676**, 15 Jan 1945. Converted to barracks ship and rec **APB 42**, renamed ***Yavapai***, 31 Mar 1945. Decomm 3 Dec 1946.
1* Iwo Jima.

LST 677 Rec **LST(M) 677**, 15 Jan 1945. Converted to barracks ship and rec **APB 43**, renamed ***Yolo***, 31 Mar 1945. Decomm 9 Aug 1946.
1* Okinawa.

LST 678 Rec **LST(M) 678**, 15 Jan 1945. Converted to barracks ship and rec **APB 44**, renamed ***Presque Isle***, 31 Mar 1945. Decomm 18 Apr 1947.
2* Iwo Jima, Okinawa.

LST 679 Decomm 24 Jun 1946. Stricken 31 Jul 1946, sold 25 May 1948; BU.
2* Leyte, Mindanao Ldgs.

LST 680 Decomm 5 Jul 1946. Stricken 28 Aug 1946, sold 14 May 1948.
3* Lingayen, Subic Bay, Mindanao Ldgs.

LST 681 Decomm 6 Sep 1946. Stricken 8 Oct 1946, sold 9 Oct 1947; BU.
3* Lingayen, Leyte, Okinawa.

No.	Builder	Launched	Comm.
LST 682	Jeffersonville	31 Jan 1944	18 Mar 1944
LST 683	Jeffersonville	7 Feb 1944	28 Mar 1944
LST 684	Jeffersonville	12 Feb 1944	3 Apr 1944
LST 685	Jeffersonville	18 Feb 1944	7 Apr 1944
LST 686	Jeffersonville	24 Feb 1944	14 Apr 1944
LST 687	Jeffersonville	28 Feb 1944	22 Apr 1944
LST 688	Jeffersonville	5 Mar 1944	27 Apr 1944
LST 689	Jeffersonville	9 Mar 1944	2 May 1944
LST 690	Jeffersonville	14 Mar 1944	6 May 1944
LST 691	Jeffersonville	23 Mar 1944	12 May 1944
LST 692	Jeffersonville	31 Mar 1944	10 May 1944
LST 693	Jeffersonville	7 Apr 1944	15 May 1944
LST 694	Jeffersonville	16 Apr 1944	19 May 1944
LST 695	Jeffersonville	24 Apr 1944	22 May 1944
LST 696	Jeffersonville	27 Apr 1944	25 May 1944
LST 697	Jeffersonville	1 May 1944	30 May 1944
LST 698	Jeffersonville	5 May 1944	3 Jun 1944
LST 699	Jeffersonville	9 May 1944	5 Jun 1944

LST 700	Jeffersonville	13 May 1944	7 Jun 1944
LST 701	Jeffersonville	18 May 1944	13 Jun 1944
LST 702	Jeffersonville	22 May 1944	19 Jun 1944
LST 703	Jeffersonville	28 May 1944	23 Jun 1944
LST 704	Jeffersonville	3 Jun 1944	27 Jun 1944
LST 705	Jeffersonville	7 Jun 1944	4 Jul 1944
LST 706	Jeffersonville	12 Jun 1944	8 Jul 1944
LST 707	Jeffersonville	16 Jun 1944	13 Jul 1944
LST 708	Jeffersonville	20 Jun 1944	17 Jul 1944
LST 709	Jeffersonville	24 Jun 1944	21 Jul 1944
LST 710	Jeffersonville	28 Jun 1944	24 Jul 1944
LST 711	Jeffersonville	3 Jul 1944	28 Jul 1944
LST 712	Jeffersonville	7 Jul 1944	2 Aug 1944
LST 713	Jeffersonville	11 Jul 1944	7 Aug 1944
LST 714	Jeffersonville	15 Jul 1944	11 Aug 1944
LST 715	Jeffersonville	20 Jul 1944	15 Aug 1944
LST 716	Jeffersonville	25 Jul 1944	18 Aug 1944
LST 717	Jeffersonville	29 Jul 1944	23 Aug 1944
LST 718	Jeffersonville	3 Aug 1944	28 Aug 1944
LST 719	Jeffersonville	8 Aug 1944	31 Aug 1944
LST 720	Jeffersonville	12 Aug 1944	4 Sep 1944
LST 721	Jeffersonville	17 Aug 1944	9 Sep 1944
LST 722	Jeffersonville	21 Aug 1944	13 Sep 1944
LST 723	Jeffersonville	25 Aug 1944	16 Sep 1944
LST 724	Jeffersonville	29 Aug 1944	22 Sep 1944
LST 725	Jeffersonville	2 Sep 1944	25 Sep 1944
LST 726	Jeffersonville	6 Sep 1944	30 Sep 1944
LST 727	Jeffersonville	10 Sep 1944	4 Oct 1944
LST 728	Jeffersonville	14 Sep 1944	10 Oct 1944
LST 729	Jeffersonville	18 Sep 1944	16 Oct 1944

Service Records:

LST 682 Decomm 30 Jul 1946. Stricken 25 Sep 1946, sold 4 Jun 1948; BU.
2* Normandy, Okinawa.

LST 683 Decomm 29 May 1946. Stricken 3 Jul 1946. Sold 26 May 1948.

LST 684 Damaged by coastal gun, Iwo Jima, 23 Feb 1945. Damaged by grounding, Okinawa, 14 Jul 1945. Went aground in typhoon at Okinawa 9 Oct 1945. Decomm 25 Nov 1945. Stricken 22 Mar 1946. Destroyed 5 Jun 1946.
3* Guam, Iwo Jima, Okinawa.

LST 685 Decomm 22 Jul 1946. †

LST 686 Decomm 10 Jul 1946. Stricken 15 Aug 1946, sold 18 Sep 1947; BU Seattle.
3* Leyte, Mindoro, Lingayen, Okinawa.

LST 687 Decomm 24 May 1946. Stricken 3 Jul 1946, sold 24 Sep 1947; BU.
4* Palau, Leyte, Lingayen, Okinawa.

LST 688 Decomm 5 Aug 1946. Stricken 25 Sep 1946, sold 17 Sep 1947; BU Seattle.
4* Palau, Leyte, Lingayen, Okinawa.

LST 689 Damaged by grounding, Okinawa, 4 Apr 1945. Decomm Mar 1946. †
1* Palau.

LST 690 Decomm 23 Jul 1946. Stricken 28 Aug 1946, sold 16 Dec 1947; BU.
2* Southern France, Okinawa.

LST 691 Decomm 14 May 1946. Stricken 19 Jun 1946, sold 13 Nov 1946.
1* Southern France.
Later history: Merchant barge *Americas.*

LST 692 Decomm Dec 1946. †
1* Southern France.

LST 693 Decomm 1 May 1946. Stricken 3 Jul 1946, sold 10 Dec 1947; BU New Orleans.
4* Leyte, Mindoro, Subic Bay, Okinawa.

LST 694 Decomm 1 Dec 1947. Stricken 23 Dec 1947. †
5* Morotai, Leyte, Lingayen, Mindanao Ldgs., Balikpapan.

LST 695 Damaged by underwater explosion (torpedoed by *I-56*) east of Leyte, 24 Oct 1944. Decomm 6 Nov 1945. Stricken 28 Nov 1945, sold 22 Mar 1946.
2* Morotai, Leyte.
Later history: Merchant barge *Sause Bros. 06.*

LST 696 Decomm 16 Jul 1946. Stricken 28 Aug 1946, sold 19 May 1948.
3* Morotai, Leyte, Lingayen.

LST 697 Decomm 12 Jul 1946. Stricken 28 Aug 1946, sold 14 Oct 1947, BU.
5* Morotai, Leyte, Lingayen, Visayan Is. Ldgs., Tarakan.

LST 698 Damaged by grounding, Okinawa, 5 Apr 1945. Decomm 26 Nov 1945. Stricken 5 Dec 1945, sold 25 Jun 1946.
3* Leyte, Lingayen, Okinawa.
Later history: Merchant *A.T.T. No.1.* Stranded on Amchitka I., Aleutians, 3 Nov 1946.

LST 699 Decomm 24 Jun 1946. Stricken 31 Jul 1946, sold 5 Dec 1947 BU.
3* Leyte, Lingayen, Mindanao Ldgs.

LST 700 Damaged in error by U.S. gunfire, northwest of Lingayen, 11 Jan and by kamikaze, 12 Jan 1945 (2 killed). Decomm 27 Jul 1946. Stricken 28 Aug 1946, sold 13 Dec 1947; BU Vancouver, Wash.
2* Leyte, Lingayen.

LST 701 Decomm 13 Jul 1946. Stricken 28 Aug 1946, sold 3 Oct 1947; BU Oakland, Calif.
3* Lingayen, Ldgs. at Nasugbu, Okinawa.

LST 702 Decomm 5 Jul 1946. Stricken 15 Aug 1946, sold 21 Oct 1947; BU Seattle.
1* Okinawa.

LST 703 Decomm 10 Jun 1946. Stricken 31 Jul 1946, sold 10 Dec 1947; BU.
3* Leyte, Subic Bay, Balikpapan.

LST 704 Damaged by coastal mortars, Leyte, 21 Oct 1944. Decomm 19 Jun 1946. Stricken 25 Sep 1946, sold 27 May 1948; BU Napa, Calif.
2* Leyte, Okinawa.

LST 705 Decomm 22 Jul 1946. Stricken 25 Sep 1946, sold 8 Dec 1947; BU Oakland, Calif.
3* Leyte, Lingayen, Mindanao Ldgs.

LST 706 Decomm 19 Jun 1946. Stricken 31 Jul 1946, sold 28 May 1948; BU.
2* Leyte, Lingayen.

LST 707 Decomm 28 May 1946. Stricken 3 Jul 1946, sold 7 May 1948.
4* Leyte, Lingayen, Subic Bay, Mindanao Ldgs.

LST 708 Decomm 28 May 1946. Stricken 3 Jul 1946, sold 28 May 1948; BU Napa, Calif.
1* Okinawa.

LST 709 Decomm 3 Jul 1946. Stricken 15 Aug 1946, sold 19 Jun 1948; BU Seattle.
4* Leyte, Palawan Ldgs., Okinawa, Visayan Is. Ldgs., Brunei.

LST 710 Damaged by U.S. gunfire in error, west of Luzon, 12 Jan 1945. Damaged by collision, Lingayen, 18 Jan 1945.
Converted to barracks ship and rec **APB 49**, renamed ***Accomac***, 1 Aug 1945. Decomm 9 Aug 1946.
1* Lingayen.

LST 711 Decomm and to Army 11 Aug 1946. Stricken 29 Sep 1947.
3* Lingayen, Mariveles-Corregidor, Tarakan.
Later history: Merchant barge *Foss 207,* renamed *Sanitary 2* 19.

LST 712 Decomm 20 May 1946. Stricken 28 Aug 1946, sold 27 May 1948; BU Napa, Calif.
2* Lingayen, Okinawa.

LST 713 Decomm 20 Jun 1946. Stricken 31 Jul 1946, sold 21 May 1948.
2* Iwo Jima, Okinawa.

LST 714 Decomm 10 May 1946, to U.S. State Department. Stricken 19 Jun 1946.
4* Leyte, Lingayen, Subic Bay, Balikpapan.

LST 715 Decomm 17 Apr 1946. To Army 28 Jun 1946. †
2* Iwo Jima, Okinawa.

LST 716 Damaged by grounding, Iwo Jima, 23 Feb 1945. Decomm and to China 12 Jun 1946.
2* Iwo Jima, Okinawa.
Later history: Renamed *Chung Chien.*

LST 717 Decomm and to China 12 Jun 1946.
1* Palawan Ldgs., Mindanao Ldgs. Tokyo Bay.
Later history: Renamed *Chung Yeh.*
LST 718 Decomm 25 Jun 1946. Stricken 31 Jul 1948, sold 18 Jun 1948; BU. Tokyo Bay.
LST 719 Decomm 12 Jul 1946. Stricken 14 Mar 1947, sold 23 Oct 1947; BU Oakland, Calif.
1* Palawan Ldgs., Mindanao Ldgs.
LST 720 Decomm 24 Jun 1946. Stricken 31 Jul 1946, sold 23 Oct 1947; BU Seattle.
2* Lingayen, Mindanao Ldgs.
LST 721 Decomm 24 Jun 1946. Stricken 15 Aug 1946, sold 8 Mar 1948.
2* Visayan Is. Ldgs., Balikpapan.
Later history: Merchant barge *Sinclair No. 5.*
LST 722 Decomm 13 Jul 1946. †
1* Palawan Ldgs., Mindanao Ldgs.
LST 723 Decomm 20 Jul 1946. Stricken 10 Jun 1947, sold 12 May 1948.
2* Iwo Jima, Okinawa.
LST 724 Damaged by kamikaze, Okinawa, 31 Mar 1945. Decomm 26 Jun 1946. Stricken 31 Jul 1946, sold 23 Sep 1947; BU.
2* Okinawa.
LST 725 Decomm 1 May 1946. Stricken 3 Jul 1946, sold 11 Dec 1947; BU New Orleans.
2* Iwo Jima, Okinawa.
LST 726 Decomm 25 Jun 1946. Stricken 31 Jul 1946, sold 26 Nov 1947; BU.
2* Iwo Jima, Okinawa.
LST 727 Damaged by grounding, Iwo Jima, 22 Mar 1945. Decomm 26 Jul 1946. Stricken 28 Aug 1946, sold 15 Jun 1948.
1* Iwo Jima.
Later history: Merchant *Stanolind 56*, renamed *R.A. McInnis* 1949, *Fort Lennox* 1970.
LST 728 Decomm 18 Jun 1946. Stricken 31 Jul 1946, sold 6 Oct 1947; BU.
1* Okinawa.
LST 729 Decomm 8 Jul 1946. Stricken 28 Aug 1946, sold 28 Oct 1947; BU Oakland, Calif.
1* Okinawa.

No.	Builder	Launched	Comm.
LST 730	Dravo Pitt.	29 Jan 1944	30 Mar 1944
LST 731	Dravo Pitt.	12 Feb 1944	30 Mar 1944
LST 732	Dravo Pitt.	19 Feb 1944	10 Apr 1944
LST 733	Dravo Pitt.	26 Feb 1944	15 Apr 1944
LST 734	Dravo Pitt.	4 Mar 1944	22 Apr 1944
LST 735	Dravo Pitt.	11 Mar 1944	26 Apr 1944
LST 736	Dravo Pitt.	18 Mar 1944	2 May 1944
LST 737	Dravo Pitt.	25 Mar 1944	6 May 1944
LST 738	Dravo Pitt.	1 Apr 1944	9 May 1944
LST 739	Dravo Pitt.	8 Apr 1944	15 May 1944
LST 740	Dravo Pitt.	8 Apr 1944	15 May 1944
LST 741	Dravo Pitt.	15 Apr 1944	19 May 1944
LST 742	Dravo Pitt.	22 Apr 1944	23 May 1944
LST 743	Dravo Pitt.	19 Apr 1944	23 May 1944
LST 744	Dravo Pitt.	29 Apr 1944	29 May 1944
LST 745	Dravo Pitt.	29 Apr 1944	31 May 1944
LST 746	Dravo Pitt.	6 May 1944	3 Jun 1944
LST 747	Dravo Pitt.	20 May 1944	15 Jun 1944
LST 748	Dravo Pitt.	13 May 1944	5 Jun 1944
LST 749	Dravo Pitt.	20 May 1944	23 Jun 1944
LST 750	Dravo Pitt.	30 May 1944	29 Jun 1944
LST 751	Dravo Pitt.	27 May 1944	26 Jun 1944
LST 752	Dravo Pitt.	3 Jun 1944	5 Jul 1944
LST 753	Dravo Pitt.	10 Jun 1944	10 Jul 1944

Service Records:
LST 730 Decomm 8 Jun 1946. Stricken 31 Jul 1946, sold 18 Dec 1947; BU Oakland, Calif.
LST 731 Rec **LST(H) 731**, 15 Sep 1945. †
2* Guam, Iwo Jima.
LST 732 Decomm 7 Jun 1946, to U.S. State Department. Stricken 19 Jul 1946.
Later history: Merchant *Wan Kuo*, renamed *Chung Shun* 1955 (Taiwan Navy).
LST 733 Decomm 28 Jun 1946. Stricken 31 Jul 1946, sold 10 Oct 1947; BU Seattle.
3* Leyte, Mindoro, Okinawa.
LST 734 Decomm 7 May 1946. Stricken 5 Jun 1946, sold 24 May 1948.
5* Palau, Leyte, Ormoc, Okinawa, Subic Bay.
LST 735 Decomm 18 Jul 1946. †
4* Saipan, Lingayen, Subic Bay, Okinawa.
LST 736 Damaged by grounding, Okinawa, 4 Apr 1945. Decomm 20 Jun 1946. Stricken 31 Jul 1946, sold 28 May 1948
4* Palau, Leyte, Subic Bay, Okinawa.
LST 737 Damaged by kamikaze, south of Ormoc, Leyte, 7 Dec 1944. Decomm and to Army 2 Nov 1946. Stricken 29 Sep 1947.
5* Palau, Leyte, Ormoc, Lingayen, Subic Bay, Okinawa.
LST 738 Damaged by kamikaze off Mindoro and sunk by U.S., 15 Dec 1944.
2* Leyte, Mindoro.
LST 739 Decomm 1 May 1946. Stricken 3 Jul 1946, sold 1 Mar 1948.
2* Leyte, Ormoc, Okinawa.
Later history: Merchant barge *TMT Georgia*, renamed *Contran, Ocean Burning No. 2.*
LST 740 Decomm 8 Mar 1946. Stricken 12 Apr 1946, sold 14 Jun 1948.
5* Morotai, Leyte, Lingayen, Mindanao Ldgs., Balikpapan.
LST 741 Decomm 9 Aug 1946. Stricken 25 Sep 1946, sold 12 May 1948.
3* Morotai, Leyte, Mindoro, Lingayen, Mindanao Ldgs.
LST 742 Decomm 26 Apr 1946. To Army 28 Jun 1946. †
3* Lingayen, Visayan Is. Ldgs., Tarakan.
LST 743 Decomm 23 Apr 1946. Stricken 19 Jun 1946, sold 23 Oct 1947; BU.
2* Mindanao Ldgs. Tarakan.
LST 744 Decomm 28 Jun 1946. Stricken 15 Aug 1946, sold 4 Mar 1948.
4* Morotai, Leyte, Lingayen, Mindanao Ldgs.
Later history: Merchant barge *Sample No. 1.*
LST 745 Decomm 9 Jul 1946. Stricken 28 Aug 1946, sold 26 Sep 1947; BU Baltimore.
3* Leyte, Subic Bay, Okinawa.
LST 746 Decomm 1 May 1946. Stricken 3 Jul 1946, sold 5 Mar 1948
4* Leyte, Mindoro, Lingayen, Mindanao Ldgs., Subic Bay.
Later history: Merchant barge *Sample No. 2*, renamed *Booth.*
LST 747 Decomm 20 Jun 1946. Stricken 31 Jul 1946, sold 21 May 1948.
2* Lingayen, Okinawa.
LST 748 Decomm 12 Mar 1946, sold 27 May 1948.
2* Leyte, Lingayen.
LST 749 Sunk by kamikaze off Mindoro, 21 Dec 1944.
1* Leyte.
LST 750 Torpedoed by Japanese aircraft off Negros I. and sunk by U.S., 28 Dec 1944.
1* Leyte.
LST 751 Decomm 21 Aug 1946. Stricken 15 Oct 1946, sold 13 Nov 1947.
2* Leyte, Lingayen.
Later history: Merchant *North Star* 1948, renamed *Santa Lucia* 1958, *Wayli* 1960, *Robina* 1961, *Sorong* 1962.
LST 752 Damaged by collision west of Mindoro, 18 Jan 1945. Decomm 7 Jun 1946. Stricken 19 Jul 1946. Sold 13 Oct 1947; BU.
2* Lingayen, Okinawa.
LST 753 Decomm 25 Jun 1946. Stricken 31 Jul 1946, sold 13 Dec 1947 sold; BU Vancouver, Wash.
3* Lingayen, Mindanao Ldgs., Balikpapan.

No.	Builder	Launched	Comm.
LST 754	Amer. Bridge	6 Jul 1944	29 Jul 1944
LST 755	Amer. Bridge	11 Jul 1944	3 Aug 1944
LST 756	Amer. Bridge	15 Jul 1944	8 Aug 1944
LST 757	Amer. Bridge	21 Jul 1944	15 Aug 1944
LST 758	Amer. Bridge	25 Jul 1944	19 Aug 1944
LST 759	Amer. Bridge	29 Jul 1944	25 Aug 1944
LST 760	Amer. Bridge	3 Aug 1944	28 Aug 1944
LST 761	Amer. Bridge	7 Aug 1944	2 Sep 1944
LST 762	Amer. Bridge	11 Aug 1944	5 Sep 1944
LST 763	Amer. Bridge	16 Aug 1944	8 Sep 1944
LST 764	Amer. Bridge	21 Aug 1944	13 Sep 1944
LST 765	Amer. Bridge	26 Aug 1944	18 Sep 1944
LST 766	Amer. Bridge	30 Aug 1944	25 Sep 1944
LST 767	Amer. Bridge	4 Sep 1944	30 Sep 1944
LST 768	Amer. Bridge	8 Sep 1944	4 Oct 1944
LST 769	Amer. Bridge	12 Sep 1944	9 Oct 1944
LST 770	Amer. Bridge	17 Sep 1944	13 Oct 1944
LST 771	Amer. Bridge	21 Sep 1944	18 Oct 1944
LST 772	Chicago Bridge	24 Oct 1944	13 Nov 1944
LST 773	Chicago Bridge	27 Oct 1944	*7 Nov 1944*
LST 774	Chicago Bridge	31 Oct 1944	20 Nov 1944

Service Records:

LST 754 Decomm 20 Jun 1946. Stricken 31 Jul 1946, sold 21 May 1948.
3* Lingayen, Mariveles-Corregidor, Mindanao Ldgs.

LST 755 Decomm and trfd to China 29 May 1946.
2* Lingayen, Mindanao Ldgs.
Later history: Renamed *Chung Hai.* R.

LST 756 Damaged by grounding, Okinawa, 4 Apr 1945. Decomm 5 Apr 1946. Stricken 17 Apr 1946, sold 6 Dec 1946.
2* Iwo Jima, Okinawa.
Later history: Merchant *Las Piedras* 1947. Wrecked at La Guiara, Venezuela, 5 Feb 1949.

LST 757 Decomm 28 May 1946. Stricken 3 Jul 1946, sold 10 May 1948.
2* Lingayen, Mindanao Ldgs.

LST 758 USCG. Decomm 13 Jul 1946. †
2* Iwo Jima, Okinawa.

LST 759 USCG. Decomm 29 Mar 1946. †
1* Okinawa.

LST 760 USCG. Damaged by coastal gun, Iwo Jima, 26 Feb 1945. Decomm 24 May 1946. Stricken 3 Jul 1946, sold 28 May 1948.
2* Iwo Jima, Okinawa.

LST 761 USCG. Decomm 19 Jul 1946. †
1* Iwo Jima.

LST 762 USCG. Decomm 1946. †
1* Okinawa.

LST 763 USCG. Decomm 29 Apr 1946. Stricken 15 Aug 1946, sold 11 Dec 1947; BU New Orleans.
2* Iwo Jima, Okinawa.

LST 764 USCG. Decomm 30 Apr 1946. Stricken 3 Jul 1946, sold 11 Dec 1947; BU New Orleans.
1* Iwo Jima.

LST 765 USCG. Decomm 29 Apr 1946. Stricken 3 Jul 1946, sold 16 Dec 1947; BU.
1* Okinawa.

LST 766 Decomm 19 Mar 1946. Stricken 5 Jun 1946, sold 24 Dec 1946.
1* Iwo Jima.
Later history: Merchant *Ling Yuan*, renamed *Chung 128* 1958

LST 767 USCG. Damaged in hurricane, 1 Dec 1945. Decomm 7 Mar 1946. Stricken 28 Mar 1946, sold May 1947.
1* Okinawa.

LST 768 USCG. Decomm 15 Apr 1946. Stricken 5 Jun 1946, sold 18 Dec 1947.
3* Iwo Jima, Okinawa, Minesweeping 1945.
Later history: Merchant barge *Humble ST-4*, renamed *World-Over ST-4* 1964, *Diamond M Offshore ST-4* 1968, *John D. Askew ST-64* 1972.

LST 769 USCG. Decomm 29 Apr 1946. Stricken 3 Jul 1946, sold 11 Dec 1947.
1* Okinawa.
Later history: Merchant *S-21* 1948, renamed *Rowan Rig No.15 +16, Fanis* BU 1976 Perama, Greece.

LST 770 USCG. Decomm 29 Apr 1946. Stricken 31 Jul 1946, sold 6 Feb 1948.
1* Okinawa.
Later history: Merchant barge *M-140.*

LST 771 USCG. Decomm 14 May 1946. Stricken 5 Jun 1946, sold 26 Sep 1947; BU Baltimore.
1* Okinawa.

LST 772 Decomm 3 Jul 1946. †
1* Okinawa.

LST 773 Completed as MTB tender, rec **AGP 16**, renamed ***Antigone***, 14 Aug 1944.

LST 774 Decomm 12 Jul 1946. Stricken 15 Aug 1946, sold 17 Sep 1947; BU.
1* Okinawa.

No.	Builder	Launched	Comm.
LST 775	Dravo Pitt.	10 Jun 1944	15 Jul 1944
LST 776	Dravo Pitt.	17 Jun 1944	20 Jul 1944
LST 777	Dravo Pitt.	24 Jun 1944	25 Jul 1944
LST 778	Dravo Pitt.	24 Jun 1944	31 Jul 1944
LST 779	Dravo Pitt.	1 Jul 1944	3 Aug 1944
LST 780	Dravo Pitt.	10 Jul 1944	7 Aug 1944
LST 781	Dravo Pitt.	15 Jul 1944	18 Aug 1944
LST 782	Dravo Pitt.	22 Jul 1944	22 Aug 1944
LST 783	Dravo Pitt.	11 Jul 1944	14 Aug 1944
LST 784	Dravo Pitt.	29 Jul 1944	1 Sep 1944
LST 785	Dravo Pitt.	5 Aug 1944	4 Sep 1944
LST 786	Dravo Pitt.	22 Jul 1944	28 Aug 1944
LST 787	Dravo Pitt.	12 Aug 1944	13 Sep 1944
LST 788	Dravo Pitt.	19 Aug 1944	18 Sep 1944
LST 789	Dravo Pitt.	5 Aug 1944	11 Sep 1944
LST 790	Dravo Pitt.	19 Aug 1944	22 Sep 1944
LST 791	Dravo Pitt.	26 Aug 1944	27 Sep 1944
LST 792	Dravo Pitt.	2 Sep 1944	2 Oct 1944
LST 793	Dravo Pitt.	2 Sep 1944	5 Oct 1944
LST 794	Dravo Pitt.	16 Sep 1944	16 Oct 1944
LST 795	Dravo Pitt.	9 Sep 1944	9 Oct 1944
LST 796	Dravo Pitt.	16 Sep 1944	20 Oct 1944
LST 797	Jeffersonville	22 Sep 1944	20 Oct 1944
LST 798	Jeffersonville	26 Sep 1944	26 Oct 1944
LST 799	Jeffersonville	3 Oct 1944	28 Oct 1944
LST 800	Jeffersonville	10 Oct 1944	2 Nov 1944
LST 801	Jeffersonville	14 Oct 1944	8 Nov 1944
LST 802	Jeffersonville	19 Oct 1944	13 Nov 1944
LST 803	Jeffersonville	23 Oct 1944	17 Nov 1944
LST 804	Jeffersonville	27 Oct 1944	22 Nov 1944
LST 805	Jeffersonville	31 Oct 1944	27 Nov 1944

Service Records:

LST 775 Decomm 15 Jul 1946, sold 11 Jun 1948.
4* Leyte, Lingayen, Subic Bay, Mindanao Ldgs.

LST 776 Decomm 18 Mar 1946. Stricken 1 May 1946, sold 16 Jan 1947.
2* Iwo Jima, Okinawa.
Later history: Merchant *San Benito* 1947.

LST 777 Decomm 19 Jul 1946. Stricken 28 Aug 1946, sold 14 May 1948 .
2* Visayan Is. Ldgs., Subic Bay.
LST 778 Damaged by U.S. gunfire in error, west of Luzon, 12 Jan 1945. Decomm 27 May 1946. Stricken 19 Jun 1946, sold 23 Oct 1947; BU Baltimore.
2* Lingayen, Mindanao Ldgs.
LST 779 Damaged by coastal mortar, Iwo Jima, 20 and by collision, 27 Feb 1945. Decomm 18 May 1946. Stricken 19 Jul 1946, sold 5 Dec 1947.
2* Iwo Jima, Okinawa.
LST 780 Decomm 13 Jun 1946. Stricken 31 Jul 1946, sold 23 Oct 1947; BU Oakland, Calif.
1* Okinawa.
LST 781 Damaged by grounding, Okinawa, 4 Apr 1945. Decomm 27 Jun 1946. Stricken 15 Aug 1946, sold 20 Dec 1947.
1* Okinawa.
Later history: Merchant barge *Humble ST-3.*
LST 782 USCG. Decomm 14 May 1946. Stricken 5 Jun 1946, sold 26 Sep 1947; BU Baltimore.
2* Iwo Jima, Okinawa.
LST 783 Decomm 22 Aug 1946. †
1* Iwo Jima.
LST 784 USCG. Decomm 29 Mar 1946. †
2* Iwo Jima, Okinawa.
LST 785 USCG.
2* Iwo Jima, Okinawa. Decomm 3 May 1946. Stricken 5 Jun 1946, sold 3 Jun 1948; BU.
LST 786 USCG. Decomm 9 Jul 1946. †
1* Okinawa.
LST 787 USCG. Damaged in collision, Iwo Jima, 28 Feb 1945. Decomm 27 May 1946. Stricken 3 Jul 1946, sold 7 May 1948.
2* Iwo Jima, Okinawa.
LST 788 USCG. Decomm 16 Apr 1946. Stricken 5 Jun 1946, sold 26 Sep 1947; BU Baltimore.
2* Iwo Jima, Okinawa.
LST 789 USCG. Decomm 29 Apr 1946. Stricken 3 Jul 1946, sold 11 Dec 1947.
2* Iwo Jima, Okinawa. Tokyo Bay.
Later history: Merchant *S-22* 1948, renamed barge *Dave Dodge* 1973.
LST 790 USCG. Rec **LST(H) 790**, 15 Sep 1945. Decomm 27 May 1946. Stricken 3 Jul 1946, sold 5 May 1948.
2* Iwo Jima, Okinawa.
LST 791 USCG. Decomm 28 May 1946. Stricken 4 Jul 1946, sold 3 Jun 1948; BU.
1* Okinawa.
LST 792 USCG. Damaged by coastal gunfire, Iwo Jima, 23 Feb 1945. Decomm 29 Apr 1946. Stricken 19 Jul 1946, sold 31 Oct 1946.
2* Iwo Jima, Okinawa.
Later history: Merchant *Marcala* 1947, renamed *Areia Blanca* 1952. Lost by grounding south of Ilheus, Brazil, 14 Aug 1954.
LST 793 USCG. Decomm 29 Apr 1946. Stricken 3 Jul 1946, sold 16 Dec 1947.
1* Okinawa.
Later history: Merchant barge *TMT Carolina.*
LST 794 USCG. Decomm 9 Jul 1946. †
1* Okinawa.
LST 795 USCG. Decomm 29 Apr 1946. Stricken 19 Jul 1946, sold 31 Oct 1946.
2* Iwo Jima, Okinawa.
Later history: Merchant *Patuca* 1947, renamed *Santa Mathilde* 1953.
LST 796 USCG. Decomm 17 Apr 1946. Stricken 19 Jun 1946, sold 22 Sep 1947.
1* Okinawa.
Later history: Merchant *Cootip,* renamed *Presidente Aleman.*
LST 797 Decomm 28 Jun 1946. Stricken; 31 Jul 1946, sold 12 Dec 1947; BU.
1* Okinawa.
LST 798 Decomm 16 Jul 1946. Stricken 15 Aug 1946, sold 17 Sep 1947; BU.
LST 799 Decomm 22 Apr 1946. To Army 6 May 1946. †
1* Okinawa.
LST 800 Decomm 1 May 1946. Stricken 3 Jul 1946; sold 22 Dec 1947.
Later history: Merchant barge *Humble ST-1,* renamed *World-Over ST-1* 1964. *Diamond M Offshore ST-61.* 1969
LST 801 Decomm 18 Jul 1946. Stricken 18 Aug 1946; to Argentina 29 Dec 1947.
1*Okinawa.
Later history: Renamed *Don Antonio* 1947, then *BDT-5 Cabo Buen Tiempo.* R 1961.
LST 802 Decomm and to Army 21 Jul 1946. †
1* Okinawa.
LST 803 †
1* Okinawa.
LST 804 Decomm 24 May 1946, to U.S. State Department. Stricken 3 Jul 1946.
1* Okinawa.
Later history: Merchant *Chung 101* 1946. To PRC Navy.
LST 805 Decomm 25 May 1946. Stricken 19 Jul 1946, sold 5 Nov 1946.
1* Okinawa.
Later history: Merchant *Chung 111,* to PRC Navy.

No.	Builder	Launched	Comm.
LST 806	Missouri Valley	7 Sep 1944	28 Sep 1944
LST 807	Missouri Valley	11 Sep 1944	3 Oct 1944
LST 808	Missouri Valley	15 Sep 1944	29 Sep 1944
LST 809	Missouri Valley	19 Sep 1944	10 Oct 1944
LST 810	Missouri Valley	21 Sep 1944	13 Oct 1944
LST 811	Missouri Valley	23 Sep 1944	18 Oct 1944
LST 812	Missouri Valley	27 Sep 1944	19 Oct 1944
LST 813	Missouri Valley	30 Sep 1944	24 Oct 1944
LST 814	Missouri Valley	4 Oct 1944	27 Oct 1944
LST 815	Missouri Valley	7 Oct 1944	30 Oct 1944
LST 816	Missouri Valley	11 Oct 1944	2 Nov 1944
LST 817	Missouri Valley	14 Oct 1944	7 Nov 1944
LST 818	Missouri Valley	18 Oct 1944	9 Nov 1944
LST 819	Missouri Valley	21 Oct 1944	14 Nov 1944
LST 820	Missouri Valley	25 Oct 1944	16 Nov 1944
LST 821	Missouri Valley	27 Oct 1944	14 Nov 1944
LST 822	Missouri Valley	1 Nov 1944	23 Nov 1944
LST 823	Missouri Valley	4 Nov 1944	28 Nov 1944
LST 824	Missouri Valley	8 Nov 1944	30 Nov 1944
LST 825	Missouri Valley	11 Nov 1944	8 Dec 1944
LST 826	Missouri Valley	14 Nov 1944	7 Dec 1944
LST 827	Missouri Valley	16 Nov 1944	12 Dec 1944
LST 828	Missouri Valley	22 Nov 1944	13 Dec 1944

Service Records:

LST 806 Decomm 20 May 1946. Stricken 19 Jul 1946, sold 20 Nov 1947.
3* Palawan Ldgs., Brunei, Minesweeping 1945.
Later history: Merchant *Chung 112.* Sunk at Yulin, Hainan I., 30 Apr 1950.
LST 807 Damaged in collision with DE *Melvin R.Nawman,* Iwo Jima, 22 Feb 1945. Decomm 27 May 1946, to U.S. State Department. Stricken 3 Jul 1946.
2* Iwo Jima, Okinawa.
LST 808 Damaged by aircraft torpedo, and kamikaze, off Ie Shima, Okinawa, 18 May 1945 (11 killed). Destroyed 11 Nov 1945.
2* Iwo Jima, Okinawa.
LST 809 Damaged by kamikaze, Iwo Jima, 21 Feb and in collision, Iwo Jima, 27 Feb 1945. Decomm 15 Jul 1946. Stricken 18 Aug 1946; sold 19 May 1948; BU.
2* Iwo Jima, Okinawa.
LST 810 Damaged by collision, Okinawa, 5 Apr 1945. Decomm 18 Jul 1946. Stricken 28 Aug 1946, sold 14 Oct 1947.
1* Okinawa.
LST 811 Decomm 26 Jun 1946. Stricken 31 Jul 1946, sold 4 Nov 1947; BU Seattle.
1* Okinawa.

LST 812 Decomm 9 May 1946. Stricken 19 Jun 1946, sold 25 May 1948.
2* Iwo Jima, Okinawa.
LST 813 Decomm 21 Jun 1946. Stricken 31 Jul 1946, sold 12 Jun 1948.
1* Okinawa.
LST 814 Damaged during beaching operations off Sasebo, Japan, 30 Dec 1945. Decomm 16 Apr 1946. Stricken 8 May 1946. Scuttled 12 Aug 1946.
1* Okinawa.
LST 815 Decomm 6 Sep 1946, sold 28 May 1948, to France.
1* Okinawa.
Later history: Renamed *Odet*, L-9005. Stricken 1 Jul 1961; reacq 1963. R 14 Aug 1969.
LST 816 Decomm 29 Jun 1946. Stricken 31 Jul 1946, sold 27 May 1948
2* Iwo Jima, Okinawa.
LST 817 Operation Crossroads. Decomm 31 Jan 1947. Stricken 7 Feb 1947; sold 25 May 1948; BU Napa, Calif.
1* Okinawa.
LST 818 Decomm 16 Jul 1946. Stricken 28 Aug 1946, sold 17 Sep 1947; BU Seattle.
1* Okinawa.
LST 819 Decomm 15 Nov 1946.†
1* Okinawa.
LST 820 Decomm 16 Jan 1946. Stricken 7 Feb 1946. Destroyed 22 Mar 1946.
1* Okinawa.
LST 821 Decomm 8 Jul 1946. †
1* Okinawa.
LST 822 Decomm 27 Jul 1946. †
1* Okinawa.
LST 823 Decomm 1 Dec 1945. Stricken 3 Jan 1946. Destroyed May 1947.
1* Okinawa.
LST 824 Decomm 15 May 1946. †
1* Okinawa.
LST 825 Decomm 22 May 1946. †
1* Okinawa.
LST 826 Damaged by grounding in typhoon, Okinawa, 9 Oct 1945, sold May 1947.
1* Okinawa.
LST 827 †
1* Okinawa.
LST 828 Decomm 22 Apr 1947. Stricken 22 May 1947. Destroyed in Marianas, 7 May 1947.
1* Okinawa.

No.	Builder	Launched	Comm.
LST 829	Amer. Bridge	26 Sep 1944	23 Oct 1944
LST 830	Amer. Bridge	30 Sep 1944	28 Oct 1944
LST 831	Amer. Bridge	6 Oct 1944	8 Nov 1944
LST 832	Amer. Bridge	11 Oct 1944	4 Nov 1944
LST 833	Amer. Bridge	16 Oct 1944	10 Nov 1944
LST 834	Amer. Bridge	20 Oct 1944	10 Nov 1944
LST 835	Amer. Bridge	25 Oct 1944	20 Nov 1944
LST 836	Amer. Bridge	29 Oct 1944	25 Nov 1944
LST 837	Amer. Bridge	3 Nov 1944	29 Nov 1944
LST 838	Amer. Bridge	8 Nov 1944	4 Dec 1944
LST 839	Amer. Bridge	12 Nov 1944	6 Dec 1944
LST 840	Amer. Bridge	15 Nov 1944	11 Dec 1944
LST 841	Amer. Bridge	20 Nov 1944	18 Dec 1944
LST 842	Amer. Bridge	24 Nov 1944	19 Dec 1944
LST 843	Amer. Bridge	29 Nov 1944	23 Dec 1944
LST 844	Amer. Bridge	3 Dec 1944	30 Dec 1944
LST 845	Amer. Bridge	7 Dec 1944	9 Jan 1945
LST 846	Amer. Bridge	12 Dec 1944	9 Jan 1945
LST 847	Amer. Bridge	17 Dec 1944	15 Jan 1945
LST 848	Amer. Bridge	21 Dec 1944	20 Jan 1945
LST 849	Amer. Bridge	30 Dec 1944	16 Jan 1945

Service Records:

LST 829 USCG. Decomm end of 1945, sold 19 Mar 1948.
1* Okinawa.
Later history: Merchant *Macau.* Sunk by fire and explosion off northeast Brazil, 21 Dec 1961.
LST 830 USCG. Decomm 29 Apr 1946. Stricken 3 Jul 1946, sold 8 Jul 1947.
1* Okinawa.
Later history: Merchant *Marplatense*.
LST 831 USCG. Decomm 15 Apr 1946, sold 19 Dec 1947.
1* Okinawa.
Later history: Merchant barge *Humble ST-2*, renamed *Bauer ST-2.*
LST 832 USCG. Decomm 30 Apr 1946. Stricken 3 Jul 1946, sold 12 Mar 1948.
1* Okinawa.
LST 833 Decomm 2 May 1946. Stricken 10 Jun 1947, sold 13 May 1948.
1* Okinawa.
Later history: Merchant barge *Joseph Zeppa.*
LST 834 Decomm 12 Sep 1946. Stricken 8 Oct 1946, sold 28 Nov 1947; BU Seattle.
1* Okinawa.
LST 835 Decomm Jan 1946. †
1* Okinawa.
LST 836 Decomm 25 Jul 1946. †
1* Okinawa.
LST 837 Decomm 28 Jun 1946. Stricken 15 Aug 1946; sold 6 Feb 1948.
1* Okinawa.
Later history: Merchant *Willie D.*
LST 838 Decomm 7 Aug 1946. †
1* Okinawa.
LST 839 Decomm 24 Jul 1946. †
1* Okinawa.
LST 840 Decomm 1 Jun 1946. †
1* Okinawa.
LST 841 Decomm 25 Jun 1946. Stricken 23 Jun 1947, sold 5 Jan 1948.
1* Okinawa.
Later history: Merchant *S-23* 1948.
LST 842 Decomm 30 Dec 1947. To Philippines 30 Dec 1947.
1* Okinawa.
Later history: Renamed *Pampanga.*
LST 843 Decomm 18 Dec 1947. To Philippines 18 Dec 1947.
1* Okinawa.
Later history: Renamed *Bulacan.*
LST 844 Damaged by grounding, Okinawa, 29 May 1945. Decomm 15 Sep 1947. Stricken 29 Sep 1947, sold 28 Jun 1948.
1* Okinawa.
Later history: Merchant *S-25* 1949.
LST 845 †
LST 846 Tokyo Bay. †
LST 847 Decomm 21 Jun 1946. Stricken 31 Jul 1946, sold 13 May 1948.
LST 848 Decomm 10 Aug 1946. †
LST 849 Decomm 13 Jun 1946. †
1* Okinawa.

No.	Builder	Launched	Comm.
LST 850	Chicago Bridge	3 Nov 1944	27 Nov 1944
LST 851	Chicago Bridge	8 Nov 1944	30 Nov 1944
LST 852	Chicago Bridge	13 Nov 1944	*24 Nov 1944*
LST 853	Chicago Bridge	17 Nov 1944	11 Dec 1944
LST 854	Chicago Bridge	20 Nov 1944	14 Dec 1944
LST 855	Chicago Bridge	27 Nov 1944	21 Dec 1944
LST 856	Chicago Bridge	1 Dec 1944	23 Dec 1944
LST 857	Chicago Bridge	6 Dec 1944	29 Dec 1944

LST 858	Chicago Bridge	11 Nov 1944	*24 Dec 1944*
LST 859	Chicago Bridge	15 Dec 1944	6 Jan 1945
LST 860	Chicago Bridge	19 Dec 1944	13 Jan 1945
LST 861	Jeffersonville	4 Nov 1944	30 Nov 1944
LST 862	Jeffersonville	9 Nov 1944	4 Dec 1944
LST 863	Jeffersonville	14 Nov 1944	9 Dec 1944
LST 864	Jeffersonville	18 Nov 1944	13 Dec 1944
LST 865	Jeffersonville	22 Nov 1944	16 Dec 1944
LST 866	Jeffersonville	27 Nov 1944	21 Dec 1944
LST 867	Jeffersonville	1 Dec 1944	18 Dec 1944
LST 868	Jeffersonville	6 Dec 1944	30 Dec 1944
LST 869	Jeffersonville	11 Dec 1944	6 Jan 1945
LST 870	Jeffersonville	15 Dec 1944	10 Jan 1945
LST 871	Jeffersonville	20 Dec 1944	18 Jan 1945
LST 872	Jeffersonville	28 Dec 1944	22 Jan 1945
LST 873	Jeffersonville	3 Jan 1945	27 Jan 1945

Service Records:

LST 850 Decomm 17 May 1946. †
1* Okinawa.

LST 851 Decomm 24 Apr 1946. Stricken 8 May 1946, sold 14 Oct 1946.
1* Okinawa.

LST 852 Completed as repair ship, rec **ARL 23**, renamed ***Satyr***, 14 Aug 1944.

LST 853 Decomm 24 Jul 1946. †
1* Okinawa.

LST 854 †
1* Okinawa.

LST 855 †

LST 856 Conversion to **ARL 25** canceled. Decomm 29 May 1946. Stricken 3 Jul 1946, sold 5 May 1948.
1* Okinawa.

LST 857 †
1* Okinawa.

LST 858 Completed as repair ship, rec **ARL 26**, renamed ***Stentor***, 14 Aug 1944.

LST 859 †
1* Okinawa.

LST 860 Decomm 1 Jun 1946. Stricken 3 Jul 1946, sold 19 Mar 1948, to France.
Later history: Renamed *Inspecteur Général Pouyanne, L-9007.* Renamed *Adour.* Damaged by explosion at Nhatrang, Indochina, 17 May 1951; not repaired.

LST 861 Operation Crossroads. Decomm 10 Mar 1947. Stricken 4 Apr 1947, sold 10 Jun 1948; BU Seattle.
1* Okinawa.

LST 862 Decomm early 1946, sold 10 Oct 1947; BU.
1* Okinawa.

LST 863 Decomm 19 Jun 1946. Stricken 31 Jul 1946, sold 13 May 1948; BU.
1* Okinawa.

LST 864 Decomm 1 May 1947. Stricken; 22 May 1947, sold 26 May 1948; BU Seattle.
1* Okinawa.

LST 865 Decomm and to Philippines 30 Dec 1947.
Later history: Renamed *Albay.*

LST 866 Decomm 27 Jun 1946. Stricken 31 Jul 1946, sold 24 Oct 1947; BU Seattle.
1* Okinawa.

LST 867 Decomm 2 Jul 1946. Stricken 31 Jul 1946, sold 25 Oct 1947; BU Seattle.

LST 868 Decomm 9 Aug 1946. Stricken 10 Jun 1947, sold 19 Dec 1947; BU Philadelphia.
1* Okinawa.

LST 869 Decomm 31 Jul 1946. Stricken 28 Aug 1946, sold 26 Dec 1947, to Argentina.
Later history: Renamed *BDT-8, Dona Micaela* or *Dona Stella* 1953, merchant *Rio Turbio* 1966.

LST 870 Decomm Jun 1946. Stricken 28 Aug 1946, sold 29 Sep 1947, to Argentina.
Later history: Renamed *BDT-1, Cabo San Bartolme.*

LST 871 Rec **LST(H) 871**, 15 Sep 1945. Decomm 4 Oct 1946. Stricken 13 Nov 1946, sold 30 Jun 1948.
Later history: Merchant barge *Humble ST-9,* renamed *Lofco ST-1* 1968.

LST 872 Decomm 8 Jul 1946. Stricken 15 Aug 1946, sold 27 Oct 1947, to Argentina.
Later history: Renamed *BDT-4, Cabo San Gonzalo.*

LST 873 Decomm 8 Aug 1946. Stricken 25 Sep 1946, sold 20 May 1948; BU Vancouver, Wash.

No.	Builder	Launched	Comm.
LST 874	Missouri Valley	25 Nov 1944	18 Dec 1944
LST 875	Missouri Valley	29 Nov 1944	22 Dec 1944
LST 876	Missouri Valley	2 Dec 1944	27 Dec 1944
LST 877	Missouri Valley	6 Dec 1944	1 Jan 1945
LST 878	Missouri Valley	9 Dec 1944	3 Jan 1945
LST 879	Missouri Valley	13 Dec 1944	5 Jan 1945
LST 880	Missouri Valley	16 Dec 1944	9 Jan 1945
LST 881	Missouri Valley	20 Dec 1944	15 Jan 1945
LST 882	Missouri Valley	23 Dec 1944	18 Jan 1945
LST 883	Missouri Valley	30 Dec 1944	23 Jan 1945
LST 884	Dravo Pitt.	30 Sep 1944	10 Oct 1944
LST 885	Dravo Pitt.	23 Sep 1944	26 Oct 1944
LST 886	Dravo Pitt.	30 Sep 1944	2 Nov 1944
LST 887	Dravo Pitt.	7 Oct 1944	7 Nov 1944
LST 888	Dravo Pitt.	14 Oct 1944	13 Nov 1944
LST 889	Dravo Pitt.	14 Oct 1944	18 Nov 1944
LST 890	Dravo Pitt.	21 Oct 1944	24 Nov 1944
LST 891	Dravo Pitt.	28 Oct 1944	27 Nov 1944
LST 892	Dravo Pitt.	28 Oct 1944	30 Nov 1944
LST 893	Dravo Pitt.	4 Nov 1944	4 Dec 1944
LST 894	Dravo Pitt.	11 Nov 1944	12 Dec 1944
LST 895	Dravo Pitt.	11 Nov 1944	16 Dec 1944
LST 896	Dravo Pitt.	18 Nov 1944	20 Dec 1944
LST 897	Dravo Pitt.	25 Nov 1944	22 Dec 1944
LST 898	Dravo Pitt.	25 Nov 1944	29 Dec 1944
LST 899	Dravo Pitt.	2 Dec 1944	1 Jan 1945
LST 900	Dravo Pitt.	9 Dec 1944	6 Jan 1945
LST 901	Dravo Pitt.	9 Dec 1944	11 Jan 1945
LST 902	Dravo Pitt.	16 Dec 1944	15 Jan 1945
LST 903	Dravo Pitt.	23 Dec 1944	20 Jan 1945
LST 904	Dravo Pitt.	23 Dec 1944	25 Jan 1945
LST 905	Dravo Pitt.	30 Dec 1944	20 Jan 1945

Service Records:

LST 874 Decomm 29 May 1946. Stricken 3 Jul 1946, sold 8 Jun 1948, to France.
1* Okinawa.
Later history: Renamed *Cheliff, L-9006.* R 1970.

LST 875 Decomm 22 Apr 1946. Stricken 19 Jul 1946; to Philippines 2 Jul 1948.
1* Okinawa.
Later history: Renamed *Misamis Oriental.*

LST 876 Decomm 28 Jun 1946. Stricken 31 Jul 1946, sold 6 Nov 1947; BU.
1* Okinawa.

LST 877 Decomm 1 May 1946. Stricken 3 Jul 1946, sold 15 Jan 1948.
1* Okinawa.
Later history: Merchant *S-24* 1948.

LST 878 Decomm 3 May 1946. Stricken 19 Jul 1946, sold 5 Nov 1947.
Later history: Merchant *Chung 114* 1948.

LST 879 Decomm 26 Jun 1946. Stricken 25 Sep 1946, sold 17 May 1948.
1* Okinawa.

LST 880 Decomm 1 Oct 1946. †

LST 881 Operation Crossroads. Decomm 14 Feb 1947. Stricken 5 Mar 1947, sold 24 Nov 1947.
Later history: Merchant *Rio Douro*, renamed *Rio dos Sinos* 1951, *Clarion* 1956, *Sao Sebastiao* 1964. Sank after fire at Rio de Janeiro, 3 Aug 1973; BU 1975.

LST 882 Decomm 5 Jul 1946. Stricken 28 Aug 1946, sold 4 Nov 1947; BU Oakland, Calif.

LST 883 Decomm and stricken 20 Apr 1946. To Army 18 Aug 1946. †
1* Okinawa.

LST 884 USCG. Damaged by coastal gunfire, Iwo Jima, 26 Feb 1945. Damaged by kamikaze, Okinawa, 31 Mar 1945 (24 killed). Decomm 16 Feb 1946. Scuttled 6 May 1946.
2* Iwo Jima, Okinawa.

LST 885 USCG. Decomm 29 Apr 1946. Stricken 3 Jul 1946, sold 16 Dec 1947.
1* Okinawa.
Later history: Merchant *Gaspedoc* 1948, renamed *Vedalin* 1968, *Witshoal* 1968.

LST 886 USCG. Decomm 10 May 1946. Stricken 19 Jun 1946, sold 20 May 1948; BU Vancouver, Wash.
2* Iwo Jima, Okinawa.

LST 887 USCG. Decomm 23 Jul 1946. †
1* Okinawa.

LST 888 Decomm 2 Sep 1946. †
1* Okinawa.

LST 889 Decomm 28 May 1946. Stricken 19 Jul 1946; sold 13 Feb 1948.
1* Okinawa.

LST 890 Damaged in collision, Okinawa, 7 Apr 1945. Decomm 24 May 1946. Stricken 3 Jul 1946, sold 10 Jun 1948; BU Vancouver, Wash.
1* Okinawa.

LST 891 Decomm 2 Jul 1946. Stricken 31 Jul 1946, sold 29 Aug 1947; BU Seattle.
1* Okinawa.

LST 892 Decomm 5 Jul 1946. Stricken 28 Aug 1946, sold 28 Oct 1947; BU Oakland, Calif.
1* Okinawa.

LST 893 Decomm 8 May 1946. Stricken 19 Jun 1946, sold 25 May 1948.

LST 894 Decomm 29 Apr 1946. Stricken 19 Jul 1946, sold 5 Dec 1947.
1* Okinawa.

LST 895 Decomm 17 Aug 1946. Stricken 12 Mar 1948, sold 10 Jan 1952.
1* Okinawa.
Later history: Merchant barge *Irrigon.*

LST 896 Went aground in typhoon at Okinawa, 9 Oct 1945. Decomm 3 Dec 1945. Destroyed 8 Mar 1946.

LST 897 Decomm 23 Jul 1946. Stricken 28 Aug 1946, sold 15 Jun 1948.
1* Okinawa.
Later history: Merchant *Stanolind 57*, renamed *Guaratinga* 1951. Lost by grounding near Santa Marta LH, 21 Jul 1954.

LST 898 Decomm 9 May 1946. To Army 25 May 1946. †
1* Okinawa.

LST 899 Decomm 15 Jul 1946. Stricken 15 Aug 1946; sold, 5 Dec 1947; BU.
1* Okinawa.

LST 900 Decomm 15 May 1946. †
1* Okinawa.

LST 901 Decomm 9 Aug 1946. †

LST 902 Decomm 3 Aug 1946. †

LST 903 Decomm 10 Sep 1946. †

LST 904 Decomm 15 Nov 1946. †
1* Okinawa.

LST 905 Decomm 11 Sep 1946. †
1* Okinawa.

Figure 9.8: *LST-913* at anchor.

No.	Builder	Launched	Comm.
LST 906	Beth. Hingham	11 Mar 1944	27 Apr 1944
LST 907	Beth. Hingham	18 Mar 1944	30 Apr 1944
LST 908	Beth. Hingham	28 Mar 1944	8 May 1944
LST 909	Beth. Hingham	3 Apr 1944	11 May 1944
LST 910	Beth. Hingham	8 Apr 1944	24 May 1944
LST 911	Beth. Hingham	12 Apr 1944	14 May 1944
LST 912	Beth. Hingham	22 Apr 1944	21 May 1944
LST 913	Beth. Hingham	26 Apr 1944	23 May 1944
LST 914	Beth. Hingham	18 Apr 1944	18 May 1944
LST 915	Beth. Hingham	3 May 1944	27 May 1944
LST 916	Beth. Hingham	29 Apr 1944	25 May 1944
LST 917	Beth. Hingham	6 May 1944	28 May 1944
LST 918	Beth. Hingham	7 May 1944	29 May 1944
LST 919	Beth. Hingham	17 May 1944	31 May 1944
LST 920	Beth. Hingham	29 May 1944	17 Jun 1944
LST 921	Beth. Hingham	2 Jun 1944	23 Jun 1944
LST 922	Beth. Hingham	7 Jun 1944	29 Jun 1944
LST 923	Beth. Hingham	11 Jun 1944	6 Jul 1944
LST 924	Beth. Hingham	17 Jun 1944	10 Jul 1944
LST 925	Beth. Hingham	21 Jun 1944	15 Jul 1944
LST 926	Beth. Hingham	24 Jun 1944	20 Jul 1944
LST 927	Beth. Hingham	28 Jun 1944	4 Jul 1944
LST 928	Beth. Hingham	5 Jul 1944	30 Jul 1944
LST 929	Beth. Hingham	8 Jul 1944	2 Aug 1944
LST 930	Beth. Hingham	12 Jul 1944	6 Aug 1944
LST 931	Beth. Hingham	19 Jul 1944	11 Aug 1944
LST 932	Beth. Hingham	22 Jul 1944	15 Aug 1944
LST 933	Beth. Hingham	26 Jul 1944	20 Aug 1944
LST 934	Beth. Hingham	29 Jul 1944	25 Aug 1944
LST 935	Beth. Hingham	5 Aug 1944	29 Aug 1944
LST 936	Beth. Hingham	9 Aug 1944	1 Sep 1944
LST 937	Beth. Hingham	12 Aug 1944	6 Sep 1944
LST 938	Beth. Hingham	15 Aug 1944	9 Sep 1944
LST 939	Beth. Hingham	23 Aug 1944	14 Sep 1944
LST 940	Beth. Hingham	26 Aug 1944	20 Sep 1944

LST 941	Beth. Hingham	30 Aug 1944	22 Sep 1944
LST 942	Beth. Hingham	6 Sep 1944	26 Sep 1944
LST 943	Beth. Hingham	9 Sep 1944	30 Sep 1944
LST 944	Beth. Hingham	13 Sep 1944	4 Oct 1944
LST 945	Beth. Hingham	16 Sep 1944	9 Oct 1944
LST 946	Beth. Hingham	20 Sep 1944	12 Oct 1944
LST 947	Beth. Hingham	23 Sep 1944	15 Oct 1944
LST 948	Beth. Hingham	28 Sep 1944	*18 Oct 1944*
LST 949	Beth. Hingham	30 Sep 1944	23 Oct 1944
LST 950	Beth. Hingham	4 Oct 1944	27 Oct 1944
LST 951	Beth. Hingham	7 Oct 1944	31 Oct 1944
LST 952	Beth. Hingham	11 Oct 1944	3 Nov 1944
LST 953	Beth. Hingham	15 Oct 1944	7 Nov 1944
LST 954	Beth. Hingham	18 Oct 1944	*10 Nov 1944*
LST 955	Beth. Hingham	22 Oct 1944	*13 Nov 1944*
LST 956	Beth. Hingham	Oct 1944	*29 Nov 1944*
LST 957	Beth. Hingham	30 Oct 1944	20 Nov 1944
LST 958	Beth. Hingham	31 Oct 1944	25 Nov 1944
LST 959	Beth. Hingham	4 Nov 1944	29 Nov 1944
LST 960	Beth. Hingham	8 Nov 1944	2 Dec 1944
LST 961	Beth. Hingham	11 Nov 1944	6 Dec 1944
LST 962	Beth. Hingham	15 Nov 1944	*9 Dec 1944*
LST 963	Beth. Hingham	18 Nov 1944	*12 Dec 1944*
LST 964	Beth. Hingham	22 Nov 1944	16 Dec 1944
LST 965	Beth. Hingham	25 Nov 1944	20 Dec 1944
LST 966	Beth. Hingham	29 Nov 1944	*22 Dec 1944*
LST 967	Beth. Hingham	2 Dec 1944	*27 Dec 1944*
LST 968	Beth. Hingham	9 Dec 1944	3 Jan 1945
LST 969	Beth. Hingham	13 Dec 1944	9 Jan 1945
LST 970	Beth. Hingham	16 Dec 1944	13 Jan 1945
LST 971	Beth. Hingham	20 Dec 1944	*15 Jan 1945*
LST 972	Beth. Hingham	22 Dec 1944	22 Jan 1945
LST 973	Beth. Hingham	27 Dec 1944	27 Jan 1945
LST 974	Beth. Hingham	31 Dec 1944	31 Jan 1945
LST 975	Beth. Hingham	6 Jan 1945	3 Feb 1945
LST 976	Beth. Hingham	10 Jan 1945	*5 Feb 1945*
LST 977	Beth. Hingham	15 Jan 1945	*8 Feb 1945*
LST 978	Beth. Hingham	20 Jan 1945	15 Feb 1945
LST 979	Beth. Hingham	23 Jan 1945	20 Feb 1945

Service Records:

LST 906 Lost by grounding off Livorno, Italy, 18 Oct 1944. Decomm 20 May 1945. Stricken 22 Jun 1945.
1* Southern France.

LST 907 Decomm 18 Oct 1946. Stricken 25 Nov 1946. To Venezuela 1946.
1* Southern France.
Later history: Renamed *Capana*, merchant *Aldebaran* 1966.

LST 908 Decomm 30 Jul 1946. Stricken 28 Aug 1946, sold 3 Oct 1947; BU Philadelphia.
4* Leyte, Mindoro, Lingayen, Subic Bay, Okinawa.

LST 909 Decomm 21 Jun 1946. Stricken 31 Jul 1946, sold 19 May 1948; BU Vancouver, Wash.
2* Lingayen, Okinawa.

LST 910 Decomm 27 Jun 1946. Stricken 31 Jul 1946, sold 3 Dec 1947; BU.
3* Surigao Strait, Lingayen, Palawan Ldgs., Subic Bay, Mindanao Ldgs., Balikpapan.

LST 911 Decomm 24 Jun 1946. Stricken 31 Jul 1946, sold 25 Sep 1947; BU Seattle.
5* Morotai, Lingayen, Leyte, Mindoro, Lingayen, Mindanao Ldgs., Balikpapan.

LST 912 Damaged by kamikaze, Lingayen, 7 Jan 1945 (4 killed). †
4* Morotai, Leyte, Lingayen, Palawan Ldgs., Mindanao Ldgs.

LST 913 Decomm 16 Jul 1946. Stricken 14 Mar 1947, sold 18 Jun 1948.
3* Southern France, Leyte, Okinawa.
Later history: Merchant barge *Kiska Island, 537* 19.

LST 914 Decomm and stricken 26 Jun 1946. To Army 28 Jun 1946. †
2* Southern France, Okinawa.

LST 915 Decomm 25 Jun 1946. Stricken 31 Jul 1946, sold 19 Jun 1948.
Later history: Merchant barge *Adak Island.*

LST 916 Decomm 5 Apr 1946. To Army 28 Jun 1946. Stricken 29 Sep 1947. Went aground in typhoon on Naha Reef, near Hong Kong, Oct 1948.
3* Leyte, Lingayen, Okinawa.

LST 917 Decomm 24 May 1946. Stricken 3 Jul 1946, sold 19 May 1948; BU Vancouver, Wash.
5* Leyte, Morotai, Lingayen, Mindanao Ldgs., Okinawa.

LST 918 Damaged by coastal defense gun, Lingayen, 11 Jan 1945. Decomm 12 Jun 1946. Stricken 31 Jul 1946, sold 18 Dec 1947; BU Oakland, Calif.
2* Leyte, Okinawa.

LST 919 Decomm 5 Aug 1946. Stricken 25 Sep 1946, sold 10 Jan 1948, to Argentina.
3* Leyte, Lingayen, Mindanao Ldgs.
Later history: Renamed *BDT-6, Cabo San Isidro.*

LST 920 Decomm 8 Jul 1946. Stricken 14 Mar 1947, sold 18 Jun 1948.
1* Okinawa.
Later history: Merchant *Stanolind 55*, renamed *Guarape* 1951.

LST 921 Torpedoed by *U-667* in Bristol Channel, 14 Aug 1944, not repaired. Decomm 20 Sep 1944. Stricken 14 Oct 1944, hulked.

LST 922 Decomm 8 Jul 1946. Stricken 28 Aug 1946, sold 13 Jun 1948; BU.
4* Lingayen, Subic Bay, Palawan Ldgs., Visayan Is. Ldgs., Brunei.

LST 923 Decomm 10 Jul 1946. Stricken 15 Aug 1946, sold 31 May 1948.
2* Lingayen, Okinawa.

LST 924 Decomm 13 Jun 1946. Stricken 3 Jul 1946. To Thailand 5 May 1947.
4* Leyte, Lingayen, Visayan Is. Ldgs., Tarakan.
Later history: Renamed *Angthong.*

LST 925 Damaged by depth charges in Japanese suicide boat attack, Lingayen, 9 Jan 1945. Decomm 26 Nov 1945. Stricken 5 Dec 1945, sold 9 May 1948; BU Seattle.
1* Lingayen.

LST 926 Decomm 14 Jun 1946. Stricken 31 Jul 1946, sold 13 Jun 1948; BU.
2* Lingayen, Okinawa.

LST 927 Decomm 20 Jul 1946. Stricken 8 Oct 1946, sold 9 Dec 1947; BU Oakland, Calif.
2* Lingayen, Mindanao Ldgs.

LST 928 Damaged by collision, Iwo Jima, 25 Feb 1945. Damaged by grounding, Iwo Jima, 16 Mar 1945. Converted to barracks ship and rec **APB 50**, renamed ***Cameron***, 1 Aug 1945. Decomm 13 Dec 1946. †
1* Iwo Jima.

LST 929 Damaged in collision, Okinawa, 18 Apr 1945. Rec **LST(H) 929**, 15 Sep 1945. Decomm and trfd to China 24 May 1946.
2* Iwo Jima, Okinawa.
Later history: Renamed *Chung 102* 1946.

LST 930 Rec **LST(H) 930**, 15 Sep 1945. Decomm 26 Jun 1946. Stricken 31 Jul 1946, sold 8 Jun 1948.
2* Iwo Jima, Okinawa.
Later history: Merchant *U 909.*

LST 931 Rec **LST(H) 931**, 15 Sep 1945. Decomm 26 Jun 1946. Stricken 31 Jul 1946, sold, 12 Jun 1948; BU.
2* Iwo Jima, Okinawa.

LST 932 Decomm 24 Jun 1946. Stricken 31 Jul 1946, sold 29 Mar 1948.
3* Visayan Is. Ldgs., Mindanao Ldgs., Okinawa.
Later history: Merchant *Esso Neuquen.* Destroyed by fire off Campana, Argentina, 21 Feb 1952. BU 1953.

LST 933 Decomm 2 Jul 1946. Stricken 15 Aug 1946, sold 25 May 1948; BU.
2* Palawan Ldgs., Mindanao Ldgs., Okinawa.
LST 934 Decomm 13 May 1946, to U.S. State Department. Stricken 19 Jun 1946.
2* Mindanao Ldgs., Visayan Is. Ldgs., Palawan Ldgs., Okinawa.
LST 935 Decomm 2 Jul 1946. Stricken 15 Aug 1946, sold 29 Aug 1947; BU Seattle.
2* Visayan Is. Ldgs., Mindanao Ldgs., Palawan Ldgs., Balikpapan.
LST 936 Decomm 17 May 1946. Stricken 5 Jun 1946, sold 12 Jun 1948; BU.
1* Mindanao Ldgs.
LST 937 Decomm 24 May 1946, to U.S. State Department. Stricken 3 Jul 1946.
2* Mindanao Ldgs., Brunei.
LST 938 2* Mindanao Ldgs., Balikpapan. †
LST 939 Damaged by collision, Okinawa, 8 Apr 1945. Decomm 22 Jun 1946. Stricken 31 Jul 1946, sold 12 Jun 1948; BU.
1* Okinawa.
LST 940 Damaged by collision, Okinawa, 5 Apr 1945 and by grounding, 8 Apr 1945. Decomm 13 Jul 1946. Stricken 28 Aug 1946, sold 13 Jun 1948; BU.
2* Iwo Jima, Okinawa.
LST 941 Decomm 1 May 1946. Stricken 3 Jul 1946, sold 27 Feb 1947.
2* Palawan Ldgs., Visayan Is. Ldgs., Brunei.
Later history: Merchant *R.W. McIlvain* 1948, renamed barge *Seadrill 11* 1965.
LST 942 Decomm 26 Jun 1946. Stricken 31 Jul 1946, sold 10 Jun 1948.
1* Visayan Is. Ldgs.
LST 943 Decomm 16 Jul 1946. Stricken 25 Sep 1946, sold 9 Oct 1947; BU Oakland, Calif.
2* Iwo Jima, Okinawa.
LST 944 Decomm 19 Dec 1945. Stricken 8 Jan 1946, sold 26 Sep 1947; BU Baltimore.
2* Iwo Jima, Okinawa.
LST 945 Decomm 16 Apr 1946. Stricken 19 Jul 1946, sold 29 May 1946.
1* Okinawa.
Later history: Merchant *Chung 103* 1946, Taiwan *Chung Kung*. R 1956.
LST 946 Decomm 25 Jun 1946. Stricken 31 Jul 1946, sold 25 May 1948.
1* Okinawa.
Later history: Merchant *Guaraciaba* 1948, renamed *Lorenco Taques* 1967, 1969 *Marvi I*. BU 1973 Rio de Janeiro.
LST 947 Decomm 16 Aug 1946. Stricken 15 Oct 1946, sold 5 Dec 1947.
1* Okinawa.
LST 948 Completed as repair ship, rec **ARL 16**, renamed ***Myrmidon***, 14 Aug 1944.
LST 949 Rec **LST(H) 949**, 15 Sep 1945. Decomm 18 Jul 1946. Stricken 25 Sep 1946, sold 30 Jun 1948.
1* Okinawa.
Later history: Merchant barge *Attu Island*.
LST 950 Rec **LST(H) 950**, 15 Sep 1945. Decomm 23 Sep 1946. Stricken 10 Jun 1947, sold 8 Mar 1948; BU Barber, N.J.
1* Okinawa.
LST 951 Rec **LST(H) 951**, 15 Sep 1945. Decomm 8 Aug 1946. Stricken 25 Sep 1946, sold 14 Jun 1948; BU.
1* Okinawa.
LST 952 Rec **LST(H) 952**, 15 Sep 1945. Decomm 1 Aug 1946. Stricken 22 Jan 1947, sold 3 Oct 1947; BU Philadelphia.
1* Okinawa.
LST 953 Decomm 12 Nov 1946. †
1* Okinawa.
LST 954 Completed as repair ship, rec **ARL 17**, renamed ***Numitor***, 14 Aug 1944.
LST 955 Completed as repair ship, rec **ARL 19**, renamed ***Patroclus***, 14 Aug 1944.
LST 956 Completed as repair ship, rec **ARB 7**, renamed ***Sarpedon***, 14 Aug 1944.
LST 957 Decomm 20 May 1946. Stricken 22 Jan 1948; sold 5 Dec 1947.
1* Okinawa.
LST 958 Decomm 14 Mar 1946. Stricken 28 Mar 1946, sold 20 Dec 1946.
1* Okinawa.
LST 959 Decomm 13 Jun 1946. Stricken 3 Jul 1946. Destroyed 10 Jun 1948.
1* Okinawa.
LST 960 Decomm 2 Jul 1946. Stricken 15 Aug 1946, sold 4 Apr 1948; BU Seattle.
1* Okinawa.
LST 961 Decomm 23 Jul 1946. Stricken 28 Aug 1946, sold 10 Dec 1947; BU Oakland, Calif.
2* Palawan Ldgs., Okinawa.
LST 962 Completed as repair ship, rec **ARL 22**, renamed ***Romulus***, 14 Aug 1944.
LST 963 Completed as repair ship, rec **ARL 24**, renamed ***Sphinx***, 14 Aug 1944.
LST 964 Decomm 27 Jun 1946. Stricken 15 Aug 1946, sold 17 Jan 1947.
Later history: Merchant *San Juan Bosco* 1948, renamed *Mar Jonico* 1965.
LST 965 Decomm 3 Jun 1946. Stricken 19 Jul 1946, sold 23 Oct 1947; BU Baltimore.
LST 966 Completed as MTB tender, rec **AGP 15**, renamed ***Callisto***, 14 Aug 1944.
LST 967 Completed as repair ship, rec **ARB 9**, renamed ***Ulysses***, 14 Aug 1944.
LST 968 Decomm 2 Jul 1946. Stricken 15 Aug 1946, sold 10 Jun 1948.
Later history: Merchant barge *Humble ST-8*, renamed *Delta Marine 8* se80.
LST 969 Decomm 12 Jul 1946. Stricken 15 Aug 1946, sold 25 Apr 1947.
Later history: Merchant *New York* 1947.
LST 970 Decomm 10 Jul 1946. Stricken 15 Aug 1946, sold 25 Apr 1947.
1* Okinawa.
Later history: Merchant *Albany* 1947, renamed *Old Point Comfort* 1957, *Atlantic* 1964.
LST 971 Completed as repair ship, rec **ARL 13**, renamed ***Menelaus***, 14 Aug 1944.
LST 972 Decomm 25 Jun 1946. Stricken 15 Aug 1946, sold 29 May 1947.
Later history: Merchant *Tucupita*, renamed *Ciudad de Panama* 1951, *Seadrill 1*.
LST 973 Decomm 24 May 1946. To Army 2 Aug 1946. Stricken 29 Sep 1947. †
LST 974 Decomm 14 May 1946, to U.S. State Department. Stricken 19 Jun 1946.
LST 975 Decomm 16 Apr 1946. To Army 28 Apr 1946. †
LST 976 Completed as repair ship, rec **ARB 8**, renamed ***Telamon***, 14 Aug 1944.
LST 977 Completed as MTB tender, rec **AGP 14**, renamed ***Alecto***, 14 Aug 1944.
LST 978 Decomm 6 Jun 1946. Stricken 3 Jul 1946, sold, 10 Dec 1947 BU.
LST 979 Decomm 5 Jul 1946. Stricken 28 Aug 1946, sold 4 Nov 1947; BU Oakland, Calif.

No.	Builder	Launched	Comm.
LST 980	Boston NYd	27 Jan 1944	26 Feb 1944
LST 981	Boston NYd	27 Jan 1944	11 Mar 1944
LST 982	Boston NYd	10 Feb 1944	19 Mar 1944
LST 983	Boston NYd	10 Feb 1944	25 Mar 1944
LST 984	Boston NYd	25 Feb 1944	1 Apr 1944
LST 985	Boston NYd	25 Feb 1944	7 Apr 1944
LST 986	Boston NYd	5 Mar 1944	14 Apr 1944
LST 987	Boston NYd	5 Mar 1944	19 Apr 1944
LST 988	Boston NYd	12 Mar 1944	25 Apr 1944
LST 989	Boston NYd	12 Mar 1944	28 Apr 1944
LST 990	Boston NYd	27 Mar 1944	1 May 1944
LST 991	Boston NYd	27 Mar 1944	6 May 1944
LST 992	Boston NYd	7 Apr 1944	10 May 1944
LST 993	Boston NYd	7 Apr 1944	12 May 1944
LST 994	Boston NYd	17 Apr 1944	17 May 1944
LST 995	Boston NYd	2 May 1944	20 May 1944
LST 996	Boston NYd	2 May 1944	23 May 1944
LST 997	Boston NYd	12 May 1944	27 May 1944
LST 998	Boston NYd	14 May 1944	29 May 1944
LST 999	Boston NYd	14 May 1944	30 May 1944
LST 1000	Boston NYd	26 May 1944	14 Jun 1944
LST 1001	Boston NYd	26 May 1944	20 Jun 1944

LST 1002	Boston NYd	8 Jun 1944	25 Jun 1944
LST 1003	Boston NYd	8 Jun 1944	*29 Jun 1944*
LST 1004	Beth. Quincy	3 Mar 1944	28 Mar 1944
LST 1005	Beth. Quincy	11 Mar 1944	6 Apr 1944
LST 1006	Beth. Quincy	11 Mar 1944	12 Apr 1944
LST 1007	Beth. Quincy	20 Mar 1944	15 Apr 1944
LST 1008	Beth. Quincy	23 Mar 1944	18 Apr 1944
LST 1009	Beth. Quincy	23 Mar 1944	22 Apr 1944
LST 1010	Beth. Quincy	29 Mar 1944	25 Apr 1944
LST 1011	Beth. Quincy	29 Mar 1944	5 May 1944
LST 1012	Beth. Quincy	8 Apr 1944	30 Apr 1944
LST 1013	Beth. Quincy	16 Apr 1944	2 May 1944
LST 1014	Beth. Quincy	16 Apr 1944	5 May 1944
LST 1015	Beth. Quincy	20 Apr 1944	8 May 1944
LST 1016	Beth. Quincy	25 Apr 1944	10 May 1944
LST 1017	Beth. Quincy	25 Apr 1944	12 May 1944
LST 1018	Beth. Quincy	6 May 1944	14 May 1944
LST 1019	Beth. Quincy	6 May 1944	17 May 1944
LST 1020	Beth. Quincy	10 May 1944	19 May 1944
LST 1021	Beth. Quincy	16 May 1944	21 May 1944
LST 1022	Beth. Quincy	16 May 1944	24 May 1944
LST 1023	Beth. Quincy	17 May 1944	26 May 1944
LST 1024	Beth. Quincy	22 May 1944	28 May 1944
LST 1025	Beth. Quincy	22 May 1944	31 May 1944
LST 1026	Beth. Quincy	2 Jun 1944	7 Jun 1944
LST 1027	Beth. Quincy	2 Jun 1944	7 Jun 1944

Service Records:

LST 980 †
1* Normandy.

LST 981 Damaged by mine off Bognor Regis, England, 5 Jun 1944. Decomm 30 Jul 1946. Stricken 28 Aug 1946, sold 12 Dec 1947; BU.
2* Normandy, Okinawa.

LST 982 Decomm 25 Apr 1946. Stricken 19 Jul 1946, sold 5 Dec 1947.
2* Normandy, Okinawa.

LST 983 †
1* Normandy.

LST 984 Decomm 25 Jun 1946. Stricken 31 Jul 1946, sold 19 Jun 1948.
Later history: Merchant barge *Humble ST-11,* renamed *Placid T-66, Green Dolphin* 1972.

LST 985 Decomm 11 Jun 1946. Stricken 3 Jul 1946, sold 13 Oct 1947; BU.

LST 986 Decomm 18 Jul 1946. Stricken 28 Aug 1946, sold 31 Oct 1947; BU Oakland, Calif.
3* Guam, Lingayen, Okinawa.

LST 987 Decomm 3 Sep 1946. †

LST 988 †
1* Southern France.

LST 989 Decomm 7 Oct 1946. Stricken 13 Nov 1946, sold 25 Jun 1948.
1* Southern France.
Later history: Merchant *Humble ST-10,* renamed *Blue Dolphin* 1972.

LST 990 Decomm 10 Jul 1946. Stricken 25 Sep 1946, sold 26 Sep 1947; BU Baltimore.
4* Palau, Leyte, Subic Bay, Okinawa.

LST 991 Decomm 3 May 1946 and sold.
5* Palau, Leyte, Lingayen, Subic Bay, Okinawa.
Later history: Merchant *Mei Ling,* renamed *Wan Chun* sunk 1952.

LST 992 Decomm 9 Aug 1946. Stricken 25 Sep 1946, sold 13 Jun 1948; BU.
1* Okinawa.

LST 993 Decomm 1 Jun 1946. †
3* Leyte, Lingayen, Tarakan.

LST 994 Decomm 31 Jul 1946. Stricken 28 Aug 1946, sold 23 Dec 1947, to Argentina.
1* Southern France.
Later history: Renamed *Dona Flora* 1947, then *BDT-7, Cabo San Pablo.* R 1964.

LST 995 Decomm 15 Aug 1946. Stricken 25 Sep 1946, sold 4 Nov 1947, to Argentina.
1* Southern France.
Later history: Renamed *Don Nicolas* 1947, then *BDT-2, Cabo San Diego.* R 1964.

LST 996 Decomm 22 Apr 1946. Stricken 8 May 1946; sold 22 Oct 1947; BU.
2* Southern France, Okinawa.

LST 997 Decomm 7 Mar 1947. Stricken 7 Apr 1947, sold 15 Jun 1948; BU Seattle.
1* Southern France.
Later history: Merchant *Wan Ming,* renamed *Wan Ming.* (Taiwanese Navy).

LST 998 Decomm 26 Jun 1946. Stricken 31 Jul 1946, sold 11 Nov 1947 to Argentina.
Later history: Renamed *Don Ernesto* 1947, then *BDT-3, Cabo San Francisco de Paula.*

LST 999 Decomm 29 Jul 1946. Stricken 25 Sep 1946, sold 3 Nov 1947; BU Seattle.
3* Leyte, Mindanao Ldgs., Okinawa.

LST 1000 Damaged by collision, Okinawa, 5 Apr and by USN gunfire in error, 6 Apr 1945. Decomm 22 Jul 1946. Stricken 28 Aug 1946, sold 13 Jun 1948; BU.
1* Okinawa.

LST 1001 Decomm 26 Feb 1946. Stricken 19 Jun 1946, sold 23 Oct 1947; BU.
1* Okinawa.

LST 1002 Decomm 22 May 1946, to U.S. State Department. Stricken 3 Jul 1946.
1* Okinawa.

LST 1003 Completed as repair ship, rec **ARL 10**, renamed ***Coronis***, 14 Aug 1944.

LST 1004 Decomm 27 Jun 1946. Stricken 7 Feb 1947, sold 16 Oct 1947; BU Seattle.

LST 1005 Damaged in beaching operations, 1946. Decomm 6 Apr 1946. Stricken 17 Apr 1946. Destroyed 8 Nov 1946.

LST 1006 Decomm 26 Jul 1946. Stricken 28 Aug 1946, sold 14 Jun 1948.
3* Leyte, Mindoro, Lingayen, Subic Bay, Okinawa.
Later history: Merchant *Stanolind 58,* renamed *Solveig* barge.

LST 1007 Decomm 2 Mar 1946. Stricken 12 Apr 1946, sold 12 Sep 1946.
1* Tarakan.
Later history: Merchant *Romano* 1947. Foundered 120 miles east of Cayenne, 24 Jun 1955.

LST 1008 Decomm 4 May 1946, to U.S. State Department. Stricken 19 Jun 1946. To China.
Later history: Museum at Qingdao, China.

LST 1009 Decomm and to Army 17 Jul 1946. Stricken 14 Mar 1947.

LST 1010 Decomm and to Army 24 Apr 1947. †
2* Southern France, Okinawa.

LST 1011 Decomm 20 Jun 1946. Stricken 31 Jul 1946, sold 12 Jun 1948; BU.
2* Southern France, Okinawa.

LST 1012 Decomm 10 Jun 1946, to U.S. State Department. Stricken 19 Jul 1946.
1* Southern France.
Later history: Merchant *Wan Pu,* renamed *Ping Yuan* 1952.

LST 1013 Decomm 11 Jun 1946, to U.S. State Department. Stricken 19 Jul 1946. BU 1947.
3* Leyte, Lingayen, Okinawa.

LST 1014 Decomm 5 Mar 1946. Stricken 17 Apr 1946, sold 12 Sep 1946.
3* Palau, Leyte, Okinawa.
Later history: Merchant *Aminoil.*

LST 1015 Decomm 6 May 1946, to U.S. State Department. Stricken 19 Jun 1946.
4* Palau, Leyte, Lingayen, Okinawa.

LST 1016 Decomm 26 Jun 1946. Stricken 31 Jul 1946, sold 9 Dec 1947; BU Oakland, Calif.
2* Mindanao Ldgs., Balikpapan.

LST 1017 Decomm 29 Jun 1946. To China 14 Dec 1946.
5* Morotai, Leyte, Lingayen, Balikpapan, Mindanao Ldgs.
Later history: Renamed *Chung Chi.* R 1993.
LST 1018 Decomm 16 Aug 1946. Stricken 23 Jun 1947, sold 24 Jun 1948; BU Seattle.
5* Morotai, Lingayen, Leyte, Mindanao Ldgs., Balikpapan.
LST 1019 Decomm 30 Jul 1946. Stricken 25 Sep 1946, sold 28 Jun 1948.
2* Southern France, Okinawa.
Later history: Merchant barge *Humble ST-12,* renamed *Exxon ST-12* 1973, *ST-12* 1979.
LST 1020 Decomm 16 Jul 1946. Stricken 28 Aug 1946, sold 13 Jun 1948; BU.
1* Southern France.
LST 1021 To UK 25 Dec 1944–29 Nov 1946. Stricken 1 Aug 1947, sold 7 Oct 1947.
1* Southern France.
Later history: Merchant *Chong Ya,* renamed *Honesta* 1957, *Prospera* 1962, *Sindhusiam* 1964.
LST 1022 Decomm 31 Dec 1947. Stricken 22 Jan 1948, sold 28 Jun 1948; BU.
1* Okinawa.
LST 1023 Decomm 19 Jul 1946. Stricken 28 Aug 1946, sold 18 Jun 1948.
Later history: Merchant barge *Humble ST-7,* renamed *Zama "M".*
LST 1024 Decomm 27 Jun 1946. Stricken 31 Jul 1946, sold 12 Mar 1948.
2* Leyte, Okinawa.
LST 1025 24 May 1946. Stricken 15 Aug 1946, sold 11 Jun 1948; BU.
4* Leyte, Visayan Is. Ldgs., Subic Bay, Tarakan.
LST 1026 Decomm 11 Aug 1946. Stricken 28 Aug 1946, sold 5 Dec 1947.
2* Leyte, Mindanao Ldgs.
LST 1027 Decomm 4 Sep 1946. Stricken 23 Apr 1947, sold 20 Jan 1947.
3* Leyte, Lingayen, Mindanao Ldgs.
Later history: Merchant *Chung 107.*

No.	Builder	Launched	Comm.
LST 1028	Boston NYd	18 Jun 1944	7 Jul 1944
LST 1029	Boston NYd	18 Jun 1944	13 Jul 1944
LST 1030	Boston NYd	25 Jun 1944	19 Jul 1944
LST 1031	Boston NYd	25 Jun 1944	25 Jul 1944
LST 1032	Boston NYd	9 Jul 1944	1 Aug 1944
LST 1033	Boston NYd	9 Jul 1944	12 Aug 1944
LST 1034	Boston NYd	4 Aug 1944	26 Aug 1944
LST 1035	Boston NYd	4 Aug 1944	1 Sep 1944
LST 1036	Boston NYd	24 Aug 1944	*16 Sep 1944*
LST 1037	Boston NYd	24 Aug 1944	*22 Sep 1944*
LST 1038	Dravo Pitt.	6 Jan 1945	5 Feb 1945
LST 1039	Dravo Pitt.	6 Jan 1945	9 Feb 1945
LST 1040	Dravo Pitt.	13 Jan 1945	13 Feb 1945
LST 1041	Dravo Pitt.	20 Jan 1945	19 Feb 1945
LST 1042	Dravo Pitt.	20 Jan 1945	22 Feb 1945
LST 1043	Dravo Pitt.	27 Jan 1945	24 Feb 1945
LST 1044	Dravo Pitt.	3 Feb 1945	2 Mar 1945
LST 1045	Dravo Pitt.	3 Feb 1945	27 Mar 1945
LST 1046	Dravo Pitt.	10 Feb 1945	28 Mar 1945
LST 1047	Dravo Pitt.	17 Feb 1945	28 Mar 1945
LST 1048	Dravo Pitt.	17 Feb 1945	28 Mar 1945

Service Records:

LST 1028 Damaged by depth charges from Japanese suicide boats, Lingayen, 9 Jan 1945. Decomm 19 Nov 1945. Stricken 5 Dec 1945, sold 17 Sep 1947; BU.
1* Lingayen.
LST 1029 Decomm 1 May 1946. Stricken 10 Jun 1947, sold 31 Oct 1946.
2* Lingayen, Okinawa.
Later history: Merchant *Barbara* 1947, renamed *Maria Cristina* 1962, *Belisco.* Wrecked south of Cidreira, Rio Grande, Brazil, 29 Oct 1963.
LST 1030 Decomm 29 May 1946. To China 17 Feb 1948.
2* Lingayen, Okinawa.
Later history: Renamed *Chung Chuan.*
LST 1031 Decomm 18 Dec 1945. Stricken 8 Jan 1946, sold 23 Oct 1947; BU Baltimore.
1* Okinawa.
LST 1032 †
2* Iwo Jima, Okinawa.
LST 1033 Rec **LST(H) 1033**, 15 Sep 1945. Decomm 1 Aug 1946. Stricken 28 Aug 1946, sold 5 Dec 1947, to China.
2* Iwo Jima, Okinawa.
Later history: Renamed *Chung Sheng.* Ran aground near Keelung, 5 Oct 1995; BU.
LST 1034 Decomm 8 Oct 1946, sold 28 Oct 1946, to Netherlands East Indies.
1* Mindanao Ldgs.
Later history: Dutch *LST V,* renamed *Steven van der Hagen, Woendi.* R.
LST 1035 Decomm 6 Jun 1946. Stricken 3 Jul 1946, sold 16 Dec 1947; BU Oakland, Calif.
2* Palawan Ldgs., Visayan Is. Ldgs., Tarakan.
LST 1036 Completed as repair ship, rec **ARL 11**, renamed ***Creon,*** 14 Aug 1944.
LST 1037 Completed as repair ship, rec **ARL 12**, renamed ***Poseidon,*** 14 Aug 1944.
LST 1038 †
1* Okinawa.
LST 1039 Decomm 21 Jun 1946. Stricken 31 Jul 1946, sold 8 Sep 1947.
1* Okinawa.
Later history: Merchant *Tinian* 1948, renamed *Iraty* 1961.
LST 1040 Decomm 23 Sep 1946, sold 5 Oct 1946, to Netherlands East Indies
1*Okinawa.
Later history: Renamed *LST III.* R
LST 1041 †
LST 1042 Decomm 9 May 1946. Stricken 19 Jun 1946.
1* Okinawa.
LST 1043 Decomm 22 Jul 1946. Stricken 28 Aug 1946, sold 10 Dec 1947; BU Oakland, Calif.
LST 1044 Decomm 28 Jun 1946. Stricken 31 Jul 1946, sold 8 Jan 1948, to Argentina.
Later history: Renamed *Dona Barbara* 1947, *BDT-10, Cabo San Pio.* R 1964.
LST 1045 Decomm 10 Jul 1946. Stricken 15 Aug 1946, sold 9 Dec 1947; BU.
LST 1046 Decomm 27 Jun 1946. Stricken 31 Jul 1946, sold 29 Oct 1947; BU Seattle.
LST 1047 Decomm 6 May 1946. To Army 25 Jun 1946. Stricken 29 Sep 1947.
Later history: Merchant barge *Charleston 337.*
LST 1048 Decomm 14 May 1946. To Army 2 Aug 1946. †

No.	Builder	Launched	Comm.
LST 1049	Dravo Pitt.	24 Feb 1945	30 Mar 1945
LST 1050	Dravo Pitt.	3 Mar 1945	3 Apr 1945
LST 1051	Dravo Pitt.	3 Mar 1945	7 Apr 1945
LST 1052	Dravo Pitt.	6 Mar 1945	15 Apr 1945
LST 1053	Dravo Pitt.	6 Mar 1945	23 Apr 1945
LST 1054	Dravo Pitt.	17 Mar 1945	17 Apr 1945
LST 1055	Dravo Pitt.	24 Mar 1945	26 Apr 1945
LST 1056	Dravo Pitt.	24 Mar 1945	2 May 1945
LST 1057	Dravo Pitt.	31 Mar 1945	7 May 1945
LST 1058	Dravo Pitt.	7 Apr 1945	16 May 1945
LST 1059	Dravo Pitt.	14 Apr 1945	17 May 1945
LST 1060	Beth. Hingham	29 Jan 1945	24 Feb 1945
LST 1061	Beth. Hingham	3 Feb 1945	1 Mar 1945
LST 1062	Beth. Hingham	6 Feb 1945	5 Mar 1945

LST 1063	Beth. Hingham	11 Feb 1945	8 Mar 1945
LST 1064	Beth. Hingham	14 Feb 1945	12 Mar 1945
LST 1065	Beth. Hingham	17 Feb 1945	16 Mar 1945
LST 1066	Beth. Hingham	21 Feb 1945	20 Mar 1945
LST 1067	Beth. Hingham	27 Feb 1945	24 Mar 1945
LST 1068	Beth. Hingham	3 Mar 1945	27 Mar 1945
LST 1069	Beth. Hingham	7 Mar 1945	31 Mar 1945
LST 1070	Beth. Hingham	9 Mar 1945	5 Apr 1945
LST 1071	Beth. Hingham	14 Mar 1945	9 Apr 1945
LST 1072	Beth. Hingham	20 Mar 1945	12 Apr 1945
LST 1073	Beth. Hingham	22 Mar 1945	17 Apr 1945
LST 1074	Beth. Hingham	27 Mar 1945	21 Apr 1945
LST 1075	Beth. Hingham	3 Apr 1945	25 Apr 1945
LST 1076	Beth. Hingham	14 Apr 1945	1 May 1945
LST 1077	Beth. Hingham	18 Apr 1945	8 May 1945
LST 1078	Beth. Hingham	25 Apr 1945	15 May 1945
LST 1079	Beth. Hingham	27 Apr 1945	22 May 1945
LST 1080	Beth. Hingham	2 May 1945	29 May 1945

Service Records:

LST 1049 Decomm 18 Jul 1946. Stricken 19 Feb 1948; sold 1 Jul 1949.

LST 1050 Decomm and to China 27 Jan 1947.
Later history: Renamed *Chung Lien.* R93.

LST 1051 Decomm 7 May 1946. Stricken 5 Jun 1946, sold 13 Jun 1948; BU.

LST 1052 Decomm 11 Jul 1946. Stricken 15 Aug 1946, sold 31 Oct 1947; BU Seattle.

LST 1053 Decomm 3 Jun 1946. Stricken 3 Jul 1946, sold 8 Jun 1948.
Later history: Merchant barge *Humble ST-6*, merchant *Mexican Pride* 1964.

LST 1054 Decomm 28 Jun 1946. Stricken 31 Jul 1946, sold 26 Nov 1947; BU.

LST 1055 Decomm and to Army 13 Feb 1947. Stricken 25 Feb 1947.
Later history: Merchant *Peter G.*, renamed *Eagle* 1953; se 1980.

LST 1056 Decomm 12 Jul 1946. Stricken 10 Jun 1947, sold 20 Jan 1947.
Later history: Merchant *Chung 108*, renamed *Chung Yeh* (Chinese Navy).

LST 1057 Decomm 5 Aug 1946. Stricken 25 Sep 1946, sold 12 Jan 1948 to Argentina
Later history: Renamed *BDT 9, Dona Stella* or *Dona Dorothea*, then *Teniente de Navio del Castillo* 1953. R 1958.

LST 1058 Decomm 30 Jul 1946. Stricken 25 Sep 1946, sold 13 Jun 1948; BU.

LST 1059 Decomm 14 Sep 1946. Stricken 23 Apr 1947, sold 20 Jan 1947.

LST 1060 Decomm 7 Sep 1946. Stricken 23 Apr 1947, sold 13 Feb 1948.
Later history: Merchant *Kun Yeep.*

LST 1061 Decomm 1 May 1946. Stricken 3 Jul 1946, sold 1 Mar 1948.
Later history: Merchant *Jobure 1948*, renamed *Auguste Weitert* 1957, *Alster* 1959, *Magallenes* 1961, *Brian Conway* 1968. BU 1969 Hong Kong.

LST 1062 Decomm 27 Jun 1946. Stricken 31 Jul 1946, sold 25 Nov 1947; BU.

LST 1063 Decomm 13 Jul 1946, sold 30 Jun 1948.
Later history: Merchant *Polaris* 1948. BU 1978 Ashtabula, Ohio.

LST 1064 Decomm 21 Aug 1946. †

LST 1065 Decomm 23 May 1946. Stricken 23 Jun 1947, sold 17 Jan 1948.
Later history: Merchant *Santa Micaela* 1948, renamed *Mar Tirreno* 1965. BU 1976 Campana, Argentina.

LST 1066 Decomm Mar 1946. †

LST 1067 Decomm 13 Aug 1946. †

LST 1068 Decomm 9 Aug 1946. †

LST 1069 Decomm 6 Aug 1946. †

LST 1070 Decomm 3 Dec 1946. Rec **AG 147**, 27 Jan 1947. †

LST 1071 Decomm 10 Jun 1946. †

LST 1072 †

LST 1073 Decomm 5 Aug 1946. †

LST 1074 Decomm 4 Sep 1946. †

LST 1075 Decomm 18 Dec 1946 and trfd to China. Stricken 12 Mar 1948.
Later history: Renamed *Chung Cheng.*

LST 1076 Decomm 13 Jun 1946. †

LST 1077 Decomm 31 Jul 1946. †

LST 1078 †

LST 1079 Decomm Mar 1946. †

LST 1080 Decomm 29 Aug 1946. †

No. Name	Builder	Launched	Comm.
LST 1081	Amer. Bridge	5 Jan 1945	30 Jan 1945
LST 1082	Amer. Bridge	26 Jan 1945	7 Feb 1945
LST 1083	Amer. Bridge	14 Jan 1945	13 Feb 1945
LST 1084	Amer. Bridge	19 Jan 1945	19 Feb 1945
LST 1085	Amer. Bridge	13 Jan 1945	21 Feb 1945
LST 1086	Amer. Bridge	28 Jan 1945	24 Feb 1945
LST 1087	Amer. Bridge	3 Feb 1945	2 Mar 1945
LST 1088	Amer. Bridge	11 Feb 1945	27 Mar 1945
LST 1089	Amer. Bridge	17 Feb 1945	28 Mar 1945
LST 1090	Amer. Bridge	24 Feb 1945	2 Apr 1945
LST 1091	Amer. Bridge	3 Mar 1945	6 Apr 1945
LST 1092	Amer. Bridge	24 Mar 1945	*19 May 1945*
LST 1093	Amer. Bridge	11 Apr 1945	*30 May 1945*
LST 1094	Amer. Bridge	21 Apr 1945	*19 Jun 1945*
LST 1095	Amer. Bridge	25 Apr 1945	*27 Jun 1945*
LST 1096	Jeffersonville	10 Jan 1945	2 Feb 1945
LST 1097	Jeffersonville	16 Jan 1945	9 Feb 1945
LST 1098	Jeffersonville	27 Jan 1945	*5 Jun 1945*
LST 1099	Jeffersonville	8 Feb 1945	*19 Jun 1945*
LST 1100	Jeffersonville	20 Feb 1945	*28 Jul 1945*
LST 1101	Missouri Valley	3 Jan 1945	26 Jan 1945
LST 1102	Missouri Valley	10 Jan 1945	29 Jan 1945
LST 1103	Missouri Valley	13 Jan 1945	31 Jan 1945
LST 1104	Missouri Valley	17 Jan 1945	8 Feb 1945
LST 1105	Missouri Valley	20 Jan 1945	13 Feb 1945
LST 1106	Missouri Valley	24 Jan 1945	16 Feb 1945
LST 1107	Missouri Valley	29 Jan 1945	21 Feb 1945
LST 1108	Missouri Valley	1 Feb 1945	27 Feb 1945
LST 1109	Missouri Valley	6 Feb 1945	28 Feb 1945
LST 1110	Missouri Valley	9 Feb 1945	7 Mar 1945
LST 1111	Missouri Valley	9 Apr 1945	*9 Jul 1945*
LST 1112	Missouri Valley	12 Apr 1945	*15 Jun 1945*
LST 1113	Missouri Valley	17 Apr 1945	*27 Jun 1945*
LST 1114	Missouri Valley	20 Apr 1945	*3 Jul 1945*

Service Records:

LST 1081 Decomm 30 Jul 1946. †

LST 1082 Decomm 5 Aug 1946. †
1* Okinawa.

LST 1083 Decomm Aug 1946. Tokyo Bay. †
1* Okinawa.

LST 1084 Decomm 13 Aug 1946. †

LST 1085 †

LST 1086 Decomm 7 Aug 1946. †

LST 1087 Decomm 11 Aug 1947. Stricken 29 Sep 1947. To Army 8 Apr 1948. †

LST 1088 Decomm 29 Aug 1946. †

LST 1089 Decomm 16 Aug 1946. †

LST 1090 Decomm 22 Jul 1946. †

LST 1091 Decomm 5 Jul 1946. †

LST 1092 Completed as aviation repair ship and rec **ARV(E) 3**, renamed ***Aventinus***, 8 Dec 1944.
LST 1093 Completed as aviation repair ship and rec **ARV(A) 5**, renamed ***Fabius***, 8 Dec 1944.
LST 1094 Completed as aviation repair ship and rec **ARV(E) 4**, renamed ***Chloris***, 8 Dec 1944.
LST 1095 Completed as aviation repair ship and rec **ARV(E) 6**, renamed ***Megara***, 8 Dec 1944.
LST 1096 Decomm 24 Aug 1946. †
1* Okinawa.
LST 1097 Decomm 19 Dec 1946. †
1* Okinawa.
LST 1098 Completed as salvage craft tender and rec **ARS(T) 1**, renamed ***Laysan Island***, 8 Dec 1944.
LST 1099 Completed as salvage craft tender and rec **ARS(T) 2**, renamed ***Okala***, 8 Dec 1944.
LST 1100 Completed as salvage craft tender and rec **ARS(T) 3**, renamed ***Palmyra***, 8 Dec 1944.
LST 1101 Decomm 6 Jun 1946. †
1* Okinawa.
LST 1102 Decomm 21 Nov 1947. †
1* Okinawa.
LST 1103 Decomm 18 Jun 1946. Stricken 23 Jun 1947, sold 17 Jun 1948.
LST 1104 Decomm 8 Jul 1946. Stricken 22 May 1947, sold 28 Apr 1947, to Argentina.
1* Okinawa.
Later history: Renamed BDT-12, later merchant *Samba*.
LST 1105 Decomm 29 May 1946. Stricken 19 Jun 1946, sold 20 May 1948.
1* Okinawa.
Later history: Merchant *Guaranesia*, renamed *Brasilia* 1959.
LST 1106 Decomm 2 Aug 1946. Stricken 8 Oct 1946, sold 13 Jun 1948; BU.
1* Okinawa.
LST 1107 Damaged by grounding, Okinawa, 10 Jul 1945. Decomm 1 May 1946. Stricken 3 Jul 1946, sold 28 Feb 1947.
Later history: Merchant *Andrew Jackson Higgins* 1948, renamed *Francis Chorin* 1955, *Punta Paramo* 1958, *Guer-Aike* 1966.
LST 1108 Decomm 15 Aug 1946. Stricken 25 Sep 1946, sold 10 Jan 1948, to Argentina.
Later history: Renamed *Dona Irma* 1948, *BDT-11, Cabo San Sebastian.* Stricken 1964
LST 1109 Decomm 6 May 1946. Stricken 19 Jun 1946, sold 13 Jun 1948; BU.
LST 1110 †
1* Okinawa.
LST 1111 Rec **AKS 16**, renamed ***Blackford***, 8 Dec 1944. Converted to barracks ship and rec **APB 45**, 6 Mar 1945. †
LST 1112 Rec **AKS 17**, renamed ***Dorchester***, 8 Dec 1944. Converted to barracks ship and rec **APB 46**, 6 Mar 1945. †
LST 1113 Rec **AKS 18**, renamed ***Kingman***, 8 Dec 1944. Converted to barracks ship and rec **APB 47**, 6 Mar 1945. †
LST 1114 Rec **AKS 19**, renamed ***Vanderburgh***, 8 Dec 1944. Converted to barracks ship and rec **APB 48**, 6 Mar 1945. †

No.	Builder	Launched	Comm.
LST 1115	Chicago Bridge	22 Dec 1944	*4 Jan 1945*
LST 1116	Chicago Bridge	28 Dec 1944	*9 Jan 1945*
LST 1117	Chicago Bridge	2 Jan 1945	*13 Jan 1945*
LST 1118	Chicago Bridge	5 Jan 1945	*18 Jan 1945*
LST 1119	Chicago Bridge	11 Jan 1945	*23 Jan 1945*
LST 1120	Chicago Bridge	16 Jan 1945	9 Feb 1945
LST 1121	Chicago Bridge	19 Jan 1945	*31 Jan 1945*
LST 1122	Chicago Bridge	24 Jan 1945	14 Feb 1945
LST 1123	Chicago Bridge	29 Jan 1945	19 Feb 1945
LST 1124	Chicago Bridge	1 Feb 1945	*3 Mar 1945*
LST 1125	Chicago Bridge	6 Feb 1945	*17 Feb 1945*
LST 1126	Chicago Bridge	9 Feb 1945	28 Feb 1945
LST 1127	Chicago Bridge	14 Feb 1945	*26 Feb 1945*
LST 1128	Chicago Bridge	19 Feb 1945	9 Mar 1945
LST 1129	Chicago Bridge	22 Feb 1945	6 Mar 1945
LST 1130	Chicago Bridge	27 Feb 1945	20 Mar 1945
LST 1131	Chicago Bridge	2 Mar 1945	*15 Mar 1945*
LST 1132	Chicago Bridge	7 Mar 1945	*19 Mar 1945*
LST 1133	Chicago Bridge	10 Mar 1945	*23 Mar 1945*
LST 1134	Chicago Bridge	16 Mar 1945	7 Apr 1945
LST 1135	Chicago Bridge	21 Mar 1945	12 Apr 1945
LST 1136	Chicago Bridge	26 Mar 1945	*6 Apr 1945*
LST 1137	Chicago Bridge	30 Mar 1945	*11 Apr 1945*
LST 1138	Chicago Bridge	5 Apr 1945	24 Apr 1945
LST 1139	Chicago Bridge	9 Apr 1945	27 Apr 1945
LST 1140	Chicago Bridge	13 Apr 1945	4 May 1945
LST 1141	Chicago Bridge	18 Apr 1945	9 May 1945
LST 1142	Chicago Bridge	23 Apr 1945	12 May 1945
LST 1143	Chicago Bridge	27 Apr 1945	*9 May 1945*
LST 1144	Chicago Bridge	2 May 1945	28 May 1945
LST 1145	Chicago Bridge	7 May 1945	*18 May 1945*
LST 1146	Chicago Bridge	11 May 1945	30 May 1945
LST 1147	Chicago Bridge	21 May 1945	*28 May 1945*
LST 1148	Chicago Bridge	23 May 1945	9 Jun 1945
LST 1149	Chicago Bridge	25 May 1945	*3 Dec 1945*
LST 1150	Chicago Bridge	30 May 1945	20 Jun 1945
LST 1151	Chicago Bridge	4 Jun 1945	*15 Jun 1945*
LST 1152	Chicago Bridge	8 Jun 1945	30 Jun 1945

Service Records:

LST 1115 Completed as repair ship, rec **ARL 20**, renamed ***Pentheus***, 14 Aug 1944.
LST 1116 Completed as repair ship, rec **ARL 21**, renamed ***Proserpine***, 14 Aug 1944.
LST 1117 Completed as repair ship, rec **ARL 27**, renamed ***Tantalus***, 14 Aug 1944.
LST 1118 Completed as repair ship, rec **ARL 28**, renamed ***Typhon***, 14 Aug 1944.
LST 1119 Completed as repair ship, rec **ARB 11**, renamed ***Diomedes***, 14 Aug 1944.
LST 1120 †
1* Okinawa.
LST 1121 Completed as repair ship, rec **ARB 10**, renamed ***Demeter***, 14 Aug 1944.
LST 1122 †
LST 1123 †
LST 1124 Completed as repair ship, rec **ARL 29**, renamed ***Amphitrite***, 14 Aug 1944.
LST 1125 Completed as M tender, rec **AGP 17**, renamed ***Brontes***, 14 Aug 1944.
LST 1126 †
LST 1127 Completed as repair ship, rec **ARB 12**, renamed ***Helios***, 14 Aug 1944.
LST 1128 Decomm 29 Jul 1946. †
LST 1129 Decomm 31 Jul 1946. †
LST 1130 Damaged by grounding at Yap, 12 Mar 1948. †
LST 1131 Completed as repair ship, rec **ARL 30**, renamed ***Askari***, 14 Aug 1944.
LST 1132 Completed as repair ship, rec **ARL 31**, renamed ***Bellerophon***, 14 Aug 1944.
LST 1133 Completed as MTB tender, rec **AGP 18**, renamed ***Chiron***, 14 Aug 1944.
LST 1134 †
LST 1135 †
LST 1136 Completed as repair ship, rec **ARL 32**, renamed ***Bellona***, 14 Aug 1944.
LST 1137 Completed as repair ship, rec **ARL 33**, renamed ***Chimaera***, 14 Aug 1944.

LST 1138 †
LST 1139 Decomm 20 Jul 1946. Stricken 15 Aug 1946, sold 30 Jun 1948. Tokyo Bay.
LST 1140 †
LST 1141 Conversion to **ARL 34** canceled 1944. †
LST 1142 Decomm 15 Nov 1946. †
LST 1143 Completed as repair ship, rec **ARL 35**, renamed ***Daedalus***, 14 Aug 1944.
LST 1144 †
LST 1145 Completed as repair ship, rec **ARL 36**, renamed ***Gordius***, 14 Aug 1944.
LST 1146 †
LST 1147 Completed as repair ship, rec **ARL 37**, renamed ***Indra***, 14 Aug 1944.
LST 1148 USCG. Decomm 11 May 1946. †
LST 1149 Completed as repair ship, rec **ARL 38**, renamed ***Krishna***, 14 Aug 1944.
LST 1150 USCG. Decomm 13 Sep 1946. †
LST 1151 Completed as repair ship, rec **ARL 39**, renamed ***Quirinus***, 14 Aug 1944.
LST 1152 USCG. †

No.	Builder	Launched	Comm.
LST 1153	Boston NYd	24 Apr 1947	3 Sep 1947
LST 1154	Boston NYd	19 Jul 1946	24 May 1949
LST 1155	Boston NYd	—	—

Displacement	2,324 tons, 6,000 f/l
Dimensions	382' (oa); 368' (wl) x 54' x 14'5""
Machinery	2 screws; GT; hp 6,000; 14 knots
Complement	178
Armament	2–5"/38, 2 twin 40mm, 6 twin 20mm AA guns

Notes: New, larger design with geared turbines, greater speed. Prominent funnel aft.

Service Records:

LST 1153 †
LST 1154 †
LST 1155 Canceled 7 Jan 1946.

LANDING SHIPS, MEDIUM

LSM 1–558	
Displacement	520 tons, 1,095 tons f/l
Dimensions	203'6" (oa); 196'6" (wl) x 34'6" x 8'4"
Machinery	2 screws; diesel, SHP 2,800; 13.2 knots
Endurance	4,900/12
Complement	59
Armament	2 twin 40mm, 4–20mm AA guns

Figure 9.9: *LSM-233*, 27 Jul 1944, showing bow doors open.

Notes: Bow doors. Carried five medium or three heavy tanks, or six LVTs; nine DUKWs and 54 troops. A total of 558 ordered; 48 completed as LSM(R), and 14 converted. Originally classified LCT(7). LSM 549–52 rec ARS(D) 1–4, 24 Apr 1945.

LANDING SHIPS, MEDIUM (ROCKET)

LSM(R) 188–95	
Displacement	961 tons f/l (188–195), 1,004 tons f/l
Dimensions	203'6" (oa); 196'6" (wl) x 34'6" x 6'6"
Machinery	2 screws; diesel, SHP 2,800; 13.2 knots
Endurance	4,900/12
Complement	81

Figure 9.10: A converted *LSM(R)* firing rockets. One of the first group converted with 5" gun on stern. Compare with *LSM(R)-409*, converted while under construction.

Figure 9.11: *LSM(R)-409*, after the war. Notice the completely different appearance from the LSM, the lack of bow doors. Five-inch mount and rocket launchers line the deck.

Armament	1–5"/38, 4–4.2" mortars, 2–40mm AA, 3–20mm, 105 rocket launchers; LSM(R) 196–99: 85 rocket launchers

LSM(R) 401–12, 501–36	
Displacement	850 tons, 1,280 tons f/l
Dimensions	203'6" (oa); 197'3" (wl) x 34'6" x 6'8"; LSM(R) 501–36: 206'3" (oa); 204'6"(wl)
Machinery	2 screws; diesel, SHP 2,800; 12.6 knots
Endurance	3,000/12
Complement	138
Armament	1–5"/38, 4–4.2" mortars, 4–40mm AA, 10 rocket launchers

Note: Automatic rocket launchers.

Builders of LSM and LSM(R):

Brown	1–125, 354–88, 459–552
Charleston NYd	126–200; 295–309, 389–413, 553–58
Dravo Wilm.	201–32, 414–46
Federal	253–94
Pullman	310–53
W. Pipe S.P.	233–52, 447–58

War Losses:

LSM 12	Broached and abandoned on coral reef, off Okinawa, 4 Apr 1945.
LSM 15	Sunk in typhoon off Okinawa, 9 Oct 1945.
LSM 20	Sunk by kamikaze in Surigao Strait, off Ormoc, 5 Dec 1944 (8 killed).
LSM 59	Sunk by Japanese aircraft off Okinawa, 21 Jun 1945 (2 killed).
LSM 135	Sunk by kamikaze off Okinawa, 25 May 1945 (11 killed).
LSM 149	Broached at Sansapor, New Guinea, and lost, 5 Dec 1944.
LSM 169	Damaged by mine in Mariveles harbor, 15 Feb 1945, not repaired.
LSM 318	Sunk by Japanese aircraft at Ormoc, 7 Dec 1944.
LSM 361	Aground in typhoon at Okinawa, 9 Oct 1945, not repaired.

LSM(R) 190 Sunk by Japanese aircraft at Okinawa, 4 Apr 1945 (13 killed).
LSM(R) 194 Sunk by kamikaze at Okinawa, 4 May 1945 (13 killed).
LSM(R) 195 Sunk by kamikaze at Okinawa, 3 May 1945 (8 killed).

LANDING CRAFT, INFANTRY (LARGE)

LCI(L) 1–1139	
Displacement	387 tons f/l, 216 tons; LCI(L) 351–1139: 246 tons
Dimensions	158'6" (oa); 153' (wl) x 23'8" x 5'8"; LCI(L) 351–1098: 159' (oa)
Machinery	2 screws; diesel; SHP 1,320; 14.4 knots
Endurance	8,700/12
Complement	LCI(L) 29; LCI(G) 70; LCI(M) 53; LCI(R) 34; LC(FF) 64
Armament	4–20mm AA; LCI(L) 351–1098: 5–20mm; LCI(G): 3–40mm AA, 10 rocket launchers; LCI(M): 3–4.2" chemical mortars, 1–40mm AA; LCI(R): 6–5" rocket launchers, 1–40mm AA; LC(FF): 5–20mm AA

Notes: Originally a British design for raiding craft. Conceived as cross-channel transport for the invasion of France. Able to make long open ocean voyages. A total of 1,139 ordered, of which 941 were completed. LCI(L) 351–1139 had higher rounded conning towers. Designed with two ramps, one on either side, but later units (641–57, 691–716, 762–80, 782–821, 866–84, 1024–33, 1068–98) had center line ramp and bow doors. Many were converted to gunboats, LCI(G); mortar ships, LCI(M); rocket ships, LCI(R); and flagships, LC(FF).

Transferred under lend-lease to the United Kingdom were LCI(L) 3–16, 33, 35, 75, 97–136, 161–87, 193, 209–18, 229, 231, 238–318, 374–91, 411, 487–512, and 537 (220 total). Transferred under lend-lease to the USSR were LCI(L) 521–27, 554, 557, 564–67, 590–93, 665–68, 671–72, 675, 943, 945–46, and 949–50 (29 total).

Figure 9.12: *LCI(L)-463*, 19 Oct 1943. Notice the gangways for unloading troops stowed on bow.

LCI(L)s Canceled:

30 Oct 1942	137–60
5 Nov 1942	197–208
6 Nov 1942	49–60
5 Jun 1944	838–44, 860–65, 902–10
16 Jun 1944	1034–51
23 Jun 1944	781, 845–59, 929–42
19 Aug 1944	717–24, 822–37, 885–901, 911–28, 1099–1139.

War Losses:

LCI(L) 1, 20, 32, 85, 91, 92, 93, 219, 232, 339, 416, 497, 553, 600, 974, 1065
LCI(G) 82, 459, 468, 474

LANDING CRAFT, SUPPORT (LARGE)

LCS(L)(3) 1–130	
Displacement	250 tons, 387 tons f/l
Dimensions	158' (oa); 153' (wl) x 23'8" x 6'6"
Machinery	2 screws; diesel, SHP 1,320; 15.5 knots
Endurance	5,500/12
Complement	78
Armament	6–40mm AA; 1–3"/50 or 1 twin 40mm, 2 twin 40mm, 4–20mm, 10 rocket launchers

Notes: Designed to provide close infire support for landing operations. Similar hull to LCI(L).

Builders of LCI and LCS:

Albina	LCI 1013–51; LCS 48–78
Brown	LCI 319–50
Commercial	LCI 725–81, 845–59, 929–942; LCS 26–47, 79–108
Consol. Orange	LCI 61–96, 943–1012
Defoe	LCI 1052–1109
Federal	LCI 161–208
Hingham	LCI 97–160
Lawley	LCI 209–38, 351–422, 658–724, 822–44, 860–65, 902–10; LCS 1–25, 109–30

Figure 9.13: *LCS(L)-25*, 26 Oct 1944. Landing craft support as completed. A variant of the landing craft infantry design.

Figure 9.14: An *LCT(5)* on maneuvers in Chesapeake Bay, 1943.

New Jersey LCI 239–318, 423–657, 782–821, 866–901, 911–28, 1110–39
NY Sbdg LCI 1–60

LANDING CRAFT, TANK

LCT(5) 1–500	
Displacement	133 tons; 285 tons f/l
Dimensions	114'2" (oa); 105' (wl) x 32'8" x 3'6"
Machinery	3 screws; diesels; SHP 675; 8 knots
Endurance	1,200/7
Complement	13; capacity: 3 to 5 tanks or 9 trucks
Armament	1 or 2 20mm AA

LCT(6) 501–1465	
Displacement	143 tons; 309 tons f/l
Dimensions	120'4" (oa); 105' (wl) x 32'8" x 3'9"
Machinery	3 screws, diesels, SHP 675, 8 knots
Endurance	1,200/7
Complement	13; capacity: 3 to 4 tanks
Armament	2–20mm AA

Notes: Transferred under lend-lease: 176 to UK, 17 to USSR.

LCT(7) 1501–2830 Rec LSM 1–336

Figure 9.15: *LST-926*. The deck is clear of ventilators.

10
TENDERS

Destroyer Tenders

Destroyer tenders were specialized ships used for servicing destroyers. They provided mobile base and repair facilities, fuel, stores, torpedoes and ammunition. The later ships were named for natural features and national parks.

Destroyer Tenders on the Navy List, 1922:

AD 2 *Melville* Decomm 9 Aug 1946. Stricken 23 Apr 1947, sold 30 Mar 1948; BU Baltimore.

AD 3 *Dobbin* Decomm 27 Sep 1946. Sold 23 Dec 1946, BU 1951. 1* Pearl Harbor (4 killed).

AD 4 *Whitney* Atlantic Fleet 1924–32. Damaged by gasoline explosion at Guantanamo, 21 Mar 1928 (2 killed). Pacific Fleet 1932–46. Decomm 22 Oct 1946. Stricken 22 Jan 1947, sold 18 Mar 1948; BU. 1* Pearl Harbor.

AD 8 *Buffalo* Decomm 15 Nov 1922. Stricken 27 May 1927, sold 28 Sep 1927.
Later history: Merchant *Sirius*. BU 1933.

Figure 10.2: *Whitney* (AD 4) was present at Pearl Harbor. Note that gun tubs have been added at bow and stern.

Figure 10.1: *Melville* (AD 2), 28 Dec 1941, the World War I veteran leaving Norfolk Navy Yard after modifications, her appearance not much changed.

Figure 10.3: *Black Hawk* (AD 9) as she appeared during World War II. Notice new radar mast and gun tubs.

AD 9 *Black Hawk* Asiatic Fleet 1922–40. Yangtze River 1926–27 and 1931–32. China 1937–39. Decomm and stricken 15 Aug 1946. BU 1948 Seattle. Masts cut down; radar mast added forward of funnel.
1* Philippines 1942.

AD 10 *Bridgeport* Decomm 3 Nov 1924. Stricken 2 Oct 1941, sold 2 Feb 1942.
Later history: Merchant *Bridgeport* 1942, to Army as hospital ship, renamed *Larkspur* 1943, Army transport *Bridgeport*, 1946. BU 1948.

AD 11 *Altair* Decomm 21 Jun 1946. Stricken 21 Jul 1946. BU 1948 Napa, Calif.

AD 12 *Denebola* Mediterranean 1922–23. Out of comm 9 Aug 1924–6 Apr 1940. Decomm 10 Apr 1946. BU 1950 Baltimore.
1* Southern France.

AD 13 *Rigel* Converted to repair ship and rec **AR 11**, 10 Apr 1941. Under conversion at Pearl Harbor, 7 Dec 1941. Recomm 7 Apr 1942. Decomm 11 Jul 1946. BU 1950 Seattle.
4* Pearl Harbor, Saidor, Western New Guinea.

Notes: Armament: AD 2: 2–5"/51, 4–3"/50, 2 twin 40mm, 8–20mm; AD 3–4: 4–5"/38, 4 twin 40mm, 16–20mm; masts cut down, radar mast added aft of bridge; AD 9: 4–3"/50, 2 twin 40mm, 16–20mm. Masts cut down; radar mast added forward of funnel; AD 11–12: 4–3"/50, 4 twin 40mm, 6 twin 20mm; AD 13:1–5"/51, 4–3"/50, 2 twin 40mm, 10–20mm.

Dixie Class

No.	Name	Builder	Laid Down	Launched	Comm.
AD 14	*Dixie*	NY Sbdg	17 Mar 1938	27 May 1939	25 Apr 1940
AD 15	*Prairie*	NY Sbdg	7 Dec 1938	9 Dec 1939	5 Aug 1940
AD 17	*Piedmont*	Tampa	1 Dec 1941	7 Dec 1942	5 Jan 1944
AD 18	*Sierra*	Tampa	31 Dec 1941	23 Feb 1943	20 Mar 1944
AD 19	*Yosemite*	Tampa	19 Jan 1942	16 May 1943	25 Mar 1944

Displacement	14,037 tons, 18,000 f/l
Dimensions	530'6" (oa); 520' (wl) x 73'4" x 25'6"
Machinery	2 screws; Parsons turbines; 4 B&W A boilers (AD 14–15), 4 A-C boilers (AD 17–19); SHP 11,000; 19.6 knots
Complement	1,262
Armament	4–5"/38, 4 twin 40mm, 23–20mm AA

Notes: Large ships built from the keel up as destroyer tenders. Similar basic design with *Fulton* class AS and *Vulcan* class AR. AD 17–19 originally ordered from Sun. Two funnels.

Service Records:

AD 14 *Dixie* Operation Crossroads. †

Figure 10.4: *Dixie* (AD 14), the first new tender of the Navy in 1940, with destroyer *Hovey* alongside. Notice that the second 5" mount is as yet unshielded.

Figure 10.5: *Prairie* (AD 15), 17 Oct 1943, with wartime modifications, including a director for the 5" guns.

AD 15 *Prairie* Damaged by fire at Argentia, Newfoundland 29 May 1942 (2 killed). †

AD 17 *Piedmont* Damaged by explosion of USS *Mount Hood* at Manus, 10 Nov 1944 (1 killed). Tokyo Bay. †

AD 18 *Sierra* †

AD 19 *Yosemite* †

Cascade Class

No.	Name	Builder	Laid Down	Launched	Comm.
AD 16	*Cascade*	W. Pipe, S.F.	17 Jul 1941	7 Jun 1942	12 Mar 1943

Displacement	11,755 tons, 16,600 f/l
Dimensions	492' (oa); 465" (wl) x 69'6" x 27'3"
Machinery	1 screw; GE turbines; 2 FW D boilers; SHP 8,500; 18.4 knots
Complement	857
Armament	2–5"/38, 3 twin 40mm, 12–20mm guns

Notes: Type C3–S1–N2. Single funnel.

Service Record:

AD 16 *Cascade* Decomm 12 Feb 1947. †
1* Okinawa.

Hamul Class

No.	Name	Builder	Laid Down	Launched	Comm.
AD 20	*Hamul*	Federal	9 Oct 1939	6 Apr 1940	14 Jun 1941
	ex-AK 30 (2 Jun 1942); ex-*Doctor Lykes* (1941), LD as *Sea Panther*				
AD 21	*Markab*	Ingalls	26 Dec 1939	21 Dec 1940	15 Jun 1941
	ex-AK 31 (2 Jun 1942); ex-*Mormacpenn* (1941), LD as *Sea Swallow*				

Displacement	14,800 tons f/l
Dimensions	492'5" (oa); 465' (wl) x 69'9" x 2'9"
Machinery	1 screw; DeLaval (AD 20 *Hamul*); GE (AD 21 *Markab*) GT; 2 FW boilers; SHP 8,500; 18.4 knots
Complement	864
Armament (as AD)	1–5"/38, 4–3"/50, 2 twin 40mm, 20–20mm (AD 20 *Hamul*), 8–20mm (AD 21 *Markab*)

Notes: Type C3–Cargo. Converted to destroyer tenders, 1942.

Service Records:

AD 20 *Hamul* Recomm as AD, 7 Jan 1943. †
1* Okinawa.

AD 21 *Markab* Recomm as AD, 27 Sep 1942. Decomm 3 Jun 1947. †

Figure 10.6: The destroyer tender *Yellowstone* (AD 27), 1950, of the Klondike class, which was built on C3 hulls.

Klondike Class

No.	Name	Builder	Laid Down	Launched	Comm.
AD 22	*Klondike*	Los Angeles	6 Dec 1943	12 Aug 1944	30 Jul 1945
AD 23	*Arcadia*	Los Angeles	6 Mar 1944	19 Nov 1944	13 Sep 1945
AD 24	*Everglades*	Los Angeles	26 Jun 1944	28 Jan 1945	23 May 1946 (completed)
AD 25	*Frontier*	Los Angeles	16 Aug 1944	25 Mar 1945	2 Mar 1946
AD 26	*Shenandoah*	Todd Tacoma	16 Sep 1944	29 Mar 1945	13 Aug 1945
AD 27	*Yellowstone*	Todd Seattle	16 Oct 1944	12 Apr 1945	16 Jan 1946
AD 28	*Grand Canyon*	Todd Tacoma	15 Nov 1944	27 Apr 1945	5 Apr 1946
AD 29	*Isle Royale*	Todd Seattle	16 Dec 1944	19 Sep 1945	2 Jul 1946 (completed)
AD 30	*Great Lakes* ex–AS 29 (12 Aug 1944)	Todd Seattle	16 Apr 1945	—	—
AD 31	*Tidewater* ex–AS 30 (12 Aug 1944)	Charleston NYd	27 Nov 1944	30 Jun 1945	19 Feb 1946 (completed)
AD 33	*Canopus* ex–AS 27 (27 Sep 1944)	Mare I. NYd	15 Mar 1945	—	—
AD 35	*Arrowhead*	Puget Sound NYd	1 Dec 1944	—	—
AD 36	*Bryce Canyon*	Charleston NYd	5 Jul 1945	7 Mar 1946	15 Sep 1950

Displacement	11,755 tons, 16,635 f/l
Dimensions	492' (oa); 465' (wl) x 69'6" x 27'3"
Machinery	1 screw; GE turbines; 2 B&W D boilers (AD 22–25) West turbines; 2 FW D boilers (AD 26–36), SHP 8,500; 18.4 knots
Complement	826
Armament	1–5"/38, 4–3"/50, 2–40mm twin, 20–20mm (AD 22–25); 2–5"/38, 4 twin 40mm, 22–20mm (AD 26–36)

Notes: AD 29–30 originally ordered from Tampa. C3-type merchant hulls built as tenders.

Service Records:

AD 22 *Klondike* Decomm 30 Nov 1946. †
AD 23 *Arcadia* Completed at Long Beach NYd. †
AD 24 *Everglades* Completed by Beth. S. Pedro. †
AD 25 *Frontier* Decomm 29 Sep 1947. †
AD 26 *Shenandoah* †
AD 27 *Yellowstone* †
AD 28 *Grand Canyon* Completed by Lake Wash. †
AD 29 *Isle Royale* Completed by Todd Tacoma. Not comm. †
AD 30 *Great Lakes* Canceled 7 Jan 1946.
AD 31 *Tidewater* No service. Decomm mid-1946. †
AD 33 *Canopus* Canceled 11 Aug 1945.
AD 35 *Arrowhead* Canceled 11 Aug 1945.
AD 36 *Bryce Canyon* Construction suspended 7 Mar 1946, resumed 14 Aug 1947. †

No.	Name	Builder	Laid Down	Launched	Comm.
AD 32	*New England* ex–AS 28 (12 Aug 1944)	Tampa	10 Aug 1945	—	—

Displacement	14,037 tons; 16,750 fl
Dimensions	529'6" (oa); 520' (wl) x 73'4" x 23'11"
Machinery	2 screws; Westinghouse GT; 4 boilers; SHP 12,000; 19.6 knots
Armament	4–5"/38, 4 twin 40mm AA

Notes: Modified *Dixie* class. Originally ordered from Phila NYd.

Service Record:

AD 32 *New England* Canceled 11 Aug 1945.

No.	Name	Formerly	Date
AD 34	*Alcor*	AR10	6 Nov 1944

SUBMARINE TENDERS

Submarine tenders provide spare parts, torpedoes, and diesel fuel, as well as quarters and recreation facilities for submarine crews. They were stationed in distant bays to provide bases for submarine operations.

Figure 10.7: The submarine tender *Canopus* (AS 9) was lost in the Philippines in 1942. Notice the 5" gun on the bow.

Figure 10.8: *Holland* (AS 3), leaving San Francisco for Australia on 22 May 1943, showing wartime modifications. Notice guns mounted on bow. A small radar mast abaft the bridge has replaced the tall foremast on the bow and the mainmast has been greatly cut down.

Figure 10.9: *Fulton* (AS 11) on 3 Jun 1944.

Submarine Tenders on the Navy List, 1922

AS 1 *Fulton* Out of comm 5 Oct 1925–2 Sep 1930. Survey service. Rec **PG 49**, 29 Sep 1930. Damaged by fire off South China Coast, 14 Mar 1934. Decomm 12 May 1934. Stricken 18 May 1935, sold 6 Jun 1935.

AS 2 *Bushnell* Converted to survey ship, Dec 1937. Rec **AG 32**, 25 Jul 1940. Renamed ***Sumner***, 23 Aug 1940. Rec **AGS 5**, 1 Dec 1943. Damaged by gunfire off Iwo Jima, 8 Mar 1945 (1 dead). Decomm 13 Sep 1946. BU 1948.
3* Pearl Harbor, Gilbert Is., Iwo Jima.

AS 3 *Holland* Comm 1 Jul 1926. Sailed from Manila to Darwin, Northern Australia, Dec 1941. Converted to repair ship, rec **ARG 18**, 25 Jun 1945. Decomm 21 Mar 1947. Armament:
2* Philippines 1942, Saipan.

AS 5 *Beaver* Yangtze River, 1931. Converted to repair ship, rec **ARG 19**, 25 Jun 1945. Decomm 17 Jul 1946, sold 5 Aug 1946; BU 1951 Baltimore.

AS 6 *Camden* Decomm 26 May 1931. Rec **IX 42**, 17 Sep 1940. Barracks ship, New York. Sold 23 Oct 1946; BU 1949 Baltimore. In 1920s, two funnels replaced by one.

AS 7 *Rainbow* Decomm 11 Jul 1925. Stricken 26 Jun 1928, sold 13 Sep 1928; BU Baltimore.

AS 8 *Savannah* Decomm 16 Dec 1926. Name canceled 15 Sep 1933. Stricken 26 Jun 1934, sold 26 Sep 1934.
Later history: Merchant *Savannah* 1934, renamed *Orbis* 1942. BU 1954 Osaka.

AS 9 *Canopus* Asiatic Fleet. Yangtze River 1931–32. China 1937–39. Damaged by Japanese bomber at Mariveles, Luzon, 29 Dec 1941. Scuttled to prevent capture off Bataan, 10 Apr 1942.
1* Philippines 1942

AS 10 *Argonne* Ex-AP 4, 1 Jul 1924. Rec **AG 31**, 25 Jul 1940.

Notes: AS 2: 1–5"/38, 4–3"/50, 8–20mm guns: AS 3: 4–5"/38, 4 twin 40mm, 12–20mm guns; AS 5: 2–5"/51, 4–3"/50, 8–20mm.

No.	Name	Builder	Laid Down	Launched	Comm.
AS 11	*Fulton*	Mare I. NYd	19 Jul 1939	27 Dec 1940	12 Sep 1941
AS 12	*Sperry*	Moore	1 Feb 1941	17 Dec 1941	1 May 1942
AS 15	*Bushnell*	Mare I. NYd	23 Dec 1941	14 Sep 1942	10 Apr 1943
AS 16	*Howard W. Gilmore*	Mare I. NYd	21 Dec 1942	16 Sep 1943	24 May1944
	ex-*Neptune* (summer 1943)				
AS 17	*Nereus*	Mare I. NYd	11 Oct 1943	12 Feb 1945	27 Oct 1945
AS 18	*Orion*	Moore	31 Jul 1941	14 Oct 1942	30 Sep 1943
AS 19	*Proteus*	Moore	15 Sep 1941	12 Nov 1942	31 Jan 1944

Figure 10.10: Submarine tender *Orion* (AS 18), *Fulton* class. Notice director for 5" guns, huge crane aft.

Displacement	15,250 tons, 18,000 f/l
Dimensions	529'6" (oa); 520' (wl) x 73'4" x 25'6"
Machinery	2 screws; GM diesel-electric; SHP 11,520; 15.4 knots
Complement	1,300
Armament	4–5"/38, 4 twin 40mm, 23–20mm guns

Notes: Large ships designed from the keel up as submarine tenders. Hulls similar to *Dixie* class AD and *Vulcan* class AR. AS 17 originally ordered from Puget Sound NYd.

Service Records:

AS 11 *Fulton* Operation Crossroads. Decomm 3 Apr 1947. †
1* Midway.

AS 12 *Sperry* †

AS 15 *Bushnell* †

AS 16 *Howard W. Gilmore* †

AS 17 *Nereus* Stripped and sank 39 Japanese submarines off Sasebo, Jan 1946. †

AS 18 *Orion* †

AS 19 *Proteus* Tokyo Bay. †

Figure 10.11: *Griffin* (AS 13), a submarine tender converted in 1941. Notice lack of radar.

No.	Name	Builder	Laid Down	Launched	Comm.
AS 13	*Griffin* ex–*Mormacpenn* (1940)	Sun	1 May 1939	11 Oct 1939	31 Jul 1941
AS 14	*Pelias* ex–*Mormacyork* (1940)	Sun	8 May 1939	14 Nov 1939	5 Sep 1941

Displacement	14,500 tons f/l
Dimensions	492' (oa); 465' (wl) x 69'6" x 24'3"
Machinery	1 screw; BS diesel; SHP 8,500; 16.5 knots
Complement	1,500
Armament	4–3"/50, 10 to 20–20mm guns

Notes: Type C3–Cargo. Acquired 1940. AS 13 *Griffin* converted by Robins; AS 14 *Pelias* by Beth. Brooklyn.

Service Records:

AS 13 *Griffin* Decomm 12 Oct 1945. †

AS 14 *Pelias* †
1* Pearl Harbor.

No.	Name	Builder	Laid Down	Launched	Comm.
AS 20	*Otus* ex–*Fred Morris* (1941)	Federal	3 Jun 1940	2 Nov 1940	19 Mar 1941

Displacement	12,930 tons
Dimensions	417'9" (oa); 395' (wl) x 60' x 20'6"
Machinery	1 screw; De Laval GT; 2 FW D boilers; SHP 4,000; 14.7 knots
Complement	644
Armament	1–5"/38, 4–3"/50 guns, 12–20mm

Notes: Acquired 1 Mar 1941. Converted cargo ship.

Service Record:

AS 20 *Otus* Sailed from Manila to Darwin, Dec 1941. Converted to repair ship, rec **ARG 20**, 25 Jun 1945. Decomm 20 Aug 1946. Sold 21 Aug 1946, stricken 25 Sep 1946; BU 1970 Portland, Ore.
1* Philippines 1941.

No.	Name	Builder	Launched	Acquired	Comm.
AS 21	*Antaeus* ex–*St. John* (1941)	Newport News	9 Jan 1932	24 Apr 1941	17 May 1941

Displacement	7,800 tons, 8,350 dsp
Dimensions	403' (oa); 400'3" (wl) x 61' x 20'2"
Machinery	2 screws; NN GT; 4 B&W hdr boilers; SHP 13,000; 20 knots
Complement	440
Armament	1–4"/50, 2–3"/50 guns

Notes: Converted passenger ship. Carried 2,100 troops as transport.

Service Record:

AS 21 *Antaeus* Caribbean 1941–42. Rec **AG 67**, 15 Sep 1943, served as transport. Converted to hospital ship at New York NYd, 28 Dec 1944; rec **AH 18** and renamed ***Rescue***, 18 Jan 1945. Decomm 29 Apr 1946, to USMC. Stricken 15 Aug 1946. BU 1953 Seattle.

No.	Name	Builder	Laid Down	Launched	Comm.
AS 22	*Euryale* ex–*Hawaiian Merchant* (1943)	Federal	12 Apr 1941	15 Apr 1943	2 Dec 1943

	7,600 tons; 15,400 tons f/l
Dimensions	492'6" (oa); 465' (wl) x 69'6" x 25'6"
Machinery	1 screw; DeLaval GT; 2 FW D boilers; SHP 8,500; 16 knots
Complement	1,403
Armament	1–5"/38, 4–3"/50, 2 twin 40mm, 22–20mm AA guns

Notes: Cargo ship converted while under construction.

Service Record:

AS 22 *Euryale* Decomm 7 Oct 1946. †

No.	Name	Builder	Laid Down	Launched	Comm.
AS 23	*Aegir*	Ingalls	31 Mar 1943	15 Sep 1943	8 Sep 1944
AS 24	*Anthedon*	Ingalls	6 May 1943	15 Oct 1943	15 Sep 1944
AS 25	*Apollo*	Ingalls	24 Jun 1943	6 Nov 1943	29 Sep 1944
AS 26	*Clytie*	Ingalls	5 Jul 1943	26 Nov 1943	18 Jan 1945

Displacement	11,760 tons, 16,500 f/l
Dimensions	492' (oa); 465' (wl) x 69'6" x 27'
Machinery	1 screw; West. GT; 2 FW D boilers; SHP 8500; 18.4 knots
Complement	1,460
Armament	1–5"/38, 4–3"/50, 2 twin 40mm, 20–20mm AA guns

Notes: Type C3–S–A2, converted while under construction.

Figure 10.12: *Anthedon* (AS 24), a submarine tender, as completed, on 24 Sep 1944; type C3–S-A2 conversion.

Service Records:

AS 23 *Aegir* Decomm 18 Oct 1946. †
AS 24 *Anthedon* Decomm 21 Sep 1946. †
AS 25 *Apollo* Decomm 12 Feb 1947. †
AS 26 *Clytie* Decomm 5 Oct 1946. †

No.	Name	Reclassified	Date
AS 27	*Canopus*	AD 33	27 Sep 1944.
AS 28	—	AD 32	12 Aug 1944.
AS 29–30	—	AD 30–31	12 Aug 1944.

SUBMARINE RESCUE VESSELS

Submarine rescue vessels were specialized ships to help submarines in distress. Each was equipped with a diving bell and rescue chamber. The first group were converted minesweepers, succeeded by the built-for-the-purpose *Chanticleer* class.

Ex–Minesweepers (Rec 12 Sep 1929)

No.	Name	Formerly	Service record
ASR 1	*Widgeon*	AM 22	Recomm 5 Mar 1923. Operation Crossroads. Decomm 5 Feb 1947. Stricken 23 Dec 1947, sold 5 Mar 1948. BU Napa, Calif.
	1* Pearl Harbor.		
ASR 2	*Falcon*	AM 28	Submarine *Squalus* rescue 1939. In collision with m/v *El Oceano* in Buzzards Bay, Mass., 14 Apr 1940. Decomm 18 Jun 1946. Stricken 19 Jul 1946, sold 12 Mar 1947; BU.
ASR 3	*Chewink*	AM 39	Recomm 13 Oct 1923. Out of comm 12 Aug 1933–12 Nov 1940. Went aground in typhoon at Tsingtao, China, 31 Aug 1939, refloated 1 Oct. Decomm 4 Feb 1947. Stricken 10 Jun 1947. Sunk as target off New London, 31 Jul 1947.
ASR 4	*Mallard*	AM 44	Decomm 10 Dec 1946. Stricken 14 Mar 1947. Sunk as target by USS *Piper*, 22 May 1947.
ASR 5	*Ortolan*	AM 45	Decomm 18 Mar 1947. Stricken 10 Jun 1947, sold 20 Aug 1947. FFU
	1* Solomons.		
ASR 6	*Pigeon*	AM 47	Yangtze River 1931–32. China 1937–39. Went aground in typhoon at Tsingtao, China, 31 Aug 1939, refloated 1 Oct. Sunk by aircraft bomb off Corregidor, 4 May 1942. (none killed)
	1* Philippines 1942.		

Armament	1–3"/50 (ASR 3), 4–20mm guns.

Figure 10.13: The submarine rescue vessel *Widgeon* (ASR 1), a converted minesweeper, at San Francisco on 29 Oct 1943. Note the rescue chamber on stern. Before the war each ASR had a fish-type symbol on the bow.

Figure 10.14: *Kittiwake* (ASR 13), a *Chanticleer*-class submarine rescue vessel completed after the war.

No.	Name	Builder	Laid Down	Launched	Comm.
ASR 7	*Chanticleer*	Moore	15 Sep 1941	29 May 1942	20 Nov 1942
ASR 8	*Coucal*	Moore	30 Sep 1941	29 May 1942	22 Jan 1943
ASR 9	*Florikan*	Moore	30 Sep 1941	14 Jun 1942	5 Apr 1943
ASR 10	*Greenlet*	Moore	15 Oct 1941	12 Jul 1942	29 May 1943
ASR 11	*Macaw*	Moore	15 Oct 1941	12 Jul 1942	12 Jul 1943
ASR 13	*Kittiwake*	Savannah	5 Jan 1945	10 Jul 1945	18 Jul 1946
ASR 14	*Petrel*	Savannah	26 Feb 1945	26 Sep 1945	24 Sep 1946
ASR 15	*Sunbird*	Savannah	2 Apr 1945	3 Apr 1946	28 Jan 1947 (delivered)
ASR 16	*Tringa*	Savannah	12 Jul 1945	25 Jun 1946	28 Jan 1947
ASR 17	*Verdin*	Savannah	—	—	—
ASR 18	*Windhover*	Savannah	—	—	—

Displacement	1,780 tons, 2,045 f/l
Dimensions	251'4" (oa); 240' (wl) x 42' x 14'10"
Machinery	1 screw; Alco diesel-electric (ASR 7–11), GM diesel-electric (ASR 13–18); SHP 3,000; 14.9 knots
Complement	102
Armament	2–3"/50, 8–20mm guns

Note: The largest tug-type vessels in the Navy; built-for-the-purpose rescue ships.

Service Records:

ASR 7 *Chanticleer* †
ASR 8 *Coucal* Operation Crossroads. †
ASR 9 *Florikan* †
ASR 10 *Greenlet* Tokyo Bay. †
ASR 11 *Macaw* Went aground in Midway Channel while attempting to assist grounded submarine *Flier*, 16 Jan 1944 and foundered, 12 Feb 1944 (5 lost).
1* Gilbert Is.
ASR 13 *Kittiwake* †
ASR 14 *Petrel* †

ASR 15 *Sunbird*	Not comm. †
ASR 16 *Tringa* †	
ASR 17 *Verdin*	Canceled 12 Aug 1945.
ASR 18 *Windhover*	Canceled 12 Aug 1945.

FORMER TUGS

No.	Name	Formerly	Reclassified	Comm. as ASR
ASR 12	*Penguin*	ATF 99	23 Sep 1943	29 May 1944 (Armament: 1–3"/50, 4–20mm guns)
ASR 19	*Bluebird*	ATF 164	7 Nov 1945	28 May 1946
ASR 20	*Skylark*	ATF 165	7 Nov 1945	Mar 1951

Service Records:

ASR 12 *Penguin*	Decomm 4 Sep 1947. †
ASR 19 *Bluebird* †	
ASR 20 *Skylark*	Not comm. †

MOTOR TORPEDO BOAT TENDERS

These tenders were converted to service PT-boat squadrons, providing spare parts and engines, supplies, and fuel.

No.	Name	Formerly	Reclassified
AGP 1	*Niagara*	PG 52	13 Jan 1943
	1* Solomons		
AGP 2	*Hilo*	PG 58	13 Jan 1943
	4* Saidor, Western New Guinea, Leyte		
AGP 3	*Jamestown*	PG 55	13 Jan 1943
	3* Solomons, Brunei		
AGP 6	*Oyster Bay*	AVP 28	8 Mar 1943
AGP 7	*Mobjack*	AVP 27	8 Mar 1943
AGP 8	*Wachapreague*	AVP 56	8 Mar 1943
AGP 9	*Willoughby*	AVP 57	8 Mar 1943
Armament	2–5"/38, 1 quad 40mm, 2 twin 40mm, 4 twin 20mm		

Figure 10.15: *Chiron* (AGP 18), an LST converted to motor torpedo boat tender, on 4 Oct 1945.

No.	Name	Formerly	Reclassified	Comm. as AGP
AGP 4	*Portunus*	LST 330	25 Jan 1943	12 Jun 1943
AGP 5	*Varuna*	LST 14	25 Jan 1943	31 Aug 1943
AGP 10	*Orestes*	LST 135	3 Nov 1943	25 Apr 1944
AGP 11	*Silenus*	LST 604	18 Dec 1943	9 Aug 1944
AGP 14	*Alecto*	LST 977	14 Aug 1944	28 Jul 1945
AGP 15	*Callisto*	LST 966	14 Aug 1944	12 Jun 1945
AGP 16	*Antigone*	LST 773	14 Aug 1944	14 May 1945
AGP 17	*Brontes*	LST 1125	14 Aug 1944	14 Aug 1945
AGP 18	*Chiron*	LST 1133	14 Aug 1944	18 Sep 1945
AGP 19	—	LST 1152	Conversion canceled	
AGP 20	*Pontus*	LST 201	21 Jul 1944	(15 Aug 1944)
Armament	2 quad 40mm, 8 twin 20mm			

Service Records:

AGP 4 *Portunus* Decomm 18 Apr 1946. Stricken 13 Nov 1946; sold 6 Feb 1948; BU 1948 Oakland, Calif.
3* Saidor, Western New Guinea, Mindanao Ldgs.

AGP 5 *Varuna* Damaged in collision with *LST-219* off Balboa, Panama, 27 Oct 1943. Decomm 4 Jan 1946. Stricken 1 May 1946, sold 31 Jul 1947.
4* Solomons, Palau, Mariveles-Corregidor, Balikpapan.
Later history: Brazilian *Guarauna*. BU 1972 Rio de Janeiro.

AGP 10 *Orestes* Damaged by kamikaze, Mindoro, 30 Dec 44 and beached (59 killed). Decomm 29 Apr 1946. Stricken 23 Apr 1947, sold 15 Mar 1948; BU.
2* Western New Guinea, Leyte.

AGP 11 *Silenus* Decomm 14 Mar 1946. Stricken 17 Apr 1946, sold 25 Jul 1947.
1* Solomons.
Later history: Merchant *Arzell III* 1948, renamed *Petrus* then *Paula* 1956. BU 1972 Brazil.

AGP 14 *Alecto* Decomm 28 Jun 1946. Stricken 28 Jun 1947. To Turkey, 10 May 1948
Later history: Renamed *Onaran*. R 1992.

AGP 15 *Callisto* Decomm 9 May 1946. Sold 15 May 1948.
Later history: Merchant *Elena*, renamed *Daytona* 1953. Foundered 75 miles off Gloucester, Mass., 20 Nov 1955.

AGP 16 *Antigone* Decomm 1946. Stricken 10 Jun 1947. Sold 6 Feb 1948; BU.

AGP 17 *Brontes* Decomm 14 Mar 1946. Sold 1 Apr 1947.
Later history: Merchant *Barbara, Diane* 1948, *Xalapa* 1956. Lost in hurricane at Manzanillo, 27 Oct 1959.

AGP 18 *Chiron* Decomm 20 Feb 1946. Sold 19 May 1947.
Later history: Merchant *Altamar* 1948. Wrecked on Manoel Luis Reef, 27 Mar 1960.

AGP 19 Conversion canceled.

AGP 20 *Pontus* USCG crew 15 Aug 1944–5 Feb 1946. Partially converted to AGP, 1943. Decomm 2 Apr 1946. Stricken 1 May 1946. BU 1947.
3* Saidor, Western New Guinea, Leyte.

No.	Name	Builder	Laid Down	Launched	Comm.
AGP 12	*Acontius*	Pusey	5 Jun 1943	12 Oct 1943	23 Jun 1944
	LD as *Cape Carthage*				
AGP 13	*Cyrene*	Pusey	14 Oct 1943	8 Feb 1944	27 Sep 1944
	LD as *Cape Farewell*				
Displacement	5,826 tons; 10,590 tons f/l				
Dimensions	413' (oa); 390' (wl) x 60' x 22'6"				

Machinery	1 screw; AC GT; 2 B&W boilers; SHP 4,000; 14 knots
Complement	289
Armament	1–5"/38, 4–40mm twin, 12–20mm guns

Note: Type C1–A.

Service Records:

AGP 12 *Acontius* Decomm 22 Mar 1946, Stricken 17 Apr 1946. BU 1965.
1* Solomons.

AGP 13 *Cyrene* Decomm 2 Jul 1946, BU 1978 Portland, Ore.

REPAIR SHIPS

Repair ships were fitted to carry out substantial repairs on damaged ships not requiring drydock, with fully-equipped machine shops and foundries. They were named for mythical characters denoting strength.

Repair Ships on the Navy List, 1922

AR 1 *Medusa* Comm 18 Sep 1924. Damaged by grounding at Manus, May 1944. Decomm 18 Nov 1947. Sold 24 Aug 1950; BU Portland.
1* Pearl Harbor.

AR 3 *Prometheus* Out of comm 4 Oct 1924–15 May 1942. Decomm 1 Jul 1946. Stricken 31 Jul 1946, sold 29 Aug 1950; BU Portland, Ore.
1* Palau.

AR 4 *Vestal* Damaged by two aircraft bombs and explosion of *Arizona* at Pearl Harbor and beached, 7 Dec 1941 (7 killed). Decomm 14 Aug 1946. Stricken 25 Sep 1946, sold 28 Jul 1950; BU Baltimore.
Armament: AR 1: 6–3"/50, 2 twin 40mm, 8–20mm guns. AR 3–4: 2–5"/51, 4–3"/50, 2 twin 40mm, 8–20mm guns.
2* Pearl Harbor, Okinawa.

No.	Name	Builder	Laid Down	Launched	Comm.
AR 5	*Vulcan*	NY Sbdg	26 Dec 1939	14 Dec 1940	14 Jun 1941
AR 6	*Ajax*	Los Angeles	7 May 1941	22 Aug 1942	30 Oct 1943
AR 7	*Hector*	Los Angeles	28 Jul 1941	11 Nov 1942	7 Feb 1944
AR 8	*Jason*	Los Angeles	9 Mar 1942	3 Apr 1943	19 Jun 1944

Displacement	16,200 tons, 8,975 dsp
Dimensions	530' (oa); 520' (wl) x 73'4" x 23'4"
Machinery	2 screws; AC GT; 4 B&W D boilers; SHP 11,000; 19.2 knots
Complement	1,058
Armament	4–5"/38, 4 twin 40mm, 23–20mm guns

Notes: Large ships built for the purpose of use as repair ships. Hulls similar to *Dixie* class AD and *Fulton* class AS with more widely spaced funnels.

Service Records:

AR 5 *Vulcan* †
1* Normandy.

AR 6 *Ajax* Damaged by fire in Marshall Is., 8 Jan 1944. †

AR 7 *Hector* †

AR 8 *Jason* Rec **ARH 1**, 15 Aug 1941. Heavy-hull repair ship. †

No.	Name	Formerly	Date
AR 10	*Alcor*	AG 34	22 Dec 1941
AR 11	*Rigel*	AD 13	10Apr 1941

Notes: AR 10rec AD 34, 6 Nov 1944. AR 11: armament: 1–5"/51, 4–3"/50, 20–40mm, 10–20mm guns.

No.	Name	Builder	Launched	Comm.
AR 9	*Delta*	Newport News	2 Apr 1941	16 Jun 1941 (as AK)
	ex-AK 29 (1 Jul 1942); ex-*Hawaiian Packer* (1941)			
AR 12	*Briareus*	Newport News	14 Feb 1941	15 Nov 1943
	ex-*Hawaiian Planter* (1943)			

Displacement	14,000 tons
Dimensions	490'6" (oa); 465'6" (wl) x 69'6" x 23'6"
Machinery	1 screw; NN GT; 2 B&W hdr boilers; SHP 8,500; 18 knots
Complement	900
Armament	1–5"/38, 4–3"/50, 2 quad 1.1"; later 2 twin 40mm, 10 twin 20mm AA guns

Notes: *Briareus* acquired 16 Feb 1943. Converted cargo ships.

Service Records:

AR 9 *Delta* Iceland 1941. Converted to repair ship 1942–43, recomm 3 Mar 1943. Tokyo Bay. Decomm 5 Mar 1947. †
2* Tunisia, Southern France.

AR 12 *Briareus* Acquired 16 Feb 1943. Decomm 15 Oct 1946. †

Figure 10.16: The old repair ship *Vestal* (AR 4) on 8 Sep 1944. Notice the small radar mast on bridge, and guns on bow.

Figure 10.17: *Briareus* (AR 12), a repair ship, 17 Feb 1944.

Figure 10.18: *Amphion* (AR 13) after the war.

Figure 10.19: *Oglala* (ARG 1), recommissioned as a repair ship. The minelayer was sunk at Pearl Harbor, salvaged, and converted.

No.	Name	Builder	Laid Down	Launched	Comm.
AR 13	*Amphion*	Tampa	20 Sep 1944	15 May 1945	30 Jan 1946
AR 14	*Cadmus*	Tampa	30 Oct 1944	5 Aug 1945	23 Apr 1946
AR 15	*Deucalion*	Tampa	15 Dec 1944	—	—
AR 16	*Mars*	Tampa	16 May 1945	—	—

Displacement	7,826 tons; 16,900 tons f/l
Dimensions	492' (oa); 465' (wl) x 69'6" x 27'6"
Machinery	1 screw; West. GT; 2 FW D boilers; SHP 8500; 16.5 knots
Complement	920
Armament	2–5"/38, 4 twin 40mm, 22–20mm guns

Notes: AR 13–16 originally ordered from Todd Tacoma; AR 15–16 originally from Newport News.

Service Records:

AR 13 *Amphion* †
AR 14 *Cadmus* †
AR 15 *Deucalion* Canceled 12 Aug 1945.
AR 16 *Mars* Canceled 12 Aug 1945.
AR 17–21 — See below

REPAIR SHIPS, INTERNAL COMBUSTION ENGINES

ARGs were named for islands

No.	Name	Formerly	Date
ARG 1	*Oglala*	CM 4	24 May 1943
ARG 18	*Holland*	AS 3	20 Sep 1945
ARG 19	*Beaver*	AS 5	25 Jun 1945
ARG 20	*Otus*	AS 20	25 Jun 1945

Notes: Armament: ARG 1: 1–5"/38, 4–3"/50, 2 twin 40mm, 8–20mm; ARG 19: 1–5"51, 4–3"/50, 8–20mm, ARG 20: 1–5"/38, 4–3"/50, 12–20mm guns.

No.	Name	Builder	Laid Down	Launched	Comm.
AR 17	—	Beth. Fairfield	17 May 1944	20 Jun 1944	*20 Jan 1945*
AR 18	—	Beth. Fairfield	7 Jun 1944	8 Jul 1944	*3 Mar 1945*
AR 19	*Xanthus* ex–*Hecla*	Beth. Fairfield	27 Jun 1944	31 Jul 1944	9 May 1945
AR 20	*Laertes* ex–*Dutiful*	Beth. Fairfield	7 Aug 1944	13 Sep 1944	24 Mar 1945
AR 21	*Dionysus* ex–*Faithful*	Beth. Fairfield	4 Sep 1944	10 Oct 1944	28 Apr 1945
ARG 2	*Luzon* LD as *Samuel Bowles*	Beth. Fairfield	8 Apr 1943	14 May 1943	12 Oct 1943
ARG 3	*Mindanao* LD as *Elbert Hubbard*	Beth. Fairfield	11 Apr 1943	13 May 1943	6 Nov 1943
ARG 4	*Tutuila* LD as *Arthur P. Gorman*	Beth. Fairfield	11 Aug 1943	12 Sep 1943	8 Apr 1944
ARG 5	*Oahu* LD as *Caleb C. Wheeler*	Beth. Fairfield	14 Aug 1943	9 Sep 1943	4 Apr 1944
ARG 6	*Cebu* LD as *Francis P. Duffy*	Beth. Fairfield	21 Sep 1943	18 Oct 1943	15 Apr 1944
ARG 7	*Culebra Island* LD as *John F. Goucher*	Beth. Fairfield	29 Oct 1943	23 Nov 1943	19 May 1944
ARG 8	*Leyte*	Beth. Fairfield	20 Jan 1944	18 Feb 1944	17 Aug 1944
ARG 9	*Mona Island*	Beth. Fairfield	10 Apr 1944	11 May 1944	17 Oct 1944
ARG 10	*Palawan*	Beth. Fairfield	10 Jul 1944	12 Aug 1944	3 May 1945

Figure 10.20: *Tutuila* (ARG 4), a Liberty Ship converted to repair ship for internal combustion engines, on 18 May 1944. This class was named for islands.

ARG 11	*Samar*	Beth. Fairfield	21 Sep 1944	19 Oct 1944	5 Jun 1945
ARG 12	*Basilan*	Beth. Fairfield	5 Feb 1944	21 Mar 1944	10 Oct 1944
	LD as *Jacques Philippe Villere*				
ARG 13	*Burias*	Beth. Fairfield	11 Feb 1944	27 Mar 1944	5 Oct 1944
	LD as *Mollie Moore Davis*				
ARG 14	*Dumaran*	Beth. Fairfield	20 Apr 1944	22 May 1944	*7 Dec 1944*
ARG 15	*Masbate*	Beth. Fairfield	1 Jul 1944	5 Aug 1944	*17 Mar 1945*
ARG 16	*Kermit Roosevelt*	Beth. Fairfield	30 Aug 1944	5 Oct 1944	31 May 1945
	ex-*Deal Island* (29 Sep 1944)				
ARG 17	*Hooper Island*	Beth. Fairfield	16 Sep 1944	18 Oct 1944	13 Jul 1945
	LD as *Bert McDowell*				
ARV 1	*Chourre*	Beth. Fairfield	20 Apr 1944	22 May 1944	7 Dec 1944
	ex-*Dumaran*, ARG 14 (22 Feb 1944)				
ARV 2	*Webster*	Beth. Fairfield	1 Jul 1944	5 Aug 1944	17 Mar 1945
	ex-*Masbate*, ARG 15 (22 Feb 1944)				

Displacement	5,801 tons; 14,350 tons (varies)
Dimensions	441'6" (oa); 416' (wl) x 56'11" x 23'
Machinery	1 screw; GM VTE; 2 B&W boilers; SHP 2500; 12.5 knots
Complement	525
Armament	1–5'/38, 3–3'/50, 2 twin 40mm, 12–20mm guns

Notes: Type EC2–S-C1. AR 17–21 built for lend-lease to Royal Navy, but 19–21 not transferred.

Service Records:

AR 17 — To UK 20 Jan 1945, renamed HMS *Assistance*. Returned 15 Aug 1946. Sold 7 Feb 1947; BU 1974.

AR 18 — To UK 3 Mar 1945, renamed HMS *Diligence*. Returned 29 Jan 1946. Stricken 20 Feb 1949; BU 1973 Kaohsiung, Taiwan.

AR 19 *Xanthus* Decomm 3 Sep 1946. †

AR 20 *Laertes* Decomm 15 Jan 1947. †

AR 21 *Dionysus* Decomm 31 Jan 1947. †

ARG 2 *Luzon* Decomm 24 Jun 1947. †

ARG 3 *Mindanao* Severely damaged by explosion of AE *Mount Hood* at Seeadler Harbor, Manus, 10 Nov 1944 (23 killed). Decomm 17 May 1947. †

ARG 4 *Tutuila* Decomm 7 Dec 1946. †

ARG 5 *Oahu* Decomm 7 Jan 1947. †
1* Philippines Raids 9/44.

ARG 6 *Cebu* Damaged by explosion of AE *Mount Hood* at Seeadler Harbor, Manus, 10 Nov 1944 (5 killed). Operation Crossroads. Decomm 30 Jun 1947. †
1* Philippines Raids 9/44.

ARG 7 *Culebra Island* Decomm 15 Jan 1947. †

ARG 8 *Leyte* Renamed ***Maui***, 31 May 1945. Decomm 30 Aug 1946.

ARG 9 *Mona Island* Went aground in typhoon at Okinawa, 8 Oct 1945. Decomm Jun 1947. †
1* Okinawa.

ARG 10 *Palawan* Decomm 15 Jan 1947. †

ARG 11 *Samar* Decomm 24 Jul 1947. †

ARG 12 *Basilan* Converted to supply and repair ship; rec **AG 68**, 14 Mar 1944. Decomm 22 Apr 1946. Stricken 22 May 1947. BU 1972 Portland, Ore.

ARG 13 *Burias* Converted to supply and repair ship; rec **AG 69**, 14 Mar 1944. Decomm 9 Apr 1946. Stricken 17 Jul 1947. BU 1970 Portland, Ore.

ARG 14 *Dumaran* Rec **ARV 1 *Chourre***, 22 Feb 1944.

ARG 15 *Masbate* Rec **ARV 2 *Webster***, 22 Feb 1944.

ARG 16 *Kermit Roosevelt* †

ARG 17 *Hooper Island* †

ARV 1 *Chourre* †

ARV 2 *Webster* Decomm 28 Jun 1946. †

AIRCRAFT MAINTENANCE SHIPS

No.	Name	Formerly	Date
ARV 1	*Chourre*	ARG 14	22 Feb 1944 †
ARV 2	*Webster*	ARG 15	22 Feb 1944 †
Armament	1–5"/38, 2–40mm twin, 1 quad 40mm, 14–20mm guns		

No.	Name	Formerly	Reclassified	Comm. as AR
ARV(E) 3	*Aventinus*	LST 1092	8 Dec 1944	30 May 1945
ARV(A) 4	*Chloris*	LST 1094	8 Dec 1944	19 Jun 1945
ARV(E) 5	*Fabius*	LST 1093	8 Dec 1944	7 Jun 1945
ARV(A) 6	*Megara*	LST 1095	8 Dec 1944	27 Jun 1945
Armament	2 quad 40mm, 6–twin 20mm guns			

Service Records:

ARV(E) 3 *Aventinus* Decomm 30 Aug 1946. †

ARV(A) 4 *Chloris* Decomm 18 Jun 1946. †

ARV(E) 5 *Fabius* Decomm 30 Aug 1946. †

ARV(A) 6 *Megara* Decomm 3 Jun 1946. †

REPAIR SHIPS, BATTLE DAMAGE

No.	Name	Formerly	Reclassified	Comm. as AR
ARB 1	*Aristaeus*	LST 329	25 Jan 1943	18 May 1943
ARB 2	*Oceanus*	LST 328	25 Jan 1943	22 May 1943

Figure 10.21: *Sarpedon* (ARB 7), a former LST converted to battle damage repair ship, on 24 Mar 1945.

ARB 3	*Phaon*	LST 15	25 Jan 1943	5 Aug 1943
ARB 4	*Zeus*	LST 132	3 Nov 1943	11 Apr 1944
ARB 5	*Midas*	LST 514	3 Nov 1943	23 May 1944
ARB 6	*Nestor*	LST 518	3 Nov 1943	24 Jun 1944
ARB 7	*Sarpedon*	LST 956	14 Aug 1944	19 Mar 1945
ARB 8	*Telamon*	LST 976	14 Aug 1944	1 Jun 1945
ARB 9	*Ulysses*	LST 967	14 Aug 1944	20 Apr 1945
ARB 10	*Demeter*	LST 1121	14 Aug 1944	3 Jul 1945
ARB 11	*Diomedes*	LST 1119	14 Aug 1944	23 Jun 1945
ARB 12	*Helios*	LST 1127	14 Aug 1944	23 Jul 1945
Armament	2 quad 40mm, 8–20mm guns			

Service Records:

ARB 1 *Aristaeus* Decomm 15 Jan 1947. †
1* Okinawa.

ARB 2 *Oceanus* Decomm Jan 1947. †
3* Palau, Iwo Jima, Okinawa.

ARB 3 *Phaon* Near miss, 24 Jun 1944 (3 killed). Operation Crossroads. Decomm 15 Jan 1947. †
3* Gilbert Is., Saipan, Tinian.

ARB 4 *Zeus* Decomm 30 Aug 1946. †

ARB 5 *Midas* Decomm Jan 1947. †
1* Leyte.

ARB 6 *Nestor* Driven aground in typhoon off Okinawa, 9 Oct 1945. Decomm 29 Nov 1945 and stricken. Hulk sold May 1947.
1* Okinawa.

ARB 7 *Sarpedon* Decomm 29 Jan 1947. †

ARB 8 *Telamon* Operation Crossroads. Decomm 20 May 1947. †

ARB 9 *Ulysses* Decomm 28 Feb 1947. †

ARB 10 *Demeter* Decomm 27 May 1947. †

ARB 11 *Diomedes* Decomm 3 Dec 1946. †

ARB 12 *Helios* Decomm 3 Dec 1946. †

HEAVY-HULL REPAIR SHIP

No.	Name	Formerly	Date
ARH 1	*Jason*	ex–AR 8	15 Aug 1941

REPAIR SHIPS, LANDING CRAFT

These were LSTs converted for specialized repairs to landing craft. The hold was converted to a machine shop, and derricks were capable of lifting small craft for repairs.

No.	Name	Formerly	Reclassified	Comm. as AR
ARL 1	*Achelous*	LST 10	13 Jan 1943	2 Apr 1943
ARL 2	*Amycus*	LST 489	13 Jan 1943	30 Jul 1943
ARL 3	*Agenor*	LST 490	13 Jan 1943	20 Aug 1943
ARL 4	*Adonis*	LST 83	26 Aug 1943	12 Nov 1943
ARL 5	—	LST 81	20 Jul 1943	—
ARL 6	—	LST 82	20 Jul 1943	—
ARL 7	*Atlas*	LST 231	3 Nov 1943	8 Feb 1944
ARL 8	*Egeria*	LST 136	3 Nov 1943	30 Mar 1944
ARL 9	*Endymion*	LST 513	3 Nov 1943	9 May 1944
ARL 10	*Coronis*	LST 1003	14 Aug 1944	28 Nov 1944
ARL 11	*Creon*	LST 1036	14 Aug 1944	27 Jan 1945
ARL 12	*Poseidon*	LST 1037	14 Aug 1944	13 Feb 1945
ARL 13	*Menelaus*	LST 971	14 Aug 1944	29 May 1945
ARL 14	*Minos*	LST 644	14 Aug 1944	1945
ARL 15	*Minotaur*	LST 645	14 Aug 1944	26 Feb 1945
ARL 16	*Myrmidon*	LST 948	14 Aug 1944	9 Mar 1945
ARL 17	*Numitor*	LST 954	14 Aug 1944	3 Apr 1945
ARL 18	*Pandemus*	LST 650	14 Aug 1944	23 Feb 1945
ARL 19	*Patroclus*	LST 955	14 Aug 1944	17 Apr 1945
ARL 20	*Pentheus*	LST 1115	14 Aug 1944	7 Jun 1945
ARL 21	*Proserpine*	LST 1116	14 Aug 1944	31 May 1945
ARL 22	*Romulus*	LST 962	14 Aug 1944	10 May 1945
ARL 23	*Satyr*	LST 852	14 Aug 1944	28 Apr 1945
ARL 24	*Sphinx*	LST 963	14 Aug 1944	10 May 1945
ARL 25	—	LST 856	Canceled	
ARL 26	*Stentor*	LST 858	14 Aug 1944	28 Apr 1945
ARL 27	*Tantalus*	LST 1117	14 Aug 1944	5 Jun 1945

Figure 10.22: *Chimaera* (ARL 33), a landing craft repair ship, after conversion on 19 Aug 1945.

ARL 28	*Typhon*	LST 1118	14 Aug 1944	18 Jun 1945
ARL 29	*Amphitrite*	LST 1124	14 Aug 1944	28 Jun 1945
ARL 30	*Askari*	LST 1131	14 Aug 1944	23 Jul 1945
ARL 31	*Bellerophon*	LST 1132	14 Aug 1944	21 Jul 1945
ARL 32	*Bellona*	LST 1136	14 Aug 1944	26 Jul 1945
ARL 33	*Chimaera*	LST 1137	14 Aug 1944	7 Aug 1945
ARL 34	—	LST 1141	Canceled	
ARL 35	*Daedalus*	LST 1143	14 Aug 1944	19 Oct 1945
ARL 36	*Gordius*	LST 1145	14 Aug 1944	14 Sep 1945
ARL 37	*Indra*	LST 1147	14 Aug 1944	2 Oct 1945
ARL 38	*Krishna*	LST 1149	14 Aug 1944	3 Dec 1945
ARL 39	*Quirinus*	LST 1151	14 Aug 1944	6 Nov 1945
ARL 40	*Remus*	LST 453	15 Aug 1944	n/a
ARL 41	*Achilles*	LST 455	21 Apr 1944	n/a
ARL 42	*Aeolus*	LST 310	Canceled	
ARL 43	*Cerberus*	LST 316	Canceled	
ARL 44	*Consus*	LST 317	Canceled	
ARL 45	*Feronia*	LST 332	Canceled	
ARL 46	*Chandra*	LST 350	Canceled	
ARL 47	*Minerva*	LST 374	Canceled	
Armament	2 quad 40mm, 8–20 mm guns			

Service Records:

ARL 1 *Achelous* Decomm 16 Jan 1947. †
2* Southern France, Okinawa.

ARL 2 *Amycus* Damaged by bomb from "friendly" aircraft, Lingayen, 29 Jan 1945 (3 killed). Decomm 15 Nov 1946. †
2* Lingayen, Hollandia.

ARL 3 *Agenor* Damaged by collision, Iwo Jima, 28 Mar 1945 again on 5 Apr 1945. Decomm 15 Nov 1946. †
4* Saipan, Guam, Tinian, Iwo Jima.

ARL 4 *Adonis* Decomm 11 Oct 1946. †
1* Normandy.

ARL 5 To UK 29 Jul 1943.
Later history: HMS *LSE-1*. Returned 21 May 1946; to Argentina 20 Aug 1947, renamed *Ingeniero Iribas*. R 1967.

ARL 6 To UK 2 Aug 1943.
Later history: HMS *LSE-2*. Returned 21 May 1946; to Argentina 20 Aug 1947, renamed *Ingeniero Gadda*. R 1960, merchant *Tierra del Fuego*. R 1967.

ARL 7 *Atlas* Decomm 13 Sep 1946. †
1* Normandy.

ARL 8 *Egeria* Damaged by kamikaze off Leyte, 12 Nov 1944. Decomm Jan 1947. †
2* Leyte, Okinawa.

ARL 9 *Endymion* Damaged by shrapnel, Okinawa, 28 Apr 1945. Damaged by torpedo by *I-36*, off Eniwetok, 21 Jun 1945. Decomm 30 Nov 1946. †
2* Palau, Okinawa.

ARL 10 *Coronis* Decomm 29 Jul 1946. †
1* Okinawa.

ARL 11 *Creon* Operation Crossroads. †
1* Balikpapan.

ARL 12 *Poseidon* Decomm 30 Nov 1946. †
1* Okinawa.

ARL 13 *Menelaus* Decomm 5 Jun 1947. †

ARL 14 *Minos* Decomm 18 Jun 1946. †

ARL 15 *Minotaur* Decomm 26 Feb 1947. †
1* Okinawa.

ARL 16 *Myrmidon* Decomm 7 Jul 1947. †

ARL 17 *Numitor* Decomm 1 Jul 1947. †

ARL 18 *Pandemus* Decomm 23 Sep 1946. †
1* Okinawa.

ARL 19 *Patroclus* Tokyo Bay. Decomm 2 Oct 1946. †

ARL 20 *Pentheus* Decomm 20 Apr 1946. †

ARL 21 *Proserpine* Decomm 18 Jan 1947. †

ARL 22 *Romulus* Decomm 12 May 1947. †

ARL 23 *Satyr* Decomm 1 Aug 1947. †
1* Okinawa.

ARL 24 *Sphinx* Operation Crossroads. Decomm 26 May 1947. †

ARL 25 Not converted.

ARL 26 *Stentor* Decomm Dec 1947. †

ARL 27 *Tantalus* Decomm 18 Jan 1947. Stricken 7 Feb 1947. To UNRRA in China.

ARL 28 *Typhon* Decomm Mar 1947. †

ARL 29 *Amphitrite* Decomm 1 Jan 1947. †

ARL 30 *Askari* †

ARL 31 *Bellerophon* †

ARL 32 *Bellona* Went aground on Kama Rocks, Iwo Jima and lost, 1 Dec 1945. Destroyed 14 May 1946.

ARL 33 *Chimaera* †

ARL 34 Not converted.

ARL 35 *Daedalus* Decomm 23 Oct 1947. †

ARL 36 *Gordius* †

ARL 37 *Indra* Decomm 6 Oct 1947. †

ARL 38 *Krishna* †

ARL 39 *Quirinus* Decomm 27 Jun 1947. †

ARL 40 *Remus* Converted May 1943. Decomm 15 Jul 1946. Stricken 15 Aug 1946. Sold 16 Dec 1947.
2* Finschhafen, Arawe.

ARL 41 *Achilles* Converted May 1943. Damaged by kamikaze, off Samar, 12 Nov 1944 (19 dead). Decomm 19 Jul 1946. To China, 8 Sep 1947.
2* Leyte, Brunei.
Later history: Renamed *Hsing An*. Burned and grounded 1949, salved by PRC, renamed *Taku Shan*.

ARL 42 *Aeolus* Conversion canceled 12 Sep 1945.

ARL 43 *Cerberus* Conversion canceled 12 Sep 1945.

ARL 44 *Consus* Conversion canceled 12 Sep 1945.

ARL 45 *Feronia* Conversion canceled 12 Sep 1945.

ARL 46 *Chandra* Conversion canceled 12 Sep 1945.

ARL 47 *Minerva* Conversion canceled 12 Sep 1945.

SEAPLANE TENDERS

Seaplane tenders were designed to service two patrol squadrons of 24 planes. They provided repair, ordnance, refueling, and quarters for the plane crews, and were named for sounds or inlets.

Figure 10.23: USS *Langley* (AV 3) in 1941. The Navy's first aircraft carrier—a converted collier, as a seaplane tender—with flight deck cut back to amidships, she was sunk in the opening months of the Pacific war.

Figure 10.24: *Patoka* (AO 9). The dirigible mooring mast was removed about 1933.

Figure 10.25: *Albemarle* (AV 5), a seaplane tender, 1944. Notice the large cranes and hangar aft, and also the radar mast amidships.

Seaplane Tender on the Navy List, 1922

AZ 1 *Wright* Atlantic Fleet 1922–25 and 1925–32. Converted from lighter-than-air tender to heavier-than-air tender and rec **AV 1**, 2 Dec 1926. Pacific Fleet 1925, 1932. Converted to headquarters ship and rec **AG 79**, 1 Oct 1944. Renamed ***San Clemente***, 1 Feb 1945. Decomm 21 Jun 1946. Stricken 1 Jul 1946. Sold 19 Aug 1948; BU.
2* Treasury Is., Western New Guinea.
Armament 6–3"/50, 1 twin 40mm, 12–20mm guns

No.	Name	Formerly	Date
AV 2	*Jason*	AC 12	21 Jan 1930
AV 3	*Langley*	CV 1	14 Jan 1937
AV 6	*Patoka*	AO 9	11 Oct 1939.

Service Records:

AV 2 *Jason* Yangtze River, 1931–32. Decomm 30 Jun 1932. Stricken 19 May 1936, sold 29 Jul 1936.
Later history: Merchant *Jason* 1936. BU 1948 Baltimore.

AV 3 *Langley* Sunk by Japanese aircraft 75 miles southeast of Tjilatjap, Java, 27 Feb 1942 (16 killed, others lost on AO *Pecos*).

AV 6 *Patoka* Rec **AO 9**, 19 Jun 1940.

No.	Name	Builder	Laid Down	Launched	Comm.
AV 4	*Curtiss*	NY Sbdg	25 Apr 1938	20 Apr 1940	15 Nov 1940
AV 5	*Albemarle*	NY Sbdg	12 Jun 1939	13 Jul 1940	20 Dec 1940

Displacement	8,671 tons, 12,053 tons f/l
Dimensions	527'4" (oa); 508' (wl) x 69'3" x 21'11"
Machinery	2 screws; NYSbdg Parsons GT; 4 B&W express boilers; SHP 12,000; 19.7 knots
Complement	1,200
Armament	4–5"/38, 3 quad 40mm, 2 twin 40mm, 2–20mm AA guns

Service Records:

AV 4 *Curtiss* Damaged by bomb and crashed plane at Pearl Harbor, 7 Dec 1941 (21 killed). Damaged by kamikaze, Okinawa, 21 Jun 1945 (41 killed). †
7* Pearl Harbor, Guadalcanal-Tulagi, Guadalcanal, Santa Cruz, Gilbert Is., Solomons, Okinawa.

AV 5 *Albemarle* Atlantic 1941–45. Operation Crossroads. †

Figure 10.26: The seaplane tender *Curtiss* (AV 4), burning after being hit by Japanese bomb at Pearl Harbor, 7 Dec 1941.

No.	Name	Builder	Laid Down	Launched	Comm.
AV 7	*Currituck*	Phila. NYd	14 Dec 1942	11 Sep 1943	26 Jun 1944
AV 11	*Norton Sound*	Los Angeles	7 Sep 1942	28 Nov 1943	8 Jan 1945
AV 12	*Pine Island*	Los Angeles	16 Nov 1942	26 Feb 1944	26 Apr 1945
AV 13	*Salisbury Sound*	Los Angeles	10 Apr 1943	18 Jun 1944	26 Nov 1945
	ex-*Puget Sound* (5 Jun 1944)				

Displacement	9,090 tons; 15.056 f/l
Dimensions	540'5" (oa); 520' (wl) x 69'3" x 22'3"
Machinery	2 screws; AC GT (AV 7 *Currituck*: NYS Parsons GT); 4 B&W express boilers; SHP 12,000; 19.2 knots
Complement	1,150
Armament	4–5"/38, 3 quad 40mm, 4 twin 40mm, 20–20mm guns

Notes: AV 7 originally ordered from NY Sbdg; AV 11–13 from Sun.

Service Records:

AV 7 *Currituck* Decomm 7 Aug 1947. †
2* Leyte, Lingayen.

Figure 10.27: *Currituck* (AV 7) on 19 Jul 1944, shortly after completion, at Philadelphia.

AV 11 *Norton Sound* †
2* Okinawa, Raids on Japan 7–8/45.
AV 12 *Pine Island* †
1* Raids on Japan 7–8/45.
AV 13 *Salisbury Sound* †

No.	Name	Builder	Laid Down	Launched	Comm.
AV 8	*Tangier* ex–*Sea Arrow* (1940)	Moore	18 Mar 1939	15 Sep 1939	25 Aug 1941
AV 9	*Pocomoke* ex–*Exchequer* (1940)	Ingalls	14 Aug 1939	8 Jun 1940	18 Jul 1941
AV 10	*Chandeleur*	W.Pipe	29 May 1941	29 Nov 1941	19 Nov 1942

Displacement	5,300 tons, 11,760 tons f/l
Dimensions	492'1" (oa); 465' (wl) x 69'6" x 23'9"
Machinery	1 screw; GE GT; DeLaval GT (8), 2 FW D boilers; SHP 8,500; 18.4 knots
Complement	1,075
Armament	1–5"/38, 4–3"/50, 4 twin 40mm, 15–20mm guns

Figure 10.28: *Tangier* (AV 8), shown here in late 1941, was a cargo ship converted to a seaplane tender.

Notes: Type C3–Cargo (S), C3–S1–B1 (10). AV 8 *Tangier* acquired 8 Jul 1940, AV 9 *Pocomoke* 16 Oct 1940.

Service Records:

AV 8 *Tangier* Decomm 5 Aug 1946. †
4* Pearl Harbor, Admiralty Is. Ldgs., Western New Guinea, Morotai.
AV 9 *Pocomoke* Decomm 10 Jul 1946. †
3* Treasury Is., Saipan, Palau.
AV 10 *Chandeleur* Decomm 12 Feb 1947. †
5* Treasury Is., Saipan, Palau, Okinawa, Raids on Japan 7–8/45.

No.	Name	Builder	Laid Down	Launched	Comm.
AV 14	*Kenneth Whiting*	Todd Tacoma	19 Jun 1943	15 Dec 1943	8 May 1944
AV 15	*Hamlin*	Todd Tacoma	19 Jul 1943	11 Jan 1944	26 Jun 1944
AV 16	*St. George*	Todd Tacoma	4 Aug 1943	14 Feb 1944	24 Jul 1944
AV 17	*Cumberland Sound*	Todd Tacoma	25 Aug 1943	23 Feb 1944	21 Aug 1944
AV 18	*Townsend*	Todd Tacoma	30 Jun 1945	—	—
AV 19	*Calibogue*	Newport News	—	—	—
AV 20	*Hobe Sound*	Newport News	—	—	—

Displacement	8,510 tons; 12,610 f/l
Dimensions	492' (oa); 465' (wl) x 69'6" x 23'9"
Machinery	1 screw; AC GT; 2 FW D boilers; SHP 8,500; 18.7 knots
Complement	1,075
Armament	2–5"/38, 2 quad 40mm, 2 twin 40mm, 16–20mm AA guns

Notes: AV 18 originally assigned to Philadelphia NYd, AV 19 to Puget Sound NYd, and AV 20 to Charleston NYd.

Service Records:

AV 14 *Kenneth Whiting* Damaged by kamikaze, Kerama Retto, Okinawa, 21 Jun 1945. Operation Crossroads. Decomm 29 May 1947. †
2* Okinawa, Raids on Japan 7–8/45.
AV 15 *Hamlin* Damaged in error by U.S. naval gunfire, Iwo Jima, 25 Feb 1945. Decomm 15 Jan 1947. †
3* Iwo Jima, Okinawa, Raids on Japan 7–8/45. Tokyo Bay.
AV 16 *St. George* Damaged by kamikaze, Okinawa, 5 May 1945 (3 killed). Damaged by kamikaze off Kerama Retto, 21 Jun 1945. Decomm 1 Aug 1946. †
1* Okinawa.
AV 17 *Cumberland Sound* Tokyo Bay. Operation Crossroads. Decomm 27 May 1947. †
AV 18 *Townsend* Canceled 11 Aug 1945.
AV 19 *Calibogue* Canceled 28 Oct 1944.
AV 20 *Hobe Sound* Canceled 28 Oct 1944.

SMALL SEAPLANE TENDERS

Ex–Minesweepers (Rec 22 Jan 1936)

No.	Name	Formerly
AVP 1	*Lapwing*	AM 1
AVP 2	*Heron*	AM 10
AVP 3	*Thrush*	AM 18

Figure 10.29: *Heron* (AVP 2), 12 Jul 1928. A "bird class" minesweeper converted to a small seaplane tender, with a Martin T3M-2 torpedo bomber being carried aft. A target is displayed behind the funnel. The star on the bow indicates her service with aviation.

AVP 4	*Avocet*	AM 19
AVP 5	*Teal*	AM 23
AVP 6	*Pelican*	AM 27
AVP 7	*Swan*	AM 34
AVP 8	*Gannet*	AM 41
AVP 9	*Sandpiper*	AM 51
Armament	2–3"/50, 4–20mm.	

Notes: *Sandpiper* converted 1919, *Teal* 1922, *Heron* 1924, *Swan* and *Gannet* 1931, but not reclassified until 1936. Forward mast removed during the war.

Service Records:

AVP 1 *Lapwing* Neutrality patrol. Stricken 19 Dec 1945. Decomm 29 Nov 1945. Sold 19 Aug 1946.

AVP 2 *Heron* Damaged by aircraft bombs off Ambon, Netherlands East Indies, 31 Dec 1941 (1 or more killed). Decomm 12 Feb 1946. To China (State Department) 25 Jul 1947.
4* Philippines 1942, Admiralty Is. Ldgs., Solomons, Leyte.

AVP 3 *Thrush* Out of comm 3 Apr 1922–31 Oct 1935 and converted. Rec **AVP 3**, 22 Jan 1936. Decomm 13 Dec 1945. Stricken 8 Jan 1946.
Later history: Merchant *Semper Paratus* 1947, renamed *Cyrenaica I* 1950. Disappeared off Mersa Matruh, Egypt, 3 Mar 1951.

AVP 4 *Avocet* Out of comm 3 Apr 1922–8 Sep 1925, converted 1932. Far East 1925–33. Went aground in typhoon at Chefoo, China, 26 Aug 1928. Decomm 10 Dec 1945. Stricken 3 Jan 1946, sold 12 Dec 1946.
1* Pearl Harbor.

AVP 5 *Teal* Converted 1922. Decomm 23 Nov 1945. Stricken 5 Dec 1945. Sold 1948.
Later history: Merchant *Teal* 1948.

AVP 6 *Pelican* Operated as Q-ship off U.S. West Coast, 1942. Decomm 30 Nov 1945. Stricken 19 Dec 1945, sold 22 Nov 1946.

AVP 7 *Swan* Decomm 13 Dec 1945. Stricken 8 Jan 1946. to USMC12 Oct 1946. FFU.
1* Pearl Harbor.

AVP 8 *Gannet* Neutrality patrol. Torpedoed and sunk by *U-653* northwest of Bermuda, 7 Jun 1942 (14 killed).

AVP 9 *Sandpiper* Damaged in collision with British m/v off Cape Farewell, 23 Jun 1943. Decomm 10 Dec 1945. Stricken 17 Apr 1946.

Note: For AVP 14–21, see AVD 1–7.

Figure 10.30: *Matagorda* (AVP 22), a small seaplane tender, with four 5" guns, 27 Sep 1943.

Figure 10.31: *Rockaway* (AVP 21), seen here on 5 Oct 1944, had only one 5" gun.

No.	Name	Builder	Laid Down	Launched	Comm.
AVP 10	*Barnegat*	Puget Sound NYd	26 Oct 1939	23 May 1941	3 Jul 1941
AVP 11	*Biscayne*	Puget Sound NYd	27 Oct 1939	23 May 1941	3 Jul 1941
AVP 12	*Casco*	Puget Sound NYd	30 May 1940	15 Nov 1941	27 Dec 1941
AVP 13	*Mackinac*	Puget Sound NYd	30 May 1940	15 Nov 1941	24 Jan 1942
AVP 21	*Humboldt*	Boston NYd	6 Sep 1940	17 Mar 1941	7 Oct 1941
AVP 22	*Matagorda*	Boston NYd	6 Sep 1940	18 Mar 1941	16 Dec 1941
AVP 23	*Absecon*	Lake Wash.	23 Jul 1941	8 Mar 1942	28 Jan 1943
AVP 24	*Chincoteague*	Lake Wash.	23 Jul 1941	15 Apr 1942	12 Apr 1943
AVP 25	*Coos Bay*	Lake Wash.	15 Aug 1941	15 May 1942	15 May 1943
AVP 26	*Half Moon*	Lake Wash.	10 Mar 1942	12 Jul 1942	15 Jun 1943
AVP 27	*Mobjack*	Lake Wash.	25 Feb 1942	2 Aug 1942	17 Oct 1943
AVP 28	*Oyster Bay*	Lake Wash.	17 Apr 1942	7 Sep 1942	17 Nov 1943
AVP 29	*Rockaway*	Associated	30 Jun 1941	14 Feb 1942	6 Jan 1943
AVP 30	*San Pablo*	Associated	2 Jul 1941	31 Mar 1942	15 Mar 1943
AVP 31	*Unimak*	Associated	15 Feb 1942	27 May 1942	31 Dec 1943

AVP 32	*Yakutat*	Associated	1 Apr 1942	2 Jul 1942	31 Mar 1944
AVP 33	*Barataria*	Lake Wash.	19 Apr 1943	2 Oct 1943	13 Aug 1944
AVP 34	*Bering Strait*	Lake Wash.	7 Jun 1943	15 Jan 1944	19 Jul 1944
AVP 35	*Castle Rock*	Lake Wash.	12 Jul 1943	11 Mar 1944	8 Oct 1944
AVP 36	*Cook Inlet*	Lake Wash.	23 Aug 1943	13 May 1944	5 Nov 1944
AVP 37	*Corson*	Lake Wash.	5 Oct 1943	16 Jul 1944	3 Dec 1944
AVP 38	*Duxbury Bay*	Lake Wash.	17 Jan 1944	2 Oct 1944	31 Dec 1944
AVP 39	*Gardiners Bay*	Lake Wash.	14 Mar 1944	2 Dec 1944	11 Feb 1945
AVP 40	*Floyds Bay*	Lake Wash.	16 May 1944	28 Jan 1945	25 Mar 1945
AVP 41	*Greenwich Bay*	Lake Wash.	18 Jul 1944	18 Mar 1945	20 May 1945
AVP 42	*Hatteras*	Lake Wash.	—	—	—
AVP 43	*Hempstead*	Lake Wash.	—	—	—
AVP 44	*Kamishak*	Lake Wash.	—	—	—
AVP 45	*Magothy*	Lake Wash.	—	—	—
AVP 46	*Matanzas*	Lake Wash.	—	—	—
AVP 47	*Metomkin*	Lake Wash.	—	—	—
AVP 48	*Onslow*	Lake Wash.	18 May 1942	20 Sep 1942	16 Dec 1943
AVP 49	*Orca*	Lake Wash.	13 Jul 1942	4 Oct 1942	23 Jan 1944
AVP 50	*Rehoboth*	Lake Wash.	3 Aug 1942	8 Nov 1942	23 Feb 1944
AVP 51	*San Carlos*	Lake Wash.	7 Sep 1942	20 Dec 1942	21 Mar 1944
AVP 52	*Shelikof*	Lake Wash.	20 Sep 1942	31 Jan 1943	17 Apr 1944
AVP 53	*Suisun*	Lake Wash.	4 Oct 1942	14 Mar 1943	13 Sep 1944
AVP 54	*Timbalier*	Lake Wash.	9 Nov 1942	18 Apr 1943	24 May 1946
AVP 55	*Valcour*	Lake Wash.	21 Dec 1942	5 Jun 1943	5 Jul 1946
AVP 56	*Wachapreague*	Lake Wash.	1 Feb 1943	10 Jul 1943	17 May 1944
AVP 57	*Willoughby*	Lake Wash.	15 Mar 1943	21 Aug 1943	18 Jun 1944
AVP 58–67	—	—	—	—	—

Displacement	1,766 tons; 2,592 tons f/l
Dimensions	310'9" (oa); 300' (wl) x 41'2" x 13'6"
Machinery	2 screws; FM diesel; SHP 6,400; 18.2 knots
Endurance	4,500/16
Complement	367
Armament	1–5"/38, 1 quad 40mm, 2 twin 40mm, 4 twin 20mm guns (AVP 12, AVP 26, AVP 34, AVP 48, AVP 49, AVP 51, AVP 52: 3–5"; AVP 22–24: 2–5"; AVP 25, AVP 30: 4–5")

Notes: Designed to replace "bird class" tenders. Named for bays and inlets. AVP 23 *Absecon* fitted with catapult and cranes for training of battleship and cruiser pilots. Early units built with two or four 5" guns.

Service Records:

AVP 10 *Barnegat* Decomm 17 May 1946.
1* North Africa.

AVP 11 *Biscayne* Converted to amphibious force flagship at Mers-el-Kebir, Algeria, May 1943. Rec **AGC 18**, 10 Oct 1944. Decomm 29 Jun 1946. To USCG 19 Jul 1946.
6* Sicily, Salerno, Anzio, Southern France, Iwo Jima, Okinawa.
Later history: Renamed USCGC *Dexter* (WAVP 385). Returned 1968.

AVP 12 *Casco* Torpedoed by Japanese submarine *Ro-61* off Attu while at anchor, and beached, 30 Aug 1942 (5 killed). Decomm 10 Apr 1947.
3* Attu, Kwajalein, Okinawa.

AVP 13 *Mackinac* Damaged by U.S. submarine gunfire in error at Ndeni Santa Cruz Is, 20 Aug 1942. Decomm Jan 1947. †
6* Guadalcanal-Tulagi, Gilbert Is., Saipan, Palau, Okinawa, Raids on Japan 7–8/45. Tokyo Bay.

AVP 21 *Humboldt* Rec **AG 121**, 30 Jul 1945, conversion to press information ship canceled, 25 Aug 1945. Decomm 19 Mar 1947. †

AVP 22 *Matagorda* Rec **AG 122**, 30 Jul 1945, conversion to press information ship canceled, 25 Aug 1945. Decomm 20 Feb 1946. †

AVP 23 *Absecon* Pilot training off Florida; damaged by exercise torpedo, off Jacksonville, 19 Feb 1945 (and other times). Decomm 19 Mar 1947. †

AVP 24 *Chincoteague* Damaged by aircraft bombs at Saboe Bay, New Guinea, 16 Jul 1943 (9 killed). Decomm 21 Mar 1946. †
6* Solomons, New Georgia Ldgs., Treasury Is., Eniwetok, Iwo Jima.

AVP 25 *Coos Bay* Damaged by collision with m/v near Eniwetok, 31 Mar 1945. Decomm 30 Apr 1946. †
2* Solomons, Treasury Is.

AVP 26 *Half Moon* Rec **AGP 6**, 8 Mar 1943. Conversion to MTB tender canceled, rec **AVP 26**, 1 May 1943. Decomm 4 Sep 1946. †
2* Morotai, Western New Guinea, Cape Sansapor, Leyte, Surigao Strait.

AVP 27 *Mobjack* Completed as MTB tender, rec **AGP 7**, 8 Mar 1943. Decomm 21 Aug 1946 and trfd to USC&GS.
3* Solomons, Western New Guinea, Balikpapan.
Later history: Renamed USC&GS *Pioneer.* BU 1966 Terminal I.

AVP 28 *Oyster Bay* Completed as MTB tender, rec **AGP 6**, 1 May 1943. Damaged by near miss bomb off Morotai, 19 Sep 1944. Decomm 26 Mar 1946. Stricken 12 Apr 1946. †
4* Saidor, Admiralty Is. Ldgs., Western New Guinea, Morotai, Leyte, Surigao Strait.

AVP 29 *Rockaway* Rec **AG 123**, 30 Jul 1945; conversion to press information ship canceled, 25 Aug 1945. Decomm 21 Mar 1946. †
1* Normandy.

AVP 30 *San Pablo* Decomm 13 Jan 1947. †
4* Finschhafen, Admiralty Is. Ldgs., Western New Guinea, Morotai, Western New Guinea, Leyte.

AVP 31 *Unimak* Decomm 23 Jul 1946. †

AVP 32 *Yakutat* Damaged by collision, Okinawa, 18 Jun 1945. Decomm 29 Jul 1946. †
4* Saipan, Palau, Okinawa, Raids on Japan 7–8/45.

AVP 33 *Barataria* Decomm 24 Jul 1946. †
1* Lingayen.

AVP 34 *Bering Strait* Decomm 21 Jun 1946. †
3* Iwo Jima, Okinawa, Raids on Japan 7–8/45.

AVP 35 *Castle Rock* Decomm 6 Aug 1946. †

AVP 36 *Cook Inlet* Decomm 31 Mar 1946. †
1* Iwo Jima.

AVP 37 *Corson* Decomm 21 Jun 1946. †

AVP 38 *Duxbury Bay* †

AVP 39 *Gardiners Bay* †
2* Okinawa, Raids on Japan 7–8/45. Tokyo Bay.

AVP 40 *Floyds Bay* †
1* Raids on Japan 7–8/45.

AVP 41 *Greenwich Bay* †

AVP 42 *Hatteras* Canceled 22 Apr 1943.

AVP 43 *Hempstead* Canceled 22 Apr 1943.

AVP 44 *Kamishak* Canceled 22 Apr 1943.

AVP 45 *Magothy* Canceled 22 Apr 1943.

AVP 46 *Matanzas* Canceled 22 Apr 1943.

AVP 47 *Metomkin* Canceled 22 Apr 1943.

AVP 48 *Onslow* Decomm Jun 1947. †
4* Saipan, Palau, Okinawa, Raids on Japan 7–8/45.

AVP 49 *Orca* Damaged by kamikaze near miss, west of Luzon, 5 Jan 1945. Operation Crossroads. Decomm 31 Oct 1947. †
4* Western New Guinea, Cape Sansapor, Leyte, Lingayen.

AVP 50 *Rehoboth* Decomm 30 Jun 1947. †

AVP 51 *San Carlos* Decomm 30 Jun 1947. †
4* Solomons, Morotai, Leyte, Surigao Strait.

AVP 52 *Shelikof* Decomm 30 Jun 1947. †
3* Okinawa, Raids on Japan 7–8/45, Saipan.

AVP 53 *Suisun* Damaged in collision with *LCT-1407*, Okinawa, 26 Jun 1945. Tokyo Bay. †
2* Okinawa, Raids on Japan 7–8/45.

AVP 54 *Timbalier* Completed at Puget Sound NYd. †
AVP 55 *Valcour* Completed at Puget Sound NYd. †
AVP 56 *Wachapreague* Converted to MTB Tender and rec **AGP 8**, 11 May 1943. Decomm 10 May 1946, to USCG 27 May 1946. Stricken 5 Jun 1946.
4* Western New Guinea, Leyte, Surigao Strait, Lingayen, Tarakan.
Later history: Renamed USCGC *McCulloch* (WAVP 386). To Vietnam 9 May 1972, renamed *Ngo Quyen*; to Philippines 1976, renamed *Gregorio de Pilar*.
AVP 57 *Willoughby* Converted to MTB tender and rec **AGP 9**, 11 May 1943. Decomm 26 Jun 1946, to USCG Stricken 19 Jul 1946.
3* Western New Guinea, Leyte, Surigao Strait, Ldgs. on Palawan I.
Later history: Renamed USCGC *Gresham* (WAVP 387). Stricken 25 Oct 1972, to Marad 21 May 1973; BU.
AVP 58–67— Canceled 19 Oct 1942.

SEAPLANE TENDERS (EX-DESTROYERS)

No.	Name	Formerly	Reclassified	Later Reclassified
AVD 1	*Childs*	DD 241	2 Aug 1940	—
AVD 2	*Williamson*	DD 244	2 Aug 1940	Rec DD 244, 1 Dec 1943
AVD 3	*George E. Badger*	DD 196	2 Aug 1940	Rec DD 196, 4 Nov 1943
AVD 4	*Clemson*	DD 186	2 Aug 1940	Rec DD 186, 1 Dec 1943
AVD 5	*Goldsborough*	DD 188	2 Aug 1940	Rec DD 188, 1 Dec 1943
AVD 6	*Hulbert*	DD 342	2 Aug 1940	Rec DD 342, 1 Dec 1943
AVD 7	*William B. Preston*	DD 344	2 Aug 1940	—
AVD 8	*Belknap*	DD 251	2 Aug 1940	Rec DD 251, 14 Nov 1943
AVD 9	*Osmond Ingram*	DD 255	2 Aug 1940	Rec DD 255, 4 Nov 1943
AVD 10	*Ballard*	DD 267	2 Aug 1940	—
AVD 11	*Thornton*	DD 270	2 Aug 1940	—
AVD 12	*Gillis*	DD 260	2 Aug 1940	—
AVD 13	*Greene*	DD 266	6 Apr 1941	Rec APD 36, 1 Feb 1944
AVD 14	*McFarland*	DD 237	2 Aug 1940	Rec DD 237, 1 Dec 1943

Armament	2–3"/50, 7 or 8 20mm guns

Note: Two forward boilers were replaced by aviation gasoline tanks. TT, guns, two funnels removed; crane and boats added. AVD 1–7 originally classified AVP 14–21; rec 1 Jul 1938.

AVIATION SUPPLY SHIPS

No.	Name	Formerly	Reclassified
AVS 1	*Supply*	IX 147	25 May 1945
AVS 2	*Fortune*	IX 146	25 May 1945
AVS 3	*Grumium*	IX 174	25 May 1945
AVS 4	*Allioth*	IX 204	25 May 1945
AVS 5	*Gwinnett*	AG 92	25 May 1945
AVS 6	*Nicollet*	AG 93	25 May 1945
AVS 7	*Pontotoc*	AG 94	25 May 1945
AVS 8	*Jupiter*	AK 43	31 Jul 1945

CATAPULT LIGHTER

No.	Builder	Laid Down	Launched	In service
AVC 1	Phila NYd	19 Feb 1940	17 Aug 1940	17 Dec 1941

Displacement	5,860 tons
Dimensions	424' (oa); 420' (bp) x 57' x 9'9"
Machinery	(unpowered)

Notes: Built for use with a large flying boat, later canceled. Designed for two screws and diesel engines, also canceled. Purpose changed to catapult test lighter. Not very successful, laid up in 1945. New catapult installed 1949, lengthened by 46'3". Stricken 18 Oct 1955, BU 1956.

Figure 10.32: *Goldsborough* (AVD 5), a flush-deck destroyer converted in 1940 to seaplane tender, 28 Jul 1943. The forward boilers were replaced with aviation fuel tanks.

Figure 10.33: The salvage vessel *Redwing* (ARS 4), 10 Oct 1942, in New York Harbor, a "bird class" minesweeper that served in the Coast Guard until 1941, when she was converted to a salvage vessel.

SALVAGE VESSELS

Names for salvage vessels were nouns or adjectives connected with salvage and repair operations

Ex–Minesweepers

No.	Name	Formerly	Reclassified
ARS 1	*Viking*	AM 32	27 Jun 1941
ARS 2	*Crusader*	AM 29	5 Aug 1941
ARS 3	*Discoverer*	AM 38	26 Aug 1941
ARS 4	*Redwing*	AM 48	5 Aug 1941
ARS 11	*Warbler*	AM 53	22 Sep 1941
ARS 12	*Willet*	AM 54	22 Sep 1941
ARS 32	*Brant*	AM 24	1 Sep 1942

Armament	ARS 1 *Viking*, ARS 3 *Discoverer*: 2–6 pdr guns; ARS 32 *Brant*: 4–20mm guns.

Service Records:

ARS 1 *Viking* Acq from USC&GS, 27 Jun 1941. In service 3 Jan 1942, loan to USMC. Civilian manned. †

ARS 2 *Crusader* Acq from USC&GS, 17 Sep 1941 and recomm. Stricken 25 Sep 1946; to USMC13 Feb 1947.
Later history: Merchant *Osprey* 1947, renamed *Victoria* 1948. BU 1952 Sunderland, England.

ARS 3 *Discoverer* Acq from USC&GS, 26 Aug 1941. In service, civilian manned. Stricken 28 Jan 1947, sold to Venezuela, 9 Jun 1947.
Later history: Renamed *Felipe Larrázabal* 1948. BU 1962.

ARS 4 *Redwing* Returned to USN 29 Aug 1941 as **ARS 4**. Recomm 28 Oct 1941. Sunk by explosion at Bizerte, Tunisia, 27 Jun 1943 (1 killed).

ARS 11 *Warbler* Civilian manned. Rec **ARS 11**, 13 Sep 1941. Stricken 10 Jun 1947. Sold 12 Aug 1947.

ARS 12 *Willet* Civilian manned. Rec **ARS 12**, 13 Sep 1941. Stricken 5 Dec 1947, sold 2 Nov 1948; BU.

ARS 32 *Brant* AM 24 1 Sep 1942 Damaged in error by U.S. naval gunfire, Sicily, 10 Aug 1943 (10 killed). Damaged in collision south of Salerno, Italy, 28 Sep 1943. Decomm 19 Dec 1945. Sold 2 Nov 1948. FFU.
3* Sicily, Salerno, Normandy.

No.	Name	Builder	Laid Down	Launched	Comm.
ARS 5	*Diver*	Basalt	6 Apr 1942	19 Dec 1942	23 Oct 1943
ARS 6	*Escape*	Basalt	24 Aug 1942	22 Nov 1942	20 Nov 1943
ARS 7	*Grapple*	Basalt	8 Sep 1942	31 Dec 1942	16 Dec 1943
ARS 8	*Preserver*	Basalt	26 Oct 1942	1 Apr 1943	11 Jan 1944
ARS 9	*Shackle*	Basalt	26 Oct 1942	1 Apr 1943	5 Feb 1944
ARS 19	*Cable*	Basalt	24 Nov 1942	1 Apr 1943	6 Mar 1944
ARS 20	*Chain*	Basalt	21 Dec 1942	3 Jun 1943	31 Mar 1944
ARS 21	*Curb*	Basalt	1 Jan 1943	24 Apr 1943	12 May 1944
ARS 22	*Current*	Basalt	2 Apr 1943	25 Sep 1943	14 Jun 1944
ARS 23	*Deliver*	Basalt	2 Apr 1943	25 Sep 1943	18 Jul 1944
ARS 24	*Grasp*	Basalt	27 Apr 1943	31 Jul 1943	22 Aug 1944
ARS 25	*Safeguard*	Basalt	5 Jun 1943	20 Nov 1943	30 Sep 1944
ARS 26	*Seize*	Basalt	28 Sep 1943	8 Apr 1944	3 Nov 1944
ARS 27	*Snatch*	Basalt	28 Sep 1943	8 Apr 1944	11 Dec 1944
ARS 33	*Clamp*	Basalt	2 Mar 1942	24 Oct 1942	23 Aug 1943
	ex–BARS 3, *Atlantic Salvor* (23 Sep 1942)				
ARS 34	*Gear*	Basalt	2 Mar 1942	24 Oct 1942	24 Sep 1943
	ex–BARS 4, *Pacific Salvor* (23 Sep 1942)				
ARS 38	*Bolster*	Basalt	20 Jul 1944	23 Dec 1944	1 May 1945
ARS 39	*Conserver*	Basalt	10 Aug 1944	27 Jan 1945	9 Jun 1945
ARS 40	*Hoist*	Basalt	13 Sep 1944	31 Mar 1945	21 Jul 1945
ARS 41	*Opportune*	Basalt	13 Sep 1944	31 Mar 1945	5 Oct 1945
ARS 42	*Reclaimer*	Basalt	11 Nov 1944	23 Jun 1945	20 Dec 1945
ARS 43	*Recovery*	Basalt	6 Jan 1945	4 Aug 1945	15 May 1946
ARS 44	*Retriever*	Basalt	31 Jan 1945	—	—
ARS 45	*Skillful*	Basalt	25 Apr 1945	—	—
ARS 46	*Support*	Basalt	7 Aug 1945	—	—
ARS 47	*Toiler*	Basalt	—	—	—
ARS 48	*Urgent*	Basalt	—	—	—
ARS 49	*Willing*	Basalt	—	—	—
BARS 1	—	Basalt	19 Feb 1942	22 Aug 1942	*20 May 1943*
BARS 2	—	Basalt	21 Feb 1942	7 Sep 1942	*1 Jul 1943*
BARS 3	See ARS 33				
BARS 4	See ARS 34				

Displacement	1,530 tons, 1,897 tons f/l
Dimensions	213'6" (oa); 207' (wl) x 39' x 14'1"
Machinery	2 screws; CB diesel-electric; SHP 3,000; 14.8 knots
Complement	120
Armament	2 twin 40mm, 6–20mm AA guns

Figure 10.34: The salvage vessel *Escape* (ARS 6).

Note: Large tug-type ships with steel hulls.

Service Records:

ARS 5 *Diver* Damaged by striking submerged object off Le Havre, 28 Dec 1944. Decomm 27 Jul 1946. †
1* Normandy.

ARS 6 *Escape* Decomm 20 Jul 1946. †

ARS 7 *Grapple* Decomm 30 Aug 1946. †
1* Leyte.

ARS 8 *Preserver* Damaged by aircraft bomb, Leyte, 20 Oct 1944. Operation Crossroads. Decomm 23 Apr 1947. †
3* Saipan, Tinian, Leyte.

ARS 9 *Shackle* Decomm 29 Jun 1946, to USCG.
3* Iwo Jima, Okinawa, Raids on Japan 7–8/45.
Later history: Renamed USCGC *Acushnet* (WAT 167). †

ARS 19 *Cable* Decomm 15 Sep 1947 and loaned to USMC. †
3* Leyte, Lingayen, Balikpapan.

ARS 20 *Chain* Went aground on Block I., N.Y., 29 Mar 1946. Decomm 9 Nov 1946. †

ARS 21 *Curb* Decomm 20 Dec 1946. Loaned to USMC 10 May 1947. †

ARS 22 *Current* Operation Crossroads. †
1* Okinawa, Raids on Japan 7–8/45.
ARS 23 *Deliver* Operation Crossroads. †
1* Okinawa.
ARS 24 *Grasp* Decomm 12 Dec 1946. †
2* Lingayen, Subic Bay, Ldgs at Nasugbu, Mariveles-Corregidor.
ARS 25 *Safeguard* Decomm 12 Dec 1947. †
1* Iwo Jima.
ARS 26 *Seize* Decomm 28 Jun 1946, to USCG.
Later history: Renamed USCGC *Yocona* (WAT 168). †
ARS 27 *Snatch* Decomm 23 Dec 1946. †
ARS 33 *Clamp* Decomm 6 May 1947. †
4* Gilbert Is., Saipan, Iwo Jima, Okinawa. Operation Crossroads.
ARS 34 *Gear* Decomm 13 Dec 1946. †
3* Saipan, Iwo Jima, Okinawa.
ARS 38 *Bolster* †
ARS 39 *Conserver* Operation Crossroads. †
ARS 40 *Hoist* †
ARS 41 *Opportune* †
ARS 42 *Reclaimer* Operation Crossroads. Decomm 23 Jun 1947. †
ARS 43 *Recovery* †
ARS 44 *Retriever* Canceled 12 Aug 1945.
ARS 45 *Skillful* Canceled 12 Aug 1945.
ARS 46 *Support* Canceled 12 Aug 1945.
ARS 47 *Toiler* Canceled 12 Aug 1945.
ARS 48 *Urgent* Canceled 12 Aug 1945.
ARS 49 *Willing* Canceled 12 Aug 1945.
BARS 1 — To UK 20 May 1943, renamed *Caledonian Salvor* (Australian).
Later history: Merchant *Caledonian Salvor* 1947, renamed *Sudbury II* 1958, *Lady Pacific* 1983. Sank after fire off Prince Rupert, British Columbia, 31 Oct 1982.
BARS 2 — To UK 1 Jul 1943, renamed *Cambrian Salvor* (Australian).
Later history: Merchant *Cambrian Salvor* 1958, renamed *Caribsche Zee* 1962, *Collinsea* 1964, *Francois C* 1971, *Ras Deira*. Hulk at Abadan; BU 1981 Pakistan.
BARS 3 — Rec **ARS 33**, 23 Sep 1942.
BARS 4 — Rec **ARS 34**, 23 Sep 1942.

No.	Name	Builder	Laid Down	Launched	Comm.
ARS 13	*Anchor*	Colberg	30 Apr 1942	13 Mar 1943	23 Oct 1943
ARS 14	*Protector*	Colberg	30 Apr 1942	27 Apr 1943	28 Dec 1943
ARS 15	*Extractor*	Colberg	16 May 1942	15 Jun 1943	3 Mar 1944
ARS 16	*Extricate*	Snow	18 Mar 1942	12 Sep 1942	27 Jul 1943
ARS 17	*Restorer*	Snow	25 Mar 1942	24 Oct 1942	6 Oct 1943
ARS 28	*Valve*	Bellingham	17 Nov 1942	10 May 1943	24 Feb 1944
ARS 29	*Vent*	Bellingham	29 Jan 1943	30 Jun 1943	7 Apr 1944
ARS 35	*Weight*	AC&F	7 Apr 1942	21 Apr 1943	14 Aug 1943
	ex–BARS 7, *Plymouth Salvor* (15 Mar 1943)				
ARS 36	*Swivel*	AC&F	28 Apr 1942	6 May 1943	6 Oct 1943
	ex–BARS 8, *York Salvor*				
BARS 5	—	Barbour	4 Apr 1942	27 Dec 1942	*9 Sep 1943*
BARS 6	—	Barbour	20 Apr 1942	20 Feb 1943	*28 Jan 1944*
BARS 7	See ARS 35				
BARS 8	See ARS 36				
BARS 9	—	Bellingham	27 Apr 1942	14 Nov 1942	*5 Nov 1943*
BARS 10	—	Bellingham	30 May 1942	23 Jan 1943	*17 Dec 1943*

Displacement	1,089 tons; 1,615 f/l
Dimensions	183'3" (oa); 174'1" (wl) x 37' x 14'8"
Machinery	2 screws; CB diesel-electric; SHP 1,200; 12 knots
Complement	65
Armament	1–3"/50, 4–20mm AA guns

Note: Wood hulls.

Service Records:

ARS 13 *Anchor* Decomm 16 Sep 1946. Stricken 13 Nov 1946, sold 23 May 1947. FFU.
1* Okinawa.
ARS 14 *Protector* Decomm 15 May 1946. Stricken 8 Oct 1946, sold 3 Jan 1947.
Later history: Merchant *Protector*, renamed *Pakistan Protector* 1952.
ARS 15 *Extractor* Torpedoed and sunk in error by U.S. submarine *Guardfish* in Philippine Sea, 24 Jan 1945 (6 killed).
ARS 16 *Extricate* Went aground in typhoon in Okinawa, 9 Oct 1945. Hulk destroyed 4 Mar 1946.
2* Southern France, Okinawa.
ARS 17 *Restorer* Decomm 6 Mar 1946. Stricken 19 Jul 1946, sold to Denmark 22 Apr 1947.
2* Anzio, Southern France.
Later history: Merchant *Vitus Bering*. BU 1951.
ARS 28 *Valve* Decomm 26 Aug 1946. Stricken 12 Mar 1948, sold 26 Jul 1948.
ARS 29 *Vent* Decomm 30 Aug 1946. Stricken 12 Mar 1948, sold 30 Jun 1948.
Later history: Merchant *Western Pioneer*, se 1983.
ARS 35 *Weight* Decomm 29 Mar 1946. Stricken 1 May 1946. Sold 1947.
2* Anzio, Southern France.
Later history: Merchant *Carol Ann*.
ARS 36 *Swivel* Decomm 4 Jun 1946. Stricken 3 Jul 1946, sold 6 Dec 1946.
1* Normandy.
Later history: Merchant *Swivel*. BU 1970 Burgeo, Newfoundland.
BARS 5 — To UK 9 Sep 1943, renamed *American Salvor*. Sold Nov 1946.
Later history: Merchant *American Salvor*, renamed *Aptopos* 1949.
BARS 6 — To UK 28 Jan 1944, renamed *Boston Salvor*. Severely damaged by flying bomb at Antwerp, 16 Mar 1945, not repaired. BU 1945.
BARS 7 — Rec **ARS 35**, 11 Jan 1943.
BARS 8 — Rec **ARS 36**, 11 Nov 1943.
BARS 9 — To UK 5 Nov 1943, renamed *Lincoln Salvor*. Sold Nov 1946.
Later history: Merchant *Agerochos*.
BARS 10 — To UK 17 Dec 1943, renamed *Southampton Salvor*. Sold Nov 1946.
Later history: Merchant *Alkimos*.
ARS 10 *Assistance* ex–*Medric*. Not acquired.

No.	Name	Builder	Launched	Acquired	Comm.
ARS 18	*Rescuer*	United Eng.	1904	6 Feb 1942	1942
	ex–*Caspar* (1942), ex–*Nushagak* (1925)				

Tonnage	739 grt
Dimensions	175'6" x 24' x (U)
Machinery	1 screw; VTE; IHP 700; 10 knots

Service Record:

ARS 18 *Rescuer* Lost by grounding on Unimak I. while attempting to refloat Russian m/v *Turksib*, 1 Jan 1943.

No.	Name	Builder	Launched	Acquired	In service
ARS 30	*Accelerate*	Kyle & Purdy	1921	2 Apr 1942	1942
	ex–*Walling* (1942), ex–*Toteco* (1930)				

Tonnage	449 grt
Dimensions	129'6" (oa) x 32' x 14'

Machinery	1 screw; compound, 1 s/e boiler; IHP 450; 12 knots;
Armament	20mm guns

Service Record:

ARS 30 *Accelerate* Civilian crew. Third ND. Stricken 7 Feb 1947, sold 28 Aug 1947.
Later history: Merchant *Marigo* 1948, renamed *Semara II* 1950, *George* 1951. RR 1997.

No.	Name	Builder	Launched	Acquired	In service
ARS 31	*Harjurand*	Cardona	1919	1 Jun 1942	1 Jun 1942

ex-*Harjurand* (1942), ex-*Margot* (1937), ex-*Tento* (1934), ex-*Camberway* (1933); ex-*Per Skogland* (1923), ex-*Olesa* (1921)

Tonnage	812 grt
Dimensions	188'6" (oa) x 32'11" x 13'6"
Machinery	1 screw; VTE; 2 s/e boilers; IHP 490, (U) knots
Armament	2–6 pdr, 2–20mm guns

Service Record:

ARS 31 *Harjurand* Estonian ship seized at Wilmington, Del., 1941. Civilian crew. Stricken 19 Jun 1946. Returned to WSA 22 May 1946.
Later history: Merchant *Dodecanese* 1946. BU 1955 Jacksonville, Fla.

No.	Name	Builder	Launched	Acquired	Comm.
ARS 37	*Tackle*	Newport News	26 Oct 1912	19 Jun 1943	5 Aug 1943

ex-*W. R. Chamberlin Jr.* (1943), ex-*Stanley Dollar* (1922), ex-*Adeline Smith* (1919)

Tonnage	2,264 grt
Dimensions	310'2" (oa); 296'5" (wl) x 44'6" x 22'6"
Machinery	2 screws; diesel-electric; HP 2,780, 10 knots
Complement	65
Armament	1–3"/50

Service Record:

ARS 37 *Tackle* Damaged by mine at Port de Bouc, France, 4 Sep 1944, while under tow of French tug *Provençal*, which sank. Rec **ARS(T) 4**, 1 Feb 1945. Rec **IX 217**, 20 Mar 1945. Decomm 13 Sep 1946. Stricken 11 Oct 1945, sold 24 Jul 1946; BU 1949, Chester, Pa.
2* Salerno, Southern France.

Figure 10.35: The *Tackle* (ARS 37), converted in 1943, served in the Mediterranean.

SALVAGE LIFTING VESSELS

No.	Name	Formerly	Reclassified	Comm. as ARS
ARS(D) 1	*Gypsy*	LSM 549	24 Apr 1945	18 Mar 1946
ARS(D) 2	*Mender*	LSM 550	24 Apr 1945	8 Mar 1946
ARS(D) 3	*Salvager*	LSM 551	24 Apr 1945	22 Mar 1946
ARS(D) 4	*Windlass*	LSM 552	24 Apr 1945	9 Apr 1946

Armament 2–20mm guns.

Note: Converted landing ships medium.

Service Records:

ARS(D) 1 *Gypsy* Operation Crossroads. †
ARS(D) 2 *Mender* Operation Crossroads. †
ARS(D) 3 *Salvager* †
ARS(D) 4 *Windlass* †

SALVAGE CRAFT TENDERS

No.	Name	Formerly	Reclassified	Comm. as AR
ARS(T) 1	*Laysan Island*	LST 1098	8 Dec 1944	5 Jun 1945
ARS(T) 2	*Okala*	LST 1099	8 Dec 1944	28 Jun 1945
ARS(T) 3	*Palmyra*	LST 1100	8 Dec 1944	28 Jul 1945

Armament 2 quad 40mm, 4–40mm, 6 twin 20mm guns.

Note: Converted landing ships tank.

Service Records:

ARS(T) 1 *Laysan Island* Decomm 21 Apr 1947. †
ARS(T) 2 *Okala* Operation Crossroads. Decomm 5 Aug 1946. Stricken 15 Oct 1946, sold 21 Aug 1947.
Later history: Merchant *Saipan*, renamed *Saipan Maru* 1953. BU.
ARS(T) 3 *Palmyra* Decomm 20 Jun 1947. †

No.	Name	Formerly	Date	Rec
ARS(T) 4	*Tackle*	ARS 37	1 Feb 1945	**IX 217**, 20 Mar 1945

NET LAYING SHIPS

These were small ships designed to lay and tend antisubmarine nets at harbor entrances. They were named for plants and trees. The ships of the *Cohoes* class were named for Civil War monitors.

No.	Name	Reclassified	Date
AN 1	*Monitor*	AP 160	2 Aug 1943
AN 2	*Montauk*	AP 161	2 Aug 1943
AN 3	*Osage*	AP 108	1 May 1943
AN 4	*Saugus*	AP 109	1 May 1943
AN 5	*Keokuk*	CM 8	25 Aug 1942

YN No.	No.	Name	Builder	Laid Down	Launched	In Service
YN 1	AN 6	*Aloe*	Lake Wash.	11 Oct 1940	11 Jan 1941	11 Jun 1941
YN 2	AN 7	*Ash*	Lake Wash.	31 Oct 1940	15 Feb 1941	1 Jul 1941

Figure 10.36: *Nutmeg* (AN 33), a net tender, on 21 Feb 1944 in Boston Harbor.

YN 3	AN 8	*Boxwood*	Lake Wash.	19 Nov 1940	8 Mar 1941	25 Jul 1941
	ex–*Birch* (16 Oct 1940)					
YN 4	AN 9	*Butternut*	Lake Wash.	11 Mar 1941	10 May 1941	3 Sep 1941
YN 5	AN 10	*Catalpa*	Comm.	24 Oct 1940	22 Feb 1941	20 Jun 1941
YN 6	AN 11	*Chestnut*	Comm.	5 Nov 1940	15 Mar 1941	25 Jul 1941
YN 7	AN 12	*Cinchona*	Comm.	24 Feb 1941	2 Jul 1941	15 Aug 1941
YN 8	AN 13	*Buckeye*	Comm.	17 Mar 1941	26 Jul 1941	5 Sep 1941
	ex–*Cottonwood* (16 Oct 1940)					
YN 9	AN 14	*Buckthorn*	General Eng.	5 Dec 1940	27 Mar 1941	21 Aug 1941
	ex–*Dogwood* (16 Oct 1940)					
YN 10	AN 15	*Ebony*	General Eng.	12 Dec 1940	3 Jun 1941	16 Sep 1941
YN 11	AN 16	*Eucalyptus*	General Eng.	31 Dec 1940	3 Jul 1941	9 Oct 1941
YN12	AN 17	*Chinquapin*	General Eng.	29 Mar 1941	15 Jul 1941	29 Oct 1941
	ex–*Fir* (16 Oct 1940)					
YN 13	AN 18	*Gum Tree*	Marietta	19 Sep 1940	20 Mar 1941	16 Sep 1941
YN 14	AN 19	*Holly*	Marietta	1 Oct 1940	17 Apr 1941	11 Oct 1941
YN 15	AN 20	*Elder*	Marietta	2 Oct 1940	19 Jun 1941	12 Nov 1941
	ex–*Juniper* (2 Oct 1940)					
YN 16	AN 21	*Larch*	Marietta	18 Oct 1940	2 Jul 1941	13 Dec 1941
YN 17	AN 22	*Locust*	Amer. Cleve.	18 Oct 1940	1 Feb 1941	13 Jul 1941
YN 18	AN 23	*Mahogany*	Amer. Cleve.	18 Oct 1940	13 Feb 1941	4 Sep 1941
YN 19	AN 24	*Mango*	Amer. Cleve.	18 Oct 1940	22 Feb 1941	18 Sep 1941
YN 20	AN 25	*Hackberry*	Amer. Cleve.	18 Oct 1940	6 Mar 1941	27 Oct 1941
	ex–*Maple* (28 Oct 1940)					
YN 21	AN 26	*Mimosa*	Amer. Cleve.	18 Oct 1940	15 Mar 1941	28 Oct 1941
YN 22	AN 27	*Mulberry*	Amer. Cleve.	18 Oct 1940	26 Mar 1941	1 Nov 1941
YN 23	AN 28	*Palm*	Amer. Lorain	18 Oct 1940	8 Feb 1941	21 Aug 1941
YN 24	AN 29	*Hazel*	Amer. Lorain	18 Oct 1940	15 Feb 1941	27 Oct 1941
	ex–*Poplar* (28 Oct 1940)					
YN 25	AN 30	*Redwood*	Amer. Lorain	18 Oct 1940	22 Feb 1941	12 Dec 1941
YN 26	AN 31	*Rosewood*	Amer. Lorain	18 Oct 1940	1 Apr 1941	13 Sep 1941
YN 27	AN 32	*Sandalwood*	Amer. Lorain	18 Oct 1940	6 Mar 1941	25 Oct 1941
YN 28	AN 33	*Nutmeg*	Amer. Lorain	18 Oct 1940	13 Mar 1941	30 Oct 1941
	ex–*Sycamore* (26 Jun 1940)					
YN 29	AN 34	*Teaberry*	Mathis	25 Oct 1940	24 May 1941	16 Mar 1942
YN 30	AN 35	*Teak*	Mathis	25 Oct 1940	7 Jul 1941	7 May 1942
YN 31	AN 36	*Pepperwood*	Mathis	25 Oct 1940	25 Aug 1941	8 Jun 1942
	ex–*Walnut* (16 Oct 1940)					
YN 32	AN 37	*Yew*	Mathis	22 May 1941	4 Oct 1941	1 Jul 1942

Displacement	560 tons, 850 f/l
Dimensions	163'2" (oa); 146' (wl) x 30'6" x 11'8"
Machinery	1 screw; diesel-electric; SHP 800; 12.5 knots
Complement	48
Armament	1–3"/50, 3 twin 20mm or 4–20mm guns

Notes: Ordered and completed as YN 1–32. Reclassified 20 Jan 1944 but most were placed in commission 1942. Some were renamed in 1940 to avoid confusion with Coast Guard lighthouse tenders.

Service Records:

AN 6 *Aloe* Decomm 3 Aug 1946. †
3* Solomons, Guam, Okinawa.

AN 7 *Ash* Decomm 13 Dec 1946. †
1* Pearl Harbor.

AN 8 *Boxwood* Decomm 13 Nov 1946. †

AN 9 *Butternut* †
1* Solomons.

AN 10 *Catalpa* Decomm 21 Oct 1946. †
2* Gilbert Is., Palau.

AN 11 *Chestnut* Decomm 7 Sep 1946. †

AN 12 *Cinchona* Decomm 6 Nov 1946. †
3* Pearl Harbor, Saipan, Tinian.

AN 13 *Buckeye* Ran aground in Subic Bay, 17 Jul 1946. Decomm 4 Mar 1947. †

AN 14 *Buckthorn* Decomm 20 Aug 1947. †

AN 15 *Ebony* Decomm 23 Mar 1946. †

AN 16 *Eucalyptus* Decomm 6 Mar 1946. †

AN 17 *Chinquapin* Decomm 6 Mar 1946. Sold 18 Nov 1946.
3* Kwajalein, Eniwetok, Saipan, Okinawa.

AN 18 *Gum Tree* Decomm 20 Jun 1946. Stricken 7 Feb 1947.
Later history: Merchant *Falcon*, renamed *Zaparita* 1948. Wrecked in Lake Maracaibo, Venezuela, Jan 1967.

AN 19 *Holly* Decomm 7 Jun 1946. †
1*Guam.

AN 20 *Elder* †
1* Gilbert Is.

AN 21 *Larch* Decomm 28 Jun 1946. Stricken 5 Mar 1947. To Turkey 10 May 1948.
Later history: Renamed *AG-4.* R 1996.

AN 22 *Locust* Decomm 8 Jul 1946. †
1* Solomons.

AN 23 *Mahogany* Went aground in typhoon at Okinawa, 14 Sep 1945. Destroyed at Guam, 19 Apr 1946.
1* Okinawa.

AN 24 *Mango* Decomm 4 Apr 1947. †
1* Balikpapan.
AN 25 *Hackberry* Decomm 12 Dec 1944 and trfd to France 13 Nov 1944.
1* Southern France.
Later history: Renamed *Araignée.* R 1977.
AN 26 *Mimosa* Decomm 27 Sep 1946. †
2* Saipan, Tinian.
AN 27 *Mulberry* †
AN 28 *Palm* Decomm 1 Jan 1947. †
AN 29 *Hazel* †
AN 30 *Redwood* Decomm 6 Jun 1947. †
AN 31 *Rosewood* Decomm 10 Jun 1946. †
AN 32 *Sandalwood* Decomm 13 Aug 1946. †
AN 33 *Nutmeg* Decomm Jan 1947. †
AN 34 *Teaberry* Decomm 19 Dec 1946. †
AN 35 *Teak* Decomm 30 Aug 1946. †
AN 36 *Pepperwood* Decomm and trfd to France, 14 Dec 1944.
1* Southern France.
Later history: Renamed *Tarentule.* R 1972.
AN 37 *Yew* Decomm 30 Nov 1944 and trfd to France.
Later history: Renamed *Scorpion.* R 1975.

YN No.	No.	Name	Builder	Laid Down	Launched	Comm.
YN 57	AN 38	*Ailanthus*	Everett	17 Nov 1942	20 May 1943	2 Dec 1943
YN 58	AN 39	*Bitterbush*	Everett	30 Nov 1942	30 Jun 1943	15 Jan 1944
	ex–*Almond* (3 Apr 1943)					
YN 59	AN 40	*Anaqua*	Everett	16 Dec 1942	16 Aug 1943	21 Feb 1944
YN 60	AN 41	*Baretta*	Everett	19 Dec 1942	9 Oct 1943	18 Mar 1944
YN 61	AN 42	*Cliffrose*	Everett	25 May 1943	27 Nov 1943	30 Apr 1944
YN 62	AN 43	*Satinleaf*	Everett	5 Jul 1943	15 Feb 1944	8 Apr 1944
YN 63	AN 44	*Corkwood*	Everett	18 Aug 1943	29 Mar 1944	16 May 1944
YN 64	AN 45	*Cornel*	Everett	9 Oct 1943	21 Apr 1944	6 Jun 1944
YN 65	AN 46	*Mastic*	Everett	27 Nov 1943	19 May 1944	4 Jul 1944
	ex–*Gingko* (17 Apr 1943)					
YN 66	AN 47	*Canotia*	Everett	16 Feb 1944	4 Jul 1944	31 Jul 1944
YN 67	AN 48	*Lancewood*	Pollock	15 Sep 1942	2 May 1943	18 Oct 1943
	ex–*Ironwood* (3 Apr 1943)					
YN 68	AN 49	*Papaya*	Pollock	2 Nov 1942	23 May 1943	1 Dec 1943
YN 69	AN 50	*Cinnamon*	Pollock	6 Nov 1942	6 Jun 1943	10 Jan 1944
	ex–*Royal Palm* (7 Dec 1943)					
YN 70	AN 51	*Silverbell*	Pollock	7 Nov 1942	19 Jun 1943	16 Feb 1944
YN 71	AN 52	*Snowbell*	Pollock	3 May 1943	14 Sep 1943	16 Mar 1944
YN 72	AN 53	*Spicewood*	Pollock	25 May 1943	6 Dec 1943	7 Apr 1944
YN 73	AN 54	*Manchineel*	Pollock	8 Jun 1943	1 Jan 1944	26 Apr 1944
	ex–*Sumac* (3 Apr 1943)					
YN 74	AN 55	*Torchwood*	Pollock	22 Jun 1943	19 Feb 1944	12 May 1944
YN 75	AN 56	*Winterberry*	Pollock	17 Sep 1943	22 Mar 1944	30 May 1944
	ex–*Tupelo* (3 Apr 1943)					
YN 76	AN 57	*Viburnum*	Pollock	9 Dec 1943	26 Apr 1944	27 Jun 1944
YN 77	AN 58	*Abele*	Barbour	8 Jan 1943	15 Jul 1943	2 Jun 1944
YN 78	AN 59	*Terebinth*	Barbour	24 Mar 1943	19 Aug 1943	5 Aug 1944
	ex–*Balm* (7 Dec 1943)					
YN 79	AN 73	—	Barbour	5 Aug 1943	11 Apr 1944	*14 Oct 1944*
YN 80	AN 74	*Boxelder*	Barbour	14 Sep 1943	20 Jul 1944	*21 Dec 1944*
YN 81	AN 60	*Catclaw*	Snow	24 Sep 1942	22 May 1943	14 Jan 1944
YN 82	AN 61	*Chinaberry*	Snow	24 Sep 1942	19 Jul 1943	12 Mar 1944
YN 83	AN 62	*Hoptree*	Snow	24 Sep 1942	14 Oct 1943	18 May 1944
YN 84	AN 63	*Whitewood*	Snow	24 Oct 1942	21 Apr 1944	17 Jul 1944
YN 85	AN 64	*Palo Blanco*	Snow	22 May 1943	17 Jun 1944	*25 Sep 1944* (as ATA)
YN 86	AN 65	*Paloverde*	Snow	19 Jul 1943	2 Sep 1944	*17 Dec 1944* (as ATA)
YN 87	AN 66	*Pinon*	AC&F	9 Mar 1943	10 Jan 1944	31 Mar 1944
YN 88	AN 75		AC&F	1 Apr 1943	8 Mar 1944	*3 Jun 1944*
YN 89	AN 76	*Satinwood*	AC&F	1 May 1943	23 May 1944	*5 Aug 1944*
YN 90	AN 77	*Seagrape*	AC&F	20 May 1943	9 Aug 1944	*30 Sep 1944*
YN 91	AN 67	*Shellbark*	Canulette	15 Jan 1943	31 Oct 1943	12 Apr 1944
YN 92	AN 68	*Silverleaf*	Canulette	3 Feb 1943	11 Dec 1943	26 May 1944
YN 93	AN 69	*Stagbush*	Canulette	9 Feb 1943	29 Jan 1944	30 Aug 1944
YN 94	AN 70	*Allthorn*	AC&F	31 Oct 1943	27 May 1944	*30 Oct 1944* (as ATA)
YN 95	AN 71	*Tesota*	AC&F	11 Dec 1943	29 Jul 1944	*16 Jan 1945* (as ATA)
YN 96	AN 72	*Yaupon*	AC&F	29 Jan 1944	16 Sep 1944	*10 Mar 1945* (as ATA)

Figure 10.37: *Hoptree* (AN 62), an *Ailanthus*-class net tender, at Mare Island, 12 Dec 1944.

Displacement	1,100 tons, 1,275 tons f/l
Dimensions	194'6" (oa); 169'2" (wl) x 37' x 13'6"
Machinery	1 screw; diesel-electric; SHP 1,200; 121 knots
Complement	56
Armament	1–3"/50, 4 twin 20mm guns

Notes: Wood hulls. Rec YN to AN 20 Jan 1944 and placed in commission. Horns on AN 63 *Whitewood* removed 1947.

Service Records:

AN 38 *Ailanthus* Went aground and lost on Pleasant I., Alaska, 26 Feb 1944.
AN 39 *Bitterbush* Decomm 4 Jan 1946.
1* Iwo Jima.
Later history: Merchant *Ciudad Bolivar.* Destroyed by fire south of Puerto Rico, 27 May 1954.
AN 40 *Anaqua* Damaged in storm off Dutch Harbor, 16 Oct 1944. Again damaged in storm off coast of Oregon, 5 Feb 1945. Decomm 7 Feb 1946. Stricken 26 Feb 1946, sold 6 Mar 1946.
Later history: Merchant *Anaqua.*

AN 41 *Baretta* Decomm 4 Apr 1946.
1* Palau.
Later history: Merchant *Baretta.* Went aground off Punta Gallines, Colombia, 5 Sep 1968. Scuttled off Curacao, 13 Feb 1972.

AN 42 *Cliffrose* Went aground in typhoon at Okinawa, 9 Oct 1945. Decomm 7 Jan 1947. Sold to China 10 Jan 1947.
2* Palau, Okinawa.

AN 43 *Satinleaf* Decomm 4 Apr 1946. Stricken 8 May 1946, sold 7 May 1947.
Later history: Merchant *Rocky River* 1949, renamed *Foundation Josephine II* 1952, *North Star IV* 1960. Lost by grounding in St. James Bay, Quebec, 14 Aug 1961.

AN 44 *Corkwood* Decomm 7 Mar 1946. Sold 18 Jun 1947. FFU.
1* Okinawa.

AN 45 *Cornel* Decomm 15 Feb 1946. Sold 1947.
Later history: Merchant *Maria Ines,* renamed *Sea Pearl* 1956. Burned off Wewak, New Guinea, 3 Jun 1957.

AN 46 *Mastic* Decomm 1 Mar 1946. Stricken 28 Mar 1946, sold 6 Jun 1947.
Later history: Merchant *Arctic Maid.* Scuttled off coast of Ecuador, 27 Jul 1975.

AN 47 *Canotia* Decomm 18 Feb 1946. Sold 21 Apr 1947. FFU.

AN 48 *Lancewood* Decomm 11 Feb 1946. Sold 3 May 1947.
1* Iwo Jima.
Later history: Merchant *Atiette,* renamed *Commandant Charcot* 1947.

AN 49 *Papaya* Decomm 31 Jan 1946. Stricken 25 Feb 1946, sold 9 Apr 1947.
2* Saipan, Tinian
Later history: Merchant *Pacific Reefer* 1950, renamed *Irma Catalina* 1956, *Mayon I* 1959, *Maigu's Luck* 1959. Destroyed by fire off Colombia 11 Feb 1964.

AN 50 *Cinnamon* Decomm 25 Mar 1947, sold to China.
1* Mindanao Ldgs.

AN 51 *Silverbell* Sold to China, 10 Jan 1947 as AGL.
1* Leyte.

AN 52 *Snowbell* Small craft training ship 1944. Collided with USS *Chinquapin* in typhoon and went aground at Okinawa, 9 Oct 1945. Decomm 5 Dec and stricken 19 Dec 1945. Blown up 14 Jan 1946.
1* Okinawa.

AN 53 *Spicewood* Decomm 20 Feb 1946. Stricken 12 Mar 1946, sold 18 Apr 1947.
1* Okinawa.
Later history: Merchant *Spicewood.* Burned and sank at Talara, Peru, 29 Jun 1961.

AN 54 *Manchineel* Decomm 11 Mar 1946. Stricken 12 Apr 1946, sold 18 Jun 1947.
Later history: Merchant *Marilyn.*

AN 55 *Torchwood* Decomm 26 Oct 1946 and trfd to China Maritime Customs Service.

AN 56 *Winterberry* Decomm 15 Feb 1946. Stricken 26 Feb 1946, sold 31 Mar 1947.
1* Okinawa.
Later history: Merchant *Trojan,* renamed *Atlantic Reefer* 1950, *Puelche* 1970, *Hawaii* 1972.

AN 57 *Viburnum* Damaged by mine at Ulithi, Micronesia, 28 Oct 1944 (2 killed). Decomm 12 Jul 1945, not repaired. Stricken 21 Jan 1946. BU 1947.

AN 58 *Abele* Decomm 1 Mar 1946. Stricken 28 Mar 1946.
2* Iwo Jima, Okinawa.
Later history: Merchant *Abele,* renamed *Superior Straits* 1954. Converted to barge 1970.

AN 59 *Terebinth* Decomm 31 Jan 1946. Stricken 26 Feb 1946, sold 23 Apr 1947.
1* Okinawa.
Later history: Merchant *Caribbean.*

AN 60 *Catclaw* Decomm 19 Apr 1946, sold to China.

AN 61 *Chinaberry* Decomm 26 Mar 1946. Stricken 5 Mar 1947, sold 27 Feb 1950. FFU

AN 62 *Hoptree* Decomm 1 Mar 1946. Sold 23 Apr 1947.
Later history: Merchant *Hop Tree.* BU 1954.

AN 63 *Whitewood* Damaged by fire at Boston, 20 May 1946. Rec **AG 129**, 14 Jan 1947. †

AN 64 *Palo Blanco* Rec **ATA 214**, 12 Aug 1944, name canceled. Decomm Sep 1945. Sold 30 Apr 1947. FFU.

AN 65 *Paloverde* Rec **ATA 215**, 12 Aug 1944, name canceled. Stricken 22 Dec 1948, sold 8 Feb 1949.
Later history: Loaned to Finn Ronne Antarctic expedition 1947 as merchant *Port of Beaumont,* renamed *Arctic Sealer* 1949.
Foundered off Canada Head, Newfoundland, 15 Apr 1963.

AN 66 *Pinon* Decomm 5 Mar 1946. Stricken 20 Mar 1946, sold 16 Apr 1947.
Later history: Merchant *Alaska Reefer.* Burned and sank off Port Townsend, Wash., 28 Aug 1961.

AN 67 *Shellbark* Decomm 19 Apr 1946 and sold to China. Stricken 1 May 1946.

AN 68 *Silverleaf* Decomm 18 Apr 1946. Stricken 5 Jun 1946, sold 31 Mar 1947; BU San Diego.
1* Iwo Jima.

AN 69 *Stagbush* Decomm 26 Mar 1946. Stricken 21 May 1946, sold 3 May 1947.
1* Okinawa.
Later history: Merchant *Anna Lucia,* renamed *Omar Babun* 1953. Went aground near Cape Hatteras, 13 May 1954, refloated. Burned at Norfolk, Va., 16 Oct 1954.

AN 70 *Allthorn* Rec **ATA 216**, 1 Aug 1944, name canceled. Sold 4 Jan 1947.
Later history: Merchant *Karna Gay,* renamed *El Sol.* BU 1968.

AN 71 *Tesota* Rec **ATA 217**, 1 Aug 1944, name canceled. Decomm 7 May 1946. Stricken 21 May 1946, sold 26 Mar 1947.
Later history: Merchant *Reina del Mar.* Burned and sank off San Martin I., Mexico, 17 Feb 1949.

AN 72 *Yaupon* Rec **ATA 218**, 1 Aug 1944, name canceled. Stricken 17 Apr 1946, sold 3 Jan 1947. FFU.

AN 73 To UK 14 Oct 1944, renamed HMS *Precept.* Returned 4 Jan 1946. Stricken 28 Mar 1946, sold 21 Mar 1947. FFU.

AN 74 *Boxelder* To UK 21 Dec 1944, renamed HMS *Precise.* Returned 14 Dec 1945. Stricken 26 Mar 1946, sold 10 Apr 1947.
Later history: Merchant *Precise.* Foundered 40 miles southeast of Puerto Cabezas, 13 Oct 1958.

AN 75 To UK 3 Jun 1944, renamed HMS *Prefect.* Returned 28 Dec 1945. Stricken 28 Mar 1946, sold 3 Apr 1947.
Later history: Merchant *Arctic Prowler,* renamed *North Star VI* 1962.

AN 76 *Satinwood* To UK 5 Aug 1944, renamed HMS *Pretext.* Returned 8 Jan 1946. Stricken 28 Mar 1946, sold 20 Jul 1947.
Later history: Merchant *John Biscoe* 1948, renamed HMNZS *Endeavour* 1956, merchant *Arctic Endeavour* 1962.
Foundered at moorings at Catalina, Newfoundland, 11 Nov 1982 and later scuttled at sea.

AN 77 *Seagrape* To UK 30 Sep 1944 renamed HMS *Preventer.* Returned 10 Jan 1946. Stricken 28 Mar 1946, sold 1 Apr 1947.
Later history: Merchant *Preventer,* renamed *Electron* 1952. Burned and sank northeast of Port Limon, Costa Rica, 28 Aug 1970.

YN	No.	No.	Name	Builder	Laid Down	Launched	Comm.
YN	97	AN 78	*Cohoes*	Commercial	15 Jun 1944	29 Nov 1944	23 Mar 1945
YN	98	AN 79	*Etlah*	Commercial	30 Jun 1944	16 Dec 1944	16 Apr 1945
YN	99	AN 80	*Suncock*	Commercial	30 Nov 1944	16 Feb 1945	5 May 1945
YN	100	AN 81	*Manayunk*	Commercial	18 Dec 1944	30 Mar 1945	25 May 1945
YN	101	AN 82	*Marietta*	Commercial	17 Feb 1945	27 Apr 1945	22 Jun 1945
YN	102	AN 83	*Nahant*	Commercial	31 Mar 1945	30 Jun 1945	24 Aug 1945
YN	103–8			Commercial	—	—	—
YN	109	AN 84	*Naubuc*	Marine Iron	31 Dec 1943	15 Apr 1944	15 Mar 1945
YN	110	AN 85	*Oneota*	Marine Iron	9 Feb 1944	27 May 1944	12 Mar 1945
YN	111	AN 86	*Passaconaway*	Marine Iron	15 Apr 1944	30 Jun 1944	27 Apr 1945
YN	112		—	Marine Iron	—	—	—
YN	113	AN 87	*Passaic*	L. D. Smith	25 Apr 1944	29 Jun 1944	6 Mar 1945
YN	114	AN 88	*Shakamaxon*	L. D. Smith	30 Jun 1944	9 Sep 1944	5 Apr 1945
YN	115	AN 89	*Tonawanda*	L. D. Smith	12 Sep 1944	14 Nov 1944	9 May 1945
YN	116–18		—	L. D. Smith	—	—	—
YN	119	AN 90	*Tunxis*	Zenith	2 May 1944	18 Aug 1944	28 Mar 1945
YN	120	AN 91	*Waxsaw*	Zenith	31 May 1944	15 Sep 1944	6 May 1945
YN	121	AN 92	*Yazoo*	Zenith	6 Jul 1944	18 Oct 1944	31 May 1945
YN		122–28	—	Zenith	—	—	—

Displacement	775 tons
Dimensions	168'6" (oa); 146' (wl) x 33'10" x 10'10"
Machinery	1 screw; diesel-electric; SHP 1,200; 12.3 knots
Complement	46
Armament	1–3"/50, 4–20mm guns

Notes: Steel hulls. YN rec to AN, 20 Jan 1944. YN 103–8, 112, 116–18, 122–28 canceled 23 Oct 1943.

Service Records:

AN 78 *Cohoes*	Decomm 3 Sep 1947. †
AN 79 *Etlah*	Operation Crossroads. Decomm 14 Mar 1947. †
AN 80 *Suncock*	Operation Crossroads. Decomm 12 Jun 1947. †
AN 81 *Manayunk*	Decomm 19 Jul 1946. †
AN 82 *Marietta*	Decomm 19 Mar 1947. †
AN 83 *Nahant*	Decomm 31 Jul 1946. †
AN 84 *Naubuc*	Decomm 6 Sep 1946. †
AN 85 *Oneota*	Operation Crossroads . Decomm 6 Feb 1947. †
AN 86 *Passaconaway*	Decomm Dec 1946. †
AN 87 *Passaic*	Decomm Mar 1947. †
AN 88 *Shakamaxon*	Operation Crossroads. Decomm 21 Apr 1947. †
AN 89 *Tonawanda*	Decomm 9 Aug 1946. †
AN 90 *Tunxis*	Decomm 30 Jun 1946. †
AN 91 *Waxsaw*	†
AN 92 *Yazoo*	†

OILERS

Oilers were naval tankers used to carry oil fuel. Facilities were developed for replenishing ships while underway at sea, and dozens of oilers were required to refuel the carrier task forces during the Pacific war. Oilers were usually named for rivers.

Oilers on the Navy List, 1922

AO 1 *Kanawha* Out of comm 18 Dec 1929–5 Jun 1934. Sunk by aircraft bombs off Tulagi, 7 Apr 1943 (19 killed).
1* Solomons.

AO 2 *Maumee* Out of comm 9 Jun 1922–2 Jun 1942. Converted to steam engines, 1942. Converted to minecraft tender and rec **AG 124**, 15 Aug 1945. Decomm 5 Nov 1946 and trfd to China.
Later history: Renamed *Omei* 1946. BU 1967.

AO 3 *Cuyama* Decomm 12 Apr 1946. FFU.
1* Okinawa.

AO 4 *Brazos* In collision with battleship *Maryland* off Pearl Harbor, 31 Jul 1940. Decomm 8 Feb 1946. FFU.
1* Okinawa.

AO 5 *Neches* Torpedoed and sunk by *I-72* west of Honolulu, 23 Jan 1942 (57 killed).

Figure 10.38: *Kanawha* (AO 1), 2 Jan 1943.

Figure 10.39: *Ramapo* (AO 12), an oiler, at Mare Island, 17 Apr 1943.

AO 6 *Pecos* China 1937–39. Sunk by Japanese aircraft south of Christmas I., 1 Mar 1942 (85 killed, including about 260 *Langley* survivors).
1* Philippines 1942.

AO 7 *Arethusa* Decomm 28 Jun 1922. Stricken 18 Mar 1927, sold 19 Jul 1927.
Later history: Storage hulk 1928.

AO 8 *Sara Thompson* Fuel storage, Cavite. Decomm 21 Jul 1933. Stricken 12 Dec 1933, sold 9 Aug 1934.
Later history: Merchant *Sara Thompson* 1934, renamed *Sarangani.*

AO 9 *Patoka* Tender for dirigible *Shenandoah* 1924; 125' mast added, removed about 1933. Out of comm 31 Aug 1933–10 Nov 1939. Rec **AV 6**, 11 Oct 1939. Rec **AO 9**, 19 Jun 1940. Converted to minecraft tender and rec **AG 125**, 15 Aug 1945. Decomm 1 Jul 1946. Stricken 31 Jul 1946, sold 15 Mar 1948; BU 1948.

AO 10 *Alameda* Damaged by explosion and fire off Cape Henry, Va., 19 Nov 1921. Decomm 29 Mar 1922. Sold 9 Aug 1922.
Later history: Merchant *Olean* 1923, renamed *Sweep* 1943. Reacquired as **IX 143**, 1944 (see p. 274).

AO 11 *Sapelo* Out of comm 14 Oct 1933–19 Aug 1940. Decomm 26 Oct 1945. Stricken 13 Nov 1945, sold 26 Jun 1946; BU.

AO 12 *Ramapo* In collision with m/v *Boren* at San Pedro, Calif., 1 Jan 1927. China 1937–39. Decomm 10 Jan 1946. Stricken 21 Jan 1946. BU Baltimore 1947.
1* Pearl Harbor.
Later history: Merchant *Ramapo* 1947. BU 1953 Vado, Italy.

AO 13 *Trinity* Out of comm 22 Dec 1922–21 Jun 1938. Decomm 28 May 1946. Stricken 3 Jul 1946, sold 5 Sep 1946.
1* Philippines 1942.
Later history: Merchant *Trinity* 1947, renamed *Seabeaver* 1951, *Asyneti* 1953. BU 1954 Briton Ferry, Wales.

AO 14 *Robert L. Barnes* Ex-AK 11. Rec **AG 27**, 1 Jul 1938.

AO 15 *Kaweah* Out of comm 15 Aug 1922–16 Dec 1940. Decomm 16 Nov 1945. BU Baltimore 1947.

AO 16 *Laramie* Out of comm 19 Jun 1922–26 Jun 1940. Torpedoed by *U-165* in Strait of Belle Isle (convoy SG-6), 27 Aug 1942 (4 killed). Decomm 16 Nov 1945. BU 1947 Baltimore.

AO 17 *Mattole* First comm 16 Jun 1940. Decomm 25 Oct 1945. Stricken 13 Nov 1945. BU 1947 Baltimore.

AO 18 *Rapidan* Out of comm 22 Jun 1922–22 Jan 1940. Damaged by mine off Charleston, S.C., 11 Sep 1943.
Decomm 17 Sep 1946. Stricken 29 Oct 1946, sold 10 Sep 1947; BU.

AO 19 *Salinas* Out of comm 20 Jun 1922–12 Jun 1926. Torpedoed by *U-106* 700 miles east of Newfoundland (convoy ON-28), 30 Oct 1941. Decomm 16 Jan 1946. Stricken 26 Feb 1946.
Later history: Merchant *Salinas* 1947. BU 1960 Hamburg.

AO 20 *Sepulga* Out of comm 15 Apr 1922–5 Feb 1940. Decomm 1 Mar 1946. Stricken 20 Mar 1946. BU 1947 Terminal I.

AO 21 *Tippecanoe* First comm 6 Mar 1940. Decomm 6 Mar 1946. Stricken 12 Apr 1946. Sold 20 Nov 1946; BU 1947 Terminal I.

Capacity	55,000 to 70,000 bbl.
Armament	AO 2–4, 11–13, 15–21 2–5"/38, 4 twin 40mm, 4 twin 20 mm guns.

No.	Name	Builder	Laid Down	Launched	Comm.
AO 22	*Cimarron*	Sun	25 Apr 1938	7 Jan 1939	20 Mar 1939
AO 23	*Neosho*	Federal	22 Jun 1938	29 Apr 1939	7 Aug 1939
AO 24	*Platte*	Beth. Sp. Pt.	14 Sep 1938	8 Jul 1939	1 Dec 1939
AO 25	*Sabine* ex-*Esso Albany*	Beth. Sp. Pt.	18 Sep 1938	27 Apr 1940	5 Dec 1940
AO 26	*Salamonie* ex-*Esso Columbia*	Newport News	5 Feb 1940	18 Sep 1940	28 Apr 1941
AO 27	*Kaskaskia* ex-*Esso Richmond* (1940)	Newport News	16 Jan 1939	29 Sep 1939	29 Oct 1940
AO 28	*Sangamon* ex-*Esso Trenton* (1940)	Federal	13 Mar 1939	4 Nov 1939	23 Oct 1940
AO 29	*Santee* ex-*Seakay* (1940)	Sun	31 May 1938	4 Mar 1939	30 Oct 1940
AO 30	*Chemung* ex-*Esso Annapolis* (1941)	Beth. Sp. Pt.	20 Dec 1938	9 Sep 1939	3 Jul 1941
AO 31	*Chenango* ex-*Esso New Orleans* (1941)	Sun	10 Jul 1938	1 Apr 1939	20 Jun 1941
AO 32	*Guadalupe*	Newport News	8 May 1939	26 Jan 1940	19 Jun 1941
AO 33	*Suwannee* ex-*Markay* (1941)	Federal	3 Jun 1938	4 Mar 1939	16 Jul 1941

Figure 10.40: *Cimarron* (AO 22), 28 Jan 1944, was one of a few oilers to mount four 5" guns with shields. Type T3–S2–A.

Displacement	7,470 tons, 25,440 tons f/l
Dimensions	553' (oa); 525' (wl) x 75' x 32'4"
Machinery	2 screws; Beth GT (AO 51–64, 97–100), Curtis GT (AO 30), GE GT (AO 28, AO33), NN GT (AO 27, AO 32), Parsons GT (AO 24–25), West. GT (AO 22, AO 29, AO 31), 4 B&W boilers (AO 22, AO 28–29, AO 31, AO 33), 4 FW boilers (AO 25, AO 27, AO 30, AO 32, 51–64, 97–100); SHP 13,500; 18.3 knots
Endurance	23,900/15
Complement	303.
Armament	1–5"/38, 4–3"/50, 4 twin 40mm, 4 twin 20mm AA (AO 25, AO 30, AO 51–64); 1–5"/38, 3–3"/50, 6–40mm AA (AO 27, AO 32); 4–5"/38, 4 twin 40mm, 4 twin 20mm AA (AO 22, AO 24, AO 26, AO 28–29)

Notes: Type T3–S2–A. Capacity: 146,000 bbl. AO 28–29, AO 31, and AO 33 converted to escort carriers.

Service Records:

AO 22 *Cimarron* In collision with destroyer *Norman Scott*, southeast of Okinawa, 4 Apr 1945. Damaged by grounding, Okinawa, 19 May 1945. †
10* Gilbert Is., Kwajalein, Eniwetok, Marianas Raid 2/44, Palau-Yap Raids 3/44, Truk Raid 4/44, Saipan, 3rd Bonins Raid, Guam, Palau, Philippines Raids 9/44, Formosa Raids 1/45, Luzon Raids 1/45, China Coast Raids 1/45, Iwo Jima, Okinawa, Fleet Raids 1945, Raids on Japan 7–8/45. †

AO 23 *Neosho* Damaged by Japanese aircraft in Coral Sea, 7 Apr 1942 and sunk on 10 Apr by destroyer *Henley* (168 killed).
2* Pearl Harbor, Coral Sea.

AO 24 *Platte* †
11* Marshall-Gilberts Raids 1942, Gilbert Is., Kwajalein, Raid on Truk, Eniwetok, Marianas Raid 2/44, Hollandia, Truk Raid 4/44, Saipan, 3rd Bonins Raid, Guam, Tinian, Palau, Philippines Raids 9/44, Iwo Jima, Okinawa, Raids on Japan 7–8/45.

AO 25 *Sabine* In collision with destroyer *Shaw*, Hawaii, 21 Nov 1941. Went aground in typhoon at Okinawa, 9 Oct 1945. †
10* Marshall-Gilberts Raids 1942, Gilbert Is., Kwajalein, Raid on Truk, Eniwetok, Marianas Raid 2/44, Palau-Yap Raids 3/44, Hollandia, Truk Raid 4/44, Saipan, 3rd Bonins Raid, Guam, Palau, Philippines Raids 9/44, Leyte, Fleet Raids 1945, Okinawa, Raids on Japan 7–8/45.

AO 26 *Salamonie* In collision with transport *Uruguay* in convoy off Bermuda, 12 Feb 1943. †
2* Leyte, Lingayen.

AO 27 *Kaskaskia* Acquired 22 Oct 1940. †
9* Gilbert Is., Kwajalein, Raid on Truk, Eniwetok, Marianas Raid 2/44, Palau-Yap Raids 3/44, Saipan, 3rd Bonins Raid, Guam, Tinian, Palau, Luzon Raids 10/44, Fleet Raids 1945, Okinawa, Raids on Japan 7–8/45. Operation Crossroads.

AO 28 *Sangamon* Acquired 22 Oct 1940. Decomm and rec **ACV 26**, 25 Feb 1942.

AO 29 *Santee* Acquired 18 Oct 1940. Decomm and rec **ACV 29**, 25 Feb 1942.

AO 30 *Chemung* Acquired by USN 5 Jun 1941. Damaged in collision with destroyer *Ingraham* which sank off Nova Scotia, 22 Aug 1942. †
2* North Africa, Southern France.

AO 31 *Chenango* Acquired by USN 31 May 1941. Decomm and rec **ACV 28**, 25 Feb 1942.

AO 32 *Guadalupe* Acquired 1 Jun 1941. Damaged in collision with oiler *Nantahala* in Luzon Strait, 9 Jan 1945. †
13* Midway, Solomons, Gilbert Is., Raid on Truk, Eniwetok, Marianas Raid 2/44, Hollandia, Truk Raid 4/44, Saipan, 3rd Bonins Raid, Guam, Bonins-Yap Raids, Palau, Philippines Raids 9/44, Luzon Raids 10/44, Formosa Raids 1/45, Luzon Raids 1/45, China Coast Raids 1/45, Iwo Jima, Fleet Raids 1945.

AO 33 *Suwannee* Acquired 26 Jun 1941. Decomm and rec **ACV 27**, 25 Feb 1942.

Figure 10.41: *Mississinewa* (AO 59), 25 May 1944, a T3 tanker, was sunk in Ulithi Lagoon, Micronesia, by a manned torpedo.

No.	Name	Builder	Laid Down	Launched	Comm.
AO 51	*Ashtabula*	Beth. Sp. Pt.	1 Oct 1942	22 May 1943	7 Aug 1943
AO 52	*Cacapon*	Beth. Sp. Pt.	16 Nov 1942	12 Jun 1943	21 Sep 1943
AO 53	*Caliente*	Beth. Sp. Pt.	2 Jan 1943	25 Aug 1943	22 Oct 1943
AO 54	*Chikaskia*	Beth. Sp. Pt.	3 Feb 1943	2 Oct 1943	10 Nov 1943
AO 55	*Elokomin*	Beth. Sp. Pt.	9 Mar 1943	19 Oct 1943	30 Nov 1943
AO 56	*Aucilla*	Beth. Sp. Pt.	25 May 1943	20 Nov 1943	22 Dec 1943
AO 57	*Marias*	Beth. Sp. Pt.	15 Jun 1943	21 Dec 1943	12 Feb 1944
AO 58	*Manatee*	Beth. Sp. Pt.	28 Aug 1943	18 Feb 1944	6 Apr 1944
AO 59	*Mississinewa*	Beth. Sp. Pt.	5 Oct 1943	28 Mar 1944	18 May 1944
AO 60	*Nantahala*	Beth. Sp. Pt.	31 Oct 1943	29 Apr 1944	19 Jun 1944
AO 61	*Severn*	Beth. Sp. Pt.	24 Nov 1943	31 May 1944	19 Jul 1944
AO 62	*Taluga*	Beth. Sp. Pt.	23 Dec 1943	10 Jul 1944	25 Aug 1944
AO 63	*Chipola*	Beth. Sp. Pt.	3 May 1944	21 Oct 1944	30 Nov 1944
AO 64	*Tolovana*	Beth. Sp. Pt.	5 Jun 1944	6 Jan 1945	24 Feb 1945
AO 97	*Allagash*	Beth. Sp. Pt.	26 Oct 1944	14 Apr 1945	21 Aug 1945
AO 98	*Caloosahatchee*	Beth. Sp. Pt.	30 Nov 1944	2 Jun 1945	10 Oct 1945
AO 99	*Canisteo*	Beth. Sp. Pt.	11 Jan 1945	6 Jul 1945	3 Dec 1945
AO 100	*Chukawan*	Beth. Sp. Pt.	25 Jan 1945	28 Aug 1945	22 Jan 1946

Service Records:

AO 51 *Ashtabula* Damaged by aircraft torpedo, Leyte, 24 Oct 1944 (none killed). Damaged in collision with tender *Thornton*, southwest of Okinawa, 5 Apr 1945. Damaged in collision with destroyer *Bristol*, 5 Aug 1945.
8* Kwajalein, Saipan, Philippine Sea, Guam, Leyte, Fleet Raids 1945, Okinawa, Raids on Japan 7–8/45.

AO 52 *Cacapon* Ran aground on Shah Allum Reef, Persian Gulf, 24 Apr 1946. †
*4 Formosa Raids 1/45, China Coast Raids 1/45, Nansei Shoto Raid 1/45, Iwo Jima, Okinawa, Fleet Raids 1945, Raids on Japan 7–8/45.

AO 53 *Caliente* †
10* Kwajalein, Palau-Yap Raids 3/44, Hollandia, Truk Raid 4/44, Saipan, 3rd Bonins Raid, Guam, Tinian, Bonins-Yap Raids, Palau, Philippines Raids 9/44, N. Luzon–Formosa Raids 10/44, Luzon Raids 10/44, Surigao Strait, Formosa Raids 1/45, China Coast Raids 1/45, Nansei Shoto Raid 1/45, Raids on Japan 7–8/45.

AO 54 *Chikaskia* †
6* Kwajalein, Philippines Raids 9/44, Luzon Raids 10/44, Formosa Raids 1/45, China Coast Raids 1/45, Nansei Shoto Raid 1/45, Iwo Jima, Fleet Raids 1945. Operation Crossroads.

AO 55 *Elokomin* †

AO 56 *Aucilla* †
5* Luzon Raids 10/44, Luzon Raids 1/45, Formosa Raids 1/45, China Coast Raids 1/45, Iwo Jima, Fleet Raids 1945, Raids on Japan 7–8/45. Operation Crossroads.

AO 57 *Marias* †
8* Saipan, Guam, Tinian, Bonins-Yap Raids, Palau, Philippines Raids 9/44, Okinawa Raid 10/44, N. Luzon–Formosa Raids 10/44, Luzon Raids 10/44, Formosa Raids 1/45, China Coast Raids 1/45, Nansei Shoto Raid 1/45, Iwo Jima, Fleet Raids 1945, Okinawa, Raids on Japan 7–8/45.

AO 58 *Manatee* †
8* Saipan, 2nd Bonins Raid, Guam, Tinian, Bonins-Yap Raids, Palau, Philippines Raids 9/44, N. Luzon–Formosa Raids 10/44, Luzon Raids 10/44, Formosa Raids 1/45, China Coast Raids 1/45, Nansei Shoto Raid 1/45, Iwo Jima, Fleet Raids 1945, Raids on Japan 7–8/45.

AO 59 *Mississinewa* Sunk by Japanese manned torpedo (Kaiten) at Ulithi, Micronesia, 20 Nov 1944 (60 killed).
4* Bonins-Yap Raids, Palau, Philippines Raids 9/44, Okinawa Raid 10/44, N. Luzon–Formosa Raids 10/44.

AO 60 *Nantahala* Damaged in typhoon in Philippine Sea, 18 Dec 1944.
6* Philippines Raids 9/44, Luzon Raids 10/44, Luzon Raids 1/45, Formosa Raids 1/45, China Coast Raids 1/45, Iwo Jima, Fleet Raids 1945, Fleet Raids 1945, Raids on Japan 7–8/45. †

AO 61 *Severn* Converted to water tanker, 1945. Operation Crossroads. †
2* Leyte, Lingayen.

AO 62 *Taluga* Damaged by kamikaze, Okinawa, 16 Apr 1945. †
4* Formosa Raids 1/45, Luzon Raids 1/45, China Coast Raids 1/45, Iwo Jima, Fleet Raids 1945, Okinawa, Raids on Japan 7–8/45.

AO 63 *Chipola* †
3* Iwo Jima, Fleet Raids 1945, Raids on Japan 7–8/45.

AO 64 *Tolovana* †
1* Okinawa. Operation Crossroads.

AO 97 *Allagash* †

AO 98 *Caloosahatchee* Sank tug *Lone Wolf* (YTB 179) in collision at Newport, R.I., 10 Dec 1946. †

AO 99 *Canisteo* †

AO 100 *Chukawan* †

No.	Name	Builder	Laid Down	Launched	Comm.
AO 34	*Chicopee* ex–*Esso Trenton* (1941)	Sun	14 May 1941	6 Sep 1941	9 Feb 1942
AO 35	*Housatonic* ex–*Esso Albany* (1941)	Sun	2 Apr 1941	2 Aug 1941	19 Feb 1942

Displacement	5,375 tons, 22,325 tons f/l
Dimensions	520' (oa); 500' (wl) x 68' x 30'9"
Machinery	1 screw; GE GT; 2 B&W boilers; SHP 9,000; 18 knots
Complement	279.
Armament	1–5"/38, 4–3"/50, 4 twin 40mm, 4 twin 20mm AA guns

Note: Capacity: 131,600 bbl.

Service Records:

AO 34 *Chicopee* Decomm 14 Feb 1946. Sold 30 Jun 1946.
4* Formosa Raids 1/45, Luzon Raids 1/45, China Coast Raids 1/45, Nansei Shoto Raid 1/45, Iwo Jima, Fleet Raids 1945, Okinawa, Raids on Japan 7–8/45.
Later history: Merchant *Esso Chattanooga* 1947, renamed *San Francisco* 1962.

AO 35 *Housatonic* Acquired by USN 9 Jan 1942. Decomm 11 Mar 1946.
5* North Africa, Formosa Raids 1/45, Iwo Jima, Fleet Raids 1945, Raids on Japan 7–8/45.
Later history: Merchant *Esso Bethlehem* 1947, renamed *Los Angeles* 1962.

Figure 10.42: *Housatonic* (AO 35), 12 Sep 1942. This is an example of a nonstandard-type conversion.

No.	Name	Builder	Laid Down	Launched	Comm.
AO 36	*Kennebec* ex–*Corsicana*	Beth. Sp. Pt.	12 Aug 1940	19 Apr 1941	4 Feb 1942
AO 37	*Merrimack* ex–*Caddo*	Beth. Sp. Pt.	12 Sep 1940	1 Jul 1941	4 Feb 1942
AO 38	*Winooski* ex–*Calusa*	Beth. Sp. Pt.	23 Apr 1941	12 Nov 1941	27 Jan 1942
AO 39	*Kankakee* ex–*Colina*	Beth. Sp. Pt.	31 Jul 1941	24 Jan 1942	4 May 1942
AO 40	*Lackawanna* ex–*Conestoga*	Beth. Sp. Pt.	27 Dec 1941	16 May 1942	10 Jul 1942
AO 48	*Neosho* ex–*Catawba*	Beth. Sp. Pt.	8 Jul 1941	23 Dec 1941	16 Sep 1942

Displacement	6,013 tons, 21,580 tons f/l
Dimensions	501'5" (oa); 488'5" (wl) x 68' x 30'9"
Machinery	1 screw; West. GT; 2 FW boilers; SHP 12,000; 16.7 knots
Complement	240–280
Armament	1–5"/38, 4–3"/50, 4 twin 40mm, 4 twin 20mm AA guns

Note: Type T2–A. Capacity 134,000 bbl.

Service Records:

AO 36 *Kennebec* †
1* North Africa.

AO 37 *Merrimack* Damaged in collision with carrier *San Jacinto*, Iwo Jima, 27 Feb 1945. †
8* North Africa, Formosa Raids 1/45, Luzon Raids 1/45, Formosa Raids 1/45, China Coast Raids 1/45, Iwo Jima, Fleet Raids 1945, Okinawa, Raids on Japan 7–8/45.

AO 38 *Winooski* Torpedoed by *U-173* off Fedala, Morocco, 11 Nov 1942. Damaged in collision, off Cotabato, Mindanao, Philippines, 22 Apr 1945. Decomm 30 Apr 1946. Stricken 8 Oct 1946, sold 10 Mar 1947.
4* North Africa, Southern France, Lingayen, Mindanao Ldgs.
Later history: Merchant *Samuel L. Fuller* 1947, renamed *Seanymph* 1963, *Meracoulosa* 1964. BU 1965 Kaohsiung, Taiwan.

AO 39 *Kankakee* †
6* Palau-Yap Raids 3/44, Saipan, Philippine Sea, Formosa Raids 1/45, China Coast Raids 1/45, Nansei Shoto Raid 1/45, Iwo Jima, Fleet Raids 1945, Okinawa, Raids on Japan 7–8/45.

AO 40 *Lackawanna* USCG. Damaged in typhoon, Philippine Sea, 5 Jun 1945. Decomm 14 Feb 1946. Stricken 1946.
9* Gilbert Is., Kwajalein, Palau-Yap Raids 3/44, Hollandia, Truk Raid 4/44, Saipan, Philippine Sea, Guam, Bonins-Yap Raids, Palau, Philippines Raids 9/44, Luzon Raids 10/44, Fleet Raids 1945, Raids on Japan 7–8/45.
Later history: Merchant *Tatarrax*, renamed *Thomas A.* 1963, *Padre Island* 1965. BU 1967 Spain.

AO 48 *Neosho* Decomm 13 Dec 1945. Stricken 3 Jan 1946.
13* Attu, Gilbert Is., Kwajalein, Palau-Yap Raids 3/44, Truk Raid 4/44, Saipan, 2nd Bonins Raid, Guam, Tinian, Palau, Philippines Raids 9/44, Luzon Raids 10/44, Formosa Raids 1/45, Nansei Shoto Raid 1/45, Iwo Jima, Hollandia, Okinawa, Raids on Japan 7–8/45.
Later history: Merchant *Tascalusa* 1947. BU 1967 Hamburg.

No.	Name	Builder	Laid Down	Launched	Comm.
AO 41	*Mattaponi* LD as *Kalkay*	Sun	9 Sep 1941	17 Jan 1942	11 May 1942
AO 42	*Monongahela* LD as *Ellkay*	Sun	3 Jan 1942	30 May 1942	11 Sep 1942
AO 43	*Tappahannock* LD as *Jorkay*	Sun	24 Dec 1941	18 Apr 1942	22 Jun 1942
AO 44	*Patuxent* LD as *Emmkay*	Sun	5 Mar 1942	25 Jul 1942	22 Oct 1942

Figure 10.43: *Patuxent* (AO 44), a type T2 tanker, refueling the destroyer *Monssen.*

Figure 10.44: *Schuylkill* (AO 76), seen here on 24 Apr 1943, had a false funnel amidships to disguise her appearance.

No.	Name	Builder	Laid Down	Launched	Comm.
AO 47	*Neches* LD as *Aekay*	Sun	12 Jun 1941	11 Oct 1941	16 Sep 1942

Displacement	6,809 tons 22,325 f/l
Dimensions	520' (oa); 500' (wl) x 68' x 30'9"
Machinery	1 screw; West. GT (AO 42, AO 44: GE), 2 B&W boilers; SHP 12,800; 17.5 knots
Complement	242
Armament	1–5"/38, 4–3"/50, 4 twin 40mm, 4 twin 20mm AA guns

Notes: Type T2–A. Capacity: 135,000 bbl.

Service Records:

AO 41 *Mattaponi* †

AO 42 *Monongahela* †
10* Solomons, Hollandia, Truk Raid 4/44, Saipan, 2nd Bonins Raid, Guam, Tinian, Philippines Raids 9/44, Luzon Raids 10/44, Formosa Raids 1/45, China Coast Raids 1/45, Nansei Shoto Raid 1/45, Iwo Jima, Okinawa, Fleet Raids 1945.

AO 43 *Tappahannock* Damaged by aircraft bomb off Tulagi, 7 Apr 1943. †
9* Solomons, Gilbert Is., Kwajalein, Philippine Sea, Guam, Tinian, Bonins-Yap Raids, Palau, Philippines Raids 9/44, N. Luzon–Formosa Raids 10/44, Luzon Raids 10/44, Fleet Raids 1945, Okinawa, Raids on Japan 7–8/45.

AO 44 *Patuxent* Damaged by fire and explosion off Iwo Jima, 17 Feb 1945. Decomm 21 Feb 1946. Stricken 12 Mar 1946. †
8* Saipan, Guam, Tinian, Philippines Raids 9/44, Luzon Raids 10/44, Formosa Raids 1/45, China Coast Raids 1/45, Nansei Shoto Raid 1/45, Iwo Jima, Fleet Raids 1945, Okinawa, Raids on Japan 7–8/45.
Later history: Merchant *David D. Irwin* 1947, renamed *Fairwind* 1985. BU 1985 Mombasa.

AO 47 *Neches* Damaged by mine off San Pedro, Calif., 21 May 1943. †
9* Gilbert Is., Kwajalein, Raid on Truk, Eniwetok, Marianas Raid 2/44, Palau-Yap Raids 3/44, Truk Raid 4/44, Palau, Philippines Raids 9/44, Luzon Raids 10/44, Formosa Raids 1/45, Luzon Raids 1/45, China Coast Raids 1/45, Nansei Shoto Raid 1/45, Iwo Jima, Okinawa, Fleet Raids 1945, Raids on Japan 7–8/45. Tokyo Bay.

No.	Name	Builder	Laid Down	Launched	Comm.
AO 49	*Suamico* LD as *Harlem Heights*	Sun	27 Sep 1941	30 May 1942	10 Aug 1942
AO 50	*Tallulah* LD as *Valley Forge*	Sun	1 Dec 1941	25 Jun 1942	5 Sep 1942
AO 65	*Pecos* LD as *Corsicana*	Sun	20 Apr 1942	17 Aug 1942	5 Oct 1942
AO 67	*Cache* LD as *Stillwater*	Sun	25 May 1942	7 Sep 1942	3 Nov 1942
AO 73	*Millicoma* LD as *King's Mountain*	Sun	4 Aug 1942	21 Jan 1943	5 Mar 1943
AO 74	*Saranac* LD as *Cowpens*	Sun	27 Aug 1942	21 Dec 1942	22 Feb 1943
AO 75	*Saugatuck* LD as *Newtown*	Sun	20 Aug 1942	7 Dec 1942	19 Feb 1943
AO 76	*Schuylkill* LD as *Louisberg*	Sun	24 Sep 1942	16 Feb 1943	9 Apr 1943
AO 77	*Cossatot* LD as *Fort Necessity*	Sun	24 Oct 1942	28 Feb 1943	20 Apr 1943
AO 78	*Chepachet* LD as *Eutaw Springs*	Sun	1 Nov 1942	10 Mar 1943	27 Apr 1943
AO 79	*Cowanesque* LD as *Fort Duquesne*	Sun	23 Nov 1942	11 Mar 1943	1 May 1943

Displacement	5,782 tons, 22,380 tons f/l
Dimensions	523'6" (oa); 503' (wl) x 68' x 30'10"
Machinery	1 screw; GE T-E; 2 B&W boilers; SHP 6,000; 15.1 knots
Complement	220–250
Armament	1–5"/38, 4–3"/50, 2 twin 40mm, 4 twin 20mm AA guns

Notes: Type T2–SE-A1. Capacity: 140,000 bbl.

Service Records:

AO 49 *Suamico* Ran aground on reef off San Pedro Bay, Philippines, 13 Jun 1945. Decomm 20 Jan 1946. Damaged by fire at Richmond, Calif., 9 Mar 1946. Stricken. Oct 1946. †
8* Solomons, Gilbert Is., Kwajalein, Saipan, Leyte, Lingayen, Iwo Jima, Okinawa, Fleet Raids 1945.

AO 50 *Tallulah* Decomm 2 Apr 1946. Stricken 3 Oct 1946. †
7* Solomons, Gilbert Is., Kwajalein, Palau-Yap Raids 3/44, Saipan, Philippine Sea, Guam, Iwo Jima, Fleet Raids 1945, Okinawa.

AO 65 *Pecos* Damaged by aircraft bomb in Mangarin Bay, Mindoro, 4 Jan 1945. Decomm 14 Mar 1946. Stricken 23 Apr 1947. †
7* Gilbert Is., Kwajalein, Saipan, Guam, Tinian, Palau, Philippines Raids 9/44, Lingayen, Okinawa, Fleet Raids 1945.

AO 67 *Cache* Torpedoed by submarine *RO-37* off Espiritu Santo, 22 Jan 1944 (1 killed). Decomm 14 Jan 1946. Stricken Jun 1946. †
8* Saipan, Tinian, Guam, Palau, Philippines Raids 9/44, Luzon Raids 10/44, Luzon Raids 1/45, Formosa Raids 1/45, China Coast Raids 1/45, Nansei Shoto Raid 1/45, Iwo Jima, Fleet Raids 1945, Raids on Japan 7–8/45.

AO 73 *Millicoma* In collision with oiler *Schuylkill* off Palau, 12 Sep 1944. Damaged in typhoon in Philippine Sea, 5 Jun 1945. Decomm 21 Feb 1946. Stricken 13 Mar 1946. †
8* Kwajalein, Tinian, Palau, Philippines Raids 9/44, Luzon Raids 10/44, Luzon Raids 1/45, Formosa Raids 1/45, China Coast Raids 1/45, Luzon Raids 1/45, Nansei Shoto Raid 1/45, Iwo Jima, Fleet Raids 1945.

AO 74 *Saranac* Damaged by aircraft bomb off Guam, 18 Jun 1944 (9 killed). Decomm 19 Jul 1946. Converted to power plant 1948. Served Army at Inchon, Korea, 1951–53. Rec **YFP 9**, 1 Sep 1954. Stricken 26 Mar 1956, sold 4 Dec 1957.
5* Gilbert Is., Palau-Yap Raids 3/44, Saipan, Leyte, Okinawa, Fleet Raids 1945.
Later history: Merchant barge *Somerset*.

AO 75 *Saugatuck* Damaged by enemy aircraft off Saipan, 18 Jun 1944 (1 killed). Went aground in typhoon at Okinawa, 9 Oct 1945. Decomm 19 Mar 1946. Stricken Oct 1946. †
7* Saipan, Guam, Tinian, Bonins-Yap Raids, Palau, Philippines Raids 9/44, Formosa Raids 1/45, Luzon Raids 1/45, China Coast Raids 1/45, Nansei Shoto Raid 1/45, Iwo Jima, Fleet Raids 1945, Raids on Japan 7–8/45.

AO 76 *Schuylkill* Damaged in collision with oiler *Millicoma* off Palau, 10 Sep 1944. Decomm 14 Feb 1946. Stricken 1946. †
7* Gilbert Is., Saipan, Guam, Tinian, Palau, Philippines Raids 9/44, Luzon Raids 10/44, Lingayen, Iwo Jima.

AO 77 *Cossatot* Decomm 7 Mar 1946. Stricken 28 Oct 1946. †
2*Fleet Raids 1945, Okinawa, Raids on Japan 7–8/45.

AO 78 *Chepachet* Decomm 15 May 1946. Stricken 1946. †
2* Leyte, Balikpapan.

AO 79 *Cowanesque* Damaged by kamikaze in San Pedro Bay, Philippines, 2 Jan 1945 (2 killed). Decomm 30 Jan 1946. †
2* Southern France, Fleet Raids 1945.

No.	Name	Builder	Laid Down	Launched	Comm.
AO 68	*Chiwawa*	Beth. Sp. Pt.	26 Feb 1942	25 Jun 1942	24 Dec 1942
	LD as *Samoset*				
AO 69	*Enoree*	Beth. Sp. Pt.	8 Apr 1942	29 Aug 1942	23 Jan 1943
	LD as *Sachem*				
AO 70	*Escalante*	Beth. Sp. Pt.	20 May 1942	29 Sep 1942	30 Jan 1943
	LD as *Shabonee*				
AO 71	*Neshanic*	Beth. Sp. Pt.	11 Jun 1942	31 Oct 1942	20 Feb 1943
	LD as *Marquette*				
AO 72	*Niobrara*	Beth. Sp. Pt.	29 Jun 1942	28 Nov 1942	13 Mar 1943
	LD as *Citadel*				

Displacement	5,650 tons, 22,030 tons f/l
Dimensions	501'8" (oa); 487'6" (wl) x 68' x 30'8"
Machinery	1 screw; Beth. GT; 2 FW boilers; SHP 7,000; 15.3 knots

Figure 10.45: *Niobrara* (AO 72), seen here on 18 Apr 1944, had a derrick crane for loading landing craft. An attack transport is passing behind.

Complement	213
Armament	1–5"/38, 4–3"/50, 4 twin 40mm, 4 twin 20mm AA guns

Notes: Type T3–S-A1. Capacity: 134,000 bbl. AO 69 *Enoree* and AO 72 *Niobrara* had a large crane for loading landing craft.

Service Records:

AO 68 *Chiwawa* Decomm 6 May 1946. Sold 1 Feb 1947.
2* Convoy UGS-6, Southern France. Tokyo Bay.
Later history: Merchant *Chiwawa*, renamed *Walter A. Sterling* 1961, *William Clay Ford* 1985, *Lee A. Tregurtha* 1989.

AO 69 *Enoree* Operation Crossroads. Decomm 27 Mar 1947. †
6* Convoy UGS-36, Saipan, Philippine Sea, 2nd Bonins Raid, Guam, Tinian, Philippines Raids 9/44, Formosa Raids 1/45, China Coast Raids 1/45, Nansei Shoto Raid 1/45, Okinawa, Fleet Raids 1945.

AO 70 *Escalante* Damaged in collision with tender *Thornton*, Okinawa, 5 Apr 1945. Decomm 12 Dec 1945. Sold 27 Jun 1946.
4* Leyte, Formosa Raids 1/45, China Coast Raids 1/45, Nansei Shoto Raid 1/45, Iwo Jima, Okinawa, Fleet Raids 1945, Raids on Japan 7–8/45.
Later history: Merchant *George MacDonald*. Foundered 50 miles off Charleston, S.C., 30 Jun 1960.

AO 71 *Neshanic* Damaged by aircraft bomb off Saipan, 18 Jun 1944 (none dead). Decomm 19 Dec 1945. Stricken 8 Jan 1946.
9* Gilbert Is., Kwajalein, Palau-Yap Raids 3/44, Truk Raid 4/44, Saipan, Guam, Tinian, Hollandia, Iwo Jima, Fleet Raids 1945, Okinawa, Raids on Japan 7–8/45.
Later history: Merchant *Gulfoil* 1947, renamed *Pioneer Challenger* 1961, *Middletown* 1963.

AO 72 *Niobrara* Decomm 24 Sep 1946. †
4* Saipan, Palau, Formosa Raids 1/45, Nansei Shoto Raid 1/45, Okinawa, Fleet Raids 1945. Tokyo Bay.

No.	Name	Builder	Laid Down	Launched	Comm.
AO 80	*Escambia*	Marinship	7 Dec 1942	25 Apr 1943	28 Oct 1943
AO 81	*Kennebago*	Marinship	9 Jan 1943	9 May 1943	4 Dec 1943
AO 82	*Cahaba*	Marinship	20 Jan 1943	19 May 1943	14 Jan 1944
	ex–*Lackawaxen*				

AO 83	*Mascoma*	Marinship	31 Jan 1943	31 May 1943	3 Feb 1944
AO 84	*Ocklawaha*	Marinship	10 Feb 1943	9 Jun 1943	9 Mar 1944
AO 85	*Pamanset*	Marinship	30 Mar 1943	25 Jun 1943	30 Apr 1944
AO 86	*Ponaganset*	Marinship	27 Apr 1943	10 Jul 1943	15 May 1944
AO 87	*Sebec*	Marinship	20 May 1943	29 Jul 1943	29 Mar 1944
AO 88	*Tomahawk*	Marinship	1 Jun 1943	10 Aug 1943	16 Apr 1944
AO 91	*Pasig*	Marinship	18 May 1944	15 Jul 1944	11 Dec 1944 (as AW)
	LD as *Mission San Xavier*				
AO 92	*Abatan*	Marinship	9 Jun 1944	6 Aug 1944	29 Jan 1945 (as AW)
	LD as *Mission San Lorenzo*				
AO 93	*Soubarissen*	Marinship	19 Jun 1944	12 Aug 1944	5 Jan 1945
	LD as *Mission Santa Ana*				
AO 94	*Anacostia*	Marinship	16 Jul 1944	24 Sep 1944	25 Feb 1945
	LD as *Mission Alamo*				
AO 95	*Caney*	Marinship	27 Jul 1944	8 Oct 1944	23 Mar 1945
	LD as *Mission Los Angeles*				
AO 96	*Tamalpais*	Marinship	18 Sep 1944	29 Oct 1944	20 May 1945
	LD as *Mission San Francisco*				
AO 101	*Cohocton*	Marinship	9 Apr 1945	28 Jun 1945	25 Aug 1945
AO 102	*Concho*	Marinship	18 Apr 1945	25 Jul 1945	—
AO 103	*Conecuh*	Marinship	25 Apr 1945	10 Aug 1945	—
AO 104	*Contoocook*	Marinship	5 May 1945	—	—

Displacement	5,782 tons, 22,380 tons f/l
Dimensions	523'6" (oa); 503' (wl) x 68' x 30'10"
Machinery	1 screw; GE T-E; 2 B&W boilers; SHP 10,000
Complement	267
Armament	1–5"/38, 4–3"/50, 4 twin 40mm, 4 twin 20mm AA guns

Notes: Type T2–SE-A2. Capacity: 140,000 bbl. AO 90 *Pasig* and AO 91 *Abatan* had large derrick cranes.

Service Records:

AO 80 *Escambia* Decomm 20 Feb 1946. Stricken Jun 1946. †
5* Truk Raid 4/44, Hollandia, Philippines Raids 9/44, Okinawa, Fleet Raids 1945, Raids on Japan 7–8/45.

AO 81 *Kennebago* Decomm 19 Jul 1946. Stricken 24 May 1947. †
6* Saipan, Guam, Tinian, Palau, Philippines Raids 9/44, N. Luzon–Formosa Raids 10/44, Luzon Raids 10/44, Surigao Strait, Formosa Raids 1/45, Luzon Raids 1/45, China Coast Raids 1/45, Nansei Shoto Raid 1/45, Raids on Japan 7–8/45.

AO 82 *Cahaba* Decomm 15 May 1946. Stricken 8 May 1947. †
8* Hollandia, Truk Raid 4/44, Saipan, Philippine Sea, Guam, Tinian, Philippines Raids 9/44, Iwo Jima, Fleet Raids 1945, Okinawa, Raids on Japan 7–8/45.

AO 83 *Mascoma* Had constant boiler trouble. Decomm 17 Dec 1945. Stricken 8 Jan 1946. †
7* Kwajalein, Saipan, Guam, Tinian, Philippines Raids 9/44, Luzon Raids 10/44, Fleet Raids 1945, Raids on Japan 7–8/45. Tokyo Bay.

AO 84 *Ocklawaha* Converted to water tanker 1945. Decomm 19 Jul 1946. Stricken 23 Apr 1947. †
2* Saipan, Guam.

AO 85 *Pamanset* Decomm 18 Mar 1946. Stricken 28 Mar 1946. †
5* Palau, Philippines Raids 9/44, N. Luzon–Formosa Raids 10/44, Luzon Raids 10/44, Formosa Raids 1/45, China Coast Raids 1/45, Nansei Shoto Raid 1/45, Iwo Jima, Raids on Japan 7–8/45.

AO 86 *Ponaganset* Converted to water tanker 1945. Decomm 26 Apr 1946. Stricken 23 Apr 1947.
2* Palau, Okinawa.
Later history: Broke in two at pier at Boston, 9 Dec 1947. Stricken 30 Jun 1948. Sold Dec 1948; BU Baltimore.

AO 87 *Sebec* Decomm 7 Feb 1946. Stricken 26 Feb 1946. †
6* Tinian, Guam, Bonins-Yap Raids, Palau, Philippines Raids 9/44, N. Luzon–Formosa Raids 10/44, Luzon Raids 10/44, Okinawa, Fleet Raids 1945, Raids on Japan 7–8/45.

AO 88 *Tomahawk* Decomm 5 Jan 1946. Stricken 21 Jan 1946. †
6* Saipan, Guam, Palau, Philippines Raids 9/44, N. Luzon–Formosa Raids 10/44, Luzon Raids 10/44, Surigao Strait, Formosa Raids 1/45, Luzon Raids 1/45, China Coast Raids 1/45, Iwo Jima, Fleet Raids 1945.

AO 91 *Pasig* Rec **AW 3**, 22 Aug 1944. Decomm Feb 1947. †

AO 92 *Abatan* Rec **AW 4**, 22 Aug 1944. 1945–46 Pacific. Decomm 27 Jan 1947. †

AO 93 *Soubarissen* Converted to water tanker 1945. Decomm May 1946 and returned to WSA. †
1* Okinawa, Fleet Raids 1945.

AO 94 *Anacostia* Decomm 16 Apr 1946. Stricken 8 May 1946. †
1* Fleet Raids 1945.

AO 95 *Caney* Decomm 27 Feb 1946. Stricken 28 Feb 1946. †
2* Okinawa, Raids on Japan 7–8/45.

AO 96 *Tamalpais* Tokyo Bay. Decomm 21 Jun 1946. Stricken 8 Jul 1946. †

AO 101 *Cohocton* Decomm 14 Jun 1946. †

AO 102 *Concho* Canceled 18 Aug 1945.
Later history: Completed as merchant *Mission Santa Ana*.

AO 103 *Conecuh* Canceled 18 Aug 1945.
Later history: Completed as merchant *Mission Los Angeles*.

AO 104 *Contoocook* Canceled 18 Aug 1945.
Later history: Completed as merchant *Mission San Francisco*.

No.	Name	Builder	Launched	Acquired	Comm.
AO 45	*Big Horn*	Sun	2 May 1936	31 Mar 1942	16 Apr 1942
	ex-*Gulfdawn* (1942)				

Displacement	7,096 grt; 4,150 tons
Dimensions	441'6" (oa); 426'4" (wl) x 64'2" x 27'6"
Machinery	1 screw; geared turbines; 2 boilers; SHP 3,080; 12.5 knots
Complement	150
Armament	2–3"/50, 2–40mm

Note: Q-ship 1942–43.

Service Record:

AO 45 *Big Horn* North Atlantic 1942–43. To USCG 17 Jan 1944 as WAO 124. Reacquired 1 Feb 1945 as **IX 207**. USCG crew. Decomm 6 May 1946. Sold 22 Nov 1946.
Later history: Merchant *C. B. Watson* 1948, renamed *R. A. Hummel* 1955, *Trinity Trader* 1958, *Oswego Trader* 1959. BU 1960 Kure.

No.	Name	Builder	Launched	Acquired	Comm.
AO 46	*Victoria*	Union	9 Apr 1917	10 Apr 1942	15 Apr 1942
	ex-*George G. Henry* (1942)				

Displacement	6,936 grt, 4,650 tons, 15,150 tons f/l
Dimensions	453' (oa); 435' (wl) x 56' x 27'11"
Machinery	1 screw; VTE; 3 Union Scotch boilers; SHP 3,200; 10 knots
Complement	175
Armament	1–5"/38, 4–3"/50, 2 twin 40mm, 4–20mm guns

Notes: Acquired at Melbourne, Australia. Served in Navy in World War I as USS *George G. Henry*. Capacity: 78,000 bbl.

Service Record:

AO 46 *Victoria* Decomm 14 Dec 1945. Stricken 8 Jan 1946.
4* Lae Ldgs., Admiralty Is. Ldgs., Hollandia, Western New Guinea.
Later history: Merchant *George G. Henry*. BU 1949 Philadelphia.

No.	Name	Builder	Laid Down	Launched	Comm.
AO 66	*Atascosa*	Sun	30 Apr 1942	7 Sep 1942	9 Nov 1942
	LD as *Esso Columbia*				

Displacement	5,730 tons, 24,660 tons f/l
Dimensions	547'3" (oa); 521' (wl) x 70' x 31'
Machinery	1/screw; West. GT; 2 B&W boilers; SHP 8,200; 15.5 knots
Complement	282
Armament	1–5"/38, 4–3"/50, 4 twin 40mm, 4 twin 20mm guns.

Note: Capacity: 156,000 bbl.

Service Record:

AO 66 *Atascosa* Decomm 21 Jan 1946. Sold 1 Jul 1946.
7* Palau-Yap Raids 3/44, Philippines Raids 9/44, Luzon Raids 10/44, Luzon Raids 1/45, Formosa Raids 1/45, China Coast Raids 1/45, Nansei Shoto Raid 1/45, Iwo Jima, Fleet Raids 1945, Raids on Japan 7–8/45.
Later history: Merchant *Esso Syracuse*. BU 1961.

No.	Name	Builder	Launched	Acquired	Comm.
AO 89	*Pasig*	Newport News	24 Nov 1917	22 Jan 1943	22 Jan 1943
	ex–*J. C. Donnell* (1943)				

Displacement	7,165 tons
Dimensions	516'6" x 68' x (U)
Machinery	1 screw; VTE; IHP 3,000; 10.25 knots
Complement	(U)
Armament	1–4" 150

Notes: Intended for use as storage tanker, not used.

Service Record:

AO 89 *Pasig* Decomm 25 Sep 1943. Stricken 11 Oct/Dec 1943.
Later history: Merchant *J. C. Donnell*. BU 1947 Baltimore.

No.	Name	Reclassified	Date
AO 90	*Shikellamy*	Rec AOG 47	15 Jul 1943

No.	Name	Builder	Keel Laid	Launched	Comm.
AO 105	*Mispillion*	Sun	14 Feb 1945	10 Aug 1945	29 Dec 1945
AO 106	*Navasota*	Sun	22 Feb 1945	30 Aug 1945	27 Feb 1946
AO 107	*Passumpsic*	Sun	8 Mar 1945	31 Oct 1945	1 Apr 1946
AO 108	*Pawcatuck*	Sun	22 Mar 1945	19 Feb 1946	10 May 1946
AO 109	*Waccamaw*	Sun	28 Apr 1945	30 Mar 1946	25 Jun 1946

Displacement	7,236 tons, 25,400 tons f/l
Dimensions	553' (oa); 525' (wl) x 75' x 32'4"
Machinery	1 screw; West. GT; 4 B&W boilers; SHP 6,750; 18 knots
Complement	304
Armament	1–5"/38, 4–3"/50, 4 twin 40mm, 4 twin 20mm guns

Notes: Type T3–S2–A3. Capacity: 146,000 bbl.

Service Records:

105 †
106 †
107 †
108 †
109 †

No.	Name	Builder	Launched	Acquired	Comm.
AO 110	*Conecuh*	Schichau	12 Jun 1937	15 Jan 1946	2 May 1946
	ex–IX 301 (1 Oct 1946); ex–*Southmark*, ex–*Dithmarschen*				

Displacement	5,730 tons, 20,000 f/l
Dimensions	584' (oa) x 72' x 30'5"
Machinery	2 screws; GT; hp 21,500; 23 knots
Complement	280
Armament	8–40mm AA guns

Notes: German naval tanker acquired as a prize after World War II. Briefly used by United Kingdom as *Southmark* 1945–46. †

GASOLINE TANKERS

These were small tankers fitted to carry high-test aviation or PT-boat fuel.

No.	Name	Builder	Keel Laid	Launched	Comm.
AOG 1	*Patapsco*	Sea-Tac Tacoma	25 May 1942	18 Aug 1942	4 Feb 1943
AOG 2	*Kern*	Sea-Tac Tacoma	25 May 1942	7 Sep 1942	9 Mar 1943
	ex–*Rappahannock* (18 Jul 1942)				
AOG 3	*Rio Grande*	Sea-Tac Tacoma	30 Jun 1942	23 Sep 1942	10 Apr 1943
AOG 4	*Wabash*	Sea-Tac Tacoma	30 Jun 1942	28 Oct 1942	10 May 1943
AOG 5	*Susquehanna*	Sea-Tac Tacoma	9 Sep 1942	23 Nov 1942	7 Jun 1943
AOG 6	*Agawam*	Cargill	7 Sep 1942	6 May 1943	18 Dec 1943
AOG 7	*Elkhorn*	Cargill	7 Sep 1942	15 May 1943	12 Feb 1944
AOG 8	*Genesee*	Cargill	22 Sep 1942	23 Sep 1943	27 May 1944
AOG 9	*Kishwaukee*	Cargill	25 Sep 1942	24 Jul 1943	27 May 1944
AOG 10	*Nemasket*	Cargill	6 Oct 1942	20 Oct 1943	16 Jun 1944
AOG 11	*Tombigbee*	Cargill	23 Oct 1942	18 Nov 1943	13 Jul 1944
AOG 48	*Chehalis*	Cargill	6 Nov 1943	15 Apr 1944	5 Dec 1944
AOG 49	*Chestatee*	Cargill	9 Dec 1943	29 Apr 1944	14 Dec 1944
AOG 50	*Chewaucan*	Cargill	23 Dec 1943	22 Jul 1944	19 Feb 1945
AOG 51	*Maquoketa*	Cargill	14 Jan 1944	12 Aug 1944	27 Feb 1945
AOG 52	*Mattabesset*	Cargill	6 Jul 1944	11 Nov 1944	9 May 1945

Figure 10.46: *Genesee* (AOG 8), a *Patapsco*-class gasoline tanker.

AOG 53	*Namakagon*	Cargill	1 Aug 1944	4 Nov 1944	18 Jun 1945
AOG 54	*Natchaug*	Cargill	15 Aug 1944	6 Dec 1944	16 Jul 1945
AOG 55	*Nespelen*	Cargill	28 Aug 1944	10 Apr 1945	9 Aug 1945
AOG 56	*Noxubee*	Cargill	17 Nov 1944	3 Apr 1945	19 Oct 1945
AOG 57	*Pecatonica*	Cargill	6 Dec 1944	17 Mar 1945	28 Nov 1945
AOG 58	*Pinnebog*	Cargill	27 Dec 1944	12 May 1945	20 Oct 1945
AOG 59	*Wacissa*	Cargill	11 Nov 1944	16 Jun 1945	20 May 1946

Displacement	1,850 tons; 4,335 tons f/l
Dimensions	310'9" (oa); 292' (wl) x 48'6" x 15'8"
Machinery	2 screws; GM diesel; SHP 3,300; 14 knots
Complement	149
Armament	4–3"/50, 12–20mm AA guns

Note: Capacity: 8,200 to 11,300 bbl.

Service Records:

AOG 1 *Patapsco* Decomm 29 May 1946. †
1* Gilbert Is.

AOG 2 *Kern* Decomm 6 Aug 1946, to Army, renamed *Y-483*. †

AOG 3 *Rio Grande* Decomm 28 Jun 1946. †
1* Western New Guinea.

AOG 4 *Wabash* Damaged by collision, Okinawa, 12 Apr 1945. To Army, 29 Jul 1946 renamed *Y-484*. Stricken 23 Apr 1947. †
2* Iwo Jima, Okinawa.

AOG 5 *Susquehanna* Decomm 15 Aug 1946, to Army, renamed *Y-485*. Stricken 23 Apr 1947. †

AOG 6 *Agawam* Loaned to Army, 1 Apr 1945–Jan 1946. †

AOG 7 *Elkhorn* †

AOG 8 *Genesee* †
1* Okinawa. Tokyo Bay.

AOG 9 *Kishwaukee* †
2* Leyte, Okinawa.

AOG 10 *Nemasket* †
2* Iwo Jima, Okinawa.

AOG 11 *Tombigbee* †
2* Iwo Jima, Okinawa. Water carrier. Operation Crossroads.

AOG 48 *Chehalis* †

AOG 49 *Chestatee* Damaged by collision near Zamboanga, Mindanao, 17 Jun 1945. Damaged by mine off Balabac I., Philippines, 27 Jul 1945 (5 killed). Decomm 8 Apr 1946. †

AOG 50 *Chewaucan* †

AOG 51 *Maquoketa* Decomm 21 Feb 1947. †

AOG 52 *Mattabesset* †

AOG 53 *Namakagon* †

AOG 54 *Natchaug* †

AOG 55 *Nespelen* †

AOG 56 *Noxubee* †

AOG 57 *Pecatonica* Decomm 7 Feb 1946. †

AOG 58 *Pinnebog* †

AOG 59 *Wacissa* Stricken 23 Apr 1947. †

No.	Name	Builder	Launched	Acquired	Comm.
AOG 12	*Halawa*	Sun	6 Apr 1929	10 Apr 1942	10 Apr 1942
	ex–*Blue Sunoco* (1942)				

Tonnage	1,588 grt, 3,650 tons f/l
Dimensions	255' (oa); 246' (wl) x 43' x 16'
Machinery	2 screws; Bessemer diesel; SHP 1,000; 8.5 knots
Complement	63
Armament	1–3"/50, 2–20mm

Note: Capacity: 17,500 bbl.

Service Record:

AOG 12 *Halawa* Engine failure at sea off Hawaii, 21 Dec 1944. Decomm 25 Oct 1945. Sold 5 Jul 1948.
Later history: Merchant *Blue Sunoco* 1948. BU 1956 Seattle.

No.	Name	Builder	Launched	Acquired	Comm.
AOG 13	*Kaloli*	Charleston Sbdg	1941	29 Apr 1942	29 Apr 1942
	ex–*Flying A* (1942)				

Tonnage	3,610 tons f/l
Dimensions	256' (oa); 246'6" (wl) x 43' x 14'10"
Machinery	2 screws; diesel; SHP 1,360; 9.5 knots
Complement	63
Armament	1–3"/50, 4–20mm

Service Record:

AOG 12 *Halawa* Decomm 7 Dec 1945. Stricken 3 Jan 1946.
Later history: Merchant *Flying A*. FFU.

No.	Name	Builder	Launched	Acquired	Comm.
AOG 14	*Aroostook*	Newport News	8 Dec 1937	1 Apr 1943	18 Apr 1943
	ex–*Esso Delivery No. 11* (1943)				

Tonnage	1,707 tons grt, 1,007 tons
Dimensions	260'6" (oa); 250' (wl) x 43'6" x 15'11"
Machinery	1 screw; diesel-electric; 10.5 knots
Complement	(U)
Armament	1–3"/50, 4–20mm

Service Record:

AOG 14 *Aroostook* Damaged by explosions during air raid on Bari, Italy, 2 Dec 1943. Decomm 18 Jan 1945 and trfd to France.
Later history: Renamed *Lac Pavin*. Stricken 1953; BU.

No.	Name	Builder	Launched	Acquired	Comm.
AOG 15	*Conasauga*	Beth. Sp. Pt.	1931	23 Mar 1943	19 Apr 1943
	ex–*New York Socony* (1943)				

Tonnage	1,540 grt, 3,100 tons f/l
Dimensions	283' (oa); 255' (wl) x 46' x 14'3"
Machinery	2 screws, diesel; 8 knots
Complement	(U)
Armament	1–3"/50, 2–20mm.

Service Record:

AOG 15 *Conasauga* Decomm 25 Dec 1944 and trfd to France.
Later history: Renamed *Lac Blanc*. Returned at Palermo, 19 Oct 1945, sold 19 Dec 1945; BU.

No.	Name	Builder	Launched	Acquired	Comm.
AOG 16	*Guyandot*	Pusey	1929	22 Mar 1943	19 Apr 1943
	ex–*Veedol No. 2* (1943)				

Tonnage	1,818 tons grt

Dimensions	255' (wl) x 44' x 18'5"
Machinery	1 screw; diesel-electric; hp 1,000, 10 knots
Complement	(U)
Armament	1–3"/50, 4–20mm

Service Record:

AOG 16 *Guyandot* Decomm 12 Jan 1945 and trfd to France.
Later history: Renamed *Lac Noir*. BU 1951.

No.	Name	Builder	Keel Laid	Launched	Comm.
AOG 17	*Mettawee*	East Coast	13 Aug 1942	28 Nov 1942	16 Aug 1943
	ex–YOG 47 (25 Mar 1943); LD as *Clearwater*				
AOG 18	*Pasquotank*	East Coast	13 Aug 1942	28 Nov 1942	26 Aug 1943
	ex–YOG 48 (25 Mar 1943); LD as *Tongue River*				
AOG 19	*Sakatonchee*	East Coast	13 Aug 1942	22 May 1943	17 Jan 1944
	ex–YOG 49 (25 Mar 1943); LD as *Soldier Creek*				
AOG 20	*Seekonk*	East Coast	13 Aug 1942	24 May 1943	10 Feb 1944
	ex–YOG 50 (25 Mar 1943); LD as *Summit Springs*				
AOG 21	*Sequatchie*	Todd Galveston	1 Jun 1943	21 Dec 1943	2 Sep 1944
	ex–YOG 51 (25 Mar 1943); LD as *Royston*				
AOG 22	*Wautauga*	Todd Galveston	14 Jun 1943	10 Jan 1944	28 Sep 1944
	ex–YOG 52 (25 Mar 1943); LD as *Conroe*				
AOG 23	*Ammonusuc*	East Coast	23 Nov 1943	25 Mar 1944	19 May 1944
AOG 24	*Sheepscot*	East Coast	15 Dec 1943	9 Apr 1944	27 Jun 1944
	ex–*Androscoggin* (4 Nov 1943)				
AOG 25	*Calamus*	East Coast	14 Mar 1944	4 May 1944	11 Jul 1944
AOG 26	*Chiwaukum*	East Coast	2 Apr 1944	4 May 1944	25 Jul 1944
AOG 27	*Escatawpa*	East Coast	17 Apr 1944	3 Jun 1944	18 Aug 1944
AOG 28	*Gualala*	East Coast	24 Apr 1944	3 Jun 1944	25 Aug 1944
AOG 29	*Hiwassee*	East Coast	3 Jul 1944	30 Aug 1944	24 Oct 1944
AOG 30	*Kalamazoo*	East Coast	7 Jul 1944	30 Aug 1944	14 Oct 1944
AOG 31	*Kanawha*	East Coast	30 Aug 1944	18 Oct 1944	23 Nov 1944
AOG 32	*Narraguagas*	East Coast	30 Aug 1944	15 Oct 1944	2 Dec 1944
AOG 33	*Ochlockonee*	East Coast	18 Oct 1944	19 Nov 1944	29 Dec 1944
AOG 34	*Oconee*	East Coast	18 Oct 1944	19 Nov 1944	12 Jan 1945
AOG 35	*Ogeechee*	East Coast	7 May 1944	30 Jun 1944	6 Sep 1944
AOG 36	*Ontonagon*	East Coast	10 May 1944	30 Jun 1944	21 Sep 1944
AOG 37	*Yahara*	East Coast	6 Jun 1944	30 Jul 1944	29 Sep 1944
AOG 38	*Ponchatoula*	East Coast	7 Jun 1944	30 Jul 1944	6 Oct 1944
AOG 39	*Quastinet*	East Coast	2 Aug 1944	24 Sep 1944	6 Nov 1944
AOG 40	*Sacandaga*	East Coast	4 Aug 1944	24 Sep 1944	9 Nov 1944
AOG 41	*Tetonkaha*	East Coast	27 Sep 1944	29 Oct 1944	8 Dec 1944
AOG 42	*Towaliga*	East Coast	29 Sep 1944	29 Oct 1944	14 Dec 1944
AOG 43	*Tularosa*	East Coast	31 Oct 1944	17 Dec 1944	10 Jan 1945
AOG 44	*Wakulla*	East Coast	31 Oct 1944	17 Dec 1944	3 Feb 1945
AOG 45	*Yacona*	East Coast	23 Nov 1944	14 Jan 1945	16 Feb 1945
AOG 46	*Waupaca*	East Coast	23 Nov 1944	4 Jan 1945	9 Feb 1945
AOG 60	*Manokin*	Todd Galveston	28 Jun 1943	25 Jan 1944	27 Oct 1944
	LD as *Rodessa*				
AOG 61	*Sakonnet*	Todd Galveston	1 May 1943	1 Dec 1943	20 Nov 1944
	LD as *Old Ocean*				
AOG 62	*Conemaugh*	East Coast	19 Dec 1944	17 Feb 1945	21 Mar 1945
AOG 63	*Klaskanine*	East Coast	21 Dec 1944	3 Feb 1945	8 Mar 1945

Figure 10.47: *Ammonusuc* (AOG 23), a gasoline tanker, in 1944. Type T1–M-A1.

Displacement	846 tons, 2,255 tons f/l
Dimensions	220'6" (oa); 212'6" (wl) x 37' x 13'
Machinery	1 screw; diesel; SHP 800; 10 knots
Complement	62
Armament	1–3"/50, 2–40mm, 3–20mm AA guns

Notes: Type T1–M-A1/A2. Capacity: 12,100 bbl.

Service Records:

AOG 17 *Mettawee* Decomm 29 Mar 1946. Returned to USMC 10 Sep 1946.
Later history: Merchant *Clearwater*. BU 1964 Terminal I.

AOG 18 *Pasquotank* Decomm 27 Mar 1946. Stricken 21 May 1946.
1* Western New Guinea.
Later history: Merchant *Tongue River*. BU 1965 Terminal I.

AOG 19 *Sakatonchee* Decomm 29 Mar 1946. Stricken 1 May 1946, sold 1 Jul 1946.
2* Western New Guinea, Balikpapan, Ldgs. on Palawan I.
Later history: Merchant *Sakatonchee*. BU 1964 Terminal I.

AOG 20 *Seekonk* Decomm 1 May 1946. Stricken 21 May 1946.
Later history: Merchant *Seekonk*. Burned at Charlottetown, Prince Edward Island, 7 Jun 1963.

AOG 21 *Sequatchie* Decomm 26 Jun 1946. Stricken 15 Aug 1946, sold 7 Oct 1946.
Later history: Merchant *Otco Bayway*, renamed *Ethel Tibbetts* 1966, *Metro Landry No. 1* 1976. BU 1981 Shediac, New Brunswick.

AOG 22 *Wautauga* Decomm 26 Apr 1947. To China, 15 Jun 1948.
Later history: Renamed *Yu Chuan*. BU 1964.

AOG 23 *Ammonusuc* USCG crew. Decomm 4 Jun 1946. Stricken 23 Apr 1947.
Later history: Merchant *Providence* 1948, renamed *Texaco Providence* 1962, *Dean Reinauer* 1967, barge *B.F.T. No. 1* 1970.

AOG 24 *Sheepscot* USCG crew. Ran aground and capsized off Iwo Jima, 6 Jun 1945. Destroyed 20 Oct 1945.

AOG 25 *Calamus* USCG crew. Went aground in typhoon at Okinawa, 9 Oct 1945. Decomm 15 May 1946. To MC, 4 Sep 1946.
1* Okinawa.
Later history: Merchant *Calamus*. BU 1964 Terminal I.

AOG 26 *Chiwaukum* USCG crew. Decomm 31 May 1946. To Turkey, 10 May 1948.
Later history: Renamed *Akpinar*. R 1985.

AOG 27 *Escatawpa* USCG crew. Went aground in typhoon at Kagoshima, Japan, 17 Sep 1945. Refloated 10 Oct 1945. Decomm 20 Mar 1946.
1* Okinawa.
Later history: Merchant *Esso Porto Alegre* 1947, renamed *Gravatai* 1959. Wrecked off Santa Catarina, Brazil, 28 Sep 1970.

AOG 28 *Gualala* USCG crew. Decomm 29 Mar 1946. Stricken 1 May 1946. To Brazil, 10 Sep 1946.
1* Balikpapan.
Later history: Renamed *Rijo*. R 1970.

AOG 29 *Hiwassee* USCG crew. Decomm 20 Feb 1946, to Army. Returned to USN, 25 Mar 1947. Sold 13 Oct 1947.
1* Okinawa.
Later history: Merchant *Tong Shui*.

AOG 30 *Kalamazoo* USCG crew. Decomm 18 May 1946. To Colombia, 26 Nov 1947.
Later history: Colombian *Blas de Lezo*. R 1965.

AOG 31 *Kanawha* USCG crew. Went aground in typhoon at Okinawa, 9 Oct 1945. Decomm 23 Mar 1946.
Later history: Merchant *Kanawha*. BU 1964 Terminal I.

AOG 32 *Narraguagas* USCG crew. Decomm 5 Mar 1946. Stricken 12 Apr 1947.
1* Okinawa.
Later history: Merchant *Esso Maracaibo*, renamed *Yurtia* 1956, *Sarita* 1961. BU 1970.

AOG 33 *Ochlockonee* USCG crew. Decomm 14 Jan 1946. Stricken 7 Feb 1946. Sold 1948.
Later history: Merchant *Tycol* 1949, renamed *Newark Getty* 1958, *Texaco No. 10* 1959, *Poling Bros. No. 10* 1969, *John P. Alban* 1975, *Vincent Tibbitts* 1975. Sunk as artificial reef off New Jersey, 5 Sep 2002.

AOG 34 *Oconee* USCG crew. Decomm 28 Mar 1946. Stricken 1 May 1946.
Later history: Merchant *Esso Rio Grande*, renamed *Piratini* 1959.

AOG 35 *Ogeechee* USCG crew. Decomm 18 Feb 1946. Stricken 12 Mar 1946.
Later history: Merchant *Ogeechee*. BU 1964 Terminal I.

AOG 36 *Ontonagon* USCG crew. Decomm 27 Feb 1946 and trfd to Army, renamed *Y-130*. Stricken 21 Sep 1946. †
1* Okinawa.

AOG 37 *Yahara* Damaged in collision with destroyer *Beale*, Okinawa, 6 Jun 1945. Decomm 21 May 1946. Stricken 19 Jul 1946. Sold 1947.
1* Okinawa.
Later history: Merchant *El-Caribe* 1947, renamed *Chrysanthi* P. 1957, *Petrobourg* 1961, *Aghia Trias* 1966.

AOG 38 *Ponchatoula* Decomm 24 Apr 1946. Stricken 31 May 1946. To USMC, 9 Sep 1946.
1* Okinawa.
Later history: Merchant *Mystic Sun* 1948.

AOG 39 *Quastinet* Decomm 16 Apr 1946. Stricken 21 May 1946. Sold 1947.
Later history: Merchant *Seagull*, renamed *Bruch* 1950. BU 1986 Huelva.

AOG 40 *Sacandaga* Went aground in typhoon at Okinawa, 8 Oct 1945. Stricken 5 Dec 1945. Hulk destroyed 25 Jan 1946.
1* Okinawa.

AOG 41 *Tetonkaha* Decomm 22 Jan 1946. Stricken 12 Mar 1946.
Later history: Merchant *Maumee Sun* 1948. BU 1972.

AOG 42 *Towaliga* Decomm 10 May 1947, to China.
Later history: Renamed *Tai Hwa*, renamed *Hsin Kao*.

AOG 43 *Tularosa* Decomm 23 Apr 1946. Stricken 21 May 1946.
Later history: Merchant *Tularosa*. BU 1964 Terminal I.

AOG 44 *Wakulla* Decomm 13 Jun 1946. Stricken 19 Jul 1946.
Later history: Merchant *Mei Nan*, renamed *Stanvac Ogan* 1948, *Sea Raven* 1963, *Mobil Service* 1967.

AOG 45 *Yacona* Decomm 20 Dec 1945. Stricken 8 Jan 1946.
Later history: Merchant *Yacona*.

AOG 46 *Waupaca* Decomm 26 Mar 1946. Stricken 1 May 1946. Sold 15 Nov 1946.
Later history: Merchant *Mei Shan*, renamed *Stanvac No. 312* 1948, *Stanvac Meifoo* 1949, *Stanvac Visayas II* 1954, *Mobil Visayas* 1962, *Lapu-Lapu Carrier* 1970.

AOG 60 *Manokin* Decomm 27 Mar 1946. Stricken 1 May 1946.
Later history: Merchant *Mei Ping*, renamed *Stanvac Selo* 1948, *Sea Horse* 1963.

AOG 61 *Sakonnet* Decomm 26 Oct 1945. Stricken 13 Nov 1945. BU 1951.

AOG 62 *Conemaugh* Decomm 26 Mar 1946. Sold 29 Mar 1946.
Later history: Merchant *Conemaugh*. BU 1964 Terminal I.

AOG 63 *Klaskanine* Decomm 25 Mar 1946, To Brazil.
Later history: Renamed *Raza*. R 1970.

No.	Name	Builder	Launched	Acquired	Comm.
AOG 47	*Shikellamy*	Beth. Wilmington	26 Mar 1921	26 Mar 1943	14 Apr 1943

ex–AO 90 (15 Jul 1943); ex–*Daniel Pierce* (1943), ex–*E. W. Sinclair* (1941)

Tonnage	4,887 grt, 10,800 tons f/l
Dimensions	391'6" (oa); 375' (wl) x 53' x 23'11"
Machinery	1 screw; VTE; SHP 2,400; 9.5 knots
Complement	62
Armament	1–5"/38, 2 twin 40mm, 8–20mm guns

Note: Capacity: 51,300 bbl.

Service Record:

AOG 47 *Shikellamy* Decomm 17 Jan 1946. Stricken 7 Feb 1946.
Later history: Merchant *Daniel Pierce* 1946. BU 1965 Guanica, Puerto Rico.

No.	Name	Builder	Keel Laid	Launched	Comm.
AOG 64	*Klickitat*	St. John's	16 Dec 1944	24 Mar 1945	14 Jul 1945
AOG 65	*Michigamme*	St. John's	30 Dec 1944	31 Mar 1945	10 Aug 1945
AOG 66	*Nanticoke*	St. John's	16 Jan 1945	7 Apr 1945	1 Sep 1945
AOG 67	*Nodaway*	St. John's	22 Jan 1945	14 Apr 1945	—
AOG 68	*Peconic*	St. John's	31 Jan 1945	14 May 1945	29 Sep 1945
AOG 69	*Petaluma*	St. John's	14 Feb 1945	5 May 1945	—
AOG 70	*Piscataqua*	St. John's	24 Mar 1945	26 May 1945	—
AOG 71	*Quinnebaug*	St. John's	2 Apr 1945	6 Aug 1945	—
AOG 72	*Sebasticook*	St. John's	9 Apr 1945	11 Aug 1945	—
AOG 73	*Kiamichi*	St. John's	16 Apr 1945	17 Aug 1945	—
AOG 74	*Tellico*	St. John's	15 May 1945	23 Aug 1945	—
AOG 75	*Truckee*	St. John's	28 May 1945	30 Aug 1945	—

Displacement	1,980 tons, 5,970 tons f/l
Dimensions	325'2" (oa); 309' (wl) x 48'2" x 19'
Machinery	1 screw; diesel; SHP 800; 10 knots
Complement	80
Armament	1–3"/50, 2–40mm, 8–20mm guns

Notes: Type T1–M-BT1. Capacity: 30,000 bbl.

Service Records:

AOG 64 *Klickitat* USCG crew. Decomm 23 Jan 1946. Stricken 7 Feb 1946.
Later history: Merchant *Capitan* 1946, renamed *Punta Loyola* 1949, *Alkene* 1964. Lost by grounding off Surigao, 9 Jan 1974.

AOG 65 *Michigamme* USCG crew. Decomm 23 Jan 1946.
Later history: Merchant *Black Bayou* 1946, Argentine *Punta Ninfas* 1949, *Moises* 1968.

AOG 66 *Nanticoke* USCG crew. Decomm 4 Jan 1946. To USMC 12 Jan 1946.
Later history: Merchant *Sugarland*, renamed *Punta Delgada* 1949 (Argentine Navy) R 1984.

AOG 67 *Nodaway* Canceled 27 Aug 1945.
Later history: Completed as merchant *West Ranch*, renamed *Dynafuel* 1946. Sunk in collision with m/v *Fernview* off Cape Cod, 14 Nov 1963.

AOG 68 *Peconic* USCG crew. Decomm 4 Jan 1946. Stricken 21 Jan 1946.
Later history: Merchant *Voshell*. †

AOG 69 *Petaluma* Canceled 29 Aug 1945.
Later history: Completed as merchant *Avoca*, renamed *Transpet* 1946. Sunk by explosion in Gulf of St. Lawrence, 29 Oct 1951.

AOG 70 *Piscataqua* Canceled 29 Aug 1945.
Later history: Completed as merchant *Louden*, renamed *Transwel* 1946, *Salamanca* 1950. BU 1967.

AOG 71 *Quinnebaug* Canceled 11 Aug 1945.
Later history: Completed as merchant *Lafitte* 1946, renamed *Transpan* 1948, *River Transport* 1960, *Don Ernesto* 1975.

AOG 72 *Sebasticook* Canceled 11 Aug 1945.
Later history: Completed as merchant *Mexia* 1946, renamed *Transpar* 1946, *Kwang Lung* 1958. BU 1961 Kaohsiung, Taiwan.

AOG 73 *Kiamichi* Canceled 29 Aug 1945.
Later history: Completed as merchant *White Castle*, renamed *Transmere* 1946, *Sancho Jimeno* (Colombian Navy).

AOG 74 *Tellico* Canceled, 29 Aug 1945 74.4% complete.
Later history: Completed as merchant *Ville Platte*, renamed *Transea* 1946, *Sea Transporter* 1956, *Sea Transport* 1959, LSCO *Petroparcel* 1971.

AOG 75 *Truckee* Canceled 29 Aug 1945.
Later history: Completed as merchant *Eola* 1947, renamed *California Standard* 1951, LSCO *Transpacific* 1970.

Figure 10.48: *Stag* (AW 1), 7 Aug 1944, was a version of the Liberty Ship that was converted to a water tanker.

Fig. 10.49: *Pasig* (AW 3), a type T2–SE-A2 water tanker, 7 Jan 1945.

DISTILLING SHIPS

No.	Name	Formerly	Date
AW 1	*Stag*	IX 128	1 Feb 1944
AW 2	*Wildcat*	IX 130	1 Feb 1944
AW 3	*Pasig*	AO 91	22 Aug 1944
AW 4	*Abatan*	AO 92	22 Aug 1944

MOBILE STATION TANKERS

Except for IX 111–130, these ships were named for Civil War ships and some captured in the Spanish-American War.

No.	Name	Builder	Keel Laid	Launched	Comm.
IX 111	*Armadillo*	Calship	24 Sep 1943	26 Oct 1943	18 Nov 1943
	LD as *Sidney Howard*				
IX 112	*Beagle*	Calship	27 Sep 1943	29 Oct 1943	20 Nov 1943
	LD as *David Rittenhouse*				
IX 113	*Camel*	Calship	30 Sep 1943	31 Oct 1943	22 Nov 1943
	LD as *William H. Carruth*				
IX 114	*Caribou*	Calship	5 Oct 1943	2 Nov 1943	25 Nov 1943
	LD as *Nathaniel B. Palmer*				
IX 115	*Elk*	Calship	9 Oct 1943	6 Nov 1943	26 Nov 1943
	LD as *William Winter*				
IX 116	*Gazelle*	Calship	11 Oct 1943	9 Nov 1943	29 Nov 1943
	LD as *Cyrus K. Holliday*				
IX 117	*Gemsbok*	Calship	13 Oct 1943	9 Nov 1943	3 Dec 1943
	LD as *Carl R. Gray*				
IX 118	*Giraffe*	Calship	14 Oct 1943	11 Nov 1943	12 Dec 1943
	LD as *Sanford B. Dole*				
IX 119	*Ibex*	Calship	16 Oct 1943	15 Nov 1943	13 Dec 1943
	LD as *Nicholas Longworth*				
IX 120	*Jaguar*	Calship	17 Oct 1943	20 Nov 1943	15 Dec 1943
	LD as *Charles T. Yerkes*				
IX 121	*Kangaroo*	Delta	28 Sep 1943	6 Nov 1943	20 Dec 1943
	LD as *Paul Tulane*				
IX 122	*Leopard*	Delta	5 Oct 1943	15 Nov 1943	26 Dec 1943
	LD as *William B. Bankhead*				

IX 123	*Mink*	Delta	20 Oct 1943	4 Dec 1943	9 Jan 1944
	LD as *Judah Touro*				
IX 124	*Moose*	Delta	1 Nov 1943	17 Dec 1943	28 Jan 1944
	LD as *Mason L. Weems*				
IX 125	*Panda*	Delta	19 Oct 1943	3 Dec 1943	6 Jan 1944
	LD as *Opie Read*				
IX 126	*Porcupine*	Delta	11 Oct 1943	24 Nov 1943	30 Dec 1943
	LD as *Leif Ericsson*				
IX 127	*Raccoon*	Delta	7 Nov 1943	23 Dec 1943	1 Feb 1944
	LD as *J.C.W. Beckham*				
IX 128	*Stag*	Delta	13 Nov 1943	7 Jan 1944	17 Feb 1944
	LD as *Norman O. Pedrick*				
IX 129	*Whippet*	Delta	31 Oct 1943	15 Dec 1943	14 Jan 1944
	LD as *Eugene W. Hilgard*				
IX 130	*Wildcat*	Delta	16 Nov 1943	7 Jan 1944	17 Feb 1944
	LD as *Leon Godchaux*				

Displacement	3,665 tons, 14,500 tons f/l
Dimensions	441'6" (oa); 416' (wl) x 56'11" x 28'4"
Machinery	1 screw; VTE; 2 B&W boilers; SHP 2,300; 11 knots
Complement	79
Armament	1–5"/38, 1–3"/50, 8–20mm AA

Notes: Type Z-ET1-S-C3. Tanker version of the Liberty Ship. IX 128 *Stag* and IX 130 *Wildcat* completed as water tankers.

Service Records:

IX 111 *Armadillo* Decomm 29 May 1946, Stricken 19 Jun 1946.
1* Okinawa.
Later history: Merchant *Dean H.*, renamed *Chris H.* 1955. BU 1972 Castellon, Spain.

IX 112 *Beagle* Decomm 13 Jun 1946. Stricken 3 Jul 1946.
1* Leyte.
Later history: Merchant *Edison Skipper* 1948, renamed *George S.* 1955, *Georgios Sideratos* 1960, *Maria G. L.* 1964. BU 1969 Hirao, Japan.

IX 113 *Camel* Decomm 22 May 1946.
1* Okinawa.
Later history: Merchant *William H. Carruth*, renamed *Penn Shipper* 1959, *Halcyon Pioneer* 1962. BU 1963 Portland, Ore.

IX 114 *Caribou* Decomm 3 May 1946.
1* Leyte.
Later history: Merchant *Nathaniel B. Palmer*, renamed *Manolito* 1953, *Manegina* 1961. BU 1962 Savona, Italy.

IX 115 *Elk* Decomm 17 May 1946.
1* Okinawa.
Later history: Merchant *William Winter*, renamed *Seapearl* 1951, *Korthi* 1953, *Andros County* 1957, *Kalamas* 1960. BU 1962 Oakland, Calif.

IX 116 *Gazelle* Decomm 9 May 1946. Returned 10 May 1946 to WSA. Stricken 21 May 1946.
2* Kwajalein, Eniwetok.
Later history: Merchant *Evistar*, renamed *Crysstar* 1949, *Chrysanthy* 1950, *Rhapsody* 1955, *Fos* 1960, *Pacific Logger* 1966. BU 1968 Taiwan.

IX 117 *Gemsbok* Decomm 30 Apr 1946. Returned 8 May 1946.
2* Kwajalein, Eniwetok.
Later history: Merchant *Alpha* 1948, renamed *Strathbay* 1951, *Columbia Trader* 1954, *Pilot Rock* 1963. BU 1966 Portland, Ore.

IX 118 *Giraffe* Decomm 17 Jun 1946, returned to WSA. Stricken 3 Jul 1946.
2* Saipan, Okinawa.
Later history: Merchant *Sanford B. Dole*, renamed *Eileen* 1950, *Seapender* 1951, *Ragnar Naess* 1953, *Ocean Daphne* 1955, *Orient Lakes* 1961. BU 1967 Hirao, Japan.

IX 119 *Ibex* Decomm 28 Jun 1946. Stricken 30 Jun 1946.
Later history: Merchant *Elderfields* 1957, renamed *Winner* 1961. Went aground in typhoon at Wakayama, 10 Sep 1965. BU 1966 Hirao, Japan.

IX 120 *Jaguar* Decomm 10 Jun 1946 and stricken.
Later history: Merchant *Harry Peer*, renamed *Tini* 1949, *Illenao* 1951. Went aground off Bombay, 4 Jun 1954. BU Bombay.

IX 121 *Kangaroo* Decomm 13 May 1946. Stricken 14 May 1946.
Later history: Merchant *Mostank*, renamed *Seabrave* 1950, *Niborio* 1954, *Andros Seafarer* 1957, *San Pablo* 1963. BU 1968 Kaohsiung, Taiwan.

IX 122 *Leopard* Decomm 21 Jun 1946. Stricken 3 Jul 1946.
Later history: Merchant *Yankee Fighter*, renamed *Fighter* 1952, *Carreto* 1954, *Zoe* 1961. BU 1965.

IX 123 *Mink* Decomm 26 Jun 1946. Stricken 19 Jul 1946.
3* Admiralty Is. Ldgs., Leyte, Lingayen.
Later history: Merchant *Judah Touro*, renamed *Seavalor* 1951, *Apikia* 1952, *Eleni V* 1953. BU 1967 Osaka.

IX 124 *Moose* Decomm 19 Apr 1946. Stricken 8 May 1946.
1* Okinawa.
Later history: Merchant *Yankee Pioneer* 1948, renamed *W. L. McCormick* 1951, *Anji* 1962. BU 1966 Hong Kong

IX 125 *Panda* Decomm 12 Jul 1946. Stricken 15 Jul 1946.
1* Leyte.
Later history: Merchant *Westport*, renamed *Pardalina* 1954, San Antonio 1963. BU 1968 Hirao, Japan.

IX 126 *Porcupine* Sunk by kamikaze in Mindoro Strait, 30 Dec 1944 (7 killed).

IX 127 *Raccoon* Decomm 10 Jul 1946. Stricken 31 Jul 1946.
Later history: Merchant *Chrysanthystar*, renamed *Jupiter* 1949, *Searanger* 1952, *Sariza* 1953, *Sara* 1963, *Asia Mariner* 1965. BU 1968 Kaohsiung, Taiwan.

IX 128 *Stag* Rec **AW 1**, 4 Feb 1944. Recomm Aug 1944. Decomm 30 Apr 1946. Stricken 8 May 1946. BU 1970 Burriana, Spain.

IX 129 *Whippet* Decomm 1 Jul 1946. Stricken 19 Jul 1946. Returned 25 Jun 1946.
2* Saipan, Okinawa.
Later history: Merchant *Eugene W. Hilgard*, renamed *Loida* 1955, *Nervion* 1964. BU 1971 Kaohsiung, Taiwan.

IX 130 *Wildcat* Rec **AW 2**, 4 Feb 1944. Recomm 15 Oct 1944. Damaged by grounding in San Pedro Bay, Philippines, 25 Apr 1945.
Decomm 17 Jan 1947. Stricken 10 Jun 1947. BU 1967 Portland, Ore.

No.	Name	Builder	Launched	Acquired	Comm.
IX 132	*Andrew Doria*	Napier Miller	13 Jun 1908	18 Aug 1944	23 Aug 1944
	ex-*Alcibiades* (1944), ex-*Jole Fassio* (1941), ex-*Sequoya* (1926), ex-*Tamarac* (1914)				

Displacement	13,800 tons f/l, 5,169 grt
Dimensions	395'4" (oa); 371'4" (wl) x 51'7" x 30'6"
Machinery	1 screw; VTE; 3 s/e Scotch boilers; SHP 1,500; 10 knots
Complement	102
Armament	1–5"/38, 3-twin 40mm, 8–20mm guns

Service Record:

IX 132 *Andrew Doria* As Italian *Jole Fassio* was scuttled at Puerto Cabello, Venezuela, 31 Mar 1941. Raised and renamed *Alcibiades*.
Decomm 28 Feb 1946, Stricken 20 Mar 1946. BU 1949 Philadelphia.
2* Admiralty Is. Ldgs., Lingayen.

No.	Name	Builder	Launched	Acquired	Comm.
IX 131	*Abarenda*	Union	29 Apr 1916	26 Feb 1944	18 Apr 1944
	ex–*Acme* (1944)				
IX 184	*Clifton*	Beth. Alameda	30 Jun 1919	31 May 1945	2 Jun 1945
	ex–*Dilworth* (1945)				
IX 185	*Stonewall*	Beth. Alameda	18 Feb 1921	16 Sep 1944	18 Sep 1944
	ex–*Frank G. Drum* (1944)				
IX 190	*Nausett*	Beth. Alameda	30 Dec 1917	Oct 1944	8 Jan 1945
	ex–*W. M. Irish* (1944), ex–*Moskva* (1944), ex–*W. M. Irish* (1943)				
IX 193	*Meredosia*	Union	1921	16 Feb 1945	16 Feb 1945
	ex–*Liebre* (1945)				
IX 214	*Yucca*	Beth. Alameda	31 Jul 1919	Feb 1945	9 Jul 1945
	ex–*Utacarbon* (9 Mar 1945), ex–*Varlaam Avanesov* (1945), ex–*Utacarbon* (1943)				

Displacement	4,600 tons, 19,410 f/l. (IX 131 *Abarenda*, 6,878 grt; IX 184 *Clifton*: 7,045 grt; IX 185 *Stonewall*: 7,048 grt, 14,230 f/l; IX 190 *Nausett*: 7,123 grt, 14,492 f/l; IX 193 *Meredosia*: 7,057 grt, IX 214 *Yucca*: 6,878 grt)
Machinery	1 screw; ; 3 s/e Scotch boilers; SHP 2,500; 10.2 knots (IX 184 *Clifton*: 2 boilers; IX 190 *Nausett*: *DeLaval GT*, 3 w/t boilers; SHP 2,000; 11 knots
Complement	120 (IX 190 *Nausett*: 83)
Armament	IX 131 *Abarenda*, none; IX 184–85, 214: 1–4"/50, 1–3"/50; IX 190: 1–5"/51, 1–3"/50; IX 193 *Meredosia*: 2–3"/50 guns

Note: Mobile floating storage tankers.

Service Records:

IX 131 *Abarenda* USCG crew. Decomm 28 Feb 1946. Stricken 20 Mar 1946. BU 1948 Shanghai.

IX 184 *Clifton* Decomm 21 Feb 1946. BU 1947 Mobile, Ala.

IX 185 *Stonewall* Decomm 17 Jan 1946. Stricken 7 Feb 1946.
Later history: Merchant *Frank G. Drum*. BU 1953 Yokohama.

IX 190 *Nausett* Not used. Decomm 12 Oct 1945. Stricken 24 Oct 1945. BU 1946 Richmond, Calif.

IX 193 *Meredosia* Damaged in collision with m/v *Abner Doubleday* at Eniwetok, 29 Jun 1945. Decomm 2 Feb 1946 and returned to WSA. Stricken 25 Feb 1946. BU 1947 Mobile, Ala.

IX 214 *Yucca* Decomm 19 Feb 1946. Stricken 12 Mar 1946. Sold 24 Jan 1947 and BU 1947 Mobile, Ala.

No.	Name	Builder	Launched	Acquired	Comm.
IX 133	*Antona*	Moore	21 Oct 1921	4 May 1944	5 May 1944
	ex–*Birkenhead* (1943)				
IX 135	*Arethusa*	Moore	1921	23 Mar 1944	23 Mar 1944
	ex–*Gargoyle* (1943)				
IX 186	*Dawn*	Moore	1 May 1920	25 Dec 1944	26 Dec 1944
	ex–*Vacuum* (1944)				

Displacement	IX 133: 6,960 grt; IX 139: 7,003 grt; IX 186: 13,581 tons f/l, 7,020 grt
Dimensions	438'6" (oa); 425' (wl) x 57' x 27'4"
Machinery	1 screw; VTE; 3 s/e Scotch boilers; SHP 3,200; 10.5 knots
Complement	72
Armament	1–4"/50, 1–3"/50

Service Records:

IX 133 *Antona* Decomm 3 May 1946. Stricken 21 Mar 1946. BU 1947 Oakland, Calif.

IX 135 *Arethusa* Decomm 16 May 1946. Stricken 5 Jun 1946. BU 1947 Oakland, Calif.
2* Leyte, Okinawa.

IX 186 *Dawn* Decomm 12 Apr 1946; BU 1947 Baltimore.

No.	Name	Builder	Launched	Acquired	Comm.
IX 134	*Arayat*	Fairfield	1918	13 Apr 1944	18 Apr 1944
	ex–*Faireno* (1944), ex–*Dentice* (1942), ex–*Adna* (1937), ex–*War Patriot* (1921)				

Displacement	12,275 tons f/l, 5,197 grt
Dimensions	431'1" (oa); 400' (wl) x 52' x 25'8"
Machinery	1 screw; VTE; 3 s/e Scotch boilers; SHP 2,500; 9.7 knots
Complement	117
Armament	1–5"/38, 3–40mm AA

Service Record:

IX 134 *Arayat* Italian tanker *Dentice* scuttled at Maracaibo, Venezuela, Jun 1940, seized 31 Mar 1941. Decomm 15 Feb 1946. Stricken 12 Mar 1946.
Later history: Merchant *Dentice* 1949. BU 1954 Vado, Italy.

No.	Name	Builder	Launched	Acquired	Comm.
IX 136	*Carondelet*	Bacini	1921	24 Feb 1944	4 Apr 1944
	ex–*Gold Heels* (1944), ex–*Brennero* (1941)				

Displacement	11,700 tons f/l, 4,946 grt
Dimensions	343' (oa); 328' (wl) x 59'4" x 24'10"
Machinery	1 screw; VTE; 2 w/t boilers; SHP 3,200; 10 knots
Complement	152
Armament	1–5"/38, 3–40mm AA

Service Record:

IX 136 *Carondelet* Italian naval tanker *Brennero*, seized at New York, 30 Mar 1941. Decomm 25 Feb 1946. Returned to Italy.

Later history: Italian Navy *Brennero*. BU 1955.

No.	Name	Builder	Launched	Acquired	Comm.
IX 137	*Celtic*	Fore River	30 Apr 1921	17 Jan 1944	17 Jan 1944
	ex–*Kerry Patch* (1944), ex–*Java Arrow* (1942)				
IX 142	*Signal*	NY Sbdg	15 May 1916	4 Apr 1944	4 Apr 1944
	ex–*Standard Arrow* (1944)				
IX 188	*Chotauk*	Fore River	23 Oct 1920	29 Nov 1944	29 Nov 1944
	ex–*American Arrow* (1944), ex–*Japan Arrow* (1942)				

Displacement	20,000 tons f/l; IX 137, IX 188: 8,327 grt; IX 142: 7,794 grt
Dimensions	485' (oa); 468' (wl) x 62'6" x 31'6"
Machinery	1 screw; VQE, 3 Scotch boilers (IX137: (1943) diesel), SHP 3,200; 10.2 knots
Complement	114
Armament	1–4"/50, 1–3"/50

Notes: IX 137 *Celtic* reengined 1943.

Service Records:

IX 137 *Celtic* USCG crew. Decomm 6 Feb 1946.
Later history: Merchant *Kerry Patch*, renamed *Radketch* 1948, *Gale* 1949, *Sugar* 1955. BU 1959 La Spezia, Italy.

IX 142 *Signal* Decomm 20 Feb 1946. BU 1947 Mobile, Ala.

IX 188 *Chotauk* Decomm 7 Feb 1946. BU 1947 New Orleans.

No.	Name	Builder	Launched	Acquired	Comm.
IX 138	*Malvern*	Armstrong	8 Dec 1900	10 May 1944	11 May 1944
	ex-*Orissa* (1944), ex-*Trottiera* (1941), ex-*Tankschindler* (1931), ex-*British Earl* (1929), ex-*Pinna* (1917)				

Displacement	13,250 tons f/l, 6,205 grt
Dimensions	436'10" (oa); 420'3" (wl) x 51'10" x 27'3"
Machinery	1 screw; VTE; 3 s/e Scotch boilers; SHP 2,300; 7 knots
Complement	84
Armament	1–4"/50, 1–3"/50.

Service Record:

IX 138 *Malvern* Italian tanker *Trottiera*, scuttled at Puerto Cabello, Venezuela, 26 Mar 1941. Decomm 16 Feb 1946.
Later history: Merchant *Orissa*. BU 1949 Shanghai.

No.	Name	Builder	Launched	Acquired	Comm.
IX 139	*Octorara*	Southwestern	1921	11 Sep 1944	11 Sep 1944
	ex-*La Purisima* (1944), ex-*Taganrog* (1944), ex-*La Purisima* (1943)				

Displacement	11,570 tons f/l, 5,091 grt
Dimensions	407'5" (oa); 392' (wl) x 51' x 25'6"
Machinery	1 screw; VTE; 3 s/e Scotch boilers; SHP 2,800; 10.5 knots
Complement	88
Armament	2–3"/50

Service Record:

IX 139 *Octorara* Acquired by USN after return from USSR on lend-lease. Decomm 8 Apr 1946; BU 1947 Mobile, Ala.

No.	Name	Builder	Launched	Acquired	Comm.
IX 140	*Quiros*	Palmers	12 Feb 1903	23 Mar 1944	23 Mar 1944
	ex-*Osmond* (1944), ex-*Alabama* (1941), ex-*Ashtabula* (1930), ex-*Graf Stroganoff* (1906)				

Displacement	20,000 tons f/l, 6,725 grt
Dimensions	442' (oa); 435' (wl) x 54'8" x 27'11"
Machinery	1 screw; VTE; 3 s/e Scotch boilers; SHP ..., 10.5 knots
Complement	97
Armament	1–4"/50, 1–3"/50, 8–20mm

Service Record:

IX 140 *Quiros* As Italian *Alabama*, beached in Lake Maracaibo, 10 Jun 1940, after attack by French cruiser *Jeanne d'Arc*. Salved by Venezuela. Decomm 7 Dec 1945, Stricken 3 Jan 1946; BU 1947 Richmond, Calif.

No.	Name	Builder	Launched	Acquired	Comm.
IX 141	*Manileno*	Bacini	1922	8 Apr 1944	—
	ex-*Polonaise* (1944), ex-*Victorian* (1941), ex-*Rapallo* (1941)				

Displacement	5,812 grt
Dimensions	395' (oa); 376'6" (wl) x 51'10" x 30'
Machinery	1 screw; VTE; 2 s/e Scotch boilers; SHP 2,400; 10 knots
Complement	70
Armament	1–4"/50, 1–3"/50.

Service Record:

IX 141 *Manileno* Italian tanker interned at Cartagena, Colombia. Decomm 7 Feb 1946. Stricken 28 Mar 1946.
Later history: Merchant *Rapallo* 1947. BU 1955 Trieste, Italy.

No.	Name	Builder	Launched	Acquired	Comm.
IX 143	*Silver Cloud*	Cramp	15 Jul 1919	12 Jul 1944	12 Jul 1944
	ex-*Sweep* (1944), ex-*Olean* (1943), ex-*USS Alameda* (AO 10) (1925)				
IX 178	*Banshee*	Cramp	3 May 1917	13 Dec 1944	25 Dec 1944
	ex-*W. C. Fairbanks* (1944), ex-*Emba* (1943), ex-*W. C. Fairbanks* (1943), ex-*Harold Walker* (1935)				

Displacement	15,333 tons f/l; IX 143: 7,118 grt; IX 178: 6,353 grt
Dimensions	446' (oa); 430' (wl) x 58' x 27'
Machinery	1 screw; VTE; 3 s/e Scotch boilers; SHP 2,800; 10.7 knots
Complement	132
Armament	1–4"/50, 1–3"/50.

Service Records:

IX 143 *Silver Cloud* Decomm 29 Mar 1946. Stricken 17 Apr 1946. BU 1947 Mobile, Ala.

IX 178 *Banshee* Returned 5 Feb 1946; stricken 25 Feb 1946. BU 1949 Shanghai.
1* Balikpapan.

No.	Name	Builder	Launched	Acquired	Comm.
IX 145	*Villalobos*	Newport News	4 Feb 1911	19 Oct 1943	10 Feb 1944
	ex-*Typhoon* (Oct 1944), ex-*Colorado* (1941), ex-*William F. Herrin* (1928)				

Displacement	12,000 tons f/l, 5,039 grt
Dimensions	400' (oa); 378' (wl) x 52' x 25'10"
Machinery	1 screw; VTE; 3 s/e Scotch boilers; SHP 2,500; 10 knots
Complement	133
Armament	1–5"/38, 3–40mm AA

Service Record:

IX 145 *Villalobos* Italian tanker seized at San Juan, Puerto Rico, 30 Mar 1941. Decomm 16 Feb 1946. Stricken 26 Feb 1946. Merchant *Typhoon*. BU in Far East 1948.
3* Gilbert Is., Kwajalein, Saipan, Guam.

No.	Name	Builder	Launched	Acquired	Comm.
IX 144	*St. Mary*	Laing	24 Oct 1918	9 Feb 1944	14 Mar 1944
	ex-*Swivel* (1944), ex-*Manzanares* (1942), ex-*Bacicin Padre* (1941), ex-*Scottish Bard* (1930), ex-*War Pundit* (1920)				

Displacement	10,800 tons f/l, 5,591 grt
Dimensions	409'8" (oa); 400' (wl) x 52'5" x 25'3"
Machinery	1 screw; VTE; 3 s/e Scotch boilers; SHP 2,800; 11 knots
Complement	97
Armament	1–4"/50, 1–3"/50

Service Record:

Italian tanker, seized at Puerto Cabello, Venezuela, 31 Mar 1941. Renamed *Clyde*, 10 Jun 1944. Damaged in collision at Hollandia, 1 Nov 1944. Decomm 9 Apr 1945. Stricken 5 May 1946.
Later history: Merchant *Swivel.* BU 1947.

No.	Name	Builder	Launched	Acquired	Comm.
IX 179	*Kenwood*	Fore River	1915	16 Nov 1944	6 Dec 1944
	ex–*Johren* (1944), ex–*Apsheron* (1943), ex–*Texas* (1943)				
IX 210	*Sea Foam*	Fore River	1917	Feb 1945	15 May 1945
	ex–*Pennsylvania* (1945)				

Displacement	IX 179: 6,368 grt; IX 210: 6,390 grt
Dimensions	416'8" (oa); 415'10" (wl) x 56; IX 210: 431'6" (oa)
Machinery	1 screw; VTE; 3 s/e Scotch boilers; SHP 2,800; 10 knots
Complement	70
Armament	IX 179: 1–4"/50, 1–3"/50; IX 210: 1–5"/38, 1–3"/50

Service Records:

IX 179 *Kenwood* Decomm 10 Jan 1946. BU 1949 Hong Kong.
IX 210 *Sea Foam* Decomm 8 Feb 1946. Stricken 26 Feb 1947. BU 1947 Mobile, Ala.

No.	Name	Builder	Launched	Acquired	Comm.
IX 187	*Belusan*	Howaldt	1920	11 Feb 1945	14 Feb 1945
	ex–*Vistula* (1945)				

Displacement	20,000 tons f/l, 8,537 grt
Dimensions	517'6" (oa); 500' (wl) x 64' x 28'4"
Machinery	2 screws; diesel; SHP 3,200; 10.5 knots
Complement	113
Armament	1–4"/50, 2–3"/50, 8–20mm

Service Record:

IX 187 *Belusan* Decomm 7 Jan 1946. Stricken 21 Jan 1946. BU 1949 Shanghai.

No.	Name	Builder	Launched	Acquired	Comm.
IX 189	*Marmora*	Ames	8 Jun 1918	13 Dec 1944	13 Dec 1944
	ex–*J. C. Fitzsimmons* (1944), ex–*Valerian Kuibyshev* (1944), ex–*J. C. Fitzsimmons* (1943), ex–*Montrolite* (1926)				

Displacement	14,000 tons f/l, 6,716 grt
Dimensions	436'6" (oa); 419'8" (wl) x 57'2" x 24'
Machinery	1 screw; VTE; 3 s/e Scotch boilers; SHP 2,800; 9 knots
Complement	88
Armament	1–4"/50, 1–3"/50, 6–20mm

Service Record:

IX 189 *Marmora* Decomm 11 Feb 1946. BU 1947 Mobile, Ala.
1* Okinawa.

No.	Name	Builder	Launched	Acquired	Comm.
IX 191	*Vandalia*	Federal	9 Feb 1921	Oct 1944	23 Dec 1944
	ex–*Walter Jennings* (1944)				
IX 218	*Guardoqui*	Federal	17 May 1921	6 Jun 1945	23 Jun 1945
	ex–*E. T. Bedford* (1945)				

Displacement	10,396 grt, 22,491 tons f/l
Dimensions	516'6" (oa); 500' (wl) x 68'1" x 28'8"
Machinery	2 screws; VTE; 3 s/e Scotch boilers; SHP 3,500; 10 knots
Complement	105
Armament	IX 191: 1–4"/50 ; 1–3"/50; IX 218: 1–4"/50; 2–3"/50

Service Records:

IX 191 *Vandalia* Went aground in typhoon at Okinawa, 9 Oct 1945. Stricken 5 Dec 1945. Hulk sold, 31 Dec 1948; BU China.
IX 218 *Guardoqui* Decomm 13 Feb 1946. Stricken 12 Apr 1946. BU 1947 Mobile, Ala.

No.	Name	Builder	Launched	Acquired	Comm.
IX 192	*Flambeau*	Sun	14 Jun 1919	8 Jan 1945	8 Jan 1945
	ex–*S. B. Hunt* (1945)				

Displacement	15,800 tons f/l, 6,840 grt
Dimensions	445' (oa); 430' (wl) x 59' x 26'6"
Machinery	1 screw; VTE; 3 s/e Scotch boilers; SHP 2,600; 10 knots
Complement	83
Armament	1–5"/51, 1–3"/50, 8–20mm

Service Record:

IX 192 *Flambeau* Decomm 5 Apr 1946. BU 1947 Baltimore.

No.	Name	Builder	Launched	Acquired	Comm.
IX 197	*Mariveles*	Baltimore	27 Mar 1920	1944	17 Apr 1945
	ex–*Jamestown* (1945), ex–*Aurora* (1942), ex–*Miller County* (1927), LD as *Berington*				
IX 213	*Serapis*	Baltimore	18 Dec 1920	9 Mar 1945	3 Aug 1945
	ex–*District of Columbia* (1945), ex–*Tuapse* (1945), ex–*District of Columbia* (1943)				

Displacement	11,478 tons f/l; IX 197: 7,050 grt; IX 213: 7,162 grt
Dimensions	450' (oa); 430' (wl) x 59' x 28'1"
Machinery	1 screw; diesel; (IX 213: GT) SHP 2,600; 10 knots
Complement	90
Armament	IX 197: 2–3"/50, 8–20mm; IX 213: 1–4"/50, 1–3"/50, 8–20mm

Service Records:

IX 197 *Mariveles* Decomm 8 Jun 1946. Stricken 10 Jun 1947. BU 1948 Shanghai.
IX 213 *Serapis* Decomm 19 Oct 1945. Stricken 1 Nov 1945. BU 1947 Richmond, Calif.

MISCELLANEOUS AUXILIARIES

Miscellaneous Auxiliaries on the Navy List, 1922

AG 1 *Hannibal* Surveying in Caribbean 1920–40. Decomm 20 Aug 1944. Stricken 16 Sep 1944. Sunk as bombing target, U.S. East Coast, 3 Mar 1945.
AG 5 *General Alava* Yangtze River, 1926–27. Decomm 28 Jun 1929. Stricken 17 Jul 1929 and sunk as target off China Coast.
AG 6 *Dubuque* See PG 17
AG 7 *Paducah* See PG 18

AG 10 *Antares* Converted to cargo ship and rec **AKS 3**, 30 Nov 1940. Decomm 2 Aug 1946. Stricken 25 Sep 1946, sold 18 Sep 1947; BU Oakland, Calif. (Armament in World War II: 2–5"/51, 4–3"/50, 8–20mm.)

2* Pearl Harbor, Okinawa.

AG 11 *Procyon* Flagship, Fleet Base Force, U.S. Battle Fleet, 1921–31. Rec **IX 38**, renamed ***Empire State***, 15 Jul 1931 and loaned to New York State. Stricken 30 Jun 1940.

Later history: Merchant training ship *American Pilot* 1940. BU 1948 Wilmington, Del.

AG 12 *Gold Star* (AK 12) Decomm 17 Apr 1946. To USMC 30 Jun 1946. Sold 1 Dec 1947; BU Seattle. (Armament: 2–5"/51, 4–3"/50, 8–20mm guns.)

1* Philippines 1942.

AG 13 *Pensacola* (AK 7) Station ship Guam 1922–25. Decomm 14 Mar 1925, sold 5 Aug 1925; BU 1932, Stockton, Calif.

AG 14 *Abarenda* AC 13 1 Jul 1924 Asiatic Fleet. Decomm and stricken 21 Feb 1926, sold 28 Feb 1926.

Later history: Merchant *Antonio*. BU 1934 Philippines.

AG 15 *Ajax* AC 14 1 Jul 1924 RS Cavite, 1921–25. Decomm and stricken 8 Jul 1925, sold 14 Aug 1925.

Later history: Merchant *Consuelo* 1925, renamed *Hua Tong* 1930. BU 1933 China.

AG 16 *Utah* BB 31 1 Jul 1931 Mobile target ship. Torpedoed and capsized at Pearl Harbor, 7 Dec 1941 (57 killed). Stricken 13 Nov 1944. (Armament: Retained main turrets without guns. Rearmed 1939 as training ship, with 4–5"/25 and 2 quad 1.1" guns; 4–5"/38 added 1941.)

1* Pearl Harbor.

AG 17 *Wyoming* BB 32 25 Apr 1932 Gunnery Training Ship. Damaged by premature shell explosion in 5" turret, 18 Feb 1937 (6 killed). Decomm 1 Aug 1947. Stricken 16 Sep 1947, sold 30 Oct 1947; BU Newark, N.J. (Armament: 6–12"/50, 16–5"/51, 8–3"/50, 4–6 pdr. Rebuilt 1945, 12" guns removed; [1945] 10–5"/38, 4–3"/50, 3 twin 40mm, 1 quad 40mm, 1–40mm sgl, 6–20mm, 2 twin 20mm, 2 Mk-17 rocket launchers.)

AG 18 *Stoddert* DD 302 30 Jun 1931 Rec **DD 302**, 16 Apr 1932.

AG 19 *Boggs* DD 136 5 Sep 1931 Rec **DMS 3**,19 Nov 1940.

AG 20 *Kilty* DD 137 5 Sep 1931 Rec **DD 137**, 16 Apr 1932.

AG 21 *Lamberton* DD 119 16 Apr 1932 Rec **DMS 2**, 19 Nov 1940.

AG 22 *Radford* DD 120 16 Apr 1923 Rec **DD 120**, 27 Jun 1932.

AG 24 *Semmes* DD 189 1 Jul 1935 Damaged in collision with British trawler *Senateur Duhamel*, which sank, off Cape Lookout, N.C. 6 May 1942. Decomm 2 Jun 1946, sold 25 Nov 1946; BU. (Armament: 1–3"/50.)

AG 27 *Robert L. Barnes* AK 11 1 Jul 1938 Captured by Japanese in damaged condition at Guam, 10 Dec 1941. Recovered by British at Singapore, Aug 1945, renamed *MTS No. 2*. BU 1950 Singapore.

AG 28 *Manley* DD 74 28 Nov 1938 Rec **APD 1**, 2 Aug 1940.

AG 31 *Argonne* AS 10 25 Jul 1940 Ex-AP 4. Base Force Flagship. Damaged by explosion of USS *Mount Hood* at Manus, 10 Nov 1944 (4 killed). Decomm 15 Jul 1946. Stricken 28 Aug 1946, sold 14 Aug 1950; BU Baltimore. (Armament: 4–5"/51, 4–3"/50, 12–20mm guns.)

1* Pearl Harbor.

AG 32 *Sumner* AS 2 25 Jul 1940 Rec **AGS 5**, 1 Dec 1943. (Armament: 1–5"/38, 4–3"/50, 8–20mm guns.)

Figure 10.50: The target ship *Utah* (AG 16), a former battleship, as converted to a target ship. Notice the turrets without guns.

No.	Name	Builder	Launched	Acquired	Comm.
AG 23	*Sequoia*	Mathis	1925	24 Mar 1931	25 Mar 1933

Displacement 105 tons

Figure 10.51: *Wyoming* (AG 17), an old battleship used as a gunnery training ship, covered with all types of guns, at Norfolk Navy Yard on 31 Mar 1945.

Figure 10.52: *Potomac* (AG 25) was a former Coast Guard cutter used as the presidential yacht. Here, on 9 Jun 1939, when President Franklin Delano Roosevelt entertained the United Kingdom's King George VI, she is flying the president's flag and the royal standard.

Dimensions	104' (oa); 99' (wl) x 18'2" x 4'6"
Machinery	2 screws; diesel; SHP 400; 12 knots
Complement	10

Note: Presidential yacht 1933–36; later used by the Secretary of the Navy. †

No.	Name	Builder	Launched	Acquired	Comm.
AG 25	*Potomac*	Manitowoc	30 Jun 1934	8 Nov 1935	2 Mar 1936
	ex-USCGC *Electra* (30 Jan 1936)				
AG 35	*Calypso*	Bath	6 Jan 1932	17 May 1941	17 May 1941
	ex-USCGC *Calypso*				

Displacement	337 tons f/l
Dimensions	165' (oa); 160'9" (wl) x 25'3" x 9'6"
Machinery	2 screws; diesel; SHP 1,340; 16 knots
Complement	44
Armament	AG 25 *Potomac*: 1–3"/23

Notes: AG 25 *Potomac* was presidential yacht; AG 35 *Calypso* tender to presidential yacht.

Service Records:

AG 25 *Potomac* Decomm 18 Nov and returned to USCG, 21 Nov 1945. Sold May 1946.
Later history: Merchant *Potomac*.

AG 35 *Calypso* Decomm 20 Jan 1942 and returned to USCG.
Later history: USCGC *Calypso* (WPC 104).

No.	Name	Builder	Launched	Acquired	Comm.
AG 26	*Cuyahoga*	NY Sbdg	27 Jan 1927	29 May 1933	1 Apr 1935
	ex-USCGC *Cuyahoga*				

Displacement	220 tons f/l
Dimensions	125' (oa); 120' (wl) x 23'6" x 9'
Machinery	2 screws; diesel; SHP 800; 13 knots
Complement	22
Armament	1–3"/23

Service Record:

AG 26 *Cuyahoga* Escort and tender to presidential yacht. Designated **AG 26**, 30 Nov 1937. Returned to USCG 17 May 1941.
Later history: USCGC *Cuyahoga* (WPC 157).

Figure 10.53: *Bear* (AG 29). Built in 1874, this ship served in the Coast Guard until 1929, and was acquired by the Navy in 1939 for Arctic service.

No.	Name	Builder	Launched	Acquired	Comm.
AG 29	*Bear*	Stephen	19 Jan 1874	11 Sep 1939	11 Sep 1939
	ex-*Bear of Oakland* (1939), ex-*USCGC Bear* (1929), ex-*Bear* (1885)				

Displacement	1,700 tons
Dimensions	198' (wl) x 28'6" x 18'3"
Machinery	1 screw; diesel; (Converted to diesel 1939.)
Armament	1 seaplane

Service Record:

AG 29 *Bear* Adm. Richard Byrd Antarctic Expedition 1933–35. Antarctic 1939–40, 1940–41. North Greenland, 1941–43. Decomm 17 May 1944. Stricken 9 Jun 1944; sold 17 Feb 1948.
Later history: Merchant *Arctic Bear*, renamed *Bear* 1962. Foundered in tow 250 miles south of Nova Scotia, 19 Mar 1963.

No.	Name	Builder	Launched	Acquired	Comm.
AG 30	*Bowditch*	Burmeister	20 Dec 1928	4 Mar 1940	1 Jul 1940
	ex-*Santa Inez* (1940)				

Displacement	7,680 tons f/l, 4,576 grt
Dimensions	386' (oa); 370' (wl) x 53'2" x 20'
Machinery	2 screws; diesel; SHP 3,500; 12 knots
Complement	406
Armament	4–3"/50, 8–20mm AA guns

Notes: Survey vessel. Sister of AP 6 *William Ward Burrows*.

Service Record:

AG 30 *Bowditch* Surveying Atlantic 1941, Central America 1942, Caribbean and western coast of South America 1943. Rec **AGS 4**, 1 Dec 1943. Operation Crossroads. Decomm 31 Jan 1947, sold 9 Jun 1948; BU 1959 Baltimore.
3* Kwajalein, Saipan, Okinawa.

No.	Name	Builder	Launched	Acquired	Comm.
AG 33	*Kaula*	Robb	28 Jun 1938	3 Jan 1941	22 Jan 1941
	ex-*Cubahama* (1941)				

Displacement	2,250 tons f/l, 932 Grt
Dimensions	266'9" (oa); 250' (wl) x 38'3" x 13'5"
Machinery	2 screws; diesel; SHP 2,240; 15.1 knots
Complement	70
Armament	1–4"/50, 2–3"/50

Notes: Ferry, Hawaii. Engines aft.

Service Record:

AG 33 *Kaula* Decomm 14 Jan 1946. Stricken 12 Mar 1946.
Later history: Merchant *Cubahama* 1946, renamed *Wandajean* 1982; RR 1993.

No.	Name	Builder	Launched	Acquired	Comm.
AG 34	*Alcor*	Federal	29 Jul 1927	3 Mar 1941	4 Sep 1941
	ex-*Dixie* (1941)				

Displacement	12,250 tons f/l, 8,188 grt
Dimensions	445'6" (oa); 427' (wl) x 60' x 25'8"
Machinery	1 screw; DeLaval ST, 4 B&W boilers; SHP 7,100; 16.5 knots
Complement	734
Armament	4–3"/50, 2–40mm AA (as AD)

Figure 10.54: *Tuluran* (AG 46), seen here in San Francisco Bay on 14 Dec 1942, was an inter-island cargo ship in the South Pacific.

Notes: Acquired from Morgan Line. Flagship, fleet train.

Service Record:

AG 34 *Alcor* Rec **AR 10**, 22 Dec 1941. Rec **AD 34**, 6 Nov 1944. Decomm 5 Aug 1946. Sold 6 Aug 1946, stricken 28 Aug 1946; BU 1950 Baltimore.

No.	Name	Builder	Launched	Acquired	Comm.
AG 36	*Manasquan*	Toledo	25 May 1918	14 Oct 1941	2 Apr 1942
	ex-*Aetna* (1941), ex-*Oscar J. Lingeman* (1937), ex-*Lake Catherine* (1925); NOTS 1918–19				
AG 45	*Taganak*	Toledo	1 Sep 1917	23 May 1942	23 Jul 1942
	ex-*Olympic* (1942), ex-*Lakeshore* (1923)				
AG 46	*Tuluran*	Toledo	3 Oct 1917	16 Oct 1942	11 Dec 1942
	ex-*Anna Schafer* (1942), ex-*C. D. Johnson III* (1934), ex-*Lake Superior* (1926)				

Displacement	2,580 tons (AG 36); 3,000 tons f/l, 2,016 grt (AG 36); 1,985 grt (AG 46), 1,877 grt (AG 45), 4,072 f/l (AG 45)
Dimensions	261' (oa); 251' (wl) x 43'6" x 18'8"
Machinery	1 screw; VTE; 2 Scotch boilers; SHP 1,200; 10 knots
Complement	56
Armament	AG 36: 1–4"/50; AG 45–46: 1–3"/50, 1–40mm, 5–20mm AA guns

Notes: Inter-island cargo ships. AG 45 *Taganak* served in Navy in World War I.

Service Records:

AG 36 *Manasquan* USCG manned. Tested first LORAN system, Jun 1942. To USCG 22 Oct 1943.
Later history: USCGC *Manasquan* (WIX 273).

AG 45 *Taganak* Southwest Pacific. Decomm 25 Mar 1946. Stricken 12 Apr 1946, sold 15 Nov 1946.
Later history: Merchant *Glento* 1947, renamed *Pilhamn* 1947, *Lulu* 1954. BU 1961 Piraeus, Greece.

AG 46 *Tuluran* Southwest Pacific. Decomm 20 Dec 1945. Stricken 8 Jan 1946. Sold 26 Dec 1946; BU 1947 Terminal I.

No.	Name	Builder	Launched	Acquired	Comm.
AG 37	*Manomet*	McDougall	22 Jun 1918	22 Sep 1941	18 Jul 1942
	ex-*John J. O'Hagan* (1941), ex-*Lake Geneva* (1925)				
AG 39	*Menemsha*	McDougall	31 Jul 1918	19 Sep 1941	20 Jan 1942
	ex-*John Gehm* (1941), ex-*Lake Orange* (1923)				

Displacement	AG 37: 1,998; AG 39: 1,991 grt
Dimensions	261' (oa); 251' (wl) x 43'6" x 18'2"
Machinery	1 screw; VTE; 2 Scotch boilers; SHP 1,200; 10 knots
Complement	105
Armament	1–5"/38, 2–4"/50, 2–20mm; AG 37: 2–3"/50, 4–20mm AA guns

Note: Weather patrol ships.

Service Record:

AG 37 *Manomet* Operated with civilian crew 1941–42. Rec **AK 51** and renamed ***Aries***, 7 Jan 1942. Iceland 1942–43. Main engine replaced 1943. South Pacific 1944–45. Decomm 28 Mar 1946. Stricken 17 Apr 1946. Sold 7 May 1947.
Later history: Merchant *Adelanto.* BU 1952 Hong Kong.

AG 39 *Menemsha* Manned by USCG. To USCG 30 Oct 1943.
Later history: USCGC *Menemsha* (WAG 274).

No.	Name	Builder	Launched	Acquired	Comm.
AG 38	*Matinicus*	Manitowoc	2 Nov 1918	27 Sep 1941	4 Aug 1942
	ex-*Saginaw* (1941), ex-*Aetna* (1937), ex-*Coperas* (1926)				

Displacement	3,550 tons f/l, 2,153 grt
Dimensions	261' (oa); 257' (wl) x 43'6" x 15'9"
Machinery	1 screw; VTE; 2 Scotch boilers; SHP 1,000; 8.5 knots
Complement	371; capacity: 265 troops (as AP; see below)
Armament	2–3"/50, 4–20mm

Service Record:

AG 38 *Matinicus* Rec **AK 52**, renamed ***Gemini***, 7 Jan 1942. Iceland area 1942–43. Rec **AP 75**, 15 Aug 1942. Pacific inter-island transport 1944–45. Decomm 8 Apr 1946. To USMC 10 Sep 1946, sold 30 Jun 1946.
1* Convoy SC-107.
Later history: Merchant *Saginaw* 1946, renamed *Ramsdal* 1948, *Transdal* 1965. BU 1968 Helsinki.

No.	Name	Builder	Launched	Acquired	Comm.
AG 40	*Monomoy*	Globe Duluth	29 Aug 1918	15 Sep 1941	24 Dec 1941
	ex-*J. Floyd Massey Jr.* (1941), ex-*Lake Arline* (1931)				

Displacement	2,084 grt
Dimensions	261' (oa); 251' (wl) x 43'8" x 19'2"
Machinery	1 screw; VTE; 2 Scotch boilers; SHP 1,200; 10 knots
Complement	105
Armament	2–3"/50, 8–20mm

Service Record:

AG 40 *Monomoy* Weather patrol. USCG manned. To USCG, 30 Oct 1943.
Later history: USCGC *Monomoy* (WAG 275).

No.	Name	Builder	Launched	Acquired	Comm.
AG 47	*Manhasset*	Beth. Sp. Pt.	1923	2 Jan 1942	8 Aug 1942
	ex-*YAG 8* (30 May 1942); ex-*Wilton* (1942)				
AG 48	*Muskeget*	Beth. Sp. Pt.	1923	29 Dec 1941	18 May 1942
	ex-*YAG 9* (30 May 1942); ex-*Cornish* (1941)				

Displacement	3,170 tons f/l, 1,827 grt

Dimensions	250' (oa); 233'6" (wl) x 40'2" x 24'3"
Machinery	1 screw; VTE; 2 s/e Scotch boilers; SHP 1,300; 11.5 knots
Complement	150
Armament	1–4"/50, 1–3"/50, 4–20mm

Notes: Weather patrol ships; Q-ships. Converted by Sullivan DD, Brooklyn.

Service Record:

AG 47 *Manhasset* To USCG 22 Oct 1943.
Later history: USCGC *Manhasset* (WAG 276)

AG 48 *Muskeget* Torpedoed and sunk by *U-755* in North Atlantic and lost without a trace, 9 Sep 1942 (117 lost).

No.	Name	Builder	Launched	Acquired	Comm.
—	*Asterion*	Newport News	9 May 1912	17 Sep 1942	22 Mar 1943
	ex-*Evelyn* (1942)				
—	*Atik*	Newport News	3 Jul 1912	12 Feb 1942	5 Mar 1942
	ex-*Carolyn* (1942), LD as *Parkgate*				

Displacement	3,209 grt, 6,610 dsp.
Dimensions	328'2" (oa); 313'7" (wl) x 46'1" x 22"9"
Machinery	1 screw; VTE; 2 Scotch boilers; IHP 1,200; 9 knots
Complement	141
Armament	4–4"/50, 8 MG

Notes: Q-ships. Given false numbers AK 100 and AK 101. Holds packed with dry pulpwood.

Service Record:

*Asterion*Made seven cruises as Q-ship. Rec **AK 63**, 25 Sep 1942. To USCG, 12 Jan 1944.
Later history: USCGC *Asterion* (WAK 123). 20 Jul 1944 decomm. Sold 14 Mar 1946; BU Baltimore.

Atik Torpedoed by *U-123* off Norfolk, Va., and blew up, 27 Mar 1942 (~141 killed, no survivors).

No.	Name	Builder	Launched	Acquired	Comm.
AG 41	*Midway*	Todd; Bklyn	1920	8 Apr 1942	10 Apr 1942
	ex-*Tyee* (1942), ex-*Oritani* (1939)				

Displacement	2,250 tons f/l, 1,362 grt
Dimensions	238'8" (oa); 272' (wl) x 33'8" x 16'9"
Machinery	1 screw; VTE; 2 Scotch boilers; SHP 1,400; 11.5 knots
Complement	86
Armament	1–3"/23

Notes: Held 300 troops. Alaska supply ship.

Service Record:

AG 41 *Midway* Renamed ***Panay***, 7 Apr 1943. Decomm 24 May 1946 and returned; sold.
Later history: Merchant *Lloyd Quinto* 1946, renamed *Rio das Antas* 1951, *Consuelo* 1955, *Hanna Lilia* 1958, *Tritao* 1958, *Imperial* I 1959, *Leblon* 1960. BU 1961 Vlissingen, Netherlands.

No.	Name	Builder	Launched	Acquired	Comm.
AG 42	*Camanga*	Albina	27 Mar 1918	25 Apr 1942	25 May 1942
	ex-*Oliver Olson* (1942), ex-*San Pedro* (1937), ex-*Point Bonita* (1923)				
AG 43	*Majaba*	Albina	22 May 1919	23 Apr 1942	13 May 1942
	ex-*El Capitan* (1942), ex-*Meriden* (1923)				
AG 66	*Besboro*	Albina	18 Oct 1918	9 Jun 1943	22 Sep 1943
	ex-*Lurline Burns* (1943), ex-*Caddopeak* (1937)				

Figure 10.55: *Camanga* (AG 42), seen here on 30 May 1943, operated as a cargo ship in the South Pacific.

Displacement	5,500 tons f/l; AG 42: 2,235 grt; AG 43: 2,227 grt; AG 66: 2,865 grt
Dimensions	300' (oa); 289' (wl) x 44' x 19'4"
Machinery	1 screw; VTE; 2 Scotch boilers; SHP 1,600; 9 knots
Complement	71; AG 42: 60
Armament	3–3"/50, 4–20mm; AG 42: 2–3"/50

Note: AG 66 could carry 340 troops.

Service Records:

AG 42 *Camanga* Decomm 10 Dec 1945.
Later history: Merchant *Oliver Olson*. Stranded at Bandon, Ore., 3 Nov 1953; BU Napa, Calif.

AG 43 *Majaba* Inter-island supply ship. Torpedoed by Japanese submarine *I-20* off Guadalcanal, beached, 7 Nov 1942. Decomm and rec **IX 102**, 1 Jul 1943. Floating headquarters at Florida I., Solomons. Out of service 14 Mar 1946.
Later history: Merchant *El Capitan*. Sank while laid up at Subic Bay, Jul 1946.

AG 66 *Besboro* Alaska supply ship. Decomm 3 May 1946. Stricken 8 Oct 1946. Sold 23 May 1947.
Later history: Merchant *Shapur* 1947, renamed *Van Hwa* 1960. BU 1960 Kaohsiung, Taiwan.

No.	Name	Builder	Launched	Acquired	Comm.
AG 44	*Malanao*	Craig Long Beach	1912	3 May 1942	3 Jun 1942
	ex-*Florence Olson* (1942), ex-*Paraiso* (1923)				

Displacement	2,250 tons f/l
Dimensions	224' (oa); 216' (wl) x 40' x 13'10"
Machinery	2 screws; VTE; 1 Scotch boilers; SHP 900; 8 knots
Complement	45
Armament	1–3"/50, 3–20mm

Notes: Island supply ship, Hawaii, Central Pacific. Engines aft.

Service Record:

AG 44 *Malanao* Decomm 18 Feb 1946. Stricken 12 Mar 1946, sold 4 Jun 1946; BU Mare I. NYd.

No.	Name	Builder	Launched	Acquired	Comm.
AG 49	*Anacapa*	Pusey	15 Feb 1919	20 Jun 1942	31 Aug 1942
	ex-*Coos Bay* (1942), ex-*Lumbertown* (1940), ex-*Castle Town* (1936)				

Displacement	7,420 tons f/l, 3,321 grt

Dimensions	335'3" (oa); 321'9" (wl) x 49'10" x 20'5"
Machinery	1 screw; VTE; 2 Scotch boilers; SHP 1600; 8 knots
Complement	155
Armament	2–4"/50, 2–3"/50; (1944) 4–3"/50; (1945) 2–3"/50, 5–20mm guns

Notes: Q-ship 1942–43. Pacific weather ship 1944. Inter-island cargo transport.

Service Record:

AG 49 *Anacapa* Decomm 21 Mar 1946. Stricken 12 Apr 1946, sold 12 Aug 1946.
Later history: Merchant *George Olson* 1947. Wrecked in tow as a barge in Columbia River, 30 Jan 1964.

No.	Name	Builder	Launched	Acquired	Comm.
AG 50	*Kopara*	Robb	30 Jul 1938	4 Aug 1942	21 Sep 1942
	ex-*AK 62* (23 Sep 1942); ex-*Kopara* (1942)				

Displacement	679 grt
Dimensions	193' (wl) x 35'8" x 13'8"
Machinery	2 screws; diesel; 12 knots
Complement	(U)
Armament	4–20mm

Notes: Interisland supply ship, Southwest Pacific.

Service Record:

AG 50 Kopara Decomm 12 Jan 1945.
1* Solomons.
Later history: Merchant *Kopara*, renamed *Sarang* 1966, *Cherry Chepat* 1968.

No.	Builder	Keel Laid	Launched
AG 51	St. Louis Sbdg	6 Jan 1944	21 Jun 1944
AG 52	St. Louis Sbdg	20 Jan 1944	14 Jul 1944
AG 53	St. Louis Sbdg	6 Mar 1944	15 Aug 1944
AG 54	St. Louis Sbdg	20 Mar 1944	29 Aug 1944
AG 55	St. Louis Sbdg	10 Apr 1944	20 Sep 1944
AG 56	St. Louis Sbdg	24 Apr 1944	4 Oct 1944
AG 57	St. Louis Sbdg	22 May 1944	20 Oct 1944
AG 58	St. Louis Sbdg	5 Jun 1944	1 Nov 1944
AG 59	St. Louis Sbdg	19 Jun 1944	22 Nov 1944
AG 60	St. Louis Sbdg	10 Jul 1944	6 Dec 1944
AG 61	St. Louis Sbdg	19 Aug 1944	20 Dec 1944
AG 62	St. Louis Sbdg	22 Sep 1944	24 Jan 1945
AG 63	St. Louis Sbdg	23 Sep 1944	31 Jan 1945
AG 64	St. Louis Sbdg	7 Oct 1944	14 Feb 1945
AG 65	St. Louis Sbdg	20 Oct 1944	24 Feb 1945

Displacement	502 tons
Dimensions	175' x 29'6" x 11'5"
Machinery	2 screws; VTE; hp 800, 9.5 knots
Complement	38
Armament	none

Notes: Ice-breaking tugs built for USSR under lend-lease. Authorized as AT 146–61. All stricken 1 Jan 1983, not returned.

Service Records:

AG 51 To USSR 21 Aug 1944 renamed *Kapitan Melekhov.* BU 1970.
AG 52 To USSR 18 Sep 1944 renamed *Kapitan Sergievskiy.* BU 1970.
AG 53 To USSR 2 Oct 1944 renamed *Letchik Cherepkov.* BU 1970.
AG 54 To USSR 24 Oct 1944 renamed *Aleksandr Suvorov.* 2 Sep 1945 ?
AG 55 To USSR 7 Nov 1944 renamed *Mikhail Kutuzov.* BU 1970.
AG 56 To USSR 17 Nov 1944 renamed *Aleksandr Nevskiy.* Scuttled in Kolyma River, 1960.
AG 57 To USSR 2 Dec 1944 renamed *Letchik Asyasimov.* BU 1961.
AG 58 To USSR 19 Dec 1944 renamed *Patriot.* BU 1972.
AG 59 To USSR 28 Dec 1944 renamed *Ivan Susanin.*
AG 60 To USSR 16 Jan 1945 renamed *Admiral Nakhimov.*
AG 61 To USSR 27 Jan 1945 renamed *Bagration.*
AG 62 To USSR 17 Feb 1945 renamed *Slava.*
AG 63 To USSR 12 Apr 1945 renamed *Pobeda.* BU 1970.
AG 64 To USSR 14 Apr 1945 renamed *Rodina.* R 1970.
AG 65 To USSR 11 Apr 1945 renamed *General Brusilov.* BU 1970.

No.	Name	Builder	Keel Laid	Launched	Comm.
AG 73	*Belle Isle*	New England	19 Sep 1944	3 Nov 1944	13 Jul 1945
AG 74	*Coasters Harbor*	New England	4 Oct 1944	17 Nov 1944	29 Jul 1945
AG 75	*Cuttyhunk Island*	New England	16 Oct 1944	26 Nov 1944	1 Sep 1945
AG 76	*Avery Island*	New England	31 Oct 1944	13 Dec 1944	31 Jul 1945
AG 77	*Indian Island*	New England	5 Nov 1944	19 Dec 1944	27 Jul 1945
AG 78	*Kent Island*	New England	19 Nov 1944	9 Jan 1945	1 Aug 1945

Displacement	5,766 tons; 14,350 tons f/l
Dimensions	441'6" (oa); 416' (wl) x 56'11" x 23'
Machinery	1 screw; VTE; 2 B&W boilers; SHP 2,500; 12.5 knots
Complement	895
Armament	1–5"/38, 4–40mm, 12–20mm AA

Notes: Type EC2–S–C1. Electronics repair ships. Converted to barracks issue ships.

Service Records:

AG 73 *Belle Isle* Decomm 30 Aug 1946. †
AG 74 *Coasters Harbor* Operation Crossroads. Decomm 3 Jul 1947.†
AG 75 *Cuttyhunk Island* Decomm 3 May 1946. †
AG 76 *Avery Island* Operation Crossroads. Decomm 26 May 1947. †
AG 77 *Indian Island* Decomm 11 May 1947. †
AG 78 *Kent Island* Decomm 22 Jun 1946. †

No.	Name	Formerly	Date	Later
AG 67	*Antaeus*	AS 21	15 Sep 1943	Rec AH 18, 18 Jan 1945
AG 68	*Basilan*	ARG 12	14 Mar 1944 †	—
AG 69	*Burias*	ARG 13	14 Mar 1944 †	—
AG 70	*Zaniah*	AK 120	14 Mar 1944	—
AG 71	*Baham*	AK 122	14 Mar 1944	—
AG 72	*Parris Island*	PCE 901	28 Apr 1944	—
AG 79	*San Clemente*	AV 1	1 Oct 1944	—
AG 80	*Du Pont*	DD 152	25 Sep 1944	—
AG 81	*J. Fred Talbott*	DD 156	25 Sep 1944	—
AG 82	*Schenck*	DD 159	25 Sep 1944	—
AG 83	*Kennison*	DD 138	1 Oct 1944	—
AG 84	*Hatfield*	DD 231	1 Oct 1944	—
AG 85	*Fox*	DD 234	1 Oct 1944	—

Figure 10.56: *Baham* (AG 71), a converted Liberty Ship, was used as a repair, distilling, and stores-issue ship.

Figure 10.57: The former destroyer *Hatfield* (AG 84), disarmed, on 2 Apr 1945. She was used for towing targets for aircraft bombing practice on the U.S. West Coast.

AG 86	*Bulmer*	DD 222	5 Jan 1945	—
AG 87	*MacLeish*	DD 220	5 Jan 1945	—
AG 90	*Henry T. Allen*	APA 15	1 Feb 1945	—
AG 91	*Dahlgren*	DD 187	1 Mar 1945	—
AG 92	*Gwinnett*	AK 185	9 Mar 1945	Rec AVS 5, 25 May 1945
AG 93	*Nicollet*	AK 199	9 Mar 1945	Rec AVS 6, 25 May 1945
AG 94	*Pontotoc*	AK 206	9 Mar 1945	Rec AVS 7, 25 May 1945
AG 95	*Litchfield*	DD 336	31 Mar 1945	—
AG 96	*Broome*	DD 210	23 May 1945	—
AG 97	*Simpson*	DD 221	23 May 1945	—
AG 98	*Ramsay*	DD 124	5 Jun 1945	—
AG 99	*Preble*	DD 345	5 Jun 1945	—
AG 100	*Sicard*	DD 346	5 Jun 1945	—
AG 101	*Pruitt*	DD 347	5 Jun 1945	—
AG 102	*Babbitt*	DD 128	10 Jun 1945	—
AG 103	*Upshur*	DD 144	30 Jun 1945	—
AG 104	*Elliot*	DD 146	5 Jun 1945	—
AG 105	*Hogan*	DD 178	5 Jun 1945	—
AG 106	*Howard*	DD 179	5 Jun 1945	—
AG 107	*Stansbury*	DD 180	5 Jun 1945	—
AG 108	*Chandler*	DD 206	5 Jun 1945	—
AG 109	*Zane*	DD 337	5 Jun 1945	—
AG 110	*Trever*	DD 339	5 Jun 1945	—
AG 111	*Hamilton*	DD 141	5 Jun 1945	—
AG 112	*Breckinridge*	DD 148	30 Jun 1945	—
AG 113	*Barney*	DD 149	30 Jun 1945	—
AG 114	*Biddle*	DD 151	30 Jun 1945	—
AG 115	*Ellis*	DD 154	30 Jun 1945	—
AG 116	*Cole*	DD 155	30 Jun 1945	—
AG 117	*Whipple*	DD 217	6 Jun 1945	—
AG 118	*McCormick*	DD 223	30 Jun 1945	—
AG 119	*John D. Ford*	DD 228	30 Jun 1945	—
AG 120	*Paul Jones*	DD 230	30 Jun 1945	—
AG 121	*Humboldt*	AVP 21	30 Jul 1945	Canceled 10 Sep 1945
AG 122	*Matagorda*	AVP 22	30 Jul 1945	Canceled 10 Sep 1945
AG 123	*Rockaway*	AVP 29	30 Jul 1945	Canceled 10 Sep 1945
AG 124	*Maumee*	AO 2	15 Aug 1945	—
AG 125	*Patoka*	AO 9	15 Aug 1945	—
AG 126	*McDougal*	DD 358	17 Sep 1945	—
AG 127	*Winslow*	DD 359	17 Sep 1945 †	—
AG 128	*Mississippi*	BB 41	15 Feb 1946 †	—
AG 129	*Whitewood*	AN 63	14 Jan 1947 †	—

Note: Flush-deck destroyers were disarmed and used for training and target towing.

AMPHIBIOUS FORCE FLAGSHIPS

No.	Name	Builder	Keel Laid	Launched	Comm.
AGC 1	*Appalachian*	Federal	4 Nov 1942	29 Jan 1943	2 Oct 1943
AGC 2	*Blue Ridge*	Federal	4 Dec 1942	7 Mar 1943	27 Sep 1943

Figure 10.58: *Catoctin* (AGC 5), an amphibious force flagship, in 1946. MC type C2–S-B1.

AGC 3	*Rocky Mount*	Federal	4 Dec 1942	7 Mar 1943	15 Oct 1943
AGC 5	*Catoctin*	Moore	14 Nov 1942	23 Jan 1943	24 Jan 1944
	ex–*Mary Whitridge* (1943)				

Displacement	7,430 tons, 13,910 tons f/l
Dimensions	459'3" (oa); 435' (wl) x 63' x 24'
Machinery	1 screw; GE GT; 2 CE boilers; SHP 6,000; 16.4 knots
Endurance	48,460/15
Complement	696
Armament	2–5"/38, 4 twin 40mm, 10 twin 20mm AA

Note: Type C2–S–B1.

Service Records:

AGC 1 *Appalachian* Decomm 21 May 1947. †
4* Kwajalein, Guam, Leyte, Lingayen.

AGC 2 *Blue Ridge* Decomm 14 Mar 1947. †
2* Leyte, Lingayen.

AGC 3 *Rocky Mount* Flag of Admirals Turner, Forrest Royal and Kinkaid. Decomm 22 Mar 1947. †
7* Kwajalein, Saipan, Tinian, Leyte, Lingayen, Tarakan, Brunei. NUC.

AGC 5 *Catoctin* Damaged by aircraft bombs off St. Topez, France, 18 Aug 1944 (6 killed). At Sevastopol, Crimea, for Yalta Conference, 1945. Had King George VI on board Jul 1944, Secretary of Defense James Forrestal Aug 1944, President Franklin Delano Roosevelt and party, Feb 1945. Decomm 26 Feb 1947. †
1* Southern France.

No.	Name	Builder	Keel Laid	Launched	Comm.
AGC 7	*Mount McKinley*	N. Carolina	31 Jul 1943	27 Sep 1943	1 May 1944
	LD as *Cyclone*				
AGC 8	*Mount Olympus*	N. Carolina	3 Aug 1943	3 Oct 1943	24 May 1944
	LD as *Eclipse*				
AGC 9	*Wasatch*	N. Carolina	7 Aug 1943	8 Oct 1943	20 May 1944
	LD as *Fleetwing*				
AGC 10	*Auburn*	N. Carolina	14 Aug 1943	19 Oct 1943	20 Jul 1944
	LD as *Kathay*				
AGC 11	*Eldorado*	N. Carolina	20 Aug 1943	26 Oct 1943	25 Aug 1944
	LD as *Monsoon*				
AGC 12	*Estes*	N. Carolina	25 Aug 1943	1 Nov 1943	9 Oct 1944
	LD as *Morning Star*				
AGC 13	*Panamint*	N. Carolina	1 Sep 1943	9 Nov 1943	14 Oct 1944
	LD as *Northern Light*				
AGC 14	*Teton*	N. Carolina	9 Nov 1943	5 Feb 1944	18 Oct 1944
	LD as *Witch of the Wave*				
AGC 15	*Adirondack*	N. Carolina	18 Nov 1944	13 Jan 1945	2 Sep 1945
AGC 16	*Pocono*	N. Carolina	30 Nov 1944	25 Jan 1945	29 Dec 1945
AGC 17	*Taconic*	N. Carolina	19 Dec 1944	10 Feb 1945	16 Jan 1946

Figure 10.59: *Wasatch* (AGC 9), an amphibious force flagship, as completed, at Norfolk Navy Yard on 31 May 1944. MC type C2–S-AJ1.

Displacement	13,910 tons f/l; AGC 7 7, 201 tons, 13,040 f/l; AGC 15 6,849 tons, 12,270 f/l
Dimensions	459'2" (oa); 435' (wl) x 63' x 24'
Machinery	1 screw; GE GT; 2 B&W boilers; SHP 6,000; 16.4 knots (AGC 15 CE boilers)
Endurance	45,948/15
Complement	696
Armament	2–5"/38, 4 twin 40mm, 14–20mm AA

Note: Type C2–S-AJ1.

Service Records:

AGC 7 *Mount McKinley* Flagship, Operation Crossroads 1946. Flagship, Operation High Jump, Antarctic, 1946. †
4* Leyte, Lingayen, Okinawa, Palau, Subic Bay.

AGC 8 *Mount Olympus* Damaged in collision with oiler *Millicoma* in Philippines Jul 1945. †
2* Leyte, Lingayen. Tokyo Bay.

AGC 9 *Wasatch* Decomm 30 Aug 1946. †
5* Morotai, Leyte, Lingayen, Mindanao, Balikpapan.

AGC 10 *Auburn* Decomm 7 May 1947. †
2* Iwo Jima, Okinawa.

AGC 11 *Eldorado* Carried Secretary Forrestal to Iwo Jima, Feb 1945; Admirals Nimitz, Halsey and Spruance, May 1945. †
2* Iwo Jima, Okinawa.

AGC 12 *Estes* Damaged in collision with cruiser *Chester*, Iwo Jima, 19 Feb 1945. †
2* Iwo Jima, Okinawa.

AGC 13 *Panamint* Operation Crossroads. Decomm Jan 1947. †
1* Okinawa.

AGC 14 *Teton* Decomm 30 Aug 1946. †
1* Okinawa. Tokyo Bay.

AGC 15 *Adirondack* †

AGC 16 *Pocono* †

AGC 17 *Taconic* †

No.	Name	Formerly	Date
AGC 4	*Ancon*	AP 66	26 Feb 1943
AGC 6	*Duane*	WAGC 33	
AGC 18	*Biscayne*	AVP 11	10 Oct 1944

Armament	2–5"/38, 3 twin 40mm, 6–20mm AA guns

Service Records:

AGC 4 *Ancon* Visited by King George VI of UK, 1944.
5* North Africa, Sicily, Salerno, Normandy, Okinawa.

AGC 18 *Biscayne*
6* Sicily, Salerno, Anzio, Southern France, Iwo Jima, Okinawa

Figure 10.60: *Biscayne* (AGC 18), a seaplane tender converted to amphibious force flagship. She served at all major landings in the Mediterranean before heading for the Pacific in 1945.

Figure 10.61: *Ancon* (AGC 4), 11 Sep 1943, at Salerno. An Italian submarine is alongside.

ICE BREAKERS

No.	Name	Builder	Keel Laid	Launched	Comm.
AG 88	*Burton Island*	W. Pipe S.P.	15 Mar 1945	30 Apr 1946	28 Dec 1946
AG 89	*Edisto*	W. Pipe S.P.	15 May 1945	29 May 1946	20 Mar 1947

Displacement	5,425 tons
Dimensions	269' (oa); 250' (wl) x 63'6" x 25'9"
Machinery	3 screws; diesel-electric; SHP 13,300; 16 knots
Complement	353
Armament	2–5"/38, 2 twin 40mm, 4 twin 20mm AA

Notes: Similar to Coast Guard "Wind" class. One screw in bow.

Service Records:

AG 88 *Burton Island* †

AG 89 *Edisto* †

SURVEYING SHIPS

No.	Name	Builder	Launched	Acquired	Comm.
AGS 1	*Pathfinder*	Lake Wash.	11 Jan 1942	3 Sep 1942	31 Aug 1942
	ex–USC&GS *Pathfinder* (1942)				

Displacement	1,523 tons; 2,175 f/l
Dimensions	229'4" (oa); 209'4" (wl) x 39' x 16'
Machinery	1 screw; DeLaval GT; 2 B&W boilers; SHP 2,000; 14.7 knots
Complement	158
Armament	2–3"/50, 6–20mm AA guns

Notes: Transferred from USC&GS.

Service Record:

AGS 1 *Pathfinder* Damaged by kamikaze off Okinawa, 5 May 1945 (1 killed). Decomm 31 Jan 1946. Returned to USC&GS 22 Aug 1946.
2* Solomons, Okinawa.
Later history: USC&GS *Pathfinder*. Sold to Philippines.1972.

No.	Name	Builder	Launched	Acquired	Comm.
AGS 2	*Hydrographer*	Spear	1928	15 Apr 1942	20 May 1942
	ex–PY 30 (4 Apr 1942); ex–*Hydrographer*				

Displacement	1,135 tons f/l
Dimensions	164'11" (oa); 143' (wl) x 31'6" x 13'10"
Machinery	1 screw; diesel-electric; SHP 650, 10 knots
Complement	92
Armament	1–3"/50, 2 twin 20mm AA guns

Notes: Acquired from USC&GS.

Service Record:

AGS 2 *Hydrographer* Newfoundland 1942, Aleutians 1943, Pacific 1943–45. Decomm and returned to USC&GS 1 Jul 1946.
3* Attu, Guam, Palau.
Later history: USC&GS *Hydrographer*.

No.	Name	Builder	Launched	Acquired	Comm.
AGS 3	*Oceanographer*	Marvel	1898	7 Apr 1942	15 Aug 1942
	ex–PG 85 *Natchez* (2 Jun 1942); ex–*Oceanographer* (1930); ex–*Corsair*				

Displacement	1,252 tons
Dimensions	304' (oa); 270' (wl) x 33' x 16'
Machinery	2 screws; VTE; IHP 4550, 14.7 knots
Complement	146
Armament	2–3"/50

Notes: Originally built as a yacht for banker J. P. Morgan.

Service Record:

AGS 3 *Oceanographer* Decomm 22 Sep 1944. Stricken 14 Oct 1944. BU.

No.	Name	Formerly	Date
AGS 4	*Bowditch*	AG 30	1 Dec 1943
AGS 5	*Sumner*	AS 2/AG 32	1 Dec 1943
AGS 6	*Derickson*	PCS 1458	27 May 1944
AGS 7	*Littlehales*	PCS 1388	20 Mar 1945
AGS 8	*Dutton*	PCS 1396	20 Mar 1945
AGS 9	*Armistead Rust*	PCS 1404	20 Mar 1945
AGS 10	*John Blish*	PCS 1457	20 Mar 1945
AGS 11	*Chauvenet*	YMS 195	20 Mar 1945

AGS 12	*Harkness*	YMS 242	20 Mar 1945
AGS 13	*James M. Gilliss*	YMS 262	20 Mar 1945
AGS 14	*Simon Newcomb*	YMS 263	20 Mar 1945
Armament	AGS 6–14 1–3"/50, 4–20mm AA guns		

Service Records:

AGS 4 *Bowditch*
3* Kwajalein, Saipan, Okinawa.
AGS 5 *Sumner*
3* Pearl Harbor, Gilbert Is., Iwo Jima.
AGS 6 *Derickson* Loaned to C&GS 17 May 1944; trfd to USC&GS 23 Nov 1948.
AGS 7 *Littlehales* †
AGS 8 *Dutton* Damaged by kamikaze, Okinawa, 27 May 1945. Rec **AGSc 8**, 29 Jul 1946. †
1* Okinawa.
AGS 9 *Armistead Rust* Decomm 9 Jun 1946. †
1* Okinawa.
AGS 10 *John Blish* Operation Crossroads. Rec **AGSc 10**, 27 Jul 1946. †
1* Okinawa.
AGS 11 *Chauvenet* Decomm 1946. Stricken 3 Jul 1946, sold 1947.
Later history: Merchant *Zipper.*
AGS 12 *Harkness* Rec **AGSc 12**, 27 Jul 1946. †
AGS 13 *James M. Gilliss* Operation Crossroads. Rec **AGSc 13**, 29 Jul 1946. †
AGS 14 *Simon Newcomb* Rec **AGSc 14**, 29 Jul 1946. †

HOSPITAL SHIPS

These were specialized ships used to evacuate the wounded and sick personnel from combat areas. They were unarmed, painted white with a green stripe on the hull and red crosses on the sides and stacks, following the guidelines of the Hague Convention. They would travel unescorted, and lit up at night. A number of hospital ships were also operated by the Army.

Hospital Ships on the Navy List, 1922

AH 1 *Relief* Pacific 1923–41, Atlantic 1941–43. Decomm 11 Jun 1946. Stricken 19 Jul 1946. Sold 23 Mar 1948; BU Baltimore.
5* Gilbert Is., Kwajalein, Saipan, Palau, Okinawa.
AH 2 *Solace* Decomm 20 Jul 1921. Stricken 6 Aug 1930, sold 6 Nov 1930; BU 1931 Baltimore.
AH 3 *Comfort* Decomm 5 Aug 1921. Sold 4 Apr 1925.
Later history: Merchant *Havana* 1925, renamed *Yucatan* 1935, *Agwileon* 1941. Army hospital ship *Shamrock* 1943. BU 1946 San Francisco.
AH 4 *Mercy* Out of commission 1 Dec 1924–1 Sep 1926. Decomm 1 Sep 1929. Loaned to U.S. Public Relief Administration, 23 Mar 1934. Stricken 20 Apr 1938, sold 16 Mar 1939; BU 1939 Baltimore.

No.	Name	Builder	Launched	Acquired	Comm.
AH 5	*Solace*	Newport News	11 Dec 1926	22 Jul 1940	8 Aug 1941
	ex-*Iroquois* (1940)				
Displacement	8,900 tons; 6,209 grt				
Dimensions	409'4" (oa); 394'6" (wl) x 62' x 20'7"				
Machinery	2 screws; NN GT; 3 FW boilers; SHP 8,500; 18 knots				
Complement	466				

Notes: Could hold 418 patients. Former Clyde Steamship Company liner.

Figure 10.62: The newly commissioned hospital ship *Solace* (AH 5) in Aug 1941.

Service Record:

AH 5 *Solace* Decomm 27 Mar 1946. Stricken 21 May 1946, sold 18 Apr 1948.
7* Pearl Harbor, Gilbert Is., Kwajalein, Saipan, Guam, Palau, Iwo Jima, Okinawa.
Later history: Merchant *Ankara* 1948. BU 1981 Aliaga, Turkey.

No.	Name	Builder	Keel Laid	Launched	Comm.
AH 6	*Comfort*	Consol. Wilm.	25 Jan 1943	18 Mar 1943	5 May 1944
AH 7	*Hope*	Consol. Wilm.	31 May 1943	30 Aug 1943	15 Aug 1944
AH 8	*Mercy*	Consol. Wilm.	4 Feb 1943	25 Mar 1943	7 Aug 1944
Displacement	11,250 tons f/l; 6,711 grt				
Dimensions	416' (oa); 395' (wl) x 60' x 24'6"				
Machinery	1 screw; J-H GT; 3 B&W boilers; SHP 4,000; 15 knots				
Complement	516				

Notes: Type C1–B. These ships had Army medical staff and could carry 700 patients.

Service Records:

Figure 10.63: The *Hope* (AH 7) carried Army medical staff. MC type C1–B.

AH 6 *Comfort* Damaged by kamikaze, Okinawa, 28 Apr 1945 (28 killed). Decomm 19 Apr 1946, to Army.
2* Leyte, Okinawa.
Later history: USAHS *Comfort.* Maine training ship, renamed *State of Maine* 1955. BU 1967 New Orleans.

AH 7 *Hope* Decomm 9 May 1946, to Army.
2* Leyte, Okinawa.
Later history: USAHS *Hope.* BU 1975 Houston.

AH 8 *Mercy* Decomm 17 May 1946. To Army 20 Jun 1946
2* Leyte, Okinawa.
Later history: USAHS *Mercy.* New York training ship, renamed *Empire State III,* 1956. BU 1970 Valencia.

No.	Name	Formerly	Date
AH 9	*Bountiful*	AP 1 *Henderson*	23 Mar 1944
AH 10	*Samaritan*	AP 5 *Chaumont*	2 Sep 1943
AH 11	*Refuge*	AP 62 *Kenmore*	24 Feb 1944
AH 18	*Rescue*	AS 21 *Antaeus*	18 Jan 1945

Note: Patients: AH 9: 477; AH 10: 394; AH 11: 626; AH 18: 792.

Service Records:

AH 9 *Bountiful*
4* Saipan, Guam, Palau, Iwo Jima, Fleet Raids 1945. Operation Crossroads.

AH 10 *Samaritan* Damaged in error by naval gunfire, Iwo Jima, 20 Feb 1945.
4* Saipan, Guam, Palau, Iwo Jima, Okinawa.

AH 11 *Refuge*
1* Southern France.

AH 18 *Rescue*
2* Okinawa, Raids on Japan 7–8/45.

No.	Name	Builder	Keel Laid	Launched	Comm.
AH 12	*Haven*	Sun	1 Jul 1943	24 Jun 1944	5 May 1945
	LD as *Marine Hawk*				
AH 13	*Benevolence*	Sun	26 Jul 1943	10 Jul 1944	12 May 1945
	LD as *Marine Lion*				
AH 14	*Tranquillity*	Sun	20 Aug 1943	25 Jul 1944	24 Apr 1945
	LD as *Marine Dolphin*				
AH 15	*Consolation*	Sun	24 Aug 1943	1 Aug 1944	22 May 1945
	LD as *Marine Walrus*				
AH 16	*Repose*	Sun	22 Oct 1943	8 Aug 1944	26 May 1945
	LD as *Marine Beaver*				
AH 17	*Sanctuary*	Sun	22 Nov 1943	15 Aug 1944	20 Jun 1945
	LD as *Marine Owl*				

Figure 10.64: *Sanctuary* (AH 17), one of six large C4–S-B2 vessels completed as hospital ships.

Displacement	11,141 tons, 15,400 tons f/l
Dimensions	510' (oa); 496' (wl) x 71'6" x 24'
Machinery	1 screw; GE GT; 2 B&W boilers; SHP 9,000; 17.5 knots
Complement	574

Notes: Type C4–S-B2. Engines aft. Designated APH 112–17, late 1945–1946. Could carry 800 patients.

Service Records:

AH 12 *Haven* Operation Crossroads. Decomm 1 Jul 1947. †

AH 13 *Benevolence* Operation Crossroads. Decomm 13 Sep 1947. †
1* Raids on Japan 7–8/45. Tokyo Bay.

AH 14 *Tranquillity* Decomm 26 Jul 1946. †
1* Raids on Japan 7–8/45.

AH 16 *Repose* †

AH 17 *Sanctuary* Decomm 15 Aug 1946. †

TRAINING AIRCRAFT CARRIERS

No.	Name	Builder	Launched	Acquired	Comm.
IX 64	*Wolverine*	Detroit	1912	12 Mar 1942	12 Aug 1942
	ex–*Seeandbee* (1942)				

Displacement	7,200 tons
Dimensions	500' (oa); 484'6" (wl) x 58'1" x 15'6"
Machinery	sidewheels; reciprocating; 12 Scotch boilers; SHP 8,000; 18 knots
Complement	325

Notes: Training aircraft carrier. Lake steamer converted at Buffalo, N.Y. Had four funnels on island.

Service Record:

IX 64 *Wolverine* Decomm 7 Nov 1945. Stricken 28 Nov 1945, sold 26 Nov 1947; BU 1948 Milwaukee, Wis.

No.	Name	Builder	Launched	Acquired	Comm.
IX 81	*Sable*	Amer. Lorain	27 Oct 1923	7 Aug 1942	8 May 1943
	ex–*Greater Buffalo* (1942)				

Displacement	6,564 tons, 7,739 Grt
Dimensions	535' (oa); 519' (wl) x 58'x 15'5"
Machinery	Sidewheels, VTE;
Complement	About 300

Notes: Lake steamer converted by American Shipbuilding, Buffalo, N.Y. Had two funnels on island.

Service Record:

IX 81 *Sable* Decomm 7 Nov 1945. Stricken 28 Nov 1945, sold 7 Jul 1948; BU Hamilton, Ont.

Figure 10.65: *Sable* (IX 81), 10 Aug 1943, was converted from a Great Lakes passenger steamer; her great length supported a flight deck to simulate that of a fleet carrier.

UNCLASSIFIED VESSELS

The IX classification became official 17 Feb 1941, but was used in Navy filing manuals as early as 1923.

Unclassified Vessels on the Navy List, 1922

IX 1 *Annapolis* Ex–PG 10. Training ship, state of Pennsylvania, 1 Apr 1920. Stricken 30 Jun 1940.
Later history: Pennsylvania training ship *Keystone State*, 1940. BU 1950.

IX 2 *Boston* Ex–protected cruiser of 1883. RS Yerba Buena, Calif., 1918–46. Renamed ***Despatch***, 9 Aug 1940. Scuttled off San Francisco, 8 Apr 1946.

IX 3 *Briarcliff* New York Naval Militia. Out of service 25 Sep 1938. Stricken 30 Dec 1938. Towed to sea and sunk off Ambrose Light, N.Y., 30 Dec 1938.

IX 4 *Cheyenne* Ex–BM 10. Training ship, Baltimore. Decomm 1 Jun 1926. Stricken 25 Jan 1937, sold 20 Apr 1939; BU.

IX 5 *Chicago* Ex–protected cruiser of 1884. Decomm 30 Sep 1923. Barracks ship, Pearl Harbor, 1923–35. Renamed ***Alton***, 16 Jul 1928. Stricken 16 Aug 1935. Foundered in tow between Honolulu and San Francisco, 8 Jul 1936.

IX 6 *Coast Battleship 4* Ex–BB 4, *Iowa*. Radio controlled target ship. Sunk as target by USS *Mississippi* off Panama, 23 Mar 1923.

IX 7 *Commodore* Training ship, Chicago. Stricken 11 Mar 1930. BU Jan 1931.

IX 8 *Cumberland* Training ship, Annapolis. Decomm 31 Oct 1946, sold 22 Jul 1947; BU 1950.

IX 9 *Dubuque* Ex–AG 6, ex–PG 17. Great Lakes, 1922–40. Rebuilt with one funnel. Reclassified **PG 17**, 4 Nov 1940. Recomm 1 Jul 1941. Training ship, Chesapeake Bay, 1941–45. Decomm 7 Sep 1945. Sold 7 Jan 1947; BU.

IX 10 *Essex* Ex–screw sloop of 1874. Training ship, Great Lakes. Stricken 27 Oct 1930, sold 23 Dec 1930. Hulk burned and sunk in Lake Superior, 14 Oct 1931.

IX 11 *Gopher* Ex–*Fern*. Damaged by ramming lock in Soulanges Canal, Quebec, 6 Aug 1923. Naval reserve, Toledo. Sank in tow in Gulf of St. Lawrence, 21 Sep 1923.

IX 12 *Hancock* Ex–AP 3. RS Pearl Harbor 1921–25. Decomm 1 Sep 1925. Stricken 10 Sep 1925, sold 21 May 1926; BU.

IX 13 *Hartford* Ex–screw sloop of 1856. Station ship, Charleston, S.C., 1912–26. Decomm 20 Aug 1926. At Washington, D.C., 1938–45.
Later history: Displayed as relic at Norfolk NYd. †

IX 14 *Hawk* Ex–PY 2. Recomm 16 Apr 1922. Great Lakes. Decomm 14 Feb 1940. Stricken 24 Sep 1941, sold 25 Feb 1942; BU Michigan City, Ind.

IX 15 *Illinois* Ex–BB 7. New York Naval Reserve 23 Oct 1921. Floating armory, 14 Feb 1924. Renamed ***Prairie State***, 23 Jan 1942. †

IX 16 *Kearsarge* Ex–BB 5. Rec **AB 1**, converted to crane ship, 5 Aug 1920. Renamed ***Crane Ship No. 1***, 6 Nov 1941.

IX 17 *Monadnock* Ex–BM 3. Stricken 2 Feb 1923, sold 24 Aug 1923; BU.

IX 18 *Nantucket* Ex–screw gunboat of 1876, ex–*Ranger*. Massachusetts as school ship. Stricken 30 Jun 1940.
Later history: USMC training ship Bay State 1940, renamed *Emery Rice*. BU 1958.

IX 19 *Newport* Ex–PG 12. New York Naval Militia, 1907–31. Stricken 12 Oct 1931, transferred to city of Aberdeen, Wash. as training ship. FFU.

IX 20 *Old Constellation* Ex–sail frigate of 1797. Renamed ***Constellation***, 24 Jul 1925. Recomm Aug 1940. Relief flagship. Atlantic Fleet. †

IX 21 *Old Constitution* Ex–sail frigate of 1797. Renamed ***Constitution***, 24 Jul 1925. Recomm 1 Jul 1931. Towed to 90 U.S. ports on tour, 1931–34. Preserved at Boston NYd. †

IX 22 *Oregon* Ex–BB 3. Museum at Portland, Oregon 1924. Stricken, 4 Nov 1942, sold, 7 Dec 1942, used as ammunition hulk at Guam. Hulk sold 15 Mar 1956 and BU.

IX 23 *Paducah* Ex–PG 18. Recomm 2 May 1922, Naval Reserve training, Great Lakes, 1922–41. Reclassified **PG 18**, 4 Nov 1940. Recomm 1941. Trained armed guard gunners, Chesapeake Bay, 1941–45. Decomm 7 Sep 1945. Sold 19 Dec 1946.
Later history: *Merchant Paducah* 1947, renamed *Geulah* 1947. BU 1950.

IX 24 *Philadelphia* Ex–cruiser 4. Housed over. Receiving ship, Puget Sound. Stricken 24 Nov 1926, sold 1 Jul 1927 and BU.

IX 25 *Reina Mercedes* Ex–Spanish cruiser. Station ship, Annapolis 1912–57. †

IX 26 *Southery* Ex–collier. RS Boston. Decomm 12 Jul 1933. Stricken 1 Sep 1933, sold 1 Dec 1933.
Later history: Merchant *Steel Barge No. 2* 1934. Foundered off Black Fish Point, Honduras, 23 Jan 1935.

IX 27 *Sturgeon Bay* Floating Armory, N.Y. Naval Militia. Decomm and stricken 7 Feb 1928, sold 5 Mar 1928; BU Milwaukee, Wis.

IX 28 *Wheeling* Ex–PG 14. Naval Reserve training, 1920–41. Stricken 28 Mar 1946, sold 5 Oct 1946.

IX 29 *Wilmette* Training ship, Great Lakes. Decomm 28 Nov 1945. Stricken 19 Dec 1945, sold 31 Oct 1946; BU 1947 Chicago.

IX 30 *Wilmington* Ex–PG 8. Great Lakes 1922–42. Renamed ***Dover***, 23 Jan 1941. Decomm 20 Dec 1945. Stricken 8 Jan 1946, sold 30 Dec 1946, BU.

IX 31 *Wolverine* Ex–sidewheel gunboat *Michigan* of 1843. Pennsylvania Naval Militia 1912–23. Transferred to city of Erie, Pa., as a relic, 1927. BU 1949.

IX 32 *Yantic* Ex–screw gunboat of 1864. Training ship, Great Lakes. Decomm 30 Jun 1926 and loaned to state of Michigan. Foundered at her dock at Detroit, Mich., 22 Oct 1929. Stricken 9 May 1930.

IX 33 *Newton* New Jersey Naval Militia 1922–41. Out of service 14 Nov 1945. Sank in Hudson River, Jan 1946. Stricken 8 Jan 1946, sold 12 Sep 1946.

No.	Name	Formerly	Reclassified	Notes
IX 35	*Stoddert*	DD 302	5 Nov 1930	Rec DD 302, 24 Apr 1931.
IX 36	*Boggs*	DD 136	11 Aug 1931	Rec AG 19, 5 Sep 1931.
IX 37	*Kilty*	DD 137	11 Aug 1931	Rec AG 20, 5 Sep 1931.
IX 38	*Empire State*	AG 11 *Procyon*	15 Jul 1931	Loaned to New York State. Stricken 30 Jun 1940.
IX 39	*Seattle*	CA 11	1 Jul 1931	—
IX 40	*Olympia*	CA 16	30 Jun 1931 †	—
IX 41	*America*	Yacht, Annapolis		Hull crushed when shed collapsed, 29 Mar 1942. Stricken 11 Oct 1945.

IX 42	*Camden*	AS 6	17 Sep 1940	—
IX 44	*DCH-1*	DD 163 *Walker*	6 Jan 1941	—
IX 45	*Favorite*	(SP-1385)	24 Oct 1940	Panama Canal tug. Stricken 19 Feb 1948.
IX 46	*Transfer*	—	—	Derrick-rigged freight lighter, New York NYd. Decomm 8 Feb 1934. Stricken 16 Sep 1945, sold 8 Apr 1946.
IX 55	*Black Douglas*	U.S. Fish and Wildlife Service	2 Jan 1942	Rec **PYc** 45, 8 Apr 1943. U.S. Fish and Wildlife Service
IX 56	—	*AT 56*	14 Jan 1942	—

MISCELLANEOUS SAILING VESSELS

No.	Name	Dimensions	Type	Built	Acquired
IX 43	*Freedom*	88' x 20'	yacht	1931	13 Sep 1940
IX 47	*Vamarie*	72' x 15'	yacht	1933	10 Mar 1936
IX 48	*Highland Light*	68' x 15'	yacht	1931	26 Oct 1940
IX 49	*Spindrift*	54' x 13'	cutter	1928	5 Dec 1940
IX 50	*Bowdoin*	75' x 20'	schooner	1921	22 May 1941
IX 52	*Cheng Ho*	94' x 23'	junk	1939	23 Jul 1941
IX 54	*Galaxy*	130' x 21'	yacht	1930	8 Sep 1941
IX 57	*Araner*	86' x 25'	ketch	1926	27 Jan 1942
IX 58	*Dwyn Wen*	93' x 20'	schooner	1906	4 Feb 1942
IX 59	*Volador*	110' x 23'	schooner	1926	2 Feb 1942
IX 60	*Seaward*	94' x 22'	schooner	1920	31 Jan 1942
IX 61	*Geoanna*	111' x 22'	yacht	1934	1 Feb 1942
IX 62	*Vileehi*	80' x 19'	ketch	1930	19 Dec 1941
IX 63	*Zahma*	80' x 21'	ketch	1915	8 Jan 1942
IX 65	*Blue Dolphin*	99' x 22'	schooner	1926	17 Mar 1942
IX 66	*Migrant*	223' x 34'	schooner	1929	21 Mar 1942
IX 67	*Guinevere*	171' x 32'	schooner	1921	24 Mar 1942
IX 68	*Seven Seas*	165' x 27'	ship	1912	10 Apr 1942
	ex–Swedish training ship *Abraham Rydberg*				
IX 69	*Puritan*	102' x 21'	schooner	1931	3 May 1942
IX 70	*Gloria Dalton*	87" x 21'	schooner	1925	11 May 1942
IX 73	*Zaca*	118' x 22'	yacht	1930	12 Jun 1942
IX 74	*Metha Nelson*	156' x 36'	schooner	1896	11 Jun 1942
IX 75	*John M. Howard*	79' x 20'	yacht	1934	2 Jul 1942
	ex–Elsie Fenimore (17 Aug 1942)				
IX 76	*Ramona*	109' x 23'	schooner	1920	15 Jul 1942
IX 77	*Juniata*	134' x 28'	schooner	1930	20 Jul 1942
IX 78	*Brave*	98' x 24'	schooner		10 Aug 1942
	ex–A. Maitland Adams				
IX 79	*El Cano*	172' x 28'	schooner	1927	8 Aug 1942
	ex–Pioneer (17 Aug 1942)				
IX 82	*Luster*	73' x 20'	ketch	1936	21 Jul 1942
	ex–Ko Asa (2 Sep 1942)				
IX 83	*Ashley*	58' x 17'	schooner	1937	29 Jul 1942
IX 84	*Congaree*	70' x 15'	yawl	1938	11 Aug 1942
IX 85	*Euhaw*	66' x 20'	yawl	1910	18 Aug 1942
IX 86	*Pocotaligo*	96' x 17'	schooner	1926	18 Aug 1942
IX 87	*Saluda*	88' x 18'	yacht	1938	31 Jul 1942
IX 88	*Wimbee*	59' x 13'	yawl	1936	30 Jul 1942
IX 89	*Romain*	84' x 20'	schooner	1937	18 Aug 1942
IX 90	*Forbes*	81' x 27'	schooner	1927	19 Aug 1942
	ex–Morning Star				
IX 91	*Palomas*	161' x 30'	schooner	1922	23 Sep 1942
	ex–Goodwill (5 Oct 1942)				
IX 92	*Liston*	62' x 21'	schooner	1923	9 Oct 1942
IX 93	*Irene Forsyte*	144' x 27'	schooner	1920	16 Nov 1942
IX 94	*Ronaki*	112' x 27'	schooner	1922	4 Nov 1942
IX 95	*Echo*	(U)	scow	1892	4 Nov 1942
IX 233	*Canandaigua*	81' x 20'	(U)	1922	20 Sep 1945
IX 234	*Eastwind*	73' x 17'	yawl	1939	1 Jun 1947

Figure 10.66: *Juniata* (IX 77), a schooner used for patrolling out of San Francisco Bay.

Note: Former merchant names not given here; known as the "Hooligan Navy."

Service Records:

IX 43 *Freedom* Annapolis. †
IX 47 *Vamarie* Annapolis. †
IX 48 *Highland Light* Annapolis. †
IX 49 *Spindrift* Annapolis. †
IX 50 *Bowdoin* Comm 16 Jun 1941. Greenland Patrol. Decomm 16 Dec 1943. Stricken 16 May 1944, sold 24 Jan 1945.
IX 52 *Cheng Ho* Fourteenth ND. Stricken 25 Feb 1946, sold 3 Feb 1947.
IX 54 *Galaxy* Underwater sound research. Out of service 25 Mar 1946. Stricken 1 May 1946, sold 20 May 1946.
IX 57 *Araner* San Diego. Decomm 1 May 1944. Returned 12 Jul 1944.
IX 58 *Dwyn Wen* Eleventh ND. Out of service 1 Apr 1943. Stricken 18 Jul 1944, sold 6 Jan 1945.
IX 59 *Volador* USCG crew. Eleventh ND. To Army, 17 Aug 1943.
IX 60 *Seaward* San Pedro, Calif. Out of service 1 Apr 1943. Stricken 18 Jul 1944, sold 6 Apr 1945.
IX 61 *Geoanna* San Pedro, Calif. In USCG, 2 Jul 1943–28 Aug 1943. To Army, *TP-249*, 3 Sep 1943.
IX 62 *Vileehi* Eleventh ND. Out of service 20 Sep 1945. Returned 27 Sep 1945. Stricken 4 Oct 1945.

IX 63 *Zahma* San Diego. Out of service 13 Apr 1943. Stricken 18 Jul 1944.
IX 65 *Blue Dolphin* Stricken 11 Jul 1945, sold 14 Sep 1945.
IX 66 *Migrant* New York City area. Decomm 3 Aug 1945. Stricken 13 Aug 1945.
Later history: Merchant *Fimbert.* Sank after engine room explosion off Cape Samana, 13 Jul 1953.
IX 67 *Guinevere* Boston, Greenland. Decomm 2 Aug 1945. Stricken 13 Aug 1945.
IX 68 *Seven Seas* Key West, Fla. Out of service 22 May 1944. Stricken 29 Jul 1944, sold 26 Jul 1945.
IX 69 *Puritan* San Diego. Out of service 27 Sep 1943. Stricken 28 Jun 1944, sold 18 Nov 1944.
IX 70 *Gloria Dalton* San Diego. Decomm 1 Oct 1943. Stricken 28 Jun 1944.
IX 73 *Zaca* California. Out of service 6 Oct 1944. Stricken 13 Nov 1944, sold 21 May 1945.
IX 74 *Metha Nelson* Los Angeles. Out of service 25 Sep 1945. Stricken 24 Oct 1945, sold 31 Oct 1946.
IX 75 *John M. Howard* Ordnance experiments, Chesapeake Bay. Decomm 9 May 1945. To MC 24 Jan 1946.
IX 76 *Ramona* San Diego. Out of service 1 Apr 1943. Stricken 28 Jul 1944, sold 5 Aug 1944.
IX 77 *Juniata* California. Out of service 1 Jan 1945.
IX 78 *Brave* Sound school training, Key West, Fla. Comm 23 Jan 1943. Decomm 14 Dec 1944. Sold 19 Sep 1946.
IX 79 *El Cano* Eleventh ND. USCG-manned training ship for merchant marine, 1939–42. Returned 23 Oct 1945.
IX 82 *Luster* Port Everglades, Fla. Out of service 24 Mar 1943. Civilian crew, loaned to marine salvage and construction firm Merritt Chapman and Scott, 23 Jan 1944. Stricken 29 Jul 1944. Returned 20 Dec 1944.
IX 83 *Ashley* Port Everglades, Fla. Stricken 16 Nov 1943, sold 5 Jan 1946.
IX 84 *Congaree* Port Everglades, Fla. Out of service 15 Mar 1943. Stricken 10 Jun 1947.
IX 85 *Euhaw* Seventh ND. Stricken 28 Jun 1944. To WSA 1 Nov 1944.
IX 86 *Pocotaligo* Seventh ND. Out of service17 Mar 1943 Stricken 28 Jun 1944, sold 14 Mar 1945.
IX 87 *Saluda* Port Everglades, Fla. Out of comm Oct 1945–20 May 1946. Experimental hydrographic service. †
IX 88 *Wimbee* Port Everglades, Fla. Out of service 17 Mar 1943. Stricken 28 Jun 1944, sold 7 Feb 1945.
IX 89 *Romain* Port Everglades, Fla. Out of service 16 Mar 1943. Stricken 28 Jun 1944, sold 3 Jan 1945.
IX 90 *Forbes* Seventh ND. Stricken 12 Aug 1943. Sold 21 Mar 1945.
IX 91 *Palomas* San Diego. Out of service 10 Aug 1946. Stricken 25 Sep 1946, sold 3 Mar 1947.
IX 92 *Liston* Fourth ND. Out of service 12 Jul 1943. Stricken 29 Jul 1944.
IX 93 *Irene Forsyte* Q-ship, North Atlantic, 1943. (Armament: 1–4"/50, 1–40mm, 1–20mm.) Decomm 16 Dec 1943, sold 18 Oct 1945.
IX 94 *Ronaki* Acq in New Zealand. Lost by grounding off east coast of Australia. 18 Jun 1943.
IX 95 *Echo* Acq in New Zealand. Supply ship, Southwest Pacific. Decomm 15 Mar 1944 and returned.
IX 233 *Canandaigua* Sank, 22 Nov 1945, raised. Sold 31 Oct 1946.
IX 234 *Eastwind* Former German yacht. †

No.	Name	Builder	Launched	Acquired	Comm.
IX 34	*Henry County*	Amer. Lorain	1919	1930	27 May 1930

Tonnage	2,490 tons
Dimensions	261'10" (oa); 251' (wl) x 43'8" x 11'2"
Machinery	1 screw, VTE
Complement	37

Service Record:

IX 34 *Henry County* Decomm 22 Aug 1930. Loan to State of California as training ship, renamed ***California State***, 23 Jan 1931. To MC 30 Jun 1940.
Later history: Merchant *Golden State* 1940, renamed *Isle of Patmos* 1948, *Santa Rosa* 1952. BU 1962 Rio de Janeiro.

No.	Name	Builder	Launched	Acquired	In service
IX 51	*Sea Otter I*	Jacobson	1941	29 May 1941	9 Jul 1941

Dimensions	80' x 12'8" x 6'8"

Service Record:

IX 57 *Sea Otter I* Out of service, 6 Nov 1941. Stricken 24 Jun 1942. BU Annapolis.

No.	Name	Builder	Launched	Acquired	In service
IX 53	*Sea Otter II*	Levingston	23 Aug 1941	26 Sep 1941	26 Oct 1941

Displacement	1,941 tons
Dimensions	254' x 38' x 10'2"
Complement	15

Note: Experimental shallow draft steamer.

Service Record:

IX 53 *Sea Otter II* Out of service 28 May 1942. To MC 26 Jun 1942. Stricken 8 May 1946.

No.	Name	Builder	Launched	Acquired	Comm.
IX 71	*Kailua* ex-*Dickenson* (1942)	Sun	17 Feb 1923	19 May 1942	5 May 1943

Displacement	1,411 tons f/l, 831 grt
Dimensions	189'9" (oa); 167'3" (wl) x 30' x 15'9"
Machinery	1 screw, VTE; IHP 800; 9.8 knots
Complement	61

Note: Cable vessel.

Service Record:

IX 71 *Kailua* Southwest Pacific 1943–44, Pearl Harbor 1944–45. Sank at moorings, Honolulu, 29 Oct 1945 and decomm. Raised and sunk as target 7 Feb 1946.

No.	Name	Builder	Launched	Acquired	In Service
IX 72	*Liberty Belle*	Harlan	1909	23 Apr 1942	1 Jan 1943

Tonnage	622 grt; 992 tons
Dimensions	200' (wl) 198'7" (bp) x 44' x 11'9"

Note: Mine warfare experimental ship.

Service Record:

IX 72 *Liberty Belle* Out of service 18 May 1944. Returned to WSA, 10 Apr 1947.

Later history: Merchant *Asbury Park*, 1948, renamed *Tolchester.*

No.	Name	Builder	Launched	Acquired	Comm.
IX 80	*Christiana* ex-*Azalea* (LHS)	Johnson	29 Nov 1890	Aug 1942	9 Nov 1942

Tonnage	600 tons
Dimensions	155' (oa); 146' (wl) x 24'3" x 12'4"
Machinery	1 screw, compound

Note: Seaplane tender.

Service Record:

IX 80 *Christiana* West Indies. Decomm 28 Jul 1945. To MC 25 Feb 1946.

No.	Name	Builder	Launched	Acquired	Comm.
IX 96	*Richard Peck*	Harlan	1892	30 Jan 1943	

Tonnage	2,906 grt
Dimensions	303.3' x 48'
Machinery	2 screws, VTE; 16.5 knots

Note: Provided electric power at Argentia, Newfoundland.

Service Record:

IX 96 *Richard Peck* Decomm 5 Nov 1943. Stricken 16 Nov 1943, sold 9 Dec 1943.
Later history: Merchant *Elisha Lee*, 1944. BU 1953 Baltimore.

No.	Name	Builder	Launched	Acquired	In service
IX 97	*Martha's Vineyard* ex-*Thelma*	Seabury	1911	11 Jan 1943	30 Mar 1943

Tonnage	141 grt
Dimensions	138' (oa) 131'9" (wl) x 16' x 8'9"(wl)
Machinery	2 screws, diesel
Complement	11

Note: Motor yacht.

Service Record:

IX 97 *Martha's Vineyard* Underwater sound experiments and training, New London, Conn. Out of service 18 Apr 1946.

No.	Name	Builder	Launched	Acquired	Comm.
IX 99	*Sea Cloud*	Germania	25 Apr 1931	7 Jan 1942	1942
	ex-*Sea Cloud*, ex-*Hussar* (1935)				

Tonnage	2,323 tons
Dimensions	316' (oa)x 49'2" x 19
Machinery	2 screws, diesel; HP 3,200; 14 knots
Complement	72
Armament	2–3" 50, 5–20mm

Note: Four-mast steel bark.

Service Record:

IX 99 *Sea Cloud* USCG weather patrol 1942. USCG crew. Decomm and returned to owner, 4 Nov 1944. Stricken 13 Nov 1944.
Later history: Merchant *Sea Cloud*, renamed *Angelita* (as Dominican Republic President Rafael Trujillo's yacht), renamed *Patria* 1964, *Antarna* 1964, *Sea Cloud of Cayman* 1974.

No.	Name	Builder	Launched	Acquired	Comm.
IX 101	*Big Chief*	Neafie	1897	5 May 1943	1943
	ex-*Big Chief* (1943), ex-*Plymouth* (1938), ex-USLHS *Iris* (1934)				

Displacement	428 tons; 358 grt
Dimensions	150' (oa); 141'8" (wl) x 30'1" x 13'4"
Machinery	1 screw, diesel; SHP 450; 11 knots

Notes: Former lighthouse tender.

Service Record:

IX 101 *Big Chief* Returned 14 Jun 1946. Striken 3 Jul 1946.
Later history: Merchant *Big Chief* 1946, renamed *B.O. Colonna* 1956. RR 1975.

No.	Name	Builder	Launched	Acquired	Comm.
IX 106	*Greyhound*	Delaware River	1 Dec 1906	30 Apr 1943	8 Aug 1943
	ex-*Yale* (19 Aug 1943), ex-USS *Yale* (1918)				

Displacement	3,818 grt
Dimensions	406'6" (oa); 386'2" (wl) x 62'6" x 18';
Machinery	Removed (was 3 screws; VTE)

Notes: Transport in World War I.

Service Record:

IX 106 *Greyhound* Decomm 31 Mar 1944. Floating barracks, Puget Sound NYd. Out of service 9 Mar 1948. Stricken 18 Jun 1948. Sold 5 Jun 1949; BU San Francisco.

No.	Name	Builder	Launched	Acquired	Comm.
IX 108	*Atlantida*	Workman	24 Apr 1924	13 Sep 1943	13 Sep 1943

Displacement	4,191 grt
Dimensions	351' (wl) x 50'3" x 20'
Machinery	1 screw, VQE

Notes: Mine warfare training ship. Merchant name retained.

Service Record:

IX 108 *Atlantida* Decomm 16 May 1944 and returned to USMC. Stricken 9 Jun 1944. Returned to owner 11 Mar 1946.
Later history: Merchant *Atlantida* 1953. BU 1960 Ghent, Belgium.

No.	Name	Builder	Launched	Acquired	In service
IX 103	*E. A. Poe*	Oregon	26 Mar 1942	18 Nov 1942	30 Aug 1943
	ex-*Edgar Allen Poe* (1942)				
IX 104	*P. H. Burnett*	Calship	10 Aug 1942	15 Jun 1943	30 Aug 1943
	ex-*Peter H. Burnett* (1943)				
IX 109	*Antelope*	Permanente 2	6 Jul 1943	4 Oct 1943	4 Oct 1943
	ex-*M. H. de Young* (1943)				
IX 215	*Don Marquis*	Calship	23 Aug 1943	31 May 1945	31 May 1945
	ex-*Don Marquis* (1945)				
IX 223	*Triana*	Calship	24 Jan 1944	24 May 1945	Jul 1945
	ex-*Elinor Wylie* (1945)				
IX 225	*Harcourt*	Calship	27 Dec 1942	22 Jun 1945	22 Jun 1945
	ex-*John M. Clayton* (1945)				
IX 226	*Araner*	Oregon	27 Dec 1942	23 Sep 1945	23 Sep 1945
	ex-*Juan de Fuca* (1945)				
IX 227	*Gamage*	Calship	8 Mar 1943	30 Jul 1945	—
	ex-*William B. Allison* (1945)				
IX 228	*Justin*	Todd-Houston	22 May 1944	2 Sep 1945	4 Sep 1945
	ex-*Gus W. Darnell* (1945)				
IX 229	*Inca*	Oregon	12 Aug 1943	30 July 1945	—
	ex-*Henry L Abbott* (1945)				

Displacement	4,023 tons; 14,500 f/l
Dimensions	441'6" (oa); 416' (wl) x 56'11" x 28'4"
Machinery	removed (IX 103–4, IX 109, IX 215); 1 screw; VTE; 2 B&W boilers; SHP 2,500
Armament	IX 203: 1–4"/50; IX 104: 1–5"/50, 1–3"/50; IX 215: 1–3"/50; 2–3"/50

Notes: Type EC2–S-C1. Liberty ships. Damaged hulls acquired by Navy for use as mobile dry cargo storage, non-self-propelled.

Service Records:

IX 103 *E. A. Poe* Torpedoed by Japanese submarine *I-21* off Noumea, New Caledonia, 9 Nov 1942; CTL. Out of service, 15 Mar 1946. Stricken 28 Mar 1946. BU 1949 Hong Kong.

IX 104 *P. H. Burnett* Torpedoed by Japanese submarine *I-21* off Sydney, 22 Jan 1943; CTL. Out of service 7 Aug and returned 8 Aug 1946, BU 1958 Terminal I.

IX 109 *Antelope* Torpedoed by Japanese submarine *I-19* off Fiji, 13 Aug 1943; CTL. Partially repaired and taken over by Navy. Used as storage hulk. Returned to WSA 3 May 1946; BU 1949 Shanghai, China.

IX 215 *Don Marquis* Burned after collision with tanker *Missionary Ridge* off Negros, Philippines, 26 Sep 1944. Returned to WSA, 30 Nov 1945. Stricken 5 Jun 1946. BU 1949 Manus I.

IX 223 *Triana* Damaged by mine off southern France, 6 Oct 1944; CTL. Decomm 21 Feb 1946 and returned to WSA. Stricken 12 Mar 1946. BU 1958 Oakland, Calif.

IX 225 *Harcourt* Damaged by Japanese aircraft bomb off Mindoro, 2 Jan 1945; CTL. Decomm 17 May 1946, to WSA. BU 1962 Portland, Ore.

IX 226 *Araner* Damaged by kamikaze off Mindoro 9 Dec 1944; torpedoed and run aground, 30 Dec 1944, CTL. Returned to WSA 22 Aug 1946. Sold 3 Mar 1948.
Later history: Seized by PRC while at Shanghai for BU 1949 . Sunk by Chinese nationalists while in tow, 20 Sep 1950.

IX 227 *Gamage* Damaged at Ulithi, Micronesia, 25 May 1945; CTL. Out of service 8 Feb 1946. Stricken 7 Apr 1946, sold 19 Feb 1948; BU 1949 China.

IX 228 *Justin* Torpedoed by Japanese aircraft off Samar, 23 Nov 1944; CTL. Decomm 23 Jan 1946 and returned to WSA. Sold 25 May 1954; BU Baltimore.
Later history: Sold. Went aground in typhoon at Hong Kong, 7 Sep 1949, total loss. BU 1951, Hong Kong.

IX 229 *Lnca* Out of service 8 Feb 1946. Stricken 12 Mar 1946. Sold 19 Feb 1948. BU China.

No.	Name	Builder	Launched	Acquired	Comm.
IX 110	*Ocelot*	Daniels	22 Feb 1919	2 Oct 1943	15 Jan 1944
	ex–*Yomachichi* (1943)				
IX 156	*City of Dalhart*	Daniels	May 1920	29 Feb 1944	2 Jun 1944
	ex–*City of Dalhart* (1944)				
IX 157	*Orvetta*	Daniels	12 Jun 1919	4 Apr 1944	7 Jun 1944
	ex–*Tampa* (1944)				
IX 216	*Unicoi*	Daniels	23 Oct 1919	20 Apr 1945	23 Apr 1945
	ex–*Unicoi* (1945), ex–*Excelsior* (1940), ex–*Unicoi*				

Displacement	IX 110: 8,747 tons f/l; IX 157: 9,471 tons f/l; IX 110: 5,868 grt; IX 156: 5,878 grt; IX 157: 5,959 grt; IX 216: 5,873 grt
Dimensions	416' (oa); 402' (wl) x 54' x 18'9"
Machinery	1 screw; diesel; SHP 3,000; 13 knots
Complement	70
Armament	1–3"/50, 1–40mm; IX 216: 1–4', 1–3"

Figure 10.67: The *Orvetta* (IX 157), seen here on 9 Jun 1944, was used mainly as a barracks ship to provide housing for personnel at advanced bases in the Pacific.

Notes: Barrack Ships; IX 216 *Unicoi*: Mobile dry storage.

Service Records:

IX 110 *Ocelot* Went aground in typhoon at Okinawa, 16 Sep 1945; refloated. Wrecked in typhoon at Okinawa, broke in two, 9 Oct 1945. Stricken 3 Jan 1946; Returned 7 Apr 1946. BU 1948 Shanghai.

IX 156 *City of Dalhart* Decomm 28 Jan 1946 and returned; sold 22 Jan 1947; BU Jacksonville, Fla.
1* Guam.

IX 157 *Orvetta* Decomm Dec 1946. Stricken 10 Jun 1947. Returned 26 Jan 1948. BU 1949 Hong Kong.

IX 216 *Unicoi* Went aground at Green I., 7 Aug 1945. Decomm 16 Apr 1946. Stricken 1 May 1946. BU 1948 San Francisco.

No.	Name	Builder	Launched	Acquired	Comm.
IX 146	*Fortune*	Doullut	Mar 1920	16 Feb 1944	19 Feb 1944
	ex–*City of Elwood* (1944)				
IX 147	*Supply*	Doullut	Jan 1921	5 Feb 1944	8 Feb 1944
	ex–*Ward* (1944), ex–*Exton* (1942), ex–*Ward* (1940)				

Displacement	13,250 tons f/l, 6,197 grt (146), 6,167 (147)
Dimensions	411'9" (oa); 395'6" (wl) x 55' x 27'2"
Machinery	1 screw; diesel; SHP 3,500; 11.8 knots
Complement	167
Armament	1–4"/50, 1–3"/50, 8–20mm

Note: Aviation stores ships.

Service Records:

IX 146 *Fortune* Rec **AVS 2**, 25 May 1945. Decomm 18 Oct 1945. BU 1946, Emeryville, Calif.

IX 147 *Supply* Rec **AVS 1**, 25 May 1945. Decomm 4 Feb 1946. BU 1948 Jacksonville, Fla.
1* Palau.

No.	Name	Builder	Launched	Acquired	In service
IX 155	*Mustang*	H. K. Hall	1899	28 Jan 1944	Apr 1944
	ex–*William H. Smith*		Pt Blakely, Wash.		

Tonnage	566 grt
Dimensions	170'4" x 37'6" x 12'8"

Note: Four–mast wood schooner

Service Record:

IX 155 *Mustang* Amphibious training, Coronado, Calif. Stricken 5 Jun 1946.

No.	Name	Builder	Launched	Acquired	Comm.
IX 167	*Leyden*	Harlan	1910	22 May 1944	1944
	ex–*Northland* (1944)				
IX 168	*Southland*	Newport News	10 Mar 1908	22 May 1944	1944
	ex–*Southland* (1944)				

Displacement	3,117 tons f/l, 2,055 grt (167), 2,081 (168)

Dimensions	305' (oa); IX 167 *Leyden*: 291'2" x 51' x 18"; IX 168 *Southland*: 283' (wl) x 52'10" x 17'
Machinery	1 screw; VTE; .. boilers; SHP 3,000; 15 knots
Armament	1–12 pdr

Notes: Details for IX 168. Cross-channel ferry.

Service Records:

IX 167 *Leyden* Decomm 23 Jul 1945. Sold 7 Nov 1946.
Later history: Merchant *Hung Chong* 1947. BU 1955 Hong Kong.

IX 168 *Southland* Decomm 23 Jul 1945. Stricken 13 Aug 1945.
Later history: Merchant *Hung Yung* 1947. BU 1955 Hong Kong.

No.	Name	Builder	Launched	Acquired	Comm.
IX 169	*President Warfield*	Pusey	7 Feb 1928	21 May 1944	21 May 1944
	ex-*APL* 16 (22 Oct 1942)				

Displacement	4,273 tons f/l, 1,814 grt
Dimensions	328' (oa); 318' (wl) x 44'1" x 16'
Machinery	1 screw; VTE; 4 Scotch boilers; SHP 2,600
Complement	70
Armament	(U)

Notes: Accommodation ship, Omaha Beach. Merchant name retained.

Service Record:

IX 169 *President Warfield* Decomm 13 Sep 1945. Stricken 11 Oct 1945. Sold 9 Nov 1946.
Later history: Merchant *President Warfield*, renamed *Exodus* 1947, 1947. Burned at Haifa, 26 Aug 1952.

No.	Name	Builder	Launched	Acquired	Comm.
IX 205	*Callao*	P. Smit	1943	15 Oct 1944	24 Jan 1945
	ex-USCG *East Breeze* (1945), ex-*Externstiene* (1944)				

Displacement	1,015 tons f/l
Dimensions	183' (oa); 175' (wl) x 30'10" x 13'11"
Machinery	1 screw; VTE; 1 Scotch boiler, SHP 750, 10 knots
Complement	78
Armament	(U)

Note: Experimental vessel.

Service Record:

IX 205 *Callao* German weather ship captured off Greenland, 15 Oct 1944. In collision with CGC *Travis* off Boston, 30 Nov 1944. †

No.	Name	Builder	Launched	Acquired	Comm.
IX 224	*Aide de Camp*	Lawley	1922	31 May 1945	18 Jun 1945
	ex-*Aide de Camp*, ex-*Poinsettia*, ex-*Ranger*, ex-*Colleen*				

Displacement	167 tons
Dimensions	110' x 18'2" x 6'
Machinery	1 screw, diesel, 400hp, 15 knots

Notes: Acquired from the Office of Scientific Research and Development; former name retained.

Service Record:

IX 224 *Aide de Camp* Out of service 2 Nov 1945. Stricken 28 Nov 1945. Sold
Later history: *Merchant Mariner II*, 1955.

No.	Name	Formerly	Reclassified	Notes
IX 98	*Moosehead*	DD 259	10 Feb 1943	—
IX 100	*Racer*	SC 501	21 Apr 1943	—
IX 102	*Majaba*	AG 43	1 Jul 1943	—
IX 105	*Panther*	SC 1470	26 Jun 1943	—
IX 107	*Zebra*	AKN 5	11 Feb 1944	—
IX 148	*North Star*	WPG 59	15 Jan 1944	ex-USCG
IX 149–54	—	—	—	Concrete barges
IX 158–64	—	—	—	Concrete barges
IX 165	*Flicker*	AM 70	20 Apr 1944	—
IX 166	*Linnet*	AM 76	20 Apr 1944	—
IX 170	*Curlew*	AM 69	1 Jun 1944	—
IX 171	*Albatross*	AM 71	1 Jun 1944	—
IX 172	*Bluebird*	AM 72	1 Jun 1944	—
IX 173	*Etamin*	AK 93	15 Jun 1944	—
IX 174	*Grumium*	AK 112	20 Jun 1944	Rec AVS 3, 25 May 1945
IX 175	*Kestrel*	AMc 5	10 Jul 1944	—
IX 176	*Kingbird*	AMc 56	10 Jul 1944	—
IX 177	*Nightingale*	AMc 149	10 Jul 1944	—
IX 180	*Flamingo*	AMc 22	17 Jul 1944	—
IX 181	*Egret*	AMc 24	17 Jul 1944	—
IX 182	*Donnell*	DE 56	15 Jul 1944	—
IX 183	*Catbird*	AM 68	15 Aug 1944	—
IX 194	*Kildeer*	AMc 21	25 Sep 1944	—
IX 195	*Goshawk*	AM 79	10 Oct 1944	—
IX 196	*Spark*	LST 340	20 Oct 1944	—
IX 198	*Cohasset*	LST 129	31 Dec 1944	—
IX 199	*Barcelo*	YP 375	15 Dec 1944	—
IX 200	*Maratanza*	YP 448	15 Dec 1944	Out of service 7 Nov 1945
IX 201	*Sterling*	YP 449	15 Dec 1944	Out of service 11 Dec 1945
IX 202	*Liberator*	AMc 87	30 Dec 1944	—
IX 203	*Agile*	AMc 111	30 Dec 1944	—
IX 204	*Allioth*	AK 109	31 Dec 1944	Rec AVS 4, 25 May 1945
IX 206	*Chocura*	PC 1124	20 Feb 1945	—
IX 207	*Big Horn*	AO 45	1 Feb 1945	—
IX 208	*Domino*	Not acquired	—	—
IX 209	*Seaward*	LST 278	15 Feb 1945	—
IX 211	*Castine*	PC 452	10 Mar 1945	—
IX 212	—	LCI(G) 396	23 Feb 1945	—
IX 217	*Tackle*	ARS(T) 4	20 Mar 1945	—
IX 219	—	Not acquired	—	—
IX 220	—	Not acquired	—	—
IX 221	*Eureka*	PC 488	25Apr 1945	—
IX 222	*Pegasus*	AK 48	15 May 1945	—
IX 230	*Tapacola*	AMc 54	10 Aug 1945	—
IX 231	*Stalwart*	AMc 105	10 Aug 1945	—

IX 232	*Summit*	AMc 106	10 Aug 1945	—
IX 300	*Prinz Eugen*	German cruiser	—	—
IX 301	*Dithmarschen*	German naval tanker	—	Rec AO 110, 1 Oct 1946

Notes: IX 300 *Prinz Eugen* was a German cruiser taken over at the end of the war. It was used as a Bikini atomic test target ship and foundered in Kwajalein lagoon, 21 Dec 1946. The ex–Japanese battleship *Nagato* and cruiser *Sakawa* were also used and sunk in the tests at Bikini, but received no Navy numbers.

11
TRANSPORT AND SUPPLY VESSELS

COLLIERS

Colliers were naval auxiliaries for carrying coal, and were phased out before the war as oil fuel replaced coal.

Colliers on the Navy List, 1922

AC 8 *Neptune* Decomm 28 Jun 1922. Stricken 14 May 1938, sold 18 Apr 1939 sold; BU Philadelphia.

AC 9 *Proteus* Decomm 25 Mar 1924 Stricken 5 Dec 1940, sold 8 Mar 1941.
Later history: Merchant *Proteus* 1941. Foundered off U.S. coast (missing after 23 Nov 1941).

AC 10 *Nereus* Decomm 30 Jun 1922. Stricken 5 Dec 1940, sold 10 Mar 1941.
Later history: Merchant *Nereus* 1941. Foundered off Nova Scotia (missing after 10 Dec 1941).

AC 11 *Orion* Decomm 18 Jun 1926. Stricken 10 Jul 1931, sold 30 Aug 1933; BU Baltimore.

AC 12 *Jason* Far East 1925–32. Aviation tender, 1925, rec **AV 2**, 21 Jan 1930.

AC 13 *Abarenda* Rec **AG 14**, 1 Jul 1924.

AC 14 *Ajax* Rec **AG 15**, 1 Jul 1924.

Figure 11.1: *Sangay* (AE 10), seen here on 11 Apr 1943, was the only ammunition ship equipped to transport mines.

AMMUNITION SHIPS

Ammunition ships were specially fitted for carrying ammunition in air-cooled compartments. They were named after volcanoes.

Ammunition Ships on the Navy List, 1922

AE 1 *Pyro* Out of comm 10 Sep 1924– 1 Jul 1939. Decomm 12 Jun 1946. Stricken 3 Jul 1946, sold 17 Jul 1946; BU Terminal I.
1* Pearl Harbor.

AE 2 *Nitro* Decomm 30 Nov 1945. Stricken 19 Mar 1948. Sold 14 Sep 1949; BU New York.
1* Southern France.
Armament: 2–5"/51, 4– 3"/50, 2 twin 40mm, 8–20mm guns.

No.	Name	Builder	Keel Laid	Launched	Comm.
AE 3	*Lassen* ex–*Shooting Star* (1940)	Tampa	24 Sep 1938	10 Jan 1940	27 Mar 1941
AE 4	*Kilauea* ex–*Surprise* (1940	Tampa	6 Nov 1939	6 Aug 1940	16 May 1941
AE 5	*Rainier* ex–*Rainbow* (1941)	Tampa	14 May 1940	1 Mar 1941	21 Dec 1941
AE 6	*Shasta* ex–*Comet* (1941)	Tampa	12 Aug 1940	9 Jul 1941	20 Jan 1942

Displacement	6,350 tons; 13,855 f/l
Dimensions	459' (oa); 435' (wl) x 63' x 26'5"
Machinery	1 screw; Nordberg diesel; SHP 6,000; 15.3 knots
Complement	280
Armament	1–5"/38, 4–3"/50, 2 twin 40mm, 8 twin 20mm AA guns

Note: Type C2–T.

Service Records:

AE 3 *Lassen* Decomm 15 Jan 1947. †
3* Palau, Fleet Raids 1945, Raids on Japan 7–8/45.

AE 4 *Kilauea* Renamed ***Mount Baker***, 17 Mar 1943. Decomm 15 Aug 1946. †

AE 5 *Rainier* Decomm 30 Aug 1946. †

AE 6 *Shasta* In collision with cruiser *Indianapolis* off Iwo Jima, 19 Feb 1945. Damaged in typhoon, Philippine Sea, 5 Jun 1945. Decomm 10 Aug 1946. †
4* Saipan, Palau, Iwo Jima, Fleet Raids 1945, Okinawa, Raids on Japan 7–8/45.

AE 7 *Maj. Gen. Henry Gibbins* Acquisition from Army canceled.

No.	Name	Builder	Keel Laid	Launched	Comm.
AE 8	*Mauna Loa*	Tampa	10 Dec 1942	14 Apr 1943	27 Oct 1943
AE 9	*Mazama*	Tampa	14 Apr 1942	15 Aug 1943	10 Mar 1944
AE 13	*Akutan*	Tampa	20 Jun 1944	17 Sep 1944	15 Feb 1945

Displacement	6,350 tons; 14,225 f/l
Dimensions	459' (oa); 435' (wl) x 63' x 26'5"
Machinery	1 screw; Nordberg diesel; SHP 6,000; 15.3 knots
Complement	281
Armament	1–5"/38, 4–3"/50, 2 twin 40mm, 8–20mm AA guns

Service Records:

AE 8 *Mauna Loa* Decomm 2 Jun 1947. †
3* Palau, Fleet Raids 1945, Raids on Japan 7–8/45.

AE 9 *Mazama* Damaged by Japanese midget submarine at Ulithi, Micronesia, 12 Jan 1945 (1 killed). Decomm 3 Aug 1946. †
2* Saipan, Raids on Japan 7–8/45.

AE 13 *Akutan* Decomm 19 Oct 1946. †
2* Okinawa, Raids on Japan 7–8/45.

No.	Name	Builder	Keel Laid	Launched	Comm.
AE 10	*Sangay* ex–*Cape Sable*	Pennsylvania	30 Oct 1941	5 Apr 1942	25 Mar 1943

Displacement	6,400 tons
Dimensions	412'3" (oa); 390' (wl) x 60' x 23'7"
Machinery	1 screw; Nordberg diesel; SHP 4,150; 14.8 knots
Complement	308
Armament	1–5"/38, 4–3"/50, 4–40mm AA guns; (1945) 1–5"/38, 3 twin 40mm, 12–20mm AA.

Notes: Type C1–A. The only AE equipped to transport mines.

Service Record

AE 10 *Sangay* Decomm 20 Jul 1947. †
2* Kwajalein, Palau.

No.	Name	Builder	Keel Laid	Launched	Comm.
AE 11	*Mount Hood* LD as *Marco Polo*	N. Carolina	28 Sep 1943	30 Nov 1943	12 Jul 1944
AE 12	*Wrangell* LD as *Midnight*	N. Carolina	21 Feb 1944	14 Apr 1944	10 Oct 1944
AE 14	*Firedrake* LD as *Winged Racer*	N. Carolina	13 Mar 1944	12 May 1944	27 Dec 1944
AE 15	*Vesuvius* LD as *Game Cock*	N. Carolina	25 Mar 1944	26 May 1944	16 Jan 1945
AE 16	*Mount Katmai*	N. Carolina	11 Nov 1944	6 Jan 1945	21 Jul 1945
AE 17	*Great Sitkin*	N. Carolina	23 Nov 1944	20 Jan 1945	11 Aug 1945
AE 18	*Paricutin*	N. Carolina	7 Dec 1944	30 Jan 1945	25 Jul 1945
AE 19	*Diamond Head*	N. Carolina	12 Dec 1944	3 Feb 1945	9 Aug 1945

Displacement	13,910 tons
Dimensions	459'2" (oa); 435' (wl) x 63' x 28'3"
Machinery	1 screw; GE GT; 2 CE boilers; SHP 6,000; 16.4 knots
Complement	267
Armament	1–5"/38, 4–3"/50, 2 twin 40mm, 8–20mm AA guns

Note: Type C2–S–AJ1.

Service Records:

AE 11 *Mount Hood* Blew up and sank in Seeadler Harbor, Manus I., 10 Nov 1944 (295 killed).

AE 12 *Wrangell* Decomm 19 Nov 1946. †
2* Iwo Jima, Fleet Raids 1945, Raids on Japan 7–8/45.

AE 14 *Firedrake* Decomm 21 Feb 1946. †
2* Okinawa, Fleet Raids 1945, Raids on Japan 7–8/45.

Figure 11.2: *Mount Hood* (AE 11), 16 Jul 1944. She was destroyed by a massive explosion at Manus in 1944, causing much damage to nearby ships.

Figure 11.3: The store ship *Arctic* (AF 7), seen at San Francisco on 29 Apr 1943, was acquired after World War I.

AE 15 *Vesuvius* Decomm 20 Aug 1946. †
2* Fleet Raids 1945, Raids on Japan 7–8/45.
AE 16 *Mount Katmai* †
AE 17 *Great Sitkin* †
AE 18 *Paricutin* †
AE 19 *Diamond Head* Decomm 23 Aug 1946. †

STORE SHIPS

Store ships were refrigerator ships for carrying fresh food and were known as "beef boats."

Store Ships on the Navy List, 1922

AF 1 *Bridge* Eastern Mediterranean 1922–23. China 1937–39. Damaged by mine off Korea, 1 Nov 1945. Decomm 27 Jun 1946. Sold 22 Dec 1947.
1* Okinawa.
Later history: Merchant *Don Jose* 1948. BU 1953 Kudamatsu, Japan.

AF 6 *Rappahannock* Decomm 10 Dec 1924. Stricken 19 Jul 1933, sold 5 Oct 1933.
Later history: Merchant *William Luckenbach* 1934, renamed *Maria C.* 1946. BU 1953 Savona.

AF 7 *Arctic* Pacific. Decomm 3 Apr 1946. Stricken 1 May 1946. Sold 19 Aug 1947; BU New Orleans.

AF 8 *Boreas* Comm 24 Mar 1941. Pacific. Decomm 15 Feb 1946. Sold 18 Jul 1946; BU Baltimore.

AF 9 *Yukon* Out of comm 14 Apr 1922–19 Jan 1940. Damaged in collision with freighter *El Mirlo* in convoy off Sydney, Nova Scotia, 23 Jul 1943. Torpedoed by *U-979* off Reykjavik and severely damaged, 22 Sep 1944. Decomm 18 Mar 1946. Stricken 17 Apr 1946. Sold 29 Jul 1946; BU Baltimore.
Armament, AF7–9 1–5"/51, 4–3"/50, 8–20mm AA guns; AF 1: [1942] 2–5"/51, 4–3"/50, 1 quad 1.1"; [1945] 1–5"/38, 4–3"/50, 1 twin 40mm, 8–20mm AA guns.

No.	Name	Builder	Keel Laid	Launched	Comm.
AF 10	*Aldebaran*	Newport News	28 Nov 1938	21 Jun 1939	14 Jan 1941
	ex-*Stag Hound* (1940)				

Displacement	13,910 tons
Dimensions	459'3" (oa); 435' (wl) x 63' x 25'10"
Machinery	1 screw; NN GT; 2 B&W boilers; SHP 6,000; 16.4 knots
Complement	287
Armament	1–5"/38, 4–3"/50, 10–20mm AA guns

Notes: Type C2. Acquired from Grace Lines 22 Dec 1940. Converted Apr–Nov 1942.

Service Record:

AF 10 *Aldebaran* †
2* Fleet Raids 1945, Raids on Japan 7–8/45.

No.	Name	Builder	Keel Laid	Launched	Comm.
AF 11	*Polaris*	Sun	25 Jul 1938	22 Apr 1939	4 Apr 1941
	ex-*Donald McKay* (1941)				

Displacement	13,910 tons
Dimensions	459'1" (oa); 435' (wl) x 63' x 25'10"
Machinery	1 screw; Sun Doxford diesel; SHP 6,000; 16.4 knots
Complement	253
Armament	1–5"/38, 4–3"/50, 10–20mm AA guns

Note: Acquired 27 Jan 1941.

Service Record

AF 11 *Polaris* North Atlantic. Decomm 18 Jan 1946. Stricken 7 Feb 1946. †
1* Convoy UGS-36.

No.	Name	Builder	Launched	Acquired	Comm.
AF 12	*Mizar*	Beth. Quincy	6 Feb 1932	2 Jun 1941	14 Jun 1941
	ex-*Quirigua* (1941)				
AF 13	*Tarazed*	Newport News	14 Nov 1931	4 Jun 1941	14 Jun 1941
	ex-*Chiriquà* (1941)				
AF 15	*Talamanca*	Newport News	15 Aug 1931	16 Dec 1941	28 Jan 1942
	ex-*Talamanca* (1942)				
AF 21	*Merak*	Beth. Quincy	23 Apr 1932	20 Mar 1942	8 May 1942
	ex-*Veragua* (1942)				

Figure 11.4:. *Ariel* (AF 22) was one of several United Fruit Company ships taken over in 1941–42.

Figure 11.5: *Calamares* (AF 18), 14 Aug 1944, served as a Navy transport during World War I.

AF 22	*Ariel*	Newport News	15 Aug 1931	24 Mar 1942	14 May 1942
	ex-*Dione* (28 Apr 1942), ex-*Jamaica* (1937), ex-*Peten* (1931), ex-*Segovia* (1931)				

Displacement	11,875 tons; 6,982 grt (AF 12, AF 21), 6,963 (AF 13, AF 15), 6,968 (AF 22)
Dimensions	446'10" (oa); 415' (wl) x 60'3" x 26'
Machinery	2 screws, GE turbo–electric, 4 B&W boilers; SHP 11,000; 18.5 knots
Complement	238
Armament	1–5"/51, 3–3"/50; 1–5"/38, 4–3"/50 (AF 12); (1945) 1–5"/38, 4–3"/50, 8 to 12 20mm AA guns

Notes: Acquired from United Fruit Company. *Antigua* (AF 17) was acquired 28 Dec 1941, never used, and canceled 26 May 1944.

Service Records:

AF 12 *Mizar* Decomm 1 Apr 1946 and returned to owner. Stricken 17 Apr 1946.
4* Saidor, Bismarck Arch., Western New Guinea, Admiralty Is., Hollandia.
Later history: Merchant *Quirigua*, renamed *Samala* 1959. BU 1964 Kaohsiung, Taiwan, Taiwan.

AF 13 *Tarazed* Decomm 4 Jan 1946 and returned. Stricken 21 Jan 1946.
1* Southern France.
Later history: Merchant *Chiriqui*, renamed *Blexen* 1957. BU 1969 Taiwan.

AF 15 *Talamanca* Decomm 29 Nov 1945. Stricken 19 Dec 1945. Returned.
Later history: Merchant *Talamanca*, renamed *Sulaco* 1958. BU 1964 Bruges.

AF 21 *Merak* Blown aground in blizzard at Reykjavik, 14 Jan 1946. Decomm 21 Jun 1946 and returned.
Later history: Merchant *Veragua*, renamed *Sinaloa* 1959, *Olancho* 1963. BU 1964 Bruges.

AF 22 *Ariel* Decomm 21 Jun 1946, returned. Stricken 3 Jul 1946.
Later history: Merchant *Jamaica*, renamed *Blumenthal* 1958. BU 1969 Taiwan.

No.	Name	Builder	Launched	Acquired	Comm.
AF 14	*Uranus*	Helsingor	21 Dec 1932	11 Aug 1941	27 Oct 1941
	ex-*Maria* (1941), ex-*Caravelle* (1938), ex-*Helga* (1935)				

Displacement	3,540 tons; 1,700 grt
Dimensions	296'6" (oa); 256' (wl) x 39'6" x 17'4"
Machinery	1 screw; 2 VTE, 2 Scotch s/e boilers; SHP 1,140, 11.5 knots
Complement	93
Armament	2–3"/50, 6–20mm AA guns

Note: Danish ship seized at New York, 31 Mar 1941.

Service Record:

AF 14 *Uranus* Ran aground off Akureyi, Iceland, 10 Apr 1943. Decomm 8 May 1946. Stricken 21 May 1946.
Later history: Merchant *Maria Dan* 1946, renamed *Michael* 1959. BU 1968 Split.

No.	Name	Builder	Launched	Acquired	Comm.
AF 16	*Pastores*	Workman	17 Aug 1913	23 Dec 1941	13 Feb 1942
AF 18	*Calamares*	Workman	2 Sep 1913	12 Dec 1941	10 Apr 1943

Displacement	13,750 tons; 7,233 grt
Dimensions	486'6" (oa); 470' (wl) x 55' x 27'4"
Machinery	2 screws; VQE; 3 Scotch s/e; 1 d/e boiler (AF 16: 3 Yarrow); SHP 6,500; 14 knots
Complement	248
Armament	1–5"/51, 4–3"/50 (AF 18: 1–5"/38), 8–20mm AA guns

Figure 11.6: *Taurus* (AF 25), shortly after commissioning on 30 Nov 1942.

Notes: Acquired from United Fruit Company. Served in NOTS during World War I. Merchant names retained.

Service Records:

AF 16 *Pastores* Decomm 14 Mar 1946. Stricken 28 Mar 1946, sold 19 Dec 1946; BU 1947 Oakland.

AF 18 *Calamares* Decomm 25 Apr 1946. Stricken 6 May 1946; BU 1948 Baltimore.

No.	Name	Builder	Launched	Acquired	Comm.
AF 19	*Roamer*	Helsingor	14 Sep 1935	22 Jul 1942	30 Aug 1942
	ex-*African Reefer* (1942), ex-*Yrsa* (1936)				

Displacement	4,600 tons f/l; 1,771 grt
Dimensions	318'6" (oa); 300' (wl) x 42'7" x 18'
Machinery	1 screw; diesel; SHP 1,850; 12 knots
Complement	114
Armament	2 3"/50, 4–20mm AA guns

Notes: Danish ship seized at New York, 5 Sep 1941. Merchant name retained.

Service Record:

AF 19 *Roamer* Southwest Pacific. Decomm 14 Jun 1946. Stricken 3 Jul 1946.
Later history: Merchant *African Reefer* 1946. BU 1963 Rotterdam.

No.	Name	Builder	Launched	Acquired	Comm.
AF 20	*Pontiac*	Nakskov	3 Oct 1936	11 May 1942	12 May 1942
	ex-*Pontiac* (1942), ex-*Australian Reefer* (1941)				

Displacement	5,410 tons f/l; 2,321 grt
Dimensions	447'10" (oa); 415' (wl) x 60' x 18'11"
Machinery	1 screw; diesel; SHP 4,300; 15.5 knots
Complement	166
Armament	2–3"/50, 2 twin 20mm.

Note: Danish ship seized at New York, 31 Mar 1941.

Service Record:

AF 20 *Pontiac* Foundered in gale off Halifax, NS, 30 Jan 1945. Refloated, 17 Feb 1945. Decomm 20 May 1945. Stricken 2 Jun 1945; BU 1948 Baltimore.

No.	Name	Builder	Launched	Acquired	Comm.
AF 23	*Cygnus*	Cammell Laird	22 Mar 1924	11 Aug 1942	31 Aug 1942
	ex–*La Perla* (1942)				

Displacement	7,170 tons f/l; 3,792 grt
Dimensions	336'3" (oa); 325' (wl) x 48' x 23'9"
Machinery	1 screw; VTE; 3 Scotch boilers; SHP 2,500, 12 knots
Complement	112
Armament	2–3"/50, 6–20mm AA guns

Service Record:

AF 23 *Cygnus* Decomm 18 Jul 1946.

Later history: Merchant *La Perla*, renamed *La Perla I* 1947, *Giuba* 1949, *Frigo Asia* 1957. BU 1970 Brazil.

No.	Name	Builder	Launched	Acquired	Comm.
AF 24	*Delphinus*	Workman	5 May 1915	11 Aug 1942	11 Aug 1942
	ex–*San Mateo* (22 Aug 1942)				

Displacement	5,230 tons f/l; 5,947 grt
Dimensions	329' (oa); 315' (wl) x 44'2" x 23'
Machinery	1 screw; VTE; 3 Scotch s/e boilers; SHP 2,500, 12 knots
Complement	107
Armament	1–4"/50, 1–3"/50, 6–20mm AA guns

Service Record:

AF 24 *Delphinus* Ran aground off New Caledonia, 17 Mar 1943. Decomm 9 May 1946. BU 1948 Mobile.

No.	Name	Builder	Launched	Acquired	Comm.
AF 25	*Taurus*	Workman	12 Aug 1921	2 Oct 1942	29 Oct 1942
	ex–*San Benito* (1942)				

Displacement	6,600 tons f/l; 3,724 grt
Dimensions	325'3" (oa); 325' (wl) x 40'4" x 23'6"
Machinery	1 screw; Thompson Houston Curtis turbine; 3 Scotch s/e boilers; SHP 2,500, 11.5 knots
Complement	114
Armament	1–4"/50, 1–3"/50, 6–20mm AA guns

Service Record:

AF 25 *Taurus* Decomm 11 Dec 1945. Stricken 3 Jan 1946.

Later history: Merchant *San Benito*. BU 1953 Mobile.

No.	Name	Builder	Launched	Acquired	Comm.
AF 26	*Octans*	Workman	1917	8 May 1943	11 Jun 1943
	ex–*Ulua* (1943)				

Displacement	11,600 tons f/l; 6,494 grt
Dimensions	440' (oa); 425' (wl) x 54'4" x 26'2"
Machinery	2 screws; VTE; 2 Scotch s/e, 2 d/e boilers; SHP 6,000; 13.5 knots
Complement	227
Armament	1–5"/38, 4–3"/50, 8–20mm AA guns

Figure 11.7: *Merapi* (AF 38), one of 17 type R1-M-AV3 ships acquired as storeships.

Service Record:

AF 26 *Octans* Decomm 6 Mar 1946. Stricken 20 Mar 1946, BU 1948 Baltimore.

No.	Name	Formerly	Date
AF 27	*Pictor*	*Platano*	
	Acquisition canceled 22 May 1944		
AF 40	*Saturn*	AK 49	10 Apr 1944

No.	Name	Builder	Keel Laid	Launched	Comm.
AF 28	*Hyades*	Gulf	10 Dec 1942	12 Jun 1943	3 Aug 1944
	LD as *Iberville*				
AF 29	*Graffias*	Gulf	17 Jun 1943	12 Dec 1943	28 Oct 1944
	LD as *Topa Topa*				

Displacement	15,300 tons f/l
Dimensions	468'8" (oa); 445' (wl) x 63' x 28'
Machinery	1 screw; GE GT; 2 B&W boilers; SHP 6,000; 15.5 knots
Complement	252
Armament	1–5"/38, 4–3"/50, 12–20mm AA guns

Note: Type C2–S–E1.

Service Records:

AF 28 *Hyades* †
AF 29 *Graffias* †

No.	Name	Builder	Keel Laid	Launched	Comm.
AF 30	*Adria*	Pennsylvania	27 Dec 1943	16 Apr 1944	26 Dec 1944
AF 31	*Arequipa*	Pennsylvania	17 Jan 1944	4 May 1944	14 Jan 1945
AF 32	*Corduba*	Pennsylvania	7 Feb 1944	11 Jun 1944	26 Jan 1945
AF 33	*Karin*	Pennsylvania	17 Apr 1944	22 Jun 1944	3 Feb 1945
AF 34	*Kerstin*	Pennsylvania	5 May 1944	16 Jul 1944	23 Feb 1945
AF 35	*Latona*	Pennsylvania	12 Jun 1944	10 Aug 1944	25 Feb 1945
AF 36	*Lioba*	Pennsylvania	23 Jun 1944	27 Aug 1944	6 Mar 1945
AF 37	*Malabar*	Pennsylvania	17 Jul 1944	17 Sep 1944	8 Mar 1945
AF 38	*Merapi*	Pennsylvania	11 Aug 1944	4 Oct 1944	21 Mar 1945

Figure 11.8: *Regulus* (AK 14), a World War I cargo steamer, on 20 Mar 1942. Although acquired in 1921, she was first commissioned in 1940 and served in the Pacific.

AF 39	*Palisana*	Pennsylvania	28 Aug 1944	21 Oct 1944	16 Apr 1945
AF 41	*Athanasia*	Pennsylvania	14 Aug 1944	12 Oct 1944	3 Apr 1945
	LD as *Stevedore Knot*				
AF 42	*Bondia*	Pennsylvania	18 Sep 1944	9 Nov 1944	17 Apr 1945
	LD as *Flemish Bend*				
AF 43	*Gordonia*	Pennsylvania	5 Oct 1944	30 Nov 1944	14 May 1945
	LD as *Whale Knot*				
AF 44	*Laurentia*	Pennsylvania	23 Oct 1944	12 Dec 1944	5 Jun 1945
	LD as *Wall and Crown*				
AF 45	*Lucidor*	Pennsylvania	1 Dec 1944	25 Jan 1945	6 Jul 1945
	LD as *Chain Splice*				
AF 46	*Octavia*	Pennsylvania	22 Nov 1944	18 Jan 1945	19 Jun 1945
	LD as *Yardarm Knot*				
AF 47	*Valentine*	Pennsylvania	7 Dec 1944	3 Feb 1945	19 Jul 1945
	LD as *Becket Bend*				

Displacement	3,139 tons; 7,435 tons f/l
Dimensions	338'6" (oa); 320' (wl) x 50' x 21'1"
Machinery	1 screw; Nordberg diesel; SHP 1,700, 11.5 knots
Complement	84
Armament	1–3"/50, 6–20mm AA guns

Note: Type R1–M–AV3.

Service Records:

AF 30 *Adria* †
1* Okinawa.

AF 31 *Arequipa* †

AF 32 *Corduba* †

AF 33 *Karin* †

AF 34 *Kerstin* †

AF 35 *Latona* †
1* Okinawa.

AF 36 *Lioba* †
1* Okinawa.

AF 37 *Malabar* †

AF 38 *Merapi* †
1* Okinawa.

AF 39 *Palisana* Decomm 22 May 1946 and returned to MC. Stricken 19 Jun 1946.
Later history: Merchant *Palisana*, renamed *Sea Harvester* 1981, *Spirit* 1985.

AF 41 *Athanasia* Went aground in fog on Nootka I., BC, 12 Oct 1945. Decomm 20 Dec 1945. Returned 8 Jan 1946.
1* Okinawa.
Later history: Merchant *Polar Pioneer* 1982.

AF 42 *Bondia* Decomm 29 Jul 1946 and returned. †
Later history: Merchant *Flemish Bend.*

AF 43 *Gordonia* Decomm 8 Jul 1946, returned to MC.
Later history: Merchant *Whale Knot.*

AF 44 *Laurentia* Decomm 18 Jun 1946 and returned to WSA. †
Later history: Merchant *Wall and Crown.*

AF 45 *Lucidor* Decomm 26 May 1946 and returned to WSA. To Army; BU 1974.
Later history: Merchant *Lucidor*, renamed *Polar Pioneer* 1967, *Mermaid* 1972, *Mochica* 1973, *Polar M.* 1977, *Caribea* 1977. Went aground at Necochea, Argentina, 24 Apr 1980.

AF 46 *Octavia* Decomm 12 Aug 1946 and returned to WSA. Stricken 8 Oct 1946.
Later history: Merchant *Yardarm Knot.* sold 1972. Damaged by grounding in Alaska waters, 15 Feb 1989, CTL. Damaged by fire, Seattle, 8 Nov 1994.

AF 47 *Valentine* Decomm 6 Aug 1946 and returned to WSA. Stricken 8 Oct 1946. †
Later history: Merchant *Pier Bend.*

CARGO SHIPS

The Navy operated many cargo ships to carry the multitude of needed specialized supplies and equipment. They were named after stars, but the later C1 type were named after U.S. counties.

Cargo Ships on the Navy List, 1922

AK 2 *Kittery* Decomm 5 Apr 1933. Stricken 11 Apr 1933; BU 1937.

AK 3 *Newport News* Decomm and stricken 1 Aug 1924, sold 4 Apr 1925.
Later history: Merchant *Arctic* 1925. BU 1937 Osaka.

AK 4 *Bath* Decomm 9 May 1922. Sold 2 Jan 1926.
Later history: Merchant *Paz* 1926, renamed *Oued Fes* 1929, *Rosa Linda* 1952. Wrecked in Abrolhos Is., Brazil, 29 Dec 1955.

AK 6 *Beaufort* Decomm 23 Dec 1925. Sold 22 Oct 1926.
Later history: Merchant *Fjorden* 1927. Wrecked off Hong Kong, 12 Apr 1933.

AK 11 *R. L. Barnes* **AO 14**, Jul 1921. Rec **AG 27**, 1 Jul 1938.

Figure 11.9: *Betelgeuse* (AK 28) was one of several fast new cargo ships converted to AKA in 1942.

AK 13 *Capella* Out of comm 1 Sep 1924–10 Nov 1938. Decomm 30 Nov 1945. To WSA Jul 1946; BU.

AK 14 *Regulus* Recomm 14 Dec 1940. Decomm 25 Mar 1946. Stricken 17 Apr 1946, sold 29 Sep 1947; BU.

AK 15 *Sirius* Decomm 26 Apr 1946. Stricken 5 Jun 1946, sold 29 Sep 1947; BU Oakland.

AK 16 *Spica* First comm 1 Mar 1940. Decomm 18 Jan 1946. Stricken 7 Feb 1946, sold 13 Jun 1947; BU.
1* Attu

AK 17 *Vega* Decomm 15 Jan 1946. Stricken 12 Mar 1946. BU Terminal I.
4* Pearl Harbor, Saipan, Guam, Palau, Okinawa.
Armament: AK 13–17One 5"/38, 4–3"/50, 8–20mm AA guns.

No.	Name	Builder	Keel Laid	Launched	Comm.
AK 19	*Procyon*	Tampa	15 Jan 1940	14 Nov 1940	8 Aug 1941
	LD as *Sweepstakes*				
AK 20	*Bellatrix*	Tampa	20 Nov 1940	15 Aug 1941	17 Feb 1942
	LD as *Raven*				
AK 21	*Electra*	Tampa	6 Mar 1941	18 Nov 1941	17 Mar 1942
	LD as *Meteor*				

Displacement	8,045 tons; 14,225 tons f/l
Dimensions	59'1" (oa); 435' (wl) x 63' x 26'5" x 64'8" x 25'10"
Machinery	1 screw; diesel; SHP 6,000; 16.5 knots
Endurance	22,600/12
Complement	370/343
Armament	1–5"/38, 4–3"/50 (AK 20); (1945) 1–5"/38, 4 twin 40mm, 14 twin 20mm AA

Notes: Type C2–T. Converted to amphibious ships.

Service Records:

AK 19 *Procyon* Acq 14 Nov 1940. Rec **AKA 2**, 1 Feb 1943. Decomm 23 Mar 1946. Stricken 12 Apr 1946.
5* North Africa, Sicily, Salerno, Southern France, Okinawa.

AK 20 *Bellatrix* Rec **AKA 3**, 1 Feb 1943. Training, U.S. West Coast, Aug 1944–Sep 1945. Decomm 1 Apr 1946. Stricken 30 Jun 1946.
4* Guadalcanal–Tulagi, Solomons, Sicily, Gilbert Is., Saipan.

AK 21 *Electra* Torpedoed by *U–173* off Casablanca, beached, 15 Nov 1942. Rec **AKA 4**, 1 Feb 1943. Decomm 19 Mar 1946. Sold 23 Mar 1947.
7* North Africa, Kwajalein, Eniwetok, Saipan, Palau, Leyte, Iwo Jima.

No.	Name	Builder	Keel Laid	Launched	Comm.
AK 22	*Fomalhaut*	Pennsylvania	28 Mar 1940	25 Jan 1941	2 May 1942
	ex–*Cape Lookout* (1941)				

Displacement	4,036 tons; 10,630 f/l
Dimensions	412'3" (oa); 390' (wl) x 61' x 23'7"
Machinery	1 screw; diesel; SHP 4,600, 16 knots
Complement	283/342
Armament	1–5"/38, 4–3"/50, 2–40mm, 10–20mm AA

Notes: Type C1–A. Converted to underway ammunition replenishment ship, 1944.

Service Record

AK 22 *Fomalhaut* Acq 16 Apr 1941. Rec **AKA 5**, 1 Feb 1943. Rec **AK 22**, 25 Aug 1944. Decomm 25 Jun 1946. †
5* Guadalcanal–Tulagi, Solomons, Saipan, Okinawa, Fleet Raids 1945.

Figure 11.10: *Saturn* (AK 49), seen here on 5 Aug 1942, was the former German *Arauca*, seized in 1941.

No.	Name	Builder	Keel Laid	Launched	Comm.
AK 18	*Arcturus*	Sun	26 Jul 1938	18 May 1939	26 Oct 1940
	ex–*Mormachawk* (1940)				
AK 23	*Alchiba*	Sun	15 Aug 1938	6 Jul 1939	15 Jun 1941
	ex–*Mormacdove* (1941)				
AK 24	*Alcyone*	Sun	12 Jan 1939	28 Aug 1939	15 Jun 1941
	ex–*Mormacgull* (1941)				
AK 25	*Algorab*	Sun	10 Aug 1939	15 Jun 1939	15 Jun 1941
	ex–*Mormacwren* (1941)				
AK 28	*Betelgeuse*	Sun	9 Mar 1939	18 Sep 1939	14 Jun 1941
	ex–*Mormaclark* (1941)				

Displacement	7,293 tons; 10,850 f/l; 6,085 grt, 14,225 tons f/l
Dimensions	459'1" (oa); 435' (wl) x 63' x 26'5"
Machinery	1 screw; diesel; SHP 6,000; 16.5 knots
Endurance	19,700/12
Complement	343
Armament	1–5"/38, 4–3"/50 (AK 24); (1945) 1–5"/38, 4 twin 40mm, 14 twin 20mm AA guns

Notes: Type C2–Cargo. Converted to amphibious ships 1941.

Service Records:

AK 18 *Arcturus* Acq 20 Sep 1940. Rec **AKA 1**, 1 Feb 1943. Decomm 3 Apr 1946. Stricken 5 Jun 1946. Sold 24 Jun 1947.
5* North Africa, Sicily, Salerno, Southern France, Okinawa.
Later history: Merchant *Star Arcturus.* BU 1971 Sakaide, Japan.

AK 23 *Alchiba* Acq 2 Jun 1941. Torpedoed twice by midget submarine from *I–16* at Lunga Point, beached; burned for five days, Guadalcanal, 28 Nov 1942. Again torpedoed off Guadalcanal, 7 Dec 1942 (3 killed). Rec **AKA 6**, 1 Feb 1943. Under repair until Jun 1945, engine trouble. Decomm 14 Jan 1946. Stricken 25 Feb 1946. Sold 1948.
2* Guadalcanal–Tulagi, Solomons, Cape Torokina.
Later history: Merchant *Tjipanas* 1948, renamed *Tong Jit* 1967. BU 1973 Whampoa.

AK 24 *Alcyone* Acq 31 May 1941. Rec **AKA 7**, 1 Feb 1943. Decomm 23 Jul 1946. Stricken 15 Aug 1946.
9* Sicily, Gilbert Is., Kwajalein, Saipan, Guam, Leyte, Lingayen, Subic Bay, Raids on Japan 7–8/45.
Later history: Merchant *Star Alcyone* 1947. BU 1969 Kaohsiung, Taiwan.

AK 25 *Algorab* Acq 6 Jun 1941. Damaged in collision with transport *Harris* off Norfolk, 11 Sep 1942 (1 killed). Rec **AKA 8**, 1 Feb 1943. Decomm 3 Dec 1945. Stricken 19 Dec 1945. Sold 17 Apr 1947.
4* North Africa, Solomons, New Georgia, Okinawa.
Later history: Merchant *Kamran*, renamed *Mongala* 1948, *Hellenic Sailor* 1954, *Aloha* 1973. BU 1974 Kaohsiung, Taiwan.

AK 28 *Betelgeuse* Acq 29 May 1941. Rec **AKA 11**, 1 Feb 1943. Decomm 15 Mar 1946, sold 27 Jun 1946.
6* Guadalcanal–Tulagi, Solomons, Sicily, Southern France, Okinawa.
Later history: Merchant *Star Betelgeuse* 1947. BU 1972 Kaohsiung, Taiwan.

No.	Name	Builder	Keel Laid	Launched	Comm.
AK 26	*Alhena*	Beth. Sp. Pt.	19 Jun 1940	18 Jan 1941	15 Jun 1941
	ex–*Robin Kettering* (1941)				

Displacement	7,151 tons; 15,080 tons f/l
Dimensions	479'8" (oa); 450' (wl) x 66'5" x 27'1"
Machinery	1 screw; Beth. GT; 2 B&W boilers; SHP 6,300, 16.5 knots
Endurance	11,000/12
Complement	446/345
Armament	1–5"/38, 4 twin 40mm, 14 twin 20mm AA

Notes: Type C2–S. Converted to amphibious ship.

Service Record:

AK 26 *Alhena* Torpedoed by *I-4* off Guadalcanal, Solomons, 29 Sep 1942 (5 killed). Rec **AKA 9**, 1 Feb 1943. Damaged by explosion of *Mount Hood* at Seeadler Harbor, 10 Nov 1944 (3 killed). Decomm 22 May 1946. Stricken 15 Aug 1946.
4* Guadalcanal–Tulagi, Solomons, Cape Torokina, Saipan, Iwo Jima.
Later history: Merchant *Robin Kettering*, renamed *Flying Hawk* 1957. BU 1971 Kaohsiung, Taiwan.

No.	Name	Builder	Keel Laid	Launched	Comm.
AK 27	*Almaack*	Beth. Quincy	14 Mar 1940	21 Sep 1940	15 Jun 1941
	ex–*Executor* (1941)				
AK 41	*Hercules*	Beth. Quincy	7 Nov 1938	18 Jul 1939	30 Nov 1942
	ex–*Exporter* (1941)				

Displacement	7,074 tons; 14,480 f/l; 15,265 tons f/l
Dimensions	473'1" (oa); 450' (wl) x 66'5" x 28'5"
Machinery	1 screw; Parsons GT; 2 B&W boilers; SHP 8,500, 18 knots
Endurance	19,345/12
Complement	426/345
Armament	1–5"/38, 4–3"/50 (AK 41: also 4 twin 40mm AA), 8–20mm

Notes: Type C3–E. *Almaack* converted to amphibious ship.

Service Records:

AK 27 *Almaack* Acq by U.S. Navy, 3 Jun 1941. Torpedoed by *U-155* west of Gibraltar, 15 Nov 1942 (4 killed). Rec **AKA 10**, 1 Feb 1943. Decomm 23 May 1946. Stricken 15 Aug 1946. .
6* North Africa, Kwajalein, Saipan, Leyte, Lingayen, Iwo Jima.
Later history: Merchant *Bunker Hill*, renamed *Excellency* 1949. BU 1970 Terminal I.

AK 41 *Hercules* Acq by U.S. Navy, 15 Jul 1941. Civilian crew 1941–42. Damaged by collision, Iwo Jima, 20 Mar 1945. Decomm 28 Jun 1946.
5* Gilbert Is., Saipan, Palau, Leyte, Iwo Jima.
Later history: Merchant *Bostonian* 1947, renamed *Exermont* 1949. BU 1971 Terminal I.

No.	Name	Reclassified	Date
AK 29	*Delta*	AR 9	1 Jul 1942
AK 30	*Hamul*	AD 20	2 Jun 1942
AK 31	*Markab*	AD 21	2 Jun 1942
AK 45	*Stratford*	AP 41	1 Aug 1941
AK 52	*Gemini*	AP 75	15 Aug 1942
AK 54	*Pollux*	AKS 4	1942
AK 62	*Kopara*	AG 50	23 Sep 1942
AK 64–69	—	AKA 15–20	1 Feb 1943

No.	Name	Formerly	Date
AK 44	*Aroostook*	CM 3	20 May 1941
AK 51	*Aries*	AG 37	7 Jan 1942
AK 52	*Gemini*	AG 38	7 Jan 1942
AK 63	*Asterion*	(no number) (see p. 279)	

Not acquired		
AK 32	*John R. R. Hannay*	from Army
AK 33	*Henry Gibbins*	from Army
AK 34	*Meigs*	from Army
AK 35	*Liberty*	from Army
AK 36	*W. R. Gibson*	from Army
AK 37	*Ludington*	from Army
AK 38	*Irvin L. Hunt*	from Army
AK 39	*Mendocino*	from Army
AK 40	*William H. Point*	from Army
AK 50	*Alcoa Pennant*	
AK 57–61	—	—

No.	Name	Builder	Keel Laid	Launched	Comm.
AK 42	*Mercury*	Federal	3 Jan 1939	15 Jul 1939	1 Jul 1942
	ex–*Mormactern* (1941), ex–*Lightning* (1940)				
AK 43	*Jupiter*	Federal	16 Mar 1939	30 Sep 1939	22 Aug 1942
	ex–*Santa Catalina* (1941), ex–*Flying Cloud* (1940)				

Displacement	7,345 tons; 13,900 tons f/l
Dimensions	459'2" (oa); 435' (wl) x 63' x 25'10"
Machinery	1 screw; GE GT; 2 B&W boilers; SHP 6,000; 16.4 knots
Complement	245
Armament	1–5"/38, 4–3"/50, 10–20mm guns

Notes: Type C2–Cargo.

Service Records:

AK 42 *Mercury* Acq 20 Jun 1941. Damaged by aircraft torpedo off Saipan, 26 Jun 1944. Converted to cargo–stores issue ship and rec **AKS 20**, 31 Jul 1945. Damaged by fire at Bristol, England, 18 Nov 1946. †
6* Kwajalein, Eniwetok, Saipan, Leyte, Subic Bay, Fleet Raids 1945.

AK 43 *Jupiter* Acq by Navy19 Jun 1941. Converted to aviation supply ship and rec **AVS 8**, 31 Jul 1945. Sank tug *Tamaroa* (YTB 136) in collision at San Francisco, 17 Jan 1946. Decomm 23 May 1947. †
6* Gilbert Is., Saipan, Palau, Leyte, Mindoro, Okinawa.

No.	Name	Builder	Launched	Acquired	Comm.
AK 46	*Pleiades*	Riuniti Palermo	1939	11 Aug 1941	25 Oct 1941
	ex–*Mangalia* (1941)				

Displacement	8,185 tons f/l
Dimensions	383'2" (oa); 361'11" (wl) x 50'11" x 21'9"
Machinery	1 screw; diesel; SHP 2,400, 12 knots
Complement	42
Armament	2–3"/50, 4–20mm AA guns

Note: Romanian ship seized at New York, 25 Jun 1941.

Service Record:

AK 46 *Pleiades* Decomm 21 Nov 1945.
2* Convoy SC–107, Southern France.
Later history: Merchant *Scepter* 1945. BU 1966 Baltimore.

No.	Name	Builder	Launched	Acquired	Comm.
AK 47	*Aquila*	Helsingor	1936	11 Aug 1941	24 Oct 1941
	ex–*Tunis* (1941)				

Displacement	4,075 tons f/l; 1,641 grt
Dimensions	288'1" (oa); 211'11" (wl) x 40'6" x 18'4"
Machinery	1 screw; diesel; SHP 1,600, 12.5 knots
Complement	156
Armament	2–3"/50, 4–20mm AA guns

Note: Danish freighter, seized 31 Mar 1941.

Service Record

AK 47 *Aquila* Decomm 9 Oct 1945. Stricken 24 Oct 1945.
Later history: Merchant *Bonanza*, renamed *Tunis* 1946, *Maria T* 1966, *Mathios* 1972. BU 1978 Piraeus.

No.	Name	Builder	Launched	Acquired	Comm.
AK 48	*Pegasus*	Helsingor	27 Dec 1939	18 Sep 1941	3 Dec 1941
	ex–*Lawrin* (1941), ex–*Rita Maersk* (1941)				

Displacement	5,070 tons f/l
Dimensions	299'11" (oa); 288' (bp) x 43'6" x 14'
Machinery	1 screw; compound; 2 Scotch boilers; SHP 1,750; 12 knots
Complement	110
Armament	1–4"/50, 1–3"/50

Note: Danish ship seized at Boston, 31 Mar 1941.

Service Record:

AK 48 *Pegasus* Damaged by fire at sea off San Juan, PR, May 1944. Rec **IX 222**, 15 May 1945. Decomm 19 Apr 1946. Stricken 1 May 1946.
Later history: Merchant *Rita Maersk* 1946, renamed *Kenneth* 1950, *Faliron* 1966, *Christina Maria* 1970. Damaged by explosion and fire off Palermo, 3 Sep 1970, CTL. Sunk as breakwater Sep 1971. BU Israel 1972.

Figure 11.11: *Deimos* (AK 78), seen here on 26 Jan 1943, was a Liberty ship used by the Navy.

No.	Name	Builder	Launched	Acquired	Comm.
AK 49	*Saturn*	Bremer Vulkan	26 May 1939	20 Apr 1942	20 Apr 1942
	ex–*Sting* (1942), ex–*Arauca* (1940)				

Displacement	5,088 tons; 9,760 tons f/l
Dimensions	423' (oa); 397' (wl) x 55'5" x 24'
Machinery	1 screw; TE; 2 LaMont boilers; SHP 5,600, 17.5 knots
Complement	205
Armament	(1945) 1–5"/38, 2–3"/50, 2–40mm, 4–20mm guns

Note: German freighter interned 1939 and seized at Port Everglades, 30 Mar 1941.

Service Record:

AK 49 *Saturn* Rec **AF 40**, 10 Apr 1944, converted to refrigerator ship. Decomm 23 Jul 1946. Stricken 15 Aug 1946. Sold 12 Sep 1972; BU 1973 Castellon, Spain.
1* Southern France.

No.	Name	Builder	Keel Laid	Launched	Comm.
AK 53	*Libra*	Federal	5 Jun 1941	12 Nov 1941	13 May 1942
	LD as *Jean Lykes*				
AK 55	*Titania*	Federal	25 Oct 1941	28 Feb 1942	27 May 1942
	LD as *Harry Culbreath*				
AK 56	*Oberon*	Federal	17 Nov 1941	18 Mar 1942	15 Jun 1942
	LD as *Delalba*, ex–*Seattle Mail*				

Displacement	6,944 tons; 11,600 f/l
Dimensions	459'2" (oa); 435' (wl) x 63' x 26'5"
Machinery	1 screw; GE GT; 2 FW boilers; SHP 6,000; 16.4 knots
Endurance	18,180/12
Complement	494/344
Armament	1–5"/38, 8–40mm AA; (1945) 1–5"/38, 4 twin 40mm, 18–20mm AA guns

Notes: Type C2–F. Converted to amphibious ships.

Service Records:

AK 53 *Libra* Rec **AKA 12**, 1 Feb 1943. †
9* Guadalcanal–Tulagi, Solomons, Battle of Guadalcanal, Solomons, New Georgia, Cape Torokina, Guam, Lingayen, Iwo Jima. Tokyo Bay.

AK 55 *Titania* In collision with transport *Lakehurst* at Safi, Morocco, 11 Nov 1942. Rec **AKA 13**, 1 Feb 1943. †
7* North Africa, Solomons, Cape Torokina, Saipan, Guam, Leyte, Lingayen, Tarakan, Balikpapan.

AK 56 *Oberon* Rec **AKA 14**, 1 Feb 1943. †
6* North Africa, Sicily, Salerno, Convoy KMF–25A, Southern France, Okinawa.

No.	Name	Builder	Keel Laid	Launched	Comm.
AK 98	*Auriga*	Consol. Wilm.	9 Jun 1942	7 Sep 1942	1 Apr 1943
	LD as *Alcoa Partner*				

Displacement	5,775 tons, 12,875 tons f/l
Dimensions	416' (oa); 395' (wl) x 60' x 27'7"
Machinery	1 screw; West. GT; 2 B&W boilers; SHP 4,000;
Complement	258
Armament	1–5"/38, 1–3"/50, 2 twin 40mm, 6–20mm AA guns

Notes: Type C1–B.

Service Record:

AK 98 *Auriga* Decomm 22 Jan 1946. Stricken 7 Feb 1946.
5* Gilbert Is., Saipan, Leyte, Subic Bay, Okinawa.
Later history: Merchant *Alcoa Partner*. BU 1970 Valencia.

No.	Name	Builder	Keel Laid	Launched	Comm.
AK 80	*Enceladus*	Penn–Jersey	14 Feb 1942	9 Oct 1942	18 Aug 1943
	LD as *Elias D. Knight*				
AK 81	*Europa*	Penn–Jersey	2 Mar 1942	7 Dec 1942	—
	LD as *William Lester*				
AK 82	*Hydra*	Penn–Jersey	11 Apr 1942	23 Jan 1943	25 Sep 1943
	LD as *Eben H. Linnell*				
AK 83	*Media*	Penn–Jersey	28 Jan 1943	29 Aug 1943	—
	LD as *Oliver R. Mumford*				
AK 84	*Mira*	Penn–Jersey	22 May 1943	31 Oct 1943	—
	LD as *William Nott*				
AK 85	*Nashira*	Penn–Jersey	1 Nov 1943	23 Apr 1944	—
	LD as *Josiah Paul*				
AK 86	*Norma*	Penn–Jersey	3 Dec 1943	4 Jun 1944	—
	LD as *Sumner Pierce*				
AK 87	*Sagitta*	Penn–Jersey	24 Jan 1944	9 Jul 1944	—
	LD as *Moses Pike*				
AK 88	*Tucana*	Penn–Jersey	24 Apr 1944	13 Sep 1944	—
	LD as *Symmes Potter*				
AK 89	*Vela*	Penn–Jersey	5 Jun 1944	15 Jan 1945	—
	LD as *Charles A. Raulett*				

Displacement	1,677 tons; 5,200 tons f/l
Dimensions	269'10" (oa); 255' (wl) x 42'6" x 20'8"
Machinery	1 screw; diesel; SHP 1,190, 10 knots
Complement	83
Armament	1–3"/50, 8–20mm AA guns

Notes: Type N3–S–A1. AK 81–89 were transferred to the Army on completion and converted to port repair ships.

Service Records:

AK 80 *Enceladus* USCG crew. Southwest Pacific. Damaged in storm southeast of Rendova, Solomons, 31 Jan 1944.
Decomm 18 Dec 1945. Sold 30 Jun 1946.

AK 81 *Europa* To Army 25 Nov 1943.
Later history: Renamed *Thomas F. Farrell Jr.* BU 1967 Baltimore.

AK 82 *Hydra* USCG crew. Decomm 19 Nov 1943, to Army.
Later history: Renamed *Madison Jordan Manchester.*

AK 83 *Media* To Army 17 Nov 1943.
Later history: Renamed *Glen Gerald Griswold.* BU 1966.

AK 84 *Mira* To Army 17 Nov 1943.
Later history: Renamed *Robert M. Emery.* Sold 1965 BU Portland, Ore.

AK 85 *Nashira* To Army 25 Apr 1944.
Later history: Renamed *Richard R. Arnold.* Sold 1965.

AK 86 *Norma* To Army 6 Jun 1944.
Later history: Renamed *Henry Wright Hurley.* BU 1970 Portland, Ore.

AK 87 *Sagitta* To Army 18 Jul 1944. †
Later history: Renamed *Marvin Lyle Thomas.*

AK 88 *Tucana* To Army 14 Sep 1944.
Later history: Renamed *Arthur C. Ely.* BU 1970 Portland, Ore.

AK 89 *Vela* To Army 17 Jan 1945. †
Later history: Renamed *Joe C. Specker.*

Figure 11.12: *Sculptor* (AK 103), another Liberty ship, seen at San Francisco on 13 Dec 1944.

Figure 11.13: *Chatham* (AK 169) was one of many C1-M-AV1 cargo ships completed for the Navy.

No.	Name	Builder	Keel Laid	Launched	Comm.
AK 70	*Crater*	Permanente #2	28 Aug 1942	8 Oct 1942	31 Oct 1942
	ex-*John James Audubon* (1942)				
AK 71	*Adhara*	Permanente #2	16 Sep 1942	27 Oct 1942	16 Nov 1942
	ex-*G. H. Corliss* (1942)				
AK 72	*Aludra*	Permanente #2	28 Oct 1942	7 Dec 1942	26 Dec 1942
	ex-*Robert T. Lincoln* (1942)				
AK 73	*Arided*	Permanente #1	20 Sep 1942	28 Oct 1942	23 Nov 1942
	ex-*Noah H. Swayne* (1942)				
AK 74	*Carina*	Permanente #1	30 Sep 1942	6 Nov 1942	1 Dec 1942
	ex-*David Davis* (1942)				
AK 75	*Cassiopeia*	Permanente #1	13 Oct 1942	15 Nov 1942	8 Dec 1942
	ex-*Melville W. Fuller* (1942)				
AK 76	*Celeno*	Permanente #2	3 Nov 1942	12 Dec 1942	2 Jan 1943
	ex-*Redfield Proctor* (1942)				
AK 77	*Cetus*	Permanente #2	21 Nov 1942	26 Dec 1942	17 Jan 1943
	ex-*George B. Cortelyou* (1943)				
AK 78	*Deimos*	Permanente #1	27 Nov 1942	28 Dec 1942	23 Jan 1943
	ex-*Chief Ouray* (1943)				
AK 79	*Draco*	Permanente #2	15 Dec 1942	19 Jan 1943	16 Feb 1943
	ex-*John M. Palmer* (1943)				
AK 90	*Albireo*	Permanente #1	17 Jan 1943	25 Feb 1943	29 Mar 1943
	ex-*John G. Nicolay* (1943)				
AK 91	*Cor Caroli*	Permanente #2	20 Feb 1943	19 Mar 1943	16 Apr 1943
	ex-*Betsy Ross* (1943)				

AK 92	*Eridanus*	Permanente #2	12 Mar 1943	9 Apr 1943	8 May 1943
	ex–*Luther Burbank* (1943)				
AK 93	*Etamin*	Permanente #2	28 Mar 1943	25 Apr 1943	25 May 1943
	ex–*Isaac Babbitt* (1943)				
AK 94	*Mintaka*	Calship	9 Feb 1943	10 Mar 1943	10 May 1943
	ex–*Ansel Briggs* (1943)				
AK 95	*Murzim*	Calship	10 Jul 1942	17 Aug 1942	14 May 1943
	ex–*Brigham Young* (1943)				
AK 96	*Sterope*	Oregon	9 Dec 1941	22 Feb 1942	11 May 1943
	ex–*James Wilson* (1943)				
AK 97	*Serpens*	Calship	10 Mar 1943	5 Apr 1943	28 May 1943
	ex–*Benjamin N. Cardozo* (1943)				
AK 99	*Bootes*	Calship	24 Apr 1943	16 May 1943	15 Jul 1943
	ex–*Thomas Oliver Larkin* (1943)				
AK 100	*Lynx*	Calship	26 Apr 1943	18 May 1943	26 Jul 1943
	ex–*Juan Bautista de Anza* (1943)				
AK 101	*Lyra*	Permanente #1	25 Apr 1943	24 May 1943	22 Jul 1943
	ex–*Cyrus Hamlin* (1943)				
AK 102	*Triangulum*	Calship	14 May 1943	6 Jun 1943	30 Jul 1943
	ex–*Eugene B. Daskam* (1943)				
AK 103	*Sculptor*	Calship	18 May 1943	10 Jun 1943	10 Aug 1943
	ex–*D. W. Harrington* (1943)				
AK 104	*Ganymede*	Permanente #2	16 May 1943	8 Jun 1943	31 Jul 1943
	ex–*James W. Nye* (1943)				
AK 105	*Naos*	Calship	8 Jun 1943	30 Jun 1943	17 Aug 1943
	ex–*William R. Nelson* (1943)				
AK 106	*Caelum*	Calship	30 Jun 1943	25 Jul 1943	22 Oct 1943
	ex–*Wyatt Earp* (1943)				
AK 107	*Hyperion*	Permanente #1	28 May 1943	24 Jun 1943	25 Aug 1943
	ex–*Christopher C. Andrews* (1943)				
AK 108	*Rotanin*	Calship	25 Jul 1943	18 Aug 1943	23 Nov 1943
	ex–*William Kelly* (1943)				
AK 109	*Allioth*	Permanente #2	30 Jul 1943	20 Aug 1943	25 Oct 1943
	ex–*James Rowan* (1943)				

Displacement	4,023 tons; 12,350 tons f/l
Dimensions	441'6" (oa); 416' (wl) x 56'11" x 28'4"
Machinery	1 screw; VTE; 2 B&W boilers; SHP 2,500, 13 knots
Complement	205
Armament	1–5"/38, 1–3"/50, 2–40mm, 6–20mm AA *or* 1–5"/38, 4–40mm, 12–20mm AA guns

Notes: Type EC2–S–C1. *Alderamin, Alkaid, Alnitah, Celeno, Crux, DeGrasse, Kenmore, Livingston, Mintaka, Naos, Prince Georges, Rotanin, Sabik, Zaurak* fitted to carry troops.

Service Records:

AK 70 *Crater* Decomm 25 Jun 1946. Sold 19 Aug 1974. BU 1978. Gandia, Spain.

AK 71 *Adhara* Damaged by dive bombers at Tulagi, 7 Apr 1943. Decomm 7 Dec 1945. Stricken 3 Jan 1946. BU 1971 Gandia, Spain.
2* Solomons, Okinawa.

AK 72 *Aludra* Torpedoed and sunk by *RO–103* off San Cristobal I., 23 Jun 1943 (2 killed).
1* Solomons.

AK 73 *Arided* Decomm 12 Jan 1946. Stricken 29 Sep 1947, sold 2 Oct 1947; BU 1962 Terminal I.

AK 74 *Carina* Damaged by suicide boat, Okinawa, 4 May 1945. Decomm 16 Oct 1945. BU 1952.
3* Solomons, Okinawa.

AK 75 *Cassiopeia* Decomm 21 Nov 1945, sunk as target by submarine *Cutlass*, 18 Jun 1961.
1* Solomons.

AK 76 *Celeno* Damaged by aircraft bombs and beached off Lunga Point, 16 Jun 1943 (15 killed). Decomm 1 Mar 1946. BU 1961 Panama City, Fla.
3* Solomons, Admiralty Is., Okinawa.

AK 77 *Cetus* Decomm 20 Nov 1945. Returned 21 Nov 1945; BU 1971 Bilbao, Spain.
2* Saipan, Okinawa.

AK 78 *Deimos* Torpedoed by *RO–103* off San Cristobal I. and sunk by US destroyer *O'Bannon*, 23 Jun 1943.
1* Solomons.

AK 79 *Draco* Decomm 28 Nov 1945 and returned to MC.
2* Guam, Okinawa.
Later history: Merchant *President Kruger* 1947, renamed *Riviera* 1951, *Effie* 1953, *President Pretorius* 1958. BU 1968 Kaohsiung, Taiwan.

AK 90 *Albireo* USCG crew. Decomm 5 Jul 1946. Stricken 31 Jul 1946.
Later history: Merchant *President Steyn*, renamed *Hidalgo* 1951, *Ocean Sailor* 1954. BU 1967 Kure.

AK 91 *Cor Caroli* USCG crew. Decomm 30 Nov 1945.
1* Guam.
Later history: Renamed *Betsy Ross*. Sunk as artificial reef off Florida, 1978.

AK 92 *Eridanus* USCG crew. Decomm 8 May 1946. Returned 15 May 1946.
1* Solomons.
Later history: Merchant *Panagiotis*, renamed *Silla* 1957. BU 1972 Masan, Korea.

AK 93 *Etamin* USCG crew, 24 May 1943–26 Jun 1944. Damaged by aircraft torpedo, Milne Bay, 27 Apr 1944. Rec **IX 173**, 15 Jun 1944. Decomm 26 Jun 1944, engines inoperable. Out of service 9 Jul 1946. Stricken 31 Jul 1946; BU 1948 Shanghai.
2* Admiralty Is., Hollandia.

AK 94 *Mintaka* USCG crew. Decomm 12 Feb 1946. Stricken 26 Feb 1946. BU 1968 Oakland, Calif.
1* Okinawa.

AK 95 *Murzim* USCG crew. Decomm 7 Jun 1946. Stricken 23 Jun 1946. BU 1973.
1* Leyte.

AK 96 *Sterope* USCG crew. Decomm 16 May 1946. Stricken 19 Nov 1947. BU 1964 Oakland.
2* Guam, Okinawa.

AK 97 *Serpens* USCG crew. Blew up and sank while loading depth charges, off Guadalcanal, 29 Jan 1945 (253 killed).
1* Solomons.

AK 99 *Bootes* Decomm 22 Apr 1946. Stricken 1 Aug 1947. BU 1973 Kaohsiung, Taiwan.
1* Hollandia.

AK 100 *Lynx* Decomm 1 Nov 1945. Stricken 16 Nov 1945. BU 1973 Panama City, Fla.
1* Okinawa.

AK 101 *Lyra* Decomm 3 May 1946.
Later history: Merchant *Virginia*, renamed *Amedeo* 1964. BU 1967 Kaohsiung, Taiwan.

AK 102 *Triangulum* Decomm 15 Apr 1946. Stricken 17 Jul 1947. BU 1973.
2* Hollandia, Leyte.

AK 103 *Sculptor* Decomm 26 Feb 1946. Stricken 12 Mar 1946.
Later history: Merchant *Dimosthenes Pantaleon*. BU 1969 Trieste.

AK 104 *Ganymede* Damaged by collision off Leyte, 27 Jul 1945. Decomm 15 Apr 1946. Stricken 1 Aug 1947. BU 1973 Kaohsiung, Taiwan.
2* Finschhafen, Hollandia.

AK 105 *Naos* Decomm 6 Dec 1945. Stricken 3 Jan 1946. BU 1971 Oakland, Calif.

AK 106 *Caelum* Decomm 30 Jul 1946. BU 1961 Everett, Wash.
1* Kwajalein.

AK 107 *Hyperion* Decomm 16 Nov 1945. BU 1963 Baltimore.
3* Solomons, Leyte, Okinawa.

AK 108 *Rotanin* Decomm 5 Apr 1946. Stricken 17 Apr 1946. BU 1966 Richmond, Calif.
1* Palau.

AK 109 *Allioth* Slightly damaged by aircraft bombs east of Peleliu, 20 Nov 1944. Rec **IX 204**, 31 Dec 1944. Converted to aviation supply ship, rec **AVS 4**, 25 May 1945. Decomm 18 May 1946. Stricken 22 May 1947. BU 1971 Gandia, Spain.

No.	Name	Builder	Keel Laid	Launched	Comm.
AK 110	*Alkes*	Permanente #2	10 Jun 1943	29 Jun 1943	29 Oct 1943
	ex-*Increase A. Lapham* (1943)				
AK 111	*Giansar*	Oregon	27 Dec 1942	19 Jan 1943	29 Oct 1943
	ex-*Thomas Ewing* (1943)				
AK 112	*Grumium*	Permanente #2	12 Nov 1942	20 Dec 1942	20 Oct 1943
	ex-*William G. McAdoo* (1943)				
AK 113	*Rutilicus*	Calship	2 Apr 1943	26 Apr 1943	30 Oct 1943
	ex-*Andrew Rowan* (1943)				
AK 114	*Alkaid*	St. Johns	13 Sep 1943	8 Nov 1943	27 Mar 1944
	ex-*William G. Sumner* (1943)				
AK 115	*Crux*	St. Johns	27 Sep 1943	16 Nov 1943	17 Mar 1944
	ex-*Peter Stuyvesant* (1943)				
AK 116	*Alderamin*	Todd–Houston	5 Oct 1943	13 Nov 1943	2 Apr 1944
	ex-*J. S. Cullinan* (1943)				
AK 117	*Zaurak*	Todd–Houston	7 Oct 1943	18 Nov 1943	17 Mar 1944
	ex-*Hugh Young* (1943)				
AK 118	*Shaula*	St. Johns	4 Oct 1943	23 Nov 1943	5 May 1944
	ex-*James Screven* (1943)				
AK 119	*Matar*	St. Johns	16 Oct 1943	30 Nov 1943	17 May 1944
	ex-*Napoleon B. Broward* (1943)				
AK 120	*Zaniah*	Todd–Houston	29 Oct 1943	12 Dec 1943	2 Sep 1944
	ex-*Anthony F. Lucas* (1943)				
AK 121	*Sabik*	Todd–Houston	8 Nov 1943	17 Dec 1943	15 Apr 1944
	ex-*William Becknall* (1943)				
AK 122	*Baham*	St. Johns	10 Nov 1943	21 Dec 1943	18 Aug 1944
	ex-*Elizabeth C. Bellamy* (1943)				
AK 123	*Menkar*	St. Johns	17 Nov 1943	31 Dec 1943	20 Jun 1944
	ex-*John White* (1944)				
AK 124	*Azimech*	Permanente #2	21 Jul 1943	11 Aug 1943	29 Oct 1943
	ex-*Mary Patten* (1943)				
AK 125	*Lesuth*	Calship	24 Mar 1943	17 Apr 1943	1 Nov 1943
	ex-*William M. Gwin* (1943)				
AK 126	*Megrez*	Calship	31 Mar 1943	23 Apr 1943	26 Oct 1943
	ex-*General Vallejo* (1943)				
AK 127	*Alnitah*	Permanente #2	10 Dec 1942	14 Jan 1943	27 Nov 1943
	ex-*John A. Logan* (1943)				
AK 128	*Leonis*	Permanente #1	21 Nov 1942	22 Dec 1942	25 Oct 1943
	ex-*Key Pittman* (1943)				
AK 129	*Phobos*	Todd–Houston	25 Sep 1943	6 Nov 1943	12 Jun 1944
	ex-*Joseph H. Kibbey* (1944)				
AK 130	*Arkab*	Delta	4 Dec 1943	22 Jan 1944	15 May 1944
	ex-*Warren Stone* (1944)				
AK 131	*Melucta*	St. Johns	21 Jan 1944	20 Mar 1944	22 Jul 1944
	ex-*Thomas A. McGinley* (1944)				
AK 132	*Propus*	St. Johns	31 Jan 1944	29 Mar 1944	12 Jun 1944
	ex-*Frederick Tesca* (1944)				
AK 133	*Seginus*	Delta	10 Jan 1944	4 Mar 1944	14 Jun 1944
	ex-*Harry Toulmin* (1944)				
AK 134	*Syrma*	Delta	10 Jan 1944	19 Feb 1944	12 Aug 1944
	ex-*Andres Almonaster* (1944)				
AK 135	*Venus*	Permanente #2	5 Jul 1942	21 Aug 1942	10 Nov 1943
	ex-*William Williams* (1943)				
AK 136	*Ara*	Calship	17 Jul 1941	14 Jan 1942	4 Jan 1944
	ex-*Daniel Boone* (1943)				
AK 137	*Ascella*	Calship	7 Jan 1943	4 Feb 1943	7 Jan 1944
	ex-*George C. Yount* (1943)				
AK 138	*Cheleb*	Permanente #1	29 Dec 1942	29 Jan 1943	1 Jan 1944
	ex-*Lyman J. Gage* (1943)				
AK 139	*Pavo*	Todd–Houston	8 Mar 1943	23 Apr 1943	14 Jan 1944
	ex-*James S. Hogg* (1943)				
AK 140	*Situla*	Oregon	9 Jan 1943	7 Feb 1943	14 Jan 1944
	ex-*John Whiteaker* (1943)				
AK 225	*Allegan*	Beth. Fairfield	21 Dec 1943	21 Jan 1944	21 Sep 1944
	ex-*Van Lear Black* (1944)				
AK 226	*Appanoose*	Beth. Fairfield	20 Jun 1944	27 Jul 1944	26 Sep 1944
	ex-*A. J. Cassatt* (1944)				

Service Records:

AK 110 *Alkes* Decomm 20 Feb 1946. Stricken 12 Mar 1946. BU 1972 Bilbao, Spain.
3* Kwajalein, Guam, Okinawa.

AK 111 *Giansar* Decomm 28 Nov 1945. Stricken 19 Dec 1945. BU 1963 Baltimore.

AK 112 *Grumium* Acq 5 Oct 1943. Rec **IX 174**, 20 Jun 1944. Converted to aviation supply ship and rec **AVS 3**, 25 May 1945. Decomm 20 Dec 1945. BU 1970 Barcelona, Spain.
1* Okinawa.

AK 113 *Rutilicus* Decomm 17 Dec 1945. Stricken 8 Jan 1946. BU 1972 Gandia, Spain.
2* Kwajalein.

AK 114 *Alkaid* Decomm 11 Mar 1946. Stricken 28 Mar 1946. BU 1965 Terminal I.
1* Okinawa.

AK 115 *Crux* Decomm 31 Jan 1946. BU 1961 Oakland, Calif.

AK 116 *Alderamin* Decomm 10 Apr 1946. Stricken 1 May 1946. BU 1965.

AK 117 *Zaurak* Decomm 12 Mar 1946. Stricken 28 Mar 1946. BU 1963 Oakland, Calif.
1* Okinawa.

AK 118 *Shaula* Damaged in typhoon in Philippine Sea, 24–25 Nov 1945. Decomm 25 Jun 1946. Stricken 19 Jul 1946.
Later history: Merchant *Olimpia.* BU 1968 La Spezia, Italy.

AK 119 *Matar* Decomm 15 Mar 1946. Stricken 31 Oct 1947; BU 1972 Richmond, Calif.
2* Palau, Okinawa.

AK 120 *Zaniah* Rec **AG 70**, 14 Mar 1944. Completed as stores–barracks–distilling ship. Damaged in typhoon at Okinawa, 16 Sep 1945. Decomm 29 Apr 1946. Stricken 22 May 1947; BU 1972 Portland, Ore.
1* Okinawa.

AK 121 *Sabik* Decomm 19 Mar 1946. Stricken 17 Apr 1946, sold Oct 1961; BU Oakland, Calif.

AK 122 *Baham* Rec **AG 71**, 14 Mar 1944 and conv to repair, distilling and stores issue ship, 10 Jan 1945. Decomm 9 Jul 1946. Sold 30 Jun 1947. BU 1972 Terminal I.

AK 123 *Menkar* USCG crew. Loran supply ship. Decomm 15 Apr 1946. BU 1962 Oakland, Calif.
1* Okinawa.

AK 124 *Azimech* Decomm 11 Dec 1945. Stricken 3 Jan 1946. BU 1972 Castellon, Spain.
1* Okinawa.

AK 125 *Lesuth* Decomm 16 Aug 1946. Stricken 17 Jul 1946. BU 1964, Richmond, Calif. Tokyo Bay.
1* Palau.

AK 126 *Megrez* Decomm 29 May 1946. Stricken 1 Aug 1947. BU 1974 Portland, Ore.

AK 127 *Alnitah* Decomm 11 Mar 1946.
Later history: To SCAJAP. Stricken 28 Mar 1946. BU 1961 Portland, Ore.

AK 128 *Leonis* Acq 11 Oct 1943. Decomm 9 Dec 1945. BU 1966 Wilmington, Del.
2* Saipan, Palau.

AK 129 *Phobos* Acq 15 Jan 1944. Decomm 22 Mar 1946. BU 1970 Oakland, Calif.

AK 130 *Arkab* Decomm 2 Jan 1946. Stricken 21 Jan 1946. BU 1971 Burriana, Spain.

AK 131 *Melucta* Decomm 13 Dec. BU 1970 Bilbao, Spain.

AK 132 *Propus* Decomm 20 Nov. 21 Nov 1945. Stricken 5 Dec 1945.
Later history: Merchant *Nicolaou Georgios*, renamed *Gabbiano* 1952. BU 1969 La Spezia, Italy.

AK 133 *Seginus* Decomm 13 Nov 1945. Stricken 28 Nov 1945.
Later history: Merchant *Kehrea*. BU 1967 Shanghai.

AK 134 *Syrma* Decomm 8 Jan 1946. Stricken 21 Jan 1946.
Later history: Merchant *San Jorge*, renamed *St. John* 1954. BU 1967 Shanghai.

AK 135 *Venus* As merchant ship, torpedoed by *I–19* off Fiji, 2 May 1943. Acq by U.S. Navy, 6 Nov 1943. Recomm 26 Sep 1944. Decomm 4 Dec 1944, repaired at Sydney. Decomm 18 Apr 1946. Stricken 19 Feb 1948. BU 1963 Oakland.
1* (as m/v).

AK 136 *Ara* Acq 3 Dec 1943. Decomm 26 Nov 1945 and returned. Stricken 5 Dec 1945. BU 1971 Bilbao, Spain.
1* Guam.

AK 137 *Ascella* Acq 30 Nov 1943. Decomm 13 Aug 1946. Stricken 22 May 1947. BU 1964 Terminal I.

AK 138 *Cheleb* Acq 1943. Decomm 25 Jul 1946. Sold 23 May 1947. BU 1978, San Jose, Calif.

AK 139 *Pavo* Decomm 30 Nov 1945. Stricken 19 Dec 1945. BU 1971 Bilbao, Spain.

AK 140 *Situla* Acq 2 Dec 1943. Decomm 23 Apr 1946. Stricken 22 Jan 1948. BU 1961 Oakland, Calif.

AK 225 *Allegan* Acq 7 Aug 1944. Damaged by kamikaze, Okinawa, 3 Jun 1945. Decomm 15 Nov 1945. Stricken 28 Nov 1945.
1* Okinawa.
Later history: Merchant *San Leonardo* 1947, renamed *Wanderer* 1951, *Valiant Force* 1959, *Wanderer* 1963, *Wanderlust* 1964, *Agathopolis* 1964. BU 1969 Osaka.

AK 226 *Appanoose* Decomm 26 Nov and returned 27 Nov 1945. Stricken 5 Dec 1945.
1* Okinawa.
Later history: Merchant *Santa Ana*. BU 1965 Yokosuka.

No.	Name	Builder	Keel Laid	Launched	Comm.
AK 221	*Kenmore*	Calship	8 May 1943	30 May 1943	14 Nov 1943
	ex–AP 162 (20 Aug 1944), ex–*James H. McClintock* (1943)				
AK 222	*Livingston*	Calship	22 Mar 1943	16 Apr 1943	10 Nov 1943
	ex–AP 163 (20 Aug 1944), ex–*Josiah D. Whitney* (1943)				
AK 223	*DeGrasse*	Oregon	31 Jan 1943	24 Feb 1943	8 Nov 1943
	ex–AP 164 (20 Aug 1944), ex–*Nathaniel J. Wyethe* (1943)				
AK 224	*Prince Georges*	Permanente #2	20 Sep 1942	30 Oct 1942	10 Nov 1943
	ex–AP 165 (20 Aug 1944), ex–*Richard March Hoe* (1943)				

Note: AK 221–24 acquired from the Army; troop carriers.

Service Records:

AK 221 *Kenmore* Decomm 1 Feb 1946. BU 1973 Kaohsiung, Taiwan.
3* Kwajalein, Saipan, Okinawa.

AK 222 *Livingston* Decomm 27 Feb 1946. BU 1973 Kaohsiung, Taiwan.
2* Kwajalein, Guam.

AK 223 *DeGrasse* Decomm 28 Mar 1946. Stricken 1 May 1946. BU 1970 Oakland, Calif.
3* Eniwetok, Saipan, Guam, Okinawa.

AK 224 *Prince Georges* Decomm 12 Apr 1946. Stricken 1 May 1946. BU 1969 Oakland, Calif.
1* Saipan.

No.	Name	Builder	Keel Laid	Launched	Comm.
AK 156	*Alamosa*	Kaiser #4	15 Nov 1943	14 Apr 1944	25 Sep 1944
AK 157	*Alcona*	Kaiser #4	27 Nov 1943	9 May 1944	15 Sep 1944
AK 158	*Amador*	Kaiser #4	27 Dec 1943	15 Jun 1944	25 Nov 1944
AK 159	*Antrim*	Kaiser #4	18 Apr 1944	17 Jul 1944	31 Oct 1944
AK 160	*Autauga*	Kaiser #4	10 May 1944	7 Aug 1944	24 Nov 1944
AK 161	*Beaverhead*	Kaiser #4	15 Jun 1944	2 Sep 1944	3 Jan 1945
AK 162	*Beltrami*	Kaiser #4	18 Jul 1944	26 Sep 1944	4 Jan 1945
AK 163	*Blount*	Kaiser #4	7 Aug 1944	19 Oct 1944	26 Jan 1945
AK 164	*Brevard*	Kaiser #4	2 Sep 1944	18 Nov 1944	19 Feb 1945

Figure 11.14: *Pollux* (AKS 4), second of the name, a cargo stores issue ship of type C2-F, after the war.

AK 165	*Bullock*	Kaiser #4	26 Sep 1944	2 Dec 1944	2 Mar 1945
AK 166	*Cabell*	Kaiser #4	20 Oct 1944	23 Dec 1944	11 Apr 1945
AK 167	*Caledonia*	Kaiser #4	20 Nov 1944	20 Jan 1945	13 Mar 1945
AK 168	*Charlevoix*	Froemming	25 Nov 1943	20 Apr 1944	1 Feb 1945
AK 169	*Chatham*	Froemming	11 Dec 1943	13 May 1944	22 Feb 1945
AK 170	*Chicot*	Froemming	22 Apr 1944	16 Jul 1944	4 Apr 1945
AK 171	*Claiborne*	Froemming	17 May 1944	3 Sep 1944	19 Apr 1945
AK 172	*Clarion*	Froemming	19 Jul 1944	22 Oct 1944	27 May 1945
AK 173	*Codington*	Froemming	5 Sep 1944	29 Nov 1944	23 Jul 1945
AK 174	*Colquitt*	Froemming	26 Oct 1944	21 Jan 1945	22 Sep 1945
AK 175	*Craighead*	Froemming	6 Dec 1944	28 Feb 1945	5 Sep 1945
AK 176	*Doddridge*	Froemming	25 Jan 1945	23 Mar 1945	—
AK 177	*Duval*	Froemming	28 Feb 1945	26 Apr 1945	—
AK 178	*Fairfield*	Kaiser #4	4 Dec 1944	6 Feb 1945	28 Mar 1945
AK 179	*Faribault*	Kaiser #4	27 Dec 1944	24 Feb 1945	20 Apr 1945
AK 180	*Fentress*	Kaiser #4	22 Jan 1945	10 Mar 1945	4 May 1945
AK 181	*Flagler*	Kaiser #4	6 Feb 1945	24 Mar 1945	18 May 1945
AK 182	*Gadsden*	Butler	3 Nov 1943	8 Apr 1944	28 Feb 1945
AK 183	*Glacier*	Butler	3 Nov 1943	22 Apr 1944	14 Apr 1945
AK 184	*Grainger*	Butler	16 Dec 1943	7 May 1944	26 Jan 1945
AK 185	*Gwinnett*	Butler	21 Dec 1943	14 May 1944	10 Apr 1945
AK 186	*Habersham*	Butler	28 Dec 1943	7 Jun 1944	12 May 1945
AK 187	*Hennepin*	Butler	29 Dec 1943	27 Jun 1944	3 Jul 1945
AK 188	*Herkimer*	Butler	10 Apr 1944	2 Jul 1944	14 Jul 1945
AK 189	*Hidalgo*	Butler	25 Apr 1944	28 Jul 1944	4 Aug 1945
AK 190	*Kenosha*	Butler	8 May 1944	25 Aug 1944	7 Sep 1945
AK 191	*Lebanon*	Butler	15 May 1944	14 Oct 1944	25 Aug 1945
AK 192	*Lehigh*	Butler	8 Jun 1944	25 Nov 1944	13 Sep 1945
AK 193	*Lancaster*	Butler	1 Jul 1944	15 Dec 1944	21 Sep 1945
AK 194	*Marengo*	Butler	4 Jul 1944	4 Dec 1944	24 Aug 1945
AK 195	*Midland*	Butler	29 Jul 1944	23 Dec 1944	17 Aug 1945
AK 196	*Minidoka*	Butler	26 Aug 1944	13 Jan 1945	—

Displacement	2,382 tons; 7,450 tons f/l; 3,805 grt
Dimensions	338'6" (oa); 320' (wl) x 50' x 21'1"
Machinery	1 screw; diesel; SHP 1,750; 11.5 knots
Complement	85
Armament	1–3"/50, 6–20mm AA guns

Note: Type C1–M–AV1.

Service Records:

AK 156 *Alamosa* Ammunition issue ship. Decomm 20 May 1946. Stricken 14 Jun 1946. BU 1972 Portland, Ore.

AK 157 *Alcona* Arctic service 1946. †

AK 158 *Amador* Ammunition issue ship. Decomm 20 Jun 1946. Stricken 19 Jul 1946.
Later history: Merchant *Skagern*, renamed *Nicolaos* 1963, *Dina* 1972, *Alkistis* 1973. BU 1980 Gadani Beach, Pakistan.

AK 159 *Antrim* Decomm 3 Apr 1946. Stricken 17 Apr 1946.
Later history: Merchant *Kars*. BU 1983 Aliaga.

AK 160 *Autauga* Decomm 24 Jun 1946. Stricken 19 Jul 1946.
Later history: Merchant *Hersilia*, renamed *Fauzia B* 1962. BU 1970 Hsinkang.

AK 161 *Beaverhead* Decomm 8 Mar 1946.
Later history: Merchant *Hera* 1947, renamed *Omar Express* 1963, *Cementos Ponce* 1967, *Vanessa* 1977.

AK 162 *Beltrami* Arctic operations 1946. †

AK 163 *Blount* Decomm 18 Apr 1946.
Later history: Merchant *Hecuba* 1948, renamed *Anna* 1963, *Panos* 1965. BU 1973 Shanghai.

AK 164 *Brevard* Decomm 3 Jul 1946.
Later history: Merchant *Zeehond*, renamed *Hestia* 1948, *Leila B.* 1962. BU 1970 Tientsin.

AK 165 *Bullock* Decomm 13 Mar 1946.
Later history: Merchant *Edirne* 1947, renamed *Adana* 1948, *Malatya* 1948. BU 1982 Aliaga.

AK 166 *Cabell* Decomm 19 Jul 1946.
Later history: Merchant *Sommen*, renamed *Donald* 1963. Foundered in Gulf of Aden, 27 Aug 1963.

AK 167 *Caledonia* Decomm 25 Mar 1946.
Later history: Merchant *Norse Captain*, renamed *Mabini* 1962, *President Quezon* 1964, *Seven Kings* 1966. BU 1980 Kaohsiung, Taiwan.

AK 168 *Charlevoix* Decomm 18 Jan 1946.
Later history: Merchant *Benny*, renamed *Benny Viking* 1959, *Benny* 1963, *Stella Oceanica* 1963, *Jasolinan* 1965, *Paraskivi* 1965. BU 1970 Castellon, Spain.

AK 169 *Chatham* Decomm 2 Apr 1946.
Later history: Merchant *Helena* 1947, renamed *Lincoln Express* 1963. Broke in two and sank off San Juan, PR, 14 Dec 1972.

AK 170 *Chicot* Decomm 18 Jul 1946. Reacquired 14 May 1947. Recomm 23 Jun 1947. †

AK 171 *Claiborne* Decomm 7 Feb 1946. To Army.
Later history: To SCAJAP. To Army, *Claiborne* to 1960. BU 1971.

AK 172 *Clarion* Decomm 13 May 1946. Returned to WSA 18 May 1946.
Later history: Merchant *Lovdal* 1947, renamed *Urubamba* 1956, *Cebu* 1969. Lost by grounding 560 milesnorth of Lima, 26 Apr 1970.

AK 173 *Codington* USCG crew. Decomm 27 Feb 1946.
Later history: To SCAJAP. Merchant *Codington*, renamed *Pohang* 1956.

AK 174 *Colquitt* To USCG 24 Sep 1945. Decomm 1 Mar 1946.
Later history: Renamed USCGC *Kukui* (WAK 186). †

AK 175 *Craighead* USCG crew. Decomm 18 Jan 1946.
Later history: Merchant *Kastamonu*. BU 1984 Aliaga.

AK 176 *Doddridge* Acquisition canceled 16 Aug 1945, completed as m/v.
Later history: Merchant *Coastal Messenger*. To U.S. State Departmentt, renamed USCGC *Courier* (WAGR 410) 1952. †

AK 177 *Duval* Acquisition canceled 16 Aug 1945, completed as m/v.
Later history: Merchant *Coastal Racer*. Reacquired as **YFP 10**, 1952. Sold 1 Sep 1974; BU 1975 Kobe.

AK 178 *Fairfield* Decomm 11 Jan 1946.
Later history: To SCAJAP. Returned to WSA. To Army, *Fairfield*.

AK 179 *Faribault* Decomm 10 Jul 1946. Returned 11 Jul 1946. Reacquired 16 May 1947. Recomm 26 Jun 1947. †

AK 180 *Fentress* Decomm 20 Feb 1946. †
Later history: To SCAJAP. To Army as *Fentress*.

AK 181 *Flagler* Went aground in typhoon at Okinawa, 9 Oct 1945. Decomm 24 Dec 1945. Stricken 29 Mar 1946. BU 1948.

AK 182 *Gadsden* Decomm 31 Jan 1946.
Later history: Merchant *Gadsden*, renamed *Yosu* 1955. BU 1980 Inchon, South Korea.

AK 183 *Glacier* Decomm 19 Feb 1946. Stricken 12 Mar 1946.
Later history: Merchant *Hydra*, renamed *Assma B* 1962. BU 1970 Hsinkang.

AK 184 *Grainger* Decomm 25 Jul 1946. Stricken 15 Aug 1946. Reacquired 9 May 1947. Recomm 12 Jun 1947. †

AK 185 *Gwinnett* Rec **AG 92**, 9 Mar 1945. Rec **AVS 5**, 25 May 1945. Decomm 11 Feb 1946. No service.
Later history: Merchant *Ste. Helene*, renamed *Prince KL* 1968. BU 1970 Hong Kong.

AK 186 *Habersham* Decomm 9 Apr 1946.
Later history: Merchant *Rosa Thorden*, renamed *Pusan* 1952, *Busan*, *Sam Dai* 1978. Damaged by engine room fire off Inchon, South Korea, 14 Apr 1979. BU 1979 Inchon.

AK 187 *Hennepin* Decomm 16 Feb 1946. †
Later history: To SCAJAP. To Army as *Hennepin.*
AK 188 *Herkimer* Decomm 1 Feb 1946. †
Later history: To SCAJAP. To Army as *Herkimer.*
AK 189 *Hidalgo* No service. Decomm 26 Apr 1946.
Later history: Merchant *Rize.* BU 1982 Aliaga.
AK 190 *Kenosha* Decomm 16 Apr 1946.
Later history: Merchant *Rio Dale* 1947, renamed *Torian* 1959, *Lars Viking* 1963, *Neptune V* 1965, *Arabdrill 2* 1967. BU 1984 Gadani Beach, Pakistan.
AK 191 *Lebanon* Decomm 15 Nov 1945. No service.
Later history: Merchant *Coastal Archer,* renamed *Rio Paraguacu* 1956, *Irazu* 1976, BU 1986 Mamonal, Colombia.
AK 192 *Lehigh* Decomm 6 Nov 1945. No service.
Later history: Merchant *Coastal Expounder,* renamed *Rio Solimoes* 1947. BU 1969.
AK 193 *Lancaster* Decomm 23 Nov 1945. No service.
Later history: Merchant *Coastal Ringleader,* renamed *Rio Pianco* 1956.
AK 194 *Marengo* Decomm 23 Nov 1945 and returned with no service.
Later history: Merchant *Coastal Spartan,* renamed drilling ship *Cyclone* 1965, *Ocean Cyclone* 1976.
AK 195 *Midland* Decomm 23 Nov 1945. No service.
Later history: Merchant *Coastal Harbinger* 1945, renamed *Union Banker* 1948. BU 1970 Kaohsiung, Taiwan.
AK 196 *Minidoka* Not acq, 25 Aug 1945 conversion canceled; completed as m/v.
Later history: Merchant *Coastal Herald,* renamed *Rio Miranda* 1956, *Mirosal* 1974. BU 1977 Vila Velha–Vitoria, Brazil.

No.	Name	Builder	Keel Laid	Launched	Comm.
AK 197	*Muscatine*	Globe Sup.	21 Dec 1943	16 Jun 1944	19 Apr 1945
AK 198	*Muskingum*	Globe Sup.	26 Jan 1944	30 Jun 1944	24 Apr 1945
AK 199	*Nicollet*	Globe Sup.	9 Feb 1944	31 Jul 1944	27 Apr 1945
AK 200	*Pembina*	Globe Sup.	23 Jun 1944	14 Oct 1944	25 May 1945
AK 201	*Pemiscot*	Globe Sup.	7 Jul 1944	18 Nov 1944	—
AK 202	*Pinellas*	Globe Sup.	9 Aug 1944	22 Dec 1944	—
AK 203	*Pipestone*	Globe Sup.	4 Dec 1944	6 Mar 1945	—
AK 204	*Pitkin*	Globe Sup.	6 Jan 1945	7 Apr 1945	—
AK 205	*Poinsett*	L. D. Smith	6 Nov 1943	22 May 1944	7 Feb 1945
AK 206	*Pontotoc*	L. D. Smith	15 Jan 1944	2 Jul 1944	22 Mar 1945
AK 207	*Richland*	L. D. Smith	15 Jan 1944	5 Aug 1944	22 Apr 1945
AK 208	*Rockdale*	L. D. Smith	15 Jan 1944	1 Oct 1944	26 Jun 1945
AK 209	*Schuyler*	L. D. Smith	27 May 1944	26 Oct 1944	18 Jul 1945
AK 210	*Screven*	L. D. Smith	11 Jul 1944	30 Nov 1944	2 Aug 1945
AK 211	*Sebastian*	L. D. Smith	10 Aug 1944	21 Dec 1944	11 Sep 1945
AK 212	*Somerset*	L. D. Smith	9 Oct 1944	21 Jan 1945	20 Sep 1945
AK 213	*Sussex*	L. D. Smith	30 Oct 1944	3 Feb 1945	20 Aug 1945
AK 214	*Tarrant*	L. D. Smith	4 Dec 1944	25 Feb 1945	18 Sep 1945
AK 215	*Tipton*	L. D. Smith	28 Dec 1944	13 Mar 1945	9 Oct 1945
AK 216	*Traverse*	L. D. Smith	25 Jan 1945	1 Apr 1945	—
AK 217	*Tulare*	L. D. Smith	8 Feb 1945	22 Apr 1945	—
AK 218	*Washtenaw*	L. D. Smith	9 Mar 1945	13 May 1945	—
AK 219	*Westchester*	L. D. Smith	21 Mar 1945	3 Jun 1945	—
AK 220	*Wexford*	L. D. Smith	12 Apr 1945	24 Jun 1945	—

Service Records:

AK 197 *Muscatine* Decomm 7 Mar 1946. Stricken 20 Mar 1946.
Later history: Merchant *Palma* 1947, renamed *Avance* 1953, *Duke KL* 1968. BU 1972 Hong Kong.
AK 198 *Muskingum* Decomm 7 Mar 1946 and trfd to Army. Stricken 5 Jun 1946. †
Later history: To SCAJAP. To U.S. Army as *Muskingum.*
AK 199 *Nicollet* Rec **AG 93**, 9 Mar 1945. Rec **AVS 6**, 25 May 1945. Decomm 17 Jun 1946, returned to WSA. Stricken 3 Jul 1946.
Later history: Merchant *Djerada.* BU 1970 Cartagena, Spain.
AK 200 *Pembina* Decomm 26 Jan 1946. Stricken 5 Jun 1946. †
Later history: To SCAJAP as *Pembina.*
AK 201 *Pemiscot* Returned without service, 31 Oct 1945. Stricken 5 Dec 1945.
Later history: Merchant *Coastal Competitor,* renamed *Rio Tubarao* 1956.
AK 202 *Pinellas* Not acq, completed as m/v.
Later history: Merchant *Coastal Stevedore,* renamed *Bahia de Matanzas* 1948. BU 1980 Alvarado, Mexico.
AK 203 *Pipestone* Not acq, completed as m/v.
Later history: Merchant *Coastal Explorer,* renamed *Putumayo* 1947, *Felipe* 1968. BU 1974 Bilbao, Spain.
AK 204 *Pitkin* Not acq, completed as m/v.
Later history: Merchant *Coastal Observer,* renamed *Rio Moçoro* 1956, *Guararapes* 1973. BU 1983.
AK 205 *Poinsett* Decomm 25 Jan and returned 29 Jan 1946. Stricken 12 Mar 1946.
1* Balikpapan.
Later history: Merchant *Carina,* renamed *Masan* 1953.
AK 206 *Pontotoc* Rec **AG 94**, 9 Mar 1945. Rec **AVS 7**, 25 May 1945. Decomm 26 Apr 1946. Stricken 8 May 1946.
Later history: Merchant *Taurus,* renamed *Tadgera* 1960, *Myriam* 1964. BU 1968 Valencia.
AK 207 *Richland* Decomm 23 Jan 1946. Stricken 7 Feb 1946. BU 1971.
AK 208 *Rockdale* Decomm 22 Mar 1946. Stricken 12 Apr 1946.
Later history: Merchant *Apollo,* renamed *Thabor* 1952, *Etienne Denis* 1960, *Hongkong Pioneer* 1962. BU 1970 Kaohsiung, Taiwan.
AK 209 *Schuyler* Decomm 22 Apr 1946.
Later history: To SCAJAP. Stricken 5 Jun 1946. Army *Schuyler.* BU 1971 Baltimore.
AK 210 *Screven* Decomm 30 Apr 1946. Stricken 8 May 1946.
Later history: Merchant *Norlindo,* to Peruvian Navy, renamed *Ilo* 1959. BU 1968 Valencia, Spain.
AK 211 *Sebastian* Decomm 14 Nov 1945 and returned, no service. Stricken 28 Nov 1945.
Later history: Merchant *Coastal Highlander,* renamed Army *Resolve* 1967.
AK 212 *Somerset* USCG crew. No service. Stricken 5 Dec 1945.
Later history: Merchant *Coastal Sentry,* later USAF *E-45-1849.*
AK 213 *Sussex* USCG crew 20 Sep 45/2 Nov 45. Recomm 27 May 1947. †
AK 214 *Tarrant* USCG crew. Decomm 21 Nov 1945 and returned. Stricken 5 Dec 1945.
Later history: Merchant *Coastal Advocate,* renamed *Rio Guapore* 1947, *Itamar* 1948, *Rio Guapore* 1952. BU 1969.
AK 215 *Tipton* USCG crew. To USCG 4 Mar 1946.
Later history: Renamed USCGC *Unalga* (WAK 185). Sold 1 Jun 1950. Merchant *Tipton.*
AK 216 *Traverse* Not acq, completed as m/v.
Later history: Merchant *Coastal Merchant,* renamed *Norlantic* 1946, *Leif Viking* 1959. Went aground off Rhode Island, 7 Jan 1962. BU.
AK 217 *Tulare* Not acq, completed as m/v.
Later history: Merchant *Coastal Challenger,* renamed *Pachitea* 1946, *Dunstan* 1954, *Sallust* 1958, *Malacca* 1959, *Tong Hong* 1963. Missing en route Kawasaki–Hong Kong 25 Oct 1967.
AK 218 *Washtenaw* Not acq, completed as m/v.
Later history: Merchant *Coastal Guide,* renamed *Sgt. George Peterson* (Army) 1947. †

AK 219 *Westchester* Not acq, completed as m/v.
Later history: Merchant *Coastal Defender*, renamed *Rio Maracana* 1956. BU 1970.

AK 220 *Wexford* Not acq, completed as m/v.
Later history: Merchant *Coastal Crusader*, renamed *Pvt. Joe R. Hastings* (Army) 1947, *Coastal Crusader* 1955.

No.	Name	Builder	Keel Laid	Launched	Comm.
AK 227	*Boulder Victory*	Permanente #1	18 Jun 1944	31 Aug 1944	12 Oct 1944
AK 228	*Provo Victory*	Permanente #1	28 Jun 1944	9 Sep 1944	18 Oct 1944
AK 229	*Las Vegas Victory*	Permanente #1	7 Jul 1944	16 Sep 1944	25 Oct 1944
AK 230	*Manderson Victory*	Permanente #1	14 Jul 1944	23 Sep 1944	3 Nov 1944
AK 231	*Bedford Victory*	Permanente #1	20 Jul 1944	30 Sep 1944	11 Nov 1944
AK 232	*Mayfield Victory*	Permanente #1	10 Aug 1944	10 Oct 1944	16 Nov 1944
AK 233	*Newcastle Victory*	Permanente #1	21 Aug 1944	17 Oct 1944	23 Nov 1944
AK 234	*Bucyrus Victory*	Permanente #1	1 Sep 1944	31 Oct 1944	29 Nov 1944
AK 235	*Red Oak Victory*	Permanente #1	9 Sep 1944	9 Nov 1944	5 Dec 1944
AK 236	*Lakewood Victory*	Permanente #1	16 Sep 1944	17 Nov 1944	11 Dec 1944

Displacement	4,420 tons; 15,580 tons f/l; 7,609 grt
Dimensions	455'3" (oa); 436'6" (wl) x 62' x 29'2"
Machinery	1 screw; West. GT; 2 FW boilers; SHP 6,000; 15.5 knots
Complement	99
Armament	1–5"/38, 1–3"/50, 2 twin 40mm, 4 twin 20mm guns

Notes: Type VC2–S–AP2. Ammunition carriers.

Service Records:

AK 227 *Boulder Victory* Damaged by mine off Palau, 20 Dec 1944. Decomm 4 Jan 1946. Stricken 21 Jan 1946. BU 1984 Kaohsiung, Taiwan.

AK 228 *Provo Victory* Decomm 10 Apr 1946. Stricken 8 May 1946. BU 1984 Taiwan.

AK 229 *Las Vegas Victory* Decomm 8 Apr 1946. BU 1994 China.
1* Okinawa, Fleet Raids 1945.

AK 230 *Manderson Victory* Decomm 10 May 1946. BU 1993 Alang, India.
1* Okinawa, Fleet Raids 1945

AK 231 *Bedford Victory* Decomm 26 Mar 1946; BU 1972 Seattle.
1* Fleet Raids 1945.

AK 232 *Mayfield Victory* Decomm 5 Apr 1946. BU 1994 China.
2* Fleet Raids 1945, Okinawa.

AK 233 *Newcastle Victory* Decomm 21 Jun 1946. Stricken 3 Jul 1946. BU 1992 Alang, India.

AK 234 *Bucyrus Victory* Decomm 24 Feb 1946. BU 1969 Hong Kong.
1* Okinawa, Fleet Raids 1945.

AK 235 *Red Oak Victory* Decomm 21 May 1946. Stricken 19 Jul 1946.
Later history: Museum at Richmond, Calif., 2002.

AK 236 *Lakewood Victory* Decomm 16 May 1946. BU 1994 China.
2* Iwo Jima, Okinawa, Fleet Raids 1945.

NET CARGO SHIPS

No.	Name	Builder	Keel Laid	Launched	Comm.
AKN 1	*Indus*	Beth. Fairfield	4 Oct 1943	29 Oct 1943	15 Feb 1944
	ex–*Theodore Roosevelt* (1943)				
AKN 2	*Sagittarius*	Beth. Fairfield	8 Nov 1943	30 Nov 1943	18 Mar 1944
	ex–*J. Fred Essary* (1943)				
AKN 3	*Tuscana*	Beth. Fairfield	5 Dec 1943	29 Dec 1943	28 Mar 1944
	ex–*William R. Cox* (1944)				
AKN 5	*Zebra*	Permanente #1	18 Mar 1943	11 Apr 1943	27 Feb 1944
	ex–IX 107 (11 Feb 1944), ex–*Matthew Lyon* (1 Oct 1943)				

Displacement	4,023 tons; 14,550 tons f/l
Dimensions	441' (oa); 416' (wl) x 56'11" x 28'4"
Machinery	1 screw; VTE; 2 B&W boilers; SHP 2,500,
Complement	228
Armament	1–5"/38, 4–40mm, 10–20mm AA guns

Note: Type EC2–S–C1.

Service Records:

AKN 1 *Indus* Decomm 20 May 1946. Returned 23 May 1946. BU 1967 Wilmington, N.C.
2* Leyte.

AKN 2 *Sagittarius* Decomm 16 Jan 1946. Stricken 7 Feb 1946. BU 1972 Castellon, Spain.
2* Saipan, Okinawa.

AKN 3 *Tuscana* Decomm 28 Jan 1946. Stricken 25 Feb 1946. BU 1968 Wilmington, N.C.
2* Saipan, Okinawa.

AKN 5 *Zebra* As m/v, Torpedoed by submarine *I–11* off Noumea 11 Aug 1943. Acq by Navy 1 Oct 1943 as **IX 107**. Decomm 21 Jan 1946. Stricken 7 Feb 1946. BU 1972 Kearny, N.J.
1* Iwo Jima.

No.	Name	Formerly	Date
AKN4	*Keokuk*	CM 8	1 Nov 1943

Service Record:

5* Sicily, Saipan, Palau, Iwo Jima, Okinawa.

GENERAL–STORES–ISSUE SHIPS

No.	Name	Builder	Keel Laid	Launched	Comm.
AKS 1	*Castor*	Federal	25 Aug 1938	20 May 1939	12 Mar 1941
	ex–*Challenge* (29 Oct 1940)				
AKS 2	*Pollux*	Federal	26 May 1939	16 Dec 1939	16 May 1941
	ex–*Comet* (1941)				

Displacement	7,350 tons; 14,440 tons f/l
Dimensions	459'2" (oa); 435' (wl) x 63' x 26'5"
Machinery	1 screw; GE GT; 2 FW boilers; SHP 6,000; 16.5 knots
Complement	207
Armament	AKS 1: 1–5"/38, 4–3"/50, 8 to 10 20mm AA guns

Note: Type C2–Cargo (S).

Service Records:

AKS 1 *Castor* Acq 23 Oct 1940. Decomm 30 Jun 1947. †
3* Pearl Harbor, Gilbert Is., Okinawa.

AKS 2 *Pollux* Acq 16 Jan 1941. Wrecked in storm off St. Lawrence, Newfoundland, 18 Feb 1942. (~200 killed).

No.	Name	Builder	Keel Laid	Launched	Comm.
AKS 4	*Pollux*	Federal	2 Oct 1941	5 Feb 1942	27 Apr 1942
	ex–AK 54, LD as *Stella Lykes*				

Displacement	7,350 tons; 14,440 tons f/l
Dimensions	459'2" (oa); 435' (wl) x 63' x 26'5"
Machinery	1 screw; GE Curtis GT; 2 FW boilers; SHP 6,000; 16.5 knots
Complement	200
Armament	1–5"/38, 4–3"/50, 10–20mm AA guns

Note: Type C2–F.

Service Record:

AKS 4 *Pollux* Operation Crossroads. †

AKS 3 *Antares* Ex–AG 10 (30 Nov 1940).

No.	Name	Builder	Keel Laid	Launched	Comm.
AKS 5	*Acubens*	Delta	25 Nov 1943	8 Jan 1944	15 Jul 1944
	ex–*Jean Louis* (1944)				
AKS 6	*Kochab*	Delta	18 Feb 1944	30 Mar 1944	4 Nov 1944
AKS 7	*Luna*	Jones	23 Apr 1943	30 Sep 1943	7 Feb 1944
	ex–*Harriet Hosmer* (1943)				
AKS 8	*Talita*	Oregon	23 Apr 1943	12 May 1943	4 Mar 1944
	ex–*Jonathan Jennings* (1943)				
AKS 9	*Volans*	New England	19 Oct 1942	2 Jan 1943	31 Mar 1944
	ex–*Edward Preble* (1943)				
AKS 10	*Cybele*	Delta	29 Aug 1944	9 Oct 1944	16 Apr 1945
	ex–*William Hackett* (1944)				
AKS 11	*Gratia*	Delta	14 Sep 1944	21 Oct 1944	5 May 1945
	ex–*John W. Draper* (1944)				
AKS 12	*Hecuba*	Delta	27 Sep 1944	6 Nov 1944	21 Apr 1945
	ex–*George W. Cable* (1944)				
AKS 13	*Hesperia*	Delta	9 Oct 1944	18 Nov 1944	1 Apr 1945
	ex–*Sam Dale* (1944)				
AKS 14	*Iolanda*	New England	9 Sep 1944	21 Oct 1944	14 Jun 1945
	ex–*William A. Dobson* (1944)				
AKS 15	*Liguria*	New England	19 Sep 1944	3 Nov 1944	12 Jul 1945

Displacement	5,240 tons; 14,550 tons f/l
Dimensions	441'6" (oa); 416' (wl) x 56'11" x 28'4"
Machinery	1 screw; VTE; 2 B&W boilers (AKS 7: CE; AKS 9: FW), SHP 2,500
Complement	195
Armament	1–5"/38, 1–3"/50, 8–20mm (AKS 5–6: 4–3"/50)

Note: Type EC2–S–C1.

Service Records:

AKS 5 *Acubens* Decomm 11 Mar 1946. Sold 20 Jun 1947, stricken 17 Jul 1947; BU 1964 Portland, Ore.

AKS 6 *Kochab* Decomm 17 Apr 1946. Stricken 22 Oct 1947. BU 1965 Richmond, Calif.
1* Okinawa.

AKS 7 *Luna* Decomm 20 Apr 1946. BU 1965 Richmond, Calif.

AKS 8 *Talita* Decomm 9 Apr 1946. Stricken 17 Jul 1947. BU 1963 Oakland, Calif.

AKS 9 *Volans* Decomm 17 Jun 1946. Stricken 17 Jul 1947. BU 1965 Oakland, Calif.

AKS 10 *Cybele* Decomm 22 Aug 1946. BU 1965 Portland, Ore. Tokyo Bay.

AKS 11 *Gratia* Decomm 1 Jul 1946. Stricken 17 Jul 1947. BU 1965 Richmond, Calif.

AKS 12 *Hecuba* Decomm 26 Mar 1946. Sold 19 Oct 1946; BU 1964 Portland, Ore.

AKS 13 *Hesperia* Operation Crossroads. Decomm 27 Feb 1947. BU 1973 Kaohsiung, Taiwan.

AKS 14 *Iolanda* Decomm 11 Jul 1946. BU 1972.

AKS 15 *Liguria* Decomm 7 Aug 1946. Sold 23 Apr 1947. BU 1974 South Korea.

Figure 11.15: *Capricornus* (AKA 57), an attack cargo ship of type C2-S-B1, after the war.

CARGO SHIPS AND AIRCRAFT FERRIES

Note: For AKV, see APV, p. 341.

ATTACK CARGO SHIPS

AKA 1	*Arcturus*	Ex–AK 18
AKA 2	*Procyon*	Ex–AK 19
AKA 3	*Bellatrix*	Ex–AK 20
AKA 4	*Electra*	Ex–AK 21
AKA 5	*Fomalhaut*	Ex–AK 22; rec AK 22, 25 Aug 1944
AKA 6	*Alchiba*	Ex–AK 23
AKA 7	*Alcyone*	Ex–AK 24
AKA 8	*Algorab*	Ex–AK 25
AKA 9	*Alhena*	Ex–AK 26
AKA 10	*Almaack*	Ex–AK 27
AKA 11	*Betelgeuse*	Ex–AK 28
AKA 12	*Libra*	Ex–AK 53
AKA 13	*Titania*	Ex–AK 55
AKA 14	*Oberon*	Ex–AK 56

Note: All rec 1 Feb 1943.

No.	Name	Builder	Keel Laid	Launched	Comm.
AKA 15	*Andromeda*	Federal	22 Sep 1942	22 Dec 1942	2 Apr 1943
AKA 16	*Aquarius*	Federal	28 Apr 1943	23 Jul 1943	21 Aug 1943
AKA 17	*Centaurus*	Federal	7 Jun 1943	3 Sep 1943	21 Oct 1943
AKA 18	*Cepheus*	Federal	26 Jul 1943	23 Oct 1943	16 Dec 1943
AKA 19	*Thuban*	Federal	2 Feb 1943	26 Apr 1943	10 Jun 1943
AKA 20	*Virgo*	Federal	9 Mar 1943	4 Jun 1943	16 Jul 1943

Displacement	6,556 tons; 13,910 tons f/l
Dimensions	459'3" (oa); 435' (wl) x 63' x 26'4"
Machinery	1 screw; GE GT; 2 CE boilers; SHP 6,000; 16.5 knots
Endurance	16,046/12
Complement	404/368
Armament	1–5"/38 *or* 4–3"/50, 2 twin 40mm, 18–20mm AA

Note: Ex–AK 64–69 (1 Feb 1943).

Service Records:

AKA 15 *Andromeda* †
5* Sicily, Salerno, Convoy KMF–25A, Southern France, Okinawa.

AKA 16 *Aquarius* USCG crew. Decomm 23 May 1946. Sold 12 Sep 1946. Stricken 13 Nov 1946.
7* Kwajalein, Guam, Palau, Leyte, Lingayen, Okinawa, Subic Bay.
Later history: Merchant *Pioneer Lake*, renamed *American Trapper* 1956. BU 1967 Kearny, N.J.

AKA 17 *Centaurus* USCG crew. Decomm 30 Apr 1946.
6* Kwajalein, Admiralty Is., Hollandia, Guam, Palau, Okinawa.
Later history: Merchant *Pioneer Bay* 1948, renamed *American Gunner* 1956. BU 1970 Burriana.

AKA 18 *Cepheus* USCG crew. Decomm 22 May 1946. Sold 17 Jan 1947.
2* Southern France, Okinawa.
Later history: Merchant *Pioneer Sea* 1947, renamed *American Hunter* 1956, *Brookville* 1966. Wrecked on reef off Honduras, 3 Apr 1968.

AKA 19 *Thuban* †
7* Gilbert Is., Kwajalein, Saipan, Tinian, Leyte, Iwo Jima, Raids on Japan 7–8/45.

AKA 20 *Virgo* †
7* Gilbert Is., Kwajalein, Hollandia, Guam, Palau, Iwo Jima, Okinawa.

Figure 11.17: *Athene* (AKA 22), 9 Oct 1944, was one of 32 type S4 vessels completed as attack cargo ships.

No.	Name	Builder	Keel Laid	Launched	Comm.
AKA 53	*Achernar*	Federal	6 Sep 1943	3 Dec 1943	31 Jan 1944
AKA 54	*Algol* ex–*James Baines* (Aug 1943)	Moore	10 Dec 1942	17 Feb 1943	21 Jul 1944
AKA 55	*Alshain*	Federal	29 Oct 1943	26 Jan 1944	1 Apr 1944
AKA 56	*Arneb* LD as *Mischief*	Moore	20 Apr 1943	6 Jul 1943	28 Apr 1944
AKA 57	*Capricornus* ex–*Spitfire* (Nov 1943)	Moore	5 May 1943	14 Aug 1943	31 May 1944
AKA 58	*Chara*	Federal	6 Dec 1943	15 Mar 1944	14 Jun 1944
AKA 59	*Diphda*	Federal	27 Jan 1944	11 May 1944	8 Jul 1944
AKA 60	*Leo*	Federal	17 Mar 1944	29 Jun 1944	30 Aug 1944
AKA 61	*Muliphen*	Federal	13 May 1944	26 Aug 1944	23 Oct 1944
AKA 62	*Sheliak*	Federal	19 Jun 1944	17 Oct 1944	1 Dec 1944
AKA 63	*Theenim*	Federal	3 Jul 1944	31 Oct 1944	22 Dec 1944
AKA 88	*Uvalde* LD as *Wild Pigeon*	Moore	27 Mar 1944	20 May 1944	18 Aug 1944
AKA 89	*Warrick* LD as *Black Prince*	Moore	7 Apr 1944	29 May 1944	30 Aug 1944
AKA 90	*Whiteside* LD as *Wings of the Morning*	Moore	22 Apr 1944	12 Jun 1944	11 Sep 1944
AKA 91	*Whitley*	Moore	2 May 1944	22 Jun 1944	21 Sep 1944
AKA 92	*Wyandot*	Moore	6 May 1944	28 Jun 1944	30 Sep 1944
AKA 93	*Yancey*	Moore	22 May 1944	8 Jul 1944	11 Oct 1944
AKA 94	*Winston*	Federal	10 Jul 1944	30 Nov 1944	19 Jan 1945
AKA 95	*Marquette*	Federal	30 Aug 1944	29 Apr 1945	20 Jun 1945
AKA 96	*Mathews*	Federal	15 Sep 1944	22 Dec 1944	5 Mar 1945
AKA 97	*Merrick*	Federal	19 Oct 1944	28 Jan 1945	31 Mar 1945
AKA 98	*Montague*	Federal	2 Nov 1944	11 Feb 1945	13 Apr 1945
AKA 99	*Rolette*	Federal	2 Dec 1944	11 Mar 1945	27 Apr 1945
AKA 100	*Oglethorpe*	Federal	26 Dec 1944	15 Apr 1945	5 Jun 1945
AKA 109	*San Joaquin*	Federal	17 Aug 1945	—	—
AKA 110	*Sedgwick*	Federal	—	—	—
AKA 111	*Whitfield*	Federal	—	—	—

Figure 11.16: *Whiteside* (AKA 90), 20 Sep 1945. This aerial views shows many small craft carried as deck cargo.

Displacement	6,470 tons; 11,130 f/l 13,910 tons f/l
Dimensions	459'2" (oa); 435' (wl) x 63' x 26'4"
Machinery	1 screw; GE GT; 2 FW boilers; SHP 6,000; 16.5 knots
Complement	429/342
Armament	1–5"/38, 4 twin 40mm, 18–20mm AA

Note: Type C2–S–B1.

Service Records:

AKA 53 *Achernar* Damaged by kamikaze, Okinawa, 2 Apr 1945 (5 killed). Damaged in collision with m/v *H. H. Raymond* off Seattle, 4 Dec 1945. †
3* Normandy, Southern France, Okinawa.

AKA 54 *Algol* Decomm 26 Nov 1947. †
2* Subic Bay, Okinawa.

AKA 55 *Alshain* †
5* Guam, Leyte, Lingayen, Subic Bay, Okinawa.

AKA 56 *Arneb* †
4* Palau, Leyte, Subic Bay, Okinawa.

AKA 57 *Capricornus* †
4* Leyte, Lingayen, Subic Bay, Okinawa.

AKA 58 *Chara* †
4* Leyte, Lingayen, Subic Bay, Okinawa.

AKA 59 *Diphda* †
1* Okinawa.

AKA 60 *Leo* Damaged in error by U.S. gunfire, Okinawa, 6 Apr and 11 Apr 1945. †
2* Iwo Jima, Okinawa.

AKA 61 *Muliphen* Damaged in collision with cruiser *Salt Lake City*, Iwo Jima, 25 Feb 1945. †
2* Iwo Jima, Okinawa.

AKA 62 *Sheliak* USCG crew. Decomm 10 May 1946. Stricken 21 May 1946.
1* Okinawa.
Later history: Merchant *Pioneer Isle*, renamed *Australian Isle* 1966, *Transluna* 1969. BU 1969 Kaohsiung, Taiwan.

AKA 63 *Theenim* USCG crew. Decomm 10 May 1946. Stricken 21 May 1946.
1* Okinawa.
Later history: Merchant *American Inventor* 1948, renamed *Pioneer Surf* 1958, *Australian Surf* 1965, *Surfer* 1968. BU 1970 Kaohsiung, Taiwan.

AKA 88 *Uvalde* Decomm 9 Nov 1946. †
1* Okinawa.

AKA 89 *Warrick*
2* Honshu Raid 2/45, Iwo Jima. †

AKA 90 *Whiteside* Damaged in collision with transport *Bayfield* off Maui, Hawaii, 14 Dec 1944. †
2* Iwo Jima, Okinawa. Tokyo Bay.

AKA 91 *Whitley* Damaged by Kamikaze, Iwo Jima, 28 Feb 1945. †
1* Iwo Jima.

AKA 92 *Wyandot* Damaged by aircraft bomb, Okinawa, 29 Mar 1945. † Damaged by collision, Okinawa, 12 Apr 1945.
1* Okinawa.

AKA 93 *Yancey* Damaged in collision with cruiser *Pensacola*, Iwo Jima, 21 Feb 1945. †
2* Iwo Jima, Okinawa.

AKA 94 *Winston* †

AKA 95 *Marquette* †

AKA 96 *Mathews* Decomm 4 Apr 1947. †

AKA 97 *Merrick* Rudder damaged by ice in Antarctica, 11 Feb 1946. Decomm 25 Jun 1946. †
1* Okinawa. Tokyo Bay.

AKA 98 *Montague* †

AKA 99 *Rolette* Operation Crossroads. Decomm Jan 1946. Returned 31 Mar 1947. Stricken 23 Apr 1947. †

AKA 100 *Oglethorpe* †

AKA 109 *San Joaquin* Canceled, 27 Aug 1945.
Later history: Completed as merchant *Santa Monica*.

AKA 110 *Sedgwick* Canceled, 27 Aug 1945.
Later history: Completed as merchant *Santa Clara*.

AKA 111 *Whitfield* Canceled, 27 Aug 1945.
Later history: Completed as merchant *Santa Sofia*.

Figure 11.18: *Starr* (AKA 67), 1 Nov 1944, a type C2-S-AJ3 attack cargo ship.

No.	Name	Builder	Keel Laid	Launched	Comm.
AKA 21	*Artemis*	Walsh-Kaiser	23 Nov 1943	20 May 1944	28 Aug 1944
AKA 22	*Athene*	Walsh-Kaiser	20 Jan 1944	18 Jun 1944	29 Sep 1944
AKA 23	*Aurelia*	Walsh-Kaiser	5 Feb 1944	4 Jul 1944	14 Oct 1944
AKA 24	*Birgit*	Walsh-Kaiser	22 Feb 1944	18 Jul 1944	28 Oct 1944
AKA 25	*Circe*	Walsh-Kaiser	6 Mar 1944	4 Aug 1944	10 Nov 1944
AKA 26	*Corvus*	Walsh-Kaiser	4 Apr 1944	24 Sep 1944	20 Nov 1944
AKA 27	*Devosa*	Walsh-Kaiser	22 May 1944	12 Oct 1944	30 Nov 1944
AKA 28	*Hydrus*	Walsh-Kaiser	19 Jun 1944	28 Oct 1944	9 Dec 1944
AKA 29	*Lacerta*	Walsh-Kaiser	5 Jul 1944	10 Nov 1944	19 Dec 1944
AKA 30	*Lumen*	Walsh-Kaiser	19 Jul 1944	20 Nov 1944	29 Dec 1944
AKA 31	*Medea*	Walsh-Kaiser	5 Aug 1944	30 Nov 1944	10 Jan 1945
AKA 32	*Mellena*	Walsh-Kaiser	25 Sep 1944	11 Dec 1944	20 Jan 1945
AKA 33	*Ostara*	Walsh-Kaiser	13 Oct 1944	21 Dec 1944	31 Jan 1945
AKA 34	*Pamina*	Walsh-Kaiser	29 Oct 1944	5 Jan 1945	10 Feb 1945
AKA 35	*Polana*	Walsh-Kaiser	11 Nov 1944	17 Jan 1945	21 Feb 1945
AKA 36	*Renate*	Walsh-Kaiser	21 Nov 1944	31 Jan 1945	28 Feb 1945
AKA 37	*Roxane*	Walsh-Kaiser	1 Dec 1944	14 Feb 1945	12 Mar 1945
AKA 38	*Sappho*	Walsh-Kaiser	12 Dec 1944	3 Mar 1945	24 Apr 1945
AKA 39	*Sarita*	Walsh-Kaiser	22 Dec 1944	23 Feb 1945	22 Mar 1945
AKA 40	*Scania*	Walsh-Kaiser	6 Jan 1945	17 Mar 1945	16 Apr 1945
AKA 41	*Selinur*	Walsh-Kaiser	18 Jan 1945	28 Mar 1945	21 Apr 1945
AKA 42	*Sidonia*	Walsh-Kaiser	1 Feb 1945	7 Apr 1945	30 Apr 1945
AKA 43	*Sirona*	Walsh-Kaiser	15 Feb 1945	17 Apr 1945	10 May 1945
AKA 44	*Sylvania*	Walsh-Kaiser	24 Feb 1945	25 Apr 1945	19 May 1945
AKA 45	*Tabora*	Walsh-Kaiser	4 Mar 1945	3 May 1945	29 May 1945
AKA 46	*Troilus*	Walsh-Kaiser	18 Mar 1945	11 May 1945	8 Jun 1945
AKA 47	*Turandot*	Walsh-Kaiser	29 Mar 1945	20 May 1945	18 Jun 1945
AKA 48	*Valeria*	Walsh-Kaiser	8 Apr 1945	29 May 1945	28 Jun 1945
AKA 49	*Vanadis*	Walsh-Kaiser	18 Apr 1945	8 Jun 1945	9 Jul 1945
AKA 50	*Veritas*	Walsh-Kaiser	26 Apr 1945	16 Jun 1945	19 Jul 1945
AKA 51	*Xenia*	Walsh-Kaiser	4 May 1945	27 Jun 1945	28 Jul 1945
AKA 52	*Zenobia*	Walsh-Kaiser	12 May 1945	6 Jul 1945	6 Aug 1945

Displacement	7,000 tons f/l; 4,087 tons; 6,800 f/l
Dimensions	426' (oa); 400' (wl) x 58' x 16'
Machinery	2 screws; West. TE, 2 Wickes boilers; SHP 6,000; 16.5 or 17.8 knots
Endurance	9500/12
Complement	304
Armament	1–5"/38, 4 twin 40mm, 12–20mm AA guns

Note: Type S4–SE2–BE1.

Service Records:

AKA 21 *Artemis* Bikini target ship. Decomm 10 Jan 1947. Stricken 25 Feb 1947. BU 1966.
1* Iwo Jima.

AKA 22 *Athene* Collided with an LST in typhoon in Tokyo Bay, 18 Sep 1945. Bikini target. Decomm 17 Jun 1946. Stricken 1 Aug 1947. BU 1966 San Francisco.
2* Iwo Jima, Okinawa.

AKA 23 *Aurelia* Decomm 14 Mar 1946. Stricken 19 Jun 1946. BU 1972.
1*Okinawa.

AKA 24 *Birgit* Decomm 15 Mar 1946. Stricken 21 May 1946. BU 1972.

AKA 25 *Circe* Decomm 20 May 1946. BU 1964.
1* Okinawa.

AKA 26 *Corvus* Decomm 29 Mar 1946. BU 1964 Mobile.
1* Okinawa.

AKA 27 *Devosa* Decomm 2 Apr 1946.
1* Okinawa.
Later history: Training ship *King's Pointer.* BU 1966 Baltimore.

AKA 28 *Hydrus* Decomm 26 Mar 1946, to N.Y. State Maritime Academy.
1* Okinawa.
Later history: Training ship *Empire State II* until 1956. BU 1964.

AKA 29 *Lacerta* Decomm 25 Mar 1946. BU 1966.
1* Okinawa.

AKA 30 *Lumen* Decomm 23 Mar 1946. BU 1964.
1* Okinawa.

AKA 31 *Medea* Decomm 24 Apr 1946. Stricken 15 Oct 1946. BU 1964 New Orleans.
1* Okinawa.

AKA 32 *Mellena* Conversion to AGS canceled, Mar 1946. Decomm 11 Jun 1946. Stricken 3 Jul 1946. Tokyo Bay.
Later history: Trfd to California State Maritime Academy, renamed *Golden Bear.* BU 1971 Terminal I.

AKA 33 *Ostara* Decomm 1 Mar 1946. Stricken 17 Apr 1946. Sold 26 Jun 1946. BU 1966 Wilmington, N.C.

AKA 34 *Pamina* Converted to surveying ship and rec **AGS 15**, renamed ***Tanner***, 15 May 1946. Tokyo Bay. †
1* Okinawa.

AKA 35 *Polana* Decomm 21 Mar 1946. Stricken 1 May 1946. Sold 25 Jun 1946; BU 1966 Kearny, N.J.

AKA 36 *Renate* Converted to surveying ship and rec **AGS 16**, renamed ***Maury***, 1 Aug 1946. †

AKA 37 *Roxane* Decomm 5 Jun 1946. Stricken 3 Jul 1946. BU 1966 Portland, Ore.

AKA 38 *Sappho* Decomm 23 May 1946. Stricken 15 Oct 1946, sold 13 Jan 1947; BU 1965 Portland, Ore.

AKA 39 *Sarita* Decomm 29 Jan 1947. Stricken 25 Feb 1947, sold 8 Jun 1966; BU Terminal I.

AKA 40 *Scania* Decomm 2 Sep 1947. Stricken 16 Sep 1947. Sold 13 Jul 1965; BU Portland, Ore.

AKA 41 *Selinur* Decomm 30 Apr 1946. Stricken 8 May 1946.
Later history: Pennsylvania training ship *Keystone State.* Laid up 1947. BU 1968 Philadelphia.

AKA 42 *Sidonia* Decomm 25 Feb 1946. Stricken 17 Apr 1946. BU 1966 Portland, Ore.

AKA 43 *Sirona* Decomm 12 Jun 1946. Stricken 3 Jul 1946.
Later history: Training ship *Yankee State.* 1947 laid up. BU 1966 Baltimore.

AKA 44 *Sylvania* Decomm 17 Dec 1946. Stricken 7 Feb 1947, sold 30 Apr 1947. BU 1964 Baltimore.

AKA 45 *Tabora* Decomm 29 May 1946. Stricken 3 Jul 1946. BU 1964 Portland, Ore.

AKA 46 *Troilus* Decomm 14 Jun 1946. Stricken 8 Jul 1946. BU 1967 Kearny, N.J.

AKA 47 *Turandot* Decomm 21 Mar 1946. Stricken 17 Apr 1947, sold 25 Jun 1946. †

AKA 48 *Valeria* Decomm 18 Mar 1946. Stricken 17 Apr 1946. BU 1967 Kearny, N.J.

AKA 49 *Vanadis* Decomm 27 Mar 1946. Stricken 5 Jun 1946. †

AKA 50 *Veritas* Decomm 21 Feb 1946. Stricken 12 Apr 1946. BU 1966.

AKA 51 *Xenia* Decomm 13 May 1946. Stricken 30 Nov 1946. To Chile 3 Dec 1946.
Later history: Renamed *Presidente Errazuriz.* R 1962.

AKA 52 *Zenobia* Decomm 7 May 1946. Stricken 30 Nov 1946. To Chile 9 Dec 1946.
Later history: Renamed *Presidente Pinto.* R 1968.

No.	Name	Builder	Keel Laid	Launched	Comm.
AKA 64	*Tolland*	N. Carolina	22 Apr 1944	26 Jun 1944	4 Sep 1944
AKA 65	*Shoshone*	N. Carolina	12 May 1944	17 Jul 1944	24 Sep 1944
AKA 66	*Southampton*	N. Carolina	26 May 1944	28 Jul 1944	8 Oct 1944
AKA 67	*Starr*	N. Carolina	13 Jun 1944	18 Aug 1944	29 Sep 1944
AKA 68	*Stokes*	N. Carolina	26 Jun 1944	31 Aug 1944	12 Oct 1944
AKA 69	*Suffolk*	N. Carolina	11 Jul 1944	15 Sep 1944	23 Oct 1944
AKA 70	*Tate*	N. Carolina	22 Jul 1944	26 Sep 1944	25 Nov 1944
AKA 71	*Todd*	N. Carolina	10 Aug 1944	10 Oct 1944	30 Nov 1944
AKA 72	*Caswell*	N. Carolina	25 Aug 1944	24 Oct 1944	13 Dec 1944
AKA 73	*New Hanover*	N. Carolina	31 Aug 1944	31 Oct 1944	22 Dec 1944
AKA 74	*Lenoir*	N. Carolina	7 Sep 1944	6 Nov 1944	14 Dec 1944
AKA 75	*Alamance*	N. Carolina	15 Sep 1944	11 Nov 1944	22 Dec 1944
AKA 76	*Torrance*	N. Carolina	1 Apr 1944	6 Jun 1944	18 Nov 1944
AKA 77	*Towner*	N. Carolina	8 Apr 1944	13 Jun 1944	3 Dec 1944

Figure 11.19: *Chaumont* (AP 5). This transport, built at Hog I., served during the interwar period.

AKA 78	*Trego*	N. Carolina	14 Apr 1944	20 Jun 1944	21 Dec 1944
AKA 79	*Trousdale*	N. Carolina	28 Apr 1944	3 Jul 1944	21 Dec 1944
AKA 80	*Tyrrell*	N. Carolina	6 May 1944	10 Jul 1944	4 Dec 1944
AKA 81	*Valencia*	N. Carolina	20 May 1944	22 Jul 1944	9 Jan 1945
AKA 82	*Venango*	N. Carolina	6 Jun 1944	9 Aug 1944	2 Jan 1945
AKA 83	*Vinton*	N. Carolina	20 Jun 1944	25 Aug 1944	3 Feb 1945
AKA 84	*Waukesha*	N. Carolina	3 Jul 1944	6 Sep 1944	23 Feb 1945
AKA 85	*Wheatland*	N. Carolina	17 Jul 1944	21 Sep 1944	3 Apr 1945
AKA 86	*Woodford*	N. Carolina	29 Jul 1944	5 Oct 1944	3 Mar 1945
AKA 87	*Duplin*	N. Carolina	18 Aug 1944	17 Oct 1944	15 May 1945
AKA 101	*Ottawa*	N. Carolina	5 Oct 1944	29 Nov 1944	8 Feb 1945
AKA 102	*Prentiss*	N. Carolina	10 Oct 1944	6 Dec 1944	11 Feb 1945
AKA 103	*Rankin*	N. Carolina	31 Oct 1944	22 Dec 1944	25 Feb 1945
AKA 104	*Seminole*	N. Carolina	7 Nov 1944	28 Dec 1944	8 Mar 1945
AKA 105	*Skagit*	N. Carolina	21 Sep 1944	18 Nov 1944	2 May 1945
AKA 106	*Union*	N. Carolina	27 Sep 1944	23 Nov 1944	25 Apr 1945
AKA 107	*Vermilion*	N. Carolina	17 Oct 1944	12 Dec 1944	23 Jun 1945
AKA 108	*Washburn*	N. Carolina	24 Oct 1944	18 Dec 1944	17 May 1945

Displacement	6,318 tons; 13,050 f/l
Dimensions	459'2" (oa); 435' (wl) x 63' x 26'4"
Machinery	1 screw; GE GT; 2 B&W boilers; SHP 6,000; 16.5 knots
Complement	374
Armament	1–5"/38, 4 twin 40mm, 16–20mm AA guns

Note: Type C2–S–AJ3.

Service Records:

AKA 64 *Tolland* Damaged in collision, Iwo Jima, 27 Feb 1945. Decomm 1 Jul 1946. Stricken 19 Jul 1946. Tokyo Bay.
2* Iwo Jima, Okinawa.
Later history: Merchant *Edgar F. Luckenbach* 1947, renamed *Blue Grass State* 1959, *Reliance Cordiality* 1970. BU 1971 Kaohsiung, Taiwan.

AKA 65 *Shoshone* Damaged in collision with cargo ship *Muliphen* at Pearl Harbor, 13 Jan 1945. Decomm 28 Jun 1946. Stricken 19 Jul 1946.
2* Iwo Jima, Okinawa.
Later history: 1947 merchant *Alameda* 1947, renamed *Hawaiian Trader* 1961, *Short Hills* 1961, *Colorado* 1964, *U.S. Mate* 1966. BU 1971 Kaohsiung, Taiwan.

AKA 66 *Southampton* Decomm 21 Jun 1946. Stricken 3 Jul 1946.
2* Iwo Jima, Okinawa.
Later history: Merchant *Flying Clipper*. BU 1971 Kaohsiung, Taiwan.

AKA 67 *Starr* Damaged in collision with cruiser *Salt Lake City*, Iwo Jima, 20 Feb 1945. Slightly damaged by suicide boat, Okinawa, 9 Apr 1945. Decomm 31 May 1946. Stricken 19 Jun 1946.
2* Iwo Jima, Okinawa.
Later history: Merchant *Indian Bear*, renamed *Lanakila* 1959, *India Bear* 1960. BU 1970 Kaohsiung, Taiwan.

AKA 68 *Stokes* Damaged in collision with LST, Iwo Jima, 2 Mar 1945. Decomm 9 Jul 1946. Stricken 19 Jul 1946.
2* Iwo Jima, Okinawa.
Later history: Merchant *Sierra* 1947, renamed *Hawaiian Banker* 1961, *Fanwood* 1962, *A. and J. Doctor Max* 1964, *Fanwood* 1964. BU 1971 Kaohsiung, Taiwan.

AKA 69 *Suffolk* Decomm 27 Jun 1946. Stricken 19 Jul 1946.
1* Okinawa.
Later history: Merchant *Southport*, renamed *American Retailer* 1961, *Alcoa Master* 1963, *Columbia Star* 1969, *Antillian Star* 1971. BU 1971 Kaohsiung, Taiwan.

AKA 70 *Tate* Decomm 10 Jul 1946. Stricken 19 Jul 1946.
1* Okinawa.
Later history: Merchant *Julia Luckenbach*, renamed *Bay State* 1960. BU 1970 Kaohsiung, Taiwan.

AKA 71 *Todd* Decomm 25 Jun 1946. Stricken 19 Jul 1946. Tokyo Bay.
Later history: Merchant *Ventura*, renamed *Hawaiian Wholesaler* 1961, *Chatham* 1961.BU 1972 Kaohsiung, Taiwan.

AKA 72 *Caswell* Decomm 19 Jun 1946.
1* Okinawa.
Later history: Merchant *Southwind*, renamed *American Surveyor* 1961. BU 1974 Philadelphia.

AKA 73 *New Hanover* Decomm 30 Jul 1946. Stricken 15 Aug 1946.
1* Okinawa.
Later history: Merchant *Alawai* 1947, renamed *Franklin Berwin* 1955, *Santa Mercedes* 1957, *Green Wave* 1960, *Sagamore Hill* 1966. BU 1970 Kaohsiung, Taiwan.

AKA 74 *Lenoir* Decomm 13 Jun 1946.
1* Okinawa.
Later history: Merchant *Margaret Lykes*, renamed *Gulf Merchant* 1947, *Del Aires* 1964, *Columbia Tiger* 1968, *Antillian Tiger* 1970. BU 1971.

AKA 75 *Alamance* Decomm 25 Jun 1946. Stricken 19 Jul 1946.
Later history: Merchant *Southstar*, renamed *American Supplier* 1961, *Alcoa Voyager* 1963, *Columbia Fox* 1969, *Antillian Fox* 1971. BU 1971 Bilbao, Spain.

AKA 76 *Torrance* Decomm 20 Jun 1946. Stricken 3 Jul 1946.
1* Okinawa.
Later history: Merchant *Alcoa Roamer* 1947, renamed *Eldorado* 1968, *Richmond* 1970, *Singapore Trader* 1971. BU 1972 Santander.

AKA 77 *Towner* Decomm 10 Jun 1946. Stricken 19 Jun 1946.
Later history: Merchant *Philippine Bear*, renamed *Kiamana* 1959, *Guam Bear* 1960. Damaged in collision with tanker *Esso Seattle* at Guam, 13 Jan 1967; scuttled off Guam 3 Jul 1967.

AKA 78 *Trego* Decomm 21 May 1946. Stricken 5 Jun 1946.
1* Okinawa.
Later history: Merchant *Mason Lykes*, renamed *Flower Hill* 1963. BU 1969 Kaohsiung, Taiwan.

AKA 79 *Trousdale* Decomm 29 Apr 1946. Stricken 8 May 1946.
1* Okinawa.
Later history: Merchant *Lafayette*, renamed *Ocean Deborah* 1954, *Green Dale* 1961. BU 1969 Kaohsiung, Taiwan.

AKA 80 *Tyrrell* Damaged by kamikaze, Okinawa, 2 Apr 1945. Decomm 19 Apr 1946. Stricken 1 May 1946.
1* Okinawa.
Later history: Merchant *California Bear*, renamed *America Bear* 1961, *Green Lake* 1962, *Oceanic Cloud* 1965. BU 1967 Kaohsiung, Taiwan.

AKA 81 *Valencia* Decomm 8 May 1946. Stricken 21 May 1946.
1* Okinawa.
Later history: Merchant *Genevieve Lykes*, renamed *Garden City* 1964. BU 1970 Kaohsiung, Taiwan.

AKA 82 *Venango* Decomm 18 Apr 1946. Stricken 1 May 1946.
1* Okinawa.
Later history: Merchant *Ponce de Leon*, renamed *Flying Eagle* 1952, *Southern Star* 1968, *Anna* 1970. BU 1971 Bilbao, Spain.

AKA 83 *Vinton* Decomm 16 Mar 1946. Stricken 5 Jun 1946.
Later history: Merchant *Gulf Shipper* 1947, renamed *President Harding* 1964, *America Bear* 1967, *Columbia Beaver* 1969. BU 1971 Kaohsiung, Taiwan.

AKA 84 *Waukesha* Decomm 10 Jul 1946. Stricken 31 Jul 1946.
Later history: Merchant *Mary Luckenbach*, renamed *Bayou State* 1960. BU 1970 Kaohsiung, Taiwan.

AKA 85 *Wheatland* Decomm 25 Apr 1946. Stricken 8 May 1946.
Later history: Merchant *Beatrice*, renamed *Bangor* 1964, *Grand Loyalty* 1968. BU 1973 Kaohsiung, Taiwan.

AKA 86 *Woodford* Decomm 1 May 1946. Stricken 8 May 1946.
1* Okinawa.
Later history: Merchant *Suzanne*, renamed *Rappahannock* 1965. BU 1973 Kaohsiung, Taiwan.

AKA 87 *Duplin* Decomm 21 May 1946.
Later history: Merchant *Kathryn*, renamed *Dearborn* 1963, *Rio Grande* 1963. BU 1971.

AKA 101 *Ottawa* Operation Crossroads. Decomm 10 Jan 1947. Stricken 14 Mar 1947.
Later history: Merchant *Andrea F. Luckenbach*. Wrecked off Kauai, Hawaii, 11 Mar 1951.

AKA 102 *Prentiss* Decomm 31 May 1946. Stricken 19 Jun 1946.
1* Okinawa.
Later history: Merchant *Alcoa Ranger*, renamed *Cortez* 1967, *Jody Re* 1969. BU 1970 Bilbao.

AKA 103 *Rankin* Decomm 21 May 1947. †
1* Okinawa.

AKA 104 *Seminole* Damaged by collision, Okinawa, 3 Aug 1945. †

AKA 105 *Skagit* Tokyo Bay. †

AKA 106 *Union* †

AKA 107 *Vermilion* †

AKA 108 *Washburn* †

TRANSPORTS

Transports were mostly passenger vessels converted to carry troops. Others were built as troopships during the war. Many were named for Marine Corps or Army generals.

Transports on the Navy List, 1922:

AP 1 *Henderson* Carried President Warren G. Harding on tour to Alaska, Jul 1923. Nicaragua 1927. Yangtze River 1927. China 1937–39. Decomm 13 Oct 1943 for conversion to hospital ship. Rec **AH 9**, renamed ***Bountiful.*** Recomm 23 Mar 1944. Operation Crossroads. Decomm 13 Sep 1946. Sold 28 Jan 1948; BU Seattle.

AP 2 *Heywood* Not built (see AP 2, below)

AP 3 *Hancock* Rec **IX 12**, 24 Apr 1922. RS Pearl Harbor 1921–25. Decomm 1 Sep 1925. Stricken 10 Sep 1925, sold 21 May 1926; BU.

Figure 11.20: *Doyen* (APA 1), seen here on 5 Sep 1943, was one of two built-for-the-purpose attack transports, named after Marine Corps generals.

Figure 11.21: *American Legion* (APA 17), an attack transport, seen here on 8 Apr 1944. It is an example of one of the many U.S. Shipping Board design 535 transports used by the Navy during the war.

AP 4 *Argonne* Converted to submarine tender at Mare I. NYd and rec **AS 10**, 1 Jul 1924. Recomm 25 Mar 1926. Converted to survey vessel and rec **AG 31**, 25 Jul 1940. Decomm 15 Jul 1946. Sold 31 Jul 1946; BU 1951 Baltimore.

AP 5 *Chaumont* China 1937–39. Decomm 28 Aug 1943 for conversion to hospital ship. Rec **AH 10**, renamed ***Samaritan***, 2 Sep 1943. Recomm 1 Mar 1944. Decomm 25 Jun 1946. Sold 29 Aug 1946; BU 1948 Oakland.

No.	Name	Builder	Keel Laid	Launched	Comm.
AP 2	*Doyen*	Consol. Wilm.	18 Sep 1941	9 Jul 1942	22 May 1943
AP 18	*Feland*	Consol. Wilm.	25 Nov 1941	10 Nov 1942	21 Jun 1943

Displacement	4,351 tons; 6,710 tons f/l
Dimensions	414'6" (oa); 405' (wl) x 56' x 18'6"
Machinery	2 screws; West. GT; 2 B&W boilers; SHP 8,000; 19 knots
Endurance	9,500/15
Complement	794/453; capacity: 1,100 troops, 16 LCVP.
Armament	4–3"/50, 2 twin 40mm, 8–20mm AA guns

Notes: Type P1–S2–L2. First built for the purpose attack transports.

Service Records:

AP 2 *Doyen* Rec **APA 1**, 1 Feb 1943. Decomm 22 Mar 1946.
6* Gilbert Is., Kwajalein, Saipan, Guam, Leyte, Lingayen, Iwo Jima.
Later history: Training ship *Bay State*. BU 1974.

AP 18 *Feland* Rec **APA 11**, 1 Feb 1943. Decomm 15 Mar 1946. Sold 27 Jun 1946; BU 1964 Portland, Ore.
6* Gilbert Is., Kwajalein, Saipan, Guam, Leyte, Iwo Jima.

No.	Name	Builder	Launched	Acquired	Comm.
AP 6	*William Ward Burrows* ex–*Santa Rita* (1940)	Burmeister	9 Feb 1929	6 Feb 1940	15 May 1940

Displacement	4,910 tons; 7,684 tons f/l; 4,576 grt
Dimensions	386' (oa); 370' (wl) x 53'2" x 20'
Machinery	2 screws; diesel; SHP 3,465; 12 knots
Complement	178; capacity: 1,340 troops.
Armament	4–3"/50, 8–20mm AA guns

Notes: Grace Liner, sistership of *Bowditch* (AG 30). Too slow for use as APA.

Service Record:

AP 6 *William Ward Burrows* Made voyages for construction and supply of Wake I., Jan–Dec 1941. Damaged by grounding off Tulagi, Solomons, 29 Aug 1942, refloated 2 Sep 1942. Decomm 16 May 1946. Stricken 15 Aug 1946, BU 1957 Long Beach, Calif.
4* Guadalcanal, Saipan, Guam, Palau, Okinawa.

No.	Name	Builder	Launched	Acquired	Comm.
AP 7	*Wharton*	NY Sbdg	20 Jul 1919	8 Nov 1939	7 Dec 1939
	ex-*Southern Cross* (1939), ex-*Sea Girt* (1921), LD as *Manmasco*				
AP 8	*Harris*	Beth. Sp. Pt.	19 Mar 1921	17 Jul 1940	19 Aug 1940
	ex-*President Grant* (1940), ex-*Pine Tree State* (1923)				
AP 9	*Zeilin*	Newport News	11 Dec 1920	17 Jul 1940	19 Aug 1940
	ex-*President Jackson* (1940), ex-*Silver State* (1922)				
AP 25	*Leonard Wood*	Beth. Sp. Pt.	17 Sep 1921	3 Jun 1941	10 Jun 1941
	ex-USAT *Leonard Wood* (1941), ex-*Western World* (1939), ex-*Nutmeg State* (1922)				
AP 26	*Joseph T. Dickman*	NY Sbdg	6 Jul 1921	27 May 1941	10 Jun 1941
	ex-USAT *Joseph T. Dickman* (1941), ex-*President Roosevelt* (1940), ex-*President Pierce* (1922), ex-*Peninsula State* (1922)				
AP 27	*Hunter Liggett*	Beth. Sp. Pt.	4 Jun 1921	29 May 1941	9 Jun 1941
	ex-USAT *Hunter Liggett* (1941), ex-*Pan America* (1939), ex-*Palmetto State* (1922)				
AP 30	*Henry T. Allen*	NY Sbdg	24 May 1919	6 Dec 1941	22 Apr 1942
	ex-USAT *Henry T. Allen* (1941), ex-*President Jefferson* (1940), ex-*Wenatchee* (1923), LD as *C. M. Schwab*				
AP 34	*J. Franklin Bell*	NY Sbdg	15 May 1920	26 Dec 1941	12 Apr 1942
	ex-USAT *J. Franklin Bell* (1941), ex-*President McKinley* (1940), ex-*Keystone State* (1922)				
AP 35	*American Legion*	NY Sbdg	11 Oct 1919	22 Aug 1941	26 Aug 1941
	ex-USAT *American Legion* (1941), ex-*American Legion* (Nov 1939), ex-*Badger State* (1919)				
AP 42	*Tasker H. Bliss*	Newport News	17 Jul 1920	19 Aug 1942	21 Sep 1942
	ex-USAT *Tasker H. Bliss* (1942), ex-*President Cleveland* (1941), ex-*Golden State* (1922)				
AP 43	*Hugh L. Scott*	Beth. Sp. Pt.	17 Apr 1920	14 Aug 1942	7 Sep 1942
	ex-USAT *Hugh L. Scott* (1942), ex-*President Pierce* (1941), ex-*Hawkeye State* (1922)				

Figure 11.22: *Tasker H. Bliss* (AP 42), 8 Oct 1942. The former liner President Cleveland sunk off Morocco in Nov 1942.

Figure 11.23: *George F. Elliott* (AP 13), 1 Jan 1942. One of five "City" liners of the Panama Pacific Line taken over in 1940, she was sunk at the start of the Guadalcanal campaign.

Displacement	21,900 tons f/l; 13,789 grt (AP 7), 14,119 (AP 8), 14,124 (AP 9), 13,869 (AP 26), 14,174 (AP 30), 14,127 (AP 34), 13,736 (AP 35), 12,568 (AP 42), 12,579 (AP 43)
Dimensions	535'2" (oa); 534' (wl) x 72' x 31'3"
Machinery	2 screws; West. GT; 8 B&W boilers; SHP 12,000; 16.5 knots; Curtis GT and Yarrow boilers (AP 8)
Endurance	13,700/15
Complement	566; capacity: 2,850 troops (AP 7); 1,400 troops, 25 LCVP (all others)
Armament	4–3"/50, 2 twin 40mm, 10–20mm AA (AP 8); 1–5"/38, 4–3"/50, 2 twin 40mm, 18–20mm AA (AP 7); AP 7, AP 34: 3"/50, 1 twin 40mm, 1 quad, 10–20mm guns;AP 30, 1945: 4–3"/50, 2 twin 40mm, 10–20mm guns

Notes: All except AP 7 *Wharton* fitted as assault ships. AP 7, AP 25, AP 27, AP 35 were Munson liners, the other from Dollar (American President) Line. They were a standard U.S. Shipping Board design, type 535. All except AP 7–9 were taken over by the Army in 1939–40 and later transferred to the Navy.

Service Records:

AP 7 *Wharton* Ran aground in Seeadler Harbor, Manus, 17 Apr 1944. Operation Crossroads. Decomm 26 Mar 1947, Stricken 4 Apr 1947; BU 1952 San Francisco.
3* Kwajalein, Eniwetok, Guam, Okinawa.

AP 8 *Harris* Damaged in collision off Monterey, Calif., Sep 1942. Rec **APA 2**, 1 Feb 1943. Decomm 16 Jul 1946, sold 20 Jul 1948; BU 1948 Wilmington, Del.
10* North Africa, Attu, Gilbert Is., Kwajalein, Saipan, Palau, Leyte, Lingayen, Subic Bay, Okinawa.

AP 9 *Zeilin* Damaged by dive bomber, Guadalcanal, 6 Nov 1942. Rec **APA 3**, 1 Feb 1943. Damaged by kamikaze, west of Luzon, 12 Jan 1945 (10 killed). Decomm 19 Apr 1946. Stricken 5 Jun 1946. BU 1948 Wilmington, Del.
8* Guadalcanal–Tulagi, Solomons, Attu, Gilbert Is., Kwajalein, Hollandia, Guam, Iwo Jima.

AP 25 *Leonard Wood* Acq by Army 1939. USCG crew. Convoy WS–12X, Halifax to Singapore, Nov 1941–Jan 1942. Rec **APA 12**, 1 Feb 1943. Decomm 22 Mar 1946. BU 1948.
8* North Africa, Sicily, Gilbert Is., Kwajalein, Eniwetok, Saipan, Palau, Leyte, Lingayen.

AP 26 *Joseph T. Dickman* Acq by Army Oct 1940. USCG crew. Convoy WS–12X, Halifax to Singapore, Nov 1941–Jan 1942. Rec **APA 13**, 1 Feb 1943. Decomm 7 Mar 1946, BU 1948 Oakland.
6* North Africa, Sicily, Salerno, Normandy, Southern France, Okinawa.

AP 27 *Hunter Liggett* Acq by Army Feb 1939. USCG crew. Rec **APA 14**, 1 Feb 1943. Decomm 18 Mar 1946, returned; BU 1948 Baltimore.
4* Guadalcanal–Tulagi, Solomons, Cape Torokina.

AP 30 *Henry T. Allen* Rec **APA 15**, 1 Feb 1943. Converted to administrative headquarters base ship, rec **AG 90**, 1 Feb 1945. Decomm 5 Feb 1946. BU 1948 Baltimore.
3* North Africa, Hollandia, Wakde.

AP 34 *J. Franklin Bell* Rec **APA 16**, 1 Feb 1943. Decomm 20 Mar 1946, BU 1948 Baltimore.
6* Attu, Gilbert Is., Kwajalein, Saipan, Tinian, Leyte.

AP 35 *American Legion* Acq by Army 19 Dec 1939. Rec **APA 17** 1 Feb 1943. Decomm 28 Mar 1946 and stricken; BU 1948 Portland, Ore.
2* Guadalcanal–Tulagi, Cape Torokina.

AP 42 *Tasker H. Bliss* Acq by Army Jul 1941. Torpedoed and sunk by *U–130* off Fedala, Morocco, 12 Nov 1942 (34 killed).
1* North Africa.

AP 43 *Hugh L. Scott* Acq by Army 31 Jul 1941. Torpedoed and sunk by *U–130* off Fedala, Morocco, 12 Nov 1942 (59 killed).
1* North Africa.

No.	Name	Builder	Launched	Acquired	Comm.
AP 12	*Heywood*	Beth. Alameda	24 Dec 1918	26 Oct 1940	19 Feb 1941
	ex–*City of Baltimore* (1940), ex–*Steadfast* (1931)				
AP 13	*George F. Elliott*	Beth. Alameda	4 Jul 1918	30 Oct 1940	10 Jan 1941
	ex–*City of Los Angeles* (1940), ex–*City of Havre* (1938), ex–*Victorious* (1931), LD as *War Haven*				
AP 14	*Fuller*	Beth. Alameda	4 Nov 1918	12 Nov 1940	9 Apr 1941
	ex–*City of Newport News* (1940), ex–*Archer* (1931), LD as *War Wave*				
AP 15	*William P. Biddle*	Beth. Alameda	20 Oct 1918	13 Nov 1940	3 Feb 1941
	ex–*City of San Francisco* (1940), ex–*City of Hamburg* (1938), ex–*Eclipse* (1931), LD as *War Surf*				
AP 16	*Neville*	Beth. Alameda	4 Jul 1918	14 Dec 1940	14 May 1941
	ex–*City of Norfolk* (1940), ex–*Independence* (1931), LD as *War Harbour.*				

Figure 11.24: *Fuller* (APA 7), 22 Mar 1944. The former liner *City of Newport News* as attack transport. Notice the LCTs on deck.

Figure 11.25: *Harry Lee* (AP 17), seen here on 14 Sep 1942, was the only one of the four American Export Line "Aces" to survive the war.

Displacement	8,789 tons; 14,450 tons f/l; 8,378 grt
Dimensions	507' (oa); 486' (wl) x 56' x 25'6"
Machinery	1 screw; De Laval turbine GT; 4 B&W boilers; SHP 9,500; 16.8 knots
Endurance	9,000/12
Complement	550; capacity: 1,150 troops, 19 LCVP.
Armament	4–3"/50, 2 twin 40mm, 8 twin 20mm AA guns

Note: Originally built as USSB freighters, converted to passenger–cargo liners in 1931 for the Baltimore Mail Line's transatlantic service, and switched to the New York–California route in 1938.

Service Records:

AP 12 *Heywood* Rec **APA 6**, 1 Feb 1943. Decomm 12 Apr 1946. BU 1957 Baltimore.
8* Guadalcanal–Tulagi, Attu, Gilbert Is., Kwajalein, Eniwetok, Saipan, Tinian, Leyte.

AP 13 *George F. Elliott* Sunk by Japanese aircraft off Tulagi, 8 Aug 1942. Dead
1* Guadalcanal–Tulagi.

AP 14 *Fuller* Damaged in collision with destroyer *Conyngham*, Guadalcanal, 2 Nov 1942. Rec **APA 7**, 1 Feb 1943. Damaged by aircraft bombs off Cape Torokina, 8 Nov 1943 (7 killed). Decomm 20 Mar 1946. BU 1958 Seattle.
9* Guadalcanal–Tulagi, Solomons, Cape Torokina, Saipan, Tinian, Palau, Leyte, Okinawa.

Figure 11.26: *Wakefield* (AP 21), the former United States Lines passenger liner *Manhattan*, after suffering a devastating fire, Sep 1942. She was rebuilt as a transport and never returned to commercial service.

AP 15 *William P. Biddle* Rec **APA 8**, 1 Feb 1943. In collision with *LST-382*, Sicily, 10 Jul 1943. Decomm 9 Apr 1946. Stricken 5 Jun 1946. BU 1957 Baltimore.
7* North Africa, Sicily, Gilbert Is., Kwajalein, Guam, Leyte, Lingayen.

AP 16 *Neville* Rec **APA 9**, 1 Feb 1943. Decomm 30 Apr 1946. BU 1957 Fieldsboro, N.J., or Wilmington, Del.
5* Guadalcanal–Tulagi, Sicily, Gilbert Is., Kwajalein, Eniwetok, Saipan.

No.	Name	Builder	Launched	Acquired	Comm.
AP 17	*Harry Lee* ex-*Exochorda* (1940)	NY Sbdg	18 Oct 1930	30 Oct 1940	27 Dec 1940
AP 50	*Joseph Hewes* ex-*Excalibur* (1942)	NY Sbdg	5 Aug 1930	8 Jan 1942	1 May 1942
AP 51	*John Penn* ex-*Excambion* (1942)	NY Sbdg	28 May 1931	8 Jan 1942	6 Apr 1942
AP 52	*Edward Rutledge* ex-*Exeter* (1942)	NY Sbdg	4 Apr 1931	7 Jan 1942	18 Apr 1942

Displacement	10,050 tons; 14,520 tons f/l; 9,359 grt
Dimensions	475'4" (oa); 450' (wl) x 61'6" x 26'4"
Machinery	1 screw; NYSbdg GT; 4 B&W boilers; SHP 7,200; 16 knots
Endurance	12,500/12
Complement	453; capacity: 1,000 troops, 15 LCVP.
Armament	1–5"/38, 4–3"/50; (AP 17, 1945) 4–3"/50, 2 twin 40mm, 18–20mm AA guns

Note: Acquired from American Export Lines; known as the "Four Aces."

Service Records:

AP 17 *Harry Lee* Rec **APA 10**, 1 Feb 1943. Decomm 9 May 1946. Returned to MC 17 Sep 1946.
7* Sicily, Gilbert Is., Kwajalein, Hollandia, Guam, Lingayen, Iwo Jima.
Later history: Merchant *Tarsus* 1948. Destroyed by fire after collision with m/v *Peter Zoranic* in Bosporus, 14 Dec 1960.

AP 50 *Joseph Hewes* Torpedoed and sunk by *U-173* off Fedala, Morocco, 11 Nov 1942 (~10 killed).
1* North Africa.

AP 51 *John Penn* Rec **APA 23**, 1 Feb 1943. Sunk by aircraft torpedo off Guadalcanal, 13 Aug 1943. (98 killed)
1* North Africa.

AP 52 *Edward Rutledge* Damaged in collision with cruiser *Philadelphia* in Hampton Roads, Va. 15 Sep 1942. Torpedoed and sunk by *U-130* off Fedala, Morocco, 12 Nov 1942 (15 killed).
1* North Africa.

No.	Name	Builder	Launched	Acquired	Comm.
AP 10	*McCawley* ex-*Santa Barbara* (1940)	Furness	8 Dec 1927	26 Jul 1940	11 Sep 1940
AP 11	*Barnett* ex-*Santa Maria* (1940)	Furness	15 Aug 1927	9 Aug 1940	25 Sep 1940

Displacement	9,750 tons; 14,080 tons f/l; 7,858 grt
Dimensions	486'6" (oa); 465' (wl) x 63'9" x 25'4"
Machinery	2 screws; diesel; SHP 8,000; 14.5 knots
Endurance	9,000/12
Complement	488; capacity: 1,400 troops, 25 LCVP.
Armament	1–5"/51, 4–3"/50 (AP 10); (AP 11, 1945) 4–3"/50, 2 twin 40mm, 10–20mm AA guns

Notes: Formerly Grace Line. Dummy forward funnel removed.

Service Records:

AP 10 *McCawley* Rec **APA 4**, 1 Feb 1943. Torpedoed by Japanese aircraft off New Georgia, 30 Jun 1943 and sunk in error by U.S. PT boats (15 killed).
5* Guadalcanal–Tulagi, Guadalcanal, Battle of Guadalcanal, New Georgia, Solomons.

AP 11 *Barnett* Damaged by bomber, Guadalcanal, 8 Aug 1942. Rec **APA 5**, 1 Feb 1943. Damaged by German aircraft off Gela, Sicily, 11 Jul 1943 (7 killed). Damaged in error by gunfire, Okinawa, 6 Apr 1945. Decomm 30 Apr 1946. Stricken 21 May 1946.
7* Guadalcanal–Tulagi, Solomons, Sicily, Salerno, Normandy, Southern France, Okinawa.
Later history: Merchant *Surriento*. BU 1966 La Spezia, Italy.

No.	Name	Builder	Launched	Acquired	Comm.
AP 19	*Catlin* ex-*George Washington* (1941)	Vulcan	10 Nov 1908	28 Jan 1941	13 Mar 1941

Displacement	10,210 tons; 23,788 grt
Dimensions	772' (oa); 698'11' (wl) x 78'3' x 23'1'
Machinery	2 screws; VQE, SHP 22,000; 11 knots
Endurance	20,000
Complement	749; capacity: 6,341 troops
Armament	4–5"/38, 4–3"/50

Notes: Too slow for naval service. Former German liner seized in 1917, laid up 1931. Extensively rebuilt 1942–43 with new oil-burning B&W boilers; single funnel replaced original two.

Service Record:

AP 19 *Catlin* Stricken 29 Sep 1941, to UK but returned because of poor engines.
Later history: Merchant *George Washington*. Returned to USMC 17 Apr 1942; to Army. USAT *George Washington*. Reboilered, conv to oil fuel 1943. Returned to MC 21 Apr 1947. Gutted by fire while laid up at Baltimore, 16 Jan 1951. BU 1951 Baltimore.

No.	Name	Builder	Launched	Acquired	Comm.
AP 20	*Munargo* ex-*Munargo* (1941)	NY Sbdg	17 Sep 1921	4 Jun 1941	12 Aug 1941

Figure 11.27: *West Point* (AP 23), 25 Jan 1944. The former *America* flagship of the United States Lines, was U.S. Maritime Commission hull number 1. She carried 350,000 troops during the war.

Fig. 11.28: *Chateau Thierry* (AP 31), 19 Sep 1942, one of two Army transports built at Hog I. that was used by the Navy. She was later used by the Army as a hospital ship.

Displacement	6,337 grt
Dimensions	432' (oa); 413'9" (wl) x 57'10" x 22'9"
Machinery	1 screw; GT; SHP 5,800; 15.5 knots
Endurance	7,000
Complement	254; capacity: 1,113 troops
Armament	1-5"/51, 4-3"/50

Notes: Acquired by Army, Mar 1941, from United Fruit Company. Was to be named *Arthur Murray*.

Service Record

AP 20 *Munargo* Decomm 18 Oct 1943 and returned to Army, 26 Oct 1943; converted to hospital ship.
Later history: Renamed USAHS *Thistle*. BU 1957 Baltimore.

No.	Name	Builder	Launched	Acquired	Comm.
AP 21	*Wakefield*	NY Sbdg	5 Dec 1931	14 Jun 1941	10 Jul 1941
	ex-*Manhattan* (1941)				
AP 22	*Mount Vernon*	NY Sbdg	20 Aug 1932	16 Jun 1941	11 Jul 1941
	ex-*Washington* (1941)				

Displacement	33,560 tons f/l; 24,289 grt
Dimensions	705' (oa); 685' (wl) x 86' x 30'9"
Machinery	2 screws; NY Sbdg GT; 6 B&W boilers; SHP 30,000; 21.5 knots
Endurance	14,000
Complement	934 (AP 21), 765 (AP 22); capacity: 7,000 troops (AP 21), 5,120 troops (AP 22)
Armament	4-5"/38, 4 quad 40mm, 32-20mm AA (AP 21); 4-5"/51, 4-3"/50, 2 twin 40mm AA (AP 22)

Notes: Formerly U.S. Lines passenger liners. 2 funnels, 2 masts.

Service Records:

AP 21 *Wakefield* Convoy WS-12X, Halifax to Singapore, Nov 1941–Jan 1942. Damaged by aircraft bomb at Singapore, 30 Jan 1942 (5 killed), while evacuating civilians. Temporary repairs at Bombay. Burned out by fire at sea in North Atlantic, 3 Sep 1942. Towed in and grounded near Halifax. Recomm 10 Feb 1944. USCG crew. Decomm 15 Jun 1946. †
1* Philippines (Singapore)

AP 22 *Mount Vernon* Convoy WS-12X, Halifax to Singapore, Nov 1941–Jan 1942. Decomm 18 Jan 1946.
Later history: Merchant *Washington* 1946. BU 1964 Kearny, N.J.

No.	Name	Builder	Launched	Acquired	Comm.
AP 23	*West Point*	Newport News	31 Aug 1939	6 Jun 1941	10 Jul 1941
	ex-*America* (1941)				

Displacement	35,440 tons f/l
Dimensions	723' (oa); 660' (wl) x 93'3' x 32'9"
Machinery	2 screws; NN GT; 6 B&W boilers; SHP 34,000; 17.5 knots
Endurance	10,000
Complement	970; capacity: 8,175 troops
Armament	4-5"/38, 4-3"/50, 4 twin 40mm, 14-20mm AA guns

Note: The largest passenger liner under the U.S. flag. Was U.S. Maritime Commission hull No. 1.

Service Record:

AP 23 *West Point* Convoy WS-12X, Halifax to Singapore, Nov 1941–Jan 1942. Evacuated civilians from Singapore, Jan 1942. Carried 350,000 troops during World War II. Decomm 28 Feb 1946. Stricken 12 Mar 1946.
Later history: Merchant *America*, renamed *Australis* 1965, *America* 1978, *Italis* 1979, *Noga* 1980, *Alferdoss* 1984, *American Star* 1993. Went aground on Fuertaventurea I. after breaking tow en route Piraeus to Phuket and broke in two, 18 Jan 1994.

No.	Name	Builder	Launched	Acquired	Comm.
AP 24	*Orizaba*	Cramp	26 Feb 1918	4 Jun 1941	15 Jun 1941
	ex-USAT *Orizaba* (1941), ex-*Orizaba* (1940)				

Displacement	11,025 tons f/l; 6,937 grt
Dimensions	443' (oa); 423' (wl) x 60' x 23'11"
Machinery	2 screws; GT; 8 s/e boilers; SHP 8,500; 16.5 knots
Endurance	6,200
Complement	323; capacity: 1,578 troops

Armament	4–5"/51; (1945) 2–5"/51, 4–3"/50, 12–20mm guns

Notes: Acquired from New York and Cuba Mail Line (Ward Line). In Navy in World War I. Merchant name retained.

Service Record

AP 24 *Orizaba* Convoy WS–12X, Halifax to Singapore, Nov 1941–Jan 1942. Damaged by German aircraft, Sicily, 11 Jul 1943. Decomm 23 Apr 1945. To Brazil 16 Jul 1945.
1* Sicily.
Later history: Renamed *Duque de Caxias.* R1960; BU 1962 Brazil.

No.	Name	Builder	Launched	Acquired	Comm.
AP 28	*Kent*	Cramp	4 Jul 1918	21 Jul 1941	21 Dec 1941
	ex-USAT *Ernest Hinds* (1941), ex-*Kent* (1941), ex-*Santa Teresa* (1936)				

Displacement	5,341 grt
Dimensions	374' (oa); 360'4" (wl) x 51'6" x 22'8"
Machinery	1 screw; VQE, s/e boilers , SHP 3,500, 13 knots
Endurance	10,000
Complement	(U); capacity: 751 troops
Armament	4–3"/50

Notes: In Navy in World War I. Acquired by the Army from the Grace Line, Apr 1941.

Service Record:

AP 28 *Kent* Decomm and returned to Army, 24 Mar 1942.
Later history: Renamed USAT *Ernest Hinds.* Went aground off Guadalcanal, 17 Dec 1942. Conv to hospital ship, Sep 1943. Returned to transport Sep 1945. BU 1957 Baltimore.

No.	Name	Builder	Launched	Acquired	Comm.
AP 29	*U. S. Grant*	Vulcan	23 Mar 1907	16 Jun 1941	30 Jan 1942
	ex-USAT *U.S. Grant* (1941), ex-*Madawaska* (1922), ex-*Konig Wilhelm II* (1917)				

Displacement	14,940 tons f/l; 9,410 grt.
Dimensions	508'2" (oa); 488' (wl) x 55'3" x 27'
Machinery	1 screw; VTE, 5 B&W boilers; SHP 6,800, 15 knots (reengined 1928)
Complement	402; capacity: 1,163 troops
Armament	7–3"/50; (1945) 1–5"/51, 4–3"/50, 8–20mm

Notes: Former German liner seized in 1917; in Navy in World War I. Acquired by Army 1922.

Service Record:

AP 29 *U. S. Grant* Decomm 14 Nov 1945 and returned. Stricken 28 Nov 1945, sold 24 Feb 1948; BU 1948 Baltimore.
1* Attu.

Figure 11.29: *Thomas Stone* (AP 59), showing damage received during the North African landings. She remained at Algiers and was never put back in service. A British P&O liner is at left.

No.	Name	Builder	Launched	Acquired	Comm.
AP 31	*Chateau Thierry*	Amer. Intl.	24 Dec 1919	15 Jul 1941	6 Aug 1941
AP 32	*St. Mihiel*	Amer. Intl.	19 Nov 1919	1941	22 Jul 1941

Displacement	9,050 tons
Dimensions	448' (oa); 437' (bp) x 58'2" x 28'
Machinery	1 screw; Curtiss GT; 6 B&W boilers; SHP 6,000; 15 knots
Endurance	7,300
Complement	253; capacity: 1247 troops
Armament	1–5"/38, 4–3"/50

Notes: Two of 12 vessels built for the Army in 1919, named after World War I battles. Acquired from the Army in 1941.

Service Records:

AP 31 *Chateau Thierry* Decomm 9 Sep 1943. Returned to Army as hospital ship.
1* Sicily.
Later history: USAHS *Chateau Thierry.* Decomm Jan 1946. BU 1957, Portland, Ore.

AP 32 *St. Mihiel* Went aground off McNamara Point, Alaska, 9 Feb 1942, and again off Turn I., Alaska, 2 Oct 1941. Decomm 16 Nov 1943. Returned to Army as hospital ship.
1* Attu.
Later history: USAHS *St. Mihiel.* Decomm Feb 1946. BU 1957.

No.	Name	Builder	Launched	Acquired	Comm.
AP 33	*Republic*	Harland	19 Dec 1903	22 Jul 1941	21 Oct 1941
	ex-USAT *Republic* (1941), *ex-Republic* (1931), ex-*President Grant* (1917)				

Displacement	29,300 tons f/l; 17,388 grt
Dimensions	615'10" (oa); 599' (wl) x 68' x 32'9"
Machinery	2 screws; VQE; 6 boilers; SHP 7,650; 12.5 knots
Endurance	10,000
Complement	712; capacity: 3,397 troops
Armament	1–5", 4–3", 4–5"/38, 2–1 pdr

Notes: Former German liner that served in Navy in World War I as *President Grant.* Acquired by Army in 1931.

Service Record:

AP 33 *Republic* Decomm 27 Jan 1945. Returned to Army 8 Feb 1945 and conv to hospital ship.
Later history: USAHS *Republic.* Sold 1951; BU San Francisco.

Figure 11.30: *Thomas Jefferson* (APA 30), a type C3 passenger cargo ship completed as an attack transport, seen at Norfolk Navy Yard, 6 Dec 1944.

Figure 11.31: *Stratford* (AP 41), 4 May 1942. This small transport operated in the South Pacific.

No.	Name	Builder	Keel Laid	Launched	Comm.
AP 37	*President Jackson*	Newport News	2 Oct 1939	7 Jun 1940	16 Jan 1942
AP 38	*President Adams*	Newport News	10 Jun 1940	31 Jan 1941	19 Nov 1941
AP 39	*President Hayes*	Newport News	26 Dec 1939	4 Oct 1940	15 Dec 1941
AP 59	*Thomas Stone*	Newport News	12 Aug 1940	1 May 1941	18 May 1942
	ex–*President Van Buren* (1942)				
AP 60	*Thomas Jefferson*	Newport News	5 Feb 1940	20 Nov 1940	31 Aug 1942
	ex–*President Garfield* (1942)				
AP 103	*President Polk*	Newport News	7 Oct 1940	28 Jun 1941	4 Oct 1943
AP 104	*President Monroe*	Newport News	13 Nov 1939	7 Aug 1940	20 Aug 1943

Displacement	10,192 tons; 14,430 f/l
Dimensions	491'10" (oa); 465' (wl) x 69'6" x 27'6"
Machinery	1 screw; NN GT; 2 B&W boilers; SHP 8,500; 18.4 knots
Endurance	10,700/15
Complement	374–500, 580 (AP 60); capacity: 1,380 troops (AP 37–39), 1,270 troops (AP 60), 2,500 troops (AP 103), 2,100 troops (AP 104); 31 LCVP.
Armament	4–3"/50, 2 twin 40mm, 14–20mm AA (AP 37–39), same but only 10–20mm (AP60), 4–3"/50, 1–5"/38, 4–3"/50, 2 twin 40mm, 10–20mm AA (AP 103–4)

Notes: Type C3–P & C. Built for the American President Line.

Service Records:

AP 37 *President Jackson* Acq 30 Jan 1941. Rec **APA 18**, 1 Feb 1943. †
8* Guadalcanal–Tulagi, Battle of Guadalcanal, Solomons, New Georgia, Cape Torokina, Guam, Iwo Jima.

AP 38 *President Adams* Rec **APA 19**, 1 Feb 1943. Damaged in collision, Iwo Jima, 27 Feb 1945. †
8* Guadalcanal–Tulagi, Battle of Guadalcanal, Solomons, New Georgia, Cape Torokina, Guam, Iwo Jima.

AP 39 *President Hayes* Acq 7 Jul 1941. Rec **APA 20**, 1 Feb 1943. †
7* Guadalcanal–Tulagi, Solomons, New Georgia, Cape Torokina, Guam, Leyte.

AP 59 *Thomas Stone* Acq by Navy 14 Jan 1942. Torpedoed by U-boat northwest of Algiers, 7 Nov 1942. Again damaged by aircraft bomb at Algiers, 25 Nov 1942, then went aground in a storm. Rec to **APA 29** canceled. Decomm 1 Apr 1944. Stricken 8 Apr 1944. BU Algiers.
1* North Africa.

AP 60 *Thomas Jefferson* Acq 1 May 1942. Rec **APA 30**, 1 Feb 1943. †
6* North Africa, Sicily, Salerno, Normandy, Southern France, Okinawa.

AP 103 *President Polk* Decomm 26 Jan 1946 and trfd to WSA 8 Aug 1946. Stricken 25 Feb 1946.
6* Gilbert Is., Kwajalein, Guam, Lingayen, Iwo Jima, Subic Bay.
Later history: Merchant *President Polk*, renamed *Gaucho Martin Fierro* 1965, *Minotauros* 1966. BU 1970 Kaohsiung, Taiwan.

AP 104 *President Monroe* Acq 18 Jul 1943. Decomm 30 Jan 1946. Stricken 12 Mar 1946. Returned to WSA 16 Nov 1946.
5* Gilbert Is., Kwajalein, Eniwetok, Guam, Iwo Jima.
Later history: Merchant *President Monroe* 1946, renamed *Marianna V* 1965. BU 1969 Hong Kong.

No.	Name	Builder	Keel Laid	Launched	Comm.
AP 40	*Crescent City*	Beth. Sp. Pt.	8 May 1939	17 Feb 1940	10 Oct 1941
	ex–*Delorleans* (1941)				
AP 58	*Charles Carroll*	Beth. Sp. Pt.	4 Sep 1941	24 Mar 1942	13 Aug 1942
	ex–*Deluruguay* (1942)				
AP 64	*Monrovia*	Beth. Sp. Pt.	26 Mar 1942	19 Sep 1942	1 Dec 1942
	ex–*Delargentino* (1942)				
AP 65	*Calvert*	Beth. Sp. Pt.	15 Nov 1941	22 May 1942	1 Oct 1942
	ex–*Delorleans* (1942)				
AP 105	*George F. Elliot*	Beth. Sp. Pt.	10 Apr 1939	16 Dec 1939	23 Sep 1943
	ex–*Delbrasil* (1943)				

Displacement	8,646 tons; 14,247 tons f/l
Dimensions	491' (oa); 465' (wl) x 65' x 26'6"
Machinery	1 screw; GE GT; 2 B&W boilers; SHP 7,800; 18.5–17.8 knots
Endurance	15,500/15

Complement	534 (AP 40), 610 (AP 58), 302 (AP 105); capacity: 1,200 troops, 26 to 30 LCVP.
Armament	4–3"/50, 6–40mm AA (AP 40); 1–5"/38, 3–3"/50, 4–40mm AA (AP 65); 1–5"/38, 4–3"/50, 2–40mm, 8–20mm (AP 64), same as AP 64 but no 40mm (AP105). (1945) 1–5"/38, 4–3"/50, 2 twin 40mm, 11–20mm (all except AP 65).

Notes: Type C3–Delta. Built for the Delta Line.

Service Records:

AP 40 *Crescent City* Acq 9 Jun 1941. Rec **APA 21**, 1 Feb 1943. †
10* Guadalcanal–Tulagi, Battle of Guadalcanal, Solomons, Treasury Is., Guam, Palau, Leyte, Okinawa.

AP 58 *Charles Carroll* Rec **APA 28**, 1 Feb 1943. Decomm 27 Dec 1946. †
6* North Africa, Sicily, Salerno, Normandy, Southern France, Okinawa.

AP 64 *Monrovia* Damaged by German aircraft, Sicily, 11 Jul 1943. Rec **APA 31**, 1 Feb 1943. Decomm 26 Feb 1947. †
8* Sicily, Gilbert Is., Kwajalein, Saipan, Guam, Leyte, Lingayen, Okinawa.

AP 65 *Calvert* Rec **APA 32**, 1 Feb 1943. Decomm 26 Feb 1947. †
8* North Africa, Sicily, Gilbert Is., Kwajalein, Eniwetok, Saipan, Tinian, Leyte, Lingayen.

AP 105 *George F. Elliot* Damaged off Okinawa, 18 Jul 1945. Decomm 10 Jun 1946, returned to WSA. Stricken 19 Jun 1946.
4* Saipan, Leyte, Lingayen, Iwo Jima.
Later history: Merchant *African Endeavor*. BU 1972 Baltimore.

No.	Name	Builder	Keel Laid	Launched	Comm.
AP 55	*Arthur Middleton* ex–*African Comet* (1942)	Ingalls	1 Jul 1940	28 Jun 1941	7 Sep 1942
AP 56	*Samuel Chase* ex–*African Meteor* (1942)	Ingalls	31 Aug 1940	23 Aug 1941	13 Jun 1942
AP 57	*George Clymer* ex–*African Planet* (1942)	Ingalls	28 Oct 1940	27 Sep 1941	15 Jun 1942

Displacement	11,040 tons; 18,000 tons f/l
Dimensions	489' (oa); 465' (wl) x 69'6" x 27'4"
Machinery	1 screw; GE GT; 2 FW boilers; SHP 8,500; 18.4 knots
Endurance	11,000/15
Complement	530; capacity: 1,500 troops, 25 LCVP
Armament	4–3"/50, 2 twin 40mm, 8–20mm AA guns

Notes: Type C3 P and C. Built for the American–South African Line, never sailed as liners. The first all-welded passenger liners.

Service Records:

AP 55 *Arthur Middleton* USCG crew. Rec **APA 25**, 1 Feb 1943. Ran aground off Amchitka I., 12 Jan 1943; refloated 9 Apr 1943. Decomm 21 Oct 1946. †
6* Gilbert Is., Kwajalein, Eniwetok, Saipan, Leyte, Lingayen, Okinawa.

AP 56 *Samuel Chase* USCG crew. Rec **APA 26**, 1 Feb 1943. Damaged by grounding off Leyte, 16 Mar 1945. Decomm 26 Feb 1947. †
5* North Africa, Sicily, Salerno, Normandy, Southern France.

AP 57 *George Clymer* Rec **APA 27**, 1 Feb 1943. Operation Crossroads. †
6* North Africa, Solomons, Cape Torokina, Guam, Leyte, Okinawa.

Not acquired		
AP 36	*John L. Clem*	from Army
AP 44	*Willard A. Holbrook*	from Army
AP 45	*Thomas H. Barry*	from Army
AP 46	*James Parker*	from Army
AP 47	*J.W. McAndrew*	from Army
AP 68	*Alameda*	

Figure 11.32: *Lafayette* (AP 53), formerly the *Normandie*, queen of the French Line, being raised at New York in 1943 after she capsized during a disastrous fire on 9 Feb 1942. The funnels were removed and all openings on the port side sealed to enable the great hull to be pumped out.

Figure 11.33: *Hermitage* (AP 54), the former Italian liner *Conte Biancamano*, seized in 1941. She carried almost 130,000 troops while in Navy service.

No.	Name	Builder	Launched	Acquired	Comm.
AP 41	*Stratford* ex–AK 45 (1 Aug 1941), ex–*Catherine* (1941), ex–*Lake Greenwood* (1920), LD as *War Mist*	Manitowoc	28 May 1918	31 Jul 1941	25 Aug 1941

Displacement	3,640 tons f/l; 2,286 grt
Dimensions	261' (oa); 251' (wl) x 43'6" x 15'7"
Machinery	1 screw; VTE; 2 Scotch boilers; SHP 1,550; 9.6 knots
Complement	132; capacity: 1,600 troops
Armament	1–3"/50, 3–40mm, 6–20mm AA guns

Service Record:

AP 41 *Stratford* South Pacific 1942–45. Decomm 17 Apr 1946. Stricken 1 May 1946.
Later history: Merchant *Granton Glen* 1947, renamed *Anne de Bretagne* 1951. BU 1956 La Spezia, Italy.

No.	Name	Builder	Launched	Acquired	Comm.
AP 53	*Lafayette*	Penhoët	29 Oct 1932	24 Dec 1941	—
	ex-*Normandie* (1942)				

Displacement	66,400 tons f/l; 83,423 grt
Dimensions	1,029'4' (oa); 961'11" (wl) x 117' x 37'6"
Machinery	4 screws; Als–Thom TE, 29 Penhoët boilers; SHP 160,000; 29 knots
Complement	(U)
Armament	(U)

Notes: Largest ship in the world when built for the French Line. Laid up in New York 1939 and taken over after Pearl Harbor. Not converted to aircraft transport because of severe damage to hull and machinery and low priority.
Service Record:

AP 53 *Lafayette* Burned and capsized at New York pier, 9 Feb 1942. Refloated 7 Aug 1943. Rec **APV 4**, 15 Sep 1943 but never converted. Stricken 11 Oct 1945, sold 3 Oct 1946; BU 1947 Kearny, N.J.

No.	Name	Builder	Launched	Acquired	Comm.
AP 54	*Hermitage*	Beardmore	23 Apr 1925	3 Apr 1942	14 Aug 1942
	ex-*Conte Biancamano* (1942)				

Displacement	24,465 tons f/l; 23,255 grt
Dimensions	655' (oa); 635'6" (wl) x 66'1" x 27'
Machinery	2 screws; GT; nine Scotch boilers; SHP 24,000; 20 knots
Endurance	7,000
Complement	909; capacity: 6,100 troops
Armament	1–5"/38, 6–3"/50, 16–20mm AA guns

Notes: Former Italian liner, interned at Balboa, Canal Zone. 2 funnels, 2 masts.
Service Record:

AP 54 *Hermitage* Decomm 20 Aug 1946. Returned to Italy May 1947.
Later history: Merchant *Conte Biancamano*. BU 1960 La Spezia, Italy.

No.	Name	Builder	Launched	Acquired	Comm.
AP 61	*Monticello*	Stab.Tecnico	29 Jun 1927	16 Apr 1942	10 Sep 1942
	ex-*Conte Grande* (1942)				

Displacement	25,000 tons f/l; 23,861 grt
Dimensions	651'10" (oa); 625' (wl) x 78'1" x 27'6"
Machinery	2 screws; Parsons GT; nine Scotch boilers; SHP 24,000
Endurance	8,740
Complement	751; capacity: 6,890 troops
Armament	1–5"/38, 6–3"/50, 16–20mm AA guns

Notes: Former Italian liner, interned in Brazil. 2 funnels, 2 masts.
Service Record:

AP 61 *Monticello* USCG crew, 6 Aug 45–22 Mar 46. Decomm 22 Mar 1946. Returned Jun 1947.
Later history: Merchant *Conte Grande* 1947. BU 1961 La Spezia, Italy.

No.	Name	Builder	Launched	Acquired	Comm.
AP 62	*Kenmore*	NY Sbdg	23 Feb 1921	11 Apr 1942	5 Aug 1942
	ex-*President Madison* (1942), ex-*President Garfield* (1940), ex-*Blue Hen State* (1923)				

Displacement	16,800 tons f/l; 10,501 grt
Dimensions	522'8" (oa); 502' bp x 62' x 26'
Machinery	2 screws; VTE; 6 Alco Scotch boilers; SHP 7,000; 14 knots
Endurance	13,000/13
Complement	1,242
Armament	1–5"/38, 4–3"/50

Service Record:

AP 62 *Kenmore* Acq from American President Line. Decomm 16 Feb 1944 for conversion to hospital ship, rec **AH 11**, renamed ***Refuge***, 24 Feb 1944. Decomm 2 Apr 1946. Stricken 8 May 1946. Sold 2 Feb 1948; BU 1948 Vancouver, Wash.

Figure 11.34: The transport *Rochambeau* (AP 63) on 5 Oct 1942. Formerly the French liner *Maréchal Joffre* of Messageries Maritimes, she was seized at Manila.

Figure 11.35: *Susan B. Anthony* (AP 72) 13 May 1942. The former Grace liner *Santa Clara* sunk during the landings in Normandy.

No.	Name	Builder	Launched	Acquired	Comm.
AP 63	*Rochambeau*	La Ciotat	14 May 1931	20 Apr 1942	27 Apr 1942
	ex–*Maréchal Joffre* (1942)				

Displacement	14,242 tons f/l; 11,732 grt
Dimensions	492' (oa); 470'10" (wl) x 63'11" x 25'3"
Machinery	2 screws; diesels; SHP 10,400; 17 knots
Endurance	9400/(U)
Complement	381; capacity: 3,015 troops
Armament	1–5"/38, 4–3"/50, 8–1.1" (later, 8–20mm)

Notes: Built for Messageries Maritimes. French liner, seized at Manila, 7 Dec 1941. Casualty evacuation ship. 2 square funnels.

Service Record:

AP 63 *Rochambeau* Decomm 17 Mar 1945. Returned to France.
Later history: Merchant *Maréchal Joffre.* BU 1960 Osaka.

No.	Name	Builder	Launched	Acquired	Comm.
AP 66	*Ancon*	Beth. Quincy	24 Sep 1938	7 Aug 1942	12 Aug 1942
	ex-USAT *Ancon* (1942), ex–*Ancon* (11 Jan 1942)				

Displacement	14,150 tons f/l; 7,201 tons; 13,144 f/l
Dimensions	493' (oa); 471'6" (wl) x 64' x 26'3"
Machinery	2 screws; Beth. GT; 2 Yarrow boilers; SHP 10,000; 17.5 knots
Endurance	9,000
Complement	707 (as AGC)
Armament	2–5"/38, 4 twin 40mm, 10 twin 20mm AA

Notes: Formerly Panama Railroad Company liner. Acquired by the Army, 11 Jan 1942. Merchant name retained.

Service Record:

AP 66 *Ancon* Converted to amphibious force flagship and rec **AGC 4**, 26 Feb 1943. Decomm 25 Feb 1946, returned to owner. Stricken 17 Apr 1946.
5* North Africa, Sicily, Salerno, Normandy, Okinawa.
Later history: Merchant *Ancon* 1946, renamed *State of Maine* 1963. BU 1973, Wilmington, Del.

No.	Name	Builder	Keel Laid	Launched	Comm.
AP 67	*Dorothea L. Dix*	Beth. Quincy	11 Nov 1939	22 Jun 1940	17 Sep 1942
	ex–*Exemplar* (1942), ex–*Empire Widgeon* (1941), ex–*Exemplar* (1941)				

Displacement	6,888 tons; 14,480 f/l
Dimensions	473' (oa); 450' (wl) x 66' x 24'
Machinery	1 screw; Beth. GT; 2 B&W boilers; SHP 8,000; 17.5 knots
Endurance	18,000/15
Complement	422; capacity: 1,680 troops
Armament	4–3"/50, 2 twin 40mm, 10–20mm AA guns

Notes: Type C3–E. Acquired 13 Sep 1942. Served as APA.

Service Record:

AP 67 *Dorothea L. Dix* Decomm 24 Apr 1946.
5* North Africa, Sicily, Normandy, Southern France, Okinawa.
Later history: Merchant *Exemplar* 1946. BU 1968 Alicante, Spain.

No.	Name	Builder	Keel Laid	Launched	Comm.
AP 69	*Elizabeth C. Stanton*	Moore	21 Sep 1939	22 Dec 1939	17 Sep 1942
	ex–*Mormacstar* (1942)				
AP 70	*Florence Nightingale*	Moore	20 Jun 1940	28 Aug 1940	17 Sep 1942
	ex–*Mormacsun* (1942)				
AP 71	*Lyon*	Ingalls	21 Aug 1939	12 Oct 1940	16 Sep 1942
	ex–*Mormactide* (1942)				
AP 76	*Anne Arundel*	Federal	18 Jul 1940	16 Nov 1940	17 Sep 1942
	ex–*Mormacyork* (1942)				

Displacement	7,980 tons; 14,907 f/l; 16120 (71)
Dimensions	492'1" (oa); 465' (wl) x 69'6" x 24'
Machinery	1 screw; DeLaval GT; 2 FW boilers; SHP 8,500; 18.4 knots
Endurance	14,000
Complement	429; capacity: 2,600 troops
Armament	4–3"/50, 2 twin 40mm, 2–40mm, 8 twin 20mm AA (AP 69, AP 71, AP 76); 1–5"/38, 4–3"/50, 6–40mm (AP 70)

Notes: Type C3–Cargo and C3–M. Served as APAs.

Service Records:

AP 69 *Elizabeth C. Stanton* Acq 13 Sep 1942. Decomm 3 Apr 1946.
5* North Africa, Sicily, Salerno, Southern France, Okinawa.
Later history: Merchant *Mormacstar* 1947, renamed *Jacqueline Someck* 1961, *National Seafarer* 1964. BU 1967 Nagasaki.

AP 70 *Florence Nightingale* In collision with transport *Thurston* off Morocco, 24 Dec 1942. Decomm 1 May 1946.
4* North Africa, Sicily, Southern France, Okinawa.
Later history: Merchant *Mormacsun*, renamed *Japan Transport* 1953, *Texas* 1959. BU 1970 Portland, Ore.

AP 71 *Lyon* Decomm 3 May 1946.
5* North Africa, Sicily, Salerno, Southern France, Okinawa.
Later history: Merchant *Mormactide*, renamed *Santa Regina* 1966. BU 1972 Kaohsiung, Taiwan.

AP 76 *Anne Arundel* Acq by Navy 13 Sep 1942. Decomm 21 Mar 1946, to WSA. Stricken 12 Apr 1946.
5* North Africa, Sicily, Normandy, Southern France, Okinawa.
Later history: Merchant *Mormacyork*. BU 1970 La Spezia, Italy.

Figure 11.36: *Storm King* (AP 171), 3 Apr 1944. Used as an APA, although never reclassified.

No.	Name	Builder	Launched	Acquired	Comm.
AP 72	*Susan B. Anthony*	NY Sbdg	14 Nov 1929	7 Aug 1942	7 Sep 1942
	ex–*Santa Clara* (1942)				

Displacement	9,055 tons; 8,183 grt
Dimensions	486' (oa); 466' (wl) x 64' x 25'2"
Machinery	2 screws; TE, SHP 12,000; 16.5 knots
Endurance	8,900
Complement	158; capacity: 2,074 troops
Armament	1–5"/38, 4–3"/50

Notes: Acquired from Grace Line. 1 of 2 original funnels removed.

Service Record:

AP 72 *Susan B. Anthony* Sunk by mine off Normandy, 7 Jun 1944.
3* North Africa, Sicily, Normandy.

No.	Name	Builder	Launched	Acquired	Comm.
AP 73	*Leedstown*	Federal	3 Oct 1932	6 Aug 1942	24 Sep 1942
	ex–*Santa Lucia* (1942)				

Displacement	9,135 grt
Dimensions	508' (oa); 484' (wl) x 72' x 25'11"
Machinery	2 screws; GE GT; 4 boilers; SHP 13,200; 20 knots
Endurance	11,000
Complement	538; capacity: 2,505 troops
Armament	(U)

Notes: Grace Line.

Service Record:

AP 73 *Leedstown* Torpedoed by *U–331*, 8 Nov and again by German aircraft near Cap Matifou, sinking off Algiers, 9 Nov 1942 (8 killed).
1* North Africa.

No.	Name	Builder	Keel Laid	Launched	Comm.
AP 74	*Le Jeune*	Blohm and Voss	15 Oct 1936	12 May 1942	12 May 1944 (as AP)
	ex–*Windhuk* (1942)				

Displacement	12,255 tons; 19,200 tons f/l; 16,662 grt
Dimensions	572'8" (oa); 541'4" (wl) x 72'2" x 26'
Machinery	2 screws; Beth GT; 3 B&W boilers; SHP 13,500, 17 knots
Endurance	10,000
Complement	626; capacity: 5,260 troops
Armament	1–5"/38, 4–3"/50, 8–40mm, 14–20mm AA guns

Notes: German liner interned in Brazil. Original engines destroyed by her crew. 1 of 2 original funnels removed.

Service Record:

AP 74 *Le Jeune* Comm 26 Mar 1943 to ferry ship from Rio de Janeiro to Norfolk, Va. Decomm 9 Feb 1948. †

No.	Name	Builder	Keel Laid	Launched	Comm.
AP 77	*Thurston*	Federal	9 Dec 1941	4 Apr 1942	19 Sep 1942
	ex–*Dauphin* (18 Sep 42), ex–*Delsantos* (16 Sep 42)				

Displacement	5,185 tons; 13,898 f/l
Dimensions	459'2" (oa); 438'5" (wl) x 63' x 23'
Machinery	1 screw; GE GT; 2 FW boilers; SHP 6,000; 16.5 knots
Endurance	19,100
Complement	456; capacity: 1,300 troops
Armament	4–3"/50, 2 twin 40mm, 10–20mm AA guns

Notes: Type C2–F. Served as APA.

Service Record:

A77 *Thurston* Damaged in collision with transport *Florence Nightingale* off Morocco, 24 Dec 1942. Decomm 1 Aug 1946. Stricken 28 Aug 1946. Sold 1948.
7* North Africa, Sicily, Convoy KMF–25A, Normandy, Southern France, Iwo Jima, Okinawa.
Later history: Merchant *Chickasaw.* Wrecked on Santa Rosa I., Calif., 7 Feb 1962.

No.	*Name*	Formerly	Date
AP 75	*Gemini*	AK 52	15 Aug 1942

No.	Name	Reclassified	Date
AP 48–49	—	APA 89–90	—
AP 78–101	—	AKA 33–55	1 Feb 1943
AP 106–109	—	LSV 1–4	21 Apr 1944
AP 160–161	—	LSV 5–6	21 Apr 1944
AP 162–166	—	AK 221–24	20 Aug 1944

No.	Name	Builder	Keel Laid	Launched	Comm.
AP 102	*La Salle*	Moore	29 Apr 1942	2 Aug 1942	31 Mar 1943
	ex–*Hotspur* (6 Apr 1943).				
AP 166	*Comet*	Moore	13 Oct 1942	21 Dec 1942	15 Feb 1944
AP 167	*John Land*	Moore	14 Nov 1942	22 Jan 1943	8 Apr 1944
AP 168	*War Hawk*	Moore	24 Dec 1942	3 Apr 1943	9 Mar 1944
AP 169	*Golden City*	Moore	16 Aug 1943	28 Oct 1943	29 May 1944
AP 170	*Winged Arrow*	Moore	26 Jan 1943	3 Apr 1943	21 Apr 1944
AP 173	*Herald of the Morning*	Moore	12 Jun 1943	14 Aug 1943	22 Apr 1944

Displacement	12,200 tons f/l 7,440 tons; 13,893 f/l AP 102 6,556 tons; 13,910 f/l
Dimensions	459'2" (oa); 435' (wl) x 63' x 23'
Machinery	1 screw; GE GT; 2 FW boilers; SHP 6,000; 16.5 knots
Endurance	18,000
Complement	276; capacity: 2,000 troops (AP 102: 1,575)
Armament	1–5"/38, 4–3"/50, 10 twin 20mm; AP 102: 1–5"/38, 4–3"/50, 12–20mm AA guns

Notes: Type C2–S–B1. Named after clipper ships. Served as APAs (except AP 102).

Service Records:

AP 102 *LaSalle* Decomm 24 Jul 1946.
8* Gilbert Is., Kwajalein, Saipan, Palau, Leyte, Lingayen, Subic Bay, Okinawa.
Later history: Merchant *Hotspur* 1947, renamed *Stonewall Jackson* 1948, *John C.* 1953. BU 1968 Taiwan.

AP 166 *Comet* Decomm 14 Aug 1946.
3* Saipan, Guam, Leyte.
Later history: Merchant *Pioneer Reef,* renamed *Australian Reef,* 1965.

AP 167 *John Land* Carried President Sergio Osmeña back to the Philippines, Oct 1944. Decomm 5 Aug 1946.
5* Saipan, Tinian, Palau, Leyte, Iwo Jima.
Later history: Merchant *Jeff Davis,* renamed *Sea Comet II* 1953, *Santa Regina* 1957, *African Gulf* 1961, *Norberto Capay* 1963, *Galicia Lee* 1968. BU 1968 Kaohsiung, Taiwan.

Figure 11.37: *Gen. George M. Randall* (AP 115) 1944, one of 11 large, two-funneled type P2 transports named after generals, designed to be converted into passenger liners at the end of the war.

AP 168 *War Hawk* Damaged in collision, Leyte, 21 Oct 1944. Damaged by kamikaze boat off Lingayen, Luzon, 9 Jan 1945 (61 killed). Decomm 12 Aug 1946. Stricken 8 Oct 1946.
3* Saipan, Guam, Leyte, Lingayen.
Later history: Merchant *War Hawk*, renamed *Ocean Dinny* 1954, *Overseas Dinny* 1966. BU 1971 Kaohsiung, Taiwan.

AP 169 *Golden City* Decomm 10 Aug 1946.
4* Guam, Leyte, Iwo Jima, Subic Bay.
Later history: Merchant *Golden City*, renamed *Ocean Eva* 1955, *Overseas Eva* 1961, *Sapphire Etta* 1965, *Cortland* 1967. BU 1973 Kaohsiung, Taiwan.

AP 170 *Winged Arrow* Decomm 12 Aug 1946. Stricken 28 Aug 1946.
4* Saipan, Tinian, Iwo Jima, Subic Bay.
Later history: Merchant *Fairhope*, renamed *Susan* 1953, *Noordzee* 1955, *Green Bay* 1959, *Winged Arrow* 1965. BU 1970.

AP 173 *Herald of the Morning* Decomm 9 Aug 1946.
5* Saipan, Palau, Leyte, Lingayen, Iwo Jima.
Later history: Merchant *Citrus Packer* 1948, renamed *Gulf Trader* 1958, *Bowling Green* 1965. BU 1973 Kaohsiung, Taiwan.

No.	Name	Builder	Keel Laid	Launched	Comm.
AP 171	*Storm King*	N. Carolina	20 Jul 1943	17 Sep 1943	4 Dec 1943
AP 175	*Starlight*	N. Carolina	9 Oct 1943	23 Dec 1943	15 Feb 1944

Displacement	6,363 tons; 13,910 f/l
Dimensions	459'2" (oa); 435' (wl) x 63' x 23'
Machinery	1 screw; GE GT; 2 FW boilers; SHP 6,000; 16.5 knots
Endurance	18,000
Complement	360; capacity: 2,000 troops
Armament	1–5"/38, 4–3"/50, 10–20mm AA guns

Notes: Type C2–S–AJ1. Used as APAs.

Service Records:

AP 171 *Storm King* Decomm 16 Aug 1946.
4* Saipan, Palau, Leyte, Iwo Jima.
Later history: Merchant *Santa Cruz*, renamed *Gulf Farmer* 1947, *Ranger* 1964. BU 1970 Kaohsiung, Taiwan.

AP 175 *Starlight* Decomm 12 Aug 1946.
4* Guam, Leyte, Lingayen, Okinawa.
Later history: Merchant *Florence Luckenbach*, renamed *Badger State* 1960. On fire 580 miles northeast of Midway, 26 Dec 1969; floundered 5 Jan 1970.

No.	Name	Builder	Keel Laid	Launched	Comm.
AP 172	*Cape Johnson*	Consol. Wilm.	28 Nov 1942	20 Feb 1943	1 Jun 1944
AP 174	*Arlington*	Consol. Wilm.	11 May 1942	10 Aug 1942	18 Apr 1944
	ex–*Fred Morris* (1944)				

Displacement	5,668 tons; 10,120 tons f/l 9,104 f/l
Dimensions	417'9" (oa); 395' (wl) x 60' x 22'3"
Machinery	1 screw; West. GT; 2 B&W boilers; SHP 4,000; 14.7 knots
Endurance	16,000
Complement	350; capacity: 1,575 troops
Armament	1–5"/38, 4–3"/50, 4–40mm, 12–20mm AA guns

Notes: Type C1–B. Used as APAs.

Service Records:

AP 172 *Cape Johnson* Acq Dec 1943. Decomm 25 Jul 1946. Returned 26 Jul 1946; BU 1963 Portland, Ore.
2* Leyte, Iwo Jima.

AP 174 *Arlington* Acq 17 Apr 1944. Training ship for auxiliary ships' crews, Seattle and San Francisco. Decomm 20 Mar 1946. Stricken 28 Mar 1946.
Later history: Merchant *Fred Morris*. BU 1965 Baltimore.

No.	Name	Builder	Keel Laid	Launched	Comm.
AP 110	*Gen. John Pope*	Federal	15 Jul 1942	21 Mar 1943	5 Aug 1943
AP 111	*Gen. A. E. Anderson*	Federal	7 Sep 1942	2 May 1943	5 Oct 1943
AP 112	*Gen. W. A. Mann*	Federal	28 Dec 1942	18 Jul 1943	13 Oct 1943
AP 113	*Gen. H. W. Butner*	Federal	23 Mar 1943	19 Sep 1943	1 Jan 1944
AP 114	*Gen. William Mitchell*	Federal	3 May 1943	31 Oct 1943	19 Jan 1944
AP 115	*Gen. G. M. Randall*	Federal	20 Jul 1943	30 Jan 1944	15 Apr 1944

Figure 11.38: *Admiral R. E. Coontz* (AP 122). Ten P2 transports named after admirals had turbo-electric machinery. After the war they were transferred to the Army and renamed after generals. The old Navy number can still be seen, although the legend on the hull reads "U.S. Army Transport."

AP 116	*Gen. M. C. Meigs*	Federal	22 Sep 1943	12 Mar 1944	3 Jun 1944
AP 117	*Gen. W. H. Gordon*	Federal	2 Nov 1943	7 May 1944	29 Jul 1944
AP 118	*Gen. W. P. Richardson*	Federal	2 Feb 1944	6 Aug 1944	2 Nov 1944
	ex–*Gen. R. M. Blatchford* (1 Jul 1944)				
AP 119	*Gen. William Weigel*	Federal	15 Mar 1944	3 Sep 1944	6 Jan 1945
	ex–*Gen. C. H. Barth* (24 Aug 1944)				
AP 176	*Gen. J. C. Breckinridge*	Federal	10 May 1944	18 Mar 1945	30 Jun 1945

Displacement	11,450 tons; 20,175 tons f/l
Dimensions	622'7" (oa); 573' (wl) x 75'6" x 25'6"
Machinery	2 screws; DeLaval GT; 4 FW boilers; SHP 17,000; 20.6 knots
Endurance	12,400
Complement	466; capacity: 5,650 troops
Armament	4–5"/38, 4 twin 40mm, 18 twin 20mm AA guns

Notes: Type P2–S2–R2. Three additional units ordered from Federal, canceled 17 Aug 1945. Named after Army generals.

Service Records:

AP 110 *Gen. John Pope* Decomm 12 Jun 1946, to Army. †
AP 111 *Gen. A.E. Anderson* †
AP 112 *Gen. W. A. Mann* †
AP 113 *Gen. H. W. Butner* †
AP 114 *Gen. William Mitchell* USCG crew. †
AP 115 *Gen. G. M. Randall* USCG crew. †
AP 116 *Gen. M. C. Meigs* USCG crew. Decomm 4 Mar 1946. †
AP 117 *Gen. W. H. Gordon* USCG crew. Decomm 11 Mar 1946, to Army. †
AP 118 *Gen. W. P. Richardson* USCG crew. Decomm 14 Feb 1946, to Army. Returned to Marad, 10 Mar 1948.
Later history: Merchant *LaGuardia*, renamed *Leilani* 1956, *President Roosevelt* 1961, *Atlantis* 1970, *Emerald Seas* 1972, *Funtastica* 1992, *Terrifica* 1992, *Sapphire Seas* 1992, *Ocean Explorer* 1998. BU 2004 India.
AP 119 *Gen. William Weigel* USCG crew. Decomm 10 May 1946, to Army. †
AP 176 *Gen. J. C. Breckinridge* USCG crew. †

No.	Name	Builder	Keel Laid	Launched	Comm.
AP 120	*Adm. W. S. Benson*	Beth. Alameda	10 Dec 1942	28 Nov 1943	23 Aug 1944
AP 121	*Adm. W. L. Capps*	Beth. Alameda	15 Dec 1942	20 Feb 1944	18 Sep 1944
AP 122	*Adm. R. E. Coontz*	Beth. Alameda	15 Jan 1943	22 Apr 1944	21 Nov 1944
AP 123	*Adm. E. W. Eberle*	Beth. Alameda	15 Feb 1943	14 Jun 1944	24 Jan 1945
AP 124	*Adm. C. F. Hughes*	Beth. Alameda	29 Nov 1943	27 Aug 1944	31 Jan 1945
AP 125	*Adm. H. T. Mayo*	Beth. Alameda	21 Feb 1944	26 Nov 1944	24 Apr 1945
AP 126	*Adm. Hugh Rodman*	Beth. Alameda	24 Apr 1944	25 Feb 1945	10 Jul 1945
AP 127	*Adm. W. S. Sims*	Beth. Alameda	15 Jun 1944	4 Jun 1945	27 Sep 1945
AP 128	*Adm. D. W. Taylor*	Beth. Alameda	28 Aug 1944	—	—
AP 129	*Adm. F. B. Upham*	Beth. Alameda	27 Nov 1944	—	—

Displacement	9,676 tons; 20,120 tons f/l
Dimensions	608'11" (oa); 573' (wl) x 75'6" x 26'6"
Machinery	2 screws; GE turbo–electric, 4 CE boilers; SHP 18,000; 19 knots
Endurance	15,000
Complement	410; capacity 5,100 troops
Armament	4–5"/38, 4 twin 40mm, 14 twin 20mm AA guns

Notes: Type P2–SE2–R1. Originally begun for the Army, but assigned to the Navy. All renamed Dec 1947.

Service Records:

AP 120 *Adm. W. S. Benson* Decomm 3 Jun 1946, to Army, renamed USAT *Gen. Daniel I. Sultan*. †
AP 121 *Adm. W. L. Capps* USCG crew. Decomm 8 May 1946, to Army, renamed USAT *Gen. Hugh J. Gaffey*. †

Figure 11.39: The transport *Gen. C. G. Morton* (AP 138), 16 Sep 1944, one of 30 type C4 ships with engines aft, built for the Navy as transports and named after Army generals.

Figure 11.40: *Europa* (AP 177), the former North German Lloyd liner seized in 1945 that served the Navy briefly, arriving in New York. Notice the Navy number on the bow.

AP 122 *Adm. R. E. Coontz* Decomm 25 Mar 1946, to Army, renamed USAT *Gen. Alexander M. Patch*. †
AP 123 *Adm. E. W. Eberle* USCG crew. Hit by Navy aircraft at Manus, 25 Mar 1945 (3 killed). Decomm 8 May 1946, to Army, renamed USAT *Gen. Simon B. Buckner*. †
AP 124 *Adm. C. F. Hughes* USCG crew. Decomm 3 May 1946, to Army, renamed USAT *Gen. Edwin D. Patrick*. †
AP 125 *Adm. H. T. Mayo* USCG crew. Decomm 26 May 1946, to Army, renamed USAT *Gen. Nelson M. Walker*. †
AP 126 *Adm. Hugh Rodman* Decomm 29 May 1946, to Army, renamed USAT *Gen. Maurice Rose*. †
AP 127 *Adm. W. S. Sims* Decomm 21 Jun 1946, to Army, renamed USAT *Gen. William O. Darby*. †
AP 128 *Adm. D. W. Taylor* Canceled 16 Dec 1944.
Later history: Completed as merchant *President Cleveland* 1947, renamed *Oriental President* 1973. BU 1974 Kaohsiung, Taiwan.
AP 129 *Adm. F .B. Upham* Canceled 16 Dec 1944.
Later history: Completed as merchant *President Wilson* 1947, renamed *Oriental Empress* 1973. BU 1974 Kaohsiung, Taiwan.

No.	Name	Builder	Keel Laid	Launched	Comm.
AP 130	*Gen. G. O. Squier*	Kaiser #2	14 May 1942	25 Nov 1942	2 Oct 1943
AP 131	*Gen. T. H. Bliss*	Kaiser #2	22 May 1942	19 Dec 1942	24 Feb 1944
AP 132	*Gen. J.R. Brooke*	Kaiser #2	29 Jun 1942	21 Feb 1943	20 Jan 1944
AP 133	*Gen. O. H. Ernst*	Kaiser #2	29 Jun 1942	14 Apr 1943	15 Jul 1944
AP 134	*Gen. R. L. Howze*	Kaiser #2	22 Jul 1942	23 May 1943	7 Feb 1944
AP 135	*Gen. W. M. Black*	Kaiser #2	26 Nov 1942	23 Jul 1943	24 Feb 1944
AP 136	*Gen. H. L. Scott*	Kaiser #2	20 Dec 1942	19 Sep 1943	3 Apr 1944
AP 137	*Gen. S. D. Sturgis*	Kaiser #2	15 Apr 1943	12 Nov 1943	10 Jul 1944
AP 138	*Gen. C. G. Morton*	Kaiser #2	20 Sep 1943	15 Mar 1944	7 Jul 1944
AP 139	*Gen. R. E. Callan*	Kaiser #2	16 Dec 1943	23 May 1944	17 Aug 1944
AP 140	*Gen. M. B. Stewart*	Kaiser #2	22 Jun 1944	15 Oct 1944	3 Mar 1945
AP 141	*Gen. A. W. Greely*	Kaiser #2	18 Jul 1944	5 Nov 1944	22 Mar 1945
AP 142	*Gen. C. H. Muir*	Kaiser #2	7 Aug 1944	24 Nov 1944	12 Apr 1945
AP 143	*Gen. H. B. Freeman*	Kaiser #2	28 Aug 1944	11 Dec 1944	26 Apr 1945
AP 144	*Gen. H. F. Hodges*	Kaiser #2	21 Sep 1944	3 Jan 1945	6 Apr 1945
AP 145	*Gen. Harry Taylor*	Kaiser #2	22 Feb 1943	10 Oct 1943	8 May 1944
AP 146	*Gen. W. F. Hase*	Kaiser #2	24 May 1943	15 Dec 1943	6 Jun 1944
AP 147	*Gen. E. T. Collins*	Kaiser #2	24 Jul 1943	22 Jan 1944	20 Jul 1944
AP 148	*Gen. M. L. Hersey*	Kaiser #2	11 Oct 1943	1 Apr 1944	29 Jul 1944
AP 149	*Gen. J. H. McRae*	Kaiser #2	13 Nov 1943	26 Apr 1944	8 Aug 1944
AP 150	*Gen. M. M. Patrick*	Kaiser #2	24 Jan 1944	21 Jun 1944	4 Sep 1944
AP 151	*Gen. W. C. Langfitt*	Kaiser #2	16 Mar 1944	17 Jul 1944	30 Sep 1944
AP 152	*Gen. Omar Bundy*	Kaiser #2	3 Apr 1944	5 Aug 1944	6 Jan 1945
AP 153	*Gen. R. M. Blatchford*	Kaiser #2	27 Apr 1944	27 Aug 1944	26 Jan 1945
AP 154	*Gen. LeRoy Eltinge*	Kaiser #2	24 May 1944	20 Sep 1944	21 Feb 1945
AP 155	*Gen. A. W. Brewster*	Kaiser #2	16 Oct 1944	21 Jan 1945	23 Apr 1945
AP 156	*Gen. D. E. Aultman*	Kaiser #2	6 Nov 1944	21 Feb 1945	20 May 1945
AP 157	*Gen. C. C. Ballou*	Kaiser #2	12 Dec 1944	7 Mar 1945	30 Jun 1945
AP 158	*Gen. W. G. Haan*	Kaiser #2	4 Jan 1945	20 Mar 1945	2 Aug 1945
AP 159	*Gen. Stuart Heintzelman*	Kaiser.#2	22 Feb 1945	21 Apr 1945	12 Sep 1945

Displacement	9,950 tons; 17,250 tons f/l
Dimensions	522'10" (oa); 496' (wl) x 71'6" x 26'6"
Machinery	1 screw; West. GT; 2 B&W boilers; SHP 9,000; 16.5 knots
Endurance	15,000
Complement	266/356; capacity: 3,823 troops
Armament	4–5"/38, 2 twin 40mm, 15 twin 20mm AA guns

Notes: Type C4–S–A1. Engines aft. Named after Army generals.

Service Records:

AP 130 *Gen. G. O. Squier* Decomm 10 Jul 1946. Stricken 18 Jul 1946, to WSA. Sold 7 Apr 1964.
1* Southern France.
Later history: Merchant *Pennmar*, renamed *Penn* 1976, *Penny* 1979.
AP 131 *Gen. T. H. Bliss* Decomm 28 Jun 1946.
Later history: Merchant *Seamar*, renamed *Caroni* 1975. BU 1979 Kaohsiung, Taiwan.
AP 132 *Gen. J. R. Brooke* Decomm 3 Jul 1946.
Later history: Merchant *Marymar* 1964, renamed *Marlin* 1976, *Mary* 1976. BU 1979 Kaohsiung, Taiwan.
AP 133 *Gen. O. H. Ernst* Decomm 13 Aug 1946.
Later history: Merchant *Calmar* 1964, renamed *Orinoco* 1975. BU 1979 Brownsville, Tex.
AP 134 *Gen. R. L. Howze* USCG crew. Decomm 1 Apr 1946, to Army. †
AP 135 *Gen. W. M. Black* USCG crew. Decomm 28 Feb 1946, to Army. †
AP 136 *Gen. H. L. Scott* USCG crew. Decomm 29 May 1946.
Later history: Merchant *Yorkmar* 1964, renamed *York Maru* 1974. BU 1974 Villanueva, Spain. Tokyo Bay.
AP 137 *Gen. S. D. Sturgis* Decomm 24 May 1946, to Army. †
AP 138 *Gen. C. G. Morton* Decomm 15 May 1946, to Army. †
AP 139 *Gen. R. E. Callan* Decomm 24 May 1946, to Army. †
AP 140 *Gen. M. B. Stewart* Decomm 24 May 1946, to Army. †
AP 137 *Gen. S. D. Sturgis* Decomm 24 May 1946, to Army. †
AP 138 *Gen. C. G. Morton* Decomm 15 May 1946, to Army. †
AP 139 *Gen. R. E. Callan* Decomm 24 May 1946, to Army. †
AP 140 *Gen. M. B. Stewart* Decomm 24 May 1946, to Army. †

Figure 11.41: *President Adams* (APA 19), an attack transport, 1944, was a C3 passenger cargo ship built for the American President Line.

Figure 11.42: *Knox* (APA 46), 9 Jan 1945, of the *Bayfield* class, type C3-S-A2.

AP 141 *Gen. A. W. Greely* USCG crew. Decomm 29 Mar 1946, to Army. †
AP 142 *Gen. C. H. Muir* USCG crew. Decomm 18 Jun 1946, to Army. †
AP 143 *Gen. H. B. Freeman* USCG crew. Decomm 4 Mar 1946, to Army. †
AP 144 *Gen. H. F. Hodges* USCG crew. Decomm 13 May 1946, to Army. †
AP 145 *Gen. Harry Taylor* Decomm 13 Jun 1946, to Army. †
AP 146 *Gen. W. F. Hase* Decomm 6 Jun 1946, to Army. †
AP 147 *Gen. E. T. Collins* Decomm 17 Jun 1946, to Army. †
AP 148 *Gen. M. L. Hersey* Decomm 1 Jun 1946, to Army, 6 Jun 1946. †
1* Leyte.
AP 149 *Gen. J. H. McRae* Decomm 27 Feb 1946, to Army. †
AP 150 *Gen. M. M. Patrick* Decomm 8 Mar 1946, to Army 11 Mar 1946. †
AP 151 *Gen. W. C. Langfitt* Decomm 6 Jun 1946, to Army. †
AP 152 *Gen. Omar Bundy* Decomm 14 Jun 1946. Stricken 8 Oct 1946.
To Army 30 Aug 1946. Returned to MarAd 12 Dec 1949.
Later history: Merchant *Portmar* 1964, renamed *Port* 1976, *Poet* 1979. Foundered in N. Atlantic, 24 Oct 1980.
AP 153 *Gen. R. M. Blatchford* Decomm 12 Jun 1946, to Army. †
AP 154 *Gen. LeRoy Eltinge* Decomm 26 May 1946, to Army. †
AP 155 *Gen. A. W. Brewster* USCG crew. Decomm 10 Apr 1946, to Army. †
AP 156 *Gen. D. E. Aultman* USCG crew. Decomm 15 Mar 1946, to Army. †
AP 157 *Gen. C. C. Ballou* Decomm 17 May 1946, to Army. †
AP 158 *Gen. W. G. Haan* Decomm 7 Jun 1946, to Army. †
AP 159 *Gen. Stuart Heintzelman* Decomm 12 Jun 1946, to Army. †

No.	Name	Builder	Launched	Acquired	Comm.
AP 177	*Europa*	Blohm and Voss	15 Aug 1928	25 Aug 1945	28 Aug 1945

Displacement	43,407 tons; 49,746 grt
Dimensions	936' (oa); 888' (wl) x 102' x 33'10"
Machinery	4 screws; GT; 20 boilers; SHP 96,800; 27 knots
Complement	(U)
Armament	none

Notes: North German Lloyd liner taken as war prize 1945. Used by German Navy as barracks ship.

Service Record:

AP 177 *Europa* Decomm 2 May 1946. Stricken 8 Jun 1946.
Later history: Merchant *Liberté* 1948. BU 1962 La Spezia, Italy.

ATTACK TRANSPORTS

Attack transports were designed to carry troops into amphibious operations, equipped to carry landing craft. Most were named after U.S. counties.

APA 1 *Doyen* Ex–AP 2
APA 2 *Harris* Ex–AP 8
APA 3 *Zeilin* Ex–AP 9
APA 4 *McCawley* Ex–AP 10
APA 5 *Barnett* Ex–AP 11
APA 6 *Heywood* Ex–AP 12
APA 7 *Fuller* Ex–AP 14
APA 8 *William P. Biddle* Ex–AP 15
APA 9 *Neville* Ex–AP 16
APA 10 *Harry Lee* Ex–AP 17
APA 11 *Feland* Ex–AP 18
APA 12 *Leonard Wood* Ex–AP 25
APA 13 *Joseph T. Dickman* Ex–AP 26
APA 14 *Hunter Liggett* Ex–AP 27
APA 15 *Henry T. Allen* Ex–AP 30, rec **AG 90**, 1 Feb 1945
APA 16 *J. Franklin Bell* Ex–AP 34
APA 17 *American Legion* Ex–AP 35
APA 18 *President Jackson* Ex–AP 37
APA 19 *President Adams* Ex–AP 38
APA 20 *President Hayes* Ex–AP 39

Figure 11.43: *Adair* (APA 91) 17 Jul 1944, a *Bayfield*-class C3 type attack transport. Notice the tall mast between the kingposts.

APA 21 *Crescent City* Ex–AP 40
APA 22 *[Joseph Hewes]* AP 50, lost before rec.
APA 23 *John Penn* Ex–AP 51
APA 24 *[Edward Rutledge]* AP 52, lost before rec.
APA 25 *Arthur Middleton* Ex–AP 55
APA 26 *Samuel Chase* Ex–AP 56
APA 27 *George Clymer* Ex–AP 57
APA 28 *Charles Carroll* Ex–AP 58
APA 29 *[Thomas Stone]* AP 59, not rec.
APA 30 *Thomas Jefferson* Ex–AP 60
APA 31 *Monrovia* Ex–AP 64
APA 32 *Calvert* Ex–AP 65

Note: All rec 1 Feb 1943.

No.	Name	Builder	Keel Laid	Launched	Comm.
APA 33	*Bayfield*	W. Pipe S.F.	14 Nov 1942	15 Feb 1943	30 Nov 1943
	ex–*Sea Bass*				
APA 34	*Bolivar*	W. Pipe S.F.	13 May 1942	7 Sep 1942	1 Sep 1943
	ex–*Sea Angel*				
APA 35	*Callaway*	W. Pipe S.F.	10 Jun 1942	10 Oct 1942	11 Sep 1943
	ex–*Sea Mink*				
APA 36	*Cambria*	W. Pipe S.F.	1 Jul 1942	10 Nov 1942	10 Nov 1943
	ex–*Sea Swallow*				
APA 37	*Cavalier*	W. Pipe S.F.	10 Dec 1942	15 Mar 1943	15 Jan 1944
APA 38	*Chilton*	W. Pipe S.F.	10 Sep 1942	29 Dec 1942	7 Dec 1943
	ex–*Sea Needle*				
APA 39	*Clay*	W. Pipe S.F.	14 Oct 1942	23 Jan 1943	21 Dec 1943
	ex–*Sea Carp*				
APA 40	*Custer*	Ingalls	19 Feb 1942	6 Nov 1942	18 Jul 1943
	ex–*Sea Eagle*				
APA 41	*DuPage*	Ingalls	20 Mar 1942	19 Dec 1942	1 Sep 1943
	ex–*Sea Hound*				
APA 42	*Elmore*	Ingalls	19 Jun 1942	29 Jan 1943	25 Aug 1943
	ex–*Sea Panther*				
APA 43	*Fayette*	Ingalls	1 Oct 1942	25 Feb 1943	14 Oct 1943
	ex–*Sea Hawk*				
APA 44	*Fremont*	Ingalls	28 Oct 1942	31 Mar 1943	23 Nov 1943
	ex–*Sea Corsair*				
APA 45	*Henrico*	Ingalls	12 Nov 1942	31 Mar 1943	26 Nov 1943
	ex–*Sea Darter*				
APA 46	*Knox*	Ingalls	4 Mar 1943	17 Jul 1943	4 Mar 1944
	ex–*Sea Scamp*				
APA 47	*Lamar*	Ingalls	31 Mar 1943	28 Aug 1943	6 Apr 1944
	ex–*Sea Porpoise*				
APA 48	*Leon*	Ingalls	6 Feb 1943	19 Jun 1943	12 Feb 1944
	ex–*Sea Dolphin*				
APA 92	*Alpine*	W. Pipe S.F.	12 Apr 1943	10 Jul 1943	22 Apr 1944
	ex–*Sea Arrow* (1943)				
APA 93	*Barnstable*	W. Pipe S.F.	6 May 1943	5 Aug 1943	22 May 1944
	ex–*Sea Snapper*				
APA 95	*Burleigh*	Ingalls	6 Jul 1943	3 Dec 1943	30 Oct 1944
APA 96	*Cecil*	W. Pipe S.F.	24 Jun 1943	27 Sep 1943	15 Sep 1944
	ex–*Sea Angler*				
APA 99	*Dade*	Ingalls	2 Sep 1943	14 Jan 1944	11 Nov 1944
	ex–*Lorain* (19 Nov 1943)				
APA 100	*Mendocino*	Ingalls	20 Sep 1943	11 Feb 1944	31 Oct 1944
APA 101	*Montour*	Ingalls	20 Oct 1943	10 Mar 1944	8 Dec 1944
APA 102	*Riverside*	Ingalls	11 Nov 1943	13 Apr 1944	18 Dec 1944
APA 104	*Westmoreland*	Ingalls	8 Dec 1943	28 Apr 1944	18 Jan 1945
APA 106	*Hansford*	W. Pipe S.F.	10 Dec 1943	25 Apr 1944	12 Oct 1944
	ex–*Gladwin* (25 Aug 1944), ex–*Sea Adder*				
APA 107	*Goodhue*	W. Pipe S.F.	7 Jan 1944	31 May 1944	11 Nov 1944
	ex–*Sea Wren*				
APA 108	*Goshen*	W. Pipe S.F.	31 Jan 1944	29 Jun 1944	13 Dec 19 44
	ex–*Sea Hare*				
APA 109	*Grafton*	W. Pipe S.F.	3 Mar 1944	10 Aug 1944	5 Jan 1945
	ex–*Sea Sparrow*				
APA 110	*Griggs*	Ingalls	1 Dec 1943	26 May 1944	14 Dec 1944
APA 111	*Grundy*	Ingalls	22 Dec 1943	16 Jun 1944	3 Jan 1945
APA 112	*Guilford*	Ingalls	19 Jan 1944	14 Jul 1944	14 May 1945
APA 113	*Sitka*	Ingalls	2 Feb 1944	23 Jun 1944	14 Mar 1945
APA 114	*Hamblen*	Ingalls	16 Feb 1944	30 Jul 1944	12 Jun 1945
APA 115	*Hampton*	Ingalls	4 Mar 1944	25 Aug 1944	17 Feb 1945
APA 116	*Hanover*	Ingalls	15 Mar 1944	18 Aug 1944	31 Mar 1945

Displacement	8,920 tons; 16,100 tons f/l
Dimensions	492' (oa); 465' (wl) x 69'6" x 26'6"
Machinery	1 screw; GE GT; 2 CE boilers; SHP 8,500, 18 knots
Endurance	10,450/12
Complement	576; capacity 1,500 troops, 24 to 26 LCVP
Armament	2–5"/38, 2 to 4 twin 40mm, 12 to 18 twin 20mm AA guns

Notes: Type C3–S–A2. AP 78–101 rec APA 33–56, 1 Feb 1943.

Service Records:

APA 33 *Bayfield* USCG crew. Operation Crossroads. †
4* Normandy, Southern France, Iwo Jima, Okinawa.

APA 34 *Bolivar* Damaged by coastal gunfire, Iwo Jima, 3 Mar 1945 (1 dead). Decomm 29 Apr 1946. Stricken 19 Jul 1946.
5* Kwajalein, Saipan, Guam, Leyte, Lingayen, Iwo Jima.
Later history: Merchant *President Van Buren* 1949, renamed P*resident Harding* 1967, *Thailand Bear* 1968, *Santa Monica* 1970. BU 1972 Kaohsiung, Taiwan.

APA 35 *Callaway* USCG crew. Damaged by kamikaze, Lingayen, Luzon, 8 Jan 1945 (29 killed). Decomm 10 May 1946. Sold 12 Sep 1946.
6* Kwajalein, Saipan, Palau, Leyte, Iwo Jima, Lingayen.
Later history: Merchant *President Harrison* 1949, renamed *President Fillmore* 1966, *Hurricane* 1968.

APA 36 *Cambria* USCG crew. †
6* Kwajalein, Eniwetok, Saipan, Tinian, Leyte, Lingayen, Okinawa.

APA 37 *Cavalier* USCG crew. Torpedoed by *RO-115* west of Bataan, Luzon, 29 Jan 1945. †
5* Saipan, Tinian, Leyte, Lingayen, Subic Bay.
APA 38 *Chilton* Damaged by kamikaze, Okinawa, 2 Apr 1945. Operation Crossroads. †
1* Okinawa.
APA 39 *Clay* Decomm 15 May 1946. Sold 12 Sep 1946.
4* Saipan, Leyte, Lingayen, Okinawa.
Later history: Merchant *President Johnson* 1948, renamed *LaSalle* 1968. BU 1974 Kaohsiung, Taiwan.
APA 40 *Custer* Decomm 24 May 1946. Stricken 1946.
7* Kwajalein, Eniwetok, Saipan, Guam, Leyte, Lingayen, Okinawa.
Later history: Merchant *Mormacmar* 1948, renamed *Santa Ana* 1967. BU 1973 Kaohsiung, Taiwan.
APA 41 *DuPage* Damaged by kamikaze, Lingayen, Luzon, 10 Jan 1945 (36 killed). Decomm 28 Mar 1946. Stricken 1946.
6* Cape Gloucester, Kwajalein, Guam, Palau, Leyte, Lingayen, Subic Bay.
Later history: Merchant *P. & T. Pathfinder*, renamed *Mormacsun* 1957, *Mormacport* 1963, *Green Port* 1964, *Pine Tree State* 1967. BU 1973 Kaohsiung, Taiwan.
APA 42 *Elmore* Damaged by aircraft bomb, Okinawa, 1 Apr 1945. Decomm 13 Mar 1946. Stricken 1946.
8* Kwajalein, Guam, Palau, Leyte, Lingayen, Subic Bay, Okinawa.
Later history: Merchant *China Transport*, renamed *Oregon* 1958, *Idaho* 1960. BU 1971.
APA 43 *Fayette* Damaged in collision, Iwo Jima, 25 Feb 1945. Decomm 6 Mar 1946. Stricken 1946.
6* Kwajalein, Guam, Palau, Leyte, Lingayen, Iwo Jima.
Later history: Merchant *Robin Gray*, renamed *Gray* 1971. BU 1971 Kaohsiung, Taiwan.
APA 44 *Fremont* †
5* Saipan, Palau, Leyte, Lingayen, Iwo Jima.
APA 45 *Henrico* Hit on bridge by kamikaze, Okinawa, 2 Apr 1945 (49 killed). Operation Crossroads. †
3* Normandy, Southern France, Okinawa.
APA 46 *Knox* Damaged in collision, Iwo Jima, 27 Feb 1945. Decomm 14 Mar 1946. Stricken 1 May 1946.
5* Saipan, Leyte, Lingayen, Iwo Jima.
Later history: Merchant *Steel Recorder* 1947, renamed *Constitution State* 1968. BU 1971 Kaohsiung, Taiwan.
APA 47 *Lamar* Decomm 7 Mar 1946. Stricken 1946.
5* Guam, Leyte, Lingayen, Subic Bay, Okinawa.
Later history: Merchant *J. L. Luckenbach*, renamed *Evergreen State* 1959. BU 1971 Kaohsiung, Taiwan.
APA 48 *Leon* Decomm 7 Mar 1946. Stricken 1 Apr 1946.
4* Saipan, Palau, Leyte, Okinawa.
Later history: Merchant *Steel Chemist*. BU 1971 Bilbao, Spain.
APA 92 *Alpine* Damaged by kamikaze, Leyte, 17 Nov 1944 (5 killed). Damaged by kamikaze, Okinawa, 1 Apr 1945 (16 killed). Decomm 5 Apr 1946. Stricken 1 May 1946.
5* Guam, Leyte, Lingayen, Subic Bay, Okinawa.
Later history: Merchant *India Mail* 1947, renamed *Transwestern* 1965; *Buckeye Pacific* 1969, *Empire Pacific* 1971. BU 1971 Kaohsiung, Taiwan.
APA 93 *Barnstable* Decomm 25 Mar 1946. Stricken 12 Apr 1946.
4* Palau, Leyte, Lingayen, Okinawa.
Later history: Merchant *Steel Fabricator*, renamed *Reliance Dynasty* 1970, *Grand Valor* 1971.
APA 95 *Burleigh* Decomm 11 Jun 1946. Stricken 3 Jul 1946.
1* Okinawa.
Later history: Merchant *Hawaiian Pilot*, renamed *Sonoma* 1961, *Noma* 1972. BU 1973 Kaohsiung, Taiwan.
APA 96 *Cecil* Decomm 24 May 1946. Stricken 1946. Tokyo Bay.
2* Iwo Jima, Okinawa.
Later history: Merchant *Steel Admiral*. BU 1973 Kaohsiung, Taiwan.
APA 99 *Dade* Decomm 25 Feb 1946. Stricken 1946.
1* Okinawa.
Later history: Merchant *Hawaiian Retailer* 1947. BU 1970 Terminal I.
APA 100 *Mendocino* Decomm 27 Feb 1946. Stricken 12 Mar 1946.
1* Okinawa.
Later history: Merchant *P. & T. Seafarer*, renamed *Mormacwind* 1957, *Santa Eliana* 1967, Eliana 1973. BU 1973 Kaohsiung, Taiwan.
APA 101 *Montour* Decomm 19 Apr. Stricken 8 May 1946.
Later history: Merchant *Steel Rover*. BU 1971 Kaohsiung, Taiwan.
APA 102 *Riverside* Decomm 27 Apr 1946. Stricken 8 May 1946.
Later history: Merchant *P. & T. Forester*, renamed *Mormacwave* 1957, *Santa Leonor* 1967. Lost by grounding in Straits of Magellan, 31 Mar 1968.
APA 104 *Westmoreland* Decomm 5 Jun 1946. Stricken 19 Jun 1946. Tokyo Bay.
Later history: Merchant *Steel King*. BU 1973 Kaohsiung, Taiwan.
APA 106 *Hansford* Decomm 14 Jun 1946. Stricken 1946.
2* Iwo Jima, Okinawa.
Later history: Merchant *Steel Apprentice*. BU 1973 Kaohsiung, Taiwan.
APA 107 *Goodhue* Damaged by kamikaze, Okinawa, 2 Apr 1945 (27 killed). Decomm 5 Apr 1946. Stricken 1946.
1* Okinawa.
Later history: Merchant *Hawaiian Citizen*. BU 1982 Kashsiung, Taiwan.
APA 108 *Goshen* Decomm 20 Apr 1946. Stricken 1946.
1* Okinawa.
Later history: Merchant *Canada Mail*, renamed *California Mail* 1963, *Lafayette* 1968. BU 1973 Kaohsiung, Taiwan.
APA 109 *Grafton* Decomm 16 May 1946. Stricken 1946.
1* Okinawa.
Later history: Merchant *Java Mail*, renamed *Carrier Dove* 1969. BU 1974 Kaohsiung, Taiwan.
APA 110 *Griggs* Decomm 27 May 1946. Stricken 19 Jun 1946.
Later history: Merchant *Mormacrey*, renamed *Santa Alicia* 1966. BU 1973 Kaohsiung, Taiwan.
APA 111 *Grundy* Decomm 8 May 1946. Stricken 1946.
Later history: Merchant *Mormacsurf*, renamed *Santa Anita* 1966. BU 1973 Kaohsiung, Taiwan.
APA 112 *Guilford* Decomm 29 May 1946. Stricken 1946.
Later history: Merchant *P. & T. Navigator* 1947, renamed *American Oriole* 1963. BU 1976 Kaohsiung, Taiwan.
APA 113 *Sitka* Decomm 14 May 1946. Stricken 5 Jun 1946.
Later history: Merchant *P. & T. Trader*, renamed *Mormacguide* 1957, *American Condor* 1965. BU 1976 Kaohsiung, Taiwan.
APA 114 *Hamblen* Decomm 1 May 1946. Stricken 1946.
Later history: Merchant *Steel Voyager* 1947. BU 1973 Kaohsiung, Taiwan.
APA 115 *Hampton* Decomm 30 Apr 1946. Stricken 1946.
Later history: Merchant *P. & T. Explorer*, renamed *American Falcon* 1963. BU 1973 Kaohsiung, Taiwan.
APA 116 *Hanover* Decomm 11 May 1946. Stricken 1946.
Later history: Merchant *Hawaiian Wholesaler* 1947, renamed *Ventura* 1961, *Entu* 1972. BU 1972 Kaohsiung, Taiwan.

No.	Name	Builder	Keel Laid	Launched	Comm.
APA 49	*Ormsby* ex-*Twilight*	Moore	21 Jul 1942	20 Oct 1942	14 Jul 1943
APA 50	*Pierce* ex-*Northern Light*	Moore	22 Jul 1942	10 Oct 1942	30 Jun 1943
APA 51	*Sheridan* ex-*Messenger*	Moore	5 Aug 1942	11 Nov 1942	31 Aug 1943

Displacement	7,300 tons, 13,893 f/l
Dimensions	459'3" (oa); 435' (wl) x 63' x 24'
Machinery	1 screw; GE GT; 2 FW boilers; SHP 6,000; 17 knots

Endurance	12,000/15
Complement	524; capacity 1,550 troops, 26 LCVP
Armament	2 5"/38, 4 twin 40mm, 14 twin 20mm AA guns

Notes: Type C2–S–B1.

Service Records:

APA 49 *Ormsby* Decomm 15 Mar 1946. Stricken 17 Apr 1946.
6* Gilbert Is., Kwajalein, Hollandia, Guam, Palau, Leyte.
Later history: Merchant *American Producer* 1947. BU 1969 Kaohsiung, Taiwan.

APA 50 *Pierce* Decomm 11 Mar 1946. Stricken 17 Apr 1946.
6* Gilbert Is., Kwajalein, Saipan, Palau, Leyte, Subic Bay, Okinawa.
Later history: Merchant *American Planter*. BU 1969.

APA 51 *Sheridan* Decomm 5 Mar 1946. Stricken 12 Apr 1946.
6* Gilbert Is., Kwajalein, Saipan, Guam, Leyte, Lingayen, Subic Bay, Okinawa. Tokyo Bay.
Later history: Merchant *Pioneer Sun* 1947, renamed *American Scientist* 1947. BU 1970 Kaohsiung, Taiwan after boiler explosion 3 Jul 1969.

No.	Name	Builder	Keel Laid	Launched	Comm.
APA 52	*Sumter* ex–*Iberville*	Gulf	3 Apr 1942	4 Oct 1942	5 Sep 1943
APA 53	*Warren* ex–*Jean Lafitte*	Gulf	19 Apr 1942	7 Sep 1942	12 Aug 1943
APA 54	*Wayne* ex–*Afoundria*	Gulf	20 Apr 1942	6 Dec 1942	27 Aug 1943
APA 94	*Baxter* ex–*Antinous*	Gulf	18 Mar 1943	19 Sep 1943	15 May 1944

Displacement	8,355 tons; 13,893 f/l
Dimensions	468'9" (oa); 445' (wl) x 63' x 23'3"
Machinery	1 screw; GE GT; 2 B&W boilers; SHP 6,000; 14.7 knots
Endurance	13,500/12
Complement	511; capacity: 1,650 troops, 26 LCVP
Armament	2–5"/38, 4 twin 40mm, 10 twin 20mm AA guns

Notes: Type C2–S–E1.

Service Records:

APA 52 *Sumter* Decomm 19 Mar 1946. Stricken 17 Apr 1946.
5* Kwajalein, Saipan, Palau, Leyte, Okinawa.
Later history: Merchant *Gateway City*. BU 1978 Hong Kong.

Figure 11.44: *Cleburne* (APA 73) 20 Mar 1945. The transport version of the type S4, with turbo-electric drive.

APA 53 *Warren* Decomm 14 Mar 1946. Stricken 17 Apr 1946.
4* Kwajalein, Guam, Palau, Leyte.
Later history: Merchant *Arizpa*. BU 1977 Brownsville, Tex.

APA 54 *Wayne* Decomm 16 Mar 1946. Stricken 17 Apr 1946.
6* Kwajalein, Guam, Palau, Leyte, Lingayen, Okinawa.
Later history: Merchant *Beauregard*. BU 1977 Kaohsiung, Taiwan.

APA 94 *Baxter* Decomm 22 Mar 1946. Stricken 12 Apr 1946.
4* Leyte, Lingayen, Okinawa, Subic Bay.
Later history: Merchant *Rival* 1946, renamed *La Salle* 1947. BU 1968 Mobile, Ala.

No.	Name	Builder	Keel Laid	Launched	Comm.
APA 55	*Windsor* ex–*Excelsior*	Beth. Sp. Pt.	23 Jul 1942	28 Dec 1942	17 Jun 1943
APA 56	*Leedstown* ex–*Wood* (17 Mar 1943), ex–*Exchequer*	Beth. Sp. Pt.	26 Aug 1942	13 Feb 1943	16 Jul 1943
APA 91	*Adair* ex–*Exchester*	Beth. Sp. Pt.	28 Jul 1943	29 Feb 1944	15 Jul 1944
APA 97	*Dauphin*	Beth. Sp. Pt.	22 Dec 1943	10 Jun 1944	23 Sep 1944
APA 98	*Dutchess*	Beth. Sp. Pt.	1 Feb 1944	26 Aug 1944	4 Nov 1944
APA 103	*Queens*	Beth. Sp. Pt.	2 Mar 1944	12 Sep 1944	16 Dec 1944
APA 105	*Shelby*	Beth. Sp. Pt.	13 Jun 1944	25 Oct 1944	20 Jan 1945

Displacement	8,276 tons; 13,143 tons f/l
Dimensions	473'1" (oa); 450' (wl) x 66' x 25'
Machinery	1 screw; Beth. GT; 2 B&W boilers; SHP 8,000; 18.5 knots
Endurance	16,000/15
Complement	467/505; capacity: 1,500 troops, 24 LCVP
Armament	2–5"/38, 2 or 4 twin 40mm, 18–20mm AA guns

Notes: Type C3–S–A3.

Service Records:

APA 55 *Windsor* Decomm 4 Mar 1946. Stricken 12 Apr 1946.
5* Kwajalein, Hollandia, Guam, Palau, Leyte.
Later history: Merchant *Paul Revere*, renamed *Expeditor* 1947. BU 1972 Kaohsiung, Taiwan.

APA 56 *Leedstown* Decomm 7 Mar 1946. Stricken 1946.
6* Kwajalein, Guam, Palau, Leyte, Lingayen, Iwo Jima.
Later history: Merchant *Minute Man*, renamed *Exilona* 1949, *Ilona* 1969. BU 1970 Kaohsiung, Taiwan.

APA 91 *Adair* Decomm 30 Apr 1946. Stricken 8 May 1946.
2* Lingayen, Okinawa.
Later history: Merchant *Express*, renamed *Press* 1970. BU 1970 Kaohsiung, Taiwan.

APA 97 *Dauphin* Decomm 3 Apr 1946. Stricken 1946.
1* Okinawa.
Later history: Merchant *Exochorda* 1948, renamed *Stevens* 1967. BU 1975 Chester, Pa.

APA 98 *Dutchess* Decomm 4 Apr 1946. Stricken 1946.
1* Okinawa.
Later history: Merchant *Excalibur*, renamed *Oriental Jade* 1965. BU Kaohsiung, Taiwan 1974.

APA 103 *Queens* Decomm 10 Jun 1946. Stricken 19 Jun 1946.
Later history: Merchant *Excambion*, renamed *Texas Clipper* 1965. Laid up 1996.

APA 105 *Shelby* Decomm 14 May. Stricken 5 Jun 1946.
1* Okinawa.
Later history: Merchant *Exeter*, renamed *Oriental Pearl* 1965. BU 1974 Kaohsiung, Taiwan.

Figure 11.45: *Sarasota* (APA 204), a *Haskell*-class Victory ship attack transport.

No.	Name	Builder	Keel Laid	Launched	Comm.
APA 57	*Gilliam*	Consol. Wilm.	30 Nov 1943	28 Mar 1944	1 Aug 1944
APA 58	*Appling*	Consol. Wilm.	7 Dec 1943	9 Apr 1944	22 Aug 1944
APA 59	*Audrain*	Consol. Wilm.	11 Dec 1943	21 Apr 1944	2 Sep 1944
APA 60	*Banner*	Consol. Wilm.	24 Jan 1944	3 May 1944	16 Sep 1944
APA 61	*Barrow*	Consol. Wilm.	28 Jan 1944	11 May 1944	28 Sep 1944
APA 62	*Berrien*	Consol. Wilm.	23 Feb 1944	20 May 1944	8 Oct 1944
APA 63	*Bladen*	Consol. Wilm.	8 Mar 1944	31 May 1944	18 Oct 1944
APA 64	*Bracken*	Consol. Wilm.	13 Mar 1944	10 Jun 1944	4 Oct 1944
APA 65	*Briscoe*	Consol. Wilm.	29 Mar 1944	19 Jun 1944	29 Oct 1944
APA 66	*Brule*	Consol. Wilm.	10 Apr 1944	30 Jun 1944	31 Oct 1944
APA 67	*Burleson*	Consol. Wilm.	22 Apr 1944	11 Jul 1944	8 Nov 1944
APA 68	*Butte*	Consol. Wilm.	4 May 1944	20 Jul 1944	22 Nov 1944
APA 69	*Carlisle*	Consol. Wilm.	12 May 1944	30 Jul 1944	29 Nov 1944
APA 70	*Carteret*	Consol. Wilm.	22 May 1944	15 Aug 1944	3 Dec 1944
APA 71	*Catron*	Consol. Wilm.	1 Jun 1944	28 Aug 1944	28 Nov 1944
APA 72	*Clarendon*	Consol. Wilm.	12 Jun 1944	12 Sep 1944	14 Dec 1944
APA 73	*Cleburne*	Consol. Wilm.	20 Jun 1944	27 Sep 1944	22 Dec 1944
APA 74	*Colusa*	Consol. Wilm.	1 Jul 1944	7 Oct 1944	20 Dec 1944
APA 75	*Cortland*	Consol. Wilm.	12 Jul 1944	18 Oct 1944	1 Jan 1945
APA 76	*Crenshaw*	Consol. Wilm.	21 Jul 1944	27 Oct 1944	4 Jan 1945
APA 77	*Crittenden*	Consol. Wilm.	31 Jul 1944	6 Nov 1944	17 Jan 1945
APA 78	*Cullman*	Consol. Wilm.	16 Aug 1944	18 Nov 1944	25 Jan 1945
APA 79	*Dawson*	Consol. Wilm.	29 Aug 1944	27 Nov 1944	4 Feb 1945
APA 80	*Elkhart*	Consol. Wilm.	13 Sep 1944	5 Dec 1944	8 Feb 1945
APA 81	*Fallon*	Consol. Wilm.	28 Sep 1944	14 Dec 1944	14 Feb 1945
APA 82	*Fergus*	Consol. Wilm.	7 Oct 1944	24 Dec 1944	20 Feb 1945
APA 83	*Fillmore*	Consol. Wilm.	19 Oct 1944	4 Jan 1945	25 Feb 1945
APA 84	*Garrard*	Consol. Wilm.	28 Oct 1944	13 Jan 1945	3 Mar 1945
APA 85	*Gasconade*	Consol. Wilm.	7 Nov 1944	23 Jan 1945	11 Mar 1945
APA 86	*Geneva*	Consol. Wilm.	18 Nov 1944	31 Jan 1945	22 Mar 1945
APA 87	*Niagara*	Consol. Wilm.	28 Nov 1944	10 Feb 1945	29 Mar 1945
APA 88	*Presidio*	Consol. Wilm.	6 Dec 1944	17 Feb 1945	9 Apr 1945

Displacement	4,247 tons; 7,081 f/l
Dimensions	426' (oa); 400' (wl) x 58' x 15'6"
Machinery	2 screws; t/e, 2 B&W boilers; SHP 6,500, 16.5 knots,
Endurance	5,256/15
Complement	370; capacity 986 troops, 13 LCVP
Armament	1–5"/38, 4 twin 40mm, 10 twin 20mm AA guns

Notes: Type S4–SE2–BD1.

Service Records:

APA 57 *Gilliam* Sunk as atomic target, Bikini, 1 Jul 1946.
2* Leyte, Okinawa.

APA 58 *Appling* Bikini target ship. Decomm 20 Dec 1946. Stricken 4 Apr 1947. BU 1968 Philadelphia.
2* Okinawa, Subic Bay.

APA 59 *Audrain* Damaged in error by U.S. gunfire, Okinawa, 7 Apr 1945. Decomm 15 May 1946. Stricken 1 Aug 1947. BU 1972 Terminal I.
1* Okinawa.

APA 60 *Banner* Bikini target ship. Decomm 27 Aug 1946. Scuttled off Kwajalein, 16 Feb 1948.
2* Lingayen, Okinawa.

APA 61 *Barrow* Bikini target ship. Decomm 28 Aug 1946. Scuttled 11 May 1948.
2* Iwo Jima, Okinawa.

APA 62 *Berrien* Damaged in collision, Iwo Jima, 1 Mar 1945. Damaged by collision, Okinawa, 11 Apr 1945. Decomm 17 May 1946. Stricken 1 Aug 1947; BU 1966 Portland, Ore.
2* Iwo Jima, Okinawa.

APA 63 *Bladen* Decomm 26 Dec 1946. †
2* Iwo Jima, Okinawa.

APA 64 *Bracken* Bikini target ship. Decomm 28 Aug 1946. Scuttled off Kwajalein, 10 Mar 1948.

APA 65 Briscoe Bikini target ship. Decomm 28 Aug 1946. Scuttled 6 May 1948. Tokyo Bay.
APA 66 *Brule* Bikini target ship. Decomm 28 Aug 1946. Scuttled 11 May 1948.
APA 67 *Burleson* Animal transport for Operation Crossroads. Decomm 9 Nov 1946. †
1* Okinawa.
APA 68 *Butte* Bikini target ship. Decomm 28 Aug 1946. Scuttled off Kwajalein, 12 May 1948.
1* Okinawa.
APA 69 *Carlisle* Sunk in first atomic test, Bikini, 1 Jul 1946.
APA 70 *Carteret* Bikini target ship. Decomm 6 Aug 1946. Sunk as target off Kwajalein, 19 Apr 1948.
2* Iwo Jima, Okinawa.
APA 71 *Catron* Bikini target ship. Decomm 29 Aug 1946. Sunk as target off Kwajalein, 6 May 1948.
1* Okinawa.
APA 72 *Clarendon* Decomm 9 Apr 1946. to WSA, 27 Jun 1946 BU 1964.
1* Okinawa.
APA 73 *Cleburne* Decomm 7 Jun 1946. Bikini target. Stricken 1947; BU 1965 Portland, Ore.
APA 74 *Colusa* Decomm 16 May 1946. Stricken Mar 1947; BU 1965.
APA 75 *Cortland* Bikini target. Decomm. Stricken 1947. BU 1966 Baltimore.
APA 76 *Crenshaw* Decomm 19 Apr 1946. Stricken 1946; BU 1964 Portland, Ore.
APA 77 *Crittenden* Bikini target. Decomm 28 Aug 1946. Scuttled off California, 6 Oct 1947.
APA 78 *Cullman* Decomm 22 May 1946. Stricken Jul 1946. BU 1965.
APA 79 *Dawson* Bikini target. Decomm 20 Sep 1946. Scuttled off Kwajalein, 19 Apr 1948.
APA 80 *Elkhart* Decomm 12 Apr 1946. Stricken 1946; BU 1964 Portland, Ore.
APA 81 *Fallon* Bikini target. Decomm 20 Sep 1946. Scuttled off Kwajalein, 11 Mar 1948.
APA 82 *Fergus* Decomm 25 Jun 1946. Stricken 1946–47. BU 1965 Portland, Ore.
APA 83 *Fillmore* Bikini target. Decomm 24 Jan 1947. Stricken 1946–47. BU 1966 Wilmington, N.C.
APA 84 *Garrard* Decomm 21 May 1946. Stricken May 1946. BU 1965 Portland, Ore.
2* Okinawa, Raids on Japan 7–8/45.
APA 85 *Gasconade* Bikini target. Decomm 28 Aug 1946. Scuttled off California 21 Jul 1948.
APA 86 *Geneva* Bikini target. Decomm 23 Jan 1947. Stricken 25 Feb 1947. BU 1966 Wilmington, N.C.
APA 87 *Niagara* Bikini target. Decomm 12 Dec 1946. Stricken 1947. BU 1950 Philadelphia.
APA 88 *Presidio* Decomm 20 Jun 1946. Stricken 1 Aug 1947. BU 1965 Portland, Ore.
1* Raids on Japan 7–8/45.

No.	Name	Builder	Launched	Acquired	Comm.
APA 89	*Frederick Funston*	Sea–Tac Tacoma	27 Sep 1941	8 Apr 1943	24 Apr 1943
APA 90	*James O'Hara*	Sea–Tac Tacoma	30 Dec 1941	15 Apr 1943	26 Apr 1943

Displacement	10,967 tons lt, 14,700 f/l
Dimensions	492' (oa); 465' (wl) x 69'6" x 27'3"
Machinery	1 screw; GT, 8 FW boilers; SHP 8,500, 16.5 knots
Endurance	13,000/15
Complement	538; capacity 2,427 troops, 27 LCVP
Armament	1–5"/38, 2–3"/50, 2 twin 40mm, 11 twin 20mm AA guns

Notes: Type C3–S1–A3. Acquired from Army. Built for Army Transport Service. Originally to be classified AP48–49.

Service Records:

APA 89 *Frederick Funston* Comm by Army 28 Oct 1942. Decomm 4 Apr 1946 and returned to Army. †
6* Sicily, Salerno, Saipan, Guam, Leyte, Lingayen, Iwo Jima.
APA 90 *James O'Hara* Comm by Army 30 Nov 1942. Damaged by kamikaze, Leyte, 23 Nov 1944. Decomm 5 Apr 1946 and returned to Army. †
7* Sicily, Salerno, Saipan, Palau, Leyte, Iwo Jima, Lingayen.

No.	Name	Builder	Keel Laid	Launched	Comm.
APA 117	*Haskell*	Calship	28 Mar 1944	13 Jun 1944	11 Sep 1944
APA 118	*Hendry*	Calship	15 Apr 1944	24 Jun 1944	29 Sep 1944
APA 119	*Highlands*	Calship	28 Apr 1944	8 Jul 1944	5 Oct 1944
APA 120	*Hinsdale*	Calship	12 May 1944	22 Jul 1944	15 Oct 1944
APA 121	*Hocking*	Calship	30 May 1944	6 Aug 1944	22 Oct 1944
APA 122	*Kenton*	Calship	13 Jun 1944	21 Aug 1944	1 Nov 1944
APA 123	*Kittson*	Calship	21 Jun 1944	28 Aug 1944	5 Nov 1944
APA 124	*LaGrange*	Calship	26 Jun 1944	1 Sep 1944	11 Nov 1944
APA 125	*Lanier*	Calship	25 Jun 1944	29 Aug 1944	22 Dec 1944
APA 126	*St. Mary's*	Calship	29 Jun 1944	4 Sep 1944	15 Nov 1944
APA 127	*Allendale*	Calship	1 Jul 1944	9 Sep 1944	22 Nov 1944
APA 128	*Arenac*	Calship	9 Jul 1944	14 Sep 1944	8 Jan 1945
APA 129	*Marvin H. McIntyre* ex-*Arlington*	Calship	13 Jul 1944	21 Sep 1944	28 Nov 1944
APA 130	*Attala*	Calship	18 Jul 1944	27 Sep 1944	30 Nov 1944
APA 131	*Bandera*	Calship	23 Jul 1944	6 Oct 1944	6 Dec 1944
APA 132	*Barnwell*	Calship	25 Jul 1944	30 Sep 1944	19 Jan 1945
APA 133	*Beckham*	Calship	27 Jul 1944	14 Oct 1944	10 Dec 1944
APA 134	*Bland*	Calship	2 Aug 1944	26 Oct 1944	15 Dec 1944
APA 135	*Bosque*	Calship	7 Aug 1944	28 Oct 1944	19 Dec 1944
APA 136	*Botetourt*	Calship	22 Aug 1944	19 Oct 1944	31 Jan 1945
APA 137	*Bowie*	Calship	28 Aug 1944	31 Oct 1944	23 Dec 1944
APA 138	*Braxton*	Calship	29 Aug 1944	3 Nov 1944	29 Dec 1944
APA 139	*Broadwater*	Calship	1 Sep 1944	5 Nov 1944	2 Jan 1945
APA 140	*Brookings*	Calship	5 Sep 1944	20 Nov 1944	6 Jan 1945
APA 141	*Buckingham*	Calship	9 Sep 1944	13 Nov 1944	23 Jan 1945
APA 142	*Clearfield*	Calship	15 Sep 1944	21 Nov 1944	12 Jan 1945
APA 143	*Clermont*	Calship	21 Sep 1944	25 Nov 1944	28 Jan 1945
APA 144	*Clinton*	Calship	27 Sep 1944	29 Nov 1944	1 Feb 1945
APA 145	*Colbert*	Calship	30 Sep 1944	1 Dec 1944	7 Feb 1945
APA 146	*Collingsworth*	Calship	6 Oct 1944	2 Dec 1944	27 Feb 1945
APA 147	*Cottle*	Kaiser Vanc.	15 Oct 1944	25 Nov 1944	14 Dec 1944
APA 148	*Crockett*	Kaiser Vanc.	18 Oct 1944	28 Nov 1944	18 Jan 1945
APA 149	*Audubon*	Kaiser Vanc.	21 Oct 1944	3 Dec 1944	20 Dec 1944
APA 150	*Bergen*	Kaiser Vanc.	25 Oct 1944	5 Dec 1944	23 Dec 1944

Displacement	6,873 tons; 10, 680 f/l
Dimensions	455' (oa); 436' (wl) x 62' x 24"
Machinery	1 screw; GT; 2 B&W boilers; SHP 8,500; 17.7 knots
Endurance	7,200/15

Complement	336; capacity 1,561 troops, 22 LCVP
Armament	1–5"/38 , 4 twin 40mm, 1 quad 40mm, 10–20mm guns

Notes: Type VC2–S–AP5. Victory ships built to transport specifications.
Service Records:

APA 117 *Haskell* Decomm 22 May 1946. Stricken 1946. BU 1973.
2* Okinawa, Subic Bay.

APA 118 *Hendry* Decomm 21 Feb 1946. Stricken Mar 1946. BU 1973.
2* Iwo Jima, Okinawa.

APA 119 *Highlands* Decomm 14 Feb 1946. Stricken 1946. BU 1973.
2* Iwo Jima, Okinawa. Tokyo Bay.

APA 120 *Hinsdale* Damaged by kamikaze, Okinawa, 31 Mar 1945 (24 killed). Decomm 8 Apr 1946. Stricken 1 May 1946. BU 1974 Rotterdam.
2* Iwo Jima, Okinawa.

APA 121 *Hocking* Decomm 10 May 1946. Stricken 1946; BU 1974.
2* Iwo Jima, Okinawa.

APA 122 *Kenton* Decomm 28 Mar 1946. Stricken 12 Apr 1946. BU 1973.
1* Okinawa.

APA 123 *Kittson* Decomm 11 Mar 1946. Stricken 1946. BU 1973.
1* Okinawa.

APA 124 *LaGrange* Damaged by kamikaze, Okinawa, 13 Aug 1945 (21 killed). Decomm 27 Oct 1945 Stricken 1946. BU 1975.
1* Okinawa.

APA 125 *Lanier* Decomm 5 Mar 1946. Stricken 1946. BU 1973.
1* Okinawa.

APA 126 *St. Mary's* Decomm 15 Feb 1946 and returned. Stricken 21 Feb 1946. BU 1975.
1* Okinawa. Tokyo Bay.

APA 127 *Allendale* Decomm 14 Mar 1946. Stricken 28 Mar 1946. BU 1989 Kaohsiung, Taiwan.
1* Okinawa.

APA 128 *Arenac* Decomm 10 Jul 1946. †
1* Okinawa.

APA 129 *Marvin H. McIntyre* Decomm 6 Jun 1946. Stricken 19 Jun 1946. BU 1973.
1* Okinawa.

APA 130 *Attala* Decomm 26 Feb 1946. Stricken 20 Mar 1946. BU 1974 Castellon, Spain.
1* Iwo Jima.

APA 131 *Bandera* Decomm 7 May 1946. Stricken 21 May 1946. BU 1973 Brownsville, Tex.

APA 132 *Barnwell* Decomm 1 Feb 1947. †

APA 133 *Beckham* Decomm 25 Apr 1946. Stricken 8 May 1946. BU Rotterdam 1974.
2* Iwo Jima, Okinawa.

APA 134 *Bland* Decomm 27 Apr 1946. Stricken 8 May 1946. BU 1973 Brownsville, Tex.

APA 135 *Bosque* Decomm 15 Mar 1946. Stricken 28 Mar 1946. Sold 9 Apr 1973; BU 1973.
1* Okinawa. Tokyo Bay.

APA 136 *Botetourt* Decomm 5 Jun 1946
Tokyo Bay. †

APA 137 *Bowie* Decomm 8 Mar and returned 14 Mar 1946. Sold 9 Apr 1973; BU.
1* Okinawa.

APA 138 *Braxton* Decomm 27 Jun 1946. Stricken 19 Jul 1946. BU 1973.

APA 139 *Broadwater* Decomm 28 Feb 1946. Stricken 20 Mar 1946. BU 1974 Brownsville, Tex.

APA 140 *Brookings* Decomm 25 Jul 1946. †

APA 141 *Buckingham* Decomm 1 Mar 1946. Stricken 20 Mar 1946. BU 1974 Brownsville, Tex.

APA 142 *Clearfield* Decomm 4 Mar 1946. Stricken 1946. BU 1973.
1* Okinawa.

APA 143 *Clermont* Decomm 1 Mar 1946. Stricken 1946. BU 1973.
1* Okinawa. Tokyo Bay.

APA 144 *Clinton* Decomm 2 May 1946. †
1* Okinawa.

APA 145 *Colbert* Struck floating mine off Okinawa, 17 Sep 1945 (3 killed). Decomm 26 Feb 1946 Stricken 1946. BU 1974.
1* Okinawa.

APA 146 *Collingsworth* Decomm 17 Mar 1946. Stricken 28 Mar 1946. BU 1983.

APA 147 *Cottle* Decomm 6 Mar 1946. Stricken 1946. BU 1973.

APA 148 *Crockett* Decomm 15 Oct 1946. †
1* Okinawa.

APA 149 *Audubon* Decomm 19 Feb 1946. Stricken Mar 1946. BU 1973.
1* Okinawa.

APA 150 *Bergen* Decomm 24 Apr 1946. Stricken 8 May 1946. BU 1973.

No.	Name	Builder	Keel Laid	Launched	Comm.
APA 151	*La Porte*	Oregon	15 May 1944	30 Jun 1944	14 Aug 1944
APA 152	*Latimer*	Oregon	19 May 1944	4 Jul 1944	28 Aug 1944
APA 153	*Laurens*	Oregon	23 May 1944	11 Jul 1944	9 Sep 1944
APA 154	*Lowndes*	Oregon	26 May 1944	18 Jul 1944	14 Sep 1944
APA 155	*Lycoming*	Oregon	30 May 1944	25 Jul 1944	20 Sep 1944
APA 156	*Mellette*	Oregon	3 Jun 1944	4 Aug 1944	27 Sep 1944
APA 157	*Napa*	Oregon	7 Jun 1944	12 Aug 1944	1 Oct 1944
APA 158	*Newberry*	Oregon	10 Jun 1944	24 Aug 1944	7 Oct 1944
APA 159	*Darke*	Oregon	14 Jun 1944	29 Aug 1944	10 Oct 1944
APA 160	*Deuel*	Oregon	17 Jun 1944	4 Sep 1944	13 Oct 1944
APA 161	*Dickens*	Oregon	21 Jun 1944	8 Sep 1944	18 Oct 1944
APA 162	*Drew*	Oregon	30 Jun 1944	14 Sep 1944	22 Oct 1944
APA 163	*Eastland*	Oregon	4 Jul 1944	19 Sep 1944	26 Oct 1944
APA 164	*Edgecombe*	Oregon	11 Jul 1944	24 Sep 1944	30 Oct 1944
APA 165	*Effingham*	Oregon	19 Jul 1944	29 Sep 1944	1 Nov 1944
APA 166	*Fond du Lac*	Oregon	25 Jul 1944	5 Oct 1944	6 Nov 1944
APA 167	*Freestone*	Oregon	4 Aug 1944	9 Oct 1944	9 Nov 1944
APA 168	*Gage*	Oregon	13 Aug 1944	14 Oct 1944	12 Nov 1944
APA 169	*Gallatin*	Oregon	24 Aug 1944	17 Oct 1944	15 Nov 1944
APA 170	*Gosper*	Oregon	29 Aug 1944	20 Oct 1944	18 Nov 1944
APA 171	*Granville*	Oregon	4 Sep 1944	23 Oct 1944	21 Nov 1944
APA 172	*Grimes*	Oregon	8 Sep 1944	27 Oct 1944	23 Nov 1944
APA 173	*Hyde*	Oregon	14 Sep 1944	30 Oct 1944	26 Nov 1944
APA 174	*Jerauld*	Oregon	19 Sep 1944	3 Nov 1944	28 Nov 1944
APA 175	*Karnes*	Oregon	24 Sep 1944	7 Nov 1944	3 Dec 1944
APA 176	*Kershaw*	Oregon	29 Sep 1944	12 Nov 1944	2 Dec 1944
APA 177	*Kingsbury*	Oregon	5 Oct 1944	16 Nov 1944	6 Dec 1944
APA 178	*Lander*	Oregon	9 Oct 1944	19 Nov 1944	9 Dec 1944
APA 179	*Lauderdale*	Oregon	14 Oct 1944	23 Nov 1944	12 Dec 1944
APA 180	*Lavaca*	Oregon	17 Oct 1944	27 Nov 1944	17 Dec 1944
APA 181–86	—	Oregon	—	—	—
APA 187	*Oconto*	Kaiser Vanc.	5 Apr 1944	20 Jun 1944	2 Sep 1944
APA 188	*Olmsted*	Kaiser Vanc.	11 Apr 1944	4 Jul 1944	5 Sep 1944
APA 189	*Oxford*	Kaiser Vanc.	17 Apr 1944	12 Jul 1944	11 Sep 1944
APA 190	*Pickens*	Kaiser Vanc.	22 Apr 1944	21 Jul 1944	18 Sep 1944
APA 191	*Pondera*	Kaiser Vanc.	28 Apr 1944	27 Jul 1944	24 Sep 1944
APA 192	*Rutland*	Kaiser Vanc.	4 May 1944	10 Aug 1944	29 Sep 1944
APA 193	*Sanborn*	Kaiser Vanc.	10 May 1944	19 Aug 1944	3 Oct 1944
APA 194	*Sandoval*	Kaiser Vanc.	16 May 1944	2 Sep 1944	7 Oct 1944
APA 195	*Lenawee*	Kaiser Vanc.	22 May 1944	11 Sep 1944	11 Oct 1944

APA 196	*Logan*	Kaiser Vanc.	27 May 1944	19 Sep 1944	14 Oct 1944
APA 197	*Lubbock*	Kaiser Vanc.	2 Jun 1944	25 Sep 1944	18 Oct 1944
APA 198	*McCracken*	Kaiser Vanc.	8 Jun 1944	29 Sep 1944	21 Oct 1944
APA 199	*Magoffin*	Kaiser Vanc.	20 Jun 1944	4 Oct 1944	25 Oct 1944
APA 200	*Marathon*	Kaiser Vanc.	4 Jul 1944	7 Oct 1944	28 Oct 1944
APA 201	*Menard*	Kaiser Vanc.	12 Jul 1944	11 Oct 1944	31 Oct 1944
APA 202	*Menifee*	Kaiser Vanc.	21 Jul 1944	15 Oct 1944	4 Nov 1944
APA 203	*Meriwether*	Kaiser Vanc.	27 Jul 1944	18 Oct 1944	7 Nov 1944

Service Records:

APA 151 *La Porte* Decomm 25 Mar 1946. Stricken 1946. Sold 9 Apr 1973; BU 1974 Brownsville, Tex.
1* Okinawa.

APA 152 *Latimer* Damaged in collision with transport *Clemson*, Lingayen, Luzon, 10 Jan 1945. Decomm 26 Feb 1947.
1* Okinawa.

APA 153 *Laurens* Decomm 10 Apr 1946. Stricken 1946. BU 1988.
2* Lingayen, Okinawa.

APA 154 *Lowndes* Decomm 17 Apr 1946. Stricken 1 May 1946.BU 1983.
2* Iwo Jima, Okinawa.

APA 155 *Lycoming* Decomm 14 Mar 1946. Stricken 1946. BU 1973.
1* Okinawa.

APA 156 *Mellette* Tokyo Bay. Decomm 25 Jun 1946. †
2* Iwo Jima, Okinawa.

APA 157 *Napa* Damaged in collision with APA *Logan*, Iwo Jima, 20 Feb 1945. Decomm 24 May 1946. BU.
1* Iwo Jima.

APA 158 *Newberry* Decomm 21 Feb 1946. Stricken 12 Mar 1946.
2* Iwo Jima, Okinawa.

APA 159 *Darke* Decomm 17 Apr 1946. Stricken 1946. BU 1974 Rotterdam.
2* Iwo Jima, Okinawa. Tokyo Bay.

APA 160 *Deuel* Decomm 17 May 1946. †
2* Iwo Jima, Okinawa. Tokyo Bay.

APA 161 *Dickens* Decomm 21 May 1946. Stricken 1946. BU 1974.
2* Iwo Jima, Okinawa. Tokyo Bay.

APA 162 *Drew* Decomm 10 May 1946. Stricken 1946. BU 1974 Brownsville, Tex.
1* Okinawa.

APA 163 *Eastland* Decomm 15 Apr 1946. Stricken 1946. BU 1974 Brownsville, Tex.
1* Okinawa.

APA 164 *Edgecombe* Decomm 31 Jan 1947. †
1* Okinawa.

APA 165 *Effingham* Decomm 17 May 1946. Stricken 1946. BU 1974.
1* Okinawa.

APA 166 *Fond du Lac* Decomm 11 Apr 1946. Stricken 1946. BU 1974 Burriana, Spain.
1* Okinawa.

APA 167 *Freestone* Decomm 17 Apr 1946. Stricken 1946. BU 1973.
1* Okinawa.

APA 168 *Gage* Decomm 26 Feb 1947. †
1* Okinawa.

APA 169 *Gallatin* Decomm 23 Apr 1946.Stricken 8 Max 1946. BU 1973

APA 170 *Gosper* Evacuation transport. Decomm 10 Apr 1946. Stricken 17 May 1946. BU 1974 Castellon, Spain.
1* Okinawa.

APA 171 *Granville* Decomm 10 May 1946. Stricken 21 May 1946. BU 1974.
1* Okinawa.

APA 172 *Grimes* Decomm 26 Feb 1947. †
1* Iwo Jima.

APA 173 *Hyde* Decomm 14 May 1946. Stricken 5 Jun 1946. BU 1973.
1* Iwo Jima.

APA 174 *Jerauld* Decomm 6 May 1946. Stricken 1946. BU 1974 Burriana, Spain.
1* Okinawa.

APA 175 *Karnes* Decomm 11 Apr 1946. Stricken May 1946. BU 1974 Castellon, Spain.
1* Okinawa.

APA 176 *Kershaw* Decomm 20 Dec 1946. †
1* Okinawa.

APA 177 *Kingsbury* Decomm 19 Apr 1946. Stricken 1 May 1946. BU 1983, Spain.
1* Iwo Jima.

APA 178 *Lander* Decomm 29 Mar 1946. Stricken 1946.
2* Iwo Jima, Okinawa.

APA 179 *Lauderdale* Decomm 25 Apr 1946. Stricken. BU 2005 Sparrows Rt..
1* Okinawa.

APA 180 *Lavaca* Decomm 31 Jan 1947. Tokyo Bay. †

APA 181–86 — Canceled 22 May 1944.

APA 187 *Oconto* Decomm 22 May 1946. Stricken 19 Jun 1946. BU 1974.
1* Okinawa.

APA 188 *Olmsted* Decomm 21 Feb 1947. †
1* Okinawa.

APA 189 *Oxford* Decomm 17 Apr 1946. Stricken 1 May 1946. BU 1974 Rotterdam.
1* Okinawa.

APA 190 *Pickens* Decomm 12 Apr 1946. Stricken 1 May 1946. BU 1974.
1* Iwo Jima, Okinawa.

APA 191 *Pondera* Decomm 6 Jun 1946. Stricken 19 Jun 1946. BU 1974 Brownsville, Tex.
1* Okinawa.

APA 192 *Rutland* Decomm 26 Feb 1947. †
2* Iwo Jima, Okinawa. Tokyo Bay.

APA 193 *Sanborn* Decomm 14 Aug 1946. †
2* Iwo Jima, Okinawa.

APA 194 *Sandoval* Damaged by kamikaze, Okinawa, 27 May 1945 (8 killed). Decomm 19 Jul 1946. †
2* Iwo Jima, Okinawa.

APA 195 *Lenawee* Decomm 3 Aug 1946. †
2* Iwo Jima, Okinawa. Tokyo Bay.

APA 196 *Logan* Damaged in collision with APA *Napa*, Iwo Jima, 20 Feb 1945. Decomm 27 Nov 1946. †
2* Iwo Jima, Okinawa.

APA 197 *Lubbock* Decomm 14 Dec 1946. †
2* Iwo Jima, Okinawa.

APA 198 *McCracken* Decomm 10 Oct 1946. †
1* Okinawa.

APA 199 *Magoffin* Decomm 14 Aug 1946. †
1* Okinawa.

APA 200 *Marathon* Damaged by piloted torpedo (kaiten), Okinawa, 21 Jul 1945. Decomm 8 May 1946. BU 1975.
2* Okinawa, Minesweeping 1945.

APA 201 *Menard* †
1* Okinawa.

APA 202 *Menifee* Decomm 31 Jul 1946. †
1* Okinawa.

APA 203 *Meriwether* Decomm 14 Aug 1946. †
1* Okinawa.

No.	Name	Builder	Keel Laid	Launched	Comm.
APA 204	*Sarasota*	Permanente #2	11 Apr 1944	14 Jun 1944	16 Aug 1944
APA 205	*Sherburne*	Permanente #2	18 May 1944	10 Jul 1944	20 Sep 1944

Figure 11.46: The high-speed transport *Belknap* (APD 34) on 27 Jul 1944 at Charleston Navy Yard. A former flush-deck destroyer previously converted to a seaplane tender. Notice the two funnels and landing craft.

APA 206	*Sibley*	Permanente #2	17 May 1944	19 Jul 1944	2 Oct 1944
APA 207	*Mifflin*	Permanente #2	15 May 1944	7 Aug 1944	11 Oct 1944
APA 208	*Talladega*	Permanente #2	3 Jun 1944	17 Aug 1944	31 Oct 1944
APA 209	*Tazewell*	Permanente #2	2 Jun 1944	22 Aug 1944	25 Oct 1944
APA 210	*Telfair*	Permanente #2	30 May 1944	30 Aug 1944	31 Oct 1944
APA 211	*Missoula*	Permanente #2	20 Jun 1944	6 Sep 1944	27 Oct 1944
APA 212	*Montrose*	Permanente #2	17 Jun 1944	13 Sep 1944	2 Nov 1944
APA 213	*Mountrail*	Permanente #2	3 Jul 1944	20 Sep 1944	16 Nov 1944
APA 214	*Natrona*	Permanente #2	30 Jun 1944	27 Sep 1944	8 Nov 1944
APA 215	*Navarro*	Permanente #2	27 Jun 1944	3 Oct 1944	15 Nov 1944
APA 216	*Neshoba*	Permanente #2	15 Jun 1944	7 Oct 1944	16 Nov 1944
APA 217	*New Kent*	Permanente #2	11 Jul 1944	12 Oct 1944	22 Nov 1944
APA 218	*Noble*	Permanente #2	20 Jul 1944	18 Oct 1944	27 Nov 1944
APA 219	*Okaloosa*	Permanente #2	8 Aug 1944	22 Oct 1944	28 Nov 1944
APA 220	*Okanogan*	Permanente #2	19 Aug 1944	26 Oct 1944	3 Dec 1944
APA 221	*Oneida*	Permanente #2	24 Aug 1944	31 Oct 1944	4 Dec 1944
APA 222	*Pickaway*	Permanente #2	1 Sep 1944	5 Nov 1944	12 Dec 1944
APA 223	*Pitt*	Permanente #2	8 Sep 1944	10 Nov 1944	11 Dec 1944
APA 224	*Randall*	Permanente #2	15 Sep 1944	15 Nov 1944	16 Dec 1944
APA 225	*Bingham*	Permanente #2	22 Sep 1944	20 Nov 1944	23 Dec 1944
APA 226	*Rawlins*	Kaiser Vanc.	10 Aug 1944	21 Oct 1944	11 Nov 1944
APA 227	*Renville*	Kaiser Vanc.	19 Aug 1944	25 Oct 1944	15 Nov 1944
APA 228	*Rockbridge*	Kaiser Vanc.	2 Sep 1944	28 Oct 1944	18 Nov 1944
APA 229	*Rockingham*	Kaiser Vanc.	11 Sep 1944	1 Nov 1944	22 Nov 1944
APA 230	*Rockwall*	Kaiser Vanc.	19 Sep 1944	5 Nov 1944	14 Jan 1945
APA 231	*Saint Croix*	Kaiser Vanc.	25 Sep 1944	9 Nov 1944	1 Dec 1944
APA 232	*San Saba*	Kaiser Vanc.	29 Sep 1944	12 Nov 1944	3 Dec 1944
APA 233	*Sevier*	Kaiser Vanc.	4 Oct 1944	16 Nov 1944	5 Dec 1944
APA 234	*Bollinger*	Kaiser Vanc.	7 Oct 1944	19 Nov 1944	9 Dec 1944
APA 235	*Bottineau*	Kaiser Vanc.	11 Oct 1944	22 Nov 1944	30 Dec 1944
APA 236	*Bronx*	Oregon	22 May 1945	14 Jul 1945	27 Aug 1945
APA 237	*Bexar*	Oregon	2 Jun 1945	25 Jul 1945	9 Oct 1945
APA 238	*Dane*	Oregon	18 Jun 1945	9 Aug 1945	29 Oct 1945
APA 239	*Glynn*	Oregon	30 Jun 1945	25 Aug 1945	17 Oct 1945
APA 240	*Harnett*	Oregon	Jul 1945	—	—
APA 241	*Hempstead*	Oregon	Jul 1945	—	—
APA 242	*Iredell*	Oregon	11 Aug 1945	—	—
APA 243	*Luzerne*	Oregon	—	—	—
APA 244	*Madera*	Oregon	—	—	—
APA 245	*Maricopa*	Oregon	—	—	—
APA 246	*McLennan*	Oregon	—	—	—
APA 247	*Mecklenburg*	Oregon	—	—	—

Service Records:

APA 204 *Sarasota* Decomm 1 Aug 1946. †
3* Lingayen, Okinawa, Subic Bay.

APA 205 *Sherburne* Decomm 3 Aug 1946. †
1* Okinawa. Tokyo Bay.

APA 206 *Sibley* Decomm 27 Nov 1946. †
2* Iwo Jima, Okinawa.

APA 207 *Mifflin* Decomm 5 Jul 1946. †
2* Iwo Jima, Okinawa.

APA 208 *Talladega* Decomm 27 Dec 1946. †
2* Iwo Jima, Okinawa. Tokyo Bay.

APA 209 *Tazewell* Decomm 27 Dec 1946. †
1* Okinawa.

APA 210 *Telfair* Damaged by kamikaze, Okinawa, 2 Apr 1945 (1 killed). Decomm 20 Jul 1946. †
1* Okinawa.

APA 211 *Missoula* Decomm 13 Sep 1946. †
1* Iwo Jima, Okinawa. Tokyo Bay.

APA 212 *Montrose* Decomm 26 Oct 1946. †
1* Okinawa.

APA 213 *Mountrail* Decomm 12 Jul 1946. †
1* Okinawa.

APA 214 *Natrona* Decomm 29 Jul 1946. †
1* Okinawa.

APA 215 *Navarro* Decomm 15 Mar 1946. †
1* Okinawa.

APA 216 *Neshoba* Decomm 4 Dec 1946. †
1* Okinawa.

APA 217 *New Kent* †
1* Okinawa.

APA 218 *Noble* †
1* Okinawa.

APA 219 *Okaloosa* †
1* Okinawa.

APA 220 *Okanogan* †
1* Okinawa.
APA 221 *Oneida* Decomm 27 Dec 1946. †
1* Okinawa.
APA 222 *Pickaway* †
1* Iwo Jima. Operation Crossroads.
APA 223 *Pitt* Decomm 9 Apr 1947. Stricken 23 Apr 1947. BU.
1* Okinawa. BU.
APA 224 *Randall* †
APA 225 *Bingham* Decomm 17 Jun and returned 18 Jun 1946. †
1* Okinawa.
APA 226 *Rawlins* Decomm 15 Nov 1946. †
1* Okinawa.
APA 227 *Renville* Operation Crossroads. HQ ship, UN Truce Committee at Batavia, Netherlands East Indies, Dec 1947. †
1* Okinawa.
APA 228 *Rockbridge* Operation Crossroads. Decomm 8 Mar 1947. †
1* Iwo Jima.
APA 229 *Rockingham* Operation Crossroads. Decomm 17 Mar 1947. †
1* Okinawa.
APA 230 *Rockwall* Operation Crossroads. Decomm 15 Mar 1947. †
1* Okinawa.
APA 231 *Saint Croix* Operation Crossroads. Decomm 7 Apr 1947. Stricken 23 Apr 1947. BU 1979.
APA 232 *San Saba* Decomm 17 Dec 1946. †
APA 233 *Sevier* Decomm 30 Apr 1947. Stricken 23 Jun 1947. BU 1980.
2* Iwo Jima, Okinawa.
APA 234 *Bollinger* Decomm 1 Apr 1947. †
1* Iwo Jima.
APA 235 *Bottineau* Operation Crossroads. Decomm 8 Mar 1947. †
1* Okinawa.
APA 236 *Bronx* †
APA 237 *Bexar* Operation Crossroads. †
APA 238 *Dane* Decomm 20 Dec 1946. †
APA 239 *Glynn* Decomm 12 Dec 1946. †
APA 240 *Harnett* Canceled 27 Aug 1945.
APA 241 *Hempstead* Canceled 27 Aug 1945.
APA 242 *Iredell* Canceled 27 Aug 1945.
Later history: Completed as *Alcoa Corsair*, renamed *Rye* 1963. BU 1963.
APA 243–47 Canceled 27 Aug 1945.

HIGH-SPEED TRANSPORTS

High speed transports were converted destroyers or destroyer escorts able to carry small units and landing craft for amphibious operations.

Ex-Destroyers

Figure 11.47: *Lloyd* (APD 63), 15 Sep 1944, as completed after conversion, in bright dazzle camouflage.

No.	Name	Formerly	Rec	Notes
APD 1	*Manley*	DD 74	2 Aug 1940	Rec **DD 74**, 25 Jun 1945.
APD 2	*Colhoun*	DD 85	2 Aug 1940	Sunk by Japanese aircraft off Guadalcanal, 30 Aug 1942.
APD 3	*Gregory*	DD 82	2 Aug 1940	Sunk by Japanese warships off Lunga Point, Guadalcanal, 5 Sep 1942.
APD 4	*Little*	DD 79	2 Aug 1940	Sunk by Japanese warships off Lunga Point, Guadalcanal, 5 Sep 1942.
APD 5	*McKean*	DD 90	2 Aug 1940	Torpedoed and sunk by Japanese aircraft off Bougainville, 17 Nov 1943.
APD 6	*Stringham*	DD 83	2 Aug 1940	Rec **DD 83**, 25 Jun 1945
APD 7	*Talbot*	DD 114	31 Oct 1942	Rec **DD 114**, 16 Jul 1945.
APD 8	*Waters*	DD 115	31 Oct 1942	Rec **DD 115**, 2 Aug 1945.
APD 9	*Dent*	DD 116	31 Oct 1942	
APD 10	*Brooks*	DD 232	1 Dec 1942	
APD 11	*Gilmer*	DD 233	22 Jan 1943	
APD 12	*Humphreys*	DD 236	1 Dec 1942	Rec **DD 236**, 20 Jul 1945.
APD 13	*Sands*	DD 243	30 Oct 1942	
APD 14	*Schley*	DD 103	2 Jan 1943	Rec **DD 103**, 5 Jul 1945
APD 15	*Kilty*	DD 137	2 Jan 1943	Rec **DD 137**, 20 Jul 1945.
APD 16	*Ward*	DD 139	2 Jan 1943	Sunk by Japanese aircraft off Ormoc, Leyte, 7 Dec 1944.
APD 17	*Crosby*	DD 164	2 Jan 1943	
APD 18	*Kane*	DD 235	2 Jan 1943	
APD 19	*Tattnall*	DD 125	24 Jul 1943	
APD 20	*Roper*	DD 147	20 Oct 1943	
APD 21	*Dickerson*	DD 157	21 Aug 1943	Damaged by kamikaze off Okinawa, 2 Apr and sunk 21 Apr 1945 (54 killed).
APD 22	*Herbert*	DD 160	1 Dec 1943	
APD 23	*Overton*	DD 239	21 Aug 1943	
APD 24	*Noa*	DD 343	10 Aug 1943	Sunk in collision with destroyer *Fullam* off New Guinea, 12 Sep 1944.
APD 25	*Rathburne*	DD 113	20 May 1944	Rec **DD 113**, 10 Jul 1945.
APD 26	*McFarland*	DD 237		Conversion canceled
APD 27	*Williamson*	DD 244		Conversion canceled
APD 28	*Hulbert*	DD 342		Conversion canceled

No.	Name	Formerly	Rec	Notes
APD 29	*Barry*	DD 248	15 Jan 1944	Damaged by kamikaze, Okinawa, 24 May 1945. Decomm 21 Jun 1945 and sunk by kamikaze while in tow as a decoy.
APD 30	*Decatur*	DD 342		Conversion canceled
APD 31	*Clemson*	DD 186	7 Mar 1944	Rec **DD 186**, 17 Jul 1945.
APD 32	*Goldsborough*	DD 188	7 Mar 1944	Rec **DD 188**, 10 Jul 1945
APD 33	*George E. Badger*	DD 196	10 Apr 1944	Rec **DD 196**, 20 Jul 1945
APD 34	*Belknap*	DD 251	22 Jun 1944	
APD 35	*Osmond Ingram*	DD 255	22 Jun 1944	
APD 36	*Greene*	DD 266	1 Feb 1944	Went aground in typhoon at Okinawa and lost, 9 Oct 1945.

Notes: Former flush-deck destroyers. Forward boilers and funnels, TT and one gun removed. Able to carry a Marine rifle company and four assault boats. Conversion of AVD 1, 7, DD 210, 221, 246, 341 canceled. Armament: 3–3"/50, 2–40mm, 5–20mm guns.

Ex–Destroyer Escorts

No.	Name	Formerly	Rec	Notes
APD 37	*Charles Lawrence*	DE 53	23 Oct 1944	
APD 38	*Daniel T. Griffin*	DE 54	23 Oct 1944	
APD 39	*Barr*	DE 576	31 Jul 1944	
APD 40	*Bowers*	DE 637	25 Jun 1945	
APD 41	*England*	DE 635	10 Jul 1945	Conversion canceled
APD 42	*Gantner*	DE 60	23 Feb 1945	
APD 43	*George W. Ingram*	DE 62	23 Feb 1945	
APD 44	*Ira Jeffery*	DE 63	23 Feb 1945	
APD 45	*Lee Fox*	DE 65	31 Jul 1944	
APD 46	*Amesbury*	DE 66	31 Jul 1944	
APD 47	*Bates*	DE 68	31 Jul 1944	Sunk by kamikazes and bomb off Okinawa, 25 May 1945 (21 killed).
APD 48	*Blessman*	DE 69	31 Jul 1944	
APD 49	*Joseph E. Campbell*	DE 70	24 Nov 1944	
APD 50	*Sims*	DE 154	25 Sep 1944	
APD 51	*Hopping*	DE 155	25 Sep 1944	
APD 52	*Reeves*	DE 156	25 Sep 1944	
APD 53	*Hubbard*	DE 211	1 Jun 1945	
APD 54	*Chase*	DE 158	28 Nov 1944	
APD 55	*Laning*	DE 159	28 Nov 1944	
APD 56	*Loy*	DE 160	23 Oct 1944	
APD 57	*Barber*	DE 161	23 Oct 1944	
APD 58	*Witter*	DE 636		Conversion canceled 15 Aug 1945.
APD 59	*Newman*	DE 205	5 Jul 1944	
APD 60	*Liddle*	DE 206	5 Jul 1944	
APD 61	*Kephart*	DE 207	5 Jul 1944	
APD 62	*Cofer*	DE 208	5 Jul 1944	
APD 63	*Lloyd*	DE 209	5 Jul 1944	
APD 64	*Scott*	DE 214		Conversion canceled 10 Sep 1945.
APD 65	*Burke*	DE 215	24 Jan 1945	
APD 66	*Enright*	DE 216	24 Jan 1945	
APD 67	*Jenks*	DE 665		Conversion canceled.
APD 68	*Durik*	DE 666		Conversion canceled.
APD 75	*Weber*	DE 675	15 Dec 1944	
APD 76	*Schmitt*	DE 676	24 Jan 1945	
APD 77	*Frament*	DE 677	15 Dec 1944	
APD 78	*Bull*	DE 693	31 Jul 1944	
APD 79	*Bunch*	DE 694	31 Jul 1944	
APD 80	*Hayter*	DE 212	1 Jun 1945	
APD 81	*Tatum*	DE 789	15 Dec 1944	
APD 82	*Borum*	DE 790		Conversion canceled.
APD 83	*Maloy*	DE 791		Conversion canceled.
APD 84	*Haines*	DE 792	15 Dec 1944	
APD 85	*Runels*	DE 793	24 Jan 1945	
APD 86	*Hollis*	DE 794	24 Jan 1945	
APD 137	*De Long*	DE 684		Conversion canceled 10 Sep 1945.
APD 138	*Coates*	DE 685		Conversion canceled 10 Sep 1945
APD 139	*Bray*	DE 709	16 Jul 1945	

Notes: Fifty type TE destroyer escorts converted, including six under construction (DE 668–73). Conversion of DE 214, 665, 666, 790, and 791 canceled. Armament: 1 5"/38, 3 twin 40mm, 6–20mm guns. Carried 162 troops.

Figure. 11.48: *APc-15*, a coastal transport, with wood hull.

Completed as Transports

No.	Name	Formerly
APD 69	*Yokes*	DE 668
APD 70	*Pavlic*	DE 669

APD 71	*Odum*	DE 670
APD 72	*Jack C. Robinson*	DE 671
APD 73	*Bassett*	DE 672
APD 74	*John P. Gray*	DE 673
APD 87	*Crosley*	DE 226
APD 88	*Cread*	DE 227
APD 89	*Ruchamkin*	DE 228
APD 90	*Kirwin*	DE 229
APD 91	*Kinzer*	DE 232
APD 92	*Register*	DE 233
APD 93	*Brock*	DE 234
APD 94	*John Q. Roberts*	DE 235
APD 95	*William M. Hobby*	DE 236
APD 96	*Ray K. Edwards*	DE 237
APD 97	*Arthur L. Bristol*	DE 281
APD 98	*Truxtun*	DE 282
APD 99	*Upham*	DE 283
APD 100	*Ringness*	DE 590
APD 101	*Knudson*	DE 591
APD 102	*Rednour*	DE 592
APD 103	*Tollberg*	DE 593
APD 104	*William J. Pattison*	DE 594
APD 105	*Myers*	DE 595
APD 106	*Walter B. Cobb*	DE 596
APD 107	*Earle B. Hall*	DE 597
APD 108	*Harry L. Corl*	DE 598
APD 109	*Belet*	DE 599
APD 110	*Julius A. Raven*	DE 600
APD 111	*Walsh*	DE 601
APD 112	*Hunter Marshall*	DE 602
APD 113	*Earhart*	DE 603
APD 114	*Walter S. Gorka*	DE 604
APD 115	*Rogers Blood*	DE 605
APD 116	*Francovich*	DE 606
APD 117	*Joseph M. Auman*	DE 674
APD 118	*Don O. Woods*	DE 721
APD 119	*Beverly W. Reid*	DE 722
APD 120	*Kline*	DE 687
APD 121	*Raymon W. Herndon*	DE 688
APD 122	*Scribner*	DE 689
APD 123	*Diachenko*	DE 690
APD 124	*Horace A. Bass*	DE 691
APD 125	*Wantuck*	DE 692
APD 126	*Gosselin*	DE 710
APD 127	*Begor*	DE 711
APD 128	*Cavallaro*	DE 712
APD 129	*Donald W. Wolf*	DE 713
APD 130	*Cook*	DE 714
APD 131	*Walter X. Young*	DE 715
APD 132	*Balduck*	DE 716
APD 133	*Burdo*	DE 717
APD 134	*Kleinsmith*	DE 718
APD 135	*Weiss*	DE 719
APD 136	*Carpellotti*	DE 720

COASTAL TRANSPORTS

No.
APc 1–115

Displacement	100 tons; 258 tons f/l
Dimensions	103'3" (oa); 98'2" (wl) x 21'3" x 9'3"
Machinery	1 screw; diesel; SHP 400; 10 knots
Complement	25; capacity: 66 troops
Armament	2–20mm

Notes: Ex–AMc 150–99. Thirty (APc 51–79, APc 97) transferred to the United Kingdom, renamed *FT 1–30*; APc 85 transferred to Ecuador. APc 84–89, 99–100, 104–7, 112, 115 canceled 3 Oct 1942.

War Losses:

APc 2 Damaged by dive bomber southwest of Arawe, New Britain, 21 Dec 1943.

APc 15 Damaged by dive bomber southwest of Arawe, New Britain, 27 Dec 1943.

EVACUATION TRANSPORTS

No.	Name	Builder	Keel Laid	Launched	Comm.
APH 1	*Tryon*	Moore	26 Mar 1941	21 Oct 1941	30 Sep 1942
	ex–*Comfort* (13 Aug 1942), ex–*Alcoa Courier*				
APH 2	*Pinkney*	Moore	3 Jun 1941	4 Dec 1941	27 Nov 1942
	ex–*Mercy* (13 Aug 1942), ex–*Alcoa Corsair*				
APH 3	*Rixey*	Moore	6 Aug 1941	30 Dec 1941	30 Dec 1942
	ex–*Hope* (13 Aug 1942), ex–*Alcoa Cruiser*				

Displacement	7,100 tons; 9,920 tons f/l
Dimensions	450' (oa); 420' (wl) x 62' x 23'6"
Machinery	1 screw; GE GT; 2 FW boilers; SHP 8,500; 18.2 knots
Complement	450; capacity 1,166 troops
Armament	1–5"/38, 4 twin 40mm, 6 twin 20mm AA guns

Notes: Type C2–S1–A1. Ordered for Alcoa Line, but requisitioned after launching. Designed to carry troops and then evacuate the wounded.

Service Records:

APH 1 *Tryon* Decomm 20 Mar 1946. Stricken 17 Apr 1946. To Army, 17 Jul 1946 renamed USAT *Sgt. Charles E. Mower.* †
6* Palau, Lingayen, Solomons, Saidor, Tinian, Leyte.

Figure 11.49: USS *Rixey* (APH 3), 12 Feb 1943, a transport fitted for the evacuation of wounded at San Francisco. These ships were not hospital ships and carried armament.

Figure 11.50: *Nueces* (APB 40), 4 Jan 1946, a barracks ship built on an LST-type hull.

APH 2 *Pinkney* Damaged by kamikaze, Okinawa, 28 Apr 1945 (32 killed). To Army, 9 Sep 1946 renamed USAT *Pvt. Elden H. Johnson.* †
4* Palau, Lingayen, Iwo Jima, Okinawa.

APH 3 *Rixey* Decomm 27 Mar 1946. To Army, 10 Sep 1946 as USAT *Pvt. William H. Thomas.* †
4* New Georgia, Guam, Leyte, Okinawa.

BARRACKS SHIPS

No.	Name	Builder	Launched	Acquired	In service
APL 1	*Edmund B. Alexander*	Harland	20 Apr 1905	1940	Jan 1941
	ex–*America* (Dec 1940), ex–*Amerika* (1917)				

Displacement	21,329 GRT
Dimensions	687' (oa); x 74' x 33'5"
Machinery	2 screws; VQE; SHP 11,000; 10 knots
Complement	(U)
Armament	(U)

Notes: Served with Navy in World War I and as a passenger liner for U.S. Lines. Barracks ship at St. Johns, Newfoundland. Returned to Army late 1941. Reboilered and converted to oil fuel, single funnel, 1942–43. Laid up 1949. BU 1957 Baltimore.

No.	Name	Builder	Keel Laid	Launched	Comm.
APB 35	*Benewah*	Boston NYd	2 Jan 1945	6 May 1945	19 Mar 1946
APB 36	*Colleton*	Boston NYd	9 Jun 1945	30 Jul 1945	27 Sep 1946
APB 37	*Echols*	Boston NYd	9 Jun 1945	30 Jul 1945	30 Dec 1947
APB 38	*Marlboro*	Boston NYd	25 Aug 1944	17 Nov 1944	18 Aug 1945
APB 39	*Mercer*	Boston NYd	25 Aug 1944	17 Nov 1944	19 Sep 1945
APB 40	*Nueces*	Boston NYd	2 Jan 1945	6 May 1945	30 Nov 1945

Displacement	4,080 tons f/l
Dimensions	328' (oa); 316' (wl) x 50' x 11'2"
Machinery	2 screws; diesels; SHP 1,600; 10 knots
Complement	141; capacity: 1,226 troops
Armament	2 quad 40mm, 8 or 12–20mm AA

Notes: LST–type hulls. APL rec APB, 8 Aug 1944.

Missing numbers were unnamed non-powered barges designated APL.

Figure 11.51: *Hammondsport* (APV 2), the former *Seatrain Havana*, a train ferry that operated between Havana and Florida.

Service Records:

APB 35 *Benewah* Decomm 30 Aug 1946. †

APB 36 *Colleton* No service, laid up. †

APB 37 *Echols* †

APB 38 *Marlboro* Decomm 30 Jan 1947. †

APB 39 *Mercer* Decomm 18 Jun 1947. †

APB 40 *Nueces* †

No.	Name	Formerly	Rec	Notes
APB 41	*Wythe*	LST 575	31 Mar 1945	Decomm 29 May 1947 †.
APB 42	*Yavapai*	LST 676	1 May 1945	Decomm 3 Dec 1946. †
APB 43	*Yolo*	LST 677	31 Mar 1945	Decomm 9 Aug 1946. †
APB 44	*Presque Isle*	LST 678	31 Mar 1945	Operation Crossroads. Decomm 18 Apr 1947. †
APB 45	*Blackford*	LST 1111	6 Mar 1945	Decomm 26 Apr 1947. †
APB 46	*Dorchester*	LST 1112	6 Mar 1945	Decomm 16 Oct 1946. †
APB 47	*Kingman*	LST 1113	6 Mar 1945	Decomm 15 Jan 1947. †
APB 48	*Vanderburgh*	LST 1114	6 Mar 1945	Decomm 30 Jan 1947. †
APB 49	*Accomac*	LST 710	1 Aug 1945	Decomm 9 Aug 1946. †
APB 50	*Cameron*	LST 928	1 Aug 1945	Decomm 13 Dec 1946. †

MECHANIZED ARTILLERY TRANSPORTS

No.	Name		Date
APM 1–8	—	Rec LSD 1–8	1 Jul 1942
APM 9	*Lakehurst*	Ex–APV 3	3 Dec 1942
APM 10–18	—	Canceled	24 Aug 1942
BAPM 1–7	—	Rec LSD 9–15	1 Jul 1942

RESCUE TRANSPORTS

No.	Name
APR 1	*Adair*
APR 2	*Berkshire*
APR 3	*Burleigh*
APR 4	*Cecil*
APR 5	*Dutchess*
APR 6	*Lorain*
APR 7	*Douglas*
APR 8	*Mendocino*
APR 9	*Montour*
APR 10	*Napa*
APR 11	*Westmoreland*

Note: All canceled 12 Mar 1943.

TRANSPORTS AND AIRCRAFT FERRIES

No.	Name	Builder	Launched	Acquired	Comm.
APV 1	*Kitty Hawk*	Sun	14 Sep 1932	25 Jun 1941	26 Nov 1941
	ex–*Seatrain New York* (1941)				
APV 2	*Hammondsport*	Sun	26 Sep 1932	2 Jul 1941	11 Dec 1941
	ex–*Seatrain Havana* (1941)				
APV 3	*Lakehurst*	Sun	26 Mar 1940	13 Oct 1942	13 Oct 1942
	ex–*Seatrain New Jersey* (1942)				

Displacement	8,061 grt; APV 1–2: 10,900 tons; 16,480 f/l
Dimensions	478' (oa); 460'6" (wl) x 63'6" x 26'3" (APV 3: 483' oa)
Machinery	1 screw; DeLaval GT; 3 B&W boilers; SHP 8,000; 16 knots
Complement	255
Armament	1–5"/38, 4– 3"/50, 2 twin 40mm, 8 twin 20mm, 16–20mm AA guns

Notes: Seatrain Lines. Converted by Tietjen and Lang, Hoboken, N.J. These railroad car ferries could also carry fully assembled aircraft in their large open holds.

Service Records:

APV 1 *Kitty Hawk* Rec **AKV 1**, 15 Sep 1943. Decomm 24 Jan 1946 and returned.
Later history: Merchant *Seatrain New York* 1947. BU 1973 Kaohsiung, Taiwan.

APV 2 *Hammondsport* Rec **AKV 2**, 15 Sep 1943. Decomm 7 Mar 1946 and returned.
Later history: Merchant *Seatrain Havana* 1947, renamed *Seatrain Savannah* 1957. BU 1973 Kaohsiung, Taiwan.

APV 3 *Lakehurst* In collision with cargo ship *Titania* at Safi, Morocco, 11 Nov 1942. Rec **APM 9**, 3 Dec 1942. Decomm, to Army 2 Aug 1943.
1* North Africa.
Later history: USAT *Lakehurst*. Merchant *Seatrain New Jersey* 1946. BU 1973 Castellon, Spain.

APV 4 *Lafayette* See AP 53

12
TUGS

OCEAN TUGS

The U.S. Navy operated tugs for service in Navy yards and fleet bases. The AT series was divided into three groups on 15 May 1944 ATF (fleet), ATO (old), and ATA (auxiliary). The unnamed rescue tugs (ATR) were a separate series. Tugs were given American Indian names—either tribes or great chiefs.

Fleet Tugs on the Navy List, 1922

AT 10 *Patapsco* Decomm 16 Jan 1925. Stricken 4 Mar 1936, sold 18 Jun 1936.
Later history: Merchant *Patapsco* 1936. BU 1953 Baltimore.

AT 11 *Patuxent* Decomm 30 Sep 1924. Loan to Bureau of Fisheries, 17 Dec 1935.
Later history: Renamed fisheries steamer *Albatross II,* 1935. Stricken 19 Jun 1938, sold 16 Mar 1939.

AT 12 *Sonoma* Sunk by kamikaze in San Pedro Bay, Leyte, 24 Oct 1944.
5* Lae Ldgs., Finschhafen, Cape Gloucester, Saidor, Admiralty Is., Hollandia, Wakde, Biak, Noemfoor I., Morotai, Leyte.

Figure 12.1: *Sciota* (AT 30), 12 Feb 1928; one of a class of 19 tugs built for the Navy in 1918. Notice seaplane hoisted on stern.

AT 13 *Ontario* Samoa 1920–41. Decomm 3 Jun 1946. Stricken 19 Jun 1946, sold 4 Apr 1947.
1* Pearl Harbor.

AT 14 *Arapaho* Decomm 6 Apr 1922. Rec **YT 121**, 31 Jan 1936. Stricken 22 Dec 1936, sold 5 May 1937.
Later history: Merchant *James E. Hughes* 1937.

AT 15 *Mohave* Ran aground near Nantasket, Mass., 13 Feb 1928. Hulk sold, 10 Apr 1928.

AT 16 *Tillamook* Mare I. NYd. Rec **YT 122**, 31 Jan 1936. Sold 28 Sep 1947.
Later history: Merchant *Tillamook* 1948. FFU.

AT 17 *Wando* Out of comm 18 Apr 1922–15 Mar 1933. Rec **YT 123**, 31 Jan 1936. Decomm 3 Jul 1946. Stricken 30 Dec 1946. Sold 5 May 1947.
Later history: Merchant *Wando* 1948. FFU.

AT 18 *Chemung* Annapolis 1921–26. Decomm 25 Oct 1926. Rec **YT 124**, 31 Jan 1936. Sold 12 Feb 1937.
Later history: Merchant *Peter C. Gallagher* 1937.

AT 19 *Allegheny* Sank at Pensacola, Florida, after being struck by propeller of USS *Orion*, 5 Jul 1922, salvaged. Decomm 10 Jul 1946. Stricken 25 Sep 1946. FFU.

AT 20 *Sagamore* Decomm 31 Aug 1946. Stricken 28 Jan 1947, sold 24 Dec 1947.
Later history: Merchant *John E. McAllister* 1948.

AT 21 *Bagaduce* Out of comm 20 Apr 1932–22 Jun 1938. Decomm 22 Jun 1946. Sold 9 Jan 1947. FFU.

AT 22 *Tadousac* Decomm 18 Oct 1924. Stricken 13 Apr 1938, sold 29 Dec 1938.
Later history: Merchant *Falcon* 1939. Reacq as **YP 515**, 1943.

AT 23 *Kalmia* Decomm 15 May 1946. Stricken 3 Jul 1946, sold 21 Jan 1947. FFU.

AT 24 *Kewaydin* Decomm 10 Dec 1945. Sold 23 Dec 1946. FFU.
1* Normandy.

AT 25 *Umpqua* Decomm 24 May 1946. Stricken 3 Jul 1946. FFU.

AT 26 *Wandank* Decomm 20 Sep 1946. Stricken 13 Nov 1946 and sold.
Later history: Merchant *W. A. Bisso,* se 1971.

AT 27 *Tatnuck* Alaska 1920–46. Decomm 12 Sep 1946. Stricken 29 Oct 1946. FFU.

AT 28 *Sunnadin* Pearl Harbor 1920 West 45. Decomm 4 Apr 1946. Stricken 8 May 1946, sold 15 Jan 1947. FFU.
1* Pearl Harbor.

AT 29 *Mahopac* 12th and 13th ND. Decomm 12 Sep 1946. Stricken. Oct 1946, sold 5 May 1947. FFU.

AT 30 *Sciota* Decomm 8 May 1946. Sold 15 Oct 1946. FFU.
AT 31 *Koka* Ran aground off San Clemente I, Calif., 7 Dec 1937. Stricken 2 Mar 1938.
AT 32 *Napa* Guam 1919–29. Out of comm 7 Jun 1929–15 Aug 1939. Scuttled off Bataan, 8 Apr 1942.
1* Philippines 1942.
AT 33 *Pinola* Out of comm 9 Jun 1922–14 Aug 1923. Decomm 31 Jan 1946. Stricken 26 Feb 1946, sold 16 Nov 1947. FFU
AT 34 *Algorma* Out of comm 3 May 1922–29 Sep 1924. Decomm 18 Jun 1946. Stricken 31 Jul 1946. FFU.
1* Normandy.
AT 35 *Carrabasset* Decomm 27 Mar 1922. To USCG, 24 May 1924.
Later history: Renamed USCGC *Carrabasset*, WYT 55. Stricken 26 Jul 1946.
AT 36 *Contocook* Decomm 27 Nov 1933. Stricken 28 Nov 1933, sold 8 Feb 1934.
Later history: Merchant *Sea Giant* 1934. In RN 1940–45.
AT 37 *Iuka* Out of comm 20 Jul 1932–23 Nov 1940. Decomm 15 Apr 1947. Sold 8 Jul 1948.
Later history: Merchant *Iuka* 1948. FFU.
AT 38 *Keosanqua* Out of comm 8 Jun 1922–1 Jul 1934. Decomm 6 May 1946. Stricken 7 Feb 1947, sold 15 Jul 1947.
1* Pearl Harbor.
Later history: Merchant *Edward J. Coyle* 1947, renamed *Commodore Straits* 1960. BU 1968 Vancouver.
AT 39 *Montcalm* Out of comm 30 Jun 1932–13 Aug 1935. Guantanamo 1939–46. Decomm 24 May 1946. Stricken 13 Jun 1946, sold 12 Feb 1947; BU.
AT 46 *Iroquois* Decomm 7 Mar 1925. Stricken 14 Oct 1927, sold 15 May 1928. FFU.
AT 49 *Piscataqua* Decomm 10 Apr 1922. Stricken 4 Aug 1930, sold 7 Jan 1931 at Manila.
Later history: Cut down to barge. Lost off Mindanao, Dec 1941.
AT 52 *Navajo* Pearl Harbor NYd. Stricken 24 Apr 1937, reinstated. Rec **IX** 56, 14 Jan 1942. Stricken 9 Feb 1946, sold 23 Nov 1948; BU.
AT 53 *Delaware* Ex-SP 467. Rec **YT 111**, 1 Jul 1921. Stricken 15 Feb 1934; sold 9 Apr 1935. FFU.
AT 55 *Genesee* Ex-SP 1116. Far East 1920–42. Scuttled off Corregidor, 5 May 1942.
1* Philippines 1942.
AT 56 *Lykens* Ex-SP 876. Decomm 9 Dec 1922. Stricken 21 Nov 1933; sold 3 Feb 1934; BU Philadelphia.
AT 58 *Undaunted* Ex-SP 1950. Rec **YT 125**, 27 Feb 1936. Rec **AT 58,** 16 Jul 1940. Decomm 1 Jul 1946. Stricken 25 Sep 1946, sold 19 Mar 1947. FFU.
AT 59 *Challenge* Ex-SP 1015. Out of comm 13 May 1922–21 Feb 1925. Rec **AT 59**, 21 Feb 1925. To **YT 126**, 31 Jan 1936. Sold 16 Oct 1946.
AT 60 *Bay Spring* Key West 1922–26. Decomm 23 Nov 1926. Rec **YNg 19** and converted to NSP gate vessel, 7 Oct 1940. In service 4th ND, 31 Jan 1941. Stricken 16 Sep 1944.
Later history: Merchant *Bay Spring*, 1946. BU 1958.
AT 61 *Cahokia* Acq from USCG, 14 May 1936. Rec **YT 135**, 1 Jan 1938. **YTB**. To USMC 8 Aug 1947.
AT 62 *Tamaroa* Acq from USCG, 14 May 1936. Rec **YT 136**, 1 Jan 1938. **YTB**. Sunk in collision with AVS *Jupiter* in San Francisco Bay, 27 Jan 1946.

Note: Surviving tugs reclassified **ATO**, 15 May 1944. Armament, World War II, AT 12–13, 19–39: 4–20mm AA guns.

No.	Name	Builder	Launched	Acquired	Comm.
AT 63	*Acushnet*	Newport News	16 May 1908	30 May 1936	1 Sep 1936

Displacement	860 tons
Dimensions	152' (oa) 145' (wl) x 29' x 13'9"
Machinery	1 screw, VTE, 2 B&W boilers; SHP 1,033; 11 knots
Complement	61
Armament	4–20mm.

Note: Acquired from USCG.

Service Record:

ATO 63 *Acushnet* Decomm 14 Dec 1945. Stricken 8 Jan 1946. Sold, BU.

No.	Name	Builder	Launched	Acquired	Comm.
AT 64	*Navajo*	Beth. Staten I.	12 Dec 1938	17 Aug 1939	26 Jan 1940
AT 65	*Seminole*	Beth. Staten I.	16 Dec 1938	15 Sep 1939	8 Mar 1940
ATF 66	*Cherokee*	Beth. Staten I.	23 Dec 1938	10 Nov 1939	26 Apr 1940
ATF 67	*Apache*	Charleston Sbdg	8 Nov 1941	6 May 1942	12 Dec 1942
ATF 68	*Arapaho*	Charleston Sbdg	8 Nov 1941	22 Jun 1942	20 Jan 1943
	ex-*Arapahoe* (5 Aug 1941)				
ATF 69	*Chippewa*	Charleston Sbdg	28 Jan 1942	25 Jul 1942	14 Feb 1943
ATF 70	*Choctaw*	Charleston Sbdg	4 Apr 1942	18 Oct 1942	21 Apr 1943
ATF 71	*Hopi*	Charleston Sbdg	5 May 1942	7 Sep 1942	31 Mar 1943
ATF 72	*Kiowa*	Charleston Sbdg	22 Jun 1942	5 Nov 1942	7 Jun 1943
ATF 73	*Menominee*	United Eng.	27 Sep 1941	14 Feb 1942	25 Sep 1942
ATF 74	*Pawnee*	United Eng.	23 Oct 1941	31 Mar 1942	7 Nov 1942
ATF 75	*Sioux*	United Eng.	14 Feb 1942	27 May 1942	6 Dec 1942
ATF 76	*Ute*	United Eng.	27 Feb 1942	25 Jun 1942	13 Dec 1942
ATF 81	*Bannock*	Charleston Sbdg	4 Aug 1942	7 Jan 1943	28 Jun 1943
ATF 82	*Carib*	Charleston Sbdg	7 Sep 1942	7 Feb 1943	24 Jul 1943
ATF 83	*Chickasaw*	United Eng.	14 Feb 1942	23 Jul 1942	4 Feb 1943

Fig 12.2: *Bannock* (ATF 81), 4 Jul 1943; a *Navajo*-class fleet tug. Later units had no stack.

ATF 84	*Cree*	United Eng.	31 Mar 1942	17 Aug 1942	28 Mar 1943
ATF 85	*Lipan*	United Eng.	30 May 1942	17 Sep 1942	29 Apr 1943
ATF 86	*Mataco*	United Eng.	27 Jun 1942	14 Oct 1942	29 May 1943
ATF 87	*Moreno*	Cramp	26 Jan 1942	9 Jul 1942	30 Nov 1942
ATF 88	*Narragansett*	Cramp	31 Jan 1942	8 Aug 1942	15 Jan 1943
AT 89	*Nauset*	Cramp	10 Jul 1942	7 Sep 1942	2 Mar 1943
ATF 90	*Pinto*	Cramp	10 Aug 1942	5 Jan 1943	1 Apr 1943
ATF 91	*Seneca*	Cramp	7 Sep 1942	2 Feb 1943	30 Apr 1943
ATF 92	*Tawasa*	Commercial	22 Jun 1942	22 Feb 1943	17 Jul 1943
ATF 93	*Tekesta*	Commercial	7 Sep 1942	20 Mar 1943	16 Aug 1943
ATF 94	*Yuma*	Commercial	13 Feb 1943	17 Jul 1943	31 Aug 1943
ATF 95	*Zuni*	Commercial	8 Mar 1943	31 Jul 1943	9 Oct 1943
ATF 96	*Abnaki*	Charleston Sbdg	28 Nov 1942	22 Apr 1943	15 Nov 1943
ATF 97	*Alsea*	Charleston Sbdg	29 Nov 1942	22 May 1943	13 Dec 1943
ATF 98	*Arikara*	Charleston Sbdg	10 Jan 1943	22 Jun 1943	5 Jan 1944
AT 99	*Chetco*	Charleston Sbdg	9 Feb 1943	20 Jul 1943	31 May 1944
ATF 100	*Chowanoc*	Charleston Sbdg	24 Apr 1943	20 Aug 1943	21 Feb 1944
ATF 101	*Cocopa*	Charleston Sbdg	25 May 1943	5 Oct 1943	25 Mar 1944
ATF 102	*Hidatsa*	Charleston Sbdg	8 Jul 1943	29 Dec 1943	25 Apr 1944
ATF 103	*Hitchiti*	Charleston Sbdg	24 Jul 1943	29 Jan 1944	27 May 1944
ATF 104	*Jicarilla*	Charleston Sbdg	25 Aug 1943	25 Feb 1944	26 Jun 1944
ATF 105	*Moctobi*	Charleston Sbdg	7 Oct 1943	25 Mar 1944	25 Jul 1944
ATF 106	*Molala*	United Eng.	26 Jul 1942	23 Dec 1942	29 Sep 1943
ATF 107	*Munsee*	United Eng.	20 Aug 1942	21 Jan 1943	30 Oct 1943
ATF 108	*Pakana*	United Eng.	1 Oct 1942	3 Mar 1943	17 Dec 1943
ATF 109	*Potawatomi*	United Eng.	19 Oct 1942	3 Apr 1943	12 Feb 1944
ATF 110	*Quapaw*	United Eng.	28 Dec 1942	15 May 1943	6 May 1944
ATF 111	*Sarsi*	United Eng.	25 Jan 1943	12 Jun 1943	24 Jun 1944
ATF 112	*Serrano*	United Eng.	6 Mar 1943	24 Jul 1943	22 Sep 1944
ATF 113	*Takelma*	United Eng.	7 Apr 1943	18 Sep 1943	3 Aug 1944
ATF 114	*Tawakoni*	United Eng.	19 May 1943	28 Oct 1943	15 Sep 1944
ATF 115	*Tenino*	United Eng.	16 Jun 1943	10 Jan 1944	18 Nov 1944
ATF 116	*Tolowa*	United Eng.	28 Jul 1943	17 May 1944	26 Dec 1944
ATF 117	*Wateree*	United Eng.	22 Sep 1943	14 Jun 1944	17 Feb 1945
ATF 118	*Wenatchee*	United Eng.	12 Jan 1944	7 Sep 1944	24 Mar 1945

Displacement	1,235 tons, 1,674 f/l
Dimensions	205' (oa) 195' (wl) x 38'6" x 15'4"
Machinery	1 screw; diesel; SHP 3,000; 16.5 knots
Complement	85
Armament	1–3"/50, 2–40mm, 2 twin 40mm AA guns

Notes: Rec **ATF**, 15 May 1944. Sturdy tugs with a single funnel. ATF 96 and later were built without a funnel.

Service Records:

AT 64 *Navajo* Torpedoed and sunk by Japanese submarine *I-39* off New Hebrides Is., 12 Sep 1943 (17 killed).
2* Rennell I.

AT 65 *Seminole* Sunk by Japanese destroyers off Tulagi, 25 Oct 1942 (1 killed).
1* Solomons.

AT 66 *Cherokee* Decomm 29 Jun 1946 and trfd to USCG.
1* North Africa.
Later history: Renamed USCGC *Cherokee* (WMEC 165). To Marad 25 Jun 1991. Reacq as target 6 Oct 1993.

AT 67 *Apache* Damaged by kamikaze, Luzon, 5 Jan 1945. Decomm 3 Dec 1946. †
4* Treasury Is. Ldgs., Cape Torokina, Saipan, Guam, Leyte, Lingayen.

AT 68 *Arapaho* Decomm 15 Jan 1947. †
4* Gilbert Is., Kwajalein, Tinian, Fleet Raids 1945.

ATF 69 *Chippewa* Decomm 26 Feb 1947. †

ATF 70 *Choctaw* Decomm 11 Mar 1947. †

ATF 71 *Hopi* †
4* Sicily, Salerno, Anzio, Southern France.

ATF 72 *Kiowa* †
1* Normandy.

ATF 73 *Menominee* Decomm 15 Nov 1946. †
5* Solomons, Green I. Ldgs., Palau, Okinawa, Raids on Japan 7–8/45.

ATF 74 *Pawnee* Decomm Jan 1947. †
4* New Georgia, Vella Lavella Ldgs., Cape Torokina, Palau, Okinawa Raid 10/44, N. Luzon–Formosa Raids 10/44, Luzon Raids 10/44.

ATF 75 *Sioux* Decomm 23 Apr 1947. †
4* Treasury Is. Ldgs., Cape Torokina, Green I. Ldgs., Iwo Jima, fleet Raids 1945. Operation Crossroads.

ATF 76 *Ute* Damaged by mine in Yangtze River near Keichow, 19 Oct 1945. Decomm 13 Jul 1946. †
3*Attu, Iwo Jima, Fleet Raids 1945, Okinawa.

ATF 81 *Bannock* Decomm 21 Feb 1947. †
2* Normandy, Okinawa.

ATF 82 *Carib* Decomm 24 Jan 1947. †

ATF 83 *Chickasaw* †
7* Kwajalein, Eniwetok, Saipan, Tinian, Leyte, Lingayen, Okinawa. Operation Crossroads.

ATF 84 *Cree* †
2* Iwo Jima, fleet Raids 1945, Okinawa.

ATF 85 *Lipan* Damaged by fire during typhoon in Pacific, 30 Sep 1945. †
3* Saipan, Guam, Okinawa.

ATF 86 *Mataco* †
5* Gilbert Is., Kwajalein, Saipan, Iwo Jima, Okinawa.

ATF 87 *Moreno* Decomm 13 Aug 1946. †
3* Sicily, Salerno, Southern France.

ATF 88 *Narragansett* Damaged by aircraft bomb at Palermo, 23 Aug 1943 (6 killed). Damaged in collision with drydock *ARDC-12* off Central America coast, 24 Feb 1945. Decomm 21 Dec 1946. †
3* Sicily, Salerno, Southern France.

AT 89 *Nauset* Sunk by German aircraft off Salerno, 9 Sep 1943 (18 killed).
2* Sicily, Salerno.

ATF 90 *Pinto* †
2* Normandy, Southern France. Decomm 11 Jul 1946.

ATF 91 *Seneca* †

ATF 92 *Tawasa* †
4* Gilbert Is., Kwajalein, Eniwetok, Saipan.

ATF 93 *Tekesta* †
6* Kwajalein, Eniwetok, Saipan, Tinian, Guam, Luzon Raids 10/44.

ATF 94 *Yuma* †
2* Noemfoor I., Iwo Jima.

ATF 95 *Zuni* Damaged by grounding, Iwo Jima, while attempting to salve *LST-727*, 23 Mar 1945 (2 killed). Decomm 29 Jun 1946, trfd to USCG.
4* Saipan, Guam, Palau, Luzon Raids 1/45, Formosa Raids 1/45, China Coast Raids 1/45, Nansei Shoto Raid 1/45, Iwo Jima.
Later history: Renamed USCGC *Tamaroa* (WMEC 166). Stricken 1 Feb 1994. Trfd to Intrepid Sea, Air, and Space Museum, New York, 28 Feb 1994.

ATF 96 *Abnaki* Sank *ATR-98* in collision off Azores, 12 Apr 1944. †

ATF 97 *Alsea* †
ATF 98 *Arikara* †
3* Normandy, Southern France, Okinawa.
AT 99 *Chetco* Completed as submarine rescue vessel. Rec **ASR 12**, renamed ***Penguin***, 23 Sep 1943. Decomm 4 Sep 1947. †
ATF 100 *Chowanoc* †
4* Leyte, Guam, Lingayen, Raids on Japan 7–8/45. Operation Crossroads.
ATF 101 *Cocopa* †
ATF 102 *Hidatsa* Damaged by mine at Mariveles, Luzon, 17 Feb 1945 (8 killed). †
2* Leyte, Mariveles-Corregidor, Subic Bay.
ATF 103 *Hitchiti* †
1* Luzon Raids 1/45, Formosa Raids 1/45, China Coast Raids 1/45, Nansei Shoto Raid 1/45, Fleet Raids 1945.
ATF 104 *Jicarilla* †
2* Iwo Jima, Okinawa. Damaged in typhoon, Philippine Sea, 18 Dec 1944. Operation Crossroads.
ATF 105 *Moctobi* †
2* Fleet Raids 1945, Raids on Japan 7–8/45. Tokyo Bay.
ATF 106 *Molala* †
5* Kwajalein, Eniwetok, Saipan, Luzon Raids 1/45, Formosa Raids 1/45, China Coast Raids 1/45, Nansei Shoto Raid 1/45, Iwo Jima, Okinawa.
ATF 107 *Munsee* †
3* Palau, Philippines Raids 9/44, Okinawa Raid 10/44, N. Luzon–Formosa Raids 10/44, Luzon Raids 10/44, Fleet Raids 1945, Okinawa. Operation Crossroads.
ATF 108 *Pakana* Damaged by gunfire, Okinawa, 27 May 1945. †
1* Guam.
ATF 109 *Potawatomi* †
2* Leyte, Lingayen.
ATF 110 *Quapaw* †
4* Morotai, Leyte, Lingayen, Ldgs. on Palawan I, Mindanao Ldgs.
ATF 111 *Sarsi* †
ATF 112 *Serrano* Completed by Pollock. †
1* Okinawa.
ATF 113 *Takelma* Damaged in collision, Leyte, 11 Feb 1945. †
ATF 114 *Tawakoni* †
2* Iwo Jima, Okinawa.
ATF 115 *Tenino* Went aground in typhoon at Okinawa, 9 Oct 1945. Decomm 17 May 1947. †
1* Okinawa.
ATF 116 *Tolowa* Completed by Pollock. Decomm 27 Jan 1947. †
ATF 117 *Wateree* Sunk on reef in typhoon at Okinawa, 9 Oct 1945 (8 killed).
ATF 118 *Wenatchee* Operation Crossroads. Decomm 19 May 1947. †
1* Raids on Japan 7–8/45. Tokyo Bay.

No.	Name	Builder	Launched	Acquired	Comm.
ATF 148	*Achomawi*	Charleston Sbdg	15 Jan 1944	14 Jun 1944	11 Nov 1944
ATF 149	*Atakapa*	Charleston Sbdg	17 Feb 1944	11 Jul 1944	8 Dec 1944
ATF 150	*Avoyel*	Charleston Sbdg	25 Mar 1944	9 Aug 1944	8 Jan 1945
ATF 151	*Chawasha*	Charleston Sbdg	7 Apr 1944	15 Sep 1944	5 Feb 1945
ATF 152	*Cahuilla*	Charleston Sbdg	16 Jun 1944	2 Nov 1944	10 Mar 1945
ATF 153	*Chilula*	Charleston Sbdg	13 Jul 1944	1 Dec 1944	5 Apr 1945
ATF 154	*Chimariko*	Charleston Sbdg	11 Aug 1944	30 Dec 1944	28 Apr 1945
ATF 155	*Cusabo*	Charleston Sbdg	28 Sep 1944	26 Feb 1945	19 May 1945
ATF 156	*Luiseno*	Charleston Sbdg	7 Nov 1944	17 Mar 1945	16 Jun 1945
ATF 157	*Nipmuc*	Charleston Sbdg	2 Dec 1944	12 Apr 1945	8 Jul 1945
ATF 158	*Mosopelea*	Charleston Sbdg	2 Jan 1945	7 May 1945	28 Jul 1945
ATF 159	*Paiute*	Charleston Sbdg	27 Feb 1945	4 Jun 1945	27 Aug 1945
ATF 160	*Papago*	Charleston Sbdg	19 Mar 1945	21 Jun 1945	3 Oct 1945
ATF 161	*Salinan*	Charleston Sbdg	13 Apr 1945	20 Jul 1945	9 Nov 1945
ATF 162	*Shakori*	Charleston Sbdg	9 May 1945	9 Aug 1945	20 Dec 1945
ATF 163	*Utina*	Charleston Sbdg	6 Jun 1945	31 Aug 1945	30 Jan 1946
ATF 164	*Yurok*	Charleston Sbdg	23 Jun 1945	15 Feb 1946	*28 May 1946*
ATF 165	*Yustaga*	Charleston Sbdg	23 Jul 1945	19 Mar 1946	*19 Jul 1946* (completed)

Service Records:

ATF 148 *Achomawi* Operation Crossroads. Decomm 10 Jun 1947. †
ATF 149 *Atakapa* Decomm 8 Nov 1946. †
ATF 150 *Avoyel* Decomm 11 Jan 1947. †
1* Minesweeping 1945.
ATF 151 *Chawasha* Decomm 30 Sep 1946. †
1* Raids on Japan 7–8/45.
ATF 152 *Cahuilla* Decomm 27 Jun 1947. †
ATF 153 *Chilula* Decomm 8 Feb 1947. †
ATF 154 *Chimariko* Decomm 31 Oct 1946. †
ATF 155 *Cusabo* Decomm 3 Dec 1946. †
ATF 156 *Luiseno* †
ATF 157 *Nipmuc* †
ATF 158 *Mosopelea* †
ATF 159 *Paiute* †
ATF 160 *Papago* †
ATF 161 *Salinan* †
ATF 162 *Shakori* †
ATF 163 *Utina* †
ATF 164 *Yurok* Completed as submarine rescue vessel. Rec **ASR 19**, 13 Nov 1945 and renamed ***Bluebird***, 7 Nov 1945. †
ATF 165 *Yustaga* Completed as submarine rescue vessel. Rec **ASR 20**, 13 Nov 1945 and renamed ***Skylark***, 7 Nov 1945. †

No.	Name	Builder	Launched	Acquired	Comm.
AT 77	*Tuscarora*	Levingston	17 Jul 1941	Jan 1941	13 Dec 1941

Displacement	530 tons lt
Dimensions	135' (oa) 123'6" (bp) x 31' x 14'2"
Machinery	1 screw, diesel, hp 1,500

Notes: Rec **YT 341**, 5 Nov 1942. Stricken 1 Sep 1961. BU 1976.

No.	Name	—
AT 78	*Carib*	Cancelled 1941
AT 79	*Yuma*	Cancelled 1941
AT 80	*Yaqui*	Cancelled 1941

No.	Name	Builder	Launched	Acquired	Comm.
AT 147	*Esselen*	Harlan	1897	18 Jun 1943	21 Aug 1943
	ex–*New York*, ex–*Catawissa*				

Displacement	800 tons, 558 grt
Dimensions	164' (oa) 157'9" (bp) x 29'
Machinery	1 screw, VTE, 1,000 hp, 11 knots
Complement	(U)

Service Record:

AT 147 *Esselen* Tenth ND, Caribbean. **Rec ATO 147**, 15 May 1944. Decomm 11 Nov 1944. Stricken 27 Nov 1944.
Later history: Merchant *New York*, renamed *Beth Tank Ship No. 2*, 1952.

No.	Name	Builder	Launched	Acquired	Comm.
AT 166	*Chetco*	Beth. Eliz.	29 Apr 1919	13 Sep 1943	24 Sep 1943
	ex–*Thomas E. Moran* (1943), ex–*Barryton* (1942)				
AT 167	*Chatot*	Beth. Eliz.	21 May 1919	16 Oct 1943	3 Nov 1943
	ex–*Buttercup* (1943).				

Displacement	554 grt
Dimensions	150' (oa) 142' (wl) x 27'7" x 15'
Machinery	1 screw, diesel-electric, 1,400 shp
Complement	47
Armament	20mm guns

Service Records:

AT 166 *Chetco* Rec **ATO 166**, 24 Apr 1945. Rec **ATA 166**, 15 May 1945. Decomm 14 Jun 1946.
2* Admiralty Is., Hollandia.
Later history: Merchant *Neptune*. Sunk in collision with m/v *Herald of the Morning* off Willapa, Washington, 16 Nov 1948.

AT 167 *Chatot* Rec **ATA 167**, 15 May 1944. Out of service 9 Feb 1945. Stricken 10 Mar 1945, to USSR.
Later history: Merchant, renamed *Albatros*. Ran aground on Western Sakhalin, 1 Jul 1947, refloated 30 Aug but later foundered in tow in Tatar Strait, 31 Aug 1947.

Ex–Minesweepers

No.	Name	Formerly	Date
ATO 131	*Bobolink*	AM 20	1 Jun 1942
	1* Pearl Harbor		
ATO 132	*Brant*	AM 24	1 Jun 1942
	3* Sicily, Salerno, Normandy		
ATO 133	*Cormorant*	AM 40	1 Jun 1942
	1* Normandy		
AT 134	*Grebe*	AM 43	1 Jun 1942
	1* Pearl Harbor		
ATO 135	*Kingfisher*	AM 25	1 Jun 1942
	1* Gilbert Is.		
ATO 136	*Oriole*	AM 7	1 Jun 1942
ATO 137	*Owl*	AM 2	1 Jun 1942
	1* Normandy		
ATO 138	*Partridge*	AM 16	1 Jun 1942
	1* Normandy		
ATO 139	*Rail*	AM 26	1 Jun 1942
	2* Pearl Harbor, Subic Bay		
ATO 140	*Robin*	AM 3	1 Jun 1942
ATO 141	*Seagull*	AM 30	1 Jun 1942
ATO 142	*Tern*	AM 31	1 Jun 1942
	1* Pearl Harbor		
ATO 143	*Turkey*	AM 13	1 Jun 1942
	1* Pearl Harbor		
ATO 144	*Vireo*	AM 52	1 Jun 1942
	6* Pearl Harbor, Midway, Solomons, Cape Sansapor, Leyte, Tarakan		
ATO 145	*Woodcock*	AM 14	1 Jun 1942
ATO 168	*Lark*	AM 21	1 Mar 1944
	2* Philippines 1942, Leyte		
ATO 169	*Whippoorwill*	AM 35	1 Mar 1944
	1* Philippines 1942		

Notes: Armament 1–3"/50, 4–20mm guns

Fig 12.3: *Owl* (ATO 137) at Norfolk Navy Yard, 17 Apr 1945. In 1942, the remaining "Bird class" minesweepers were reclassified as fleet tugs.

No.	Reclassified	Date
AT 119–27	ATR 41–49	31 Jul 1942
AT 128–30	BAT 3-5	15 Apr 1942
AT 146	ATR 9	05 Jan 1943

AUXILIARY OCEAN TUGS

ATR No.	ATA No.	Builder	Keel Laid	Launched	Comm.
43	ATA 121	Levingston	7 Sep 1942	19 Oct 1942	29 May 1943
44	ATA 122	Levingston	19 Oct 1942	27 Nov 1942	10 Jun 1943
45	ATA 123	Levingston	21 Nov 1942	20 Dec 1942	30 Jun 1943
46	ATA 124	Levingston	27 Nov 1942	3 Jan 1943	24 Jul 1943
47	ATA 125	Levingston	21 Dec 1942	29 Jan 1943	12 Aug 1943
90	ATA 146	Gulfport	29 May 1942	23 Oct 1942	20 Jan 1943
97	ATA 170	Gulfport	9 Apr 1943	21 Aug 1943	7 Dec 1943
98	(171)	Gulfport	3 Jun 1943	6 Nov 1943	18 Jan 1944
99	ATA 172	Gulfport	24 Aug 1943	25 Nov 1943	23 Feb 1944
100	ATA 173	Gulfport	7 Nov 1943	12 Mar 1944	12 Apr 1944
101	ATA 174	Levingston	5 Oct 1943	18 Nov 1943	20 Jul 1944

Fig 12.4: *ATA-177.* Designated as auxiliary ocean tugs, these vessels were not named until 1948.

102	ATA 175	Levingston	9 Dec 1943	29 Jan 1944	3 Aug 1944
103	ATA 176	Levingston	30 Jan 1944	1 Mar 1944	19 Aug 1944
104	ATA 177	Levingston	27 Apr 1944	5 Jun 1944	2 Sep 1944
105	ATA 178	Levingston	20 May 1944	15 Jun 1944	15 Sep 1944
106	ATA 179	Levingston	22 May 1944	30 Jun 1944	22 Sep 1944
107	ATA 180	Levingston	5 Jun 1944	14 Jul 1944	27 Sep 1944
108	ATA 181	Levingston	15 Jun 1944	27 Jul 1944	7 Oct 1944
109	ATA 182	Levingston	30 Jun 1944	5 Aug 1944	16 Oct 1944
110	ATA 183	Levingston	14 Jul 1944	16 Aug 1944	26 Oct 1944
111	ATA 184	Levingston	27 Jul 1944	29 Aug 1944	6 Nov 1944
112	ATA 185	Levingston	5 Aug 1944	11 Sep 1944	17 Nov 1944
113	ATA 186	Levingston	16 Aug 1944	18 Sep 1944	24 Nov 1944
114	ATA 187	Levingston	29 Aug 1944	29 Sep 1944	7 Dec 1944
115	ATA 188	Levingston	11 Sep 1944	12 Oct 1944	14 Dec 1944
116	ATA 189	Levingston	18 Sep 1944	19 Oct 1944	20 Dec 1944
117	ATA 190	Levingston	20 Sep 1944	26 Oct 1944	1 Jan 1945
118	ATA 191	Levingston	12 Oct 1944	7 Nov 1944	12 Jan 1945
119	ATA 192	Levingston	19 Oct 1944	15 Nov 1944	22 Jan 1945
120	ATA 193	Levingston	26 Oct 1944	24 Nov 1944	1 Feb 1945
121	ATA 194	Levingston	7 Nov 1944	4 Dec 1944	14 Feb 1945
122	ATA 195	Levingston	15 Nov 1944	14 Dec 1944	26 Feb 1945
123	ATA 196	Levingston	24 Nov 1944	21 Dec 1944	6 Mar 1945
124	ATA 197	Levingston	4 Dec 1944	6 Jan 1945	15 Mar 1945
125	ATA 198	Levingston	14 Dec 1944	17 Jan 1945	19 Mar 1945
126	ATA 199	Gulfport	27 Nov 1943	22 Aug 1944	20 Oct 1944
127	ATA 200	Gulfport	4 Jul 1944	8 Sep 1944	31 Oct 1944
128	ATA 201	Gulfport	3 Aug 1944	23 Sep 1944	22 Nov 1944
129	ATA 202	Gulfport	24 Aug 1944	10 Oct 1944	8 Dec 1944
130	ATA 203	Gulfport	10 Sep 1944	26 Oct 1944	1 Jan 1945
131	ATA 204	Gulfport	25 Sep 1944	9 Nov 1944	18 Jan 1945
132	ATA 205	Gulfport	12 Oct 1944	26 Nov 1944	30 Jan 1945
133	ATA 206	Gulfport	26 Oct 1944	14 Dec 1944	10 Feb 1945
134	ATA 207	Gulfport	10 Nov 1944	4 Jan 1945	1 Mar 1945
135	ATA 208	Gulfport	27 Nov 1944	19 Jan 1945	19 Mar 1945
136	ATA 209	Gulfport	15 Dec 1944	2 Feb 1945	2 Apr 1945
137	ATA 210	Gulfport	5 Jan 1945	15 Feb 1945	18 Apr 1945
138	ATA 211	Gulfport	20 Jan 1945	3 Mar 1945	3 May 1945
139	ATA 212	Gulfport	3 Feb 1945	20 Mar 1945	21 May 1945
140	ATA 213	Gulfport	16 Feb 1945	9 Apr 1945	31 May 1945

Displacement	835 tons
Dimensions	143' (oa); 134'6" (wl) x 33'10" x 13'2"
Machinery	1 screw; diesel-electric; SHP 1,500; 13 knots
Complement	45
Armament	1–3"/50, 2–20mm guns

Notes: ATR 97–140 rec ATA 170–213, 15 May 1944. ATR 98 lost before reclassification.

Service Records:

ATA 121 Decomm 9 Apr 1946. †

ATA 122 Sold 19 Sep 1947 to Chile.
1* Okinawa.
Later history: Renamed *Lautaro.* Sold to Urvguay 1992, renamed *San Jose*

ATA 123 Decomm 26 Nov 1947. †

ATA 124 Operation Crossroads. Sold 23 Jul 1947 to Argentina.
1* Okinawa.
Later history: Renamed *Diaguita.* Sold 1979

ATA 125 Sold 24 Dec 1946.
2* Normandy, Southern France.
Later history: Merchant *Joseph H. Moran* 1947, renamed *Joseph H. Moran II* 1948, *Dragon* 1949, *Joseph H. Moran II* 1953, *Dragon* 1959, *Utrecht* 1968, *Hippopotame* (French Navy).

ATA 146 Sold 19 Oct 1947.
Later history: Merchant *Eugene F. Moran,* renamed *Sea Ranger* 1949, *Buckeye* 1971. Sunk by Vietcong batteries in Mekong River, 2 Feb 1975.

ATA 170 Sold 22 Jan 1947.
2* Normandy, Southern France.
Later history: Merchant *Leon.* BU 1990 Greece.

ATR 98 (ATA 171) Sunk in collision with fleet tug *Abnaki,* Azores, 12 Apr 1944.

ATA 172 Stricken/to Panama Canal, 20 Feb 1947.
2* Normandy, Southern France.

ATA 173 Sold 3 Jul 1947.
Later history: Merchant *Dom Luiz,* renamed *Alpertucho* 1987. se 1992.

ATA 174 Decomm 16 Jan 1947. †

ATA 175 Decomm 8 Nov 1946. †

ATA 176 Decomm 30 Jun 1947. †

ATA 177 Sold 29 Sep 1947 to Chile.
Later history: Renamed *Lientur.* R. 1984.

ATA 178 Decomm 23 Dec 1947. †

ATA 179 Decomm 10 Oct 1947. †
1* Visayan Is. Ldgs.

ATA 180 Operation Crossroads. Stricken 30 Mar 1948.
Later history: Merchant *Horizon.*

ATA 181 Went aground in typhoon at Okinawa, 15 Oct 1945.
1* Okinawa.

ATA 182 Decomm 26 Nov 1946. †

ATA 183 Decomm 22 Oct 1946. †

ATA 184 Decomm 24 Jun 1946. †

ATA 185 †
1* Okinawa. Operation Crossroads.

ATA 186 †

ATA 187 †
1* Okinawa. Operation Crossroads.

ATA 188 †
1* Okinawa.

ATA 189 Decomm 29 Aug 1947. †

ATA 190 †
1* Okinawa.

ATA 191 Went aground in typhoon at Okinawa, 9 Oct 1945. Destroyed 31 Dec 1945.

ATA 192 †
1* Okinawa. Operation Crossroads.

ATA 193 Decomm 1 Sep 1946. †
1* Okinawa.
ATA 194 †
ATA 195 †
ATA 196 †
ATA 197 †
ATA 198 †
ATA 199 Decomm 25 Aug 1947. †
ATA 200 Sold 29 Sep 1947.
1* Okinawa.
Later history: To Chile, renamed *Leucoton.* Went aground off Valdivia and lost, 15 Aug 1965.
ATA 201 †
ATA 202 Decomm 27 Feb 1947. †
1* Okinawa.
ATA 203 Decomm 20 Oct 1946. †
2* Okinawa, Minesweeping 1945.
ATA 204 Decomm 26 Nov 1947. †
ATA 205 Decomm Jan 1947. Tokyo Bay. †
ATA 206 Decomm 4 Oct 1946. †
ATA 207 Decomm 19 Sep 1947. †
ATA 208 †
ATA 209 †
ATA 210 †
ATA 211 †
ATA 212 Decomm 20 Dec 1946. †
ATA 213 †

No.	Builder	Keel Laid	Launched	Comm.
ATA 219	Levingston	21 Dec 1944	31 Jan 1945	5 Dec 1945
ATA 220	Levingston	6 Jan 1945	9 Feb 1945	5 Dec 1945
ATA 221	Levingston	17 Jan 1945	18 Feb 1945	11 Dec 1945
ATA 222	Levingston	31 Jan 1945	8 Mar 1945	31 Dec 1945
ATA 223	Levingston	9 Feb 1945	17 Mar 1945	31 Jan 1946
ATA 224	Levingston	28 Feb 1945	31 Mar 1945	13 Feb 1946
ATA 225	Levingston	8 Mar 1945	13 Apr 1945	7 Mar 1946
ATA 226	Levingston	31 Mar 1945	12 May 1945	21 Mar 1946
ATA 227	Levingston	13 Apr 1945	26 May 1945	4 Apr 1946
ATA 228	Levingston	1 May 1945	9 Jun 1945	25 Apr 1946
ATA 229–33	Levingston	—	—	—
ATA 234	Gulfport	3 Mar 1945	7 May 1945	11 Dec 1945
ATA 235	Gulfport	21 Mar 1945	19 May 1945	6 Dec 1945
ATA 236	Gulfport	10 Apr 1945	6 Jun 1945	3 Dec 1945
ATA 237	Gulfport	8 May 1945	23 Jun 1945	27 Dec 1945
ATA 238	Gulfport	21 May 1945	2 Jul 1945	8 Feb 1946

Displacement	800 tons f/l
Dimensions	143' (oa) x 33' x 14'2"
Machinery	1 screw; diesel-electric; hp 1,500; 12.5 knots
Endurance	3,000/12.5
Complement	45
Armament	1–3"/50

Notes: ATA 219–38 were planned for lend-lease to USSR.
Service Records:
ATA 219 Sold 24 Jul 1946.
Later history: Merchant *Titan*, renamed *Wilvin* 1974.
ATA 220 Sold 31 Jul 1946.
Later history: Merchant *Samuel J. Dark.*
ATA 221 To USSR, renamed MB-44, 9 Apr 1946. Renamed MB-24, 1949. BU 1965.
ATA 222 To USSR, renamed MB-43, 19 Apr 1946. Renamed MB-25, 1949. BU 1973.
ATA 223 Sold 23 May 1946.
Later history: Merchant *Ono*, renamed *Lucky, Terry M.*
ATA 224 Sold 23 May 1946.
Later history: Merchant *Ahi*, renamed *Wolverine* 19...
ATA 225 To USSR. Probably renamed MB-26. Sold 9 May 1947.
ATA 226 Sold 3 Jul 1947 to France.
Later history: Renamed *Ténace.* R 1972.
ATA 227 Sold 18 Jul 1947 to Argentina.
Later history: Renamed *Chiriguano.*
ATA 228 Sold 18 Jul 1947 to Argentina.
Later history: Renamed *Sanaviron.* R 1997.
ATA 229 Canceled 13 Aug 1945. Completed as *Moi*, renamed *CC 9.*
ATA 230 Canceled 13 Aug 1945. Completed as *G. W. Codrington.*
ATA 231–33 Canceled 13 Aug 1945.
ATA 234 Sold 26 Mar 1947 to Brazil.
Later history: Renamed *Tritão.*
ATA 235 Sold 26 Mar 1947 to Brazil.
Later history: Renamed *Tridente.*
ATA 236 Sold 22 Apr 1947 to Brazil.
Later history: Renamed *Triunfo.* (Note: Authoritative sources also say ATA-236 and ATA-237 became merchant tugs *Vencedor* and *Vengador.*)
ATA 237 Sold 22 Apr 1947.
ATA 238 Sold 23 Jun 1947.
Later history: Merchant *Noord Holland* 1948.

No.	Formerly	Date	Comm as ATA
ATA 214	AN 64	12 Aug 1944	25 Sep 1944
ATA 215	AN 65	12 Aug 1944	17 Dec 1944
ATA 216	AN 70	12 Aug 1944	30 Oct 1944
ATA 217	AN 71	12 Aug 1944	16 Jan 1945
ATA 218	AN 72	12 Aug 1944	10 Mar 1945

Note: Net layers completed as auxiliary tugs, names canceled. Armament: 2–40mm, 2 or 3 20mm AA guns.

RESCUE TUGS

ATR 1–40
ATR 50–89

Displacement	1,312 tons
Dimensions	165'5" (oa) 155' (wl) x 33'4" x 15'10"
Machinery	2 screws; VTE; 2 boilers; SHP 1,600; 12.2 knots
Complement	52
Armament	1–3"/50, 2–20mm guns

Notes: ATR 17–20 trfd to UK; 80 built.

War Loss

ATR 15 Lost by grounding, Normandy 19 Jun 1944.

No.	Formerly	Date
ATR 41–42	AT 119–20	31 Jul 1942
ATR 43–47	ATA 121–25	31 Jul 1942
ATR 48–49	AT 126–27	31 Jul 1942
ATR 90	BAT 2	30 Sep 1942

No.	Reclass	Date
ATR 43–47	ATA 121–25	15 May 1944
ATR 90	ATA 146	15 May 1944
ATR 97–140	ATA 170–213	15 May 1944

Fig 12.5: *ATR-14.* One of 79 unnamed rescue tugs built.

Lend-Lease Tugs

Lend-Lease No.	Builder	Keel Laid	Launched	Completed
ATR 41	Levingston	8 Aug 1942	7 Sep 1942	*19 Apr 1943*
ATR 42	Levingston	7 Sep 1942	10 Oct 1942	*3 May 1943*
ATR 48	Levingston	3 Jan 1943	7 Feb 1943	*31 Aug 1943*
ATR 49	Levingston	29 Jan 1943	1 Mar 1943	*2 Oct 1943*
ATR 91	Levingston	31 Mar 1943	13 May 1943	*22 Oct 1943*
ATR 92	Levingston	6 Apr 1943	18 May 1943	*13 Nov 1943*
ATR 93	Levingston	19 Apr 1943	11 Jun 1943	*7 Dec 1943*
ATR 94	Levingston	14 May 1943	30 Jun 1943	*21 Dec 1943*
ATR 95	Levingston	11 Jun 1943	23 Jul 1943	*18 Jan 1944*
ATR 96	Levingston	1 Jul 1943	18 Aug 1943	*27 Jan 1944*
BAT 1	Gulfport	16 Mar 1942	15 Aug 1942	*22 Dec 1942*
BAT 2	Gulfport	29 May 1942	23 Oct 1942	—
BAT 3	Levingston	25 Oct 1941	15 Jun 1942	*15 Jun 1942*
BAT 4	Levingston	25 Dec 1941	28 Mar 1942	*23 Oct 1942*
BAT 5	Levingston	19 Feb 1942	15 May 1942	*10 Aug 1942*
BAT 6	Levingston	30 Mar 1942	5 Jun 1942	*28 Aug 1942*
BAT 7	Defoe	15 Nov 1941	8 Apr 1942	*6 Jun 1942*
BAT 8	Defoe	21 Nov 1941	21 May 1942	*29 Jun 1942*
BAT 9	Defoe	10 Apr 1942	1 Jul 1942	*30 Jul 1942*
BAT 10	Defoe	22 May 1942	12 Aug 1942	*14 Sep 1942*
BAT 11	Levingston	18 May 1942	18 Jul 1942	*12 Oct 1942*
BAT 12	Levingston	17 Jun 1942	7 Aug 1942	*23 Nov 1942*
BAT 13	Gulfport	2 Sep 1942	1 Jan 1943	*18 Feb 1943*
BAT 14	Gulfport	30 Oct 1942	21 Feb 1943	*10 Apr 1943*

Displacement	783 tons
Dimensions	143' (oa); 135' (bp) x 33'3" x 14'9"
Machinery	1 screw; diesel; bhp 2,400; 14 knots
Complement	34
Armament	1–3"/50, 2–20mm

Notes: Lend-lease to UK. Transferred on completion.

Service Records:

ATR 41 To UK, renamed HMS *Advantage.* Returned 19 Feb 1946. Sold 24 Sep 1946.
Later history: Merchant *Ming 309.* BU 1965.

ATR 42 To UK, renamed HMS *Aspirant.* Returned 20 Mar 1946. Sold 18 Nov 1947.
Later history: Merchant *Vivi.*

ATR 48 To UK, renamed HMS *Mindful.* Returned 13 May 1946. Sold 18 Nov 1947.
Later history: Merchant *Gay Moran,* renamed *Sea Lion* 1949, *Harry J. Mosser* 1955, *Margaret Walsh* 1957, *Margaret Foss* 1966, *CC 7* 1968.

ATR 49 To UK, renamed HMS *Vagrant.* Returned 20 Mar 1946. Sold 10 Nov 1947.
Later history: Merchant *Marion Moran,* renamed *Mary Elizabeth* 1964, *Ann Lee* 1971, *Wilbie* 1972, *Columbia I* 1982. BU 1983 Manila.

ATR 91 To UK, renamed HMS *Patroclus.* Returned 20 Jun 1946. Sold 18 Nov 1947.
Later history: Merchant *Kevin Moran,* renamed *Mohawk* 1960; se 1992.

ATR 92 To UK, renamed HMS *Athlete.* Sunk by mine off Livorno, Italy, 17 Jul 1945.

ATR 93 To UK, renamed HMS *Flare.* Returned 13 Apr 1946. Sold 24 Sep 1946.
Later history: Merchant *Ming 301,* renamed *Hongkongdocks.* BU 1972 Hong Kong.

ATR 94 To UK, renamed HMS *Flaunt.* Returned 13 Apr 1946. Sold 24 Sep 1946.
Later history: Merchant *Ming 102,* renamed *Ming 302* 1951, *Sui Jiu 203* 1986.

ATR 95 To UK, renamed HMS *Cheerly.* Returned 19 Feb 1946. Sold 24 Sep 1946. FFU.

ATR 96 To UK, renamed HMS *Emphatic.* Returned 13 Apr 1946. Sold 5 Dec 1947.
Later history: To Philippines, renamed *Ifugao.*

BAT 1 To UK, renamed HMS *Oriana.* Returned 13 Apr 1946. Sold 13 Mar 1948.
Later history: Merchant *Ocean Pride* 1948, renamed *Pan America* , *Zeeland* 1956, *Ras Adar* 1964 (Tunisian Navy).

BAT 2 Rec **ATR 90**, 30 Sep 1942.

BAT 3 To UK, renamed HMS *Favourite.* Returned 27 Mar 1946. Sold 18 Oct 1946.
Later history: Merchant *Susan A. Moran* 1946, renamed *Eugene F. Moran* 1947, *Monsanto* 1947, *Monte Branco* 1976.

BAT 4 To UK, renamed HMS *Integrity.* Returned 19 Feb 1946. Sold 2 Oct 1948.

BAT 5 To UK, renamed HMS *Lariat.* Returned 19 Feb 1946. Sold 17 Sep 1946.
Later history: Merchant *Ming 308.*

BAT 6 To UK, renamed HMS *Masterful.* Returned 11 Mar 1946. Sold 10 Nov 1947.
Later history: Merchant *Eugenia M. Moran,* renamed *Comanche* 1960.

BAT 7 To UK, renamed HMS *Aimwell.* Returned 30 Mar 1946. Sold 14 Mar 1948.
Later history: Merchant *Patricia Moller* 1948, renamed *Golden Cape* 1952, *Hawkeye* 1971. Sunk by Vietcong batteries in Mekong River, 2 Feb 1975.

BAT 8 To UK, renamed HMS *Bold.* Returned 1 Jun 1946. Sold 2 Oct 1948.

BAT 9 to UK, renamed HMS *Destiny.* Returned 13 Apr 1946. Sold 14 Mar 1948.
Later history: Merchant *Frosty Moller,* renamed *Christine Moller* 1950, *Oceanus* 1951, *Gele Zee* 1953, *Atlas* 1964, *Atlas II* 1975.

BAT 10 To UK, renamed HMS *Eminent.* Returned 13 Apr 1946. Sold 24 Sep 1946.
Later history: Merchant *Ming 305.*

BAT 11 To Australia, renamed HMAS *Reserve.*
Later history: Merchant *Pacific Reserve* 1964, renamed *Polaris* 1970.

BAT 12 To Australia, renamed HMAS *Sprightly.*
Later history: Merchant *Sprightly* 1970. BU 1992 Alang, India.

BAT 13 To Australia, renamed HMAS *Tancred.*
Later history: Merchant *Tancred* 1947.

BAT 14 To UK, renamed HMS *Weazel.* Returned 11 Mar 1946. Sold 17 Sep 1946.
Later history: Merchant *Ming 106.*

13
U.S. COAST GUARD

The U.S. Coast Guard came into existence in 1915 as an agency of the Treasury Department, a merger between the Revenue Cutter Service and the Lifesaving Service. Its ships were divided into three categories: first- or second-class cruising cutters, harbor cutters, and launches (later called patrol boats). Originally cutters had no numbers. Building numbers were assigned; these are noted with prefix CG but these were not used in service. Service numbers were assigned in 1941 as noted below.

Between 1920 and 1933 the Coast Guard, in addition to its ordinary duties, was fully involved in preventing the illegal import of liquor into the United States. A "war" at sea took place among the Coast Guard and numerous others intent on bringing the banned products in by sea. In order to patrol the coasts, including the inland Great Lakes, the Coast Guard expanded by building and acquiring numerous new cutters. The *Corwin-*, *Active-*, and *Thetis-*class cutters and numerous patrol boats were built to combat the rum runners. A number of old but fast destroyers were borrowed from the U.S. Navy, and many captured rum runners were also put into service. The Coast Guard maintained that it was not enforcing prohibition but only preventing smuggling.

Cutters were defined by their length. Vessels over 100' were named while those under had only numbers. On 1 Jul 1939 the Lighthouse Service was taken over by the Coast Guard, and its tenders became Coast Guard cutters. In 1941 larger cutters were assigned a number preceded by the letter *W*. On 1 Nov 1941 the Coast Guard became part of the Navy, and sometime later in 1942 cutters were identified by the Navy type designations prefixed with the letter *W*. At first the Navy prefixed the designations with the letter *G*, but later all Coast Guard vessels were assigned the *W* designation. Craft under 100 feet long were designated by a five-digit number of which the first two numbers indicated the length.

During the war the Coast Guard operated about 400 cutters and 4,000 small craft. In addition Coast Guard personnel manned some 300 Navy ships and 300 ships operated by the Army. In 1941, ten large cutters were given to the United Kingdom under lend-lease. The Greenland Patrol was started on 1 Jun 1941 with the cutters *Comanche* and *Raritan* and the schooner USS *Bowdoin*, to protect U.S. interests in that area. Large cutters were well suited as convoy escorts in the North Atlantic, and two were lost. Sixty 83' patrol boats were used at Normandy, and thirty were sent to the Pacific. The Coast Guard built and maintained the LORAN (long range navigation) system, at the time a top secret project. Some of the new buoy tenders were assigned to service the LORAN stations.

The Coast Guard reverted to the Treasury Department on 1 Jan 1946.

COAST GUARD CUTTERS ON THE LIST, 1922:

Name	Service Record
James Guthrie	Rebuilt 1893. Sold 24 Feb 1942.
Bear	Sold 3 May 1929.
	Later history: Merchant *Bear of Oakland.* Acq by USN as **AG 29**, 11 Sep 1939.
Morrill	Sold 12 Dec 1928.
	Later history: Merchant *Evangeline* 1929. se 1931.
Apache	Decomm 10 Dec 1937, to U.S. War Department. Converted 1944 to radio communication ship at Sydney, Australia.

Figure 13.1: *Tallapoosa* (WPG 52) in peacetime white paint; she served in the Bering Sea Patrol, then operated out of Savannah during the war.

Comanche	Went adrift in Gulf of Mexico after fire, 22 Jul 1927. Sold 13 Nov 1930.
	Later history: Merchant *Comanche* 1931, renamed *Turquino*, 1933. RR 1951.
Gresham	Sold 19 Jan 1935. Merchant *Gresham*. Reacquired as **WPG 85**, 21 Jan 1943. Poor condition. Decomm 7 Apr 1944. Sold 7 May 1944. (Armament: 2–3"/50, 4–20mm guns.)
	Later history: Merchant *T. V. McAllister*, renamed *Trade Winds* 1947, illegal immigrant ship to Palestine as *Hatikvah*. BU 1951 Haifa.
Manning	Decomm 22 May 1930. Sold 6 Dec 1930.
Algonquin	Sold 23 Sep 1931. Acq by USN as **YAG-29**, 1943.
Onondaga	Sold 16 Sep 1924.
	Later history: Merchant barge, lost in 1955.
Seminole	Decomm 17 Dec 1934. Sold 1937.
	Later history: Merchant *Seminole* 1937.
Tuscarora	Decomm 1 May 1936. Sold 1937.
	Later history: Merchant *Tuscarora*.
Pamlico	**WPR 57**. New Bern, N.C. Decomm 6 Sep 1946. Sold 7 Jul 1947.
	Later history: Merchant *C.W. Curlett* 1948, renamed *William Dea*. SE 1974.
Snohomish	Sold 1 Dec 1934.
	Later history: Merchant *Snohomish* 1935, renamed *Mataras* (ASR, Argentine Navy), 1948. R 1952.
Seneca	Decomm 21 Mar 1936. Sold 2 Sep 1936.
	Later history: MC training ship *Keystone State*, 1941. BU 1949.
Acushnet	Sank schr *George L. Elsley Jr.* in collision in fog in Nantucket Sound, 28 Feb 1932. To Navy 30 May 1936.
	Later history: USS *Acushnet* (**AT 63**). Stricken 8 Jan 1946.
Yamacraw	Decomm 11 Dec 1937.
	Later history: Merchant *Rescue* 1938, renamed *Pemex XV*, 1948. BU 1968 Mexico.
Unalga	Northeast Pacific 1913–30. **WPG 53**. Decomm 10 Oct 1945. Sold 19 Jul 1946. (Armament: 2–3"/50 guns.)
	Later history: Merchant *Ulua*, illegal immigrant ship to Palestine 1947 as *Haim Arlosoroff*.
Ossipee	Great Lakes, 1936–45. **WPR 50**. Decomm 6 Dec 1945. Sold 18 Sep 1946.
Tallapoosa	**WPG 52**. Decomm 8 Nov 1945. Sold 22 Jul 1946. (Armament: 2–3"/50 guns.)
	Later history: Merchant *Santa Maria*. SE 1990.

River Boats

Kankakee Sold 1936.

Yocona Sold 2 Nov 1925.

Tampa Class (240')

CG	No.	Name	Builder	Keel Laid	Launched	Comm.
36	WPG 48	*Tampa*	General Eng.	27 Sep 1920	19 Apr 1921	15 Sep 1921
37	WPG 45	*Haida*	General Eng.	27 Sep 1920	19 Apr 1921	26 Oct 1921
38	WPG 47	*Mojave*	General Eng.	20 Apr 1921	7 Sep 1921	12 Dec 1921
39	WPG 44	*Modoc*	General Eng.	20 Apr 1921	1 Oct 1921	14 Jan 1922

Figure 13.2: The cutter *Modoc* (WPG 46), seen here on 12 Jan 1945, witnessed the air attack on the German battleship *Bismarck*, 24 May 1941.

Displacement	1,780 tons, 1,955 f/l
Dimensions	240' (oa); 220' (wl) x 39' x 16'6"
Machinery	1 screw; TE; 2 B&W boilers; SHP 2,600; 16 knots
Endurance	3,500/15
Complement	122
Armament	2–5"/51, 2–6 pdr; (1942) added 1–3"/50; (1945) 2–5"/51, 2–3"/50, 4–20mm AA guns.

Notes: First cutters with turbo-electric drive.

Service Records:

WPG 48 *Tampa* Boston 1922, New York 1932, Mobile 1938. Helped rescue survivors from m/v *Morro Castle* off New Jersey, 8 Sep 1934. North Atlantic convoys. Decomm 1 Feb 1947. Sold 22 Sep 1947.
Later history: Merchant *Rigel Kent*. BU 1951 Savona, Italy.

WPG 45 *Haida* Bering Sea, Alaska. Decomm 13 Feb 1947. Sold 20 Jan 1948.

WPG 47 *Mojave* Fort Lauderdale, Fla. In collision with m/v *T. K. Bentley* at Gloucester, Mass., 8 Oct 1928. Decomm 3 Jul 1947. Sold 14 Feb 1948.

WPG 44 *Modoc* Wilmington, N.C., and Greenland. Decomm 1 Feb 1947. Sold 30 Jun 1947.
Later history: Merchant *Amalia V* 1948, renamed *Machala* 1950. BU 1964 Guayaquil.

Northland

CG	No.	Name	Builder	Keel Laid	Launched	Comm.
44	WPG 49	*Northland*	Newport News	16 Aug 1926	5 Feb 1927	14 May 1927

Displacement	1,785 tons
Dimensions	216'7" (oa);; 200' (wl) x 39' x 16'9"
Machinery	1 screw; diesel-electric; SHP 1,000; 11 knots
Endurance	10,200/11
Complement	107
Armament	2–6 pdr; (1941) 2–3"/50, 4–20mm AA guns

Notes: Reinforced for ice; welded hull. Had full sail rig (brigantine) until 1936. Carried 1 aircraft.

Service Record:

WPG 49 *Northland* U.S. West Coast and Bering Sea to 1938. Captured German radio stations in northern Greenland, Jul–Sep 1944. Disabled by ice, 1 Sep 1944. Decomm 27 Mar 1946. Sold 3 Jan 1947.

Figure 13.3: *Champlain* (CG 48), seen here in the 1930s, was one of ten *Lake* class cutters. She was transferred to the United Kingdom in 1941 and renamed *Sennen*.

2* Greenland.
Ship captured: Norwegian sealer *Buskoe* off Greenland, 12 Sep 1941.
Later history: Merchant *Northland*, illegal immigrant ship to Palestine 1947, renamed *Elath* (Israeli Navy) 1948, *Matzpen* BU 1962.

Chelan (Lake) Class (250')

CG No.	Name	Builder	Keel Laid	Launched	Comm.
45	*Chelan*	Beth. Quincy	14 Nov 1927	19 May 1928	5 Sep 1928
46	*Pontchartrain*	Beth. Quincy	29 Nov 1927	16 Jun 1928	13 Oct 1928
47	*Tahoe*	Beth. Quincy	22 Sep 1927	12 Jul 1928	8 Nov 1928
48	*Champlain*	Beth. Quincy	23 May 1928	11 Oct 1928	24 Jan 1929
49	*Mendota*	Beth. Quincy	20 Jun 1928	27 Nov 1928	23 Mar 1929
50	*Itasca*	General Eng.	—	16 Nov 1929	12 Jul 1930
51	*Sebago*	General Eng.	—	15 Jan 1930	2 Sep 1930
52	*Saranac*	General Eng.	—	12 Apr 1930	2 Oct 1930
53	*Shoshone*	General Eng.	—	11 Sep 1930	10 Jan 1931
54	*Cayuga*	United Staten I.	—	8 Oct 1931	22 Mar 1932

Displacement	1,662 tons, 2,075 f/l
Dimensions	256' (oa); 239' (wl) x 42' x 16'
Machinery	1 screw; turbo-electric; 2 B&W boilers; SHP 3,350; 17.3 knots
Endurance	8,000/12
Complement	97
Armament	1–5"/51, 1–3"/50, 2–6 pdr.; (1941) 2–3"/50.

Notes: Modified *Tampa* class, with cruiser stern. Transferred to Royal Navy under lend-lease 1941.

Service Records:

45 *Chelan* Seattle, then Boston. To UK 2 May 1941.
Later history: Renamed HMS *Lulworth*. Returned 12 Feb 1946. Sold 23 Oct 1947.

46 *Pontchartrain* Norfolk, then New York. To UK 30 Apr 1941.
Later history: Renamed HMS *Hartland*. Sunk by gunfire from French destroyer *Typhon* and shore batteries at Oran, Algeria, 8 Nov 1942.

47 *Tahoe* Bering Sea, then New Bedford, Mass. In collision with m/v *Silvermaple* at Oakland, Calif., 9 Jul 1932. To UK 30 Apr 1941.
Later history: Renamed HMS *Fishguard*. Returned 27 Mar 1946. Sold 24 Oct 1947.

48 *Champlain* Stapleton, N.Y. To UK 12 May 1941.
Later history: Renamed HMS *Sennen*. Returned as **WPG 319**, renamed ***Champlain***, 27 Mar 1946. †

49 *Mendota* Norfolk. Cadet practice ship. To UK 30 Apr 1941.
Later history: Renamed HMS *Culver*. Torpedoed and sunk by *U-105* in North Atlantic, 31 Jan 1942.

50 *Itasca* Honolulu, then San Diego. To UK 31 May 1941.
Later history: Renamed HMS *Gorleston*. Returned as **WPG 321**, renamed ***Itasca***, 23 Apr 1946. †

51 *Sebago* New York, then Norfolk. To UK 12 May 1941.
Later history: Renamed HMS *Walney*. Sunk by gunfire from French destroyers *Epervier* and *Tramontane* and shore batteries at Oran, Algeria, 8 Nov 1942.

52 *Saranac* Galveston. To UK 30 Apr 1941.
Later history: Renamed HMS *Banff*. Returned as **WPG 164**, renamed ***Sebec***, 27 Feb 1946. Renamed ***Tampa***, 27 May 1947. †

53 *Shoshone* Bering Sea. To UK 20 May 1941.
Later history: Renamed HMS *Landguard*. BU 1949 Colombo, Ceylon.

54 *Cayuga* Boston. Spanish Civil War (Sqn 40T), Sep 1936–1937. To UK 12 May 1941.
Later history: Renamed HMS *Totland*. Returned as **WPG 163**, renamed ***Mocoma***, May 1946. †

Escanaba Class (165' [A])

CG	No.	Name	Builder	Keel Laid	Launched	Comm.
55	WPG 77	*Escanaba*	Defoe	—	17 Sep 1932	23 Nov 1932
56	WPG 75	*Algonquin*	Pusey	—	25 Jul 1934	20 Oct 1934
57	WPG 76	*Comanche*	Pusey	—	6 Sep 1934	16 Dec 1934
58	WPG 78	*Mohawk*	Pusey	—	23 Oct 1934	19 Jan 1935
59	WPG 79	*Onondaga*	Defoe	—	2 Aug 1934	11 Sep 1934
60	WPG 80	*Tahoma*	Defoe	—	5 Sep 1934	22 Oct 1934

Displacement	1,005 tons f/l
Dimensions	165' (oa); 150' (wl) x 36' x 13'6"

Figure 13.4: *Tahoma* (WPG 80), 14 Jul 1942, a cruising class cutter.

Machinery	1 screw; GT; 2 boilers; SHP 1,500; 12.5 knots
Endurance	2,500/12
Complement	62; (1945) 98
Armament	2–3"/50, 3–20mm AA guns.

Notes: Steel hulls, strengthened for ice breaking. Modified *Tallapoosa* design.

Service Records:

WPG 77 *Escanaba* Boston. Sunk by explosion in North Atlantic, 13 Jun 1943 (101 killed).

WPG 75 *Algonquin* Portland, Me., Greenland. Decomm 18 Apr 1947. Sold 15 Nov 1948, BU.

WPG 76 *Comanche* South Greenland. Decomm 29 Jul 1947. Sold 10 Nov 1948.
Later history: Merchant *Relief* 1949, renamed *Hampton Roads* 1967, *Virginia* 1976. At Patriots Point Maritime Museum, Mt. Pleasant, S.C., to 1991.

WPG 78 *Mohawk* Boston. Decomm 8 Jan 1948. Sold 1 Nov 1948.
Later history: Merchant pilot *Philadelphia.* To museum at Wilmington, Del., 1974–90. FFU.

WPG 79 *Onondaga* Alaska. Decomm 24 Jul 1947. †

WPG 80 *Tahoma* Boston and Greenland. Decomm 18 Sep 1947. †

Figure 13.5: *Alexander Hamilton* (WPG 34), seen here on 27 Dec 1941, was the only Treasury class cutter lost during the war. She reassumed her full name to avoid confusion with the destroyer *Hamilton.*

Figure 13.6: The cutter *Spencer* (WPG 36), 3 May 1944, an example of the ships of the Treasury class, which made excellent convoy escorts.

Figure 13.7: *Bibb* (WAGC 31), 29 Jan 1945, after conversion to amphibious force flagship.

TREASURY CLASS (327')

CG	No.	Name	Builder	Keel Laid	Launched	Comm.
65	WPG 32	*George W. Campbell*	Phila. NYd	1 May 1935	3 Jun 1936	22 Oct 1936
66	WPG 35	*Samuel D. Ingham*	Phila. NYd	1 May 1935	3 Jun 1936	6 Nov 1936
67	WPG 33	*William J. Duane*	Phila. NYd	1 May 1935	3 Jun 1936	16 Oct 1936
68	WPG 37	*Roger B. Taney*	Phila. NYd	1 May 1935	3 Jun 1936	19 Dec 1936
69	WPG 34	*Alexander Hamilton*	New York NYd	11 Sep 1935	10 Nov 1936	4 Mar 1937
70	WPG 36	*John C. Spencer*	New York NYd	11 Sep 1935	6 Jan 1937	13 May 1937
71	WPG 31	*George M. Bibb*	Charleston	15 Aug 1935	14 Jan 1937	19 Mar 1937

Displacement	2,216 tons; 2,750 f/l
Dimensions	327' (oa); 308' (wl) x 41' x 15'
Machinery	2 screws; GT; 2 boilers; SHP 5,250; 19.5 knots
Endurance	4,200/19 or 7,012/12
Complement	123; (1945) 262
Armament	2–5"/51, 2–6 pdr; (1941) 3–5"/51, 3–3"/50; (1945) 2–5"/38, 3 twin 40mm, 4 to 8 20mm guns (WPG 37 *Taney*: 4–5").

Notes: All carried aircraft before World War II. Converted to amphibious force flagships (AGC), 1944. Very successful class. Three additional units were to be ordered to replace the *Ossipee*, *Tallapoosa*, and *Unalga*, but for economy reasons they were built as units of the *Owasco* class. Names were shortened after completion.

Service Records:

WPG 32 *George W. Campbell* Renamed ***Campbell***, Jun 1937. Pacific 1945. †
3* Convoy ON-166, Convoy UGS-40.
Submarine sunk: *U-606* in Mid-Atlantic, 22 Feb 1943 (damaged by ramming).

WPG 35 *Samuel D. Ingham* Renamed ***Ingham***, Jun 1937. †
4* Convoy SC-121, Subic Bay, Mindanao Ldgs., Visayan Is. Ldgs.
Submarine sunk: *U-626* in Mid-Atlantic, 15 Dec 1942.

WPG 33 *William J. Duane* Renamed ***Duane***, Jun 1937. †
3* Convoy HX-233, Convoy UGS-38, Southern France.
WPG 37 *Roger B. Taney* Renamed ***Taney***, Jun 1937. †
3* Pearl Harbor, Convoy UGS-38, Okinawa.
WPG 34 *Alexander Hamilton* Renamed ***Hamilton***, Jun 1937; renamed ***Alexander Hamilton***, 12 Jan 1942. Torpedoed by *U-132* 29 Jan and foundered in tow off Reykjavik, 30 Jan 1942 (26 killed).
WPG 36 *John C. Spencer* Renamed ***Spencer***, Jun 1937. Went aground in San Pedro Bay, Leyte, 7 Dec 1944. †
9* Convoy ON-166, Convoy SC-121, Convoy HX-233, Leyte, Brunei, Ldgs. at Nasugbu, Ldgs. on Palawan I., Visayan Is Ldgs., Mindanao Ldgs.
Submarines sunk: *U-225* in Mid-Atlantic, 21 Feb 1943; *U-175* southwest of Ireland, 17 Apr 1943 (1 killed).
WPG 31 *George M. Bibb* Renamed ***Bibb***, Jun 1937. Pacific 1945. †
2* Convoy SC-121, Okinawa.

Owasco Class

No.	Name	Builder	Keel Laid	Launched	Comm.
WPG 39	*Owasco* LD as *Oneida*	W. Pipe	17 Nov 1943	18 Jun 1944	18 May 1945
WPG 40	*Winnebago*	W. Pipe	1 Dec 1943	2 Jul 1944	21 Jun 1945
WPG 41	*Chautaqua*	W. Pipe	22 Dec 1943	14 May 1944	4 Aug 1945
WPG 42	*Sebago* LD as *Wachusett*	W. Pipe	7 Jun 1943	28 May 1944	20 Sep 1945
WPG 43	*Iroquois*	W. Pipe	19 Jun 1944	22 Oct 1944	9 Feb 1946
WPG 44	*Wachusett* LD as *Huron*	W. Pipe	3 Jul 1944	5 Nov 1944	23 Mar 1946
WPG 64	*Escanaba* LD as *Otsego*	W. Pipe	25 Oct 1944	23 Mar 1945	20 Mar 1946
WPG 65	*Winona*	W. Pipe	8 Nov 1944	22 Apr 1945	19 Apr 1946
WPG 66	*Klamath*	W. Pipe	13 Dec 1944	2 Sep 1945	19 Jun 1946
WPG 67	*Minnetonka* LD as *Sunapee*	W. Pipe	26 Dec 1944	21 Nov 1945	11 Jul 1946
WPG 68	*Androscoggin*	W. Pipe	30 Dec 1944	16 Sep 1945	26 Sep 1946
WPG 69	*Mendota*	Curtis Bay	5 Jul 1943	29 Feb 1944	2 Jun 1945
WPG 70	*Pontchartrain* LD as *Okeechobee*	Curtis Bay	5 Jul 1943	29 Feb 1944	28 Jul 1945

Displacement	1,563 tons, 2,010 f/l
Dimensions	254' (oa); 245' (bp) x 43' x 17'
Machinery	1 screw; TE; 2 boilers; SHP 4,000; 16 kts
Endurance	5,800/19
Complement	276
Armament	4–5"/38, 2 quad 40mm, 4–20mm guns

Notes: Ordered as CG 105–17, to replace "Lake" class. Large armament for their size, but units completed after the war did not receive full wartime armament.

Service Records:

WPG 39 *Owasco* †
WPG 40 *Winnebago* †
WPG 41 *Chautauqua* †
WPG 42 *Sebago* †
WPG 43 *Iroquois* †
WPG 44 *Wachusett* †
WPG 64 *Escanaba* †
WPG 65 *Winona* †
WPG 66 *Klamath* †
WPG 67 *Minnetonka* †
WPG 68 *Androscoggin* †
WPG 69 *Mendota* †
WPG 70 *Pontchartrain* †

No.	Name	Builder	Launched	Acquired	Comm.
WPG 59	*North Star*	Berg	1932	1941	14 May 1941

Displacement	1,435 grt, 2,200 f/l
Dimensions	225' (oa); 216'2" (bp) x 41' x 16'6"
Machinery	1 screw; diesel; bhp 1,500; 13 knots
Endurance	9,000/11
Complement	133
Armament	2–3"/50, 6–20mm, 1 aircraft

Notes: Wood hull. Acquired from the U.S. Department of the Interior. Name retained.

Service Record:

WPG 59 *North Star* Greenland. Trapped and damaged by ice, Jul 1943. To Navy 15 Jan 1944.

Later history: USS *North Star* (IX 148). Merchant *North Star*, se 1954.

Figure 13.8: *Winnebago* (WPG 40), 23 Jun 1947, an *Owasco* class cutter.

Figure 13.9: *North Star* (WPG 59), seen here on 9 Nov 1942, was acquired from the U.S. Department of the Interior for service in Arctic waters.

No.	Name	Builder	Launched	Acquired	Comm.
WPG 122	*Nourmahal*	Germania	1928	1940	21 Aug 1940

Displacement	1,969 grt, 3,200 f/l
Dimensions	264'10" (oa); 251'6" (bp) x 41'6" x 18'5"
Machinery	2 screws; diesel; bhp 3,200; 13.7 knots
Endurance	12,700/13
Complement	107
Armament	2–4"/50; (1945) 1–4"/50, 6–20mm guns

Notes: Converted to weather station. Former name retained.

Service Record:

WPG 122 *Nourmahal* Escort duty 1942–43. To USN as **PG 72,** 16 Jun 1943. Returned to USCG, 12 Jan 1944. Decomm 30 May 1946, laid up. Burned and sank at Texas City, Tex., 23 Nov 1964.

No.	Name	Builder	Launched	Acquired	Comm.
WPG 181	*Cobb*	Delaware River	21 Apr 1906	1943	20 Jul 1943
	ex–*Governor Cobb* (2 Aug 1943)				

Displacement	2,522 grt, 3,500 f/l
Dimensions	300'8" (oa); x 55' x 19'
Machinery	3 screws; geared turbines; 6 Scotch boilers; SHP 5,000; 14.7 knots
Endurance	3,300/14.7
Complement	123
Armament	2–5"/38, 6–20mm

Notes: Used as helicopter test ship, 1944. Had machinery failures.

Service Record:

WPG 181 *Cobb* Decomm 31 Jan 1946. Sold 6 Mar 1947; BU 1947 Chester, Pa.

No.	Name	Builder	Launched	Acquired	Comm.
WPG 182	*Bodkin*	Pusey	May 1914	1942	—
	ex–*Burke* (1 Jun 1943), ex–*Nokomis*, ex-USS *Nokomis* (SP 109, PY 6)				

Displacement	1,000 tons f/l
Dimensions	243' (oa); x 31'7" x 10'6"
Machinery	2 screws; VTE, 2 B&W boilers; SHP 2,000; 16 knots
Complement	118
Armament	never armed

Notes: Conversion at Curtis Bay suspended because of poor condition. Had served in Navy in World War I.

Service Record:

WPG 182 *Bodkin* Conversion canceled 15 Jul 1943. BU 1944.

No.	Name	Builder	Launched	Acquired	Comm.
WPG 183	*Mayflower*	Thompson	1896	6 Sep 1943	20 Oct 1943
	ex–*Butte* (15 Aug 43), ex–*Mayflower* (31 Jul 42), ex–PY 1				

Displacement	2,690 tons
Dimensions	320'7" (oa); 276' (wl) x 37' x 19'10"
Machinery	2 screws; VTE; 2 boilers; SHP 2,400; 12 knots
Endurance	4,800/12
Complement	153
Armament	1–5"/51, 2–3"/50, 6–20mm guns

Notes: Used for radar training. Former presidential yacht acquired for war service.

Service Record:

WPG 183 *Mayflower* Decomm 1 Jul 1946. Sold 8 Jan 1947.
Later history: Merchant *Mayflower*, renamed *Malla* 1948.

No.	Name	Builder	Launched	Acquired	Comm.
WPG 284	*Sea Cloud*	Germania	25 Apr 1931	1942	4 Apr 1942
	ex–*Sea Cloud*, ex–*Hussar* (1935)				

Displacement	2,323 grt, 3,077 f/l
Dimensions	316' (oa); x 49'2" x 19'
Machinery	2 screws; diesel; SHP 1600; 12 knots
Endurance	20,000/12
Complement	186
Armament	2–3"/50, 5–20mm guns

Notes: Four masted yacht, masts removed in CG service.

Service Record:

WPG 284 *Sea Cloud* To USN, 9 Apr 1943 as *Sea Cloud* (IX 99). Decomm 4 Nov 1944, rtnd to USCG, sold.
Later history: Merchant *Angelita*, renamed *Patria* then *Antarna.*

DESTROYERS

CG-1	*Cassin*	DD 43
CG-2	*Conyngham*	DD 58
CG-3	*Cummings*	DD 44
CG-4	*Downes*	DD 45
CG-5	*Ericsson*	DD 56
CG-6	*McDougal*	DD 54
CG-7	*Porter*	DD 59
CG-8	*Ammen*	DD 35
CG-9	*Beale*	DD 40
CG-10	*Burrows*	DD 29
CG-11	*Fanning*	DD 37
CG-12	*Henley*	DD 39
CG-13	*Jouett*	DD 41
CG-14	*McCall*	DD 28
CG-15	*Monaghan*	DD 32
CG-16	*Patterson*	DD 36
CG-17	*Paulding*	DD 22
CG-18	*Roe*	DD 24
CG-19	*Terry*	DD 25
CG-20	*Trippe*	DD 33
CG-21	*Davis*	DD 65

Figure 13.10: *Paulding* (CG 17), one of the old destroyers that served in the Coast Guard during Prohibition to combat rum runners.

CG-22	*Shaw*	DD 68
CG-23	*Tucker*	DD 57
CG-24	*Wainwright*	DD 62
CG-25	*Wilkes*	DD 67
CG-15	*Abel P. Upshur*	DD 193
CG-16	*George E. Badger*	DD 196
CG-17	*Herndon*	DD 198
CG-18	*Hunt*	DD 194
CG-19	*Welborn C. Wood*	DD 195
CG-20	*Semmes*	DD 189

Note: These were destroyers acquired from the Navy to enforce Prohibition 1924. All were stationed at New York; New London, Connecticut; and Boston. A second group of "flush-deckers" was taken over in 1930 repeating earlier numbers. The *Paulding* was damaged in a severe storm off Cape Cod, losing a funnel, 27 Feb 1927. She rammed and sank submarine *S-4* in a collision, 17 Dec 1927. All were returned upon the repeal of Prohibition in 1933. For dates and details see pp. 46, 47, 51.

PATROL VESSELS

Acquired Vessels

Name	Built	GRT	Dimensions	Acquired
Carolina	1906	—	57' x 13'	1906; sold 3 Aug 1922
Valiant	1905	—	42' x 9'	1919; sold 28 Jul 1922
	ex–*Virginia*			
Coquet	1906	120	58' x 18'	1 Mar 1918; returned 15 May 1919
	ex–*Coquet*			
Alexander Hamilton	1896	1,000	168' x 36'	1 Jul 1921; **WIX 272**; sold 30 Dec 1944.
	ex–USS *Vicksburg* (PG 11)			
Lexington	1897	234	115' x 22'	30 Dec 1922; sold 4 Nov 1924
	ex–*Lexington* (USA), ex–*Lexington* (Massachusetts State Police)			
Wayanda	—	—	—	21 Oct 1924; sold 1935
	ex–*Col. William H. Baldwin* (USA)			
Colfax	1921	—	—	27 Oct 1924; sold 7 Dec 1928
	ex–*Gen. Rufus Ingalls* (USA)			
Pickering	1921	—	128'6" x 28'	Oct 1924; decomm 7 Dec 1928
	ex–*Brig. Gen. O. S. Allison*			
Argus	1921	—	128'6" x 28'	1 Dec 1924; decomm 1 Nov 1929
	ex–*Major E. Pickett* (USA)			
Gen. George Gibson	—	—	—	31 Oct 1924; sold 7 Jan 1927
	ex–USLHS			
Gen. Ludington	—	—	—	20 Jan 1925; sold 11 Mar 1927
	ex–USLHS , ex–*Gen. M. I. Ludington*			
Leopard	1920	176	94' x 24'	6 Jun 1926; sold 18 May 1935

Note: *Wayanda, Colfax, Argus,* and *Pickering* had concrete hulls.

Name	Formerly	Acquired	Fate
Carrabassett	AT 35	13 Oct 1924.	**WAT 55**. Decomm 26 Jul 1946.
Redwing	AM 48	11 Oct 1924.	Returned to USN 5 Aug 1941.

Name	Builder	Launched	Comm.
Corwin	Defoe	21 Oct 1925	—
Dallas	Defoe	29 Oct 1925	—
Dexter	Defoe	3 Nov 1925	—
Eagle	Defoe	11 Nov 1925	—
Forward	Defoe	7 Nov 1925	14 Nov 1925
Gallatin	Defoe	10 May 1926	—
Mahoning	Defoe	15 May 1926	—
Nansemond	Defoe	1 Jun 1926	—
Naugatuck	Defoe	6 Jun 1926	—
Patriot	Defoe	12 Jun 1926	—
Perry	Defoe	1 Jul 1926	—
Petrel	Defoe	16 Jul 1926	—
Wolcott	Defoe	26 Jul 1926	—

Displacement	210 tons f/l
Dimensions	99'8" (oa) x 23' x 8'
Machinery	2 screws; diesel; bhp 330; 9 knots
Endurance	2,492/9
Complement	17
Armament	1–3"/23

Notes: A 100' class. Steel hull, designed for inshore work to combat "rum runners" during Prohibition. Bay and sound tenders. *Forward, Nansemond,* and *Petrel* modified for aids-to-navigation work, 1941.

Service Records:

Corwin Decomm 29 Feb 1936. To USN 11 May 1936, **YP-62**. Sold 14 Aug 1946.

Dallas Decomm 10 Jan 1936. To USN 16 May 1936, **YP-61**. Sold 14 Aug 1946.

Dexter Sank rum runner *I'm Alone* off Louisiana, 22 Mar 1929. Decomm 31 Jan 1936. To USN 19 May 1936, **YP-63**. Sold 2 Jul 1946.
Later history: Merchant *Kingfisher*, renamed *Jamaica II, Trinidad* se 1974.

Eagle Decomm 29 Feb 1936. To USN 16 May 1936, **YP 64**. Sold 8 May 1946.
Later history: Merchant *Eagle.*

Forward Rec **WAGL 160**, 1942. Decomm 14 Aug 1947, sold 9 Sep 1947.
Later history: Merchant *Stanolind 27*, renamed *Forward*, se 1998.

Gallatin Decomm 1934. To USN 1934, **YP-42**. Sold 6 Dec 1946.
Later history: Merchant *Orca*; se 1974.

Mahoning To USN 1934, **YP-41**. Sold 16 Jan 1947.
Later history: Merchant *Mahoning*, se 1948.

Nansemond Renamed ***Phlox***, 1 Sep 1941. Rec **WAGL 161**, 1942.
Later history: Merchant *Salvor*, renamed *Big Red.* Lost 1970.

Naugatuck Decomm and trfd to USN 23 Dec 1935, **YP-56**. Sold 19 Nov 1946.
Later history: Merchant *Shamrock, E. D. Smith, Sea Eagle*, se 1978.

Patriot To USN 24 Aug 1936, **YT-127**. Rec **YP-69**, 1 Mar 1938. Sold 20 Nov 1946.

Perry Decomm 31 Dec 1937.

Petrel Portland, Me. Renamed ***Pine***, 1 Jul 1940. Rec **WAGL 162**, 1942. sold 15 Jul 1948.

Later history: Merchant *Pine*, renamed *Mighty Red*; se 1974.

Wolcott Decomm 10 Feb 1936. Trfd to U.S. Army Corps of Engineers.

Later history: Merchant *Pacific*, renamed *Willamette Pacific* 1977, then *Imagineer*, *Friendship*.

Active Class (125')

No.	Name	Builder	Launched	Comm.
WPC 125	*Active*	NY Sbdg	30 Nov 1926	13 Jan 1927
WPC 126	*Agassiz*	NY Sbdg	30 Nov 1926	20 Jan 1927
WPC 127	*Alert*	NY Sbdg	30 Nov 1926	27 Jan 1927
WPC 128	*Antietam*	NY Sbdg	30 Nov 1926	25 Jan 1927
WPC 129	*Bonham*	NY Sbdg	30 Nov 1926	29 Jan 1927
WPC 130	*Boutwell*	NY Sbdg	27 Jan 1927	21 Feb 1927
WPC 131	*Cahoone*	NY Sbdg	27 Jan 1927	21 Feb 1927
WPC 132	*Cartigan*	NY Sbdg	27 Jan 1927	3 Mar 1927
WPC 134	*Crawford*	NY Sbdg	27 Jan 1927	21 Feb 1927
WPC 157	*Cuyahoga*	NY Sbdg	27 Jan 1927	3 Mar 1927
WPC 135	*Diligence*	NY Sbdg	27 Jan 1927	22 Feb 1927
WPC 136	*Dix*	NY Sbdg	27 Jan 1927	5 Mar 1927
WPC 137	*Ewing*	NY Sbdg	15 Mar 1927	26 Mar 1927
WPC 138	*Faunce*	NY Sbdg	15 Mar 1927	1 Apr 1927
WPC 139	*Frederick Lee*	NY Sbdg	15 Mar 1927	5 Apr 1927
WPC 140	*General Greene*	NY Sbdg	14 Feb 1927	7 Apr 1927
WPC 141	*Harriet Lane*	NY Sbdg	30 Nov 1926	4 Jan 1927
WPC 142	*Jackson*	NY Sbdg	14 Feb 1927	14 Mar 1927
WPC 143	*Kimball*	NY Sbdg	25 Apr 1927	7 May 1927
WPC 144	*Legare*	NY Sbdg	14 Feb 1927	17 Mar 1927
WPC 145	*Marion*	NY Sbdg	15 Mar 1927	6 Apr 1927
WPC 146	*McLane*	NY Sbdg	22 Mar 1927	8 Apr 1927
WPC 133	*Montgomery*	NY Sbdg	22 Mar 1927	4 Apr 1927
WPC 147	*Morris*	NY Sbdg	4 Apr 1927	19 Apr 1927
WPC 148	*Nemaha*	NY Sbdg	4 Apr 1927	19 Apr 1927
WPC 149	*Pulaski*	NY Sbdg	4 Apr 1927	20 Apr 1927
WPC 150	*Reliance*	NY Sbdg	18 Apr 1927	26 Apr 1927
WPC 151	*Rush*	NY Sbdg	18 Apr 1927	27 Apr 1927
WPC 152	*Tiger*	NY Sbdg	18 Apr 1927	3 May 1927
WPC 153	*Travis*	NY Sbdg	18 Apr 1927	29 Apr 1927
WPC 154	*Vigilant*	NY Sbdg	25 Apr 1927	3 May 1927
WPC 155	*Woodbury*	NY Sbdg	2 May 1927	11 May 1927
WPC 156	*Yeaton*	NY Sbdg	2 May 1927	10 May 1927

Figure 13.11: *Yeaton* (WPC 156), 6 Aug 1942; this 125' chaser type was built in 1927 to enforce Prohibiton.

Displacement	220 tons
Dimensions	125' (oa); 120' (wl) x 23'6" x 9'
Machinery	2 screws; diesel; bhp 500/800; 12 knots
Endurance	2,500/12
Complement	22
Armament	1–3"/23, 2–20mm guns

Notes: Builder was briefly named American Brown-Boveri at the time. Offshore patrol vessels designed to combat rum runners. Reengined in late 1930s. *Active*, *Colfax*, *Crawford*, *Ewing*, *Harriet Lane*, *Legare*, *McLane*, *Vigilant*, *Diligence*, and *Woodbury* served as buoy tenders 1941–42. A very successful class.

Service Records:

WPC 125 *Active* Greenland, then Caribbean SF. †

WPC 126 *Agassiz* Damaged in collision with m/v *Prince George* in fog off Cape Ann, 7 Jul 1928. Caribbean SF. †

WPC 127 *Alert* Western SF. †

WPC 128 *Antietam* Eastern SF. Renamed ***Bedloe***, 1 Jun 1943. Foundered in hurricane off North Carolina, 14 Sep 1944 (26 lost).

WPC 129 *Bonham* Northwest SF. †

WPC 130 *Boutwell* Gulf SF. †

WPC 131 *Cahoone* Sank suspected rum runner *James E.* in accidental collision off Long I., 30 Oct 1929. Helped rescue survivors of m/v *Morro Castle* off N.J., 8 Sep 1934. Western SF. †

WPC 132 *Cartigan* Eastern SF. Laid up 1946–47. †

WPC 134 *Crawford* Caribbean SF. Decomm 15 Aug 1947. †

WPC 157 *Cuyahoga* To USN, 29 May 1933. Rec **AG 26**, 30 Nov 1937. Returned to USCG, 17 May 1941. Caribbean SF. †

WPC 135 *Diligence* Western SF. †

WPC 136 *Dix* Caribbean SF. †

WPC 137 *Ewing* ASW training, San Diego. Laid up 1947. †

WPC 138 *Faunce* Greenland. †

WPC 139 *Frederick Lee* Greenland. †

WPC 140 *General Greene* Eastern SF. †

WPC 141 *Harriet Lane* Eastern SF. Decomm 29 Apr 1946. Sold 16 Jun 1948.

Later history: Merchant *Humble AC-4*, renamed *Snipe*, then *Roy-Von* 1973; se 1974.

WPC 142 *Jackson* Eastern SF. Foundered in hurricane off North Carolina coast, 14 Sep 1944 (21 lost).

WPC 143 *Kimball* Training ship, Merchant Marine Academy, New York, 1939. Eastern SF. †

WPC 144 *Legare* Rammed and sank rum runner *Symor* off Nantucket, 4 Apr 1931. Caribbean SF. †

WPC 145 *Marion* Caribbean SF. †

WPC 146 *McLane* †

1* Western SF.

Submarine sunk: Claimed *RO-32* off Ketchikan, Alaska, 9 Jul 1942 (identification wrong, no sub sunk).

WPC 133 *Montgomery* Renamed ***Colfax***, 1 Apr 1933. Caribbean SF. †

WPC 147 *Morris* Training, San Diego. †

WPC 148 *Nemaha* Laid up 1935–36. Northwest SF. Decomm 21 Jul 1947. Sold 14 Jun 1948.

Later history: Merchant *Nemaha*, renamed *Sea Monarch II* 1952, *Le Roi* 1958, *International Tug* 1968, *Emerson I*, *Den Den*. se 1992.

WPC 149 *Pulaski* Western SF. Decomm 4 Dec 1946. Sold 14 Jul 1948.

Later history: Merchant *Pulaski*, renamed *Cementos No.1* 1957; se 1992.

WPC 150 *Reliance* Hawaiian SF. Decomm 8 Aug 1947. †
1* Pearl Harbor.
WPC 151 *Rush* Sunk in collision with m/v *J. A. Moffett Jr.* in Ambrose Channel, N.Y., 29 Dec 1927; salved. Caribbean SF. Decomm 21 Aug 1947. Sold 6 Jul 1948.
Later history: Merchant tug *Humble AC-1*, renamed *Vitow I* 1964; se 1974.
WPC 152 *Tiger* Hawaiian SF. Decomm 12 Nov 1947. Sold 14 Jun 1948.
1* Pearl Harbor.
Later history: Merchant *Tiger* 1949, renamed *Cherokee* 1968, *Polar Merchant* 1976; se 1992.
WPC 153 *Travis* Greenland. In collision with m/v *East Breeze* off Halifax, Nova Scotia, 30 Nov 1944. †
WPC 154 *Vigilant* Gulf SF. †
WPC 155 *Woodbury* Gulf SF. Decomm 11 Dec 1946. Sold 6 Jul 1948.
Later history: Merchant tug *Humble AC-3* 1947, renamed *Challenge* 1963, *Challenge 1* 1972; se 1992.
WPC 156 *Yeaton* Caribbean SF. †

Thetis Class (165' [B])

CG	No.	Name	Builder	Keel Laid	Launched	Comm.
P-1	WPC 115	*Thetis*	Bath	19 May 1931	9 Nov 1931	27 Nov 1931
P-2	WPC 103	*Aurora*	Bath	6 Jun 1931	28 Nov 1931	21 Dec 1931
P-3	WPC 104	*Calypso*	Bath	7 May 1931	6 Jan 1932	16 Jan 1932
P-4	WPC 106	*Daphne*	Bath	15 May 1931	29 Jan 1932	12 Feb 1932
P-5	WPC 109	*Hermes*	Bath	20 May 1931	23 Feb 1932	7 Mar 1932
P-6	WPC 110	*Icarus*	Bath	23 Jul 1931	19 Mar 1932	1 Apr 1932
P-7	WPC 114	*Perseus*	Bath	6 Aug 1931	11 Apr 1932	27 Apr 1932
P-8	WPC 100	*Argo*	Mathis	—	12 Nov 1931	6 Jan 1933
P-9	WPC 108	*Galatea*	Mathis	—	10 Dec 1932	3 Feb 1933
P-10	WPC 102	*Atalanta*	Lake Union	—	16 Jun 1934	20 Sep 1934
P-11	WPC 101	*Ariadne*	Lake Union	—	21 Jul 1934	9 Oct 1934
P-12	WPC 105	*Cyane*	Lake Union	—	30 Aug 1934	25 Oct 1934
P13	WPC 107	*Dione*	Manitowoc	—	30 Jun 1934	5 Oct 1934
P-14	WPC 187	*Electra*	Manitowoc	—	30 Jun 1934	25 Oct 1934
P-15	WPC 113	*Pandora*	Manitowoc	—	30 Jun 1934	1 Nov 1934
P-16	WPC 116	*Triton*	Marietta	—	7 Jul 1934	20 Nov 1934
P-17	WPC 112	*Nike*	Marietta	—	7 Jul 1934	24 Oct 1934
P-18	WPC 111	*Nemesis*	Marietta	—	7 Jul 1934	10 Oct 1934

Figure 13.12: *Aurora* (WPC 103), 5 Jan 1943; this 165' submarine chaser type was built in 1931.

Displacement	337 tons
Dimensions	165' (oa); 169'9" (wl) x 25'3" x 9'6"
Machinery	2 screws; diesel; bhp 1,340; 16 knots
Endurance	1,750/14
Complement	44
Armament	1–3"/23; (1945) 2–3"/50, 2–20mm

Notes: Originally designed to enforce Prohibition laws. Very successful and retained for a long time in service.

Service Records:

WPC 100 *Argo* Newport, R.I. †
WPC 101 *Ariadne* Alameda, Calif. Laid up 1946–49. †
WPC 102 *Atalanta* Bering Sea. †
WPC 103 *Aurora* Bering Sea. †
WPC 104 *Calypso* To USN 17 May 1941 as *Calypso* (AG 35). Returned 20 Jan 1942. Norfolk, Va. Decomm 18 Jul 1947. †
WPC 105 *Cyane* Ketchikan. †
WPC 106 *Daphne* Alameda, Calif. †
WPC 107 *Dione* Norfolk, Va. †
WPC 187 *Electra* to USN 8 Nov 1935.
Later history: USS *Potomac* (AG 25). Returned 21 Nov 1945. Decomm 23 May 1946. Merchant *Potomac*.
WPC 108 *Galatea* Key West, Fla. †
WPC 109 *Hermes* San Pedro, Calif. Sold 16 May 1958. †
WPC 110 *Icarus* New York. Decomm 21 Oct 1946. †
1* sub
Submarine sunk: *U-352* off Cape Hatteras, 9 May 1942.
WPC 111 *Nemesis* St. Petersburg, Fla. Damaged in collision with m/v *Felipe de Neve* off Point Judith Light, R.I., 11 Jan 1945. †
1*
WPC 112 *Nike* Gulfport, Miss. †
1*
WPC 113 *Pandora* Key West, Fla. †
WPC 114 *Perseus* Juneau, Alaska, and San Diego. †
WPC 115 *Thetis* Key West, Fla. Decomm 1 Jul 1947. †
1* sub
Submarine sunk: *U-157* north of Havana, 13 Jun 1942.
WPC 116 *Triton* Key West, Fla. †

PATROL BOATS

No.	W-	Class (feet)	Number Built	Year	Dimensions	Tons	HP	Speed (in Knots)
CG-100–302	74300–350	74	203	1924–25	74'11" x 13'8" x 4'	37	400	13.5
CG-400–405	78300–305	78	6	1931	78'9" x 14'5" x 4'	43	1,070	21.7
CG-406–414	80300–308	80	9	1937	80'9" x 15'8" x 4'	52	1,600	25
CG-439–441	72005, 72300–301	72	3	1933–37	72' x 15'2" x 3'9"	27	1,600	34
CG-442–443	65300–301	65	2	1937	65' x 14' x 3'9"	30	1,600	28
CG-450–499, 600–34	83300–529	83	230	1938–42	83' x 16' x 4'6"	50	1,200	23.5

Notes: CG numbers discontinued in 1942 and replaced by five-digit numbers using the length as the first two digits. Thus, CG-119 became W-74300. The 83' class numbers started with W-83300 and ended with 83529. Sixty of the 83' patrol boats served at Normandy. All were armed with 1–20mm gun.

Losses

CG-111 Burned, 7 Mar 1931.
CG-113 Sunk in collision, 25 Jul 1928.
CG-114 Lost after collision with a Navy boat off Atlantic City, N.J., 16 Nov 1925.
CG-126 Stranded in storm in Narragansett Bay, Mass., 10 Feb 1926.
CG-134 Foundered in gale off Nantucket, 11 Oct 1925.
CG-188 Lost in hurricane, Sep 1928.
CG-230 Lost in hurricane, Sep 1928.
CG-256 Wrecked on Spanish Cay, Calif., 12 Oct 1933.

W-74327 Rammed and sunk by submarine *Thornback* off Portsmouth, N.H., 10 Nov 1944. (ex-CG-211)
W-83301 Sunk in typhoon at Okinawa, 9 Oct 1945.
W-83306 Sunk in typhoon at Okinawa, 9 Oct 1945.
W-83415 Sank after being damaged on wreckage in storm off Normandy, 21 Jun 1944.
W-83421 Sunk in collision with *SC 1330* off Great Isaac Light, Bahamas, 29 Jun 1944.
W-83471 Foundered in storm off Normandy, 21 Jun 1944.

AIR-SEA RESCUE BOATS

In 1945, 70 wood submarine chasers were transferred from the Navy to the Coast Guard for air-sea rescue duties. They were given bird names beginning with *Air* such as *Air Brant.* Because of a shortage of Coast Guard personnel, few were put into service. Most were kept in reserve and sold by 1948.

Figure 13.13: *CG-83306*, a standard 83' patrol boat.

CONVERTED YACHTS

No.	Name	Builder	Launched	Acquired	Comm.
WPY 175	*Marita*	Smiths Dock	5 Nov 1918	Nov 42	30 Jan 1943
	ex-*Marita* (1942), ex-*Kaspar* (1925), ex-*Seghill* (1922), ex-HMS *Kilmacrennan* (1920)				

Displacement	632 grt, 1,450 f/l
Dimensions	183' (oa); 172'2" (bp) x 30' x 17'
Machinery	1 screw; VTE; 1 boiler; SHP 700; 7 knots
Complement	85
Armament	2–3"/50, 4–20mm.

Notes: Built as British "Kil" class gunboat.

Service Record:

WPY 175 *Marita* Training ship. Decomm 13 Nov 1944. Sold 3 May 1945.
Later history: Merchant *Marita*, renamed *Tela* 1948. BU 1964 Guayaquil, Ecuador.

Figure 13.14: *Marita* (WPY 175). Used for training at Little Creek, Virginia, it was built as a "Kil" class gunboat for the Royal Navy during World War I.

No.	Name	Builder	Built	Comm	GRT	Dimensions (oa);	Machinery
WPYc 158	*Wicomico*	Robins	1914	14 Oct 1942	303	175' x 23'6" x 12'8"	1/diesel
	ex–*Catoctin* (16 Aug 1943), ex–*Dupont*, ex–*Saelmo*, ex–USS *Kwasind* (1917), ex–*Nokomis*						
WPYc 159	*Micawber*	Nevins	1925	8 Jul 1942	153	110' x 20'" x 6'8"	2/diesel
	ex–*Ottilie*, ex–*Nevada*						
WPYc 337	*Nellwood*	Pusey	1929	26 Mar 1943	244	126'1" x 21'11" x 9'	2/diesel
	ex–*Nellwood II*, ex–*Murdona*, ex–*Acania*						
WPYc 343	*Blanco*	Beth. Wilm.	1923	20 Aug 1942	198	120' x 24'10" x 6'10"	1/diesel
	ex–*Atlantic*, ex–*Moby Dick*						
WPYc 345	*Madalan*	Martinolich	1928	1 Apr 1943	357	147'6" x 30'2" x 14'9"	1/diesel
WPYc 346	*Bedford*	Lawley	1913	28 Jul 1942	201	164'6" x 18' x 7'	1/VTE
	ex–*Condor*, ex–*Gipsy Jo*, ex–*Athero*, ex–*Gem*, ex–*Gem* (SP 41), ex–*Gem*						
WPYc 348	*Thalassa*	Ditchburn Boats	1930	5 Feb 1943	138	100' x 18' x 5'6"	2/diesel
WPYc 352	*Boulder*	(Boston)	1906	4 Dec 1942	55	104'6" x 13'7" x 7'	1/diesel
	ex–*Elkhorn*						
WPYc 369	*Blanchard*	Pusey	1910	20 Aug 1942	101	118' x 15' x 5'6"	2/gasoline
	ex–*Nedra B.*, ex–*Alacrity*, ex–SP-206, ex–*Alacrity*						
WPYc 386	*Gertrude L. Thebaud*	Story	1930	24 Dec 1942	137	133' x 25'2" x 12'2"	1/diesel

Notes: *Bedford, Blanchard,* and *Wicomico* served in Navy in World War I. Armament, *Wicomico* 1–3"/50; *Nellwood* 1–6 pdr, 2–20mm; *Madalan* 2–20mm.

Service Records:

158 *Wicomico* Newport, R.I. Decomm Jun 1945.

159 *Micawber* Wood hull yacht. Gulf SF. Decomm 5 Jul 1945. Sold 18 Feb 1946.

337 *Nellwood* Converted to fireboat 1944. Training ship. Decomm 15. Nov 1946. Sold 23 Sep 1947.
Later history: Merchant *Nellwood II*, renamed *Acania*. se 1998.

343 *Blanco* Steel two-mast schooner. Gulf SF. Decomm 31 Oct 1945.
Later history: Merchant *Atlantic*, renamed *AA Jakkula, Luisa, Linda Lee, Lover Boy*.

345 *Madalan* Training ship. Decomm 7 Jul 1945. Returned 16 Oct 1945.
Later history: Merchant *Madalan*. Foundered at moorings, Cape Verde Is., 1957.

346 *Bedford* Steel hull yacht. Gulf SF. To USN 22 Jan 1943, renamed USS ***Perserverance*** (PYc 44).

348 *Thalassa* Wood yacht, training ship. Decomm 3 Jul 1945. Returned 26 Jun 1946.
Later history: Merchant *Thalassa*. Foundered off Vigo, Spain 31 Dec 1948.

352 *Boulder* Fishing boat. Atlantic City, N.J. Decomm 15 Jun 1943 .

369 *Blanchard* Steel hull yacht. Gulf SF. Decomm 25 Nov 1943.

386 *Gertrude L. Thebaud* Wood fishing schooner. Gloucester, Mass. Decomm 10 Feb 1944 and returned.
Later history: Merchant *Gertrude L. Thebaud*. Wrecked at LaGuiara, Venezuela, 6 Feb 1948.

DISTRICT PATROL VESSELS (TRAWLERS AND WHALERS)

No.	Name	Builder	Built	Comm	GRT	Dimensions (oa)	Machinery
WYP 163	*Atak*	Bath	1937	14 Jun 1942	243	128' x 23'5" x 11'8"	1/diesel
	ex–*Winchester*						
WYP 164	*Aivik*	Bath	1936	24 Jun 1942	251	128' x 23'5" x 11'8"	1/diesel
	ex–*Arlington*						
WYP 165	*Arvek*	Beth. Quincy	1936	16 Jul 1942	172	110'3" x 22'1" x 10'6"	1/diesel
	ex–*Triton*						
WYP 166	*Amarok*	General	1938	31 Jul 1942	251	128' x 24'1" x 12'7"	1/diesel
	ex–*Lark*, ex–*Greyhound One*						
WYP 167	*Arluk*	Beth. Quincy	1934	16 Jul 1942	172	110'3" x 22'1" x 10'6"	1/diesel
	ex–*Atlantic*						
WYP 168	*Aklak*	Beth. Quincy	1941	16 Jul 1942		170 116' x 22'5" x 10'6"	1/diesel
	ex–*Weymouth*						
WYP 169	*Nanok*	Snow	1941	7 Jun 1942	220	120' x 23'5" x 12'	1/diesel
	ex–*North Star*						
WYP 170	*Natsek*	Snow	1941	19 Jun 1942	225	116'9" x 23'6" x 11'8"	1/diesel
	ex–*Belmont*						
WYP 171	*Nogak*	Snow	1940	7 Jul 1942	176	111' x 23'6" x 11'8"	1/diesel
	ex–*St. George*						
WYP 172	*Alatok*	Cochrane	1922	22 Aug 1942	386	150'3" x 25' x 13'5"	1/VTE
	ex–*Hekla*, ex–*Sea Hawk*						
WYP 173	*Kodiak*	Duthie	1912	9 Mar 1943	148	106'10" x 19'2" x 12'4"	1/VTE
WYP 174	*Caddo*	Moran	1907	9 Mar 1943	151	103" x 17'7" x 11'8"	1/steam
	ex–*Tanginak*, ex–*Tyee Junior*						
WYP 312	*EM-Brusstar*	(Baltimore)	1902	25 Jan 1943	202	130'7" x 20' x 9'6"	1/steam
	ex–*William S. Brusstar*						

WYP 314	*EM-Covington*	Davis	1923	17 Feb 1943	263	129'11" x 22'4" x 10'	2/diesel
	ex–*William T. Covington Jr.*						
WYP 318	*EM-Vernon McNea*	Colonna	1904	9 Mar 1943	265	136' x 22' x 10'5"	1/diesel
	ex–*A. Vernon McNeal*, ex–*Charles J. Colonna*						
WYP 320	*EM-Conant*	Abbott	1919	25 Jan 1943	260	124'4" x 22'3" x 10'1"	1/steam
	ex–*Henry W. Conant*, ex–*Sprite*, ex–*John R. Baylis*						
WYP 322	*EM-Reed*	(Pocomoke City, Md.)	1899	11 Dec 1942	167	122'2" x 19'8" x 9'7"	1/diesel
	ex–*E. Warren Reed*						
WYP 323	*EM-Margaret*	Rappahannock	1912	28 Dec 1942	268	128' x 23'3" x 11'4"	1/diesel
	ex–*Margaret*, ex–SP-328						
WYP 325	*EM-Humphreys*	Humphreys	1919	26 Jan 1943	211	126'1' x 20'7" x 9'7"	1/diesel
	ex–*H. R. Humphreys*						
WYP 328	*EM-Rowe*	Tull	1901	25 Jan 1943	218	132'5" x 20'9" x 10'9"	1/diesel
	ex–*W. R. Rowe*, ex–*R. B. Douglas*						
WYP 329	*EM-Pelican*	Portland Sbdg	1919	4 Jun 1943	384	163' x 25' x 13'3"	1/VTE
	ex–*Pelican*						
WYP 330	*EM-Seabird*	Portland Sbdg	1919	1 Apr 1943	384	163' x 25' x 13'3"	1/VTE
	ex–*Seabird*						
WYP 333	*EM-Wilcox*	Palmer	1911	8 Sep 1943	247	132' x 22'3" x 10'7"	1/diesel
	ex–*Rowland H. Wilcox*, ex–*P.V. VII*						
WYP 340	*Bronco*	Akers	1930	7 Dec 1942	249	123'1" x 23'9" x 13'2"	1/U
	ex–*Star XVIII*						
WYP 341	*Belmont*	Akers	1929	14 Dec 1942	249	123'1" x 23'9" x 13'2"	1/U
	ex–*Thorarinn*						
WYP 342	*Bodega*	Akers	1929	21 Nov 1942	249	123'1" x 23'9" x 13'2"	1/U
	ex–*Thordr*						
WYP 353	*EM-Dow*	Humphreys	1924	24 Jun 1943	241	134'3" x 21'7" x 10'8"	1/diesel
	ex–*Annie Dow*						
WYP 356	*EM-Joe*	Humphreys	1922	9 Jun 1943	241	134'3" x 21'7" x 10'8"	1/diesel
	ex–*Little Joe*						
WYP 354	*EM-Warren Edwards*	Abbott	1918	5 Jul 1943	231	152'2" x 21' x 10'2"	1/diesel
	ex–*E. Warren Edwards*						
WYP 357	*EM-Edwards*	Davis	1912	24 Jun 1943	343	143'4" x 24' x 11'6"	1/diesel
	ex–*Wilbert A. Edwards*, ex–SP-315						
WYP 358	*EM-Messick*	Smith & McCoy	1911	24 Jun 1943	326	131'8" x 23'5" x 12'5"	1/diesel
	ex–*W. L. Messick*, ex–SP-322						
WYP 360	*EM-Euphane*	Tull	1902	23 Mar 1943	168	124' x 20'4" x 9'3"	1/diesel
	ex–*Helen Euphane*, ex–SP-403						
WYP 361	*EM-Northumberland*	(Pocomoke City, Md.)	1897	8 Mar 1943	169	134'2" x 20'2" x 9'3"	1/diesel
	ex–*Northumberland*						
WYP 362	*EM-Pocahontas*	Abbott	1914	22 Jan 1943	345	139'7" x 24'2" x 11'5"	1/steam
	ex–*Pocahontas*, ex–*David W. Burbage*						
WYP 363	*EM-Stephen McKeever*	Palmer	1911	19 Jul 1943	223	128' x 22'2" x 10'	1/diesel
	ex–*Stephen W. McKeever Jr*, ex–SP-1169						
WYP 373	*Bellefonte*	Rice	1926	6 Apr 1944	341	178'9" x 24' x 14'10"	1/diesel
	ex–*Albatross III* (F&WS), ex–*Harvard*						
WYP 377	*Thorgaut*	Framnes	1939	28 Dec 1942	313	135'9" x 25'6" x 14'9"	1/steam
WYP 378	*Thoris*	Framnes	1936	25 Jan 1943	305	134' x 25'6" x 13'9"	1/steam
WYP 379	*Ottern*	Smiths Dock	1937	5 Apr 1943	361	138' x 26'4" x 14'8"	1/steam
WYP 380	*Globe Eight*	Moss	1936	29 Dec 1942	297	136' x 25'3" x 13'2"	1/steam
	ex–*Globe VIII*						
WYP 381	*Globe*	Moss	1937	5 Apr 1943		130'1" x 25'2" x 13'3"	1/steam
	ex–*Globe IX*						
WYP 382	*Pol*	Nylands	1936	25 Feb 1943	338	142' x 25'9" x 14'8"	1/steam
	ex–*Pol VII*						
WYP 383	*Thorfinn*	Akers	1929	25 Jan 1943	249	123'1" x 23'9" x 13'2"	1/U
WYP 384	*Thorfjell*	Kaldnaes	1934	25 Jan 1943	313	126'1" x 25'1" x 14'2"	1/steam

Figure 13.15: *Atak* (WYP 163), 20 Jun 1942, one of many trawlers acquired for the Greenland Patrol.

Figure 13.16: *Kodiak* (WYP 173), 10 Mar 1943, a steel-hulled whaler acquired in 1943 and assigned to Ketchikan, Alaska.

Note: Trawlers and whalers taken over for temporary duty.

Service Records:

163 *Atak* Greenland. Decomm 15 Jul 1944. Returned 1 Aug 1944.
Later history: Merchant *Winchester*, renamed *Winchester II* 1971, *Winchester* 1980, *Crystal and Katie*; se 1998.

164 *Aivik* Greenland. Decomm 21 Jul 1944. Returned 11 Sep 1944.
Later history: Merchant *Arlington*; se 1954.

165 *Arvek* Greenland. Decomm 29 Jul 1944. Returned 17 Aug 1944.
Later history: Merchant *Triton*.

166 *Amarok* Greenland. Decomm and returned 5 Feb 1944.
Later history: Merchant *Lark*, *Pattyjean*; se 1954.

167 *Arluk* Greenland. Decomm and returned 6 Jul 1944.
Later history: Merchant *Atlantic*.

168 *Aklak* Greenland. Decomm 10 Mar 1944. Sold 5 Apr 1944.
Later history: Merchant *Weymouth*; se 1954.

169 *Nanok* Greenland. Decomm 25 Jul 1944. Returned 14 Sep 1944.

170 *Natsek* Greenland. Missing in snowstorm off Greenland, Dec 1942 (24, all lost).

171 *Nogak* Greenland Decomm and returned 24 Jul 1944.
Later history: Merchant *St. George*, se 1954.

172 *Alatok* Greenland. Decomm 27 Dec 1943. Returned 13 Mar 1944.
Later history: Merchant *Belmont*.

173 *Kodiak* Ketchikan, Alaska. Decomm 16 Mar 1944. Returned 20 Apr 1944.
Later history: Merchant *Kodiak*.

174 *Caddo* Returned 16 Mar 1944.
Later history: Merchant *Tanginak*.

312 *EM-Brusstar* Decomm and returned 16 Jun 1943.
Later history: Merchant *William S. Brusstar*; se 1954.

314 *EM-Covington* Reengined 1942. San Juan, Puerto Rico. Decomm 30 Jun 1943. Returned 7 Jul 1943.
Later history: Merchant *William T. Covington Jr.*; se 1954.

318 *EM-Vernon McNeal* San Juan, Puerto Rico. Decomm 22 Feb 1944. Returned 13 Mar 1944.
Later history: Merchant *A. Vernon McNeal*. BU 1971.

320 *EM-Conant* Decomm 16 Nov 1943. Returned 1 Dec 1943.
Later history: Merchant *Henry W. Conant*; se 1954.

322 *EM-Reed* Decomm 8 Mar 1943. Returned 15 Mar 1943.
Later history: Merchant *E. Warren Reed*; se 1954.

323 *EM-Margaret* Eastern SF. Decomm 7 Jun 1943. Returned 24 Jun 1943.
Later history: Merchant *Margaret*; se 1954.

325 *EM-Humphreys* Decomm and returned 27 Mar 1944.
Later history: Merchant *H. R. Humphreys*; se 1954.

328 *EM-Rowe* Decomm 9 Jun 1943. Returned 5 Jul 1943.
Later history: Merchant *W. R. Rowe*.

329 *EM-Pelican* Decomm 6 Aug 1943. Returned 14 Mar 1946.
Later history: Merchant *Pelican*; se 1954.

330 *EM-Seabird* Decomm 22 Nov 1943. Returned 19 Jul 1944.
Later history: Merchant *Sea Bird*; se 1954.

333 *EM-Wilcox* Foundered in hurricane off Nags Head, N.C., 29 Sep 1943 (1 lost).

340 *Bronco* Decomm 30 Jun 1945. Returned 20 Nov 1946.
Later history: Merchant *Star XVIII*, renamed *Finback* 1949. Went aground off Comfort Head, Labrador, 26 Jul 1961.

341 *Belmont* Balboa, Canal Zone. Decomm 18 Oct 1945. Sold 20 Nov 1946.

342 *Bodega* Went aground off Cristobal, Panama Canal, 20 Dec 1943.

353 *EM-Dow* Went aground in gale off Mayaguez, Puerto Rico, 14 Oct 1943.

356 *EM-Joe* Decomm 22 Feb 1944. Returned 6 Mar 1944.
Later history: Merchant *Little Joe*; se 1954.

354 *EM-Warren Edwards* Decomm 1 Oct 1943. Returned 1 Nov 1943.
Later history: Merchant *E. Warren Edwards*; se 1954.

357 *EM-Edwards* Decomm 15 Mar 1944. Returned 24 Mar 1944.
Later history: Merchant *Wilbert A. Edwards*

358 *EM-Messick* Decomm 2 Mar 1944. Returned 13 Mar 1944.
Later history: Merchant *W.L. Messick*; se 1954.

360 *EM-Euphane* Decomm 22 Nov 1943. Returned 29 Dec 1944.
Later history: Merchant *Helen Euphane*; se 1954.

361 *EM-Northumberland* Decomm 1 Mar 1944. Returned 20 Mar 1944.
Later history: Merchant *Northumberland*; se 1954.

362 *EM-Pocahontas* Eastern SF. Decomm 13 Nov 1943. Returned 23 Mar 1945.
Later history: Merchant *Pocahontas*; se 1954.

363 *EM-Stephen McKeever* Decomm 3 Dec 1943. Returned 29 Dec 1943.
Later history: Merchant *Stephen W. McKeever Jr.*; se 1954.

373 *Bellefonte* Returned to F&WS, 22 Aug 1944.
Later history: F&WS *Albatross III* 1944; merchant, renamed *Nyleve* 1963. Went aground at Roman Key, Cuba, 28 Mar 1969.

377 *Thorgaut* Western SF. Decomm and returned 3 Jul 1943.
Later history: Merchant *Thorgaut*, *Berg Karl* 1955.

378 *Thoris* Western SF. Decomm and returned 7 Jul 1943.

379 *Ottern* Decomm and returned 7 Jul 1943.
Later history: Merchant *Ottern*, renamed *Jadar* 1964, *Moflag Senior*.

Figure 13.17: *EM-Messick* (WYP 358), 1942. A number of fishing boats were acquired for patrolling the Atlantic Coast.

380	*Globe Eight*	Decomm and returned 4 Jul 1943.
	Later history: Merchant *Globe VIII.*	
381	*Globe*	Decomm 7 Jul 1943. Returned 9 Jul 1943.
382	*Pol*	Western SF. Decomm and returned 7 Jul 1943.
	Later history: Merchant *Pol VII.* BU 1965.	
383	*Thorfinn*	Returned 2 Jul 1943.
	Later history: Merchant *Thorfinn*, renamed *Norman II* 1952.	
384	*Thorfjell*	Decomm 2 Jul 1943.

EX–SUBMARINE CHASERS

No.	Name	Builder	Acquired or Comm.
WSC 335	*Boone*	NY Yacht	Comm 14 Aug 1942. Decomm 6 Dec 1945. Sold 8 Mar 1946
	ex–SC 229		
WSC 336	*Blaze*	NY Yacht	Acq 18 Aug 1942. Decomm 25 Sep 1944. Sold 8 Mar 1946
	ex–SC 231		
WSC 365	*Bowstring*	NY Yacht	Comm 7 Jul 1943. Decomm 22 Dec 1944. Sold 6 Jan 1945
	ex–*Sea Rover*, ex–*Allen*, ex–SC 238		
WSC 372	*Belleville*	Lawley	Acq 20 Mar 1943. Decomm 30 Jun 1945. Sold 2 May 1946.
	ex–*Liberty II*, ex–SC 258		
WIX 375	*Bonneville*	Rocky River	Comm 5 Mar 1943. Training ship. Damaged in collision, 20 Jul 1945. Decomm 22 Sep 1945.
	ex–*Islander*, ex–USCGC *Cook*, ex–SC 438		

Displacement	167 ton f/l
Dimensions	110' (oa) x 14'9" x 5'8"
Machinery	3 screws, gasoline; SHP 600; 14 knots (WIX 375: 2 screws, diesel; bhp 160; 13 knots)
Complement	(U)
Armament	1–3"/23 (WIX 375: 1–1 pdr.)

Note: Built as submarine chasers in World War I.

ICEBREAKERS

No.	Name	Builder	Keel Laid	Launched	Comm.
WAGL 38	*Storis*	Toledo Sbdg	14 Jul 1941	4 Apr 1942	30 Sep 1942
	ex–*Eskimo* (1942)				

Displacement	1,715 tons f/l
Dimensions	230' (oa); x 43'2" x 15'
Machinery	1 screw; diesel-electric; bhp 1,800, 13 knots
Endurance	11,300/12.5
Complement	148
Armament	2–3"/50, 4–20mm, 1 aircraft

Notes: Designed as supply ship for Greenland area. Ordered as CG 82.

Service Record:

WAGL 38 *Storis* †
1* Greenland.

No.	Name	Builder	Keel Laid	Launched	Comm.
WAGB 83	*Mackinaw*	Toledo Sbdg	20 Mar 1943	6 Mar 1944	20 Dec 1944
	ex–*Manitowoc*				

Displacement	5,200 tons f/l
Dimensions	290' (oa); x 74'4" x 19'
Machinery	3 screws (1 forward), diesel-electric; SHP 12,000; 16 knots
Complement	144
Armament	none

Notes: Wind class adapted for Great Lakes, with mild steel hull rather than high tensile steel. Ordered as CG 121.

Service Record:

WAGB 83 *Mackinaw* †

No.	Name	Builder	Keel Laid	Launched	Comm.
WAGB 278	*Northwind*	W. Pipe S.P.	9 Jul 1942	28 Dec 1942	26 Feb 1944
WAGB 279	*Eastwind*	W. Pipe S.P.	23 Jun 1942	6 Feb 1943	3 Jun 1944
WAGB 280	*Southwind*	W. Pipe S.P.	20 Jul 1942	8 Mar 1943	15 Jul 1944
WAGB 281	*Westwind*	W. Pipe S.P.	24 Aug 1942	31 Mar 1943	18 Sep 1944
WAGB 282	*Northwind*	W. Pipe S.P.	10 Jul 1944	25 Feb 1945	28 Jul 1945

Figure 13.18: *Northwind* (WAG 282), 10 Feb 1944. This was the second ship of that name, the first having been transferred to the Soviet Union.

Displacement	6,515 tons f/l
Dimensions	269' (oa); x 63'6" x 25'9"
Machinery	3 screws (1 forward), diesel-electric; SHP 12,000; 16.8 knots
Endurance	50,000/11
Complement	316
Armament	4–5"/38, 3 quad 40mm, 6–20mm, 1 aircraft

Notes: Built to provide access to ice-bound military bases in Greenland. Bow screw later removed, SHP 10,000. Three transferred to USSR under lend-lease were returned 1950–51. Ordered as CG 96–99, 184.

Service Records:

WAGB 278 *Northwind* To USSR 26 Feb 1944.
Later history: Renamed *Severni Veter*. Returned 19 Dec 1951. †
WAGB 279 *Eastwind* Captured German weather station, east Greenland, 4 Oct 1944. Captured German trawler *Externstiene* off Greenland, 15 Oct 1944. †
1* Greenland.
WAGB 280 *Southwind* To USSR 23 Mar 1945.
1* Greenland.
Later history: Renamed *Kapitan Belusov*. Returned 13 Apr 1950. †
WAGB 281 *Westwind* To USSR 21 Feb 1945.
Later history: Renamed *Severni Polius*. Returned 19 Dec 1951. †
WAGB 282 *Northwind* †

CABLE-LAYING VESSEL

No.	Name	Builder	Launched	Acquired	Comm.
WARC 58	*Pequot*	NY Sbdg	13 Feb 1909	1922	1 May 1922
	ex–*Gen. Samuel M. Mills*				

Displacement	1,130 tons f/l.
Dimensions	166'6" (oa); 154' (wl) x 32' x 10'
Machinery	2 screws; vertical compound; 2 FW boilers; SHP 345; 13 knots
Complement	53
Armament	1–3"/50, 2–20mm.

Notes: Former Army mine planter.

Service Record:

WARC 58 *Pequot* To USN, 1 Nov 1941. Decomm 8 Dec 1946. Sold.

TUGS

Coast Guard Tugs 1922

Guthrie Portland, Me. Decomm 24 Oct 1941. Sold 24 Feb 1942.
Hudson Decomm 3 May 1935. Sold 1940.
Later history: Merchant *Hudson*. Foundered in St. Johns River, Fla., 19 Dec 1946.
Calumet Renamed ***Tioga***, 1934. **WYT 74**. Baltimore. Decomm 14 Oct 1946.
Later history: Sold 22 Mar 1947, merchant *John F. Drews*, renamed *William J. Dugan* 1967, *Spanky Paine* 1991; se 1998.
Golden Gate **WYT 94**. San Francisco. Decomm 22 Nov 1945. Sold 8 Apr 1947.
Winnisimmet **WYT 84**. Norfolk. Decomm Oct 1945. Sold 22 Jul 1946.
Later history: Merchant *Sophia* 1947, renamed *Bullhead*, *David C. Winslow*; se 1980.
Wissahickon Sold 1935.
Later history: Merchant *Atlas* 1936; se 1980.
Mackinac Sold Jun 1941.
Later history: Merchant *Patricia* 1941, renamed *William T. Moore*, *George J. Murphy*, 1966.
Arcata Decomm 31 Jan 1936 and sold.
Later history: Merchant *Patricia Foss* 1936.
Davey **WYT 81**. New Orleans. Decomm 17 Jul 1945.
Later history: Merchant *David* 1945, renamed *Kingston*; se 1974.
Tioga Sold 26 Apr 1930.
Later history: Merchant *Absley* 1930; se 1935.
Manhattan **WYT 95**. New York. Damaged when rammed by m/v *Guayaquil* in New York harbor, 13 Apr 1932 (1 killed). Decomm 30 Jan 1947. Sold 28 Jul 1947.
Later history: Merchant *Hazel* 1947. Scuttled off Florida, Jun 1971.

Name	Builder	Launched	Acquired	Comm.
Cahokia	Providence Eng.	Aug 1920	7 Dec 1921	—
	ex–*Bayside*			
Kickapoo	Beth. Elizabethport	20 Nov 1918	31 Oct 1921	21 Jan 1922
	ex–*Baldridge*			
Mascoutin	Northwest; Green Bay	11 Oct 1919	31 Oct 1921	—
	ex–*Pylos*			
Saukee	Northwest; Green Bay	12 Jul 1919	31 Oct 1921	—
	ex–*Vallonia*			
Tamaroa	Beth. Elizabethport	1919	31 Oct 1921	—
	ex–*Bartolomé*			

Displacement	840 tons; *Cahokia*: 426 grt
Dimensions	157'4" (oa); 142' (bp) x 35' x 14'6"
Machinery	1 screw; VTE; 2 Scotch boilers; SHP 1,000; 11.5 knots
Endurance	2,300/11
Complement	38
Armament	2–1 pdr

Notes: Shipping Board tugs, acquired 1921.

Service Records:

Cahokia Eureka, Calif. To USN 14 May 1936.
Later history: USS *Cahokia* (AT 61), merchant *Cahokia*; se 1954.
Kickapoo Rec **WAGL 56**, 1942. Buzzards Bay, Mass.; Rockland, Me. Rebuilt 1920s. Decomm 24 Aug 1945. Sold 7 Jul 1947.
Mascoutin Norfolk, Va. Sold 5 Jun 1936.
Later history: Merchant *Henry W. Card* 1937. RR 1959.
Saukee Key West, Fla. Sold 1935.
Later history: Merchant *Trojan*, 1937. BU 1948 Norfolk, Va.
Tamaroa San Pedro, Calif. Decomm 10 Oct 1935. To USN 14 May 1936.
Later history: USS *Tamaroa* (AT 62). Sunk in collision with USS *Jupiter*, San Francisco, 27 Jan 1946. Merchant *Tamaroa*; se 1954.

Name	Builder	Launched	Acquired
Raritan	Harlan	1905	1 Dec 21
	ex–*Immigrant*		

Displacement	220 tons grt

Dimensions	103' x 22'8" x 12' (check data)

Notes: Acquired from U.S. Department of Labor.

Service Record:

Raritan: Sold 1938c.

Later history: Merchant *Henry Lee.*

VESSELS ACQUIRED FROM THE NAVY

Name	USN	Fate
Chattahoochee	Ex–YT 62	17 Jul 1924 Sold
Chautaqua	Ex–YT 59	Sold
Chenango	Ex–YT 58	31 Jul 1923 Sold
Chicopee	Ex–YT 65	Sold
Chillicothe	Ex–YT 85	31 Oct 1925 Sold
Chincoteague	Ex–YT 52	20 Mar 1925 Sold
Chippewa	Ex–YT 60	—
Choptank	Ex–YT 51	20 Mar 1925 Sold
Chowan	Ex–YT 75	22 Jul 1924
Chulahoma	Ex–YT 66	19 Sep 1933 Sold

CG	No.	Name	Builder	Keel Laid	Launched	Comm.
40	WAT 54	*Shawnee*	General Eng.	5 May 1920	15 Nov 1921	8 Mar 1922

Displacement	900 tons f/l, 558 grt
Dimensions	158'3" (oa); x 30' x 13'10"
Machinery	1 screw; VTE; 2 B&W boilers; SHP 1,400; 13 knots
Endurance	2,340/12
Complement	43
Armament	2–1 pdr; (1945) 2–20mm

Service Record:

40 WAT 54 *Shawnee* Eureka, Calif. Western SF. Decomm 21 Nov 1946. Sold 28 Nov 1947.

Later history: Merchant *Novo Bandeirante.*

CG	No.	Name	Builder	Keel Laid	Launched	Comm.
61	WYT 86	*Calumet*	Charleston NYd		28 Sep 1934	3 Dec 1934
62	WYT 87	*Hudson*	Portsmouth NYd		Oct 1934	31 Oct 1934
63	WYT 88	*Navesink*	Charleston NYd		28 Sep 1934	5 Jan 1935
64	WYT 89	*Tuckahoe*	Charleston NYd		28 Sep 1934	30 Jan 1935

Displacement	290 tons f/l
Dimensions	110'" (oa); x 24' x 12'6"
Machinery	1 screw; diesel-electric; SHP 800; 13 knots
Endurance	1,400/12
Complement	16
Armament	none; (1945) 2–20mm

Notes: Ice-breaking capability. Very successful class.

Service Records:

WYT 86 *Calumet* Norfolk, Va. †
WYT 87 *Hudson* New York, Baltimore. †
WYT 88 *Navesink* New York, Norfolk, Va. †
WYT 89 *Tuckahoe* New Orleans. †

CG	No.	Name	Builder	Keel Laid	Launched	Comm.
72	WYT 93	*Raritan*	Defoe		23 Mar 1939	11 Apr 1939
73	WYT 92	*Naugatuck*	Defoe		23 Mar 1939	12 Apr 1939
74	WYT 90	*Arundel*	Gulfport		24 Jun 1939	6 Jul 1939
75	WYT 91	*Mahoning*	Gulfport		22 Jul 1939	7 Aug 1939
86	WYT 60	*Manitou*	Curtis Bay	20 May 1942	29 Sep 1942	15 Feb 1943
87	WYT 61	*Kaw* ex–*Kennebec*	Curtis Bay	9 May 1942	6 Oct 1942	1 Mar 1943

Displacement	328 tons
Dimensions	110' (oa); x 26'5" x 12'
Machinery	1 screw; diesel-electric; SHP 1,000; 13 knots
Endurance	1,600/12
Complement	16
Armament	1–20mm

Notes: Repeat *Calumet* class. *Manitou* and *Kaw* had different engines.

Service Records:

WYT 93 *Raritan* Greenland. †
WYT 92 *Naugatuck* Philadelphia. †
WYT 90 *Arundel* Greenland. †
WYT 91 *Mahoning* New York. †
WYT 60 *Manitou* Boston, Greenland. †
WYT 61 *Kaw* Portland, Me. †

CG	No.	Name	Builder	Keel Laid	Launched	Comm.
118	WYT 71	*Apalachee*	Bushey	17 Nov 1942	29 Apr 1943	26 Nov 1943
119	WYT 72	*Yankton*	Bushey	26 Oct 1942	29 Apr 1943	26 Jan 1944
120	WYT 73	*Mohican*	Bushey	10 Nov 1942	16 Jun 1943	29 Feb 1944
126	WYT 96	*Chinook*	Bushey	10 Nov 1942	16 Jun 1943	24 Mar 1944
127	WYT 97	*Ojibwa*	Bushey	25 Jan 1943	10 Sep 1943	7 Apr 1944

Figure 13.19: *Arundel* (WYT 90), 24 Jun 1942, a Coast Guard tug.

128	WYT 98	*Snohomish*	Bushey	25 Jan 1943	10 Sep 1943	2 May 1944
129	WYT 99	*Sauk*	Bushey	25 Jan 1943	10 Sep 1943	25 May 1944

Displacement	384 tons f/l
Dimensions	110' (oa); x 26'5" x 11'6"
Machinery	1 screw; diesel-electric; SHP 1,000; 12 knots
Endurance	2,000/10
Complement	16
Armament	2–20mm

Notes: Modified *Arundel* class.

Service Records:

WYT 71 *Apalachee* Baltimore. †
WYT 72 *Yankton* Philadelphia. †
WYT 73 *Mohican* New York. †
WYT 96 *Chinook* Boston. †
WYT 97 *Ojibwa* Boston. †
WYT 98 *Snohomish* Boston. †
WYT 99 *Sauk* New York. †

WEATHER PATROL SHIPS (ACQUIRED FROM THE NAVY)

No.	Name	Navy No.	Acquired
WAG 273	*Manasquan*	AG 36	22 Oct 1943. Damaged in collision at dock with AGL *Cactus,* 12 Jun 1943. Gunnery practice ship 1943–45. Decomm 22 Feb 1945. Sold 11 Mar 1946.
WAG 274	*Menemsha*	AG 39	30 Oct 1943. Gunnery training ship 1943–45. Decomm 24 Sep 1945. Sold 6 Mar 1947.
WAG 275	*Monomoy*	AG 40	22 Oct 1943. Decomm 12 Oct 1945. Sold 13 Feb 1951.
WAG 276	*Manhasset*	AG 47	22 Oct 1943. Decomm 15 Oct 1945. Sold 16 Oct 1946.
WAK 123	*Asterion*	AK 63	12 Jan 1944. Decomm 20 Jul 1944. Sold 14 Mar 1946, BU.
WAO 124	*Big Horn*	AO 45	17 Jan 1944. Returned to USN as IX 207, 1 Feb 1945.

Armament: WAG 274– 75: 1–5"/38, 2–4"/50, 2–3"/50, 8–20mm; WAG 276: 2–4"/50, 4–20mm. See *TK.*

CARGO SHIPS

No.	Name	Builder	Acquired	Built	GRT
WAK 169	*Nettle* ex–FS 396	Ingalls Decatur	1 Oct 1947	1945	550
WAK 170	*Trillium* ex–FS 397	Ingalls Decatur	23 Aug 1946	1945	550
WAK 185	*Unalga* ex–*Tipton* (AK 215)	L. D. Smith	21 Oct 1946	1945	3,805
WAK 186	*Kukui* ex–*Colquitt* (AK 174)	Froemming	Mar 1946	1945	3,805

Notes: *Nettle* and *Trillium* acquired from Army.

Service Record:

WAK 169 *Nettle* †
WAK 170 *Trillium* †
WAK 185 *Unalga* †
WAK 186 *Kukui* †

MISCELLANEOUS VESSELS

No.	Name	Builder	Built	Comm	GRT	Dimensions (oa)	Machinery
WIX 180	*MacNichol* ex–*David G. MacNichol,* ex–*William H. Hoyt,* ex–*Stratford*	(Bridgeport, Conn.)	1891	5 Jul 1942	98	100'6" x 22'1" x 7'	1/steam
WIX 184	*Alexander Graham Bell*	Oregon	1942	7 Oct 1944	7,176	441'7" x 57' x 27'	1/VTE
WIX 271	*Atlantic*	Townsend	1903	1 Apr 1941	303	185' x 29'6" x 17'6"	1/VTE
WIX 272	*Beta* ex–*Alexander Hamilton,* ex–USS *Vicksburg* (PG 11)	Bath	1896	1 Jul 1921	—	—	—
WIX 283	*Danmark*	Nakskov	1933	12 May 1942	777	188'6" x 33' x 14'9"	1/diesel
WIX 338	*Navigation* ex–*Navigation* (1942), ex–*Alida* (1935), ex–*Victoria Mary,* ex–*All Alone*	(Boston)	1922	19 Jan 1942	212	134'9" x 20' x 9'9"	2/diesel
WIX 339	*Tyrer* ex–*Tyrer* (1938), ex–*Waleda II*	Mathis	1928	—	149	125'11" x 19' x 8'8"	2/diesel
WIX 347	*Bison* ex–*Beaufort* (22 Jul 1943), ex–*President*	Globe	1910	3 Feb 1943	730	185' x 45'6" x 7'3"	1/steam
WIX 375	*Bonneville*	See above, p. 364.					

Service Records:

WIX 180 *MacNicol* FFU.

WIX 184 *Alexander Graham Bell* Liberty ship damaged by mine off Naples, 17 Apr 1944. Used for testing of lifesaving devices. Returned 28 Dec 1944. BU 1962.

WIX 271 *Atlantic* Three-masted steel schooner. Served in USN in World War I as *SP-251*. Cadet training ship. Sold 10 Sep 1948.

WIX 272 *Beta* Hulk, barracks ship. Former Navy gunboat. Decomm 30 Dec 1944. Sold 28 Mar 1946.

WIX 283 *Danmark* Danish square-rigged training ship visiting the United States in 1940 and used by USCG for training. Name retained. Training ship, New London. Returned to Denmark 26 Sep 1945.
Later history: Training ship *Danmark*; se 2006.

WIX 338 *Navigation* Acq from U.S. Bureau of Marine Inspection and Navigation. Loaned to USN 19 Jan 1942.
Later history: USS *Sard* (PYc 23). Decomm 29 Jul 1944. Sold 10 Jan 1946.

WIX 339 *Tyrer* Acq from U.S. Bureau of Marine Inspection. Returned.
Later history: Merchant *Tyrer, Catherine-Tek.*

WIX 347 *Bison* Floating barracks, Curtis Bay, Md. Decomm 17 Jun 1946. Sold 19 Mar 1947.
Later history: Merchant *President.*

LIGHTHOUSE TENDERS

Merged with the U.S. Coast Guardin 1939; all surviving ships became Coast Guard cutters. **WAGL** numbers assigned 1942.

Lighthouse Tenders in Service with the U.S. Lighthouse Service, 1922

Name	Service Record
Pansy	Sold 29 Jan 1933. Merchant *Mayfair.* RR 1980s.
Holly	Sold 4 Dec 1931. Merchant barge *Wright No. 1.* RR 1944.
Madroño	Sold 11 Oct 1927. Merchant *Madrono* 1929, to Army 1944, renamed *Col. Charles L. Willard.*
Zizania	Sold 15 Jan 1925. Merchant *Zizania,* 1926. Acq by USN, ***Adario,*** YNT 25, 9 Aug 1943, rec YTM 743, 1944. Sold 1947; Merchant *Adario.*
Marigold	**WAGL** 235. Great Lakes (Detroit). Decomm 3 Oct 1945. Sold 19 Oct 1946.
	Later history: Merchant dredge *Miss Mudhen II;* se 1974.
Azalea	Sold 13 Dec 1933. Merchant *Christiana,* 1933. To USN 1942, rec IX 80.
Amaranth	**WAGL 201**. Great Lakes (Duluth). Decomm 29 Sep 1945. Sold 19 Oct 1946.
	Later history: Merchant *South Wind,* renamed *Ocean Transport No.45,* 1957.
Columbine	Sold 22 Jul 1927. Merchant *Columbine.* BU 1939.
Lilac	Sold 3 Mar 1925. Merchant *Elma.* RR 1938.
Maple	Sold 29 Oct 1933. Merchant *Nichols No. 6, McLain No. 300.* RR 1948.
Mangrove	**WAGL 232**. Charleston, S.C. Decomm 22 Aug 1946. Sold 6 Mar 1947.
Mayflower	**WAGL 236**. Norfolk, Va. Renamed ***Hydrangea,*** 15 Aug 1943. Decomm and sold, 8 Oct 1945.
Iris	Sold 21 Jun 1934.
	Later history: Merchant *Plymouth,* renamed *Big Chief* 1938. Aquired by USN as 101, 5 May 1943. Army in World War II, renamed *B. O. Colonna,* 1956. BU 1973.
Heather	Trfd to U.S. War Department, 6 Sep 1940.
	Later history: Renamed *FS-534.* Merchant *Mahamaya,* 1949. BU 1955 Bombay.
Hyacinth	**WAGL 221**. Great Lakes (Milwaukee). Decomm 15 Nov 1945. Sold 19 Oct 1946.
	Later history: Merchant *Hyacinth;* se 1954.
Larkspur	**WAGL 226**. Mobile, Ala. Decomm 10 Jan 1946. Sold 19 Feb 1946.
	Later history: Merchant *Larkspur.* Foundered northeast of Sydney, Nova Scotia, 20 Aug 1948.
Sumac	Sold 1937. Used as fueling barge.
	Later history: Merchant *Oscar Lehtinen.* BU 1957.
Juniper	Sold 22 Dec 1932.
	Later history: Merchant *Aubrey L. Hodgins;* se 1964.
Crocus	**WAGL 210**. Great Lakes (Toledo). Decomm 13 Jul 1946.
Magnolia	**WAGL 231**. Mobile, Ala. Sunk in collision with m/v *Marguerite Le Hand* off Mobile, 25 Aug 1945 (1 killed).
Ivy	Decomm 6 Nov 1940. Sold 25 Apr 1941.
Aspen	**WAGL 204**. Great Lakes (Sault Ste. Marie, Mich.). Decomm 25 Jan 1947. Sold 26 Jan 1948.
Sunflower	**WAGL 247**. Galveston, Tex. Decomm 10 Jan 1946. Sold 19 Feb 1947.
Anemone	**WAGL 202**. Woods Hole, Mass. To Philippines 1 Jul 1947. Stricken 1957; trfd to Philippines 1947.
Cypress	**WAGL 211**. Charleston, S.C. Decomm 20 Aug 1946. Sold 18 Mar 1947.
	Later history: Merchant *Cypress,* renamed *Drafin* 1952. BU 1969 La Spezia, Italy.
Hibiscus	**WAGL 218**. Portland, Me. Damaged by fire and beached, Argentia, Nfld., 28 May 1942. Decomm 3 Sep 1946. Sold 26 Jun 1947.
Kukui	**WAGL 225**. Honolulu, Hawaii. Decomm 1 Feb 1946. Sold 8 Apr 1947.
	1* Pearl Harbor.
Manzanita	**WAGL 233**. Astoria, Ore. Decomm 19 Nov 1946. Sold 30 Apr 1947.
Orchid	**WAGL 240**. Portsmouth, Va. To Philippines 1 Dec 1945.
Sequoia	**WAGL 243**. San Francisco, Calif. To Philippines 1 Jul 1947.
Tulip	**WAGL 249**. Went aground in hurricane at New London, Conn., 21 Sep 1938. Staten I., N.Y. To Philippines 5 Jul 1947
Camellia	**WAGL 206**. New Orleans. Decomm 18 Aug 1947. Sold 29 Dec 1947.
	Later history: Dominican *Capotillo.*
Rose	**WAGL 242**. Lengthened 1936. Astoria, Ore. Decomm 15 Oct 1947. Sold 14 Jun 1948.
	Later history: Merchant *Northern Express,* renamed *Chenega* 1954. RR 1979.
Palmetto	**WAGL 265**. Charleston, S.C. †
Cedar	**WAGL 207**. Ketchikan, Alaska. †

Shrub **WAGL 244**. Bristol, R.I. Decomm 1 Jul 1947. Sold 29 Dec 1947.
Later history: Merchant *Shrub*. Foundered off Bahamas, Mar 1963.

Armament: *Hibiscus, Sequoia*: 1–3"/50, 3–20mm; *Magnolia, Anemone, Cypress, Orchid, Tulip*: 1–3"/23, 2–20mm; *Kukui*: 5–20mm; *Sunflower*: 1–20mm. *Manzanita, Mangrove, Larkspur, Cedar, Rose*: 2–20mm.

RIVER TENDERS

Goldenrod Used by U.S. Army Corp of Engineers. Sunk by ice at Cincinnati. Sold 5 Dec 1924.
Dandelion Sold Oct 1927. Sunk in collision with towboat *Herbert Hoover* at Cairo, Ill., Feb 1929.
Oleander Sold 1926. Used as fueling barge.

LAUNCHES

Daisy Sold 19 Mar 1928.
Water Lily Sold 2 Jul 1930. Merchant *Water Lily*. RR 1944.
Clover Sold 1935.
Woodbine Sold 30 Oct 1933. Merchant *Woodbine*, se 1935.
Fern Sold 19 Sep 1934. Merchant *Fern*, renamed *S. D. Mason*. To Army in World War II, renamed *FS-551*.
Laurel Sold 1931.
Birch Sold 8 Sep 1932.
Pine Sold 1939.
Cosmos Sold 24 Jun 1936.
Poinsettia Destroyed by explosion and fire at Key West, Fla., 27 Dec 1928.

No.	Name	Builder	Keel Laid	Launched	Comm.
WAGL 215	*Hawthorn*	Consol. NY	14 Jan 1920	18 Jun 1921	28 Dec 1921
WAGL 239	*Oak*	Consol. NY	14 Jan 1920	28 Jun 1921	31 Dec 1921

Displacement	875 tons
Dimensions	160' (oa); 149' (bp) x 30' x 9'6"
Machinery	1 screw; VTE; 1 boiler; SHP 700; 8 knots
Endurance	1,750/8
Complement	27
Armament	1–3"/23, 1–20mm

Note: Bay and sound tenders.

Service Record:

215 *Hawthorn* New London, Conn. †
239 *Oak* Staten I., N.Y. †

No.	Name	Builder	Keel Laid	Launched	Comm.
WAGL 269	*Aster*	Flechas (Pascagoula)	1921	16 Dec 1921	17 Jan 1922

Displacement	109 tons f/l
Dimensions	75'10" (oa); x 21'8" x 5'7"
Machinery	2 screws; diesel; bhp 90; 7.8 knots
Complement	8
Armament	none

Notes: Wood hull. Small bay tender.

Service Record:

WAGL 269 *Aster* Mobile, Ala. Decomm 24 Jan 1946. Sold 2 Oct 1946.

No.	Name	Builder	Launched	Comm.
WAGL 200	*Acacia* ex–*Gen. John P. Story*	Fabricated	11 Sep 1919	14 Apr 1927
WAGL 222	*Ilex* ex–*Gen. Edmund Kirby*	Fabricated	4 Oct 1919	1924
WAGL 229	*Lotus* ex–*Col. Albert Todd*	Fabricated	31 Jan 1919	1924
WAGL 230	*Lupine* ex–*Gen. W. P. Randolph*	Fabricated	11 Nov 1919	14 Apr 1927
WAGL 245	*Speedwell* ex–*Col. John V. White*	Fabricated	29 Apr 1920	23 Apr 1923
WAGL 246	*Spruce* ex–*Col. Garland N. Whistler*	Fabricated	15 Jan 1920	22 Dec 1923

Displacement	1,130 tons f/l.
Dimensions	172'6" (oa); x 32' x 11'6"
Machinery	2 screws; compound; 2 boilers; SHP 1,000; 11 knots
Endurance	1,800/10
Complement	44
Armament	1–3"/50, 2–20mm.

Notes: Former Army mine planters, acquired in 1922, and converted to as tenders.

Service Records:

200 *Acacia* San Juan, Puerto Rico. Sunk by gunfire from *U-161* north of Curacao, 15 Mar 1942 (none lost).
222 *Ilex* Portland, Me. Decomm 17 Apr 1947. Sold 14 Oct 1947. **Later history:** Merchant *Ilex* 1948. Beached in Kingman Cove, Nfld, after fire, 28 Oct 1948.
229 *Lotus* Chelsea, Mass. 1943, San Juan, Puerto Rico. 5 Nov 1946 decomm. Sold 11 Jun 1947.
230 *Lupine* San Francisco, Calif. Decomm 7 Jan 1947. Sold 28 Nov 1947.
245 *Speedwell* Portsmouth, Va. Decomm 19 Jun 1947. Sold 30 Dec 1947. **Later history:** Merchant *Santa Patricia*, 1948. BU 1956 Jacksonville.
246 *Spruce* San Juan, Puerto Rico. Decomm 28 Jun 1946. To USC&GS, 17 May 1950.

No.	Name	Builder	Keel Laid	Launched	Comm.
WAGL 205	*Beech*	Southern	—	1926	Jan 1928

Displacement	255 tons f/l
Dimensions	103' (oa); x 23' x 9'
Machinery	1 screw; diesel; bhp 300; 8 knots
Endurance	2,000/6
Complement	22
Armament	none

Note: Intended for use on Lake Champlain.

Service Record:

WAGL 205 *Beech* Staten I., N.Y. †

No.	Name	Builder	Keel Laid	Launched	Comm.
WAGL 250	*Violet*	Manitowoc	1929	12 Apr 1930	1930
WAGL 227	*Lilac*	Pusey	15 Nov 1932	26 May 1933	1933
WAGL 237	*Mistletoe*	Pusey	1939	1938 15 Sep	1939

Displacement	799 tons f/l

Dimensions	173'4" (oa); 163'6" (bp) x 32' x 11'
Machinery	2 screws; VTE; 2 boilers; SHP 1,000; 11.5 knots
Endurance	1,800/7
Complement	41
Armament	1–3"/50, 2–20mm

Note: Coastal tenders.

Service Records:

250 *Violet* Baltimore †
227 *Lilac* Edgemoor, Del. †
237 *Mistletoe* Portsmouth, Va.†

No.	Name	Builder	Keel Laid	Launched	Comm.
WAGL 208	*Columbine*	Moore	1931	23 Jul 1931	21 Oct 1931
WAGL 228	*Linden*	Merrill Stevens	26 Sep1930	7 Mar 1931	22 Jul 1931
WAGL 254	*Wistaria*	United DD	1932	3 Feb 1933	Mar 1933

Displacement	323 tons
Dimensions	121'4" (oa); x 25' x 8'
Machinery	1 screw; diesel-electric; SHP 240; 9 knots
Endurance	1,600/8
Complement	28
Armament	none

Notes: Steel hulls. Bay and sound tenders.

Service Records:

208 *Columbine* San Francisco †
228 *Linden* Washington, N.C. †
254 *Wistaria* Baltimore, Md. †

No.	Name	Builder	Keel Laid	Launched	Comm.
WAGL 219	*Hickory*	Bath	24 Aug 1932	9 Feb 1933	Mar 1933

Displacement	400 tons f/l
Dimensions	131'4" (oa); x 24'6" x 10'
Machinery	1 screw; VTE; 1 boiler, SHP 500; 10 knots
Endurance	1,700/9.4
Complement	41
Armament	2–20mm

Note: Coastal tender.

Service Record:

WAGL 219 *Hickory* Staten I., N.Y. †

No.	Name	Builder	Keel Laid	Launched	Comm.
WAGL 248	*Tamarack*	Manitowoc	—	1934	1934

Displacement	400 tons f/l
Dimensions	124'4" (oa); 111'8" (bp) x 30'3" x 8'
Machinery	1 screw; diesel; bhp 450, 9.8 knots
Endurance	8,000/8
Complement	32
Armament	none

Service Record:

WAGL 248 *Tamarack* Great Lakes (Manitowoc, Wis.). †

No.	Name	Builder	Keel Laid	Launched	Comm.
WAGL 203	*Arbutus*	Pusey	1932	25 Mar 1933	1933

Displacement	997 tons
Dimensions	174'7" (oa); x 33' x 14'
Machinery	2 screws; VTE; 2 boilers; SHP 1000; 11.3 knots
Endurance	1,950/11
Complement	41
Armament	1–3"/23, 2–20mm

Service Record:

WAGL 203 *Arbutus* Woods Hole, Mass. †

No.	Name	Builder	Keel Laid	Launched	Comm.
WAGL 217	*Hemlock*	Berg	1933	23 Jan 1934	1934

Displacement	1,005 tons
Dimensions	174'6" (oa); 163'6" (bp) x 32' x 13'3"
Machinery	2 screws; VTE; 2 boilers; SHP 1,000; 11.3 knots
Endurance	1,950/11
Complement	74
Armament	2–3"/23, 4–20mm.

Note: *Hemlock* designed for service in Alaskan waters, double bottom.

Service Record:

WAGL 217 *Hemlock* Ketchikan, Alaska †

No.	Name	Builder	Keel Laid	Launched	Comm.
WAGL 220	*Hollyhock*	Defoe	13 Apr 1936	24 Mar 1937	7 Aug 1937
WAGL 252	*Walnut*	Moore	5 Dec 1938	1939	27 Jun 1939
WAGL 212	*Fir*	Moore	7 Jan 1939	22 Mar 1939	1 Oct 1940

Displacement	885 tons
Dimensions	174'10" (oa); 163'6" (bp) x 32' x 11'3"
Machinery	2 screws; VTE; 2 boilers; SHP 1,000; 12 knots
Endurance	2,500/10
Complement	74
Armament	**WAGL** 252 *Walnut*: 2–3"/50, 4–20mm; **WAGL** 212 *Fir*: 1–6 pdr, 2–20mm.

Figure 13.20: *Laurel* (**WAGL** 292), one of many buoy tenders built for the Coast Guard in 1942–43.

Note: Coastal tenders.

Service Record:

220 *Hollyhock* Great Lakes (Milwaukee, Wis.). †
252 *Walnut* Honolulu, Hawaii †
1* Pearl Harbor.
212 *Fir* Seattle, Wash. †

No.	Name	Builder	Keel Laid	Launched	Comm.
WAGL 238	*Narcissus*	Mathis	1938	4 Feb 1939	1939
WAGL 255	*Zinnia*	Mathis	1938	4 Feb 1939	1939
WAGL 234	*Maple*	Marine Iron	1938	29 Apr 1939	Jun 1939

Displacement	375 tons f/l
Dimensions	122'2" (oa); x 27' x 7'
Machinery	2 screws; diesel; bhp 430; 9 knots
Endurance	3,000/8
Complement	43
Armament	none

Service Records:

238 *Narcissus* Portsmouth, Va. †
255 *Zinnia* Edgemoor, Del. †
234 *Maple* Great Lakes (Ogdensburg, N.Y.). †

No.	Name	Builder	Keel Laid	Launched	Comm.
WAGL 224	*Juniper*	Mathis	1939	18 May 1940	1 Oct 1940

Displacement	794 tons f/l
Dimensions	177' (oa); x 32' x 8'7"
Machinery	2 screws; diesel-electric; SHP 900; 12.5 knots
Endurance	7,000/11
Complement	38
Armament	1–3"/50, 2–20mm

Notes: Last lighthouse tender built for U.S. Lighthouse Service. Prototype of *Cactus* class. Three were planned.

Service Record:

WAGL 224 *Juniper* Key West, Fla. †

CG	No.	Name	Builder	Keel Laid	Launched	Comm.
76	WAGL 270	*Cactus*	Marine Iron	31 Mar 1941	25 Nov 1941	1 Sep 1942
88	WAGL 62	*Balsam*	Zenith	25 Oct 1941	15 Apr 1942	14 Oct 1942
89	WAGL 289	*Woodbine*	Zenith	2 Feb 1942	3 Jul 1942	17 Nov 1942
90	WAGL 290	*Gentian*	Zenith	3 Oct 1941	23 May 1942	3 Nov 1942
91	WAGL 277	*Cowslip*	Marine Iron	16 Sep 1941	11 Apr 1942	17 Oct 1942
92	WAGL 291	*Laurel*	Zenith	17 Apr 1942	4 Aug 1942	24 Nov 1942
93	WAGL 292	*Clover*	Marine Iron	3 Dec 1941	25 Apr 1942	8 Nov 1942
102	WAGL 295	*Evergreen*	Marine Iron	15 Apr 1942	3 Jul 1942	30 Apr 1943
103	WAGL 296	*Sorrel*	Zenith	26 May 1942	28 Sep 1942	15 Apr 1943
130	WAGL 300	*Citrus*	Marine Iron	29 Apr 1942	15 Aug 1942	30 May 1943
131	WAGL 301	*Conifer*	Marine Iron	6 Jul 1942	3 Nov 1942	1 Jul 1943
132	WAGL 302	*Madrona*	Zenith	6 Jul 1942	11 Nov 1942	30 May 1943
133	WAGL 303	*Tupelo*	Zenith	15 Aug 1942	28 Nov 1942	30 Aug 1943

Displacement	935 tons f/l
Dimensions	180' (oa); x 37' x 12'
Machinery	1 screw; diesel-electric; SHP 1,000; 13 knots
Endurance	12,000/12
Complement	80
Armament	1–3"/50, 2 to 4–20mm

Notes: First group 180A. Ice-breaking capability.

Service Records:

270 *Cactus* Boston, Mass. Damaged in collision with USCGC *Manasquan* at Boston, 14 Jun 1943. †
62 *Balsam* †
1* Okinawa.
289 *Woodbine* †
2* Saipan, Okinawa.
290 *Gentian* Cape May, N.J. †
277 *Cowslip* Boston, Mass. †
291 *Laurel* Boston, Mass.; Greenland †
292 *Clover* Alaska †
295 *Evergreen* Charleston, S.C., and Boston †
296 *Sorrell* Greenland †
300 *Citrus* Greenland; Ketchikan, Alaska †
301 *Conifer* Boston †
302 *Madrona* Miami †
303 *Tupelo* Boston, South Pacific †

CG	No.	Name	Builder	Keel Laid	Launched	Comm.
104	WAGL 297	*Ironwood*	Curtis Bay	2 Nov 1942	16 Mar 1943	4 Aug 1943
138	WAGL 305	*Mesquite*	Marine Iron	20 Aug 1942	14 Nov 1942	27 Aug 1943
139	WAGL 306	*Buttonwood*	Marine Iron	5 Oct 1942	30 Nov 1942	24 Sep 1943
140	WAGL 307	*Planetree*	Marine Iron	4 Dec 1942	20 Mar 1943	4 Nov 1943
141	WAGL 308	*Papaw*	Marine Iron	16 Nov 1942	19 Feb 1943	12 Oct 1943
142	WAGL 309	*Sweetgum*	Marine Iron	21 Feb 1943	15 Apr 1943	20 Nov 1943

Displacement	935 tons f/l

Dimensions	180' (oa); x 37' x 12"
Machinery	1 screw; diesel-electric; SHP 1,200; 13 knots
Endurance	12,000/12
Complement	80
Armament	1–3"/50, 4–20mm

Notes: Group 180B. Ice-breaking capability.

Service Records:

297 *Ironwood* South Pacific †
305 *Mesquite* Southwest Pacific †
306 *Buttonwood* South Pacific †
307 *Planetree* Seattle †
308 *Papaw* South Pacific. Damaged by explosion (probably mine) in southern Palau Is., 24 Dec 1944. †
2* Saipan, Palau
309 *Sweetgum* Miami †

CG	No.	Name	Builder	Keel Laid	Launched	Comm.
149	WAGL 388	*Basswood*	Marine Iron	21 Mar 1943	20 May 1943	12 Jan 1944
150	WAGL 390	*Blackhaw*	Marine Iron	16 Apr 1943	18 Jun 1943	17 Feb 1944
152	WAGL 394	*Hornbeam*	Marine Iron	19 Jun 1943	14 Aug 1943	14 Apr 1944
153	WAGL 398	*Redbud*	Marine Iron	21 Jul 1943	11 Sep 1943	2 May 1944
154	WAGL 401	*Sassafras*	Marine Iron	16 Aug 1943	5 Oct 1943	23 May 1944
157	WAGL 391	*Blackthorn*	Marine Iron	21 May 1943	20 Jul 1943	27 Mar 1944
165	WAGL 403	*Spar*	Marine Iron	13 Sep 1943	2 Nov 1943	12 Jun 1944
166	WAGL 402	*Sedge*	Marine Iron	6 Oct 1943	27 Nov 1943	5 Jul 1944
167	WAGL 405	*Sweetbrier*	Marine Iron	3 Nov 1943	30 Dec 1943	26 Jul 1944
168	WAGL 404	*Sundew*	Marine Iron	29 Nov 1943	8 Feb 1944	24 Aug 1944
169	WAGL 400	*Salvia*	Zenith	24 Jun 1943	15 Sep 1943	19 Feb 1944
170	WAGL 399	*Sagebrush*	Zenith	15 Jul 1943	30 Sep 1943	1 Apr 1944
171	WAGL 392	*Bramble*	Zenith	2 Aug 1943	23 Oct 1943	22 Apr 1944
172	WAGL 389	*Bittersweet*	Zenith	16 Sep 1943	11 Nov 1943	11 May 1944
173	WAGL 396	*Mallow*	Zenith	10 Oct 1943	9 Dec 1943	6 Jun 1944
174	WAGL 397	*Mariposa*	Zenith	25 Oct 1943	14 Jan 1944	1 Jul 1944
175	WAGL 393	*Firebush*	Zenith	12 Nov 1943	3 Feb 1944	20 Jul 1944
176	WAGL 395	*Iris*	Zenith	10 Dec 1943	18 May 1944	11 Aug 1944
177	WAGL 406	*Acacia* ex–*Thistle* (15 Mar 1944)	Zenith	16 Jan 1944	7 Apr 1944	1 Sep 1944
178	WAGL 407	*Woodrush*	Zenith	4 Feb 1944	28 Apr 1944	22 Sep 1944

Displacement	935 tons f/l
Dimensions	180' (oa); x 37' x 12"
Machinery	1 screw; diesel-electric; SHP 1,200; 13 knots
Endurance	12,000/12
Complement	80
Armament	1–3"/50, 4–20mm

Notes: Group 180C. Ice-breaking capability.

Service Records:

388 *Basswood* Hawaii †
390 *Blackhaw* Charleston †
391 *Blackthorn* San Pedro, Calif. †
394 *Hornbeam* Woods Hole, Mass. †
309 *Redbud* Miami †
401 *Sassafras* Western Pacific †
403 *Spar* Woods Hole, Mass. †
402 *Sedge* Guam, Okinawa, Shanghai †
405 *Sweetbrier* †
1* Okinawa.
406 *Sundew* Manitowoc, Wis. †
400 *Salvia* Portsmouth, Va. †
399 *Sagebrush* San Juan, Puerto Rico
392 *Bramble* San Pedro, Calif. Damaged in collision with *FS-252* while docked at Seward, Alaska, 13 Jun 1945. †
389 *Bittersweet* Ketchikan †
396 *Mallow* San Francisco †
397 *Mariposa* Staten I., N.Y. †
393 *Firebush* Staten I., N.Y. †
395 *Iris* Galveston †
406 *Acacia* Detroit †
407 *Woodrush* Duluth, Minn. †

ACQUIRED VESSELS

No.	Name	Builder	Launched	Acquired
WAGL 177	*Almond* ex–*La Salle*	Toledo Sbdg	1922	11 Dec 1942
WAGL 176	*Arrowwood* ex–*Cadillac*	Great Lakes	1928	15 Dec 1942

Displacement	677 tons f/l; 1148 grt (176), 677 grt (177)
Dimensions	161'10" (oa); x 56' x 13'6"
Machinery	1 screw; compound; 1 boiler; SHP 1,700; 10 knots
Endurance	1,220/9
Complement	39
Armament	none

Notes: Ferryboats, converted 1942. Great Lakes.

Service Records:

177 *Almond* Decomm 29 Sep 1945. Sold 31 Aug 1946.
Later history: Merchant *LaSalle.* BU 1952 Cleveland.
176 *Arrowwood* Decomm 29 Sep 1945. Sold 11 Jul 1946.
Later history: Merchant *Cadillac*, renamed *Lady Hamilton* 1952.

No.	Name	Builder	Launched	Comm.
WAGL 178	*Chaparral* ex–*Halcyon*	Great Lakes	1925	4 Dec 1942

Displacement	405 grt

Dimensions	161' (oa); x 45' x 14'4"
Machinery	1 screw; VTE; 1 boiler, SHP 800; 9 knots
Complement	42
Armament	none

Notes: Converted ferryboat. Great Lakes.

Service Record:

WAGL 178 *Chaparral* Decomm 8 Feb 1946. Sold 12 Dec 1946.
Later history: Merchant *Treasure Unlimited* 1952, renamed *Newfoundland Cruiser* 1961. Wrecked at Cape Dorset, Baffin I., 15 Sep 1963.

No.	Name	Builder	Acquired	Comm.
WAGL 367	*Blackrock* ex–*The Boys*	(Morehead City, N.C.)	1924	17 Jun 1943

Displacement	230 tons f/l
Dimensions	114' (oa); 112' (bp) x 19'6" x 8'
Machinery	1 screw; diesel; bhp 300, 12 knots
Endurance	3,240/10
Complement	15
Armament	none

Notes: Caribbean. Decomm 31 Mar 1944 for conversion, recomm 23 Feb 1945.

Service Record:

WAGL 367 *Blackrock* †

INLAND AND RIVER TENDERS

No.	Name	Builder	Launched	Comm.
WAGL 214	*Greenbrier*	Ward Eng.	19 Sep 1922	20 Jun 1924

Displacement	350 grt, 440 tons f/l
Dimensions	164'6" (oa); 140' (bp) x 32'6" x 4'
Machinery	sternwheel; steam; 3 boilers; SHP 500; 10 knots
Complement	26

Notes: Steel hull. Ohio River.

Service Record:

WAGL 214 *Greenbrier* Decomm 19 Sep 1947. Sold 19 Apr 1948.
Later history: Merchant *Mississippi*; se 1974.

No.	Name	Builder	Keel Laid	Launched	Comm.
WAGL 253	*Willow*	Dubuque	1924	26 Jul 1926	4 Oct 1927

Displacement	1,070 tons f/l
Dimensions	200' (oa); x 65' x 6'6"
Machinery	sidewheels, steam, 6 boilers; SHP 800; 7.5 knots
Complement	22

Service Record:

WAGL 253 *Willow* Memphis, Tenn. Damaged in collision with *LST-841*, 15 Dec 1944. To U.S. War Department (CofE), 1 Mar 1945.
Later history: Merchant *Willow* (Spanish); se 1998.

No.	Name	Builder	Keel Laid	Launched	Comm.
WAGL 251	*Wakerobin*	Dravo Pitt.	1925	1926	15 Apr 1927

Displacement	900 grt; 622 tons f/l
Dimensions	182' (oa); 153'6" (bp) x 43' x 4'2"
Machinery	sternwheel; steam; 2 boilers; SHP 550; 9 knots
Complement	36

Service Record:

WAGL 251 *Wakerobin* Memphis. Sold to U.S. War Department (CofE), 20 Apr 1955

No.	Name	Builder	Launched	Acquired	Comm.
WAGL 216	*Alder*	(U)	1917	Mar 1924	1930

Displacement	80 tons f/l
Dimensions	72' (oa) x 16' x 7'6"
Machinery	1 screw; diesel; bhp 110, 8 knots
Endurance	875/8
Complement	9

Notes: Wood hull. Exploded and sank, June 1929, raised and rebuilt.

Service Record:

WAGL 216 *Alder* Ketchikan, Alaska. Decomm 11 Dec 1947. Sold 14 Jun 1948.
Later history: Merchant *Acme*, renamed *Lummi* 1960. Foundered at sea off Baja California, 15 Nov 1960.

No.	Name	Builder	Launched	Comm.
WAGL 223	*Althea*	New London	24 Feb 1930	30 Apr 1930
WAGL 266	*Poinciana*	Electric Boat	7 Jun 1930	8 Jul 1930

Displacement	120 tons
Dimensions	80'9" (oa) x 19' x 3'8"
Machinery	2 screws; diesel, bhp 220, 7 knots
Endurance	875/6
Complement	9

Notes: Steel hulls.

Service Records:

223 *Althea* Fort Pierce, Fla. †
266 *Poinciana* Fort Lauderdale, Fla. †

No.	Name	Builder	Keel Laid	Launched	Comm.
WAGL 258	*Cherry*	L. D. Smith	1931	24 Dec 1931	19 May 1932

Displacement	202 tons
Dimensions	86'3" (oa) x 22' x 9'6"
Machinery	1 screw; diesel, bhp 300, 9 knots
Endurance	1600/8
Complement	10

Service Record:

WAGL 258 *Cherry* Great Lakes (Buffalo, NY) †

No.	Name	Builder	Keel Laid	Launched	Comm.
WAGL 263	*Myrtle*	Dubuque	1932	30 Sep 1932	1932

Displacement	186 tons f/l
Dimensions	92'8" (oa) x 23' x 6'
Machinery	2 screws; diesel; bhp 220; 8 knots

Endurance	980/5
Complement	11

Service Record:

WAGL 263 *Myrtle* Galveston, Tex. †

No.	Name	Builder	Keel Laid	Launched	Comm.
WAGL 288	*Dahlia*	Great Lakes	1933	15 Jun 1933	Aug 1933

Displacement	160 tons f/l
Dimensions	81'2" (oa) x 21' x 9'
Machinery	1 screw; diesel; bhp 235; 10 knots
Endurance	1,027/7;
Complement	10

Service Record.

WAGL 288 *Dahlia* Great Lakes (Detroit) †

No.	Name	Builder	Keel Laid	Launched	Comm.
WAGL 267	*Rhododendron*	Commercial	1934	16 Mar 1935	12 Apr 1935

Displacement	140 tons f/l
Dimensions	81' (oa) x 20' x 6'
Machinery	2 screws; diesel; bhp 240; 9 knots
Complement	10

Service Record.

WAGL 267 *Rhododendron* Vancouver Wash. †

No.	Name	Builder	Keel Laid	Launched	Comm.
WAGL 261	*Jasmine*	Dravo Pitt.	26 Dec 1934	26 Mar 1935	May 1935
WAGL 257	*Bluebonnet*	Dubuque	—	1939	4 Nov 1939

Displacement	184 tons f/l
Dimensions	91'4" (oa); 82' (bp) x 23' x 6'
Machinery	2 screws; diesel; bhp 440; 9 knots
Endurance	570/8
Complement	11

Service Records:

261 *Jasmine* New Orleans, La. †
257 *Bluebonnet* Galveston, Tex. †

No.	Name	Builder	Launched	Comm.
WAGL 213	*Goldenrod*	Dubuque	1937	2 Jun 1938
WAGL 241	*Poplar*	Dubuque	1939	—

Displacement	193 tons f/l
Dimensions	103'6" (oa) x 24' x 4'6"
Machinery	2 screws; diesels, bhp 400; 9 knots;
Complement	15

Note: Tunnel-stern propellers.

Service Records:

WAGL 213 *Goldenrod* †
WAGL 241 *Poplar* †

No.	Name	Builder	Launched	Comm.
WAGL 260	*Elm*	Defoe	—	1 Apr 1938
WAGL 256	*Birch*	General Ship	1939	—

Displacement	69 tons 77 f/l; *Birch*: 76 tons, 137 f/l
Dimensions	72'4" (oa) x 17'6" x 5'
Machinery	2 screws; diesel; bhp 330; 9 knots
Endurance	900/8
Complement	9

Service Records:

WAGL 260 *Elm* Atlantic City, N.J. †
WAGL 256 *Birch* St. Petersburg, Fla. †

No.	Name	Builder	Launched	Comm.
WAGL 262	*Azalea* ex–*Minneapolis* (1 Feb 1942)	(Grafton Ill.)	1915	12 Nov 1940
WAGL 209	*Cottonwood* ex–*Le Clair* (U.S. War Department)	(Grafton, Ill.)	1915	1939

Displacement	**WAGL** 262: 352 tons f/l; **WAGL** 209: 243 tons f/l
Dimensions	**WAGL** 262: 149'9" (oa) x 34'4" x 4'6"; **WAGL** 209: 151' (oa); x 34'8" x 5'
Machinery	sternwheel; steam; 1 boiler; SHP 320; 8 knots
Complement	36

Notes: Acquired from U.S. War Departmentt.

Service Records:

WAGL 262 *Azalea* Decomm 6 May 1946. Sold 14 Nov 1946.
WAGL 209 *Cottonwood* Decomm 25 May 1946. Sold 1 May 1947.

CG	No.	Name	Builder	Keel Laid	Launched	Comm.
77	**WAGL** 259	*Dogwood*	Dubuque	Jul 1940	16 Jun 1941	17 Sep 1941
78	**WAGL** 268	*Sycamore*	Dubuque	1940	16 Jun 1941	9 Sep 1941
94	**WAGL** 63	*Forsythia*	Avondale	24 Nov 1941	15 Apr 1942	15 Feb 1943

Displacement	230 tons f/l
Dimensions	113'9" (oa) x 26' x 5'
Machinery	2 screws; diesels; bhp 400; 10 knots
Complement	24

Service Records:

WAGL 259 *Dogwood* †
WAGL 268 *Sycamore* †
WAGL 63 *Forsythia* †

CG	No.	Name	Builder	Launched	Comm.
80	**WAGL** 264	*Oleander*	Jeffersonville	24 May 1941	20 Sep 1941

Displacement	80 tons f/l
Dimensions	73' (oa) x 18' x 5'
Machinery	2 screws; diesels, bhp 300, 9 knots
Complement	9

Service Record:

WAGL 264 †

CG	No.	Name	Builder	Keel Laid	Launched	Comm.
100	**WAGL** 293	*Cosmos*	Dubuque	19 Feb 1942	11 Nov 1942	5 Dec 1942
101	**WAGL** 294	*Barberry*	Dubuque	20 Apr 1942	14 Nov 1942	3 Jan 1943
122	**WAGL** 298	*Rambler*	Dubuque	7 Dec 1942	6 May 1943	26 May 1943
123	**WAGL** 299	*Brier*	Dubuque	5 Aug 1942	6 May 1943	2 Jul 1943
180	**WAGL** 316	*Primrose*	Dubuque	26 Nov 1943	18 Aug 1944	23 Oct 1944
181	**WAGL** 315	*Smilax*	Dubuque	26 Nov 1943	18 Aug 1944	1 Nov 1944
185	**WAGL** 317	*Verbena*	Dubuque	20 Mar 1944	2 Oct 1944	13 Nov 1944
186	**WAGL** 313	*Bluebell*	Birchfield	20 Mar 1944	28 Sep 1944	24 Mar 1945

Displacement	178 tons f/l
Dimensions	100' (oa) x 24' x 5'
Machinery	2 screws; diesels; bhp 330; 10 knots
Endurance	2,400/8;
Complement	16

Note: Bay and sound tenders.

Service Records:

WAGL 293 *Cosmos* St. Petersburg, Fla. †
WAGL 294 *Barberry* Morehead City, N.C. †
WAGL 298 *Rambler* New Orleans. †
WAGL 299 *Brier* Charleston, S.C. †
WAGL 316 *Primrose* Charleston, S.C. †
WAGL 315 *Smilax* Fort Pierce, Fla. †
WAGL 317 *Verbena* Coinjock, N.C. †
WAGL 313 *Bluebell* Vancouver, Wash. †

CG	No.	Name	Builder	Keel Laid	Launched	Comm.
134	**WAGL** 304	*Fern*	Peterson/ Hacker	1 Jul 1942	6 Nov 1942	19 Nov 1942

Displacement	350 tons f/l
Dimensions	115' (oa); x 31' x 8'
Machinery	3 screws; diesels; bhp 960; 10 knots
Complement	24

Note: Built with detachable ice plow (CG 136).

Service Record:

134 **WAGL** 304 *Fern* †

CG	No.	Name	Builder	Keel Laid	Launched	Comm.
179	**WAGL** 311	*Sumac*	Peterson/ Hacker	13 Mar 1944	14 Oct 1944	11 Nov 1944

Displacement	350 tons f/l
Dimensions	114'6" (oa) x 30'6" x 9'
Machinery	3 screws; diesels; bhp 960; 11.3 knots
Complement	24

Service Record:

179 **WAGL** 311 *Sumac* †

CG	No.	Name	Builder	Keel Laid	Launched	Comm.
143	**WAGL** 285	*Foxglove*	Dubuque	9 Nov 1944	19 Jul 1945	1 Oct 1945

Displacement	385 tons f/l
Dimensions	114' (oa) x 26' x 6'
Machinery	3 screws; diesels; bhp 600; 9 knots
Complement	22

Service Record:

143 **WAGL** 285 *Foxglove* St. Louis, Mo. †

No.	Name	Builder	Keel Laid	Launched	Comm.
WAGL 310	*Lantana*	Peterson/ Hacker	21 Mar 1943	18 Oct 1943	6 Nov 1943

Displacement	273 tons f/l
Dimensions	80' (oa) x 30' x 6'
Machinery	3 screws; diesel; bhp 495; 9 knots
Complement	17

Service Record:

WAGL 310 *Lantana* †

No.	Name	Builder	Launched	Comm.
WAGL 179	*Jonquil* ex–*Lucinda Clark*	(Harbor Pt, Mo.)	1937	6 Jan 1943

Displacement	107 grt
Dimensions	76' (oa); 73' (bp) x 22'7" x 4'8"
Machinery	2 screws; semidiesel; bhp 360

Note: Towboat.

Service Record:

WAGL 179 *Jonquil* St. Louis, Mo. Returned 1 Dec 1943.
Later history: Merchant *Lucinda Clark*. se 1974.

CG	No.	Name	Builder	Keel Laid	Launched	Comm.
125	**WAGL** 286	*Clematis*	Peterson	20 Jul 1943	15 May 1944	28 Jul 1944
126	**WAGL** 287	*Shadbush*	Peterson	20 Jul 1943	15 May 1944	20 Jul 1944

Displacement	80 tons f/l
Dimensions	73'6""(oa) x 18'10" x 3'6"
Machinery	2 screws; diesels; bhp 150; 9.6 knots
Endurance	3,300/6.4
Complement	8

Service Records:

125 **WAGL** 286 *Clematis* †
126 **WAGL** 287 *Shadbush* †

No.	Name	Builder	Keel Laid	Launched	Comm.
WAGL 408	*Aster*	Martinolich	1943	1943	Apr 1944
WAGL 409	*Thistle*	Martinolich	20 Jun 1943	1943	1 Sep 1943

Displacement	80 tons f/l
Dimensions	106'3" (oa); 85'8" (bp) x 30'9" x 8'
Machinery	2 screws; diesels; bhp 270; 7.5 knots
Endurance	3,300/6.4
Complement	10

Note: Former Army barges.

Service Records:

WAGL 408 *Aster* †
WAGL 409 *Thistle* †

HARBOR CUTTERS AND LAUNCHES

In Service, 1922

Advance Renamed ***AB-1***, 6 Nov 1923. Damaged by gasoline explosion at Sault Ste. Marie, Mich., 27 May 1924, salvaged. Sold 1940.
Arrow Renamed ***AB-2***, 6 Nov 1923. To USSB, 18 Mar 1925.
Cossack Renamed ***AB-3***, 6 Nov 1923. Destroyed by fire at Miami, 8 May 1925.
Dare Renamed ***AB-4***, 6 Nov 1923. Sold 17 Jul 1924.
Dash Renamed ***AB-5***, 6 Nov 1923. Sold 19 Sep 1933.
Delmarva Renamed ***AB-22***, 6 Nov 1923. RR 1934.
Guide To USSB, 5 Aug 1926
Guard Decomm 17 Feb 1943 and sold.
Kangaroo Renamed ***AB-6***, 6 Nov 1923. Sold 1 Oct 1932.
Lookout Renamed ***AB-7***, 6 Nov 1923. Sold 19 Sep 1933.
Messenger Renamed ***AB-8***, 6 Nov 1923. Sold Feb 1931.
Patrol Renamed ***AB-28***, 1938. Decomm 1940.
Penrose Sold 15 Jul 1924.
Pioneer Renamed ***AB-9***, 6 Nov 1923. RR 1934.
Relief Renamed ***AB-10***, 6 Nov 1923.
Scout Renamed ***AB-11***, 6 Nov 1923. Decomm 15 Mar 1930 and sold.
Search Renamed ***AB-12***, 6 Nov 1923. Renamed CGC-12, 1939. Decomm 1940.
Sentinel Renamed ***AB-13***, 6 Nov 1923. RR 1939.
Tulare Renamed ***AB-14***, 6 Nov 1923. RR 1935.
Tybee Renamed ***AB-15***, 6 Nov 1923. Sold 25 Sep 1930.
Venture Sold 6 Aug 1923. Was to be renamed ***AB-16***.
Vidette Sold 20 Mar 1925.
Vigilant Renamed ***AB-17***, 6 Nov 1923. Stricken 1940.
Voyager Renamed ***AB-18***, 6 Nov 1923. RR 1936.

UNITED STATES COAST & GEODETIC SURVEY

In service 1923:		
Bache	1902	Sold 30 Apr 1927.
Hydrographer	1901	Sold 1928.
Explorer	1904	trfd to National Youth Authority 1939.
Surveyor	1917	Sold 1936.
Lydonia	1912	Pacific and Atlantic Sold 1947.
Natoma	1913	Sold 1934.
Ranger	1910	Sold 21 Dec 1931.

Name	Formerly	Date	Disposition
Pioneer	ex–AM 29 *Osprey*	7 Apr 1922	To USN 17 Sep 1941 as **ARS 2**, renamed ***Crusader***.
Discoverer	ex–AM 36 *Auk*	7 Apr 1922	To USN 26 Aug 1941 as **ARS 3**, as ***Discoverer***.
Guide	ex–AM 32 *Flamingo*	7 Apr 1922	To USN 27 Jun 1941 as **ARS 1**, renamed ***Viking***.
Guide	ex–*Caronia*	1941	To USN 16 Mar 1942 as PYc 11, renamed ***Andradite***
Pioneer	ex–*Argus* PY 14	17 Sep 1941	Returned to USN 16 Mar 1942

Name	Builder	Launched	Comm.
Hydrographer	Spear	1928	

Displacement	1,135 tons f/l
Dimensions	164'11" (oa) 143' (wl) x 31'6" x 13'10"
Machinery	1 screw, diesel-electric, SHP 650, 10 knots
Complement	92
Armament	1-3"/50, 2-20mm twin AA guns (WWII)

Notes: To USN 15 Apr 1942 as **PY 30**, rec **AGS 2,** 4 Apr 1942. Newfoundland 1942, Aleutians 1943, Pacific 1943-45. Decomm and rtnd to USC&GS 1 Jul 1946.

3* Attu, Guam, Palau.

Name	Builder	Launched	Acquired	Comm.
Oceanographer	Marvel ex–*Corsair*	1898	1930	

Displacement	1,252 tons
Dimensions	304' (oa) 270' (wl) x 33' x 16'
Machinery	2 screws, VTE, 14.7 knots
Complement	146
Armament	2-3"/50

Notes: To USN 7 Apr 1942 as **PG 85**, renamed ***Natchez***. Rec **AGS 3** & renamed ***Oceanographer***, 2 Jun 1942. Decomm 22 Sep 1944. Stricken 14 Oct 1944; BU.

Name	Builder	Laid Down	Launched	Comm.
Explorer	Lake Washington		Mar 1940	

Displacement	1,800 tons
Dimensions	219'6 (oa) 193'8" (bp) x 38 x 16
Machinery	1 screw, turbine, SHP 2,200,
Complement	(U)
Armament	(U)

Notes: Served in Aleutians. †

Name	Builder	Laid Down	Launched	Comm.
Pathfinder	Lake Washington.		11 Jan 1942	31 Aug 1942

Displacement	1,523 tons ; 2,175 f/l
Dimensions	229'4" (oa) 209'4" (wl) x 39' x 16'
Machinery	1 screw, DeLaval GT, 2 B&W boilers, SHP 2,000, 14.7 knots
Complement	158
Armament	2-3"/50, 6-20mm AA guns (WWII)

Notes: To USN 3 Sep 1942 as **AGS 1**. Damaged by kamikaze off Okinawa, 5 May 1945 (1 killed). Decomm 31 Jan 1946. Rtnd to USC&GS 22 Aug 1946. †

2* Solomons, Okinawa.

SMALL VESSELS

IN SERVICE 1923

Name	Formerly	Built	Acquired	Fate
Audwin	SP-451	1911	27 Mar 1919	Sold 1927.
Helianthus	SP-585	1912	28 Mar 1919	Sold 1939
Wildcat	SP-879	1915	14 Apr 1919	Sold 1941.
Elsie III	SP-708	1912	21 Apr 1919	Sold 1944.
Mikawe	SP-309	1916	24 Apr 1919	Training ship. Destroyed by fire 27 Oct 1939
Marindin				Sold 1944.
Mitchell				Sold 1944.

Ogden				Sold 1944.	
Rodgers				Sold 1944.	

Name	Builder	Built	Acquired	Dimensions	Fate
Echo	Portsmouth NYd	1902	1928	65 x 15 x 7	Sold 1938
	ex–YFB 132				
Westdahl	(Portland, Ore)	1929		77.5 x 15.5 x 7.5	Sold 1946
Gilbert	L.D.Smith	1929		77.5 x 16.5 x 7.5	†
Lester Jones	Astoria Marine	1940		88 x 21 x 8	†
George D. Cowie	Great Lakes Boat	1933	1941	103 x 18.5 x 6.8	†
	ex–Perkins (1942), *ex–Rhea III*				
Pratt	Tacoma Boat	1937	1941	78.1 x 20.3 x 9	Returned to USN 1942
	ex–YP 96, *ex–Midnight Sun*				
Wainwright	Robinson Marine	1942		66 x 14.8 x 3.5	†
Hilgard	Robinson Marine	1942		66 x 14.8 x 3.5	†
Sosbee	Hodgson Bros.	1945		68 x 16.6 x 5.5	†

ACQUIRED FROM US COAST GUARD 1933-34

Name	Formerly	Built	Acquired	Dimensions	Fate
Dickins	CG-144	1925	1933	75 x 13.6 x 4	Returned to USCG 1935
Welker	CG-179	1925	15 Jan 1934	75 x 13.7 x 4	To US Army 1937.
Faris	CG 223	1924	Jun 1933	75 x 13.6 x 7	Sold 1946
Miller	CG 198	1925	15 Jan 1934	75 x 13.6 x 4	Returned 1935
Davidson	CG 242	1925	1933	75 x 13.6 x 4	Returned 1935
Pratt	CG 295	1924	1933	75 x 13,5 x 4	Disc 1937
Ritter	CG 145	1925	1933	75 x 13.6 x 4	Returned 1935

ACQUIRED FROM USN 1945-46

Name	Formerly	Built	Acquired
Bowen	SC-1361	1943	3 Oct 1945 †
Stirni	SC-1358	1943	30 Sep 1946 †
Parker	SC-1277	1943	30 Sep 1946 †
Bowie	PCS-1405	1943	9 Aug 1946 †
Derickson	PCS-1458 (AGS 6)	1943	17 May 1944 †
Hodgson	PCS-1450	1943	9 Aug 1946 †
Pioneer	AGP 7 *Mobjack*	1942	21 Aug 1946 †

APPENDIX I NAVY CONSTRUCTION PROGRAM, NAVY STRENGTH

BY FISCAL YEAR

1924 CA 24–25; PR 2–8
1925 SS 166–168
1927 CA 26–31
1929 CA 32–36; SS 169
1930 CA 38; CV 4
1931 CA 37; DD 348–351; SS 170–171
1932 DD 352–355
1933 CA 39, 44; CL 40–43; CV 5–6; DD 356–363, 364–379; PG 50–51; SS 172–175
1934 CA 45; CL 46–48; DD 381, 383, 384–385, 380–393; SS 176–181
1935 CV 7; CL 49–50; DD 394–396, 397–408; SS 182–187
1936 DD 409–420; SS 188–193
1937 BB 55–56; DD 421–428; SS 194–197; AD 14; AV 4

BY DATES ORDERED

FY 1939 Oct 1938+: BB 57–60; CV 8; CL 51–54; DD 429–436 SS 198–203; CM 5; AM 55–56; AD 15; AS 11; AT 64–66; AV 5; AVP 10–11. Also PC 449–453; PT 1–20; PTC 1–12; AVC 1

FY 1940 Jul 1939+: BB 61–62; CL 55–56; DD 437–444; SS 204–211; AR 5; AVP 12–13

FY 1941 Jun 1940: BB 63–64; CV 12; CL 57–58; DD 453–458, 461–464; SS 212–214, 228–230; AM 57; AS 12; AV 7; AVP 21–22

Jul 1940 (Expansion Program I): CV 9–11; CA 68–71; CL 59–67; DD 445–452, 455–460, 465–482; SS 215–221; 231–239; 253–258

Sep 1940 (Expansion Program II): BB 65–71; CV 13–19; CB 1–6; CA 72–75; CL 76–98; DD 483–597; SS 222–227, 240–252, 259–282; CM 6–7; AM 58–65; AD 17–19; AN 1–4; AOG 1–4; APA 1, 11; AR 6–8; AS 15–19; ASR 7–11; AVP 23–32

Dec 1940: CL 99–100; DD 598–644

Apr 1941: AM 82–131; PC 542–577; PT 45–68; AT 67–76; DD 645–648; SS 283–284

Jun 1941+ (Lend-Lease): BARS 1–5; BYMS 1–30; BPT 21–52; BAPM 1–7; BARS 6–10; BAT 1–14

Sep 1941: PC 578–627; SC 628–675; PT 71–102

FY 1942 Aug 1941+: AT 81–95; BDE 1–50; BAM 1–32; LSD 1–8; ARS 13–17; AM 136–165; SC 676–775; PC 776–825; PT 103–138; BYMS 31–80

Dec 1941 (Expansion Program): CV 20–21; CL 101–102; DD 649–665; SS 285–307

Jan 1942 (Maximum War Effort): DE 51–300; (Mar 42) AM 166–313; PCE 827–976; SC 977–1076; PC 1077–1265; YMS 135–409; APM 9–18; LST 1–300; ARS 28–29; AT 119–127; APR 1–11; ATR 10–40; WPG 72–84; AOG 6–11; ARS 19–27; AT 96–118; AVP 33–67

Apr 1942: CVE 52–54; AD 22–26; AE 8–9; AO 51–64; AS 23; AV 14–17; SS 308–313

Jun 1942: SS 315–434

FY 1943 Aug 1942: CVB 41–44; CV 31–40; CA 122–138; CL 103–121; DD 692–791; DE 301–720; LST 301–490; LCIL 1–350; APc 51–89

Jun 1942: DD 666–691, 792–808

Aug 1942: PT 259–367; SC 1266–1375; PC 1376–1465; CVE 55–104

Nov 1942: ATR 50–89

Jan 1943: CVE 105–119

Nov 1942: DE 721–800; PF 3–102

Mar 1943: LST 491–621; LCIL 423–542

FY 1944 Jun 1943: CV 45–47; CA 139–142; CL 143–149; DD 809–890; SS 435–544; DE 801–1005

Nov 1943: AD 16–29; AE 13; AOG 48–59; AR 13–16; ARS 38–49; AS 27–30; ST 148–165; AV 18–20

Jul 1943: LSD 16–27; LST 511–739; LCIL 543–892

Sep–Oct 1943: LSM 1–230

Dec 1943: LST 754–828; LSM 253–353; LCIL 845–929; LST 829–1028

Jan 1944: CVE 120–127

Mar–Apr 1944: LST 1029–1130; LSM 354–458; LCIL 1110–1139; LCSL 1-60; APB 35–40

May–Nov 1944: LST 1131–1152; LSM 459–558; LCSL 61–130; AO 97–109; AOG 62–75; ATA 219–138; AG 88–89

FY 1945 Feb 1945: CVB 56–57; CV 50–55; CVE 128–139; CA 150–153; CL 154–159; DD 891–926; SS 545–562

Source: Adapted from Stephen S. Roberts, "U.S. Navy Shipbuilding Programs during World War II," *Warship International* 3 (1981): p. 218. Dates are approximate or represent the start of the period; cancellations are not noted.

NAVY STRENGTH: SHIPS ON HAND AND BUILDING

	1 Jan 1942		1 Jan 1943		1 Jan 1944		1 Jan 1945		1 Jan 1946		
Type	On Hand	Building	On Hand	Building	On Hand	Building	On Hand	Building	On Hand	Building	
BB	17	15	20	11	22	4	23	2	23	1	
CV	7	16	4	35	10	19	16	13	21	6	
CVB						3		3	2	1	
CVL					9	2	8	2	8	2	
CVE	1	15	12	85	35	51	65	21	79	4	
CB		6		6		3	2	1	2	1	
CA	18	8	14	25	16	25	17	27	24	9	
CL	20	38	26	43	32	43	43	25	45	8	
DD	173	206	229	267	335	222	371	132	354	43	
DM	8		8		8		20		12		
DMS	18		18		17		28		23		
APD	6		5		20		26		5		xDD
DE		300		800	230	394	376	10	327	4	
APD							39	41	93		xDE
SS	113	94	133	187	178	241	238	64	206	21	

Source: U.S. Department of the Navy, Office of Chief of Naval Operations, *Combatant Shipbuilding 1-1-42 to 7-1-46* (Washington, D.C.: U.S. Department of the Navy, 1946), 41–1000.

VESSELS TRANSFERRED UNDER LEND-LEASE

To Brazil: 8 DE; 8 PC; 8 SC; 1 AP; 1 YF; 1 YR
To Cuba: 12 WYP
To Dominican Republic: 3 WYP
To Ecuador: 1 PY; 1 APc
To France: 1 CVE; 5 DE; 32 PC; 50 SC; 31 YMS; 3 AN; 3 AOG; 3 YO; 2 YTB; 19 YTL; 2 YW
To Greece: 4 LST; 1 PC; 8 YMS; 5 APc
To Mexico: 3 SC; 2 WYP
To Netherlands: 1 PC; 1 PT
To Norway: 1 PC; 3 SC; 8 YMS
To Panama: 2 WYP
To Peru: 6 WYP; 2 YT
To United Kingdom: 38 CVE; 50 DD; 78 DE; 9 SS; 32 AM; 150 YMS; 20 PF; 14 PGE; 15 PCE; 5 AN; 30 APc; 2 AR; 2 ARL; 6 ARS; 13 AT; 14 ATR; 120 LST; 220 LCI(L); 187 LCT; 10 WPG; 2 YO; 2 YT (includes ships transferred to other countries, listed herein; also 9 DD to USSR, 1 SS to Poland)
To USSR: 1 CL; 34 AM; 28 PF; 36 RPC; 202 PT; 26 PTC; 76 SC; 30 LCI(L); 17 LCT; 15 AG; 3 WAGB; 43 YMS; 4 YR
To Uruguay: 1 PC
To Venezuela: 4 WYP
To Yugoslavia: 8 PT

APPENDIX II
NAVY TYPE DESIGNATIONS

Note: * designates unused or discontinued by 1945.

Capital Ships

BB Battleship
BM Monitor*

Aircraft Carriers

CV Aircraft Carrier
CVB Large Aircraft Carrier
CVE Escort Aircraft Carrier
CVL Light Aircraft Carrier
CVS Seaplane Carrier

Cruisers

CA Heavy Cruiser
CB Large Cruiser
CC Battle Cruiser*
CF Flying-Deck Cruiser*
CL Light Cruiser

Destroyers

DD Destroyer
DE Destroyer Escort
DL Destroyer Leader*

Submarines

SC Cruiser Submarine*
SF Fleet Submarine*
SM Submarine Minelayer
SS Submarine

Mine Vessels

ACM Auxiliary Minelayer
AM Minesweeper
AMb Base Minesweeper
AMc Coastal Minesweeper
AMC(U) Coastal Minesweeper (Underwater Locator)
CM Minelayer
CMc Coastal Minelayer
DM Destroyer Minelayer
DMS High Speed Minesweeper

Patrol Vessels

PC Submarine Chaser (173')
PC(C) Submarine Chaser, Control
PCE Escort
PCE(C) Escort, Control
PCE(R) Escort (Rescue)
PCS Submarine Chaser (136')
PCS(C) Submarine Chaser, Control
PE Eagle
PF Frigate
PG Gunboat
PGM Motor Gunboat
PR River Gunboat
PT Motor Torpedo Boat
PTC Motorboat, Submarine Chaser
PY Yacht
PYc Coastal Yacht
SC Submarine Chaser (110')
SC(C) Submarine Chaser Control

Auxiliaries

AB Crane Ship
ABD Advance Base Dock

ABSD Advance Base Sectional Dock
AC Collier*
ACV Aircraft Escort Vessel* (later CVE)
AD Destroyer Tender
AE Ammunition Ship
AF Storeship
AFD Mobile Floating Drydock
AG Miscellaneous Auxiliary
AGC Amphibious Force Flagship
AGD Seagoing Dredge*
AGL Lighthouse Tender
AGP Motor Torpedo Boat Tender
AGS Surveying Ship
AGSc Coastal Surveying Ship
AH Hospital Ship
AK Cargo Ship
AKA Attack Cargo Ship
AKD Deep-Hold Cargo Ship*
AKN Net Cargo Ship
AKS General Stores Issue Ship
AKV Cargo Ship and Aircraft Ferry
AL Lightship
AN Net Tender
AO Oiler
AOG Gasoline Tanker
AP Transport
APA Attack Transport
APB Barracks Ship (Self-Propelled)
APC Cavalry Transport*
APc Coastal Transport
APD High-Speed Transport
APF Administration Flagship*
APG Supporting Gunnery Flagship*
APH Evacuation Transport
APL Barracks Ship; Labor Transport
APM Mechanized Artillery Transport
APN Nonmechanized Artillery Transport*
APP Troop Barge, Class A*
APR Rescue Transport*
APS Submarine Transport
APT Troop Barge, Class B*
APV Transport and Aircraft Ferry
AR Repair Ship
ARB Battle Damage Repair Ship
ARC Cable Repairing or Laying Ship
ARD Floating Dry Dock
ARDC Floating Dry Dock, Concrete
ARG Repair Ship, Internal Combustion Engine
ARH Heavy Hull Repair Ship
ARL Landing Craft Repair Ship
ARM Heavy Machinery Repair Ship*
ARS Salvage Vessel
ARS(D) Salvage Lifting Vessel
ARS(T) Salvage Craft Tender
ARV(A) Aircraft Repair Ship (Aircraft)
ARV(E) Aircraft Repair Ship (Engine)
AS Submarine Tender
ASR Submarine Rescue Vessel
AT Oceangoing Tug*
ATA Auxiliary Ocean Tug
ATF Fleet Tug
ATO Fleet Tug (Old)
ATR Rescue Tug
AV Seaplane Tender
AVC Catapult Lighter
AVD Seaplane Tender, Destroyer
AVG Aircraft Escort Vessel* (later CVE)
AVP Seaplane Tender, Small
AVR Aircraft Rescue Vessel
AVS Aviation Supply Ship
AW Distilling Ship
AWK Water Tanker
AZ Airship Tender*
IX Unclassified

Landing Ships and Craft

LC(FF) Landing Craft, Flotilla Flagship
LCI(G) Landing Craft, Infantry (Gunboat)
LCI(L) Landing Craft, Infantry (Large)
LCI(R) Landing Craft, Infantry (Rocket)
LCM Landing Craft, Mechanized
LCP Landing Craft, Personnel
LCS(L) Landing Craft, Support (Large)
LCT Landing Craft, Tank
LCV Landing Craft, Vehicle
LCVP Landing Craft, Personnel
LSD Landing Ship, Dock
LSM Landing Ship, Medium
LSM(R) Landing Ship, Medium (Rocket)
LST Landing Ship, Tank
LST(H) Landing Ship, Tank (Evacuation)
LSV Landing Ship, Vehicle
LVT Landing Vehicle, Tracked

District Craft

YA Ash Lighter
YAG District Auxiliary, Miscellaneous
YC Open Lighter
YCF Car Float
YCV Aircraft Transportation Lighter
YCK Open Cargo Lighter
YD Floating Derrick
YDG Degaussing Vessel
YDT Diving Tender
YE Ammunition Lighter
YF Covered Lighter
YFB Ferryboat; Launch
YFD Floating Dry Dock
YFT Torpedo Transportation Lighter
YG Garbage Lighter
YH Ambulance Boat
YHB Houseboat
YHT Heating Scow
YLA Open Landing Lighter
YM Dredge
YMS Motor Minesweeper

YMT	Motor Tug
YN	Net Tender
YNg	Gate Vessel
YNT	Net Tender (Tug)
YO	Fuel Oil Barge
YOG	Gasoline Barge
YOS	Oil Storage Barge
YP	District Patrol Vessel
YPD	Pile Driver
YPK	Pontoon Stowage Barge
YR	Floating Workshop
YRC	Rescue Chamber
YRD	Floating Workshop, Dry Dock
YS	Stevedoring Barge
YSD	Seaplane Wrecking Derrick
YSP	Salvage Pontoon
YSR	Sludge Removal Barge
YT	Harbor Tug
YTB	Harbor Tug, Big
YTM	Harbor Tug, Medium
YTL	Harbor Tug, Little
YTT	Torpedo Testing Barge
YW	Water Barge

Prefixes

B	British Lend-Lease
E	Experimental
O	Obsolete
R	Russian Lend-Lease
W	Coast Guard (Originally G)
X	Converted

Fig. App.2.1. Puget Sound Navy Yard at Bremerton, Wash.; an aerial view during the 1930s. L to R: *Crane Ship No. 1* (ex-battleship *Kearsarge*); a heavy cruiser; *Lexington* (CV 2) in dry dock; two *New Mexico*–class BBs; *California*-class and *Maryland*–class BBs; two destroyers, and target ship *Utah* (AG 16).

APPENDIX III
WORLD WAR II OPERATIONS

Short Title	Dates	Action
Admiralty Is.	29 Feb–17 Apr 1944	Landings in Admiralty Islands, Los Negros Island
Anzio	22 Jan–1 Mar 1944	Landings at Anzio and Nettuno
Arawe	15 Dec 1943–1 Mar 1944	Landings at Arawe, New Britain
Arctic Convoys	16 Dec 1941–27 Feb 1943	Russian convoy operations
Attu	11 May–2 Jun 1943	Landings on Attu
Badoeng Strait	19–20 Feb 1942	Battle of Badoeng Strait
Balikpapan	15 Jun–20 Jul 1945	Landings at Balikpapan, Borneo
Biak	27 May–21 Jun 1944	Landings on Biak Island, Schouten Islands off New Guinea
1st Bonins Raid	15–16 Jun 1944	First raid on Bonin Islands, Iwo Jima, and Chichi Jima
2nd Bonins Raid	24 Jun 1944	Second raid on Bonin Islands, Iwo Jima, and Pagan Island
3rd Bonins Raid	3–4 Jul 1944	Third raid on Bonin Islands, Iwo Jima, and Chichi Jima
4th Bonins Raid	4–5 Aug 1944	Fourth raid on Bonin Islands and Chichi Jima
Bonins-Yap Raids	31 Aug–8 Sep 1944	Raids on Bonin Islands, Yap, Iwo Jima, and Ulithi
Brunei	7 Jun–15 Jul 1945	Landings in Brunei Bay, Borneo
Buka Bombard.	31 Oct–1 Nov 1943	Bombardment of Buka, Bougainville
Buka Raid	1–2 Nov 1943	Raid on Buka
Cape Esperance	11–12 Oct 1942	Battle of Cape Esperance
Cape Gloucester	26 Dec 1943–1 Mar 1944	Landings at Cape Gloucester, New Britain
Cape St. George	24–25 Nov 1943	Battle of Cape St. George
Cape Sansapor	30 Jul–31 Aug 1944	Landings at Cape Sansapor, New Guinea

Short Title	Dates	Action
Cape Torokina	1 Nov–15 Dec 1943	Landings at Cape Torokina, Bougainville
Casablanca	8 Nov 1942	Actions off Casablanca
China Coast Raids 1/45	12–16 Jan 1945	Raids on China Coast, French Indochina, Hainan, and Hong Kong
Choiseul Ldgs.	28 Oct–4 Nov 1943	Landings on Choiseul Island
Convoy HX-229	16–18 Mar 1943	Halifax, Nova Scotia to UK
Convoy HX-233	16–18 Apr 1943	Halifax, Nova Scotia to UK
Convoy KMF-25A	6 Nov 1943	UK to North Africa
Convoy KMS-31	11 Nov 1943	UK to North Africa
Convoy MKS-21	13 Aug 1943	North Africa to UK
Convoy ON-67 (N. Atl.)	21–26 Feb 1942	UK to North America
Convoy ON-166 (N. Atl.)	20–25 Feb 1943	UK to North America
Convoy SC-107	3–8 Nov 1942	Halifax, Nova Scotia to UK
Convoy SC-121	3–10 Mar 1943	Halifax, Nova Scotia to UK
Convoy TAG-18	1–6 Nov 1942	Trinidad to Guantanamo
Convoy UC-1	22–24 Feb 1943	UK to Caribbean
Convoy UGS-6	12–18 Mar 1943	US to North Africa/ Mediterranean
Convoy UGS-36	1 Apr 1944	Mediterranean
Convoy UGS-37	11–12 Apr 1944	Mediterranean
Convoy UGS-38	20 Apr 1944	Mediterranean
Convoy UGS-40	11 May 1944	Mediterranean
Coral Sea	4–8 May 1942	Battle of the Coral Sea
Eastern Solomons	23–25 Aug 1942	Battle of the Eastern Solomon Islands
Elba	17 Jun 1944	Landings on Elba
Empress Augusta Bay	1–2 Nov 1943	Battle of Empress Augusta Bay

Short Title	Dates	Action
Eniwetok	17 Feb–2 Mar 1944	Landings on Eniwetok
Finschhafen	22 Sep 1943–17 Feb 1944	Landings at Finschhafen, New Guinea
Fleet Raids 1945	17 Mar–11 Jun 1945	Raids in support of Okinawa landings
Formosa Raids 1/45	3–21 Jan 1945	Raids on Formosa
Gilbert Is.	13 Nov–8 Dec 1943	Landings in Gilbert Islands (Makin and Tarawa)
Green I. Ldgs.	15–19 Feb 1944	Landings on Green Island off New Guinea
Battle of Guadalcanal	12–15 Nov 1942	Naval battle of Guadalcanal
Guadalcanal-Tulagi	7–9 Aug 1942	Landings on Guadalcanal and Tulagi, and Savo Island battle
Guam	12 Jul–15 Aug 1944	Landings on Guam
Hollandia	21 Apr–1 Jun 1944	Landings at Hollandia, New Guinea
Honshu Raids 2/45	15 Feb–16 Mar 1945	Raids on Honshu and Nansei Shoto
Iwo Jima	15 Feb–16 Mar 1945	Landings on Iwo Jima
Iwo Jima Bombard.	11 Nov 1944–24 Jan 1945	Bombardments of Iwo Jima
Jaluit Attack	20 Feb 1944	Raid on Jaluit
Java Sea	27 Feb 1942	Battle of the Java Sea
Kavieng Raid 1943	25 Dec 1943	Raid on Kavieng, New Ireland
Kavieng Raid 1/44	1 and 4 Jan 1944	Raids on Kavieng, New Ireland
Kolombangara	12–13 Jul 1943	Battle of Kolombangara
Komandorski Is.	26 Mar 1943	Battle of the Komandorski Islands
Kula Gulf	5–6 Jul 1943	Battle of Kula Gulf
Kurile Is.	1 Feb 1944–11 Aug 1945	Operations in Kurile Islands
Kwajalein	29 Jan–8 Feb 1944	Landings on Kwajalein and Majuro
Lae Ldgs.	4–22 Sep 1943	Landings at Lae, on Huon Peninsula
Leyte	10 Oct–29 Nov 1944	Landings on Leyte
Lingayen	4–18 Jan 1945	Landings in Lingayen Gulf
Luzon Raids 10/44	15 Oct–16 Dec 1944	Raids on Luzon, Manila area
Luzon Raids 1/45	6–7 Jan 1945	Raids on Luzon
Makassar Strait	23–24 Jan 1942	Battle of Makassar Strait, Balikpapan
Reinforcement of Malta	14–21 Apr and 3–6 May 1942	Reinforcement of Malta
Marcus I. Raid	4 Mar 1942	Raid on Marcus Island
Marcus I. Raid 1943	31 Aug 1943	Raid on Marcus Island
Marcus I. Raid 10/44	9 Oct 1944	Marcus Island raid and bombardment

Short Title	Dates	Action
Marianas Raid 2/44	21–22 Feb 1944	Raid on Mariana Islands, Saipan, Tinian, Rota, and Guam
Mariveles-Corregidor	14–28 Feb 1945	Landings at Mariveles and Corregidor
Marshall-Gilbert Raids 1942	1 Feb 1942	Raid on Marshall and Gilbert Islands
Midway	3–6 Jun 1942	Battle of Midway
Mindanao Ldgs.	8 Mar–20 Jul 1945	Landings at Zamboanga, Mindanao Island
Mindoro	12–18 Dec 1944	Landings on Mindoro
Minesweeping 1945	1945	Minesweeping Operations, Far East
Morotai	11 Sep 1944–9 Jan 1945	Landings on Morotai Island
N. Luzon–Formosa Raids 10/44	11–14 Oct 1944	Raids on North Luzon and Formosa
Nansei Shoto Raids 1/45	22 Jan 1945	Raids on Nansei Shoto, Ryukyu Islands
Ldgs. at Nasugbu	31 Jan–10 Feb 1945	Landings at Nasugbu, Luzon
New Georgia	20 Jun–31 Aug 1943	Landings on New Georgia and Rendova
Noemfoor I.	2 Jul–23 Jul 1944	Landings on Noemfoor Island, off Dutch New Guinea
Normandy	6–25 Jun 1944	Landings in Normandy
North Africa	8–11 Nov 1942	Landings in Morocco and Algeria
Raid on Norway	2–6 Oct 1943	Raid on Norwegian coast
Okinawa Raid 10/44	10 Oct 1944	Raids on Okinawa and Ryukyu Islands
Okinawa	24 Mar–30 Jun 1945	Landings on Okinawa
Ormoc	7–13 Dec 1944	Operations in Ormoc Bay
Palau	6 Sep–14 Oct 1944	Landings in Palau, Peleliu
Palau-Yap Raids 3/44	30 Mar–1 Apr 1944	Raids on Palau, Yap, Ulithi, and Woleai, Caroline Islands
Palau-Yap Raids 7/44	25–27 Jul 1944	Raids on Palau, Yap, Ulithi, Sorol, Fais, and Ngulu
Ldgs. on Palawan I.	28 Feb–10 Mar 1945	Landings at Puerta Princesa, Palawan Island
Pearl Harbor	7 Dec 1941	Japanese attack on Pearl Harbor
Philippines 1941–42	8 Dec 1941–6 May 1942	Defense of the Philippines
Philippines Raids 9/44	9–24 Sep 1944	Raids on Philippines, Luzon
Philippine Sea	19–20 Jun 1944	Battle of the Philippine Sea
Rabaul and Kavieng Bombard.	18 Feb 1944	Raid on Rabaul and Kavieng
1st Rabaul Raid	5 Nov 1943	First Raid on Rabaul
2nd Rabaul Raid	11 Nov 1943	Second Raid on Rabaul
Raids on Japan 7–8/45	10 Jul–15 Aug 1945	Third Fleet Raids on Japan

Short Title	Dates	Action
Rennell Island	29–30 Jan 1943	Battle of Rennel Island
Sabang Raid	19 Apr 1944	Raid on Sabang, Sumatra
Saidor	2 Jan–1 Mar 1944	Landings at Saidor, New Guinea
Saipan	11 Jun–10 Aug 1944	Landings on Saipan
Salamaua-Lae Raid	10 Mar 1942	Salamaua–Lae raid
Salerno	9–21 Sep 1943	Landings on Salerno
Santa Cruz	26 Oct 1942	Battle of the Santa Cruz Islands
Shortland I. Raid	1 Nov 1943	Raid on Shortland Island
Sicily	9 Jul–17 Aug 1943	Landings in Sicily
Soerabaja Raid	17 May 1944	Raid on Soerabaja, Java
Solomons	7 Aug 1942–15 Mar 1945	Consolidation of Solomon Islands
Southern France	15 Aug–25 Sep 1944	Landings in southern France
Subic Bay	29–31 Jan 1945	Landings at Zambales and Subic Bay
Surigao Strait	24–26 Oct 1944	Battle of Surigao Strait, Leyte Gulf
TG 21.11	13 Jun–6 Aug 1943, 22 Apr–29 May 1944	Task Group 21.11
TG 21.12	20 Apr–20 Jun 1943, 27 Jun–31 Jul 1943, 7 Mar–26 Apr 1944	Task Group 21.12
TG 21.13	12 Jul–13 Aug 1943, 11 Nov–29 Dec 1943	Task Group 21.13
TG 21.14	27 Jul–10 Sep 1943, 25 Sep–9 Nov 1943, 2 Dec 1943–Jan 1944	Task Group 21.14
TG 21.15	24 Mar–11 May 1944	Task Group 21.15
TG 21.16	16 Feb–31 Mar 1944	Task Group 21.16
TG 22.3	13 May–19 Jun 1944	Task Group 22.3
TG 22.5	3 Jun–22 Jul 1944	Task Group 22.5
Tarawa raid	18 Sep 1943	Raid on Tarawa, Makin & Abemama, Gilbert Islands
Tarakan	27 Apr–29 May 1945	Landings on Tarakan Island, Borneo
Tassafaronga	30 Nov–1 Dec 1942	Battle of Tassafaronga
Tinian	24 Jul–1 Aug 1944	Landings on Tinian
Treasury Is. ldgs	27 Oct–6 Nov 1943	Landings on Treasury Islands
Raid on Truk	16–17 Feb 1944	Raid on Truk
Truk raid 4/44	29 Apr–1 May 44	Raid on Truk & Ponape, Caroline Islands
Tunisia	8 Nov 42–9 Jul 1943	Support of Tunisian operations
Vella Gulf	6–7 Aug 1943	Battle of Vella Gulf
Vella Lavella	15 Aug–16 Oct 1943	Landings on Vella Lavella
Visayan Is. raids 10/44	20 Oct–11 Nov 1944	Raids on Visayan Is., Panay, Masbate, Cebu & Negros Islands 10/44
Visayan Is. ldgs	1 Mar–20 Apr 1945	Masbate, Panay, Cebu, Visayan Island landings
Wakde	17 May–21 Jun 1944	Landings at Wakde and Sarmi, New Guinea
Wake I. raid 1942	24 Feb 1942	Wake Island raid
Wake I. raid 1943	5–6 Oct 1943	Raid on Wake Island
Wewak-Aitape	14–24 Jul 1944	Landings at Erwak and Aitape

Note: Short title is the form used in service records for individual ships

The following were not 'operations' entitled to battle star awards:

Magic Carpet	Sep 1945–Mar 1946	Operation to bring troops home by use of large combatant vessels
Operation Crossroads	1–30 Jul 1946	Atomic bomb tests at Bikini
Tokyo Bay	2 Sep 1945	Present in Tokyo Bay for signing of Japanese surrender on USS *Missouri*

APPENDIX IV
LIST OF SHIPBUILDERS

Name	Location
Abbott	Shipbuilding Co., Milford, Del.
Abrams	Walter E. Abrams Shipyard, Inc., Halesite, Long Island, N.Y.
AC&F	American Car & Foundry Co., Wilmington, Del.
Akers	Akt. Akers Mekaniske Verksted, Oslo, Norway
Albina	Albina Engine & Machine Works, Portland, Ore.
Ambridge	American Bridge Co., Ambridge, Pa.
Amer. Cleve.	American Ship Building Co., Cleveland, Oh.
Amer. Cruiser	American Cruiser Co., Inc., Detroit, Mich.
Amer. Intl.	American International Shipbuilding Co., Hog Island, Pa.
Amer. Lorain	American Ship Building Co., Lorain, Oh.
American Brown Boveri	*See* NYSbdg
Ames	Ames Shipbuilding & Dry Dock Co., Seattle, Wash.
Annapolis Yt.	Annapolis Yacht Yard, Annapolis, Md. (formerly Trumpy)
Armstrong	Sir W. G. Armstrong, Whitworth & Co. Ltd., Walker, Newcastle-upon-Tyne, England
Associated	Associated Shipbuilders, Harbor Island, Seattle and Lake Union, Wash.
Astoria Marine	Astoria Marine Construction Co., Astoria, Ore.
Avondale	Avondale Marine Ways, Avondale, La.
Bacini	Societa Esercizio Bacini, Riva Trigosa (near Genoa), Italy
Ballard	Ballard Marine Railway Co., Inc., Seattle, Wash.
Baltimore	Baltimore Dry Dock & Shipbuilding Co., Baltimore, Md.
Barbour	Barbour Boat Works, New Bern, N.C.
Basalt	Basalt Rock Co., Inc., Napa, Calif.
Bath	Bath Iron Works Co., Bath, Me.
Beardmore	W. Beardmore & Co., Dalmuir, Scotland
Bellingham	Bellingham Shipyards Co., Bellingham, Wash.

Name	Location
Berg	Berg Shipbuilding Co., Seattle, Wash.
Beth. Alameda	Bethlehem-Alameda Shipyard, Alameda, Calif.
Beth. Eliz.	Bethlehem Shipbuilding Co., Elizabeth City, N.J.
Beth. Fairfield	Bethlehem-Fairfield Shipyard, Inc., Baltimore, Md.
Beth. Quincy	Bethlehem Shipbuilding Corp., Quincy, Mass.
Beth. S. Fran.	Bethlehem Steel Co., San Francisco, Calif.
Beth. S. Pedro	Bethlehem Steel Co., San Pedro, Calif.
Beth. Sp. Pt.	Bethlehem-Sparrows Point Shipyard, Sparrows Point, Md.
Beth. Staten I.	Bethlehem Steel Co., Staten Island, N.Y.
Beth. Wilm.	Bethlehem Shipbuilding Corp., Wilmington, Del.
Birchfield	Birchfield Boiler Co., Inc., Tacoma, Wash.
Blohm & Voss	Blohm & Voss, Hamburg, Germany
Boston NYd	Boston Naval Shipyard, Boston, Mass.
Bremer Vulkan	Schiffbau & Maschinenfabrik Bremer Vulkan, Vegesack, Germany
Brown	Brown Shipbuilding Co., Houston, Tex.
Burger	Burger Boat Co., Manitowoc, Wis.
Burmeister	A/S Burmeister & Wain's Maskin og Skibsryggeri, Copenhagen, Denmark
Bushey	Ira S. Bushey & Sons, Inc., Brooklyn, N.Y.
Butler	Walter Butler Shipbuilders, Inc., Superior, Wis.
Calderwood	Calderwood Yacht Yard, Inc., Manchester, Mass.
Calship	California Shipbuilding Corp., Terminal Island, Los Angeles, Calif.
Camden	Camden Shipbuilding & Marine Railway Co., Camden, Me.
Cammell Laird	Cammell, Laird & Co. Ltd., Birkenhead, England
Campbell	Campbell Machine Co., San Diego, Calif.
Can. Vickers	Canadian Vickers Ltd., Montreal, Que.
Canulette	Canulette Shipbuilding Co., Slidell, La.
Cardona	SA Astilleros Cardona, Barcelona, Spain

Name	Location
Cargill	Cargill, Inc., Savage, Minn.
Charleston	Charleston Shipyards, Inc., Charleston, S.C.
Charleston NYd	Charleston Naval Shipyard, Charleston, S.C.
Charleston Sbdg	Charleston Shipbuilding & Dry Dock Co., Charleston, S.C.
Chicago Bridge	Chicago Bridge & Iron, Seneca, Ill.
La Ciotat	Societé Provençale de Constructions Navales, La Ciotat, France
Cochrane	Cochrane & Sons, Selby, England
Colberg	Colberg Boatworks, Stockton, Calif.
Collingwood	Collingwood Shipyards Ltd., Collingwood, Ont.
Colonna	Charles J. Colonna Shipyard, Berkley, Va.
Commercial	Commercial Iron Works, Portland, Ore.
Consol. NY	Consolidated Shipbuilding Corp., Morris Heights, New York, N.Y.
Consol. Orange	Consolidated Steel Corp., Orange, Tex.
Consol. Wilm.	Consolidated Steel Corp., Wilmington Yard, Los Angeles, Calif.
Consolidated	Consolidated Steel Corp., Craig Yard, Long Beach, Calif.
Cook Welton	Cook, Welton & Gemmell Ltd., Beverley, England
Craig LB	Craig Shipbuilding Co., Long Beach, Calif.
Craig Toledo	Craig Shipbuilding Co., Toledo, Ohio
Cramp	William Cramp & Sons Ship & Engine Building Co., Philadelphia, Pa.
Crown	John Crown & Sons Ltd., Sunderland, England
Curtis Bay	United States Coast Guard Yard, Curtis Bay, Md.
Dachel-Carter	Dachel-Carter Shipbuilding Corp., Benton Harbor, Mich.
Daniels	Oscar Daniels Co., Tampa, Fla.
Davis	M. M. Davis & Sons, Inc., Solomons, Md.
Daytona Beach	Daytona Beach Boat Works, Inc., Daytona Beach, Fla.
Defoe	Defoe Shipbuilding Co., Bay City, Mich.
Delaware Bay	Delaware Bay Shipbuilding Co., Leesburg, N.J.
Delaware River	Delaware River Iron & Ship Building Works, Chester, Pa.
Delta	Delta Shipbuilding Co., New Orleans, La.
Detroit	Detroit Shipbuilding Co., Wyandotte, Mich.
Dingle Boat	Dingle Boat Works, St. Paul, Minn.
Ditchburn Boats	Ditchburn Boats Ltd., Orillia, Ont., Canada
Donovan	Donovan Contracting, Burlington, Vt.
Dooleys Basin	Dooleys Basin & Dry Dock, Inc., Fort Lauderdale, Fla.
Doullut	Doullut & Williams Shipbuilding Co., New Orleans, La.
Dravo Pitt.	Dravo Corp., Neville Island, Pittsburgh, Pa.
Dravo Wilm.	Dravo Corp., Wilmington, Del.
Dubuque	Dubuque Boat & Boiler Co., Dubuque, Iowa
Duthie	J. F. Duthie & Co., Seattle, Wash.
East Coast	East Coast Shipyards, Inc., Bayonne, N.J.
Elco	Electric Boat Co., Elco Works, Bayonne, N.J.
Electric Boat	Electric Boat Co., Groton, Conn.
Elizabeth City	Elizabeth City Shipyard, Elizabeth City, N.C.
Erie Concrete	Erie Concrete & Steel Supply Co., Erie, Pa.

Name	Location
Everett	Everett Pacific Shipbuilding & Dry Dock Co., Everett, Wash.
Fabricated	Fabricated Ship Corp., Milwaukee, Wis.
Fairfield	Fairfield Shipbuilding & Engineering Co. Ltd., Glasgow, Scotland
Federal	Federal Shipbuilding & Dry Dock Co., Kearny and Newark, N.J.
Fellows Stewart	Fellows & Stewart, Wilmington, Calif.
Fisher Boat	Fisher Boat Works, Inc., Detroit, Mich.
Fore River	Fore River Shipbuilding Co., Quincy, Mass.
Flechas	M. M. Flechas, Pascagoula, Miss.
Fleming	Fleming & Ferguson Ltd., Paisley, Scotland
Foundation	Foundation Co., Savannah, Ga.
Framnes Mek.	Akt. Framnes Mek. Vaerksted, Sandefjord, Norway
Froemming	Froemming Bros., Inc., Milwaukee, Wis.
Fulton SYd	Fulton Shipyards, Antioch, Calif.
Furness	Furness Shipbuilding Co., Haverton Hill-on-Tees, England
General Eng.	General Engineering & Dry Dock Co., Alameda, Calif.
Germania	Schiff- und Maschinenbau AG "Germania," Kiel, Germany
Gibbs Gas	Gibbs Gas Engine Co., Jacksonville, Fla.
Globe Duluth	Globe Shipbuilding Co., Duluth, Minn.
Globe Sup.	Globe Shipbuilding Co., Superior, Wis.
Grangemouth	Grangemouth Dockyard Ltd., Grangemouth, England
Grebe	Henry C. Grebe & Co., Chicago, Ill.
Great Lakes	Great Lakes Engineering Works, Ecorse, Mich.
Greenport	Greenport Basin & Construction Co., Greenport, Long Island, N.Y.
Gulf	Gulf Shipbuilding Corp., Mobile and Chickasaw, Ala.
Gulf Mad.	Gulf Shipbuilding Corp., Madisonville, La.
Gulf Marine	Gulf Marine Ways, Inc., Galveston, Tex.
Gulfport	Gulfport Boiler & Welding Works, Port Arthur, Tex.
H. K. Hall	H. K. Hall, Port Blakely, Wash.
Harbor Boat	Harbor Boat Building Co., Terminal Island, Calif.
Harlan	Harlan & Hollingsworth Corp., Wilmington, Del. (*also* Beth. Wilm.)
Harland	Harland & Wolff Ltd., Belfast, Northern Ireland
Harris Parsons	Harris & Parsons, Greenwich, R.I.
Helsingor	A/S Helsingörs Jernskibs-og Maskinbyggeri, Elsinore, Denmark
Herreshoff	Herreshoff Manufacturing Co., Bristol, R.I.
Higgins	Higgins Industries, Inc., New Orleans, La.
Hiltebrant	Hiltebrant Dry Dock Co., Kingston, N.Y.
Hingham	Bethlehem-Hingham Shipyard, Inc., Hingham, Mass.
Hodgson	Hodgdon Bros, East Boothbay, Me.
Howaldt	Howaldtswerke AG, Kiel, Germany
Huckins	Huckins Yacht Corp., Jacksonville, Fla.
Humphreys	Humphreys Shipbuilding Corp., Keyport, N.J.
Humphreys Marine	Humphreys Marine Railway, Inc., Weems, Va.
Ingalls	Ingalls Shipbuilding Corp., Pascagoula, Miss.
Ingalls Decatur	Ingalls Shipbuilding Corp., Decatur, Ala.

Name	Location
Inland Waterway	Inland Waterways, Inc., Duluth, Minn.
Island Dock	Island Dock, Inc., Kingston, N.Y.
Jacob	Robert Jacob, Inc., City Island, N.Y.
Jacobson	Jacobson's Shipyard, Inc., Oyster Bay, Long Island, N.Y.
Jeffersonville	Jeffersonville Boat & Machine Co., Inc., Jeffersonville, Ind.
Johnson	Johnson Foundry & Marine Co., New York, N.Y.
Jones	J. A. Jones Construction Co., Panama City, Fla.
Kaiser #2	Kaiser Co., Richmond Yard No. 2, Richmond, Calif.
Kaiser #4	Kaiser Co., Richmond Yard No. 4, Richmond, Calif.
Kaiser Rich.	Kaiser Co., Richmond, Calif.
Kaiser Vanc.	Kaiser Co., Vancouver, Wash.
Kaldnaes	Kaldnaes Mek. Verksted, Topnsberg, Norway
Kiangnan	Kiangnan Dock & Engineering Works, Shanghai
Kingston	Kingston Shipbuilding Co. Ltd., Kingston, Ont.
Kneass	George W. Kneass Co., San Francisco, Calif.
Knutson	Thomas Knutson Ship Building Co., Halesite, Long Island, N.Y.
Krupp	Fried. Krupp Germaniawerft AG, Kiel, Germany
Kruse & Banks	Kruse & Banks Shipbuilding Co., North Bend, Ore.
Kyle & Purdy	Kyle & Purdy, City Island, N.Y.
Laing	Sir James Laing & Sons Ltd., Sunderland, England
Lake Union	Lake Union Dry Dock, Inc., Seattle, Wash.
Lake Wash.	Lake Washington Shipyards, Hoquiam, Wash.
Larson	Al Larson Boat Shop, Inc., Terminal Island, Calif.
Lawley	George Lawley & Son Corp., Neponset, Mass.
Le Blanc	Le Blanc Ship Building Co. Canada
Levingston	Levington Ship Building Co., Orange, Tex.
Liberty	Liberty Dry Dock, Inc., Brooklyn, N.Y.
Los Angeles	Los Angeles Ship Building & Dry Dock Co., San Pedro, Calif. (later Todd Shipyards)
Luders	Luders Marine Construction Co., Stamford, Conn.
Lynch	Lynch Shipbuilding Co., San Diego, Calif.
Manitowoc	Manitowoc Shipbuilding, Inc., Manitowoc, Wis.
Mare I. NYd	Mare Island Naval Shipyard, Vallejo, Calif.
Marietta	Marietta Manufacturing Co., Point Pleasant, W.V.
Marine Iron	Marine Iron & Ship Building Co., Duluth, Minn.
Marinship	Marinship Corp., Sausalito, Calif.
Martinac	J. W. Martinac Ship Building Corp., Tacoma, Wash.
Martinolich	Martinolich Shipbuilding Co., San Francisco, Calif.; Tacoma; Los Angeles; San Diego
Marvel	T. S. Marvel & Co., Newburgh, N.Y.
Mathis	John H. Mathis Co., Camden, N.J.
J. E. Matton	John E. Matton & Son, Waterford, N.Y.
McDougall	McDougall-Duluth Co., Duluth, Minn.
Merrill Stevens	Merrill Stevens Shipbuilding Co. Jacksonville, Fla.
Midland	Midland Shipbuilding Co. Ltd., Midland, Ont.
Missouri Valley	Missouri Valley Bridge & Iron Co. Evansville, Ind. & Leavenworth, Kans.
Mojean Ericsson	Mojean & Ericsson, Tacoma, Wash.
Moore	Moore Dry Dock Co., Oakland, Calif.
Moran	Moran Bros., Seattle, Wash.

Name	Location
Morton	Morton Engineering & Dry Dock Co. Ltd., Quebec, Que.
Moss	Akt. Moss Vaerft & Dokk, Moss, Norway
Nakskov	Nakskov Skibsvaerft A/S, Nakskov, Denmark
Napier Miller	Napier & Miller Ltd., Glasgow, Scotland
Nashville	Nashville Bridge Co., Nashville, Tenn.
N. Carolina	North Carolina Shipbuilding Co., Wilmington, N.C.
Neafie	Neafie & Levy, Philadelphia, Pa.
Nevins	Henry B. Nevins, Inc., City Island, N.Y.
New England	New England Shipbuilding Corp., South Portland, Me.
New Jersey	New Jersey Ship Building Corp., Barber, N.J.
New Jersey DD	New Jersey Drydock and Transportation Corp., Elizabeth, N.J.
New London	New London Ship & Engine Co., Groton, Conn.
New York NYd	New York Naval Shipyard, Brooklyn, N.Y.
Newport News	Newport News Shipbuilding & Dry Dock Co., Newport News, Va.
Norfolk NYd	Norfolk Navy Yard, Portsmouth, Va.
Northwestern	Northwestern Shipbuilding Co., South Bellingham, Wash.
NY Sbdg	New York Shipbuilding Corp., Camden, N.J.
NY Yacht	New York Yacht Co., Morris Heights, N.Y.
Nylands	Nylands Verksted, Oslo, Norway
Oregon	Oregon Shipbuilding Corp., Portland, Ore.
Palmer	R. Palmer & Son, Noank, Conn.
Palmers	Palmers Shipbuilding & Iron Co. Ltd. Hebburn, Newcastle-upon-Tyne, England
Penhoët	S. A. des Chantier & Ateliers de Saint-Nazaire, Chantier de Penhoët, St. Nazaire, France
Penn-Jersey	Penn-Jersey Ship Building Corp., Camden, N.J.
Pennsylvania	Pennsylvania Shipyards, Inc., Beaumont, Tex.
Perkins Vaughan	Perkins & Vaughan, Wickford, R.I.
Permanente #1	Permanente Metals Corp., Yard No. 1, Richmond, Calif.
Permanente #2	Permanente Metals Corp., Yard No. 2, Richmond, Calif.
Peterson	Peterson Boat Works, Sturgeon Bay, Wis.
J. Peterson	Julius Peterson, Inc., Nyack, N.Y.
Peterson/Hacker	Peterson & Haecker Ltd., Blair, Neb.
Peyton	Peyton Co., Newport Beach, Calif.
Phila. NYd	Philadelphia Navy Yard, Philadelphia, Pa.
Pollock	Pollock Stockton Shipbuilding Co., Stockton, Calif.
Portland Sbdg	Portland Shipbuilding Co., Portland, Ore.
Portsmouth NYd	Portsmouth Naval Shipyard, Portsmouth, N.H.
Providence Eng.	Providence Engineering Co., Providence, R.I., and City Island, N.Y.
Puget Sound Bridge	Puget Sound Bridge & Dredging Co., Seattle, Wash.
Puget Sound NYd	Puget Sound Naval Shipyard, Bremerton, Wash.
Pullman	Pullman Standard Car Mfg. Co., Chicago, Ill.
Pusey	Pusey & Jones Corp., Wilmington, Del.
Quincy Adams	Quincy Adams Yacht Yard, Inc., Quincy, Mass.
Ramage	Ramage & Ferguson Ltd., Leith, Scotland
Rappahannock	Rappahannock Marine Railway, Weems, Va.
Rice	Rice Brothers Corp., East Boothbay, Me.
Riuniti Palermo	Cantieri Navali Riuniti, Palermo, Italy

Name	Location
Robb	Henry Robb Ltd., Leith, Scotland
Robins	Robins Dry Dock Co., Brooklyn, N.Y.
Robinson Marine	Robinson Marine Construction Co., Benton Harbor, Mich.
W. A. Robinson	W. A. Robinson, Inc., Ipswich, Mass.
Rocky River	Rocky River Dry Dock Co., Rocky River, Ohio
Russell Erie	Russell Erie Basin Shipyard, Brooklyn, N.Y.
Sample	Frank L. Sample Jr., Boothbay Harbor, Me.
San Diego Marine	San Diego Marine Construction Co., San Diego, Calif.
Savannah	Savannah Machine & Foundry Co., Savannah, Ga.
Schichau	F. Schichau GmbH, Elbing, Germany
Seabrook	Seabrook Shipyards, Seabrook, Tex.
Sea-Tac Tacoma	Seattle-Tacoma Shipbuilding Corp., Tacoma, Wash.
Sea-Tac Seattle	Seattle-Tacoma Shipbuilding Corp., Seattle, Wash.
Seattle Sbdg	Seattle Shipbuilding & Dry Dock Co., Seattle, Wash.
Simms Bros.	Simms Brothers, Dorcheseter, Mass.
P. Smit	NV Machinfabrieken Scheepswerf van P.Smit, Jun., Rotterdam, Netherlands
L. D. Smith	Leatham D. Smith Ship Building Co., Sturgeon Bay, Wis.
Smith & McCoy	Smith & McCoy, Norfolk, Va.
Smith's Dock	Smith's Dock Co. Ltd., South Bank, England
Snow	Snow Shipyards, Inc., Rockland, Me.
South Coast	South Coast Co., Newport Beach, Calif.
Southern	Southern Shipyard Corp., Newport News, Va.
Southwestern	Southwestern Shipbuilding Corp., San Pedro, Calif.
Spear	Spear Engineering Works, Norfolk, Va.
St. John's	St. John's River Shipbuilding Co., Jacksonville, Fla.
St. Louis Sbdg	St. Louis Ship Building & Steel Co., St. Louis, Mo.
Stab. Tecnico	Stabilimento Tecnico Triestino, Trieste, Italy
Stadium	Stadium Yacht Basin, Inc., Cleveland, Ohio
Staten I.	Staten Island Shipbuilding Co., Port Richmond, Staten Island, N.Y.
Stephen	A. Stephen & Sons Ltd., Glasgow, Scotland
W. F. Stone	William F. Stone & Son, Oakland, Calif.
Story	A. D. Story, Essex, Mass.
Sullivan	Sullivan Dry Dock & Repair Corp., Brooklyn, N.Y.
Sun	Sun Shipbuilding & Dry Dock Co., Chester, Pa.
Tacoma Boat	Tacoma Boat Building Co., Tacoma, Wash.

Name	Location
Tampa	Tampa Shipbuilding Co., Tampa, Fla.
Thompson	J. & G. Thompson, Clydebank, Glasgow, Scotland
Todd Bklyn	Todd Shipyards Corp., Brooklyn, N.Y.
Todd Galveston	Todd Shipyards Corp./Todd-Galveston Dry Dock, Inc., Galveston, Tex.
Todd Houston	Todd Houston Shipbuilding Corp., Houston, Tex.
Todd L.A.	Todd Shipyards Corp., San Pedro, Calif.
Todd Seattle	Todd Shipyards Corp./Todd-Pacific Shipyard, Inc., Seattle, Wash.
Todd Tacoma	Todd Pacific Shipyards, Inc., Tacoma, Wash.
Toledo	Toledo Shipbuilding Co., Toledo, Ohio
Trumpy	Jonathan Trumpy & Son, Annapolis, Md. (later Annapolis Yacht)
Tull	E. James Tull, Pocomoke City, Md.
Union	Union Iron Works, San Francisco, Calif.
United DD	United Dry Dock, Inc., Staten Island, N.Y.
United Eng.	United Engineering Works, Alameda and San Francisco, Calif.
United Staten I.	United Shipyards, Inc., Mariner's Harbor, Staten Island, N.Y. (*also* Beth. Staten I.)
Ventnor Boat	Ventnor Boat Corp., Ventnor, N.J.
Victory	Victory Shipbuilding Co., Newport Beach, Calif., and Holland, Mich.
Vineyard Sbdg	Vineyard Shipbuilding, Milford, Del.
Vosper	Vasper Ltd., Portsmouth, England
Vulcan	Vulcan Werke, Stettin, Germany
Walsh-Kaiser	Walsh-Kaiser Co., Providence, R.I.
Ward Eng.	Chas. Ward Engineering Works, Charleston, W. Va.
Weaver	Weaver Shipyards, Orange, Tex.
Westergard	Wetergard Boat Works, Inc., Biloxi, Miss.
Western Boat	Western Boat Building Co., Tacoma, Wash.
W. Pipe S.F.	Western Pipe & Steel Co., San Francisco, Calif.
W. Pipe S.P.	Western Pipe & Steel Co., San Pedro, Calif.
Wheeler	F. W. Wheeler & Co., West Bay City, Mich.
Wheeler Sbdg	Wheeler Shipbuilding Corp., Whitestone, Long Island, N.Y.
Willamette	Willamette Iron & Steel Corp., Portland, Ore.
Wilmington Boat	Wilmington Boat Works, Inc., Wilmington, Calif.
Winslow	Winslow Marine Railway Shipbuilding Co., Winslow, Wash.
Workman	Workman, Clark & Co. Ltd., Belfast, Northern Ireland
Zenith	Zenith Dredge Co., Duluth, Minn.

BIBLIOGRAPHY

JOURNALS

Marine News (Journal of the World Ship Society)
Warship International (Journal of the International Naval Research Organization)

BOOKS IN SERIAL PUBLICATION

American Bureau of Shipping. *American Bureau of Shipping Record.* Houston, Tex.: American Bureau of Shipping; various editions, 1870–1954.

Fahey, James C. *The Ships and Aircraft of the United States Fleet.* Annapolis, Md.: United States Naval Institute/Washington D.C.: Ships and Aircraft; various editions, 1939–1946.

Jane's Fighting Ships.

Lloyd's Register of Shipping, London.

Lloyd's Register of American Yachts. New York: Lloyd's Register; various editions, 1870–1941.

Starke, Tony, and Schell, William. *Register of Merchant Ships.* England: WSS; various editions, 1890–1939.

U.S. Coast Guard. *Merchant Vessels of the United States.* Washington, D.C.: U.S. Government Printing Office; various editions, 1870–1944.

U.S. Navy. *Ships Data U.S. Naval Vessels.* Washington, D.C.: U.S. Government Printing Office; various editions, 1921–1949.

BOOKS

Alden, John D. *Flush Decks and Four Pipes.* Annapolis, Md.: United States Naval Institute, 1965.

———. *The Fleet Submarine in the U.S. Navy.* Annapolis, Md.: Naval Institute Press, 1979.

Bauer, K. Jack, and Roberts, Stephen S. *Register of Ships of the U.S. Navy, 1775–1990: Major Combatants.* Westport, Conn.: Greenwood, 1991.

Berezhnoy, S. S. *Flot SSSR Korabli I Suda Lendlisa.* St. Petersburg, Russia: Velen, 1994.

Canney, Donald L. *U.S. Coast Guard and Revenue Cutters 1790–1935.* Annapolis, Md.: Naval Institute Press, 1995.

Charles, Roland W. *Troopships of World War II.* Washington, D.C.: Army Transportation Association, 1947.

Cooney, David M. *A Chronology of the United States Navy: 1775–1965.* New York: Franklin Watts, 1965.

Friedman, Norman. *U.S. Battleships: An Illustrated Design History.* Annapolis, Md.: Naval Institute Press, 1985.

———. *U.S. Cruisers: An Illustrated Design History.* Annapolis, Md.: Naval Institute Press, 1984.

———. *U.S. Destroyers: An Illustrated Design History.* Annapolis, Md.: Naval Institute Press, 1982.

———. *U.S. Small Combatants.* Annapolis, Md.: Naval Institute Press, 1987.

Grover, David H. *U.S. Army Ships and Watercraft of World War II.* Annapolis, Md.: Naval Institute Press, 1987.

Lenton, H. T. *British and Empire Warships of the Second World War.* London: Greenhill, 1998.

Mitchell, Donald W. *History of the Modern American Navy.* New York: Alfred A. Knopf, 1946.

Morison, Samuel Eliot. *History of United States Naval Operations in World War II*, 15 vols. Boston, Little Brown, 1947–1962.

Peterson, Douglas. *United States Lighthouse Service Tenders, 1840–1939.* Annapolis, Md.: Eastwind, 2000.

Raven, Alan. *Fletcher-Class Destroyers.* Annapolis, Md.: Naval Institute Press, 1989.

Scheina, Robert L. *U.S. Coast Guard Cutters and Craft of World War II.* Annapolis, Md.: Naval Institute Press, 1982.

U.S. Maritime Commission. *Permanent Report of Completed Ship Construction Contracts*, Washington, D.C.: U.S. Government Printing Office, 1948.

U.S. Navy. *Dictionary of American Naval Fighting Ships*, 8 vols. Washington, D.C.: Naval Historical Center, Department of the Navy, 1959–1981.

———. *Navy and Marine Corps Awards Manual.* Navpers 15,790 (Rev. 1953).

———. *Naval Vessel Register, 25 January 1946*, Washington, D.C.: U.S. Government Printing Office, 1946.

———. *Contracts Awarded Private Shipyards for Construction of Naval Vessels since 1 January 1934.* Washington, D.C.: U.S. Government Printing Office, 1946.

U.S. Navy Office of the Chief of Naval Operations, *Combatant Shipbuilding 1-1-1942 to 7-1-1946*, Washington, D.C.: U.S. Government Printing Office, 1947.

Willoughby, Malcolm T., *The U.S. Coast Guard in World War II.* Annapolis, Md.: United States Naval Institute, 1957.

WEBSITES

http://www.navsource.org
http://uboat.net
http://www.ibilio.org/hyperwar/USN

INDEX

THE NAVY OF WORLD WAR II PLAN OF THE BOOK

INDEX FOR VOL. 4 THE NAVY OF WORLD WAR II 1922–1946

ERRATA

In *The New Navy, 1883–1922*, the fourth volume of the U. S. Navy Warship Series by Paul H. Silverstone, Figure 4.4 on page 37 of the torpedo boat *Porter* (TB 6), 1897 should be the photo below:

Figure 4.6 on page 38 of the large torpedo boat *Stringham* (TB 19), 1907 should be:

We sincerely regret any inconvenience this may have caused you.

Taylor and Francis Group, LLC

#RT718X/0415978718